Lecture Notes in Computer Science   11999

More information about this series at http://www.springer.com/series/7410

Jianying Zhou · Xiapu Luo ·
Qingni Shen · Zhen Xu (Eds.)

Information and Communications Security

21st International Conference, ICICS 2019
Beijing, China, December 15–17, 2019
Revised Selected Papers

 Springer

Editors
Jianying Zhou 🆔
Singapore University of Technology
and Design
Singapore, Singapore

Qingni Shen 🆔
Peking University
Beijing, China

Xiapu Luo 🆔
The Hong Kong Polytechnic University
Kowloon, Hong Kong

Zhen Xu
Institute of Information Engineering
Beijing, China

ISSN 0302-9743   ISSN 1611-3349   (electronic)
Lecture Notes in Computer Science
ISBN 978-3-030-41578-5   ISBN 978-3-030-41579-2   (eBook)
https://doi.org/10.1007/978-3-030-41579-2

LNCS Sublibrary: SL4 – Security and Cryptology

This Springer imprint is published by the registered company Springer Nature Switzerland AG
The registered company address is: Gewerbestrasse 11, 6330 Cham, Switzerland

Preface

This book contains the papers that were selected for presentation and publication at the 21st International Conference on Information and Communications Security (ICICS 2019) – which was held in Beijing, China, December 15–17, 2019. ICICS 2019 was organized by the School of Software and Microelectronics, Peking University, the Institute of Information and Engineering, Chinese Academy of Sciences, and the Institute of Software, Chinese Academy of Sciences.

ICICS, which was launched in Beijing in 1997, aims at bringing together leading researchers and practitioners from both academia and industry to exchange their experiences and insights related to computer and communications security. We organized ICICS 2019 in the same venue as ICICS 1997, to commemorate late Prof. Sihan Qing, a cybersecurity pioneer and a founder of ICICS.

This year's Program Committee (PC) consisted of 73 members with diverse backgrounds and broad research interests. In response to the call for papers, 199 papers were submitted to the conference. The number of submissions was among the top in ICICS history. The review process was double-blind, and the papers were evaluated on the basis of their significance, novelty, and technical quality. Most papers were reviewed by three or more PC members. The PC meeting was held electronically, with intensive discussion over a period of two weeks. Finally, 47 papers were selected for presentation at the conference (with an acceptance rate of 23.6%).

This year we set the best paper and best student paper awards for the first time with a monetary prize generously sponsored by Springer. The paper "Prototype-based Malware Traffic Classification with Novelty Detection" authored by Lixin Zhao, Lijun Cai, Aimin Yu, Zhen Xu, and Dan Meng received the best paper award. Two papers shared the best student paper award: "AADS: A Noise-Robust Anomaly Detection Framework for Industrial Control Systems" authored by Maged Abdelaty, Roberto Doriguzzi-Corin, and Domenico Siracusa; and "Automated Cyber Threat Intelligence Reports Classification for Early Warning of Cyber Attacks in Next Generation SOC" authored by Wenzhuo Yang and Kwok-Yan Lam. These papers received very positive comments by the reviewers, and we appreciated their contributions to ICICS 2019.

This year we had two outstanding keynote talks: "Towards Leakage Resilient User Authentication" presented by Prof. Robert Deng from Singapore Management University, Singapore, and "Can't You Hear Me Knocking: Novel Security and Privacy Threats to Mobile Users" by Prof. Mauro Conti from University of Padua, Italy. Our deepest gratitude to Robert and Mauro for their excellent presentations.

ICICS 2019 was made possible by the joint efforts of many individuals and organizations. We sincerely thank the authors of all submissions. We are grateful to all the PC members for their great effort in reading, commenting, debating, and finally selecting the papers. We thank all the external reviewers for assisting the PC in their particular areas of expertise. We also thank the ICICS Steering Committee, the general chairs (Qingni Shen and Zhen Xu), the publicity chairs (Qi Li and Weizhi Meng), the publication chair (Dongmei Liu), and the Local Organizing Committee. Finally, we thank everyone else, speakers and session chairs, for their contribution to the program of ICICS 2019.

We would also like to thank the sponsors for their generous support: Ali, TCG, Microsoft, Intel, AWS, 360, Neusoft, Nationz Technology, Octa Innovation, SANGFOR, China International Talent Exchange Foundation, and Springer.

December 2019

Jianying Zhou
Xiapu Luo

Organization

ICICS 2019

21st International Conference on Information and Communications Security

Beijing, China
December 15–17, 2019

Organized by
School of Software and Microelectronics, Peking University, China
Institute of Information Engineering, Chinese Academy of Sciences (CAS)
Institute of Software, Chinese Academy of Sciences (CAS)

Supported by
International Talent Exchange Foundation, China

Steering Committee Chair

Jianying Zhou	SUTD, Singapore

Steering Committee

Robert Deng	Singapore Management University, Singapore
Dieter Gollmann	Hamburg University of Technology, Germany
Javier Lopez	University of Malaga, Spain
Qingni Shen	Peking University, China
Zhen Xu	Institute of Information Engineering, CAS, China

Honorary General Chair

Changxiang Shen	Academician of China Engineering Academy, China

General Chairs

Qingni Shen	Peking University, China
Zhen Xu	Institute of Information Engineering, CAS, China

Program Chairs

Jianying Zhou	SUTD, Singapore
Xiapu Luo	The Hong Kong Polytechnic University, China

Publicity Chairs

Qi Li   Tsinghua University, China
Weizhi Meng   Technical University of Denmark, Denmark

Publication Chair

Dongmei Liu   Microsoft, China

Program Committee

Chuadhry Mujeeb Ahmed   SUTD, Singapore
Cristina Alcaraz   University of Malaga, Spain
Dinh Tien Tuan Anh   SUTD, Singapore
Man Ho Au   The Hong Kong Polytechnic University, China
Joonsang Baek   University of Wollongong, Australia
Tegawendé F. Bissyandé   University of Luxembourg, Luxembourg
Zhenfu Cao   East China Normal University, China
Xiaolin Chang   Beijing Jiaotong University, China
Kai Chen   Institute of Information Engineering, CAS, China
Liqun Chen   University of Surrey, UK
Songqing Chen   George Mason University, USA
Ting Chen   UEST, China
Xiaofeng Chen   Xidian University, China
Zhong Chen   Peking University, China
Yueqiang Cheng   Baidu USA X-Lab, USA
Sherman S. M. Chow   The Chinese University of Hong Kong, China
Mauro Conti   University of Padua, Italy
Jintai Ding   University of Cincinnati, USA
Xuhua Ding   Singapore Management University, Singapore
Jose Maria de Fuentes   Universidad Carlos III de Madrid, Spain
Debin Gao   Singapore Management University, Singapore
Xing Gao   University of Memphis, USA
Angelo Genovese   University of Milan, Italy
Dieter Gollmann   Hamburg University of Technology, Germany
Stefanos Gritzalis   University of the Aegean, Greece
Le Guan   University of Georgia, USA
Jinguang Han   Queen's University of Belfast, UK
Chenglu Jin   New York University, USA
Sokratis Katsikas   NTNU, Norway
Dong Seong Kim   University of Queensland, Australia
Qi Li   Tsinghua University, China
Shujun Li   University of Kent, UK

Zhou Li	University of California, Irvine, USA
Giovanni Livraga	University of Milan, Italy
Javier Lopez	University of Malaga, Spain
Kangjie Lu	University of Minnesota Twin Cities, USA
Bo Luo	University of Kansas, USA
Daisuke Mashima	Advanced Digital Sciences Center, Singapore
Weizhi Meng	Technical University of Denmark, Denmark
Jiang Ming	The University of Texas at Arlington, USA
Chris Mitchell	Royal Holloway, University of London, UK
Atsuko Miyaji	Osaka University, Japan
Jianbing Ni	University of Waterloo, Canada
Jianting Ning	Singapore Management University, Singapore
Roberto Di Pietro	Hamad Bin Khalifa University, Qatar
Giovanni Russello	The University of Auckland, New Zealand
Pierangela Samarati	University of Milan, Italy
Qingni Shen	Peking University, China
Chunhua Su	University of Aizu, Japan
Purui Su	Institute of Software, CAS, China
Hung-Min Sun	National Tsing Hua University, Taiwan
Kun Sun	George Mason University, USA
Pawel Szalachowski	SUTD, Singapore
Qiang Tang	LIST, Luxembourg
Ding Wang	Peking University, China
Haining Wang	Virginia Tech, USA
Lingyu Wang	Concordia University, Canada
Shuai Wang	HKUST, China
Weiping Wen	Peking University, China
Jia Xu	Singtel/Trustwave, Singapore
Jun Xu	Stevens Institute of Technology, USA
Yu Yu	Shanghai Jiao Tong University, China
Toshihiro Yamauchi	Okayama University, Japan
Tsz Hon Yuen	The University of Hong Kong, China
Chao Zhang	Tsinghua University, China
Fan Zhang	Zhejiang University, China
Junjie Zhang	Wright State University, USA
Rui Zhang	Institute of Information Engineering, CAS, China
Tianwei Zhang	Nanyang Technological University, Singapore
Yang Zheng	SUTD, Singapore
HongSheng Zhou	Virginia Commonwealth University, USA
Yajin Zhou	Zhejiang University, China
Yongbin Zhou	Institute of Information Engineering, CAS, China

Additional Reviewers

Alhebaishi, Nawaf
Anagnostopoulos, Marios
Branco, Pedro
Cai, Quanwei
Cao, Jiahao
Case, Benjamin
Cecconello, Stefano
Chang, Deliang
Chen, Jiageng
Chen, Joann
Cui, Handong
Diamantopoulou, Vasiliki
Dong, Shuaike
Dou, Yi
Du, Minxin
Feng, Pengbin
Gao, Yiwen
Ghosal, Amrita
Gu, Xiaolan
Halder, Subir
Hamedani, Kian
Han, Zhaoyang
Hao, Shuai
He, Xu
Homoliak, Ivan
Hou, Ruomu
Huang, Hui
Jia, Yanxue
Jia, Yunhan
Jin, Lin
Junming, Ke
Karopoulos, Georgios
Karybali, Irene
Karyda, Maria
Kim, Jongkil
Lai, Jianchang
Lakshmanan, Sudershan
Li, Juanru
Li, Wenjuan
Li, Yanyin
Li, Zengpeng
Lin, Yan
Lin, Yun

Liu, Guannan
Liu, Mingxuan
Lou, Xin
Lu, Chaoyi
Lu, Xingye
Ma, Haoyu
Ma, Hui
Meng, Guozhu
Mimoto, Tomoaki
Myloth Josephlal, Edwin Franco
Navarin, Nicolò
Nieto, Ana
Ntantogian, Christoforos
Okumura, Shinya
Oqaily, Alaa
Pang, Chengbin
Peiyuan, Zong
Peng, Le
Phuong, Tran Viet Xuan
Poh, Geong Sen
Polato, Mirko
Rios, Rubén
Roman, Rodrigo
Rubio, Juan E.
Shao, Jun
Sharma, Vishal
Shen, Jun
Shen, Tianxiang
Song, Qiyang
Sun, Pengfei
Tabiban, Azadeh
Takano, Yuuki
Tan, Glenice
Tan, Heng Chuan
Thao, Tran Phuong
Tian, Guohua
Tian, Jianwen
Tian, Yangguang
Turrin, Federico
Venugopalan, Sarad
Viet Xuan Phuong, Tran
Wan, Shengye
Wang, Chenyu

Wang, Cong
Wang, Hao
Wang, Haoliang
Wang, Jiafan
Wang, Jianfeng
Wang, Jingwei
Wang, Shu
Wang, Weizheng
Wang, Xinda
Wang, Yujue
Wang, Yunling
Wu, Ge
Wu, Huangting
Wu, Mingli
Wu, Pengfei
Wu, Qianhong
Xin, Xianrui
Xu, Fenghao

Xu, Shengmin
Xue, Lei
Ye, Quanqi
Yu, Miao
Yu, Ruotong
Yu, Zuoxia
Zhang, Qian
Zhang, Xiaoyu
Zhang, Yicheng
Zhang, Yiming
Zhang, Yinghui
Zhao, Wenjia
Zhao, Yue
Zheng, Mengce
Zheng, Yu
Zhu, Hong
Zhu, Zhiqing
Zuo, Cong

Contents

Applied Cryptograph

Internet Security

Machine Learning Security

Machine Learning Privacy

Web Security

Steganography and Steganalysis

Malware Analysis and Detection

Prototype-Based Malware Traffic Classification with Novelty Detection

Lixin Zhao[1,2], Lijun Cai[1], Aimin Yu[1(✉)], Zhen Xu[1], and Dan Meng[1]

[1] Institute of Information Engineering, Chinese Academy of Sciences, Beijing, China
{zhaolixin,cailijun,yuaimin,xuzhen,mengdan}@iie.ac.cn
[2] School of Cyber Security, University of Chinese Academy of Sciences,
Beijing, China

Abstract. Automated malware classification using deep learning techniques has been widely researched in recent years. However, existing studies addressing this problem are always based on the assumption of closed world, where all the categories are known and fixed. Thus, they lack robustness and do not have the ability to recognize novel malware instances. In this paper, we propose a prototype-based approach to perform robust malware traffic classification with novel class detection. We design a new objective function where a distance based cross entropy (DCE) loss term and a metric regularization (MR) term are included. The DCE term ensures the discrimination of different classes, and the MR term improves the within-class compactness and expands the between-class separateness in the deeply learned feature space, which enables the robustness of novel class detection. Extensive experiments have been conducted on datasets with real malware traffic. The experimental results demonstrate that our proposed approach outperforms the existing methods and achieves state-of-the-art results.

Keywords: Malware classification · Convolutional Neural Network · Novelty detection

1 Introduction

Malware has long been one of the major security threats in the cyber space. They are responsible for a large number of malicious activities such as identity theft, Phishing, and Distributed Denial of Service (DDoS) attacks. As the carrier of Internet communication, network traffic plays an important role in malware detection.

The malware detection can be accomplished at different levels of detail. Most of current network security devices use signature based techniques, which rely on a database of known malware samples. They search for distinct patterns to characterize the malware. These techniques are able to achieve high precision and low number of false alerts, but their detection ability is bounded to the known samples and patterns included in the database. Another category of

© Springer Nature Switzerland AG 2020
J. Zhou et al. (Eds.): ICICS 2019, LNCS 11999, pp. 3–17, 2020.
https://doi.org/10.1007/978-3-030-41579-2_1

techniques is machine learning based detection. The main goal of this kind of techniques is to build a classification model that can identify different types of malware. According to whether labels are needed during model training, they can work in unsupervised or supervised ways. The unsupervised methods are typically used to detect new threats. They use cluster based mechanisms and assume that samples from the same class are closer to each other than those belonging to different classes in feature space. Unfortunately, this may not hold true in higher-dimensional feature space such as network traffic data. Hence, unsupervised methods often suffer from lower precision which limits their practical usefulness. By contrast, the supervised methods train classifiers under the supervision of known malicious samples and achieve better efficacy results. Thus they are more widely used in the field of malware detection, especially after the emergence of deep learning techniques. However, when building classifiers, existing studies are often based on the assumption of closed world that all the categories appear in the testing phase have already appeared in the training phase. This assumption, which does not conform to the actual situation, limits their detection capabilities to known categories of malware and reduces their detection accuracy. The above facts highlight the need to build a robust classifier for both known classes classification and novel class detection.

In this paper, we propose an effective prototype-based approach for malware traffic classification in the open world setting, where traffic from unknown or novel malware may emerge in the testing phase. In our approach, Convolutional Neural Network (CNN) is applied to learn feature representation for each network flow (i.e., continuous packets with same 5-tuple *(ip_src, port_src, ip_dst, port_dst, protocol)*). At the top of CNN, multiple prototypes, each of which can be viewed as the mean of each class in the deeply learned feature space, are assigned to represent different classes. The classification is performed by finding the nearest prototype in the feature space. Here, from the perspective of probability, our approach projects samples into a low-dimensional feature space and makes the samples of each category obey Gaussian distribution, and the prototype act as the mean of Gaussian distribution for each category. We design a new objective function, which contains two terms namely distance based cross entropy loss (DCE) and metric regularization (MR). The former one ensures that different classes are discriminable. The latter one enables the closeness between samples and their respective prototypes. Moreover, it can also improve the within-class compactness and expand the between-class separateness in the learned feature space, which makes the representation more suitable for novelty detection. Under the supervision of our objective function, the CNN along with the prototypes can be learned jointly from the raw network data.

In summary, this paper has the following major contributions:

- we propose a new prototype-based approach for malware traffic classification. The newly proposed objective function motivates the CNN to extract more discriminative features for network flows, which makes the model more robust and suitable for unknown or novel malware traffic detection.

 - we conduct extensive experiments to evaluate our approach on public malware traffic datasets. The experimental results show significant improvement compared to existing state-of-the-art malware traffic classification methods.

2   Related Work

2.1   Malware Traffic Detection and Classification

The topic of malware traffic detection and classification have long been concerned by researchers. Traditionally, flow level statistical features combined with various machine learning algorithms such as SVM, Random Forest, Logistic Regression and so on are tend to be used for malware detection and classification [1,2,4,5,18,21]. They think that the flow statistical patterns like packet size, inter-packet time, transmitted bytes etc. presented by different applications are distinguishable. However, this may not hold true, because this coarse-grained statistical features lead to large within-class scatter and small between-class separation. Thus, it is hard to construct classifiers with high accuracy. Recently, deep learning techniques have achieved great success in the field of computer vision and speech. Attracted by their powerful ability of representation learning, researchers start trying to use deep learning based techniques to solve the problem of malware traffic detection and classification [9,12,15,16,20,24]. Compared to traditional flow statistical features, the features learned by deep neural network are more discriminative. Unfortunately, to our best knowledge, all the existing relevant studies perform classification under the assumption of closed world that all the categories are known and fixed. Therefore, they can not correctly classify the traffic data generated by previously unknown malware.

2.2   Prototype Learning

Prototype indicates an average or best exemplar of a category, and it can provide a concise representation for the entire category of instances [11]. A typical method of prototype learning is K-Nearest-Neighbor (KNN) [6]. To reduce the huge computing and storage costs for KNN, a technique called learning vector quantization (LVQ) is proposed by [10]. Afterwards, a great number of variations of LVQ are proposed by researchers. For prototype learning, most of studies accomplished by optimizing the customized objective function like in [7,8,17,22,23]. In addition, some researchers have also combined prototype learning with probabilistic models and neural networks for classification task [3]. Different from previous works, we learn prototypes to distinguish different categories on one hand, and make the feature representations have small within-class diversity and large between-class separation that are more suitable for novel class detection on the other hand.

3   Proposed Approach

3.1   Problem Formalization

Given a training dataset $D = \{(x_1, y_1), (x_2, y_2), ..., (x_n, y_n)\}$, where $x_i \in \mathbb{R}^d$ is a training instance and $y_i \in Y = \{1, 2, ..., k\}$ is the label of x_i. In the testing phase, the labels of an open dataset $D_0 = \{(x_i, y_i)\}_{i=1}^{\infty}$ need to be predicted, where $y_i \in Y_0 = \{1, 2, ..., k, ..., K\}$ with $K > k$. Our goal is to learn a robust classifier $C : x \rightarrow Y' = \{1, 2, ..., k, novel\}$, where the option *novel* indicates that the label was unseen in the training phase and thus the corresponding instances are from unknown malware.

3.2   Approach Overview

Recent research work has successfully demonstrated the superiority of deep neural network with regard to classification performance on high-dimensional data. In addition, The flexibility of network design and training facilitates the feature learning by utilizing custom loss functions. Thus, we employ a CNN to learn more discriminative feature representation for each raw input. Specifically, given an input x, the deeply learned features are denoted as $f(x; \theta)$, where θ denotes the parameters of the CNN. For purpose of obtaining distinguishing characteristics of class from training instances so that it has the ability to detect novel class, we define and maintain a class-distribution of instances, what we call a *prototype*, as $P_i = \frac{1}{|\Psi_i|} \Sigma_{x \in \Psi_i} f(x, \theta)$, for each observed class y_i. The symbol Ψ_i in the formula above denotes the training instances belonging to class y_i.

In the training phase, the CNN and the prototypes $P = \{P_i\}$ are jointly trained based on raw input data. In the testing phase, instances are classified by nearest prototype matching, that is, a testing instance is labeled as the class of the prototype that has the smallest Euclidean distance from it. This is different from the traditional CNN which employs a softmax layer for linear classification on the learned features.

3.3   Objective Function Definition

Since the similarity between the instances and the prototypes are measured by Euclidean distance, we naturally think of using a distance based loss function to train the CNN model over the training data. Considering that for a given instance x, the smaller the distance between $f(x, \theta)$ and the prototype P_i, the greater the probability that it belongs to class y_i. Hence, the probability of an instance x belonging to the class y_i can be measured as follows.

$$p(x \in y_i | x) \propto -||f(x, \theta) - P_i||_2^2 \tag{1}$$

Furthermore, we normalize the distance measure in Eq. 1 to satisfy the sum-to-one property of the probability and further define it as:

$$p(y_i | x) = \frac{exp(-\gamma ||f(x, \theta) - P_i||_2^2)}{\Sigma_{j=1}^{k} exp(-\gamma ||f(x, \theta) - P_j||_2^2)} \tag{2}$$

where k is the number of observed classes in the training dataset and γ is a hyper-parameter that controls the strength of distance used. Based on the probability of $p(y_i|x)$, we can define the Distance based Cross Entropy (DCE) as follows.

$$L_{DCE}(x; \theta, P) = -logp(y_i|x) \tag{3}$$

From Eq. 1–3, we can observe that minimizing the DCE loss decreases the distance between the instance x and the prototype P_i associated with it.

The DCE loss defined above performs classification based on the distance measurement between sample and prototype, and it would make sure that samples from different classes are discriminable. However, CNN training based solely on this loss may lead to over-fitting, because distribution information from samples of a class is included in a prototype, and the corresponding samples in the class may contain noise, which is a common situation in network traffic data. In order to alleviate this and make the learned feature representation more robust, we propose to impose a new metric regularization term on the learned features. This metric regularization term enforces the CNN model to be more discriminative so that the feature representations have small within-class scatter and large between-class separation. Specifically, we expect that the distances between similar samples (i.e., from same class) are smaller than those between dissimilar ones (i.e., from different classes). To this end, we explicitly constrain the distances between the similar samples and prototypes (i.e., they share same class) to be smaller than an up-threshold τ_1, and urge the distances between dissimilar samples and prototypes (i.e., they belong to different classes) to be larger than a down-threshold τ_2. That is,

$$\begin{cases} ||f(x, \theta) - P_i||_2^2 < \tau_1, label(x) = label(P_i), \\ ||f(x, \theta) - P_i||_2^2 > \tau_2, label(x) \neq label(P_i). \end{cases} \tag{4}$$

Obviously, τ_2 should be larger than τ_1.

To reduce the number of free parameters, we introduce an intermediate threshold parameter τ and a margin α. We can simplify the constraint in (4) by setting $\tau_1 = \tau - \alpha$ and $\tau_2 = \tau + \alpha$ as follows:

$$\alpha - \bar{y}(\tau - ||f(x, \theta) - P_i||_2^2) < 0 \tag{5}$$

where $\bar{y} \in \{-1, 1\}$ indicates whether instance x and prototype P_i share the same class or not. In Eq. 5, the scale of α should be comparable to the value of $\tau - ||f(x, \theta) - P_i||_2^2$, so we further transform Eq. 5 into Eq. 6.

$$\alpha - \bar{y}(1 - \frac{||f(x, \theta) - P_i||_2^2}{\tau}) < 0 \tag{6}$$

Hence, we can select the value of margin α from $(0, 1)$. By applying this constrain to each similar and dissimilar pair between prototype and sample, we define the metric regularization term using hinge loss function, which is formulated as follows:

$$L_{MR}(x; \theta, P) = \Sigma_{i=1}^k h(\alpha - \bar{y}(1 - \frac{||f(x, \theta) - P_i||_2^2}{\tau})) \tag{7}$$

where $h(x) = max(0, x)$ is the hinge loss function and k is the number of classes in the training dataset.

Finally, our objective function is the combination of the DCE loss term and MR term, which is defined as follows:

$$J = min(L_{DCE}(x; \theta, P) + \lambda L_{MR}(x; \theta, P))$$
$$= min(-logp(y_i|x) + \lambda \Sigma_{i=1}^k h(\alpha - \bar{y}(1 - \frac{||f(x, \theta) - P_i||_2^2}{\tau}))) \qquad (8)$$

where λ is a tradeoff parameter that controls the relative importance of the two terms. From the perspective of probability, we can regard the MR term as maximum-likelihood regularization like [13,14]. Obviously, this optimization problem can be solved by Stochastic Gradient Descent (SGD) method.

3.4   Novel Class Detection

Traditional softmax based classifiers make partition for the whole feature space, and any sample from unseen classes will certainly be projected to some region under the partition. Thus, these samples will still be labeled as some known classes in the training dataset. This closed world property limits its detection for novel class.

In our approach, we adopt a threshold based nearest prototype matching mechanism for classification of known classes and rejection for novel class. We give a threshold T_i, which is determined based on the training data, for each known class y_i in the training dataset. Since the samples of each class approximately follow Gaussian distribution in the learned feature space, and the prototypes are the means of the samples in each class. We define the threshold T_i for class y_i as the average distance between all samples in class y_i and the prototype P_i plus a generalization interval. It is can be formulated as follows:

$$T_i = \mu(y_i) + \eta\sigma(y_i)$$
$$= \frac{1}{|\Psi_i|}\Sigma_{x \in \Psi_i}||f(x, \theta) - P_i||_2^2 + \eta std(\{||f(x, \theta) - P_i||_2^2, \forall x \in \Psi_i\}) \qquad (9)$$

where Ψ_i is the training set of class y_i, η is a generalization coefficient for the generalization interval term. Particularly, the generalization interval is defined as the sample standard deviation of $\{||f(x, \theta) - P_i||_2^2, \forall x \in \Psi_i\}$.

In the testing phase, each testing instance x is firstly projected to the learned feature space using the trained CNN. Then, we compute the squared Euclidean distance $S_{x,i}$ from $f(x, \theta)$ to prototype P_i for each class y_i, and we find the minimum $S_{x,i}$ with the corresponding class y_i. Here, we denote them as $\hat{S}_x$ and $\hat{y}$. Also, we denote the corresponding threshold for class $\hat{y}$ as $\hat{T}$ without loss of generality. Finally, the prediction label for instance x can be given by:

$$y = \begin{cases} \hat{y}, & \hat{S}_x \leq \hat{T}, \\ -1, & \hat{S}_x > \hat{T}. \end{cases} \qquad (10)$$

where $y = -1$ indicates that the instance x is determined to come from a novel class.

4   Experimental Evaluation

Table 1. Statistics of datasets MCFP and USTC-TFC2016.

MCFP	Flows	USTC	Flows
Artemis	12654	Geodo	1000
Sennoma	10003	Htbot	1000
Dynamer	11777	Miuref	1000
Tinba	12862	Neris	1000
Ursnif	11000	Nsisay	1000
CCleaner	11538	Shifu	1000
Miner	9864	Virut	1000
Downloader	10239	Zeus	1000
CoreBot	9892		
Dridex	11319		
Total	111148	Total	8000

4.1   Datasets

MCFP dataset. We use the malware traffic data maintained by the Malware Capture Facility Project[1] as one of the two malware traffic datasets to evaluate our approach. The captured traffic of various malware is kept in separated pcap files, from which we randomly selected 10 kinds of malware to build the MCFP dataset. There are more than 100 thousands network flows in total after the raw traffic is parsed. We mainly evaluate and compare the performance of our approach with existing relevant methods on this dataset.

USTC-TFC2016 dataset. This dataset[2] is mainly used to evaluate our approach's ability to detect novel classes. The original version of this dataset contains 10 kinds of malware traffic which are kept in separated pcap files like MCFP. We manually exclude 2 kinds of malware namely Tinba and Cridex that have already existed in the MCFP. Then, we parse the raw traffic and select 1000 flows uniformly at random from each one of the rest 8 kinds of malware to build this dataset. The detailed statistics of the datasets are listed in Table 1.

---

[1] Malware Capture Facility Project (https://www.stratosphereips.org/datasets-malware) is responsible for making the long-term captures. This project is continually obtaining malware and normal data to feed the Stratosphere IPS.
[2] https://github.com/yungshenglu/USTC-TFC2016.

4.2   Implementation Details

Preprocessing. In our approach, we classify malware traffic at flow granularity. Considering that only fixed-size input is accepted by CNN while the flow lengths are often varied, we transform raw network flows of varying lengths to satisfy the input structure of CNN. Specifically, we keep the first 32 packets of each flow, and for each packet, we keep the first 512 bytes starting from transport layer header. Zero will be padded if the flow length is less than 32 packets or the IP packet length is less than 512 bytes. After this transformation, each flow is represented as a matrix with size 32 × 512. To obtain a better performance, we normalize all the packet bytes in the matrix by dividing them by 255, the maximum value of a byte, and then resize the normalized matrix to 128 × 128.

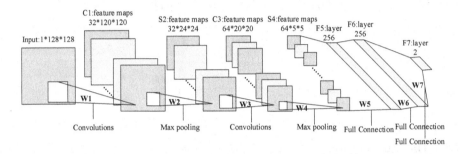

Fig. 1. The CNN architecture used in our approach. It is composed of two convolution layers, two max-pooling layers and three fully connected layers.

CNN Architecture. The architecture of CNN used for feature learning in our work is shown in Fig. 1. The layers of the CNN comprise a convolutional layer C_1 with 32 feature maps, a max pooling layer S_2, a second convolutional layer C_3 with 64 feature maps, a second max pooling layer S_4, and three fully connected layers F_5, F_6 and F_7 with 256 units, 256 units and 2 units respectively. The sizes of the kernels for the C_1 and C_3 are 9 × 9 and 4 × 4 respectively.

Parameter Settings. For our CNN model training, the learning rate is set to 0.001, the weight decay is set to 0.0005 and the minibatch size is 64. For the hyper-parameters settings, we set the strength parameter $\gamma = 1.0$ in the DCE loss term, $\tau = 10$, $\alpha = 0.5$ respectively in the MR term, and we set the generalization coefficient $\eta = 3$ for novelty detection. The tradeoff parameter λ in the final objective function is set to 0.5.

4.3   Evaluation Metrics

Three commonly used metrics including precision, recall and overall accuracy are adopted to quantitatively evaluate and compare the classification results.

The precision and recall are computed for per class as follows:

$$precision = \frac{TP}{TP + FP}, recall = \frac{TP}{TP + FN} \tag{11}$$

Besides, the overall accuracy is defined as the number of correctly classified samples, regardless of which class they belong to, divided by the total number of testing samples.

4.4 Evaluation Results and Comparisons

We compare the performance of our approach with the following relevant methods that focus on malware traffic detection and classification.

- [1]: Flow statistical features with various machine learning methods are applied for encrypted malware traffic classification. We choose Random Forest algorithm with enhanced features for comparison, which works best as described in [1]. Particularly, we excluded the TLS related features from the enhanced feature set, because they are missing in most of the flows in our datasets.
- [9]: A deep learning method works on handcrafted features for intrusion detection.
- [24]: A CNN-based malware traffic classification method for representation learning. We use the tools provided by them to parse and preprocess the raw pcap files in our dataset to satisfy the input structure of their model. The flow number generated by each file is slightly different from ours. We ignore this difference and just focus on the per class precision, recall and overall accuracy.

Since to our best knowledge, all the existing relevant studies perform traffic classification under assumption of closed world, which means that they can not deal with the novel class in the testing data (i.e., all the samples from novel classes will be classified into known classes). Thus, we compare the classification performance of different methods on known classes only (a closed world scenario). The comparison is performed on the MCFP dataset and all the results are achieved through 5-fold cross testing.

The comparison results are detailed in Table 2, from which we can observe that traditional machine learning algorithm with flow statistical features [1] perform poorly on diverse malware traffic flows, because the within-class compactness and between-class separateness can not be obtained by coarse-grained flow statistical features. Similar classification performance is obtained by applying deep learning techniques on the handcrafted features, because the final feature representations used for classification are learned from the low-dimensional handcrafted features in an unsupervised manner, which make them not robust enough. By contrast, methods using CNN as feature extractor provide better performance than traditional statistical based approach. This indicates that deep neural network can learn superior features from high-dimensional traffic data. Furthermore, our approach (column DCE+MR in Table 2) consistently outperforms [24] in per class precision, recall and overall accuracy. This result can be mainly attributed to the use of prototypes in the learned feature space. In addition, we also evaluate the performance of model that is trained under the supervision of DCE loss term only (column DCE in Table 2). The results indicate that the MR term can prevent over-fitting and make the deeply learned features more robust.

Table 2. Classification results comparison on MCFP dataset. All the classifications are performed in a closed world setting. [1], [9], [24] are the comparing works. DCE+MR denotes our proposed work and DCE denotes that CNN is trained using DCE loss term only. All the results are obtained through 5-fold testing.

%	[1]			[9]			[24]			DCE			DCE+MR		
	pre.	rec.	acc.	pre.	rec.	acc.	pre.	rec.	acc.	pre.	rec.	acc.	pre.	rec.	acc.
Arte.	79.8	82.1	80.2	85.5	86.1	80.6	95.6	90.4	90.7	90.5	91.0	91.8	99.0	99.1	**99.2**
Senn.	86.6	78.3		76.7	82.5		96.3	97.2		96.7	98.0		99.3	99.1	
Dyna.	82.2	79.2		83.4	79.1		92.1	94.6		93.4	95.3		99.1	99.2	
Tinba	89.2	80.9		85.7	81.1		90.3	89.8		95.7	89.7		99.6	99.0	
Ursnif	86.8	76.4		87.1	79.0		89.9	92.9		97.1	94.4		99.1	99.1	
CCle.	70.8	88.1		76.2	85.5		90.2	90.4		96.2	91.1		99.2	99.4	
Miner	85.8	75.2		78.8	76.9		95.1	95.1		88.9	96.8		99.4	99.3	
Down.	71.4	77.7		81.1	77.2		88.2	84.9		81.2	81.8		99.5	99.2	
Core.	79.9	84.8		78.2	81.9		86.3	88.5		98.2	98.5		99.6	99.1	
Drid.	72.6	77.7		75.2	73.7		84.7	83.5		82.1	83.4		100	99.4	

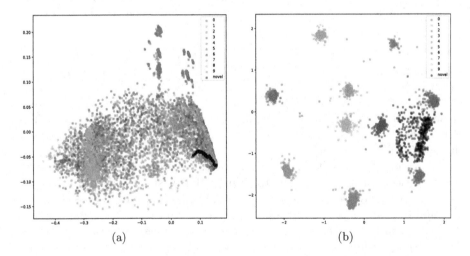

(a)   (b)

Fig. 2. Intuitive display of data distribution before and after projection. (a) data distribution in the original feature space. (b) data distribution in the deeply learned feature space. We can see that, more discriminative features are learned and they are robust to novel class samples.

Novel Class Detection Evaluation. To test the performance of our approach in the presence of novel classes (an open world scenario), we perform a 5-fold cross testing on the MCFP dataset, meanwhile, all the samples in USTC-TFC2016 dataset are used as novel class data in each fold testing. Thus, the number of output classes extends from N to N+1. An intuitive display of the sample distributions before and after projection are shown in Fig. 2. Here, the CNN model used to transform the raw inputs is selected from one in 5-fold cross testing. For the raw inputs in Fig. 2(a), we project them onto 2-dimensional feature space using Principal Component Analysis (PCA) method provided by the library scikit-learn [19]. The samples from novel classes are denoted as black circles, and samples from 10 known classes are denoted by circles of other colors. Obviously, from Fig. 2(b) we can see that samples from different classes have distinct clusters in the deeply learned feature space, and samples from novel classes are well separated from other clusters which helps novel class detection.

Table 3 lists the test results of our approach. We can see that all the precision, recall and overall accuracy are still kept high for both the known classes and novel class. This indicates that under the supervision of our objective function (DCE+MR), more discriminative features can be learned and they are also robust enough for the samples from novel classes. Similar to the results in Table 2, the performance of DCE is not as good as DCE+MR, which once again confirms the importance of the MR term. In addition, we have manually checked the misclassified samples in the novel classes and found that most of them are short flows (i.e., number of packets are less than 6). That means a large number of zeros are padded to represent each flow, which do not contribute to distinguish different flows.

Table 3. Novel class detection performance. All the classifications are performed in an open world setting, where all the samples in the USTC-TFC2016 dataset are used as novel class samples in each testing fold. DCE+MR denotes our proposed work and DCE denotes that CNN is trained using DCE loss term only. All the results are obtained through 5-fold testing.

%	DCE			DCE+MR		
	pre.	**rec.**	**acc.**	**pre.**	**rec.**	**acc.**
Arte.	80.4	88.6	80.5	95.3	98.4	**96.7**
Senn.	75.4	85.5		94.6	98.0	
Dyna.	78.7	87.7		96.3	98.3	
Tinba	85.8	88.7		97.1	98.4	
Ursnif	79.1	82.3		97.0	98.2	
CCle.	80.2	91.9		95.9	98.2	
Miner	80.8	85.3		97.7	97.9	
Down.	77.1	81.0		93.5	98.0	
Core.	81.0	90.4		95.5	97.9	
Drid.	79.0	82.8		95.9	98.2	
Novel	81.3	62.5		99.1	92.5	

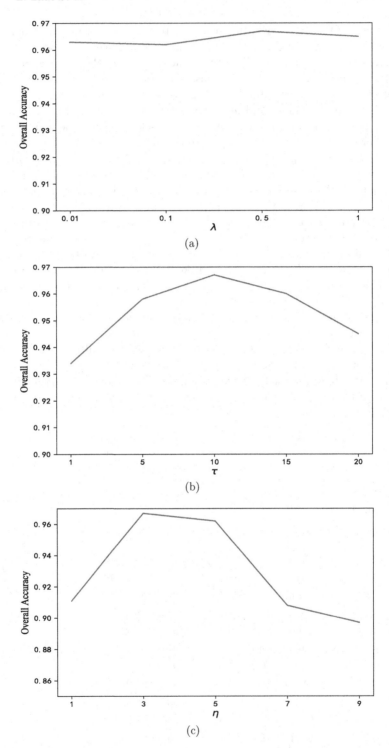

Fig. 3. The influence of hyper-parameters λ, τ and η on classification performance.

The Influence of Hyper-parameters. The λ used for balancing the importance of DCE loss term and MR term in our objective function, the τ used in the MR term, and the η used for novel class detection are the three main hyper-parameters in our approach. To test their sensitivity, we vary these hyper-parameters and observe the influence on classification performance. Here, we evaluate the classification performance in the open world scenario based on the overall accuracy metric. Firstly, we vary the value of λ from the set of $\{0.01, 0.1, 0.5, 1\}$ and the results are shown in Fig. 3(a), from where we can see that the change of λ has little influence on the overall accuracy as it remains basically unchanged. Then, we vary the value of τ from the set of $\{1, 5, 10, 15, 20\}$ and the results are shown in Fig. 3(b). We can see from the Fig. 3(b) that too small a value of τ may drop the classification performance, since the deeply learned features are not discriminative enough among different classes, while too large a value of τ may lead to over-fitting, which will drop the classification performance as well. Finally, we vary the value of η from the set of $\{1, 3, 5, 7, 9\}$ and the results are shown in Fig. 3(c). In Fig. 3(c), we can see that the value of η has a clear impact on the overall accuracy. If η is too small, many of samples from known classes will be misclassified as novel class. Conversely, if the η is too large, a large proportion of novel class samples will be misclassified as existing classes. All the results shown in the Fig. 3(a)–3(c) are obtained through 5-fold testing.

5 Conclusion

In this paper, we propose a new prototype-based malware traffic classification approach with novel class detection ability. It breaks the closed world assumption that all the categories are known and fixed, which is the basis of the existing relevant studies. Our approach directly learns a prototype for each class and then perform classification based on nearest prototype matching. A new objective function is proposed to increase the within-class compactness and expand the between-class separateness so that the deeply learned features are discriminative enough to novel class samples. We conduct extensive experiments to evaluate our approach in both the closed world and open world scenarios using two public datasets with real malware traffic. The experimental results show the superiority of our approach compared with existing studies.

Acknowledgements. This work is supported by the strategic Priority Research Program of Chinese Academy of Sciences, Grant No. XDC02040200.

References

1. Anderson, B., McGrew, D.: Machine learning for encrypted malware traffic classification: accounting for noisy labels and non-stationarity. In: Proceedings of the 23rd ACM SIGKDD International Conference on Knowledge Discovery and Data Mining, pp. 1723–1732. ACM (2017)

2. Bekerman, D., Shapira, B., Rokach, L., Bar, A.: Unknown malware detection using network traffic classification. In: 2015 IEEE Conference on Communications and Network Security (CNS), pp. 134–142. IEEE (2015)
3. Bonilla, E.V., Robles-Kelly, A.: Discriminative Probabilistic Prototype Learning (2012)
4. Celik, Z.B., Walls, R.J., McDaniel, P., Swami, A.: Malware traffic detection using tamper resistant features. In: MILCOM 2015–2015 IEEE Military Communications Conference, pp. 330–335. IEEE (2015)
5. Chen, Z., et al.: Machine learning based mobile malware detection using highly imbalanced network traffic. Inf. Sci. **433**, 346–364 (2018)
6. Cover, T., Hart, P.: Nearest neighbor pattern classification. IEEE Trans. Inf. Theory **13**(1), 21–27 (1967)
7. Decaestecker, C.: Finding prototypes for nearest neighbour classification by means of gradient descent and deterministic annealing. Pattern Recogn. **30**(2), 281–288 (1997)
8. Huang, Y.-S., et al.: A simulated annealing approach to construct optimized prototypes for nearest-neighbor classification. In: Proceedings of 13th International Conference on Pattern Recognition, vol. 4, pp. 483–487. IEEE (1996)
9. Javaid, A.Y., Niyaz, Q., Sun, W., Alam, M.: A deep learning approach for network intrusion detection system. In: EAI International Conference on Bio-inspired Information & Communications Technologies (2016)
10. Kohonen, T.: Learning vector quantization. In: Kohonen, T. (ed.) Self-Organizing Maps. Springer Series in Information Sciences, vol. 30, pp. 175–189. Springer, Heidelberg (1995). https://doi.org/10.1007/978-3-642-97610-0_6
11. Kuncheva, L.I., Bezdek, J.C.: Nearest prototype classification: clustering, genetic algorithms, or random search? IEEE Trans. Syst. Man Cybern. Part C Appl. Rev **28**(1), 160–164 (1998)
12. Li, Z., Qin, Z., Huang, K., Yang, X., Ye, S.: Intrusion detection using convolutional neural networks for representation learning. In: Liu, D., Xie, S., Li, Y., Zhao, D., El-Alfy, E.-S.M. (eds.) ICONIP 2017, Part V. LNCS, vol. 10638, pp. 858–866. Springer, Cham (2017). https://doi.org/10.1007/978-3-319-70139-4_87
13. Liu, C.-L., Sako, H., Fujisawa, H.: Discriminative learning quadratic discriminant function for handwriting recognition. IEEE Trans. Neural Networks **15**(2), 430–444 (2004)
14. Liu, C.-L., Sako, H., Fujisawa, H.: Effects of classifier structures and training regimes on integrated segmentation and recognition of handwritten numeral strings. IEEE Trans. Pattern Anal. Mach. Intell. **26**(11), 1395–1407 (2004)
15. Marín, G., Casas, P., Capdehourat, G.: Rawpower: deep learning based anomaly detection from raw network traffic measurements. In: Proceedings of the ACM SIGCOMM 2018 Conference on Posters and Demos, pp. 75–77. ACM (2018)
16. Marín, G., Casas, P., Capdehourat, G.: Deepsec meets rawpower-deep learning for detection of network attacks using raw representations. ACM SIGMETRICS Perform. Eval. Rev. **46**(3), 147–150 (2019)
17. Miller, D., Rao, A.V., Rose, K.: A global optimization technique for statistical classifier design. IEEE Trans. Signal Process. **44**(12), 3108–3122 (1996)
18. Narudin, F.A., Feizollah, A., Anuar, N.B., Gani, A.: Evaluation of machine learning classifiers for mobile malware detection. Soft Comput. **20**(1), 343–357 (2016)
19. Pedregosa, F., et al.: Scikit-learn: machine learning in Python. J. Mach. Learn. Res. **12**(Oct), 2825–2830 (2011)
20. Radford, B.J., Apolonio, L.M., Trias, A.J., Simpson, J.A.: Network traffic anomaly detection using recurrent neural networks. arXiv preprint arXiv:1803.10769 (2018)

21. Saad, S., et al.: Detecting P2P botnets through network behavior analysis and machine learning. In: 2011 Ninth Annual International Conference on Privacy, Security and Trust, pp. 174–180. IEEE (2011)
22. Sato, A., Yamada, K.: Generalized learning vector quantization. In: Advances in Neural Information Processing Systems, pp. 423–429 (1996)
23. Sato, A., Yamada, K.: A formulation of learning vector quantization using a new misclassification measure. In: Proceedings of the Fourteenth International Conference on Pattern Recognition (Cat. No. 98EX170), vol. 1, pp. 322–325. IEEE (1998)
24. Wang, W., Zhu, M., Zeng, X., Ye, X., Sheng, Y.: Malware traffic classification using convolutional neural network for representation learning. In: 2017 International Conference on Information Networking (ICOIN), pp. 712–717. IEEE (2017)

Evading API Call Sequence Based Malware Classifiers

Fenil Fadadu, Anand Handa$^{(\boxtimes)}$, Nitesh Kumar, and Sandeep Kumar Shukla

C3i Center, Department of CSE, Indian Institute of Technology, Kanpur, India
{fenilk,ahanda,niteshkr,sandeeps}@cse.iitk.ac.in

Abstract. In this paper, we present a mimicry attack to transform malware binary, which can evade detection by API call sequence based malware classifiers. While original malware was detectable by malware classifiers, transformed malware, when run, with modified API call sequence without compromising the payload of the original, is effectively able to avoid detection. Our model is effective against a large set of malware classifiers which includes linear models such as Random Forest (RF), Decision Tree (DT) and XGBoost classifiers and fully connected NNs, CNNs and RNNs and its variants. Our implementation is easy to use (i.e., a malware transformation only requires running a couple of commands) and generic (i.e., works for any malware without requiring malware specific changes). We also show that adversarial retraining can make malware classifiers robust against such evasion attacks.

Keywords: Adversarial machine learning · Evasion attacks · API call sequence · Dynamic analysis

1 Introduction

Pitfalls of signature-based malware detection gave rise to cloud-based analysis and white-listing [13]. While signature-based detection remains the first line of defense, malware detection can be automated by analysing them in the cloud-based backend, extracting relevant features from a known set of malware, and training a machine learning classifiers which can generalize well for new and unseen malware [5].

It is possible to systematically exploit machine learning models and evade detection by such models. These exploits consist of methods of slightly but carefully modifying the sample under test, resulting in misclassification by the model (also referred to as the target model) even though the unmodified sample was classified correctly. Such modified samples are called adversarial examples. Over time, researchers presented novel ways of generating adversarial examples [3]. Researchers also come up with countermeasures to make machine learning more robust against such adversarial examples [14].

Majority of the work on generating adversarial examples to attack machine learning based classifiers, is limited to image classification. However, images are

© Springer Nature Switzerland AG 2020
J. Zhou et al. (Eds.): ICICS 2019, LNCS 11999, pp. 18–33, 2020.
https://doi.org/10.1007/978-3-030-41579-2_2

fundamentally different from executables. An image consists of a fixed set of pixels, and each pixel is an integer value that varies over a wide range of possible values. Generating adversarial examples for image classification typically involves slightly modifying pixel values, which results in misclassification. A slight modification in malware may adversely affect malware functionality to the point of making it useless. Therefore methods to generate adversarial examples for image classification are not directly transferable to malware domain.

It is not practical to assume too much information about the target model that we are trying to attack. While an adversary might be able to observe outputs (i.e., malicious or benign labels for submitted executables) of a commercial anti-malware product, internal specifications of such models are well-kept secrets. Researchers generate adversarial examples in 'black-box' setting to make their attack practical. While exact black-box setting varies across different work, typically researchers try to assume the least possible information about the target classifier.

To the best of our knowledge, Grosse et al. [6]'s work is the first one to craft adversarial examples for malware classifiers in a black box setting. Static features are extracted, and a substitute model is trained for Android malware. Extracted features include permissions, hardware components, API calls, network addresses. Information about the substitute model is used to generate adversarial examples systematically. Limitations of generating adversarial examples in malware domain are observed – specifically, modifying anything in malware can cause it to lose its functionality. Malware modification is restricted only to the addition of new features instead of removing or changing features that are already present. Misclassification rates of 60%-80% were achieved for different classifiers in [6].

1.1 Problem Statement

Given a machine learning classifier f that uses dynamic API calls as features and a set of malware M that is correctly getting classified by f, our objective is to find a systematic method to modify each $m \in M$ such that modified malware m' corresponding to each m can evade detection by f with high probability. The method should not use any information about f other than the fact that it used API call sequences as features and the method should be generic enough to work uniformly across each $m \in M$ without requiring specific changes to the method for different malware.

1.2 Contribution of This Work

This paper makes the following contributions.

- We demonstrate a systematic and automatic method to evade detection by API call sequence based malware classifiers while still preserving its malicious functionality.

- Unlike previous work, which requires generating malware-specific configuration files, our implementation is generic and removes the overhead of per-malware configuration files.
- We show that adversarial malware generated by our method can be used to retrain the classifiers to make them robust against such evasion attacks.
- In this work, we show the evasion at two different levels - feature level, in which during the execution of malware we keep on generating adversarial sequences and executable level, in which we use IAT hooking to modify an executable.

Rest of the paper is organized as follows: Sect. 2 describes our design and implementation of our attack. Section 3 describes evaluation results. Section 4 describes related work in the area of adversarial example generation. Section 5 concludes the work and talks about future work.

2   Proposed Methodology

2.1   Preparing Target Models

We generate adversarial examples for a malware classifier that uses API call sequence made by an executable during the execution. We call it the target model. We assume the target model as a black-box, i.e., we do not use any information about the target model in designing our attack except for the fact that it uses API calls as its features. We do not exploit any property of the model directly but analyse benign and malware executables and try to mimic benign like behavior in malware executables by using elementary techniques. While similar works propose complex methods, we will justify our reasoning behind using elementary techniques. First, we test our methodology by generating adversarial sequences for already extracted sequences and show that it can produce results comparable to previous work. Then we test it by modifying the malware which when executed, will dynamically produce adversarial sequence to evade detection. In both cases, we evaluate our adversarial examples against the target models.

Dataset Collection and Feature Extraction. Malicious executables are collected from CDAC Mohali [12], and some malware repositories including Malshare [11] and VirusShare [17]. Malware are submitted to Virustotal. Virustotal is an ensemble of more than 70 Antivirus engines. Only files which get a malware tag from at least one engine are filtered for the training set. Finally, we are left with 20, 000 binaries having 10, 000 malware and 10, 000 benignware.

To extract the features, executables in the dataset are executed in Cuckoo sandbox for 30 s each. The configuration for creating a sandbox environment are 3.4 GHz Intel Core i7 processor, 100 GB storage, and 4 GB primary memory. We use Windows 7 as the host operating system for the Cuckoo sandbox. Cuckoo generate reports comprising of analysis results in the JSON format. We use scripts to extract the API call sequence from Cuckoo reports. To truly capture the malicious activity, the firewall and updates in our host machine are disabled, which would make the system vulnerable to as many exploits as possible.

Classification. We have trained eight different models namely Random Forest, Decision Tree, XGBoost, Neural Network (NN), Convolutional Neural Network (CNN), Standard Recurrent Neural Network (RNN) and its two variants; Gated Recurrent Unit Network (GRU) and Long Short-Term Memory Network (LSTM). We implement the non-linear models using Keras deep learning library in Python [1] and linear models using scikit-learn library [2]. We use 70% data for the training purpose and 30% data for the testing purpose. To minimize the risk of overfitting, we use 10 fold cross-validation for linear models. Each model takes a sequence of 300 API calls at a time, which is also referred to as its window size. Since ASCII API names cannot be given directly as input, we map each API to a unique integer in the range of (0,300). Each ASCII API name is integer encoded using the same mapping which is then given as input to the model. Analysed malware consists of a good mixture of different types of malware, including TrojanDropper, TrojanDownloader, Worm, Trojan, Virus, Virtool, PWS, and Backdoor. Table 1 show the accuracy % for various models when used on our dataset.

Table 1. Target model accuracies

Classifier type	Accuracy (%)
NN	94.65%
CNN	94.66%
RNN	92.93%
GRU	93.56%
LSTM	94.27%
Random Forest	92.77%
Decision Tree	88.77%
XGBoost	90.26%

2.2 Evasion of Target Model

Till now, the target model is trained using the API call sequences. Now, we try to evade the prepared target model using two categories of implementation, which are feature level evasion and executable level evasion.

Feature Level Evasion. Let us denote the set of all API calls by A. Let us denote the set of all l-length sequences of integer-encoded API calls by S_l.

Let us denote the target classifier by a function f which takes a sequence of integer encoded API calls as input and returns a binary value; 1 if it is malware and 0 if it is benign. Mathematically,

$$f : S_l \to \{0, 1\} \tag{1}$$

N-gram is a sequence of n API calls. A single API call is referred to as unigram; a sequence of two is referred to as bigram; a sequence of three is referred to as trigram and so forth. Let us denote the set of all N-grams of APIs by NG, the domain of malicious executables by M and the domain of benign executables by B. Each domain comprises of elements where each element is a sequence of API calls made by an executable of that domain. Let us introduce a Fraction Function F, defined as

$$F : \{M, B\} \times NG \to \mathbb{R} \tag{2}$$

For a $d \in \{M, B\}$ and an $ng \in NG$,

$$F(d, ng) = \frac{\text{Number of sequences in d having } ng \text{ as a subsequence}}{\text{Number of sequences in d}}$$

Here subsequence means continuous sequence of API calls and not to be confused with subsequence as in Longest Common Subsequence. For example, $F(M, ng)$ is a fraction of malware whose API call sequence has ng as a subsequence.

The idea is to start with S, $f(S) = 1$ (malware), and iteratively modify it till we get a sequence S' such that $f(S') = 0$ (benign). Since modifying already present API calls in S can fatally harm malware functionality, we restrict ourselves to only additive modifications, i.e., we can only add new API calls without changing anything in the already present ones.

Algorithm 1. Feature Level Attack

Input: $\mathbf{f}$(Model), $\mathbf{x}$(Input API call sequence of length l), $\mathbf{A}$(Set of API calls), $\perp$(Concatenation operation)

1: $\mathbf{x}^* \leftarrow \mathbf{x}$
2: **while** f($\mathbf{x}^*$) = malicious **do**
3:     $i \leftarrow random(0, l - 1)$
4:     $api \leftarrow \arg\max_{api \in A}(F(B, x^*[i] \perp api) - F(M, x^*[i] \perp api))$
5:     $x^* \leftarrow x^*[1 : i] \perp api \perp x^*[i + 1 : l - 1]$
6: **end while**

Algorithm 1 describes our approach. At each iteration, we randomly select index i, and add an API $api \in A$, which maximizes the Fraction Function difference between benign and malware domain. The motivation is to introduce a feature which is more probable to occur in benign executables than in malicious ones, mimicking benign behavior in a malicious sequence. The iterative heuristic is inspired by Rosenberg et al. [15]'s work. Next section presents the detailed arguments about why our additive modification will preserve malicious functionality.

One could argue that iterative loop in Algorithm 1 goes on till it changes classification model's decision which makes it unclear whether the choice of API call in step 4 is significant at all or decision randomly changes at some point due to exhaustive iterations. While Rosenberg et al. [15]'s work does not provide any explanation about it, our result section provides detailed analysis showing that choice of API calls in step 4 is actually significant from the perspective of the target model.

Executable Level Evasion: The idea is to enhance the malware executables such that they mimic benign behavior. It is achieved by making malware periodically call smartly chosen API calls in between the original API calls so that overall sequence looks more like benign. The extra code, which is referred to as adversarial code, is attached to the malware whose job is to follow the original API call sequence of malware and periodically make smartly chosen API calls in between. It requires us to periodically transfer control back and forth between the original malware code and adversarial code. It is achieved by hooking Import Address Table (IAT) of Portable Executables (PE). Once the adversarial code gets control, it should observe previously made API calls and choose an adversarial call to make. Once it chooses an API call to make, it must make that call, which will be a dynamic choice. Once it performs its job, it must transfer control back to the original code.

IAT Hooking: The external calls to runtime libraries are funneled through an indirect jump to the address specified in the Import Address Table (IAT). Our implementation plays with this IAT entry to periodically transfer control to the adversarial code. Typically these IAT entries contain the address of the corresponding API in the loaded runtime libraries. However, our implementation makes sure that it points to a specific location in the adversarial code instead. This specific location is unique to each API.

Let us understand the design with the help of an example. Figure 1 shows a call to `CreateFile`. The call transfers control to a jump instruction in IAT. However, our implementation modifies its corresponding IAT entry such that at runtime instead of jumping to `CreateFile` in `Kernel32.dll`, it jumps to some location in the adversarial code. This process of diverting control flow is typically referred to as IAT hooking. Our IAT hooking implementation serves two purposes; firstly, it helps in keeping track of which API calls are made, and secondly it can periodically transfer control to adversarial code. We extend an Open Source framework IAT Patcher [19] to automatically hook malware executables en-masse. Figure 1 shows that the arguments are pushed before the call instruction. When control returns to the original code, it expects `CreateFile` to be executed from `kernel32.dll` and the return value is set.

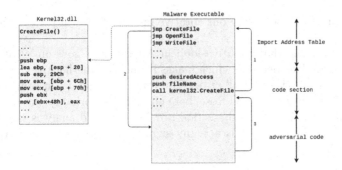

Fig. 1. Architecture of IAT hooks

Preserving Malware Functionality: An IAT hook will redirect control in adversarial code to an identical looking function (API). `CreateFileA` is a Windows API which is declared in `Kernel32.dll` as:

```
1 HANDLE  CreateFileA (
2 LPCSTR                FileName ,
3 DWORD                 DesiredAccess ,
4 DWORD                 ShareMode ,
5 LPSECURITY_ATTRIBUTES SecurityAttributes ,
6 DWORD                 CreationDisposition ,
7 DWORD                 FlagsAndAttributes ,
8 HANDLE                TemplateFile
9 );
```

Our framework will patch the IAT entry of `CreateFileA` with address of `wrap_CreateFileA` function which is defined in the adversarial code as:

```
1  HANDLE  wrap_CreateFileA (
2  LPCSTR          FileName ,
3  DWORD           DesiredAccess ,
4  DWORD           ShareMode ,
5  LPSECURITY_ATTRIBUTES SecurityAttributes ,
6  DWORD           CreationDisposition ,
7  DWORD           FlagsAndAttributes ,
8  HANDLE          TemplateFile
9  )
10 {
11    HANDLE return_val = CreateFileA (FileName ,
12    DesiredAccess ,ShareMode , SecurityAttributes ,
13    CreationDisposition , FlagsAndAttributes ,
14    TemplateFile );
15    // logic to book-keep API call made by
16    the original code
17    // logic to make smartly chosen API call
18    return return_val
19 }
```

One can make the following observations in the above discussion. Redirection of control flow due to IAT hooking happens to a function having identical arguments and return values, i.e., from `CreateFileA` to `wrap_CreateFileA`. Control will return to the original malware code when `wrap_CreateFileA` returns. `wrap_CreateFileA` would pass received arguments to a call to `CreateFileA` and would store the return value received. In the end `wrap_CreateFileA` will return the value originally returned by the call to `CreateFileA`. Arguments received in `wrap_CreateFileA`, and the return value of the call to `CreateFileA` is never modified during the execution of `wrap_CreateFileA`.

These observations support our argument that when control returns to the original code in step 3 in Fig. 1, it receives return value identical to what it would have received in the absence of IAT hook. However, the execution of adversarial code between steps 2 and 3 in Fig. 1 can change machine state and can make malware behavior unpredictable. Here the state is referring to the combined state of registers, memory and secondary storage. It is easy to see that malware functionality will remain preserved if no state change happens in between steps 2 and 3. Since we control the implementation of the adversarial code, we can control what kind of state changes occur during the execution of that code. We argue that malware functionality will remain preserved in all possible state changes that can happen during the execution of adversarial code by exhaustively going through all possible state changes that can occur.

- **Register state changes:** All Windows APIs use the `__stdcall` calling convention as opposed to `__cdecl` which is the default C/C++ calling conventions. The hook functions also use `__stdcall` calling convention. As control flow redirection happens in the form of a function call and return, both caller and callee will take respective responsibility of saving and restoring necessary register state information at the time of the call and return respectively, and we do not need to take care of it explicitly.
- **Primary and secondary memory state changes:** Memory state can change in one of the following cases.
    1. **Memory accesses on stack and heap:** Although adversarial code implementation allocates memory on the stack, as per the calling convention (`__stdcall`), callee function automatically takes the responsibility of cleaning up the stack. Adversarial code implementation never directly modifies the allocated memory location through pointers. Heap modifications are limited to newly allocated memory regions in adversarial code. Any change in these memory regions cannot change the malware behavior because it would never access it.
    2. **Resource handles:** In Windows, a process owns handles to a diverse set of resources including open files, sockets, special objects, devices, registry keys, processes, and threads. Accessing these handles can change memory state. For example, accessing a handle to an open file and reading from it or writing to it can modify the memory state. So we do not access any handles owned by original malware code, and always open/access/close handles that are not used by original malware code.

3. **Page replacements:** Adversarial code's memory access lead to page replacements which can result in memory state changes, but there is no reason that it can lead to malware behavior change.

Special Case of GetProcAddress(): Apart from directly calling Windows APIs, an executable can get a pointer to an API by calling `GetProcAddress` and then it can directly jump to that address instead of funneling through indirect jump described in IAT hooking. We will not be able to hook these function calls using IAT hooking. Using GetProcAddress is common practice by both malicious as well as benign executables. We are still able to redirect control flow as executables can only get such pointers using `getProcAddress`, and we can still hook `getProcAddress`. We modify the hook for `getProcAddress` such that instead of returning the address of the original function, it will return the address of that function's hook which is part of the adversarial code.

Choice and Dynamic Invocation of an API Call: Our target model utilizes the set of all the API calls that appear at least once in our dataset, which turns out to be slightly more than 300. Since it is a black-box setting, we can not assume the set of API calls used by the target model as part of our attack. Set of API calls used by our adversarial code consists of 200 API calls taken from Microsoft documentation. It makes our attack stronger than that of Rosenberg et al. [15] as their attack uses the information about the set of API calls used by the target model to exploit the target model. The choice of API call remains the same as our feature level implementation. Once a choice is made, the adversarial code must dynamically make that call. It is achieved by having a generic interface which can invoke any of the 200 functions. Following is a snippet from our generic interface implementation.

```
 1  void make_adversrial_call(string apiname)
 2  {
 3      ...
 4      if(apiname == "GetUserNameA"){
 5          CHAR lpBuffer[128];
 6          DWORD cbBuffer;
 7          GetUserNameA(lpBuffer, &cbBuffer);
 8      }
 9      ...
10  }
```

Here 'CHAR' and 'DWORD' are Windows defined data types. One can observe that all the necessary arguments need to be declared (also initialized in some cases) before making the call.

To conclude, our design uses a combination of IAT hooking and a generic function invoking interface to insert benign-looking API calls during malware execution periodically. It is a best-effort approach, which means that though it does not guarantee a 100% success rate, it can significantly decrease the probability of being detected by a target model.

3   Experimental Results and Comparison

We use the following metrics to evaluate our implementation.

1. **Effectiveness**: We use same effectiveness metric as Rosenberg et al. [15]'s work which defines effectiveness as *"the number of malware samples in the test set which were detected by the target classifier, for which the adversarial sequences generated by the given algorithm were misclassified by the same classifier."*

$$effectiveness = \frac{|\{f(x) = Malicious \wedge f(x') = Benign\}|}{|\{f(x) = Malicious\}|}$$

2. **Time taken**: It is the time taken to modify one sequence such that it gets misclassified iteratively.

3.1   Feature Level Evasion Results

To the best of our knowledge, Rosenberg et al.'s work is the only work which has done comparable work. Their work does not show the time taken by their approach for a single example. Our work takes less than 1 s to generate an adversarial sequence. Table 2 shows the effectiveness comparison of our results with the reported effectiveness. We are able to achieve comparable results to Rosenberg et al. while greatly simplifying the method. At each iteration, choice of API call in their work requires taking derivative of the loss function and back-propagating gradients through layers by applying the chain rule of derivation. Compared to that our fraction function greatly reduces the complexity of code written to choose an API call.

Table 2. Effectiveness results for feature and executable level implementation

Classifier type	Feature level evasion		Executable level evasion
	Rosenberg et al.	Our work	Our work
NN	95.66%	100.00%	81.30%
CNN	100.00%	100.00%	83.26%
RNN	100.00%	100.00%	89.90%
GRU	100.00%	100.00%	91.79%
LSTM	99.99%	100.00%	91.29%
Random Forest	-	100.00%	87.36%
Decision Tree	-	100.00%	85.35%
XGBoost		100.00%	81.85%

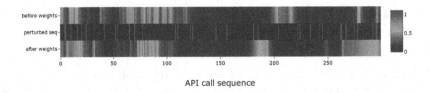

Fig. 2. Heat-map for attention to the input 300 API calls

To show that choice of API call in step 4 of Algorithm 1 is actually significant, we added an additional attention layer to our LSTM network after the
LSTM layer and analysed attention weights corresponding to each of the 300
APIs. First, we plotted a heatmap of one random API call sequence before and
after perturbation by Algorithm 1. Figure 2 shows a heat-map with 300 columns
and 3 rows. Each column refers to one of the 300 API calls in the sequence. Top
and bottom rows depict weights (magnified by 100 times) corresponding to each
API call before and after perturbation by Algorithm 1 respectively. More is the
weight; more attention is to be given to that API. Middle row depicts the API
call sequence where each red column corresponds to perturbed API call inserted
by Algorithm. One can observe that perturbation leads to a change in attention, and noticeable attention is given to perturbed APIs. To back our claim,
we empirically analysed 3000 perturbed API call sequences to know how important the target model considers perturbed API calls. We find that the average
proportion of perturbed API calls in the perturbed sequence is 23.6%. But if
we only consider top 10% API calls based on the importance, the proportion of
perturbed API calls increases to 32.5%, i.e., we see 37% rise in the proportion
of perturbed API calls.

3.2 Executable Level Evasion Results

An executable, whether malicious or benign, contains quite a lot of conditional
jump instructions whose branching decision is made at run time. We find that
there are conditional jumps in a typical malware whose jump decision depends
on a number of factors, including operating system version, the value of a particular registry entry, or the presence of a particular vulnerability. These conditions
will vary across different execution environments across different systems, which
would result in variation in the overall API call sequence across different executions. Our work does not make any such assumptions and works well even
if API call sequence changes significantly. Also, our approach uses elementary
mathematics, which is primitive enough to attach to malware binaries without
introducing severe bugs.

Our results are shown in Table 2. To summarize, the attack is not as effective
at the executable level because of the way we added API calls. In feature level,
we are completely unconstrained and can add API calls at any given location,
and we can keep on adding API calls in no particular sequence till we get a

misclassification. Whereas at Executable level we can only add API calls in the temporal order.

3.3   Comparison to Previous Work

We have found three shortcomings of Rosenberg et al.'s work. First, it involves analysing a malicious file in a Virtual Machine snapshot, extracting API call sequence, generating adversarial sequence corresponding to the original sequence and giving it as a configuration file to the modified malware. When modified malware is run again in the same Virtual Machine, it traces configuration file and inserts adversarial API calls such that generated API call sequence matches with the one present in the configuration file. It might work if modified malware is executed in the same machine as original malware. If modified malware is executed in a different machine, it might result in different API call sequence than that made by original malware, and it won't match anymore with the configuration file generated previously. To understand this, consider typical API calls under Windows including but not limited to directory traversals, network retries, listening events. The occurrence of these API calls can change from execution to execution. Also consider variations in different machines, including version changes, or presence of particular software that malware tries to exploit. All these things can lead to change in the API call sequence made by the malware, which could make the behavior of modified malware unpredictable.

Second, in their work, malware is analysed for 1 min, and adversarial sequence is generated corresponding to the original sequence. Modified malware, when run will only be able to generate an adversarial sequence for that one minute sequence and if anti-malware product analyses that malware for more than one minute, it might be able to detect it easily.

Third, their work has an overhead of generating configuration files for each malware under consideration individually.

Our work gets rid of all three shortcomings by dynamically choosing API calls to make at execution time. The simplicity of the code (argmax over fraction function) to choose API call in Algorithm 1 makes it possible to put it directly as a part of executable and invoking it whenever an adversarial API call needs to be chosen rather than relying on configuration files. Also, adversarial sequences will keep on generating till malware is running, unlike their work, which would stop generating adversarial sequence after 1 min or so.

3.4   Adversarial Retraining

Retraining on adversarially crafted inputs has shown to defend against such evasive techniques in previous works. Adversarially crafted inputs are generated against target classifier, and target classifier is retrained using these inputs. To evaluate our models against adversarial retraining, we add 3,000 adversarial sequences to our original training set. We retrain our target models using the updated training set. We evaluate adversarially trained models against another test set of 5,000 adversarially crafted sequences made by modified malware.

Table 3 shows the results. Retraining on adversarial examples work turns out to be effective in our case. Our attack is based on the frequency analysis, which can be done in many other ways. For adversarial retraining to work, it has to know all such techniques or at least similar techniques. Adversarial retraining might not work if frequency analysis is done differently for training and testing.

Table 3. Evasion effectiveness after adversarial retraining

Classifier type	Effectiveness
NN	0.00%
CNN	0.00%
RNN	0.04%
GRU	0.00%
LSTM	0.00%
Random Forest	0.00%
Decision Tree	0.00%
XGBoost	0.00%

4   Related Work

In [7], the authors use a machine learning model that uses a binary feature vector corresponding to API calls made by the executable being classified. They use a linear classifier. The evader changes the feature vector at a cost measured by the number of values changed in the binary vector. Their classifier does not consider API call sequences but only the use of an API as a feature. However, they mention that other types of features such as call sequences can be similarly considered for evasion. They show that as they increase the number of changes done by the evader to the feature vector, the evasion rate increases and the classifier accuracy comes down from 95% to 43%. To enhance the robustness of their classifier against this kind of attacks, they reformulate their classification problem with a regularization term and show that an evader's success rate drastically reduces at a given evasion cost. Our work shows the success of our evasion techniques for both linear classifiers and non-linear ones, including deep network architectures.

In [8], four commercial anti-virus products, and two machine learning based malware classifiers were put to the test against evasion techniques including byte sequence occlusion by replacing byte sequences in malware by sequences from benign-ware and replacing shellcode by return-oriented programming. They show that such modifications can mislead binary n-gram based classifier and deep convolutional network-based classifiers. However, their evasions were more misleading for anti-virus products than the machine learning based classifiers.

Their goal was not to find effective evasion techniques but to create a framework to compare various anti-malware products against evasive adversaries.

In [10], the authors use the insertion of byte sequences in the malware and successfully evade the convolutional network-based classifier with an evasion rate of 99.21%. Since the modifications are at the end of the binary file or unused parts of sections and found through fast gradient sign method after embedding of the byte sequence of the binary to a differential domain, their success rate in evading is above 99%. However, this method will only work for CNN or similar classifier - not likely to succeed in linear classifiers. They show that the convolution activations move away from malware features to the added byte sequences while processing the modified malware - which leads to the success of evasion.

In [18] authors introduce a genetic algorithm based modification of PDF files infected with malware using features from benign pdf files - and get a 100% evasion against two well known successful classifiers for detecting PDF malware. For every step of modification, they check that they do not lose the malicious functionality of the file.

In [4], authors use a reinforcement learning based evader - defender game-like setting to achieve evasion, but their evasion rate is low (around 15–25% evasion rate). They only manipulate static features such as section names, section deletion, adding phantom library functions in the import address table, etc.

Kreuk et al. [9] generate adversarial examples for a whole binary classifier. Such classifier takes a byte sequence of executables as inputs. The authors modify byte values by restricting modifications to a new section of some bytes in the executable. These bytes do not take part in the execution of malware in any way. Although they achieve a misclassification rate of 100%, such an attack might be easy to circumvent by removing unused sections from the executable.

In [16], the authors talk about distillation defense, ensemble defense, and weight decay defenses. The ensemble defense seems to work the best for them. However, in our work, since evasion seems to mislead all kinds of classifiers, it is unlikely to be defeated by ensemble defense.

All the previous work try to evade detection for classifiers based on static features. To the best of our knowledge, Rosenberg et al. [15] is the first work that evades detection by malware classifiers trained on dynamic features. We consider attacks targeting dynamic features based malware classifiers more severe than static features as static features based models can also be evaded by polymorphic and metamorphic techniques. Our work targets model trained using API call sequence made during the execution of Windows executables. We successfully modify the sequence such that the modified sequence will be classified as benign. This work, like most of the other works, restricts itself to only additive modifications to features. Apart from the limitations described individually, a lot of the work, except Rosenberg et al., has a common limitation that writers do not back the validity of their approach by actually modifying malware and limits their experiments on only extracted features. An adversarial scheme's credibility lies in whether a malware running in a target detection environment, can reproduce the modified feature level behavior or not. Anything can go wrong while modifying the executable and things that seem feasible while working with abstract features might not even be possible to reproduce by modifying executable.

On the other hand, Rosenberg et al.'s work has a severe hidden assumption that target execution environment is completely known in their black-box setting. Dynamic behavior of malware can change due to changes in execution environment including a change in operating system version, change in registry keys and its corresponding values, presence or absence of some software component (e.g., whether macros are enabled in Microsoft Office), or content of any file that malware is accessing. Their attack will easily fail if such changes occur. Secondly, their work also depends on a configuration file which needs to be changed for each new malware.

In conclusion, our work addresses the following challenges which are not addressed by Rosenberg et al.'s work. Firstly, an adversarial attack must be resilient to a slight change in the target execution environment, which includes changes in operating system version, presence, absence or slight modification in registry keys, presence or absence of a particular software (e.g. Microsoft Office) or any kind of change that can result in the change of the API call sequence. Secondly, An adversarial attack implementation should be generic and should not require any specific change for different malware. Our work addresses these issues, and present an attack in a stronger black-box environment than the one assumed by Rosenberg et al.'s work.

5   Conclusion and Future Work

In this work, we demonstrate an attack that can evade API call sequence based malware classifiers. To perform this attack, we generate eight target machine learning models that use dynamic features based on API call sequences. The models are trained using 300 API call sequences. We present two categories of evasion techniques on the target models. One is feature level evasion, and the other is executable level evasion. For feature level evasion the effectiveness of the attack on all target models is 100%, and for executable level evasion, the highest effectiveness of the attack is 91.79%. In our work, we also implement a defense mechanism for evasion attacks using adversarial retraining for all the eight models. Similar techniques can be applied to evade classifiers that use features other than API call sequences. A unified framework can be developed that can modify malware to evade detection from multiple types of classifiers by mimicking benign behavior. Future work involves making malware detection schemes robust to such mimicry attacks. All the code and dataset are available upon request from the authors for artifact validation.

References

1. Keras: The python deep learning library (2019). https://keras.io/
2. scikit-learn: Machine learning in python (2019). https://scikit-learn.org/stable/

3. Akhtar, N., Mian, A.: Threat of adversarial attacks on deep learning in computer vision: a survey. IEEE Access **6**, 14410–14430 (2018)
4. Anderson, H.S., Kharkar, A., Filar, B., Roth, P.: Evading Machine Learning Malware Detection. Black Hat, Las Vegas (2017)
5. Arp, D., Spreitzenbarth, M., Hubner, M., Gascon, H., Rieck, K., Siemens, C.: Drebin: effective and explainable detection of android malware in your pocket. In: NDSS, vol. 14, pp. 23–26 (2014)
6. Backes, M., Manoharan, P., Grosse, K., Papernot, N.: Adversarial perturbations against deep neural networks for malware classification. The Computing Research Repository (CoRR) (2016)
7. Chen, L., Ye, Y., Bourlai, T.: Adversarial machine learning in malware detection: arms race between evasion attack and defense. In: 2017 European Intelligence and Security Informatics Conference (EISIC), pp. 99–106. IEEE (2017)
8. Fleshman, W., Raff, E., Zak, R., McLean, M., Nicholas, C.: Static malware detection and subterfuge: Quantifying the robustness of machine learning and current anti-virus. In: 2018 13th International Conference on Malicious and Unwanted Software (MALWARE), pp. 1–10. IEEE (2018)
9. Kreuk, F., Barak, A., Aviv-Reuven, S., Baruch, M., Pinkas, B., Keshet, J.: Adversarial examples on discrete sequences for beating whole-binary malware detection. arXiv preprint arXiv:1802.04528 (2018)
10. Kreuk, F., Barak, A., Aviv-Reuven, S., Baruch, M., Pinkas, B., Keshet, J.: Deceiving end-to-end deep learning malware detectors using adversarial examples. arXiv preprint arXiv:1802.04528 (2018)
11. Malshare (2019). https://malshare.com/
12. Mohali, C.: (2019). https://cdac.in/index.aspx?id=mohali
13. Nachenberg, C., Seshadri, V., Ramzan, Z.: An analysis of real-world effectiveness of reputation-based security. In: Proceedings of the Virus Bulletin Conference (VB) (2010)
14. Paudice, A., Muñoz-González, L., Gyorgy, A., Lupu, E.C.: Detection of adversarial training examples in poisoning attacks through anomaly detection. arXiv preprint arXiv:1802.03041 (2018)
15. Rosenberg, I., Shabtai, A., Rokach, L., Elovici, Y.: Generic black-box end-to-end attack against state of the art API call based malware classifiers. In: Bailey, M., Holz, T., Stamatogiannakis, M., Ioannidis, S. (eds.) RAID 2018. LNCS, vol. 11050, pp. 490–510. Springer, Cham (2018). https://doi.org/10.1007/978-3-030-00470-5_23
16. Stokes, J.W., Wang, D., Marinescu, M., Marino, M., Bussone, B.: Attack and defense of dynamic analysis-based, adversarial neural malware detection models. In: MILCOM 2018–2018 IEEE Military Communications Conference (MILCOM), pp. 1–8. IEEE (2018)
17. VirusShare (2019). https://virusshare.com/
18. Xu, W., Qi, Y., Evans, D.: Automatically evading classifiers, pp. 21–24 (2016)
19. Zade, H.: Persistent IAT hooking (2018). https://github.com/hasherezade/IAT_patcher

UBER: Combating Sandbox Evasion via User Behavior Emulators

Pengbin Feng[1](✉), Jianhua Sun[2], Songsong Liu[1], and Kun Sun[1]

[1] George Mason University, Fairfax, VA, USA
{pfeng4,sliu23,kun3}@gmu.edu
[2] College of William and Mary, Williamsburg, VA, USA
jianhua@cs.wm.edu

Abstract. Sandbox-enabled dynamic malware analysis has been widely used by cyber security teams to handle the threat of malware. Correspondingly, malware authors have developed various anti-sandbox techniques to evade the analysis. Most of those evasion techniques are well studied and can be defeated with appropriate mitigation strategies. However, one particular technique is usually overlooked and can be extremely effective in defeating sandbox-based malware analysis, i.e., usage artifacts analysis. This technique leverages a variety of system artifacts that are expected to exist in a real system as a result of typical user activities for sandbox environment identification. To tackle this drawback of lacking authentic system artifacts in existing sandbox designs, in this paper we propose a novel system UBER for automatic artifact generation based on the emulation of real user behavior. Instead of cloning real usage artifacts or directly simulating user behaviors, UBER generalizes the user's computer usage pattern with an abstract behavior profile, employs the profile to guide the simulation of user actions and the generation of artifacts, and then clones the system with generated artifacts into the sandbox environment. We implement a prototype of UBER and verify the effectiveness of the generated artifacts. The experimental results further demonstrate that UBER can effectively mitigate the system artifacts based sandbox evasion and significantly increase the difficulty for the attacker to distinguish the sandbox from the real user system.

Keywords: Malware analysis · Evasive malware · Anti-analysis · Virtualization

1 Introduction

Malware sandboxes have become a highly desirable and widely utilized tool through which most cyber security teams regularly perform malware analysis. They can provide effective analysis of malware by monitoring its runtime behaviors at various levels. Sandboxes allow inexperienced analysts to identify malicious features, which could not be obtained through malware reverse engineering.

© Springer Nature Switzerland AG 2020
J. Zhou et al. (Eds.): ICICS 2019, LNCS 11999, pp. 34–50, 2020.
https://doi.org/10.1007/978-3-030-41579-2_3

In addition, many security companies adopt sandboxes for unknown downloads analysis [1–3].

However, the arm race between attacker and defender never stops. As cyber security teams begin to rely more and more on sandbox-based dynamic analysis, malware authors have begun to develop ever-more sophisticated evasion techniques to circumvent sandboxes. Specific environment indicators, such as system settings [4], analysis instrumentation files or drivers [5], user-like mouse clicking and scrolling movements [11] and derived sandbox configuration [10], as well as timing attacks [6], CPU virtualization [8] and process introspection [7] could be adopted by malware to identify sandbox environments.

Many of these evasion techniques have been identified and well documented by security teams. Furthermore, researchers have proposed several mitigation approaches, such as state modification, multi-platform record&replay and bare metal analysis, to make sandbox environment indistinguishable from the real system [9]. However, all these anti-sandbox techniques are ineffective in mitigating usage artifacts analysis based sandbox evasion [17], which leverages user usage artifacts to determine whether malware is running on actual system or sandbox.

In this paper, we seek to tackle the drawback of lacking real user activity related system artifacts in existing sandbox systems. One straightforward strategy is to construct the sandbox by directly cloning the real user system. However, there are several limitations with this approach. First, copying artifacts from real user system could potentially threat user privacy. Second, the artifacts in the cloned system would become outdated eventually without consistent user interactions, and it is unrealistic to clone the real system for each analysis. Another alternative strategy is to directly simulate real user interactions within the sandbox environment. Although this approach does not suffer from privacy issues, it is unclear whether the generated artifacts are sufficiently, as many artifacts are accumulated through the history of persistent user access. Motivated by these two strategies, we propose a novel architecture, the User Behavior Emulator (UBER), which employs a user behavior profile to generate "real" user activities. Specifically, instead of cloning artifacts from real system or directly simulating user behaviors, UBER generalizes the user's computer usage pattern into an abstract behavior profile, emulates the user actions based on the profile to generate system artifacts, and finally copies the generated artifacts to the sandbox environment.

The main intuition behind the proposed strategy is that simulating user actions from usage pattern allows to faithfully replicate real user behavior, thus generating realistic usage artifacts. For example, in a Windows system, multiple artifacts, such as the registry entries, the system logs and the cached files, could be generated due to real user actions. Due to the considerations of user privacy, UBER only records a user's application usage times with the tracker software (e.g. ManicTime[1]) to generalize usage pattern. For the application operation,

---

[1] https://www.manictime.com/.

UBER relies on the statistics data from public websites (e.g. Alex[2], Google Trends[3]) and performs generic user actions, such as accessing top sites, searching common terms. Thus, UBER generates realistic artifacts based on specific usage pattern with generic operations. These artifacts collectively present a holistic profile of the system usage pattern.

To avoid runtime conflicts between the malware and UBER, we deploy UBER on one always-on system, which is cloned to the malware analysis sandbox on demand. In this way, the sandbox environment is rendered indistinguishable from the real system. Since there is clear distinction of system artifacts between a sandbox system running specialized analysis software and the real system, the artifacts in the cloned system will become obsolete eventually without persistent real user actions. Therefore, UBER uses a scheduler to perform the cloning regularly so that the artifacts are not outdated. Given that a sandbox-based malware analysis system is usually rolled back to its initial state after each malware analysis [10], UBER mainly replaces this initial state with the always-on system that possesses the most up-to-date and realistic artifacts.

To demonstrate the effectiveness of the proposed architecture, we implement a prototype of UBER with python script. To assess the usefulness of the generated artifacts, we deploy UBER on a virtual machine with fresh installed Windows Operating System (OS), and manually operate the cloned fresh virtual machine as "real system" simultaneously. After running these two systems for one month, we compare the artifacts accumulation process of them. Overall comparable amounts of system artifacts are accumulated in both systems, which indicates that UBER can effectively generate realistic artifacts through the emulation of real user operations.

In conclusion, this paper makes the following contributions:

- We present a comparative study of the malware sandbox evasion techniques that leverage system artifacts indicating normal usage for sandbox detection.
- As a countermeasure, we propose the User Behavior Emulators (UBER) for realistic usage artifacts generation based on the predefined user profile without violating user privacy. UBER manages to create high-fidelity sandbox environments that are indistinguishable from real systems.
- We implement a prototype of UBER and our evaluation results demonstrate its effectiveness in mitigating the system artifacts based sandbox evasion.

2   Threat Model

Sandbox evasion malware usually leverages a variety of techniques to determine whether it is running in a sandbox before performing malicious behavior. This kind of malware would camouflage as "benign" through executing normal function when identifying sandbox system. The ability of hindering malware analysis could greatly harm the effectiveness of current computer system defense

---

[2] https://www.alexa.com/topsites.
[3] https://trends.google.com/trends/.

mechanisms. In this paper, we focus on the sandbox evasion malware that leverages system artifacts indicating normal user usage to distinguish the sandbox environments from the real systems. In general, UBER aims at preventing the malware from distinguishing a sandbox system from the real system through usage artifacts analysis.

3   System Design

To defeat the sandbox evasion with usage artifacts analysis, we develop a user behavior emulation system UBER for automatic artifacts generation. Figure 1 shows the system architecture of UBER.

In the following, we first give an overview of UBER and then elaborate on the design details. **Data Collector** gathers the raw user data (e.g., the web access log) which characterizes user behavior. **User Profile Generator** performs statistical and correlation analysis on the raw data to generate an abstract profile that serves as a generalized representation of typical user activities and outputs a configuration file that describes the user profile. This configuration file is then fed to the **Artifact Generation OS**, which uses the **Event Generator** to create events following the configuration and executes them via the **Event Executor**. Finally, continuous operation of the **Event Generator** results in various seemingly "real" system artifacts in the **Artifact Generation OS**, which can then be cloned to create the malware sandbox analysis environment with realistic OS image.

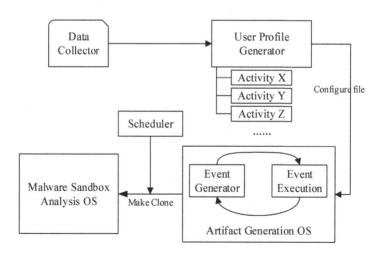

Fig. 1. UBER architecture

3.1   Data Collector

This component gathers the information needed to derive the user profile. First, it records the user's application usage times with a tracker software and then categorizes each application into the activity types defined by UBER. Second, it collects useful information from several public web usage repositories to define the operations of each activity type. In this paper, we define the activity types according to an individual's real computer usage experience in combination with public stats of popular web[4] and application activities[5]. As an example, we collect data from public statistics website (e.g. Alexa, Google Trends) to construct generic user web activities.

3.2   User Profile Generator

This component translates the information gathered by **Data Collector** into various user activities. It outputs a configuration file that defines how the emulation software will perform user actions. Particularly, the configuration file consists of the application and web usage behavior with corresponding execution probabilities, which are derived from a statistical analysis of the information collected by **Data Collector**. These probability values indicate the likelihood that a user would perform specific activities (application or web).

Figure 2 shows an example of configure file which represents one common staff who regularly starts to work approximately at 8am and 1pm of everyday. In this configure file, the web browsing usage of 60 indicates that this particular

```
# System usage (Start Time,Duration)
    onTimes: 0800+0100-0100,210
    onTimes: 1300+0030-0030,270
# Activity type of user (Type,Probability)
    ActivityTypes: web,60|app,40
# Sub-activities for Web Activity
    WebActivityTypes: searching,60|webmail,20|new,10|miscellaneous,10
# Sub-activities for App Activity
    AppActivityTypes: productivity,70|Leisure,20|miscellaneous,10
# Browsers for Web Activity
    Browsers: iexplore,10|chrome,50|firefox,40
# WebSites for Sub-activities of Web Activity
    SearchSites: www.google.com,70|www.bing.com,30
    WebMailSites: mail.google.com,60|outlook.live.com/mail,20|mail.yahoo.com,20
    NewsSites: www.cnn.com,60|www.bbc.com,20|www.foxnews.com,10
    MiscSites: (Pull from Alex)
# Actions for Sub-activities of Web Activity
    SearchTerms: (Pull from Google Trend)
```

Fig. 2. Configure file example

---

[4] https://www.infoplease.com/science-health/internet-statistics-and-resources/most-popular-internet-activities.

[5] https://www.microsoft.com/en-us/store/most-popular/apps/pc.

user will likely spend approximately 60% of computer usage time performing web browsing task.

3.3 Artifact Generation OS

The Artifact Generation OS directly runs the emulation software to generate realistic usage artifacts. Furthermore, to keep system artifacts up-to-date, the emulation software is executed continuously based on the configuration file. This software consists of two modules: **Event Selector** and **Event Executor**. We do not execute the malware on this OS to eliminate runtime conflicts. To maintain the applicability of the artifacts, the virtual machine (VM) running this OS is never reverted to the previous snapshots. In the following, we first introduce the artifacts we have identified that characterize the usage history of a real system, and then present the workflow of the **Event Selector** and **Event Executor**.

System Artifacts. We identify and collect a multitude of useful system artifacts that can be leveraged by the malware to differentiate the sandbox from the real system. Table 1 presents a list of the system usage artifacts used in our experiments.

Table 1. A list of system artifacts

Category	Artifacts	Description
File system	Downloaded files	# of download files in computer
Browser	Total URLs visited	# of unique visited URLs
	Unique domains	# of unique visited domains
	Cookies	# of cookie in browsers
	CookiesTime	# of days since first cookies
	Bookmarks	# of bookmarks in browsers
	Temporary internet files	# of temporary files generate by browser
Network	ARP entries	# of ARP entries
	DNS records	# of DNS resolver entries
	Bytes sent	# of count data sent
	Active connections	# of active TCP/UDP connections
Registry	MUI Cache	# of MUI entries
	Userassist entries	# of Userassist entries
	MRU entries	# of MRU entries
	Registry size	Size of registry (in bytes)
System	System log entries	# of system events
	Application log entries	# of application events

File System: Typically, a variety of files are created and modified during the normal usage of a computer system.

Browser: A user's daily browsing also generates multiple traces that indicate the browser usage history. In particular, normal browser usage usually results in abundant other files such as the temporary internet files, bookmarks and cookies. These files serve as a strong indicator of the regular browser usage, which can be used by the malware to identify normal user activities. Furthermore, the stored bookmarks and cookies in the browser could serve the same purpose as the temporary internet files.

Network: Various network related artifacts are associated with an authentic system. The amount, type and variety of network information from a sandbox system will be vastly different from the real system that has been used to browse web sites, execute various client applications and install OS/application updates.

Registry: The Windows Registry contains a lot of information about the computer system and its usage. Among these, three registry items, Userassist, Most Recently Used (MRU) and MUICache keys, are particularly informative. Userassist keys contain information about the applications accessed via the GUI. Most Recently Used (MRU) keys contain information of the recently accessed or saved files, such as zip files (.zip), text files (.txt) or graphic files (.jpg, .png, etc.). MUICache key is another way to determine the software previously run on the system. Due to the running specialized analysis software and the lacking of abundant operations, fairly limited number of these registry entries are accumulated in the sandbox systems.

System: The event logs of the Windows systems contain plenty of information about the current state and past usage of the system. Event log records various types of events, such as the application, security, setup and update, etc. Considering that the event categories are diverse among different systems, we only enumerate the number of the application and system events to generalize usage pattern.

Event Selector and Event Executor. The workflow of the **Event Selector** and **Event Executor** is illustrated in Fig. 3.

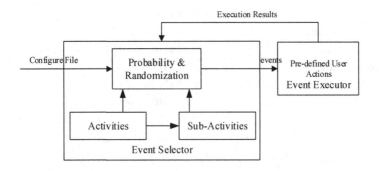

Fig. 3. Workflow of event selector and event executor

Event Selector: This module makes decisions on which events will be performed according to the configuration file. Each event generates different subsequent events which are based on the output of each primary event. The Probability and Randomization function within this module mainly takes probabilities and additional variables provided by the configure file to select the activities and the corresponding sub-activities. This function mainly determines the event to be executed based on the probability that indicates which and how user actions will be performed. In this paper, event represents specific behaviors of sub-activity.

The Probability and Randomization function works by following the Algorithm 1. This function takes configuration file, the predefined activity /sub-activity types as inputs, and outputs the list of selected events based on the usage pattern. It firstly loads configuration file to obtain the probability and average duration of the activities and sub-activities. Then, it selects the activity and further sub-activity according to corresponding probability. Finally, it selects specific new sub-activity based on the operation results of sub-activity. In the above process, we record the time of each sub-activity and activity and make sure these times do not exceed the limits defined in the configuration file.

Algorithm 1. Probability and Randomization function

Input: Configuration file of user profile, $config$; Predefined user activity types, $types$; Predefined sub-activity types, $subtypes$;
Output: Selected event list, E;
1: Loading user profile from $config$ to $User$;
2: $E = \emptyset$;
3: **while** $sys.runtime{<}User.sys.time$ **do**
4:     select $type$ from $types$ based on $User.type.probability$;
5:     **while** $type.runtime{>}User.type.time$ **do**
6:         select another $type$ from $types$;
7:     **while** $type.runtime{<}User.type.time$ **do**
8:         selects $subtype$ from $type.subtypes$;
9:         **while** $subtype.runtime{>}User.subtype.time$ **do**
10:            select another $subtype$ from $type.subtypes$;
11:         **while** $subtype.runtime{<}User.sbutype.time$ **do**
12:            perform operation of $subtype$;
13:            $E = E \cup subtype$;
14:            Obtain $results$ from $subtype$ operation;
15:            **while** $results$ contains $subtype_{new}$ **do**
16:                perform operation of $subtype_{new}$;
17:                $E = E \cup subtype_{new}$;
18:                Obtain $results$ from $subtype_{new}$ operation;
19:            Recording runtime for each $subtype$;
20:         Recording runtime for each $type$;
        return E;

Event Executor: This module is responsible for executing the events determined by the **Event Selector**. Each event performs predefined user actions.

Event Selector provides all the variables needed to perform corresponding actions. The outputs of these actions, such as results returned from a particular web search, are then returned to the **Event Selector** to make a new decision. Once the new decision is made, it is returned to the **Event Executor** module again and the process continues.

3.4   Malware Sandbox Analysis OS

The Malware Sandbox Analysis OS is where the malware is executed and the runtime information is gathered to derive the behavior of mawlare. It is a real-time clone of the **Artifact Generation OS** including the already generated realistic artifacts, leading to the inability of malware identifying the analysis environments. The emulation software should not be executed on this VM, as the software would compete resources with the malware, influence the obtained malicious features and even interfere with subsequent analysis. Furthermore, malware can further evade detection through identifying the execution of the emulation software.

3.5   Scheduler

The Scheduler is responsible for creating a copy of the **Artifact Generation OS** that is used as the malware analysis sandbox. Once copied, the configurations of the **Malware Sandbox Analysis OS** sandbox are also updated to use the most recent OS image. The copy process can be done in several minutes, which allows a newly updated VM to be used before each analysis. However, performing a VM copy for each analysis significantly increases the analysis time and may not be feasible in practice. An alternative solution is to clone the VM following a schedule (e.g. daily) or use a service to monitor the analysis system usage and replicate the VM during the system downtime. Our implementation of UBER performs the cloning on schedule when the malware analysis sandbox is idle.

4   Implementation

We implemented a prototype of UBER on Window OS using python script. UBER uses python packages selenium [20], pywin32 [21] and pywinauto [22] to implement the automated control of the browser and other applications. The implementation architecture is shown in Fig. 4. We recruit several volunteers and collect their computer application usage pattern via using the application usage tracker software ManicTime and then obtain generalized user profiles. Although these profiles represent realistic computer usage pattern, they may not be universally suitable. Taking the configuration file and the data from Google Trends and Alexa sites, UBER randomly selects the browser or application activity and further selects sub-activities to emulate user operations.

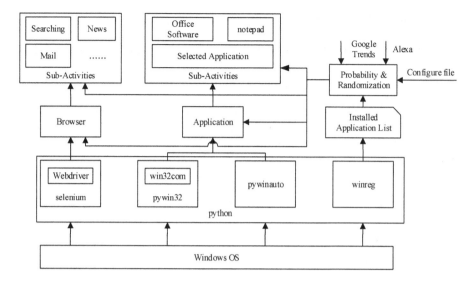

Fig. 4. Implementation process of UBER

To emulate realistic user activities, UBER performs all user interactions including scrolling, mouse clicking and keyboard input in human-like speed. In addition, UBER emulates user behavior based on user profile which ensures the execution of web and application activities in human-like habits and ways. We manually parse the commonly accessed website, e.g., such as Google, Bing, CNN, and BBC, to help UBER extract meaningful URLs from the searching results and news pages. For example, UBER selects Internet Explorer browser to perform Google search. It employs the method "$find\_elements\_by\_xpath("// * [@id =' rso']/div/div//*/div[@class =' rc']/div[1]/a")$" provided by selenium to extract effective Google searching results. Then, UBER selects one or multiple result pages to browser. We also manually parse the GUI elements from popular applications such as Notepad and PDF reader to help UBER perform realistic operations. Moreover, it also extracts the text paragraphs from the pre-chosen websites and then performs text editing using applications such as Office Word and Notepad. To determine the application to be executed, UBER looks up the Windows registry items to extract installed application list, and then randomly selects one.

5 Evaluation

In this section, we first demonstrate the differences of system usage artifacts between the sandbox environments and the real systems. We then evaluate the effectiveness of UBER in artifacts generation and comparison with other mitigation strategies.

5.1 Artifacts Difference

We implement an automation script with NirSoft[6] to collect the artifacts introduced in Sect. 3.3 from the Windows OS. Specifically, we use the script to collect the artifacts from multiple available sandbox systems and real user systems. Table 2 shows the average values of each artifact for the two categories of systems along with their differences. We can see that there exists clear distinction in these artifacts between a sandbox system and a real system. This demonstrates that the identified artifacts can serve as strong indicators of the sandbox environment, which can be exploited by the malware to differentiate a sandbox from the real system.

5.2 Measurement

To assess the effectiveness of UBER in defeating artifacts analysis-based sandbox evasion, we extracted the artifacts from several VMs with fresh installations of Windows OSes as baseline. They include Windows 10, Windows 7, Windows Vista, Windows 8, Windows 8.1 and Windows XP, which covers all available Windows versions commonly used by normal users, according to a recent statistical report [19]. In this experiment, the host system is a PC installing Ubuntu 18.04 LTS, and is featured with Intel Xeon(R) E5-2620 CPU @ 2.40GHz x 12 and 16 GB memory. The VMs are deployed using VirtualBox 6.0, each of which is configured with 3 vCPUs and 4GB memory.

The objective of this experiment is to demonstrate that the artifact values from the sandbox systems are indistinguishable from the real systems once we deploy UBER in the sandboxes. Specifically, We deploy UBER on the VMs with freshly installed OSes, which serve as the sandbox systems as previously mentioned. As for comparison, we manually operate another set of cloned VMs that represent "real systems" with normal user access. We then continuously run these machines for one month and use our automatic script to calculate the artifacts values from these systems. The results are summarized in Table 3. We observe that the sandbox systems with UBER deployed have comparable amount of artifacts accumulated as real systems we manually access. Although there is variation of the artifact values between these two systems, they both possess realistic usage artifacts. In particular, the values of "CookiesTime" and "Arp Entries" in both systems are the same since they are created on the same day and stay in the same LAN network. In Table 3, the "Cookies" and "DNS Records" may be quite different among these two systems, this is mainly caused by that UBER accesses different URLs from real users. However, the malware cannot identify sandbox environment only through the different of URL access pattern because of it exists huge difference among different users. In conclusion, UBER is able to faithfully emulate real user operations and generate realistic artifacts in the sandboxes to make them indistinguishable from real systems.

---

[6] https://www.nirsoft.net/.

Table 2. Artifacts difference between Sandbox and Real System

Artifacts	Sandbox	Real systems	Difference
Downloaded files	0	27	27
Total URLs visited	3	301	298
Unique domains	1	55	54
Cookies	0	71	71
CookiesTime	N/A	310	310
Bookmarks	0	921	921
Temporary internet files	0	851	851
Arp entries	0	13	13
DNS records	0	44	44
Bytes sent	2,731,035	43,007,337	40,276,302
Active connections	8	54	46
MUI cache	2	211	209
Userassist entries	33	62	29
MRU entries	57	433	376
Registry size	52,521,688	73,218,690	20,697,002
System log entries	774	1715	841
Application log entries	293	1290	997

Table 3. Artifacts comparison between baseline, baseline with UBER and baseline with user operation

Artifacts	Baseline	Baseline + User operation	Baseline + UBER
Downloaded files	0	27	34
Total URLs visited	3	1786	1766
Unique domains	1	373	354
Cookies	5	31	55
CookiesTime	0.8	30	30
Bookmarks	0	151	164
Temporary internet files	19	57	55
Arp entries	8	8	8
DNS records	8	10	14
Bytes sent	2,124,684	5,225,592	5,012,932
Active connections	6	50	46
MUI cache	14	26	24
Userassist entries	43	73	74
MRU entries	17	128	136
Registry size	87,030,444	92,026,650	91,356,255
System log entries	813	845	921
Application log entries	694	1124	1208

5.3   Comparison with Other Mitigation Solutions

A variety of mitigation solutions have been proposed to combat malware sandbox evasion. Ether [23] provides a hypervisor-based analysis environment, which employs hardware-assisted virtualization to remove the emulation and software indicators. BareCloud [24] proposes a bare-metal analysis environment, which runs on real hardware devices and is able to provide transparent analysis. It executes malware in different analysis environments to investigate the evasion behaviors. The bare-metal method manages to create high-fidelity sandbox environment by eliminating the virtualization-related artifacts. However, these two mitigation methods are ineffective when encountering sandbox evasion malwares that utilize system artifacts. Due to the lack of real user activities, the system artifacts indicating past user access are seldomly generated in the sandbox systems. As a countermeasure, we propose UBER to generate realistic usage artifacts through user behavior emulation, which is orthogonal but complementary to existing mitigation solutions.

6   Limitations and Discussions

UBER is not a complete solution to counter sandbox evasion. When combined with existing mitigation solutions, it is an indispensable complement to create authentic sandbox systems that highly resemble real systems.

Data Collection. The effectiveness of UBER depends on the collected data. It is usually sufficient to create realistic user profiles with generic operations from the publicly available data. However, if one malware targets a specific individual or organization, generic profiles may be invalid. Defining user profiles of specific targets could be used to hurdle this kind of targeted malwares.

Software Specific Artifacts. UBER generates the most commonly identified user artifacts by emulating the relevant activities. This approach is not applicable to generating artifacts associated with proprietary, customized or otherwise less popular software. These softwares usually generate their own unique artifacts. To defeat the sandbox evasion that utilizes these software specific artifacts, we can modify UBER to emulate the software usage to generate those unique artifacts.

UBER Detection. The execution of UBER in the **Artifact Generation OS** could also leave footprints, which can in turns be exploited by the malware to identify the sandbox. These footprints could be eliminated by removing the python because UBER is implemented all through python scripts. Moreover, the supporting software for sandbox deployment may generate traces. To alleviate this, we can adopt the techniques employed by the malware to conceal the emulation behaviors. In the case where UBER produces fixed patterns in the generated artifacts, we can adjust the installation and operation of UBER (e.g., randomizing the activity selection) to reduce the likelihood of sandbox identification.

Validation of Artifacts. As stated in Spotless Sandboxes [17], the lack of normal usage in existing sandbox analysis system makes its environmental characteristics be very different from real system. UBER tries to fix this defects through user behavior emulation. In this paper, we verify that the generated usage artifacts are similar to real system in terms of statistical features. In fact, the attack surface of usage artifacts is huge. With the evolution of evasion techniques, malware could identify sandbox environment by leveraging a variety of artifacts, or even validating the content of artifacts like the correctness of documents. Therefore, we plan to integrate methods like FORGE [26] into UBER to generate validated artifacts for confusing malware in the future.

7 Related Work

Sandbox Evasion. There is a wide variety of literature outlining both sandbox evasion techniques and corresponding mitigation strategies. Chen et al. [14] points out the widely application of sandbox evasion in nowadays advanced persistent threat (APT). Dilshan [11] provides an overview of the most common methods resisting sandbox evasion. Hassan et al. [12] details one common evasion technique: delaying malicious behavior execution to evade sandbox-based dynamic analysis. Chailytko et al. [13] lists many sandbox evasion techniques as well as ways to defeat them. These techniques include identifying features created by sandbox environment, configuration files, communication channels and other unique traces the analysis software would leave. Aim at countering usage artifacts analysis based evasion techniques, this paper proposes an anti-evasion technique through user behavior emulation, which could make complement to existing anti-evasion strategies.

Emulation. When emulation is discussed, it typically regards to hardware emulation liking testing applications on different platforms, or software emulation to identify function bugs and other deficiencies in software. Kruegel [15] discussed some ways of sandbox evasion towards hardware emulation through virtualization, as well as methods to subvert them. Kaur et al. [16] and Renu et al. [18] both introduce one of the components of UBER, the selenium web driver. In these papers, emulation and replication software is for quality control and software development functionality. However, UBER takes another way and applies these emulation software to trick malware of "realistic" execution environment.

System Artifacts. The identification of historical usage artifacts on one system has been recognized as sandbox evasion techniques. Spotless Sandboxes [17] identified many common, and easily accessible, historical usage artifacts generated by OS through normal user activities. Spotless Sandboxes found that the type of activities conducted on a sandbox OS varies greatly from a typical system, so do the generated artifacts. UBER follows this idea and tries to make up this defects by generating "real" historical artifacts through user activities emulation based on predefined usage pattern.

8   Conclusion

With the widely application of sandbox-based malware analysis, ever-more sophisticated evasion techniques have been developed by malware authors to evade the sandbox. Among them, one effective approach is to leverage various artifacts generated during the normal usage of a system, which cannot be mitigated by state-of-the-art defense strategies. In this paper, we investigate the useful system artifacts and propose a novel anti-evasion system UBER, which can effectively generate realistic usage artifacts based on predefined user profile. We implement a prototype of UBER and our evaluation indicates that UBER can generate artifacts through user behavior emulation. We do not intend to defeat all sandbox evasion techniques with UBER. Nevertheless, UBER serves as an essential supplement to the existing anti-evasion arsenal. Furthermore, UBER is flexible to leverage tailored user behavior data to construct user profiles of specific individuals or organizations, which can further improve its capability of handling increasingly sophisticated and targeted sandbox evasion techniques. In the future, we plan to integrate UBER into real-world malware analysis systems (e.g., Cuckoo Sandbox [25]) to build up high-fidelity sandbox environment.

Acknowledgements. This work is partially supported by ONR grants N00014-16-1-3214, N00014-16-1-3216, and N00014-18-2893.

References

1. McAfee Advanced Threat Defense, Advanced detection for stealthy, zero-day malware. https://www.mcafee.com/enterprise/en-us/products/advanced-threat-defense.html. Accessed 14 Aug 2019
2. Symantec Content - Malware Analysis, Detect and block advanced threats that elude traditional analysis with multiple-layer inspection and customizable sandboxing. https://www.symantec.com/products/atp-content-malware-analysis. Accessed 14 Aug 2019
3. FireEye Malware Analysis, Safely execute and analyze malware in a secure environment. https://www.fireeye.com/solutions/malware-analysis.html. Accessed 14 Aug 2019
4. Lindorfer, M., Kolbitsch, C., Milani Comparetti, P.: Detecting environment-sensitive malware. In: Sommer, R., Balzarotti, D., Maier, G. (eds.) RAID 2011. LNCS, vol. 6961, pp. 338–357. Springer, Heidelberg (2011). https://doi.org/10.1007/978-3-642-23644-0_18
5. Chen, X., Andersen, J., Mao, Z.M., Bailey, M., Nazario, J.: Towards an understanding of anti-virtualization and anti-debugging behavior in modern malware. In 2008 IEEE International Conference on Dependable Systems and Networks With FTCS and DCC (DSN), pp. 177–186. IEEE (2008)
6. Brengel, M., Backes, M., Rossow, C.: Detecting hardware-assisted virtualization. In: Caballero, J., Zurutuza, U., Rodríguez, R.J. (eds.) DIMVA 2016. LNCS, vol. 9721, pp. 207–227. Springer, Cham (2016). https://doi.org/10.1007/978-3-319-40667-1_11

7. Blackthorne, J., Bulazel, A., Fasano, A., Biernat, P., Yener, B.: AVLeak: finger-printing antivirus emulators through black-box testing. In: 10th USENIX Work-shop on Offensive Technologies (WOOT 16) (2016)
8. Alwabel, A., Shi, H., Bartlett, G., Mirkovic, J.: Safe and automated live malware experimentation on public testbeds. In: 7th Workshop on Cyber Security Experimentation and Test (CSET 14) (2014)
9. Bulazel, A., Yener, B.: A survey on automated dynamic malware analysis evasion and counter-evasion: PC, mobile, and web. In: Proceedings of the 1st Reversing and Offensive-Oriented Trends Symposium, p. 2. ACM (2017)
10. Yokoyama, A., et al.: SandPrint: fingerprinting malware sandboxes to provide intelligence for sandbox evasion. In: Monrose, F., Dacier, M., Blanc, G., Garcia-Alfaro, J. (eds.) RAID 2016. LNCS, vol. 9854, pp. 165–187. Springer, Cham (2016). https://doi.org/10.1007/978-3-319-45719-2_8
11. Keragala, D.: Detecting malware and sandbox evasion techniques. SANS Inst. InfoSec Read. Room **16**, 1–25 (2016)
12. Mourad, H.: Sleeping your way out of the sandbox. SANS Inst. InfoSec Read. Room **1**(1), 1–21 (2015)
13. Chailytko, A., Skuratovich, S.: Defeating sandbox evasion: how to increase the successful emulation rate in your virtual environment. In: ShmooCon 2017 (2017)
14. Chen, P., Desmet, L., Huygens, C.: A study on advanced persistent threats. In: De Decker, B., Zúquete, A. (eds.) CMS 2014. LNCS, vol. 8735, pp. 63–72. Springer, Heidelberg (2014). https://doi.org/10.1007/978-3-662-44885-4_5
15. Kruegel, C.: Full system emulation: achieving successful automated dynamic analysis of evasive malware. In: Proceedings BlackHat USA Security Conference, pp. 1–7 (2014)
16. Kaur, H., Gupta, G.: Comparative study of automated testing tools: selenium, quick test professional and testcomplete. Int. J. Eng. Res. Appl. **3**(5), 1739–1743 (2013)
17. Miramirkhani, N., Appini, M.P., Nikiforakis, N., Polychronakis, M.: Spotless sandboxes: evading malware analysis systems using wear-and-tear artifacts. In: 2017 IEEE Symposium on Security and Privacy (SP), pp. 1009–1024. IEEE (2017)
18. Renu, P., Temkar, R.: Intelligent testing tool: selenium web driver. Int. Res. J. Eng. Technol. (IRJET) **4**(6), 1920–1923 (2017)
19. GlobalStats - Desktop Windows Version Market Share Worldwide. https://gs.statcounter.com/os-version-market-share/windows/desktop/worldwide. Accessed 14 Aug 2019
20. Python package selenium. https://pypi.org/project/selenium. Accessed 14 Aug 2019
21. Python package pywin32. https://pypi.org/project/pywin32/. Accessed 14 Aug 2019
22. Python package pywinauto. https://pypi.org/project/pywinauto/. Accessed 14 Aug 2019
23. Dinaburg, A., Royal, P., Sharif, M., Lee, W.: Ether: malware analysis via hardware virtualization extensions. In: Proceedings of the 15th ACM Conference on Computer and Communications Security, pp. 51–62. ACM (2008)
24. Kirat, D., Vigna, G., Kruegel, C.: Barecloud: bare-metal analysis-based evasive malware detection. In: 23rd USENIX Security Symposium (USENIX Security 14), pp. 287–301 (2014)

25. Cuckoo, Automated Malware Analysis. https://cuckoosandbox.org/. Accessed 14 Aug 2019
26. Chakraborty, T., Jajodia, S., Katz, J., Picariello, A., Sperli, G., Subrahmanian, V.S.: FORGE: a fake online repository generation engine for cyber deception. IEEE Trans. Dependable Secur. Comput. **1**(1), 1–16 (2019)

IoT and CPS Security

AADS: A Noise-Robust Anomaly Detection Framework for Industrial Control Systems

Maged Abdelaty[1,2]([⊠]), Roberto Doriguzzi-Corin[1], and Domenico Siracusa[1]

[1] Fondazione Bruno Kessler, Trento, Italy
{mabdelaty,rdoriguzzi,dsiracusa}@fbk.eu
[2] University of Trento, Trento, Italy

Abstract. Deep Neural Networks are emerging as effective techniques to detect sophisticated cyber-attacks targeting Industrial Control Systems (ICSs). In general, these techniques focus on learning a "normal" behavior of the system, to be then able to label noteworthy deviations from it as anomalies. However, during operations, ICSs inevitably and continuously evolve their behavior, due to e.g., replacement of devices, workflow modifications, or other reasons. As a consequence, the quality of the anomaly detection process may be dramatically affected with a considerable amount of false alarms being generated. This paper presents AADS (Adaptive Anomaly Detection in industrial control Systems), a novel framework based on neural networks and greedy-algorithms that tailors the learning-based anomaly detection process to the changing nature of ICSs. AADS efficiently adapts a pre-trained model to learn new changes in the system behavior with a small number of data samples (i.e., time steps) and a few gradient updates. The performance of AADS is evaluated using the Secure Water Treatment (SWaT) dataset, and its sensitivity to additive noise is investigated. Our results show an increased detection rate compared to state of the art approaches, as well as more robustness to additive noise.

Keywords: Anomaly detection · Domain shift · Few-shot learning · Industrial control networks

1 Introduction

Cyber-attacks against Industrial Control Systems (ICSs) are extremely dangerous. They not only cause service downtime or material losses in industrial production, but also have a negative impact on the daily life of citizens.

A notable example is the blackout attack against the Ukrainian power grid perpetrated in late 2015 [20] using the BlackEnergy (BE) malware. The attackers intruded remotely into the computers of three regional power distribution companies in a coordinated attack. They executed a malicious code to alter the firmware

© Springer Nature Switzerland AG 2020
J. Zhou et al. (Eds.): ICICS 2019, LNCS 11999, pp. 53–70, 2020.
https://doi.org/10.1007/978-3-030-41579-2_4

of specific control devices and to instruct unscheduled disconnections from servers. The attack affected thousands of users and left them without electricity.

Another example is the Stuxnet worm used to attack the Iranian nuclear program [24] in 2010. The worm infected the code running inside the Programmable Logic Controllers (PLCs), collecting information on the ICS and damaging the centrifuges inside the plant by repeatedly changing their rotation speed.

These harmful attacks have motivated the development of intrusion detection solutions for ICSs. Among the different approaches proposed in the scientific literature, a popular and powerful technique is called one-class classification. At the training stage, solutions based on one-class classification build the model of the normal behavior of the ICS (the class of "normality"). At the production stage, the detection system uses the model to verify whether the behavior of the live system matches the expected normal behavior. Deviations from the normality, usually determined through thresholds on the classification error, are flagged as anomalies.

These algorithms have the advantage of detecting any abnormal behavior, including zero-days anomalies/attacks and faulty devices. However, real-world ICSs are dynamic and noisy environments, where the processes and workflows are often changed based on new production requirements, and where various sources of noise, in particular, the electromagnetic noise, can interfere with the communication within the ICS. In such a scenario, the main challenges are: timely updating the model of normality upon changes in the production workflow, and periodically updating the thresholds used for the detection. Previous works either do not tackle such challenges [16,22], or require highly specialized human intervention to update the parameters of the model [13].

This paper tackles the aforementioned challenges by proposing AADS (Adaptive Anomaly Detection in industrial control Systems). AADS combines a greedy approach and a neural network to model the normal behavior of the ICS. AADS implements the *few-time-steps* learning algorithm based on the few-shot learning paradigm [2,4] to quickly update the model with the latest changes. The proposed framework employs an adaptive detection threshold to minimize the false alarms caused by noisy communication between the devices in the ICS.

We evaluated AADS using the data collected from the SWaT testbed, a water treatment testbed for research in the area of cybersecurity [12,15]. Such a dataset comprises a training set containing only normal records, and a test set with normal and anomalous records. The anomalies in the test set are real-world attacks targeting the integrity and the availability of the testbed [23]. AADS has been compared with state-of-the-art solutions in terms of anomaly detection accuracy and robustness to Gaussian noise. To the best of our knowledge, AADS is the first approach proposed in the ICS domain based on the one-class classification that tackles the problem of timely updating the model of normality according to operational and environmental changes.

The contributions of this paper can be summarized as follows:

- A neural network designed following the *wide and deep* model, previously used in other contexts [10]. A wide branch in the neural network is used

to efficiently memorize the existing relations between the different features, while a deep branch generalizes the model to unknown relations.
- The few-time-steps learning algorithm that quickly re-trains the neural network to learn new characteristics of the normal behavior upon changes in the ICS.
- An adaptive technique that dynamically tunes the detection threshold based on the classification error observed on the live ICS, hence taking into account unexpected noise conditions in the communication channels between devices.

The rest of this paper is organized as follows: Sect. 2 reviews state-of-the-art works on anomaly detection in ICSs. The problem statement is presented in Sect. 3. Section 4 introduces the proposed anomaly detection framework. Experimental setup and the evaluation results are presented in Sect. 5. Finally, we conclude this paper and point to possible future directions in Sect. 6.

2 Related Work

This section reviews recent research studies on anomaly detection in ICSs. Particular attention is given to those works focussing on water treatment plants and validated using the SWaT dataset, as their performance is discussed in Sect. 5 for state-of-the-art comparison.

Due to the lack of labeled data, solutions for anomaly detection in ICSs are typically based on unsupervised learning. In [13], Goh et al. present an approach based on a Recurrent Neural Network (RNN) and the Cumulative Sum (CuSum) technique to detect the anomalies. CuSum sets upper and lower control limits for the prediction error in each sensor and actuator. An anomaly is detected when the prediction error is outside such limits. Besides suffering from a high false-positive rate, the main limitation of this approach is that it requires an expert human intervention to tune and update the CuSum limits.

Kravchik et al. [16] propose a solution for detecting anomalies using convolutional and recurrent neural networks. The key aspect of this work is the proposed statistical approach for anomaly detection based a normalized value of the prediction error. The normalization is computed by using the mean and standard deviation of the prediction error of the benign samples recorded during the normal operations of the water treatment plant, as recorded in the SWaT dataset. However, the authors do not explain how such statistical properties are updated in the case of changes in the production environment, quite frequent in real-world environments, such as the replacement of a sensor with a new model or the variation of operation parameters of one or more actuators.

The anomaly detection solution proposed in [6] is based on an Multilayer Perceptron (MLP) and relies on a threshold applied to a weighted sum of the prediction errors of all sensors and actuators. Low weights are assigned to those devices whose normal behaviors are hard to predict. However, this can lead to false negatives for attacks and anomalies involving such devices.

TABOR [22] is an anomaly detection solution validated on the SWaT dataset. TABOR combines three different models, namely: Probabilistic Deterministic

Finite Automaton (PDFA), and a Bayesian Network (BN). The final anomaly detection is based on a combination of results from the two models. Also, in this case, the authors do not address the problem of updating the model in case of changes in the normal operations of the ICS. Updating the model here appears significantly cumbersome due to the complex characterization of the interaction between sensors and actuators needed to build the model.

In summary, a common drawback of these works is that they are not flexible enough to quickly and efficiently adapt to changes in the production environment. In a water treatment plant, examples of such changes are: increasing the size of a water tank or replacing a motorized valve with another with different operation modes. Instead, our approach is based on a novel algorithm called *few-time-steps*, presented in Sect. 4.4, that fine-tunes the neural network according to the changes in the normal behavior of the ICS. The proposed algorithm uses a small amount of data to update the weights of the neural network and requires minimal human intervention.

3   Problem Statement

Unsupervised anomaly detection solutions for ICSs are usually built using the so-called *one-class classification* technique. The basic idea is to build a model of the normal behavior of the industrial process and to consider anomaly every event that does not fit the model. The main challenge with such approaches is dealing with the so-called *domain shift*, in which a model trained on a source distribution is used in the context of a different (but related) target distribution. Generally, the domain shift problem originates from a variation in measurements or their meaning across both training and test sets [14,19]. The tangible effect of these variations is an increase of false alarms generated by the anomaly detection system due to normal events classified as anomalies.

In an ICS scenario, we can observe the *domain shift* when the distribution of readings from control devices change over the time due to modifications (even minimal) in the control system such as the installation of new devices, or changes in the operation modes and firmware updates on existing devices.

The *domain shift* problem is present in the SWaT dataset, where we can observe changes in the normal behaviour of some devices across the training and test sets. For instance, during the normal operation, the pump $P102$ has a single state on the training set $P102 \in \{1\}$, then it takes an additional "normal" state on the test set $P102 \in \{1, 2\}$. Also, the probability distribution of some sensors changes between the two sets. For example, in the training set the output of the Analyzer Indication Transmitter $AIT201 \in [251, 272]$, while in the test set $AIT201 \in [168, 267]$ with a substantial different distribution, as illustrated in Fig. 1. Another non-trivial and representative example is the presence of redundant devices, such as the redundant pump P102 in the SWaT testbed. A redundant pump is always off until the primary pump stops working unexpectedly. In this case, the PLC turns on the redundant pump instantaneously to take over the work of the primary pump. If such a process is not covered in the

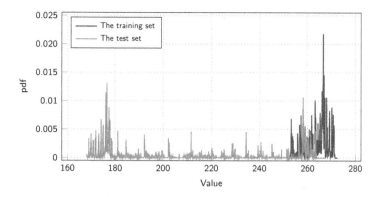

Fig. 1. The probability density function for sensor AIT201. It provides an indication about changes in the normal behavior between the training set and the test set.

training set, the forecasting model will consider the operations of the redundant pump as anomalies.

The characterization of the normal behavioral evolvement is still a challenge for the implementation of the anomaly detection solutions in real-world systems [17,18]. Current research in anomaly detection in ICSs have tackled the domain shift problem by only focusing on adjusting the parameters of the detection algorithms, as explained before in Sect. 2. However, we argue that tuning the detection parameters without updating the model of normality is not sufficient to cope with dynamic environments such as ICSs.

In the next section, we present our solution for anomaly detection in ICSs that encompasses a lightweight technique, called *few-time-steps learning*, which is inspired by the few-shot learning paradigm [2,26]. The *few-time-steps learning* technique updates the initial model of the industrial process throughout its evolvement in the hardware and software configuration, hence minimizing the number of false positives caused by the domain shift phenomena.

4   The AADS Framework

AADS defines a model of the normal behavior of the ICS combining a neural network with a database-like approach. Deep learning techniques are used to characterize the continuous readings of sensors, whose values are usually sampled by a PLC very frequently, while the database memorizes the states of actuators, as commanded by the PLC. AADS includes the few-time-steps learning algorithm to update the model based on the normal behavioral evolvement of the ICS. The detection of anomalies is determined with a threshold that is automatically adjusted using the prediction error.

4.1   Anomaly Detection in Sensors

The normal behavior of sensors is modeled by means of a wide and deep neural network. The architecture of the proposed neural network, shown in Fig. 2 and detailed in Table 1, is inspired by the recommender system introduced in [10], where the authors jointly trained wide and deep neural networks to recommend apps based on the user's query and preferences. Our neural network has two goals, memorization through the wide branch and generalization through the deep branch. Memorization means learning the relationship between feature-pairs in the training set, hence recording the co-occurrence of combinations of sensors values. Generalization means the ability to explore relationships that did not exist in the training set.

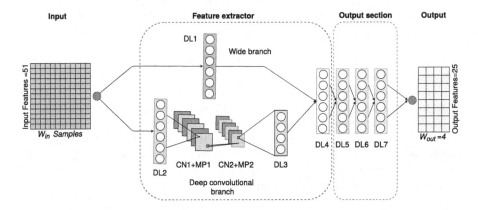

Fig. 2. Architecture of the wide and deep neural network. The prediction of the sensors states is computed combining the information from both sensors and actuators.

Neural Network Architecture. The design presented below is tailored to the SWaT testbed; however, it can be generalized to other ICSs. The SWaT testbed consists of 25 sensors (e.g., flow meters, level transmitters, pH analyzers) and 26 actuators (e.g., pumps, motorized valves).

The neural network takes as input an array X of data samples collected during a time window of length W_{in} seconds, corresponding to W_{in} samples, as the dataset was collected at a sampling rate of one sample per second. The size of X is $m \times W_{in}$, where m is the number of features for each sample representing the state of 25 sensors and 26 actuators taken at time t. Please note that we use the features from both sensors and actuators because the behavior of the sensors depends on their current states and the actions taken by actuators. The output Y is the predicted readings from sensors during a future time window W_{out}. The two time-windows W_{in} and W_{out} are separated by a time interval called horizon H. This separation prevents the forecasting model from copying the last values of the input time window W_{in} into W_{out}, as pointed out by the authors of [6].

As shown in Fig. 2, the neural network architecture comprises two convolutional layers and seven fully connected layers. The fully connected layer *DL1* defines the so-called *wide branch* used for the memorization of the normal state of sensors and actuators using cross products between the input features.

The deep branch provides the level of generalization necessary for correctly handling the events not covered in the training set, aiming to minimize the prediction error in the case of new input states. The deep branch is formed with a sequence of one fully connected layer (*DL2*), two one-dimensional convolutional layers (*CN1* and *CN2*) each one followed by a max-pooling layer (*MP1* and *MP2*), and finally an additional fully connected layer (*DL3*). Layer *DL2* transforms the input size by increasing the size by a factor of three, acting as a feature enrichment technique. As shown in other works (e.g., [16]), one-dimensional Convolutional Neural Networks (CNNs) are particularly suited for modeling time series data. The purpose of layers *CN1* and *CN2* is to model the data collected from sensors and actuators in a specific time window. For max pooling, we down-sample the output of each convolutional layer using a pool size 2×2. The final fully connected layer *DL3* re-shapes the output of the deep branch to allow its concatenation with the output of the wide branch.

Both branches are aggregated in another fully connected layer (*DL4*) followed by a dense output section consisting of the three fully connected layers *DL5*, *DL6* and *DL7*. The output section learns the most relevant information from the aggregation layer in order to predict the normal behaviour of sensors.

Each fully connected layer can be described as $Y = ReLU(\mathbf{W}^T X + \mathbf{b})$, where Y is the output, X input, $\mathbf{W}$ is an array of weights the model learns during the training, and $\mathbf{b}$ is the bias. As per convention for neural networks, we introduce non-linearity in the model by using the rectified linear activation function $ReLU(x) = max\{0, x\}$. Similarly, the convolutional layers can be described as $Y_k = ReLU(Conv(X, \mathbf{W}_k, \mathbf{b}_k))$, where Y_k is the output of the convolution on the input X using the kth filter with weights $\mathbf{W}_k$ and bias $\mathbf{b}_k$.

Cost Function. The neural network presented above has been trained to minimize the Mean Square Error (MSE) cost function by iteratively updating all the weights and biases contained within the model. The cost function computes the error between the prediction of the model and the corresponding observed sensor values. Hence, minimizing the cost, we reduce the prediction error. At the training stage, the cost function for a batch size of s samples (i.e., s different time windows) can be formally written as:

$$c = \frac{1}{s} \sum_{t=1}^{s} \left(\frac{1}{m_{se}} \sum_{i=1}^{m_{se}} (Y_t[i] - \tilde{Y}_t[i])^2 \right) \tag{1}$$

where $Y_t[i]$ is the predicted value for sensor i at sample t (i.e. time-step t), while $\tilde{Y}_t[i]$ is the corresponding observed sensor value. m_{se} is the number of sensors in the ICS (25 in the case of the SWaT testbed).

Table 1. AADS wide and deep neural network.

Layer	Trainable parameters	Output shape
Input – Array of shape $[m = 51, W_{in}]$	–	$[m, W_{in}]$
Wide branch		
Fully connected (DL1)+ReLU	$4 + W_{in} \cdot 4$	$[m, 4]$
Deep branch		
Fully connected (DL2)+ReLU	$180 + W_{in} \cdot 180$	$[F, 180]$
Convolution1D (CN1)+ReLU – 64 kernels of shape $[m, 2]$ – $(1, 1)$ stride, no padding	$64 \cdot (m \cdot 2 + 1)$	$[64, 179]$
MaxPooling1D (MP1) – $(64, 2)$ pool-size	–	$[64, \lfloor \frac{179}{2} \rfloor] = [64, 89]$
Convolution1D (CN2)+ReLU – 128 kernels of shape $[64, 2]$ – $(1, 1)$ stride, no padding	$128 \cdot (64 \cdot 2 + 1)$	$[128, 88]$
MaxPooling1D (MP2) – $(128, 2)$ pool-size	–	$[128, \frac{88}{2}] = [128, 44]$
Fully connected (DL3)+ReLU	$4 + 128 \cdot 4$	$[44, 4]$
Concatenation of Wide and Deep branches	–	$[F + 44, 4] = [95, 4]$
Fully connected (DL4)+ReLU	$80 + 95 \cdot 80$	$[80, 4]$
Output section		
Fully connected (DL5)+ReLU	$65 + 80 \cdot 65$	$[65, 4]$
Fully connected (DL6)+ReLU	$50 + 65 \cdot 50$	$[50, 4]$
Fully connected (DL7)+ReLU	$25 + 50 \cdot 25$	$[25, 4]$
Output	–	$[m_{se} = 25, W_{out} = 4]$

4.2   Anomaly Detection in Actuators

Actuators in the SWaT testbed include pumps and motorized valves. The pumps are arranged in pairs of primary and redundant hot-standby pumps. A redundant pump is turned on only in the case the respective primary pump stops working. This operational mode complicates building a forecasting model that predicts the actuator states, as some actuators (such as the redundant pumps), are rarely used during the normal operations. As a consequence, after experiencing several prediction errors using Deep Learning (DL)-based approaches due to lack of records, we designed a light and straightforward greedy approach based on querying a database containing all the normal actuator states. The database entries are 26-tuples, each one containing an ordered combination of states of the 26 actuators in the SWaT testbed. The database, denoted as A in this paper, is filled with all the 146 combinations labeled as normal in the SWaT training set. An example of tuple is provided in Table 2.

Table 2. Example of tuple in the database of actuators normal states.

Actuator labels	MV101	P101	P102	MV201	P201	...	P501	P502	P601	P602	P603
Tuple	2	2	1	2	1	...	2	1	1	1	1

At testing time, the combinations in the test set with no occurrences in the training set are marked as anomalies, as explained in Sect. 4.3.

4.3 Detection Logic

Given an observation time window $W_t = [t, t + W_{out}]$ of W_{out} samples, the objective is to determine whether an anomaly is present in the sensors and actuators values observed in W_t. For the actuators, AADS checks whether the W_{out} observed combinations are present in the database A built at the training stage. An anomaly is reported when none of the W_{out} combinations belongs to A. In the case of the sensors, the observed values are compared with those predicted by the wide and deep neural network presented in Sect. 4.1. A threshold T on the MSE is used to perform the comparison. More precisely, a sequence of W_{out} sensors samples observed starting from time t determines an anomaly when $\mathrm{MSE}_t > T$.

To reduce the false positives caused by sudden changes in the underlying physical process (as also reported in [16]), AADS reports an anomaly at time t only if the anomaly condition has been continuously observed for W_{anom} sampling intervals:

$$L_t = \begin{cases} 1, & \text{if } \mathrm{MSE}_i > T \, \forall i \in [t - W_{anom}, t] \\ 1, & \text{if } \nu_i \notin A \, \forall i \in [t - W_{anom}, t] \\ 0, & \text{otherwise} \end{cases} \tag{2}$$

where ν_i is the combination of the actuators values observed at time i, while $L_t = 1$ defines the anomaly condition at time t. W_{anom} is one of the hyperparameters used to tune AADS, as reported in Sect. 5.

4.4 Few-Time-Steps Learning

The few-time-steps algorithm has been designed to easily update a trained instance of AADS in a production environment.

The algorithm updates the database A and tunes the output section of the pre-trained wide and deep neural network upon a false alarm. When a false alarm is caused by changes in the normal operating condition of the ICS (e.g., changes in the hardware/software configurations), it can be recognized by the operator and used to update the neural network model. While state-of-the-art approaches need expert human intervention to fine-tune the detection threshold and other hyperparameters, the few-time-step approach only requires the operator to inform AADS about the false alarms.

Algorithm 1. Few-time-steps learning algorithm

1: μ_{init} ← load the pre-trained model;
2: μ_u ← freeze all parameters of μ_{init} except layers $DL5, DL6$ and $DL7$;
3: **for each** t **do**
4:     **if** $L_t == 1$ **and** L_t is false alarm **then**
5:         **for** $i \in [t - W_{anom}, t]$ **do**
6:             **if** $\nu_i \notin A$ **then**
7:                 $A = A \cup \nu_i$;
8:             **end if**
9:         **end for**
10:        l ← compute MSE for time steps in $[t - W_{anom}, t]$;
11:        **if** $l > T$ **then**
12:            epochs ← number of fine-tuning epochs;
13:            **for** epoch **in** epochs **do**   // Loop to fine-tune the dense output section
14:                l ← compute MSE for time steps in $[t - W_{anom}, t]$;
15:                Do one SGD step to minimize l;
16:                μ_u ← update parameters of layers $DL5, DL6$ and $DL7$;
17:            **end for**
18:        **end if**
19:    **end if**
20: **end for**

In lines 5–9 of Algorithm 1, we add the new combinations of the actuator states to database A, while in lines 10–18, we fine-tune the output section of the neural network. Specifically, in line 15, the Stochastic Gradient Descend (SGD) [11] is employed to fine-tune the output section through multiple gradient steps. We calculate the prediction loss for the data samples collected during the time interval $[t - W_{anom}, t]$ and that caused the false alarm. The optimizer minimizes this loss by tuning the parameters of the output layers $DL5, DL6$, and $DL7$. After 100 optimization steps (around 250 ms in total on our testing environment described in Sect. 5.1), the updated model μ_u replaces the previous one in the anomaly detection process. The idea of weights fine-tuning is quite similar to basic few-shot learning [26].

4.5   Threshold Selection

The industrial environments are usually subject to various sources of noise. In particular, the electromagnetic noise can interfere with the communication within the ICS, hence compromising the operations of anomaly detection systems [8, 27]. The main challenge is finding the correct threshold needed to classify an event either as anomaly or as normal activity. Previous works tackled this problem empirically, by tuning the threshold at test time as a hyper-parameter [6, 13, 16]. While this technique produces good results in the laboratory when using static datasets such as SWaT, online systems can hardly afford long threshold tuning sessions for updating the thresholds upon new noise levels. Instead, we use an adaptive technique that dynamically tunes the threshold based on the prediction error observed on a set of normal records.

In our implementation, AADS uses the initial threshold $T = T_0$ computed as the maximum validation error observed during the training of the model with the normal records. Every record with a prediction error greater than T_0 is classified as an anomaly. In a second phase, T is updated by using a set of normal records, called threshold set, collected during the ICS operations. Similarly to what done by Singh et al. in the context of anomaly detection in smart homes [25], T is computed as $T = \mu + \sigma$, where μ and σ are the mean and the standard deviation of the prediction error obtained on the threshold set. In this regard, the mean μ roughly estimates the threshold for the prediction error above which a record is anomalous. The standard deviation is added to reduce the false positives, particularly frequent in noisy communication systems.

In our experiments, we use a portion of the SWaT test set as our threshold set to update the value of T. We demonstrate the effectiveness of this solution in the next section, where we compare the performance of AADS and a state-of-the-art solution by using increasing levels of additive noise.

5   Experimental Evaluation

This section presents the experimental setup and the results obtained after applying the few-time-steps learning to detect anomalies in the SWaT dataset.

5.1   Experimental Setup

AADS has been implemented in PyTorch 1.0 [7] and validated using a Singularity container [9] running in a shared machine configured with 24 shared CPU, 64 GB virtual RAM and an NVIDIA 12 GB K80 GPU.

Prior to our experiments, we normalized the 51 features of the SWaT dataset between 0 and 1. Moreover, we empirically chose the hyper-parameter values based on the results of a preliminary tuning. For the input time window W_{in}, the learning rate α and the dropout probability δ, we adopted a grid search strategy to explore the set of hyper-parameters using F1 score as the performance metric. Specifically, we experimented using $W_{in} \in \{50, 60, 70, 90, 120\}$, SGD with $\alpha \in \{0.1, 0.01, 0.001\}$ and decay on plateau, and $\delta \in \{0.1, 0.2, 0.3, 0.4, 0.5\}$. On the other hand, the output time window and the horizon have been set based on the setup used by Shalyga et al. in [6].

The final set of hyper-parameters that maximizes the F1 score is the following:

$$W_{in} = 60, \ W_{out} = 4, \ H = 50, \ W_{anom} = 50, \ \alpha = 0.01, \ \delta = 0.4$$

These hyper-parameters are kept constant throughout our experiments presented below in this section.

5.2   Methodology

As per convention in the literature, we evaluate AADS using the following metrics:

$$Pr = \frac{TP}{TP + FP} \quad Re = \frac{TP}{TP + FN} \quad F1 \; Score = 2 \cdot \frac{Pr \cdot Re}{Pr + Re}$$

where $Pr = Precision$, $Re = Recall$, $F1 = F1 \; Score$, $TP = True \; Positives$, $FP = False \; Positives$, $FN = False \; Negatives$. Such metrics allow us to assess the overall performance of the proposed framework as well as to compare AADS with the state-of-the-art.

We also measure the sensitivity of AADS to noise. It is worth recalling that industrial control systems operate in hostile environments [21], where the communication channels are often subject to interference (e.g., in the case of employing wireless communication devices [3]). For evaluation purposes we add Gaussian noise to sensor readings of the SWaT dataset with mean $\mu = 0$ and standard deviation $\sigma \in \{1, 2, 3, 5, 10, 15\}$. The noise distribution and the values of μ and σ have been selected based on similar assumptions made in other works [8, 27] regarding the noise in communication channels of networked control systems.

In this research, we do not evaluate the robustness of AADS against adversarial noise, i.e., the noise added to the communication channels by an attacker intending to perturb the detection accuracy. Indeed, the defense against adversarial attacks in ICS is a complex problem, and its discussion is outside the scope of this work.

The validation presented below is divided into three different experiments. In Experiment 1, we compare the performance of AADS with three relevant works in the state-of-the-art in terms of precision, recall, F1 score, and the number of attacks correctly detected. In Experiments 2 and 3, we evaluate the robustness of AADS to additive noise applied on the SWaT training and test sets, and we compare the results with the framework proposed in [16].

5.3   Experiment 1: Detection Accuracy

AADS matches existing state-of-the-art detection accuracy on the SWaT test set, while correctly recognizing 33 out of 36 attacks in the test set (see Table 3). It is worth noting that AADS also detects a higher rate of attacks during their execution (97% against 93% of [16]), hence allowing the operator to activate the adequate countermeasures more promptly. A full comparison between AADS, [16] and the other three state-of-the-art solutions considered in this experiment is provided in Table A.1 of Appendix A.

To measure the contribution of the few-time-steps algorithm to the detection accuracy of AADS, we repeated the experiment disabling the algorithm. As the SWaT test set contains normal records that are not present in the training set, the model of normal behavior built with the training set leads to several false positives and, more precisely, to a low F1-score measure of 0.66. Instead, when

Table 3. A comparison between our results and state of the art. In brackets, the number of attacks detected after their end.

Architecture	Precision	Recall	F1	Detected attacks
AADS	0.866	0.861	0.863	33(1)
MLP [6]	0.967	0.696	0.812	25
CNN [16]	0.867	0.854	0.860	31(2)
TABOR [22]	0.861	0.788	0.823	24

enabling the few-time-steps algorithm, the database of actuators combinations and the weights of the output section of the neural network model are updated with new information of the normal behavior available in the test set, leading to a higher detection accuracy.

The update process is fast. In fact, with our setup, the execution of one cycle of the few-time-step algorithm with 50 samples takes 2.7 ms on average. In an online system, the algorithm can be triggered by the operator upon identifying a false alarm. It is important to stress that this is the only requirement for the operator, unlike other solutions where an in-depth knowledge of the underlying algorithms is necessary to update thresholds or other parameters.

5.4 Experiment 2: Additive Noise on the Test Set

In this experiment, we measure the robustness of AADS to synthetic noise added to the sensors readings in the SWaT test set. In our experiments, we generate various levels of white Gaussian noise by varying the standard deviation $\sigma \in \{1, 2, 3, 5, 10, 15\}$, and we compare AADS with our implementation of the CNN proposed in [16]. Figure 3 shows the values of F1-score and number of detected attacks as functions of σ.

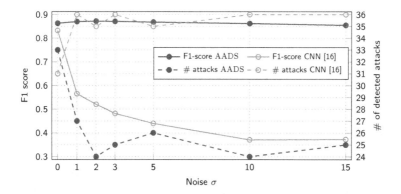

Fig. 3. Performance after adding Gaussian noise to the test set.

The solid line with filled circles in the figure shows that the detection accuracy of AADS does not decrease, even in the presence of noise. This is thanks to the mechanism presented in Sect. 4.5, which dynamically tunes the detection threshold based on the prediction error. However, the number of detected attacks drops from 33 with no noise, to 24 with $\sigma = 2$ and $\sigma = 10$ (dashed line with filled circles in the figure).

On the other hand, the performance of the state of the art approach drops drastically (solid line with empty circles). This is mainly due to the statistical approach and to the static threshold employed to detect the anomalies, empirically selected as the value $T \in [1.8, 3]$ that maximizes the F1-score. The low values of the F1-Score for $\sigma > 0$ are due to a low precision measure (around 0.31 on average), meaning that the CNN classifies most of the records as anomalies, mostly false positives. This is the reason why the 36 attacks in the SWaT test set are almost all correctly classified (dashed line with empty circles). However, as everything looks like an anomaly, in a real-world deployment, the output of the CNN would be unusable.

5.5   Experiment 3: Additive Noise on both Training and Test Sets

In a real-world scenario, the data used to build the model of normal behavior can also be affected by noise. Here, we repeat the experiment presented in Sect. 5.4 by adding white Gaussian noise not only to the test set, but also to the sensors records in the training set before training the neural network. The results are presented in Fig. 4.

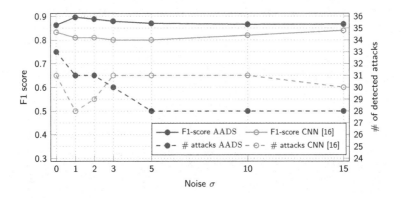

Fig. 4. Performance after adding Gaussian noise to both training and test set.

Adding noise to the training records allows AADS to build a more precise representation of the normal behavior under noisy conditions. The benefits are observed for both AADS and the CNN used for comparison in terms of more stable F1-score measure (solid lines in Fig. 4). However, AADS is less prone to false alarms, with a precision measure of 0.97 on average compared to 0.80 on average obtained with the CNN.

Also, in this experiment, we can notice an increase in the number of attacks detected by the CNN when increasing the standard deviation of the Gaussian noise. Although less prominent than in experiment 2, this behavior is a consequence of the static threshold adopted in [16], which causes an increase in the total number of true and false positives.

6 Conclusion

In this paper, we have presented AADS, a framework for anomaly detection in Industrial Control Systems (ICSs) grounded on the one-class classification paradigm. AADS has been designed to mitigate two major problems affecting similar solutions proposed in the state-of-the-art literature. The first, called *domain shift*, can be observed when changes in the normal behaviour of the ICS are not correctly handled by the detection system. The results are usually an increase in the number of false alarms. The second problem is caused by the electromagnetic noise affecting the communication within the ICSs, which prevents the detection system from segregating the anomalies from normal operations correctly.

We have tackled the aforementioned problems by introducing a fast and automated mechanism for updating the model of the ICS based on the detected false alarms caused by changes in the normal behaviour, such as planned updates in the hardware and software configuration. Additionally, AADS dynamically adjusts the detection threshold using the statistical properties of small sets of normal records. With respect to state-of-the-art results, AADS detects a larger number of attacks and is more robust to noisy data samples.

In a real-world deployment, the operator would be only required to recognize the false alarms and to signal them to AADS, unlike other solutions where an in-depth knowledge of the underlying algorithms is necessary to update thresholds or other parameters. In this regard, minimizing the human intervention without exposing the system to poisoning attacks is an interesting direction for future research.

We also plan to improve the threshold selection method, by studying how to apply a dedicated threshold to each sensor/actuator. Finally, we are interested in extending our threat to model stealthy attacks [5] and in analysing the robustness of AADS to adversarial machine learning attacks [1].

Acknowledgment. The authors would like to thank the Center for Research in Cyber Security at the Singapore University of Technology and Design for providing the SWaT dataset.

Appendix A   Point Recall Comparison

Table A.1. Recall for each attack in the SWaT dataset.

Attack scenario[1]	Attack description	MLP [6]	TABOR [22]	CNN [16]	**AADS**
1	Open MV-101	0	0.049	0.995	0.953
2	Turn on P-102	0.764	0.930	1	1
3	Increase LIT-101 by 1 mm every second	0	0	0.225[2]	0.296
4	Open MV-504	0	0.328	0	0
6	Set value of AIT-202 at 6	0.952	0.995	0.903	0.903
7	Water level LIT-301 increased above HH	0.909	0	1	0.012
8	Set value of DPIT as <40 kpa	0.984	0.612	1	0.969
10	Set value of FIT-401 at >0.7	0.976	0.994	1	0.931
11	Set value of FIT-401 at 0	0.989	0.998	1	1
13	Close MV-304	0	0	0	0
14	Do not let MV-303 open	0	0	0	0.012
16	Decrease water level LIT-301 by 1 mm each second	0.60	0	0.236	0
17	Do not let MV-303 open	0	0.597	0.631	0.539
19	Set value of AIT-504 at 16 uS/cm	0.97	0.004	0[2]	0.434
20	Set value of AIT-504 at 255 uS/cm	0	0.997	1	0.973
21	Keep MV-101 on continuously; set value of LIT-101 at 700 mm	0.98	0.083	0.907	0.908
22	Stop UV-401; set value of AIT502 at 150; force P-501 to remain on	0.978	0.998	1	0.958
23	Set value of DPIT301 at >0.4 bar; keep MV302 open, P602 closed	0.711	0	1	0.954
24	Turn off P-203 and P-205	0.918	0	0.169	0.225
25	Set value of LIT-401 at 1000; P402 is kept on	0.294	0	0.019	0.899
26	P-101 is turned on continuously; set value of LIT-301 at 801 mm	0.998	0.999	1	0.766
27	Keep P-302 on; set value of LIT401 at 600 mm until 1:26:01	0	0.196	0.063	0.547
28	Close P-302	0.0324	0.936	1	1
29	Turn on P-201; turn on P-203; turn on P-205	0.87	0	0	0[2]
30	Turn P-101 and MV-101 on; set value of LIT-101 at 700 mm;	0.834	0.999	1	1
31	Set LIT-401 at less than L	0.786	0	0.303	0.626
32	Set LIT-301 at above HH	-	0	0.935	0.838
33	Set LIT-101 at above H	-	0.890	0.883	0.151
34	Turn P-101 off	0.331	0.990	0.6	0.01
35	Turn P-101 off; keep P-102 off	0.84	0.258	0	0.042
36	Set LIT-101 at less than LL	0.808	0.889	0.878	0.9
37	Close P-501; set value of FIT-502 at 1.29 at 11:18:36	0.842	0.998	0.895	0.915
38	Set value of AIT402 at 260; set value of AIT502 at 260	0.767	0.996	0.864	1
39	Set value of FIT-401 at 0.5; set value of AIT-502 at 140 mV	0.836	0.369	0.908	1
40	Set value of FIT-401 at 0	0.784	0.997	1	1
41	Decrease LIT-301 value by 0.5 mm per second	0	0	0.638	0.626

[1] Identifiers of attack scenarios from the SWaT dataset documentation [15].
[2] The attack is detected after its end.

References

1. A. Erba, et al.: Real-time evasion attacks with physical constraints on deep learning-based anomaly detectors in industrial control systems. arXiv preprint arXiv:1907.07487 (2019)
2. A. Nichol, et al.: On First-Order Meta-Learning Algorithms. arXiv e-prints arXiv:1803.02999, March 2018
3. Galloway, B., et al.: Introduction to Industrial Control Networks. IEEE Commun. Surv. Tutor. **15**(2), 860–880 (2013). https://doi.org/10.1109/SURV.2012.071812.00124
4. Finn, C., et al.: Model-agnostic meta-learning for fast adaptation of deep networks. In: Proceedings of the 34th International Conference on Machine Learning, vol. 70, pp. 1126–1135. JMLR. org (2017)
5. Ahmed, C.M., et al.: Noise matters: using sensor and process noise fingerprint to detect stealthy cyber attacks and authenticate sensors in CPS. In: Proceedings of the 34th Annual Computer Security Applications Conference, pp. 566–581. ACM (2018)
6. Shalyga, D., et al.: Anomaly Detection for Water Treatment System based on Neural Network with Automatic Architecture Optimization. arXiv e-prints arXiv:1807.07282, July 2018
7. Facebook: Pytorch (2019). https://pytorch.org/
8. Goodwin, G., et al.: Architectures and coder design for networked control systems. Automatica **44**(1), 248–257 (2008)
9. Kurtzer, G., et al.: Singularity: Scientific containers for mobility of compute. PloS One **12**(5), e0177459 (2017)
10. Cheng, H., et al.: Wide and deep learning for recommender systems. In: Proceedings of the 1st Workshop on Deep Learning for Recommender Systems, pp. 7–10. ACM (2016)
11. Sutskever, I., et al.: On the importance of initialization and momentum in deep learning. In: International Conference on Machine Learning, pp. 1139–1147 (2013)
12. iTrust: Secure Water Treatment. https://itrust.sutd.edu.sg/testbeds/secure-water-treatment-swat/
13. Goh, J., et al.: Anomaly detection in cyber physical systems using recurrent neural networks. In: 2017 IEEE 18th International Symposium on High Assurance Systems Engineering (HASE), pp. 140–145. IEEE (2017)
14. Quionero-Candela, J., et al.: Dataset Shift in Machine Learning. The MIT Press, Cambridge (2009)
15. Aung, K.M.: Secure Water Treatment Testbed (SWaT): An Overview. Technical report, iTrust (2015)
16. Kravchik, M., et al.: Detecting cyber attacks in industrial control systems using convolutional neural networks. In: Proceedings of the 2018 Workshop on Cyber-Physical Systems Security and PrivaCy, pp. 72–83. ACM (2018)
17. Pavol, M., et al.: Adaptive network security through stream machine learning. In: Proceedings of the ACM SIGCOMM 2018 Conference on Posters and Demos, pp. 4–5. ACM (2018)
18. Pavol, M., et al.: Stream-based machine learning for network security and anomaly detection. In: Proceedings of the 2018 Workshop on Big Data Analytics and Machine Learning for Data Communication Networks, pp. 1–7. ACM (2018)
19. Wang, M., et al.: Deep visual domain adaptation: a survey. Neurocomputing **312**, 135–153 (2018)

20. NCCIC/ICS-CERT: Cyber-attack against ukrainian critical infrastructure (2016). https://ics-cert.us-cert.gov/alerts/IR-ALERT-H-16-056-01
21. ODVA: Technology overview series: EtherNet/IP. Technical report, ODVA (2016)
22. Lin, Q., et al.: Tabor: A graphical model-based approach for anomaly detection in industrial control systems. In: Proceedings of the 2018 on Asia Conference on Computer and Communications Security, pp. 525–536. ACM (2018)
23. Adepu, S., et al.: Generalized attacker and attack models for cyber physical systems. In: 2016 IEEE 40th Annual Computer Software and Applications Conference (COMPSAC), vol. 1, pp. 283–292. IEEE (2016)
24. Karnouskos, S.: Stuxnet worm impact on industrial cyber-physical system security. In: IECON 2011–37th Annual Conference of the IEEE Industrial Electronics Society, pp. 4490–4494. IEEE (2011)
25. Singh, S., et al.: SH-SecNet: an enhanced secure network architecture for the diagnosis of security threats in a smart home. Sustainability 9(4), 513 (2017)
26. Chen, W.Y., et al.: A Closer Look at Few-shot Classification. arXiv e-prints arXiv:1904.04232, April 2019
27. Zhan, X.S., et al.: Performance analysis of networked control systems with snr constraint. Int. J. Innov. Comput. Inf. Control 8(12), 8287–8298 (2012)

Characterizing Internet-Scale ICS Automated Attacks Through Long-Term Honeypot Data

Jianzhou You[1,2], Shichao Lv[1,2], Yichen Hao[3], Xuan Feng[1,2], Ming Zhou[1,2], and Limin Sun[1,2(✉)]

[1] Beijing Key Laboratory of IoT Information Security Technology, IIE CAS, Beijing, China
{youjianzhou,lvshichao,fengxuan,zhouming,sunlimin}@iie.ac.cn
[2] School of Cyber Security, University of Chinese Academy of Sciences, Beijing, China
[3] School of Big Data and Software Engineering, Chongqing University, Chongqing, China
20161638@cqu.edu.cn

Abstract. Industrial control system (ICS) devices with IP addresses are accessible on the Internet and become an essential part of critical infrastructures. The adoption of ICS devices also yields cyber-attacks targeted specific port based on proprietary industrial protocols. However, there is a lack of comprehensive understanding of these ICS threats in cyberspace. To this end, this paper uniquely exploits active interaction on ICS-related ports and analysis of long-term multi-port traffic in a first attempt ever to capture and comprehend ICS automated attacks based on private protocols. Specially, we first propose a minimal-interaction scheme for ICS honeypot(MirrorPot), which can listen on any port and respond automatically without understanding the protocol format. Then, we devise a pre-processing algorithm to extract requests payload and classify them from long-term honeypot-captured data. Finally, to better characterize the ICS attacks based on private industrial protocols, we propose a Markov state transition model for describing their attack complexity. Our experiments show that there are several unknown probing methods have not been observed by previous works. We concur that our work provides a solid first step towards capturing and comprehending real ICS attacks based on private protocols.

Keywords: ICS honeypot · Automated attacks · Private protocol

1 Introduction

With the networking trend for the industry, more and more industrial control system (ICS) devices appear online with little security measures. Today, ICS has become an essential part of the country's critical infrastructure, such as

J. Zhou et al. (Eds.): ICICS 2019, LNCS 11999, pp. 71–88, 2020.
https://doi.org/10.1007/978-3-030-41579-2_5

power grids, gas pipelines, and even aerospace. Computer network modernizes conventional industry by ICS devices, like Remote Terminal Units(RTUs), Programmable Logic Controllers (PLCs) and Intelligent Electronic Devices (IEDs). ICS devices use the Transport Control Protocol and Internet Protocol (TCP/IP) stack to exchange data, but additional security concerns may rise by this convergence. The supervisory control and data acquisition (SCADA) [4] is one of the most commonly used types of modern industrial control systems. It is developed as a universal means of remote access to a variety of local control modules. ICS devices could be from different manufacturers and allowed access through standard industrial protocols, such as S7comm [41], Modbus/TCP [37], and EtherNet/IP [20]. Engineers can control large-scale processes that include multiple sites and work over vast distances [5]. Although some organization has updated their protocols to a secure version [29], the renewal cycle of ICS devices is still too long to apply the update in time. Therefore, industrial protocols used in online devices do not typically require authentication to execute commands on a control device remotely [36]. Nmap [18] and more recently ZMap [10] are used to identify vulnerabilities and characterize ICS online devices by sending crafted packets towards IPV4 network hosts automatically. Moreover, Shodan [3], a search engine that crawls the Internet for devices, provides search services by listing available industrial devices.

Honeypots are commonly defined as "an information system resource whose value lies in unauthorized or illicit use of that resource" [35]. Obviously, the interaction towards system resources is the core of a honeypot. Although most of the honeypot tools integrate the default interaction capability, their main contribution is designing a software framework for users to simulate or deploy the resource more easily, such as Honeyd [26], Cowrie [23], Conpot [28], Opencanary [27]. Moreover, some new honeypot frameworks were proposed to adapt to application fields, like wireless network [40], social network [22], blockchain network [33].

When it comes to specific services, no matter how the framework changes, the library used for interaction is the decisive factor for honeypot [39]. These libraries are the realizations of specific communication protocols, which can be divided into two fractions: common protocols and private protocols. Common protocols set the standard to build common services, such as SSH, HTTP, and FTP. Their libraries are often official and consistent with each other. Specific to ICS honeypots, unlike the fully transparent common protocols, industrial protocols often partly or entirely private due to the customization by various manufacturers. There are usually not official libraries for most of the industrial protocols to build ICS services. Building unknown heterogeneity ICS services consume a lot of human and material resources due to the difficulties in the operation of reverse engineering and purchasing physical ICS devices. Purchasing physical ICS devices to build honeypot is not affordable, let alone covering all the specific industrial protocols. Therefore, there is not enough dataset and methodology for attack analysis based on unknown industrial protocols, particularly for small manufacturers. It is a big challenge for ICS honeypots and this dilemma forced us to seek an innovative way to capture threat data for ICS devices.

Thus, we propose a minimal-interaction scheme supporting interactions on any port and respond automatically without understanding the protocol format. Due to the attack surface of ICS devices, we only focus on automated attacks based on industrial protocols. Our goal is to capture and analyze attack sequences to take the first look at those unknown ICS attacks based on private protocols. As a result, it is enough for an ICS honeypot to use a minimal-interaction scheme. In our experiment, we specify 26 ports, which include default ports of multiple ICS private protocols and some special ports as control groups.

Overall, the major contributions of this work are summarised as follows,

– Designing a novel minimal-interaction scheme for ICS honeypots and deployed seven instances for 418 days.
– Proposing a preprocessing algorithm to (1) filter noise, (2) extract 78 910 unique ICS-related sessions and (3) provide a probability model based on request entropy to distinguish between common attacks around ICS-related ports (common attacks) and proprietary ICS attacks towards specific port (proprietary attacks).
– Characterizing common attacks and proprietary attacks using Markov state transition graphs.

The remainder of the paper is structured as follows. Section 2 surveys related work. Section 3 elaborates on our methodology. Section 4 details our data analysis and characterization. Section 5 discusses ICS attack patterns based on the Markov transition graph, and finally, Scct. 6 concludes.

2   Related Work

There is a long history of developing analysis and interaction libraries for industrial protocols. It is the prerequisite for understanding the ICS network. The first ICS Honeypot project [25] was developed by the Cisco Critical Infrastructure Assurance Group (CIAG). Released in March of 2004, it combines Honeyd [26] and custom Modbus library to simulate a programmable logic controller (PLC). Conpot [28] is a low-interaction industrial honeypot, introduced by the Honeynet Project, that integrated modbus-tk, BACpype library, and customized S7 library. Most of the researches regard default libraries in Conpot as a baseline, either increase the interaction level of specific protocols [6,42] or optimize network deployment structure [2,13,19,21]. As Table 1 shows, ICS honeypots focus primarily on S7comm, Modbus, IEC104, Bacnet, ENIP, which caused by the existence of opensource libraries, such as SNAP7[1], modbus-tk[2], BACpype[3], Conpot-s7[4], cpppo[5].

---

[1]   http://snap7.sourceforge.net/.
[2]   https://github.com/ljean/modbus-tk.
[3]   https://github.com/JoelBender/bacpypes.
[4]   https://github.com/mushorg/conpot/tree/master/conpot/protocols/s7comm.
[5]   https://github.com/pjkundert/cpppo.

Table 1. Libraries used in ICS honeypot

Library	Updated	Language	Related work
S7comm			
CryPLH*	Aug-2014	/	[6]
HosTaGe-ics*	Apr-2016	/	[38]
SNAP7	May-2019	C/C++	[8,14]
Conpot-s7	Aug-2019	Python	[7,21]
Xpot*	Oct-2016	/	[16]
Modbus			
modbus-tk	Aug-2019	Python	[7,21,34]
pymodbus	Apr-2019	Python	[30,32,34]
Bacnet			
bacpypes	Apr-2019	Python	[7,21]
IEC-61850			
SHaPe*	Jan-2015	/	[15]
OpenMUC	Dec-2018	C	[13,19]
ENIP			
cpppo	Jul-2019	Python	[2]

*means the library is not open-source

The aforementioned researches are limited by libraries, and thus restrict the research scope into some popular protocols. To capture and analyze attacks based on unknown protocols, Vlad et al. [31] built ICS services in passive mode to analyze global ICS threat related to Modbus, IEC-104, DNP3, and ICCP. But their honeynet could only receive a one-off request without response. Therefore they cannot be indexed by Shodan. The most similar related work to ours [11] describes the authors' experiences with network telescopes to detect global probing of CPS. In contrast, our work uses a minimal-interaction scheme that does not have such library-based limitations and can complement existing interaction approaches by extending the coverage of private protocols. And we uniquely built large amounts of unknown ICS services to capture persistent connection traffic and gives a comprehensive understanding of ICS threats by describing attack patterns in detail with the Markov transition graph.

3   Methodology

As shown in Fig. 1, this section makes a detailed description of our methodology of honeypot design, preprocessing algorithm and Markov state transition graph that aim at (1) capturing multi-port ICS attacks at Internet-scale, (2) cleansing raw data and characterizing the packets to make preparations for practical analysis on attack pattern, (3) describing the attack patterns of common attacks and proprietary attacks.

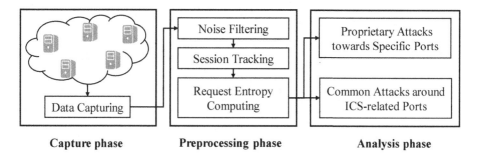

Fig. 1. Methodology overview

3.1 Honeypot Architecture

Build Unknown ICS Services. Industrial protocols run as application-layer services over standardized TCP/IP protocols. ICS devices use them to send configurations and control commands for interacting with one another [12]. The basic idea of our minimal-interaction scheme is to construct the response for each port and return the payload in the original format as passed in the request. Although industrial protocols have different packet structures to encapsulate their payload, those automated attacks confirm the response by matching the ICS header and function code [17]. Therefore, we build ICS services on TCP/UDP sockets with the copied payload. In short, our honeypot generates the response purely based on the request, but not parse it. The advantage of the minimal-interaction scheme is illustrated with an example from the test of an open-source ICS-related Nmap scripts[6]. Generally, device services can be identified by '-sV' command and device attributes can be identified by custom scripts using '–script' command. As Table 2 shows, on the one hand, responding with null will lead to difficulties in determining the service version. On the other hand, responding with a fixed string like 'OK' will mislead Nmap to identify a service as a wrong service type. What's more, 'Null' and 'OK' scheme are both incapable of responding to custom scripts. And Fig. 2 shows, responding with copied payload can successfully deceive automated scripts to some degree. We selected 26 ports for different ICS services. The rationale for this selection stems from the fact that those ports are widely used in a lot of ICS devices and cover well-known manufacturers, such as Siemens, Schneider. Building services and capturing traffic are achieved with individual components for every protocol.

Is minimal-interaction scheme enough for capturing ICS automated attacks? We believe the answer is yes. Unlike the traditional computing devices, ICS devices are heterogeneous and customized by different manufacturers. The realization mechanism of their interaction is often private. It is the essential reason why is it difficult to realize ICS honeypots and why are the ICS automated attacks mostly very simple. Due to the attack surface of ICS devices, most of

---

[6] ICS Protocol Detect Nmap Script, https://github.com/cckuailong/ICS-Protocal-Detect-Nmap-Script.

Table 2. Test results from different schemes

Nmap command	Interaction scheme	Test results
nmap -sV -p 1911 [IP]	No Response(Null)	SERVICE: mtp?
	Responding with 'OK'	SERVICE: zabbix
	Responding with Copied Payload	SERVICE: Niagara Fox
nmap -p 1911 –script fox-info [IP]	No Response(Null)	fox-info: Null
	Responding with 'OK'	fox-info: Null
	Responding with Copied Payload	fox-info: shown in Fig. 2(C)

Fig. 2. Comparison of different interaction schemes using 'fox-info.nse' nmap script

the automated attacks are launched using private protocol, and ultimately try to send simple requests for device information without authentication or get login credentials. The payload header is often considered as the protocol identifier by scripts to confirm the service types. Our goal is to capture the activities of automated scripts and extract the attack sequences from them. Therefore, interaction with attackers is not complicated and just reply a response to prevent the request thread from blocking. As a result, minimal-interaction scheme is enough for capturing ICS automated attacks.

Data Capture and Collection. To avoid loss of potentially-revealing information, data capturing is realized at two levels. On the one hand, raw traffic is recorded as ".pcap" files at the network level. On the other hand, the interaction data is recorded in the log at the application level. Each honeypot transmitted captured traffic to a central server periodically. Having all traffic captured at multiple locations for a long time enables us to gain enough data based on private protocols around the world.

Deployment. We deployed 7 instances to collect ICS automated attacks. Table 3 summarizes our experimental setup and honeypots scattered across countries. In an attempt to make the honeypots popular, we tried to host the honeypots at Internet Service Providers(ISP) providing static IP addresses. Most honeypots were deployed in 2016. The longest duration of our honeypots is 418 days, and the setup was not changed during our experiments, especially 2016-12-13 to 2018-2-4.

Table 3. Setup of MirrorPot experiments

No	Location	Deployed	IP Addr	Duration
1	London (UK)	2016/10/10	139.*.*.*	17 days
2	Shanghai (CN)	2016/10/17	218.*.*.*	10 days
3	Beijing (CN)	2016/12/13	123.*.*.*	477 days
4	Beauharnois (CA)	2016/12/14	198.*.*.*	257 days
5	Los Angeles (US)	2017/01/10	23.*.*.*	29 days
6	San Diego (US)	2017/07/4	71.*.*.*	35 days
7	Dalian (CN)	2018/06/15	43.*.*.*	16 days

3.2 Preprogressing Algorithm and Request Entropy Model

For better handling of captured data, the traffic is fragmented into packets. Each packet contains source IP, source port, destination IP, destination port, and payload. Because honeypot instances were hosted on remote server rooms by cloud service providers, the captured traffic may contain the noise generated by daily operation and maintenance. In order to wipe out the noise, we have adopted a variety of filtering to narrow down the scope of the source host and removed intranet probing and misoperation activities from the traffic.

To infer the attack pattern more exactly, we introduce the concept of request entropy, which used to quantify the concentration of attacks. We formulate and compute two metrics that aim at measuring the degree of dispersion among ports and inspecting how much variety we see in the request payloads. The first metric is the request entropy of packet numbers. Let $D = \{d_1, d_2, d_3, ..., d_k\}$ represent the set of unique ports exposed by MirrotPot and D_i a subset of those targeted by source packet s_i. The idea behind this metric stems from the fact that a malicious source will access a destination at random [9]. Thus, the model estimates the distribution of a port d_k capturing such a source packet s_i as

$$P_{counts}(s_i \rightarrow d_k) = \frac{n_s(d_k)}{\sum_{\forall d_j \in D_i} n_s(d_j)} \tag{1}$$

where $n_s(d_k)$ is the number of packets s_i that have accessed d_k. The second metric is the request entropy of packet types. As mentioned in Sect. 3.1, the payload header is typically used to make inferences related to specific protocol traffic.

We group attack packets by the first 4 bytes of request payloads. That is, the packets of each group share the same header. Thus, the model estimates the distribution of a port d_k capturing such a source packet s_i in the group as

$$P_{type}(s_i \rightarrow d_k) = \frac{m_s(d_k)}{\sum_{\forall d_j \in D_i} m_s(d_j)} \tag{2}$$

where $m_s(d_k)$ is the number of packet types sharing the same header as s_i that have accessed d_k. Algorithm 1 operates honeypot-captured data based on packet-based parameters. First, it extracts effective sessions from traffic flows. Second, it provides an effective mechanism to group attack packets. Due to the request entropy, packets are divided into common attacks and proprietary attacks by a threshold. We enforce the value here, which proved to be correct by manual verification. These two attack patterns will be explained in detail in Sect. 5.

Algorithm 1. Preprocessing and packet classification algorithm

---

Input:
    List of ICS Service Ports, $IcsPorts$; List of honeypot IPs, $HoneyIP$;
    Threshold value, T_{th};
    The honeypot-captured traffic flows, $Flows$;
    (*The minimum unit of Flows is packet which contains ip.src, port.src, ip.dst, port.dst and payload*)

Output:
    Proprietary attack Flag, $Proprietary\_flag$;
  1: $PacketGroup = [Port1, Port2, ..., Port26]$;
  2: **for** $packet \in Flows$ **do**
  3:    **if** $ip.dst \in HoneyIP$ **then**
  4:      **if** $payload \neq null$ **then**
  5:        $PacketGroup \leftarrow packets.GroupBy(port.dst)$;
  6:      **end if**
  7:    **end if**
  8: **end for**
  9: **for** $packets \in PacketGroup$ **do**
10:    $UniquePackets = packets.deduplication()$;
11:    **for** $packet \in UniquePackets$ **do**
12:      $Proprietary\_flag \leftarrow 0$;
13:      **if** $P_{counts}(s_i \rightarrow d_k) \cdot P_{type}(s_i \rightarrow d_k) > T_{th}$ **then**
14:        $Proprietary\_flag = 1$;
15:      **end if**
16:    **end for**
17: **end for**

3.3 Markov Chain Representation of the Attack Pattern

The attack pattern is concealed in continuous packets of Algorithm 1 output. Therefore, in this section, we mainly discuss how to generate a state transition graph based on these packet sequences. A Markov chain is a stochastic process with the Markov property, defining serial dependence only between adjacent periods (as in a "chain"). It can be utilized to describe systems that follow a chain of linked events, where what happens next depends only on the current state of the system. The Markov chain model consists of multiple variables, including the nodes set S representing individual request types, the edge set E used to connect the nodes representing the correlation between request types, the transition probability set T representing the probability of transferring from the current state to the next state. Introduce the Markov process, consider the next state is are only relevant to the current state, but not relevant to the previous state. The transition probability can be expressed as:

$$p(x_{i+1}|x_i, x_{i-1}, ..., x_1) = p(x_{i+1}|x_i) \tag{3}$$

Therefore, the probability value can be computed by the proportion of occurrence number for adjacent requests transferring. Since the Markov chain can effectively model the discrete-time random variables or stochastic processes, we use it to describe the causal knowledge in the request sequences. As shown in Fig. 3, each state in the chain should be a state for the attack process. To describe the process more completely, we have added two new states. The "Start" state represent the begin of a unique attack sequence. The "Stop" state represent the end of a unique sequence. Other states are defined by unique request payloads. The transition between states indicates the conditional probability that the attacker will transfer from the current state to the next state. Moreover, the Markov property requires that the sum of all transition probabilities for a given state must equal to 1.

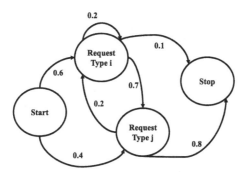

Fig. 3. Markov chain representation of attack patterns

4   Results

In this section, we present the results of our analysis of the traffic captured by our honeypots. In particular, we focus on two aspects: (a) the distribution of attack for each port, (b) the characteristics of ICS automated attacks.

4.1   General Overview

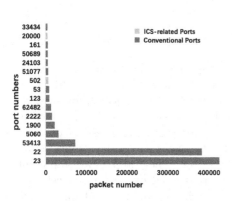

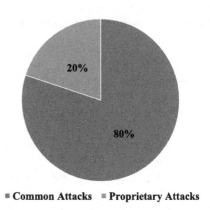

Fig. 4. Packets captured by each port   Fig. 5. Distribution of ICS-related attacks

MirrorPots were port scanned at an almost constant pace during the whole duration of the experiments. Even though only ICS-related ports were exposed, the
conventional probing is still the most frequent one, probably caused by a large
number of real-world objects are connected to the Internet using conventional
protocols. With 89.5% of all observed packets, TCP is the dominant protocol,
followed by UDP(1.1%) and ICMP(9.4%), we total captured 56 643 490 attack
attempts and 1 493 389 of them at least contain a payload. Even though honeypots are not entirely passive on ICS-related ports and encourage connecting
hosts to exchange more packets, only 5.3%(78 910) of them were captured from
the exposed ports.

Figure 4 shows the number of attacks with packet payloads for each destination port (Top 16). Port 22(SSH) and 23(Telnet) are the most active ports
with nearly quintuple the third. It indicated that ssh-based and telnet-based
attempts are widespread in the wild. Also, the third-place port 53413 is well
known as the Netcore/Netis routers backdoor, which is caused by an open UDP
port listening at port 53413 in the router. Thus, it is a strong indication that
the IoT-related attacks are the most frequent ones, probably caused by the enormous success of such attacks against smart devices. Among the top 16 ports, only
port 502(Modbus) and port 20000(DNP3) are ICS-related. Modbus was designed
in 1979 to control and monitor Modicon (now Schneider Electric) PLCs. The
protocol quickly became the de facto standard for industrial networks. Modbus has also been seen in building infrastructure, transportation, and energy
management systems. Distributed Network Protocol (DNP3) was developed by
GE-Harris Canada (formerly known as Westronic, Inc.) in 1990 and was subsequently widely deployed by electrical and water companies. Although attacks on
ICS-related ports are not many, there is still some significant threat intelligence
among them.

4.2   Packets Classification and Inference

After a brief analysis of holistic data, we will now turn to effective ICS automated attacks. We define the ICS attacks as common attacks and proprietary attacks by Algorithm 1, then give an overview of attacks by the attack sources, attack repetition, and coverage scale on ports. Figure 5 depicts the outcome of the execution of the proposed model on ICS-related packets with payloads. Our findings revealed that 20% of packets belong to proprietary attacks.

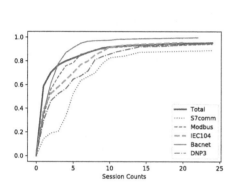
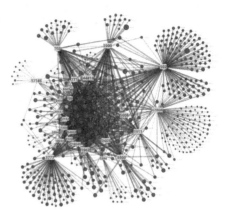

Fig. 6. Session counts based on typical industrial protocols

Fig. 7. Connection relation between source IP and exposed ports

Attack Sources. There are 2710 unique source IP addresses, including 2147 common attacks and 857 proprietary attacks. Although not a reliable indicator (since attackers can easily tunnel through IPs located anywhere in the world), we also gathered statistics on the location of source IPs. Moreover, we found that 90% of the connections originated in China, US, Germany, Switzerland, Netherlands, and UK. Apart from MirroPot locations, major attacks origin from Germany, Switzerland, and the Netherlands.

Attack Repetition. We further investigated how often honeypots (i.e., an IP address) were attacked, as shown in Fig. 6. More than 50% of IP sources appeared only once; a further 30% appeared twice. 90% of the IP sources appeared less than 26 times, hardly one time for each port. It means that the vast majority of attacks are one-off operations, and in many cases, the proprietary attacks in the wild is a non-persistent threat. These observations may be biased due to the total session counts, so we have repeated the measurements on some single ports. Figure 6 includes the comparison of S7comm, Modbus, IEC104, Bacnet, and DNP3 protocols. Interestingly, while these protocols showed a similar trend, these ports seem to be more attractive with more interactions over once. As plotted on the figure, the S7comm seems relatively unique. 80% of the IP sources appeared more than four times, and 20% of them even contacted honeypot more than ten times probably because S7comm is a private protocol of Siemens, the leading German engineering company.

Coverage Scale on Ports. In an attempt to understand the preferences and coverage scale of the ICS attacks, we inspected how much variety we see in the request payloads. The more adversaries vary their requests, the clearer the intention is on ICS devices. Indeed, the previously inferred ICS-related sessions appear to originate from common sources. To prove its correctness, we extract the connection relation between source IP and each exposed port. Figure 7 provides a holistic depiction of the connection relations, where the yellow nodes represent exposed ports, the purple nodes represent the unique source IP, and the nodes/edges weigh represent the number of packets received. One can notice the appearance of a large source IP cluster shared by nearly all the 26 ports, which illustrates that most attackers treat these ports equally importantly. The large cluster may well be the source of ICS-related probing script, who is searching for ICS devices in the wild automatically. Apart from that, port 102, 502, 1911, 37777, 47808, 20000 linked distinctly with there own single-destination cluster, which illustrates that these ports are higher value than others.

Following the observation from above, those sources which have a broad coverage scale on ports mainly refer to some device search engines, like Shodan. They searched Internet-connected devices and shared their findings to the public. Interestingly, 5 of our MirrorPot instances were listed on the website of Shodan and marked with "Industrial Control System". It also demonstrates that our honeypots are effective.

5   Attack Patterns on ICS-Related Ports

Based on the above results, we elaborate on attack patterns using the Markov transition graph. To verify our work, we made a detailed comparison of some results on well-known industrial protocols. Moreover, we extract a large number of proprietary attacks that have not been observed by previous works.

5.1   Common Attacks Around ICS-Related Ports

On ICS-related ports, there are some attacks without a strong purpose, which dubbed as common attacks around ICS-related ports. They can be easily finger-printed and extracted using the request entropy model. Common attacks have no specific destination ports but access ports in a large range. Figure 8 shows typical common attacks around ICS-related ports. Each node is tagged by protocol parsing tools. We found that "HTTP/1.1" was the most popular attack pattern, followed by "RPC proc-0", "TLS SSLv1 Client Hello", "Mongo test .$cmd server-Status". In addition to these conventional protocol request, there are some hex codes, such as "0x0d0a0d0a", "0x446d6454" and "0x48454c50". Common attacks are related to the intention that detect service version on specific ports, because these payloads are very similar to Nmap detection using '-sV' command. It also

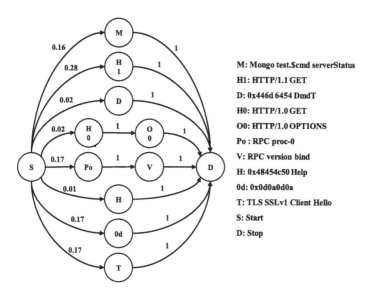

Fig. 8. Attack pattern of common attacks around ICS-related ports

reflects the technical maturity of attacks based on conventional protocols and the preferences for web-based attacks and database attacks.

5.2   Proprietary Attacks Based on Well-Known Industrial Protocols

In order to verify our request entropy model, this section mainly explains the data quality of Mirrorpot and introduces some new findings. In view of the number of industrial protocols and the complexity of interactions, we select two well-known proprietary industrial protocols (Modbus and S7comm) as samples. Both of them can be parsed by Wireshark [24], a free and open-source packet analyzer. By manual verification, we found that the S7comm(COTP) packets classified as common attacks are another type of attack based on conventional protocols, called MMS protocol (Microsoft Media Server Protocol). Moreover, the Modbus packets classified as common attacks are marked with "Malformed Packet" by Wireshark. It indicates that those packets are not valid requests, like "0x5700000000111107".

To validate the capture performance, the analysis results of these parsed protocols can be compared against the baseline: an Internet-wide view of ICS devices [21]. The latter launched 20 instances of Conpot, so-called high-interaction honeypots, to probing activities for ICS devices. As shown in Table 4, MirrorPot has enough number of instances and longer durations of the experiment than the baseline experiment. In every point of view, the Modbus traffic captured by MirrorPot has better quality than the baseline experiment. Besides, we reveal some new attackers' intentions, such as "Read Coils", "Read Holding Registers" and "Read File Record". We can safely claim that the proposed MirrorPot has similar capabilities to Conpot, or even better.

Table 4. Comparison of capture performance between mirropot and conpot

	Conpot	MirrorPot
Duration	10 weeks	418 days
Instances	20	7
Modbus Connections	1954	17353
BACnet Connections	520	1950
S7comm Connections	2778	10382(COTP)
Modbus fuction(0x01)	Captured	Captured
Modbus fuction(0x03)	Captured	Captured
Modbus fuction(0x11)	None	Captured
Modbus fuction(0x14)	None	Captured
Modbus fuction(0x2B)	None	Captured
COTP connection 0x102	Captured	Captured
COTP connection 0x200	Captured	Captured
S7comm system status list	Captured	None

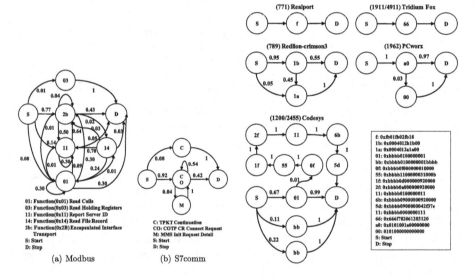

Fig. 9. Attack pattern of well-known industrial protocols

Fig. 10. Attack pattern of unparsed private protocols

Figure 9(a) shows that the typical ICS attack pattern mostly contains several start directions and shares multiple paths, like Modbus. The graph can reveal facts and show the transition relationship of each attack. Take Modbus as an example, and we can be directly aware of the high-complexity attack pattern. The sensitive operations function "0x14" is highly dependent on previous requests. We can speculate that previous requests are commonly used to check devices information and prepare for sensitive operations. Besides Modbus, some private industrial protocols use an authentication mechanism based on underlying protocols. In that case, MirrorPot can not capture the data from the complete application layer. As Fig. 9(b) shows, due to the failure of COTP handshakes, MirrorPot never receives a complete S7comm packet. However, fortunately, underlying protocols also indicate some valuable operations.

Table 5. Overview 1 of proprietary attacks on each port

Industrial protocol	Port number	Proprietary attack identifier
S7comm	102	0x0300;0x0502
Modbus	502	0x0000;···
RealPort	771	0xfb01
Redlion-crimson3	789	0x0004
Codesys	1200	0xbbbb
Tridium Fox	1911	0x666f
PCworx	1962	0x0101
GPRS Tunneling	2123	0x3201
GPRS Tunneling	2152	/
IEC104	2404	0x6804
Codesys	2455	0xbbbb
GPRS Tunneling	3386	0x3201
Tridium Fox	4911	0x666f

Table 6. Overview 2 of proprietary attacks on each port

Industrial protocol	Port number	Proprietary attack identifier
melsec-q-udp	5006	0x5700
melsec-q-tcp	5007	0x7b01
Hart IP	5094	0x0100
OMRON FINS	9600	0x4649;0x8000
Vxworks WDB	17185	0x1111
GE SRTP	18245	0x1a09
DNP3	20000	0x0564;
ProConOS	20547	0xcc01
Lantronix	30718	0x0001
Profinet	34962	/
Dahua	37777	0xc100;0xa001; 0xa400;0xa400
ENIP	44818	0x6300
Bacnet	47808	0x810a

5.3 Proprietary Attacks Based on Private Protocols

For those unparsed industrial protocols, we can not understand the specific meaning of payloads. Thus, we propose the Markov state transition model to describe their attack process and features. Then we can infer something useful from them. As Tables 5 and 6 shows, we extracted the proprietary attacks identifier for each port. We can speculate that proprietary attacks based on various private protocols have widely existed. Although most of them only contain one single attack path with a unique request, there are still a large number of valid interactions for specific ICS devices.

There are various industrial protocols available online [1]. We select five protocols from them. As shown in Fig. 10, these attack patterns are relatively simple. For Realport, Tridium Fox and PCworx, the attack pattern contains only one single path, which indicates that there are not sophisticated script-based attacks or there are some authentication mechanisms for them. For Redlion-crimson3 and Codesys, the attack pattern is similar to Modbus, which means attackers have a good understanding of these protocol specifications. Especially for Codesys, it is evident that attackers have the capacity to find Codesys devices and exploit the devices according to their demand.

6   Conclusion

The industrial protocols in use today were designed over twenty years ago and were initially intended for closed, serial systems. However, despite the lack of built-in security, these protocols have been layered on top of Ethernet and TCP/IP to support long-distance communication, which leads to remote attacks based on private industrial protocols. In this paper, we first design MirrorPot that tracks ICS script-based attacks. We deploy seven honeypots for 418 days to reveal the attack pattern based on private protocols. Second, we devise a pre-processing algorithm for filtering non-ICS interaction traffic and extract unique attack payloads. Finally, through the analysis of the Markov state transition graph, we find more than 20 common attack patterns on ICS-related ports, which contains little unique request and single transition path. We characterized what ICS attackers query for based on private industrial protocols. Similar to the well-known industrial protocols like Modbus, different proprietary attacks launched by various scripts due to the disparities in understanding the protocols. Based on the good performance in private industrial protocols, we believe MirrorPot is a realistic option for researchers to capture ICS-related activities at Internet-wide and a good baseline for evaluating the capture performance of ICS honeypots.

Acknowledgement. The research presented in this paper is supported by the National Key R&D Program of China (Grant No. 2018YFB0803402), Strategic Priority Research Program of the Chinese Academy of Sciences (Grant No. XDC02020500), Key Program of National Natural Science Foundation of China (Grant No. U1766215), National Natural Science Foundation of China (Grant No. 61702503).

References

1. Andreeva, O., et al.: Industrial Control Systems and Their Online Availability (2016)
2. Antonioli, D., Agrawal, A., Tippenhauer, N.O.: Towards high-interaction virtual ICS honeypots-in-a-box. In: Proceedings of ACM Workshop on Cyber-Physical Systems Security and Privacy (2016)
3. Bodenheim, R., Butts, J., Dunlap, S., Mullins, B.: Evaluation of the ability of the shodan search engine to identify internet-facing industrial control devices. Int. J. Crit. Infrastruct. Prot. **7**(2), 114–123 (2014)
4. Boyer, S.A.: SCADA: Supervisory Control and Data Acquisition. International Society of Automation, Research Triangle (2009)
5. Boys, W.: Back to basics: SCADA. Automation TV: Control Global-Control Design (2009)
6. Buza, D.I., Juhász, F., Miru, G., Félegyházi, M., Holczer, T.: CryPLH: protecting smart energy systems from targeted attacks with a PLC honeypot. In: Cuellar, J. (ed.) SmartGridSec 2014. LNCS, vol. 8448, pp. 181–192. Springer, Cham (2014). https://doi.org/10.1007/978-3-319-10329-7_12
7. Cao, J., Li, W., Li, J., Li, B.: DiPot: a distributed industrial honeypot system. In: Qiu, M. (ed.) SmartCom 2017. LNCS, vol. 10699, pp. 300–309. Springer, Cham (2018). https://doi.org/10.1007/978-3-319-73830-7_30

8. Ding, C., Zhai, J., Dai, Y.: An improved ICS honeypot based on SNAP7 and IMUNES. In: Sun, X., Pan, Z., Bertino, E. (eds.) ICCCS 2018, Part I. LNCS, vol. 11063, pp. 303–313. Springer, Cham (2018). https://doi.org/10.1007/978-3-030-00006-6_27

9. Durumeric, Z., Bailey, M., Halderman, J.A.: An internet-wide view of internet-wide scanning. In: Proceedings of USENIX Security Symposium (USENIX Security) (2014)

10. Durumeric, Z., Wustrow, E., Halderman, J.A.: ZMap: fast internet-wide scanning and its security applications. In: Presented as part of the 22nd {USENIX} Security Symposium ({USENIX} Security 13), pp. 605–620 (2013)

11. Fachkha, C., Bou-Harb, E., Keliris, A., Memon, N.D., Ahamad, M.: Internet-scale probing of CPS: inference, characterization and orchestration analysis. In: Proceedings of Annual Network and Distributed System Security Symposium (NDSS) (2017)

12. Feng, X., Li, Q., Wang, H., Sun, L.: Characterizing industrial control system devices on the internet. In: Proceedings of IEEE International Conference on Network Protocols (ICNP) (2016)

13. Gunathilaka, P., Mashima, D., Chen, B.: Softgrid: a software-based smart grid testbed for evaluating substation cybersecurity solutions. In: Proceedings of the 2nd ACM Workshop on Cyber-Physical Systems Security and Privacy, pp. 113–124. ACM (2016)

14. Holczer, T., Félegyházi, M., Buttyán, L.: The design and implementation of a PLC honeypot for detecting cyber attacks against industrial control systems (2015)

15. Kołtyś, K., Gajewski, R.: Shape: a honeypot for electric power substation. J. Telecommun. Inf. Technol. **4**, 37–43 (2015)

16. Lau, S., Klick, J., Arndt, S., Roth, V.: Poster: towards highly interactive honeypots for industrial control systems. In: Proceedings of the 2016 ACM SIGSAC Conference on Computer and Communications Security, pp. 1823–1825. ACM (2016)

17. Li, Q., Feng, X., Wang, H., Sun, L.: Understanding the usage of industrial control system devices on the internet. IEEE Internet Things J. **5**(3), 2178–2189 (2018)

18. Lyon, G.F.: Nmap Network Scanning: The Official Nmap Project Guide to Network Discovery and Security Scanning. Insecure, Sunnyvale (2009)

19. Mashima, D., Chen, B., Gunathilaka, P., Tjiong, E.L.: Towards a grid-wide, high-fidelity electrical substation honeynet. In: 2017 IEEE International Conference on Smart Grid Communications (SmartGridComm), pp. 89–95. IEEE (2017)

20. Metcalfe, R.M., Boggs, D.R.: Ethernet: distributed packet switching for local computer networks. Commun. ACM **19**(7), 395–404 (1976)

21. Mirian, A., et al.: An internet-wide view of ICS devices. In: Proceedings of IEEE Annual Conference on Privacy, Security and Trust (PST) (2016)

22. Nisrine, M., et al.: A security approach for social networks based on honeypots. In: 2016 4th IEEE International Colloquium on Information Science and Technology (CiSt), pp. 638–643. IEEE (2016)

23. Oosterhof, M.: Cowrie honeypot. https://www.cowrie.org/. Accessed 16 Sept 2019

24. Orebaugh, A., Ramirez, G., Beale, J.: Wireshark & Ethereal Network Protocol Analyzer Toolkit. Elsevier, Amsterdam (2006)

25. Pothamsetty, V., Franz, M.: SCADA honeynet project: building honeypots for industrial networks. SCADA Honeynet Proj. **15**. http://scadahoneynet.sourceforge.net/. Accessed 16 Sept 2019

26. Provos, N.: Honeyd-a virtual honeypot daemon. In: 10th DFN-CERT Workshop, Hamburg, Germany, vol. 2, p. 4 (2003)

27. Research., T.A.: Opencanary. http://opencanary.org. Accessed 16 Sept 2019
28. Rist, L., Vestergaard, J., Haslinger, D., Pasquale, A., Smith, J.: Conpot ICS/SCADA honeypot. Honeynet Project (conpot. org) (2013)
29. Schneider Electric USA, Inc.: Modbus/TCP security. http://modbus.org/docs/MB-TCP-Security-v21_2018-07-24.pdf. Accessed 15 Sept 2019
30. Serbanescu, A.V., Obermeier, S., Yu, D.Y.: A flexible architecture for industrial control system honeypots. In: 2015 12th International Joint Conference on e-Business and Telecommunications (ICETE), vol. 4, pp. 16–26. IEEE (2015)
31. Serbanescu, A.V., Obermeier, S., Yu, D.Y.: ICS threat analysis using a large-scale honeynet. In: Proceedings of International Symposium for ICS & SCADA Cyber Security Research (2015)
32. Serbanescu, A.V., Obermeier, S., Yu, D.-Y.: A scalable honeynet architecture for industrial control systems. In: Obaidat, M.S., Lorenz, P. (eds.) ICETE 2015. CCIS, vol. 585, pp. 179–200. Springer, Cham (2016). https://doi.org/10.1007/978-3-319-30222-5_9
33. Shi, L., Li, Y., Liu, T., Liu, J., Shan, B., Chen, H.: Dynamic distributed honeypot based on blockchain. IEEE Access 7, 72234–72246 (2019). https://doi.org/10.1109/ACCESS.2019.2920239
34. Simões, P., Cruz, T., Proença, J., Monteiro, E.: Specialized honeypots for SCADA systems. In: Lehto, M., Neittaanmäki, P. (eds.) Cyber Security: Analytics, Technology and Automation. ISCA, vol. 78, pp. 251–269. Springer, Cham (2015). https://doi.org/10.1007/978-3-319-18302-2_16
35. Spitzner, L.: Honeypots: catching the insider threat. In: 19th Annual Computer Security Applications Conference, 2003, Proceedings, pp. 170–179. IEEE (2003)
36. Stouffer, K., Falco, J., Scarfone, K.: Guide to industrial control systems (ICS) security. NIST Spec. Publ. 800(82), 16–16 (2011)
37. Swales, A., et al.: Open modbus/TCP specification. Schneid. Electric 29. http://www.dankohn.info/projects/Fieldpoint_module/Open_ModbusTCP_Standard.pdf. Accessed 15 Sept 2019
38. Vasilomanolakis, E., Srinivasa, S., Cordero, C.G., Mühlhäuser, M.: Multi-stage attack detection and signature generation with ICS honeypots. In: NOMS 2016–2016 IEEE/IFIP Network Operations and Management Symposium, pp. 1227–1232. IEEE (2016)
39. Vetterl, A., Clayton, R.: Bitter harvest: systematically fingerprinting low-and medium-interaction honeypots at internet scale. In: 12th {USENIX} Workshop on Offensive Technologies ({WOOT} 18) (2018)
40. Wafi, H., Fiade, A., Hakiem, N., Bahaweres, R.B.: Implementation of a modern security systems honeypot honey network on wireless networks. In: 2017 International Young Engineers Forum (YEF-ECE), pp. 91–96. IEEE (2017)
41. Wiens, T.: S7comm wireshark dissector plugin (2014)
42. Zhao, C., Qin, S.: A research for high interactive honepot based on industrial service. In: Proceedings of IEEE International Conference on Computer and Communications (ICCC) (2017)

Cloning Vulnerability Detection in Driver Layer of IoT Devices

WeiPeng Jiang[1,2], Bin Wu[1,2(✉)], Zhou Jiang[3], and ShaoBo Yang[4]

[1] State Key Laboratory of Information Security, Institute of Information Engineering, Chinese Academy of Sciences, Beijing, China
{jiangweipeng,wubin}@iie.ac.cn
[2] School of Cyber Security, University of Chinese Academy of Sciences, Beijing, China
[3] School of Computer and Software, Nanjing University of Information Science and Technology, Nanjing, China
[4] School of Software, North University of China, Taiyuan, China

Abstract. With the spread of the Internet of Things (IoT), the IoT operating systems have correspondingly increased and brought more potential security risks. For instance, it is not hard to find that many driver layer codes in IoT operating systems could come directly from open source projects, where the vulnerabilities would also be propagated. These vulnerabilities could leak sensitive information and even lead to arbitrary code execution. However, existing clone detecting tools have limitations, especially for clones with minor modifications. In this paper, we propose a method that can detect not only exact clones, but also clones with additions, deletions, and partial modifications. The proposed method uses code patches and program slicing to get precisely fingerprint of the restructured clones. Then the fingerprint matching is achieved through a greedy-based optimization algorithm. Afterwards, the detecting tool called RCVD is implemented based on the proposed method. Finally, the experimental results indicate that the method has a significant effect on detecting restructured cloning vulnerabilities. By this means, the Orange Pi and WisCam have been detected dozens of clone-caused vulnerabilities in the code of driver.

Keywords: Code clone detection · IoT operating system · Restructured cloning vulnerability · Fingerprint matching · Program slicing

1 Introduction

Unlike traditional PC terminals, the IoT hardware devices are more diverse, and most of whose operating systems are platform-customized [14]. This character results in a large increase in the number of IoT operating systems, while the codes of these operating systems have high similarity. Considering two similar IoT devices A and B, if the operating system used by A already has mature open source code, then B's author can quickly generate a customized operating system from A's operating system by simply modifying the source codes. (such as the driver layer, file system or the architecture-related code). At the same time, vulnerabilities in the open source operating system code would also

© Springer Nature Switzerland AG 2020
J. Zhou et al. (Eds.): ICICS 2019, LNCS 11999, pp. 89–104, 2020.
https://doi.org/10.1007/978-3-030-41579-2_6

be introduced into B, which are the so called clone-caused vulnerabilities [3]. Although the open source code will be patched after the vulnerability is disclosed, a large number of previous researches [1, 7–13] show that developers rarely upgrade and maintain the cloned codes, leaving great security threats.

There exists a bunch of approaches to detect code clone. The earlier tools include CCFinder [4] by Kamiya et al. and Deckard [5] by Jiang et al. The main goal of these tools is to detect similarities between codes, while the vulnerabilities are seldom concerned. Li et al. [19] first noticed the copy-paste related bugs in the operating system, and implemented the tool CP-Miner to detect such bugs. The research about cloning vulnerabilities has been on the rise since 2007, with the appearing of optimized algorithm [18] and various tools [1–3, 6–9, 11]. These tools detect cloning vulnerabilities from different granularity, and make use of Abstract Syntax Tree (AST), Program Dependence Graph (PDG), etc. to characterize the fingerprint of vulnerabilities. In addition, detecting methods based on machine learning [2, 3, 10] have also emerged.

These researches provide us with a variety of detection methods. However, they cannot effectively detect restructured cloning vulnerabilities in IoT driver layer codes. The restructured cloning vulnerability represents clone with additions, deletions, or partially modifications that retains the vulnerability. The mentioned detecting tools only treat the exact same syntax as clones, thus they tend to miss this kind of vulnerabilities. According to this paper, the state-of-the-art tool VUDDY just detects 9 exact and renamed clones in Orange Pi, while there are 8 restructured clones that remain invisible to VUDDY. However, the proposed method can detect all the restructured clones and 5 exact and renamed clones with the precision about 86%.

The main contributions of this paper are as follows:

Vulnerability Fingerprint Based on Program Slicing. The security patches of vulnerable codes are used to locate the position of the key codes related to vulnerability and the vulnerable code fragments are obtained by taking advantage of static program slicing. These code fragments could be considered as the minimal part of code which can characterize a vulnerability.

Greedy-Based Algorithm for Fingerprint Matching. The fingerprint is generated by the granularity of line, so it is necessary to compare the fingerprint with the target code line by line, which is time consuming. Therefore, we use greedy-based algorithm to match the fingerprint, ensuring that the detection time is linear with the lines of tested code and the number of fingerprints.

Restructured Cloning Vulnerabilities Detector. Basing on VUDDY [1] and joern [21], the proposed method is called Restructured Cloning Vulnerabilities Detector (RCVD). When it comes to the evaluation of the method, the empirical results show that it can effectively detect the exact, renamed and restructured cloning vulnerabilities.

The remainder of the paper is organized as follows: Sect. 2 gives a brief introduction to code clone detection and program slicing. Then we proposed our method in Sect. 3. Moreover, we evaluate our method in Sect. 4, and introduce the related work about vulnerable code clone detection in Sect. 5. At last, we conclude this paper in Sect. 6.

2 Background

In this section, a general introduction to some common concepts and the process of code clone detection is given first, followed by the demonstration of the program slicing technique.

2.1 Code Clone Detection

Clone Type. A code fragment is recognized as a cloned one if it satisfies several given definition of similarity [17]. Currently widely accepted types of code clone mainly include four types [1]:

Type-1: Exact Clones. The code is copied directly without any modifications.
Type-2: Renamed Clones. These are syntactically identical clones except for the modification of identifiers, literals, types, whitespace, layout and comments.
Type-3: Restructured Clones. Based on the cloning of Type-2, copied code fragments are further modified such as added, deleted or modified statements. The proposed method covers Type-1, Type-2 and Type-3 clones.
Type-4: Semantic Clones. The two code fragments implement the same function and have the same semantics, but their grammars are different.

Now, most of the researches are focus on first three types. For the fact that vulnerabilities are sensitive to grammars, two pieces of code with the same function may not have the same vulnerabilities. Although Yamaguchi, et al. [22] propose the method to detect Type-4 clones, their method relies heavily on costly operations, and the accuracy of detection is not precisely given in their analysis.

Detection Granularity. Different detection methods apply different granularities, which influences the accuracy of detection result. At present, the code clone detection is mainly composed of five different granularities [1].

Token: This is the smallest meaningful unit that makes up a program. For example, in the statement 'int x;' three tokens exist: 'int', 'x' and ';'.
Line: This is a sequence of tokens delimited by a new-line character.
Function: This is a collection of consecutive lines that perform a specific task.
File: This contains a set of functions.
Program: This is a collection of files.

Detection Method. The common detection method includes two stages: feature generation and clone matching. At the first stage, features are extracted from code database, which usually includes hash [1], code gadgets [3], tokens [4] and patches [8]. Then the features are generally considered as fingerprints that represent the target codes. The second stage is to compute the similarity between fingerprints and tested codes, where the similarity algorithm used also has two types: precise matching (i.e. VUDDY matches the exact hash) and fuzzy matching (i.e. SourcererCC has a similarity threshold). In this paper, this two-stage method is adapted with precise matching.

2.2 Program Slicing

Program slicing is a technique for extracting code snippets from a target program, which would affect specific data. The specific data may consist of variables, processes, objects or anything that users are interested in. It has been seeing a rapid development since the original definition by Weiser [15]. At first, slicing is static, and could only be applied to the source code. Then Korel and Laski [16] introduced dynamic slicing, which works on a specific execution of the program.

Typically, the program slicing is based on a slicing criterion, which consists of a pair <p, V>, where p is a program point and V is a subset of program variables [23]. In addition, program slicing includes backward and forward ways. A backward slice consists all statements that the slicing criteria may depend on, while a forward slice includes all statements depending on the slicing criterion.

There are two major kinds of approaches in program slicing. The first method is based on iteration of dataflow equations. It first computes directly relevant statements for each node in the CFG (Control Flow Graph), and then the indirectly relevant statements. The process stops when there are no more relevant statements. The second method slices via graph reachability, which is also the most popular method. The detail of this method is shown in algorithm 1. *PDG* is the Program Dependence Graph of target code, n is the node to be sliced. Output S is the result of slicing. DominatorList (*PDG*, n) represents all the dominator node of n in the PDG. If node m is the dominator node of n, then it is obvious that the entire path from entry point of *PDG* to node n must pass through node m.

Algorithm 1. Program slicing via graph reachability

Input: *PDG*, n
Output: S
Slice(*PDG*, n)
{
1.   Put n in S
2.   **for** i in DominatorList(*PDG*, n) **do**
3.   **if** i **not** in S **then**
4.   put i in S
5.   **for** j in DominatorList(*PDG*, i) **do**
6.   Slice(*PDG*, j)
7.   **end for**
8.   **else**
9.   **return**
10.   **end if**
11. **end for**
}

The method base on graph reachability is more intuitive, easy to calculate and more practical. Therefore, this method is also applied for program slicing in the proposed method.

3   Method

The main idea of RCVD is to use code patches and program slicing to obtain code fragments related to vulnerabilities and then abstract the code fragments into precisely fingerprint.

3.1   Overall Structure

There are two stages in RCVD as shown in Fig. 1: fingerprint database generating and clone detection. The first stage includes the establishment of vulnerability database, program slicing and fingerprint generating. The second stage includes code preprocessing and fingerprint matching. The details of each sub-step are described in the following figure.

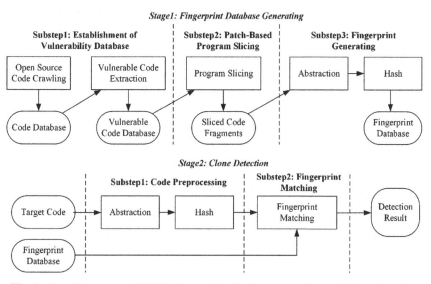

Fig. 1.   Overall structure of RCVD: fingerprint database generating and clone detection.

3.2   Establishment of Vulnerability Database

Code Collection.   First, the source code database is formed by collecting open source projects. In order to retrieve the information about vulnerabilities more conveniently, the codes are crawled from open source projects hosted on GitHub, which also makes it easier to get patch information from the commit history.

Vulnerability Code Extraction.   Then the vulnerability related codes need to be extracted to form the vulnerable code database. The commit history in git contains the information about code patching and vulnerabilities. Therefore, we could take advantage of vulnerability related keywords to retrieve them. After that, the vulnerable codes, patches and the type of vulnerabilities are saved as the vulnerable code database.

3.3 Patch-Based Program Slicing

The driver layer codes in IoT operating system have a large amount of restructured clone that current methods cannot effectively detect. Obviously, it is impossible to detect these clones with granularity of Function or higher. The granularity of Token will discard a lot of information about program, thus it is not suitable for detecting clone-caused vulnerabilities. Therefore, we propose taking the Line as granularity and use program slicing to get the discontinuous code fragments, which would preserve the vulnerability related codes better, not only in order to detect the exact and renamed clones, but also to detect the restructured clones.

To determine the slicing criterion, the most intuitive idea is that the codes added or deleted in the patches are related to the vulnerability. However, we could only get the variables related to vulnerability from added codes, while the actual lines of relevant code are not available. Thus utilizing patches with added codes may introduce codes unrelated to vulnerability, which would greatly increase false positive. Therefore, we only take the deleted code as the slicing criterion and retrieve the corresponding forward slices and backward slices. Table 1 is a simple example of double free, which is patched in Linux v5.3-rc7. We take the deleted 1556 line as the slicing criterion, and get seven lines of code as the result.

Table 1. Snippet of the code with double free patched in Linux v5.3-rc7 and the result of patch-based program slicing

Commit	If 'fb_alloc_cmap()' fails, 'fbi->pseudo_palette' is freed and 'fb_alloc_cmap()' will return code less than zero. This leads to a double free of 'fbi->pseudo_palette'.

Patch	```@@ -1553,7 +1553,6 @@ static int au1200fb_init_fbinfo(struct au1200fb_device *fbdev)```
	
	```1553 if (fb_alloc_cmap(&fbi->cmap,```
	``` AU1200_LCD_NBR_PALETTE_ENTRIES, 0) < 0) {```
	```1554 print_err("Fail to allocate colormap (%d```
	``` etries)",```
	```1555 AU1200_LCD_NBR_PALETTE_ENTRIES);```
	```1556 - kfree(fbi->pseudo_palette);```
	```1557 return -EFAULT;```
	```1558 }```

Sliced Code	```1. struct fb_info *fbi = fbdev->fb_info;```
	```2. fbi->fbops = &au1200fb_fb_ops;```
	```3. bpp = winbpp(win->w[fbdev->plane].mode_winctrl1);```
	```4. fbi->pseudo_palette = kcalloc(16, sizeof(u32),```
	``` GFP_KERNEL);```
	```5. if (!fbi->pseudo_palette) {```
	```6. if (fb_alloc_cmap(&fbi->cmap,```
	``` AU1200_LCD_NBR_PALETTE_ENTRIES, 0) < 0) {```
	```7. kfree(fbi->pseudo_palette);```

3.4 Fingerprint Generation

Abstraction. In order to eliminate the impact of renamed clones, we need to abstract the code fragments [1]. First, the parameters from the arguments of function are all replaced with symbol FPARAM. Then all the local variables that appear in the body of a function are substituted with symbol LVAR. Next, the data types are all replaced with symbol DTYPE. Last, the names of called function are substituted with symbol FUNCCALL.

The slice results may only contain a few lines of code, which may lead to a large number of false positive. Therefore, two intuitive indicators are proposed for filtering: the lines of sliced code and the percentage of the lines of sliced code to the total lines of the function. For example, if a function has 10 lines and the sliced code contains 3 lines, then the percentage is 30%. In the process of fingerprint generation, those fingerprints that are too short or take a small percentage will be ignored.

Hash. Directly comparison between two lines of code maybe time consuming, so it is necessary to covert the code to a shorter string. Moreover, two different lines of code need to be completely different after conversion and the cost should be minimized. Therefore, hash algorithm would be an ideal choice. Furthermore, the comparison aims at finding the exact vulnerability which requires precise matching between the hash values of each line. Since MD5 hash algorithm is naturally suitable for the requirement, it is then employed in this process. We calculate the MD5 for each line of code to generate the fingerprint. An example for abstraction and hash is shown in Table 2.

Table 2. The result of abstraction and fingerprint generation for the sliced code in **Table 1**

Abstraction	1.DTYPE*LVAR=FPARAM->fb_info;
	2.LVAR->fbops=&au1200fb_fb_ops;
	3.LVAR=FUNCCALL(win->w[FPARAM-
	    >plane].mode_winctrl1);
	4.LVAR->pseudo_palette=
	    FUNCCALL(16,sizeof(DTYPE),GFP_KERNEL);
	5.if(!LVAR->pseudo_palette){
	6.if(FUNCCALL(&LVAR-
	    >cmap,AU1200_LCD_NBR_PALETTE_ENTRIES,0)<0){
	7.FUNCCALL(LVAR->pseudo_palette);

Fingerprint	1.388d86029226687be5c9c1615fd35699 2.68df8e9ba0be6a602fff2d6e053d96b2 3.a3de00e7f6f0aeb7d0b895280f6ba768 4.729c49af63ff5c6939027f0cc97fc504 5.c0d99c692805f1e2356fab0fc9f27155 6.52352f2bd0966543686470c3a7221748 7.f4bc70d18fa8d5272d3c45e658039350

3.5 Greedy-Based Fingerprint Matching Algorithm

Normally, once the target code contains the subsequence, which is the same as one of the fingerprints, it's not hard to conclude that the target code may contain vulnerability. In other words if a fingerprint is the subsequence of target code, then the target code is likely to have the same vulnerability with this fingerprint. Therefore, fingerprint matching can be treated as a problem of the existence of subsequence. At present, greedy algorithm is usually used to solve such problems. We also propose a greedy-based matching algorithm to realize the process of matching.

Algorithm 2. Greedy-based matching algorithm

Input: C, F
Output: matching result R
1. L_c = length of C
2. L_f = length of F
3. R = False
4. **if** $L_c < L_f$ **then**
5. R = False
6. **else**
7. $m = 0$
8.   **for** $n = 0, 1, \ldots, Lc$ **do**
9.   **if** $C[n] == F[m]$ **then**
10. $m = m + 1$
11.   **end if**
12.   **if** $m == L_f$ **then**
13. R = True
14.   **break**
15.   **end if**
16.   **end for**
17. **end if**
18. **Output** R

Algorithm 2 introduces the pseudocode for matching algorithm. C is the target code and F is the fingerprint. The output R will be *True* if code C contains the fingerprint F, else it will be *False*. If the length of C is less than the length of F, it's impossible for C to match the F. If the nth element of C is the same as the mth element of F, the n and m will increase by one at the same time. Otherwise, only n will increase. If F is completely matched, then the fingerprint matching is considered as successful and returns *True*. From Algorithm 2, it's explicit that the time complexity is independent of fingerprint length and it has a linear relationship with the lines of code and the number of fingerprints.

4 Experimental Evaluation

In order to prove the effectiveness of our method for detecting restructured clones, RCVD is implemented. Since the deep learning based detecting tool VulDeePecker does not open its source code, RCVD would only be compared with ReDeBug and VUDDY.

4.1 Experimental Setup

System Environment. The execution and detection performance of RCVD are evaluated by conducting experiments on a machine running Ubuntu 18.04, with a 32-core Intel Xeon E5-2620 CPU operating at 2.10 GHz, 16 GB RAM, and 500G HDD.

Dataset and Keywords. In order to detect the restructured clone in driver layer codes of IoT operating systems, the source code of Linux is collected from GitHub for fingerprint generating. What's more, the source code of OrangePiRDA_kernel and WisCam are chosen for detection. The Orange Pi [24] is a commercial IoT device with its own operating system that can be used as a computer, wireless server, HD player, and so on. WisCam [26] is ultra-low-cost Modular Based Evaluation Kit to help the developer to design Wi-Fi video product with Linux OS. Moreover, the source code of their operating system can be obtained from GitHub. As for the vulnerable code retrieving, two different keyword lists are applied. The first list contains keywords related to popular vulnerabilities including use-after-free, double free, heap-based buffer overflow, stack-based buffer overflow, integer overflow, OOB, out-of-bounds read and out-of-bounds write. The second one is Common Vulnerabilities and Exposures (CVE) [25] list as used in VUDDY.

Metrics. Normally, excessive false positives in vulnerability detection will increase the workload of manual audit, and we hope to find vulnerabilities as many as possible. Therefore, the evaluation of detecting tools mainly uses precision ($P = \frac{TP}{TP+FP}$) and false negative rate ($FNR = \frac{FN}{FN+TP}$). Let TP be the number of sames with vulnerabilities detected correctly, FP be the number of samples with false vulnerabilities detected. As it is very challenging to find literally every vulnerability (including unknown vulnerabilities) in the target program, we cannot easily determine false negatives. Therefore, we count FN by comparing different detection results. For example, FN is the number of TP clones detected by other tools rather than RCVD.

4.2 RCVD vs ReDeBug

First, RCVD is compared with ReDeBug, which can also detect restructured clones. The code of Linux and keywords related to popular vulnerabilities are used to retrieve the vulnerable code. For RCVD, let's set the minimum of sliced codes to 6, and set the percentage of sliced codes more than 30%. As a result, the proposed method gets 790 fingerprints. For ReDeBug, it gets 8443 patches using its default parameters (n-gram of 4 lines).

The detection results are shown in Fig. 2. Surprisingly, ReDeBug can only detect the same one exact clone in both projects while RCVD detects 114 exact and restructured clones. After analyzing the detection results that missed by ReDeBug, it turns out that ReDeBug could not deal with Type-2 clones with slight modifications in variable names or data types. The abstraction in RCVD is resistant to these modifications therefore it can detect much more than ReDeBug. Although ReDeBug claims that it can detect Type-3 clones, it cannot find any restructured cloning vulnerabilities while RCVD finds 35 in this experiment.

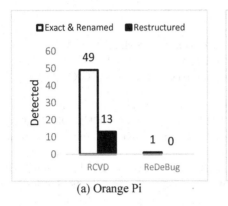
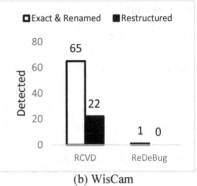

(a) Orange Pi   (b) WisCam

Fig. 2. Detection results for different types of clones in RCVD and ReDeBug

The precision and FNR of two tools is further illustrated as Table 3. RCVD could detect much more clones than ReDeBug with a rather high precision and low FNR. The only vulnerability missed by RCVD is due to the length of sliced codes is less than 6. The 89% and 94.6% precision of RCVD in two projects indicate that it is more effective than ReDeBug. However, ReDeBug is much faster than RCVD. The matching algorithm in the proposed method determined that the detection time keeps a linear relationship with the lines of target code, thus it takes a rather long time to detect codes of 10M lines.

Table 3. Detection results of RCVD and ReDeBug

Tools	Time(s)	Detected	TP	FP	FN	P	FNR
Detection results for OrangePiRDA_kernel (about 10M lines of code)							
RCVD	3598	**69**	**62**	7	1	**89.9%**	**1.5%**
ReDeBug	980	4	1	**3**	62	25%	99.1%
Detection results for WisCam (about 10M lines of code)							
RCVD	4268	**92**	**87**	5	1	**94.6%**	**1.1%**
ReDeBug	819	4	1	**3**	87	25%	98.9%

4.3 RCVD vs VUDDY

Then RCVD was compared with the state-of-the-art tool VUDDY. The code of Linux and CVE list are used to retrieve vulnerable codes. For the reason that the amount of vulnerable codes retrieved by CVE list is relatively small, the minimum percentage is set as 10% and the minimum length is set as 5, and finally it gets 194 fingerprints. VUDDY does not provide the complete tool, but provides an online service, thus the codes and results could only be detected and filtered with the CVEs appeared in Linux. In addition, VUDDY does not provide the exact detection time in their online service.

Figure 3 shows the test results for different types of clones. RCVD detects 14 restructured cloning vulnerabilities in total, in contrast, VUDDY can detect none of them due to its design. After analyzing these 14 cases, some negligible modifications are found to be enough to prevent VUDDY from detecting. The most typical example is in function atl2_probe of Orange Pi, it just adds a semicolon after the 'switch' statement without any other changes. As for the exact and renamed clones, VUDDY detects 20 clones while RCVD can only detect 12 clones, let alone missing 8 of them. This is because the fingerprints are filtered in advance.

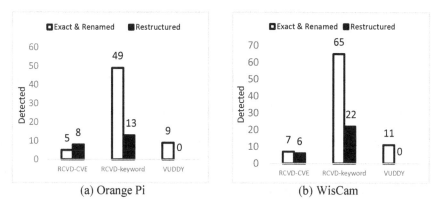

(a) Orange Pi   (b) WisCam

Fig. 3. Detection results for different types of clones in RCVD and VUDDY

Through the comparison with detection results of keyword in Fig. 3, we could infer that the number of detected vulnerabilities is positively related to the number of fingerprints. Given the items in database are ample enough, RCVD could always detect more vulnerabilities. Additionally, if third-party users customize the cloned codes and introduce extra vulnerability, the newly emerged vulnerability would still be detected as long as the corresponding fingerprints exist in our database.

VUDDY abandons the detection of Type-3 in exchange for accurate detection of Type-1 and Type-2 clones. RCVD implements the detection of Type-3 even though the users customize the code. Frankly it's hard to conclude which kind of vulnerability is more severe, all we can see is RCVD's improvement in numbers of total detected clones compared with VUDDY and ReDeBug. After all, since there's no existing detecting tools that can handle this problem with practical resources, it would be our further work to find the breakthrough. Correspondingly, as shown in Table 4, RCVD detects more clones than VUDDY in Orange Pi and WisCam with a high precision, so it is reasonable to believe that RCVD has more advantages in detecting vulnerabilities.

4.4 Case Study

There was a use-after-free vulnerability caused by race condition in Linux v5.3, which was cloned by Orange Pi in the module of wireless shown in Table 5. It only changed the

Table 4. Detection results of RCVD and VUDDY

Tools	Times(s)	Detected	TP	FP	FN	P (%)	FNR (%)
Detection results for OrangePiRDA_kernel (about 10M lines of code)							
RCVD	1253	**15**	**13**	2	**4**	86.6	**30.7**
VUDDY	Not Known	9	9	**0**	8	**100**	47.1
Detection results for WisCam (about 10M lines of code)							
RCVD	1764	**16**	**13**	3	**4**	81.3	**23.5**
VUDDY	Not Known	11	11	**0**	6	**100**	35.3

function, which named `min_t` to `min`, while retained the vulnerability. RCVD detects it correctly with the fingerprint in Sect. 4.2.

A tiny race window could result in a use-after-free bug of the `current_beacon`. Since `current_beacon` is not locked, several threads may obtain it at the same time. During the execution of function `b43_write_beacon_template`, if other threads release `current_beacon`, then use-after-free occurs when `current_beacon` is used. Unfortunately, Orange Pi retains the vulnerability without any patches. We could exploit this vulnerability to launch denial of service attack or execute arbitrarily code remotely on Orange Pi through its wireless module. However, VUDDY and ReDeBug cannot detect it, leaving a significant security risk to the operating system.

5   Related Work

As we all know, the earlier clone detecting tool is CCFinder [4] proposed in 2002. It measured the similarity of the sequence of tokens by a suffix-tree algorithm, which is computationally costly and consumes a large amount of memory. SourcererCC [20] uses a bag-of-tokens strategy to manage minor to specific changes in clones, which allows it to detect Type-3 clone. However, it is mainly designed to measure similarity and is not suitable for vulnerable code clone detection. Li etc. proposed the CP-Miner [19], the first vulnerable code clone detector. It parses a program and compares the token sequence with a heuristic algorithm. It can be seen that the early tools are still at the exploratory stage, with relatively high complexity.

Then the related researches begin to increase gradually and so as the tools. SecureSync [6] uses two models: xASTs and xGRUMs, which use AST and directed graphs to describe the vulnerabilities caused by code base reuse and API reuse. CBCD [7] utilizes PDG to parse the vulnerability code, and divides the graph into sub-graphs with a small number of nodes, finds vulnerability through the isomorphic matching algorithm of the graph. ReDeBug [8] uses a sliding window algorithm for Token streams and a Bloom filter to find clones of vulnerability code. It supports large amount of code detection and has high detection efficiency, but it cannot cope with Type-2 clone. CLORIFI

Table 5. Use-after-free vulnerability in Linux v5.3 and OrangePiRDA_kernel

| Vulnerable function in Linux drivers/net/wireless/ b43/main.c | ```
@@ -1601,12 +1601,26 @@ static void
b43_write_beacon_template(struct b43_wldev *dev, u16
   ram_offset, u16 shm_size_offset){
1     unsigned int rate;
2     u16 ctl;
3     int antenna;
4     struct ieee80211_tx_info *info =
5         IEEE80211_SKB_CB(dev->wl->current_beacon);
6     bcn = (const struct ieee80211_mgmt
7         *)(dev->wl->current_beacon->data);
8     len = min_t(size_t, dev->wl->current_beacon->len,
9         0x200 - sizeof(struct b43_plcp_hdr6));
10    rate = ieee80211_get_tx_rate(dev->wl->hw,
11        info)->hw_value;
12    b43_write_template_common(dev, (const u8 *)bcn,
13        len, ram_offset, shm_size_offset, rate);
14    ...
``` |
| The cloned code in OrangePiRDA _kernel drivers/net/wireless/ b43/main.c | ```
static void b43_write_beacon_template(struct b43_wldev
   *dev, u16 ram_offset, u16 shm_size_offset){
1     unsigned int i, len, variable_len;
2     const struct ieee80211_mgmt *bcn;
3     const u8 *ie;
4     bool tim_found = false;
5     unsigned int rate;
6     u16 ctl;
7     int antenna;
8     struct ieee80211_tx_info *info =
9         IEEE80211_SKB_CB(dev->wl->current_beacon);
10    bcn = (const struct ieee80211_mgmt
11        *)(dev->wl->current_beacon->data);
12    len = min((size_t) dev->wl->current_beacon->len,
13        0x200 - sizeof(struct b43_plcp_hdr6));
14    rate = ieee80211_get_tx_rate(dev->wl->hw,
15        info)->hw_value;
16    b43_write_template_common(dev, (const u8 *)bcn,
17        len, ram_offset, shm_size_offset, rate);
18    ...
``` |

[9] uses the n-token algorithm to process the input code and uses the Bloom filter to find clones of the vulnerability code. It also verifies the vulnerability with concolic test to reduce false positives. However, it cannot detect Type-2 clone either. CVdetector [10] traverses the grammar of vulnerability code fragments, constructs vulnerability feature matrix and feature vector of key nodes by analysis tree, and detects various types of vulnerability codes by applying clustering algorithm. This method implemented a linear relationship between overhead and amount of code.

In order to improve the effect of detector for different vulnerabilities, VulPecker [2] combines Token, AST, PDG and etc., extracts vulnerability fragment features according to its type, selects corresponding algorithms from similarity comparison algorithms, and detects the reuse of vulnerability code by using support vector machine. It improves the accuracy of detection, but brings about a large computational overhead. VUDDY

[1] focuses on Type-1 and Type-2, and generates the fingerprint with the granularity of Function. It utilizes the abstraction to eliminate the influence of renamed clone, which is also applied to this paper. In addition, there are detection methods based on machine learning. Lin etc. [13] extract the features from AST and use LSTM to learn the representation. VulDeePecker [3] is the first to use deep learning for testing. It extracts features automatically but can only handle with the vulnerabilities about API.

Through the introduction of the development of vulnerable code cloning detection technology, we can infer that it is an inevitable trend to extract code fragments or features by program analysis. Compared with code clone detection, the vulnerable code detection needs more information about semantic or grammar. Therefore, the proposed method uses program slicing based on patches to obtain the vulnerability related code fragments, which is not achieved by previous work. In addition, the proposed matching algorithm achieves a linear relationship between time complexity and the lines of target code.

6   Conclusion

In this paper, the method of cloning vulnerability detection is discussed. Applying program slicing and greedy-based matching algorithm to code similarity-based method, the tool for restructured cloning vulnerability detection is implemented with low false negative and high precision on IoT driver layer codes. It sacrifices some detection accuracy and realizes a better detection of reconstructed clones. Experiment shows that although RCVD introduces some false positive, it could detect 49 restructured cloning vulnerabilities totally while other two tools cannot detect. In addition, it could detect exact and renamed clones, which also proves the adaptability of this method to different types of clone. It's reasonable to believe RCVD can be a realistic solution for the security of IoT operating systems.

So far, the work can also be extended in multiple directions. Firstly, semantic analysis can be used to solve the false positive introduced by patches. In addition, extending the fingerprint database and proposing faster algorithm for fingerprint matching would be of great value. Moreover, the quality of fingerprints may also be improved.

Acknowledgements. This work was supported by the National Key R&D Program of China under Grant No. 2017YFC0821705, National Key R&D Program of China under Grant No. 2019QY(Y)0602 and National Natural Science Foundation of China under Grant No. U1536202.

References

1. Kim, S., Woo, S., Lee, H., Oh, H.: Vuddy: a scalable approach for vulnerable code clone discovery. In: 2017 IEEE Symposium on Security and Privacy (SP), pp. 595–614. IEEE, May 2017
2. Li, Z., Zou, D., Xu, S., Jin, H., Qi, H., Hu, J.: VulPecker: an automated vulnerability detection system based on code similarity analysis. In: Proceedings of the 32nd Annual Conference on Computer Security Applications, pp. 201–213. ACM, December 2016
3. Li, Z., et al.: VulDeePecker: a deep learning-based system for vulnerability detection. In: Proceedings of the 25th Annual Network and Distributed System Security Symposium, San Diego, California, USA (2018)

4. Kamiya, T., Kusumoto, S., Inoue, K.: CCFinder: a multilinguistic token-based code clone detection system for large scale source code. IEEE Trans. Software Eng. **28**(7), 654–670 (2002)
5. Jiang, L., Misherghi, G., Su, Z., Glondu, S.: Deckard: scalable and accurate tree-based detection of code clones. In: Proceedings of the 29th International Conference on Software Engineering, pp. 96–105. IEEE Computer Society, May 2007
6. Pham, N.H., Nguyen, T.T., Nguyen, H.A., Wang, X., Nguyen, A.T., Nguyen, T.N.: Detecting recurring and similar software vulnerabilities. In: Proceedings of the 32nd ACM/IEEE International Conference on Software Engineering-Volume 2, pp. 227–230. ACM, May 2010
7. Li, J., Ernst, M.D.: CBCD: Cloned buggy code detector. In: Proceedings of the 34th International Conference on Software Engineering, pp. 310–320. IEEE Press, New Jersey, June 2012
8. Jang, J., Agrawal, A., Brumley, D.: ReDeBug: finding unpatched code clones in entire os distributions. In: 2012 IEEE Symposium on Security and Privacy, pp. 48–62. IEEE, May 2012
9. Li, H., Kwon, H., Kwon, J., Lee, H.: CLORIFI: software vulnerability discovery using code clone verification. Concurrency Comput. Pract. Experience **28**(6), 1900–1917 (2016)
10. Gan, S., Qin, X., Chen, Z., Wang, L.: Software vulnerability code clone detection method based on characteristic metrics. J. Softw. **26**(2), 348–363 (2015)
11. Liu, Z., Wei, Q., Cao, Y.: Vfdetect: a vulnerable code clone detection system based on vulnerability fingerprint. In: 2017 IEEE 3rd Information Technology and Mechatronics Engineering Conference (ITOEC), pp. 548–553. IEEE, October 2017
12. Nishi, M.A., Damevski, K.: Scalable code clone detection and search based on adaptive prefix filtering. J. Syst. Softw. **137**, 130–142 (2018)
13. Lin, G., et al.: Cross-project transfer representation learning for vulnerable function discovery. IEEE Trans. Ind. Inform. **14**(7), 3289–3297 (2018)
14. Zhang, Z.K., Cho, M.C.Y., Wang, C.W., Hsu, C.W., Chen, C.K., Shieh, S.: IoT security: ongoing challenges and research opportunities. In: 2014 IEEE 7th International Conference on Service-Oriented Computing and Applications, pp. 230–234. IEEE, November 2014
15. Weiser, M.: Program slicing. In: Proceedings of the 5th International Conference on Software Engineering, pp. 439–449. IEEE Press, New Jersey, March 1981
16. Korel, B., Laski, J.: Dynamic slicing of computer programs. J. Syst. Softw. **13**(3), 187–195 (1990)
17. Roy, C.K., Cordy, J.R., Koschke, R.: Comparison and evaluation of code clone detection techniques and tools: a qualitative approach. Sci. Comput. Program. **74**(7), 470–495 (2009)
18. Jiang, L., Su, Z., Chiu, E.: Context-based detection of clone-related bugs. In: Proceedings of the the 6th Joint Meeting of the European Software Engineering Conference and The ACM SIGSOFT Symposium on The Foundations of Software Engineering, pp. 55–64. ACM, September 2007
19. Li, Z., Lu, S., Myagmar, S., Zhou, Y.: CP-Miner: a tool for finding copy-paste and related bugs in operating system code. In: OSdi, vol. 4, no. 19, pp. 289–302, December 2004
20. Sajnani, H., Saini, V., Svajlenko, J., Roy, C.K., Lopes, C.V.: Sourcerercc: scaling code clone detection to big-code. In: 2016 IEEE/ACM 38th International Conference on Software Engineering (ICSE), pp. 1157–1168. IEEE, May 2016
21. joern. https://joern.readthedocs.io
22. Yamaguchi, F., Lindner, F., Rieck, K.: Vulnerability extrapolation: assisted discovery of vulnerabilities using machine learning. In: Proceedings of the 5th USENIX Conference on Offensive Technologies, pp. 13. USENIX Association, August 2011
23. Xu, B., Qian, J., Zhang, X., Wu, Z., Chen, L.: A brief survey of program slicing. ACM SIGSOFT Softw. Eng. Notes **30**(2), 1–36 (2005)

24. Orange Pi. http://www.orangepi.org/
25. Common Vulnerabilities and Exposure. https://cve.mitre.org/index.html
26. WisCam. https://www.rakwireless.com/en/WisKeyOSH/WisCam

Impact of Multiple Reflections on Secrecy Capacity of Indoor VLC System

Jian Chen and Tao Shu$^{(\boxtimes)}$

Auburn University, Auburn, AL 36849, USA
{jzc0111,tzs0058}@auburn.edu

Abstract. While visible light communication (VLC) is expected to have a wide range of applications in the near future, the security vulnerabilities of this technology have not been well understood so far. In particular, due to the extremely short wavelength of visible light, the VLC channel presents several unique characteristics than its radio frequency counterparts, which impose new features on the VLC security. Taking a physical-layer security perspective, this paper studies the intrinsic secrecy capacity of VLC as induced by its special channel characteristics. Different from existing models that only consider the specular reflection in the VLC channel, a modified Monte Carlo ray tracing model is proposed to account for both the specular and the diffusive reflections, which is unique to VLC. Based on this model the upper and the lower bounds of the VLC secrecy capacity are derived, which allow us to evaluate the VLC communication confidentiality against a comprehensive set of factors, including the locations of the transmitter, receiver, and eavesdropper, the VLC channel bandwidth, the ratio between the specular and diffusive reflections, and the reflection coefficient. Our results reveal that due to the different types of reflections, the VLC system becomes more vulnerable at specific locations where strong reflections exist.

Keywords: Physical layer security · Indoor VLC · Multipath reflection · Secrecy capacity

1 Introduction

Visible light communication (VLC), which integrates communication and illumination, has now become a very active research topic in the area of wireless communication. Compared with its radio frequency (RF) counterparts, VLC enjoys many nice features, such as license free, interference free, reusable spectrum, wider bandwidth, higher transmission rate, higher energy efficiency and so on. Because of these nice features, VLC has been considered to be a promising and urgently-needed solution for offloading the crowded RF traffic in 5G systems.

While VLC is expected to have a wide range of applications in the near future, the security vulnerabilities of this technology have not been well understood so far. In typical VLC systems, data is transmitted by modulating the output intensity of the emitters, and the data signal is captured using photo-diodes as receivers. Contrary to the initial belief that VLC is intrinsically secure because

© Springer Nature Switzerland AG 2020
J. Zhou et al. (Eds.): ICICS 2019, LNCS 11999, pp. 105–123, 2020.
https://doi.org/10.1007/978-3-030-41579-2_7

the propagation of visible light is directive and can be confined within a closed space, recent studies have revealed that this is not necessarily true, especially in public areas [12,21]. Without any sort of wave-guiding transmission media, the light illumination that a VLC link piggybacks on is diffusive in most real-world applications, which makes VLC links inherently susceptible to eavesdropping by an unintended receiver in the same room. This broadcast threat applies to most public indoor environments, such as libraries, meeting rooms, shopping centers or aircrafts. Even worse, eavesdropping from outside of the room is possible when there are windows on the wall [6,12,32].

In particular, due to the extremely short wavelength of visible light (0.38 ∼ 0.69 μm), the VLC channel presents several unique features than its RF counterparts. For example, a VLC channel is a mix of both specular reflection and diffuse reflection, which allows a VLC signal to be overheard (or seen) at much more locations than a RF signal, even when an eavesdropper is outside the main-lobe of the intended VLC communication. As a result, in contrast to the conventional multipath RF channel, a VLC channel is no longer a discrete sequence of a small number of signal paths, but rather a continuous combination of signal paths reflected by the entire environment. Such a drastic change on channel characteristics imposes new security features on VLC communication, and requires a different method to investigate than its well-studied RF counterparts.

With that in mind, in this work we attempt to investigate the intrinsic confidentiality of VLC communication as induced by its special channel characteristics. We consider the issue of communication confidentiality, because eavesdropping has been foreseen as the most common threat faced by VLC communications once they are deployed [6,13,21]. In contrast to many existing confidentiality studies that take measures at upper layers of the network protocol stack, such as access control, password protection, and end-to-end encryption, our investigation takes a physical-layer security perspective and targets at the fundamental issue of VLC channel's secrecy capacity, by characterizing how easily a VLC signal would be overheard when it is transmitted over the channel. Note that our study aims at understanding the intrinsic security limits faced by the VLC signal itself, which is independent from any cryptographic measures that could be added on the upper layers. In practice, our study may lead to a better design of VLC transceivers that possess certain built-in eaversdropping-proofness, and may be used orthogonally with upper-layer cryptographic methods to further enhance the security of VLC systems.

So far, the study on the secrecy capacity of VLC in the literature is still quite preliminary. Most of the existing models consider the VLC channel as a wiretap channel under line of sight, and have ignored the different types of signal reflections on the channel. In contrast, our study in this paper aims to exploit the unique characteristics of VLC channel in calculating its secrecy capacity. To the best of our knowledge, this is the first work that considers the impact of both the specular and the diffusive reflections on secrecy capacity of indoor VLC. More specifically, the main contributions of our study are as follows:

1. We consider both the specular and diffusive reflections using the Monte Carlo ray tracing approach.

2. We propose an analytical approach to synthesize the VLC channel impulse response using gamma probability distribution function fitting.
3. We propose a simple way to calculate the secrecy capacity when considering multiple reflections.
4. We analyze how multiple reflections affects the secrecy capacity for an indoor VLC system with a transmitter, a legitimate receiver, and an eavesdropper.

The reminder of this paper is organized as follows. Section 2 describes the related work. VLC system models are presented in Sect. 3, Sect. 4, and Sect. 5, respectively. Experimental design are presented in Sect. 6. Evaluations and Discussions are analyzed in Sect. 7, followed by Conclusions in Sect. 8.

2   Related Work

While the research on VLC has achieved significant development in many fields, such as channel modelling [5,7,11,15], modulation [35], channel estimation [8,27,30], and channel capacity analysis [17,28], the security aspect of VLC has not been well understood so far. Existing research on VLC security is preliminary, as evidenced by the limited number of related works and the narrow scope of problems addressed in the literature. In [21], the authors discussed different scenarios of VLC sniffing, and the results of the experiment suggested that VLC channels should not be considered intrinsically secure. Yin and Haas also confirmed the vulnerabilities of multiuser VLC networks by providing an analytical framework to characterize the secrecy performance [33]. Actually due to the broadcast feature of VLC, an unintended receiver within the same communication room may receive the information without being noticed, and this kind of threat could even apply to a scenario that the unintended receiver from outside of the room could eavesdrop merely through the windows or door gaps. The feasibility of such an attack was verified in [32], where an attacker outside a room was able to accurately figure out the program being played on a TV set in the room just by observing the change of light intensity illuminated by the TV through the window. Eavesdropping outside the direct beam of the light was also verified by testbed in [12].

For most cases of securing a VLC system, conventional cryptographic methods have been implemented at upper layers of the protocol stack to provide data confidentiality, integrity, and authenticity for VLC applications [1,2,24]. But it is facing great challenges with the elevated capability of computation. As a promising complement to it, physical layer security, mainly represented by non-cryptographic methods, exploits the noise and the structure of the VLC channel to limit the amount of information that can be overheard by unauthorized eavesdroppers [19,22,34].

From an information-theoretic point of view, the physical-layer security was first introduced by Wyner as a wiretap channel model [31]: an eavesdropper sniffs a degraded signal from the main channel. The secrecy capacity is derived as the difference between the information capacity for the two channels. Different with RF communication, which is typically modeled as a Gaussian broadcast channel with an average power constraint at the transmitter side, the signal in VLC is typically modulated onto the intensity of the emitted light, it must satisfy average, peak as well as non-negative amplitude constraints, imposed by practical illumination requirements [17,25,28]. Due to the fundamental differences, results on the secrecy capacity obtained for RF networks can not be directly applied to VLC networks.

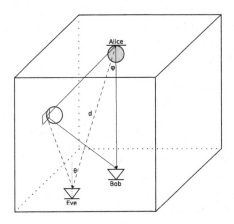

Fig. 1. A typical indoor VLC network system with Alice, Bob and Eve considering reflections.

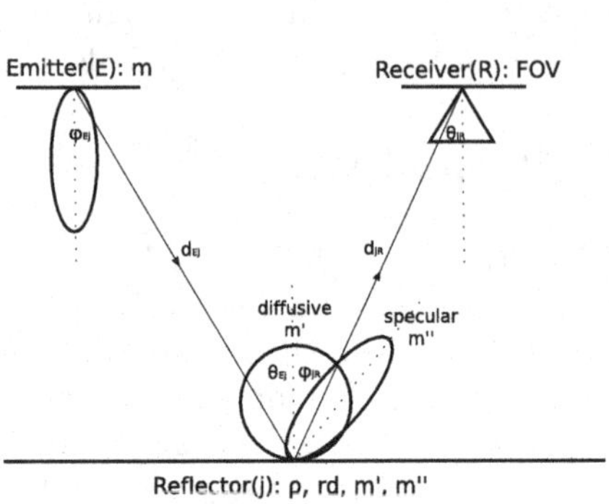

Fig. 2. Reflection pattern is described by Phong's model.

By considering one transmitter, one legitimate user and one eavesdropper in a VLC system, lower and upper bounds on the secrecy capacity of the amplitude-constrained Gaussian wiretap channel was recently studied in [29], with the use of the derived capacity lower and upper bounds in [23]. Mostafa et al. analyzed the achievable secrecy rate for single-input single-output (SISO) and multiple-input single-output (MISO) scenarios, and proposed various beamforming and jamming schemes to enhance the confidentiality of VLC links [22]. In addition, Arfaoui et al. derived in closed-form the achievable secrecy rate as a function of the discrete input distribution for wiretap channel under the amplitude constraints of the input signal [3,4]. To address the issue of a priori knowledge of locations or channel state information of eavesdropper, in [9,10], Cho et al. investigated the secrecy connectivity in VLC in the presence of randomly located eavesdroppers, and they also study how the multipath reflections affect the secrecy outage probability. However, when considering the multipath reflections, they only deal with the impact of the main channel without considering of the inter-symbol interference from multipath reflections.

3   VLC Channel Modelling

In a typical indoor VLC system (Fig. 1), data signal is transmitted by modulating the output intensity of the emitter (Alice), and then it is captured using simple photo-diodes as receivers (Bob or Eve). As the indoor optical wireless channel is significantly different from the RF channel, statistical propagation models developed for the RF, which characterize the multipath fading, can't be directly applied to VLC. Accounting for the multiple types of reflections in the indoor VLC system requires a distinct channel modeling that is able to capture the unique characteristics of a VLC channel. In particular, a VLC channel response could be decomposed into the line of sight (LOS) path component and the non-line of sight (NLOS) path component, which are described respectively as follows.

According to [15], the emitter source is modeled as a generalized Lambertian radiation pattern

$$P(m, \phi) = \frac{m+1}{2\pi} \cos^m(\phi) \tag{1}$$

where m is the Lambertian order defining the radiation lobe, which specifies the directivity of the source, ϕ is the angle between the initial direction of ray and the direction of maximum power, which specifies the emitting angle. The coefficient $(m+1)/2\pi$ ensures that integrating radiation intensity pattern over the surface of a hemisphere can obtain the source power. $m = 1$ corresponds to a traditional Lambertian source.

So, the LOS path gain can be calculated as

$$h_{LOS} = P(m, \phi) A_D \cos(\theta) \frac{1}{d^2} \delta(t - \frac{d}{c}) \tag{2}$$

where A_D is the detecting surface area of the receiver, θ is the incident angle between incident light and the receiver normal direction, product of both gives the effective collection area of the receiver. d is the LOS distance between the emitter and receiver, which depicts the geometric attenuation. Dirac delta function gives the time delay.

Multipath channel gain due to the reflections by the walls was studied in [5]. The proposed deterministic model calculated the reflection channel gain by partitioning a wall into many elementary reflectors and summing up the impulse response contributions from different reflectors as secondary sources until reaching the time limit. However, there is a problem with this model, in that they only take into account diffusive reflection and can't simulate specular reflection when light reaches a wall. In reality, for grazing incidence there is strong specular reflection with quite different behavior. If there are polished surface, such as windows or mirrors, the specualar reflection is dominant over diffusive reflection. In order to consider the high specular reflection of smooth surfaces, here we use the Phong's model to approximate the reflection patterns (Fig. 2), considered as the sum of the diffusive component and the specular component [18,27]. In this model, the surface characteristics are defined by two parameters: the percentage of incident signal that is reflected diffusely r_d and the directivity of the specular component of the reflection m''. Due to the high attenuation, in this paper, we consider only the first reflection since the channel gain of the higher order reflections is small enough to be neglected [27].

So, the NLOS path gain can be described as

$$h_{NLOS} = \sum_{j=1}^{n} P(m, \phi_{Ej}) \Delta A \cos(\theta_{Ej}) \frac{1}{d_{Ej}^2} \rho \left[r_d P(m', \phi_{jR}) + (1 - r_d) P(m'', \phi_{jR} - \theta_{Ej}) \right]$$
$$A_D \cos(\theta_{jR}) \frac{1}{d_{jR}^2} \delta \left(t - \frac{d_{Ej} + d_{jR}}{c} \right)$$

(3)

where the wall is divided into n grid reflectors, each of which has an area of ΔA, ρ is the surface reflection coefficient, m' gives the directivity of the diffusive reflection component and m'' gives the directivity of the specular reflection component, ϕ and θ represent emitting angle and incident angle, respectively.

Therefore, the channel gain considering both the LOS and NLOS can be described as

$$H = h_{LOS} + h_{NLOS}.$$

(4)

We use a modified Monte Carlo ray-tracing statistical approach to numerically calculate the channel impulse response, as explained later in the experimental section.

4   Channel Impulse Response Fitting and Synthesizing

Although the channel impulse response with multiple reflections could be numerically calculated using different approaches, there is lacking an analytical expression for it in current literature. The main drawback of the numerical methods is their excessive computational time complexity. Due to the additional NLOS reflections, numerical computation of the impulse response of a single VLC channel turns out to be very time consuming, and it becomes even more prohibitive when one needs to calculate the channel response as a function of the VLC link location over the entire communication space, e.g., to characterize the spatial distribution of the VLC channel secrecy capacity. Therefore, for the very first time, we propose a fast analytical approach to synthesize channel impulse response using gamma probability distribution function fitting.

When analyzing the numerically calculated channel impulse response (Fig. 3(a)), we notice that it could be divided into two distinct components, LOS and NLOS. The LOS component is a scalar channel gain related to the propagation attenuation of the VLC signal over the distance between the transmitter and the receiver, and can be easily calculated according to the channel model and system geometry. On the other hand, however, the NLOS component is much more complicated, as it presents some time-series structure, as shown in Fig. 3(b), where the NLOS impulse response has been normalized by the total NLOS light intensity. Based on the fact that the integral of the normalized NLOS time series equals to one, we hypothesize that this time series can be fitted analytically by some probabilistic distribution function. Physically, this hypothesis reflects the insight that the NLOS channel response is actually the distribution of the reflected light power over different time delays [26]. To verify our hypothesis, we have tested a number of probabilistic distribution functions, among which the gamma distribution turns out to be the most promising one for the fitting.

A gamma distribution can be parameterized in terms of a shape parameter α and a rate parameter β. The corresponding probability density function (PDF) in the shape-rate parametrization is

$$f(x; \alpha, \beta) = \frac{\beta^\alpha x^{\alpha-1} e^{-\beta x}}{\Gamma(\alpha)}; \quad x > 0; \alpha, \beta > 0 \tag{5}$$

where $\Gamma(\alpha)$ is the gamma function. Given a numerically computed NLOS channel response, its fitted gamma distribution expression (i.e., the fitted parameters (α, β)) can be obtained by nonlinear regression. For instance, Fig. 3(c) plots the fitted gamma distribution function for the numerically calculated and normalized NLOS channel impulse response in Fig. 3(b). The fitting in this case turns out to be very accurate according to the mean square error ($mse < 0.0002$). To graphically assess how well the numerical calculation matches with the fitted gamma distribution, a scatter quantile-quantile (Q-Q) plot is shown in Fig. 3(d), where the calculated set (X) and fitted set (Y) of quantiles are plotted against each other. The cross points (+) are referred to as percentiles, below which a certain proportion of the data fall. Ideally, if X and Y quantiles come from the same distribution, then all + marks should be aligned along the diagonal line (the red line in the figure). Indeed, it can be observed in Fig. 3(d) that most of the + marks are aligned well with the diagonal line, except a couple exceptions, which are just a little off the diagonal line. This observation confirms that the fitted gamma distribution matches reasonably well with the numerical calculations. In order to statistically verify the accuracy of gamma fitting for more general cases, we compared the calculated NLOS channel response against their gamma fitting outcomes in Figs. 3(e) and (f) for 2401 VLC channels, which are taken over a 49-by-49-grid area with a distance interval of 0.1 m per grid, in an indoor VLC communication environment. According to the spatial distribution of the mse in Fig. 3(e) and the mse histogram and cumulative density function (CDF) in Fig. 3(f), it can be observed that more than 2200 (i.e., over 90% of the tested VLC channels) channel impulse responses fitting achieve mse less than 0.0005. This exemplifies the accuracy and reliability of the proposed gamma distribution fitting in general cases.

Now we can analytically express the channel impulse response as a LOS scalar plus a NLOS gamma distribution, for which the key parameters include LOS intensity I_{LOS}, NLOS intensity I_{NLOS}, the time delay Δt between NLOS and LOS, α, and β. Based on the fitted channel response parameters, the channel impulse response at a given receiver location can be represented analytically as

$$H = I_{LOS}\delta(t - \frac{d}{c}) + I_{NLOS}f(t - \frac{d}{c} - \Delta t; \alpha, \beta) \tag{6}$$

where $\frac{d}{c}$ is the light propagation delay between the transmitter and the receiver by following the LOS path, and f is the Gamma distribution function. The fitted analytic model allows us to efficiently obtain the channel impulse response at an arbitrary location, rather than time-consuming numerical calculations.

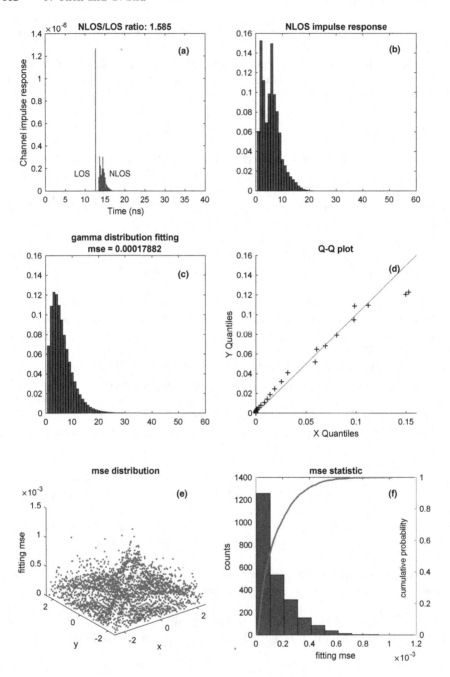

Fig. 3. A typical example of channel impulse response fitting. (a) a numerically calculated channel impulse response with LOS and NLOS; (b) the NLOS impulse response normalized with total NLOS intensity; (c) the fitted NLOS impulse response; (d) Q-Q plot to evaluate the fitting result; (e) fitting mse spatial distribution over the experimental area; (f) fitting mse statistic from e.

5   Secrecy Capacity Analysis

Consider an indoor VLC system consisting of a transmitter Alice, an intended receiver Bob, and an eavesdropper Eve, as shown in Fig. 1. Due to the diffusive and specular reflections of light, the signal transmitted from Alice to Bob may also be overheard by Eve. The received signals at Bob and Even can be represented respectively by

$$\begin{cases} Y_B = H_B X + Z_B, Z_B \sim N(0, \sigma_B^2) \\ Y_E = H_E X + Z_E, Z_E \sim N(0, \sigma_E^2) \end{cases} \tag{7}$$

where X denotes the transmitted light intensity from Alice, H_B and H_E denote the main channel gain, defined between Alice and Bob, and the eavesdropping channel gain, defined between Alice and Eve, respectively. Z_B and Z_E are zero-mean additive white Gaussian noise (AWGN) at Bob and Eve, respectively, which are assumed to be independent from each other. The variance of noise $\sigma_k^2 (k = B, E)$ is given by [16]

$$\sigma_k^2 = \sigma_{thermal}^2 + \sigma_{shot}^2 + W_{ISI} \tag{8}$$

where $\sigma_{thermal}^2$ and σ_{shot}^2 denote variances of the thermal noise in the receiver electronic circuits and the shot noise caused by ambient illumination from other light sources, respectively. These two noises are well modeled by an additive white Gaussian process. W_{ISI} denotes the inter-symbol interference (ISI) caused by the multiple reflections in a VLC channel, which may become significant under high

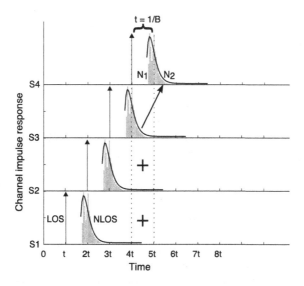

Fig. 4. Impact of ISI on system model caused by reflection. S stands for Symbol, t stands for inter symbol time interval.

symbol transmission rate. This is illustrated in Fig. 4, where the ISI for symbol 4 (S4) accounts for the accumulated power from all previous symbols (S1, S2, S3) over S4's reception window $[4t, 5t]$, where $t = 1/B$ is the reception time duration of a symbol at the receiver and B is simply the symbol rate of the VLC channel (binary intensity modulation is assumed). From this figure, it is clear that the received signal power and the ISI of a symbol (light pulse) can be calculated by partitioning the channel impulse response into two parts according to the symbol's reception window: The first part, denoted by N_1 in the figure, accounts for the first t seconds of the channel response inside the reception window, as measured beginning from the LOS component. The integral of N_1 contributes to the received signal power of the symbol. On the other hand, the second part, denoted by N_2 in the figure, includes all the remainder outside the reception window, whose integral amounts to the ISI (W_{ISI}) to the received symbol. So, H_k and σ_k^2 can be represented by

$$\begin{cases} H_k = N_1^{(k)} \\ \sigma_k^2 = \sigma_{thermal}^2 + \sigma_{shot}^2 + N_2^{(k)} \end{cases} \quad k = B, E. \tag{9}$$

where $N_1^{(k)}$ and $N_2^{(k)}$ are the integral of N_1 and N_2 defined w.r.t. the channel response at receiver k, respectively.

According to [29], the secrecy capacity C in this VLC network can be mathematically expressed as

$$C = \max_{f_X(x)} [I(X; Y_B) - I(X; Y_E)], s.t. \begin{cases} \int_0^A f_X(x)dx = 1; & 0 \leq X \leq A \\ E(X) = \int_0^A x f_X(x)dx = \xi A; & \xi \in (0, 1] \end{cases} \tag{10}$$

where $f_X(x)$ denotes the PDF of X, $I(X; Y)$ denotes the mutual information between two variables X and Y. A denotes the maximum peak optical intensity of the transmitter, ξ is the dimming target. For a practical system, the maximum optical intensity will be constrained by A and the dimmable average optical intensity will be constrained by ξ to satisfy the consistent illumination requirements.

Since the secrecy capacity is related to the information capacity of the communication channel, before determining the secrecy capacity in VLC networks it is essential to obtain the information capacity of the VLC channel with average, peak and non-negative constraints. However, to the best of our knowledge, the exact information capacity of the VLC channel with such constraints still remains unknown, even for the simplest SISO case, except that some lower and upper bounds have been derived [23,29]. In this paper, as we aim to study the impact of multiple reflections on secrecy capacity, our analysis will be based on the lower and upper bounds of the secrecy capacity. In particular, accounting for the new structure of the received signal and ISI (Eq. (9)) as induced by the multiple types of reflections in the VLC channel, and by following a similar derivation process in [29], we obtain a new set of lower bound and upper bound on the VLC channel secrecy capacity when the diffusive reflection and the specular reflection in the channel are considered. For simplicity when deriving the lower bound of secrecy capacity, we chose the average-to-peak optical intensity ratio $\xi = 0.5$ and re-wrote the objective function in Eq. (10) in entropy as

$$C = \max_{f_X(x)}[\mathcal{H}(Y_B) - \mathcal{H}(Y_E)] - \mathcal{H}(Y_B|X) + \mathcal{H}(Y_B|X) \tag{11}$$

then using the entropy power inequality in [14], the lower bound can be derived as

$$C \geq \frac{1}{2}\ln\left[\frac{3\sigma_E^2(H_B^2 A^2 + 2\pi e\sigma_B^2)}{2\pi e\sigma_B^2(H_E^2\xi^2 A^2 + 3\sigma_E^2)}\right]. \tag{12}$$

The dual expression of the secrecy capacity is employed when deriving the upper bound as in [23]. Given an arbitrary conditional PDF $g_{Y_B|Y_E}(y_B|y_E)$, we have the relative entropy equation

$$\begin{aligned}
&I(X;Y_B|Y_E) + E_{XY_E}D(f_{Y_B|Y_E}(y_B|Y_E)\|g_{Y_B|Y_E}(y_B|Y_E)) \\
&= E_{XY_E}D(f_{Y_B|XY_E}(y_B|X,Y_E)\|g_{Y_B|Y_E}(y_B|Y_E)).
\end{aligned} \tag{13}$$

According to the non-negative property of the relative entropy, we have

$$I(X;Y_B|Y_E) \leq E_{XY_E}D(f_{Y_B|XY_E}(y_B|X,Y_E)\|g_{Y_B|Y_E}(y_B|Y_E)). \tag{14}$$

Considering the constrains in Eq. (10), we can find an unique PDF $f_{X'}(x)$ that maximizes $I(X;Y_B|Y_E)$, which will lead to the secrecy capacity

$$C \leq E_{X'Y_E}D(f_{Y_B|XY_E}(y_B|X,Y_E)\|g_{Y_B|Y_E}(y_B|Y_E)). \tag{15}$$

Table 1. Numerical calculation parameters

	Parameter	Value
Room	Room size	$5 \times 5 \times 3\,\text{m}^2$
	Reflection coefficient (ρ)	0.8
	Diffusive percentage (r_d)	75%
Emitter	Emitter height	3 m
	Emitted optical power	1 W
	Number of rays	68000
	Modulation bandwidth	500 MHz
	Lambertian order (m, m', m'')	(1, 1, 250)
Receiver	Receiver height	0.85 m
	Receiver effective area	$10^{-4}\,\text{m}^2$
	Receiver FOV	$60°$
	Resolution (Δt)	0.2 ns

Using the principle of dual expression of the secrecy capacity and following a similar derivation process in [29], the upper bound can be derived as

$$
C \leq \frac{1}{2}ln \left[\frac{\left(\frac{H_E^2}{H_B^2}\sigma_B^2 + \sigma_E^2 \right) (H_B^2 A^2 \xi + \sigma_B^2)}{\sigma_B^2 \left(H_E^2 A^2 \xi + 2\frac{H_E^2}{H_B^2}\sigma_B^2 + \sigma_E^2 \right) \left(1 + \frac{H_E^2 \sigma_B^2}{H_B^2 \sigma_E^2} \right)} \right]. \tag{16}
$$

6   Numerical Experiment Design

To simplify our analysis, but without loss of generality, we design an indoor VLC environment with 5 m in length, 5 m in width, and 3 m in height. Similar to Fig. 1, the emitter is fixed at the center of ceiling and the receiver is placed on the receiver plane with a height of 0.85 m that is close to the height of a regular desk. We partition the receiver plane into small grid area with length of 0.1 m, resulting in 49-by-49-grid points taken as potential receiver location. Additional parameters assumed in the calculation are listed in Table 1. The default parameter value will be taken from the table hereafter if not specified.

We use a modified Monte Carlo ray tracing model from [20, 27] for numerical calculation of the channel impulse response. Our calculation is implemented using Matlab R2017a. Firstly, a large number of rays are randomly generated according to the radiation pattern from the emitter. When a ray impinges on a wall, the reflection point is converted into a new optical source, so a new ray is generated with the same distribution as the reflection pattern of that wall. In order to consider both the specular and diffusive reflections, when a ray arrives at the wall, a random number in the range (0, 1) is generated. If the generated number is smaller than the diffusive percentage r_d, the reflection for this ray is determined to be purely diffusive; otherwise, it becomes a specular reflection. After each reflection the power of the ray is reduced by the reflection coefficient of the wall. Since this model implements both diffusive and specular reflections, so it can represent real world scenarios more plausibly.

Then for each of the calculated 2401 channel impulse responses from 49-by-49-grid receivers, we use the nonlinear regression model in Matlab to fit the NLOS part of channel impulse response as gamma probability distribution. Once we get the seven key parameter sets, including receiver location coordinates, LOS intensity, NLOS intensity, the time delay Δt between NLOS and LOS, α, and β, the synthesized channel impulse response could be substituted into Eqs. (12) and (16) to calculate the corresponding secrecy capacity lower and upper bound. In order to quantitatively present the secrecy capacity bounds, we set the dimming target ξ as 0.5 during calculation.

7   Evaluations and Discussions

In order to test the key factors that impact the secrecy capacity, we create different scenarios by changing the locations of Bob and Eve, shown as in Fig. 5.

It shows the planimetric position of Alice (yellow illuminant), Bob (black triangle), and Eve (empty triangle), with Alice locates on the ceiling, Bob and Eve locates on the receiver plane. In the following subsections, some additional numerical results are provided to show the security performance of the indoor VLC system with multiple reflections considered.

7.1 Spatial Characteristics of Secrecy Capacity

Since the channel impulse response could be synthesized at any possible location in the indoor VLC system, the spatial character of secrecy capacity can be calculated accordingly. Figure 7 shows the spatial characteristics of secrecy capacity bounds calculated for Eve locating at each grid point with an spatial interval of 0.01 m, when Alice locates at A_1 and Bob locates at B_1. The upper two panels depict the spatial pattern of the upper bound and lower bound, both of which present similar spatial characteristics. Those red region show the vulnerable area of the VLC system, where the secrecy capacity approaches zero. They are mostly either following the diagonal line of the experimental plane or nearby the walls. The strong reflections from two adjacent walls might account for this quincunx pattern of the vulnerable zone. When receiver is approaching the walls, the intensity of NLOS part increases significantly, and it could become as strong as, or even stronger than, the intensity of LOS part. It would partially explain those vulnerable areas nearby the walls. The bottom two panels show the horizontal and diagonal cross section of the spatial secrecy capacity bounds. The relative quantity of secrecy capacity bounds is increasing from center to edge as Eve is getting far away from Bob. It's worthwhile to point out that there is a secrecy capacity cutoff on both sides, and it turns out to be result of the fixed modulation bandwidth as approaching the walls, which will be discussed in the next subsection. In real world application, it is also consistent with our real life experience as we always want the intended receiver placed at location with the best communication channel. When we have the main communication channel set up, the spatial characteristics would be used to identify the possible vulnerable area where eavesdropping likely takes place, which could be exploited to counter data sniffing. Based on the limited vulnerable area, additional detection mechanism could be instrumented to tell when an eavesdropping attack is under way.

7.2 Secrecy Capacity vs. Modulation Bandwidth

When considering the impact of multiple reflections on secrecy capacity, inter-symbol time interval (i.e., reception time duration of a symbol) is another significant factor for calculating ISI on secrecy capacity. It is determined by the reciprocal of symbol rate, as stated in Sect. 5. For simplicity, the binary intensity modulation is assumed during calculation, so the symbol rate is equivalent to modulation bandwidth if neglecting roll off factor. As long as the modulation bandwidth is determined, the inter-symbol time interval for each receiver at different location will be fixed as the same. However, the time delay from

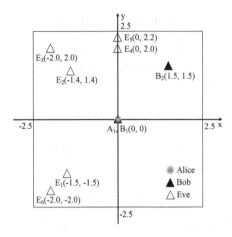 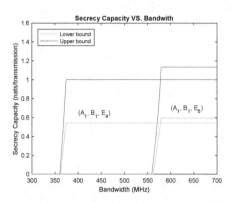

Fig. 5. Planimetric locations of Alice, Bob, and Eve for different experimental scenarios. A_x refers to Alice, B_x refers to Bob, and E_x refers to Eve.

Fig. 6. Secrecy capacity bounds changes with modulation bandwidth when Alice locates at A_1, Bob locates at B_1, and Eve locates at E_4 and E_5.

LOS to NLOS for channel impulse response of each receiver at different location will be different because of the different reflection path. So, given a location of receiver, if we change the modulation bandwidth, the impact on secrecy capacity will be identified once the inter-symbol time interval becomes comparable to the time delay from LOS to NLOS for channel impulse response. Figure 6 shows the change of secrecy capacity bounds with the bandwidth when Alice locates at A_1, Bob locates at B_1, and Eve locates at E_4 and E_5, respectively.

As we move Eve from E_4 to E_5, the eavesdropping channel is degraded, so there is an increase of secrecy capacity as expected. From both scenarios, we see a step function shaped change of secrecy capacity when increasing the modulation bandwidth. This is because for a given location of Eve, the time delay from LOS to NLOS for channel impulse response is determined, there is an increase of secrecy capacity as increase of bandwidth when the inter-symbol time interval is approaching the time delay. Once the inter-symbol time interval gets less than the time delay, the secrecy capacity will get saturated. It acts like a cutoff frequency of secrecy capacity due to the impact of reflections. This cutoff frequency varies for each location of Eve, and it increases as Eve getting far away from the center. It could partially explain the drastic drop or rise of secrecy capacity nearby the walls as we discussed in previous subsection (Fig. 7), because we used 500 MHz fixed modulation bandwidth for those scenarios. So, when we deploy a VLC system, we will have to consider not only the quality of the communication channel, but also the modulation bandwidth, as a higher modulation bandwidth would eliminate the feasibility of eavesdropping nearby the reflector, even though it could be far away from the main communication channel.

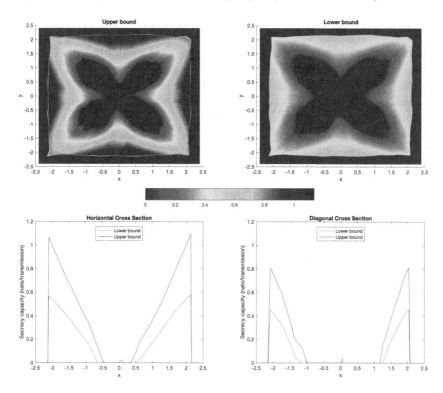

Fig. 7. Spatial characteristics of secrecy capacity bounds when Alice locates at A_1, Bob locates at B_1, and Eve locates at any place.

7.3   Secrecy Capacity vs. Diffusive Percentage

As discussed before, each reflection is supposed to be comprised of specular and diffusive reflections depending on the roughness of the wall. Intuitively, the more rough the wall is, the more diffusive part the reflection will contain. As the increase of the diffusive percentage, we would expect to see the corresponding increase of secrecy capacity, which is verified in Fig. 8 when Alice locates at A_1, Bob locates at B_1, and Eve locates at E_6. Since the numerically calculated channel impulse response using statistic approach for a given location varies from time to time, We calculate secrecy capacity bounds ten times for each diffusive percentage, and get the 95% confidence interval. There is a distinct increasing trend with larger uncertainty as the increase of diffusive percentage. Obviously, it would be difficult for eavesdropper to sniff effective data when most of the emitted energy are diffusely reflected. As a testbed exemplification in [12], different flooring materials (e.g., acrylic glass, vinyl plank, glazed tile, carpet, and laminate flooring) result in variable decoding bit error rate for eavesdropper, which imposes potential eavesdropping vulnerability. Thus, for indoor VLC system implementation, the construction material and design should be taken into consideration in case of security vulnerability.

7.4 Secrecy Capacity vs. Reflection Coefficient

On the other hand, when considering the property of the wall, the reflection coefficient is another significant factor that could impact the intensity of reflection. As for each reflection, the total emitted energy would be reduced by the reflection coefficient. Figure 9 shows the change of secrecy capacity with the reflection coefficient when Alice locates at A_1, Bob locates at B_1, and Eve locates at E_6. We can see a decreasing trend of the secrecy capacity with the increase of reflection coefficient, which is consistent with our intuition that high reflection coefficient would generate strong reflection and result in secrecy vulnerability. Considering the feasibility of vulnerability due to the high reflection coefficient, it would suggest to choose materials with low reflection coefficient to reduce the impact of reflections on secrecy capacity when designing an indoor VLC system. But in the real world application, according to [18], since the VLC uses a wide spectrum in $380 \sim 750\,\mathrm{nm}$, spectral reflectance of indoor reflector (e.g., ceiling, floor, plaster wall, plastic wall) varies a lot, which will make the design of indoor VLC system more complicated by inducing spectrum information.

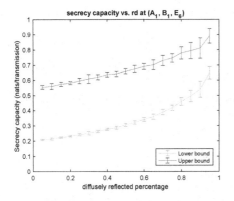
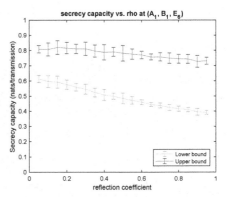

Fig. 8. Secrecy capacity bounds change with the percentage of diffusive reflection when Alice locates at A_1, Bob locates at B_1, and Eve locates at E_6. Error bar represent 95% confidence interval.

Fig. 9. Secrecy capacity bounds change with the reflection coefficient when Alice locates at A_1, Bob locates at B_1, and Eve locates at E_6. Error bar represent 95% confidence interval.

8 Conclusions

In this paper, the impact of multiple reflections on secrecy capacity of indoor VLC system is investigated. Base on the established indoor VLC system model with three entities, the system security performance is evaluated against a comprehensive set of factors, including the locations of the transmitter, receiver, and eavesdropper, the VLC channel bandwidth, the ratio between the specular and diffusive reflections, and the reflection coefficient, according to the calculated lower and upper secrecy capacity bounds. Both the specular reflection and diffusive reflection are considered in the system model, as the increase of the specular reflection part, the VLC system becomes more vulnerable. The spatial characteristics of secrecy capacity are also discussed, which could be used to identify possible vulnerable areas. Due to the addition of LOS and NLOS components, we have found areas with strong reflections, which makes feasible that if an eavesdropper located on those areas, he could sniff data at least partially due to reflection. The possible sniffing attack could also be used as an exploit on insidious attacks such as blocking and spoofing in future complex systems.

Acknowledgments. This work is supported in part by U.S. National Science Foundation (NSF) under grants CNS-1837034, CNS-1745254, CNS-1659965, and CNS-1460897. Any opinions, findings, conclusions, or recommendations expressed in this paper are those of the author(s) and do not necessarily reflect the views of NSF.

References

1. Al-Moliki, Y.M., Alresheedi, M.T., Al-Harthi, Y.: Robust key generation from optical OFDM signal in indoor VLC networks. IEEE Photonics Technol. Lett. **28**(22), 2629–2632 (2016). https://doi.org/10.1109/LPT.2016.2609683
2. Al-Moliki, Y.M., Alresheedi, M.T., Al-Harthi, Y.: Secret key generation protocol for optical OFDM systems in Indoor VLC networks. IEEE Photonics J. **9**(2), 1–15 (2017). https://doi.org/10.1109/JPHOT.2017.2667400
3. Arfaoui, M.A., Ghrayeb, A., Assi, C.: On the achievable secrecy rate of the MIMO VLC Gaussian wiretap channel. In: 2017 IEEE 28th Annual International Symposium on Personal, Indoor, and Mobile Radio Communications (PIMRC), pp. 1–5, October 2017. https://doi.org/10.1109/PIMRC.2017.8292592
4. Arfaoui, M.A., Ghrayeb, A., Assi, C.: Secrecy rate closed-form expressions for the SISO VLC wiretap channel with discrete input signaling. IEEE Commun. Lett. **22**(7), 1382–1385 (2018). https://doi.org/10.1109/LCOMM.2018.2829479
5. Barry, J.R., Kahn, J.M., Krause, W.J., Lee, E.A., Messerschmitt, D.G.: Simulation of multipath impulse response for indoor wireless optical channels. IEEE J. Sel. Areas Commun. **11**(3), 367–379 (1993). https://doi.org/10.1109/49.219552
6. Blinowski, G.J.: The feasibility of launching rogue transmitter attacks in indoor visible light communication networks. Wireless Pers. Commun., 1–19 (2017). https://doi.org/10.1007/s11277-017-4781-3
7. Carruthers, J.B., Carroll, S.M.: Statistical impulse response models for indoor optical wireless channels. Int. J. Commun. Syst. **18**(3), 267–284 (2005). https://doi.org/10.1002/dac.703
8. Chen, X., Jiang, M.: Adaptive statistical Bayesian MMSE channel estimation for visible light communication. IEEE Trans. Signal Process. **65**(5), 1287–1299 (2017). https://doi.org/10.1109/TSP.2016.2630036
9. Cho, S., Chen, G., Chun, H., Coon, J.P., O'Brien, D.: Impact of multipath reflections on secrecy in VLC systems with randomly located eavesdroppers. In: 2018 IEEE Wireless Communications and Networking Conference (WCNC), pp. 1–6, April 2018. https://doi.org/10.1109/WCNC.2018.8377184
10. Cho, S., Chen, G., Coon, J.P.: Secrecy analysis in visible light communication systems with randomly located eavesdroppers. In: 2017 IEEE International Conference on Communications Workshops (ICC Workshops), pp. 475–480, May 2017. https://doi.org/10.1109/ICCW.2017.7962703

11. Chowdhury, M.I.S., Zhang, W., Kavehrad, M.: Combined deterministic and modified monte carlo method for calculating impulse responses of indoor optical wireless channels. J. Lightwave Technol. **32**(18), 3132–3148 (2014). https://doi.org/10.1109/JLT.2014.2339131
12. Classen, J., Chen, J., Steinmetzer, D., Hollick, M., Knightly, E.: The spy next door: eavesdropping on high throughput visible light communications. In: Proceedings of the 2nd International Workshop on Visible Light Communications Systems, VLCS 2015, pp. 9–14. ACM, New York (2015). https://doi.org/10.1145/2801073.2801075
13. Classen, J., Steinmetzer, D., Hollick, M.: Opportunities and pitfalls in securing visible light communication on the physical layer. In: Proceedings of the 3rd Workshop on Visible Light Communication Systems, VLCS 2016, pp. 19–24. ACM, New York (2016). https://doi.org/10.1145/2981548.2981551
14. Cover, T.M., Thomas, J.A.: Elements of Information Theory. Wiley, New York (2012)
15. Ghassemlooy, Z., Popoola, W., Rajbhandari, S.: Optical Wireless Communications: System and Channel Modelling with MATLAB. CRC Press, Boca Raton (2012)
16. Komine, T., Nakagawa, M.: Fundamental analysis for visible-light communication system using LED lights. IEEE Trans. Consum. Electron. **50**(1), 100–107 (2004). https://doi.org/10.1109/TCE.2004.1277847
17. Lapidoth, A., Moser, S.M., Wigger, M.A.: On the capacity of free-space optical intensity channels. IEEE Trans. Inf. Theory **55**(10), 4449–4461 (2009). https://doi.org/10.1109/TIT.2009.2027522
18. Lee, K., Park, H., Barry, J.R.: Indoor channel characteristics for visible light communications. IEEE Commun. Lett. **15**(2), 217–219 (2011). https://doi.org/10.1109/LCOMM.2011.010411.101945
19. Liu, X., Wei, X., Guo, L., Liu, Y., Zhou, Y.: A new eavesdropping-resilient framework for indoor visible light communication. In: 2016 IEEE Global Communications Conference (GLOBECOM), pp. 1–6, December 2016. https://doi.org/10.1109/GLOCOM.2016.7841521
20. Lopez-Hernandez, F., Perez-Jimenez, R., Santamaria, A.: Ray-tracing algorithms for fast calculation of the channel impulse response on diffuse IR wireless indoor channels. Opt. Eng. **39**(10), 2775–2780 (2000)
21. Marin-Garcia, I., Ramirez-Aguilera, A.M., Guerra, V., Rabadan, J., Perez-Jimenez, R.: Data sniffing over an open VLC channel. In: 2016 10th International Symposium on Communication Systems, Networks and Digital Signal Processing (CSNDSP), pp. 1–6, July 2016. https://doi.org/10.1109/CSNDSP.2016.7573963
22. Mostafa, A., Lampe, L.: Securing visible light communications via friendly jamming. In: 2014 IEEE Globecom Workshops (GC Wkshps), pp. 524–529, December 2014. https://doi.org/10.1109/GLOCOMW.2014.7063485
23. Mostafa, A., Lampe, L.: Physical-layer security for MISO visible light communication channels. IEEE J. Sel. Areas Commun. **33**(9), 1806–1818 (2015). https://doi.org/10.1109/JSAC.2015.2432513
24. Mukherjee, A.: Secret-key agreement for security in multi-emitter visible light communication systems. IEEE Commun. Lett. **20**(7), 1361–1364 (2016). https://doi.org/10.1109/LCOMM.2016.2558562
25. Ozel, O., Ekrem, E., Ulukus, S.: Gaussian wiretap channel with amplitude and variance constraints. IEEE Trans. Inf. Theory **61**(10), 5553–5563 (2015). https://doi.org/10.1109/TIT.2015.2459705
26. Perez-Jimenez, R., Berges, J., Betancor, M.J.: Statistical model for the impulse response on infrared indoor diffuse channels. Electron. Lett. **33**(15), 1298–1300 (1997). https://doi.org/10.1049/el:19970866

27. Rodríguez Pérez, S., Pérez Jiménez, R., López Hernández, F., González Hernández, O., Ayala Alfonso, A.: Reflection model for calculation of the impulse response on IR-wireless indoor channels using ray-tracing algorithm. Microw. Opt. Technol. Lett. **32**(4), 296–300 (2002). https://doi.org/10.1002/mop.10159
28. Wang, J., Hu, Q., Wang, J., Chen, M., Wang, J.: Tight bounds on channel capacity for dimmable visible light communications. J. Lightwave Technol. **31**(23), 3771–3779 (2013). https://doi.org/10.1109/JLT.2013.2286088
29. Wang, J., Lin, S., Liu, C., Wang, J., Zhu, B., Jiang, Y.: Secrecy capacity of indoor visible light communication channels. In: 2018 IEEE International Conference on Communications Workshops (ICC Workshops), pp. 1–6, May 2018. https://doi.org/10.1109/ICCW.2018.8403760
30. Wu, D., Ghassemlooy, Z., Le-Minh, H., Rajbhandari, S., Chao, L.: Channel characteristics analysis of diffuse indoor cellular optical wireless communication systems. In: 2011 Asia Communications and Photonics Conference and Exhibition (ACP), pp. 1–6, November 2011. https://doi.org/10.1117/12.905663
31. Wyner, A.D.: The wire-tap channel. Bell Syst. Tech. J. **54**(8), 1355–1387 (1975). https://doi.org/10.1002/j.1538-7305.1975.tb02040.x
32. Xu, Y., Frahm, J.M., Monrose, F.: Watching the watchers: automatically inferring TV content from outdoor light effusions. In: Proceedings of the 2014 ACM SIGSAC Conference on Computer and Communications Security, CCS 2014, pp. 418–428. ACM, New York (2014). https://doi.org/10.1145/2660267.2660358
33. Yin, L., Haas, H.: Physical-layer security in multiuser visible light communication networks. IEEE J. Sel. Areas Commun. **36**(1), 162–174 (2018). https://doi.org/10.1109/JSAC.2017.2774429
34. Zaid, H., Rezki, Z., Chaaban, A., Alouini, M.S.: Improved achievable secrecy rate of visible light communication with cooperative jamming. In: 2015 IEEE Global Conference on Signal and Information Processing (GlobalSIP), pp. 1165–1169, December 2015. https://doi.org/10.1109/GlobalSIP.2015.7418381
35. Zhang, D., Hranilovic, S.: Bandlimited optical intensity modulation under average and peak power constraints. IEEE Trans. Commun. **64**(9), 3820–3830 (2016). https://doi.org/10.1109/TCOMM.2016.2592519

Road Context-Aware Intrusion Detection System for Autonomous Cars

Jingxuan Jiang[1], Chundong Wang[2(✉)], Sudipta Chattopadhyay[2], and Wei Zhang[1]

[1] School of Control Science and Engineering, Shandong University, Jinan, China
jingxuan_jiang@mail.sdu.edu.cn, davidzhang@sdu.edu.cn
[2] Singapore University of Technology and Design, Singapore, Singapore
cd_wang@outlook.com, sudipta_chattopadhyay@sutd.edu.sg

Abstract. Security is of primary importance to vehicles. The viability of performing remote intrusions to the in-vehicle network has been manifested. For unmanned autonomous cars, limited work has been done to detect such intrusions, while existing intrusion detection systems (IDSs) embrace limitations against strong adversaries. We hence consider the very nature of autonomous car and leverage the *road context* to design a novel IDS, named *R*oad context-*a*ware *IDS* (RAIDS). Given an autonomous car driving along continuous roads, road contexts and genuine frames transmitted on the car's in-vehicle network should resemble a regular and intelligible pattern. RAIDS employs a lightweight machine learning model to extract road contexts from sensory information (e.g., camera images and sensor values) used to control the car. With the road context, RAIDS validates corresponding frames observed on the in-vehicle network. Anomalous frames that substantially deviate from road context will be discerned as intrusions. We have built a prototype of RAIDS with neural networks, and done experiments on a Raspberry Pi with extensive datasets and meaningful intrusion cases. Evaluations show that RAIDS significantly outperforms state-of-the-art IDS without any road context by up to 99.9% accuracy and short response time.

Keywords: Autonomous car · Road context · Intrusion detection

1 Introduction

Security is critical for vehicles. A modern automobile embodies a protocol, like the prevalent Control Area Network (CAN) [11], for in-vehicle communications among its electrical subsystems, such as the steering wheel, brake, and engine, each of which is monitored and controlled through an electronic control unit (ECU). Researchers managed to manifest concrete intrusions to ECUs of manned

---

This work was done when J. Jiang was an intern at Singapore University of Technology and Design.

© Springer Nature Switzerland AG 2020
J. Zhou et al. (Eds.): ICICS 2019, LNCS 11999, pp. 124–142, 2020.
https://doi.org/10.1007/978-3-030-41579-2_8

vehicle to cause a breakdown or traffic accident [3,6,12,25]. Today, many practitioners and researchers are developing self-driving autonomous cars, which, undoubtedly, demand particular care for security and safety [14,17]. However, limited work has been done on designing an intrusion detection system (IDS) for the in-vehicle network of autonomous car. Existing IDSs even have limitations against strong adversaries. Take the state-of-the-art CIDS [6] for example. In accordance with its knowledge of all existing ECUs, CIDS tracks down anomalies when an original ECU stops sending frames or an ECU belonging to adversaries injects frames. Nevertheless, CIDS should be oblivious of a compromised ECU sending forged frames. If a strong adversary can manipulate an original ECU to deliver fake frames, CIDS would malfunction as the fingerprint of the ECU is not peculiar. As a result, such an attack model is beyond the capability of CIDS.

There is a fact that has not been considered in designing IDS to protect in-vehicle network: all frames transmitted on the CAN bus are generated due to the decisions made by the vehicle driver and it is the *road context* that guides a driver to make those decisions. Human drivers have highly individualized experiences and habits, and react differently to the same road context, like a stop sign or a road bend. It is hence impractical to design an IDS with road context for manned vehicles. By contrast, an autonomous car is orthogonal to manned vehicles concerning the very nature of 'driver'. In an autonomous car, decisions are made by a well-trained self-driving model upon dynamic road contexts obtained through multiple sensors [2,4]. Therefore, the road context and corresponding control signals, which eventually result in frames transmitted on the CAN bus, shall resemble a regular and intelligible pattern. Given an intrusion with forged frames upon continuous road contexts, a violation of the pattern can be perceivable.

Motivated by this observation, we develop a holistic IDS, i.e., *R*oad context-*a*ware **IDS** (**RAIDS**), for autonomous cars to detect anomalous CAN frames forged by strong adversaries. Main ideas of RAIDS are summarized as follows.

- RAIDS is a two-stage framework that mainly consists of two neural networks to extract road context from sensory information (e.g., images taken by cameras, distances to front objects, etc.) and validate the genuineness of CAN frames, respectively, for the purpose of intrusion detection. Both neural networks are designed to be lightweight and efficient regarding the computational resources of an in-vehicle embedded computing system.
- To extract road contexts, the neural network at the first stage of RAIDS processes camera images and other sensory information that are concurrently used by the self-driving model to control the car. The second stage of RAIDS is a binary classifier that verifies whether the frames observed on the CAN bus are abnormal or not with regard to the extracted road contexts.

We have built a prototype of RAIDS[1]. A convolutional neural network (CNN) makes the backbone of RAIDS's first stage for extracting and abstracting road contexts from camera images. The second stage of RAIDS mainly leverages linear

---

[1] The source code of RAIDS is available at https://github.com/cd-wang/RAIDS.

layers to efficiently discern anomalous CAN frames with extracted road context. To evaluate RAIDS, we follow state-of-the-art work [21] and implement an IDS that learns from historical CAN frames without road context. We run both IDSs in a Raspberry Pi with extensive datasets. On defending two types of intrusions, i.e., abrupt and directed intrusions, RAIDS substantially outperforms the IDS without road context by up to 99.9% accuracy and short response time.

The rest of this paper is as follows. In Sect. 2, we present the background and related works of RAIDS. In Sect. 3, we show the motivation and attack model for RAIDS. In Sect. 4, we detail the design of RAIDS. In Sect. 5, we present the evaluation results of RAIDS, and conclude the paper in Sect. 6.

2   Background and Related Works

IDS. Multiple IDSs have been proposed targeting the in-vehicle network [6, 11,13,15,19]. An automobile is made of multiple electrical subsystems, each of which has an ECU to communicate with other subsystems to control the vehicle. ECUs encapsulate data in frames and put them on the CAN bus. A CAN frame contains no identity information of sender or receiver for simplicity. The lack of identity in CAN frames facilitates adversaries in fabricating hazardous messages. Worse, modern vehicles are being connected to the outside world via multiple channels, which leave exploitable attack vectors for adversaries to leverage.

Many IDSs analyze normal CAN frames to detect anomalous ones. Müter and Asaj [15] found that CAN frames are more 'regular' than frames found on computer networks, which leads to a relatively low *entropy* for CAN frames. Hence injecting or dropping CAN frames should increase the entropy of in-vehicle network and in turn expose an intrusion. Song et al. [19] worked in a similar fashion but used the time interval between CAN frames to inspect suspicious frames. Taylor et al. [21] emphasized on the data carried in CAN frames and proposed a recurrent neural network (RNN)-based anomaly detector. Their RNN is trained with historical normal CAN frames to predict forthcoming frames and apprehend abnormal ones. Nonetheless, their experiments for detecting anomalous frames were done by manually flipping unused bits of data in a CAN frame to emulate an 'unusual case'. Such a manipulation is irrational as skilled adversaries must have a good knowledge of transmitted data and tend to fabricate meaningful but harmful frames. Wasicek et al. [25] proposed to learn the 'intra-vehicle context' by collecting the values of multiple sensors installed in a vehicle's subsystems and building reference models to detect anomalies. Note that their 'context' is the internal context inside a vehicle, not road context. Meanwhile, Cho and Shin [6] proposed Clock-based IDS (CIDS) that used the clock skew of ECUs to fingerprint them. Leveraging the unique clow skew of each ECU, CIDS can not only detect the occurrence of intrusions, but also locate the compromised ECU.

Autonomous Car and Neural Network. We consider an autonomous car that is computer-controlled most of the time except for emergency cases, such as an intrusion to in-vehicle network. Multiple sensors are installed to control an autonomous car, including cameras, ultrasonic distance sensors, radar, etc.

Such sensory information reflects and resembles real-world road context, and advises the self-driving model to generate control signals. Control signals are transformed to data encapsulated in frames transmitted on the CAN bus.

Numerical sensor values, like the distance to front objects, are computer-readable and can be directly utilized by the self-driving model of autonomous car. The camera images, however, must be processed to acquire high-level informative properties. Nowadays, neural networks have emerged as the mainstream approach that deals with images for self-driving. For example, the convolutional neural network (CNN) has been proved to be effective in extracting image features to maneuver the autonomous car [2,10]. A CNN makes use of convolutional layers that apply multiple kernels to extract embedded visual features. A kernel is a small matrix of numbers. An image can be viewed as a large matrix that comprises many small sub-matrices with the kernel size. Convolutional layer *convolves* each kernel over sub-matrices to do matrix multiplication. The output of a convolutional layer is thus a feature map that bundles results of convolving multiple kernels. In a CNN, feature maps of several convolutional layers, after being computed through hidden layers for reduction of computations and avoidance of overfitting, will eventually make a vector that resembles the features per image. Such a feature vector is expressive and meaningful in image understanding [4].

3   Problem Formulation

Motivation. Most IDSs were designed regarding human-driven vehicles. Many technology giants, startups, and academic researchers are developing autonomous cars, which, undoubtedly, demand particular care for security and safety.

Limited work has been done on detecting intrusions to the in-vehicle network of autonomous car. Worse, state-of-the-art IDSs embrace limitations against strong adversaries. For example, CIDS [6] is able to detect intrusions when a foreign ECU injects messages or an existing ECU stops sending messages based on its knowledge of fingerprints (i.e., clock skews) of ECUs. However, if adversaries compromise an ECU to send fake messages, CIDS will be ineffective as the fingerprint is not suspicious. CIDS should be oblivious of compromised ECUs sending fake messages. Such intrusion cases are beyond the capability of CIDS.

In practical, CAN frames are generated when drivers encounter dynamic road contexts. Assume that a stop sign is ahead. A driver must decelerate and then stop the car for a moment. The ECU of accelerator accordingly produces CAN frames with decreasing speed values. Fig. 1(a) and (b) illustrate how two human drivers react when they move towards a stop sign. One driver gradually reduces speed. The other one does so only when being close to the stop sign. Because human drivers have different experiences and habits, they have different reactions that entail distinct CAN frames.

When a car is controlled by a well-trained self-driving model, its behaviors should be smooth and stable. As shown by Fig. 1(c), an autonomous car shall start to reduce speed on spotting a stop sign and steadily slow down in

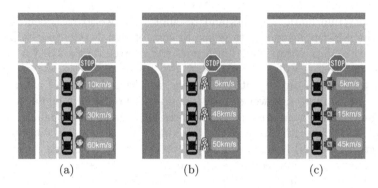

(a)   (b)   (c)

Fig. 1. An illustration of reactions of human-driven and autonomous cars on a stop sign: (a) Human-driven car 1; (b) Human-driven car 2, and (3) Autonomous car

order to approach the stop line. This results in CAN frames with consistently decreasing speed values. Concretely, the road context (i.e., a stop sign) and CAN frames (i.e., decreasing speed values) construct a regular and consistent pattern for autonomous car. Assume that adversaries compromise the accelerator of autonomous car and continually put CAN frames with non-decreasing speed values. These abnormal frames are easy to be ruled out as they significantly deviate from the pattern supposed for a stop sign.

To sum up, given a specific road context, the consequential CAN frames generated by an autonomous car are regular and predictable. If we monitor ongoing road context and validate against observed CAN frames, anomalous frames shall be detectable. This observation motivates us to design a new IDS.

Attack Model. Several network connections exist in an automobile to help it communicate with the outside world. These connections yet provide attack vectors for adversaries to exploit. We assume that strong adversaries further have good knowledge of in-vehicle network, including the format and frequency of CAN frames issued by an ECU, and also manage to force an ECU to encapsulate and send their data in CAN frames. With such knowledge, adversaries are able to remotely access and manipulate critical ECUs of an autonomous car, such as the steering wheel, brake, and accelerator. In this paper, we consider an attack model that is beyond the capability of state-of-the-art IDSs, i.e., *forgery attack*.

The process of a forgery attack is as follows. Once adversaries compromise an ECU, they first intercept the normal frames sent and received by the ECU to study the ECU's behavior and data format. Then adversaries start forging and sending CAN frames strictly with the original frequency. The data put in forged frames is yet made either inappropriate or opposite due to the malicious intentions of adversaries. For example, upon a left turn, adversaries may replace CAN frames of the steering wheel with right turn angles so as to wreck the car.

Forgery attack has two variants.

– *Abrupt intrusion*: adversaries abruptly place anomalous CAN frames with abnormal data at a random time to cause a disorder.

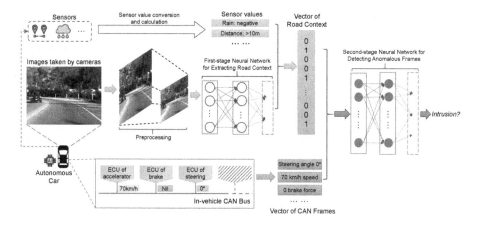

Fig. 2. An illustration of RAIDS's architecture

- *Directed intrusion*: adversaries monitor the road context at runtime and, upon a specific scenario, like a road bend or traffic light, place anomalous CAN frames that significantly violate the road context.

Assuming the autonomous car is unaware of any intrusion, the impact of directed intrusion is more detrimental, as the CAN frames it imposes shall inflict a sudden flip to the vehicle's state, like the aforementioned right turn upon a left turn.

4 RAIDS

4.1 Overview of RAIDS

The essence of RAIDS is to leverage the ongoing road context to validate whether CAN frames on the in-vehicle network are normal or not for an autonomous car. If CAN frames closely match the corresponding road context, RAIDS deems that there is no security threat. Otherwise, RAIDS will report an intrusion.

Figure 2 illustrates the architecture of RAIDS. As shown by the leftmost of Fig. 2, the ongoing road context is reflected by a variety of sensory information, such as the distances to surrendering objects and camera images showing the front scene. Numerical sensory information is computer-readable while camera images must be processed. The self-driving model depends on sensory information to decide how to maneuver the autonomous car. Such sensory information is also delivered to RAIDS. RAIDS is mainly composed of two neural networks. One neural network is responsible for processing the camera images which cannot be instantly utilized. The image is first preprocessed through techniques like normalization and centering. Then RAIDS uses one neural network, as shown at the central part of Fig. 2, to extract and abstract image features. These image features will be concatenated with other numerical sensory information to make a vector of road context. On the other hand, as illustrated by the lower half of Fig. 2, the self-driving model produces control signals upon the sensory information, which eventually conveys a number of CAN frames transmitted on the in-vehicle network. These CAN frames are formulated into another vector that is fed along with the vector of road context as two inputs to the second neural network of RAIDS. As shown by the rightmost of Fig. 2, with well-trained parameters learned from historical road contexts and CAN frames, the second neural network shall tell whether abnormal frames emerge on the CAN bus or not. RAIDS immediately informs the self-driving model once an anomaly is detected.

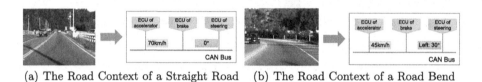

(a) The Road Context of a Straight Road   (b) The Road Context of a Road Bend

Fig. 3. An illustration of the impact of road context on CAN frames

If an intrusion is reported, RAIDS suggests that the self-driving model should (1) first disable external network connections to block remote adversaries, (2) stop the vehicle for emergency if possible, and (3) raise a switch request to human driving. These steps aim to mitigate the impact of intrusions.

4.2   Road Context

We define the road context as *the information an autonomous car is encountering when it is cruising.* In summary, the road context includes but is not limited to, (1) road conditions, like traffic lights, the bend, joint, and fork of roads, (2) pedestrians, vehicles, obstacles, and bumps around the car, (3) weather conditions, like the rain, fog, and snow, and (4) the sunrise, sunset, and tunnel lights. These road contexts are perceived by sensors installed in the car, including cameras, ultrasonic distance sensors, water sensor, etc.

The road context determines control signals issued by the self-driving model. Different road contexts entail different signals, which in turn generate different CAN frames. Figure 3 instantiates the impact of road curves on the control signal. As shown in Fig. 3(a), on a highway that is straight, the self-driving model demands the autonomous car to move straightforward and run at a velocity of 70km/h. By contrast, upon a road bend as illustrated in Fig. 3(b), the framework shall decrease the car's velocity to 45 km/h and turn to the left with an angle of 30°. Assuming that on the road shown in Fig. 3(b), a frame with a steering angle of 0° for moving straightforward, rather than the rational frame of left turn with 30°, emerges on the CAN bus, an intrusion should have taken place because the anomalous frame is not congruent with the ongoing road context.

CAN frames are ever-changing due to dynamic road contexts from time to time. The tight relation between road context and CAN frames indicates that road context must be exploited as a crucial parameter to detect intruions initiated onto the in-vehicle network. We hypothesize that the self-driving model of autonomous car is intact and always makes wise and regular decisions upon dynamic road contexts. In other words, an autonomous car is a contrast to manned vehicles in which human drivers may behave inconsistently from time to time even regarding the same road context. In addition, we note that the focus of this paper is on detecting security threats imposed by adversaries onto ECUs and in-vehicle network of a self-driving automobile. Readers may refer to other studies for the vulnerability exploration of deep learning models that drive a vehicle [20,24] and intrusion detections for the traffic systems [8].

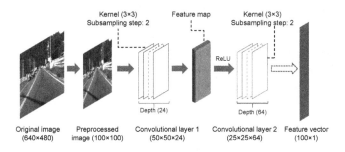

Fig. 4. The architecture of RAIDS's CNN

4.3   Extracting Road Context

We first extract the road context to use it for intrusion detection. As a matter of fact, most of the road context is reflected by the front scene that autonomous car is facing, including the aforementioned road condition, traffic light and weather. Such a scene is tracked by multiple sensors. Numerical sensory information, like the distance to front objects, can be directly utilized by RAIDS since they are both human- and computer-readable. The images captured by cameras, however, need to be converted into a format that RAIDS can deploy. As a result, the difficulty of obtaining road context lies in how to process camera images.

As mentioned in Sect. 2, the feature vector obtained in a deep neural network is a promising abstraction of road context contained in an image for RAIDS to leverage for intrusion detection. Concretely, we construct a CNN as the backbone of the first stage of RAIDS to extract and abstract the road context from camera images. Figure 4 sketches the architecture of the CNN employed by RAIDS to process images. It mainly consists of two convolutional layers. After being preprocessed, the first convolutional layer would apply 24 kernels, each of which is 3×3 with a subsampling step[2] of 2, to generate a feature map

---

[2] A subsampling of 2 means that the convolutional layer moves each kernel by 2, rather than 1, when sliding over the large matrix of image, to reduce the dimensionality of feature map but without losing important information of the image. So the size of feature map for one kernel is $\frac{100}{2} \times \frac{100}{2} = 50 \times 50$.

(50 × 50 × 24). This feature map goes through a rectified linear unit (ReLU), which is the activation function used in our implementation, and then reaches the second convolutional layer. The second convolutional layer applies 64 kernels, each of which also has 3 × 3 size with a subsampling step of 2. The second feature map is hence 25 × 25 × 64, and would entail a feature vector of 100 × 1 after passing one dropout layer and two dense layers.

Figure 5 exemplifies the feature maps visualized after two convolutional layers for two images from Udacity dataset [23] when they are being processed by the CNN of RAIDS. A comparison between Fig. 5(a) and (b) confirms that different road contexts lead to different intermediate features. In the end, the feature vector of each image would be assembled with numerical sensor values into a new vector as one of the inputs to the second stage of RAIDS.

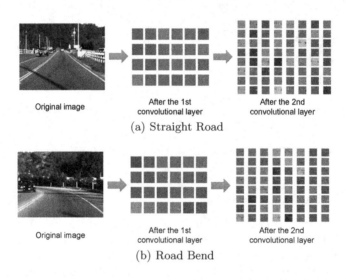

Original image   After the 1st   After the 2nd
convolutional layer   convolutional layer

(a) Straight Road

Original image   After the 1st   After the 2nd
convolutional layer   convolutional layer

(b) Road Bend

Fig. 5. An illustration of extracting features from images by RAIDS's CNN

The CNN extracting image features for RAIDS works synchronously with the self-driving model of autonomous car, because RAIDS should verify CAN frames produced by the self-driving model on the same road context. RAIDS's CNN is simpler than the self-driving model's. The reason is twofold. First, the self-driving model does not terminate with image features but has to accordingly do further computations to determine control signals subsuming left or right steering with a degree, acceleration with a velocity, brake with a force, etc. Second, the feature vector generated by the CNN of RAIDS can be coarse-grained as long as they are sufficiently accurate for detecting intrusions at the second stage of RAIDS.

4.4   Intrusion Detection with Road Context

After obtaining the vector of road context and CAN frames corresponding to the road context, we can establish a model between them by learning over historical records of road contexts and CAN frames. With the model, RAIDS validates whether observed CAN frames approximately match the newly-arrived image and sensor values. A substantial discrepancy would lead to a report of intrusion.

As historical records of sensory information and CAN frames are known as normals, how to detect intrusions on the in-vehicle network regarding road context turns to be a problem of developing a supervised learning model to check CAN frames upon forthcoming sensory information. Assume that N items of sensory information are used for training. The ith sensory information ($0 \leq i < N$) has a vector of road context r_i obtained from the first stage of RAIDS. Still for the ith sensory information, CAN frames issued by ECUs like steering wheel, accelerator, and brake have been collected and presented in a vector c_i. In the perspective of supervised learning, we can make a label λ_i ('1' for normal and '0' for anomaly) for r_i and c_i. Given these N tuples forming a training dataset,

$$\{\langle r_0, c_0, \lambda_0 \rangle, \langle r_1, c_1, \lambda_1 \rangle, ..., \langle r_i, c_i, \lambda_i \rangle, ..., \langle r_{N-1}, c_{N-1}, \lambda_{N-1} \rangle\}, \tag{1}$$

RAIDS's supervised learning attempts to seek out a model,

$$g(r_i, c_i) \approx \lambda_i, (0 \leq i < N). \tag{2}$$

Or put in another way,

$$g : \boldsymbol{R} \times \boldsymbol{C} \to \boldsymbol{\Lambda}, \tag{3}$$

in which $\boldsymbol{R}$, $\boldsymbol{C}$, and $\boldsymbol{\Lambda}$ are the domain spaces of road contexts, CAN frames, and labels, respectively.

The function g should be one that the best describes the relationship between $\boldsymbol{R}$, $\boldsymbol{C}$, and $\boldsymbol{\Lambda}$. For a new element of $\boldsymbol{R} \times \boldsymbol{C}$, which will be forthcoming road context r_x and its corresponding vector of CAN frames v_x, RAIDS computes $g(r_x, v_x)$ and obtains a label λ_x. If λ_x is '0', RAIDS deems there would be no intrusion at that moment. Otherwise, RAIDS informs the self-driving model of a possible intrusion on the CAN bus. Consequently, the second stage of RAIDS is formatted as a problem of binary classification. In the prototype of RAIDS, we build a classifier that is mainly composed of two linear layers. There are two reasons to do so. First, r_i, v_i, and λ_i are numerical vectors. Linear layers are sufficient to speculate their relationship. Second, linear layers bring about relatively simpler computations, which are especially efficient concerning the response time of IDS and the computational resources of an embedded computing system.

4.5   Training and Testing

We have built the first and second stages of RAIDS[3] with a CNN and a binary classifier, respectively, based on Keras [7] and PyTorch [16] frameworks. We follow an end-to-end learning fashion [2] to train RAIDS. The loss function is BCELoss (Binary Cross-Entropy loss) provided by PyTorch for binary classification [18]. We would use six datasets to evaluate RAIDS (more details can

---

[3] The source code of RAIDS is available at https://github.com/cd-wang/RAIDS.

be found in Sect. 5). In each dataset, we use 70% images and CAN frames for training while the 30% remainders are used for the purpose of testing. We note that because datasets have different image sizes, RAIDS would have different implementation variants to deal with respective datasets.

5   Evaluation

We have performance evaluations to answer three questions.

Q1. Does RAIDS achieve high accuracy in intrusion detection? Is the performance of RAIDS stable over different datasets?

Q2. How is the efficacy of RAIDS? Does it cost reasonable response time to detect an intrusion in an embedded computing system?

Q3. Is RAIDS effective in detecting intrusions under more difficult road contexts. e.g., nighttime road conditions?

5.1   Evaluation Setup

Datasets. We have used six datasets from five sources. Their descriptions are presented in Table 1. Except Udacity_sim with images recorded in a synthesized simulator, all other datasets were collected in the real world. They all contain a large number of records with images and data conveyed in CAN frames.

Road Context. We place emphasis on the road conditions reflected by camera images, such as lane lines, road bends, and turns. There are two reasons to do so. First, not all datasets provide numerical sensor values. Second, less sensory information imposes more challenges in precisely obtaining road context.

At the standpoint of adversaries, we would focus on intrusions onto the steering wheel. The reason is threefold. First, the steering angle is one vital control signal for autonomous car and attracts wide attention for research. Second, the steering angle is ever-changing along the road while the control signals from accelerator and brake remain relatively stable for a moving vehicle. Figure 6 sketches two curves for the steering angle and vehicle speed at runtime, respectively, with one Udacity sub-dataset (HMB_6). It is evident that the curve of vehicle speed is much smoother than that of steering angle. Therefore, an intrusion to compromise steering angle is more difficult to be detected. Third, some datasets, like Chen_2017 and Chen_2018, only include the runtime values of steering angle.

Intrusions. We consider forgery attacks in evaluation. We have performed abrupt and directed intrusions to the steering angles with each dataset. In contrast to existing works that encapsulated meaningless data in CAN frames or fabricated artificial CAN frames, our intrusions generate a CAN frame with an allowable value that yet does not match the ongoing road context. The rightmost two columns of Table 1 brief how we manipulate steering angles to produce abrupt and directed intrusion cases. Note that six datasets have different ranges

Table 1. The datasets and intrusions used to evaluate RAIDS

Datasets	Sources	Genuine steering angle ranges in radian	Manipulations of abrupt intrusion	Manipulations of directed intrusion
Udacity	Udacity self-driving challenge [23]	[−2.05, 1.90]	Randomly select 30% images and for an image, add or subtract a random value in [0.1, 0.9] to its corresponding angle	Select the largest 15% and smallest 15% angles. Flip the sign of a selected angle if its absolute value is larger than 0.3. If not, add or subtract a random value in [0.5, 1]
Udacity_sim	Udacity simulator [22]	[−0.94, 1.00]		
Apollo	Road Hackers platform in Baidu Apollo Project [1]	[−0.38, 0.21]	Randomly select 30% images and for an image, add or subtract a random value in [0.08, 0.5] to its corresponding angle	
Chen_2017	Recorded by Sully Chen in 2017 and 2018, respective [5]	[−1.99, 0.55]	Randomly select 30% images and for an image, add or subtract random value in [0.2, 0.9] to its corresponding angle	
Chen_2018		[−2.01, 0.68]		
Comma.ai	Comma.ai highway driving [9]	[−1.64, 1.29]	Randomly select 30% images and for an image, add or subtract a random value in [0.25, 1] to its corresponding angle	

for steering angles. For example, for the HMB_6 sub-dataset of Udacity shown by Fig. 6(a), steering angles fall in [−0.17, 0.11] while the range for Chen_2018 is [−1.99, 0.55]. For each dataset, we apply appropriate values to modify the steering angles so as to make intrusion cases that are not trivial to be perceived.

Competitor. We implement an IDS without considering the road context (referred to as IDS_wo_rc) for comparison. It is identical to the start-of-the-art IDS proposed by Taylor et al. [21]. IDS_wo_rc depends on learning CAN frames with RNN to determine whether an arriving frame contains genuine data or not. For IDS_wo_rc, 70% of each dataset is used for training while 30% is for testing, the same as what we do with RAIDS. For both RAIDS and IDS_wo_rc, training is performed in a Linux server while testing is done in a Raspberry Pi 3 Model B+. Python 3.5 is installed in the server and Raspberry Pi. We assume that an embedded system with Raspberry Pi's computing powers is within the in-vehicle network gateway [11] where an IDS resides to protect the in-vehicle network.

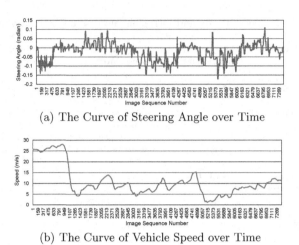

(a) The Curve of Steering Angle over Time

(b) The Curve of Vehicle Speed over Time

Fig. 6. Curves of steering angle and vehicle speed with Udacity's HMB_6 dataset

Metrics. The main metric we use to compare RAIDS and IDS_wo_rc is the detection accuracy in testing, i.e., the ratio of detected normal and intrusion cases against overall cases. A higher detection accuracy means a better effectiveness of IDS. We also measure the ratios of undetected intrusion cases as well as false alarms by which an IDS wrongly labels a normal CAN frame to be anomalous. To study the efficiency of RAIDS, we record the average and maximum response time RAIDS spends in processing all cases of a dataset.

5.2   Detection Accuracy

Detection Accuracy. Figure 7 summarizes the detection accuracies of RAIDS and IDS_wo_rc with six datasets under abrupt and directed intrusions. The first observation obtained from Fig. 7 is that, RAIDS consistently achieves high detection accuracies across different datasets under both abrupt and directed intrusions. In particular, the highest accuracy for RAIDS is 99.9% with Apollo under directed intrusion while its lowest accuracy is 89.5% with Comma.ai under abrupt intrusion. IDS_wo_rc's highest accuracy is 84.5% with Apollo under directed intrusion while its lowest accuracy is 71.8% with Comma.ai under abrupt intrusion. The significant gap between RAIDS's and IDS_wo_rc's accuracies confirms the high effectiveness of RAIDS. RAIDS leverages the road context for intrusion detection while IDS_wo_rc solely relies on the data of historical CAN frames to apprehend the newly-arrived CAN frame. As shown in Fig. 6(b), the runtime volatile curve of steering angle alone is difficult to be modeled, unless it is associated with corresponding road context, like what RAIDS does. So the model built by IDS_wo_rc lacks reliability. RAIDS, nonetheless, extracts a feature vector of road context from each image and involves it for validating corresponding CAN frames. RAIDS thus establishes a sound model that maps a specific road context, like a road bend, to CAN frames. In summary, if adversaries put frames with abnormal data on the CAN bus, the unreliable model of IDS_wo_rc is ineffective in identifying the anomaly; however, on account of using road context, RAIDS has a much higher likelihood of detecting the intrusion.

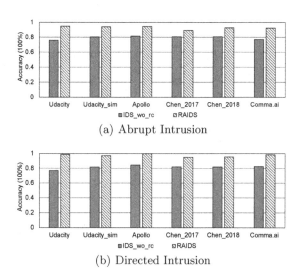

(a) Abrupt Intrusion

(b) Directed Intrusion

Fig. 7. The accuracies of two IDSs under two types of intrusions with six datasets

The second observation obtained from Fig. 7 is that the detection accuracy under directed intrusion is consistently higher than that under abrupt intrusion, especially for RAIDS. For example, with Udacity, Apollo and Comma.ai datasets, the accuracy of RAIDS under directed intrusion is 4.0%, 5.4% and 7.2% higher than that under abrupt intrusion, respectively. As mentioned, directed intrusion should be more hazardous than abrupt intrusion because the former intends to incur a sudden change at a specific occasion onto the in-vehicle communications. Such a sudden change yet brings in more significant violation to ongoing road context, which exactly matches the capability of RAIDS and can be easily captured. This explains why RAIDS yields higher detection accuracy under directed intrusion. Also, as shown in Fig. 6(a), there exist dramatic increase and decrease of steering angle at runtime in reality. Consequently, IDS_wo_rc does not raise much difference in accuracy, i.e., at most 5.4% with Apollo.

Unreported Intrusions. We also record the percentages of detected and unreported intrusions as well as detected normals and false alarms for six datasets under two types of intrusions. These results help us gain a deeper understanding of the accuracies of RAIDS and IDS_wo_rc. They are detailed in Fig. 8. Let us first focus on the percentages of detected intrusion cases as the percentage of false alarms are generally low. One observation is that, in all 16 diagrams, RAIDS detects most of the intrusion cases while IDS_wo_rc even cannot report half of

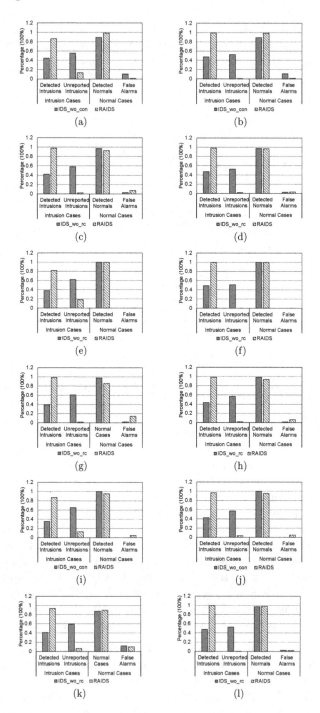

Fig. 8. The percentages of unreported intrusions and false alarms for two IDSs under abrupt and directed intrusions: (a) and (b) for Udacity; (c) and (d) for Udacity_sim; (e) and (f) for Apollo; (g) and (h) for Chen_2017; (i) and (j) for Comma.ai.

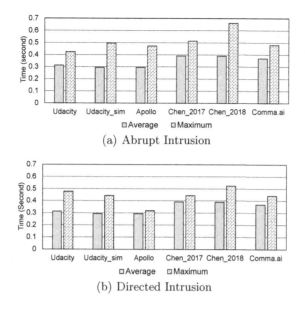

(a) Abrupt Intrusion

(b) Directed Intrusion

Fig. 9. The average and maximum response time of RAIDS under two intrusions

them. For example, in Fig. 8(i), the percentages of detected and unreported intrusion cases are 87.2% and 12.8%, respectively, for RAIDS with Chen_2018 under abrupt intrusion; however, they are 35.0% and 65.0% for IDS_wo_rc, respectively. In other words, without road context, IDS_wo_rc ignores many intrusion cases. This in turn justifies the importance of road context in intrusion detection. In addition, as to Apollo with the aforementioned 99.9% accuracy under directed intrusion, Fig. 8(f), tells that there is hardly unreported intrusion or false alarm. This reaffirms the highest accuracy achieved by RAIDS.

Second, let us make a comparison between abrupt and directed intrusions. Take Chen_2018 for example again with Fig. 8(i) and (j). The percentage of detected intrusion cases for RAIDS increases from 87.2% under abrupt intrusion to 96.5% under directed intrusion. Such an increase confirms that directed intrusion is likely to incur intrusion cases that are easier to be perceived. Comparatively, the percentage of detected intrusion cases for IDS_wo_rc jumps from 35.0% under abrupt intrusion to 42.5% under directed intrusion. Although the difference is considerable (42.5% − 35.0% = 7.5%), it is less than that of RAIDS (96.5% − 87.2% = 9.3%). These numbers agree with the second observation we have with Fig. 7, and explain why the accuracy of IDS_wo_rc does not increase as much as that of RAIDS from abrupt intrusion to directed intrusion.

5.3   Response Time

With Raspberry Pi, we have measured the response time of RAIDS in detecting intrusions for six datasets. The two diagrams in Fig. 9 capture the average and maximum response time of processing all records of images and corresponding CAN frames under abrupt and directed intrusions, respectively. The results shown in Fig. 9 state that none of the average response time is greater than 0.40 s. More important, the maximum response time, which meas the worst-case response time, is mostly no greater than 0.52 s, except with Chen_2018 for which RAIDS cost 0.66 s under abrupt intrusion. Concretely, the short response time justifies the efficiency of RAIDS.

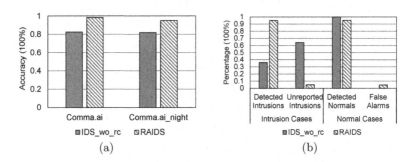

Fig. 10. A comparison between daytime and nighttime datasets for RAIDS: (a) Detection accuracy and (b) Unreported intrusions and false alarms with Comma.ai_night

The average response time does not deviate much from the maximum response time because each record contains almost the same quantity of data, i.e., image and CAN frames, for RAIDS to handle. The marginal deviation is mainly caused by other running programs and system scheduling in a real embedded computing system. Note that we have used an economical Raspberry Pi for testing. The computational resources of Raspberry Pi include an inexpensive 1.4 GHz ARM CPU and 1 GB DRAM. With regard to employing RAIDS in real-world autonomous cars, a more powerful embedded system with high-end CPU and larger RAM space could be leveraged to reduce the response time, which surely improves the efficiency and applicability of RAIDS.

5.4 The Impact of Daytime and Night

It is non-trivial to extract meaningful features from nighttime images due to the generally low visibility of road conditions. Comma.ai provides a sub-dataset with nighttime images and CAN frames (referred to as Comma.ai_night). We have done abrupt and directed intrusions with it. Due to space limitation, we present the results under directed intrusion. Figure 10(a) captures the comparison of IDS_wo_rc's and RAIDS's accuracies between daytime Comma.ai and nighttime Comma.ai_night. The accuracy of IDS_wo_rc does not fluctuate much since it is oblivious of the change of day and night. Nevertheless, due to the weaker perception of road context at night, the accuracy of RAIDS drops by 3.3%.

A comparison between Fig. 8(l) for Comma.ai and Fig. 10(b) for Comma.ai_night shows that, the percentages of unreported intrusions and false alarms for RAIDS increase by 4.6% and 2.7%, respectively. Thus, a bit more mistakes (undetected intrusions and false alarms) were made due to the relatively obscure nighttime road contexts. This explains the accuracy drop of RAIDS for nighttime images.

6   Conclusion

In this paper, we investigate how to effectively detect intrusions to the in-vehicle communications of autonomous car. In an autonomous car, a self-driving model reads sensory information reflecting ever-changing road contexts and generates control signals that are eventually transformed into CAN frames. We accordingly develop RAIDS. RAIDS extracts and abstracts road contexts from sensory information into a feature vector. It then leverages such an expressive feature vector of road context to assert the genuineness of observed CAN frames. We have built a prototype for RAIDS through lightweight neural networks, and evaluated it in an embedded computing system with extensive datasets. Experimental results confirm that RAIDS achieves up to 99.9% accuracy with short response time.

Acknowledgements. The authors appreciate the pioneering attempts done by Tanya Srivastava and Pryanshu Arora. This work is partially supported by the Ministry of Education of Singapore under the grant MOE2018-T2-1-098 and Singapore University of Technology and Design under the grant SRIS17123.

References

1. Apollo.auto: Roadhackers platform in Baidu Apollo project, April 2018. http:// data.apollo.auto/static/pdf/road_hackers_en.pdf
2. Bojarski, M., et al.: End to end learning for self-driving cars. arXiv preprint arXiv:1604.07316 (2016)
3. Checkoway, S., et al.: Comprehensive experimental analyses of automotive attack surfaces. In: Proceedings of the 20th USENIX Conference on Security, USENIX Security 2011, pp. 77–92. USENIX Association, Berkeley (2011)
4. Chen, C., Seff, A., Kornhauser, A., Xiao, J.: DeepDriving: learning affordance for direct perception in autonomous driving. In: Proceedings of the 2015 IEEE International Conference on Computer Vision (ICCV), ICCV 2015, pp. 2722–2730. IEEE Computer Society, Washington (2015)
5. Chen, S.: Sully Chen's driving datasets (2017 & 2018), April 2018. https://github. com/SullyChen/driving-datasets
6. Cho, K.T., Shin, K.G.: Fingerprinting electronic control units for vehicle intrusion detection. In: Proceedings of the 25th USENIX Security Symposium, USENIX Security 2016, pp. 911–927. USENIX Association, Austin (2016)
7. Chollet, F., et al.: Keras: deep learning for humans, February 2019. https://keras.io
8. Chowdhury, A., Karmakar, G., Kamruzzaman, J., Saha, T.: Detecting Intrusion in the Traffic Signals of an Intelligent Traffic System. In: Naccache, D., et al. (eds.) ICICS 2018. LNCS, vol. 11149, pp. 696–707. Springer, Cham (2018). https://doi. org/10.1007/978-3-030-01950-1_41

9. Comma.ai: The Comma.ai driving dataset, October 2016. https://github.com/commaai/research

10. He, K., Zhang, X., Ren, S., Sun, J.: Deep residual learning for image recognition. In: 2016 IEEE Conference on Computer Vision and Pattern Recognition (CVPR), pp. 770–778, June 2016

11. Hoppe, T., Kiltz, S., Dittmann, J.: Security threats to automotive CAN networks-practical examples and selected short-term countermeasures. Reliab. Eng. Syst. Saf. **96**(1), 11–25 (2011). Special Issue on Safecomp 2008

12. Kang, M.J., Kang, J.W.: Intrusion detection system using deep neural network for in-vehicle network security. PLoS ONE **11**(6), e0155781 (2016)

13. Kleberger, P., Olovsson, T., Jonsson, E.: Security aspects of the in-vehicle network in the connected car. In: 2011 IEEE Intelligent Vehicles Symposium (IV), pp. 528–533. IEEE, June 2011

14. Koscher, K., et al.: Experimental security analysis of a modern automobile. In: 2010 IEEE Symposium on Security and Privacy, pp. 447–462. IEEE (2010)

15. Müter, M., Asaj, N.: Entropy-based anomaly detection for in-vehicle networks. In: 2011 IEEE Intelligent Vehicles Symposium (IV), pp. 1110–1115, June 2011

16. Paszke, A., Gross, S., Chintala, S., Chanan, G.: PyTorch, February 2019. https://pytorch.org/

17. Petit, J., Shladover, S.E.: Potential cyberattacks on automated vehicles. IEEE Trans. Intell. Transp. Syst. **16**(2), 546–556 (2015)

18. PyTorch: PyTorch BCELoss function, February 2019. https://pytorch.org/docs/stable/nn.html

19. Song, H.M., Kim, H.R., Kim, H.K.: Intrusion detection system based on the analysis of time intervals of CAN messages for in-vehicle network. In: Proceedings of the 2016 International Conference on Information Networking (ICOIN), ICOIN 2016, pp. 63–68. IEEE Computer Society, Washington (2016)

20. Su, J., Vargas, D.V., Sakurai, K.: One pixel attack for fooling deep neural networks. IEEE Trans. Evol. Comput. **23**, 828–841 (2019)

21. Taylor, A., Leblanc, S., Japkowicz, N.: Anomaly detection in automobile control network data with long short-term memory networks. In: IEEE International Conference on Data Science and Advanced Analytics (DSAA), pp. 130–139, October 2016

22. Udacity: Udacity's self-driving car simulator, July 2017. https://github.com/udacity/self-driving-car-sim

23. Udacity: The Udacity open source self-driving car project, April 2018. https://github.com/udacity/self-driving-car

24. Wang, B., et al.: Neural cleanse: identifying and mitigating backdoor attacks in neural networks. In: 2019 IEEE Symposium on Security and Privacy (SP), pp. 1–16, May 2019

25. Wasicek, A., Pesé, M.D., Weimerskirch, A., Burakova, Y., Singh, K.: Context-aware intrusion detection in automotive control systems. In: 5th Embedded Security in Cars (ESCar 2017), June 2017

Enterprise Network Security

Automated Cyber Threat Intelligence Reports Classification for Early Warning of Cyber Attacks in Next Generation SOC

Wenzhuo Yang and Kwok-Yan Lam[✉]

School of Computer Science and Engineering, Nanyang Technological University,
Singapore, Singapore
wenzhuo001@e.ntu.edu.sg, kwokyan.lam@ntu.edu.sg

Abstract. Serving as a facility to collect and analyze security data, monitor anomaly activities, Security Operation Center (SOC) provides defense measures to protect the enterprise and government system from malicious intrusion. As the cyber attacks are increasingly sophisticated and harmful, it becomes a global trend to share cyber threat intelligence (CTI) between SOCs and other security departments. Security analysts can get a comprehensive understanding of diverse cyber attacks' features and make early warning and quick response for potential attacks by CTI analysis. More CTI reports generation and frequent CTI sharing cause an urgent need for much higher analysis efficiency capacity that traditional SOC does not have. Facing the big data challenge and limited professional security analysts resources, next generation SOC (NG-SOC) should emphasize greatly on processing security data like CTI reports automatically and efficiently through data mining and machine learning techniques. This paper presents a practical and efficient approach for gathering the large quantities of CTI sources into high-quality data and enhancing the CTI analysis ability of NG-SOC. Specifically, we first propose a multi-classification framework for CTI reports by combining two document embedding models and six machine learning classifiers respectively to group the same and similar threat reports together before they are analyzed. We collect 25092 CTI reports from open sources and label the reports based on their threat types and attack behaviors. Experiment results show that three classifiers can achieve higher prediction accuracy, which makes it applicable to process the massive volume of CTI reports efficiently for security analysts in NG-SOC and give early warning to help related users take proactive countermeasures to mitigate hidden costs or even avoid potential cyber attacks.

Keywords: Cyber security · Cyber threat intelligence · Text classification · Machine learning

© Springer Nature Switzerland AG 2020
J. Zhou et al. (Eds.): ICICS 2019, LNCS 11999, pp. 145–164, 2020.
https://doi.org/10.1007/978-3-030-41579-2_9

1   Introduction

Cyber security is gaining more and more significance on the national agenda. One of the issues of cyber security is the need for monitoring systems and detecting attacks, which is a problem with ever-increasing scope and complexity. A reliable and efficient security department that can mitigate or protect the enterprises and countries from the intrusion of cyber attacks plays a more and more important role in security defense. Since 1988, the first computer emergency response team (CERT) was built to detect and defend incidents at Carnegie Mellon University (CMU). Then SOC, another more technical focused and broader extend security organization of CERT came out. SOC is an institution that collects and analyzes security data from networks, specific servers and databases on a daily basis, monitors anomaly activities and provides security services like protection tactics to the specific users.

Though security organizations like CERT and SOC can monitor and respond to cyber attacks, it is challenging to fight against the increasingly sophisticated threats only relying on traditional heuristic and signature-based measures [29]. The attack time speeds up, more threat variants appear than before, and attacks belonging to the same threat type tend to initiate invasion by analogous approaches that exploit systems with the same vulnerabilities causing huge losses in a large scale. A famous example is that two ransomwares WannaCry and Petya [27] consecutively attacked many Microsoft Windows-based systems in May and June 2017. Though Microsoft had released patches for the vulnerability in April 2017, many computers of hospitals, schools and companies still had been attacked. It is because these organizations did not know the ransomware and their systems were unpatched. Besides, multi-vectored and multi-staged cyber attacks including advanced persistent threats (APT), polymorphic threats, zero-day threats and composite threats [29] increase the pressure on the defender. Countries and companies who are not familiar with the features of the emerging and existing cyber attacks are easily attacked. Therefore, SOCs and other security departments pay more and more attention to threat information sharing and proactive defense.

Serving as an approach for providing early warning of possible attacks, cyber threat intelligence (CTI) analytics helps recognize existing and emerging cyber attacks in an more efficient manner, which allows targeted users to make quick countermeasures to protect their systems and important information. CTI records threat static attributes like alias, reported time, MD5 hashes, affected systems and so on. CTI also contains threat dynamic attributes like specific attack behaviors. CTI can be used to extract threat actions like tactics, techniques and procedures (TTPs) of the cyber attacks by natural language processing (NLP) and information retrieval (IR) techniques for understanding the attack cycle [9]. It can also be applied to extract the indicators of comprise (IOCs) of attacks for efficient unstructured CTI text gathering [12,31]. There are many countries willing to exchange security intelligence and share the successful detection method, which aims at defeating cyber attacks and mitigating hidden costs effectively. Many security companies and organizations release threat intelligence reports and blogs on the open source to provide convenience to the users. These CTI documents also benefit SOC as a new source to help the analysts grasp the attributes of different attacks much easier and faster than before and give the targeted enterprises guidance to make early security defense decisions.

CTI can be collected from different sources, one important way is the open source (also publicly available source). VirusShare is one of the open sources that had merged more than 34 million threat samples from different security scanning engines or platforms by August 2019. There exists large volume of CTI data that need to be collected and analyzed in the big data society. Besides, the global trend of CTI sharing is also bound to generate large amounts of data which traditional SOC cannot afford to ignore but yet may not have the capacity to handle. Apart from the big data issue, there exists a data redundancy problem. Many same or similar CTI documents are uploaded at different times and some threat reports with different names may have the same attributes. These situations are common on websites like ThreatExpert, Symantec, McAfee, 360 Netlab Blog. Lacking professional security analysts in SOC and the increasing capability of capturing network information in the big data society make it become a key challenge for next generation SOC (NG-SOC) to efficiently gather and automatically filter the massive amount of CTI information. Facing the challenges of big data and data redundancy problem, NG-SOC should apply more machine-based techniques to automatically collect, classify and analyze security data then determine whether a cyber system would be a likely target of some emerging threats so that to devise prioritized reactive countermeasures promptly.

Many machine learning and data mining algorithms show an ability of processing and analyzing data automatically and efficiently. Support vector machine (SVM) is used in [9] to classify CTI relevant and irrelevant articles for filtering the unrelated data. Several different machine learning techniques are used to categorize different cyber attacks from Open Source Intelligence (OSINT) data [20]. Deliu et al. [3] utilized Latent Dirichlet Allocation (LDA) and SVM to automatically filter the large volume of unrelated data and collect the CTI data from hacker forums. Classifying CTI sources before they are analyzed is necessary to save the human and computing resources of the security organizations. Inspired by these works, we try to use machine learning methods to classify the unprocessed CTI from publicly available sources to improve the efficiency of CTI analysis.

When dealing with CTI documents, there exists another challenge. The cyber threat intelligence reports are in textual format. An efficient and suitable "translation tool" is needed to transfer the CTI texts into machine-readable language. Because most machine learning classification algorithms require fixed-length numeric representations to be the input of the models. There are many text representation methods. A typical representative of one-hot encoding is bag of words (BOW), which constructs a dictionary first for all the tokens in the corpus and then builds a matrix for all the documents [7]. This method is simple to use but ignores the semantics of the texts and tends to produce sparse matrices that waste storage space. We have tried to use another approach, topic modeling algorithms like LDA [2] to cluster the CTI reports by the document-topic distribution. But the words that describe different threats are too similar in the reports since most of them are security-related words. It is difficult to classify the reports by the similar topic words generated from LDA model. Then inspired by [11], we choose one of the states of the art text representation algorithms— paragraph vectors, also known as doc2vec, to represent the various length CTI documents by fixed-length vectors to fit the requirement of machine learning classifiers. Doc2vec is an unsupervised deep learning approach that learns knowledge and the semantic relations among words in the documents through deep neural networks in an efficient way. The similarity of different words and documents can be shown in a multidimensional vector space. Detailed techniques will be explained later in the paper.

In this paper, we present an approach for speeding up the CTI report analysis process of NG-SOC. The key objectives are to automatically process CTI reports, summarize the massive number of such reports into a machine-readable data structure and group the repeated documents and similar threat documents together. Specifically, the contributions of this paper are as follows:

- We investigate different open sources threat intelligence documents, collecting 25092 threat intelligence reports from ThreatExpert for text classification. Then we use a semi-automatic method to label the collected CTI data by Jaro-Winkler Distance algorithm.
- Different CTI sources own different attributes, so selecting predefined features is time-consuming and not universal to different types of dataset. So we firstly propose to combine document embedding and machine learning classifiers to group the CTI documents for solving the big data and data redundancy problems.
- The previous works related to CTI are mainly about how to extract useful indicators or develop CTI sharing tools. But works of effectively gathering the CTI and filtering the large quantities of data to high-quality knowledge are limited or with low classification accuracy. We apply multi-class classification to group the same CTI documents or similar threats together before they are analyzed. We have trained six classifiers by supervised machine learning algorithms, including K-Nearest Neighbors (KNN), Logistic Regression (LR), Decision Tree (DT), Support Vector Machines (SVM), LinearSVM (LSVM), Multiple Layer Perception Neural Networks (MLP-NN) to classify the CTI reports and using 10 fold cross validation in the experiment to compare their performance. Three classifiers achieve reasonable classification accuracy above 90%.

We want to speed up the cyber security analysis process to improve the efficiency of the CTI analytics and make NG-SOC has the ability to handle big data automatically. It's of great significance to develop the theory for automatically analyzing such threat information. This will help companies and individual users get early advice from NG-SOC to determine whether they are potential targets of a specific threat and take proactive defense to mitigate hidden costs or even prevent the invasion in the future.

This paper proceeds as follows: Sect. 2 shows the relevant technique background, Sect. 3 introduces the whole framework of the proposed method. Section 4 presents the experiment design and results analysis. Section 5 then reviews the related works. Finally, Sect. 6 makes a conclusion and summarizes the future work.

2 Background

2.1 Security Operations Center

The typical security operations center (SOC) is supervised by security experts for detecting anomalous activities and analyzing the security data from networks, servers and databases of a specific company to provide protection measures about defending potential attacks on a daily basis. SOC is always developing to cope with the changing challenges and it has experienced different generations [16,17]. SOC has changed from using single, simple and passive response measures to applying diverse, systematic and proactive defense in the evolutionary process.

However, the attackers also keep updating their intrusion methods and many new threat variants come out. Besides the internal data, next generation security operations center (NG-SOC) should collect external data to grasp the emerging threat trend and find the relationship between the known and unknown threats to provide more powerful and efficient countermeasures to the target users. The explosive growth of data amount and increasingly sophisticated threats both require that NG-SOC should emphasize more on proactive defense with the help of cyber threat intelligence [1]. In NG-SOC, security analysts should get technical details and understand the attack cycles by CTI analysis to prevent unauthorized access and protect the data confidentiality of the company.

2.2 Cyber Threat Intelligence

In 2013, an analyst from Gartner called Rob McMillan described CTI as "evidence-based knowledge, including context, mechanisms, indicators, implications and actionable advice, about an existing or emerging menace or hazard to assets that can be used to inform decisions regarding the subject's respond to that menace or hazard" [13]. As the description, CTI is evidence-based knowledge. It is textual information that can provide detailed attributes of an attack and help the users detect the attacks and make decisions against threats.

CTI can be collected from different sources, including open sources or public CTI feeds, community or industry groups as information sharing and analysis centers, external sources such as media reports and news, security systems (IDS, firewall, endpoint), CTI-specific vendors and so on. As reported in the CTI survey of SANS 2019 [21], open source or public CTI feeds are the most popular CTI data gathering sources. The main reason is that open source data is easy to access and costs little. It is easy to manage the unprocessed CTI data and realize reasonable allocation of resources by classifying them into sub-types based on their threat types and attack behaviors.

2.3   Threat Intelligence Reports

In this study, we focus on improving the CTI classification work efficiency before they have been processed. As mentioned, we choose the open source cyber threat intelligence because they are easy to access at low cost. We have investigated some publicly available websites like ThreatExpert, Symantec, McAfee and 360 Netlab Blog that can provide the users with cyber threat intelligence service. The CTI sources from these websites can be summarized as two types:

Type 1 source: automatic scanning service and intelligence reports providers, e.g. ThreatExpert (now owned by Symantec) and Symantec (see Fig. 1), where users can test whether a file is infected or contains some threats by uploading the document onto the websites. Technical threat intelligence reports can be seen in this kind of source. The reports are organized with a consistent content format. The features and behaviors of the malware are described clearly based on one specific threat in each report.

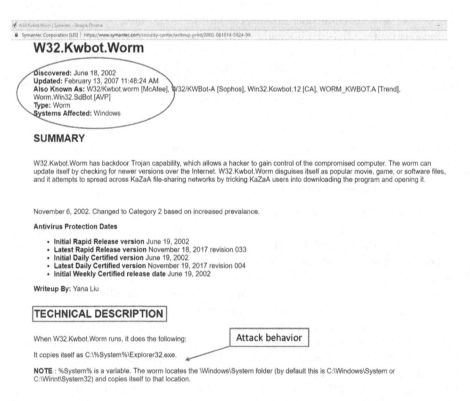

Fig. 1. An example of cyber threat intelligence report from Symantec.

Type 2 source: cyber security news and threat intelligence blogs providers, e.g. 360 Netlab Blog and threatpost. These websites show the cyber security news and summary the attributes of a kind of threat and some technical details. Threat intelligence information from this type of sources tends to present the content in a narrative way. This kind of source can help analysts get more background information. We use the CTI reports of type 1 source in our work because they contain more technical details, own consistent format and focus one specific threat rather than a general category, which ensures the quality of CTI.

As mentioned in the introduction, the challenges for threat analysis are the big data and redundancy problem. As one of the main sources of CTI data, the above problem also exists in open source websites. The main purpose of this work is to build a model that can classify the threat intelligence documents according to their threat types to help the SOC team members save security analysis time to give early warnings of potential cyber attacks. Since the CTI reports are text files, text representation methods are needed to transfer the text into numeric representation of fixed-length as the input of the machine learning classifiers [11]. We will introduce the background of text representation in the following sections.

2.4   Text Representation

Bag of Words. Bag of words (BOW) is a model that is often mentioned in information retrieval and text analysis. It is a simple but effective way to represent the occurrence of different words in a sentence or document. In BOW, a text is regarded as a "bag", the words in this text are treated as elements in the "bag". There is a dictionary to index all the words that appear at the target texts and only the counts of the words are indicated [7]. Though it is easy to implement and effective, BOW ignores the order and semantics of the words in the text [11]. It is not flexible, as the length of the vector is equal to the number of words in the vocabulary. If the size of the vocabulary changes, the dimension of the vector also needs to change. There will be many zeros to generate sparse vectors if the size of the vocabulary is large. The three shortcomings are solved by a new text representation approach, word2vec [14,15].

Word2vec. Using word vectors standing for different words in a sentence has been studied in many works. In 2013, Mikolov et al. [14] proposed two new log-linear word2vec models with low computational complexity to learn the distributed representations of the words. One of the models is continuous bag-of-words (CBOW), it can predict a word based on its surrounding words in the documents. Another model is continuous skip-gram model, contrary to CBOW, can learn the word vectors of the context words by making a specific word as the input of the model.

Word2vec is a model trained by a three-layer neural networks. This model learns the relation between different words in a sentence based on a large amount of data and each word is represented as a multidimensional vector. The similarity between different words can be learned through the model. Famous examples are that after being trained by a huge volume of data, the word2vec model can learn the knowledge that "king" to "queen" is like "man" to "woman" and different countries to their capitals show similar vector mapping relations. As our dataset is textual format, we need to apply method like word2vec that can transfer the CTI reports into fixed-length vectors. Word2vec is a good way to represent the word by multidimensional vector and show word similarity by mining the semantics from many sentences. But for representing documents by vectors, a more suitable approach is needed.

Doc2vec. Paragraph Vector (PV) in [11], also known as doc2vec, is an unsupervised method that converts variable-length pieces of texts to fixed-length vectors based on the idea of word2vec. In word2vec algorithm, each word is represented as a word vector $(\mathbf{w_1}, \mathbf{w_2}, \mathbf{w_3}, ..., \mathbf{w_N})$, and a matrix $\mathbf{W}$ is built up by the word vector columns. The difference is that doc2vec adds a new matrix $\mathbf{D}$ to index the paragraph vectors. $\mathbf{D}$ can be regarded as another special word, it can also be considered as the theme of a document. Doc2vec also has two models like word2vec, called Distributed Memory version of Paragraph Vector (PV-DM) and Distributed Bag of Words of Paragraph Vector (PV-DBOW) respectively. We will show the detail of how to train the doc2vec models in Sect. 3.

3   Framework of Proposed Method

In this section, we explain the whole work process of our proposed method for threat intelligence report classification, including data collection, class labeling, data preprocessing, text vectorization and classifier training.

3.1   Data Collection

As mentioned in the background, we choose open source threat intelligence documents from ThreatExpert [26]. We collected 25092 cyber threat intelligence reports from ThreatExpert, which are recorded from August to November, 2016. There are 3473 documents without a clear threat type. Before classification, there exist 1712 threats and their reports numbers ranging from 1 to 9914 (as shown in Fig. 2). We found that there are many repeated reports for "W32.Kwbot.Worm", so we remove 8500 same reports of this type to balance the data. We extract alias files from ThreatExpert for grouping the threat intelligence reports based on whether the CTI reports have the same alias, which will provide convenience in the next step for class labeling.

3.2   Class Labeling

In our work, we choose the threat intelligence reports from ThreatExpert mainly because the reports of this source own unified content structure (refer to Fig. 1),

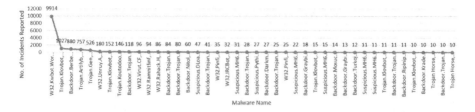

Fig. 2. Threat intelligence reports (number of the same reported threats >= 10) distribution on ThreatExpert.

which describes the malware attributes like discovered or updated time, threat names, threat type, file MD5 hashes, SHA-1, size, alias, and technical details. According to the naming rules of ThreatExpert (or Symantec now), we can know some threats' threat type and attack target system from their names, e.g. "W32.Kwbot.Worm", "Trojan-Spy", "Adware.MokeAd". The prefix in a threat name shows its affected platform or threat type, suffix will be used to indicate the variants information and some number may demonstrate the threat size. So we can know or infer the threat types of most reports from their names. For the reports who do not show threat type from their names, we can manually label them based on the content of the reports.

First, we use string distance algorithm—Jaro-Winkler Distance [10] to determine whether threat names are similar. Threats with the same or similar names are considered as the same group and the corresponding CTI reports are labeled as the same class. Then, the malware aliases are extracted from reports for labeling the reports with the same alias. For example, the three reports with different ID, file 44, file 472 and file 6684 have the same alias for "Mal/Behav-009" (bold letters) in Table 1. We still use Jaro-Winkler Distance to cluster reports with the same aliases. Threats with the same aliases or similar aliases that belong to the same threat type are given the same labels. After the first two steps, most of the reports are labeled. We manually label the remaining reports as new classes or the same classes as the labeled data based on their contents. Their contents give the technical details about their attack behavior, which can provide information to help us label these reports. Finally, we get 101 categories. These labels will be considered as benchmarks when evaluating the experiment results of different text classifiers.

Table 1. Example of three different reports show the same alias.

CTI Report ID	Alias
44	**Mal/Behav-009, Mal/Behav-009**, Trojan-Banker.Win32.Banbra
472	Trojan-Downloader.Win32.Banload, **Mal/Behav-009, Mal/Behav-009**
6684	Win32.SuspectCrc, **Mal/Behav-009, Mal/Behav-009**, Suspicious.MH690

3.3   Data Preprocessing

The threat intelligence reports we collected are HTML files, so we remove the HTML signals and convert them into TXT files first. For the convenience of the later process, we then merge the 25092 documents into one TXT file.

Filtration. In this stage, we remove unimportant content or interference information including punctuation, stop words, non-alphabetical tokens, roman numerals, hexadecimals, URL and declaration of the web-pages. Words that consist of less than three letters are removed. We also ignore tokens like "system, bytes..." that have high document frequency but are less meaningful to save storage space and reduce the computational complexity.

Tokenization. Because there are malware behavior descriptions that are relevant to the modification or generation of system paths and have file names in the technical details of the reports. While doing tokenization, we keep the paths and file names together with the punctuation as the original format, e.g. keeping "hkey_local_machine\software" and "mydailyhoroscope.exe" as special tokens. By doing this, we can group the threats with similar behavior.

Lemmatization. We do lemmatization in the last step of our data preprocessing to transfer the tokens into lowercase and revert them to the base or dictionary form. This step can also decrease the number of tokens to save space and improve computational efficiency.

3.4   Text Vectorization

As mentioned, there are two models of doc2vec algorithm. We compare the two models of doc2vec by a comparative experiment before the main classification experiment and choose PV-DBOW to transfer the processed threat intelligence reports into numeric representations. The processed TXT file is converted to CSV file. We retrain a new doc2vec model based on our dataset because there are many domain-specific words. The model is trained for thirty epochs and all the texts are converted into vectorized features with 300 dimensions.

Doc2vec applies stochastic gradient descent and backpropagation neural networks [23] to train the word vectors and paragraph vectors then get word matrix $\mathbf{W}$ and paragraph matrix $\mathbf{D}$ respectively. Two softmax weight parameters U and b of the model will be got from the training process. A binary Huffman tree [8] construct the hierarchical softmax, which is used to encode the input texts in a fast way. When predicting the PV of a new document, gradient descent is used again for calculate $\mathbf{D_{new}}$ until the values of $\mathbf{W}$, U, and b becoming steady. This is the training process of Distributed Memory version of Paragraph Vector (PV-DM), which is similar to CBOW in word2vec. Distributed Bag of Words of Paragraph Vector (PV-DBOW) model learns weight parameters but ignores $\mathbf{W}$. A text window is utilized to randomly pick words to train the classifier in each iteration of stochastic gradient descent. Compared with PV-DBOW, PV-DM takes up more storage space to memory all word vectors but often performs higher prediction accuracy according to the authors' experiment in [11]. But we choose PV-DBOW in this work based on a comparative experiment result.

3.5   Classifier Training

We use supervised learning to train the CTI classifiers in our work. After preprocessing and transferring the reports into numerical representations, we get a 25083×300 dimension feature matrix $\mathbf{X}$ and a 25083×1 dimension label vector $\mathbf{Y}$. All the instances can be represented as $(\mathbf{x}^{(1)}, \mathbf{y}^{(1)}), (\mathbf{x}^{(2)}, \mathbf{y}^{(2)}), ..., (\mathbf{x}^{(25083)}, \mathbf{y}^{(25083)})$, with each $\mathbf{x}$ consists of 300 values. We have chosen the following six classification algorithms to train the CTI reports classifiers.

K-Nearest Neighbors. K-Nearest Neighbors (KNN) is one of the most commonly used classification technique. We choose it because KNN shows good performance for checking the similarity between different instances by a simple algorithm. In the training process, KNN first sets the number of k and chooses an instance A to compute the distance between A and other labeled instances. The nearest k instances of A are selected and if most of the instances belong to threat type i over the k nearest neighbors, A will be assigned as label i. We use Minkowski distance rather than Euclidean distance in our work to compute the distance between different instances because our feature matrix is more than two dimensions.

Decision Tree. Decision Tree (DT) is a rule-based classification algorithm. When training a classifier, DT classifies the reports from the root nodes and down to the sub-nodes. The label will be known by making decisions according to the rules of different nodes until the leaf nodes. We have 300-dimensional data and train the model using the Gini index. Each dimension is regarded as an attribute and the rule in each node is learned by computing the Gini index. The classifier is trained first by splitting data based on the condition of the root node and leaf node, then prune it to avoid overfitting.

Logistic Regression. Logistic Regression (LR) is a binary classifier at first to identify whether a sample belongs to a specific class or not (whether y_{pre} is equal to 1 or not) with the predict hypothesis representation as Eq. (1).

$$h_\theta(x) = \frac{1}{1 + e^{-\theta^{\mathrm{T}}\mathbf{x}}} \tag{1}$$

Where θ is the parameter vector can be learned from the training process. The prediction value y_{pre} of a sample is decided by a threshold α. If $h_\theta(x)$ is larger than α, y_{pre} is equal to the positive class **1**. Otherwise, y_{pre} belongs to the non-positive class **0**. LR can also be used for multi-class classification by "one-vs-rest" principle. This means classifier $h_{\theta}^{(i)}(x)$ will be trained for every class **i**. A sample will be classified for many times until $y_{pre}^{(i)}$ maximize the value of $h_{\theta}^{(i)}(x)$.

Support Vector Machine. Support vector machine (SVM) is another popular algorithm that can be used for text classification. The main target of SVM is to find a hyperplane, also called decision boundary in machine learning, that can maximize the margin in Fig. 3 to better classify the data. Figure 3 shows an example of linear SVM whose decision boundary is linear. B_1 and B_2 are two decision boundaries. b_{11} and b_{12} is a pair of hyperplanes for B_1. The distance between the two hyperplanes is the margin. We can see from Fig. 3 that the margin of B_1 is bigger than B_2. The goal of SVM is to get the maximum margin, which is equal to $\frac{2}{\|\mathbf{w}\|^2}$. The boundary with bigger margin has a better generalization error than the one with a smaller margin [28], which means that the boundary with bigger margin will not be affected very much when there is some small interference near the two hyperplanes. In our work, we train two kinds of SVM classifiers, one is Linear SVM and another one is SVM with Gaussian radial basis function (RBF) kernel [19].

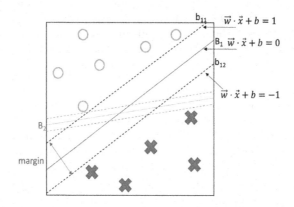

Fig. 3. An example for Linear SVM.

Multi-Layer Perceptron Neural Networks. Multi-Layer Perceptron Neural Networks (MLP-NN) is a model that can train non-linear classifiers. There will be three main modules in this model, including input, hidden layers and output as shown in Fig. 4. We use X and Y to denote the input and output result respectively. The features are represented as x_1 to x_{300} in one text instance. Arrows between input and output are called linkages. Each linkage will be assigned a random weight when the neural network training algorithm starts. In Fig. 4, the light yellow neurons consist of two hidden layers in this MLP-NN model. The value of each input neuron multiple the corresponding weight and add together, the sum s is sent to the next layer. a_{11} denotes the first value of the first hidden layer beside the bias value 1. It is calculated by the activation function with s as input. We use "relu" activation that **a** is equal to the maximum value between 0 and **s** in our experiment.

MLP-NN can learn the deep relation between the input and output with more than one hidden layer, and it is a flexible model that can adjust the activation function and neuron numbers in each layer according to the learning performance. But more parameters will be generated than the other five classification algorithms.

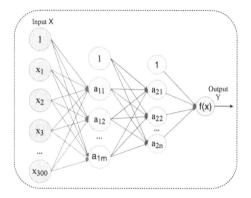

Fig. 4. An example for MLP-Neural Networks with two hidden layers.

4   Experiments

In this section, we show the experiment results of the six trained classifiers and compare their performance by different evaluation approaches. Before comparing the performance of the six classifiers, we implement another experiment to evaluate the capability of the two doc2vec models. Later we analyze the two experiment results and make a summary.

We use doc2vec python package in gensim [22] to train a new model for representing the CTI documents and apply packages in scikit learn library [18] to train our classifiers with Python 3.7.2. We tune the parameters for SVM with RBF kernel, "C = 10, gamma = 10", and C is equal to 10 for LSVM also. We use 100000 for the parameter C in LR. C is a parameter that controls the degree of regularization to mitigate overfitting, the smaller, the stronger of the effect. Two hidden layers for MLP-NN with 300 and 100 neurons respectively are settled for a better prediction result and not too slow computing speed. We use the default settings in scikit learn for the other parameters of the six classifiers. We use recall, precision and F score to evaluate the performance of the different classifiers in our experiments.

4.1   Experiment Results

We first evaluate the two models PV-DM and PV-DBOW of doc2vec by comparing their performance combined with the six mentioned classifiers and choose the better one for the later experiment. We trained the two doc2vec models both for 30 epochs, and randomly split our dataset into two parts, 70% training set and 30% testing set. The experiment result can be seen in Table 2 that PV-DBOW is much better than PV-DM for the data we collected.

Table 2. Compare the two doc2vec models: PV-DM and PV-DBOW combined with the six classifiers.

	PV-DM			PV-DBOW		
	Recall	Precision	F Score	Recall	Precision	F score
KNN	0.7385	0.7180	0.7219	0.9088	0.8937	0.8991
DT	0.5648	0.5676	0.5659	0.8622	0.8695	0.8653
LR	0.7684	0.7705	0.7673	0.8998	0.8795	0.8871
LSVM	0.7612	0.7506	0.7371	0.8909	0.8620	0.8677
SVM (RBF)	0.5934	0.3521	0.4419	0.9095	0.8867	0.8959
MLP-NN	0.7944	0.7813	0.7872	0.9039	0.8832	0.8899

Based on the first experiment result, we select the PV-DBOW algorithm to convert the threat intelligence reports into vector features as the input of the six classifiers, including K-Nearest Neighbors (KNN), Decision Tree (DT), Logistic Regression (LR), Support Vector Machines (SVM), Linear SVM (LSVM), Multiple Layer Perception Neural Networks (MLP-NN). In the second experiment, 10-fold cross validation is used to split our dataset into 10 equal parts, and train each classifier for ten times. Every tenth of the data is treated as the testing data for a time during each training process for a specific classifier. We can get average evaluation scores to judge the six models in a more convincing way by using this cross validation method.

Table 3 shows the result of the second experiment. We can see that SVM with RBF kernel achieves the highest recall at 90.76%. KNN and MLP-NN also have good performance for getting higher recalls, precisions and F scores and more stable classification accuracy based on the ten times training. The results of DT are not as good as other classification models but still not too bad.

4.2   Experiment Analysis

In the first experiment, the performance of PV-DM is not as good as PV-DBOW. In the original paper, the authors who proposed doc2vec show that the ability of PV-DM is better in the case that meaning of the whole text should be learned. But in our study, PV-DBOW performs better maybe because all the texts are

Table 3. Experiment results of the six classification models with PV-DBOW algorithm on the data collected from ThreatExpert from August to November, 2016.

Classification model	Recall	Precision	F score
PV-DBOW + KNN	0.9063 ± 0.0281	0.8907 ± 0.0357	0.8961 ± 0.0329
PV-DBOW + DT	0.8593 ± 0.0420	0.8640 ± 0.0438	0.8606 ± 0.0430
PV-DBOW + LR	0.8979 ± 0.0300	0.8769 ± 0.0393	0.8847 ± 0.0354
PV-DBOW + LSVM	0.8860 ± 0.0284	0.8539 ± 0.0396	0.8615 ± 0.0337
PV-DBOW + SVM(RBF)	0.9076 ± 0.0280	0.8816 ± 0.0360	0.8916 ± 0.0333
PV-DBOW + MLP-NN	0.9027 ± 0.0282	0.8905 ± 0.0335	0.8923 ± 0.0312

highly related with threat analysis, the words have been used are similar. Another reason may be that learning the accurate meaning and the relations among the words needs more data to train the model. We will try it later to check this. PV-DBOW is a model that ignores the order of the whole text but uses a window to learn the semantic relations between different words. It consumes less storage space and the code for PV-DBOW use less time to tune than PV-DM. For the second experiment, SVM (RBF), MLP-NN and KNN all show good performance with recall more than 90% and KNN uses the least training time. Decision tree classifier has a recall of 85.93% as the lowest one among the six classifiers. Because its classification method is rule-based, and the decision conditions for DT are abstract numbers instead of specific semantic description in this work.

Combining the two experiment results, we can see that there is a most obvious change of the prediction accuracy of SVM (RBF) classifier when transform the document representation model from PV-DM to PV-DBOW. We also spend the most time to tune the parameters of SVM (RBF) than other models. So we conclude that SVM with RBF kernel is much more sensitive to the parameters' change and is easy to overfit when tuning the parameters just for pursuing the best prediction score blindly without considering the stability of the classifier. In summary, our proposed method that applying the doc2vec algorithm to vectorize the CTI texts and then using machine learning models to classify the reports has a quite good performance and makes it possible to process the documents automatically and efficiently. This method can classify the huge amount of CTI reports based on their threat types and attack behaviors, which will save a lot of time for security analysts to do the further analysis works in security organizations like SOC.

5 Related Works

In this chapter, we first review the threat analysis works that deal with data in textual format. Then we review the existing CTI analysis works that are related with our project.

5.1   Security Analysis Based on Textual Dataset

As many security data from network traffic, system or network logs and publicly available sources are in textual format, the approaches of handling text data have been studied and applied in many research works for security analysis. In 2007, Elovici et al. [4] presented a system called eDare to detect the unknown malicious code in network traffic using three ML techniques: decision tree, Bayesian networks, artificial neural network. They extracted n-grams and Win32 executables Portable Executable header as the feature. Their experiment results show that the advantage of using ML algorithms as plug-ins is obvious and the final detection decision with significantly higher accuracy compared with the previous works. Gegick et al. [5] also used text-mining techniques, but they applied NLP to mine the bug report instead of the source code.

Another work proposed an approach to extract access control policies (ACP) from natural-language (NL) software documents and make annotations in the sentences with semantic meaning [30]. Three evaluations show that their approach, called Text2Policy, has good performance in identifying ACP sentences and with the accuracy of 86.3% in extracting ACP rules and 81.9% for extracting action steps, respectively. In 2014, Scandariato et al. [24] used bag-of-words and two machine learning classifiers (Naive Bayes and Random Forest) to analyze the source code and forecast whether a software component is vulnerable. The first two experiments show their model has good performance to predict vulnerabilities but the third indicates that they need more features of different applications to build a merged prediction model.

The above works all use different text representation methods to transfer the textual security-related data to machine-readable languages and then apply ML techniques to accelerate the threat analysis process. Facing the CTI data, we also try to use text representation approaches to vectorize them first. But different to the mentioned works, we use the doc2vec algorithm to transfer the CTI reports in to fixed-length vectors directly instead of defining some features and extracting the predefined features, which is more efficient and universal to data collected from different sources.

5.2   Cyber Threat Intelligence Analysis

There exist many works for explaining what CTI is and what it can be used for. As introduced in background, cyber threat intelligence (CTI) is textual knowledge, also evidence-based knowledge [13] collected from huge amount security dataset and combined with the intelligence of human. According to the survey of SANS in 2015 [25], the usage and definitions of CTI are stated and the report shows that many organizations are trying to develop tools that can integrate CTI information easier and faster. Because they have seen the ability of CTI analysis for improving threat detection accuracy and speeding up attack response time. Another survey reviews the different types of threat intelligence especially technical threat intelligence and describes the current status of CTI sharing [29]. The authors of this work also found that the unstructured format and redundancy problems limit the further development of CTI.

Most of the existing research works about CTI analysis focus on extracting indicators of compromise (IOCs) or tactics, techniques and procedures (TTPs). IOCs and TTPs are key information in CTI that can help the security analysts find the interrelationships among cyber attacks from different sources and know the features and attack actions of the threats. In [12], Liao et al. presented a solution called *iACE* to extract IOCs in CTI and gather the huge amount of technical articles that contain IOCs by mining the relation between OpenIOCs through a graph similarity method. *iACE* can recover a large amount of IOCs and convert them into machine-readable format fully automatically by using graph mining to analyze the dependency graphs constructed from sentences of interest. Their evaluation shows that *iACE* has good performance when applied to 71000 articles over 13 years, which is helpful as the first step for fully automated cyber threat intelligence gathering. Though the work shows high accuracy and coverage, there are still errors or missing analysis for some IOCs. This is mainly due to the limitation of the optical character recognizer tools. Besides, better preprocessing is needed to filter original polluted contents. In another work of extracting IOCs from technical articles and industry reports [31], Zhu and Dumitras used NLP techniques to represent target features applied the extracted information to construct malicious actions of different stages of the attack chain. They want to prevent cyber attacks by analyzing the attack steps. Husari et al. also used NLP techniques, but they extracted the predefined threat action from CTI reports. Then they converted threat action into a threat sharing standard language by *STIX 2.1* and constructed the TTPs for defending the cyber attacks in a timely manner [9]. They evaluated their tool by 17000 threats reports from Symantec and got 84% precision and 82% recall on average.

There are some research works about collecting CTI data from different sources. Ghazi et al. collected threat intelligence documents from open source, but they collected both unstructured and structured data. They applied named entity recognition (NER) and combined machine learning method to train a model to extract the predefined entities with the precision about 70% [6]. Deliu et al. utilized SVM and LDA to extract CTI from hacker forums for getting relevant and actionable intelligence in an efficient way [3]. In the work of [20], the authors applied seven machine learning models and used 1432 attacks to train classifiers for identifying cyber attackers from open source intelligence. They just simply classify the attacks and the accuracy is not as high as our works.

Unlike most of the existing works, we focus on classifying the CTI documents before they are analyzed to extract technical or tactical indicators. This will make the analysis more efficient and save more human and computing resources. We propose the method for automated processing threat intelligence documents by combining the doc2vec algorithms and machine learning classifiers to improve the efficiency of documents analytics for NG-SOC. The experiment results are better than the previous CTI classification works. Based on the result, security analysts can analyze and summarize the attributes and behavior of different kinds of threats without wasting too much time reading all the reports.

6 Conclusion and Future Work

The traditional protection mechanism of a system can automatically discover low-level threats and make quick reactions. However, the more sophisticated cyber threats the more difficult it is for the system to make early warnings automatically. If with limited knowledge of the emerging threats, the situation is very severe. Besides, the attackers may use the same method to attack different institutions at different times. Therefore, integrating different cyber threat resources and accelerate the CTI analysis process are extremely urgent.

The main goal of this work is to present our effort in proposing an automatic approach for processing, grouping and extracting information from cyber threat intelligence sources for NG-SOC to realize high efficiency on data analytics and facilitate proactive defense. The experiment results show that the proposed CTI documents classification methods perform well with the highest prediction recall at 91%. Utilizing the document representation models to represent the texts as vectors is a satisfactory way to map the words and documents to numeric representations. It can not only fit the machine learning classifiers input requirement but also realize dimension reduction for documents with many words. Selecting a better classification model after experiments to reorganize the reports with the same or similar threat type together can save much time for threat intelligence analysis, especially in today's data fast-growing society. Based on the threat intelligence reports classification results, the analysts can analyze the threat attributes much easier and faster. Security organizations can give the companies or individual users early warning to make a decision and then help them take proactive defense to mitigate the cost or even avoid the occurrence of a cyber attack.

However, open source is just one way among all the sources that can provide CTI data. Though combining doc2vec algorithm with machine learning techniques can help us classify cyber threat intelligence reports with the uniform format, further work like collecting more different types of CTI documents from different origins, utilizing standard threat language like $STIX2.1$ to construct a threat operation platform containing different indicators and historical events of different threats still need to be realized. More different CTI data sources and analysis techniques need to be studied for doing a more comprehensive analysis in the future to promote the better defense of cyber attacks.

Acknowledgments. This research work is partially supported and funded by the SPIRIT Smart Nation Research Centre, School of Computer Science and Engineering, Nanyang Technological University (Account No: M4082416.020.706922).

References

1. Barros, A., Chuvakin, A.: How to plan, design, operate and evolve a SOC (2016)
2. Blei, D.M., Ng, A.Y., Jordan, M.I.: Latent dirichlet allocation. J. Mach. Learn. Res. **3**(Jan), 993–1022 (2003)
3. Deliu, I., Leichter, C., Franke, K.: Collecting cyber threat intelligence from hacker forums via a two-stage, hybrid process using support vector machines and latent dirichlet allocation. In: 2018 IEEE International Conference on Big Data (Big Data), pp. 5008–5013. IEEE (2018)
4. Elovici, Y., Shabtai, A., Moskovitch, R., Tahan, G., Glezer, C.: Applying machine learning techniques for detection of malicious code in network traffic. In: Hertzberg, J., Beetz, M., Englert, R. (eds.) KI 2007. LNCS (LNAI), vol. 4667, pp. 44–50. Springer, Heidelberg (2007). https://doi.org/10.1007/978-3-540-74565-5_5
5. Gegick, M., Rotella, P., Xie, T.: Identifying security bug reports via text mining: an industrial case study. In: 2010 7th IEEE Working Conference on Mining Software Repositories (MSR 2010), Cape Town, South Africa, pp. 11–20. IEEE, IEEE Computer Society (2010)
6. Ghazi, Y., Anwar, Z., Mumtaz, R., Saleem, S., Tahir, A.: A supervised machine learning based approach for automatically extracting high-level threat intelligence from unstructured sources. In: 2018 International Conference on Frontiers of Information Technology (FIT), Islamabad, Pakistan, pp. 129–134. IEEE Computer Society (2018)
7. Harris, Z.S.: Distributional structure. Word **10**(2–3), 146–162 (1954)
8. Huffman, D.A.: A method for the construction of minimum-redundancy codes. Proc. IRE **40**(9), 1098–1101 (1952)
9. Husari, G., Al-Shaer, E., Ahmed, M., Chu, B., Niu, X.: TTPDrill: automatic and accurate extraction of threat actions from unstructured text of CTI sources. In: Proceedings of the 33rd Annual Computer Security Applications Conference, Orlando, FL, USA, pp. 103–115. ACM (2017)
10. Kambhampati, S., Knoblock, C.A. (eds.): Proceedings of IJCAI-03 Workshop on Information Integration on the Web (IIWeb 2003), Acapulco, Mexico, 9–10 August 2003 (2003)
11. Le, Q., Mikolov, T.: Distributed representations of sentences and documents. In: International Conference on Machine Learning, Beijing, China, pp. 1188–1196. JMLR.org (2014)
12. Liao, X., Yuan, K., Wang, X., Li, Z., Xing, L., Beyah, R.: Acing the IOC game: toward automatic discovery and analysis of open-source cyber threat intelligence. In: Proceedings of the 2016 ACM SIGSAC Conference on Computer and Communications Security, Vienna, Austria, pp. 755–766. ACM (2016)
13. McMillan, R.: Definition: threat intelligence. Gartner 2013 (2013)
14. Mikolov, T., Chen, K., Corrado, G., Dean, J.: Efficient estimation of word representations in vector space. arXiv preprint arXiv:1301.3781 (2013)
15. Mikolov, T., Sutskever, I., Chen, K., Corrado, G.S., Dean, J.: Distributed representations of words and phrases and their compositionality. In: Advances in Neural Information Processing Systems, Lake Tahoe, Nevada, United States, pp. 3111–3119. MIT Press (2013)
16. Muniz, J., McIntyre, G., AlFardan, N.: Security Operations Center: Building, Operating, and Maintaining Your SOC. Cisco Press, Indianapolis (2015)

17. Packard, H.: 5G/SOC: SOC generations. HP ESP Security Intelligence and Operations Consulting Services (2013). http://www.cnmeonline.com/myresources/hpe/docs/HP_ArcSight_WhitePapers_5G-SOC_SOC_Generations.PDF. Accessed 25 Aug 2019

18. Pedregosa, F., et al.: Scikit-learn: machine learning in python. J. Mach. Learn. Res. **12**, 2825–2830 (2011)

19. Platt, J., et al.: Probabilistic outputs for support vector machines and comparisons to regularized likelihood methods. Adv. Large Margin Classif. **10**(3), 61–74 (1999)

20. Pournouri, S., Zargari, S., Akhgar, B.: Predicting the cyber attackers; a comparison of different classification techniques. In: Jahankhani, H. (ed.) Cyber Criminology. ASTSA, pp. 169–181. Springer, Cham (2018). https://doi.org/10.1007/978-3-319-97181-0_8

21. Rebekah Brown, R.M.L.: The evolution of cyber threat intelligence (CTI): 2019 SANS CTI survey, February 2019. https://www.sans.org/reading-room/whitepapers/threats/paper/38790. Accessed 25 Aug 2019

22. Řehůřek, R., Sojka, P.: Software framework for topic modelling with large corpora. In: Proceedings of the LREC 2010 Workshop on New Challenges for NLP Frameworks, Valletta, Malta, pp. 45–50. ELRA, May 2010. http://is.muni.cz/publication/884893/en

23. Rumelhart, D.E., Hinton, G.E., Williams, R.J., et al.: Learning representations by back-propagating errors. Cogn. Model. **5**(3), 1 (1988)

24. Scandariato, R., Walden, J., Hovsepyan, A., Joosen, W.: Predicting vulnerable software components via text mining. IEEE Trans. Software Eng. **40**(10), 993–1006 (2014)

25. Shackleford, D.: Who's using cyberthreat intelligence and how? SANS Institute (2015)

26. Shevchenko, S.: Welcome to threatexpert blog!, February 2008. http://blog.threatexpert.com/2008/02/welcome-to-threatexpert-blog.html. Accessed 25 Aug 2019

27. Symantec: Petya ransomware outbreak: Here's what you need to know, December 2017. https://www.symantec.com/blogs/threat-intelligence/petya-ransomware-wiper. Accessed 25 Aug 2019

28. Tan, P.N., et al.: Introduction to Data Mining. Pearson Education India, New Delhi (2007)

29. Tounsi, W., Rais, H.: A survey on technical threat intelligence in the age of sophisticated cyber attacks. Comput. Secur. **72**, 212–233 (2018)

30. Xiao, X., Paradkar, A., Thummalapenta, S., Xie, T.: Automated extraction of security policies from natural-language software documents. In: Proceedings of the ACM SIGSOFT 20th International Symposium on the Foundations of Software Engineering, p. 12. ACM (2012)

31. Zhu, Z., Dumitras, T.: ChainSmith: automatically learning the semantics of malicious campaigns by mining threat intelligence reports. In: 2018 IEEE European Symposium on Security and Privacy (EuroS&P), London, United Kingdom, pp. 458–472. IEEE (2018)

HeteroUI: A Framework Based on Heterogeneous Information Network Embedding for User Identification in Enterprise Networks

Meng Li[1,2], Lijun Cai[1(✉)], Aimin Yu[1(✉)], Haibo Yu[1], and Dan Meng[1]

[1] Institute of Information Engineering, Chinese Academy of Sciences, Beijing, China
{limeng1995,cailijun,yuaimin,yuhaibo,mengdan}@iie.ac.cn
[2] School of Cyber Security, University of Chinese Academy of Sciences,
Beijing, China

Abstract. User identification process is an important security guard towards discovering insider threat and preventing unauthorized access in enterprise networks. However, most existing user identification approaches based on behavior analysis fail to capture latent correlations between multi-domain behavior records due to the lack of a panoramic view or the disability of dealing with heterogeneous data. In light of this, this paper presents HeteroUI, a framework based on heterogeneous information network embedding for user identification in enterprise networks. In our model, multi-domain heterogeneous behavior records are first transformed into a heterogeneous information network, then the embeddings of entities will be trained iteratively according to a joint objective combining with local and global components for more accurate user identification. Experimental results on the CERT insider threat dataset r4.2 demonstrate that HeteroUI exhibits excellent performance in discovering user identities with the mean average precision reaching over 98%. Besides, HeteroUI has a certain contribution to inferring potential insiders in a multi-user and multi-domain environment.

Keywords: User identification · Heterogeneous information network embedding · Joint objective · Latent correlations

1 Introduction

With the evolution of insider threat, user identification plays a more and more significant role in protecting information assets of enterprise networks. Existing user identification mechanisms only work at the start of login. Such as password input, fingerprint recognition, which can be easily cracked or deceived by inputting the password obtained in an illegal way, or using a fingerprint model. By contrast, user and entity behavior analysis (UEBA) [1] based approaches are attracting the eyes of researchers because they have the following certain

© Springer Nature Switzerland AG 2020
J. Zhou et al. (Eds.): ICICS 2019, LNCS 11999, pp. 165–180, 2020.
https://doi.org/10.1007/978-3-030-41579-2_10

advantages. (1) It is hard to be stolen or imitated since everyone has its own behavioral features. (2) It provides continuous identity authentication during the whole login session.

In order to accurately confirm the identity of a user through behavior analysis, analysts need to extract comprehensive and appropriate features from a mess of behavior records, then compare the similarity between the current behavior and the historical behavior model as the basis for identification. Existing approaches can be classified into two types. Some of them typically focus on a particular domain or specific behavior records, such as file access analysis, which lacks a panoramic view required to build a comprehensive behavior model. Others usually rely on feature engineering to aggregate behavior features from different domains, which require artificial empirical knowledge and neglect the latent correlations between multi-domain behaviors. As a result, it is a mounting challenge to provide an automatic and reliable solution that takes correlation information into consideration for user identification in a multi-user and multi-domain environment.

Behavior records in enterprise networks are mostly formatted by structured log events, making it even harder to capture latent correlations. In recent years, the extensive research of heterogeneous network representation learning has provided us with a good perspective to solve this problem. Heterogeneous information network (HIN) [2] is an effective tool for dealing with multi-domain heterogeneous data, because it contains multiple types of nodes and/or edges. We can obtain rich structural and semantic information by mining the interactions between entities within a heterogeneous information network.

Motivated by the excellent performance of HIN in many varied tasks, this paper proposes HeteroUI, a framework for user identification in enterprise networks. Specifically, we first transform behavior records into a heterogeneous information network, where each node represents an event of a particular type and each edge interprets the relationship between entities. Then we train the embeddings of entities iteratively through a joint objective combining with local and global components: (1) the local component focuses on interactions between each user and it's behavior entities, aiming to learn user's normal behavior pattern. (2) the global component utilizes meta paths [3] to capture latent correlations between different types of entities in the whole network. By combining both components, the learned embeddings can better preserve proximities and semantic information, thus paving the way for subsequent prediction and analysis. To the best of our knowledge, applying HIN to learn user behavior model as well as inferring potential insiders based on audit logs has not been extensively studied yet. The contributions of this paper are summarized as follows:

1. We present a framework called HeteroUI that is able to process multi-domain heterogeneous behavior records and take the interaction between different domains into consideration for user identification.
2. HeteroUI is an innovative attempt to combine with local and global embedding models for comprehensive user characterization. We designed a customized neural network for local embedding and performed meta paths

selection for global embedding so that HeteroUI can be more suitable for this task.

3. We propose a mechanism based on similarity calculation to deal with suspicious cases. Once a potential insider is identified, HeteroUI can provide valuable clues for forensic analysis.
4. We conduct a series of experiments on the CERT dataset r4.2. The results demonstrate that HeteroUI achieves superior performance compared with three baselines in inferring potential insiders.

2 Related Work

The relevant efforts on user identification in enterprise networks mainly encompass three aspects as follows:

Data Pre-processing. Raw logs and behavior records are always manifested in various formats. To deal with inconsistent log data from different sources, Tuor et al. [4] accumulated counts of 408 "activities" a user has performed over some fixed time window (e.g. 24 h) and enumerate them in the form of tree structure, Pei et al. [5] leveraged raw log parsers to extract specific fields from each input entry for log correlation. To facilitate event correlation analysis, HeteroUI follows a similar way to [5] that utilizes a set of pre-defined fields to capture pivotal information of each behavior record, but unlike previous efforts, HeteroUI regards fields of each normalized behavior record as unique entities to build heterogeneous information network for multi-domain event correlation.

Behavior Modeling. Establishing normal behavior model is necessary for user identification. Early research tends to exploit behavior data from a particular domain. For example, in order to protect important files against theft or destroy, Wang et al. [6] try to construct file behavior model using file access path and file action in two dimensions of time and space. However, the accuracy of these methods is usually disappointing for lacking a panoramic view. Other work focuses on aggregating inconsistent log data from heterogeneous tracking sources to build comprehensive user profile. Tuor et al. [4] try to create multi-dimensional numeric feature vectors by merging categorical user attribute features and continuous "count" features for user representation and then feed them into the neural network. These feature-driven approaches are meritorious with the help of artificial empirical knowledge, but they usually neglect the latent correlations among multi-domain behaviors. HeteroUI addresses this issue by leveraging a joint embedding objective function combining with local and global models following the idea of Chen et al. [7], which can learn representations of entities with rich structural and semantic information automatically.

Forensic Analysis. Traditional user identification methods can only judge whether the current behaviors belong to a specific user without relevant clues of potential operational users and fine-grained suspicious behaviors, which is not quite enough. Thus, it is imperative to provide actionable intelligence or pertinent evidence for forensic analysis. In recent years, workflow construction has been studied largely for anomaly diagnosis, such as in [8]. However, they are prone to high cost of overhead and severe delay. HeteroUI avoids the pitfall by leveraging a similarity calculation mechanism, which allows us to provide relevant clues about a potential insider to security officers in time for further investigation.

The proposed framework HeteroUI extends existing embedding methods and employs a task-guided embedding model involving the three collaborative aspects mentioned above.

3   Preliminaries

In this section, we first introduce the concept of heterogeneous information networks and meta paths, then introduce the embedding representation of entities and the user identification problem.

3.1   Heterogeneous Information Network

Definition 1. *Heterogeneous Information Network (HIN) is defined as a graph $G = (V, E)$ in which nodes and edges between them can have various types. Nodes are mapped to their type by a node mapping function $g_v : V \rightarrow A$ where A is the set of all node types and similarly an edge mapping function $g_e : E \rightarrow R$ maps edges to their type where R is the set of all possible edge types. By definition we have $|A| > 1$ or $|R| > 1$. Furthermore, $S_G = (A, R)$ denotes the network schema.*

Figure 1 shows the network schema we formulated in this paper to represent multi-domain behavior records. It is centered by a super node PC, the informative types of behavior records collected from this PC can be represented as its neighboring nodes. The node types A in this task include PC, user, file, HTTP, email, logon, and device, while the set of edge types R includes $pc \overset{visit}{\rightarrow} file$, $pc \overset{contact}{\rightarrow} email$, and so on.

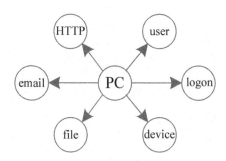

Fig. 1. Network schema of the heterogeneous information network. Each node denotes a node type, and each edge denotes an edge type.

Definition 2. *Meta Paths in HIN define higher-order relations between two node types. Having the network schema $S_G = (A, R)$, a meta path schema is demonstrated as $A_1 \xrightarrow{R_1} A_2 \xrightarrow{R_2} ... \xrightarrow{R_m} A_{m+1}$.*

Different meta paths will lead to different semantic meanings. For example, in network schema Fig. 1, the meta path $PC \xrightarrow{contact} email \xleftarrow{contact} PC$ can capture latent correlation between two PCs which have a same email recipient. However, there can be infinite potential meta paths given a network schema. In this paper, we only consider length-1 paths in the original network and length-2 meta paths and perform meta paths selection to find the optimal set of them.

3.2 Representation Learning on HIN

Definition 3. *Given a heterogeneous information network denoted as a graph $G = (V, E)$. Representation learning aims to learn a function $f : V \to R^d$ that projects each node $v \in V$ to a vector in a d-dimensional space R^d, where $d \ll |V|$.*

Throughout this paper, we use a matrix U to represent the embedding table for nodes. The size of the matrix is $N \times d$, where N is the total number of nodes (including all node types), and d is the number of dimensions. So the feature vector for node n is denoted as u_n, which is a d-dimensional vector.

3.3 Problem Definition

Unlike other user identification methods that model this task as a binary classification problem, our proposed HeteroUI regards it as a ranking prediction task. For a PC p, when a new period of behavior records are provided, we refer to the user account that appeared in these records as "the observed user". While our model will return a rank of predicted users based on these behaviors.

In a normal scenario, we hope the observed user is top-ranked in the predicted user list. This indicates an excellent user characterization and identification ability of our model. However, if the observed user doesn't appear at the top of the list, which is called "a suspicious case", we consider the observed user to be a potential insider. In this case, a severe deviation occurs between the observed user's current behavior pattern and his/her normal behavior pattern.

4   The HeteroUI Framework

Figure 2 shows an overview of the HeteroUI framework. HeteroUI is structured hierarchically, which consists of four layers (data preparation layer, construction layer, joint training layer, and detection layer, respectively), detailed in the following subsections.

- **Data Preparation layer.** This layer maintains a multi-domain historical events database and preprocesses new behavior records. The input of this layer is a set of behavior records in a new time period of a certain PC, we refer to the user account that appeared in these records as the observed user Q. The output of this layer is a window of the historical behavior records for all PCs and the normalized new behaviors records of a certain PC, denoted by training set S and test set C respectively.

- **Construction layer.** In this layer, we try to construct the heterogeneous information network G with all kinds of entities (PC, file, email, etc.) based on S following the network schema in Fig. 1. The output of this layer is a randomly initialized embedding table U for all entities in G.
- **Joint Training layer.** This layer maps each node of network G into a d-dimensional vector through a joint objective combining with local and global embedding models. After the iterative training process, we use the user predictor to perform prediction on the test set C.
- **Detection layer.** This layer determines whether the observed user Q is suspicious by comparing it with the predicted user candidates. If suspicious, HeteroUI provides relevant clues to security officers for forensic analysis.

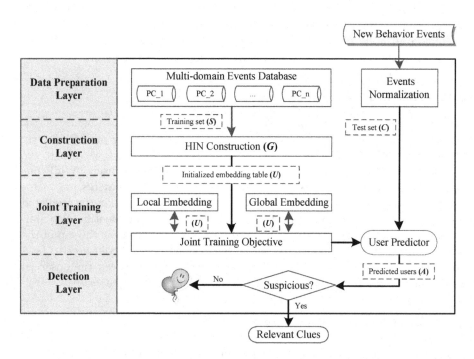

Fig. 2. Overview of HeteroUI. The flow of execution is indicated by arrows. The output of each layer is shown in the parentheses (i.e. S, C, U, A).

4.1 Data Preparation Layer

The multi-domain events database stores the normalized historical behavior records for all PCs in the whole enterprise chronologically, which serves as the behavioral baseline for building normal user models. The raw behavior records in a new time period of a PC contain five types of event types, including logon, file, email, HTTP, and device. In this paper, we assume that each PC corresponds to one user. Thus we can get the only user account as our inspected target from these behavior records, denoted by the observed user Q.

When the new behavior records arrive, the data preparation layer is responsible for parsing and normalizing them using network-specific configuration information. To capture the pivotal information of each event, HeteroUI parses an event record into several pre-defined fields as shown in Table 1, where each field is normalized for self-identifying. For example, the subject is normalized as a user identifier and the object is normalized as a behavior identifier. In particular, for logon events, we use timestamp as its behavior identifier because we are more concerned about the time period when the user logs on. As timestamp is continuous, we partition the value range into several segments such that a large amount of continuous value is reduced to a smaller set of discrete intervals.

Table 1. Pre-defined fields for an event.

Field	Explanation
Subject	The initiator of the event (i.e. a user)
Device	Device where the event took place (i.e. a pc)
Object	The receptors of the event (e.g. files, urls, emails)
Timestamp	Time when the event took place

4.2 Construction Layer

The main purpose of the construction layer is to build a suitable HIN based on the training set S. The training set contains historical behavior data for all PCs, meaning that we will construct the HIN including all of their information, and learn their behavior patterns simultaneously in the training process. The heterogeneous information network G is constructed following the network schema defined in Fig. 1. For each PC, denoted by p, we represent its neighbors in the network G as $X_p = \left\{ X_p^{(1)}, X_p^{(2)}, ..., X_p^{(T)} \right\}$, where $X_p^{(T)}$ is a set of neighbor nodes in t^{th} node type. And we use a_p to denote the true user of p.

4.3 Joint Training Layer

The joint training layer maps each node of network G into a d-dimensional vector through a joint objective combining with local and global embedding models, then use the user predictor to perform prediction on the test set C.

The local embedding model focuses on interactions between super node p and its neighboring nodes, aiming to embed regular user behavior patterns. While the global embedding model utilizes meta paths to capture latent correlations between different types of entities. The principles and architectures of them are introduced separately as below.

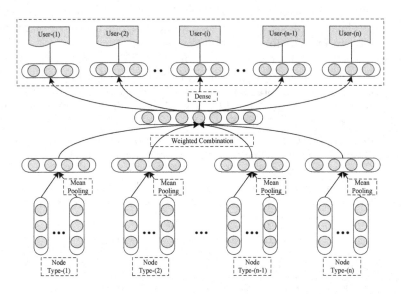

Fig. 3. Local embedding architecture for user identification.

Local Embedding. Figure 3 shows the architecture of the local embedding model. With the embedding table U as input, the local embedding model needs to build feature representation for super node p based on its observed neighbors in the network G gradually, then rank the candidate users based on dot product similarity. Details of this process are as follows.

Forward Training: There are two stages of aggregation to build up the feature representation of a super node p based on node embeddings.

In the first stage, it builds a feature vector for each of the tth node type by averaging node embeddings in $X_p^{(t)}$ (see Eq. 1).

$$V_p^{(t)} = \sum_{n \in X_p^{(t)}} u_n / \left| X_p^{(t)} \right|$$ (1)

where $V_p^{(t)}$ is the feature representation of the tth node type (e.g. email node type), and u_n is the nth node embedding (e.g. email node).

In the second stage, it builds the feature representation of super node p using a weighted combination of feature vectors of different node types (see Eq. 2).

$$V_p = \sum_t w_t V_p^{(t)}$$ (2)

Ranking: After obtaining the feature representation of super node p, we are able to rank candidate users (e.g. user a) based on the dot product operation. The similarity score is defined as follows:

$$S\left(p,a\right) = u_a^T V_p = u_a^T \left(\sum_t w_t V_p^{(t)}\right) \tag{3}$$

Backward Propagation: To learn the parameter U and W, we adopt stochastic gradient descent (SGD) [9] based on the max-margin objective. For each pair of positive sample (p,a) and negative sample $\left(p, a'\right)$, the hinge loss is defined as:

$$max\left(0, S(p, a') - S\left(p, a\right) + \xi\right) \tag{4}$$

where ξ is a positive number usually referred as margin [10]. A loss penalty will incur if the score of positive pair (p,a) is not at least ξ larger than the score of (p, a').

Global Embedding. Most of the existing network embedding models are based on the idea that embeddings of nodes can be learned by neighbor prediction, which is to predict the neighborhood given a node (i.e. the linking probability $P(j|i)$ from node i to node j). In order to embed latent correlations among nodes induced by meta paths, our global embedding model generalizes existing network embedding techniques [11] following the neighbor prediction framework. Details of this process are as follows.

Forward Training: Given a network schema $S_G = (A, R)$, the potential meta paths can be infinite. When considered a specific embedding task, we have to select a limited number of useful meta paths. This process will be discussed later, and we assume a set of meta paths R has been selected for now. Then we begin to model the conditional neighbor distribution of nodes. Note that the neighbor distribution of nodes will be conditioned on both the node i and the given path type r, which is defined as Eq. 5:

$$p\left(j|i; r\right) = \frac{exp\left(u_i^T u_j\right)}{\sum_{j' \in DST(r)} exp\left(u_i^T u_j\right)} \tag{5}$$

where u_i is the embedding of node i, and $DST(r)$ denotes the set of all possible nodes in the destination side of path r.

Considering that the number of nodes of $DST(r)$ may be very large and the evaluation of Eq. 5 can be prohibitively expensive, we apply negative sampling [12] and form the following approximation term:

$$\log \hat{P}(j|i; r) \approx \log \sigma \left(u_i^T u_j + b_r\right)$$
$$+ \sum_{l=1}^{k} \mathbb{E}_{j' \sim P_n^r(j')} \left[\log \sigma \left(-u_i^T u_{j'} - b_r\right)\right] \tag{6}$$

where j' is the negative node sampled from a pre-defined noise distribution $P_n^r(j')$ for path r, and a total of k negative nodes are sampled for each positive node i. Furthermore, a bias term b_r is added to adjust densities of different paths.

Backward Propagation: To learn the parameters U and b_r, we also adopt stochastic gradient descent (SGD) [9] with the goal of maximizing the likelihood function.

Joint Training. Local and global embedding models capture different perspectives of a network, which motives us to combine them in a unified objective. The joint training objective uses a weighted linear combination of the two components with a regulation term (see Eq. 7).

$$f = (1 - \omega) f_{local} + \omega f_{global} + \lambda \sum_i \|u_i\|_2^2 \tag{7}$$

where $\omega \in [0, 1]$ is a trade-off factor for local and global components. When $\omega = 0$, only local embedding is used; and when $\omega = 1$, only global embedding is used. The regularization term is added to avoid overfitting.

Meta Paths Selection: Now we introduce the meta paths selection. Specifically, we employ two steps to select relevant paths in a greedy fashion: (1) Single path performance. We run HeteroUI with a single path at a time, then rank all the candidate paths according to their performance. (2) Greedy additive path selection. We add each path into the selected pool following the ranking and run HeterUI for each additive combination. The paths set R with the best performance will be used.

The joint training process will be performed iteratively. For each iteration, we sample an embedding model based on the Bernoulli distribution with ω as the parameter, then perform the training process and update the embedding table U and relevant parameters.

Finally, we use the well-trained user predictor to perform prediction on the test set C and pass the output A to the detection layer, the result is a ranking of potential users corresponding to the inspected behaviors.

4.4   Detection Layer

As of now, we have obtained the prediction result A of the test set C. The last step is to determine whether the observed user Q is suspicious by comparing it with the predicted user candidates.

First, we need to set a threshold as the cutoff in the prediction output. In this work, we consider the observed user Q to be normal if it is among the top K predicted users with high probabilities. Otherwise, we consider Q as a potential insider. Under this circumstances, HeteroUI calculates the dot product similarity scores between each behavior entity and the real user entity in turn, and rank the scores in ascending order, the top-ranked behaviors can be provided to security officers as clues for forensic analysis. Note that the model can be incrementally updated to accommodate changes in users' normal behaviors.

5 Experimental Evaluation

In this section, we are dedicated to evaluating the performance of the proposed framework. Firstly, we demonstrate the superiority of the joint embedding model in user characterization in normal scenarios and perform parameter tuning. Then we compare HeteroUI with three baseline approaches in inferring potential insiders under three insider threat scenarios. Finally, we provide details on meta paths selection and case study for forensic analysis.

5.1 Dataset

The CERT dataset[1] was published by Carnegie Mellon University for insider threat detection. We utilized the r4.2 dataset for our evaluation which contains three insider threat scenarios covering 70 insiders.

In our work, five types of events (HTTP, logon, file, device, and email) are used to construct heterogeneous information networks. We extracted four sub-datasets for our experiments, denoted by D0, D1, D2, D3, reflecting the normal scenario and each of the three insider threat scenarios respectively. Table 2 summarizes the four sub-datasets.

Table 2. Dataset statistics.

Dataset	Number of users	Number of insiders	Number of events
D0	980	0	345472
D1	992	23	1727360
D2	992	16	3238801
D3	975	9	647769

5.2 Evaluation Metrics

Under normal scenarios, we adopt commonly used ranking metric: mean Average Precision at K (mAP@K) to reflect the accuracy of top-ranked users. This metric evaluates the effect of HeteroUI on user characterization, which is a prerequisite for the model to catch potential insiders. The mAP@K can be computed as mean of AP@K for each query[2] in the test time period. Defined by the follows:

$$AP@K = \sum_{k=1}^{K} p(k) * rel(k) \tag{8}$$

where $p(k)$ is the precision at cut-off k in the return list. If the true user appears after the kth position, $p(k) = 0$, otherwise, $p(k) = 1/k$. $rel(k)$ is an indicator that says whether the kth position is the true user $(rel(k) = 1)$ or not $(rel(k) = 0)$.

---

[1] https://resources.sei.cmu.edu/library/asset-view.cfm?assetid=508099.
[2] A query means a set of new behavior records for a certain PC to be inspected.

Under insider threat scenarios, we use standard metrics of precision, recall, and F1-score to show the performance of HeteroUI and three baselines in inferring potential insiders. Specifically, $Precision = TP/(TP + FP)$, $Recall = TP/(TP+FN)$ and $F1-score = 2*(Precision*Recall)/(Precision+Recall)$, where TP, FP, FN are true positive, false positive and false negative, respectively. In this case, the TP means the number of true suspicious cases captured by our model.

5.3   Parameter Study

In this subsection, we use D0 to study the hyper-parameter ω, which is the trade-off term of the joint training objective, as well as the dimension d of the embedding vector. The result is shown in Fig. 4. As we can see that the best performance is obtained when we use $\omega = 0.7$ and $d = 128$. We also demonstrate the rationality of the joint training objective compared with using a single embedding model. From Fig. 4(c) we can see that the mAP@5 is improved by more than 10%, which shows the excellent performance of our model in discovering user identities in normal scenarios, and this is a basis for insider threat detection.

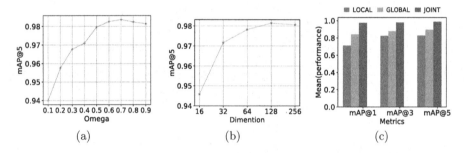

(a)   (b)   (c)

Fig. 4. Hyper-parameters selection and performance comparison. (a) Choice of different combining factor. (b) Dimension of embedding vectors. (c) Performance comparison between HeteroUI and single embedding models.

5.4   Comparative Experiments

For a comprehensive evaluation, we experimented with HeteroUI as well as three baselines as follows:

- **Feature-based method.** Considering a pair of $(PC, user)$ as a sample, we treat the user identification task as a supervised classification task. Referring to the existing work [4,13,14], we extract a total of 25 numerical features from all types of user behaviors. For the supervised algorithm, we consider Random Forests (RF) and use grid search to find its best hyper-parameters.

- **Embedding-based method.** Pre-training has been found useful to improve neural network based supervised learning [15]. So instead of training local embedding model from randomly initialized embedding table, we first pre-train the embedding of nodes using global embedding model, then initialize the local embedding training with pre-trained embedding vectors.
- **LSTM-based method.** LSTM networks are renowned for their ability to remember history information using the memory gate. Following part of the work in [4], we first create multi-dimensional feature vectors by merging categorical user attribute features and continuous "count" features for user representation and then feed them into the LSTM networks.

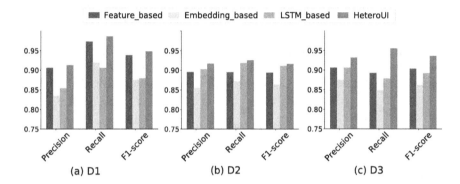

Fig. 5. The performance of HeteroUI and three baseline methods on D1–D3 datasets.

Figure 5 shows the performance of these methods on D1, D2, and D3 respectively. For all the approaches, we explored the parameter space and choose the best. As for the threshold of the detection layer, a smaller K may reduce the precision rate, while a larger K will reduce the recall rate to some extent. We performed experiments on the D1 dataset and set $K = 5$ to make a trade-off.

Our proposed HeteroUI outperforms three baselines in various degrees across all scenarios. For example, for the dataset D1, the precision of HeteroUI is 92%, improved by 1%, 8%, and 6%, compared with the feature-based, embedding-based and LSTM-based methods respectively. The recall of HeteroUI is 98%, improved by 1%, 7%, and 8% in comparison. We believe this is mainly due to the fact that HeteroUI properly models multi-domain heterogeneous behavior data and uses the global embedding model to take the correlation information into account. Besides, we also performed meta paths selection for this specific task. From Fig. 5 we also observe that the feature-based method has good precision in all scenarios. Maybe it can be explained through the RF's resistance to class imbalance in training data [16]. In the second malicious scenarios, the LSTM-based method manifests a remarkable precision and recall over the other two baselines. Further research discovered that the duration of malicious activities in the second scenario is much longer, about eight weeks on average.

And LSTM-based method can better capture the correlations in historical records. The embedding-based method has a pathetic precision in all datasets, we conjecture this is due to overfitting. Although the performance of our proposed HeteroUI fluctuates slightly in different malicious scenarios, they all remained at a stable level and thus has the potential to detect less typical anomalies.

5.5   Details

This section reveals the result of the meta paths selection and provides a case study on forensic analysis of suspicious circumstances.

Meta Paths Set. We first report experimental results for meta paths selection since the selected meta paths are used in the joint training layer. We mainly consider 15 types of meta paths to capture different semantic information. Figure 6 shows the results of single path performance and performance improvement when adding them in a greedy fashion. Note that only paths that can help improve the user identification task are shown in the figure. In the end, we choose five meta paths for our experiments: user2url, user2email, url2email, url2dev, file2dev.

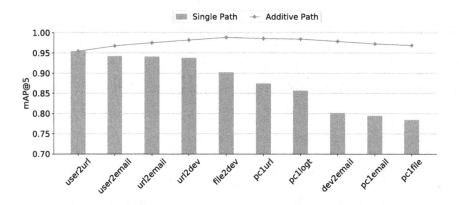

Fig. 6. The performance of single paths and the additive selection.

Case Study. In this subsection, we show a case study to demonstrate the performance of HeteroUI in forensic analysis. We select one of the insiders "AAF0535" that appeared in D2 on July 9, 2010, which has been successfully detected, and display the top 5 of the suspicious entities list HeteroUI has provided. Detailed in Table 3.

Among the list, the real anomalous behaviors are bolded. As there are a total of 11 real anomalous behaviors of "AAF0535" on July 9, 2010, it can be seen that about half of them are covered and three of them are top-ranked. This indicates that HeteroUI has certain guiding significance for event-level forensic analysis. In practice, it can be combined with other anomaly detection models for conjoint analysis.

Table 3. Ranking of suspicious entities of "AAF0535".

Ranking	Suspicious entities
1	http://northropgrumman.com/WboUhagvat572113271.aspx
2	Jaime_Carey@raytheon.com
3	http://linkedin.com/WboUhagvat1479839504.aspx
4	http://slate.com/1933_Atlantic_hurricane_season/05z/jrngure696245205.jsp
5	http://job-hunt.org/WboUhagvat919122234.html

6   Limitations

Our proposed HeteroUI aims to capture potential insider threats based on heterogeneous audit log data from multiple sources, but we do not make a comparison with mature industrial solutions, such as Darkrace.

Besides, the experiments are all based on specific insider threat scenarios in the standard CERT dataset. Therefore, we cannot fully demonstrate the effectiveness of our model in real scenarios.

In the next step, we will compare with these systems and adjust our model in combination with other available information to meet the needs of real-world scenarios, and make our proposed HeteroUI a better system with superior performance in practical applications.

7   Conclusion

This paper presents HeteroUI, a framework for user identification in enterprise networks. HeteroUI first transforms multi-domain behavior records into a heterogeneous information network, then learn embeddings of nodes iteratively through a joint objective combining with local and global components for user identification. Once a suspicious case is identified, HeteroUI is able to provide relevant clues in real-time for forensic analysis. Extensive experiments have demonstrated the superior performance of HeteroUI compared with existing baselines.

In future work, we will try other types of behavior entities and consider attribute information to improve the precision of our model and generalize it into real-world scenarios. Besides, the distributed architecture will also be considered for parallel processing to improve the executive efficiency of the framework.

Acknowledgments. This research was supported by the National Key R&D Program of China (No. 2016YFB0801001). We thank our shepherd Shujun Li for his valuable feedback.

References

1. Shashanka, M., Shen, M.Y., Wang, J.: User and entity behavior analytics for enterprise security. In: 2016 IEEE International Conference on Big Data (Big Data), pp. 1867–1874. IEEE (2016)

2. Shi, C., Li, Y., Zhang, J., Sun, Y., Philip, S.Y.: A survey of heterogeneous information network analysis. IEEE Trans. Knowl. Data Eng. **29**(1), 17–37 (2016)
3. Sun, Y., Han, J., Yan, X., Yu, P.S., Wu, T.: PathSim: meta path-based top-K similarity search in heterogeneous information networks. Proc. VLDB Endowment **4**(11), 992–1003 (2011)
4. Tuor, A., Kaplan, S., Hutchinson, B., Nichols, N., Robinson, S.: Deep learning for unsupervised insider threat detection in structured cybersecurity data streams. In: Workshops at the Thirty-First AAAI Conference on Artificial Intelligence (2017)
5. Pei, K., et al.: HERCULE: attack story reconstruction via community discovery on correlated log graph. In: ACSAC, pp. 583–595 (2016)
6. Wang, J., Cai, L., Yu, A., Zhu, M., Meng, D.: TempatMDS: a masquerade detection system based on temporal and spatial analysis of file access records. In: 2018 17th IEEE International Conference on Trust, Security and Privacy in Computing and Communications/12th IEEE International Conference on Big Data Science and Engineering (TrustCom/BigDataSE), pp. 360–371. IEEE (2018)
7. Chen, T., Sun, Y.: Task-guided and path-augmented heterogeneous network embedding for author identification. In: Proceedings of the Tenth ACM International Conference on Web Search and Data Mining, pp. 295–304. ACM (2017)
8. Du, M., Li, F., Zheng, G., Srikumar, V.: Deeplog: Anomaly detection and diagnosis from system logs through deep learning. In: Proceedings of the 2017 ACM SIGSAC, CCS, pp. 1285–1298 (2017)
9. Bottou, L.: Large-scale machine learning with stochastic gradient descent. In: Proceedings of COMPSTAT 2010, pp. 177–186. Physica-Verlag HD (2010)
10. Bordes, A., Usunier, N., Garcia-Duran, A., Weston, J., Yakhnenko, O.: Translating embeddings for modeling multi-relational data. In: Advances in Neural Information Processing Systems, pp. 2787–2795 (2013)
11. Tang, J., Qu, M., Mei, Q.: Pte: predictive text embedding through large-scale heterogeneous text networks. In: Proceedings of the 21th ACM SIGKDD International Conference on Knowledge Discovery and Data Mining, pp. 1165–1174. ACM (2015)
12. Mikolov, T., Sutskever, I., Chen, K., Corrado, G.S., Dean, J.: Distributed representations of words and phrases and their compositionality. In: Advances in Neural Information Processing Systems, pp. 3111–3119 (2013)
13. Bhattacharjee, S.D., Yuan, J., Jiaqi, Z., Tan, Y.P.: Context-aware graph-based analysis for detecting anomalous activities. In: 2017 IEEE International Conference on Multimedia and Expo (ICME), pp. 1021–1026. IEEE (2017)
14. Le, D.C., Zincir-Heywood, A.N.: Machine learning based insider threat modelling and detection. In: 2019 IFIP/IEEE Symposium on Integrated Network and Service Management (IM), pp. 1–6. IEEE (2019)
15. Erhan, D., Bengio, Y., Courville, A., Manzagol, P.A., Vincent, P., Bengio, S.: Why does unsupervised pre-training help deep learning? J. Mach. Learn. Res. **11**(Feb), 625–660 (2010)
16. Dittman, D. J., Khoshgoftaar, T. M., Napolitano, A.: The effect of data sampling when using random forest on imbalanced bioinformatics data. In: 2015 IEEE International Conference on Information Reuse and Integration, pp. 457–463. IEEE (2015)

CTLMD: Continuous-Temporal Lateral Movement Detection Using Graph Embedding

Suya Zhao[1,2], Renzheng Wei[1,2], Lijun Cai[1], Aimin Yu[1(✉)], and Dan Meng[1]

[1] Institute of Information Engineering, Chinese Academy of Sciences, Beijing, China
{zhaosuya,weirenzheng,cailijun,yuaimin,mengdan}@iie.ac.cn
[2] School of Cyber Security, University of Chinese Academy of Sciences, Beijing, China

Abstract. Lateral movement technology is widely used in complex network attacks, especially in advanced persistent threats (APT). In order to evade the detection of security tools, attackers usually use the legal credentials retained on the compromised hosts to move laterally between computers across the enterprise intranet for searching valuable information. However, attackers cannot acquire the information about the normal action patterns of intranet users. So even the savviest attacker will "blindly move" in the intranet, making his lateral movement usually different from the typical users' behavior. In order to identify this potential malicious lateral movement, we proposes a Continuous-Temporal Lateral Movement Detection framework *CTLMD*. The remote and local authentication events are represented as a *Path Connection Graph* and a *Bipartite Graph* respectively. We extract normal lateral movement paths with time constraints while abnormal lateral movement paths are generated based on several attack scenarios. Finally, we define multiple path features using graph embedding methods to complete the follow-up classification task. We evaluate our framework by using injected attack data in real enterprise network dataset (LANL). Our experimental results show that the proposed framework can classify normal and malicious lateral movement paths well with the highest AUC of 92%. Meanwhile, the framework can detect the lateral movement state timely and effectively.

Keywords: Lateral movement detection · Graph embedding · Enterprise intranet security

1 Introduction

In recent years, the form of cyber-attacks has been characterized by high level, continuity and concealment. At the same time, most attackers no longer aim to destroy the target network or infrastructure, but stealing confidential data or

This work was supported by the National Key R&D Program of China (2016YFB0801001).

© Springer Nature Switzerland AG 2020
J. Zhou et al. (Eds.): ICICS 2019, LNCS 11999, pp. 181–196, 2020.
https://doi.org/10.1007/978-3-030-41579-2_11

core intellectual property becomes their priority tasks. So enterprise networks are the hardest hit areas where these cyber-attacks and data breaches occur frequently [1,2].

Research [3] shows that 80% time of an attack is spent during lateral movement. Therefore, lateral movement stage is also the place where an attacker is most easily detected. However, Lateral Movement Detection (**LMD**) still faces with many challenges. Firstly, there are no fixed features to detect LMD. Secondly, attackers usually pretend to be normal users, which is difficult to attract the attention of the IT administrator because they only check the failed login, and do not track the successful login [4]. Finally, data sets related to LMD are rare, which makes it hard to construct effective attack detection models using supervised machine learning methods.

Considering a common scenario: an employee starts his work in one day. First, he needs to log in his host. Then following the previous working mode he logs in other remote hosts to conduct business. However, the attacker is unfamiliar with the intranet structure and the lateral movement patterns of normal users, so he can only lateral move randomly to obtain assets information as many as possible. Therefore, the lateral movement caused by attackers often differs from typical user behavior and even from typical administrator behavior [5].

Based on the above experience, we propose an assumption in our work: the familiarity of lateral movement paths generated by normal operations of internal users should be far greater than the familiarity of lateral movement paths generated by attackers through random walking. In other words, it measures the extent to which the authentication events co-occur more than by chance or are independent.

In summary, this paper makes the following contributions:

1. We propose a continuous-temporal lateral movement detection framework (**CTLMD**) to classify the lateral movement paths. CTLMD analyzes lateral movement from two behavioral perspectives at the same time: remote transfer behavior and local login behavior.
2. We use two graph embedding methods CTDNE [6] and BiNE [7] separately to represent vertexes in a dimensionless way, so we can quantitatively study the lateral movement paths appearing in similar contexts in the latent space and understand them in a more meaningful and measurable way.
3. In order to generate paths dataset, we use the breadth-first algorithm and time constraints to search all normal lateral movement paths and inject malicious paths data based on two attack scenarios.
4. We evaluate our method based on a real enterprise data (LANL). The result shows that CTLMD can classify two type paths effectively and monitor the status of intranet lateral movement paths in real-time.

The rest of this paper is organized as follows. Section 2 reviews related work. Section 3 defines two graph structures to represent the authentication data. Section 4 overviews the framework we proposed and its components in detail. In Sect. 5, we evaluate our framework in public dataset. Finally, we summarize the paper and discuss limitations and future work outline in Sect. 6.

2   Related Work

2.1   Lateral Movement Detection

Traditional intrusion detection methods based on intrusion detection system (IDS), visualization strategies, honeypot or honeynet methods and system call are used to find solutions to internal problems [8].

There are many studies on risk reduction ferry strategies to prevent LMD. Johnson [9] proposes a risk indicator with graph analytic metric to measure the potential vulnerability of intranet to attacks that use lateral movement. Pope [10] introduces a network partitioning method with dynamic authentication bipartite graphs using the mitigation strategy to reduce the number of nodes accessible from certain starting nodes.

The above methods are usually implemented by selecting a set of edges to delete, which not fully utilize the nature of the intranet represented by these authentication data and do not detect attacks of abnormal lateral movement.

There are lots of work focusing on the abnormal login behavior of users or hosts in lateral movement. Kent [11] creates a Person's Authentication Graphs (PASs) for each user, then classify three types of users using machine learning. Siadati [12] develops the concept of a *Network Login Structure* that specifies normal logins within intranet to detect credential-based lateral movement. Eberle [13] proposes a graph-based internal threat detection method to discover suspicious insider activity by identifying abnormal subgraphs.

This kind of user- or host-based anomaly detection is effective, but often ignores the possible association between successive malicious operations at multiple times. Only a small part of works try to detect the lateral movement paths.

Hogan [14] attempts to find lateral movements by finding paths from outside the network to high-value IPs. However, this work does not discuss how well the approach does at detecting lateral movements.

2.2   Graph Embedding Application in Security

Graph embedding methods are inspired by the idea of words embedding in Natural Language Processing (NLP). As shown in Fig. 1, nodes' degree in the authentication connection graph satisfies the power law distribution.

Xu [15] proposes a prototype called Gemini using struct2vec to detect cross-platform binary code similarity. Ding [16] develops an assembly code representation learning model named Asm2Vec. It can learn both lexical semantic relationships and the vector representation of assembly functions at the same time. Song [17] proposes a graph-based deep learning approach DeepMem to automatically generate embedding vector representations for kernel objects and recognize these objects. It is important for collecting evidence of malicious or criminal behaviors.

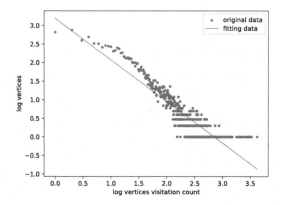

Fig. 1. The power low distribution of nodes' degree in authentication graph.

2.3   Closest Work

Work [18] designs a new graph embedding method to detect lateral movement. However, their task is only to detect abnormal hosts without analyzing the association between authentication events.

Based on the assumption that attackers' propagation speed is slower than the benign management tasks' in the intranet, work [19] proposes a malicious and benign lateral paths generation method based on the SIS virus propagation model. They inject malicious data into the public data set. In our work, we learn from the attack scenario construction of malicious lateral movement in this work to get abnormal data.

Dong [20] proposes GID, an efficient graph-based intrusion detection technique that can identify abnormal event sequences from massive heterogeneous process traces. We refer to their definition of time constraints for constructing normal sequences and use it on lateral movement paths.

3   Graph Structure Definition

We represent the interaction between login entities in intranet over a period of time as a collection of log events in temporal order $E = \{event_i \mid i = 1, 2, \ldots, k\}$, where $event_i$ is consist of 5-tuple [source user, source host, destination user, destination host, timestamp]:

$$event_i = (srcU_i, \ srcH_i, \ dstU_i, \ dstH_i, \ t_i) \tag{1}$$

Table 1 provides several examples of login events. We define a set of intranet users $U = \{u_1, u_2, \ldots, u_n\}$ and set $H = \{h_1, h_2, \ldots, h_m\}$ means hosts in the intranet. $t_i \in \mathbb{R}^+$ is the set of timestamp attributes of events.

To better characterize login events, we analyze lateral movement from two behavioral perspectives: constructing a path connection homogeneous graph with timestamps to analyze remote transfer behavior and a <users, hosts> bipartite heterogeneous graph to analyze local login behavior.

Table 1. Several examples of authentication event logs with time order.

Event	srcU	srcH	dstU	dstH	t
$event_1$	u_1	h_1	u_1	h_2	1
$event_2$	u_2	h_2	u_1	h_3	2
$event_3$	u_1	h_2	u_1	h_3	3
$event_4$	u_1	h_3	u_3	h_4	5

3.1 Path Connection Graph

In order to better formalize the interaction between remote login action [source entity →destination entity], we convert login events as a directed homogeneous graph with timestamp attribute. Both source entity and destination entity consist of a unique pair of flags $\langle u_i, h_i \rangle$.

Definition 1 (Temporal Path Connection Graph). *Given a graph $G_T = (V_T, E_T, \mathcal{T})$, let V_T be a set of login entities and $E_T \subseteq V_T \times V_T \times \mathbb{R}^+$ be the set of temporal edges. Function $\mathcal{T} : E \to \mathbb{R}^+$ maps each edge to a list of timestamp. At the finest granularity, each edge $e_i^T = (v_p, v_q) \in E_T$ may be assigned a time list $[t_1, t_2, \ldots, t_k] \in \mathbb{R}^+$.*

Definition 2 (Temporal Lateral Movement Path). *In G_T, a temporal path $l = (V_l, E_l)$ is a sequence of vertices $\langle v_1, v_2, \ldots, v_k \rangle$ such that edge $\langle v_i, v_{i+1} \rangle \in E_l$ for $1 \le i < k - 1$.*

As Fig. 2a shows, G_T provides the relevant login entities involved in each potential lateral movement path. A path with connectivity in a directed graph can directly help the security response team to increase or decrease the importance of security alter or related entity surveys. Obviously, the lateral movement path l as defined a subgraph of G_T.

3.2 Bipartite Graph

In addition to the obvious remote login connection, authentication logs also contain the local login action [user → host]. In order to analyze the similarity between users and the similarity between hosts respectively, we represent login events as a bipartite heterogeneous graph like Fig. 2b to mine the implicit information of users and hosts.

Definition 3 (Bipartite Graph). *Given a graph $G_B = (U, H, E_B)$, $E_B \subseteq U \times H$ represents a directed connection between users and hosts. Edges in E_B form a $|U| \times |H|$ weight matrix W. For each none-negative weight $w_{ij} \in W$ represents the login times between user u_i and host h_j.*

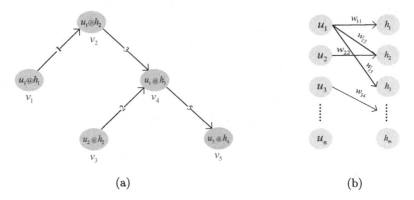

(a)   (b)

Fig. 2. We represent the authentication logs as two forms of graph. (a) is graph G_T for remote login behavior. (b) is graph G_B for local login behavior.

3.3 Problem Formulation

In this paper, we transform the LMD into a binary classification problem of paths. Given a lateral movement path $l \in L$, our goal is to find a mapping function $f(l) \to \{0, 1\}$.

4 Detection Framework

Figure 3 is the architecture and workflow of TLMD. It mainly consists of two phases: *Graph Preprocessing Unit* and *Anomaly Detection Unit*. We will explain each unit in detail in the following subsections.

4.1 Graph Preprocessing Unit

The main work of this unit it to preprocess the historical authentication data and represent the data into two types of graphs. And then we embed nodes of

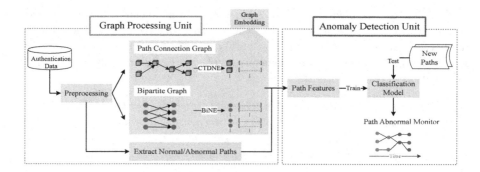

Fig. 3. The general framework of **CTLMD**.

graphs into low-dimensional vectors for later calculation. Meanwhile, we extract normal lateral movement paths based on graph G_T and generate malicious lateral movement paths according to attack scenarios for the down-stream construction of classification model.

Paths Generation. This part is mainly responsible for abstracting all normal lateral movement paths and injecting attack paths.

Normal Lateral Movement Abstract. One of the innovations of our work is how to define normal lateral movement paths. A straight forward way to generate candidate paths is to apply time constraints with breadth-first search in G_T.

Definition 4 (Time Constraints of l). *Given a lateral movement path $l = (V_l, E_l, T)$ with time, the normal path must satisfy the time constraint:* $0 \leq T(v_{i+1}, v_{i+2}) - T(v_i, v_{i+1}) \leq \Delta t$ *for* $1 \leq i < (k-1)$, *which means normal relevant events happen in time order and over a short period of time.*

Attack Scenario Simulation. Due to the scarcity of real malicious lateral movement data, we construct negative paths data based on two types of attack scenarios that is often employed by attackers, which inspired by the random walk model of web page link jump [21] and work [12,19]. We consider the following assumptions about attacks of two types:

* *Scenario-1 Remote Jump.* When attackers have compromised an intranet, they may exploit software vulnerabilities to deploy malicious code to establish tunnels between infected machines. If users suddenly start logging in hosts that they have never been visited before and generate new suspicious lateral movement paths, this situation usually indicates that users' certificate passwords have been stolen or the machines have been controlled by a Trojan. Moreover, attackers usually leave backdoors in the APT attack ending phase to have long-term control over target hosts that have been compromised. So attackers may try to create a new user in the target host.

In this scenario, we combine $\langle user, host \rangle$ pairs randomly to generate some new login entities on the malicious lateral movement paths. Some connections about login entities are also generated by random jump. This kind of negative paths thus generated is never seen in graph G_T.

* *Scenario-2 Random Walk.* After the initial intrusion, attackers will move as much as possible to expand the area of control. The most common way for attackers to move is stealing credentials that have been saved on the compromised hosts. Dunagan [22] refers to the process of repeatedly using stolen credentials to access additional computers as an *identity snowball* attack. This may not be noticed by IT administrators or security testing products because they only check for failed logins, not successful logins. However, even the most savvy attackers will perform "blindly move" in intranet. So the negative paths generation is random and without time constraints as Fig. 4.

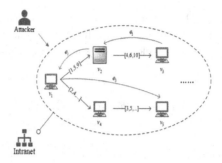

Fig. 4. The attacker enters the enterprise intranet with random walk to obtain assets information as far as possible without pattens.

Graph Embedding. One of the difficulties of our work is how to measure the familiarity of a lateral movement path. To effectively solve this problem, we use two graph embedding methods to map nodes into d-dimensional vectors respectively. Moreover, we can use the trained node vectors to directly calculate the similarity of the new path and realize real-time monitoring.

– *CTDNE.*

For the path connection graph G_T, we choose CTDNE algorithm to embed nodes with satisfying time constraints. Finally CTDNE gets the d-dimensional vector v_i representation of each login entity v_i.

The embedding for static networks is usually realized by random walk to get training corpus. Then the corpus is handed over to the model such as Skip-Gram to get the graph embedded. However, random walk method does not take into account the time order in which edges appear. For example, a message propagating in a network is directed, but an unconstrained random walk may result in a reverse corpus.

CTDNE constraint each random walk must conform to the temporal order in which edges occur, thereby capturing the graph's timing information into sequences of random walks. The addition of time series information has less embedded uncertainty, so its performance on traditional tasks is better than algorithms such as DeepWalk [23] and LINE [24].

– *BiNE.*

BiNE is a graph embedding algorithm specifically for bipartite graphs, which mapping two types of nodes into d-dimensional vectors.

One of BINE's contributions is it distinguishes between explicit and implicit relationships of bipartite graph. We use the BiNE algorithm to embed the <users, hosts> bipartite graph G_B. Finally we get the vector representation u_i and h_j of the user u_i and the host h_j respectively.

4.2 Anomaly Detection Unit

How to measure the familiarity of lateral movement path is the key part of our work. We consider that the higher the familiarity of the path, the higher the similarity between the elements on the path. Assigning similarity scores to each user/host indicates the similarity between the host and the user. On the other hand, it can interpret the correlation based on the transfer relationship between the login entities on the path. For example, when the similarity score of the user and the login host on the path is significantly different from previous, it indicates that the lateral movement is not a common pattern.

Based on the login entity embedding vector v and the user host embedding vector u, h in the previous step, we extract the following features to represent the current state of each path $l(V_l, E_l, T)$:

Path Edge Features. CTDNE calculates the vector of the login entity v based on the path connection graph. So we define 4 features to represent the similarity of the path edge: average $simE\_avg_l$, range $simE\_rg_l$, inter-quartile Range $simE\_iqr_l$ and average absolute deviation sim_mad_l. The edge similarity set of path l is $simE_l = \{sim_i = \cos(v_i, v_{i+1}) \mid i = 1, 2, \ldots, |V_l| - 1\}$. The path edge features are defined as following:

$$simE\_avg_l = \frac{\sum_{i=1}^{|V_l|-1} sim_i}{|E_l|} \tag{2}$$

$$simE\_rg_l = \max(simE_i) - \min(simE_i) \tag{3}$$

$simE\_iqr_l$ is defined as the difference between the 75% and 25% in the samples. Compared to the range feature based on only the two extreme values, $simE\_iqr_l$ measures 50% dispersion of the sample center.

$simE\_mad_l$ is defined as the median of the absolute value of the difference between a single sample and overall median. It can better measure the discrete case of the set value distribution.

Login Entity Features. For each login entity v in path l is equivalent to a edge of the user u_i connecting the host c_j in bipartite graph G_B. So we use the possibility that BiNE predicts whether an edge should exit or not to indicate whether the login entity in the path l is normal. For each path $l = \langle v_1, v_2, \ldots, v_k \rangle$, we define the normal probably of each login entity is p_i. The average possibility of path l is:

$$p_l = \frac{\sum_{i=1}^{|V_l|} p_i}{|V_l|} \tag{4}$$

User Features. In general, normal users move laterally with a fixed task pattern. We assume that the similarity between users on the normal lateral movement path should be higher than that between users on the random movement path which may caused by attackers. The average similarity $simU_l$ between users of path l is:

$$simU_l = \frac{\sum_{i=1}^{|U_l|-1} \cos(\boldsymbol{u_i}, \boldsymbol{u_{i+1}})}{|E_l|} \tag{5}$$

Host Features. The definition of average Host similarity $simC_l$ of path l is similar to $simU_l$:

$$simC_l = \frac{\sum_{j=1}^{|C_l|-1} \cos(\boldsymbol{c_j}, \boldsymbol{c_{j+1}})}{|E_l|} \tag{6}$$

5   Experiment and Result

5.1   Experiment Setup

Dataset. To evaluate CTLMD, we use authentication data from Los Alamos National Laboratory [25]. The full dataset covers 58 days of real authentication activity from LANL's network with 1,648,275,307 total events among 12,425 users and 17,684 computers. Each record in the authentication events has the form time, source user, destination user, source computer, destination computer, authentication type, logon type, authentication orientation, success/failure.

Data Preprocessing. CTLMD only needs the first five fields to form graphs and generate the lateral movement paths. At the same time, we filter out some noisy data like data with logout direction and the login failure events. Some users and hosts in the intranet are only connected to a fixed number of objects. In this case, it is difficult for attackers to move to network backbone. So we only use the largest connected subgraph of the path connection graph everyday.

Baseline. We compare *CTLMD* with the following methods to illustrate the advantages of CTLMD.

- **LSTM-based.** LSTM models are now widely used in machine learning tasks such as time series analysis and sequences anomaly detection using memory gates [26]. For the LSTM-based sequences detection, we use normal paths data from previous days to train and classify subsequent paths.
- **Feature Engineering.** In order to verify the effectiveness of the graph embedding algorithm, we extracted several common graph features of the lateral moving path: the sum of the edge weight and the average of node degrees etc.

Evaluation Metrics. Common evaluation metrics are as follows:

- *Acc.* Accuracy is the most intuitive performance measure and it is simply a ratio of correctly predicted observation to the total observations.
- *Pre.* Precision is the ratio of correctly predicted positive observations to the total predicted positive observations.
- *R.* Recall is the ratio of correctly predicted positive observations to the all observations in actual class.
- F_1. It takes both true positives and true negatives into account. In other words, it is the weighted average of Precision and Recall.
- *Auc.* The area under the curve ROC is an evaluation index to measure the pros and cons of the binary classification model.

5.2 Static Training and Test

There are abnormal login events in the first 30 days of LANL, so we select 11 days of the normal authentication events on day 30–40 to analysis and extract normal lateral movement paths separately.

The length distribution of paths on each day is shown in Fig. 5a. Obviously, day 31–32, 38–39 are weekends when the normal paths are less than work days'. On a working day as Fig. 5b, the most common path length is 3 and the longest is 4 to 6, which is consistent with the working lateral movement pattern of intranet users.

In order to get the vector representation of various types of nodes in advance, we choose a week data in day 26–32 and remove the abnormal login events to construct graph G_T and graph G_B. Two sub-tasks for graph edge prediction are designed to adjust the optimal parameters of BiNE and CTDNE algorithms as shown in Table 2 below, so that the accuracy of each task can reach 90%. It can guarantee that vectors of users and hosts can best represent the graph structure relationship while dimensionality reduction.

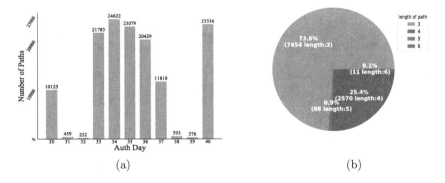

Fig. 5. Some analysis of LANL data. (**a**) shows the normal movement paths number of day 30–40 when $\Delta t = 3$ h. (**b**) is the length distribution of paths in working day 30.

For the following machine learning task, we choose the logistic regression (LR) model to classify normal paths or malicious paths. The experimental data included 137073 normal lateral movement paths which satisfy the time constraint in directed graph and 130803 malicious lateral movement paths generated by simulated attack scenarios. We use 80% of path data sets as the training set and the remaining 20% is used as the test set.

Results. The following are the results of classification experiments and comparative experiments.

There are some hyper-parameters in our method, but most of them already selected in sub-prediction tasks of BiNE and CTDNE. One of the most important parameters is Δt. It determines which paths can represent the normal lateral movement behavior of users in the intranet.

Table 3 is the classify results of different hyper-parameter Δt. Obviously, the result is better when $\Delta t = 3$ h. Because the longer the interval of login events is, the more accurate the extracted normal path pattern will be and the better the familiarity of the lateral movement generated by normal users login action will be described. So, it will be easier to distinguish from abnormal paths generated by attackers. The ROC curves are shown as Fig. 6a.

To better demonstrate the validity of the framework, we compared CTLMD with LSTM-based method and the traditional feature engineering classification. The ROCs are shown as Fig. 6b that CTLMD performs best. LSTM model structure is too complex and there is a risk of overfitting and high computational cost. So CTLMD has better performance for classify paths data in new days. The result of Feature Engineering illustrates that simple graph features can not distinguish two types of paths well.

Figure 7 is the correlation analysis heat map of path features and the path label. As seen from the figure, the similarity of path edges directly extracted by embedding vectors of CTDNE algorithms all contributed to the classification of paths to some extent. Feature 5 and Feature 6 is the similarity of users and hosts in the path, which indicates that the possibility of frequent change of login account or host is relatively small during one lateral movement action.

Table 2. The hyper-parameters of BiNE and CTDNE.

Parameter	Meaning	Value
$\alpha = \beta$	Trade-off parameter in BiNE	0.01
γ	Trade-off parameter in BiNE	1
ws	Size of skip-gram window in BiNE and CTDNE	2
d	Embedding vector dimension	128

Table 3. Experimental results of CTLMD about different hyper-parameter Δt.

	Acc	Pre	R	F_1	AUC
$\Delta t = 1\,\mathrm{h}$	0.87	0.82	0.84	0.83	0.88
$\Delta t = 3\,\mathrm{h}$	**0.91**	**0.85**	**0.90**	**0.87**	**0.92**

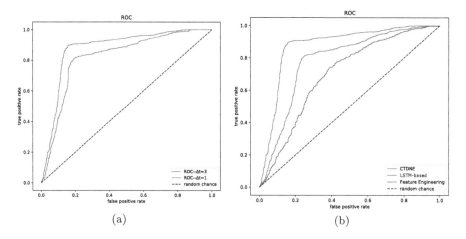

(a)   (b)

Fig. 6. The results of static experiment. **(a)** is the ROC curves with $\Delta t = 1\,\mathrm{h}$ and $\Delta t = 3\,\mathrm{h}$. **(b)** is the ROC curves of CTLMD, LSTM-based and Feature Engineering.

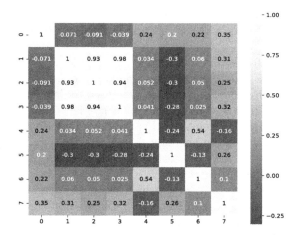

Fig. 7. Correlation analysis heat map of path features.

5.3   Dynamic Monitoring

Since the vector representation of Intranet nodes have been trained with the static graphs of historical data, we can directly use node vectors to calculate the similarity of various paths in the follow-up real-time monitoring of the status of lateral movement paths. At the same time, the CTLMD uses the trained classifier to detection whether the lateral movement path is malicious in real time.

Figure 8 illustrates the real-time change of path similarity more vividly. We choose a normal lateral movement path *C3412\$@DOM1_C1798, C3412\$@ DOM1_C3412, U42@DOM1_C3412, U42@DOM1_C561, U42@DOM1_C1025, U42@DOM1_C529* to calculate the similarity during the path generating on day 40. At time t_6 we add a new login entity at the end of the path. It is obvious that the similarity is directly reduced to 0.5 below.

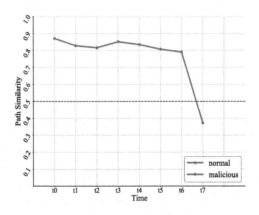

Fig. 8. A visualization example for real-time lateral movement monitoring.

6   Conclusion

We presents a new framework **CTLMD** for detecting lateral movement in intranet. In our work, the authentication events are represented as two graph structures. Two graph embedding methods are used to define a variety of path similarity features to represent the path familiarity. The follow-up paths detection can invoke the previously embedded vectors representation, which provides efficient support for large-scale anomaly detection. Moreover, we propose two attack scenarios and path time constraints first time, which provide a new possibility for lateral movement detection.

Looking at attack movement action in relation to each other can provide researchers and practitioners with invaluable insights into the *modus operandi* of attackers, highlighting important trends in the way attacks are conducted. So, security analysts must build intranet intelligence to understand how users and hosts communicate in the intranet and the typical mode used in the event of credential abuse to reduce lateral movement attacks.

However, the attack scenarios proposed in our work cannot include all attacks related to lateral movement. In future work, we will consider more reasonable attack scenarios and improve the extraction of path features to better characterize lateral movement behavior of users.

References

1. Morgan, J.P.: Chase Hack Affects 76 Million Households. https://dealbook. nytimes.com/2014/10/02/jpmorgan-discovers-further-cyber-security-issues/. Accessed 30 May 2019
2. Home Depot Hackers Exposed 53 Million Email Addresses. http://www.wsj.com/ articles/home-depot-hackers-used-password-stolen-from-vendor-1415309282. Accessed 1 June 2019
3. Smokescreen Technologies Pvt. Ltd.: Top 20 Lateral Movement Tactics. https://www.smokescreen.io/wp-content/uploads/2016/08/Top-20-Lateral-Movement-Tactics.pdf. Accessed 3 July 2019
4. How Do Threat Actors Move Deeper Into Your Network. http://about-threats. trendmicro.com/cloud-content/us/ent-primers/pdf/tlp_lateral_movement.pdf. Accessed 10 July 2019
5. Zeadally, S., Yu, B., Jeong, D.H., Liang, L.: Detecting insider threats: solutions and trends. Inf. Secur. J. Glob. Perspect. **21**(3), 183–192 (2012)
6. Nguyen, G.H., Lee, J.B., Rossi, R.A., Ahmed, N.K., Koh, E., Kim, S.: Continuous-time dynamic network embeddings. In: Companion Proceedings of the Web Conference 2018, Lyon, pp. 969–976. IWWWCSC (2018). https://doi.org/10.1145/ 3184558.3191526
7. Gao, M., Chen, L., He, X., Zhou, A.: BiNE: bipartite network embedding. In: Ann, A. (ed.) The 41st International ACM SIGIR Conference on Research & Development in Information Retrieval, New York, pp. 715–724. ACM (2018). https://doi. org/10.1145/3209978.3209987
8. Detecting malicious lateral movement across a computer network. http://www. freepatentsonline.com/20180367548.pdf. Accessed 14 May 2019
9. Johnson, J.R., Hogan, E.A.: A graph analytic metric for mitigating advanced persistent threat. In: 2013 IEEE International Conference on Intelligence and Security Informatics, Seattle, pp. 129–133. IEEE (2013). https://doi.org/10.1109/ISI.2013. 6578801
10. Pope, A., Tauritz, D., Kent, A.: Evolving bipartite authentication graph partitions. IEEE Trans. Dependable Secure Comput. **16**(1), 58–71 (2017)
11. Kent, D., Liebrock, M., Neil, C.: Analyzing user behavior within an enterprise network. Comput. Secur. **48**(1), 150–166 (2015)
12. Siadati, H., Memon, N.: Detecting structurally anomalous logins within enterprise networks. In: Proceedings of the 2017 ACM SIGSAC Conference on Computer and Communications Security, Texas, pp. 1273–1284. ACM (2017). https://doi.org/10. 1145/3133956.3134003
13. Eberle, W., Graves, J., Holder, L.: Insider threat detection using a graph-based approach. J. Appl. Secur. Res. **6**(1), 32–81 (2010)
14. Hogan, E., Johnson, J.R., Halappanavar, M.: Graph coarsening for path finding in cybersecurity graphs. In: Proceedings of the Eighth Annual Cyber Security and Information Intelligence Research Workshop, Tennessee, p. 7. ACM (2013). https://doi.org/10.1145/2459976.2459984

15. Xu, X., Liu, C., Feng, Q., Yin, H., Song, L., Song, D.: Neural network-based graph embedding for cross-platform binary code similarity detection. In: Proceedings of the 2017 ACM SIGSAC Conference on Computer and Communications Security, Dallas, pp. 363–376. ACM (2017). https://doi.org/10.1145/3133956.3134018
16. Ding, S., Fung, B., Charland, P.: Asm2Vec: boosting static representation robustness for binary clone search against code obfuscation and compiler optimization. In: Proceedings of the 2019 IEEE Symposium on Security and Privacy, San Francisco, pp. 38–55. IEEE (2019). https://doi.org/10.1109/SP.2019.00003
17. Song, W., Yin, H., Liu, C., Song, D.: DeepMem: learning graph neural network models for fast and robust memory forensic analysis. In: Proceedings of the 2018 ACM SIGSAC Conference on Computer and Communications Security, Toronto, pp. 606–618. ACM (2018). https://doi.org/10.1145/3243734.3243813
18. Chen, M., Yao, Y., Liu, J., Jiang, B., Su, L., Lu, Z.: A novel approach for identifying lateral movement attacks based on network embedding. In: 2018 IEEE International Conference on Parallel & Distributed Processing with Applications, Ubiquitous Computing & Communications, Big Data & Cloud Computing, Social Computing & Networking, Sustainable Computing & Communications (ISPA/IUCC/BDCloud/SocialCom/SustainCom), Melbourne, pp. 708–715. IEEE (2018). https://doi.org/10.1109/BDCloud.2018.00107
19. Bohara, A., Noureddine, M., Fawaz, A., Sanders, W.: An unsupervised multi-detector approach for identifying malicious lateral movement. In: 2017 IEEE 36th Symposium on Reliable Distributed Systems (SRDS), Hong Kong, pp. 224–233. IEEE (2017). https://doi.org/10.1109/SRDS.2017.31
20. Dong, B., et al.: Efficient discovery of abnormal event sequences in enterprise security systems. In: Proceedings of the 2017 ACM on Conference on Information and Knowledge Management, Singapore, pp. 707–715. ACM (2017). https://doi.org/10.1145/3132847.3132854
21. Junlin, Z.: Search Engine: Detailed Core Technology, 1st edn. Publishing House of Electronics Industry, Beijing (2012)
22. Dunagan, J., Zheng, A.X., Simon, D.R.: Heat-ray: combating identity snowball attacks using machine learning, combinatorial optimization and attack graphs. In: Proceedings of the 22nd ACM Symposium on Operating Systems Principles, , Montana, pp. 305–320. ACM (2009). https://doi.org/10.1145/1629575.1629605
23. Perozzi, B., Al-Rfou, R., Skiena, S.: DeepWalk: online learning of social representations. In: Proceedings of the 20th ACM SIGKDD International Conference on Knowledge Discovery and Data Mining, New York, pp. 701–710. ACM (2014). https://doi.org/10.1145/2623330.2623732
24. Tang, J., Qu, M., Wang, M., Zhang, M., Yan, J., Mei, Q.: Line: large-scale information network embedding. In: Proceedings of the 24th International Conference on World Wide Web, Florence, pp. 1067–1077. ACM (2015). https://doi.org/10.1145/2736277.2741093
25. Kent, D.: Cyber security data sources for dynamic network research. In: Dynamic Networks and Cyber-Security, pp. 37–65 (2016)
26. Buda, T.S., Caglayan, B., Assem, H.: DeepAD: a generic framework based on deep learning for time series anomaly detection. In: Phung, D., Tseng, V.S., Webb, G.I., Ho, B., Ganji, M., Rashidi, L. (eds.) PAKDD 2018. LNCS (LNAI), vol. 10937, pp. 577–588. Springer, Cham (2018). https://doi.org/10.1007/978-3-319-93034-3_46

Software Security

VulHunter: An Automated Vulnerability Detection System Based on Deep Learning and Bytecode

Ning Guo[1], Xiaoyong Li[1(✉)], Hui Yin[2], and Yali Gao[1]

[1] Key Laboratory of Trustworthy Distributed Computing and Service (BUPT),
Ministry of Education, Beijing, China
lixiaoyong@bupt.edu.cn
[2] College of Computer Science and Engineering, Shandong University of Science
and Technology, Qingdao, China

Abstract. The automatic detection of software vulnerability is undoubtedly an important research problem. However, existing solutions heavily rely on human experts to extract features and many security vulnerabilities may be missed (i.e., high false negative rate). In this paper, we propose a deep learning and bytecode based vulnerability detection system called Vulnerability Hunter (VulHunter) to relieve human experts from the tedious and subjective task of manually defining features. To the best of knowledge, we are the first to leverage bytecode features to represent vulnerabilities. VulHunter uses the bytecode, which is the intermediate representation output by the source code, as input to the neural networks and then calculate the similarity between the target program and vulnerability templates to determine whether it is vulnerable. We detect SQL injection and Cross Site Scripting (XSS) vulnerabilities in PHP software to evaluate the effectiveness of VulHunter. Experimental results show that VulHunter achieves more than 88% (SQL injection) and 95% (XSS) F1-measure when detecting a single type of vulnerability, as well as more than 90% F1-measure when detecting mixed types of vulnerabilities. In addition, VulHunter has lower false positive rate (FPR) and false negative rate (FNR) than existing approaches or tools. In practice, we apply VulHunter to three real PHP software (SEACMS, ZZCMS and CMS Made Simple) and detect five vulnerabilities in which three have not been disclosed before.

Keywords: Vulnerability detection · Deep learning · Bytecode

1 Introduction

Nowadays, nearly all information systems and business applications have built software-based applications. However, because of their existing security vulnerabilities which may be uncovered and unexploited, software are exposed to attacks, which will have a highly negative impact on users. According to the

© Springer Nature Switzerland AG 2020
J. Zhou et al. (Eds.): ICICS 2019, LNCS 11999, pp. 199–218, 2020.
https://doi.org/10.1007/978-3-030-41579-2_12

2018 Application Security Statistics Report from WhiteHat [3], more than 60% of applications have long been in a vulnerable environment. Thus, security experts have developed various solutions to detect vulnerabilities quickly and efficiently.

Vulnerability detection technology can be divided into three types depending on whether the program is running or not: dynamic analysis, static analysis, and mixed analysis [27]. The dynamic analysis method examines a program's behavior while it is running in a given environment. Essentially, dynamic analysis adopts an approach similar to that of a real attacker, and many commercial and open-source tools [2,4,15] and studies [16–19] have been proposed. The static analysis method detects program vulnerabilities without executing it. Usually, the static method analyzes the control logic and data flow of the program, and combines data statistics and feature recognition to determine whether the program has a vulnerability. Many systems and studies for this purpose have been conducted, including open source tools [1,10], commercial tools [5,9], and academic research projects [23,28,32,33]. Mixed analysis is a combination of dynamic and static analysis.

However, existing static solutions for vulnerability detection demonstrate over-reliance on expert experience and extract only surface source code features. The features of the source code are strongly related to the writing style of the code. The same vulnerability may appear in different source code, resulting in poor generalization of the neural networks. To address these technical challenges, we propose a vulnerability detection system called Vulnerability Hunter (VulHunter), which uses deep learning to calculate the similarity of bytecode features. We use bidirectional LSTM to build a neural network that can input two vectors and output a similarity value. We use graph-based static analysis methods to extract the code slices associated with the vulnerabilities and then transform them into bytecode slices, which are a lower-level representation of the code. In Sect. 4.3, we further demonstrate the effectiveness of the bytecode through experiments and explain it. We use PHP as a sample language to demonstrate the effectiveness of our proposed approach. The PHP source code is split into bytecode slices and word2vec [14] is used to transform them into vectors that can be fed to neural networks. The vulnerability templates are bytecode slices that have been processed, and each template represents a specific vulnerability. There are multiple templates for each vulnerability. The trained neural networks calculate the similarity between the target program and vulnerability templates to determine whether there are any vulnerabilities. In the experiment, we mainly detect SQL injection and XSS vulnerabilities, and there are 160 and 208 templates for the two vulnerabilities respectively. To verify the effectiveness of the system, we evaluate VulHunter on three open source PHP software: SEACMS, ZZCMS and CMS Made Simple. Five vulnerabilities were successfully detected, and three of them were discovered for the first time.

In summary, the contributions of this paper can be highlighted as follows.

- To the best of our knowledge, we are the first to apply bytecode to represent vulnerability features and employ graph-based static analysis methods to extract bytecode slice, which is the smallest unit of vulnerability representation. The bytecode slice is converted from a few lines of source code associated with the vulnerability to accurately represent and locate the vulnerability.

- We propose a deep learning based approach to detect vulnerabilities. Different from other existing studies which directly determine whether the target program has a vulnerability, our neural networks are mainly leveraged to calculate the similarity of the target program and the vulnerability templates. When the value of similarity exceeds a certain threshold, it will determine that the target program is vulnerable, which effectively improves the accuracy and recall rate of the system.
- A comprehensive experimental study on three real sample collections is performed to compare with the state-of-art vulnerability detection approaches. The promising experimental results demonstrate that our developed system VulHunter which integrate our proposed method outperforms other alternative vulnerability detection techniques. The code, data sets and vulnerability templates of this work is publicly available at https://github.com/Xmansec/VulHunter.

The remainder of this paper is organized as follows. In Sect. 2, we provide background on software vulnerability detection. In Sect. 3, we detail our methodology for detecting vulnerabilities and our improved technique for representing vulnerable features. In Sect. 4 we describe the results of our experiments for detecting SQL injection and XSS vulnerabilities in PHP software. At the same time, we show results of comparison with other approaches and tools. In Sect. 5, we introduce some previous work related to this paper. Finally, we conclude the paper in Sect. 6.

2   Background

Here, we provide the background relevant to software vulnerability detection. First, we give some examples of SQL injection and XSS vulnerabilities in Sect. 2.1. Then, In Sect. 2.2, we introduce the graph-based static software analysis methods. In Sect. 2.3, we discuss bytecode and its component in PHP. Finally, in Sect. 2.4, we cover background on Bi-LSTM neural networks.

2.1   SQL Injection and XSS Vulnerabilities

In this paper, we use SQL injection and XSS vulnerabilities to verify the effectiveness of the system. SQL injection refers to a class of code-injection attacks in which data provided by the user is included in an SQL query in such that part of the user's input is treated as SQL code [24]. Figure 1(a) shows an SQL injection vulnerability example in PHP source code. In the example, an attacker can craft a link that paired the single quotes of *id* and injects an arbitrary SQL such as http://www.xxx.com/?id=-1' union select database() −+. With this link, the attacker may obtain the name of the database. Cross-Site Scripting (XSS)

```
1 <?php
2 $id=$_GET['id'];
3 $sql="SELECT * FROM users WHERE id='$id'";
4 // exploit
5 $result=mysql_query($sql);
6 $row = mysql_fetch_array($result);
7 echo $row;
8 ?>
```

```
1 <?php
2 $data = $_GET['id'];
3 $data = urldecode($data);
4 //exploit
5 echo "<div ". $data ."= bob />" ;
6 ?>
```

(a) SQL injection

(b) XSS

Fig. 1. Examples of SQL injection and XSS vulnerability.

is one of the ten most critical web software security risks. There are three forms of XSS: reflected, stored and DOM XSS. Figure 1(b) shows a reflected XSS vulnerability example in PHP source code. In the example, an attacker can craft a link that injects malicious HTML and JavaScript code into the front page such as   *http://www.xxx.com/?id=><*script>*alert(document.cookie)*</script><. This link pops up a window showing the *cookies* of the current website.

2.2   Graph-Based Static Analysis

Graph-based static analysis refers to modeling program properties as graphs such as control-flow graphs (CFG), data-flow graphs (DFG) and program-dependence graphs (PDG) [27]. These techniques rely on building a model of bugs by a set of nodes in the graphs to identify bugs in a program. In this paper, we use a graph-based static analysis methods for code slicing, which is an important step in data processing. There are already some well-known algorithms to implement it [26,30]. These methods can help us analyze the program, build a static graph of the program, and extract the code related to the vulnerability. Therefore, we do not need to analyze the entire program file, and can more accurately represent and locate the vulnerability.

2.3   Bytecode

Bytecode is a form of instruction set designed for efficient execution by a software interpreter. It is an intermediate representation output by programming language implementations to ease interpretation or to reduce hardware and operating system dependence by allowing the same code to run cross-platform. Bytecode often directly executes on a virtual machine that further compiled bytecode into machine code for improving performance. Thus, the bytecode is a kind of code between the source code and the machine code, which can represent the semantic information of the code at a lower-level. Given its performance advantage, many languages first convert the source code into bytecode and then transform it into machine code or execute it directly in the virtual machine, such as Java, Python, and PHP.

2.4   Bi-LSTM

Many different types of neural networks have been successfully applied in numerous fields. The neural networks used in VulHunter are Bidirectional Long Short-Term Memory (Bi-LSTM) networks, which is a type of Recurrent Neural Networks (RNN). The problem of vanishing gradients is a key motivation behind the application of the LSTM cell [20,21,25], which consists of a state that can be read, written, or reset via a set of programmable gates. The multiplicative gates allow LSTM memory cells to store and access information over long time periods, thereby mitigating the vanishing gradients problem. For example, as long as the input gate remains closed (i.e., it has an activation near 0), the activation of the cell will not be overwritten by the new inputs arriving in the network and can be made available to the net much later in the sequence by opening the output gate [22]. However, even LSTM is insufficient for vulnerability detection because the argument(s) of a program may be affected by earlier or later statements. This result suggests that unidirectional LSTM can not learn enough vulnerability features and that we should use Bi-LSTM. Figure 5 shows a brief structure of neural networks in VulHunter.

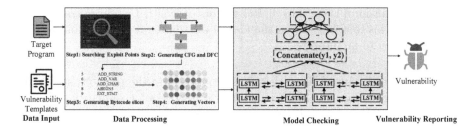

Fig. 2. Overview of VulHunter. It has two inputs, four data processing steps, one model checking step, and one output.

3   Methodology

In this section, we describe the methodology for our system to detect vulnerabilities (SQL injection and XSS) in PHP source code. In Sect. 3.1, we give an overview of VulHunter for vulnerability detection and elaborate its steps. In Sect. 3.2, we describe how to locate suspicious exploit points and generate bytecode slices from source code. In Sect. 3.3, we discuss the method to transform bytecode slices into vectors. In Sect. 3.4 we describe how to use Bi-LSTM networks in VulHunter. In Sect. 3.5, we present a formula for similarity calculation.

3.1   Overview of VulHunter

This subsection is an overview of VulHunter. Figure 2 shows the steps of methodology. VulHunter converts target program, along with the vulnerability templates, to digital vector during data processing phase. The neural networks calculate the similarity between the vulnerability templates and target program in model check phase. When the value of the similarity exceeds a certain threshold, the target program is deemed vulnerable. The following is a detailed process of the vulnerability detection.

Data Processing

- Step 1: Search for exploit points from source code, which are usually some functions or specific code (HTML tags). These points are necessary but not sufficient conditions for the existence of vulnerabilities.
- Step 2: Based on the exploit points found in Step 1, we generate CFG and DFG. Usually the input is the beginning of the graph, and the output is the end of the graph. Some of the edges in the figure are the path of the vulnerability execution.
- Step 3: According to the graph generated by Step 2, we use graph-based static analysis methods to generate code slices, which are just some code related to suspicious exploit points, such as variable declarations, function calls. And then we transform code slices to bytecode slices. Bytecode slices are the smallest unit that represents a vulnerability in this paper.
- Step 4: Bytecode slices generated by Step 3 are split into tokens by a tokenizer and then transform them into digital vectors of length L and pre-train with word2vec. This tool is based on the idea of distributed representation, which maps a token to an integer.

Model Checking. Input the target vector obtained in the previous step and vulnerability templates into the trained neural networks for similarity calculation. Finally, use the value of the similarity to determine whether it is vulnerable.

3.2   Generating Bytecode Slices

In this subsection, we describe the details how to convert the PHP source code into bytecode slices that corresponds to step 1 to step 3 of Fig. 2. A program file

Table 1. Suspicious exploit points related to SQL injection and XSS. The suspicious exploits of the SQL injection vulnerability are mainly functions that execute SQL, and the XSS vulnerability is related to various *HTML tags* (e.g., $<a>$, $<div>$) in addition to output functions.

Vulnerability	Suspicious exploit points
SQL injection	mysql_connect mysql_pconnect mysql_change_user mysql_query mysql_error mysql_set_charset mysql_unbuffered_query pg_connect pg_pconnect pg_execute pg_insert pg_put_line pg_query pg_select pg_send_query pg_set_client_encoding pg_update sqlite_open sqlite_poen sqlite_query sqlite_array_query sqlite_create_function sqlite_create_aggregate sqlite_exec mssql_connect mssql_query sqlsrv_connect sqlsrv_query odbc_connect odbc_exec
XSS	echo print printf print_r var_dump *HTML tags*

has numerous lines of code, but only a small part is related to the vulnerability. Thus, we need to use a more concise and accurate method to represent the vulnerability, not the entire file.

Searching Exploit Points. To generate bytecode slices, we must first examine for exploit points. The point referring to the vulnerability are finally triggered. It may be some functions or specific code (HTML tags). In the examples of this paper, we focus primarily on functions related to SQL execution and front-end display, such as *mysql_query()* and *echo* in Fig. 1. Table 1 summaries the suspicious exploit points related to SQL injection and XSS vulnerabilities in PHP.

Generating CFG and DFG. Code slices consists of a number of lines of code generating by graph-based static analysis methods. We construct graph based on control flow and data flow. The input is the beginning of the graph, and the output is the end. There are usually several methods to input data. First, data can be obtained from HTTP(S) communication; second, data are from the files; finally, data are from the database. For the first case, HTTP(S) methods are generally used, such as GET, POST and PUT. For the second case, it is generally related to the file uploaded by the user. In the third case, the data of the user has usually been stored in the database, which is more likely to cause secondary SQL injection or stored XSS. Figure 3 shows the details of the whole process. The source code is represented as a structured graph, then the execution path related to the vulnerability is determined. Finally, the code on the execution path is extracted.

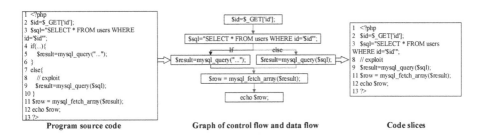

| Program source code | Graph of control flow and data flow | Code slices |

Fig. 3. Modified example of Fig. 1(a), in which the program has a SQL injection vulnerability. In this example, the code slices consists of five statements, namely lines 2, 3, 9, 11 and 12 of the program. When the program executes the *$result=mysql_query($sql)* in *else* code block, the vulnerability would be exploited, which is indicated by the red arrow. We extract these lines of the program to generate code slices. (Color figure online)

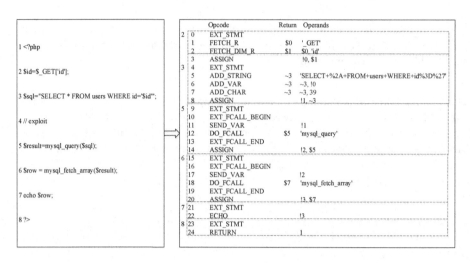

Fig. 4. Code slices and its corresponding bytecode slices. Each line of source code corresponds to several lines of bytecode. The variable name is automatically replaced, for example: !0 = $id, !1 = $sql, !2 = $result, !3 = $row.

Generating Bytecode Slices. In this step, we transform the code slices into bytecode slices by using VLD [13]. Although there are certain specifications and standards for programming, different programmers still have varying programming habits. In other words, the same vulnerability is likely to have multiple different representation at the source code level. Learning common vulnerability features is difficult from the perspective of source code. Bytecode is an more abstract representation of program. Neural networks can learn lower-level features to avoid overfitting. Figure 4 shows code slices (showed in Fig. 3) and its corresponding bytecode slices.

3.3 Transforming Bytecode Slices into Vectors

In this section, we transform the bytecode slices into digital vectors that corresponds to step 4 of Fig. 2. Given that bytecode conversion has completed tasks, such as removing comments and replacing variable names, excess data preprocessing is unnecessary. However, some operands are URL-encoded (e.g., third line of Fig. 4), so they are decoded first. Each bytecode slice needs to be encoded into a digital vector. For this purpose, we transform bytecode slices into token sequence, and each opcode follows the corresponding operations. All tokens would be split by space. For example, third line of Fig. 4:

$$\$sql = \text{``}SELECT * FROM users WHERE id = `\$id' \text{''};$$

Whose bytecode slices are

$$4 \quad EXT\_STMT$$
$$5 \ ADD\_STRING \ \ \tilde{} \ 3 \ \ `SELECT+\%2A+FROM+$$
$$users+WHERE+id\%3D\%27{'}$$
$$6 \quad ADD\_VAR \quad \tilde{} \ 3 \ \tilde{} \ 3, \ !0$$
$$7 \quad ADD\_CHAR \quad \tilde{} \ 3 \ \tilde{} \ 3, \ 39$$
$$8 \quad ASSIGN \quad \quad !1, \ \tilde{} \ 3$$

They can be represented by a sequence of 17 tokens:

"EXT_STMT", *"ADD_STRING"*, *"SELECT"*, *"*"*, *"FROM"*, *"users"*, *"WHERE"*, *"id"*, *"ADD_VAR"*, *"~ 3"*, *"!0"*, *"ADD_CHAR"*, *"~ 3"*, *"39"*, *"ASSIGN"*, *"!1"*, *"~ 3"*

This practice leads to a large corpus of tokens. In order to transform these tokens into digital vectors, we use tokenizer to encode each token into a unique number, which represents the position of token in the entire vector space.

Bytecode slices may have different numbers of tokens, so that corresponding digital vectors may have different length. Bi-LSTM takes equal-length vectors as input, so we need to make an adjustment. For this purpose, we introduce a parameter L as the fixed length of vectors corresponding to bytecode slices. There are two cases: when a vector is shorter than L, we pad zeros in the beginning of the vector; when a vector is longer than L, we delete the beginning part of the vector. We first determine the suspicious exploit points and then track the input forward, so the later tokens are crucial. This parts of the vector are retained when padding and deleting.

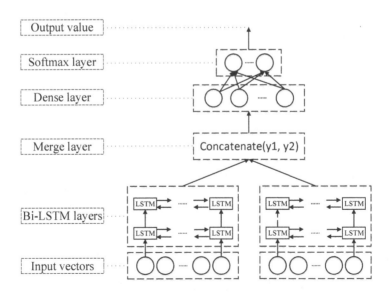

Fig. 5. A brief structure of Bi-LSTM neural networks. It evaluates the similarity of two vectors and products the result. The Bi-LSTM layers can propagate errors both forward and backward to avoid vanishing gradients problem.

3.4   Building Bi-LSTM Neural Networks

The core of our method is to calculate the similarity of bytecode between vulnerability templates and target program. Therefore, neural networks need to be able to receive two inputs and produce one output. Figure 5 shows the structure of neural networks, which has a number of Bi-LSTM layers, a merge layer, a dense layer, and a softmax layer. The Bi-LSTM layers contain some complex LSTM cells, with two directions (forward and backward). The merge layer concatenates the outputs of the two Bi-LSTM layers and combines them into a single tensor. The dense layer reduces the number of dimensions of the vectors received from the Bi-LSTM layers. The softmax layer takes the low-dimension vectors received from the dense layer as input, and is responsible for representing and formatting the classification result, which provides feedback for updating the neural network parameters in the learning phase.

3.5   Similarity Calculation

The same types of vulnerabilities may have many different subtypes, which indicate various causes of the vulnerabilities. Therefore, we use a vulnerability template to represent a subtype of vulnerability. The target program and vulnerability templates are then used as inputs of the neural networks to calculate the mean of similarity, denoted as S:

$$S = \frac{\sum_{i=1}^{N} BLNN(T_i, P)}{N} \tag{1}$$

where N is the number of vulnerability templates, $BLNN$ is Bi-LSTM neural networks, T_i is a template for a subtype of a vulnerability, and P is target program. The output of $BLNN$ is number between 0 (dissimilar) and 1 (similar). When the value of S exceeds a certain threshold (we set it to 0.5), the target program is considered to be vulnerable.

4   Experiments and Results

In the following section, we detail of our experimental steps and results. In Sect. 4.1, we give the evaluation metrics. In Sect. 4.2, we describe the process of data preprocessing and model training. In Sect. 4.3, we use VulHunter to detect signal or mixed vulnerabilities and compare results with other methods and tools. Final, we use VulHunter in practice.

4.1   Evaluation Metrics

Precision, recall, F1-measure, false negative rate (FNR), and false positive rate (FPR) are the five metrics to evaluate vulnerability detection system. A confusion matrix is used to calculate these parameters. In the confusion matrix, true positive (TP) is the number of samples with vulnerabilities detected correctly.

False positive (FP) is the number of samples without vulnerabilities detected incorrectly. True negative (TN) is the number of samples without vulnerabilities undetected. False negative (FN) is the number of samples with vulnerabilities undetected.

– Precision (P) shows how many vulnerabilities detected by system are actual vulnerabilities. The higher P is, the lower false alarm is:

$$P = \frac{TP}{TP + FP} \qquad (2)$$

– Recall (R) shows the percentage of detected vulnerabilities versus all vulnerabilities presented. We want a high R value:

$$R = \frac{TP}{TP + FN} \qquad (3)$$

– F1-measure (F1) is the harmonic mean of precision and recall. We also aim for a high F1-measure value:

$$F1 = 2\frac{P \cdot R}{P + R} \qquad (4)$$

– The FNR measures the ratio of false negative vulnerabilities to the entire population of samples that are vulnerable. We want a low FNR value:

$$FNR = \frac{FN}{FN + TP} \qquad (5)$$

– The FPR measures the ratio of false positive vulnerabilities to the entire population of samples that are not vulnerable. We also want a low FPR value:

$$FPR = \frac{FP}{FP + TN} \qquad (6)$$

4.2 Data Preprocessing and Model Training

Description of Datasets. Our experiments are mainly based on SQL injection and XSS vulnerabilities numbered CWE-89 and CWE-79 in common weakness enumeration (CWE) [6], which is a community-developed list of common software security weaknesses. The PHP code data comes mainly from NVD [7], which contains vulnerability programs in production software, and SARD [11], which has many vulnerability cases. In NVD and SARD, each program or case has a CWE ID that indicates which type of vulnerability it belongs to. In total, we collected 18,989 programs, of which 912 have SQL injection vulnerabilities and 4,352 have XSS vulnerabilities. The rest are the invulnerable programs without a known vulnerability, of which 7,992 are related to SQL injection and 5,733 are related to XSS. We used ten-fold cross-validation, using 90% of the data as a training set and 10% as a test set. The PHP source code obtained from NVD is vulnerable, and the programs obtained from SARD have been marked as "bad" or "good". Thus we do not need to manually mark them as vulnerable or invulnerable.

Table 2. Statistics of the three datasets

Dataset	Bytecode slices	Vulnerable bytecode slices	Invulnerable bytecode slices
SQL-SET	8904	912	7992
XSS-SET	10085	4352	5733
MIX-SET	18989	5264	13725

Data Preprocessing. We transform source code into bytecode slices according to steps 1 to 3 in 3.1 selection and then divide the dataset into the following three parts: SQL injection vulnerability set, XSS vulnerability set, and mixed types of vulnerabilities set (i.e., the sum of the first two sets). Table 2 summarizes the number of bytecode slices in datasets. In the SQL-SET dataset, there are 1,032,509 tokens, of which 182 are different; in the XSS-SET dataset, there are 510,252 tokens, of which 168 are different. The MIX-SET is sum of SQL-SET and XSS-SET. These symbolic representations are encoded into digital vectors for training neural networks.

Training Neural Networks. We use the three datasets in Table 2 to train neural networks and find the best parameters. The training process of the four main parameters of *number of Bi-LSTM layer, batch_size, dropout* and *epoch* is shown in Fig. 6. The selection of each parameter mainly refers to the F1-measure value and the training time. The more the number of Bi-LSTM layers, the more complex the neural networks are, which may increase the system's performance and uptime. Figure 6(a) shows the process of changing the F1-measure and number of seconds pre epoch as the number of Bi-LSTM layers increases. When the number of Bi-LSTM layers is 2, the F1-measure is the highest and the number of seconds per epoch is also low, so the number of Bi-LSTM layers is set to 2. Similarly, batch_size is set to 256, dropout is set to 0.2, and epoch is set to 20.

4.3 Vulnerability Detection

In this selection, we verify the vulnerability detection capability of VulHunter and compare with other vulnerability detection approaches or tools. We select three open source tools called RIPS [9], sonarqube [12], phpcs-security-audit [8], and a state-of-the-art systems called VulDeePecker [28]. RIPS, sonarqube, and phpcs-security-audit are all PHP vulnerability detection tools recommended by OWASP and widely used. VulDeePecker is a deep learning-based vulnerability detection system proposed by Li et al. [28]. RIPS, sonarqube, and phpcs-security-audit can directly detect PHP source code. VulDeePecker was originally designed to detect buffer error vulnerability and resource management error vulnerabilities in C/C++ programs. For a fair comparison, we construct neural networks

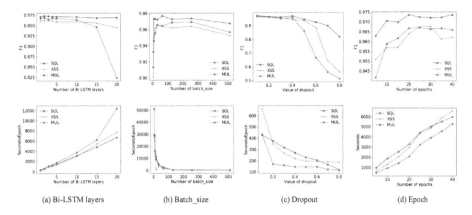

(a) Bi-LSTM layers   (b) Batch_size   (c) Dropout   (d) Epoch

Fig. 6. Parameter selection. This picture consists of four parts, (a) number of Bi-LSTM layer, (b) batch_size, (c) dropout, and (d) epoch, which all show the trend of F1- measure and time as parameters change. The time of (a), (b), and (c) is the number of seconds per epoch, and the time of the last part (d) is the number of seconds that all epochs add up.

according to VulDeePecker's design steps and retrain by our datasets. Table 3 shows the detection results of the system.

First, Let's analyze the results of Vulhunter. Its performance is better at detecting XSS vulnerabilities than detecting SQL injection vulnerabilities due to the imbalance of SQL-SET dataset. The ratio of vulnerable bytecode slices to the invulnerable in the XSS-SET dataset is approximately 0.76:1. However, the ratio in the SQL-SET dataset is 0.11:1. We have also observed that detection of mixed types of vulnerabilities is also less effective than XSS vulnerabilities detection. The precision and F1-measure on the MIX-SET dataset are lower than those on the XSS-SET. For mixed-type vulnerability detection, the neural networks trained by MIX-SET may also identify a vulnerability as another type of vulnerability, in addition to possibly erroneously determining whether target program is vulnerable. These all increase the probability of producing errors. Further, we observed that recall rate is very high and the FPR is very low in the detection results of the three datasets. And the code with and without the vulnerability often only differ between one statement and even a few characters, which indicates that neural networks can distinguish very small vulnerability features.

Second, we find that VulHunter and VulDeePecker are better than other approaches or tools. That is to say, the deep learning-based algorithm for vulnerability detection is effective. We observed that RIPS, sonarqube and phpcs-security-audit have very similar results on all three datasets, with higher recall, FPR, and lower F1-measure (sonarqube is slightly superior to other two). VulHunter and VulDeePecker have more than 80% F1-measure, and both FPR and FNR are below 10%. The highest F1-measure of the other three tools is only 60.21%, but the highest FPR is 100%. Their detection relies mainly on rules

Table 3. Results of comparing with other approaches or tools

Approaches or tools	P(%)	R(%)	F1(%)	FPR(%)	FNR(%)
SQL-SET					
RIPS	13.60	95.65	23.16	69.88	4.35
Sonarqube	12.98	40.22	19.62	31.00	59.78
Phpcs-security-audit	10.60	97.83	19.13	94.88	2.17
VulDeePecker	**86.02**	86.96	86.86	**1.63**	13.04
VulHunter	78.63	**100.0**	**88.04**	3.13	**0.00**
XSS-SET					
RIPS	43.51	97.71	60.21	96.51	2.29
Sonarqube	41.79	43.81	42.78	46.42	56.19
Phpcs-security-audit	42.06	95.41	58.39	100.0	4.59
VulDeePecker	90.04	**97.25**	93.51	8.19	**2.75**
VulHunter	**99.02**	92.22	**95.50**	**0.70**	7.78
MIX-SET					
RIPS	31.42	75.78	44.41	63.58	24.22
Sonarqube	24.44	62.12	35.08	73.85	37.88
Phpcs-security-audit	29.89	94.70	45.43	85.43	5.30
VulDeePecker	76.43	95.47	84.89	8.19	4.53
VulHunter	**85.76**	**97.99**	**91.44**	**6.26**	**2.01**

defined by human experts, and FPs are easily generated when the code of the vulnerability is not very different from the code without the vulnerability.

Third, we observed that VulHunter is better than VulDeePecker in most cases. VulHunter has the highest precision (97.67% in XSS-SET and 85.76% in MIX-SET) and F1-measure (95.13% in SQL-SET, 96.77% in XSS-SET, and 91.44% in MIX-SET). This result can be explained from three aspects.

- We transform the source code into bytecode slices and then use vectors at the bytecode level to represent the vulnerability features. A lot of redundant information, such as comments, custom variable names, is automatically processed after the source code is converted to bytecode, thereby avoiding the over-fitting problem caused by different writing styles.
- After converting the program to bytecode we can see many implicit functions that are not in the source code. This means that we can find more exploit execution paths from bytecode and extract more features, so it can avoid many false negatives.
- We determine whether there is a vulnerability based on the similarity between the target program and vulnerability templates calculated by the neural networks. Templates can preserve the features of the vulnerability so that the neural networks only focus on the calculation of similarity. The template-based similarity calculation method can flexibly cope with variants of different vulnerabilities, and it only needs to add corresponding templates when encountering new vulnerability types.

Using VulHunter in Practice. To further demonstrate the use of VulHunter, we used VulHunter to detect three software developed by PHP: SEACMS, ZZCMS, and CMS Made Simple (CMSMS). These software versions are recently released. According to the data processing steps, we extracted 681, 2,351, and 2,495 suspicious exploit points from three software and then generated byte-code slices. Subsequently, We use VulHunter to detect vulnerabilities and manually verified the results to determine that five of the vulnerabilities were real. Table 4 shows the details of the vulnerability detection results. CVE-2018-19350, CVE-2018-19349, and CVE-2018-20464 are vulnerabilities that have not been published before. They were first discovered and marked in bold in the table. CVE-2018-14962 and CVE-2018-5963 are also real vulnerabilities but have been published by other security researchers.

Table 4. Vulnerabilities detected in real software

CVE-ID	Type	Software	Version
CVE-2018-19350	XSS	SEACMS	6.6.4
CVE-2018-19349	SQL Injection	SEACMS	6.6.4
CVE-2018-14962	XSS	ZZCMS	8.3
CVE-2018-5963	XSS	CMSMS	2.2.8
CVE-2018-20464	XSS	CMSMS	2.2.8

5 Related Work

Vulnerability detection technology is divided into three types: static analysis, dynamic analysis, and mixed analysis [27]. Table 5 shows recent technologies on vulnerability detection. Static analysis is divided into two types: graph-based static analysis and static analysis with data modeling. These technologies has been used by other researchers. For example, Song et al. proposed a method called BitBlaze, which has a static analysis component that can detect vulnerabilities using CFG, DFG and weakest precondition calculation, called Vine [31]. Yamaguchiet et al. proposed a novel and comprehensive representation of source code called *code property graph* that merges concepts of abstract syntax trees, classic program analysis, program dependence graphs, and control flow graphs, as well as help user to model templates for common vulnerabilities with graph traversals [33]. Nguyen et al. propose an enhanced form of CFG known as lazy-binding CFG to produce image-based representation. This technology works well for malware detection [29].

Table 5. Summary of recent technologies on vulnerability detection

Methods	Technologies	Advantages	Disadvantages
Static analysis	Graph-based static analysis	High code coverage	Lack of run-time information
	Static analysis with data modeling		
Dynamic analysis	Fuzzing: AFL, AFLFast, AFLGo, etc.	Fast	Low code coverage
	DTA: DTA, TEMU, DTA++, etc.		
Mixed analysis	Concolic: DART, CUTE, Driller	Fast, high code coverage	Path explosion

6   Conclusions and Future Work

In this paper, we present VulHunter, an automated vulnerability detection system based on deep learning and bytecode. With graph-based static analysis methods, VulHunter can find the code related to the vulnerability and then transform it into bytecode slices that represent the vulnerability well. Bytecode slices are transformed to digital vectors as inputs of neural networks. Our neural networks are different from existing algorithms for direct classification, which can determine whether the target program is vulnerable by calculating similarity between target program and vulnerability templates. Experimental results show that VulHunter achieves 88.04%, 95.50% and 91.44% F1-measure for SQL injection, XSS and mixed types vulnerabilities detection respectively, which are the highest value compared with other approaches or tools. We also tried to use VulHunter to detect three real PHP software (i.e., SEACMS, ZZCMS and CMS Made Simple). Note that three of the five vulnerabilities found have not been published before.

For the future work, we will further the research from two aspects. For one thing, we found that existing automated vulnerability detection methods are powerless for complex vulnerabilities. Complex vulnerabilities have very long ROC-Chains (Return Oriented Programming Chain) and are often associated with multiple files. Therefore, it is difficult to analyze the structure and data information of the program. In the future, we will continue to study the application of deep learning in complex vulnerability detection. For another, due to some indeed limitations of the static analysis method itself, the system is difficult to detect for the vulnerabilities that can occur in execution. For example, some overflow vulnerabilities are easier to detect through dynamic fuzzing techniques. Thus, we will further study the application of deep learning in dynamic vulnerability detection, which can detect the vulnerabilities that only occurs in execution.

Acknowledgments. This work was supported by NSFC-General Technology Fundamental Research Joint Fund (No. U1836215), and the National Key R&D Program of China (No. 2016QY03D0605).

A   Appendices

A.1   LSTM Networks

Long short term memory networks, usually just called LSTMs, are a special kind of RNN, capable of learning long-term dependencies. LSTMs contain a complex structure called LSTM cells, which are briefly reviewed below and referred to [25] for greater details.

Each LSTM cell uses a forget gate f (i.e., the state flow of the cell), an input gate i (i.e., the input data), and an output gate o (i.e., the output of module) to control the data flow through the neural networks. Figure 7 shows the detailed structure of the LSTM cell.

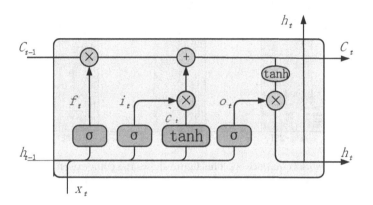

Fig. 7. LSTM cell

The forget gate looks at h_{t-1} and x_t, and outputs a number between 0 and 1, which represents how many percentages of C_{t-1} are retained. The value of f_t at the time t is:

$$f_t = \sigma(W_f[h_{t-1}, x_t] + b_f) \tag{7}$$

The input gate has two parts. First, a Sigmoid layer outputs i_t that decides which values will update. Next, a *tanh* layer creates a vector of new candidate values, $\widetilde{C}_t$, that could be added to the state. The values of i_t and $\widetilde{C}_t$ at the time t are:

$$i_t = \sigma(W_i[h_{t-1}, x_t] + b_i) \tag{8}$$

$$\widetilde{C}_t = tanh(W_c[h_{t-1}, x_t] + b_c) \tag{9}$$

And then the new cell state C_t is:

$$C_t = f_t \odot C_{t-1} + i_t \odot \widetilde{C}_t \tag{10}$$

The output gate is based on Sigmoid layer value o_t and new cell state C_t to calculate the output h_t. The o_t and h_t at the time t are calculated as follows:

$$o_t = \sigma(W_o[h_{t-1}, x_t] + b_o) \tag{11}$$

$$h_t = o_t \odot tanh(C_t) \tag{12}$$

where σ denote Sigmoid function $\frac{1}{1+exp(-x)}$, $tanh$ denote the hyperbolic tangent function $\frac{exp(x)-exp(-x)}{exp(x)+exp(-x)}$ and $\odot$ denote the element-wise multiplication, h_{t-1} is output of cell at the time $t-1$, C_{t-1} is state of cell at the time $t-1$, x_t is input of cell at time t, W_f, W_i, W_o, W_C are the weight matrices with the forget gate, the input gate, the output gate, and the cell state input, and b_f, b_i, b_o, b_C are bias items of the forget gate, the input gate, the output gate, and the cell state input.

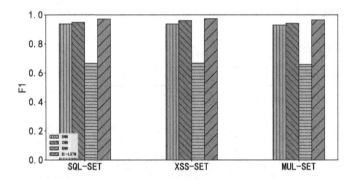

Fig. 8. Neural networks comparison. This figure shows the comparison of DNN (green), CNN (red), RNN (orange), and Bi-LSTM (blue) on the SQL-SET, XSS-SET, and MIX-SET datasets. The ordinate is F1-measures, and the values shown in the figure are the highest values that can be achieved by each network. (Color figure online)

A.2   Neural Networks Comparison

We compared three other types of neural networks: DNN, CNN, and RNN. Similarly, they are all adjusted to determine the best F1-measure. Figure 8 shows the comparison of the best F1-measures for the four neural networks on three datasets. The F1-measures of the four networks are Bi-LSTM, CNN, DNN, and RNN from high to low. The F1-measures of CNN and DNN are not much different at only 0.02 to 0.04 lower than Bi-LSTM. But the value of RNN on the three data sets is only 0.66, which is most likely caused by the vanishing gradients problem (or, exploding gradient problem).

References

1. Flawfinder (2015). http://www.dwheeler.com
2. Acunetix (2018). https://www.acunetix.com
3. Application security statistics report (2018). https://www.whitehatsec.com/blog/2018-whitehat-app-sec-statistics-report/

4. Burpsuit (2018). https://portswigger.net/burp
5. Checkmarx (2018). https://www.checkmarx.com
6. Common weakness enumeration (2018). https://cwe.mitre.org/index.html
7. National vulnerability database (2018). https://www.nist.gov
8. Phpcs-security-audit (2018). https://github.com/FloeDesignTechnologies/phpcs-security-audit
9. RIPS (2018). https://www.ripstech.com
10. Rough audit tool for security (2018). https://code.google.com/archive/p/rough-auditing-tool-for-security
11. Software assurance reference dataset (2018). https://samate.nist.gov/SRD/index.php
12. Sonarqube (2018). https://www.sonarqube.org/
13. Vulcan logic dumper (2018). https://derickrethans.nl/projects.html
14. Word2vec (2018). https://radimrehurek.com/gensim/models/word2vec.html
15. WPScan (2018). https://wpscan.org
16. Bau, J., Bursztein, E., Gupta, D., Mitchell, J.C.: State of the art: automated black-box web application vulnerability testing. In: Security and Privacy, pp. 332–345 (2010)
17. Doupé, A., Cavedon, L., Kruegel, C., Vigna, G.: Enemy of the state: a state-aware black-box vulnerability scanner. In: Usenix Security Symposium (2012)
18. Doupé, A., Cova, M., Vigna, G.: Why johnny can't pentest: an analysis of black-box web vulnerability scanners. In: International Conference on Detection of Intrusions and Malware, and Vulnerability Assessment, pp. 111–131 (2010)
19. Duchene, F., Groz, R., Rawat, S., Richier, J.L.: XSS vulnerability detection using model inference assisted evolutionary fuzzing. In: IEEE Fifth International Conference on Software Testing, Verification and Validation, pp. 815–817 (2012)
20. Gers, F.A., Schmidhuber, J., Cummins, F.: Learning to forget: continual prediction with LSTM. Neural Comput. **12**(10), 2451–2471 (2000)
21. Gers, F.A., Schraudolph, N.N., Schmidhuber, J.: Learning precise timing with LSTM recurrent networks. J. Mach. Learn. Res. **3**(1), 115–143 (2003)
22. Graves, A.: Long short-term memory. In: Supervised Sequence Labelling with Recurrent Neural Networks. Studies in Computational Intelligence, vol. 385. Springer, Heidelberg (2012). https://doi.org/10.1007/978-3-642-24797-2_4
23. Grieco, G., Grinblat, G.L., Uzal, L., Rawat, S., Feist, J., Mounier, L.: Toward large-scale vulnerability discovery using machine learning. In: ACM Conference on Data and Application Security and Privacy, pp. 85–96 (2016)
24. Halfond W G J, Viegas J, O.A.: A classification of SQL injection attacks and countermeasures (2006)
25. Hochreiter, S., Schmidhuber, J.: Long short-term memory. Neural Comput. **9**, 1735–1780 (1997)
26. Horwitz, S., Reps, T., Binkley, D.: Interprocedural slicing using dependence graphs. ACM SIGPLAN Not. **39**(4), 229–243 (2004)
27. Ji, T., Yue, W., Chang, W., Xi, Z., Wang, Z.: The coming era of alphahacking? A survey of automatic software vulnerability detection, exploitation and patching techniques. In: IEEE Third International Conference on Data Science in Cyberspace (2018)
28. Li, Z., et al.: VulDeePecker: a deep learning-based system for vulnerability detection (2018)
29. Nguyen, M.H., Le, N.D., Xuan, M.N., Quan, T.T.: Auto-detection of sophisticated malware using lazy-binding control flow graph and deep learning. Comput. Secur. **76**, 128–155 (2018)

30. Sinha, S., Harrold, M.J., Rothermel, G.: System-dependence-graph-based slicing of programs with arbitrary interprocedural control flow. In: International Conference on Software Engineering (1999)
31. Song, D., et al.: BitBlaze: a new approach to computer security via binary analysis. In: International Conference on Information Systems Security, pp. 1–25 (2008)
32. William Melicher, A.D.: Riding out DOMSday: Toward detecting and preventing DOM cross-site scripting (2018)
33. Yamaguchi, F., Golde, N., Arp, D., Rieck, K.: Modeling and discovering vulnerabilities with code property graphs. In: Security and Privacy, pp. 590–604 (2014)

Deep Learning-Based Vulnerable Function Detection: A Benchmark

Guanjun Lin[1], Wei Xiao[2], Jun Zhang[1(✉)], and Yang Xiang[1]

[1] School of Software and Electrical Engineering, Swinburne University of Technology, Hawthorn, Melbourne, VIC 3122, Australia
junzhang@swin.edu.au
[2] School of Computer Science and Engineering, Changchun University of Technology, Changchun, Jilin Province, China

Abstract. The application of Deep Learning (DL) technique for code analysis enables the rich and latent patterns within software code to be revealed, facilitating various downstream tasks such as the software defect and vulnerability detection. Many DL architectures have been applied for identifying vulnerable code segments in recent literature. However, the proposed studies were evaluated on self-constructed/-collected datasets. There is a lack of unified performance criteria, acting as a baseline for measuring the effectiveness of the proposed DL-based approaches. This paper proposes a benchmarking framework for building and testing DL-based vulnerability detectors, providing six built-in mainstream neural network models with three embedding solutions available for selection. The framework also offers easy-to-use APIs for integration of new network models and embedding methods. In addition, we constructed a real-world vulnerability ground truth dataset containing manually labelled 1,471 vulnerable functions and 1,320 vulnerable files from nine open-source software projects. With the proposed framework and the ground truth dataset, researchers can conveniently establish a vulnerability detection baseline system for comparison and evaluation. This paper also includes usage examples of the proposed framework, aiming to investigate the performance behaviours of mainstream neural network models and providing a reference for DL-based vulnerability detection at function-level.

Keywords: Vulnerability detection · Neural network · Function-level detection

1 Introduction

Deep Learning (DL), a breakthrough technique which has achieved promising results in many fields such as image processing and natural language processing (NLP), has also been widely applied for software code analysis [3] and for vulnerability detection [17,18,20,21]. Various DL architectures, including the Multi-Layer Perceptron (MLP) [10,29], the Convolutional Neural Network

© Springer Nature Switzerland AG 2020
J. Zhou et al. (Eds.): ICICS 2019, LNCS 11999, pp. 219–232, 2020.
https://doi.org/10.1007/978-3-030-41579-2_13

(CNN) [11,16,27,32], and the Long-Short Term Memory (LSTM) [18,20,21] have been adopted for learning latent vulnerable code patterns from different software code representations (e.g., the Abstract Syntax Trees (ASTs) or the Control Flow Graphs (CFGs)). However, the aforementioned approaches were evaluated on self-constructed/-collected datasets, and/or compared with conventional code analysis methods. There is a lack of a unified benchmarking dataset for evaluating the effectiveness of these DL-based approaches and there is also the absence of a baseline system which can be easily replicated to act as a reliable performance metric for comparison and evaluation.

In this paper, we take a step forward to bridge this gap by proposing a benchmarking framework based on Keras [7] with TensorFlow [2] backend, providing one-click execution scripts for establishing a DL-based baseline system for vulnerability detection. The framework encapsulates six mainstream neural network models and can be easily extended to support different code embedding schemes and neural models. We also constructed a vulnerability dataset at two levels of granularity i.e., the file-level and the function-level. The dataset is labeled based on the information provided by the Common Vulnerabilities and Exposures (CVEs)[1] and the National Vulnerability Database (NVD)[2], which are publicly available vulnerability data repositories. With this dataset and the proposed framework, a DL-based baseline system for vulnerability detection can be conveniently established for performance comparison and evaluation. We have published the proposed framework and dataset at Github[3]. In summary, the contributions of this paper are two-fold:

- We developed a modularized benchmarking framework encapsulating six mainstream neural network models and two different code embedding schemes, providing one-click execution for building and testing vulnerability detection models. To guarantee the extendability, the framework offers APIs for easy integration of more neural network models and to support more code embedding solutions.
- We constructed a real-world vulnerability ground truth dataset for performance evaluation of vulnerability detection solutions. We manually checked nine open-source projects across 1,089 popular releases and labelled/collected 1,471 vulnerable and 59,297 non-vulnerable source code functions. We also record 1,320 vulnerable and 4,460 non-vulnerable files.

The rest of this paper is organized as follows: Sect. 2 reviews the existing studies which applied DL techniques for vulnerability detection. Section 3 details the design and implementation of the proposed framework. We also introduce our proposed dataset and the known datasets in this field. In Sect. 4, we provide case studies to demonstrate how the proposed framework facilitates the building of the baseline systems using the different datasets. Section 5 concludes the paper.

---

[1] https://cve.mitre.org/.

[2] https://nvd.nist.gov/.

[3] https://github.com/DanielLin1986/Function-level-Vulnerability-Detection.

2   Related Work

The successes of neural techniques in many areas, particularly in the field of NLP, motivated researchers to apply neural networks for code analysis for the detection of software defects and vulnerabilities. Early researchers adopted fully connected networks (a.k.a the Deep Neural Networks (DNNs) or the MLP) for detecting vulnerabilities in PHP applications [29], Linux programs [10] and Android applications [9,23]. Nevertheless, the approaches proposed by these studies are task-/project-specific. Thus, no performance comparison was made among these studies.

Later studies generally built on the assumption that software code contains semantics and syntactic resembling the natural languages. Therefore, ideas and techniques from the NLP field have been applied for learning code semantics indicative of software vulnerabilities. The CNN (e.g., the text-CNN [13]), which can learn high-level representations from small context windows, has been applied for detecting vulnerabilities at assembly level [16] and at source code function-level [11,27]. Another line of studies applied variants of Recurrent Neural Network (RNN) (e.g., the bidirectional LSTM network) for learning vulnerable code patterns [17–21]. The authors assumed that the vulnerable code semantics could be revealed by analyzing a long-range code context which could be achieved by using the LSTM network.

Most recently, researchers proposed more expressive models by constructing complex network structures. Wu et al. [32] added convolutional layers on top of an LSTM network for identifying vulnerable Linux programs. Le et al. [15] built their model on a Maximal Divergence Sequential Auto-Encoder (MDSAE) for extracting representations from sequences of machine instructions. Choi et al. [6] and Sestili et al. [28] applied the memory network [30,31] for detecting buffer overflow vulnerabilities. However, due to each study using self-constructed/-collected dataset, there was no systematic performance comparison conducted across different approaches to indicate their effectiveness.

3   Benchmarking Framework

In this section, we introduce the design of the proposed benchmarking framework and our proposed dataset which can be utilized for establishing a baseline system for vulnerability detection. We also suggest a new metric for evaluating the performance vulnerability detectors.

3.1   Architecture and Implementation

Fig. 1 illustrates the modularized implementation of the proposed framework. It consists of three modules: the code encoding/embedding module, the training module and test module. It is a common practice to convert text/code tokens to vector representations so that they are acceptable by the underlying Machine Learning (ML) algorithms. More importantly, we aim at preserving the text/code

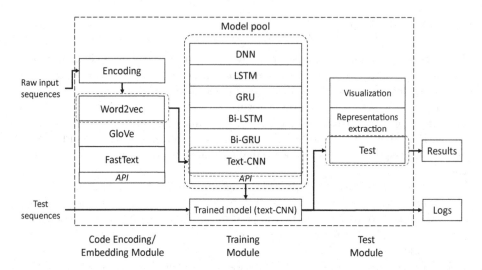

Fig. 1. The proposed benchmarking framework consists of three modules: the code encoding/embedding module, the training module and the test module. In the training phase, it allows users to choose different embedding schemes and different neural network models for building vulnerability detectors. In the test phase, it enables users to test the trained network model or to obtain representations from an arbitrary layer of a trained network. The framework provides APIs for easy integration of word/code embedding schemes and neural network models.

semantics while converting the text/code tokens to meaningful vector representations which we call the embeddings. The encoding/embedding module is built to serve this purpose. The module wraps mainstream word embedding schemes to enable the textual inputs i.e., the raw input code sequences to be converted to meaningful embeddings when we plot these embedding in a vector space, the semantically similar code tokens will be in close proximity in that vector space. This allows the neural network models to learn from a rich source. At this stage, the framework encapsulates three popular word embedding models: the Word2vec [22] model, the GloVe [24] model and FastText model [5].

In the training phase, the training module allows users to choose one of the built-in neural network models from the model pool for building a vulnerability detector. The framework provides six mainstream neural models: the DNN, the text-CNN and four RNN variants (i.e., the LSTM [12], the Gated Recurrent Unit (GRU) [14], and their bidirectional forms (the Bi-LSTM and the Bi-GRU)). During the test phase, users can feed the test data to a trained model and obtain detection results. The results are provided in a user-friendly format, including the confusion matrix and a CSV file recording the provability of each test sample containing the vulnerable code. Additionally, users can use trained neural networks as feature generators for generating neural representations from an arbitrary layer of a network. With this functionality, the generated representations can be used as features for downstream tasks (e.g., to train a random forest classifier). The test module also provides Keras APIs for visualizing training/validation processes and supports TensorBorad[4] logging system.

The framework provides one-click execution Python scripts, allowing users to invoke different modules of the framework to accomplish various tasks by specifying script arguments/parameters. For example, users can specify arguments such as *–train* or *–test* to switch the framework to training or test model. In addition, the script arguments allow users to select different built-in code embedding schemes and network models. A configuration file which contains plain text parameters is provided to offer more detailed options for model performance optimization. Users can either use the default settings for model training or customize the training process by fine-tuning the training settings and model hyperparameters.

We also provide easy-to-use APIs so that users can easily integrate new embedding schemes or implement their network models for training. The embedding API requires a Python dictionary object known as the *embedding index*. It is a table containing mappings between code tokens and the corresponding vector representations learned by the embedding method. The network model API accepts a Python class whose constructor takes one parameter which is the instance of the configuration file. Any models implemented using Keras or TensorFlow can be encapsulated in a Python class and invoked by the framework.

3.2   Dataset

The Proposed Dataset. The dataset we construct consists of nine popular open-source software projects written in C programming language, as listed in Table 1. It provides dual-granularity labelled samples, namely the vulnerable and non-vulnerable labels at function and file level. The vulnerable functions and files are labelled based on the description of the NVD and CVE web pages. In this paper, we focus on the vulnerabilities disclosed in the open-source projects because their source code is publicly available.

Typically, a vulnerability description on the NVD/CVE page specifies the exact location of the vulnerable code fragments in a particular version of a program. If the vulnerable code fragments are within a function boundary, we download the corresponding version of the source code of the program and label the source code function as vulnerable. Meanwhile, we label the file which contains the vulnerable function as vulnerable. A vulnerable file can contain at least one vulnerable function. For example, the vulnerable code fragments can span across multiple functions but they are within a file boundary, we only label the file as vulnerable. On the cases where the vulnerability description does not mention the location of vulnerable code fragments, we check the program's Github and search the commit messages using the CVE ID as the keyword. We read through the commit message(s) of the returned result and identify the commit(s) that contain(s) the fix of the CVE. By analyzing the *diff* files, we identify the code fragment(s) associated with the CVE fix and the *diff* files allow us to track

---

[4] https://www.tensorflow.org/guide/summaries_and_tensorboard.

Table 1. The number of vulnerable and non-vulnerable functions/files involved in the nine open-source projects in the proposed dataset.

Open-source projects	File-level		Function-level	
	# of non-vulnerable files collected	# of vulnerable files labeled	# of non-vulnerable functions collected	# of vulnerable functions labeled
Asterisk	862	84	17,755	94
FFmpeg	553	293	5,552	249
HTTPD	248	141	3,850	57
LibPNG	34	44	577	45
LibTIFF	94	151	731	123
OpenSSL	867	150	7,068	159
Pidgin	448	42	8,626	29
VLC Player	616	45	6,115	44
Xen	738	370	9,023	671
Total	**4,460**	**1,320**	**59,297**	**1,471**

the code prior to the fix. Then, we download the code before the fix and label them accordingly. By using this method, we can label some vulnerable files and functions which are not clearly described on the NVD and CVE pages. For the vulnerabilities which are not related to any functions or files (e.g., vulnerabilities caused due to the misconfiguration or incorrect settings). We simply discard these CVEs.

To collect the non-vulnerable files and functions, we download the latest release of the software projects at the time of writing. We assume that all the known vulnerability records in the CVE and NVD have been fixed in the latest release of a software project. To obtain the non-vulnerable files, we exclude the vulnerable files (despite these files have been fixed in the latest version) and use the remaining files as the non-vulnerable files. To obtain the non-vulnerable functions, we collect all the functions from the non-vulnerable files and label them as non-vulnerable.

The Synthetic Dataset. The synthetic vulnerability datasets provided by the Software Assurance Reference Dataset (SARD) project [1] contains artificially constructed test cases to simulate known vulnerable source code settings and patterns. The project consists of stand-alone test suits for C/C++ and Java, which are known as the Juliet Test Suites [4]. Each test site contains one main function so that the code can be compiled. In this paper, we collected all the C test cases from the SARD project and extracted 100,000+ functions from the test cases, forming a large synthetic function pool, as shown in Table 2.

The proposed dataset and the SARD project dataset form the base for benchmarking the proposed DL-based vulnerability detection framework. We aim to provide case studies of our framework and evaluate the performance behaviours of each neural network model on the proposed dataset containing real-world vulnerability samples and the SARD dataset having only synthetic samples.

Table 2. The number of vulnerable and non-vulnerable functions extracted from the SARD project.

Dataset	# of test cases	# of vulnerable C functions	# of non-vulnerable C functions
The SARD project	64,099	83,710	52,290

3.3 Performance Metrics

Precision, recall and F1-score are mainstream performance metrics for measuring the success of classification tasks. However, in the vulnerability detection scenario, one may face the severe data imbalance issue since there are significantly more non-vulnerable samples than the vulnerable ones in practice. For instance, the ratio of non-vulnerable functions to vulnerable ones is approximately 40 in our proposed dataset. Using metrics such as precision and recall would underestimate the detector's performance because the classifier tends to fit the data distribution of the majority class and by default, it uses the 0.5 as the decision boundary in the cases of binary classification. Therefore, in this paper, we apply the top-k percentage precision ($P@K\%$) and top-k percentage recall ($R@K\%$) as the metrics for evaluating the performance of vulnerability detectors. Similar metrics are usually adopted in the context of information retrial system such as search engines for measuring how many relevant documents are acquired in all the top-k retrieved documents [8]. We use these metrics in the vulnerability detection context to simulate a practical case where the number of functions to be retrieved for inspection accounted for a small proportion of total functions due to the constraints of time and resources.

In the vulnerability detection context, the top-k percentage refers to a list of retrieved functions accounted for $k\%$ of the total functions in the test set which are ordered by their probabilities of being vulnerable. The $P@K\%$ denotes the proportion of actual vulnerable functions identified by the detector in the top-$k\%$ retrieved function list. The $R@K\%$ refers to the proportion of actually found vulnerable functions which are in the top-$k\%$ returned function list. For measuring the vulnerable class, the $P@K\%$ and $R@K\%$ can be calculated using following equations:

$$P@K\% = \frac{TP@k\%}{TP@k\% + FP@k\%}, \quad R@K\% = \frac{TP@k\%}{TP@k\% + FN@k\%}, \tag{1}$$

where TP@$k\%$ is the true positive samples which are the actual vulnerable functions identified by the detector when retrieving $k\%$ most likely vulnerable functions. For example, there are 10,000 functions in a test set. After prediction, we examine 1% ($k = 1$) of the total functions which are the most likely to be vulnerable. That is, we retrieve top 100 functions ranked by their probability of being vulnerable and identify how many of these functions are actually vulnerable. Similarly, the FP@$k\%$ denotes the false vulnerable functions found by the

Table 3. The number of vulnerable and non-vulnerable functions partitioned on two datasets: the proposed dataset and the SARD dataset.

Dataset	Training set		Validation set		Test set	
	# of vul. functions	# of total functions	# of vul. functions	# of total functions	# of vul. functions	# of total functions
The proposed dataset	883	36,458	294	12,155	294	12,155
The SARD dataset	20,941	45,000	7,119	15,000	6,940	15,000

detector when returning $k\%$ most probable vulnerable functions. The FN@$k\%$ refers to the true vulnerable samples missed by the detector when returning $k\%$ functions.

4   Evaluation

This section evaluates the proposed benchmarking framework using the afore-mentioned real-world dataset and the SARD synthetic dataset for establishing baseline systems.

4.1   Experiment Settings and Environment

We set up two baseline systems using the proposed framework on two datasets. The first baseline system uses our constructed dataset, consisting of nine real-world open-source projects. It aims to investigate how the neural network models perform in a real-world scenario where severe data imbalance issue existed. The second baseline system uses the synthetic function samples from the SARD dataset. We extract functions from the test cases of the SARD project and randomly selected a subset of functions to form the dataset. The second baseline system aims to examine the behaviour of neural network models in an ideal scenario, so the dataset should not have data imbalance issue.

In this paper, we build the vulnerability detector at function-level and the Word2vec embedding scheme is chosen for embedding the code tokens. We use all the samples from our proposed dataset. For the SARD project, we randomly selected 35,000 vulnerable and 40,000 non-vulnerable C function samples from the test cases downloaded from the SARD data repository[5]. For both datasets, we partition the samples into the training, validation and test sets with the ratio of 6:2:2. The number of vulnerable and non-vulnerable samples in each set is listed in Table 3. For all the neural network models applied for case studies, we use the Stochastic Gradient Descent (SGD) optimizer with all default settings provided by Keras and the loss function to minimize is the binary cross-entropy.

---

[5] https://samate.nist.gov/SARD/testsuite.php#sardsuites.

The neural models were implemented using *Keras* (version 2.2.4) [7] with a *TensorFlow* backend (version 1.13.1) [2]. The Word2Vec embedding software was provided by the *gensim* package (version 3.4.0) [26] using all default settings. The computational system used was a server running CentOS Linux 7 with two Physical Intel(R) Xeon(R) E5-2690 v3 2.60GHz CPUs and 256GB RAM with NVIDIA GTX 1080Ti GPUs.

4.2 Case Studies – The Bi-LSTM Network

In this case, we build the vulnerability detector using Bi-LSTM network and perform training and test on two datasets – the proposed dataset and the SARD dataset. We partition them into three sets according to Table 2. The Bi-LSTM network we design has seven layers. The first layer is the Word2vec embedding layer which converts the input code sequences to meaningful embedding vectors. The second and the third layers are bidirectional LSTM layers each of which contains 64 LSTM cells. A bidirectional layer contains a forward and a backward LSTM network so that the combined output can obtain information from both the preceding and succeeding context simultaneously. This allows the Bi-LSTM network to facilitate the learning of vulnerable code patterns which are associated with multiple lines of code [18,21]. We concatenate the output of the LSTM networks of two directions and use a pooling layer for downsampling features. The last three layers of the network are dense layers, aiming to further converge the outputs to a single probability.

As the results are shown in Table 4, the Bi-LSTM network achieved better performance on the synthetic samples from the SARD dataset. When retrieving less than 50% of functions ranked by the probability of being vulnerable, the detector could identify all the vulnerable functions. When returning 50% of functions, all the vulnerable functions were found (represented by a 100% recall). In contrast, the Bi-LSTM network underperformed on the proposed dataset consisting of real-world function samples. When retrieving 1% of total functions which were considered being vulnerable, only 54% were actually vulnerable. However, when returning 20% of total functions, 87% of actual vulnerable functions could be identified and 99% of vulnerable function were found when retrieving only 50% of functions.

Table 4. The comparative results of the Bi-LSTM network on two datasets when retrieving different percentages of function samples ordered by their probabilities of being vulnerable.

Dataset	Precision and recall calculated when top $k\%$ functions were retrieved							
	1%		10%		20%		50%	
	Precision	Recall	Precision	Recall	Precision	Recall	Precision	Recall
The proposed dataset	54%	22%	18%	75%	10%	87%	5%	99%
The SARD dataset	100%	2%	100%	22%	100%	43%	93%	100%

4.3   Case Studies – The Text-CNN

Using the identical data partition setting mentioned in the previous case study, we build the vulnerability detector using the text-CNN implemented by Kim [13]. The only difference is that the convolution layer we use contains only 16 filters with four different sizes being 3, 4, 5 and 6, respectively. A filter can extract features from a small context window and various filters of different sizes are able to obtain different levels of features from the code sequences. This is different from the Bi-LSTM network which learns the long-range contextual dependencies from the code through the LSTM cells in the bidirectional structure. The filters of the text-CNN focus on extracting local features from small code contexts. Subsequently, the extracted features are passed to the pooling layers. After the pooling layers, the three dense layers are converted the features to a single probability.

Table 5. The comparative results of the text-CNN on two datasets when retrieving different percentages of function samples ordered by their probabilities of being vulnerable.

Dataset	Precision and recall calculated when top $k\%$ functions were retrieved							
	1%		10%		20%		50%	
	Precision	Recall	Precision	Recall	Precision	Recall	Precision	Recall
The proposed dataset	70%	29%	20%	81%	11%	90%	5%	97%
The SARD dataset	100%	2%	100%	22%	100%	43%	91%	98%

Table 5 shows the results of using text-CNN as the vulnerability detector. Similar to the results achieved by the Bi-LSTM network, the text-CNN performed well on the SARD dataset. The only difference between the Bi-LSTM network and the text-CNN on the SARD dataset is that when retrieving 50% of potentially vulnerable functions, the text-CNN could correctly identify 98% of actual vulnerable functions in the test set. Compared to the result achieved by the Bi-LSTM network (being 100%), the text-CNN underperformed. However, on our proposed dataset containing real-world samples, the text-CNN outperformed the Bi-LSTM network when returning less than 20% of the vulnerable functions. In particular, when retrieving 1% of vulnerable functions, the text-CNN could find 29% of total vulnerable functions. In contrast, the Bi-LSTM could identify only 22% of total vulnerable ones.

4.4   Case Studies – The DNN

Keeping the data partition setting unchanged, we build the vulnerability detector using the network containing fully connected layers i.e., the DNN. In contrast to the Bi-LSTM network and the text-CNN, the DNN is a generic structure not specifically designed for processing sequential data nor for spatial data. It is also "input structure-agnostic". Namely, the network can take data of different formats as inputs [25]. A DNN consists of multiple dense layers which map the inputs to space where data of different classes are more separable. In a sense, dense layers can be used to learn a non-linear function (with the non-linearity introduced by the activation functions) which better fits the complex and latent patterns of the data.

The DNN we use contains 6 layers. Identical to the Bi-LSTM network and the text-CNN, the first layer is the embedding layer for converting the code sequences to meaningful embeddings. The second layer flattens the outputs of the embedding layer so that the outputs can be 2-D tensors acceptable by the subsequent dense layers. The first dense layer contains 128 neurons. The number of the neurons in the second layer reduces to half and the same settings are applied for the third layer. The last layer has only one neuron which converges the outputs of the previous layer to a single probability.

Table 6. The comparative results of the DNN on two datasets when retrieving different percentages of function samples ordered by their probabilities of being vulnerable.

Dataset	Precision and recall calculated when top k% functions were retrieved							
	1%		10%		20%		50%	
	Precision	Recall	Precision	Recall	Precision	Recall	Precision	Recall
The proposed dataset	44%	18%	15%	62%	10%	80%	5%	96%
The SARD dataset	100%	2%	100%	22%	100%	43%	93%	100%

Table 6 lists the results of using DNN as the vulnerability detector on both the SARD and the proposed datasets. In contrast to the Bi-LSTM network and the text-CNN, the DNN underperformed on the proposed real-world dataset, achieved only 44% precision and 18% recall when retrieving 1% of the total functions which are most likely vulnerable. However, when retrieving 50% of the total functions, the performance of DNN was identical to that of the Bi-LSTM network and the text-CNN. On the SARD dataset, the DNN performed similarly compared with the other two networks.

4.5   Discussion

This section discusses the possible causes of the performance behaviours of the three network structures described in the aforementioned case studies. As shown in Tables 4, 5 and 6, when using the SARD dataset which consists of synthetic function samples, all the networks achieved similar and satisfactory performance. In contrast, the same networks underperformed on the proposed real-world dataset. The underlying reason is that the synthetic function samples are artificially constructed, following a template-like coding format. Therefore, the vulnerable and non-vulnerable code patterns can be easily learned and differentiated by the chosen neural networks. Whereas, the proposed dataset contains real-world function samples from open-source projects among which the code structure and logic vary significantly. Thus, the vulnerable code patterns are diverse and hidden in the complex code logic, which are difficult to be captured by the neural network models.

When using the proposed real-world dataset, different network structures exhibited varying performance behaviours, demonstrating that network structures of different types have different capacities in terms of learning vulnerable code patterns. Compared with the Bi-LSTM network and the text-CNN, the DNN underperformed on the proposed real-world dataset. This indicated that the DNN which contains only the fully connected dense layers was less effective for learning the characteristics of the potentially vulnerable code. Nonetheless, the Bi-LSTM network and the text-CNN which are specifically designed for processing sequential and spatial data (i.e., the code sequences in our context) facilitated the learning of vulnerable code patterns, resulting in more accurate vulnerability detection on the real-world samples. The Bi-LSTM network which has bidirectional LSTM layers and the text-CNN which equips with multiple filters, are capable of handling the contextual dependencies among the elements in a sequence. Noticeably, the text-CNN achieved the best performance on the proposed dataset when retrieving less than 20% of the total functions. This revealed that the high-level features which were extracted from small context windows by the filters of the text-CNN contributed to more effective learning of vulnerable code patterns.

5   Conclusion and Future Work

In conclusion, we propose a DL-based framework, providing easy-to-use Python scripts for building/testing vulnerability detectors. To evaluate the usability of the framework and the performance of the built-in neural networks, we apply two datasets for a comprehensive benchmark. The first dataset is the SARD dataset containing synthetic vulnerability samples and the second one is a real-world vulnerability dataset which we manually constructed by labelling more than 1,300 vulnerable files and functions. We performed three case studies using the DNN, the Bi-LSTM network and the text-CNN network. The experiments showed that their performance behaviours were identical on the SARD synthetic dataset, indicating that the network structures were not an important variable affecting the performance on the synthetic vulnerability samples. Nevertheless, the performance behaviours of the three networks on the proposed real-world dataset revealed that the network models which were context-aware i.e., the text-CNN and the Bi-LSTM networks facilitated the detection of the real-world vulnerable samples.

The proposed real-world vulnerability dataset is still in a preliminary stage, requiring further effort to improve. Our future work will focus on collecting vulnerable and non-vulnerable code at binary-level, since many software tools are closed-source. Additionally, the current dataset does not include the patched vulnerabilities as the non-vulnerable samples. Being able to differentiate the vulnerabilities from their patched versions can be a key performance metric for evaluating the effectiveness of the deep learning-based detectors. Thus, obtaining the patched vulnerable functions and files should also be our future work. Furthermore, we will continue to label more vulnerable samples and meanwhile, adding vulnerability type and severity information to the labeled vulnerabilities so that the dataset can be more useful to the research in this field.

References

1. Software assurance reference dataset project. https://samate.nist.gov/SRD/ (2019). Accessed: 20 Aug 2019
2. Abadi, M., et al.: Tensorflow: a system for large-scale machine learning. In: OSDI, vol. 16, pp. 265–283 (2016)
3. Allamanis, M., Barr, E.T., Devanbu, P., Sutton, C.: A survey of machine learning for big code and naturalness. ACM Comput. Surv. (CSUR) 51(4), 81 (2018)
4. Black, P.E., Black, P.E.: Juliet 1.3 Test Suite: Changes From 1.2. US Department of Commerce, National Institute of Standards and Technology (2018)
5. Bojanowski, P., Grave, E., Joulin, A., Mikolov, T.: Enriching word vectors with subword information. arXiv preprint arXiv:1607.04606 (2016)
6. Choi, M.J., Jeong, S., Oh, H., Choo, J.: End-to-end prediction of buffer overruns from raw source code via neural memory networks. arXiv preprint arXiv:1703.02458 (2017)
7. Chollet, F., et al.: Keras. https://github.com/fchollet/keras (2015)
8. Manning, C.D., Raghavan, P., Schütze, H.: Introduction to Information Retrieval. Cambridge University Press, Cambridge (2009)
9. Dong, F., Wang, J., Li, Q., Xu, G., Zhang, S.: Defect prediction in android binary executables using deep neural network. Wireless Pers. Commun. 102(3), 2261–2285 (2018)
10. Grieco, G., Grinblat, G.L., Uzal, L., Rawat, S., Feist, J., Mounier, L.: Toward large-scale vulnerability discovery using machine learning. In: Proceedings of the Sixth ACM Conference on Data and Application Security and Privacy, pp. 85–96. ACM (2016)
11. Harer, J.A., et al.: Automated software vulnerability detection with machine learning. arXiv preprint arXiv:1803.04497 (2018)
12. Hochreiter, S., Schmidhuber, J.: Long short-term memory. Neural Comput. 9(8), 1735–1780 (1997)
13. Kim, Y.: Convolutional neural networks for sentence classification. arXiv preprint arXiv:1408.5882 (2014)
14. Kostadinov, S.: Understanding GRU networks, December 2017. https://www.towardsdatascience.com. Accessed 30 Apr 2019
15. Le, T., et al.: Maximal divergence sequential autoencoder for binary software vulnerability detection. In: Proceedings of the 7th International Conference on Learning Representations (2018)
16. Lee, Y.J., Choi, S.H., Kim, C., Lim, S.H., Park, K.W.: Learning binary code with deep learning to detect software weakness. In: KSII The 9th International Conference on Internet (ICONI) 2017 Symposium (2017)
17. Li, Z., et al.: SySeVR: A framework for using deep learning to detect software vulnerabilities. arXiv preprint arXiv:1807.06756 (2018)
18. Li, Z., et al.: VulDeePecker: a deep learning-based system for vulnerability detection. In: Proceedings of NDSS (2018)

19. Lin, G., et al.: Software vulnerability discovery via learning multi-domain knowledge bases. IEEE Transactions on Dependable and Secure Computing (2019). https://doi.org/10.1109/TDSC.2019.2954088
20. Lin, G., Zhang, J., Luo, W., Pan, L., Xiang, Y.: POSTER: vulnerability discovery with function representation learning from unlabeled projects. In: Proceedings of the 2017 SIGSAC Conference on CCS, pp. 2539–2541. ACM (2017)
21. Lin, G., et al.: Cross-project transfer representation learning for vulnerable function discovery. IEEE Trans. Ind. Inform. **14**(7), 3289–3297 (2018)
22. Mikolov, T., Chen, K., Corrado, G., Dean, J.: Efficient estimation of word representations in vector space. arXiv preprint arXiv:1301.3781 (2013)
23. Peng, H., Mou, L., Li, G., Liu, Y., Zhang, L., Jin, Z.: Building program vector representations for deep learning. In: Zhang, S., Wirsing, M., Zhang, Z. (eds.) KSEM 2015. LNCS (LNAI), vol. 9403, pp. 547–553. Springer, Cham (2015). https://doi.org/10.1007/978-3-319-25159-2_49
24. Pennington, J., Socher, R., Manning, C.: GloVe: global vectors for word representation. In: Proceedings of the 2014 Conference on Empirical Methods in Natural Language Processing (EMNLP), pp. 1532–1543 (2014)
25. Ramsundar, B., Zadeh, R.B.: TensorFlow for Deep Learning: From Linear Regression to Reinforcement Learning. O'Reilly Media, Inc., Newton (2018)
26. Řehůřek, R., Sojka, P.: Software Framework for Topic Modelling with Large Corpora. In: Proceedings of the LREC 2010 Workshop on New Challenges for NLP Frameworks, ELRA, Valletta, Malta, pp. 45–50, May 2010. http://is.muni.cz/publication/884893/en
27. Russell, R., et al.: Automated vulnerability detection in source code using deep representation learning. In: 2018 17th IEEE International Conference on Machine Learning and Applications (ICMLA), pp. 757–762. IEEE (2018)
28. Sestili, C.D., Snavely, W.S., VanHoudnos, N.M.: Towards security defect prediction with AI. arXiv preprint arXiv:1808.09897 (2018)
29. Shar, L.K., Tan, H.B.K.: Predicting common web application vulnerabilities from input validation and sanitization code patterns. In: 2012 Proceedings of the 27th IEEE/ACM International Conference on Automated Software Engineering, pp. 310–313. IEEE (2012)
30. Sukhbaatar, S., Weston, J., Fergus, R., et al.: End-to-end memory networks. In: Advances in Neural Information Processing Systems, pp. 2440–2448 (2015)
31. Weston, J., Chopra, S., Bordes, A.: Memory networks. arXiv preprint arXiv:1410.3916 (2014)
32. Wu, F., Wang, J., Liu, J., Wang, W.: Vulnerability detection with deep learning. In: 2017 3rd IEEE International Conference on Computer and Communications (ICCC), pp. 1298–1302. IEEE (2017)

Automatic Demirci-Selçuk
Meet-in-the-Middle Attack on SKINNY
with Key-Bridging

Qiu Chen[1,2,3], Danping Shi[1,2,3(✉)], Siwei Sun[1,2,3], and Lei Hu[1,2,3]

[1] State Key Laboratory of Information Security, Institute of Information
Engineering, Chinese Academy of Sciences, Beijing, China
{chenqiu,shidanping,sunsiwei,hulei}@iie.ac.cn
[2] Data Assurance and Communication Security Research Center,
Chinese Academy of Sciences, Beijing, China
[3] School of Cyber Security, University of Chinese Academy of Sciences,
Beijing, China

Abstract. Demirci-Selçuk meet-in-the-middle ($\mathcal{DS}$-MITM) attack is an effective and generic method for analyzing iterative block ciphers. It reaches the best results on attacking AES in the single-key model. In ASIACRYPT 2018, a tool for finding $\mathcal{DS}$-MITM attack automatically based on general constraint programming was put forward, which can not only enumerate $\mathcal{DS}$-MITM distinguishers, but also partly automate the key-recovery process. However, the constraint programming models generated by this tool do not consider the key-bridging technique, which has been shown to be effective in reducing the complexities of many cryptanalytic attacks. In this work, we build a general constraint model for SKINNY-128–384 (the same target as the ASIACRYPT 2018 paper) integrated with the key-bridging technique. As a result, the time complexity of the key-recovery attack on SKINNY-128–384 is significantly reduced from $2^{382.46}$ to $2^{366.28}$.

Keywords: Demirci-Selçuk meet-in-the-middle attack · Constraint programming · MILP · Key-bridging · SKINNY

1 Introduction

The Demirci-Selçuk meet-in-the-middle ($\mathcal{DS}$-MITM) attack [8] was first introduced at FSE 2008 to attack the Advanced Encryption Standard (AES) [7]. The distinguisher employed in a $\mathcal{DS}$-MITM attack exploits the highly restricted range of a sequence of differences produced by the encryption of a set of carefully constructed plaintexts, and therefore is differential in nature. The $\mathcal{DS}$-MITM attack is progressively improved with a series of novel techniques (multiset tabulation, differential enumeration, and key-bridging, etc.), and eventually sets the record for cryptanalysis of AES in the single-key model [9–11,14,24]. Besides, the $\mathcal{DS}$-MITM attack has been applied to many block ciphers [4,12,13,22,23,27] and some generic structures [18,33].

© Springer Nature Switzerland AG 2020
J. Zhou et al. (Eds.): ICICS 2019, LNCS 11999, pp. 233–247, 2020.
https://doi.org/10.1007/978-3-030-41579-2_14

To facilitate the evaluation of the security of block ciphers against the $\mathcal{DS}$-MITM attack, automatic searching tools are developed by the community. In [9,10], Derbez and Fouque presented a tool implemented in C/C++, which identifies $\mathcal{DS}$-MITM attacks on a target with dedicated search algorithms. Another tool based on general constraint programming was proposed at ASIACRYPT 2018 by Shi et al. [27]. In this approach, the problem of finding good attacks is converted into general constraint programming (GCP) models (MILP, SAT/SMT, or classic CP), and the resolution (the task of finding desired attacks) is delegated to off-the-shelf optimizers, which keeps the cryptanalysts focusing on stating the problem at a higher level without bothering the details of how to solve it [5,15,16,26,28–30,32]. Despite this attractive feature, current constraint programming based tools suffer from several important drawbacks.

In [27], the attacks are built with two strategies. In the first strategy, valid $\mathcal{DS}$-MITM distinguishers of a target are enumerated in advance by listing all solutions of the underlying GCP model that only describes the distinguisher part. Then key-recovery attacks are built upon these distinguishers, from which we can pick the optimal one. In practice, we typically impose some heuristic conditions on the distinguishers since a complete listing is often infeasible. In the second strategy, the GCP model takes the key-recovery part into account and produces key-recovery attacks directly. However, current modeling methodology only deals with basic key-recovery techniques without considering the key-bridging technique, leaving a space for further improvement with manual analysis.

The so-called key-bridging technique was firstly employed in the context of $\mathcal{DS}$-MITM attack by Dunkelman et al. in ASIACRYPT 2010 [14]. In brief, the key-bridging technique exploits the relations of the subkey words created by the key schedule algorithm to reduce the amount of information to be guessed. This is a generic technique which can be applied in many key-recovery attacks based on statistical distinguishers [4,19,25,31].

Our contributions. In this work, according to the tweakey schedule of SKINNY-128–384, we integrate the key-bridging technique into the constraint programming based framework for automatic $\mathcal{DS}$-MITM cryptanalysis proposed at ASIACRYPT 2018 by introducing more types of variables into the constraint system to describe the relations of the subkey bytes. With this approach, we automatically and successfully find an $\mathcal{DS}$-MITM attack on SKINNY-128–384, where the number of key bytes to be guessed in the key-recovery is decreased from 47 to 45 and thus the overall time complexity of the attack is significantly reduced by a factor of $2^{16.18}$.

Interestingly, it turns out that the distinguisher used in this *improved* attack is *inferior* to the one used in [27] if we do not consider the key-recovery. This fact shows the importance of considering distinguishers and key-recovery attacks as a whole to avoid missing optimal attacks.

Organization. In Sect. 2, we give a brief description of our target SKINNY-128–384. The constraint programming based method for automatic $\mathcal{DS}$-MITM cryptanalysis is reviewed in Sect. 3. In Sect. 4 we extend the constraint programming based framework with the so-called key-bridging technique, apply it to SKINNY-128–384 and report on improved results. We conclude in Sect. 5 with some open questions.

2   The SKINNY Family of Block Ciphers

SKINNY [2] is a family of lightweight tweakable block ciphers designed based on the TWEAKEY framework [21], which have been employed in the construction of several authenticated encryption schemes and hash functions participating the NIST lightweight cryptography competition [1,3,17,20].

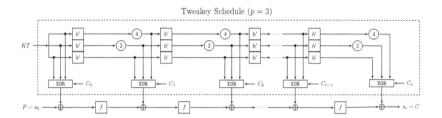

Fig. 1. The tweakey schedule and encryption process of SKINNY-128–384.

As in the ASIACRYPT 2018 work [27], our target is SKINNY-128–384 (the version of 128-bit block size and 384-bit tweakey). The high level structure of the tweakey schedule and how the sub-tweakeys(KT) step into the encryption process is depicted in Fig. 1.

To be more specific, the internal state of the encryption process of SKINNY-128–384 is arranged into a 4×4 matrix whose entries are 8-bit bytes. SKINNY-128–384 has three 128-bit tweakey registers named as TK1, TK2, and TK3, and its tweakey schedule are depicted in Fig. 2, where $s = 8$ and $P_T = [9, 15, 8, 13, 10, 14, 12, 11, 0, 1, 2, 3, 4, 5, 6, 7]$.

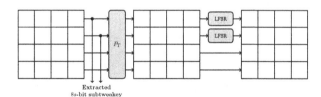

Fig. 2. The tweakey schedule of SKINNY-128–384, and there is no LFSR for TK1.

The round function of SKINNY is composed of SubCells (SC), AddConstants (AC), AddRoundTweakey (ART), ShiftRows (SR), and MixColumns (MC), which is illustrated in Fig. 3.

Finally, we refer the reader to [2] for a more detailed description of SKINNY-128–384.

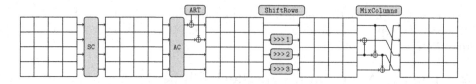

Fig. 3. The round function of SKINNY.

3   Constraint Programming Aided $\mathcal{DS}$-MITM Analysis

In this section, we give a general description of the $\mathcal{DS}$-MITM analysis, and recall how to model the attack with general constraint programming. We refer the reader to [27] for a more systematic exhibition of the topic.

3.1   The $\mathcal{DS}$-MITM Attack

In a $\mathcal{DS}$-MITM attack, a cipher E is decomposed into three consecutive keyed permutations as $E = E_2 \circ E_1 \circ E_0$. As in most key-recovery attacks based on statistical distinguishers, a $\mathcal{DS}$-MITM distinguisher is placed at E_1, the key bits involved in E_2 and E_0 are guessed to peel off the outer rounds (E_2 and E_0) surrounding E_1, such that the distinguishing property can be tested against the current key guess. Guesses that fulfill the distinguishing property are kept as candidate keys. Therefore, the key to understand the $\mathcal{DS}$-MITM attack is to understand the mechanism of its distinguishers.

Definition 1 ($\delta_{\mathcal{A}}$-set [6])**.** *A $\delta_{\mathcal{A}}$-set is a set of data in $\mathbb{F}_{2^8}^{16}$ traversing all possible values at the byte positions indicated by $\mathcal{A}$, while keeping the value at the remaining byte positions constant.*

Note that for the sake of simplicity, we confine our definition over $\mathbb{F}_{2^8}^{16}$, which is enough for our purpose. A $\mathcal{DS}$-MITM distinguisher is a chosen-plaintext distinguisher of a keyed permutation $E_1(\cdot)$. Given a $\delta_{\mathcal{A}}$-set $\{U^0, U^1, \cdots, U^{N-1}\}$ with N plaintexts, we can obtain the corresponding ciphertexts $\{V^0, V^1, \cdots, V^{N-1}\}$. Let us extract the sequence of differences

$$\Delta_{E_1}^{\mathcal{A} \to \mathcal{B}} = [V^0[\mathcal{B}] \oplus V^1[\mathcal{B}], V^0[\mathcal{B}] \oplus V^2[\mathcal{B}], \cdots, V^0[\mathcal{B}] \oplus V^{N-1}[\mathcal{B}]],$$

where $\mathcal{B}$ indicates which bytes are taken out from $V^j = E_1(U^j)$. If the value of the sequence $\Delta_{E_1}^{\mathcal{A} \to \mathcal{B}}$ can be determined by d c-bit words, then there are at most 2^{cd} possible values for the sequence. While for a random permutation F, $\Delta_F^{\mathcal{A} \to \mathcal{B}}$ have $2^{c|\mathcal{B}|(2^{c|\mathcal{A}|}-1)}$ possible values. If $2^{cd} < 2^{c|\mathcal{B}|(2^{c|\mathcal{A}|}-1)}$, the keyed permutation E_1 can be distinguished from the random permutation F. Therefore, a $\mathcal{DS}$-MITM distinguisher of E_1 can be regarded as a triple $(\mathcal{A}, \mathcal{B}, \mathsf{Deg}_{E_1}(\mathcal{A}, \mathcal{B}))$, where $d = \mathsf{Deg}_{E_1}(\mathcal{A}, \mathcal{B})$ is called the $(\mathcal{A}, \mathcal{B})$-degree of E_1.

Given a distinguisher $(\mathcal{A}, \mathcal{B}, \mathrm{Deg}_{E_1}(\mathcal{A}, \mathcal{B}))$, we can perform a key-recovery attack on $E = E_2 \circ E_1 \circ E_0$ as follows. First, we precompute all the 2^{cd} possible values of the differential sequence $\Delta_{E_1}^{\mathcal{A} \to \mathcal{B}}$ and store them in a look-up table $\mathbb{T}$. Then we prepare a set of plaintexts with the potential to create a $\delta_{\mathcal{A}}$-set with the encryption of E_0.

At this point, we can guess the key information k_{E_0} involved in E_0 to produce the hypothetic $\delta_{\mathcal{A}}$-set, and collect the corresponding plaintexts and ciphertexts. Next, we guess the necessary key information k_{E_2} involved in E_2 to decrypt the collected ciphertexts and compute the hypothetic differential sequence $\Delta_{E_1^{-1}}^{\mathcal{A} \to \mathcal{B}}$. If the computed value of the sequence is in the look-up table $\mathbb{T}$, we keep the guess of k_{E_0} and k_{E_2} as a candidate, otherwise, the guess is discarded.

3.2 Programming the $\mathcal{DS}$-MITM Attack with Constraints

As described in [27], to model the $\mathcal{DS}$-MITM attack with constraint programming, we independently introduce three types of 0–1 variables for each word (in this work it is always a byte) of the states involved in E_1. The sets of variables of type-X, type-Y, and type-Z are denoted by $\mathrm{Vars}(X)$, $\mathrm{Vars}(Y)$, and $\mathrm{Vars}(Z)$, respectively. Similarly, we introduce two sets of variable of type-M and type-W for E_0 and E_2. Now, we are ready to impose the constraints:

- Impose a set of constraints over $\mathrm{Vars}(X)$ to describe the so-called *forward differential*.
- Impose a set of constraints over $\mathrm{Vars}(Y)$ to describe the so-called *backward determination relationship*.
- Impose a set of constraints over $\mathrm{Vars}(Z)$ linking $\mathrm{Vars}(X)$ and $\mathrm{Vars}(Y)$ such that a type-Z variable is equal to 1 if and only if the corresponding type-X and type-Y variables are 1 simultaneously.
- Impose a set of constraints over $\mathrm{Vars}(M)$ to describe the so-called *backward differential*.
- Impose a set of constraints over $\mathrm{Vars}(W)$ to describe the so-called *forward determination relationship*.

The solutions of $\mathrm{Vars}(X)$, $\mathrm{Vars}(Y)$, and $\mathrm{Vars}(Z)$ determine the shape of the $\mathcal{DS}$-MITM distinguisher, while $\mathrm{Vars}(M)$ and $\mathrm{Vars}(W)$ indicate the key information involved in the outer rounds.

Note that the model can be built with MILP, SAT/SMT, or classic CP according to the situation. In [27], Shi et al. applied the CP-based automatic tool with MILP to analyze SKINNY-128–384, and a 10.5-round distinguisher was identified, based on which a key-recovery attack on 22-round SKINNY-128–384 is constructed. However, the models given in [27] are blind to the relationship between the key information involved in E_0 and E_2. Therefore, if one wants to take the key-bridging technique into account, he has to perform it manually according to the attack produced by the tool.

4   Constraint Programming for SKINNY-128–384 with Key-Bridging

In this section, we show how to extend the constraint programming based framework proposed at ASIACRYPT 2018 [27] for automatic $\mathcal{DS}$-MITM cryptanalysis by integrating the key-bridging technique into it.

The method for modeling the distinguisher part and outer rounds follows the procedure described in Sect. 3. Hence we omit the details and refer the reader to [27] for more information. Here we only review the meaning of the solution of the CP model constructed for SKINNY-128–384 in [27].

The solution of the original CP model gives a $\mathcal{DS}$-MITM distinguisher and indicates which subkey bytes should be guessed when a key-recovery attack is performed based on the distinguisher.

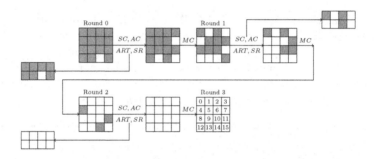

Fig. 4. The sample solution for E_0 with $\mathcal{A} = [13]$.

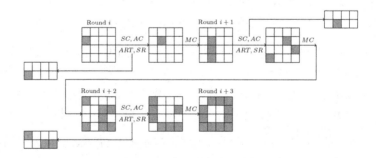

Fig. 5. The sample solution for E_2 with $\mathcal{B} = [4]$, where $i = r_0 + r_1$.

For example, Figs. 4 and 5 give the sample solutions for E_0 and E_2 (only the segment relevant to guessed subkeys are extracted), which indicates that we should guess 10 subkey bytes involved in E_0, and 5 subkey bytes involved in E_2. In fact, the objective function of the original model is to minimize the number of subkey bytes. However, the actual number of guessed bytes can be different with key-bridging technique.

4.1 Modeling the Key-Bridging

In SKINNY-128–384, the $3 \times 128 = 384$-bit master key is loaded into three 128-bit tweakey registers TK1_0, TK2_0, and TK3_0, where each register can be conceptually regarded as a 4×4 matrix. The round function of the tweakey schedule transforms the registers TK1_i, TK2_i, and TK3_i into TK1_{i+1}, TK2_{i+1}, and TK3_{i+1}. In each round, the first two rows of $\text{SK}_i = \text{TK1}_i \oplus \text{TK2}_i \oplus \text{TK3}_i$ (8 bytes in total) are extracted as a subkey and are exclusive-ored into the state.

According to the tweakey schedule algorithm of SKINNY-128–384, with the knowledge of three bytes $\text{TK1}_0[j]$, $\text{TK2}_0[j]$ and $\text{TK3}_0[j]$ of the master key for some $j \in \{0, \cdots, 15\}$, one can derive $\text{SK}_i[l_{i,j}]$, where $l_{i,j} = P_T^{-i}[j]$, and P_T^{-i} means the operation that the inverse operation P_T^{-1} is applied for i times. We define $\Omega(j)$ to be the set of all subkey bytes that can be derived from the knowledge of $\text{TK1}_0[j]$, $\text{TK2}_0[j]$ and $\text{TK3}_0[j]$. Then we have

$$\Omega(j) = \{\text{SK}_0[l_{0,j}], \text{SK}_1[l_{1,j}], \text{SK}_2[l_{2,j}], \cdots : l_{i,j} = P_T^{-i}[j]\},$$

and $\Omega(0) \cup \Omega(1) \cup \cdots \cup \Omega(15)$ covers all $\text{SK}_i[j]$.

The objective function of the original constraint programming model [27] constructed for $E = E_2 \circ E_1 \circ E_0$ is set to minimize the number of guessed $\text{SK}_i[j]$. This configuration is heuristic in nature, and the real number of bytes have to be guessed can be much smaller when the key-bridging technique is considered.

Let the number of rounds of E_0, E_1, and E_2 be r_0, r_1, and r_2 respectively, and let $\mathcal{G}^{\text{SK}}$ be the set of all $\text{SK}_i[j]$'s that should be guessed according to the solution of the CP model. Then we have

$$(\Omega(0) \cap \mathcal{G}^{\text{SK}}) \cup \cdots \cup (\Omega(15) \cap \mathcal{G}^{\text{SK}}) = \mathcal{G}^{\text{SK}}.$$

Let us see how to guess to fully derive $\Omega(j) \cap \mathcal{G}^{\text{SK}}$ for each $j \in \{0, \cdots, 15\}$. First, for a given j, with the knowledge of $\text{TK1}_0[j]$, $\text{TK2}_0[j]$ and $\text{TK3}_0[j]$, $\Omega(j)$ can be fully determined. Hence if $|\Omega(j) \cap \mathcal{G}^{\text{SK}}| \geq 3$, we can guess the three bytes $(\text{TK1}_0[j], \text{TK2}_0[j]$ and $\text{TK3}_0[j])$ of $\Omega(j)$ to determine $\Omega(j) \cap \mathcal{G}^{\text{SK}}$. If $|\Omega(j) \cap \mathcal{G}^{\text{SK}}| \leq 2$, we can guess the $|\Omega(j) \cap \mathcal{G}^{\text{SK}}|$ bytes of $\Omega(j) \cap \mathcal{G}^{\text{SK}}$. If we set

$$\rho_j = \begin{cases} |\Omega(j) \cap \mathcal{G}^{\text{SK}}|, & 0 \leq |\Omega(j) \cap \mathcal{G}^{\text{SK}}| \leq 2 \\ 3, & 2 < |\Omega(j) \cap \mathcal{G}^{\text{SK}}| \leq r_0 + r_2 \end{cases}, \tag{1}$$

the number of bytes to be guessed is $\sum_{j=0}^{15} \rho_j$. Therefore, taking key-bridging into account, we should minimize $\sum_{j=0}^{15} \rho_j$ in the model instead of minimizing the number of bytes in $\mathcal{G}^{\text{SK}}$ as was done in [27].

Next, we show how to model ρ_j. According to Eq. (1), the range of ρ_j is $\{0, 1, 2, 3\}$. For each j, we introduce three 0–1 variables α_j, β_j, and γ_j for ρ_j such that $\rho_j = \alpha_j + \beta_j + \gamma_j$, and

$$\begin{cases} \alpha_j = 0 & \text{if } |\Omega(j) \cap \mathcal{G}^{\text{SK}}| < 3, \\ \beta_j = 0 & \text{if } |\Omega(j) \cap \mathcal{G}^{\text{SK}}| < 2, \\ \gamma_j = 0 & \text{if } |\Omega(j) \cap \mathcal{G}^{\text{SK}}| < 1. \end{cases} \tag{2}$$

Let $\eta_j = |\Omega(j) \cap \mathcal{G}^{\text{SK}}|$, Eq. (2) can be described by the following linear inequalities

$$\begin{cases} \eta_j - 3\alpha_j \geq 0, \\ \eta_j - (r_0 + r_2 - 2)\alpha_j - 2 \leq 0, \\ \eta_j - 2\beta_j \geq 0, \\ \eta_j - (r_0 + r_2 - 1)\beta_j - 1 \leq 0, \\ \eta_j - \gamma_j \geq 0, \\ \eta_j - (r_0 + r_2)\gamma_j \leq 0. \end{cases} \tag{3}$$

Finally, we can set the objective function to minimize $\sum_{j-0}^{15} \rho_j$.

4.2 Improved $\mathcal{DS}$-MITM Attack on SKINNY-128–384

By solving the model built according to the previous section, we identify a new 22-round $\mathcal{DS}$-MITM attack on SKINNY-128–384 with a 10.5-round distinguisher

$$(\mathcal{A}, \mathcal{B}, \text{Deg}(\mathcal{A}, \mathcal{B})) = ([14], [13], 45)$$

which is visualized in Fig. 6. The time complexity of the precomputation is $2^{8 \times 45} \times 2^8 \times \frac{45}{16 \times 22} C_E \approx 2^{365.03} C_E$, and the memory complexity is $(2^8 - 1) \times 8 \times 2^{8 \times 45} \approx 2^{370.99}$ bits, where C_E is the time complexity of one 22-round encryption. The subkey bytes that should be guessed are shown in Fig. 8, which are derived automatically by the model according to the values of the type-M and type-W variables depicted in Fig. 7. Also, from Fig. 7, we can see that the data complexity of the attack is $2^{8 \times 12} = 2^{96}$ chosen plaintexts.

Note that in Fig. 8, there are 53 subkey bytes marked with orange, meaning that a naive strategy needs to guess 53 bytes. However, our model with key-bridging awareness automatically finds out that we only needs to guess 45 bytes to determine all these 53 bytes. Therefore, the time complexity of the one-line key-recovery phase can be estimated as $2^{8 \times 45} \times 2^8 \times \frac{107}{16 \times 22} C_E \approx 2^{366.28} C_E$, while the time complexity of the previously best attack is $2^{382.46} C_E$ [27].

The visualization of correlation among subkeys is depicted in Fig. 9.

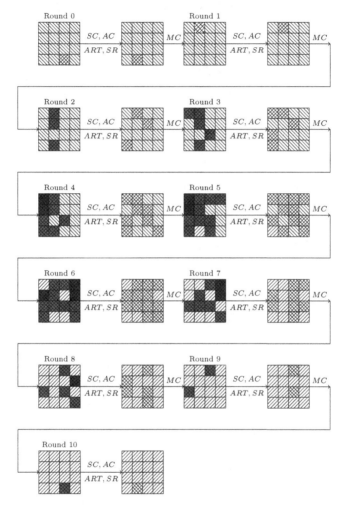

Fig. 6. The distinguisher $(\mathcal{A}, \mathcal{B}, \mathsf{Deg}(\mathcal{A}, \mathcal{B}))$ of SKINNY with $\mathcal{A} = [14]$, $\mathcal{B}=[13]$, and $\mathsf{Deg}(\mathcal{A}, \mathcal{B}) = 45$. The bytes marked with forward slashes and backward slashes show *forward differential* and *backward determination relationship* respectively. The bytes marked with red color are those need to be guessed, and the bytes marked with blue color are those should have been guessed but removed by cipher-specific constraints [27]. (Color figure online)

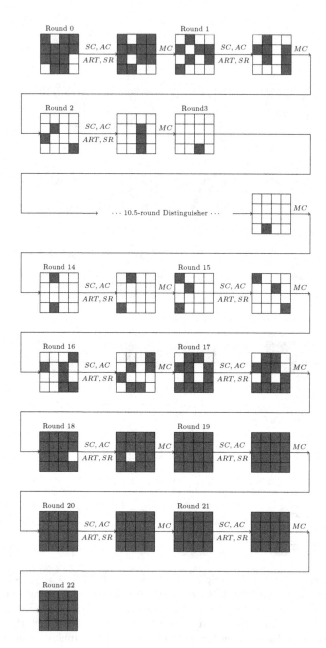

Fig. 7. Key-recovery attack of 22-round SKINNY based on the distingisher in Fig. 6, where the bytes marked with red color in the first 3 rounds indicate the *backward differential*, and the in the last 8.5 rounds the bytes marked with red color indicate the *forward determination relationship* in key-recovery. (Color figure online)

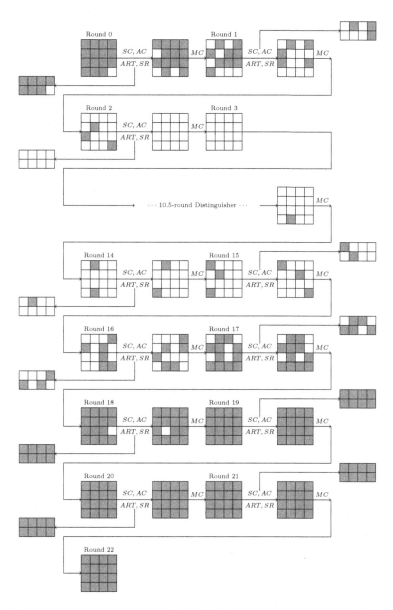

Fig. 8. The solution for our model of $\mathcal{DS}$-MITM key-recovery attack on SKINNY-128–384, where the subkey bytes should be known are marked with orange color. (Color figure online)

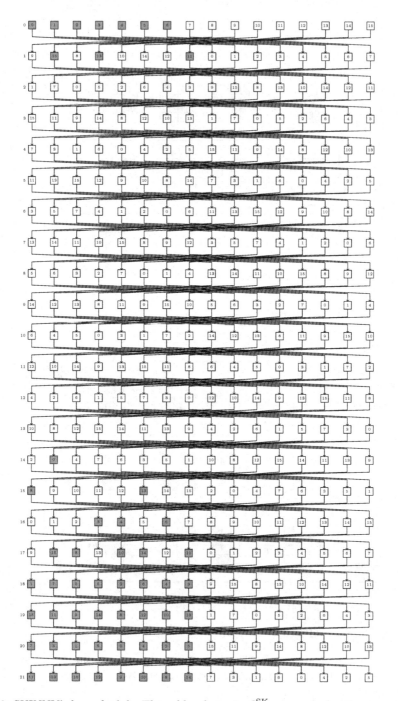

Fig. 9. SKINNY's key schedule. The subkey bytes in $\mathcal{G}^{\mathrm{SK}}$ are marked with green color, and the bytes derived from the same master key bytes share the same index. (Color figure online)

5   Conclusion

In the analysis of SKINNY-128–384, we extend the constraint programming based framework for automatic $\mathcal{DS}$-MITM cryptanalysis by taking the key bridging technique into account. As a result, we successfully identify an improved attack. At this point, we would like to propose some open questions. Since the tweakey schedule algorithm of SKINNY-128–384 is completely linear, the model for key bridging is relatively easy to establish. Is it possible to build a general constraint programming model for ciphers with non-linear key schedule?

Acknowledgments. The work is supported by the National Natural Science Foundation of China (61802400, 61772519, 61732021, 61802399), the National Key R&D Program of China (Grant No.2018YFA0704704), the Chinese Major Program of National Cryptography Development Foundation (Grant No. MMJJ20180102), and the Youth Innovation Promotion As-sociation of Chinese Academy of Sciences.

References

1. Andreeva, E., Lallemand, V., Purnal, A., Reyhanitabar, R., Roy, A., Vizár, D.: ForkAE v. Submission to NIST Lightweight Cryptography Project (2019)
2. Beierle, C., et al.: The SKINNY family of block ciphers and its low-latency variant MANTIS. In: Robshaw, M., Katz, J. (eds.) CRYPTO 2016. LNCS, vol. 9815, pp. 123–153. Springer, Heidelberg (2016). https://doi.org/10.1007/978-3-662-53008-5_5
3. Bellizia, D., et al.: Spook: sponge-based leakage-resilient authenticated encryption with a masked tweakable block cipher. Submission to NIST Lightweight Cryptography Project (2019)
4. Biryukov, A., Derbez, P., Perrin, L.: Differential analysis and meet-in-the-middle attack against round-reduced TWINE. In: Leander, G. (ed.) FSE 2015. LNCS, vol. 9054, pp. 3–27. Springer, Heidelberg (2015). https://doi.org/10.1007/978-3-662-48116-5_1
5. Cui, T., Jia, K., Fu, K., Chen, S., Wang, M.: New automatic search tool for impossible differentials and zero-correlation linear approximations. IACR Cryptol. ePrint Archive **2016**, 689 (2016)
6. Daemen, J., Knudsen, L., Rijmen, V.: The block cipher square. In: Biham, E. (ed.) FSE 1997. LNCS, vol. 1267, pp. 149–165. Springer, Heidelberg (1997). https://doi.org/10.1007/BFb0052343
7. Daemen, J., Rijmen, V.: The Design of Rijndael. AES - The Advanced Encryption Standard. Springer, Information Security and Cryptography (2002). https://doi.org/10.1007/978-3-662-04722-4
8. Demirci, H., Selçuk, A.A.: A meet-in-the-middle attack on 8-round AES. In: Fast Software Encryption, 15th International Workshop, FSE 2008, Lausanne, Switzerland, 10–13 February 2008, Revised Selected Papers. pp. 116–126 (2008)
9. Derbez, P., Fouque, P.: Exhausting demirci-selçuk meet-in-the-middle attacks against reduced-round AES. In: Fast Software Encryption - 20th International Workshop, FSE 2013, Singapore, 11–13 March 2013. Revised Selected Papers. pp. 541–560 (2013)

10. Derbez, P., Fouque, P.-A.: Automatic search of meet-in-the-middle and impossible differential attacks. In: Robshaw, M., Katz, J. (eds.) CRYPTO 2016. LNCS, vol. 9815, pp. 157–184. Springer, Heidelberg (2016). https://doi.org/10.1007/978-3-662-53008-5_6

11. Derbez, P., Fouque, P., Jean, J.: Improved key recovery attacks on reduced-round AES in the single-key setting. In: Advances in Cryptology - EUROCRYPT 2013, 32nd Annual International Conference on the Theory and Applications of Cryptographic Techniques, Athens, Greece, 26–30 May 2013. Proceedings, pp. 371–387 (2013)

12. Derbez, P., Perrin, L.: Meet-in-the-middle attacks and structural analysis of round-reduced PRINCE. In: Leander, G. (ed.) FSE 2015. LNCS, vol. 9054, pp. 190–216. Springer, Heidelberg (2015). https://doi.org/10.1007/978-3-662-48116-5_10

13. Dong, X., Li, L., Jia, K., Wang, X.: Improved attacks on reduced-round camellia-128/192/256. In: Nyberg, K. (ed.) CT-RSA 2015. LNCS, vol. 9048, pp. 59–83. Springer, Cham (2015). https://doi.org/10.1007/978-3-319-16715-2_4

14. Dunkelman, O., Keller, N., Shamir, A.: Improved single-key attacks on 8-round AES-192 and AES-256. In: Advances in Cryptology - ASIACRYPT 2010–16th International Conference on the Theory and Application of Cryptology and Information Security, Singapore, 5–9 December 2010. Proceedings. pp. 158–176 (2010)

15. Fu, K., Wang, M., Guo, Y., Sun, S., Hu, L.: Milp-based automatic search algorithms for diff erential and linear trails for speck. IACR Cryptol. ePrint Archive 2016, 407 (2016)

16. Gerault, D., Minier, M., Solnon, C.: Using constraint programming to solve a cryptanalytic problem. In: Proceedings of the Twenty-Sixth International Joint Conference on Artificial Intelligence, IJCAI 2017, Melbourne, Australia, 19–25 August 2017, pp. 4844–4848 (2017)

17. Guo, J., Iwata, T.: SIV-Rijndael 256 Authenticated Encryption and Hash Family. Submission to NIST Lightweight Cryptography Project (2019)

18. Guo, J., Jean, J., Nikolić, I., Sasaki, Y.: Meet-in-the-middle attacks on generic feistel constructions. In: Sarkar, P., Iwata, T. (eds.) ASIACRYPT 2014. LNCS, vol. 8873, pp. 458–477. Springer, Heidelberg (2014). https://doi.org/10.1007/978-3-662-45611-8_24

19. Hao, Y., Bai, D., Li, L.: A meet-in-the-middle attack on round-reduced mcrypton using the differential enumeration technique. In: Au, M.H., Carminati, B., Kuo, C.-C.J. (eds.) NSS 2014. LNCS, vol. 8792, pp. 166–183. Springer, Cham (2014). https://doi.org/10.1007/978-3-319-11698-3_13

20. Iwata, T., Khairallah, M., Minematsu, K., Peyrin, T.: Romulus v1. Submission to NIST Lightweight Cryptography Project (2019)

21. Jean, J., Nikolić, I., Peyrin, T.: Tweaks and keys for block ciphers: the TWEAKEY framework. In: Sarkar, P., Iwata, T. (eds.) ASIACRYPT 2014. LNCS, vol. 8874, pp. 274–288. Springer, Heidelberg (2014). https://doi.org/10.1007/978-3-662-45608-8_15

22. Li, L., Jia, K., Wang, X.: Improved single-key attacks on 9-round AES-192/256. In: Fast Software Encryption - 21st International Workshop, FSE 2014, London, UK, 3–5 March 2014. Revised Selected Papers. pp. 127–146 (2014)

23. Li, L., Jia, K., Wang, X., Dong, X.: Meet-in-the-middle technique for truncated differential and its applications to CLEFIA and camellia. In: Leander, G. (ed.) FSE 2015. LNCS, vol. 9054, pp. 48–70. Springer, Heidelberg (2015). https://doi.org/10.1007/978-3-662-48116-5_3

24. Li, R., Jin, C.: Meet-in-the-middle attacks on 10-round AES-256. Des. Codes Crypt. 80(3), 459–471 (2016)

25. Lin, L., Wu, W., Zheng, Y.: Automatic search for key-bridging technique: applications to LBlock and TWINE. In: Peyrin, T. (ed.) FSE 2016. LNCS, vol. 9783, pp. 247–267. Springer, Heidelberg (2016). https://doi.org/10.1007/978-3-662-52993-5_13

26. Sasaki, Y., Todo, Y.: New impossible differential search tool from design and cryptanalysis aspects. In: Coron, J.-S., Nielsen, J.B. (eds.) EUROCRYPT 2017. LNCS, vol. 10212, pp. 185–215. Springer, Cham (2017). https://doi.org/10.1007/978-3-319-56617-7_7

27. Shi, D., Sun, S., Derbez, P., Todo, Y., Sun, B., Hu, L.: Programming the Demirci-Selçuk meet-in-the-middle attack with constraints. In: Peyrin, T., Galbraith, S. (eds.) ASIACRYPT 2018. LNCS, vol. 11273, pp. 3–34. Springer, Cham (2018). https://doi.org/10.1007/978-3-030-03329-3_1

28. Shi, D., Sun, S., Sasaki, Y., Li, C., Hu, L.: Correlation of quadratic boolean functions: cryptanalysis of all versions of full MORUS. In: Advances in Cryptology - CRYPTO 2019–39th Annual International Cryptology Conference, Santa Barbara, CA, USA, August 18–22, 2019, Proceedings, Part II. pp. 180–209 (2019)

29. Sun, S., et al.: Analysis of aes, skinny, and others with constraint programming. IACR Trans. Symmetric Cryptol. **2017**(1), 281–306 (2017)

30. Sun, S., Hu, L., Wang, P., Qiao, K., Ma, X., Song, L.: Automatic security evaluation and (Related-key) differential characteristic search: application to SIMON, PRESENT, LBlock, DES(L) and other bit-oriented block ciphers. In: Sarkar, P., Iwata, T. (eds.) ASIACRYPT 2014. LNCS, vol. 8873, pp. 158–178. Springer, Heidelberg (2014). https://doi.org/10.1007/978-3-662-45611-8_9

31. Wang, Y., Wu, W.: Improved multidimensional zero-correlation linear cryptanalysis and applications to LBlock and TWINE. In: Susilo, W., Mu, Y. (eds.) ACISP 2014. LNCS, vol. 8544, pp. 1–16. Springer, Cham (2014). https://doi.org/10.1007/978-3-319-08344-5_1

32. Xiang, Z., Zhang, W., Bao, Z., Lin, D.: Applying MILP method to searching integral distinguishers based on division property for 6 lightweight block ciphers. In: Cheon, J.H., Takagi, T. (eds.) ASIACRYPT 2016. LNCS, vol. 10031, pp. 648–678. Springer, Heidelberg (2016). https://doi.org/10.1007/978-3-662-53887-6_24

33. Zhao, S., Duan, X., Deng, Y., Peng, Z., Zhu, J.: Improved meet-in-the-middle attacks on generic feistel constructions. IEEE Access **7**, 34416–34424 (2019)

System Security

SecFlush: A Hardware/Software Collaborative Design for Real-Time Detection and Defense Against Flush-Based Cache Attacks

Churan Tang[1,2], Zongbin Liu[1], Cunqing Ma[1(✉)], Jingquan Ge[1,2], and Chenyang Tu[1]

[1] State Key Laboratory of Information Security, Institute of Information Engineering, CAS, Beijing, China
{tangchuran,liuzongbin,macunqing,gejingquan,tuchenyang}@iie.ac.cn
[2] School of Cyber Security, University of Chinese Academy of Sciences, Beijing, China

Abstract. In recent years, cache attacks against micro architectures have posed a daunting threat to modern processors such as x86 and ARM. Of the attacks, flush-based cache attacks have attracted increasing attention from researchers due to their low noise, high resolution and high efficiency. However, existing defenses against flush-based cache attacks have some problems such as lack of platform versatility, high overhead, and low detection accuracy. In this study, we find that flush-based cache attacks have a fundamental feature of flushing a cache line multiple times at regular intervals. Based on this feature of flush-based cache attacks, we propose a hardware/software collaborative design of real-time safeguard on the ARM-FPGA embedded SoC, called SecFlush. SecFlush detects attacks using a hardware monitoring module, and defends against attacks by prohibiting malicious processes from performing flush operations in a kernel driver. It also provides a flush API for users to call the driver. The experimental results show that SecFlush can reduce the success rate of flush-based cache attacks to less than 1% within 6.01 ms. The evaluation results show that the time overhead is only about 5%–21%.

Keywords: Cache attack · Spectre attack · Hardware/Software collaboration · Real-Time detection and defense · ARM-FPGA embedded SoC

1 Introduction

As a variety of mobile terminals such as smart phones, wearable devices, and in-vehicle devices carry more and more private data in our lives, security and

Supported by the National Key R&D Program of China (No. 2016YFB0801002) and the National Natural Science Foundation of China (No. 61902398).

J. Zhou et al. (Eds.): ICICS 2019, LNCS 11999, pp. 251–268, 2020.
https://doi.org/10.1007/978-3-030-41579-2_15

privacy issues on these devices are becoming increasingly important. Since mobile terminal devices are mostly based on ARM cores, how to protect private data used on ARM has become an urgent problem. If no protection is provided, there will be serious security risks such as buffer overflow and side channel attacks.

Side channel attacks nowadays can collapse the strongest of crypto-algorithms and pose a great threat to network and system security. Cache side channel attacks are a specific type of implementation-level attacks that exploit the different access times within the memory hierarchy to retrieve sensitive data. They were first proposed by Kocher in 1996 [18]. As a micro-architecture attack, its departure point is the difference in access time between cache and memory. Attackers use the difference to collect the state of the cache and guess sensitive information.

In the past few years, cache attacks have made significant achievements on both x86 and ARM processors. They can be separated into three categories: time-driven attacks [2,8,10,22], trace-driven attacks [1,9,19,30] and access-driven attacks [13,16,20,23,27]. Access-driven attacks are the main stream attack methods, which include Evict+Time, Prime+Probe, Flush+Reload, Evit+Reload, and Flush+Flush attacks. Spectre [17] and Meltdown [21] attacks are new types of attacks that combine CPU micro-architecture vulnerabilities with cache attacks. Their targets are not limited to encryption keys, but all private data in the kernel, so they are more powerful than other cache attacks.

At the initial stage of cache attack studies, time-driven cache attacks were performed on encryption algorithms, but these attacks introduced great quantity of noise. Later on, more fine-grained access-driven attacks were proposed, in which the evict operation was the main technical means. However, this method is complicated and noisy because of the obscure eviction strategy. In 2011, Gullasch et al. introduced the flush instruction clflush into cache attacks on x86 processors and retrieved AES keys [20]. Flushing means writing the data in the cache back to memory, and quickly clearing contents of a cache line. Cache attacks such as Flush+Reload [27], Flush+Flush [13], Spectre [17] and Meltdown attacks [21] all need to perform the flush operation, so we refer to them as 'flush-based cache attacks'. Nowadays, due to their high efficiency and high resolution, flush-based cache attacks have gradually become the trend of cache attacks.

There are many state-of-the-art countermeasures against cache attacks. Because the nature of cache attacks is the uneven time of accessing data, the existing defense schemes are mainly built on three ideas: eliminating imbalance [14,15,24], isolating [12,25,29], and detecting malicious processes [3,11,28]. However, they have the following shortcomings.

- **Interference with normal processes or lack of versatility:** Eliminating imbalances is to eliminate the time differences between cache hits and cache misses by injecting noise and constant time instructions. However, noise injections have low efficiency because they interfere with normal processes. On the other hand, constant time instructions do not have hardware or software versatility.

- **Performance loss in time or space:** The idea of isolation is to isolate time or space among processes. If different processes cannot share cache, the attack process cannot affect the normal processes. However, not sharing can result in a lot of performance loss in time or space.
- **High false negatives and false positives:** Detecting malicious processes means identifying malicious behavior by collecting runtime data against an attack. However, such real-time monitoring is usually slow to detect malicious behavior, prone to false negatives and false positives, and often unable to defend against attacks trying to avoid detection.

In this paper, we analyze the general characteristics of the attack processes, especially of the flush operation, and find that flush-based cache attacks always flush a cache line multiple times at regular intervals. Based on this essential feature, we propose a real-time safeguard, SecFlush, that can detect malicious flush behaviors through a hardware design, and defend against the flush-based cache attacks by prohibiting malicious processes from executing flush operations in the kernel driver. Finally, we verify the effectiveness of our defense scheme by performing two flush-based cache attacks, Flush+Reload and Spectre.

Our hardware-based detection has the advantages of fast calculation, high efficiency and convenient timing. What's more, because we focus on the root cause of flush-based cache attacks, it is difficult for attackers to evade the hardware detection mechanism. More importantly, since the flush operation is one of the operations indispensable to flush-based cache attacks, flush-based attacks that cannot flush will fail. Therefore, it is also difficult for attackers to evade the software defense mechanism.

Contributions. Our contributions are summarized as follows:

- We analyze the general characteristics of flush-based cache attacks and propose a hardware/software co-design of real-time safeguard, SecFlush, that uses hardware to detect anomalies and software to defend against attacks.
- We perform Flush+Reload attack, Spectre attack and SecFlush safeguard on the ARM-FPGA embedded SoC platform.
- We verify the effectiveness of the SecFlush defense mechanism and evaluate the detection time and the performance overhead.

Outline. The rest of this paper is organized as follows. Section 2 introduces some basic concepts of the cache structure under ARM on Zynq-7000 SoC and flush-based cache attacks. Section 3 describes the flush features of flush-based cache attacks. Section 4 proposes our system design for hardware detection of anomalies and software defense against attacks. Section 5 conducts detailed experiments to verify the effectiveness of the SecFlush safeguard. In Sect. 6 we evaluate the detection time and the performance overhead. We discuss the implications and future work in Sect. 7. Finally, Sect. 8 concludes this paper.

2   Preliminaries

2.1   The Cache Architecture Under ARM on Zynq-7000 SoC

Cache is located between CPU and memory. Its main purpose is to alleviate the problem that the CPU's calculation speed is inconsistent with the memory access speed. In order to enhance system performance, modern CPUs employ cache to buffer frequently used data in small and fast internal memories. However, since cache is shared by all processes, it is the relevant point of memory data. Therefore, cache is one of the main targets of side channel attacks. As cache speeds up the access to data and instructions, an attacker can use timing measurements to infer the data processed by other applications.

In our study, we used Xilinx Zc706 Evaluation Board of Zynq-7000 SoC. The cache of this ARM Cortex-A9 MPCore processor is divided into L1 and L2 levels. The processor has two CPU cores, each CPU core has a 64KB L1 cache, including 32KB instruction cache and 32KB data cache. The instruction cache and the data cache can work simultaneously. L2 cache mixes instructions and data. It is shared between two CPU cores, and the capability is 512 KB [5,6].

2.2   Flush-Based Cache Attacks

Flush-based cache attacks are mainly divided into two types, general cache attacks and cache attacks combined with micro-architecture vulnerabilities. In the two kinds of flush-based cache attacks, the following two techniques are typical.

Flush+Reload Attack. The Flush+Reload attack was proposed by Yarom and Falkner in 2014 [27]. This is a high-precision and low-noise attack which exploits the availability of shared memory, especially the shared libraries between the attacker and the victim program. Flush+Reload works as follows.

1. Flush a specific cache line.
2. Call an encryption program.
3. Re-access the cache line and time it. If the time is short, then there is a cache hit, thus the victim program has accessed the cache line during execution.

Spectre Attack. The Spectre attack was proposed by Kocher in 2018 [17]. It combines cache attacks such as Flush+Reload with the vulnerability that the processor speculatively executes at the conditional branch, greatly increasing the ability of cache attacks. There are five main steps.

1. Flush a lot of cache lines to prepare an initial state of cache.
2. Flush the destination address of the branch instruction out of cache, so that the CPU performs branch prediction.
3. Incorrectly induce branch predictor multiple times using input that satisfies the conditional branch.

4. Using input that does not satisfy the conditional branch, the program makes a false prediction and extracts sensitive data into the cache.
5. Access cache lines and time. If the access time is short, then the cache line is hit, thus it is sensitive data.

3 Feature Detection of Flush-Based Cache Attacks

3.1 Feasibility of Feature Detection

In order to ensure cache consistency, that is, data in the memory is consistent with data in the cache, it is necessary to flush all cache lines rapidly, whether in DMA, multi-core heterogeneous processors or symmetric multi-processor architecture. These are scenarios of normal flush. On the other hand, due to branch predictor training or encryption, flush-based cache attacks will perform flush operations at certain time intervals. What's more, attackers usually flush cache lines multiple times to increase the success rate.

Flush-based cache attacks use flush to evict cache lines, thus flush is an indispensable step in flush-based cache attacks. If we can identify the features of the flush operation, we can detect all flush-based cache attacks in time.

3.2 Features of Flush+Reload and Spectre Attacks

In order to identify the characteristics of the attack process, we implemented Flush+Reload attack and Spectre attack on the ARM Cortex-A9 core. Then, we collected the time intervals of the flush operation in the two attacks, and plotted the relationship between the time intervals and the number of times in Fig. 1. We refer to these time intervals as loops. Table 1 shows the average values of different flush loops. The data is uniformly stipulated to the Global Timer frequency of 333 MHz which will be introduced in Sect. 4.

LoopFR is the time interval between flush operations in Flush+Reload attack. It refers to the process of flushing data in T-table out of cache, calling AES encryption, re-accessing the data and timing. LoopFR is a malicious loop. We collect 256 sets of LoopFR data and plot LoopFR in blue curve.

With regard to Spectre attack, we take Kocher's POC code as an example [17]. The following three cycles can be identified. LoopSP1 is the time interval between the previous time the attacker flushes cache lines and the next time he does so while he is preparing an initial state. Normal programs flush rapidly in the same way. LoopSP2 is the time interval between the time when the attacker flushes the destination address of the branch instruction out of the cache and the next time he does it. Put it another way, LoopSP2 refers to the whole process of the attacker performing the branch prediction training several times and executing attacks. LoopSP3, as we define it, refers to a complete Spectre attack, including 256 LoopSP1s, 30 LoopSP2s, access to cache lines and timing.

We collected 10240 sets of LoopSP1 data, 1200 sets of LoopSP2 data, 40 sets of LoopSP3 data and plotted the loops. In Fig. 1, LoopSP1 is displayed

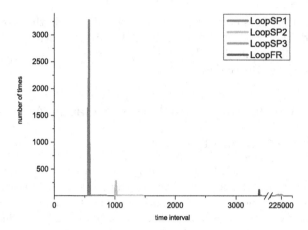

Fig. 1. Flush features of Flush+Reload attack and Spectre attack. The data is uniformly stipulated to the Global Timer frequency of 333 MHz. (Color figure online)

as red, which has the shortest time. It is a normal flush; Because of training branch predictor, LoopSP2, shown as green, takes a longer time than LoopSP1. LoopSP2 is a malicious flush; LoopSP3, shown as pink, has the longest time. We think LoopSP3 is the maximum time interval for flush-based cache attacks to perform flush operations, so a loop longer than LoopSP3 is safe.

Table 1. The average time interval for different flush loops. The data is uniformly stipulated to the Global Timer frequency of 333 MHz and in clock units.

Flush loop	Average time intervals
Spectre LoopSP1	570
Spectre LoopSP2	1,019
Flush+Reload LoopFR	3,385
Spectre LoopSP3	224,943

3.3 Detect Malicious Process

All flush-based cache attacks have the fundamental feature of flushing caches at regular intervals. Although the loops of different attacks such as LoopSP2 and LoopFR have different values, the values are all within a certain range. So we set two thresholds $T1$ and $T2$, so that all malicious loops fall within the thresholds. Therefore, the value of $T1$ should be between LoopSP1 and LoopSP2, and the value of $T2$ should be between LoopFR and LoopSP3.

In addition, we also set a threshold of *malicious_number* to determine malicious process. In order to prevent false positives, we decide that only processes with malicious flush times greater than *malicious_number* are considered to be malicious processes.

In order to obtain accurate statistics of the keys, the Flush+Reload attack requires multiple encrypting. In order to induce the branch predictor to make erroneous predictions, the Spectre attack requires multiple branch prediction training. We believe that the process which trains or encrypts more than 5 times is a malicious process. As to the final threshold selection, *malicious_number* is specified as 5.

4   Proposed Scheme

4.1   System Architecture

Figure 2 shows the overall system architecture, which is divided into three levels. User layer: user processes, three timer APIs, flush API, and Monitor. Operating system layer: three Timer Drivers and FlushDefender. Hardware layer: Global Timer, PMCCNTR Timer and caches are the modules that come with the system. New Timer and FlushDetector are the modules we implement using the FPGA and they are connected to system via the AXI-GP interface. The yellow modules of FlushDetector and FlushDefender represent the components of SecFlush.

Users can call Timer Drivers and FlushDefender through Timer APIs and Flush API. Timer Drivers are used to obtain precise current time, which can be obtained by calling Global Timer, PMCCNTR Timer or New Timer. FlushDetector is a hardware detection module that records the basic data of each flush operation, such as current time and the process's pid. It compares the recorded data with features of flush-based cache attacks to infer whether the process performs an attack. The basic function of FlushDefender is to quickly flush L1 and L2 cache lines. What's more, FlushDefender can detect abnormalities by calling FlushDetector. If FlushDefender gets an alarm from FlushDetector, it will record the current process as a malicious process, and defend against the flush-based cache attack by disabling the malicious process from performing flush operations. Additionally, it reports the malicious process's pid to Monitor via netlink. Monitor is a user-level application that receives messages from the kernel layer.

4.2   Detect Attacks

FlushDetector detects cache attacks through hardware based on the basic features of the flush-based cache attacks. Since the hardware can easily record time, no additional timers are needed. Algorithm 1 shows its working steps. *Flush_counter* is the frequency of malicious flushes of the current process. *Clock_counter* is increased by one in each clock, which shows the current time.

First, FlushDetector receives the pid of the current process from axi bus as *current_pid* and start working. Then, it clears an axi bus register called *alarm*,

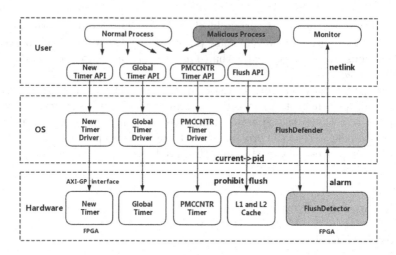

Fig. 2. Overall system architecture.

records the current time as *last_time*, and calculates the *time_interval* of the current process flushing. If the *time_interval* is between *T1* and *T2*, then there is a malicious flush, and *flush_counter* is incremented by one. If *flush_counter* is equal to *malicious_number*, **alarm** is pulled high. If *time_interval* is less than *T1*, *flush_counter* remains unchanged. If *time_interval* is greater than *T2*, there is no attack and *flush_counter* is cleared.

Algorithm 1. FlushDetector Hardware Module.

Input: *clk, rstn, s_axi_wdata*
Output: *alarm*

1 *clock_counter = clock_counter + 1* in each clock;
2 *current_pid = s_axi_wdata*;
3 *alarm= 0*;
4 *last_time = clock_counter*;
5 *time_interval = clock_counter - last_time*;
6 **if** *T1 <time_interval <T2* **then**
7 | *flush_counter = flush_counter + 1*;
8 | **if** *flush_counter == malicious_number* **then**
9 | | *alarm = 1*;
10 | **end**
11 **else if** *time_interval <T1* **then**
12 | *flush_counter = flush_counter*;
13 **else**
14 | *flush_counter = 0*;
15 **end**

4.3 Defend Against Attacks

Since there is no user layer flush command on ARM Cortex-A9 MPCore, we designed the FlushDefender kernel driver module. FlushDefender implements the basic functions of flushing L1 and L2 cache lines quickly. The ARM processor provides registers for cleaning cache hierarchy, CP15 coprocessor and PL310 cache controller [4,7]. In FlushDefender, we use CP15 coprocessor to flush L1 cache line, and the input address is a virtual address. We use PL310 cache controller to flush L2 cache line, and the input address is a physical address. Moreover, FlushDefender interacts with hardware and user layers to defend against flush-based cache attacks. The detailed working steps are shown in Algorithm 2.

First, FlushDefender gets *current_pid* from the kernel's pointer *current*. Then, it writes *current_pid* to a bus register via *iowrite32()* function, calling FlushDetector to detect attacks. The virtual address is then converted to a physical address. Next, if the current process is not a malicious process, FlushDetector cleans and invalidates L1 and L2 data cache lines. Then, we propose two defense methods. The first method is to read the value of the specific bus register *alarm* by *ioread32()* function, which is the detection result of FlushDetector. If the *alarm* register is pulled high, the current process is logged as a malicious process and the *malicious_pid* is sent to Monitor via *send_usrmsg()* function of netlink mechanism. We call this approach 'hardware alarm register defense'. Another method is to trigger an interrupt through *alarm* register, then record the malicious process and alarm the Monitor in an interrupt service routine. We call this method 'hardware interrupt defense'.

4.4 Precise Timing

Precision Timers can record the time of accessing data, accordingly determine a cache hit or miss. We implement three kernel drivers and their APIs for accurate timing operations, namely PMCCNTR Timer, Global Timer and New Timer. PMCCNTR Timer and Global Timer are the timers that come with the system, New Timer is a timer we implement using the FPGA. They are described in detail below.

PMCCNTR Timer. The full name of PMCCNTR is Performance Monitors Cycle Counter Register, which can be used to count the clocks of a processor [4]. PMCCNTR Timer clock frequency is 667M. Its counting process is shown in Algorithm 3.

Algorithm 2. FlushDefender Kernel Driver Module.

Input: virtual address of the cache line to be flushed
Output: *malicious_pid*

1 *current_pid = current−>pid*;
2 use the *iowrite32()* function to write *current_pid* to the axi bus register, **alarm**, calling FlushDetector;
3 convert the virtual address to a physical address;

4 **if** *current_pid != malicious_pid* **then**
5   /*flush the cache line begin*/;

6   run dsb instruction;
7   run isb instruction;
8   turn off IRQ and FIQ interrupts;

9   /*clean and invalidate the Level 1 data cache line*/;
10   select the Level 1 data cache;
11   clean and invalidate the Level 1 data cache by the cache line aligned virtual address;

12   /*clean and invalidate the Level 2 data cache line*/;
13   force write-through behavior and disable cache linefill;
14   clean the Level 2 cache line by the physical address;
15   invalidate the Level 2 cache line by the physical address;
16   run dsb instruction;
17   enable write-back behavior and cache linefill;
18   perform the Level 2 cache sync operation;
19   run dsb instruction;
20   run isb instruction;

21   turn on IRQ and FIQ;
22   run dsb instruction;
23   run isb instruction;
24   /*flush the cache line end*/

25 **end**

26 /*hardware alarm register defense*/;
27 use the *ioread32()* function to read **alarm** register to see if there is an attack;
28 **if** **alarm** *== 1* **then**
29   *malicious_pid = current_pid*;
30   send the *malicious_pid* from kernel to the Monitor using *send_usrmsg()* function;
31 **end**

32 /*hardware interrupt defense*/;
33 trigger an interrupt through the **alarm** register;
34 /*inside the interrupt service routine*/;
35 *malicious_pid = current_pid*;
36 send the *malicious_pid* from kernel to the Monitor using *send_usrmsg()* function;
37 /*inside the interrupt service routine*/;

Algorithm 3. PMCCNTR Timer.

Output: current time
1 enable all counters and export of events;
2 enable PMCCNTR and PMNx event counters;
3 clear the overflow bits of PMCCNTR and PMNx event counters;
4 read current time from CP15 coprocessor;
5 transfer time from the kernel to user space via *copy_to_user()* function;
6 disable all counters;
7 reset all counters;
8 disable export of events;

Global Timer. Global Timer is a global timer that comes with the ARM Cortex-A9 MPCore. It has a 64-bit register that records current high-precision time [4]. Global Timer clock frequency is 333M. Its counting process is shown in Algorithm 4.

New Timer. New Timer is the hardware peripheral timer we implement through FPGA, running at system frequency which can be set manually. It is incremented by one per clock. Similar to Global Timer, New Timer also has a 64-bit register to record current time. We set the clock frequency of New Timer to 50 M. Also, the counting process is shown in Algorithm 4.

Algorithm 4. Global Timer and New Timer.

Output: current time
1 ioremap the physical address to a virtual address;
2 time[0] = ioread32(virtual address);
3 time[1] = ioread32(virtual address + 4);
4 current time = (time[1] ≪ 32) | time[0];
5 transfer 8 bytes of time from kernel to user space via the *copy_to_user()* function;

---

5   Experiments and Results

5.1   Experiment Setup

Our experimental platform is ARM-FPGA Embedded SoC. Specifically, it is Xilinx Zc706 Evaluation Board of the Zynq-7000 SoC, which combines ARM Cortex-A9 MPCore (dual-core) with FPGA [26]. The device type is xc7z045ffg900-2. Embedded Linux kernel version is linux-xlnx-xilinx-v2015.4, cross compiler is arm-xilinx-linux-gnueabi, and gcc version is 4.6.1.

5.2 Flush+Reload Attack

We attacked OpenSSL T-table implementation of AES encryption primitive, which is vulnerable to cache attacks [23]. The principle of attack is as follows: In the first round of encryption, the process needs to look up T0[x0] in the T-table. Since the key is all zeros, x0 = k0 ⊕ p0 = 0 ⊕ p0 = p0, T0[p0] will be loaded into the cache when the encryption program is executed. Next, we record a 16*16 matrix, the horizontal axis is the first byte of the plaintext, p0. The vertical axis is the first address of the cache line to be flushed in the T-table, probe. P0 is increased from 0 to 240, and the step size is 16. Probe is increased from &T0[0] to &T0[240], and the step size is the size of a cache line, i.e. 64bits. The matrix records the number of cache line hits after encrypting the plaintext containing p0 1000 times. Therefore, if the attack is successful, the data on the (p0, &T0[p0]) matrix element is the largest, that is, the data on the main diagonal of the matrix is the largest.

Figure 3 shows the comparison experiments of Flush+Reload attack using PMCCNTR Timer, Global Timer, New Timer and the comparison experiments

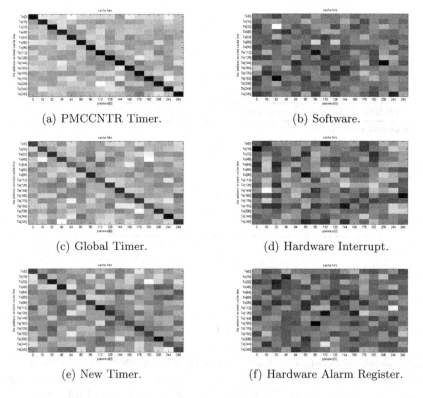

Fig. 3. Comparison experiments of the Flush+Reload attack and defenses. Subgraphs (a), (c), and (e) are matrix diagrams of the attack. The timers are PMCCNTR Timer (667 MHz), Global Timer (333 MHz) and New Timer (50 MHz). Subgraphs (b), (d), and (f) are matrix diagrams of defenses, and they are protected by software, hardware interrupt, and hardware alarm register methods. The timer is Global Timer (333 MHz).

of defenses using software, hardware interrupt, and hardware alarm register methods. There are six matrix diagrams with 16 * 16 small squares. The horizontal axis is p0, the vertical axis is probe, and the shade of the square color represents the number of cache hits. Therefore, if the attack is successful, the color of the square on the main diagonal is the darkest.

In order to verify the effectiveness of the SecFlush safeguard, we used PMC-CNTR Timer (667 MHz), Global Timer (333 MHz) and New Timer (50 MHz) to perform Flush+Reload attack. The results of Flush+Reload attack are shown in Fig. 3(a), (c), and (e). We can see from the results of the experiments that the color of the main diagonal in the three subgraphs is more and more diffcult to identify. Since in terms of frequency, PMCCNTR Timer>Global Timer>New Timer, we can conclude that the higher the frequency of a timer, the higher the accuracy of the time, the more obvious the effect of an attack will be.

In addition to the hardware interrupt and hardware alarm register methods, we also used a software method to implement the detection and defense mechanism of Algorithms 1 and 2 for comparison. Based on Global Timer (333 MHz), we defended against Flush+Reload attack using three methods: software, hardware interrupt, and hardware alarm register. The defense results are shown in Fig. 3(b), (d), and (f). It can be seen that the shade levels of the three matrix diagrams all become random, showing that the three methods can reduce the Flush+Reload attack to less than 0.1%.

5.3 Spectre Attack

We ported Spectre attack to the ARM-FPGA embedded SoC [17]. The attack was successful with all three timers. Figure 4(a) shows the 10 * 10 secret bytes obtained by Spectre attack. They are "a...a" to "j...j". The timer was Global Timer (333 MHz).

We verified the effectiveness of the SecFlush safeguard. Specifically, we determine the success rate of the attack based on the number of secret bytes extracted by CPU conditional branch prediction. The defense results are shown in Fig. 4(b), (c), (d). We can see that software and hardware alarm register defense methods can reduce the attack success rate to less than 0.1%. However, the hardware interrupt defense method cannot handle the malicious process so timely. Sometimes the first byte of the attack will succeed, with a success rate of less than 1%. We suspect that this is due to speculative execution. What's more, because the time difference between LoopSP1 and LoopSP2 is less than that between LoopSP1 and LoopFR, the attack features of Spectre are less obvious than that of Flush+Reload, so the Spectre attack is more difficult to detect timely.

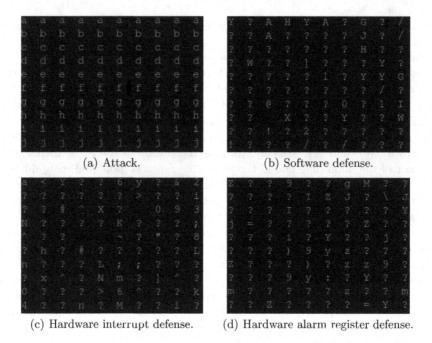

(a) Attack.   (b) Software defense.

(c) Hardware interrupt defense.   (d) Hardware alarm register defense.

Fig. 4. Comparison experiments of the Spectre attack and defenses. The timer is Global Timer (333 MHz). Subgraphs (a) is the result of the attack, attacking out 100 bytes. Subgraphs (b) is the result of using software defense, attacking out 0 byte. Subgraphs (c) is the result of using hardware interrupt defense, attacking out 1 byte, "a". Subgraphs (d) is the result of defense using the hardware alarm register, attacking out 0 byte.

6   Evaluation

6.1   Detection Time

Since cache attacks are high-speed attacks, if an attack cannot be detected in time, there may be false negatives. Therefore, the detection mechanism needs to meet the real-time requirements. Table 2 reports the detection time for Flush+Reload and Spectre attacks using three defense methods: software, hardware interrupt, and hardware alarm register. Detection time is defined as the period of time from when the cache attack is initiated to when the Monitor receives an alarm. We use Global Timer (333 MHz) for timing. As can be seen from Table 2, in terms of the time being detected, Spectre attack is larger than Flush+Reload attack. The experiments show that our detection scheme can detect attacks within 6.01 ms, and achieve the purpose of real-time detection.

Table 2. Detection time for Flush+Reload and Spectre attacks using software, hardware interrupt, and hardware alarm register defense methods. Global Timer (333 MHz) is used for timing. The numbers are in clock units.

Attack	Software	Interrupt	Alarm register
Flush+Reload	132,357 (0.40 ms)	91,534 (0.27 ms)	80,660 (0.24 ms)
Spectre	1,048,560 (3.15 ms)	2,001,042 (6.01 ms)	1,065,915 (3.20 ms)

6.2 Performance Overhead

We choose undefended flush time as a benchmark to evaluate the performance overhead. We use New Timer (50 MHz) for timing. Figure 5 is the time distribution of 1000 flush operations performed by undefended (red line), software (pink line), hardware interrupt (black line), and hardware alarm register (blue line) defense schemes respectively. As can be seen from Fig. 5, in the undefended scenario, the overhead of flushing L1 and L2 is just 2.236 µs. The hardware interrupt defense has the least time overhead, about 5% larger than the benchmark. The hardware alarm register defense and the software defense are 21% and 27% larger than the benchmark, respectively.

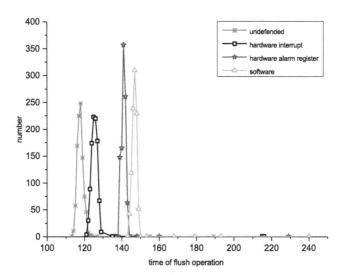

Fig. 5. Time distribution of undefended and software, hardware interrupt, hardware alarm register defense schemes for performing flush operations. The timer is New Timer of 50 MHz. (Color figure online)

7   Discussion and Future Work

7.1   Potential Smart Attacks

There may be some clever attacks trying to bypass SecFlush, such as slowing down the attack so that the time between two flushes is greater than *T2*. But if the attacker attempts to do this, he will not succeed in the attack. Because the data in the cache has the feature of temporal locality, what lies in the cache is data that has recently been used. Thus, slowing down attacks will cause data in the cache to undergo changes so large that the attacker cannot observe the cache state he expected for previously. This means that the attacker cannot get data he needs and the attack will have no chance of success.

7.2   Architectural Improvements

Modern processors have instructions or registers for flushing, such as the clflush instruction on the Intel x86 processor, the DC CIVAC instruction on the ARMv8-A processor, and the CP15 coprocessor, PL310 cache controller on the ARMv7-A processor, which makes processors vulnerable to flush-based cache attacks. Although our secure flushing is implemented by modifying the ARM MPCore hardware peripherals on the ARM-FPGA embedded SoC, we propose that our implementation of the flush API can be put into the processor's hardware architecture as a reference for designing more optimized **FLUSH** instructions.

8   Conclusion

This paper designs the hardware/software collaborative safeguard, SecFlush, on the ARM-FPGA embedded SoC. Flush-based cache attacks have a fundamental feature of periodic flushing at certain intervals. SecFlush takes advantage of this feature to detect attacks in hardware and defend against attacks by prohibiting malicious processes from performing flush operations in software. The experimental results show that SecFlush can accurately defend against flush-based cache attacks in a short period of time with low performance overhead.

References

1. Acıiçmez, O., Koç, Ç.K.: Trace-driven cache attacks on AES (Short Paper). In: Ning, P., Qing, S., Li, N. (eds.) ICICS 2006. LNCS, vol. 4307, pp. 112–121. Springer, Heidelberg (2006). https://doi.org/10.1007/11935308_9
2. Acıiçmez, O., Schindler, W., Koç, Ç.K.: Cache based remote timing attack on the AES. In: Abe, M. (ed.) CT-RSA 2007. LNCS, vol. 4377, pp. 271–286. Springer, Heidelberg (2006). https://doi.org/10.1007/11967668_18
3. Alam, M., Bhattacharya, S., Mukhopadhyay, D., Bhattacharya, S.: Performance counters to rescue: a machine learning based safeguard against micro-architectural side-channel-attacks. IACR Cryptology ePrint Archive **2017**, 564 (2017)

4. ARM: ARM architecture reference manual: Armv7-a and armv7-r edition. https://developer.arm.com/docs/ddi0406/c/arm-architecture-reference-manual-armv7-a-and-armv7-r-edition. Accessed 2014
5. ARM: ARM CPU cortex-a9: Widely deployed multicore processor. https://www.arm.com/products/silicon-ip-cpu/cortex-a/cortex-a9. Accessed 2012
6. ARM: Cortex-a9 technical reference manual. https://developer.arm.com/docs/ddi0388/latest. Accessed 2012
7. ARM: Pl310 cache controller technical reference manual. https://developer.arm.com/docs/ddi0246/a. Accessed 2007
8. Bernstein, D.J.: Cache-timing attacks on AES. http://cr.yp.to/papers.html#cachetiming (2005)
9. Bertoni, G., Zaccaria, V., Breveglieri, L., Monchiero, M., Palermo, G.: AES power attack based on induced cache miss and countermeasure. In: International Conference on Information Technology: Coding and Computing (ITCC 2005)-Volume II. vol. 1, pp. 586–591. IEEE (2005)
10. Bonneau, J., Mironov, I.: Cache-collision timing attacks against AES. In: Goubin, L., Matsui, M. (eds.) CHES 2006. LNCS, vol. 4249, pp. 201–215. Springer, Heidelberg (2006). https://doi.org/10.1007/11894063_16
11. Chiappetta, M., Savas, E., Yilmaz, C.: Real time detection of cache-based side-channel attacks using hardware performance counters. Appl. Soft Comput. **49**, 1162–1174 (2016)
12. Gruss, D., Maurice, C., Fogh, A., Lipp, M., Mangard, S.: Prefetch side-channel attacks: bypassing SMAP and kernel ASLR. In: Proceedings of the 2016 ACM SIGSAC Conference on Computer and Communications Security, pp. 368–379. ACM (2016)
13. Gruss, D., Maurice, C., Wagner, K., Mangard, S.: Flush+Flush: a fast and stealthy cache attack. In: Caballero, J., Zurutuza, U., Rodríguez, R.J. (eds.) DIMVA 2016. LNCS, vol. 9721, pp. 279–299. Springer, Cham (2016). https://doi.org/10.1007/978-3-319-40667-1_14
14. Gueron, S.: Intel's new AES instructions for enhanced performance and security. In: Dunkelman, O. (ed.) FSE 2009. LNCS, vol. 5665, pp. 51–66. Springer, Heidelberg (2009). https://doi.org/10.1007/978-3-642-03317-9_4
15. Gueron, S.: Intel® advanced encryption standard (AES) new instructions set. Intel Corporation (2010)
16. Gullasch, D., Bangerter, E., Krenn, S.: Cache games - bringing access-based cache attacks on AES to practice. In: 2011 IEEE Symposium on Security and Privacy, pp. 490–505. IEEE, May 2011. https://doi.org/10.1109/SP.2011.22
17. Kocher, P., et al.: Spectre attacks: exploiting speculative execution, 1–19. CoRR abs/1801.01203 (2019)
18. Kocher, P.C.: Timing attacks on implementations of diffie-hellman, RSA, DSS, and other systems. In: Koblitz, N. (ed.) CRYPTO 1996. LNCS, vol. 1109, pp. 104–113. Springer, Heidelberg (1996). https://doi.org/10.1007/3-540-68697-5_9
19. Lauradoux, C.: Collision attacks on processors with cache and countermeasures. WEWoRC **5**, 76–85 (2005)
20. Lipp, M., Gruss, D., Spreitzer, R., Maurice, C., Mangard, S.: Armageddon: cache attacks on mobile devices. In: 25th USENIX Security Symposium (USENIX Security 2016), pp. 549–564. USENIX Association, Austin (2016)
21. Lipp, M., et al.: Meltdown: reading kernel memory from user space. In: 27th USENIX Security Symposium (USENIX Security 2018), pp. 973–990. USENIX Association, Baltimore (2018)

22. Neve, M., Seifert, J.P., Wang, Z.: A refined look at Bernstein's AES side-channel analysis. In: Proceedings of the 2006 ACM Symposium on Information, Computer and Communications Security, pp. 369–369. ACM (2006)

23. Osvik, D.A., Shamir, A., Tromer, E.: Cache attacks and countermeasures: the case of AES. In: Pointcheval, D. (ed.) CT-RSA 2006. LNCS, vol. 3860, pp. 1–20. Springer, Heidelberg (2006). https://doi.org/10.1007/11605805_1

24. Page, D.: Defending against cache-based side-channel attacks. Inf. Secur. Tech. Rep. **8**(1), 30–44 (2003)

25. Waldspurger, C.A.: Memory resource management in VMW are ESX server. ACM SIGOPS Oper. Syst. Rev. **36**(SI), 181–194 (2002)

26. XILINX: Zynq-7000 all programmable SOC technical reference manual (v1.12.2). https://www.xilinx.com/support/documentation/user_guides/ug585-Zynq-7000-TRM.pdf. Accessed 2018

27. Yarom, Y., Falkner, K.: Flush+reload: a high resolution, low noise, l3 cache side-channel attack. In: 23rd USENIX Security Symposium (USENIX Security 2014), pp. 719–732. USENIX Association, San Diego (2014)

28. Zhang, T., Zhang, Y., Lee, R.B.: CloudRadar: a real-time side-channel attack detection system in clouds. In: Monrose, F., Dacier, M., Blanc, G., Garcia-Alfaro, J. (eds.) RAID 2016. LNCS, vol. 9854, pp. 118–140. Springer, Cham (2016). https://doi.org/10.1007/978-3-319-45719-2_6

29. Zhang, Y., Reiter, M.K.: Düppel: retrofitting commodity operating systems to mitigate cache side channels in the cloud. In: Proceedings of the 2013 ACM SIGSAC Conference on Computer & Communications Security, pp. 827–838. ACM (2013)

30. Zhao, X.J., Wang, T.: Improved cache trace attack on AES and CLEFIA by considering cache miss and s-box misalignment. IACR Cryptology ePrint Archive **2010**, 56 (2010)

CDAE: Towards Empowering Denoising in Side-Channel Analysis

Guang Yang[1,2], Huizhong Li[1,2], Jingdian Ming[1,2], and Yongbin Zhou[1,2(✉)]

[1] State Key Laboratory of Information Security, Institute of Information Engineering, Chinese Academy of Sciences, Beijing, China
{yangguang2,lihuizhong,mingjingdian,zhouyongbin}@iie.ac.cn
[2] School of Cyber Security, University of Chinese Academy of Sciences, Beijing, China

Abstract. Side-Channel Analysis (SCA) plays a crucial role in hardware security evaluation. However, side-channel acquisitions (a.k.a. traces) usually contain noises that often impose negative effects on key-recovery efficiency. In this paper, we propose convolutional denoising autoencoder (CDAE) for noise reduction in SCA. CDAE is composed of multiple layers of convolution operators, learning an end-to-end mapping from noisy traces to clean traces by minimizing the ℓ_2 loss of noisy-clean trace pairs. The convolutional layers capture the abstraction of the traces while eliminating noises. We argue that CDAE is very suitable for profiled SCA especially when the attacker has a large amount of traces in the offline profiling phase. Once the network training is done, our denoising network can be applied to individual new noisy traces for the attacker to launch online attacks. To validate the effectiveness of our method, we train CDAE to denoise traces and then perform Template Attacks (TA) in three high noise jamming scenarios, including unprotected (GPU and FPGA based) and protected (MCU based) AES implementations. Our method can significantly outperform the state-of-the-art Singular Spectrum Analysis (SSA) denoising method on both information theoretic metrics and security metrics. Results show that CDAE achieves at least $\sim 4\times$ Signal-to-Noise Ratio (SNR) gain, thus TA with denoising preprocessing requires at most 50% of the traces in the attack phase.

Keywords: Side-channel analysis · Convolutional denoising autoencoder · Preprocessing tool · Security evaluation · Deep learning

1 Introduction

For the past two decades, Side-Channel Analysis (SCA) has attracted much attention in the embedded security areas. SCA succeeds in the fact that physical leakages of a cryptographic device depend on the internally used secret key. By passively monitoring physical leakages, such as execution time [8], power consumption [7], and electromagnetic emission [1], the attacker can recover the

© Springer Nature Switzerland AG 2020
J. Zhou et al. (Eds.): ICICS 2019, LNCS 11999, pp. 269–286, 2020.
https://doi.org/10.1007/978-3-030-41579-2_16

secret information without tampering with the system. This property makes SCA become a serious practical threat to cryptographic embedded systems.

To perform a successful SCA against embedded cryptographic implementations, several steps are generally required.

- Good measurement. Measurements with too much noise usually result in a failure of SCA. For instance, the position and inclination angle of the electromagnetic probe is quite sensitive to acquire good-quality physical leakages (e.g. electromagnetic emission).
- Preprocessing. After the measurement step, traces are sent to preprocessing, including trace synchronization, denoising, and feature selection. All these efforts aim at facilitating SCA efficiency.
- Modeling. In this step, the attacker builds models to extract information from the leakages. Profiled (i.e. supervised) and non-profiled (i.e. unsupervised) attacks are often used according to the attacker's ability.
- Exploitation. After the modeling, the attacker can launch a key enumeration algorithm using the extracted leakage characteristics to find the right key.

Generally, for the last two steps, there are already a plethora of distinguishers in the toolbox, including profiled attacks and non-profiled attacks. There have been studies shown that modeling and exploitation of side-channel leakages are close to optimal [5], but the evaluation of measurement setups and preprocessing methods have still great research potential. From this perspective, the preprocessing step is of great importance, especially when targeting modern embedded systems and System-on-Chip devices with parallel computing and high clock frequencies. Indeed, noise is a fundamental ingredient for most countermeasures against SCA. First of all, electronic noise naturally exists in cryptographic devices, especially for hardware implementations (e.g. FPGA), which may drown out useful side-channel informations. Secondly, measurements are usually inevitably mixed with much environmental noise, which brings more difficulty to SCA. Finally, to protect the cryptographic device from SCA, manufacturers often protect their products with artificial algorithm noise, such as masking and hiding. As a result, various noises significantly reduce the Signal-to-Noise Ratio (SNR) of side-channel leakages and consequently, increase the attack complexity in terms of computational time and number of traces needed for a successful attack.

For the above reasons, a number of denoising methods have been proposed to reduce noises in side-channel traces after the acquisition. Le et al. [9] use fourth-order cumulant to reduce noise in SCA. In [3,17], wavelet-based denoising methods are proposed targeting noise components of high frequency. Other filtering-based methods are also investigated, such as Kalman filter [18] and Fourier Transform [13]. These sophisticated filtering-based methods generally benefit from acquisition devices with a high sampling rate. Moreover, their parameters sometimes are ad-hoc which needs prior knowledge of the device, thus decreasing the generality. The state-of-the-art denoising methods include Singular Spectrum Analysis (SSA) [4] and Independent Component Analysis (ICA) [11]. However, ICA takes at least N traces to recover one original trace made of N sources, which is impractical in profiled attacks because it significantly reduces the amount of traces for profiling. SSA can be applied to single measurement (compared with ICA) and is insensitive to sampling rate (compared with filtering-based methods), which makes it a robust tool for denoising preprocessing. However, SSA denoises each trace independently by decomposition and reconstruction of one trace at a time, thus lacking the overall noise distribution estimation of the whole trace set.

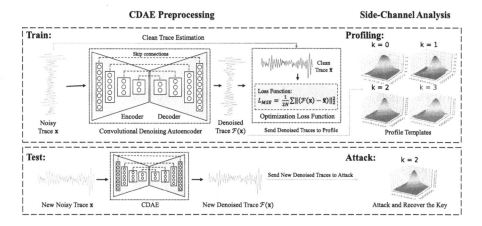

Fig. 1. The overall workflow of CDAE and its application in profiled SCA.

Thus, a question arises from the above situation: *how far can we reach for the task of denoising in SCA, especially when we obtain a large amount of traces in profiled attacks?* In this paper, we report for the first time that deep learning based denoising can significantly outperform the existing denoising methods in profiled SCA. Specifically, we achieve this by training the convolutional denoising autoencoder (CDAE) to learn a special non-linear mapping from noisy traces to clean traces in the profiling phase. Once the training is done, the denoising network can be applied as a black box, which takes a single noisy trace in and gets a single clean trace out. From the realistic evaluator's point of view, our method is a good frontend preprocessing tool that only aims at denoising, where the backend SCA distinguishers benefit key recover efficiency without any special changes to the algorithms. Noted that deep learning based profiled attacks predict key probability more or less in a black-box manner, while CDAE only denoises traces and leaves the attacker free to exploit leakages and recover the key. The overall workflow of CDAE and its deployment in SCA are described in Fig. 1. The contributions of this paper are summarized as follows:

- We propose a Convolutional Denoising Autoencoder (CDAE) based denoising method for preprocessing in profiled SCA. Unlike classic denoising approaches that are motivated by signal processing aspects, our method is a *data-driven* approach which is adaptive to the target implementation. The method is easy to deploy, where the network is built on standard encoder-decoder architectures with symmetric skip connections and trained by minimization of the ℓ_2 loss between noisy traces and clean traces.

- To estimate the clean traces, we design a noisy-clean training pair generation algorithm to provide the CDAE with noisy traces as input and estimated clean traces as output. The algorithm is suitable for unprotected and masking scenarios.
- We validate the effectiveness of our method under three high noise jamming scenarios. Experiments show that our method has at most 20 times SNR gain and 10 times TA efficiency gain with respect to the number of traces.

2 Backgrounds

Notations. In the rest of this paper, we use capital letters for random variables and small caps for their realizations. Vectors and matrices are denoted with bold notations, functions with sans serif fonts and sets with calligraphic ones.

2.1 Side-Channel Analysis

Side-Channel Analysis (SCA) aims at exploiting noisy observations of the cryptographic implementation to recover its secret key. Usually, the divide-and-conquer strategy is applied to separately recover different subkey bytes of the secret key. For instance, the attacker recovers an 8-bit subkey byte one at a time iteratively to recover the whole 128-bit secret key in AES-128 cryptographic implementations.

Profiled SCAs are the most powerful ones that assume the attacker can priorly use an open copy of the target device to offline learn the leakage distribution in a supervised way and to online attack the target device with the learned models. In profiling phase, the attacker has a device with knowledge about the secret key and acquires N traces $\mathcal{X}_{\text{profiling}} = \{\mathbf{x}_i\}_{i=1}^N$. Each trace $\mathbf{x}_i$ is corresponding to sensitive variable $v_i = \phi(p_i, k)$ in one encryption (or decryption) with known key $k \in \mathcal{K}$, plaintext (or ciphertext) p_i and priori leakage model ϕ (e.g. Hamming weight). In this work, we consider the traces measured from power consumption or electromagnetic radiation using probes with an oscilloscope. Once the acquisition is done, the attacker profiles suitable models and computes the estimation of probability:

$$\Pr[\mathbf{x}|V = v], \tag{1}$$

from a profiling set $\{\mathbf{x}_i, v_i\}_{i=1}^N$.

The most widely used profiled attack is Template Attacks (TA) [2]. The attacker estimates conditional probability Eq. (1) by assuming that $\mathbf{x}$ follows a multivariate Gaussian distribution and estimating the average trace $\bar{\mathbf{x}}$ and the covariance matrix Σ for each possible sensitive variable v. Equation (1) then turns into:

$$\Pr[\mathbf{x}|V = v] = \frac{\exp(-\frac{1}{2} \cdot (\mathbf{x} - \bar{\mathbf{x}})^\top \cdot \Sigma^{-1} \cdot (\mathbf{x} - \bar{\mathbf{x}}))}{\sqrt{(2\pi)^N \cdot |\Sigma|}}. \tag{2}$$

The pooled and reduced techniques can be sometimes useful by replacing covariance matrices by averaging covariance matrix and identity matrix. Notice that the attacker can launch a High Order Template Attack (HOTA) if the leakage exist in high order moments of sample points, such as defeating mask countermeasures.

In the attack phase, the attacker acquires a small new set of traces $\mathcal{X}_{\text{attack}} = \{\mathbf{x}_i\}_{i=1}^{Q}$ with a fixed unknown key k^*. With the help of the established models, the attacker can easily calculate the estimated posterior probabilities d_k among $|\mathcal{K}|$ guesses via the Bayes' Theorem, then select the key that maximizes it following the Maximum Likelihood strategy:

$$k^* = \arg\max_{k \in \mathcal{K}} \prod_{i=1}^{Q} \frac{\Pr[\mathbf{x} = \mathbf{x}_i | v_i = \phi(p_i, k)] \cdot \Pr[v_i = \phi(p_i, k)]}{\Pr[\mathbf{x} = \mathbf{x}_i]}. \tag{3}$$

Equation (3) stands only when acquisitions are independent which is a practical condition in reality.

2.2   Evaluation Metrics

In this work, we follow the methodology in [4] to evaluate the denoising effect. The evaluation of a cryptographic implementation usually lies in two aspects. From the information theory perspective, one should know how much leakage information is leaking from the device under test (DUT). From the security perspective, one should know how easy it is to exploit the leakage information by the attacker. In the context of this paper, we use the information theoretic metrics to evaluate the denoising effect, which is independent of the attacker. Afterward, real profiled attacks are launched to evaluate the efficiency gain with respect to the number of traces due to the denoising preprocessing. The two types of metrics are introduced briefly below.

Information Theoretic Metrics. Information theoretic metrics are used to accurately and quantitatively measure the amount of leakages from the DUT. The Signal-to-Noise Ratio (SNR) is a common choice for this purpose. SNR is the ratio of signal variance and noise variance. For a observation $\mathbf{x}$ at time t of an event v, it is defined as:

$$\text{SNR} = \frac{\hat{\text{Var}}[\hat{\text{E}}[\mathbf{x}[t]|v]]}{\hat{\text{E}}[\hat{\text{Var}}[\mathbf{x}[t]|v]]}, \tag{4}$$

where $\hat{\text{E}}$ and $\hat{\text{Var}}$ denote the sample mean and variance from the trace set, respectively. SNR quantifies the amount of leakage information of a single point in traces. The higher the SNR, the more information is leaked. Another general approach is Pearson's correlation coefficient (PCC) which measures the correlation between observation $\mathbf{x}$ and event v, it is defined as:

$$\text{PCC} = \frac{\hat{\text{Cov}}[\mathbf{x}[t], v]}{\sqrt{\hat{\text{Var}}[\mathbf{x}[t]] \cdot \hat{\text{Var}}[v]}}, \tag{5}$$

where $\hat{\mathrm{Cov}}$ denotes the sample covariance from the trace set. The improvement of PCC and SNR would improve the success rate of the attack.

Security Metrics. To further evaluate the denoising effect, it is necessary to put it in real side-channel attacks to see how much information gain can the attacker exploit after denoising preprocessing. The guessing entropy (GE) [19] is a commonly used security metric for SCA. Given Q amount of traces in the attacking phase, the attacker estimates the key guessing vector $\mathbf{k}_{guess} = [k_1, k_2, \ldots, k_{|\mathcal{K}|}]$ in the decreasing order, where $|\mathcal{K}|$ is the size of keyspace. The GE is the average rank of true key k^* in $\mathbf{k}_{guess}$.

3   The Proposed Preprocessing Method

3.1   Denoising Network Architecture

Researchers have applied deep neural networks to multiple denoising tasks, e.g. image denoising [12] and speech enhancement [10], in which encoder-decoder network is often used as a common choice. Among all the deep learning based denoising methods, we prefer deep feed-forwarded convolutional denoising autoencoder (CDAE) as the basic architecture of the denoising network. The network is composed of multiple layers of convolution and deconvolution operators, learning end-to-end mapping $\mathcal{F}$ from noisy traces to clean traces. The network architecture is detailed in Fig. 2. The *Conv encoder* (yellow blocks in Fig. 2) consists of convolutional layers acting as feature extractor, which captures the abstraction of traces while eliminating noises. The *Conv decoder* (green blocks in Fig. 2) consists of deconvolutional layers to recover clean trace details. Unless otherwise specified, the convolutional kernel size is 3 and the number of kernels is $\{16, 32, 64, 128, 128, 64, 32, 16, 1\}$. Symmetric skip connections are linked for convolutional and deconvolutional layers for faster converges and passing traces details from the convolutional layers to deconvolutional layers. Specifically, we use four convolutional layers and four deconvolutional layers. Each layer is activated by *LeakyReLU* function and then fed into *BatchNormalization* layer. *Max-Pooling* and *UpSampling* are used to extract trace details and control the feature map size.

For the training of denoising network, firstly we use Algorithm 1 and Algorithm 2 in Sect. 3.2 to generate noisy-clean training pairs and normalize the noisy traces and clean traces into $[-1, 1]$ range with min-max normalization. Then the training pairs are fed into the network with 90% for training and 10% for validation in case of over-fitting. During the training, the network weights are recorded for the best validation loss and an early stopping threshold of 10 epochs which monitors the validation loss and stops the training if the loss doesn't fall.

Once the training is done we reconstruct the network with the best-recorded weights. We feed the network with noisy trace sets $\mathcal{X}_{\text{profiling}}$ and $\mathcal{X}_{\text{attack}}$, then we can obtain the denoised trace sets $\mathcal{F}(\mathcal{X}_{\text{profiling}})$ and $\mathcal{F}(\mathcal{X}_{\text{attack}})$. Finally, we inverse the min-max normalization to rescale the traces to the original range. It should

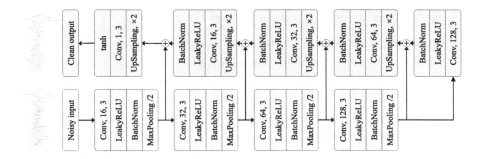

Fig. 2. The architecture of the proposed denoising network. (Color figure online)

be pointed out that the denoising process remains a black box to the backend attacker who launches a key recovery attack. This means that the attacker can select different tools (e.g. TA) to launch a profiled SCA with denoised trace sets $\mathcal{F}(\mathcal{X}_{\text{profiling}})$ and $\mathcal{F}(\mathcal{X}_{\text{attack}})$.

3.2   Clean Trace Estimation

To train a denoising autoencoder, one should feed the network with noise corrupted data as input and the ground truth as output so the network can learn the denoising mapping by optimizing the loss of noisy-clean training pairs. However, unlike the denoising task in image processing and other applications, the ground truth (i.e. clean trace) in SCA is never been promised as priori. The truth is, due to the physical limitation of measurement, the attacker only gets plenty of quite noisy traces for profiling. More specifically, at time t, the noisy trace $\mathbf{x}$ of sensitive variable v consists of clean trace part and noise part, which can be described as:

$$\mathbf{x}[t] = f_t(v) + \varepsilon_t = \overbrace{f_t(\phi(p,k))}^{\text{Clean trace}} + \overbrace{\varepsilon_t}^{\text{Noise}}, \tag{6}$$

where v is the sensitive variable (i.e. class label), f_t is a time-dependent function mapping from v to actual leakage which is hard to defined mathematically, ϕ is a priori leakage model (e.g. identity function), ε_t is a time-dependent and v-independent noise.

To tackle the barrier of unknown clean trace, the most intuitive but effective way is to take the average trace as the estimation of clean trace. Average trace is a proper approximation of clean trace under Gaussian noise assumption. Equation (7) describes sample mean $\hat{\mathrm{E}}[\mathbf{x}[t]|v]$ related to sensitive variable v at time t:

$$\hat{\mathrm{E}}[\mathbf{x}[t]|v] = \hat{\mathrm{E}}[f_t(v)|v] + \hat{\mathrm{E}}[\varepsilon_t|v]. \tag{7}$$

Since $f_t(v)$ is not a variable for certain v at time t, substitute $\hat{\mathrm{E}}[f_t(v)|v] = f_t(v)$ for Eq. (7), then Eq. (6) turns into:

$$\mathbf{x}[t] = \overbrace{\hat{\mathrm{E}}[\mathbf{x}[t]|v] - \hat{\mathrm{E}}[\varepsilon_t|v]}^{\text{Clean trace}} + \overbrace{\varepsilon_t}^{\text{Noise}}. \tag{8}$$

Consider continuous time, then we can extend Eq. (8) to:

$$\mathbf{x} = \overbrace{\bar{\mathbf{x}} - \bar{\varepsilon}}^{\text{Clean trace}} + \overbrace{\varepsilon}^{\text{Noise}}, \tag{9}$$

where $\bar{x}$ is the sample average trace, $\bar{\varepsilon}$ is the noise mean.

Traditional assumption is ε follows a zero mean multivariate Gaussian distribution. Then $\bar{\mathbf{x}} = \mathbf{x} - \varepsilon$ is the unbiased estimation of clean trace because $\bar{\varepsilon} = \mathbf{0}$. In this paper, we make no assumption about the noise. Under such circumstances, $\bar{\mathbf{x}} = \mathbf{x} + \bar{\varepsilon} - \varepsilon$ is biased estimation of clean trace in Eq. (9) because $\bar{\varepsilon}$ could be non-zero and biased. Albeit biased, $\bar{\mathbf{x}}$ can still be treated as the clean trace. Since ε is independent to sensitive variable v, then $\bar{\varepsilon}$ stays stable for every trace $\mathbf{x}$ with different sensitive variables. Considering profiled attack is essentially a classification task, to estimate the clean trace for each class (sensitive variable) is equivalent to estimate the within-class center, which is important for some classifiers. As long as the clean trace is discriminative, the biased clean trace is also discriminative which is sufficient for classification.

Unprotected Scenario. For profiled SCA against unprotected implementations, the estimation of the clean trace is simple and straightforward. The clean trace of each class[1] is the sample mean from traces within the class. Once the clean trace is estimated, we can generate training pairs for the denoising autoencoder as described in Algorithm 1.

Algorithm 1. Noisy-clean training pair generation for unprotected implementation

---

Input: profiling set $\mathcal{X}_{\text{profiling}} = \{\mathbf{x}_i\}_{i=1}^N$, sensitive variable set $\mathcal{V} = \{v_i\}_{i=1}^N$
Output: noisy-clean training set $\mathcal{X}_{\text{train}} = \{(\mathbf{x}_i, \bar{\mathbf{x}}_i)\}_{i=1}^N$
1: Initialize clean trace set $\mathcal{S}$ as empty set
2: **for all** $v \in GF(2^8)$ **do**
3:    Calculate average trace $\bar{\mathbf{x}} = \hat{\mathrm{E}}[\mathbf{x}|v]$
4:    Append $\bar{\mathbf{x}}$ into $\mathcal{S}$
5: **end for**
6: Initialize $\mathcal{X}_{\text{train}}$ as empty set
7: **for all** $\mathbf{x}_i \in \mathcal{X}_{\text{profiling}}$ **do**
8:    $\bar{\mathbf{x}}_i = \mathcal{S}[v_i]$
9:    Append $(\mathbf{x}_i, \bar{\mathbf{x}}_i)$ into $\mathcal{X}_{\text{train}}$
10: **end for**
11: **return** $\mathcal{X}_{\text{train}} = \{(\mathbf{x}_i, \bar{\mathbf{x}}_i)\}_{i=1}^N$

---

[1] Totally 256 classes for AES implementation in this paper because there are 256 elements in Galois field $GF(2^8)$.

Masked Scenario. For profiled SCA against masking implementations, the estimation of clean trace follows the same methodology. In 1st-order masked scenario, the trace $\mathbf{x} = \mathbf{x}_v \| \mathbf{x}_m$ horizontally contains two independent part: (1) masked sensitive variable part $\mathbf{x}_v$, where $v = \phi(p, k, m)$ and m is the mask, (2) mask part $\mathbf{x}_m$. For each part, the trace component is as follows:

$$\mathbf{x}_v[t] = \overbrace{f_t(\phi(p, k, m))}^{\text{Clean trace}} + \overbrace{\varepsilon_t}^{\text{Noise}}, \tag{10}$$

$$\mathbf{x}_m[t] = \overbrace{g_t(\varphi(m))}^{\text{Clean trace}} + \overbrace{\epsilon_t}^{\text{Noise}}. \tag{11}$$

According to the discussion in Sect. 3.2, $\bar{\mathbf{x}}_v$ and $\bar{\mathbf{x}}_m$ are biased estimation as follows:

$$\bar{\mathbf{x}}_v = \mathbf{x}_v + \bar{\varepsilon} - \varepsilon, \tag{12}$$

$$\bar{\mathbf{x}}_m = \mathbf{x}_m + \bar{\epsilon} - \epsilon. \tag{13}$$

Algorithm 2 illuminates how to generate noisy-clean training pairs for 1st-order masking implementation.

Algorithm 2. Noisy-clean training pair generation for 1st-order masking implementation

---

Input: profiling set $\mathcal{X}_{\text{profiling}} = \{\mathbf{x}_{v,i} \| \mathbf{x}_{m,i}\}_{i=1}^N$, sensitive variable set $\mathcal{V} = \{v_i\}_{i=1}^N$, mask set $\mathcal{M} = \{m_i\}_{i=1}^N$

Output: noisy-clean training set $\mathcal{X}_{\text{train}} = \{(\mathbf{x}_i, \bar{\mathbf{x}}_i)\}_{i=1}^N$

1: Clip $\mathcal{X}_{\text{profiling}}$ into sensitive variable part $\mathcal{X}_{\text{pv}} = \{\mathbf{x}_{v,i}\}_{i=1}^N$ and mask part $\mathcal{X}_{\text{pm}} = \{\mathbf{x}_{m,i}\}_{i=1}^N$
2: Initialize clean trace sets $\mathcal{S}_v$ and $\mathcal{S}_m$ as empty set
3: **for all** $v, m \in GF(2^8)$ **do**
4:    Calculate average trace $\bar{\mathbf{x}}_v = \hat{\mathbb{E}}[\mathbf{x}_{v,i}|v]$ and average trace $\bar{\mathbf{x}}_m = \hat{\mathbb{E}}[\mathbf{x}_{m,i}|m]$
5:    Append $\bar{\mathbf{x}}_v, \bar{\mathbf{x}}_m$ into $\mathcal{S}_v, \mathcal{S}_m$ respectively
6: **end for**
7: Initialize $\mathcal{X}_{\text{train}}$ as empty set
8: **for all** $\mathbf{x}_i \in \mathcal{X}_{\text{profiling}}$ **do**
9:    $\bar{\mathbf{x}}_i = \mathcal{S}_v[v_i] \| \mathcal{S}_m[m_i]$
10:    Append $(\mathbf{x}_i, \bar{\mathbf{x}}_i)$ into $\mathcal{X}_{\text{train}}$
11: **end for**
12: **return** $\mathcal{X}_{\text{train}} = \{(\mathbf{x}_i, \bar{\mathbf{x}}_i)\}_{i=1}^N$

3.3   Objective Function

The input of our network is a noisy trace $\mathbf{x} = \bar{\mathbf{x}} - \bar{\varepsilon} + \varepsilon$. Discriminative denoising networks aim to learn a highly non-linear mapping function $\mathcal{F}(\mathbf{x}) \approx \bar{\mathbf{x}}$ to predict the clean trace. We employ Euclidean distance (i.e. ℓ_2 loss) between clean and denoised traces as objective function.

ℓ_2 **Loss.** The network is trained using the back-propagation algorithm with mean-square error (MSE) as error-criterion. Stochastic gradient descent over a mini-batch is used to update the network parameters.

$$L(\Theta)_{\text{MSE}} = \frac{1}{2N} \sum_{n=1}^{N} \|\mathcal{F}(\mathbf{x};\Theta) - \bar{\mathbf{x}}\|_2^2 \tag{14}$$

In Eq. (14), N is the size of mini batch, $\mathcal{F}(\mathbf{x};\Theta)$ is the output (i.e. denoised trace) of the network and Θ collectively represents the learnable weights and bias parameters in the network. The Θ can be obtained as:

$$\Theta \triangleq \arg\min_{\Theta} L(\Theta). \tag{15}$$

Connection with SCA. Our denoising network with ℓ_2 distance-based objective function can be explained as the optimization step of profiled SCA in theory. Recall Eq. (4) of SNR, the optimization of $L(\Theta)$ is equivalent to reduce the variance of noise $\hat{\mathbb{E}}[\hat{\text{Var}}[\mathcal{F}(\mathbf{x})[t]|v]]$. Hence in information theoretic metrics, the SNR and PCC of denoised traces will increase.

From the attacker's point of view, after the denoising preprocessing, the denoised traces are more closed to the within-class center, which makes the classification easier. For example, TA uses Mahalanobis distance $(\mathcal{F}(\mathbf{x}) - \bar{\mathbf{x}})^\top$ $\Sigma^{-1}(\mathcal{F}(\mathbf{x}) - \bar{\mathbf{x}})$ to make discriminative predictions. When Σ is identity, the Mahalanobis distance will reduce to Euclidean distance which is $L(\Theta)_{\text{MSE}}$. That is explained why the reduced TA performs well in our experiments.

4   Experimental Results

4.1   Experimental Setup

To evaluate the efficiency of the CDAE framework in the context of profiled SCA, three different (software and hardware) platforms have been considered. Since denoising is our main concern, we specially choose the following target devices with considerable high noise: (1) our home-made AES parallel implementation on GPU, (2) public dataset DPAv2 of AES parallel implementation on FPGA and (3) public dataset ASCAD of 1st-order masking AES implementation on AVR microcontroller. SNR and PCC are used as evaluation metrics from the information theoretic point of view, to measure the information gain after denoising[2]. Guessing entropy (GE) is used to evaluate how much attack efficiency gains for a real attacker with the help of our denoising method. Specifically, we run the Template Attacks (TA), reduced Template Attack (TA.r) and

---

[2] We stress that the information gain remains consistency in $\mathcal{F}(\mathcal{X}_{\text{profiling}})$ and $\mathcal{F}(\mathcal{X}_{\text{attack}})$ since early-stopping is used to prevent over-fitting.

pooled Template Attack (TA.p) 100 times with randomly selected sub-samples of attack set for evaluation. For each attack, we pre-select $\{5, 25, 50\}$ PoIs with the highest PCC and record the best results of the minimum number of traces to achieve $GE < 2$. Singular Spectrum Analysis (SSA) [4] is used as a state-of-the-art denoising preprocessing method in profiled SCA for comparison. It should be noted we strictly follow the algorithm and recommended parameter setting of SSA in [4].

In this work, all experiments are conducted on an Intel(R) Xeon(R) CPU E5-2667 v4 @3.20GHz 32 core machine with two NVIDIA TITAN Xp GPUs. We use the Keras library (version 2.2.2) with the TensorFlow library (version 1.10.0) as the backend for CNN. All the data and code are available at https:// github.com/fr4nky4ng/CDAE-Towards-Empowering-Denoising-in-SCA.

4.2 Results on Unprotected AES Parallel Implementation on GPU (AES_GPU)

Graphics Processing Unit (GPU) has been widely used for general-purpose computing, including computationally-intensive algorithms such as the cryptographic algorithms. Recent works [6] show that GPU based cryptographic implementation is vulnerable by non-profiled attacks through electromagnetic side-channels. In [6], up to 11,000 traces are needed to perform the non-profiled attack, which indicates the noise in traces is very high. We target an NVIDIA GeForce GT620 graphics card (GPU) connected to the host with a PCIe bus. The AES parallel implementation (32 threads in a warp) and trace acquisition details are stated in [6]. We use the same trace set as in [6] and make it publicly available at https://github.com/fr4nky4ng/AES_GPU.

We aim at the leakage operation of the last round 16th byte register writing: $v = \text{Sbox}^{-1}[c[16] \oplus k^*]$, where $c[16]$ is the 16th ciphertext byte. Each trace contains 350 relevant sampling points. There are 34,511 traces for profiling and 5,000 traces for the attack. We call this homemade dataset AES_GPU in brief. The training pair is generated by Algorithm 1. During the network training, we use *Adam* optimizer with a learning rate of 0.001. The mini-batch size is 256 and the maximum iterative epoch is 100. We stop the training at epoch 49 where over-fitting occurs.

Results. We examine SNR and PCC of denoised traces from our method, SSA method and original noisy traces as shown in Fig. 3. It can be seen that our method significantly improved the SNR and PCC on the points of interest (PoI). For instance, at point 276, the peak SNR and PCC are significantly improved by 20 times and 4.5 times respectively.

Detailed power distribution at PoI 276 can be found in Appendix A Fig. 6. Kernel density estimation (KDE) [14] is used to estimate the probability density function of the power, where each colored line represents the KDE of one class because there are 256 classes in $GF(2^8)$. After denoising, the power distribution is more scattered and discriminative because the variance of the noise is suppressed.

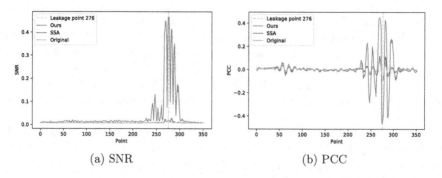

(a) SNR (b) PCC

Fig. 3. Comparison of SNR and PCC.

In general, higher SNRs should translate into more successful attacks. This has been practically verified by running TA and evaluating the Guessing Entropy of true key. In Table 1, only 40–50 denoised traces are necessary to reach GE < 2, which gains up to a factor of 10. With the help of GPU acceleration, The preprocessing time of CDAE $Time_{pre} = 1m57s$ is faster compared to 6 min of the SSA Python implementation.

Table 1. Results on AES_GPU.

Method	SNR	PCC	GE			$Time_{pre}$
			TA	TA.r	TA.p	
Original	0.020	0.098	650	700	80	0 s
SSA [4]	0.029	0.117	>1000	540	60	6 m12 s
Ours	**0.466**	**0.468**	**50**	**40**	**45**	**1 m57 s**

4.3　Results on Unprotected AES Hardware Implementation on FPGA (DPAv2)

The second dataset is from the DPA Contest v2 (DPAv2) on the public website [20]. It provides measurements of an unprotected hardware parallel implementation of the AES-128 algorithm on the SASEBO GII FPGA board. We pre-select leakage related to consecutive 1000 points for each trace. Previous works [15] showed the most suitable leakage operation is the register writing in the last round: $v = \text{Sbox}^{-1}[c[12] \oplus k^*] \oplus c[8]$, where $c[12]$ and $c[8]$ are 12th and 8th ciphertext bytes. In our experiment, there are 90,000 traces for profiling and 10,000 for attack. The training pair is generated by Algorithm 1. The convolutional kernel size is 11 in CDAE because the length of traces in DPAv2 is longer. We use *Adam* optimizer with learning rate 0.0001. The mini-batch size is 256 and the maximum iterative epoch is 100. We stop the training at epoch 90 where over-fitting occurs.

Results. As shown in Fig. 4, our method improves the SNR and PCC of the original traces at a factor of 4.2 and 1.8 respectively, where the SSA only improves the SNR and PCC at a factor of 1.4 and 1.2. An interesting phenomenon is that the traces denoised by our method still maintain the leakage characteristics. The curve of SNR/PCC is not changed but only enhanced, in comparison sharp fluctuations can be observed on the SNR/PCC of SSA denoised traces. Our method only amplifies the SNR and PCC, which is a good advantage for the backend attacker who doesn't want the leakage distribution interfered.

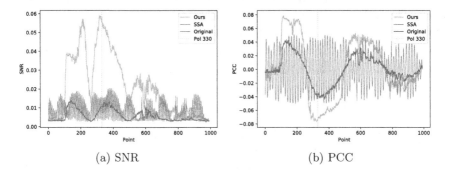

(a) SNR   (b) PCC

Fig. 4. Comparison of SNR and PCC.

The detailed power distribution is shown in Appendix A Fig. 7. The traces of DPAv2 are quite noisy due to 16 S-boxes are implemented in parallel and we only target one S-box. The sensitive variables of the other 15 S-boxes would be seen as noise. After denoising preprocessing, the power of $v = 0$ (the black line stands alone in Fig. 7) is more discriminative than before.

The further attack results of TA in Table 2 show the improvement of information gain translate into the efficiency gain of TA. Only 450 denoised traces are needed to recover the key, where SSA and original traces need 800 and 950 traces. Considering the total amount of traces is large (100,000 traces), our method takes 17 min for preprocessing which is acceptable. For comparison, SSA takes 52 min for denoising all 100,000 traces.

Table 2. Results on DPAv2

Method	SNR	PCC	GE			Time$_{pre}$
			TA	TA.r	TA.p	
Original	0.014	0.044	>3000	950	2400	0 s
SSA [4]	0.020	0.051	**2240**	800	1500	52 m22 s
Ours	**0.059**	**0.078**	>3000	**450**	**1000**	**17 m41 s**

4.4 Results on Masking AES Software Implementation on ATMega8515 (ASCAD)

Finally, we test our method on the public ASCAD database [16]. ASCAD is introduced for providing a benchmark to evaluate deep learning based SCA. The dataset is measured from the electromagnetic radiations of a masking AES software implementation on an 8-bit AVR microcontroller (ATMega8515). Each trace has 700 sampling points which contain information on the masked S-box output: $v = \text{Sbox}(p[3] \oplus k[3]) \oplus r[3]$ and S-box output mask: $m = r[3]$, where $p[3]$ is the 3rd plaintext byte. There are 50,000 traces for profiling and 10,000 for attack. The training pair is generated by Algorithm 2. The weight factor in loss is the sum of the SNRs on both parts. We use *Adam* optimizer with learning rate 0.0001. The mini-batch size is 256 and the maximum iterative epoch is 100. We stop the training at epoch 75 where over-fitting occurs.

Results. A careful observation of Fig. 5 shows that the SNR and PCC of the mask part on the left side and the masked S-box output part on the right side are both improved after using our denoising network. For the masked S-box output part, the peak SNR and PCC of v are improved by 5.9 times and 1.04 times respectively. For the mask part, the peak SNR and PCC of m are improved by 1.60 times and 1.26 times respectively. Interestingly, the noise level of both parts is reduced simultaneously at one single training. However, the denoising effect of the masked S-box output part is more effective. because the SNR of original traces on this part is higher than on the mask part, the network pays more attention to this part to minimize ℓ_2 loss. SSA fails to denoise the traces because of SNR and PCC both decrease.

A detailed look of the power distribution at point 517 of the masked S-box output part and point 156 of the mask part is shown in Appendix A Fig. 8. At point 517 of masked S-box output v and 156 of mask m, we notice that the distribution is Gaussian-like. After denoising, the distributions of 256 classes are scattered. This means the variance of the noise is suppressed and the signals are more distinguishable which is good for profiled attacks.

We use PCA-TA (use PCA to extract principal components then launch TA) and High Order Template Attacks (HOTA) as a benchmark test. The reason is two-fold: (1) Since ASCAD traces are measured from a 1st-order masking AES implementation, it is natural to use HOTA to generate the 2nd-order moments and then perform TA. (2) According to the experiments in [16], PCA-TA is utilized as recommended profiled attacks, even better than CNN based profiled attacks for synchronized ASCAD traces.

The denoising and attack results are shown in Table 3. It only takes 13 min 45s to train and denoise all 60000 traces for CDAE. We can find that PCA-TA is only suitable when using the covariance matrix. For all the PCA-TA and HOTA, our method takes the least traces (A minimum of 160) to reach GE less than 2. For both attacks, SSA fails and GE decreases slowly, even worse than attacking results without preprocessing.

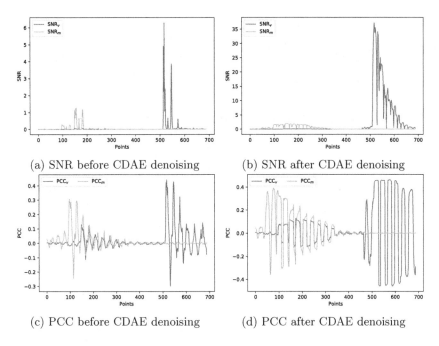

(a) SNR before CDAE denoising   (b) SNR after CDAE denoising

(c) PCC before CDAE denoising   (d) PCC after CDAE denoising

Fig. 5. Comparison of SNR and PCC (The results of SSA are omitted in the figure for clarity because SSA fails and the SNR and PCC are not improved).

Table 3. Results on ASCAD.

Method	SNR_v/SNR_m	PCC_v/PCC_m	GE						Time
			PCA			HO			
			TA	TA.r	TA.p	TA	TA.r	TA.p	
Original	6.29/1.27	0.44/0.31	310	Failed	Failed	Failed	600	600	0 s
SSA [4]	1.56/0.94	0.37/0.26	Failed	Failed	Failed	Failed	1750	5000	15 m 52 s
Ours	**37.2/2.03**	**0.46/0.39**	**160**	Failed	Failed	**7000**	**400**	**500**	**13 m 45 s**

5   Conclusion

In this paper, we propose CDAE as novel denoising preprocessing tool in the context of profiled SCA for the first time. In particular, we validate the effectiveness of CDAE under three high noise jamming circumstances with quite a high noise level and show that our method can significantly outperform the state-of-the-art SSA denoising method on both information theoretic metrics and security metrics. Unlike classic denoising methods, our method is a *data-driven* approach which learns the unique noise distribution to adaptively reduce the noise of the DUT. We argue that CDAE is very suitable for profiled attacks especially when the attacker has a large amount of traces in the offline profiling phase. Once the network training is done, our denoising network can be applied to individual traces for the attacker to launch online attacks. We demonstrate that the ℓ_2 loss is a special case of Mahalanobis distance which is the foundation of TA. It would be interesting to use Mahalanobis distance as the objective function of our denoising network, in order to directly develop a neural network enhanced Template Attacks.

Acknowledgment. This work was supported in part by the National Natural Science Foundation of China (No. 61632020) and Beijing Natural Science Foundation (No. 4192067).

Appendix A. Kernel Density Estimation of Univariate Distribution at PoI

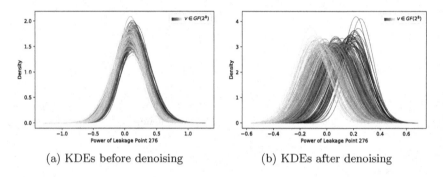

(a) KDEs before denoising   (b) KDEs after denoising

Fig. 6. Power distribution of sensitive variable v at PoI 276 (256 classes). (Color figure online)

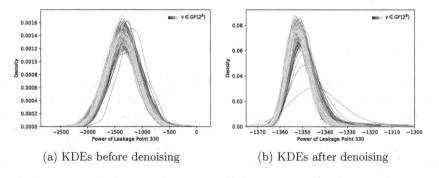

(a) KDEs before denoising   (b) KDEs after denoising

Fig. 7. Power distributions of sensitive variable v at PoI 330 (256 classes). (Color figure online)

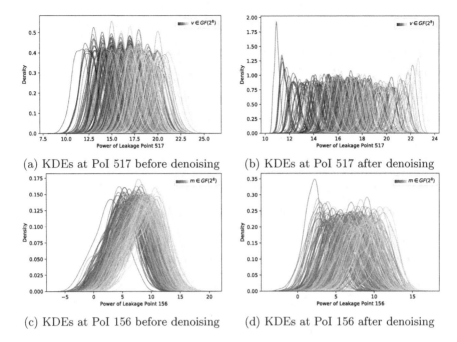

(a) KDEs at PoI 517 before denoising   (b) KDEs at PoI 517 after denoising

(c) KDEs at PoI 156 before denoising   (d) KDEs at PoI 156 after denoising

Fig. 8. Power distributions of masked Sbox output v at PoI 517 and mask m at PoI 156. (Color figure online)

References

1. Agrawal, D., Archambeault, B., Rao, J.R., Rohatgi, P.: The EM side—channel(s). In: Kaliski, B.S., Koç, K., Paar, C. (eds.) CHES 2002. LNCS, vol. 2523, pp. 29–45. Springer, Heidelberg (2003). https://doi.org/10.1007/3-540-36400-5_4
2. Chari, S., Rao, J.R., Rohatgi, P.: Template attacks. In: Kaliski, B.S., Koç, K., Paar, C. (eds.) CHES 2002. LNCS, vol. 2523, pp. 13–28. Springer, Heidelberg (2003). https://doi.org/10.1007/3-540-36400-5_3
3. Charvet, X., Pelletier, H.: Improving the DPA attack using wavelet transform. In: NIST Physical Security Testing Workshop, vol. 46 (2005)
4. Merino Del Pozo, S., Standaert, F.-X.: Blind source separation from single measurements using singular spectrum analysis. In: Güneysu, T., Handschuh, H. (eds.) CHES 2015. LNCS, vol. 9293, pp. 42–59. Springer, Heidelberg (2015). https://doi.org/10.1007/978-3-662-48324-4_3
5. Durvaux, F., Standaert, F.-X., Veyrat-Charvillon, N.: How to certify the leakage of a chip? In: Nguyen, P.Q., Oswald, E. (eds.) EUROCRYPT 2014. LNCS, vol. 8441, pp. 459–476. Springer, Heidelberg (2014). https://doi.org/10.1007/978-3-642-55220-5_26
6. Gao, Y., Zhang, H., Cheng, W., Zhou, Y., Cao, Y.: Electro-magnetic analysis of GPU-based AES implementation. In: Proceedings of the 55th Annual Design Automation Conference, p. 121. ACM (2018). https://doi.org/10.1145/3195970.3196042

7. Kocher, P., Jaffe, J., Jun, B.: Differential power analysis. In: Wiener, M. (ed.) CRYPTO 1999. LNCS, vol. 1666, pp. 388–397. Springer, Heidelberg (1999). https://doi.org/10.1007/3-540-48405-1_25

8. Kocher, P.C.: Timing attacks on implementations of Diffie-Hellman, RSA, DSS, and other systems. In: Koblitz, N. (ed.) CRYPTO 1996. LNCS, vol. 1109, pp. 104–113. Springer, Heidelberg (1996). https://doi.org/10.1007/3-540-68697-5_9

9. Le, T.H., Clédière, J., Servière, C., Lacoume, J.L.: Noise reduction in side channel attack using fourth-order cumulant. IEEE Trans. Inf. Forensics Secur. 2(4), 710–720 (2007). https://doi.org/10.1109/TIFS.2007.910252

10. Lu, X., Tsao, Y., Matsuda, S., Hori, C.: Speech enhancement based on deep denoising autoencoder. In: Interspeech, pp. 436–440 (2013)

11. Maghrebi, H., Prouff, E.: On the use of independent component analysis to denoise side-channel measurements. In: Fan, J., Gierlichs, B. (eds.) COSADE 2018. LNCS, vol. 10815, pp. 61–81. Springer, Cham (2018). https://doi.org/10.1007/978-3-319-89641-0_4

12. Mao, X., Shen, C., Yang, Y.B.: Image restoration using very deep convolutional encoder-decoder networks with symmetric skip connections. In: Advances in Neural Information Processing Systems, pp. 2802–2810 (2016)

13. Meynard, O., Réal, D., Flament, F., Guilley, S., Homma, N., Danger, J.L.: Enhancement of simple electro-magnetic attacks by pre-characterization in frequency domain and demodulation techniques. In: 2011 Design, Automation & Test in Europe, pp. 1–6. IEEE (2011)

14. Parzen, E.: On estimation of a probability density function and mode. Ann. Math. Stat. 33(3), 1065–1076 (1962)

15. Picek, S., Heuser, A., Jovic, A., Bhasin, S., Regazzoni, F.: The curse of class imbalance and conflicting metrics with machine learning for side-channel evaluations (2018). https://doi.org/10.13154/tches.v2019.i1.209-237

16. Prouff, E., Strullu, R., Benadjila, R., Cagli, E., Dumas, C.: Study of deep learning techniques for side-channel analysis and introduction to ascad database. IACR Cryptology ePrint Archive 2018, 53 (2018)

17. Souissi, Y., Elaabid, M.A., Debande, N., Guilley, S., Danger, J.L.: Novel applications of wavelet transforms based side-channel analysis. In: Non-Invasive Attack Testing Workshop (2011)

18. Souissi, Y., Guilley, S., Danger, J.l., Mekki, S., Duc, G.: Improvement of power analysis attacks using Kalman filter. In: 2010 IEEE International Conference on Acoustics, Speech and Signal Processing, pp. 1778–1781. IEEE (2010). https://doi.org/10.1109/ICASSP.2010.5495428

19. Standaert, F.-X., Malkin, T.G., Yung, M.: A unified framework for the analysis of side-channel key recovery attacks. In: Joux, A. (ed.) EUROCRYPT 2009. LNCS, vol. 5479, pp. 443–461. Springer, Heidelberg (2009). https://doi.org/10.1007/978-3-642-01001-9_26

20. TELECOM ParisTech SEN research group: DPA Contest, 2nd edn., 2009–2010. http://www.DPAcontest.org/v2/

Practical Evaluation Methodology of Higher-Order Maskings at Different Operating Frequencies

Yuguang Li[1(✉)], Ming Tang[2], Pengbo Wang[2], Yanbin Li[3], and Shan Fu[1,4]

[1] China Academy of Information and Communications Technology, Beijing, China
{liyuguang,fushan}@caict.ac.cn
[2] School of Cyber Science and Engineering, Wuhan University, Wuhan, China
m.tang@126.com, wpb2011@whu.edu.cn
[3] College of Information Science and Technology, Nanjing Agricultural University, Nanjing, China
lyb9205@163.com
[4] Beijing University of Posts and Telecommunications, Beijing, China

Abstract. FPGA is widely used in the cryptographic devices, such as security co-processor and crypto engine, due to its high speed and customizability. Side-channel analysis is the state-of-the-art method which could recover the secret information in the FPGA through measuring and analysing the power consumption or the electromagnetic radiation. Therefore, side-channel analysis may lead to a potential threat of the security of FPGA. We find that an excessively high operating frequency could cause a pretty serious security vulnerability in the FPGA implementation of a cryptographic algorithm with side-channel countermeasures. And then, how to evaluate the security of the implementation at different operating frequencies is an important question in the practical application. After investigating the physical reason of the information leakage of the FPGA, we propose a generic evaluation methodology derived from CPA and MIA that can be utilized to analyze the security of FPGA implementation of a cryptographic algorithm with side-channel countermeasures at different operating frequencies. By this methodology, the evaluator only needs to collect the measurements when the FPGA operates at an arbitrary frequency rather than collecting the measurement of all possible frequencies exhaustively. Finally, several experiments in an FPGA with AES cryptographic algorithm protected with a masking countermeasure are conducted to illustrate the feasibility of this methodology.

Keywords: FPGA · Side-channel analysis · Operating frequency · Higher-order masking

1 Introduction

FPGA is widely used in the cryptographic device, such as security co-processor and crypto engine, due to its high speed and customizability. Physical Attack is

© Springer Nature Switzerland AG 2020
J. Zhou et al. (Eds.): ICICS 2019, LNCS 11999, pp. 287–304, 2020.
https://doi.org/10.1007/978-3-030-41579-2_17

one of the most powerful kinds of attack against cryptographic devices, which do not targets the algorithm itself but attempt to recover information about the secret by attacking the implementation of the algorithm. In the past decade years, Side-Channel Attacks (SCAs) [5,6,10–12,24] have become a threatening physical analysis method of the cryptographic device, which gain the secret through measuring the power consumption, electromagnetic radiation or other side channel information. Masking [2,7,18,20,22,23] is one of the most efficient algorithm-based countermeasures in SCAs. The goal of the masking is to make the physical power consumption of a cryptographic device independent of the intermediate value of the cryptographic algorithm, and it is achieved by randomizing these intermediate values. However, though the masking scheme is considered secure theoretically, it still has many vulnerabilities due to weak implementations.

Glitches can be seen as unwilling transitions in a combinational circuit. Due to the uncontrolled glitches occurring in the masked circuit, the FPGA implementation of maskings faces many challenges [14,15]. However, the security risks induced by glitches can be eliminated with Threshold Implementation (TI) [4,19]. TI ensures the security of first order masking scheme in presence of glitches. Considering the development of TI, the security risks induced by glitches could be mitigated. Thus we do not concentrate on the vulnerabilities derived from glitches in this paper.

Besides glitches, the vulnerabilities caused by the other aspects of the implementation of the masking schemes have been studied. Moradi et al. [17] have studied the information leakage caused by an amplified setup in hardware cryptographic devices. They have discussed that the operating frequency of the real circuit and the measurement setup have an impact on the vulnerability of the masking schemes. The paper shows that an inappropriate operating frequency of a cryptographic device can cause severe security problems. However, the theoretical relationship between the quantity of leakage and the operating frequency of the cryptographic device is still uncertain. In this paper, we try to construct an evaluation methodology which can be utilized to detect the information leakage of the masked circuit operating at different frequencies.

In the aspect of leakage detection or evaluation, Welch's T-test [16], Correlation Power Analysis (CPA) distinguisher [5] and Mutual Information Analysis (MIA) distinguisher [3] are extensively used. Durvaux et al. [8] studied the features of different detection methods and proposed an improved t-test and an innovative correlation-based method. The leakage detection methods can be used to detect the Points-Of-Interests (POIs) [9], which is a complementary task in most side-channel attacks. In this paper, we focus on evaluating the quantity of the leakage that can be utilized to perform an attack successfully under the premise of knowing these POIs.

After studying the feature of the side-channel leakage of FPGA in depth, we notice that the quantity of information leakage has a direct relationship with the operating frequency. When the evaluator performs univariate MIA or CPA on FPGA implementation of masking schemes, the number of traces will decrease with the operating frequency becoming higher. Besides, the FPGA circuit can be attacked by MIA or CPA easily when the circuit operates at a high frequency (e.g. 48 MHz, 24 MHz). However, the circuit is secure when the operating frequency is rather low (e.g. 2 MHz). So the security of the FPGA implementation of masking schemes has a significant relationship with the operating frequency, so selecting an appropriate operating frequency is significant for the designer of a masking scheme, especially when implemented with FPGA.

We propose a generic methodology that can be used for side-channel leakage evaluation on FPGA, by which the designer or the implementor of a masking scheme can evaluate the security and estimate the number of traces needed to successfully attack the FPGA implementation of this scheme when the circuit operates at different frequencies. Moreover, the evaluator only needs to collect the measurements when the FPGA operates at an arbitrary frequency rather than collecting the measurement of all possible frequencies exhaustively. Also, this methodology is appropriate for real applications (e.g. smart card, IoT devices) that work at any operating frequency though it's rather high.

2 Preliminaries

2.1 Measurement Setup

All practical experiments in this paper are conducted with the SASEBO-GII board [1], which is equipped with a Xilinx Virtex-5 FPGA chip. The SASEBO-GII board is specially designed for the side-channel analysis on the cryptographic design implemented with FPGA. Figure 1 partly shows the shape of the power consumption of a FPGA implementing an AES cryptographic algorithm, where the cycle of the AES can be obviously identified.

Physical power consumption traces are collected by means of a KEYSIGHT InfiniiVision DSOX3034A digital oscilloscope at a sampling rate of 2GSa/s and a bandwidth limit of 20 MHz to reduce the environmental noise.

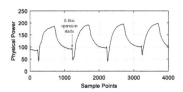

Fig. 1. SASEBO-GII (Xilinx Virtex-5 FPGA) physical power trace of AES.

2.2 CPA and MIA Distinguishers

In this section, we introduce the notations throughout this paper. We use bold capital letters for matrixes and bold small letters for vectors. The detailed description of the notation is shown in Table 1. Moreover, we introduce some background information about MIA and CPA distinguishers, which are the fundamentals of the proposed methodology in this paper.

Table 1. Notations

Notations	Descriptions
k	Vector of key hypothesis
k_{guess}	Key guess
k_c	Correct key
k_w	Wrong key
P	Random plaintext
ρ	Correlation coefficient
$\text{Cov}(X, Y)$	Covariance of X and Y
$\Pr(X = x)$	Probability that $X = x$
m	Number of power consumption traces
s	Time samples
T	Matrix of physical power consumption traces
t'_m	Row m of T, that is, the mth traces
t_s	Column s of T, that is, vector of point s (a particular time instant) in different traces
$t_{m,s}$	The power consumption value at row m column s of T
D	Matrix of differential power consumption traces, the meanings of d'_m, d_s and $d_{m,s}$ are similar to t'_m, t_s and $t_{m,s}$
P	Matrix of reconstructed power consumption traces, the meanings of p'_m, p_s and $p_{m,s}$ are similar to t'_m, t_s and $t_{m,s}$
$SBox(x)$	AES S-box function
F	Set of valid operating frequencies of cryptographic devices
f	Operating frequency
$|\cdot|$	Number of elements in a set
t_c	Length of clock cycle, which is equals to $\frac{1}{f}$
τ	Duration of differential power consumption traces d'_m

Leakage Model: $L(x)$ denotes the information leakage when $x = I(k_{guess}, P)$, where $k_{guess} \in k$ is the key guess, k is the set of the key hypothesis, P is a random plaintext, I denotes the computation of intermediate value. In the real cryptographic device, P is a random number in $GF(2^n)$, where n is the length of the plaintext block, information leakage $L(x) = L_M[I(k_{guess}, P)]$, where L_M denotes the leakage model, which is an estimation of L.

Correlation Power Analysis (CPA) Distinguisher: T denotes the matrix of physical power consumption traces (size $m \times s$), where m is the number of traces and s is the number of time samples. t_s denotes the column s of T (i.e. The vector of point s in different traces). CPA distinguisher $\rho(t_s, L(x))$ denotes the correlation between t_s and $L(x)$.

$$\rho(X, Y) = \frac{\text{cov}(X, Y)}{\sigma_X \sigma_Y},$$

where $\text{cov}(X, Y)$ represents the covariance of X and Y, σ_X and σ_Y denote the standard deviation of X and Y respectively.

Mutual Information Analysis (MIA) Distinguisher: MIA distinguisher $\text{MI}(t_S, L(x))$, which is similar to CPA, denotes the mutual information of t_s and $L(x)$. The mutual information can be calculated as follows:

$H(X)$ denotes the entropy of a random variable X, and $H(X|Y)$ denotes the conditional entropy of X given another variable Y, then $H(X)$ and $H(X|Y)$ can be expressed as:

$$H(X) = -\sum_i \Pr(X = x_i) \log \Pr(X = x_i),$$

$$H(X|Y) = -\sum_{i,j} \Pr(X = x_i, Y = y_j)$$
$$\log \Pr(X = x_i | Y = y_j).$$

The mutual information can be expressed as:

$$MI(X, Y) = H(X) - H(X|Y).$$

3   Vulnerability of Masked Circuits

In a masked circuit, the information leakage generated at a specific clock cycle still exists at the next several clock cycles, we call this phenomenon the *persistence of leakage*. The concept of the persistence of leakage is similar to the memory effect which is mentioned in [17], however, it can be observed without an amplified setup which is necessary to the memory effect. The persistence of leakage can be utilized to describe the physical reason and feature of the information leakage and explain why the results of CPA or MIA are changed when the operating frequency is altered. Besides, the concept of the persistence of leakage is the foundation of the evaluation methodology proposed in this paper. Though provably secure, a masking scheme can be vulnerable due to the persistence of leakage.

Figure 2 shows the main process of AES cryptographic algorithm, where the S-box is unmodified in the original algorithm without masking countermeasures.

Figure 3 shows the masking scheme which is proposed by Regazonni [22], where the mask and plaintext are manipulated in a similar manner. From Fig. 3 we can see that the mask and the output of the AddRoundKey, which is called the intermediate value, are the inputs of the masked S-box, if these processes are parallel in the implementation, the circuit is vulnerable to zero-offset attack [25].

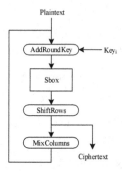

Fig. 2. Main process of AES cryptographic algorithm

Thus the mask and intermediate value cannot be manipulated in parallel due to safety factors. The most practical method to solve this problem is to process the mask and the intermediate value in different clock cycles. However, there may occur some security problems due to the persistence of leakage though the mask and the intermediate value are processed in serial, especially in continuous cycles. Figure 4 shows the main process of RSM masked S-box, which is part of the whole masking scheme proposed by Nassar [18]. The RSM masking scheme is secure against zero-offset attack. However, if the scheme is implemented where the mask and the intermediate value are processed in continuous cycles, there may also be a high-order leakage due to the persistence of leakage.

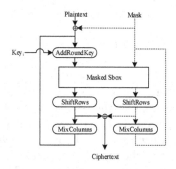

Fig. 3. Main process of Regazzoni masking scheme

Therefore, we conducted several experiments to verify the vulnerabilities from the persistence of leakage and identified the information leakage that can be utilized to perform univariate attacks with our measurement setup, from which we can see that the persistence of leakage is widespread in the real circuit.

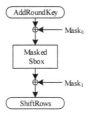

Fig. 4. Main process of RSM masked S-box

3.1 Persistence of Leakage

To analyze the persistence of leakage, the experiment is conducted on the AES hardware implementation of the Regazonni masking scheme. For the purpose of the experiments is to verify the existence of the persistence of leakage, the implementation is a single round of AES where the S-boxes are executed serially. The univariate MIA is utilized to analyze the power consumption of the implementation. Each differential power trace is computed with the Hamming weight of the intermediate value unaltered, which depends on the actual data. So differential power traces indicate the data-dependent portion which can be seen as the information leakage in physical power consumption traces. We utilize the differential power trace to verify the effect of the persistence of leakage on the cryptographic circuit. Differential power consumption D can be calculated as follows:

$$T_j = \{t_i \,|\, HW[I(k_c, P_i)] = j\},$$

$$d'_j = \lim_{|T_j| \to \infty, |T_0| \to \infty} (\frac{\sum\limits_{t \in T_j} t}{|T_j|} - \frac{\sum\limits_{t \in T_0} t}{|T_0|}), \tag{1}$$

where T_j is a set of physical power consumption traces t with the same Hamming weight j of the intermediate value. $|\cdot|$ denotes the number of elements in a set.

The differential power consumption D_1 and D_2 are calculated with intermediate values $I_1 = x_1 \oplus SBox(x_1)$ and $I_2 = x_2 \oplus SBox(x_2)$ respectively, where x_1 and x_2 denote two inputs of the AES S-box. The result is shown as Fig. 5, and two peaks correspond to two sets of differential power consumption traces D_1 and D_2. From Fig. 5 we can see that the peak of D_1 continues to the position of D_2 due to the influence of the persistence of leakage, and two peaks overlap in a single clock cycle. Thus, higher-order leakage that can be utilized to perform univariate attacks is generated in this situation.

3.2 Cause of Persistence of Leakage and Power Consumption of FPGA

In this paper, we try to investigate the information leakage from the power consumption of FPGA, so the feature of the power consumption traces is a significant problem. According to [13], FPGA can be seen as a CMOS circuit, and the power consumption of CMOS circuits is the sum of static power consumption and the dynamic power consumption. The major part of the power consumption in CMOS circuits is the dynamic power consumption, and it has a direct relationship with the data that is processed by the CMOS circuit, so the dynamic power consumption is the crucial factor that generates the information leakage.

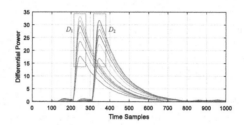

Fig. 5. The traces in two boxes correspond to two sets of differential power consumption traces D_1 and D_2, and each trace corresponds to a row of D_1 or D_2.

The main reason for the dynamic power consumption is the charging current of the output capacitance C_L. Therefore, the persistence of leakage can be seen as a result of the charging time of C_L. The charging time of C_L depends on the voltage, the resistance and the capacitance of the CMOS circuit which have no relationship with the operating frequency, so it remains unchanged when the operating frequency of the FPGA is altered. Therefore, the duration τ of the persistence of leakage does not depend on the operating frequency.

4   Evaluation Methodology

The duration τ keeps constant if the power consumption traces collected with unaltered measurement setup. With the measurement setup in this paper, τ is approximately 6 ns. The power consumption D of different shares overlap in a single clock cycle. Then the masked circuit generates higher-order leakages. As shown in Fig. 5, the operating frequency f influences the distance t_c between two peaks of D_1 and D_2 instead of the duration τ that one peak decreases to zero. So the overlapping area of different shares becomes larger with f increasing and the masked circuit is easier to be attacked. However, the exact relationship between f and the quantity of the information leakage is still unclear.

The power consumption traces collected under a specific f cannot be utilized to evaluate the information leakage if f is changed. To evaluate the security of the masking scheme implemented with different operating frequencies F, the evaluator has to collect the power consumption traces after altering the implementation with different f every time. If the evaluator is to evaluate the security of the masking scheme implemented with $|F|$ different operating frequencies, he has to alter the implementation $|F|$ times, where $|\cdot|$ denotes the number of elements in a set. The total number of traces needed is as follows:

$$N_{total} = \sum_{f \in F} N_f,$$

where N_f is the number of traces needed to perform the evaluation with a certain f. This process consumes plenty of extra time.

We proposed a generic evaluation methodology that can be utilized to analyze the security of the masked circuit at different operating frequencies more easily. The evaluator can acquire and analyze a series of power consumption traces at different operating frequencies by this methodology after simply collecting N_f (instead of N_{total}) physical power consumption traces once. Through this methodology, the designer of a higher-order masking scheme can revise the implementation or select an appropriate operating frequency of the cryptographic device. The detailed description of the methodology is stated as follows.

As shown in Fig. 5, the differential power consumption D decreases exponentially after reaching the peak. It can be assumed that the persistence of leakage disappears when the differential power decreases to zero. We utilize curve fitting to depict the trend how D decreases. The result is as follows:

$$p_{x,s} = g(x)e^{-\alpha s}, \tag{2}$$

where $p_{x,s}$ is the reconstructed power consumption in time sample s when the intermediate value equals to x, $g(x)$ denotes a function with the independent variable x, and α is a constant. We assume that the power leakage in the real circuit satisfies the Hamming weight model (or the Hamming distance model), then $g(x)$ can be expressed as follows:

$$g(x) = Amp \circ HW(x), \tag{3}$$

where Amp is an amplify function which is related to the feature of the physical power consumption, and it can be acquired by profiling. Then D can be rewritten as:

$$d_{x,s} = Amp \circ HW(x)e^{-\alpha s}. \tag{4}$$

In the real masked circuit, the shares of sensitive values are processed in adjacent clock cycles. For the shares x_1 and x_2 we have $x = x_1 \oplus x_2$, and from Eqs. (2), (3) we have:

$$p_{x_1,s} = Amp \circ HW(x_1)e^{-\alpha s}, \tag{5}$$

$$p_{x_2,s} = Amp \circ HW(x_2)e^{-\alpha(s+\frac{1}{f})}. \tag{6}$$

Due to the persistence of leakage, the power consumption of the operation of two shares overlaps. The reconstructed power consumption P of the masked circuit can be expressed as:

$$P = P_1 + P_2 + P_{noise}, \tag{7}$$

where P_{noise} is the noise in the power consumption that satisfies Gaussian distribution and $P_{noise} \sim N(\mu_{noise}, \sigma_{noise}^2)$. P_1 and P_2 represent the matrixes that consist of $p_{x_1,s}$ and $p_{x_1,s}$ respectively.

From Eqs. (5), (6), (7), the element $p_{x,s}$ of the reconstructed power consumption P can be expressed as:

$$
\begin{aligned}
p_{x,s} = {} & Amp \circ HW(x_1)e^{-\alpha s} \\
& + Amp \circ HW(x_2)e^{-\alpha(s+\frac{1}{f})} + P_{noise}.
\end{aligned}
\tag{8}
$$

The leakage in the real circuit is:

$$
L(x) = HW(x) = HW(x_1 \oplus x_2).
\tag{9}
$$

When MIA is utilized to analyze the second-order masking scheme, from Eqs. (8), (9), we have:

$$
\begin{aligned}
MI(\boldsymbol{p}_s, L(x)) = {} & MI(Amp \circ HW(x_1)e^{-\alpha s} \\
& + Amp \circ HW(x_2)e^{-\alpha(s+\frac{1}{f})} + P_{noise}, \\
& HW(x_1 \oplus x_2)).
\end{aligned}
\tag{10}
$$

However, When CPA is utilized to analyze the scheme, the power consumption p_s should be preprocessed. From Eqs. (8), (9), we have:

$$
\begin{aligned}
\rho(\boldsymbol{p}_s^*, L(X)) = {} & \rho(Pre(Amp \circ HW(x_1)e^{-\alpha s} \\
& + Amp \circ HW(x_2)e^{-\alpha(s+\frac{1}{f})}) + P_{noise}, \\
& HW(x_1 \oplus x_2)).
\end{aligned}
\tag{11}
$$

where $\boldsymbol{p}_s^* = Pre(\boldsymbol{p}_s)$ and Pre is the preprocessing function [21].

According to Eq. (10), we consider the operating frequency f as an independent variable and study the theoretical correlation between f and MI. The function Amp and the coefficient α are acquired by profiling. The result is shown in Fig. 6 regardless of P_{noise} and there is a positive correlation between f and MI. It is obvious that the masked circuit leaks more information and it is more feasible to be attacked with the operating frequency of the device increasing.

We study the correlation between f and ρ by the approach which is the same as the one used in MIA. The preprocessing function that we select is as follows:

$$
Pre(\boldsymbol{p}) = \prod_{i=1}^{n} (p_i - \overline{\boldsymbol{p}})^2,
$$

where $\boldsymbol{p}$ is a vector with n elements, p_i represents the element of $\boldsymbol{p}$, $i = 1, 2, ..., n$, $\overline{\boldsymbol{p}}$ denotes the mean of all elements of $\boldsymbol{p}$. This function is appropriate for the univariate CPA attack since it only concerns the power consumption at a single time instant.

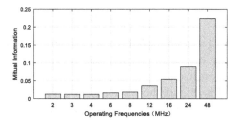

Fig. 6. Theoretical relation between operating frequencies and mutual information.

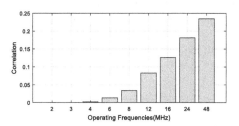

Fig. 7. Theoretical relation between operating frequencies and correlation.

Algorithm 1. Measurement reconstruction

Input:

The physical power consumption traces T_c at a certain frequency f_c;

Output:

Several sets of power consumption P_f of the cryptographic device operated at frequency f such that $f \in F$;

1: Acquire $d_{x,s}$ from Eq. 1;

2: $d_{x,s}$ can be expressed as $d_{x,s} = Amp \circ HW(x)e^{-\alpha s}$

3: **for all** f such that $f \in F$ **do**

4: $\quad P_f = Amp \circ HW(x_1)e^{-\alpha s} + Amp \circ HW(x_2)e^{-\alpha(s+\frac{1}{f})}$;

5: **end for**

6: **return** P_f;

The correlation between f and ρ is shown in Fig. 7, we can see that there is still a positive correlation between f and ρ.

From what we have discussed above, the power reconstruction flow of the proposed evaluation methodology is stated as Algorithm 1:

After acquiring the power consumption traces P_f, the analyser should calculate the mutual information MI or the correlation ρ based on Eq. (10) or Eq. (11), then find the vulnerability of the masked circuit operating at different frequencies. The analyser is able to revise the design and implementation or select an appropriate operating frequency of the cryptographic device by this methodology.

5   Experiments

To verify the feasibility of this methodology and identify the relationship between the operating frequency of the cryptographic device and the quantity of the information leakage, we utilize the proposed evaluation methodology to analyze the leakage in the ideal case and the real case respectively.

The experiment is conducted on the hardware implementation of the Regazonni masking scheme. The implementation is a single round of AES where the S-boxes of the mask and the intermediate value are executed serially. The masking scheme is implemented at the operating frequency of 24 MHz. Up to 300,000 traces were collected, and each of the traces contains 1,000 time samples (10 clock cycles).

After calculating from Eq. 2, the differential power consumption D is shown in Fig. 8.

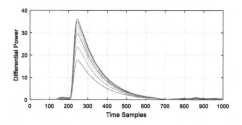

Fig. 8. Differential power consumption. Each trace corresponds to a row of D.

We collected the power consumption traces at a certain operating frequency f_c of 24 MHz, and then the reconstructed power consumption traces P at the other operating frequency f_o can be acquired based on Eq. (8). An example of P (65,536 rows) with f of 12 MHz is shown in Fig. 9, where each trace corresponds to a row of P. In this scenario, the power consumptions of two shares overlap (on the shaded area in Fig. 9) in a single clock cycle and leak sensitive information which can be analyzed by univariate MIA.

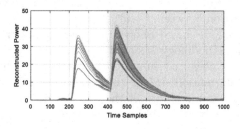

Fig. 9. Reconstructed power consumption. The power consumptions of two shares overlap on the shaded area.

5.1 Ideal Case

In the ideal case, P_{noise} can be regarded as zero. We selected several valid operating frequencies F to acquire the power consumption P_f, where $f \in F$ and $F = \{2, 3, 4, 6, 8, 12, 16, 24, 48\}$ MHz. We utilized MIA to analyze P_f under different f.

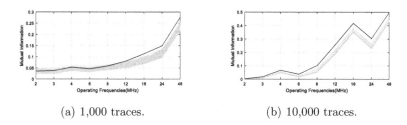

(a) 1,000 traces.   (b) 10,000 traces.

Fig. 10. Results of univariate MIA in the ideal case when the number of traces reaches (a) 1,000 or (b) 10,000

To illustrate the relationship between the operating frequency and the quantity of the information leakage, we give two examples of the results when the number of traces reaches 1,000 and 10,000 respectively, which are shown in Fig. 10(a) and (b). The correct key is plotted in black, while all other keys are plotted in gray. We can see that when the number of traces reaches 1,000, the leakage is detected if $f \in \{12, 16, 24, 48\}$ MHz, and when the number of traces reaches 10,000, the leakage cannot be detected only if $f = 2$ MHz.

To illustrate the relationship between the number of traces and the quantity of the information leakage, we give two examples of the results when the operating frequency is 3 MHz and 24 MHz respectively, which are shown in Fig. 11(a) and (b). From what we can see, given $f = 3$ MHz, the leakage is detected when the number of traces reaches 6,000. Given $f = 24$ MHz, the leakage is detected when the number of traces reaches 800.

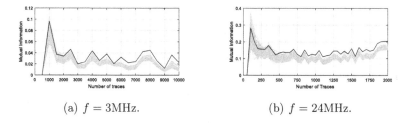

(a) $f = 3$ MHz.   (b) $f = 24$ MHz.

Fig. 11. Results of univariate MIA in the ideal case when the operating frequency f is (a) 3 MHz or (b) 24 MHz.

5.2   Real Case

The real case is to estimate the number of traces to perform an attack in the real-world situation successfully.

We performed the analysis on the reconstructed power consumption $P_{noise,f}$ where the noise is considered. At first we calculate the SNR of the physical power consumption T. The variance of signals in time sample s can be calculated as follows:

$$\sigma^2_{Signal,s} = \sum (d_{m,s} - \overline{d_s})^2,$$

where $\overline{d_s}$ denotes the mean of all elements in vector d_s, and $d_{m,s}$ denotes each element in d_s. The variance of the noise of time sample s in every trace can be calculated as follows:

$$\sigma^2_{noise,s} = \sum (t^{(I)}_{m,s} - \overline{t^{(I)}_s})^2,$$

where $t^{(I)}_s$ denotes a vector of the sample s in each trace with the same intermediate value I. We assume that $\sigma^2_{noise,s}$ is independent of I, so I can be chosen randomly. $\overline{t^{(I)}_s}$ denotes the mean of all elements in vector $t^{(I)}_s$ and $t^{(I)}_{m,s}$ denotes each element in $t^{(I)}_s$. Then the SNR of the physical power consumption can be calculated as follows:

$$\text{SNR} = 10 \cdot \log \frac{\sigma^2_{Signal,s}}{\sigma^2_{noise,s}}. \tag{12}$$

After acquiring the SNR of the physical power consumption, we add noise to P_f to acquire the power consumption in a real-world scenario with Algorithm 2. In our measurement setup, the SNR of the physical power consumption T that calculated from Eq. 12 is 4.68 db. So we add noise to P_f with SNR of 4.68 db, and then acquired the noisy power consumption $P_{noise,f}$, where $f \in \{2, 3, 4, 6, 8, 12, 16, 24, 48\}$ MHz.

Algorithm 2. Noise adding

Input:
   Power consumption P_f;
Output:
   Noisy power consumption $P_{noise,f}$;
1: Acquire $\sigma^2_{noise,s} = \sum (t^{(I)}_{m,s} - \overline{t^{(I)}_s})^2$;
2: **for all** f such that $f \in F$ **do**
3:     $P_{noise,f} = P_f + P_{noise}$ where $P_{noise} \sim N(0, \sigma^2_{noise,s})$;
4: **end for**
5: **return** P_f;

We performed univariate MIA on $P_{noise,f}$ with the same approach utilized in the ideal case. Two examples of the results are shown in Fig. 12(a) and (b) when the number of traces reaches 1,000 and 10,000 respectively. The correct key is plotted in black, while all other keys are plotted in gray. We can see that when the number of traces reaches 1,000, the leakage is detected if $f \in \{24, 48\}$ MHz, and when the number of traces reaches 10,000, the leakage is detected if $f \in \{8, 12, 16, 24, 48\}$ MHz.

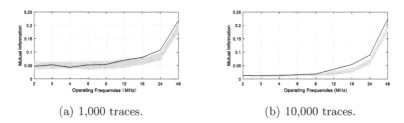

(a) 1,000 traces.   (b) 10,000 traces.

Fig. 12. Results of univariate MIA in the real case when the number of traces reaches (a) 1,000 or (b) 10,000.

Two examples of the results are shown in Fig. 13(a) and (b) when the operating frequency is 3 MHz and 24 MHz respectively. From what we can see, given $f = 3$ MHz, the leakage cannot be detected even when the number of traces reaches 50,000. However, given $f = 24$ MHz, the leakage is detected when the number of traces reaches 1500.

5.3   Final Results

The persistence of leakage has a significant influence on the security of masking schemes, and there is a direct relationship between the influence and the operating frequency of the cryptographic device. Besides the MIA analysis, we utilized the same method to perform the CPA analysis on the circuit. The final results of the experiments are shown in Table 2, where f denotes the operating frequency, and N_{MIA} or N_{CPA} denotes the number of traces required to detect the leakage successfully in the ideal case, while $N_{MIA,noise}$ or $N_{CPA,noise}$ denotes the number of traces required in the real case. $N+$ means that the correct key cannot be recovered when the number of traces reaches N.

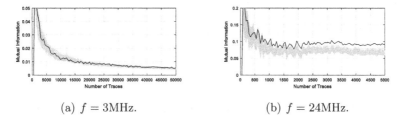

(a) $f = 3$MHz.   (b) $f = 24$MHz.

Fig. 13. Results of univariate MIA in the real case when the operating frequency f is (a) 3 MHz or (b) 24 MHz.

Table 2. Experimental results

f (MHz)	N_{MIA}	$N_{MIA,noise}$	N_{CPA}	$N_{CPA,noise}$
2	10^7+	10^7+	10^7+	10^7+
3	6000	10^5+	10^7+	10^7+
4	2100	27500	10^5+	10^7+
6	2300	16000	10^5+	10^5+
8	1300	9700	10^5+	10^5+
12	1000	2800	92500	10^5+
16	900	1600	72800	90100
24	800	1500	45580	34000
48	700	800	14800	24300

According to the results of these experiments, we can draw a conclusion that the masked circuit is easier to be attacked since the number of traces decreases when the frequency becomes larger. Besides, the masked circuit generates information leakage in the ideal case although the operating frequency is rather low, while it is relatively safe in the real case. For example, in the ideal case, when the operating frequency $f = 3$ MHz, the correct key can be recovered by MIA if the number of traces reaches 6000. However, in the real case, when the operating frequency $f \leq 3$ MHz, the correct key cannot be recovered by MIA even if the number of traces reaches 100,000.

The reason for these results is as follows: When f increases, the length of the clock cycle t_c decreases accordingly. However, the duration τ of the differential power consumption trace is unaffected. Thus, the overlapping area of the power consumption of different shares becomes larger, and the masked circuit is easier to be attacked with f increasing. Besides, when the attacker performs higher-order univariate MIA or CPA attacks, the number of traces will decrease with the operating frequency becoming higher. So a high operating frequency leads to the vulnerability of the masking scheme. The noise in the real case is another significant factor that influences the efficiency of attacks.

However, a rather low operating frequency has a significant influence on the efficiency of the cryptographic device. There is a tradeoff between the efficiency and the safety of the cryptographic device. Thus, it is important for the designer of masking schemes to select an appropriate operating frequency to keep the masked circuit invulnerable.

6   Conclusion

In this paper, we find that an excessively high operating frequency could cause a pretty serious security vulnerability in the FPGA implementation of a cryptographic algorithm with side-channel countermeasures, especially masking. After investigating the physical reason of the information leakage of the FPGA, we propose a generic evaluation methodology derived from CPA and MIA that can be utilized to analyze the security of FPGA implementation of a cryptographic algorithm with masking countermeasure at different operating frequencies.

By this methodology, the evaluator is able to quantitatively assess the security of the FPGA in side-channel aspect and come to a conclusion of what range of the operating frequency of the FPGA is secure. Furthermore, the evaluator only needs to collect the measurements when the FPGA operates at an arbitrary frequency rather than collecting the measurement of all possible frequencies exhaustively, which makes this methodology totally feasible in practice.

References

1. AIST: Side-channel attack standard evaluation board (SASEBO). http://www.risec.aist.go.jp/project/sasebo/
2. Akkar, M.-L., Giraud, C.: An implementation of DES and AES, secure against some attacks. In: Koç, Ç.K., Naccache, D., Paar, C. (eds.) CHES 2001. LNCS, vol. 2162, pp. 309–318. Springer, Heidelberg (2001). https://doi.org/10.1007/3-540-44709-1_26
3. Batina, L., Gierlichs, B., Prouff, E., Rivain, M., Standaert, F.X., Veyrat-Charvillon, N.: Mutual information analysis: a comprehensive study. J. Cryptol. **24**(2), 269–291 (2011)
4. Bilgin, B., Gierlichs, B., Nikova, S., Nikov, V., Rijmen, V.: A more efficient AES threshold implementation. In: Pointcheval, D., Vergnaud, D. (eds.) AFRICACRYPT 2014. LNCS, vol. 8469, pp. 267–284. Springer, Cham (2014). https://doi.org/10.1007/978-3-319-06734-6_17
5. Brier, E., Clavier, C., Olivier, F.: Correlation power analysis with a leakage model. In: Joye, M., Quisquater, J.-J. (eds.) CHES 2004. LNCS, vol. 3156, pp. 16–29. Springer, Heidelberg (2004). https://doi.org/10.1007/978-3-540-28632-5_2
6. Chari, S., Rao, J.R., Rohatgi, P.: Template attacks. In: Kaliski, B.S., Koç, K., Paar, C. (eds.) CHES 2002. LNCS, vol. 2523, pp. 13–28. Springer, Heidelberg (2003). https://doi.org/10.1007/3-540-36400-5_3
7. Coron, J.-S.: Higher order masking of look-up tables. In: Nguyen, P.Q., Oswald, E. (eds.) EUROCRYPT 2014. LNCS, vol. 8441, pp. 441–458. Springer, Heidelberg (2014). https://doi.org/10.1007/978-3-642-55220-5_25
8. Durvaux, F., Standaert, F.-X.: From improved leakage detection to the detection of points of interests in leakage traces. In: Fischlin, M., Coron, J.-S. (eds.) EUROCRYPT 2016. LNCS, vol. 9665, pp. 240–262. Springer, Heidelberg (2016). https://doi.org/10.1007/978-3-662-49890-3_10
9. Durvaux, F., Standaert, F.-X., Veyrat-Charvillon, N., Mairy, J.-B., Deville, Y.: Efficient selection of time samples for higher-order DPA with projection pursuits. In: Mangard, S., Poschmann, A.Y. (eds.) COSADE 2014. LNCS, vol. 9064, pp. 34–50. Springer, Cham (2015). https://doi.org/10.1007/978-3-319-21476-4_3
10. Fu, S., et al.: Multi-byte power analysis: a generic approach based on linear regression. IEEE Access **6**, 67511–67518 (2018)
11. Gierlichs, B., Batina, L., Tuyls, P., Preneel, B.: Mutual information analysis. In: Oswald, E., Rohatgi, P. (eds.) CHES 2008. LNCS, vol. 5154, pp. 426–442. Springer, Heidelberg (2008). https://doi.org/10.1007/978-3-540-85053-3_27

12. Kocher, P., Jaffe, J., Jun, B.: Differential power analysis. In: Wiener, M. (ed.) CRYPTO 1999. LNCS, vol. 1666, pp. 388–397. Springer, Heidelberg (1999). https://doi.org/10.1007/3-540-48405-1_25

13. Mangard, S., Oswald, E., Popp, T.: Power Analysis Attacks: Revealing the Secrets of Smart Cards, vol. 31. Springer, New York (2008)

14. Mangard, S., Popp, T., Gammel, B.M.: Side-channel leakage of masked CMOS gates. In: Menezes, A. (ed.) CT-RSA 2005. LNCS, vol. 3376, pp. 351–365. Springer, Heidelberg (2005). https://doi.org/10.1007/978-3-540-30574-3_24

15. Mangard, S., Pramstaller, N., Oswald, E.: Successfully attacking masked AES hardware implementations. In: Rao, J.R., Sunar, B. (eds.) CHES 2005. LNCS, vol. 3659, pp. 157–171. Springer, Heidelberg (2005). https://doi.org/10.1007/11545262_12

16. Mather, L., Oswald, E., Bandenburg, J., Wójcik, M.: Does my device leak information? An *a priori* statistical power analysis of leakage detection tests. In: Sako, K., Sarkar, P. (eds.) ASIACRYPT 2013. LNCS, vol. 8269, pp. 486–505. Springer, Heidelberg (2013). https://doi.org/10.1007/978-3-642-42033-7_25

17. Moradi, A., Mischke, O.: On the simplicity of converting leakages from multivariate to univariate. In: Bertoni, G., Coron, J.-S. (eds.) CHES 2013. LNCS, vol. 8086, pp. 1–20. Springer, Heidelberg (2013). https://doi.org/10.1007/978-3-642-40349-1_1

18. Nassar, M., Souissi, Y., Guilley, S., Danger, J.L.: RSM: a small and fast countermeasure for AES, secure against 1st and 2nd-order zero-offset SCAs. In: Proceedings of the Conference on Design, Automation and Test in Europe, pp. 1173–1178. EDA Consortium (2012)

19. Nikova, S., Rechberger, C., Rijmen, V.: Threshold implementations against side-channel attacks and glitches. In: Ning, P., Qing, S., Li, N. (eds.) ICICS 2006. LNCS, vol. 4307, pp. 529–545. Springer, Heidelberg (2006). https://doi.org/10.1007/11935308_38

20. Oswald, E., Mangard, S., Pramstaller, N., Rijmen, V.: A side-channel analysis resistant description of the AES S-box. In: Gilbert, H., Handschuh, H. (eds.) FSE 2005. LNCS, vol. 3557, pp. 413–423. Springer, Heidelberg (2005). https://doi.org/10.1007/11502760_28

21. Prouff, E., Rivain, M., Bevan, R.: Statistical analysis of second order differential power analysis. IEEE Trans. Comput. **58**(6), 799–811 (2009)

22. Regazzoni, F., Wang, Y., Standaert, F.X., et al.: FPGA implementations of the AES masked against power analysis attacks. In: Proceedings of COSADE, vol. 2011, pp. 56–66 (2011)

23. Tang, M., Guo, Z., Heuser, A., Ren, Y., Li, J., Danger, J.L.: PFDA flexible higher-order masking scheme. IEEE Trans. Comput. Aided Des. Integr. Circuits Syst. **36**(8), 1327–1339 (2017)

24. Tang, M., et al.: A generic TC-based method to find the weakness in different phases of masking schemes. Tsinghua Sci. Technol. **23**(5), 574–585 (2018)

25. Waddle, J., Wagner, D.: Towards efficient second-order power analysis. In: Joye, M., Quisquater, J.-J. (eds.) CHES 2004. LNCS, vol. 3156, pp. 1–15. Springer, Heidelberg (2004). https://doi.org/10.1007/978-3-540-28632-5_1

Authentication

Privacy-Preserving eID Derivation
for Self-Sovereign Identity Systems

Andreas Abraham[1]([envelope]), Felix Hörandner[1], Olamide Omolola[1],
and Sebastian Ramacher[2]

[1] Graz University of Technology, Graz, Austria
{andreas.abraham,felix.hoerandner,olamide.omolola}@iaik.tugraz.at
[2] AIT Austrian Institute of Technology, Vienna, Austria
sebastian.ramacher@ait.ac.at

Abstract. As centralized identity management solutions amass identity data, they increasingly become attractive targets for cyber attacks,
which entail consequences for users that range from service disruptions
to exposure of sensitive user data. Self-sovereign identity (SSI) strives to
return the control over identity data to the users by building on decentralized architectures. However, the adoption of SSI systems is currently
hampered by a lack of qualified identity data that satisfies the services'
requirements. Additionally, there is a gap w.r.t the user's privacy: Intermediate components (e.g., importers or SSI network nodes) learn the
users' sensitive attributes during the derivation of eID data.

In this work, we present a decentralized eID derivation concept that
preserves the users' privacy while maintaining the data's trustworthiness
without revealing the plain data to any component outside the users' control. Our proposed system also enables users to selectively disclose only
relevant parts of the imported identity assertion according to the service's requirements. We also implement and evaluate a proof-of-concept
to demonstrate the feasibility and performance of our concept.

Keywords: Qualified electronic identity · Self-Sovereign Identity ·
Distributed ledger · Identity derivation · Distributed trust · Privacy

1 Introduction

Online services need to identify and authenticate users in order to authorize
them and to provide a personalized experience. These services rely on digital
identities [9], which combine identity attributes with means to authenticate the
users. To offer sensitive services, for example in the context of eGovernment, the
employed identities may need to satisfy additional requirements, which are captured by qualified electronic identities (eIDs) [22]. These qualified eIDs provide
assurance of the attributes' correctness, bind the eID to the related person, and
ensure uniqueness.

S. Ramacher—Work done while the author was with Graz University of Technology.

© Springer Nature Switzerland AG 2020
J. Zhou et al. (Eds.): ICICS 2019, LNCS 11999, pp. 307–323, 2020.
https://doi.org/10.1007/978-3-030-41579-2_18

Companies and governments created their own identity management (IdM) solutions to enroll and maintain their users' digital identities or eIDs. Centralized systems accumulate huge amounts of (sensitive) data about their users, which, of course, attract attackers aiming to misuse or sell the stolen data, as exemplified by two recent incidents: Attackers stole sensitive data of 143 million users from Equifax [23] and information of 50 million users from Facebook [20]. The problem of centralized IdM systems is that users are not in full control over their identity data.

SSI and eIDs. The concept of self-sovereign identity (SSI) systems [4,25,30] tackles this issue by making users the sovereign owners of their identities. SSI extends on user-centric identity management [32], where the identity data is kept in the users' domain, by employing distributed ledger technology (DLT) and decentralized public key infrastructure (DPKI), which enables service providers (SPs) to verify the authenticity and trustworthiness of data provided by the user. However, SSI systems currently lack qualified eID data, which represents a hurdle for their wide-spread adoption. One promising approach to enrich SSI systems with qualified eID data is to develop a derivation process that imports qualified eID data from existing sources. Such a derivation process not only needs to translate between different data formats and protocols used in the existing eID system and the SSI system but also has to maintain the data's trustworthiness.

Related Work. eID derivation and the import into an SSI system has seen recent progress with conceptually different approaches. Firstly, centralized approaches, such as ARIES and LIGHTest[1], rely on a centralized component to perform the derivation and import the transformed data into the SSI system. In the ARIES ecosystem, a new trusted identity provider (IdP) is introduced for each domain [8]. Similarly, LIGHTest adds a second IdP on top of existing IdPs. Consequently, users and SPs need to place a high amount of trust in these central services. Secondly, to reduce these trust requirements, Abraham et al. [2] proposed a decentralized derivation process for qualified eIDs. In their concept, a network of nodes ensures that the qualified data has been transformed correctly. Technically, the nodes run an extended version of the redundant byzantine fault tolerance (RBFT) [6] protocol, where the nodes perform the identity data transformation, and – if the transformation was performed correctly – generate a multi-signature [17]. This efficiently-verifiable multi-signature signifies that the derivation has been performed correctly and that the data can be accepted as a qualified eID.

However, for all these derivation approaches, preserving the users' privacy was beyond their scope: The intermediate parties involved in the transformation process (e.g. centralized importer or network nodes) access the users' eID attributes in plain. Additionally, when authenticating to a SP and providing required attributes, users are forced to hand over the whole transformed identity document which may expose more attributes than strictly required by the SP.

---

[1] https://www.aries-project.eu/, https://www.lightest.eu/.

Our Contribution. In this paper, we propose a decentralized eID derivation concept for SSI systems that tackles the above-presented privacy issues while maintaining the trustworthiness of the transformed data.

Privacy-Preserving Derivation. Our derivation concept combines state-of-the-art cryptographic mechanisms to preserve privacy so that no intermediate party can access the users' identity data in plain: Users generate non-interactive zero-knowledge (NIZK) proofs that they correctly transformed their identity assertions issued by existing eID systems. In an attestation process, the network of SSI nodes verifies the validity of the proof, without ever learning the plain values. After reaching a consensus, the nodes generate a multi-signature which serves as an attestation that the resulting data has been correctly derived from a valid qualified eID.

Selective Disclosure. Our concept also enables users to selectively disclose only a subset of the attributes originally contained in the issued identity assertion. Therefore, users are able to only reveal the minimal data required by the SP. In our concept, users generate a second NIZK proof, which states that the disclosed attributes were part of the original identity assertion without revealing the whole assertion.

Revocation. This work also considers the issues of revoking obsolete eID data. We propose to utilize the features of a distributed ledger (DL) to reduce the dependence on a single point of failure (e.g., a central party that maintains a revocation list). To address privacy concerns, the revocation list only stores commitments of identity assertions rather than the sensitive data itself.

Implementation and Evaluation. To underline the feasibility of our concept, we implemented a proof-of-concept (PoC) and used it to perform benchmarks in real-world scenarios, such as the derivation and attestation process for eID data as well as selective disclosure of attributes to a SP.

2 Background

This section describes background technologies. We recall relevant cryptographic mechanisms in Appendix A.

The **Self-Sovereign Identity (SSI)** model presents a new IdM concept, which grants the owners of digital identities complete control over their data. Looking at the evolution of identity models [32], SSI can be seen as the next step after the user-centric model with the advantage of not having to trust a central authority. SSIs ensure the security and privacy of users' identity data, full portability of the data, no central authorities, and data integrity. Consequently, only the owners of the data can alter their identity data. SSI is a relatively new concept which does not provide a strict architectural definition but rather conceptional requirements. Mühle et al. [25] have presented the architecture of such SSI system and identified identification, authentication, verifiable claims and attribute storage as essential components of SSI.

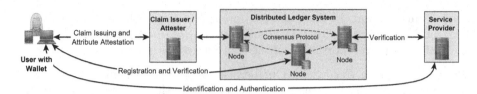

Fig. 1. High-level overview of an SSI system including main actors.

From a **technical perspective** and as depicted in Fig. 1, one of the core building blocks of an SSI system is the DL which serves as decentralized public key infrastructure (DPKI) and provides properties such as immutability and transparency. An SSI system requires identifiers which do not depend on an issuing party, such as a decentralized identifier (DID). Users create such identifiers and register them at the DL. Then, trusted claim issuers attest attributes of a user. As users in such a system should be in full control. The users' identity data, DIDs, and private key material are stored in the users' domain, whereas the public information of a user is stored on the ledger, including public keys and revocation information. When performing authentication at a SP, this SP can then verify the users' claims ownership as well as attestations.

DIDs [29] are designed and used to enable SSIs because they don't depend on a central issuing party. They are URLs that provide a way for trustworthy interactions with its subject. DIDs redirect to DID Documents stored on a DL. These Documents contain three major sections: service endpoints, verification methods, and proof purposes. Service endpoints are URIs pointing to a service provided by a DID subject. Verification methods describe cryptographic methods that can be used with proof purposes to prove, e.g., the integrity of the DID Document or the relationship of an entity to the DID. DID Documents optionally contain public key(s) of the DID subject.

Systems maintaining a (DL) rely on a **consensus mechanism**. Software bugs, administrator mistakes or faulty hardware parts can introduce faults into systems that require high availability. Such faults are called Byzantine faults, which include service interruption and unexpected behavior among others. A Byzantine fault tolerance protocol (BFT) [14] is a replication algorithm for building fault-tolerant systems. The Robust BFT (RBFT) protocol is an extension that provides acceptable performance when faults occur [6]. This is achieved by executing multiple instances of the BFT protocol simultaneously, and each of the instances has a primary replica operating on different machines, all instances get the same client requests.

3   Concept

This section presents our concept to derive qualified eIDs, issued by an existing eID system, into an SSI system without relying on a central trusted party while preserving the users' privacy. This derivation process builds a chain of trust

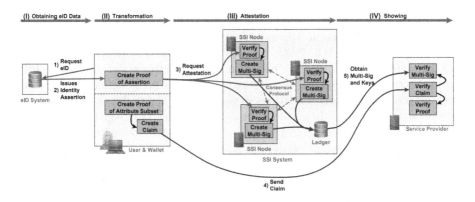

Fig. 2. Actors and main processes of our eID derivation process.

starting with the identity data issued by an existing traditional eID system via an SSI system to the final receiver, which overall facilitates and simplifies the adoption of SSI systems. Figure 2 depicts the architecture including all involved actors as well as the steps of the eID derivation process.

3.1 Actors

Our architecture consists of the following actors, depicted in Fig. 2: (1) The **users** aim to import their existing eID into an SSI system to use these eID data for authentication towards service providers. (2) The **existing eID system** holds qualified identity data about the user. Examples include governmental IdM systems that were rolled out to enable digital administration processes. (3) Users install a **wallet** software in their domain, which maintains private key material as well as the users' identity data. These identity data are cryptographically linked to the key-pair by utilizing DIDs. Therefore, the owner of the secret key can prove the ownership of the identity data. (4) **SSI systems** utilize distributed ledger technologies (DLT) to maintain their users' identities without the need for a central trusted authority. In SSI systems, nodes are holding a copy of the ledger and perform a consensus protocol to agree on which data should be written to the ledger. The ledger serves as a DPKI; it only stores public information, such as public keys within DID documents, whereas sensitive identity data are stored off-ledger. (5) Users eventually want to get access to a **service provider** (SP). The SPs require users to authenticate themselves by presenting ownership of identity attributes to grant access to the service.

3.2 eID Derivation Process

Our generic eID derivation process consists of four main processes: *obtaining eID data* from an existing eID system, the *transformation* to a format supported by the SSI system, *attestation* by the SSI system, and the *showing* of the attributes to SPs. Below, we describe these processes and map them to Protocol 1.

Throughout the protocol, we require digital signatures and NIZK proofs, which we formally discuss in Appendix A. The signatures ensure the authenticity of the identity data. For the NIZK proof system, we need to define the relations that guarantee that the user is in possession of an identity assertion from an IdP and knows that corresponding attributes. We will informally define the relations here and present the precise relations in Sect. 4 since they inherently depend on the choice of algorithms. In general, our goal is to show that – given a signature on an encoding of the attributes – one knows the attributes without revealing them. Put in the language of the NIZK proof systems, we design a relation R expressing that fact. So, let σ be a signature on some encoding $\mathcal{E}^2$ of the attributes $A = \{a_1, \ldots, a_n\}$ valid for a public key pk. We say that $(\sigma, A) \in R$ if and only if $\mathsf{Verify}(\sigma, \mathsf{pk}, \mathcal{E}(A)) = 1$.

During the showing of the attributes, some of the attributes are sent in plain to the service, and the user proves knowledge of the remaining attributes. In this case we have publicly known attributes $A_p = \{a_1, \ldots, a_m\}$ and secret attributes $A_s = \{a_{m+1}, \ldots, a_n\}$ with $A = A_p \cup A_s$, and we define the relation R_p as $((\sigma, A_p), A_s) \in R_p$ if and only if $\mathsf{Verify}(\sigma, \mathsf{pk}, \mathcal{E}(A_p \cup A_s)) = 1$.

(I) Obtaining eID Data. Initially, the user operating her wallet imports her eID data from an existing eID system. The wallet communicates with the eID system through an identity protocol where the user performs identification and authentication. With the user's consent, the eID system issues an identity assertion of the user's data. This identity assertion includes the user's DID, which binds the identity data to the user. Additionally, the eID system adds a random value (e.g., in our case 256-bit) to prevent guessing attacks when only showing subsets of the assertion to SPs (c.f. Sect. 4). Finally, the assertion is issued to the user's wallet.

(II) Transformation. The identity assertion not only needs to be transformed into a data format supported by the SSI system, but also must remain trustworthy. As the attributes must not be exposed to the SSI system, we employ NIZK proofs. The user's wallet generates a proof that (a) the identity assertion is valid, and (b) the user's attributes are certified by this assertion.

(III) Attestation. With the proof, the user is able to convince the SSI system's nodes that the transformation has been performed correctly. The nodes record on the ledger that they have checked the derivation's correctness and that the identity assertion's data were qualified.

To ensure that rogue nodes cannot write a corrupted record to the ledger, the SSI system performs a consensus protocol between the nodes. Convinced nodes generate a signature, and hand the result to the other participating nodes. After the nodes received and checked a sufficient number of signatures, they aggregate the single signatures into a multi-signature. This multi-signature serves as a means of attestation and therefore assures SPs that the data correlates to the sender and a qualified eID source issued the data. A transaction is written to the ledger, which contains the signature of the identity assertion, the multi-signature

---

^{2} For example, $\mathcal{E}$ would encode the attributes as SAML v2 identity assertion [27].

In the following, let Π_R and Π_{R_p} be a NIZK proof systems for relations R and R_p with previously set up common reference strings crs_R and crs_{R_p}, respectively. Let Σ be a signature scheme and Σ_M be a multi signature scheme.

(I) Obtaining eID Data:

    on user's wallet

      1. requests eID data from existing IdP (with authentication)

    on IdP

      2. issues/returns a signature on the identity assertion, i.e. $\sigma \leftarrow \Sigma.\mathsf{Sign}(\mathsf{sk}_{\mathsf{IdP}}, A)$ for attributes $A = \{a_1, \ldots, a_n\}$

(II) Transformation:

    on user's wallet

      1. create NIZK proof $\pi \leftarrow \Pi_R.\mathsf{Proof}(\mathsf{crs}_R, \sigma, A)$ and send proof π and σ

(III) Attestation:

    on each node s (in set S selected by SSI system) in consensus protocol

      1. verify proof $\Pi_R.\mathsf{Verify}(\mathsf{crs}_R, \sigma, \pi)$ and abort if verification fails

      2. create signature as acceptance: $\sigma_s \leftarrow \Sigma_M.\mathsf{Sign}(\mathsf{sk}_s, \sigma)$

      3. send σ_s to all other participating nodes

      4. verify signatures from other nodes s', $\Sigma_M.\mathsf{Verify}(\mathsf{pk}_{s'}, \sigma, \sigma_{s'})$, and abort if verification fails

      5. aggregate all multi-signature parts: $\sigma_M \leftarrow \Sigma_M.\mathsf{ASigs}((\mathsf{pk}_{s'}, \sigma_{s'})_{s' \in S}, \sigma)$

      6. write transaction to ledger, $T \leftarrow (\sigma, \sigma_M, S)$, and send transaction id to user

(IV) Showing:

    on user's wallet

      1. create NIZK proof $\pi_S \leftarrow \Pi_{R_p}.\mathsf{Proof}(\mathsf{crs}_{R_p}, (\sigma, A_p), A_s)$ for a set of private attributes $A_s = \{a_i\} \subset A$ and public attributes $A_p = A \setminus A_s$

      2. send verifiable claim $\mathsf{cl} \leftarrow (\mathsf{DID}, A_p, \sigma, \pi_S, c)$ and $\sigma \leftarrow \Sigma.\mathsf{Sign}(\mathsf{sk}_U, \mathsf{cl})$ that includes a challenge c of the SP

    on SP

      3. verify signature on claim: $\Sigma.\mathsf{Verify}(\mathsf{pk}, \mathsf{cl}, \sigma)$ with pk looked up from ledger

      4. verify proof π_S: $\Pi_{R_p}.\mathsf{Verify}(\mathsf{crs}_{R_p}, (\sigma, A_p), \pi_S)$

      5. lookup from ledger: derivation transaction $T \leftarrow (\sigma, \sigma_M, S)$

      6. verify multi-signature σ_M: $\Sigma_M.\mathsf{AVerify}(\Sigma_M.\mathsf{APKs}((\mathsf{pk}_s)_{s \in S}), \sigma, \sigma_M)$

Protocol 1: Derivation protocol.

as well as a list of participating nodes, to be later used to verify the attestation. In Protocol 1, we assume that the used multi-signatures are unique, i.e. any two aggregated signatures over the same signature parts result in the same value so that all SSI nodes arrive at the same aggregated signature which they add to their ledgers. Otherwise, the nodes need to agree on one multi-signature.

(IV) Showing. To get access to a service, the user needs to authenticate herself and provide a set of identity attributes. This process is split into three parts: Firstly, we rely on SSI concepts to demonstrate ownership of a DID via a challenge-response protocol. Secondly, we use a multi-signature as an attestation that the derivation process has been performed correctly. Thirdly, we achieve selective disclosure of identity attributes by employing additional NIZK proofs.

The user selects which attributes should be disclosed to the SP. Next, the wallet generates a NIZK proof that these attributes are contained in the original identity assertion. This proof, the selected subset of attributes, and a SP-defined challenge are placed into a verifiable credential including a signature of the user over the verifiable credential. The signed credential is sent to the SP.

The SP initially verifies the ownership of the transmitted data by obtaining the user's public key registered at the SSI system and verifying whether the user was able to generate a verifiable claim that contains a previously chosen challenge. Then, the SP verifies the attestation that the derivation has been performed correctly by verifying the nodes' multi-signature which is recorded on the ledger. In the final verification step, the SP verifies the proof stating that the disclosed attributes are contained in the original identity assertion.

Revocation. Despite the great benefits of privacy-preserving technologies for the user, such technologies also create challenges when it comes to revocation: Only the user and the existing eID system can access the data in plain and are therefore able to detect changes. This section describes two possible approaches to implement the revocation process by relying either on the user or the existing eID system.

One approach is to make users responsible to manually re-import changed identity data and revoke obsolete attributes. To reduce the burden on the user, we propose that the user's wallet periodically checks whether the user's data are still up to date by requesting the data from the existing eID system. For example, OpenID Connect allows the relying party (i.e., wallet) to access the user information over a long period of time by repeatedly refreshing the access token.

Alternatively, the existing eID system can be made responsible to report when changes in its users' data require revocation of issued identity assertions. While this approach might require changes at the eID system, the users are taken out of the loop, which reduces the risk of (intentionally) forgotten updates, which overall increases the reliability of data.

The SSI system holds the revocation list. The user's wallet or existing eID system instructs the SSI system to record information about revoked identity assertions on the ledger. During authentication, the SPs verify the revocation status of an identity assertion against the distributed revocation list.

Our revocation approach (1) eliminates the central point of failure of the revocation list holder since the DL is utilized, and (2) improves privacy since the revocation process is designed so that intermediaries (e.g., SSI network or the origin identity system) cannot learn from the metadata.

4   Concrete Instantiation

As discussed in Sect. 3, we prove knowledge of a message signed by the IdP and that the signature verifies for this message. Therefore, we require that the signature schemes allow us to prove knowledge of a signed message or parts thereof efficiently. However, in almost any practically used signature scheme messages are hashed using SHA2 or SHA3. The problem is that proving pre-images of those hashes is relatively expensive in runtime and proof size. Until proof systems for typical hash functions get more efficient without designing low complexity versions,[3] we focus on signature schemes with hash functions where knowledge of pre-images is efficiently provable. Changing the signature scheme on existing IdMs is trivial from a technical perspective since they support more than one signature scheme by default and allow the addition of new schemes.

As shown by Fuchsbauer and Pointcheval [18] as well as Chase et al. [16], Waters' signatures [31] work particularly well in conjunction with non-interactive zero-knowledge proofs. More specifically, the NIZK proof system Π_{cF} [18] enables us to show knowledge of the hash pre-image for Waters' signature. So, we instantiate our architecture using Waters' signatures and Π_{cF} as well as BLS signatures [11] on the validator side.[4]

Before we go into details, we want to note that the verification algorithm of Waters' signature scheme is in particular well suited (cf. Appendix A). Indeed, if we rewrite the hash function $H(m) = u_0 \cdot \prod_{i=1}^{n} u_i^{m_i}$ as used in the signature scheme to $F = \mathcal{F}(m) = u_0^{-1} \cdot H(m)$ and given a signature σ on m, the verification equation has no other dependency on the message other than F. As a consequence of [18], we know that F does not leak any information on the message m. Therefore, we can reformulate the relations as follows: if the signature σ is valid w.r.t. F, i.e. for $\sigma = (\alpha, \beta)$ the equation $e(\alpha, g) \cdot e(u_0 \cdot F, \beta) = e(g_2, \mathsf{pk})$ holds true, then we can simply define the relation such that $(F, A) \in R'$ if and only if $F = \mathcal{F}(\mathcal{E}(A))$. Thus, we obtain an equivalent relation that is easier to prove. Note though that when using Π_{cF}, the relation is implicitly extended with bit commitments to each bit of the message. If $m = \mathcal{E}(A) = m_1 \| \dots \| m_n$, then $((F, c_1, \dots, c_n), (m, r_1, \dots, r_n)) \in R'$ if and only if $F = \mathcal{F}(m) \wedge \bigwedge_{i=1}^{n} c_i = \mathsf{Com}(m_i; r_i)$. Therefore, we will use this relation and the corresponding variant for partially public attributes.

The hash function H has another useful property: Given a message $m = m_1 \| m_2$, we can decompose $H(m)$ into parts that only depend on m_1 and m_2, respectively, i.e. $H(m) = u_0 \cdot \mathcal{F}_1(m_1) \cdot \mathcal{F}_2(m_2)$. This fact is useful when we consider the attributes encoded in an identity assertion. In particular, this observation helps if the encoding $\mathcal{E}$ introduces publicly known data, e.g. XML formatting in SAML [27], that is completely independent of the attributes. There is no need to prove those bits.

(I) Obtaining eID data. The user authenticates herself towards the IdP. After successfully authentication, the IdP creates an identity assertion σ for attributes $A = \{a_1, \dots, a_n\}$ by signing an encoded version of the attributes,[5] $\sigma \leftarrow \mathsf{Waters.Sign(sk, A)}$, which is forwarded to the user.

(II) Transformation. The user receives the signature σ and verifies it using the IdP's public key pk, that is $\mathsf{Waters.Verify(pk, A, \sigma)} = 1$. Now, to produce

---

[3] For example, see [3,15,21] for recent progress in both areas.

[4] With the choice of BLS as multi-signature scheme, we follow Abraham et al. [2]. Thus, the validator nodes do not need a secure random number generator for signing.

[5] We slightly abuse notion and use A instead of always specifying the encoding $\mathcal{E}$.

the proof, the user computes $F = \mathcal{F}(A) = u_0^{-1} \cdot H(A)$ and commitments c_i to each bit of the encoding of A. Then, it produces a proof π w.r.t. relation R: $\pi \leftarrow \Pi_R.\mathsf{Proof}(\mathsf{crs}_R, (F, c_1, \ldots, c_n), (A, r_1, \ldots, r_n))$. It sends $(\sigma, F, c_1, \ldots, c_n, \pi)$ to the nodes for attestation.

(III) Attestation. Each node $s \in S$ receives the identity assertion $\sigma = (\alpha, \beta)$, F, the commitments $c_1, \ldots, c_n$ and the corresponding proof π. First, they verify that signature w.r.t. $u_0 \cdot F$ by checking $e(\alpha, g) \cdot e(u_0 \cdot F, \beta) = e(g_2, \mathsf{pk})$ for the IdP's public key pk. Secondly, they verify the proof, i.e. $\Pi_R.\mathsf{Verify}(\mathsf{crs}_R, \sigma, \pi) = 1$. If the proof is valid, they produce BLS signatures $\sigma_s \leftarrow \mathsf{BLS.Sign}(\mathsf{sk}_s, F)$. The signatures are then exchanged between the nodes, and if they all verify, the signatures are aggregated to $\sigma_M \leftarrow \mathsf{BLS.ASigs}((\mathsf{pk}_s, \sigma_s)_{s \in S}, F)$ and (F, σ_M, S) is written to the ledger.

(IV) Showing. To show some attributes $A_p \subset A$ to a service, the user computes a proof as in the transformation step, however now only $A_s = A \setminus A_p$ are kept secret and proofs are relative to relation R_p, i.e. $\pi_s \leftarrow \Pi_{R_p}.\mathsf{Proof}(\mathsf{crs}_{R_p}, (F', c_1', \ldots, c_{n'}'), (A_s, r_1', \ldots, r_{n'}'))$ where $F' = F \cdot \mathcal{F}_p(A_p)^{-1} = \mathcal{F}_s(A_s)$ and the commitments c_i' are picked based on the choice of attributes. The user then sends $(A_p, F, c_1', \ldots, c_{n'}', \pi_s)$ to the service, which checks whether $\mathsf{BLS.AVerify}(\mathsf{BLS.APKs}((\mathsf{pk}_s)_{s \in S}), F, \sigma_M) = 1$ and $\Pi_{R_p}.\mathsf{Verify}(\mathsf{crs}_{R_p}, (F \cdot \mathcal{F}_p(A_p)^{-1}, c_1', \ldots, c_{n'}'), \pi_s) = 1$ hold. We note that it suffices to write F to the ledger, since the validator nodes already verified the signature. Similarly, it suffices to store F in the revocation list. This makes it also easier for IdPs to revoke identity assertions. Otherwise, they would have to store the randomness used in the Sign algorithm of the Waters signature scheme to recreate σ or store σ itself.

Furthermore, recall that one of the attributes is selected uniformly at random and never shown to the validator nodes or the services. Hence, we can interpret $H(m)$ and $\mathcal{F}(m)$, respectively, as unconditionally hiding commitment to m which already contains the randomness. The proofs can then be seen as a proof of knowledge of the opening to that commitment.

Security Analysis. We also give an informal security analysis and present the intuition for the security of our system. We consider the two main security properties of the system: First of all, users must not be able to present an assertion to the validator nodes that was not signed by the IdP or where they do not have knowledge of the attributes contained in the assertion. Assuming that an adversary would be able to convince the validator nodes otherwise – provided that there are enough honest nodes available to ensure the correct functioning of the RBFT protocol – the adversary is either able to produce a forgery of the Waters' signature scheme or produce a proof without knowing any witness. The former would break unforgeability of the Water's signature scheme and the latter would break soundness of Π_{cF}. Similarly, when users authenticate to an SP, a user must not be able to authenticate itself if the attributes are not known or the assertion was not checked by the validator network. Again, an adversary being able to do so would break soundness of the proof system or the unforgeability of BLS signatures.

Table 1. Average and standard deviation of benchmark results (in ms) to generate and verify signatures, proofs and showings, and to aggregate BLS signatures.

Benchmark	Generation	Verification
BLS signature	1.36 ± 0.49	1.35 ± 0.50
BLS aggregation	1.19 ± 0.63	(as above)
Waters signature	3.98 ± 4.85	1.44 ± 0.52
Proof	2507.20 ± 74.10	25.10 ± 3.06
Showing of family name	2324.86 ± 97.76	24.36 ± 4.60
... full name	2136.48 ± 108.50	22.68 ± 3.75
... full name & birth date	1851.39 ± 100.32	20.14 ± 3.03

Second, neither SPs nor the validator nodes should be able to learn any of the hidden attributes. Assume that an adversary would be able to reveal one of the attributes that were not revealed by the users itself. Given that an adversary only gets to see the unconditionally-hiding commitment F and the corresponding proof, presenting the hidden attributes would mean that the adversary broke the zero-knowledge property of the proof system.

5 Benchmarks and Evaluation

To show the feasibility of our proposed architecture, we implemented a PoC based on the Java Pairing-Based Cryptography library (JPBC) [13]. Parameters were chosen according to recent estimations for 100-bit security [24]. We focus on the implementation and evaluation of the schemes discussed in Sect. 4, as these have to be employed in addition to the SSI system and its consensus protocol.

We measured different stages of our derivation process when transforming a SAML identity assertions of roughly 6 KB in size. The assertions we used for testing include the full name and date of birth among others as attributes. The benchmarks were executed on a year 2014 laptop using an Intel i5-4300U CPU at 1.90 GHz with 8 GB RAM running under Ubuntu 18.10. The results shown in Table 1 represent the average run times and standard deviation over 1000 runs. We measured (1) signing and verification of Waters and BLS signatures, (2) aggregation of 100 BLS signatures and the corresponding public keys without additional signature verification, (3) time needed to generate and verify NIZK proofs of knowledge of the attributes, and (4) generation and verification of proofs to selectively disclose different subset of attributes.

The results show that it is feasible to apply our concept to real-world scenarios. Both BLS and Waters signature generation, as well as verification, are very fast on our benchmark laptop. Aggregation of BLS signatures is also very fast. The generation of proofs is the most expensive task performed by the user's device. Nevertheless, a proof only has to be generated infrequently: once when deriving (or re-importing) the eID data and once when showing the data to a

SP. Note that the showing proofs can be reused for various SPs thereby amortizing the proof calculation time. Of course, we expect these times to improve further when deployed on more powerful hardware or implemented with highly optimized bilinear pairing libraries such as RELIC [5].

6 Discussion

Benefits. Our concept enables to import qualified eID data into an SSI system. The imported data are still trustworthy even though the data format has changed. This is ensured by (1) the proof which is calculated to prove the ownership of an identity assertion. (2) The validator network attests the correctness of the proof as well as the ownership of the related identity assertion by applying multi-signature of all verifying nodes. (3) The user selects the attributes she wants to disclose and generates a proof that ensures that these attributes are part of the original assertion.

Our concept further increases the applicability of the SSI system: Since it supports qualified eID data, the SSI system can be applied to use cases where the SP has high trust requirements on the derived eID data.

Our work also improves privacy for eID derivation as follows: (1) Intermediate parties cannot access the identity data in plain. (2) The user can perform selective attribute disclosure when authenticating towards an SP. (3) The revocation process is performed by storing the commitment to the identity assertion on the ledger. Thus, the validator network does not learn anything about the user.

This concept further enables the decoupling of trust relationships. The SPs do not have to directly trust the originator. Instead, we can build up a chain-of-trust connecting various eID systems via the SSI system indirectly with the SPs. The main benefit is that the SSI system can derive eID data from various eID systems, while the SPs do not have to establish explicit trust relationships with these eID systems.

Contrast to Centralized eID Derivation. eID attribute derivation is considered in projects such as ARIES, where eIDs data is derived using the user's passport. After a registration officer verifies the user's identity with her passport, the credentials are issued onto the mobile phone application. LIGHTest has its main focus on a cross-domain trust infrastructure that combines different trust domains and provides verification of electronic transactions across national borders. The National Institute of Standards and Technology (NIST) specified a guideline [26] for deriving eID credential from a smart card, the personal identity verification (PIV) card, to a mobile device. All these projects rely on a trusted central party that is responsible for the derivation. Also, this trusted central party gets access to the user's identity data in plain.

Our work tackles these issues by providing an eID derivation approach that is based on decentralized trust – without a trusted central party – and additionally in a fully privacy-preserving manner. No intermediary can access the plain user's identity data.

Contrast to Decentralized eID Derivation. The eID derivation concept proposed by Abraham et al. [2] shifts trust from a central authority by distributing the trust to the validator network. This validator network performs the actual transformation and attests the transformation's correctness by creating a multi-signature. While their work successfully enables to import qualified eID data, a number of privacy issues remain: In the transformation process, the identity assertion's signature is verified, which requires to access the data in plain and. Also, the importer agent, an intermediate party responsible for the communication between existing IdM and SSI system, performs the revocation process, which requires to stores the user' identity data. Besides the privacy issues, having to trust an intermediate party raises concerns.

Our work tackles the issues mentioned above. In the extended RBFT protocol, the nodes verify the proof and attests its correctness. During the derivation process, no intermediates have access to plain identity data. The revocation process utilizes the DL as the storage location for the revocation information which solves trust issues and responsibilities w.r.t. the importer agent as well as increasing data privacy.

Contrast to Anonymous Credential Systems. Attribute-based anonymous credentials systems describe a class of cryptographic schemes enabling anonymous authentication. Such a system consists of a user, an organization, and a verifier. The user obtains a credential on potentially multiple attributes from an organization and later presents this credential to a verifier. The user may select a subset of attributes to be revealed, while the verifier does not learn any information about the other attributes. Yet, the verifier can still be sure the shown attributes are authentic. In a multi-show credential system, a user can additionally perform an arbitrary number of unlinkable showings. Credential systems have been deployed in U-Prove [28] and idemix [12].

We note that ideas from credential systems transfer to our setting. Indeed, our construction borrows some ideas that are used in constructions of credentials, e.g. from [7]. Credential systems, however, do not handle the transformation of the attributes, which is the main goal and benefit of our system. Also, our design only has minimal impact on the IdPs.

7   Conclusion

In this work, we have proposed a concept for privacy-preserving eID attribute derivation into an SSI system without depending on a central trusted party while still maintaining trust in the derived data. In comparison to related work, our decentralized concept not only eliminates the single point of failure of centralized systems but also improves upon privacy concerns by ensuring that no intermediate components (i.e. SSI nodes) outside the users' domain get access to plain identity data. Within our concept, a network of SSI nodes attests the ownership and validity of derived eID data. Multiple nodes verify NIZK proofs generated by the users, and after reaching consensus, generate multi-signatures as attestation. The resulting attestation, as well as additional NIZK proofs, enable users to selectively disclose attribute of issued identity data towards a SP. Our revocation process utilizes the DLT as the storage location for the revocation information without leaking the users' attributes.

We also presented a concrete instantiation of our concept with suitable technologies and benchmarked the resulting system. Our PoC implementation demonstrates the feasibility and efficiency of the concept. Even though the calculation of NIZK proof is relatively expensive, it only has to be performed once when importing (or re-importing) the eID data.

In summary, our concept can be used to enrich SSI systems with eID data, which makes it possible to integrate with SPs that have high requirements towards the user's data, without sacrificing privacy or relying on a single point of failure.

A Cryptographic Assumptions and Primitives

We recall the standard notion of digital signature schemes.

Definition 1 (Signature Scheme). *A signature scheme Σ is a triple* (KeyGen, Sign, Verify) *of PPT algorithms, which are defined as follows:*

KeyGen(1^κ): *This algorithm takes a security parameter κ as input and outputs a secret (signing) key* sk *and a public (verification) key* pk.

Sign(sk, m): *This algorithm takes a secret key* sk *and a message m as input and outputs a signature σ.*

Verify(pk, m, σ): *This algorithm takes a public key* pk, *a message m and a signature σ as input and outputs a bit $b \in \{0, 1\}$.*

We require a signature scheme to be correct and to provide existential unforgeability under adaptively chosen message attacks (EUF-CMA).

For the concrete instantiations we need bilinear groups, which are generated by BGGen taking a security parameter 1^κ as input and returning bilinear group description including groups $\mathbb{G}$ and $\mathbb{G}_T$ of prime order q, a Type-1[6] pairing $e \colon \mathbb{G} \times \mathbb{G} \to \mathbb{G}_T$ and a generator g of $\mathbb{G}$. The Waters' signature scheme [31] is depicted in Scheme 1, which is secure under the computational Diffie-Hellman assumption (CDH).

Setup(1^κ):   Run BG $\leftarrow$ BGGen(1^κ), choose basis elements $(g_2, u_0, \ldots, u_n) \xleftarrow{R} \mathbb{G}^{n+2}$, and define $H \colon \{0,1\}^* \to \mathbb{G}$ as $H(M) = u_0 \cdot \prod_{i=1}^n u_i^{m_i}$. Return pp $\leftarrow$ (BG, H).
KeyGen(pp):   Choose $x \xleftarrow{R} \mathbb{Z}_q$, set pk $\leftarrow g^x$, sk $\leftarrow g_2^x$, and return (sk, pk).
Sign(sk, m):   Choose $r \xleftarrow{R} \mathbb{Z}_q^\times$, set $\alpha \leftarrow$ sk $\cdot H(m)^r$, $\beta \leftarrow g^{-r}$, and return $\sigma \leftarrow (\alpha, \beta)$.
Verify(pk, m, σ):   Parse σ as (α, β), and verify whether $e(\alpha, g) \cdot e(H(m), \beta) = e(g_2, \text{pk})$.

Scheme 1: Waters' signature scheme.

---

[6] Any design for Type-1 can be transformed into a Type-3 one [1] for efficiency.

Furthermore, we are interested in an extension of signature schemes to multi-signature schemes. In this case, signatures on the same message w.r.t. some public keys, can be aggregated into one compact signature which is valid w.r.t. an aggregated public key. We define such signatures following the definition of Drijvers et al. [17]:

Definition 2 (Multi-Signature Scheme). *A multi-signature scheme Σ_M extends a signature scheme with PPT algorithms* (APKs, ASigs, AVerify), *which are defined as follows:*

APKs$(\mathsf{pk}_1, \ldots, \mathsf{pk}_n)$: *This algorithm takes n public keys $(\mathsf{pk}_i)_{i=1}^n$ as input and outputs an aggregated public key pk_M.*

ASigs$((\mathsf{pk}_1, \sigma_1), \ldots, (\mathsf{pk}_n, \sigma_n), m)$: *This algorithm takes signatures $(\sigma_i)_{i=1}^n$ on the message m and the corresponding public keys $(\mathsf{pk}_i)_{i=1}^n$, and outputs an aggregated signature σ_M on the message m or $\perp$ on error.*

AVerify$(\mathsf{pk}_M, m, \sigma_M)$: *This algorithm takes an aggregated public key pk_M, a message $m \in \mathcal{M}$ and an aggregated signature σ_M as input and outputs a bit $b \in \{0, 1\}$.*

The BLS signature scheme [11] is a prominent example of a signature scheme that can be extended to a multi-signature [10].

Finally, we recall a standard definition of non-interactive zero-knowledge proof systems. Let $L \subseteq \mathsf{X}$ be an **NP**-language with associated witness relation R so that $L = \{x \mid \exists w : R(x, w) = 1\}$.

Definition 3 (NIZK). *A non-interactive proof system Π is a tuple of algorithms* (Setup, Proof, Verify), *which are defined as follows:*

Setup(1^κ): *This algorithm takes a security parameter κ as input, and outputs a common reference string* crs.

Proof(crs, x, w): *This algorithm takes a common reference string* crs, *a statement x, and a witness w as input, and outputs a proof π.*

Verify(crs, x, π): *This algorithm takes a common reference string* crs, *a statement x, and a proof π as input, and outputs a bit $b \in \{0, 1\}$.*

We require such proof system to be complete (all proofs for statements in the language verify), sound (a proof for a statement outside the language verifies only with negligible probability) and zero-knowledge (proof reveals no information on the witness). We are especially interested in proof systems for statements of the form $F = \mathcal{F}(m_1 \| \ldots \| m_n) \wedge \bigwedge_{i=1}^n c_i = \mathsf{Com}(m_i; r_i)$ where $\mathcal{F}$ is derived from the hash function H used in Waters' signature scheme, i.e. $H(m) = u_0 \cdot \mathcal{F}(m)$. Secondly, for commitments, i.e. Com,[7] we use Groth-Ostrovsky-Sahai commitments [19]. We can now define the relation R_{cF} as

$$((F, c_1, \ldots, c_n), (m_1, \ldots, m_n, r_1, \ldots, r_n)) \in R_{cF} \Leftrightarrow$$

$$F = \mathcal{F}(m_1 \| \ldots \| m_n) \wedge \bigwedge_{i=1}^n c_i = \mathsf{Com}(m_i; r_i)$$

and denote the corresponding proof system based on [18] as Π_{cF}, which is complete, sound and zero-knowledge.

---

[7] We slightly abuse notation and assume that Com only returns the commitment.

References

1. Abe, M., Hoshino, F., Ohkubo, M.: Design in Type-I, run in Type-III: fast and scalable bilinear-type conversion using integer programming. In: Robshaw, M., Katz, J. (eds.) CRYPTO 2016, Part III. LNCS, vol. 9816, pp. 387–415. Springer, Heidelberg (2016). https://doi.org/10.1007/978-3-662-53015-3_14
2. Abraham, A., Theuermann, K., Kirchengast, E.: Qualified eID derivation into a distributed ledger based IdM system. In: TrustCom/BigDataSE, pp. 1406–1412. IEEE (2018)
3. Albrecht, M.R., et al.: Feistel structures for MPC, and more. In: Sako, K., Schneider, S., Ryan, P.Y.A. (eds.) ESORICS 2019. LNCS, vol. 11736, pp. 151–171. Springer, Cham (2019). https://doi.org/10.1007/978-3-030-29962-0_8
4. Allen, C.: The Path to Self-Sovereign-Identity (2016). http://www.lifewithalacrity.com/2016/04/the-path-to-self-soverereign-identity.html. Accessed 15 Feb 2019
5. Aranha, D.F., Gouvêa, C.P.L.: RELIC is an Efficient LIbrary for Cryptography. https://github.com/relic-toolkit/relic
6. Aublin, P., Mokhtar, S.B., Quéma, V.: RBFT: redundant byzantine fault tolerance. In: ICDCS, pp. 297–306. IEEE Computer Society (2013)
7. Belenkiy, M., Chase, M., Kohlweiss, M., Lysyanskaya, A.: Non-interactive anonymous credentials. ePrint 2007, 384 (2007)
8. Bernabe, J.B., Skarmeta, A., Notario, N., Bringer, J., David, M.: Towards a privacy-preserving reliable European identity ecosystem. In: Schweighofer, E., Leitold, H., Mitrakas, A., Rannenberg, K. (eds.) APF 2017. LNCS, vol. 10518, pp. 19–33. Springer, Cham (2017). https://doi.org/10.1007/978-3-319-67280-9_2
9. Bertino, E., Takahashi, K.: Identity Management: Concepts, Technologies, and Systems. Artech House, Norwood (2010)
10. Boldyreva, A.: Threshold signatures, multisignatures and blind signatures based on the gap-Diffie-Hellman-group signature scheme. In: Desmedt, Y.G. (ed.) PKC 2003. LNCS, vol. 2567, pp. 31–46. Springer, Heidelberg (2003). https://doi.org/10.1007/3-540-36288-6_3
11. Boneh, D., Lynn, B., Shacham, H.: Short signatures from the Weil pairing. In: Boyd, C. (ed.) ASIACRYPT 2001. LNCS, vol. 2248, pp. 514–532. Springer, Heidelberg (2001). https://doi.org/10.1007/3-540-45682-1_30
12. Camenisch, J., Herreweghen, E.V.: Design and implementation of the *idemix* anonymous credential system. In: ACM CCS, pp. 21–30. ACM (2002)
13. Caro, A.D.: JPBC. http://gas.dia.unisa.it/projects/jpbc/index.html
14. Castro, M., Liskov, B.: Practical Byzantine fault tolerance and proactive recovery. ACM Trans. Comput. Syst. 20(4), 398–461 (2002)
15. Chase, M., et al.: Post-quantum zero-knowledge and signatures from symmetric-key primitives. In: ACM CCS, pp. 1825–1842. ACM (2017)
16. Chase, M., Kohlweiss, M.: A new hash-and-sign approach and structure-preserving signatures from DLIN. In: Visconti, I., De Prisco, R. (eds.) SCN 2012. LNCS, vol. 7485, pp. 131–148. Springer, Heidelberg (2012). https://doi.org/10.1007/978-3-642-32928-9_8
17. Drijvers, M., Gorbunov, S., Neven, G., Wee, H.: Pixel: multi-signatures for consensus. ePrint 2019, 514 (2019)
18. Fuchsbauer, G., Pointcheval, D.: Proofs on encrypted values in bilinear groups and an application to anonymity of signatures. In: Shacham, H., Waters, B. (eds.) Pairing 2009. LNCS, vol. 5671, pp. 132–149. Springer, Heidelberg (2009). https://doi.org/10.1007/978-3-642-03298-1_10

19. Groth, J., Ostrovsky, R., Sahai, A.: Non-interactive zaps and new techniques for NIZK. In: Dwork, C. (ed.) CRYPTO 2006. LNCS, vol. 4117, pp. 97–111. Springer, Heidelberg (2006). https://doi.org/10.1007/11818175_6
20. Isaac, M., Frenkel, S.: Facebook security breach exposes accounts of 50 million users (2018). https://www.nytimes.com/2018/09/28/technology/facebook-hack-data-breach.html. Accessed 04 June 2019
21. Katz, J., Kolesnikov, V., Wang, X.: Improved non-interactive zero knowledge with applications to post-quantum signatures. In: ACM CCS, pp. 525–537. ACM (2018)
22. Lenz, T., Alber, L.: Towards cross-domain eID by using agile mobile authentication. In: TrustCom/BigDataSE/ICESS, pp. 570–577. IEEE Computer Society (2017)
23. Mathews, L.: Equifax data breach impacts 143 million Americans (2017). https://www.forbes.com/sites/leemathews/2017/09/07/equifax-data-breach-impacts-143-million-americans/. Accessed 04 June 2019
24. Menezes, A., Sarkar, P., Singh, S.: Challenges with assessing the impact of NFS advances on the security of pairing-based cryptography. In: Phan, R.C.-W., Yung, M. (eds.) Mycrypt 2016. LNCS, vol. 10311, pp. 83–108. Springer, Cham (2017). https://doi.org/10.1007/978-3-319-61273-7_5
25. Mühle, A., Grüner, A., Gayvoronskaya, T., Meinel, C.: A survey on essential components of a self-sovereign identity. Comput. Sci. Rev. **30**, 80–86 (2018)
26. NIST: SP 800-157. Guidelines for Derived Personal Identity Verification (PIV) Credentials (2014)
27. OASIS: SAML (security assertion markup language) specifications. http://saml.xml.org/saml-specifications. Accessed 13 Apr 2019
28. Paquin, C., Zaverucha, G.: U-prove cryptographic specification v1.1 (revision 3) (2013). https://www.microsoft.com/en-us/research/publication/u-prove-cryptographic-specification-v1-1-revision-3/
29. Reed, D., Sporny, M., Longley, D., Allen, C., Grant, R., Sabadello, M.: Decentralized Identifiers (DIDs) v0.9 (2018). https://w3c-ccg.github.io/did-spec/
30. Sovrin Foundation: Sovrin: A Protocol and Token for Self-Sovereign Identity and Decentralized Trust (2018). https://sovrin.org/wp-content/uploads/Sovrin-Protocol-and-Token-White-Paper.pdf
31. Waters, B.: Efficient identity-based encryption without random oracles. In: Cramer, R. (ed.) EUROCRYPT 2005. LNCS, vol. 3494, pp. 114–127. Springer, Heidelberg (2005). https://doi.org/10.1007/11426639_7
32. Zwattendorfer, B., Zefferer, T., Stranacher, K.: An overview of cloud identity management-models. In: WEBIST (1), pp. 82–92. SciTePress (2014)

Provably Secure Group Authentication in the Asynchronous Communication Model

Zhe Xia[1,2]([✉]), Lein Harn[3], Bo Yang[4], Mingwu Zhang[5,6], Yi Mu[7], Willy Susilo[8], and Weizhi Meng[9]

[1] School of Computer Science, Wuhan University of Technology, Wuhan, China
xiazhe@whut.edu.cn
[2] Guangxi Key Laboratory of Trusted Software,
Guilin University of Electronic Technology, Guilin, China
[3] Department of Computer Science and Electronic Engineering,
University of Missouri-Kansas City, Kansas City, USA
harnlein@gmail.com
[4] School of Computer Science, Shaanxi Normal University, Xi'an, China
byang@snnu.edu.cn
[5] School of Computers, Hubei University of Technology, Wuhan, China
csmwzhang@gmail.com
[6] State Key Laboratory of Cryptology, Beijing, China
[7] Fujian Provincial Key Laboratory of Network Security and Cryptology,
College of Mathematics and Informatics, Fujian Normal University, Fuzhou, China
ymu.ieee@gmail.com
[8] School of Computing and Information Technology, University of Wollongong,
Wollongong, Australia
wsusilo@uow.edu.au
[9] DTU Compute, Technical University of Denmark, Copenhagen, Denmark
weme@dtu.dk

Abstract. Authentication is one of the most fundamental services in information security. Compared with traditional authentication methods, group authentication enables a group of users to be authenticated at once rather than authenticating each user individually. Therefore, it is preferred in the group-oriented environment, such as multicast/conference communications. While several group authentication schemes have been proposed over the past few years, no formal treatment for this cryptographic problem has ever been suggested. Existing papers only provide heuristic evidences of security and some of these schemes have later been found to be flawed. In this paper, we present a formal security model for this problem. Our model not only captures the basic requirement in group authentication that an adversary cannot pretend to be a group member without being detected, but also considers some desirable features in real-world applications, such as re-use of the credentials in multiple authentication sessions and allowance for users to exchange messages through asynchronous networks. We then introduce an efficient group authentication scheme where its security can be reduced to some well-studied complexity theoretic assumptions.

© Springer Nature Switzerland AG 2020
J. Zhou et al. (Eds.): ICICS 2019, LNCS 11999, pp. 324–340, 2020.
https://doi.org/10.1007/978-3-030-41579-2_19

1   Introduction

Authentication is the process of confirming whether someone or something is who or what it claims itself to be. It is a crucial security service in information security. In traditional authentication methods, only two parties are involved. One is the prover and the other is the verifier. The verifier will accept the prover's identity if the prover can prove that it has knowledge of the credential. However, such a one-to-one authentication model will become inefficient in the group-oriented environment. For example, suppose there are n users in the group and each user wants to verify every other user's identity. In this case, every user needs to perform the one-to-one authentication $n-1$ times, and the total number of authentications required across the entire group is $O(n^2)$, which is quadratic to the number of users.

Instead, when using group authentication [12], each user acts both roles of the prover and the verifier, and all users in the group are authenticated at once. The authentication is carried out in the many-to-many fashion and it outputs one of the two possible outcomes: either all users belong to the same group or there exists some non-members. Therefore, group authentication is sufficient if all users are group members, and even if there exists some non-members, it still can be used as a pre-processing step before applying traditional authentication methods to identify those non-members. Considering that a lot of applications nowadays are group-oriented, e.g. multicast/conference communications, group authentication is a useful tool in modern cryptography.

In general, a group authentication scheme works as follows. The group manager (GM) generates a number of credentials, and sends each of these credentials to a user in the group. In the authentication stage, every participating user uses her credential to compute a token and broadcasts it. Subsequently, every user can use the revealed information to verify whether all users are belonging to the same group. Apart from the basic requirement that an adversary should not be able to pretend to be a group member without being detected, some additional features are highly desirable in real-world applications: (1) re-use of the credentials in multiple authentication sessions, and (2) allowance for users to broadcast their tokens through asynchronous networks. Note that both these features help to make the scheme more practical. For example, the multiple usage of credentials avoids the cumbersome processes of distributing credentials before every authentication session, and the asynchronous networks are much easier to be established than the synchronous ones, especially in the distributed environment such as the Internet of Things (IoT). However, these two features also make the design of group authentication schemes more challenging. In one aspect, multiple usage of credentials in different authentication sessions requires that the token leaks no useful information of the corresponding credential. In another aspect, since the adversary in the asynchronous communication model can always wait until all other users having revealed their tokens and then fabricate her token using these revealed ones, it is required that the revealed tokens should not enable anyone to compute a new valid token without the corresponding credential.

Over the past few years, a number of group authentication schemes have been proposed in the literature [6, 8, 10, 12, 15–18]. However, the underlying formal security treatment is still lagging. Most of the existing schemes only justify their security by heuristic arguments, and some of these schemes have later been found to be flawed [1]. In this paper, our purpose is to direct the research of group authentication towards the paradigm of provable security. In this approach, one first identifies the cryptographic problem to solve and defines a formal security model for this problem. The model should be rich enough to capture both the adversary's and the players' capabilities, but it should not be overly restrictive to preclude efficient protocols from being constructed. Within this model, one further defines the security goals to clarify precisely what it means for a scheme to be secure. With these preliminaries at hand, one can strictly prove that a proposed scheme has achieved the claimed security goals. Normally, this is done via a security reduction, demonstrating that if any attack can successfully breach the security goals in the proposed scheme, this attack can be employed as a subroutine to violate some well-believed complexity theoretic assumptions.

1.1   Related Works

Group authentication was first introduced by Harn [12], and this technique has been demonstrated to enjoy computational advantages over traditional authentication methods in the group environment [22]. However, Ahmadian et al. [1] have shown recently that Harn's scheme suffers a security flaw. Specifically, an adversary in the asynchronous communication model can impersonate a group member without being detected. The main reason for this attack is that the security properties in Harn's scheme are only justified by heuristic arguments rather than formal security proofs. It was conjectured that the adversary needs to recover all the polynomials in order to fabricate a valid token. However, she can use a clever method, called the *linear subspace attack*, to construct a linear subspace spanned by the already revealed tokens and then fabricate a new valid token without reconstructing the polynomials. This flaw also demonstrates a well-known basic principle in information security that formal security analysis is crucial for the design of security protocols since intuitions might be faulty sometimes.

Based on Harn's work, several group authentication schemes have been proposed over the last few years. Some of these schemes tried to achieve slightly different features as in Harn's scheme. For example, Chien [6] renovated Harn's idea using pairing. The benefit is that the credentials can be used in multiple trials in case the authentication fails, but it can only work in the synchronous communication model. Liu et al. [16] introduced a group authentication scheme for the resource restrained environment. Different from Harn's scheme, the authentication is done by checking whether the interpolation of credentials returns a polynomial with the expected degree rather than checking whether the interpolation returns the correct value. But Liu's scheme has not considered asynchronous networks neither. Mahalle et al. [17] introduced a group authentication scheme for the Internet of Things, and they replace secret sharing schemes used in Harn's scheme by threshold Paillier cipher [23]. Li et al. [15] extended Harn's group authentication scheme so that it could further establish pairwise secret keys among the authenticated users. The key agreement function is achieved using Diffie-Hellman key exchange [7] based on elliptic curve cryptography. Guo et al. [10] and Elmouaatamid et al. [8] independently investigated how group authentication schemes can be designed with cheater detection, so that the non-members can be identified when the group authentication fails. Note that this is a feature not enjoyed in Harn's scheme, but neither of these two schemes handles asynchronous networks. Miao et al. [18] introduced a group authentication scheme that is suitable for the asynchronous communication model, but it has not considered re-use of credentials in multiple authentication sessions.

In the literature, some other techniques may also seem to be closely related to group authentication schemes. However, there exists some trivial differences between them, making these techniques unsuitable to solve the group authentication problem. For example, Bellare et al. [2] introduced an *authenticator* that can transform any message-driven protocol secure against a passive adversary into a corresponding protocol secure against an active adversary. Later, Katz et al. [14] extended it into the multi-user setting so that any group-oriented message-driven protocol can be transformed into an authenticated one. However, this technique mainly focuses on authenticating messages rather than authenticating entities. Hence, it is inappropriate for group authentication. Group authenticated key exchange schemes [3,4,13] have been designed to provide a group of users with a shared secret key which can be later used to achieve multicast message confidentiality or multicast data integrity. Moreover each user can be assured that only the group member will obtain the shared key. However, the authentication and the key exchange are intertwined with each other in this technique. Hence, it will be inefficient if it is used to solve the group authentication problem.

1.2 Our Contributions

In this paper, we first present a formal security model for the group authentication problem. Our model not only captures the basic requirement that an adversary cannot pretend to be a group member without being detected, but also considers some disirable features in real-world applications, such as re-use of the credentials in multiple authentication sessions and allowance for users to exchange messages through asynchronous networks. We then modify and extend Harn's scheme [12] using the anonymous veto networks [11], resulting an efficient group authentication scheme where its security can be reduced to some reasonable and well-defined complexity theoretic assumptions. Hence, the proposed scheme is capable of immunising Ahmadian's attack [1] as well as any unforeseen threat that can be captured in our security model.

1.3 Organisation of the Paper

The rest of this paper is organised as follows. In Sect. 2, we outline some preliminaries. The models and definitions for group authentication are described in

Sect. 3. In Sect. 4, we present the proposed scheme and formally prove its security using our security model. Finally, we discuss some possible extensions and conclude in Sect. 5.

2   Preliminaries

2.1   Notations

In this paper, we assume that all participants are probabilistic polynomial time (PPT) algorithms with respect to the security parameter λ. We use standard notations for probabilistic algorithms and experiments. For example, if A is a probabilistic algorithm, then $A(x_1, x_2, \ldots)$ is denoted as the result of running A on inputs x_1, x_2, etc. We denote $y \leftarrow A(x_1, x_2, \ldots)$ as the experiment of assigning y as $A(x_1, x_2, \ldots)$. If S is a finite set, then we denote $x \overset{R}{\leftarrow} S$ as the operation of picking an element uniformly from S. Moreover, $\Pr[x \leftarrow S; y \leftarrow T; \ldots : p(x, y, \ldots)]$ is denoted as the probability that the predicate $p(x, y, \ldots)$ will be true after the ordered execution of the algorithms $x \leftarrow S, y \leftarrow T$, etc. A function $\epsilon(\cdot) : \mathbb{N} \to \mathbb{R}^+$ is called negligible if for all $c > 0$, there exists a k_0 such that $\epsilon(k) < 1/k^c$ for all $k > k_0$.

2.2   Building Blocks

Here, we briefly describe some building blocks that are used to construct our proposed group authentication scheme. Denote G as a finite cyclic group in which the discrete logarithm assumption holds, and g as a generator of G. The order of G is a large prime q, where $|q| = \mathsf{poly}(\lambda)$ for some polynomial $\mathsf{poly}(\cdot)$. In the rest of this paper, we assume that all operations are modulo q unless otherwise stated.

Schnorr Identification Algorithm [19]. This technique serves as a zero-knowledge proof that proves the knowledge of a random value $x \in \mathbb{Z}_q$ within g^x, without revealing x. It works as follows:

- The prover selects a value $r \overset{R}{\leftarrow} \mathbb{Z}_q$ and sends the commitment $w = g^r$ to the verifier.
- The verifier selects a challenge $c \overset{R}{\leftarrow} \mathbb{Z}_q$ and sends c back to the prover.
- The prover computes the response $s = r + xc$ and sends s to the verifier.
- The verifier checks whether $g^s = wy^c$.

Obviously, the above protocol satisfies *correctness*. To see that it satisfies *robustness*: in order to make the verification $g^s = wy^c$ successful, the prover needs to output a value $s \in \mathbb{Z}_q$ such that the equation $s = r + xc$ holds. If the prover does not have the knowledge of x, the probability of outputting such a value s is exactly $1/q$, which is negligible with respect to the security parameter λ. This is because x is assumed to be uniformly distributed in $\mathbb{Z}_q$. The above protocol also satisfies *honest verifier zero-knowledge*, because the prover can "rewind" the honest verifier to simulate the proof by setting $w = g^s y^{-c}$. Moreover, using Fiat-Shamir heuristics [9], the above protocol can be transformed into a non-interactive zero-knowledge proof.

Anonymous Veto Networks (AV-nets) [11]. This technique was introduced by Hao and Zieliński in 2006, aiming to provide an efficient solution to the dining cryptographers problem [5] (i.e. how to send a boolean-OR bit anonymously from a group of users). It is a two-round protocol with very low computational load and bandwidth usage per user. It assumes that there exists an authenticated broadcast channel, and all the messages are exchanged through this channel. Suppose n users are participating, the protocol works as follows:

- **Round 1.** Each user U_i selects a value $x_i \xleftarrow{R} \mathbb{Z}_q$ and broadcasts g^{x_i}. U_i also proves that she has the knowledge of x_i without revealing it. Note that such a proof can be generated using the Schnorr Identification Algorithm introduced above. When this round finishes, every user computes:

$$g^{y_i} = \prod_{j=1}^{i-1} g^{x_j} / \prod_{j=i+1}^{n} g^{x_j}$$

- **Round 2.** Every user broadcasts a value $g^{x_i y_i}$ and proves the knowledge of x_i within $g^{x_i y_i}$ without revealing it. Now, we have the property that:

$$\prod_{i=1}^{n} g^{x_i y_i} = 1$$

To see that the above property always holds: by definition $y_i = \sum_{j<i} x_j - \sum_{j>i} x_j$, hence we have:

$$\sum_i x_i y_i = \sum_i \sum_{j<i} x_i x_j - \sum_i \sum_{j>i} x_i x_j$$
$$= \sum \sum_{j<i} x_i x_j - \sum \sum_{i<j} x_i x_j$$
$$= \sum \sum_{j<i} x_i x_j - \sum \sum_{j<i} x_j x_i$$
$$= 0$$

Moreover, the broadcast value g^{x_i} does not reveal x_i assuming that the discrete logarithm assumption holds in G. And because x_i is randomly selected in $\mathbb{Z}_q$, the value $g^{x_i y_i}$ will be randomly distributed in G.

Shamir Secret Sharing [21]. This technique can be used to share the secret value $s \in \mathbb{Z}_q$ among a number of users, so that either to learn the secret or destroy it, the adversary has to corrupt multiple of these users instead of a single one. Therefore, it enhances both secrecy and availability of the sensitive information. Shamir secret sharing works as follows. In the dealing phase, the dealer first selects a random polynomial $f(x) = a_0 + a_1 x + \cdots + a_{t-1} x^{t-1}$ over $\mathbb{Z}_q$ with degree $t - 1$, where $a_0 = s$. Then the dealer sends the shares $s_i = f(x_i)$ to each user through some secure channel. Here $\{x_1, x_2, \ldots, x_n\}$ are public parameters associate with the users that are pairwise different. In the reconstruction phase, any subset Ω ($|\Omega| \geq t$) of these users can reconstruct the secret s by Lagrange interpolation: $s = \sum_{i \in \Omega} s_i \mathcal{L}_i$, where $\mathcal{L}_i = \prod_{j \in \Omega, j \neq i} \frac{x_j}{x_j - x_i}$ is called the Lagrange coefficient.

3   Models and Definitions

3.1   The Participants

There are four types of participants in group authentication schemes:

- *Group manager* (GM). The GM initialises the protocol and generates credentials for the users. In any authentication protocol, the user needs to possess some secret that is unknown to the others. Hence, the GM is assumed to be honest in the protocol.
- *Users.* Each of the n users will receive a credential from the GM, and they will use their credentials to participate in the group authentication. Note that the credentials can be used multiple times in different group authentication sessions.
- *Inside adversary.* The inside adversary $\mathcal{A}_I$ controls at most $t - 1$ users, where t is the threshold such that $t > n/2$. $\mathcal{A}_I$ can obtain these users' internal states. $\mathcal{A}_I$'s purpose is to learn some secret information (i.e. the secret of GM or the credentials possessed by some uncorrupted users), or to pass the group authentication by herself.
- *Outside adversary.* The outside adversary $\mathcal{A}_O$ does not own any valid credential generated by the GM, but her purpose is to impersonate a group member in the group authentication without being detected.

3.2   Communication Model

We assume that there exists a secure channel between the GM and every user, so that the credentials can be distributed securely. Moreover, we assume that every participant is connected to a broadcast channel, where any message sent through this channel can be heard by the other participants within some specified time bound. Note that the broadcast channel is only assumed to be asynchronous, such that messages sent from the uncorrupted users to the corrupted ones can be delivered relatively fast, in which case, the adversary can wait for the messages of the uncorrupted users to arrive, then decide on her computation and communication, and still get her messages delivered to the honest users on time. With these assumptions, we can focus our description without considering the low level technical details. Note that both these channels can be implemented using standard cryptographic techniques such as encryptions and digital signatures.

3.3   System Model

The group authentication scheme is specified by the following four randomised algorithms: Init, Dist, Comp, Auth.

- The initialisation algorithm Init is run by the GM. Init takes as inputs the security parameter λ; it outputs the system parameters params.
- The distribution algorithm Dist is run by the GM. Dist takes as inputs the system parameters params and the number of users n; it outputs a set of credentials $\{s_1, s_2, \ldots, s_n\}$. These credentials are sent to U through the secure channel, where U denotes the set of all legitimate group members.
- The computation algorithm Comp is run by every user. Comp takes as inputs the system parameters params, the session index σ, the set of participated users Ω and a credential s_i; it outputs a token c_i through the broadcast channel.
- The group authentication algorithm Auth is run by the participated users. Auth takes as inputs the system parameters params, the session index σ and a set of tokens $\{c_i\}_{i \in \Omega}$; it outputs 1 if $|\Omega| \geq t$ and Ω only contains legitimate group members, and it outputs 0 otherwise.

3.4   Security Model

We first describe the security properties for group authentication schemes informally and justify why these properties are necessary.

- *Correctness.* If a subset Ω of users are participating in the group authentication, where $|\Omega| \geq t$ and they are all legitimate group members, then the group authentication will be successful.
- *Secrecy.* The inside adversary $\mathcal{A}_I$ cannot learn any secret information in the group authentication, including the secret of the GM and the credentials possessed by the uncorrupted users. Note that this is a necessary requirement for the protocol to be used multiple times. This property is captured as follows: we prove that there exists a PPT simulator $\mathcal{S}$ that can simulate $\mathcal{A}_I$'s view in the real run of the protocol just using the public information, and it is infeasible to distinguish the simulated protocol from the real one. Because the simulated protocol contains no secret information, this proves that no secret has been leaked in the real run of the protocol. Otherwise, the leaked secret can be used to distinguish the simulated transcripts from the ones in the real run of the protocol.
- *No forgery.* The inside adversary $\mathcal{A}_I$ cannot pass the group authentication by herself. To capture that $\mathcal{A}_I$ may have already learned some historic information in the previous group authentication sessions, we provide $\mathcal{A}_I$ with an oracle $\mathcal{O}$ that can be used to query the group authentication service, and $\mathcal{A}_I$ can query $\mathcal{O}$ polynomial number of times. It is required that $\mathcal{A}_I$ still cannot pass the group authentication by herself in a new session.
- *No impersonation.* The outside adversary $\mathcal{A}_O$ cannot impersonate a group member without being detected, even if $\mathcal{A}_O$ computes her token after seeing all other users' tokens in the asynchronous networks.

The above security properties can be formalised as follows:

Definition 1 (Correctness). *A group authentication scheme is said to have the correctness property if we have:*

$$\Pr\Big[\text{params} \leftarrow \text{Init}(\lambda); \{s_i\}_{i \in U} \leftarrow \text{Dist}(\text{params}, n) \quad ;$$
$$c_i \leftarrow \text{Comp}(\text{params}, \sigma, \Omega, s_i)|_{i \in \Omega} \quad :$$
$$\text{Auth}(\text{params}, \sigma, \{c_i\}_{i \in \Omega}) = 1\Big] = 1$$

In the above expression, $\Omega \subseteq U$ and $|\Omega| \geq t$.

Definition 2 (Secrecy). *A group authentication scheme is said to have the secrecy property if we have:*

$$\text{View}_{\mathcal{A}_I}(\text{Real}_\Pi(\lambda, \text{params})) \cong_c \text{View}_{\mathcal{A}_I}(\text{SIM}_{\mathcal{S}}(\lambda, \text{params}))$$

In the above expression, $\text{View}_{\mathcal{A}_I}(\text{Real}_\Pi(\lambda, \text{params}))$ is denoted as $\mathcal{A}_I$'s view in the real run of the protocol Π, $\cong_c$ means computationally indistinguishable, and $\text{View}_{\mathcal{A}_I}(\text{SIM}_{\mathcal{S}}(\lambda, \text{params}))$ is denoted as $\mathcal{A}_I$'s view of the transcripts simulated by a PPT simulator $\mathcal{S}$ with only public information as inputs.

Definition 3 (No forgery). *A group authentication scheme is said to have the no forgery property if we have:*

$$\Pr\Big[\text{params} \leftarrow \text{Init}(\lambda); \{s_i\}_{i \in U} \leftarrow \text{Dist}(\text{params}, n) \quad ;$$
$$T \leftarrow \mathcal{A}_I^{\mathcal{O}}(\text{params}, \sigma, \{s_i\}_{i \in U_{\mathcal{A}}}) \quad :$$
$$\sigma \notin \Sigma \wedge \text{Auth}(\text{params}, \sigma, T) = 1\Big] < \epsilon(\lambda)$$

In the above expression, $U_{\mathcal{A}}$ denotes the users that are controlled by $\mathcal{A}_I$, such that $U_{\mathcal{A}} \subset U$ and $|U_{\mathcal{A}}| \leq t - 1$. $\mathcal{O}$ denotes an oracle that is used to query the group authentication service, and Σ records all the session indexes which have been queried.

Definition 4 (No impersonation). *A group authentication scheme is said to have the no impersonation property if we have:*

$$\Pr\Big[\text{params} \leftarrow \text{Init}(\lambda); \{s_i\}_{i \in U} \leftarrow \text{Dist}(\text{params}, n) \quad ;$$
$$c_i \leftarrow \text{Comp}(\text{params}, \sigma, \Omega \cup \{\mu\}, s_i)|_{i \in \Omega} \quad ;$$
$$c_\mu \leftarrow \mathcal{A}_O(\text{params}, \sigma, \Omega \cup \{\mu\}, \{c_i\}_{i \in \Omega}) \quad :$$
$$\text{Auth}(\text{params}, \sigma, \{c_i\}_{i \in \Omega \cup \{\mu\}}) = 1\Big] < \epsilon(\lambda)$$

In the above expression, $\mathcal{A}_O$ is assumed to impersonate the user U_μ, where $\mu \notin \Omega$.

3.5   Computational Assumptions

We assume that the following assumptions hold. Note that they are well-believed assumptions that are widely used in designing cryptographic protocols.

Definition 5 (Discrete logarithm (DL) assumption). *Given the description of the finite cyclic group G, where $|G| = q$ and g is a generator of G. The discrete logarithm assumption implies that there exists a negligible function $\epsilon(\cdot)$ such that for all PPT adversaries $\mathcal{A}_{DL}$, we have:*

$$\Pr[x \xleftarrow{R} \mathbb{Z}_q; x^* \leftarrow \mathcal{A}_{DL}(G, q, g, g^x) : x^* = x] < \epsilon(\lambda)$$

Definition 6 (Decisional Diffie-Hellman (DDH) assumption). *Given the description of the finite cyclic group G, where $|G| = q$ and g is a generator of G. Select $x \xleftarrow{R} \mathbb{Z}_q$, $y \xleftarrow{R} \mathbb{Z}_q$, and $z \xleftarrow{R} \mathbb{Z}_q$. The decisional Diffie-Hellman assumption implies that there exists a negligible function $\epsilon(\cdot)$ such that for all PPT adversaries $\mathcal{A}_{DDH}$, we have:*

$$|\Pr[\mathcal{A}_{DDH}(G, q, g, g^x, g^y, g^{xy}) = 1] - \Pr[\mathcal{A}_{DDH}(G, q, g, g^x, g^y, g^z) = 1]| < \epsilon(\lambda)$$

Definition 7 (Preimage resistant hash function). *Given the description of a hash function $\mathsf{H} : \mathcal{D} \rightarrow \mathcal{R}$, where $\mathcal{D}$ and $\mathcal{R}$ denote H's domain and range respectively. The hash function H is said to be preimage resistant if there exists a negligible function $\epsilon(\cdot)$ such that for all PPT adversaries $\mathcal{A}_{PR}$, we have:*

$$\Pr[x \xleftarrow{R} \mathcal{D}, x^* \leftarrow \mathcal{A}_{PR}(\mathsf{H}(x)) : \mathsf{H}(x^*) = \mathsf{H}(x)] < \epsilon(\lambda)$$

Note that preimage resistant hash function can be constructed from any one-way permutation or one-way function.

4   The Proposed Scheme

4.1   The Scheme

Our proposed group authentication scheme works as follows:

- Init : Denote H as a preimage resistant hash function. GM first selects a cyclic group G with prime order q, and generates l independent generators of the group $g_i \xleftarrow{R} G$ for $i \in \mathbb{Z}_l$. It is required that the discrete logarithm $\log_{g_i} g_j$ is unknown for any $i, j \in \mathbb{Z}_l$. GM then selects the secret $s \xleftarrow{R} \mathbb{Z}_q$, and computes $\mathsf{H}(g_i{}^s)$ for $i \in \mathbb{Z}_l$. GM associates the pairwise different integers $\{x_1, x_2, \ldots, x_n\}$ with the group members. Finally, GM outputs the system parameters $\mathsf{params} = (\mathsf{H}, G, q, \{g_i\}_{i \in \mathbb{Z}_l}, \{\mathsf{H}(g_i{}^s)\}_{i \in \mathbb{Z}_l}, \{x_i\}_{i \in \mathbb{Z}_n})$.
- Dist : GM selects a random polynomial $f(x) = a_0 + a_1 x + \ldots + a_{t-1} x^{t-1}$ over $\mathbb{Z}_q$ with degree $t - 1$, such that $a_0 = s$. GM then computes the credentials $s_i = f(x_i)$, and sends them to the group members through the secure channel.

- Comp : In the σ-th session, every participating user in Ω first selects $u_i \xleftarrow{R} \mathbb{Z}_q$ and broadcasts $g_\sigma{}^{u_i}$. Then, each user computes:

$$g_\sigma{}^{v_i} = \prod_{j \in \Omega, j < i} g_\sigma{}^{u_j} / \prod_{j \in \Omega, j > i} g_\sigma{}^{u_j}$$

As follows, every user computes and broadcasts her token as:

$$c_i = g_\sigma{}^{s_i \mathcal{L}_i} \cdot g_\sigma{}^{u_i v_i}$$

  where $\mathcal{L}_i = \prod_{j \in \Omega, j \neq i} \frac{x_j}{x_j - x_i}$ is the Lagrange coefficient.
- Auth : In the σ-th session, every user can verify whether all the users are legitimate group members by checking:

$$H(\prod_{i \in \Omega} c_i) = H(g_\sigma{}^s)$$

4.2   Security Analysis

Theorem 1. *The proposed group authentication scheme satisfies the correctness property.*

Proof. If $\Omega \subseteq U$ and $|\Omega| \geq t$, the Lagrange interpolation implies that $s = \sum_{i \in \Omega} s_i \mathcal{L}_i$ where $\mathcal{L}_i = \prod_{j \in \Omega, j \neq i} \frac{x_j}{x_j - x_i}$ is the Lagrange coefficient. Moreover, because the AV-nets enjoy the property $\prod_{i \in \Omega} g_\sigma{}^{u_i v_i} = 1$, we have:

$$\prod_{i \in \Omega} c_i = \prod_{i \in \Omega} g_\sigma{}^{s_i \mathcal{L}_i} \cdot \prod_{i \in \Omega} g_\sigma{}^{u_i v_i} = g_\sigma{}^{\sum_{i \in \Omega} s_i \mathcal{L}_i} = g_\sigma{}^s$$

Therefore, the equation $H(\prod_{i \in \Omega} c_i) = H(g_\sigma{}^s)$ will hold, and the authentication will be successful.

Theorem 2. *The proposed group authentication scheme satisfies the secrecy property, assuming the DL assumption holds in G.*

Proof. Denote $\mathsf{Real}_\Pi(\lambda, \mathsf{params})$ as the real run of the protocol Π and $\mathsf{SIM}_\mathcal{S}(\lambda, \mathsf{params})$ as the protocol simulated by a PPT simulator $\mathcal{S}$ with only public information as inputs.
    $\underline{\mathsf{Real}_\Pi(\lambda, \mathsf{params})}$:

- Init: GM generates and outputs the system parameters:

$$\mathsf{params} = (H, G, q, \{g_i\}_{i \in \mathbb{Z}_l}, \{H(g_i{}^s)\}_{i \in \mathbb{Z}_l}, \{x_i\}_{i \in \mathbb{Z}_n})$$

- Dist: GM computes the credentials $s_i = f(x_i)$, and sends them to the group members through the secure channel. Without loss of generality, we assume that the credentials $\{s_1, s_2, \ldots s_{t-1}\}$ are learnt by the inside adversary $\mathcal{A}_I$.

- Comp: In the σ-th session, every participating user in Ω selects $u_i \xleftarrow{R} \mathbb{Z}_q$ and broadcasts $g_\sigma{}^{u_i}$. Then, each user computes

$$g_\sigma{}^{v_i} = \prod_{j \in \Omega, j < i} g_\sigma{}^{u_j} / \prod_{j \in \Omega, j > i} g_\sigma{}^{u_j}$$

and broadcasts her token $c_i = g_\sigma{}^{s_i \mathcal{L}_i} \cdot g_\sigma{}^{u_i v_i}$. In this algorithm, $\mathcal{A}_I$ learns $\{u_1, u_2, \ldots, u_{t-1}\}$ that are selected by the corrupted users as well as all the broadcast values.
- Auth: In the σ-th session, everyone verifies whether $H(\prod_{i \in \Omega} c_i) = H(g_\sigma{}^s)$.

$\underline{SIM_\mathcal{S}(\lambda, params)}$:

- Init: The simulator $\mathcal{S}$ outputs the system parameters:

$$params = (H, G, q, \{g_i\}_{i \in \mathbb{Z}_l}, \{H(g_i{}^s)\}_{i \in \mathbb{Z}_l}, \{x_i\}_{i \in \mathbb{Z}_n})$$

- Dist: $\mathcal{S}$ sends the credentials $\{s_1, s_2, \ldots s_{t-1}\}$ to the inside adversary $\mathcal{A}_I$.
  Comp: Denote $k = |\Omega|$. In the σ-th session, $\mathcal{S}$ randomly selects k values $\{u'_1, u'_2, \ldots, u'_k\}$ from $\mathbb{Z}_q$ and broadcasts $g_\sigma{}^{u'_i}$ for $i \in \{1, 2, \ldots, k\}$. $\mathcal{S}$ sends $\{u'_1, u'_2, \ldots, u'_{t-1}\}$ to $\mathcal{A}_I$. $\mathcal{S}$ then randomly selects $k - 1$ values $\{c'_1, c'_2, \ldots, c'_{k-1}\}$ from G, and computes $c'_k = \prod_{i \in \Omega} c_i / \prod_{i=1}^{k-1} c'_i$. Then, $\mathcal{S}$ broadcasts the tokens $\{c'_1, c'_2, \ldots, c'_k\}$.
- Auth: In the σ-th session, everyone verifies whether $H(\prod_{i \in \Omega} c'_i) = H(g_\sigma{}^s)$.

We now demonstrate that it is infeasible for the inside adversary $\mathcal{A}_I$ to distinguish the transcripts in these two protocols. In the Init algorithm, the same public parameters params are published in both protocols. In the Dist algorithm, the same credentials $\{s_1, s_2, \ldots, s_{t-1}\}$ are learnt by $\mathcal{A}_I$ in both protocols. In the Comp algorithm, both sets $\{u_1, u_2, \ldots, u_{t-1}\}$ and $\{u'_1, u'_2, \ldots, u'_{t-1}\}$ are randomly distributed in $\mathbb{Z}_q$, and all the broadcast values are randomly distributed in G. In Auth, the algorithm will be successful in both protocols. Therefore, $\mathcal{A}_I$ cannot distinguish between $Real_\Pi(\lambda, params)$ and $SIM_\mathcal{S}(\lambda, params)$, because all these algorithms in $\mathcal{A}_I$'s view are indistinguishable. In other words, we have:

$$View_{\mathcal{A}_I}(Real_\Pi(\lambda, params)) \cong_c View_{\mathcal{A}_I}(SIM_\mathcal{S}(\lambda, params))$$

Moreover, based on the DL assumption, $\mathcal{A}_I$ cannot learn any secret information of s from the public information $\prod_{i \in \Omega} c_i = g_\sigma{}^s$. Hence, our modified scheme satisfies the secrecy property.

Theorem 3. *The proposed group authentication scheme satisfies the no forgery property, assuming that H is a preimage resistant hash function and the DL assumption holds in G.*

Proof. Denote X as the event that $\mathcal{A}_I$ can predict the value $g_\sigma{}^s$ from the public parameters params, and Y as the event that $\mathcal{A}_I$ has learnt some secret information through querying the oracle $\mathcal{O}$. Denote F as the event that $\mathcal{A}_I$ outputs a successful forgery. Then we have:

$$\begin{aligned} \Pr[\mathsf{F}] &= \Pr[\mathsf{F}|\mathsf{X} \vee \mathsf{Y}] \cdot \Pr[\mathsf{X} \vee \mathsf{Y}] + \Pr[\mathsf{F}|\overline{\mathsf{X}} \wedge \overline{\mathsf{Y}}] \cdot \Pr[\overline{\mathsf{X}} \wedge \overline{\mathsf{Y}}] \\ &\le \Pr[\mathsf{X} \vee \mathsf{Y}] + \Pr[\mathsf{F}|\overline{\mathsf{X}} \wedge \overline{\mathsf{Y}}] \\ &\le \Pr[\mathsf{X}] + \Pr[\mathsf{Y}] + \Pr[\mathsf{F}|\overline{\mathsf{X}} \wedge \overline{\mathsf{Y}}] \end{aligned}$$

In the above expression, $\overline{\mathsf{X}}$ and $\overline{\mathsf{Y}}$ denote the complements of X and Y, respectively. Because the hash function H is assumed to be preimage resistant, we have $\Pr[\mathsf{X}] < \epsilon_1(\lambda)$ for some negligible function $\epsilon_1(\cdot)$. Moreover, Theorem 2 implies that the real run of the protocol Π does not leak any secret information to $\mathcal{A}_I$. And the hybrid argument [20] further implies that $\mathcal{A}_I$ does not learn any secret information even if she has queried the oracle $\mathcal{O}$ polynomial number of times. Hence, we have $\Pr[\mathsf{Y}] < \epsilon_2(\lambda)$, for some negligible function $\epsilon_2(\cdot)$. Finally, we analyse the probability $\Pr[\mathsf{F}|\overline{\mathsf{X}} \wedge \overline{\mathsf{Y}}]$. In this case, $\mathcal{A}_I$ needs to guess the value $g_\sigma{}^s$. Because s is randomly distributed in $\mathbb{Z}_q$ and $\mathcal{A}_I$ only controls at most $t - 1$ group members, the probability of guessing g_σ^s correct in each trial is exactly $1/q$. Recall that $\mathcal{A}_I$ can try polynomial number of times, we have $\Pr[\mathsf{F}|\overline{\mathsf{X}} \wedge \overline{\mathsf{Y}}] = Q/q$, where Q denotes the number of trials $\mathcal{A}_I$ has made. Putting the above analyses together, we have:

$$\begin{aligned} \Pr[\mathsf{F}] &\le \Pr[\mathsf{X}] + \Pr[\mathsf{Y}] + \Pr[\mathsf{F}|\overline{\mathsf{X}} \wedge \overline{\mathsf{Y}}] \\ &< \epsilon_1(\lambda) + \epsilon_2(\lambda) + Q/q \\ &\le \epsilon(\lambda) \end{aligned}$$

for some negligible function $\epsilon(\cdot)$. Therefore, our modified scheme satisfies the no forgery property.

Theorem 4. *The proposed group authentication scheme satisfies the no impersonation property, assuming that H is a preimage resistant hash function and the DDH assumption holds in G.*

Proof. Denote X as the event that $\mathcal{A}_O$ can predict the value $g_\sigma{}^s$ from the public parameters params or $\mathcal{A}_O$ can find a targeted collision x^* in G such that $x^* \ne g_\sigma{}^s$ but $\mathsf{H}(x) = \mathsf{H}(g_\sigma{}^s)$, and F as the event that $\mathcal{A}_O$ can impersonate a group member without being detected. Then we have:

$$\begin{aligned} \Pr[\mathsf{F}] &= \Pr[\mathsf{F}|\mathsf{X}] \cdot \Pr[\mathsf{X}] + \Pr[\mathsf{F}|\overline{\mathsf{X}}] \cdot \Pr[\overline{\mathsf{X}}] \\ &\le \Pr[\mathsf{X}] + \Pr[\mathsf{F}|\overline{\mathsf{X}}] \end{aligned}$$

Firstly, based on the assumption that H is a preimage resistant hash function, we have $\Pr[\mathsf{X}] < \epsilon_1(\lambda)$ for some negligible function $\epsilon_1(\cdot)$.

Next, we analyse the probability $\Pr[\mathsf{F}|\overline{\mathsf{X}}]$. In this case, we define two games which are played between the outside adversary $\mathcal{A}_O$ and the challenger. These games are denoted as Game j for $j = 0, 1$. Game 0 is with respect to our proposed scheme where the event X does not happen. We then modify the challenger to obtain Game 1. For $j = 0, 1$, we define W_j as the event that $\mathcal{A}_O$ successfully impersonate a group member in Game j. We will show that $|\Pr[W_0] - \Pr[W_1]| < \epsilon_2(\lambda)$ for some negligible function $\epsilon_2(\cdot)$ and $\Pr[W_1] = Q/q$, where Q denotes the polynomial number of trials $\mathcal{A}_O$ has made. Therefore, it follows that $\Pr[F|\overline{X}]$ is negligible.

Game 0.

- Init: the challenger outputs the system parameters:

$$\text{params} = (H, G, q, \{g_i\}_{i \in \mathbb{Z}_l}, \{H(g_i{}^s)\}_{i \in \mathbb{Z}_l}, \{x_i\}_{i \in \mathbb{Z}_n})$$

- Dist: the challenger computes the credentials $s_i = f(x_i)$ for $i \in \mathbb{Z}_n$, and sends them to the group members through the secure channel.
- Comp: in the σ-th session, every group member in Ω computes and broadcasts the token $c_i = g_\sigma{}^{s_i \mathcal{L}_i} \cdot g_\sigma{}^{u_i v_i}$, where $|\Omega| = t$. Afterwards, $\mathcal{A}_O$ computes and broadcasts her token c_{t+1}. Note that in this algorithm, since the specification of H is publicly known, anyone can evaluate H by herself. For example, any participating user, including the outside adversary $\mathcal{A}_O$, can keep querying H by inputting x_i, and H will output $y_i = H(x_i)$ to this user. Moreover, because it is already assumed that H is preimage resistant, none of the user will get an output $y_i = H(g_\sigma{}^s)$ such that the corresponding value x_i can be used to pass the authentication.
- Auth: it is verified whether $H(\prod_i^{t+1} c_i) = H(g_\sigma{}^s)$.

The game outputs 1 if the verification is successful and 0 otherwise.

Game 1.

In Game 1, the modification only comes in the Comp algorithm, while all the other algorithms remain unchanged.

- Comp: in the σ-th session, every group member in Ω, except the i^*-th group member $i^* \in \Omega$, computes and broadcasts the token $c_i = g_\sigma{}^{s_i \mathcal{L}_i} \cdot g_\sigma{}^{u_i v_i}$, where $|\Omega| = t$. The i^*-th group member selects $r_{i^*} \xleftarrow{R} \mathbb{Z}_q$ and broadcasts the token as $c_{i^*} = g_\sigma{}^{s_i \mathcal{L}_i} \cdot g_\sigma{}^{r_{i^*}}$ instead. Afterwards, $\mathcal{A}_O$ computes and broadcasts her token c_{t+1}. In this step, the participating users can query the hash function H exactly the same as in Game 0.

We then describe an efficient adversary $\mathcal{A}_{DDH}$ that uses $\mathcal{A}_O$ as a subroutine, such that:

$$|\Pr[W_0] - \Pr[W_1]| = \text{Adv}_{\mathcal{A}_{DDH}}^{\text{DDH}}$$

where $\text{Adv}_{\mathcal{A}_{DDH}}^{\text{DDH}}$ denotes $\mathcal{A}_{DDH}$'s advantages in solving the DDH problem. Given the description of the group G with generator g_σ as well as two random values $g_\sigma{}^{u_i}$ and $g_\sigma{}^{v_i}$, $\mathcal{A}_{DDH}$'s purpose is to distinguish $g_\sigma{}^{u_i v_i}$ from $g_\sigma{}^{r_{i^*}}$. We denote p_0 and p_1 as the probability that $\mathcal{A}_{DDH}$ outputs 1 in these two cases, respectively. $\mathcal{A}_{DDH}$ runs our proposed scheme Π where the event X does not happen, and outputs 1 if the corresponding game outputs 1. If $\mathcal{A}_{DDH}$ receives $g_\sigma{}^{u_i v_i}$, she is running Game 0, hence $p_0 = \Pr[W_0]$. If $\mathcal{A}_{DDH}$ receives $g_\sigma{}^{r_{i^*}}$, she is running Game 1, hence $p_1 = \Pr[W_1]$. Therefore, we have

$$|\Pr[W_0] - \Pr[W_1]| = |p_0 - p_1| = \text{Adv}_{\mathcal{A}_{DDH}}^{\text{DDH}}$$

Based on the DDH assumption, $\mathsf{Adv}^{\mathsf{DDH}}_{\mathcal{A}_{DDH}} < \epsilon_2(\lambda)$ for some negligible function $\epsilon_2(\cdot)$. Hence, we have $|\mathsf{Pr}[W_0] - \mathsf{Pr}[W_1]| < \epsilon_2(\lambda)$ as required.

In Game 1, $\mathcal{A}_O$'s hope to impersonate a group member without being detected is to output a token c_{t+1}, such that the value $\prod_{i=1}^{t+1} c_i$ happens to equal $g_\sigma{}^s$. Because the token c_{i*} is randomly distributed in G and it is independent of $g_\sigma{}^s$, the probability that the equation $\prod_{i=1}^{t+1} c_i = g_\sigma{}^s$ holds in each trial is exactly $1/q$. Recall that $\mathcal{A}_O$ can try polynomial number of times, we have $\mathsf{Pr}[W_1] = Q/q$, where Q denotes the number of trials $\mathcal{A}_O$ has made.

Putting the above analyses together, we have $\mathsf{Pr}[\mathsf{F}] < \epsilon_1(\lambda) + \epsilon_2(\lambda) + Q/q$, which is negligible. This finishes the proof that our proposed scheme satisfies the no impersonation property.

4.3   Efficiency Analysis

The computational costs in our proposed scheme are very low. In the Init algorithm, apart from selecting the group G and the required random values, GM computes l modular exponentiations in G and evaluates the hash function l times. In the Dist algorithm, GM selects a random polynomial $f(x)$ over $\mathbb{Z}_q$ with degree $t-1$, and evaluates $f(x)$ at n different points. When using the Horner's rule, every evaluation of $f(x)$ takes $t-1$ multiplications and t additions in $\mathbb{Z}_q$, and each credential is a value in $\mathbb{Z}_q$. In the Comp algorithm, each user broadcasts 2 values in G in two separate rounds. This process requires at most $n+2$ modular exponentiations and n modular multiplications in G. Note that the Lagrange coefficients can be pre-computed beforehand. In the Auth algorithm, each user performs at most n modular multiplications in G and evaluates the hash function once.

5   Conclusion

In this paper, we revisited the research of group authentication schemes and we have contributed in the following two aspects: (1) we have presented a formal security model for the group authentication problem; and (2) we have introduced an efficient and provably secure group authentication scheme in our security model. However, there are also a number of areas that we have not covered, and we would like to leave them as future works.

Proofs Based on Simulation. There are two distinct approaches to defining security for cryptographic protocols: *simulation proof* and *reduction proof*. The former is more intuitive because it models security of the targeted problem via an ideally trusted third party. However, the definitions will become complicated once all details are filled in. In contrast, the reduction proof yields definitions that are simpler to describe and easier to work with. However, the adequacy for modelling the problem is less clear. In this paper, we followed the latter approach, and it is still open how to provide formal security treatment for group authentication using the simulation proof.

Dynamic Groups. Most of the existing group authentication schemes, including the one presented in this paper, only consider a static group in which the group members are fixed throughout the entire lifetime of the protocol. However, in many real-world applications, the group members may change dynamically, e.g. some users may join or leave the group. Defining the formal security model and investigating efficient designs for group authentication schemes that support the dynamic environment are also interesting research topics.

Acknowledgement. This work was partially supported by the National Natural Science Foundation of China (Grant No. 61572303, 61772326, 61672010, 61872087) and Guangxi Key Laboratory of Trusted Software (Grant No. KX201908). We are very grateful to the anonymous reviewers for their valuable comments on the paper.

References

1. Ahmadian, Z., Jamshidpour, S.: Linear subspace cryptanalysis of Harn's secret sharing-based group authentication scheme. IEEE Trans. Inf. Forensics Secur. **13**(2), 502–510 (2018)
2. Bellare, M., Canetti, R., Krawczyk, H.: A modular approach to the design and analysis of authentication and key exchange protocols. In: Proceedings of the Thirtieth Annual ACM Symposium on Theory of Computing, pp. 419–428. ACM (1998)
3. Bresson, E., Chevassut, O., Pointcheval, D., Quisquater, J.-J.: Provably authenticated group Diffie-Hellman key exchange. In: Proceedings of the 8th ACM conference on Computer and Communications Security, pp. 255–264. ACM (2001)
4. Bresson, E., Manulis, M.: Securing group key exchange against strong corruptions. In: Proceedings of the 2008 ACM Symposium on Information, Computer and Communications Security, pp. 249–260. ACM (2008)
5. Chaum, D.: The dining cryptographers problem: unconditional sender and recipient untraceability. J. Cryptol. **1**(1), 65–75 (1988)
6. Chien, H.-Y.: Group authentication with multiple trials and multiple authentications. Secur. Commun. Netw. **2017**, 7 (2017)
7. Diffie, W., Hellman, M.: New directions in cryptography. IEEE Trans. Inf. Theory **22**(6), 644–654 (1976)
8. Elmouaatamid, O., Lahmer, M., Belkasmi, M.: Group authentication with fault tolerance for internet of things. In: Sabir, E., García, A.A., Ghogho, M., Debbah, M. (eds.) UNet 2017. LNCS, vol. 10542, pp. 299–307. Springer, Cham (2017). https://doi.org/10.1007/978-3-319-68179-5_26
9. Fiat, A., Shamir, A.: How To prove yourself: practical solutions to identification and signature problems. In: Odlyzko, A.M. (ed.) CRYPTO 1986. LNCS, vol. 263, pp. 186–194. Springer, Heidelberg (1987). https://doi.org/10.1007/3-540-47721-7_12
10. Guo, C., Zhuang, R., Yuan, L., Feng, B.: A group authentication scheme supporting cheating detection and identification. In: 2015 Ninth International Conference on Frontier of Computer Science and Technology (FCST), pp. 110–114. IEEE (2015)
11. Hao, F., Zieliński, P.: A 2-round Anonymous Veto protocol. In: Christianson, B., Crispo, B., Malcolm, J.A., Roe, M. (eds.) Security Protocols 2006. LNCS, vol. 5087, pp. 202–211. Springer, Heidelberg (2009). https://doi.org/10.1007/978-3-642-04904-0_28

12. Harn, L.: Group authentication. IEEE Trans. Comput. **62**(9), 1893–1898 (2013)
13. Katz, J., Shin, J.S.: Modeling insider attacks on group key-exchange protocols. In: Proceedings of the 12th ACM Conference on Computer and Communications Security, pp. 180–189. ACM (2005)
14. Katz, J., Yung, M.: Scalable protocols for authenticated group key exchange. J. Cryptol. **20**(1), 85–113 (2007)
15. Li, J., Wen, M., Zhang, T.: Group-based authentication and key agreement with dynamic policy updating for MTC in LTE-a networks. IEEE Internet Things J. **3**(3), 408–417 (2016)
16. Liu, Y., Sun, Q., Wang, Y., Zhu, L., Ji, W.: Efficient group authentication in RFID using secret sharing scheme. Cluster Comput. **22**, 1–7 (2018)
17. Mahalle, P.N., Prasad, N.R., Prasad, R.: Novel threshold cryptography-based group authentication (TCGA) scheme for the internet of things (IoT) (2014)
18. Miao, F., Jiang, H., Ji, Y., Xiong, Y.: Asynchronous group authentication. Chin. J. Electron. **26**(4), 820–826 (2017)
19. Schnorr, C.-P.: Efficient signature generation by smart cards. J. Cryptol. **4**(3), 161–174 (1991)
20. Shafi, G., Micali, S.: Probabilistic encryption. J. Comput. Syst. Sci. **28**(2), 270–299 (1984)
21. Shamir, A.: How to share a secret. Commun. ACM **22**(11), 612–613 (1979)
22. Su, W.-T., Wong, W.-M., Chen, W.-C.: A survey of performance improvement by group-based authentication in IoT. In: 2016 International Conference on Applied System Innovation (ICASI), pp. 1–4. IEEE (2016)
23. Xia, Z., Yang, X., Xiao, M., He, D.: Provably secure threshold paillier encryption based on hyperplane geometry. In: Liu, J.K., Steinfeld, R. (eds.) ACISP 2016. LNCS, vol. 9723, pp. 73–86. Springer, Cham (2016). https://doi.org/10.1007/978-3-319-40367-0_5

AGE: Authentication Graph Embedding for Detecting Anomalous Login Activities

Renzheng Wei[1,2], Lijun Cai[1], Aimin Yu[1(✉)], and Dan Meng[1]

[1] Institute of Information Engineering, Chinese Academy of Sciences, Beijing, China
{weirenzheng,cailijun,yuaimin,mengdan}@iie.ac.cn
[2] School of Cyber Security,
University of Chinese Academy of Sciences, Beijing, China

Abstract. Detecting anomalies in login activities is a critical step in response to credential-based lateral movement attacks. Although attackers with compromised credentials can impersonate legal users and move laterally between computers without triggering the alarm, his login activities would likely deviate from the users' normal patterns. We propose AGE, an **A**uthentication **G**raph **E**mbedding based anomalous login activities detection system. The goal of authentication graph embedding is to capture comprehensive relationships that facilitate the construction of user profiles. Specifically, the user profiles contain three types of features: the *familiarity*-related features, the *similarity*-related features, and the lateral movement *walks*-related features. To evaluate AGE thoroughly, we use our synthetic malicious lateral movement traces as well as red team activities provided by CMU-CERT. Extensive experiments show that AGE achieves good performance and outperforms the baseline methods. Moreover, we also design experiments that will help us understand the authentication graph embedding.

Keywords: Anomalous login activities detection · Authentication graph embedding · Lateral movement · User profiling

1 Introduction

Lateral movement is the key stage of Advanced Persistent Threats (APTs). After establishing a foothold, attackers move laterally in networks to collect valuable information. Even though a number of advanced hacking techniques (e.g., remote exploits) can be used in lateral movement, their effects are overrated [12]. Instead, attackers tend to use the compromised passwords or credentials (obtained by social engineering, pass the hash, etc.) to impersonate legal users and log on to computers. Doing this, attackers can avoid the detection of the security system and make defense difficult. In recent years, this type of attack (also known as the credential-based attack) has been widely adopted in many instances of APTs, including the 2011 RSA data breach [20] and 2014 JPMorgan Chase data breach [18].

© Springer Nature Switzerland AG 2020
J. Zhou et al. (Eds.): ICICS 2019, LNCS 11999, pp. 341–356, 2020.
https://doi.org/10.1007/978-3-030-41579-2_20

User login activities are recorded in the form of authentication event logs. Such log data can provide great insights into the user's normal login behavior. Given the authentication event logs, the goal is to identify the anomalous login activities which are the signs of malicious lateral movement. Behavior-based anomaly detection methods are very suitable for this task. Because behavior-based methods can identify the deviation from the norm and detect the unseen anomalies by modeling the user's normal login activities. Traditional behavior-based methods typically use statistical features to train a classifier as the normal login behavior model. However, simple statistical features can hardly capture complex relationships among entities in authentication event logs, such as community information and lateral movement path attributes. Researchers, therefore, try to mine the complex relationships by first transforming raw authentication event logs into the graph [10,13], since the graph is a data structure which is good at capturing dependencies relationship among nodes.

Recently, many behavior-based anomaly detection methods have started to model normal behavior patterns from the graph. For example, some efforts [2,7, 13] propose to apply graph theoretic approaches to discover suspicious activities. In these works, researchers have exploited basic graph attributes to represent users' normal authentication patterns [13]. And they have tried to mine communities [2] or subgraphs [7] so that they can find the users who do not belong to any community or the users who have changed their behavior patterns. Additionally, to detect malicious lateral movement, the characteristics of paths on the graph have been analyzed [3]. However, there exist two challenges in these existing graph-based anomalous behavior detection approaches: (1) most of these methods focus on mining useful relationships depend on the particular task. So the relationships in the graph may not be fully preserved. (2) The existing methods are susceptible to the noise in the user behavior logs.

To overcome challenges mentioned above, we propose an **A**uthentication **G**raph **E**mbedding (AGE for short) based anomalous login activities detection system. We first construct a graph using raw authentication event logs, which is the authentication graph, to represent login activities. Then, we make use of the graph embedding technique to capture relationships in the authentication graph as much as possible. Specifically, in our work, the relationships among source computers, destination computers and user accounts (In the following of this paper, user and user account can be used interchangeably), should be preserved into the embedding vectors. Next, we extract various features, which are the user profiles of normal login activities, using the embedding vector. At last, we train a classifier using these features to detect anomalous login activities.

The novelty of our approach is that we take advantage of the outcome of the popular graph embedding technique to extract features that represent the normal user profile in login activities. Based on the embedding vector, we construct user profile through three types of features: the *familiarity*-related features, the *similarity*-related features and the lateral movement *walks*-related features. The *familiarity*-related features measure the relationship between user and computer; the *similarity*-related features measure the relationship between computers.

They are mainly used for finding community information in the authentication graph; the lateral movement *walks*-related features are mainly used for representing path characteristics, which are important for detecting malicious lateral movement.

We evaluate the effectiveness of our approach on the CMU-CERT dataset. Note that red team activities provided by CERT only contain short term anomalous login activities. We have to test whether our approach can detect the deviation from the user's normal profile in a long term perspective. Because the malicious lateral movement can maintain persistence in network for a long time. For this purpose, we design an algorithm to generate malicious lateral movement traces. Experiments show that our approach can achieve satisfactory results and outperform baseline methods. Additionally, for evaluating the effectiveness of authentication graph embedding, we design two experiments that are related to the final anomalous login activities detection goal. The results of the two experiments can help us understand the output of the authentication graph embedding.

1.1 Contributions and Road Map

In summary, the contributions of this paper are as follows.

- We propose an authentication graph embedding based anomalous login activities detection system. We devise a user profile of login activities, taking into account three types of features: the *familiarity*-related, the *similarity*-related and the lateral movement *walks*-related.
- We evaluate our proposed approach on CERT-scenario3 and CERT-LM dataset and demonstrate its capability of detecting anomalous login activities.
- We design two experiments related to the final anomalous login activities detection goal. And the results of the experiments can help us understand and evaluate the authentication graph embedding.

The remaining sections of this paper are organized as follows. An overview of our system framework is described in Sect. 2. Section 3 mainly details the user profile constructing methods. Section 4 presents the overall experiment results, and details the evaluation methods of authentication graph embedding at last. Section 5 surveys previous related works. Section 6 concludes the paper.

2   Overview and Architecture

In this paper, we mainly focus on the credential-based malicious lateral movement where attackers steal the credentials and impersonate legal users. The assumption is that during lateral movement attackers' login activities would be likely inconsistent with normal user login patterns. The goal of our proposed method is to detect login activities that deviate from the expected norm of user profiles. In this section, we first introduce some necessary notations. Then we present the system architecture.

2.1   Definitions

Authentication Graph. Assuming a set of N_U users $\{s_{u_1}, \ldots, s_{u_{N_U}}\}$ and associated N_H computers $\{s_{h_1}, \ldots, s_{h_{N_N}}\}$ in authentication event logs. We denote the authentication graph as $G = \{V, E\}$, where users and computers are two types of vertices. The authentication graph is constructed by adding a set of E edges $\{(i, j)\}$ between user nodes and computer nodes over a time period $[0, T)$. $G = \{V, E\}$ is a bipartite graph. Additionally, we also denote the authentication graph as $G \in \{w_{ij}\}^{N_U \times N_H}$, where w_{ij} is the number of authentication events from user i to computer j within period of $[0, T)$.

PAS (Person's Authentication Subgraph) [13]. A user u's PAS represents the user's login activities over a time period $[0, T)$. The nodes of PAS are a set of computers that the user u has logged on over a time period $[0, T)$. The edges of PAS can be regarded as the user u's lateral movement traces.

User Profile. We denote user u's profile as $p_u = \{x_1, \ldots, x_i, \ldots, x_m\}$, where x_i is a feature extracted for representing one or more characteristics of u's normal login activities.

2.2   System Architecture

The framework of our AGE-based anomalous login activities detection system is presented in Fig. 1. The key components of the system are authentication graph embedding and user profile generating. Firstly, the raw authentication event logs are transformed into the graph $G \in \{w_{ij}\}^{N_U \times N_H}$ by authentication graph generator. Then the authentication graph embedding algorithm maps each node to a vector $v \in \mathbb{R}^d$, where d is the dimensionality of the v. Based on the embedding vector, we construct user profiles by extracting three types of features: familiarity-related, similarity-related and lateral movement-related. Finally, an anomaly detection model is trained using the user profile.

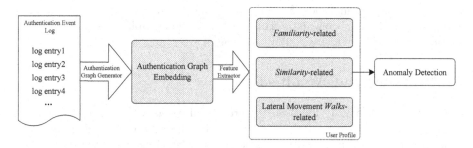

Fig. 1. The proposed framework for detecting anomalous user behavior within enterprise networks.

3   Methodology

We propose the methodology for the task of detecting anomalous user login activities. We first introduce the mechanism of authentication graph embedding, which illustrates how the relationships are well preserved in vectors. Then we present three types of extracted features in detail.

3.1   Authentication Graph Embedding

The goal of authentication graph embedding is to encode each node into a low-dimension vector while preserving relationships among nodes in graph G. For example, if the user u and the computer h co-occur many times in authentication events, then the graph embedding algorithm will make the embedding vectors v_u and v_h closer in the embedding space. The graph embedding algorithm is detailed below.

The process of authentication graph embedding is divided into two stages: (1) random walk to generate node sequences set X, where each sequence $x = (s_1, \ldots, s_M) \in X$ consists of user nodes and computer nodes; (2) learn a d-dimensional representation $v_{s_i} \in \mathbb{R}^d$ for each unique user s_u and computer s_h. Specifically, the Skip-Gram model [14] is used to learn node embedding vector by maximizing the objective function $\mathcal{L}$ over the sequence set X. $\mathcal{L}$ is defined as follows:

$$\mathcal{L} = \sum_{s \in S} \log P(N(s)|s), \tag{1}$$

where S is the vocabulary consisting of unique nodes which represent users and computers; $N(s)$ is the set of neighborhoods of node $s \in S$; $P(N(s)|s)$ is the probability of observing nodes from the neighborhood of the given source node s, which is defined using a $softmax$ unit

$$P(n_i|s) = \frac{\exp(v_{n_i}'^T v_s)}{\sum_{s'=1}^{|S|} \exp(v_{s'}'^T v_s)}, \tag{2}$$

where $n_i \in N(s)$, v and v' are two d-dimensional representation of the node s. v is what we ultimately want, namely the embedding vector of node s. From the definition of objective function $\mathcal{L}$, we can see that after the convergence of the Skip-Gram model, embedding vectors of nodes that often occur together in the same context of X are closer than others.

3.2   Generating User Profile

Graph embedding vectors are very suitable for calculating similarities between entities, whether these entities belong to the same type or not. We use the inner product of two embedding vectors as the similarity measurement. The similarity between entities i and j is defined as:

$$sim(i, j) = v_i \cdot v_j. \tag{3}$$

We present the characteristics of a user u's normal login activities from three aspects: the *familiarity* between u and computers in u's PAS, the *similarity* between computers in the u's PAS, and the characteristics of lateral movement *walks* in PAS.

Familiarity Features. We define two features, f_{min} and f_{mean}, which are used to measure the *familiarity* of the user u to computers h in PAS. Specifically, f_{min} and f_{mean} can be calculated as follows:

$$f_{min}(u) = \min_i(sim(u, h_i)), \tag{4}$$

$$f_{mean}(u) = \frac{1}{|H_u|} \sum_{i=1}^{|H_u|} sim(u, h_i), \tag{5}$$

where H_u is the set of computers in user u's PAS, h_i is a computer in the H_u, $|H_u|$ is the number of computers in H_u.

Similarity Features. The next feature, $f_{dispersion}$, measures the degree of dispersion of computers belong to user u's PAS. We compute the value of this feature as follows:

$$f_{dispersion}(u) = \frac{\sum_{h_i,h_j \in H_u, i \neq j} sim(h_i, h_j)}{|H_u| \times (|H_u| - 1)}. \tag{6}$$

In addition, we further extract a feature, f_{scope}, to quantify the scope of a user's login activities in networks. The value of f_{scope} is defined as the maximum distance between the centroid of PAS embedding v_{h_o} and each computer embedding v_{h_i}, $h_i \in H_u$. Note that the maximum distance is calculated using the minimum inner product similarity.

$$f_{scope}(u) = \min_i(sim(h_i, h_o)), \tag{7}$$

The motivation of including these two features, $f_{dispersion}$ and f_{scope}, is that the dispersion and the scope of user's login activities are likely influenced by the attacker malicious authentication behavior.

Lateral Movement *Walk* Features [3]. We define the *walk* to be a path of user's lateral movement in PAS. The length of a *walk* in PAS is defined as the sum of weights on the *walk* paths. Then the maximum and interquartile range (IQR) of lengths of all *walks* are computed as the lateral movement *walk* features, which is denoted as f_{lm_max} and f_{lm_iqr}. The IQR measures the dispersion of the central 50% of all *walks* lengths. The motivation of including these two features is that a user's normal lateral movement behavior usually has invariant *walk* attributes. We believe that the existence of attackers who pursue the maximum gains through the compromised user account is likely to cause deviations from theses two *walk* attributes.

All of the features that are used for generating user profile are listed in Table 1.

3.3 Anomaly Detection

We train a classifier as the anomaly detector to identify anomalous login activities. Given a test sample, the anomaly detector can output an anomaly score. The assumption is that all user profiles used for training do not include anomalous login activities. Note that several classifiers like One-Class SVM (OCSVM), local outlier factor [4], Principal component analysis (PCA) [27] can be used as our anomaly detector. We have compared the performance of different classifiers in Sect. 4.2.

Table 1. Summary of features.

Features name		Description
Familiarity Features	f_{min}	Minimum *familiarity* between user and computers
	f_{mean}	Mean *familiarity* between user and computers
Similarity Features	$f_{dispersion}$	The *dispersion* degree of computer in a user's PAS
	f_{scope}	The *scope* of a user's PAS
Lateral Movement *Walk* Features	f_{lm_max}	The maximum length of lateral movement *walks*
	f_{lm_iqr}	The IQR of lengths of lateral movement *walks*

4 Experiments

4.1 Dataset

In this section, we evaluate the proposed method using insider threat CERT r4.2 dataset [8]. This dataset contains multisource activity logs (i.e., user login, emails, files access, website visiting, and removable devices usage.) of 1000 users and 1003 computers. In this work, we use only user login activities (in the *logon.csv*), from which the authentication graph and PASs are generated. Additionally, users' meta-data (e.g., the department, team, and role of the user) provided in *LDAP* directory is also used to understand embedding. CERT is a synthetic dataset and its red team contains five synthetic attack scenarios. Unfortunately, only one scenario (scenario 3) contains the credential-based attacks. Therefore, to properly evaluate the proposed approach, we synthesize malicious lateral movement traces and inject them into the normal authentication event logs.

Malicious Lateral Movement Trace Generation. Inspired by the lateral movement chain generation algorithm proposed in [3], we adapt the SIS model [23] to simulate malicious lateral movement traces. When an attacker has compromised a computer in the network, the event that the attacker logged on the next computer is a Poisson process with a rate λ. λ controls the speed of lateral movement in networks. The speed of attackers should not be too fast, or the alarm will be triggered. We tune λ to ensure that the speed of attackers' lateral movement is slower than that of normal behavior, such as the administrator's regular maintenance.

The pseudo-code of generating malicious lateral movement traces is shown in Algorithm 1.[1] Given a user u's PAS, the output of Algorithm 1 is a set of simulated authentication events of malicious lateral movement. We then inject these malicious events into u's normal login activities. We set the *explore_rate* to balance the **exploration** and **exploitation** of attackers' next movement. The meaning of *explore_rate* is explained as follows. When an attacker compromised a user account u, he can exploit all computers in the PAS with fewer risks. On the other hand, to obtain more valuable information, the attacker also tries to explore other computers in networks that do not belong to PAS. We tune *explore_rate* to simulate different lateral movement behavior of attackers.

4.2   Experiment Results and Comparison Study

Experiment Setup. We train the authentication graph embedding model using 5 months of login data without any red team activities, from January to May 2010. The hyperparameters of authentication graph embedding are set as follows. The dimensionality of the embedding vector is set to be $d = 60$. It is a good trade-off between accuracy and efficiency, as a higher embedding dimensionality does not improve too much accuracy, but it requires a longer time to train and to compute inner product similarity. The context window size of the Skip-Gram model is set to $m = 1$. Starting from each node in the graph, we iterate 10 walks, each of which has a fixed length of $l = 200$. The p is set to 0.1, while the q is set to 2.0.

We evaluate our approach in two aspects, which are the abilities to discovery short term and long term anomalies. We believe that both types of anomalies may be a sign of lateral movement attacks. For the task of detecting short term anomalous login activities, we employ authentication events of 68 days. We generate the profile for each user's one-day login activities. In other words, a user's one day profile is a data sample to be fed into classifiers. In this way, we have in total of 46629 samples. In this dataset (CERT-scenario3), there are 20 positive samples which are generated from 10 malicious users' login activities provided by the red team of CERT. We train a classifier (i.e., OCSVM with Gaussian kernel) as the normal login activity model using 45609 benign samples which are randomly selected. The remaining 1000 benign samples and all of the 20 positive samples are used for the test.

---

[1] We implement Algorithm 1 at https://github.com/WeiieW-cas/Malicious-Lateral-Movement-Traces-Generation.

Algorithm 1. Malicious Lateral Movement Trace Generation

Input:
   Authentication Graph $G = \{V, E\}$, User u's PAS, λ, $explore\_rate$, $start\_time$, end_time

Output:
   $Event(t, u, c)$

1: $V_c := \emptyset$
2: $visited(v) := False, \forall v \in V$
3: $t := start\_time$
4: $v_{start} :=$ RandomSelectNode(PAS)
5: $Event := (t, u, v_{start})$
6: $visited(v_{start}) := True$
7: **while** $t \leq end\_time$ **do**
8:    Sleep for $\tau \sim Exp(\lambda)$
9:    Let $t = t + \tau$
10:   Let $rand = $ Random(0,1)
11:   **if** $rand \leq explore\_rate$ **then**
12:      Random compromise a computer v' that is NOT in user u's PAS (explore):
         Select v' from $\{v'|v' = (\neg visited(v')) \wedge v' \notin PAS\}$
13:   **else**
14:      Random compromise a computer v' in user u's PAS to compromise (exploit):
         Select v' from $\{v'|(v,v') \in \varepsilon, \forall v \in V_c\}$
15:   **end if**
16:   $Event := Event \cup (t, u, v')$
17:   $visited(v') := True$
18:   $\varepsilon := \varepsilon \backslash \{e \in E|e = (v, v') \in E, \forall v \in V_c\}$
19:   $\varepsilon := \varepsilon \cup \{e \in E|e = (v', i) \in E, \forall i \in V\}$
20:   $V_c := V_c \cup \{v'\}$
21:   $v = v'$
22: **end while**

For evaluating the detection of long term anomalies, which are most likely a sign of malicious lateral movement, we use login activities of 5 consecutive months. The data of the first 4 months is used to train a classifier, and the last month's data is used for the test. And no red team activities provided by CERT are in it. We inject into login activities of the last month the malicious lateral movement traces which are generated using Algorithm 1. In Algorithm 1, λ is set to 0.0003, $explore\_rate$ is set to 0.1. We randomly select 20 users' login activities to be inserted the synthetic attack traces. A user's one month profile is a data sample. In this dataset (CERT-LM), there are in total 4952 samples and 20 of them are malicious. Similar to the short term anomaly detection, we train a model using 3972 benign samples. The remaining samples including 20 anomalous samples are used for the test. The details of these two datasets are shown in Table 2.

Table 2. Set up of login data sets.

Dataset	Sample description	Number of samples	
		Training data	Test data
CERT-scenario3 (short term)	User's one day data as a sample	45609 benign	1000 benign; 20 malicious
CERT-LM (long term)	User's one month data as a sample	3972 benign	980 benign; 20 malicious

Overall Experiment Results. We evaluate our approach using a number of different metrics, including AUC (Area Under the ROC Curve), F1-score and recall. Besides the AGE mentioned before, we have implemented a clustering-based AGE method: AGE-Clustering. In AGE-Clustering, before training a classifier using all user profiles, we employ K-Means to partition the samples. For each cluster, we then train a classifier as the anomaly detector. For comparison, we have implemented the approach proposed in [13], named Basic-AG in Table 3. We also demonstrate whether simple baseline methods would be enough for the task of detecting anomalous user login activities. Specifically, we have implemented Oddball and PCA in Python 3.6 by using libraries like scikit-learn, numpy, and so forth. Table 3 shows the results of our AGE based approaches compared to other methods.

We can see from Table 3, our AGE based methods outperform other methods in both CERT-scenario3 and CERT-LM. The performances of our AGE based methods in CERT-LM are better than that in CERT-scenario3. This result shows that our AGE based methods have a strength to detect long term anomalies, which are an important sign of malicious lateral movement.

Table 3. Results comparison on two datasets.

Dataset	Method	AUC	F1-score	Recall
CERT-scenario3	Oddball	0.9502	0.8101	100%
	PCA	0.9212	0.8738	95%
	Basic-AG [13]	0.9755	0.9198	100%
	AGE	**0.9802**	0.9384	100%
	AGE-Clustering	0.9780	**0.9387**	100%
CERT-LM	Oddball	0.8763	0.7807	90%
	PCA	0.8198	0.7077	95%
	Basic-AG [13]	0.8876	0.8970	95%
	AGE	**0.9998**	**0.9818**	100%
	AGE-Clustering	0.9897	0.9801	100%

Next, we change λ and *explore_rate* of Algorithm 1, and evaluate the performance of AGE in the face of various types of malicious lateral movement. We vary λ while keeping *explore_rate* fixed. The result is shown in Fig. 2(a). Similarly, we vary *explore_rate* while keeping λ fixed and show the result in Fig. 2(b). Results show that the performance of AGE gradually improves as the attackers move faster or are more willing to explore. This result is consistent with the intuition.

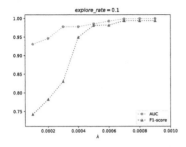 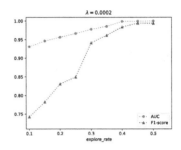

(a) Varying λ to simulate the speed changing of attacker's lateral movement.

(b) Varying *explore_rate* to simulate the changing in risk taking of attackers.

Fig. 2. Performances of AGE in the face of various types of malicious lateral movement.

We claim that the user profile constructed using authentication graph embedding is good at representing normal user behavior. Traditional one-class classifiers can directly be used to achieve satisfactory results. To verify this conclusion, we compare several classifiers: OCSVM with Gaussian kernel and linear kernel, PCA and local outlier factor. The result is shown in Fig. 3. All of these four classifiers achieve good performance using the profiles that are constructed based on authentication graph embedding vectors.

At last, we design an experiment to compare the representation ability of AGE based features and count-based features. It is obvious that many relationships in authentication event logs can be captured by both these two types of features. For example, the frequency (count-based feature) at which a user u logs on to a computer h can reflect the familiarity relationship between u and h. Unfortunately, not all relationships represented by AGE based features can be directly substituted for the count-based features. Specifically, only the features related to *familiarity* can be obtained by counting. For the sake of fairness, we only compare the *familiarity* features, which is f_{min} and f_{mean}, with the corresponding count-based features. Given these two different types of features, we chose PCA as the anomaly detector, and compare the performance on the task of detecting anomalous login activities. The CERT-scenario3 dataset is used for the comparison. Concretely, in the training feature matrix of PCA, each row represents a user, while each column represents a computer. For AGE based training matrix, the value of each cell is the *familiarity* value computed using Eqs. (3) and (4). For the count-based training matrix, the value of each cell is the number of logins. The anomaly detection results are shown in Fig. 4. It can be seen that the performance of using AGE based features outperforms that of count-based features.

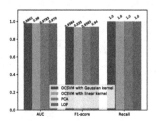
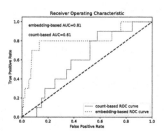

Fig. 3. Performances of four AGE based classifiers on CERT-scenario3 dataset.

Fig. 4. The comparative results of AGE based *familiarity* against count-based one.

4.3 Understanding and Evaluating the Authentication Graph Embedding

In this section, we understand and evaluate the effectiveness of authentication graph embedding through two experiments. Specifically, these two intermediate tasks are used to examine whether the relationships between computers and between users are preserved or not.

Relationships Between Computers. The embedding vectors of computers are expected to encode the relationship between computers, which is the computer community information. Only when the computer community information is well encoded in the vectors, can the features like scope and dispersion be meaningful. We demonstrate this by computing the average inner product similarities between computers from different communities. The result is reported in Table 4. In Table 4, the community label of each computer is assigned as its functional unit (The functional unit names have been abbreviated), which is inferred from the CERT LDAP file. From Table 4, we can observe that average inner product similarities between computers of the same community are much higher compared to similarities between computers of different communities. This result shows that the computer community information is well encoded in the learned embedding vectors.

Relationships Between Users. Similar to the experiment above, to evaluate if user community information is captured by embedding vectors, we also compute average inner product similarities between users of different functional units. The results are reported in Table 5. From Table 5, it can be observed that inner product similarities between users of the same functional unit are much higher compared to similarities between users of different functional units. So, this result shows that the user community information is also well encoded in the learned embedding vectors.

Table 4. Inner product similarities between different hosts communities.

Community	Admin	Finance	Manu	P&C	R&E	S&M
Admin	**4.8423**	4.4069	4.3868	4.4602	4.4305	4.1011
Finance		**6.1064**	4.3360	4.5092	4.3811	4.3251
Manu			**4.4152**	4.3529	4.3421	4.1361
P&C				**6.5514**	4.3750	4.2563
R&E					**4.4512**	4.3510
S&M						**4.3610**

Table 5. Inner product similarities between different users communities.

Community	Admin	Finance	Manu	P&C	R&E	S&M
Admin	**5.4521**	5.0671	5.1254	4.5489	5.0410	5.0662
Finance		**7.4847**	5.1512	4.4386	5.0061	4.9951
Manu			**5.4042**	4.6789	5.1491	5.1411
P&C				**5.4864**	4.5170	4.5233
R&E					**5.1542**	5.0400
S&M						**5.1810**

5   Related Work

In this section, we review previous related works including malicious lateral movement detection, credential-based attacks detection, masquerade detection, and so forth. Methods commonly followed in the literature have two main steps: feature extraction and modeling. In the first step, the distinctive features describing a user's normal behavior are processed and extracted. In the second step, these features are used to learn a classifier as the normal behavior model. Generally, the first step determines the final performance of the anomaly detection system and has become the focus of recent researches. Existing methods extract features representing a user's behavioral characteristics from different perspectives.

Many works extract raw features from various types of logs related to login activities. Goncalves et al. [9] selected count-based features describing the characteristics of the user's authentication activities, such as the number of authentication tries. However, these features are not able to identify credential-based attacks because attackers with compromised credentials would not log in by trial-and-error. Zhang et al. [28] inspected the authentication logs in university settings. They extracted the geographic location features and timing features. These features are specially designed for detecting university account abuse.

Recently, several graph-based methods [2,3,11,13,16] have been proposed to mine various relationships among entities in behavior logs. To detect malicious lateral movement, researchers focus on finding abnormal communities [16] or common structures [17] in the behavior logs (i.e., authentication event logs, network traffic logs, and audit logs.). A typical attack scenario of these works is that attackers have taken control of a computer within a network using social engineering such as phishing attack [1,6,26], they then attempt to lateral movement [25] to obtain more valuable information. To detect this type of attack, the monitor tools that can process large amounts of logs are needed. As a result, these tools produce large and heterogeneous behavior data. And it makes the task of detecting anomalous activities difficult. To deal with this type of data, several neural network-based methods [5,21,22] are proposed. However, neural network models are too "deep" to be trained and too "dark" to be interpretable.

There are two previous papers which are similar to our work. First, Kent et al. [13] proposed to use the authentication graph to analyze user behavior. They extracted features based on authentication graph attributes, including graph density, vertex count and edge count, etc. However, the representation ability of their statistical features is limited. To comprehensively represent the more complicated relationships, our work extracts the embedding-based features to generate user profiles. The embedding-based features not only can describe the structural attributes of the authentication graph but also can measure various relationships between entities in authentication event logs. Second, Siadati et al. [17] detected anomalous logins in enterprise networks. They have analyzed the real authentication event log and claimed that there exist structural login patterns in it. However, the pattern mining algorithm they proposed can not discover other patterns besides the structural ones. The dataset used in [17] has not been public, so we can not make a comparison.

We review the honeywords [24] methods which can directly detect malicious login activities. In this paper, however, we focus on detecting the activities generated by the attacker who already owns the credentials. We also review the continuous authentication methods. Most of these methods rely on the biometric trait(s) [19], such as the face information [15]. However, collecting the biometric information requires specified devices and these will increase the cost and bring high overhead.

6   Conclusion

We proposed a novel approach for detecting anomalous user login activities based on authentication graph embedding. We made use of the graph embedding algorithm to learn the representation of the authentication events. We then constructed user profiles base on the embedding vector. We evaluated the proposed approach in the tasks of detecting both short and long term anomalous login activities, which are the signs of malicious lateral movement.

Acknowledgements. This work is supported by the strategic Priority Research Program of Chinese Academy of Sciences, Grant No. XDC02040200.

References

1. Banjo, S.: Home depot hackers exposed 53 million email addresses. Wall Street J. (2014)
2. Bhattacharjee, S.D., Yuan, J., Jiaqi, Z., Tan, Y.P.: Context-aware graph-based analysis for detecting anomalous activities. In: 2017 IEEE International Conference on Multimedia and Expo (ICME), pp. 1021–1026. IEEE (2017)
3. Bohara, A., Noureddine, M.A., Fawaz, A., Sanders, W.H.: An unsupervised multi-detector approach for identifying malicious lateral movement. In: 2017 IEEE 36th Symposium on Reliable Distributed Systems (SRDS), pp. 224–233. IEEE (2017)
4. Breunig, M.M., Kriegel, H.P., Ng, R.T., Sander, J.: LOF: identifying density-based local outliers. ACM SIGMOD Rec. **29**, 93–104 (2000)
5. Brown, A., Tuor, A., Hutchinson, B., Nichols, N.: Recurrent neural network attention mechanisms for interpretable system log anomaly detection. In: Proceedings of the First Workshop on Machine Learning for Computing Systems, p. 1. ACM (2018)
6. Business insider: how the hackers broke into Sony and why it could happen to any company (2014). http://www.businessinsider.com/how-the-hackers-broke-into-sony-2014-12
7. Eberle, W., Graves, J., Holder, L.: Insider threat detection using a graph-based approach. J. Appl. Secur. Res. **6**(1), 32–81 (2010)
8. Glasser, J., Lindauer, B.: Bridging the gap: a pragmatic approach to generating insider threat data. In: 2013 IEEE Security and Privacy Workshops, pp. 98–104. IEEE (2013)
9. Gonçalves, D., Bota, J., Correia, M.: Big data analytics for detecting host misbehavior in large logs. In: 2015 IEEE Trustcom/BigDataSE/ISPA, vol. 1, pp. 238–245. IEEE (2015)
10. Hagberg, A., Lemons, N., Kent, A., Neil, J.: Connected components and credential hopping in authentication graphs. In: 2014 Tenth International Conference on Signal-Image Technology and Internet-Based Systems, pp. 416–423. IEEE (2014)
11. Javed, M.: Detecting credential compromise in enterprise networks. Ph.D. thesis, UC Berkeley (2016)
12. Joyce, R.: Disrupting nation state hackers. USENIX Association, San Francisco, January 2016
13. Kent, A.D., Liebrock, L.M., Neil, J.C.: Authentication graphs: analyzing user behavior within an enterprise network. Comput. Secur. **48**, 150–166 (2015)
14. Mikolov, T., Sutskever, I., Chen, K., Corrado, G.S., Dean, J.: Distributed representations of words and phrases and their compositionality. In: Advances in Neural Information Processing Systems, pp. 3111–3119 (2013)
15. Niinuma, K., Jain, A.K.: Continuous user authentication using temporal information. In: Biometric Technology for Human Identification VII, vol. 7667, p. 76670L. International Society for Optics and Photonics (2010)

16. Oprea, A., Li, Z., Yen, T.F., Chin, S.H., Alrwais, S.: Detection of early-stage enterprise infection by mining large-scale log data. In: 2015 45th Annual IEEE/IFIP International Conference on Dependable Systems and Networks, pp. 45–56. IEEE (2015)

17. Siadati, H., Memon, N.: Detecting structurally anomalous logins within enterprise networks. In: Proceedings of the 2017 ACM SIGSAC Conference on Computer and Communications Security, pp. 1273–1284. ACM (2017)

18. Silver-Greenberg, J., Goldstein, M., Perlroth, N.: JPMorgan chase hack affects 76 million households. New York Times **2** (2014)

19. Traore, I.: Continuous Authentication Using Biometrics: Data, Models, and Metrics: Data, Models, and Metrics. IGI Global, Hershey (2011)

20. TrendMicro: Apt myths and challenges. https://blog.trendmicro.com/trendlabs-security-intelligence/infographic-apt-myths-and-challenges/. Accessed 4 April 2012

21. Tuor, A., Kaplan, S., Hutchinson, B., Nichols, N., Robinson, S.: Deep learning for unsupervised insider threat detection in structured cybersecurity data streams. In: Workshops at the Thirty-First AAAI Conference on Artificial Intelligence (2017)

22. Tuor, A.R., Baerwolf, R., Knowles, N., Hutchinson, B., Nichols, N., Jasper, R.: Recurrent neural network language models for open vocabulary event-level cyber anomaly detection. In: Workshops at the Thirty-Second AAAI Conference on Artificial Intelligence (2018)

23. Van Mieghem, P.: The N-intertwined SIS epidemic network model. Computing **93**(2–4), 147–169 (2011)

24. Wang, D., Cheng, H., Wang, P., Yan, J., Huang, X.: A security analysis of honeywords. In: NDSS (2018)

25. Weiss, N.E., Miller, R.S.: The target and other financial data breaches: frequently asked questions. In: Congressional Research Service, Prepared for Members and Committees of Congress, February, vol. 4, p. 2015 (2015)

26. Wikipedia: Phishing – Wikipedia, the free encyclopedia (2019). http://en.wikipedia.org/w/index.php?title=Phishing&oldid=892015701. Accessed 14 April 2019

27. Wold, S., Esbensen, K., Geladi, P.: Principal component analysis. Chemometr. Intell. Lab. Syst. **2**(1–3), 37–52 (1987)

28. Zhang, J., et al.: Safeguarding academic accounts and resources with the university credential abuse auditing system. In: IEEE/IFIP International Conference on Dependable Systems and Networks (DSN 2012), pp. 1–8. IEEE (2012)

Applied Cryptograph

A Multi-Group Signature Scheme from Lattices

Tian Qiu[1,2], Lin Hou[1,2(✉)], and Dongdai Lin[1,2]

[1] State Key Laboratory of Information Security,
Institute of Information Engineering, Chinese Academy of Sciences, Beijing, China
{qiutian,houlin,ddlin}@iie.ac.cn
[2] School of Cyber Security, University of Chinese Academy of Sciences,
Beijing, China

Abstract. Group signature allows group members to sign on behalf of *the group* anonymously, and incorporate some tracing mechanism to identify the actual signer. Multi-group signature (MGS), introduced by Ateniese and Tsudik (FC'99), is a proper generalization of group signature. It allows signers to sign messages anonymously on behalf of *multiple groups* and has extensive applications in electronic commerce. However, all existing MGS schemes are from classical assumptions and will be insecure once quantum computers come true.

In this paper, we propose the first MGS scheme in the lattice setting which is also the first quantum-resistant proposal. The keystone of our work is a zero-knowledge argument of knowledge (ZKAoK) system of *different* syndromes of the *same* vector based on the work by Libert et al. (Asiacrypt'16) and Ling et al. (PKC'18). With additional signing and encryption layers, our ZKAoK allows the signer to prove memberships in multiple groups simultaneously, which is the key issue on the MGS construction, and it can be of independent interest. For security proofs, we formalize the MGS model in the framework of Bellare et al. (CT-RSA'05).

Keywords: Public-key cryptography · Group signature · Multi-Group Signature · Lattice-based cryptography · Zero-Knowledge Argument of Knowledge

1 Introduction

Group signature is an important privacy-oriented primitive as proposed by Chaum and van Heyst [9], and finds extensive applications in the real world, such as e-commerce, TCG, anonymous online communications, etc. It allows group members to sign on behalf of the group without leaking out their identities, except that some tracing authority can identify the actual signer of any suspected signature.

Up to now, many generalized notions of group signatures were proposed, such as group blind signatures [21], hierarchical group signatures [29], sub-group

© Springer Nature Switzerland AG 2020
J. Zhou et al. (Eds.): ICICS 2019, LNCS 11999, pp. 359–377, 2020.
https://doi.org/10.1007/978-3-030-41579-2_21

signatures [3] and *multi-group signatures* [3]. Multi-group signatures (MGS) was first introduced by Ateniese and Tsudik in the multiple group setting. It allows a signer simultaneously in multiple groups to sign messages on behalf of these groups anonymously. This notion has important application in the field of e-commerce, here is an example: In a bank, some loan contracts need to be signed by an authorized loan officer who is also a notary public. If Alice is a member of these independent groups (loan officers and notaries public), she can sign the document representing these groups and convince verifiers that she is a single entity in both groups. Ateniese and Tsudik also proposed the first MGS construction from CS97 [8] based on number-theoretic assumptions, where an additional proof is generated to claim that several group signatures are produced by the same signer.

In the early years, many elegant group signature schemes based on classic assumptions flourished, e.g. [2,6,7]; however, with the rapid development of quantum computing, researchers turn to seek proposals for post-quantum security[1]. Lattice-based cryptography [1] thus becomes a hot topic, and it has other advantages such as the worst-case to the average-case reduction and so on. Specifically, Gordon et al. [12] proposed the first lattice-based group signature scheme; Libert et al. [16] suggested the first scheme from lattice assumptions supporting dynamic joining; del Pino et al. [27] gave the currently most practical scheme. Besides, there are several other lattice-based schemes [15,17,19,25] featuring in efficiency or functionality. However, to our knowledge, there is no multi-group signature scheme from lattice assumptions.

Overall, it may seem simple to generalize regular group signatures into the multi-group setting, in the meaning that it can be done by additionally proving the signer belongs to different groups from the perspective of general constructions. However, in concrete schemes, generating non-interactive zero-knowledge (NIZK) for the membership of group is the most intricate part and proving extra things would perplex this issue further. In MGS, the key issue for the signer is proving memberships in multiple groups simultaneously. The idea in [3] is that a signer claims the membership in two groups by proving the equality of two double discrete logarithms. As we show here, there are some issues to be addressed if one aims to use this idea in the lattice setting. In lattice-based cryptography, one could prove in zero-knowledge (ZK) that different ciphertexts are encryptions on the same message using Stern-like protocol [16,30]. Unfortunately, in multi-group setting, identities of the signer are distinct in different groups, which means the ciphertext part of her group signature are encryptions on different plaintexts. This restriction prevents straightforward adaptation of Stern's protocol. Therefore, in order to construct a lattice-based multi-group signature scheme, we have to solve the problem that, given different ciphertexts on different messages, how to prove the relationship among those messages without exposing them.

---

[1] In this work, the post-quantum security is only considered in the classical random oracle model, rather than quantum random oracle model. This is in the same spirit as in many other work, such as [16,17,27].

Related Work. Traceable signature [14] is a variant notion of groups signature. It allows the leakage of some trapdoor with respect to some member to link all signatures produced by him. Benjumea et al. [5] extended this notion to the multi-group setting, namely fair traceable multi-group signatures.

Libert et al. [16] abstracted Stern's protocol [28] to cover many relations in lattice-based cryptography and constructed a statistical ZKAoK for the abstract relation. In particular, they proposed a signature scheme and a dynamic group signature scheme from it. Recently, Ling et al. [20] proposed the first constant size group signature scheme from Libert et al.'s abstract Stern-like protocol, where the sizes of signature and public key are independent of the group size. Following the sign-encrypt-proof paradigm, the group member encrypts her identity and proves in ZK her possession of a membership certificate which contains her secret key with a valid signature from the issuer, and the well-formedness of that ciphertext.

Our Contributions and Main Techniques. In this paper, we give the first lattice-based multi-group signature scheme. The key observation is that different syndromes are *linkable* if they are computed from the same short vector. However, when it comes to privacy applications such as group signatures, things turn to complex, because in such case, not only that vector but also all syndromes should be kept secret as user's identities.

To this end, we construct a zero-knowledge argument of knowledge (ZKAoK) of linkable syndromes. The main technique is reducing that relation to an instance of the abstract Stern-like protocol [16]. With additional signing and encryption layers, this ZKAoK allows the prover to convince the verifier that she possesses valid signatures on corresponding linkable syndromes and the ciphertexts of these syndromes are well-performed. Therefore, we prove in ZK the relationship among different plaintexts only given their encryptions and obtain the underlying zero-knowledge protocol for MGS.

Here we briefly describe our MGS scheme and the detailed construction is shown in Sect. 5. Firstly the user chooses a short secret vector $\mathbf{x}$ and computes two syndromes $p_1 = \mathbf{B}_1 \cdot \mathbf{x}$ and $p_2 = \mathbf{B}_2 \cdot \mathbf{x}$. Then she sends p_1 to the issuer of group G_1 and p_2 to the issuer of group G_2 respectively. These issuers return a signature on the syndrome independently and register her as a group member. The user generates ciphertexts for her syndromes. Moreover, she utilizes the protocol in Sect. 3.2 to prove in ZK that she owns a short secret vector, some different syndromes calculated from it (thus are linkable), valid signatures on these syndromes and the given ciphertexts are correct encryptions on her syndromes. The protocol is repeated $\kappa = \omega(\log \lambda)$ times to realize negligible soundness error and made non-interactive by the Fiat-Shamir heuristic [11]. Given a valid multi-group signature, any verifier is convinced that the signer belongs to several groups at the same time. For security parameter λ and the number of groups t, our scheme has public key size $\widetilde{\mathcal{O}}(t \cdot \lambda)$, signing key size $\widetilde{\mathcal{O}}(t \cdot \lambda)$ and signature size $\widetilde{\mathcal{O}}(t \cdot \lambda)$.

At last but not least, in the framework of Bellare et al. [4], we formalize a model for MGS under which the security of our scheme can be proved. It allows users to join multiple groups independently and sign on behalf of those groups. Besides, its security naturally covers that of the regular case as well as the most distinguishing feature of MGS, namely linkability across different groups. This property implies that signers in multiple groups are able to claim her memberships simultaneously with some proof, and it is infeasible for other unqualified members to produce valid message MGS pairs.

Paper Organizations. In Sect. 2, we primarily fix notations and introduce some difficult problems on lattices and some techniques. In Sect. 3, we introduce a ZKAoK for proving multiple linkable syndromes. We turn to formalize the model of MGS in Sect. 4 as well as its security requirements. In Sect. 5, we provide concrete construction of MGS from lattice assumptions with security analysis. Sect. 6 concludes this paper.

2 Preliminaries

Notations. Let $x\|y$ denote the concatenation of two binary strings x and y, and let $\|x\|$ denote the Euclidean norm of a vector x. If S is a finite set, we denote the cardinality (number of elements) of S by $|S|$, and denote uniformly choosing a random element s from S by $s \xleftarrow{\$} S$. If $n \in \mathbb{N}$, then $[n] - \{1, 2, \cdots, n\}$. If A is a randomized algorithm then $z \leftarrow A(x, y, \cdots)$ denotes the operation of running A on inputs $x, y, \cdots$ and outputting z. For $q \in \mathbb{N}$, $\mathbb{Z}_q$ denotes the standard group of integers modulo q. Let $[a]_3$ denote $a \bmod 3$. Throughout this paper, we let λ denote the security parameter.

2.1 Lattice

Definition 1 (Lattice). *Let $\boldsymbol{B} = \{b_1, \ldots, b_n\}$ be n ($\leqslant m$) linearly independent vectors in $\mathbb{R}^m$. The lattice generated by $\boldsymbol{B}$, denoted by $\mathcal{L}(\boldsymbol{B})$, is the set of all the integer linear combination of the vectors in $\boldsymbol{B}$, and the set $\boldsymbol{B} \in \mathbb{R}^{m \times n}$ is called the basis of $\mathcal{L}(\boldsymbol{B})$. Namely, $\mathcal{L}(\boldsymbol{B}) = \{\sum_{i=1}^{n} x_i b_i \mid x_i \in \mathbb{Z}\} = \{\boldsymbol{B}x \mid x \in \mathbb{Z}^n\}$.*

We consider lattice problems restricted to ideal lattices [24,26] and focus on rings of the form $R = \mathbb{Z}[X]/(\Phi_{2n}(X))$ and $R_q = (R/qR)$, where n is a power of 2, $q \geq 3$ is a positive integer, $\Phi_{2n}(X) = X^n + 1$ is the cyclotomic polynomial of degree n, and let $\mathbb{Z}_q = [-\frac{q-1}{2}, \frac{q-1}{2}]$. For a ring element $v = v_0 + v_1 \cdot X + \cdots + v_{n-1} \cdot X^{n-1} \in R_q$, let $\tau(v) = (v_0, v_1, \cdots, v_{n-1})^T \in \mathbb{Z}_q^n$ denote its coefficient, and for $\mathbf{v} = (v_1, v_2, \cdots, v_m)^T \in R_q^m$, let $\tau(\mathbf{v}) = (\tau(v_1)\|\tau(v_2)\| \cdots \|\tau(v_m)) \in \mathbb{Z}_q^{mn}$.

Define rot be a ring homomorphism that maps a ring element to a integer matrix: for $a \in R_q$, $\mathsf{rot}(a) = [\tau(a)|\tau(a \cdot X)| \cdots |\tau(a \cdot X^{n-1})] \in \mathbb{Z}_q^{n \times n}$. For a vector $\mathbf{A} = [a_1|a_2| \cdots |a_m] \in R_q^{1 \times m}$, $\mathsf{rot}(\mathbf{A}) = [\mathsf{rot}(a_1)|\mathsf{rot}(a_2)| \cdots |\mathsf{rot}(a_m)] \in \mathbb{Z}_q^{n \times mn}$. Moreover, for $y = a \cdot v$ over R_q, we have $\tau(y) = \mathsf{rot}(a) \cdot \tau(v) \bmod q$. For $y = \mathbf{A} \cdot \mathbf{v}$ over R_q, $\tau(y) = \mathsf{rot}(\mathbf{A}) \cdot \tau(\mathbf{v}) \bmod q$.

For $a = a_0 + a_1 \cdot X + \cdots + a_{n-1} \cdot X^{N-1} \in R$, we define its infinity norm $\|a\|_\infty = \max_i(|a_i|)$ and for $\mathbf{b} = (b_1, b_2, \cdots, b_m)^T \in R^m$, define $\|\mathbf{b}\|_\infty = \max_j(\|b_j\|_\infty)$.

Definition 2 ($\text{RSIS}_{n,m,q,\beta}$ **Problem** [22,26]). *Given a uniformly random matrix* $\mathbf{A} = [a_1|a_2|\cdots|a_m] \in R_q^{1\times m}$, *find a non-zero vector* $\mathbf{x} = (x_1, x_2, \cdots, x_m)^T \in R^m$ *such that* $\mathbf{A} \cdot \mathbf{x} = 0$ *and* $\|\mathbf{x}\|_\infty \leq \beta$.

As shown in [22], for $m > \frac{\log q}{\log(2\beta)}, \gamma = 16\beta mn \log^2 n$, and $q \geq \frac{\gamma\sqrt{n}}{4\log n}$, the $\text{RSIS}_{n,m,q,\beta}$ problem is at least as hard as SVP_γ^∞ in any ideal in the ring R.

Definition 3 ($\text{RLWE}_{n,m,q,\chi}$ **Problem** [23]). *Let* $n, m \geq 1, q \geq 2$, *and let* χ *be a probability distribution on* R. *For* $s \in R_q$, *let* $A_{s,\chi}$ *be the distribution obtained by sampling* $a \xleftarrow{\$} R_q$ *and* $e \leftarrow \chi$, *and outputting* $(a, b = a \cdot s + e) \in R_q \times R_q$. *Given* m *independent samples* $(a_i, b_i) \in R_q \times R_q$ *where every sample is chosen from* $A_{s,\chi}$ *or the uniform distribution, distinguish which is the case with non-negligible advantage.*

Let $q = \text{poly}(n)$ be a prime power, $B = \widetilde{\mathcal{O}}(n^{5/4})$ be an integer and χ be a B-bounded distribution on R. Then, for $\gamma = n^2(q/B)(nm/\log(nm))^{1/4}$, the $\text{RLWE}_{n,m,q,\chi}$ problem is at least as hard as SVP_γ^∞ in any ideal in the ring R [23].

2.2 Some Techniques

Decompositions. [18] These techniques are used to decompose B-bounded ring elements to ring vectors whose coefficients in $\{-1, 0, 1\}$.

For $B \in \mathbb{N}$, define $\delta_B := \lfloor \log_2 B \rfloor + 1$ and compute $B_j = \lfloor \frac{B+2^{j-1}}{2^j} \rfloor$ for $j \in [\delta_B]$. Decompose $v \in [B]$ as the following procedure:

1. $v' := v$;
2. For j = 1 to δ_B do: (a) If $v' \geq B_j$ then $v^{(j)} := 1$, else $v^{(j)} := 0$; (b) $v' := v' - B_j \cdot v^{(j)}$;
3. Output $\text{idec}_B(v) = (v^{(1)}, v^{(2)}, \cdots, v^{(\delta_B)})^T$.

For $B \in [1, \frac{q-1}{2}]$, define the ring decomposition function rdec_B as follows that maps a ring element $a \in R_q$ where $\|a\|_\infty \leq B$ to a vector $\mathbf{a} \in R^{\delta_B}$ such that $\|\mathbf{a}\|_\infty \leq 1$:

1. For $\tau(a) = (a_0, a_1, \cdots, a_{n-1})^T$, compute $\mathbf{w}_i = \sigma(a_i) \cdot \text{idec}_B(|a_i|) = (w_{i,1}, w_{i,2}, \cdots, w_{i,\delta_B})^T \in \{-1, 0, 1\}^{\delta_B}$ where $\sigma(a_i) = -1$ if $a_i < 0$; $\sigma(a_i) = 0$ if $a_i = 0$; $\sigma(a_i) = 1$ if $a_i > 0$;
2. Let $\mathbf{w} = (\mathbf{w}_0\|\mathbf{w}_1\|\cdots\|\mathbf{w}_{n-1}) \in \{-1, 0, 1\}^{n\delta_B}$ and compute $\mathbf{a} \in R^{\delta_B}$ s.t. $\tau(\mathbf{a}) = \mathbf{w}$;
3. Output $\text{rdec}_B(a) = \mathbf{a}$.

For $\mathbf{v} = (v_1, v_2, \cdots, v_m)^T \in R^m$, $\|\mathbf{v}\|_\infty \leq B$, let $\text{rdec}_B(\mathbf{v}) = (\text{rdec}_B(v_1) \|\text{rdec}_B(v_2)\| \cdots \|\text{rdec}_B(v_m))$.

Define matrices $\mathbf{H}_B \in \mathbb{Z}^{n\times n\delta_B}$ and $\mathbf{H}_{m,B} \in \mathbb{Z}^{nm\times nm\delta_B}$ as

$$\mathbf{H}_B = \begin{bmatrix} B_1\ B_2\ \cdots\ B_{\delta_B} & & \\ & \ddots & \\ & & B_1\ B_2\ \cdots\ B_{\delta_B} \end{bmatrix} \text{ and } \mathbf{H}_{m,B} = \begin{bmatrix} \mathbf{H}_B & & \\ & \ddots & \\ & & \mathbf{H}_B \end{bmatrix}.$$

Thus $\tau(a) = \mathbf{H}_B \cdot \tau(\mathsf{rdec}_B(a)) \bmod q$ and $\tau(\mathbf{v}) = \mathbf{H}_{m,B} \cdot \tau(\mathsf{rdec}_B(\mathbf{v}))$. For simplicity, when $B = \frac{q-1}{2}$, we abbreviate rdec_B and $\mathbf{H}_B$ to rdec and $\mathbf{H}$.

Permutations. [20] Here are some permutation techniques applied for tuples, and we would use them in Stern-like protocol.

For $z \in \{-1, 0, 1\}$, denote z by a tuple $\mathsf{enc}_3(z) = ([z+1]_3, [z]_3, [z-1]_3)^T \in \{-1, 0, 1\}^3$, and any vector $\mathbf{v} = (v^{(-1)}, v^{(0)}, v^{(1)})^T \in \mathbb{Z}^3$ can be permuted as $\pi_e(\mathbf{v}) = (v^{([-e-1]_3)}, v^{([-e]_3)}, v^{([-e+1]_3)})^T$ with $e \in \{1, 0, 1\}$. We have $\mathbf{v} = \mathsf{enc}_3(z) \Leftrightarrow \pi_e(\mathbf{v}) = \mathsf{enc}_3([z+e]_3)$.

Further, denote $\mathbf{z} = (z_1, z_2, \cdots, z_u)^T$ as $\mathsf{enc}(\mathbf{z}) = (\mathsf{enc}_3(z_1) \| \mathsf{enc}_3(z_2) \| \cdots \| \mathsf{enc}_3(z_u)) \in \{-1, 0, 1\}^{3u}$, and permute $\mathbf{v} = (\mathbf{v}_1 \| \mathbf{v}_2 \| \cdots \| \mathbf{v}_u) \in \mathbb{Z}^{3u}$ into $\Pi_{\mathbf{e}}(\mathbf{v}) = (\pi_{e_1}(\mathbf{v}_1) \| \mathbf{v}_2 \| \cdots \| \pi_{e_u}(\mathbf{v}_u))$, with $\mathbf{e} = (e_1, e_2, \cdots, e_u)^T \in \{-1, 0, 1\}^u$. We have the following equation for $\mathbf{z}, \mathbf{e} \in \{-1, 0, 1\}^u$:

$$\mathbf{v} = \mathsf{enc}(\mathbf{z}) \Leftrightarrow \Pi_{\mathbf{e}}(\mathbf{v}) = \mathsf{enc}([\mathbf{z}+\mathbf{e}]_3) \tag{1}$$

For any $(t, z) \in \{0, 1\} \times \{-1, 0, 1\}$, denote it as $\mathsf{ext}(t, z) = (\bar{t} \cdot [z+1]_3, t \cdot [z+1]_3, \bar{t} \cdot [z]_3, t \cdot [z]_3, \bar{t} \cdot [z-1]_3, t \cdot [z-1]_3)^T$, and the vector $\mathbf{v} = (v^{(0,-1)}, v^{(1,-1)}, v^{(0,0)}, v^{(1,0)}, v^{(0,1)}, v^{(1,1)}) \in \mathbb{Z}^6$ can be permuted as follows with $b \in \{0, 1\}$, $e \in \{-1, 0, 1\}$:

$$\psi_{b,e}(\mathbf{v}) = (v^{(b,[-e-1]_3)}, v^{(\bar{b},[-e-1]_3)}, v^{(b,[-e]_3)}, v^{(\bar{b},[-e]_3)}, v^{(b,[-e+1]_3)}, v^{(\bar{b},[-e+1]_3)})^T.$$

$\mathbf{v} = \mathsf{ext}(t, z) \Leftrightarrow \psi_{b,e}(\mathbf{v}) = \mathsf{ext}(t \oplus b, [z+e]_3)$ with $t, b \in \{0, 1\}$, $z, e \in \{-1, 0, 1\}$.

For $(\mathbf{t}, \mathbf{z}) = (t_0, t_1, \cdots, t_{c_d-1}, z_1, z_2, \cdots, z_u)^T \in \{0, 1\}^{c_d} \times \{-1, 0, 1\}^u$, define $\mathsf{mix}(\mathbf{t}, \mathbf{z}) = (\mathsf{enc}(\mathbf{z}) \| \mathsf{ext}(t_0, z_1) \| \cdots \| \mathsf{ext}(t_0, z_u) \| \cdots \| \mathsf{ext}(t_{c_d-1}, z_1) \| \cdots \| \mathsf{ext}(t_{c_d-1}, z_u))$, and the permutation for $\mathbf{v} = (\mathbf{v}_{-1} \| \mathbf{v}_{0,1} \| \cdots \| \mathbf{v}_{0,u} \| \cdots \| \mathbf{v}_{c_d-1,1} \| \cdots \| \mathbf{v}_{c_d-1,u}) \in \mathbb{Z}^{3u+6uc_d}$ is $\Phi_{\mathbf{b},\mathbf{e}}(\mathbf{v}) = (\Pi_{\mathbf{e}}(\mathbf{v}_{-1}) \| \psi_{b_0,e_1}(\mathbf{v}_{0,1}) \| \cdots \| \psi_{b_0,e_u}(\mathbf{v}_{0,u}) \| \cdots \| \psi_{b_{c_d-1},e_1}(\mathbf{v}_{c_d-1,1}) \| \cdots \| \psi_{b_{c_d-1},e_u}(\mathbf{v}_{c_d-1,u}))$ with $\mathbf{b} = (b_0, b_1, \cdots, b_{c_d-1})^T \in \{0, 1\}^{c_d}$, $\mathbf{e} = (e_1, e_2, \cdots, e_u) \in \{-1, 0, 1\}^u$. Then the following equivalence relation holds:

$$\mathbf{v} = \mathsf{mix}(\mathbf{t}, \mathbf{z}) \Leftrightarrow \Phi_{\mathbf{b},\mathbf{e}}(\mathbf{v}) = \mathsf{mix}(\mathbf{t} \oplus \mathbf{b}, [\mathbf{z}+\mathbf{e}]_3). \tag{2}$$

2.3 An Abstraction of Stern's Protocol [16]

Let K, L, q be positive integers, where $L \geq K$ and $q \geq 2$. Let VALID be a subset of $\{-1, 0, 1\}^L$ and suppose that $\mathcal{S}$ is a finite set such that one can associate every $\phi \in \mathcal{S}$ with a permutation Γ_ϕ of L elements, satisfying the following conditions:

$$\begin{cases} \mathbf{w} \in \mathsf{VALID} \Leftrightarrow \Gamma_\phi(\mathbf{w}) \in \mathsf{VALID} \\ \text{If } \mathbf{w} \in \mathsf{VALID} \text{ and } \phi \text{ is uniform in } \mathcal{S}, \text{ then } \Gamma_\phi(\mathbf{w}) \text{ is uniform in VALID} \end{cases} \tag{3}$$

Define the abstract relation as

$$\mathrm{R_{abstract}} = \{(\mathbf{M}, \mathbf{u}), \mathbf{w} \in \mathbb{Z}_q^{K \times L} \times \mathbb{Z}_q^K \times \mathsf{VALID} : \mathbf{M} \cdot \mathbf{w} = \mathbf{u} \bmod q\}.$$

Here is a Stern-like protocol $\langle \mathcal{P}, \mathcal{V} \rangle$ for the relation where the string commitment scheme COM is statistically hiding and computationally binding:

1. **Commitment**: $\mathcal{P}$ samples a mask vector $\mathbf{r}_w \xleftarrow{\$} \mathbb{Z}_q^L$, a permutation $\phi \xleftarrow{\$} S$ and randomness ρ_1, ρ_2, ρ_3 for COM. The she sends CMT $= (C_1, C_2, C_3)$ to $\mathcal{V}$ where $C_1 = \mathsf{COM}(\phi, \mathbf{M} \cdot \mathbf{r}_w \bmod q; \rho_1)$, $C_2 = \mathsf{COM}(\Gamma_\phi(\mathbf{r}_w); \rho_2)$, $C_3 = \mathsf{COM}(\Gamma_\phi(\mathbf{w} + \mathbf{r}_w \bmod q); \rho_3)$.
2. **Challenge**: $\mathcal{V}$ sends a challenge $Ch \leftarrow \{1, 2, 3\}$ to $\mathcal{P}$.
3. **Response**: Depending on Ch, $\mathcal{P}$ sends RSP computed as follows:
   - $Ch = 1$: Let $\mathbf{t}_w = \Gamma_\phi(\mathbf{w})$, $\mathbf{t}_r = \Gamma_\phi(\mathbf{r}_w)$, and RSP $= (\mathbf{t}_w, \mathbf{t}_r, \rho_2, \rho_3)$.
   - $Ch = 2$: Let $\phi_2 = \phi, \mathbf{w}_2 = \mathbf{w} + \mathbf{r}_w \bmod q$ and RSP $= (\phi_2, \mathbf{w}_2, \rho_1, \rho_3)$.
   - $Ch = 3$: Let $\phi_3 = \phi, \mathbf{w}_3 = \mathbf{r}_w$ and RSP $= (\phi_3, \mathbf{w}_3, \rho_1, \rho_2)$.

and the **Verification** is proceeded by $\mathcal{V}$ as follows when she receives RSP:

- $Ch = 1$: Check $\mathbf{t}_w \in \mathsf{VALID}, C_2 = \mathsf{COM}(\mathbf{t}_r; \rho_2), C_3 = \mathsf{COM}(\mathbf{t}_w + \mathbf{t}_r \bmod q; \rho_3)$
- $Ch = 2$: Check $C_1 = \mathsf{COM}(\phi_2, \mathbf{M} \cdot \mathbf{w}_2 - \mathbf{u} \bmod q; \rho_1), C_3 = \mathsf{COM}(\Gamma_{\phi_2}(\mathbf{w}_2); \rho_3)$.
- $Ch = 3$: Check $C_1 = \mathsf{COM}(\phi_3, \mathbf{M} \cdot \mathbf{w}_3; \rho_1), C_3 = \mathsf{COM}(\Gamma_{\phi_3}(\mathbf{w}_3); \rho_2)$.

Theorem 1 ([16]). *Assume that* COM *is a statistically hiding and computationally binding string commitment scheme. Then, the above protocol is a statistical* ZKAoK *with perfect completeness, soundness error $2/3$, and communication cost $\mathcal{O}(L \log q)$. In particular:*

1. *Input $(\mathbf{M}, \mathbf{u})$, $\exists$ a polynomial-time simulator who can output an accepted transcript that is statistically close to that produced by the real prover.*
2. *There exists a polynomial-time knowledge extractor that, on Input a commitment* CMT *and 3 valid responses $(\mathsf{RSP1}, \mathsf{RSP2}, \mathsf{RSP3})$ to all 3 possible values of the challenge Ch, $\exists$ a polynomial-time knowledge extractor who can output a $\mathbf{w}' \in$* VALID *such that $\mathbf{M} \cdot \mathbf{w}' = \mathbf{u} \bmod q$.*

2.4 Ducas-Micciancio Signature Scheme [10]

$\mathsf{Setup}(1^\lambda)$: On the security parameter λ, the trusted party chooses the public parameters $\{n, q, k, R, R_q, \ell, m, \overline{m}, d, c_0, c_1, \cdots, c_d, B, \beta\}$ and initialize the state $S \in \mathbb{Z}$ to 0, where $n = \mathcal{O}(\lambda)$ being a power of 2, modulus $q = \widetilde{\mathcal{O}}(\lambda)$ where $q = 3^k$ for some $k \in \mathbb{Z}^+$. Let $R = \mathbb{Z}[X]/(X^n + 1)$, $R_q = R/qR$, $\ell = \lfloor \log \frac{q-1}{2} \rfloor + 1$, $m \le 2\lceil \log q \rceil + 2$ and $\overline{m} = m + k$. Let real constant $c > 1$ and $\alpha_0 \ge 1/(c-1)$, integer $d \ge \log_c(\omega(\log(n)))$ and strictly increasing integer sequence $c_0, c_1, \cdots, c_d$ with $c_0 = 0, c_i = \lfloor \alpha_0 c^i \rfloor$ for $i \in [d]$. Set integer bounds $\beta = \widetilde{\mathcal{O}}(n)$, $B = \widetilde{\mathcal{O}}(n^{5/4})$. The verification key pk consists of $\{\mathbf{A}, \mathbf{F}_0 \in R_q^{1 \times \overline{m}}, \{\mathbf{A}_{[j]}\}_{j=0}^d \in R_q^{1 \times k}, \mathbf{F}, \mathbf{F}_1 \in R_q^{1 \times \ell}, u \in R_q\}$. The signing key is the trapdoor matrix $\mathbf{R} \in R_q^{m \times k}$.
$\mathsf{Sign}(\mathsf{pk}, \mathbf{R}, p)$: On the message $p \in R_q$, the signer with $\mathbf{R}$ proceeds as follows.

1. Set $t = (t_0, t_1, \cdots, t_{c_d-1}) \in \{0, 1\}^{c_d}$, where $S = \Sigma_{j=0}^{c_d-1} 2^j \cdot t_j$. Update S to $S + 1$.
2. Sample $\mathbf{r} \in R^{\overline{m}}$ such that $\|\mathbf{r}\|_\infty \le \beta$.
3. Use $\mathbf{R}$, produce a ring vector $\mathbf{v} = (\mathbf{s}\|\mathbf{z}) \in R^{\overline{m}+k}$ such that

$$\mathbf{A}\cdot\mathbf{s}+\mathbf{A}_{[0]}\cdot\mathbf{z}+\Sigma_{i=1}^d\mathbf{A}_{[i]}\cdot t_{[i]}\cdot\mathbf{z} = \mathbf{F}\cdot\mathsf{rdec}(\mathbf{F}_0\cdot\mathbf{r}+\mathbf{F}_1\cdot\mathsf{rdec}(p))+u, \text{ where } \|\mathbf{v}\|_\infty \leq \beta \tag{4}$$

4. Output $(t, \mathbf{r}, \mathbf{v})$ as the signature on p.

Verify($\mathsf{pk}, p, (t, \mathbf{r}, \mathbf{v})$): On the message-signature pair $(p, (t, \mathbf{r}, \mathbf{v}))$, anyone with pk can run this algorithm and output 1 if the Eq. (4) holds. Otherwise, output 0.

3 The ZKAoK Systems

In this section, we introduce our ZKAoK for linkable syndromes which would be the keystone of our MGS scheme. Combining it with the zero-knowledge protocol in [20], we obtain a ZKAoK with signing and encryption layers which serves as underlying ZKAoK for multi-group signatures.

3.1 A ZKAoK System for Linkable Syndromes

In this section, we design a ZKAoK system which allows $\mathcal{P}$ to prove in ZK that she owns *multiple* syndromes with respect to *the same* secret short value (see Definition 4 for formal description). Our ZKAoK construction is embedded in the proof of Theorem 2.

Definition 4. $R_{ls} = \{(\mathbf{B}^1, \mathbf{B}^2 \in R_q^{1\times m}), \mathbf{x} \in R^m, p^1, p^2 \in R_q : \mathbf{B}^k \cdot \mathbf{x} - p^k = 0, \|\mathbf{x}\|_\infty \leq 1\}$

Theorem 2. *If* COM *is a statistically hiding and computationally binding string commitment scheme, there exists an interactive protocol which is a statistical* ZKAoK *for the relation* R_{ls} *with perfect completeness, soundness error* $2/3$, *and communication cost* $\mathcal{O}(L_0 \log q)$.

Proof. Using Decomposition technique in Sect. 2.2, we rewrite conditions in R_{ls} as

$$[\mathsf{rot}(\mathbf{B}^k)] \cdot \tau(\mathbf{x}) - [\mathbf{H}] \cdot \tau(\mathsf{rdec}(p^k)) = \mathbf{0}^n \bmod q \tag{5}$$

where $\tau(\mathbf{x}) \in \{-1, 0, 1\}^{nm}$, $\tau(\mathsf{rdec}(p^k)) \in \{-1, 0, 1\}^{n\ell}$, and they can be integrated into one equation:

$$\begin{pmatrix} \mathsf{rot}(\mathbf{B}^1) & -\mathbf{H} & \mathbf{0} \\ \mathsf{rot}(\mathbf{B}^2) & \mathbf{0} & -\mathbf{H} \end{pmatrix} \cdot \begin{pmatrix} \tau(\mathbf{x}) \\ \tau(\mathsf{rdec}(p^1)) \\ \tau(\mathsf{rdec}(p^2)) \end{pmatrix} = \begin{pmatrix} \mathbf{0}^n \\ \mathbf{0}^n \end{pmatrix} \bmod q \tag{6}$$

which satisfies the form $\mathbf{M}_0 \cdot \mathbf{w}_0 = \mathbf{u}_0 \bmod q$, where $\mathbf{M}_0$ contents all public matrices of (5) in square brackets $[\cdot]$, $\mathbf{u}_0 = (\mathbf{0}^n\|\mathbf{0}^n)$ and $\mathbf{w}_0 = (\tau(\mathbf{x})\|\tau(\mathsf{rdec}(p^1))\|\tau(\mathsf{rdec}(p^2))) \in \{-1, 0, 1\}^{nm+2n\ell}$.

Using Permutation technique in Sect. 2.2, we extend the vector $\mathbf{w}_0$ into $\mathbf{w}_0' = \mathsf{enc}(\mathbf{w}_0) \in \{-1, 0, 1\}^{L_0}$ where $L_0 = 3nm + 6n\ell$, and add some zero-columns to $\mathbf{M}_0$ in proper positions to get matrix $\mathbf{M}_0' \in \mathbb{Z}_q^{2n\times L_0}$ such that $\mathbf{M}_0'\cdot\mathbf{w}_0' = \mathbf{M}_0\cdot\mathbf{w}_0$.

Now we define a VALID set of all vectors $\mathbf{v}_0' \in \{-1,0,1\}^{L_0}$ where $\exists\, \mathbf{v}_0 \in \{-1,0,1\}^{(m+2\ell)n}$, s.t. $\mathbf{v}_0' = \mathsf{enc}(\mathbf{v}_0)$ and there exists an element $\mathbf{f}_0 \in \mathcal{S}_0 = \{-1,0,1\}^{(m+2\ell)n}$, such that for every $\mathbf{v}_0' \in \{-1,0,1\}^{L_0}$, the permutation $\mathbf{f}_0$ transforms $\mathbf{v}_0'$ into $\varPi_{\mathbf{f}_0}(\mathbf{v}_0')$. Due to the Eq. (1), $\mathbf{w}_0'$ belongs to the VALID set, and it is clear that the VALID set and the permutation set $\mathcal{S}_0$ satisfy the conditions (3). Therefore, we reduce the statement of **linkable syndromes** to an instance of the abstract Stern's protocol in Sect. 2.3.

Let COM be the KTX commitment scheme from [13], which is statistically hiding and computationally binding if (R)SIS problem is hard. Then $\mathcal{P}$ and $\mathcal{V}$ interact with each other following the protocol in Sect. 2.3 with public input $(\mathbf{M}_0', \mathbf{u}_0')$ from $(\mathbf{B}^1, \mathbf{B}^2)$ and $\mathcal{P}$'s secret input $\mathbf{w}_0' \in \mathsf{VALID}$ from $(\mathbf{x}, p^1, p^2)$. From Theorem 1, this protocol is a statistical ZKAoK for the relation R_{ls} with perfect completeness, soundness error $2/3$, and communication cost $\mathcal{O}(L_0 \log q)$.

3.2 The Underlying ZKAoK System for MGS

In this section, we add signing and encryption layers. With authentication on her linkable syndromes by respective group issuers, the user gains memberships in these groups and becomes a certified group member. Those syndromes are regarded as the user's identities in corresponding groups. Specifically, the Ducas-Micciancio signature scheme [10] and the extended LPR encryption scheme [23] are considered, and accordingly, we define the following relation:

Definition 5. $\mathrm{R}_{mgs} = \big\{ \big(\{\mathbf{B}^k, \mathbf{A}^k, \mathbf{F}_0^k, \{\mathbf{A}_{[j]}^k\}_{j=0}^d, \mathbf{F}^k, \mathbf{F}_1^k, u^k, a^k, b_1^k, b_2^k, c_1^k,$ $c_2^k\}_{k=1,2}), \mathbf{x}, \{p^k, t^k, \mathbf{r}^k, \mathbf{v}^k, \{g_i^k, \mathbf{e}_{i,1}^k, \mathbf{e}_{i,2}^k\}_{i=1,2}\}_{k=1,2}\big)$ where

$$\begin{cases} \mathbf{B}^k \in R_q^{1\times m}, \mathbf{A}^k, \mathbf{F}_0^k \in R_q^{1\times \overline{m}}, \{\mathbf{A}_{[j]}^k\}_{j=0}^d \in R_q^{1\times k}, \mathbf{F}^k, \mathbf{F}_1^k \in R_q^{1\times \ell}, u^k \in R_q \\ a^k, b_1^k, b_2^k \in R_q^\ell, \mathbf{c}_1^k = (\mathbf{c}_1^k, \mathbf{c}_1^k) \in R_q^\ell \times R_q^\ell, \mathbf{c}_2^k = (\mathbf{c}_2^k, \mathbf{c}_2^k) \in R_q^\ell \times R_q^\ell \\ \mathbf{x} \in R^m, p^k \in R_q, t^k \in \{0,1\}^{cd}, \mathbf{r}^k \in R^{\overline{m}}, \mathbf{v}^k \in R^{\overline{m}+k}, g_1^k, g_2^k \in R, \mathbf{e}_{1,1}^k, \mathbf{e}_{1,2}^k, \mathbf{e}_{2,1}^k, \mathbf{e}_{2,2}^k \in R^\ell \end{cases}$$

satisfy the following equations

$$\mathbf{B}^k \cdot \mathbf{x} = p^k \text{ and } \|\mathbf{x}\|_\infty \leq 1 \tag{7}$$

$$\mathbf{A}_t^k \cdot \mathbf{v}^k = \mathbf{F}^k \cdot \mathsf{rdec}(\mathbf{F}_0^k \cdot \mathbf{r}^k + \mathbf{F}_1^k \cdot \mathsf{rdec}(p^k)) + u^k, \text{ where} \|\mathbf{r}^k\|_\infty \leq \beta, \|\mathbf{v}^k\|_\infty \leq \beta \tag{8}$$

$$\mathbf{c}_i^k = (\mathbf{c}_{i,1}^k, \mathbf{c}_{i,2}^k) = (a^k \cdot g_i^k + \mathbf{e}_{i,1}^k, b_i^k \cdot g_i^k + \mathbf{e}_{i,2}^k + \lfloor q/4 \rfloor \cdot \mathsf{rdec}(p^k)) \tag{9}$$

Theorem 3. *If COM is a statistically hiding and computationally binding string commitment scheme, there exists an interactive protocol which is a statistical ZKAoK for the relation R_{mgs} with perfect completeness, soundness error $2/3$, and communication cost $\mathcal{O}(L \log q)$.*

Proof. Using techniques in Sect. 2.2, Eqs. (8) and (9) can be rewritten as

$$[\mathsf{rot}(\mathbf{A}_{[0]}^k) \cdot \mathbf{H}_{k,\beta}] \cdot \mathbf{z}^{k*} + \sum_{i=1}^d \sum_{j=c_{i-1}}^{c_i-1} [\mathsf{rot}(\mathbf{A}_{[i]}^k \cdot X^j) \cdot \mathbf{H}_{k,\beta}] \cdot t_j^k \cdot \mathbf{z}^{k*} + [\mathsf{rot}(\mathbf{A}^k) \cdot \mathbf{H}_{\overline{m},\beta}] \cdot \mathbf{s}^{k*} +$$
$$[\mathsf{rot}(\mathbf{F}_0^k) \cdot \mathbf{H}_{\overline{m},\beta}] \cdot \mathbf{r}^{k*} + [\mathsf{rot}(\mathbf{F}_1^k)] \cdot \tau(\mathsf{rdec}(p^k)) - [\mathsf{rot}(\mathbf{F}^k) + \mathbf{H}] \cdot \tau(\mathbf{y}^k) = \tau(u^k) \bmod q \tag{10}$$

$$\begin{bmatrix} \mathrm{rot}(a_1^k) \cdot \mathbf{H}_B \\ \vdots \\ \mathrm{rot}(a_\ell^k) \cdot \mathbf{H}_B \end{bmatrix} \cdot \tau(\mathrm{rdec}_B(g_i^k)) + [\mathbf{H}_{\ell,B}] \cdot \tau(\mathrm{rdec}_B(e_{i,1}^k)) = \tau(\mathbf{c}_{i,1}^k) \bmod q \quad (11)$$

$$\begin{bmatrix} \mathrm{rot}(b_{i,1}^k) \cdot \mathbf{H}_B \\ \vdots \\ \mathrm{rot}(b_{i,\ell}^k) \cdot \mathbf{H}_B \end{bmatrix} \cdot \tau(\mathrm{rdec}_B(g_i^k)) + [\mathbf{H}_{\ell,B}] \cdot \tau(\mathrm{rdec}_B(e_{i,2}^k)) + \lfloor q/4 \rfloor \cdot \tau(\mathrm{rdec}(p^k)) = \tau(\mathbf{c}_{i,2}^k) \bmod q$$

$$(12)$$

where $\mathbf{z}^{k*} = \tau(\mathrm{rdec}_\beta(\mathbf{z}^k)) \in \{-1,0,1\}^{nk\delta_\beta}$, $\mathbf{s}^{k*} = \tau(\mathrm{rdec}_\beta(\mathbf{s}^k)) \in \{-1,0,1\}^{n\overline{m}k\delta_\beta}$, $\mathbf{r}^{k*} = \tau(\mathrm{rdec}_\beta(\mathbf{r}^k)) \in \{-1,0,1\}^{n\overline{m}k\delta_\beta}$, $\tau(\mathrm{rdec}(p^k)) \in \{-1,0,1\}^{n\ell}$.

Then we integrate (5) and (10–12) into one equation of the form $\mathbf{M} \cdot \mathbf{w} = \mathbf{u} \bmod q$, where $\mathbf{M}$ contents all public matrices in square brackets $[\cdot]$ of (5) (10–12) and $\mathbf{w} = (\mathbf{w}_1 \| \mathbf{w}_2 \| \mathbf{w}_3)$

$$\begin{cases} \mathbf{w}_1 = (\mathbf{z}^{1*} \| t_0^1 \cdot \mathbf{z}^{1*} \| \cdots \| t_{c_d-1}^1 \cdot \mathbf{z}^{1*}) \in \{-1,0,1\}^{(c_d+1)nk\delta_\beta}; \\ \mathbf{w}_2 = (\mathbf{z}^{2*} \| t_0^2 \cdot \mathbf{z}^{2*} \| \cdots \| t_{c_d-1}^2 \cdot \mathbf{z}^{2*}) \in \{-1,0,1\}^{(c_d+1)nk\delta_\beta}; \\ \mathbf{w}_3 = (\tau(\mathbf{x}) \| \mathbf{s}^{1*} \| \mathbf{r}^{1*} \| \tau(\mathbf{y}^1) \| \tau(\mathrm{rdec}(p^1)) \| \mathbf{g}_1^{1*} \| \mathbf{g}_2^{1*} \| \mathbf{e}_{1,1}^{1*} \| \mathbf{e}_{1,2}^{1*} \| \mathbf{e}_{2,1}^{1*} \| \mathbf{e}_{2,2}^{1*} \| \mathbf{s}^{2*} \| \mathbf{r}^{2*} \| \tau(\mathbf{y}^2) \| \\ \qquad \tau(\mathrm{rdec}(p^2)) \| \mathbf{g}_1^{2*} \| \mathbf{g}_2^{2*} \| \mathbf{e}_{1,1}^{2*} \| \mathbf{e}_{1,2}^{2*} \| \mathbf{e}_{2,1}^{2*} \| \mathbf{e}_{2,2}^{2*}) \in \{-1,0,1\}^{nm+(\overline{m}k\delta_\beta+\ell+\delta_B+2\ell\delta_B)4n}. \end{cases}$$

Next we extend the vector $\mathbf{w}$ into $\mathbf{w}' = (\mathbf{w}_1' \| \mathbf{w}_2' \| \mathbf{w}_3') = (\mathrm{mix}(t^1, \mathbf{z}^{1*}) \| \mathrm{mix}(t^2, \mathbf{z}^{2*}) \| \mathrm{enc}(\mathbf{w}_3)) \in \{-1,0,1\}^L$, where $L = L_1 + L_2 + L_3$, $L_1 = L_2 = (c_d+1)3nk\delta_\beta$, $L_3 = 3nm + (\overline{m}k\delta_\beta+\ell+\delta_B+2\ell\delta_B)12n$, and add some zero-columns to $\mathbf{M}$ in proper positions to get matrix $\mathbf{M}' \in \mathbb{Z}_q^{2n \times L}$ such that $\mathbf{M}' \cdot \mathbf{w}' = \mathbf{M} \cdot \mathbf{w}$. Now we define a $\overline{\mathsf{VALID}}$ set of all vectors $\mathbf{v}' = (\mathbf{v}_1' \| \mathbf{v}_2' \| \mathbf{v}_3') \in \{-1,0,1\}^{L_1+L_2+L_3}$ where

1. $\exists\, t_1 \in \{0,1\}^{c_d}$, $\mathbf{z}_1 \in \{-1,0,1\}^{nk\delta_\beta}$, s.t. $\mathbf{v}_1' = \mathrm{mix}(t_1, \mathbf{z}_1)$;
2. $\exists\, t_2 \in \{0,1\}^{c_d}$, $\mathbf{z}_2 \in \{-1,0,1\}^{nk\delta_\beta}$, s.t. $\mathbf{v}_2' = \mathrm{mix}(t_2, \mathbf{z}_2)$;
3. $\exists\, \mathbf{v}_3 \in \{-1,0,1\}^{nm+(\overline{m}k\delta_\beta+\ell+\delta_B+2\ell\delta_B)4n}$, s.t. $\mathbf{v}_3' = \mathrm{enc}(\mathbf{v}_3)$

and there exists an element $\phi = (b_1, e_1, b_2, e_2, f) \in \mathcal{S} = \{0,1\}^{c_d} \times \{-1,0,1\}^{nk\delta_\beta} \times \{0,1\}^{c_d} \times \{-1,0,1\}^{nk\delta_\beta} \times \{-1,0,1\}^{nm+(\overline{m}k\delta_\beta+\ell+\delta_B+2\ell\delta_B)4n}$, such that for every $\mathbf{v}' = (\mathbf{v}_1' \| \mathbf{v}_2' \| \mathbf{v}_3') \in \{-1,0,1\}^{L_1+L_2+L_3}$, the permutation Γ_ϕ transforms $\mathbf{v}'$ into

$$\Gamma_\phi(\mathbf{v}') = (\Psi_{b_1,e_1}(\mathbf{v}_1') \| \Psi_{b_2,e_2}(\mathbf{v}_2') \| \Pi_f(\mathbf{v}_3')) \quad (13)$$

Due to the Eqs. (1), (2), $\Gamma_\phi(\mathbf{v}')$ belongs to the $\overline{\mathsf{VALID}}$ set, and it is clear that the $\overline{\mathsf{VALID}}$ set and the permutation set $\mathcal{S}_0$ satisfy the conditions in Sect. 2.3. Therefore, we reduce the statement of **multiple groups** to an instance of the abstract Stern's protocol.

Based on the above preparation, we obtain the public input $(\mathbf{M}, \mathbf{u})$ of the interactive protocol from $(\{\mathbf{B}^k, \mathbf{A}^k, \mathbf{F}_0^k, \{\mathbf{A}_{[j]}^k\}_{j=0}^d, \mathbf{F}^k, \mathbf{F}_1^k, u^k, a^k, b_1^k, b_2^k, \mathbf{c}_1^k, \mathbf{c}_2^k\}_{k=1,2})$ and $\mathcal{P}$'s secret input $\mathbf{w} \in \overline{\mathsf{VALID}}$ from $(\mathbf{x}, \{p^k, t^k, \mathbf{r}^k, \mathbf{v}^k,$

$\{g_i^k, \mathbf{e}_{i,1}^k, \mathbf{e}_{i,2}^k\}_{i=1,2}\}_{k=1,2})$. Let COM be the commitment scheme from [13], which is statistically hiding and computationally binding if the RSIS problem is hard. Then $\mathcal{P}$ and $\mathcal{V}$ interact with each other following the protocol in Sect. 2.3. From Theorem 1, this protocol is a statistical ZKAoK for the relation R_{mgs} with perfect completeness, soundness error $2/3$, and communication cost $\mathcal{O}(L \log q)$.

4   A Model for Multi-Group Signatures

In this section, we formalize the security model of multi-group signatures in the framework of Bellare et al. [4]. Without loss of generality, in this paper, we only deal with the double-group case, where there are two groups G^1 and G^2. Note that the multi-group case can be extended from this case, as argued in [3]. For $\mathsf{T} \subseteq \{1,2\}$, set $\mathsf{G}^{\mathsf{T}} := \cap_{k \in \mathsf{T}} \mathsf{G}^k$.

For an $\mathcal{MGS}$ model, it should cover the linkability across different groups, which requires that signatures produced by the same signer of different groups on the same message are linkable and any pair of signatures generated by different signers cannot be linked; moreover it should satisfy the requirements of regular group signatures naturally when it degrades to the single group case. It is shown in Sect. 4.2 that these requirements are captured by the correctness and traceability.

4.1   Syntax

Formally, a multi-group signature scheme $\mathcal{MGS}$ is a tuple of seven algorithms $\mathcal{MGS} = (\mathsf{MGKg}, \mathsf{MUKg}, \langle \mathsf{Join}, \mathsf{Issue} \rangle, \mathsf{MGSig}, \mathsf{MGVf}, \mathsf{Open}, \mathsf{Judge})$:

- MGKg: On input the security parameter $\lambda \in \mathbb{N}$, This algorithm generates two triples $(\mathsf{gpk}^1, \mathsf{ik}^1, \mathsf{ok}^1)$, $(\mathsf{gpk}^2, \mathsf{ik}^2, \mathsf{ok}^2)$ independently, where gpk^k, ik^k, ok^k is the group public key, the issuer's secret key and the opener's secret key in group G^k respectively.

- MUKg: This algorithm takes as inputs the security parameter λ, as well as an argument $\mathsf{T} \subseteq \{1,2\}(\mathsf{T} \neq \emptyset)$ indicating which group(s) the user wants to join. It outputs one single secret key $\mathsf{usk}[i]$ for user i, along with her public key(s) $\mathbf{upk}[i] := \{\mathsf{upk}^k[i]\}_{k \in \mathsf{T}}$.

- $\langle \mathsf{Join}, \mathsf{Issue} \rangle$: This protocol involves two interactive algorithms Join and Issue. User i runs the Join algorithm with private input $\mathsf{upk}^k[i]$, while the issuer in group G^k runs the Issue algorithm with private input ik^k, for $k \in \mathsf{T}$. Once the protocol is executed successfully, user i becomes a member in G^k, and the final state of Join is the group signing key $\mathsf{gsk}^k[i]$ w.r.t. G^k; the final state of Issue is recorded as an entry $\mathsf{reg}^k[i]$ in the registration table $\mathbf{reg}^k$ administrated by the issuer in G^k.

- MGSig: After joining the group(s) G^k for $k \in \mathsf{T}$, the member i runs the signing algorithm with inputs the group public key(s) $\{\mathsf{gpk}^k\}_{k \in \mathsf{T}}$, her secret signing key(s) $\{\mathsf{gsk}^k[i]\}_{k \in \mathsf{T}}$, and a message $M \in \{0,1\}^*$. In turn, this algorithm outputs a signature Σ on message M and the tag T.

- MGVf: On the message-signature pair (M, Σ) along with tag $\mathsf{T} \subseteq \{1, 2\}$, anyone has access to $\{\mathsf{gpk}^k\}_{k \in \mathsf{T}}$ can run this deterministic verification algorithm, and gets returned by one bit b. If $b = 1$, it indicates that Σ is a valid signature on M for group(s) $\{\mathsf{G}^k\}_{k \in \mathsf{T}}$; otherwise it outputs 0.
- Open: For any valid message-signature pair (M, Σ) w.r.t. the tag T, the opener in group G^k for $\mathsf{k} \in \mathsf{T}$ can run this deterministic algorithm with input the group public key gpk^k, her secret opening key ok^k, registration table $\mathbf{reg}^k$, and gets an identity i with proof τ^k.
- Judge: After receiving a message-signature pair (M, Σ) along with $\mathsf{T} \subseteq \{1, 2\}$, $\mathsf{k} \in \mathsf{T}$, an opening result (i, τ^k), anyone has access to gpk^k, $\mathsf{upk}^k[i]$ and $\mathbf{reg}^k$ can run this deterministic verification algorithm, and gets returned by one bit b. If $b = 1$, it indicates that the opening result is correct; otherwise it outputs 0.

4.2 Correctness and Security Definitions

Oracles. Following the approach in [4], we give several oracles which are suitable for the multiple group setting. Especially, the MSig can produce an MGS on behalf of some group(s) and the Ch_b oracle can be used only if these two identities come from the same group(s). Besides, we recall a set MSet to record some message-signature pairs, a set HU for honest users and a set CU for corrupted users. For simplicity, we set $\mathsf{AddU} = \{\mathsf{AddU}^1, \mathsf{AddU}^2\}$, $\mathsf{CrptU} = \{\mathsf{CrptU}^1, \mathsf{CrptU}^2\}$, $\mathsf{SndToI} = \{\mathsf{SndToI}^1, \mathsf{SndToI}^2\}$, $\mathsf{SndToU} = \{\mathsf{SndToU}^1, \mathsf{SndToU}^2\}$.

$\mathsf{AddU}^k(i)$: add honest user i into G^k and return upk.

$\mathsf{CrptU}^k(i, upk)$: corrupt member $i \in \mathsf{G}^k$ and set upk as its public keys $\mathsf{upk}^k[i]$.

$\mathsf{SndToI}^k(i, M_{in})$: for corrupted member $i \in \mathsf{G}^k$, the adversary utilizes SndToI^k oracle to engage in a group-joining protocol with the honest issuer providing the oracle with $i \in \mathsf{G}^k$ and M_{in}. If it completes successfully, the oracle returns M_{out} to the adversary and stores $\mathbf{reg}^k[i]$ to $\mathbf{reg}^k$ as the final state of Issue^k.

$\mathsf{SndToU}^k(i, M_{in})$: assume that the adversary has corrupted the issuer in G^k and uses SndToU^k oracle to engage in a group-joining protocol with user i providing the oracle with i and M_{in}. If it completes successfully, i becomes a member in $\mathsf{HU} \cap \mathsf{G}^k$ and this oracle returns M_{out} to the adversary and sets $\mathsf{gsk}^k[i]$ the final state of the Join^k algorithm.

$\mathsf{USK}(i)$: obtain all secret keys of member i.

$\mathsf{RReg}(i)$: read the information of i in $\mathbf{reg}^1$ and $\mathbf{reg}^2$ via the RReg oracle.

$\mathsf{WReg}(i, \rho)$: write or modify the contents of i as ρ in $\mathbf{reg}^1$ and $\mathbf{reg}^2$.

$\mathsf{MSig}(i, M, \mathsf{T})$: obtain an MGS generated by the member i on a message M corresponding to $\{\mathsf{G}^k\}_{k \in \mathsf{T}}$.

$\mathsf{Ch}_b(i_0, i_1, M, \mathsf{T})$: it is specialized in the anonymity experiment where the adversary chooses a non-empty set $\mathsf{T} \subseteq \{1, 2\}$, a pair of identities $i_0, i_1 \in \mathsf{HU} \cap \mathsf{G}^\mathsf{T}$ with a message M. This oracle randomly chooses one bit b and returns an MGS on M generated by i_b and records message-signature pairs in MSet.

$\mathsf{Open}(M, \Sigma)$: identify the signer of a message-signature pair $(M, \Sigma) \notin \mathsf{MSet}$.

Correctness. We define the correctness of an $\mathcal{MGS}$ scheme that the signatures generated by honest members satisfy the following conditions (Fig. 1):

1. the signatures are valid;
2. the signer would be traced correctly in every group;
3. all proofs generated by openers can be verified publicly.

Definition 6 (Correctness). *A multi-group signature scheme $\mathcal{MGS}$ is correct if for any adversary $\mathcal{A}$, the following advantage function is negligible in λ*

$$\mathbf{Adv}^{\mathsf{corr}}_{\mathcal{MGS},\mathcal{A}}(\lambda) = \Pr[\mathbf{Expt}^{\mathsf{corr}}_{\mathcal{MGS},\mathcal{A}}(\lambda) = 1]$$

$\mathbf{Expt}^{\mathsf{corr}}_{\mathcal{MGS},\mathcal{A}}(\lambda)$

1 : $(\{\mathsf{gpk}^k, \mathsf{ik}^k, \mathsf{ok}^k\}_{k=1,2}) \xleftarrow{\$} \mathsf{MGKg}(1^\lambda)$; $\mathsf{CU} \leftarrow \emptyset$; $\mathsf{HU} \leftarrow \emptyset$; $(i, M, \mathsf{T}) \xleftarrow{\$} \mathcal{A}(\mathsf{gpk}^1, \mathsf{gpk}^2 : \mathsf{AddU}(\cdot), \mathsf{RReg}(\cdot))$

2 : **if** $i \notin \mathsf{HU}$ **then return** 0; **if** $\mathsf{gsk}^k[i] = \varepsilon$ for at least one $k \in \mathsf{T}$ **then return** 0

3 : $\Sigma \leftarrow \mathsf{MGSig}(\{\mathsf{gpk}^k\}_{k\in\mathsf{T}}, \{\mathsf{gsk}^k[i]\}_{k\in\mathsf{T}}, M, \mathsf{T})$; **if** $\mathsf{MGVf}(\{\mathsf{gpk}^k\}_{k\in\mathsf{T}}, M, \Sigma, \mathsf{T}) = 0$ **then return** 1

4 : $(j^k, \tau^k) \leftarrow \mathsf{Open}(\mathsf{gpk}^k, \mathsf{ok}^k, M, \Sigma, \mathsf{reg}^k, \mathsf{T})$ for $k \in \mathsf{T}$; **if** $i \neq j^k$ for at least one $k \in \mathsf{T}$ **then return** 1

5 : **if** $\mathsf{Judge}(\mathsf{gpk}^k, M, \Sigma, \mathsf{upk}^k[i], i, \tau^k, \mathsf{T}) = 0$ **then return** 1 **else return** 0

$\mathbf{Expt}^{\mathsf{trace}}_{\mathcal{MGS},\mathcal{A}}(\lambda)$

1 : $(\{\mathsf{gpk}^k, \mathsf{ik}^k, \mathsf{ok}^k\}_{k=1,2}) \xleftarrow{\$} \mathsf{MGKg}(1^\lambda)$; $\mathsf{CU} \leftarrow \emptyset$; $\mathsf{HU} \leftarrow \emptyset$;

2 : $(M, \Sigma, \mathsf{T}) \xleftarrow{\$} \mathcal{A}(\{\mathsf{gpk}^k, \mathsf{ok}^k\}_{k=1,2} : \mathsf{AddU}, \mathsf{SndToI}, \mathsf{RReg}, \mathsf{USK}, \mathsf{CrptU})$

3 : **if** $\mathsf{MGVf}(\{\mathsf{gpk}^k\}_{k\in\mathsf{T}}, M, \Sigma, \mathsf{T}) = 0$ **then return** 0; $(i, \tau^k) \leftarrow \mathsf{Open}(\mathsf{gpk}^k, \mathsf{ok}^k, M, \Sigma, \mathsf{T}, \mathsf{reg}^k)$ for $k \in \mathsf{T}$

4 : **if** $i \notin \mathsf{G}^\mathsf{T}$ or $\mathsf{Judge}(\mathsf{gpk}^k, M, \Sigma, \mathsf{T}, \mathsf{upk}^k[i], i, \tau^k) = 0$ for $k \in \mathsf{T}$ **then return** 1 **else return** 0

$\mathbf{Expt}^{\mathsf{nf}}_{\mathcal{MGS},\mathcal{A}}(\lambda)$

1 : $(\{\mathsf{gpk}^k, \mathsf{ik}^k, \mathsf{ok}^k\}_{k=1,2}) \xleftarrow{\$} \mathsf{MGKg}(1^\lambda)$; $\mathsf{CU} \leftarrow \emptyset$; $\mathsf{HU} \leftarrow \emptyset$;

2 : $(M, \Sigma, \mathsf{T}, i, \{\tau^k\}_{k\in\mathsf{T}}) \xleftarrow{\$} \mathcal{A}(\{\mathsf{gpk}^k, \mathsf{ik}^k, \mathsf{ok}^k\}_{k=1,2} : \mathsf{SndToU}, \mathsf{WReg}, \mathsf{MSig}, \mathsf{USK}, \mathsf{CrptU})$

3 : **if** $\mathsf{MGVf}(\{\mathsf{gpk}^k\}_{k\in\mathsf{T}}, M, \Sigma, \mathsf{T}) = 0$ **then return** 0

4 : **else if** all of the following is true **then return** 1 **else return** 0 :

5 : $\bullet$ $i \in \mathsf{HU} \cap \mathsf{G}^\mathsf{T}$, $\mathsf{gsk}^k[i] \neq \varepsilon$ and $\mathsf{Judge}(\mathsf{gpk}^k, M, \Sigma, \mathsf{T}, \mathsf{upk}^k[i], i, \tau^k) = 1$ for all $k \in \mathsf{T}$,

6 : $\bullet$ $\mathcal{A}$ never queries $\mathsf{USK}(i)$ or $\mathsf{MSig}(i, M, \mathsf{T})$

$\mathbf{Expt}^{\mathsf{anon}-b}_{\mathcal{MGS},\mathcal{A}}(\lambda)$

1 : $(\{\mathsf{gpk}^k, \mathsf{ik}^k, \mathsf{ok}^k\}_{k=1,2}) \xleftarrow{\$} \mathsf{MGKg}(1^\lambda)$; $\mathsf{CU} \leftarrow \emptyset$; $\mathsf{HU} \leftarrow \emptyset$; $\mathsf{MSet} \leftarrow \emptyset$

2 : $r \xleftarrow{\$} \mathcal{A}(\{\mathsf{gpk}^k, \mathsf{ik}^k\}_{k=1,2}) : \mathsf{Ch}_b, \mathsf{Open}, \mathsf{SndToU}, \mathsf{RReg}, \mathsf{WReg}, \mathsf{USK}, \mathsf{CrptU})$

3 : **if** $r == b$ **then return** 1

4 : **else return** 0

Fig. 1. Security experiments

Traceability. The traceability of $\mathcal{MGS}$ means that it should be infeasible for the adversary to output a valid message MGS pair (M, Σ) with tag T, which satisfies at least one of the following conditions, unless some issuer or opener is fully corrupted.

1. Σ traces to a member i not in $\mathsf{G^T}$, which means there is no matching information of i in $\mathbf{reg}^k$ for at least one $k \in \mathsf{T}$;
2. Σ traces to an honest member $i \in \mathsf{G^T}$, whose $\mathsf{reg}^k[i] \in \mathbf{reg}^k$ for all $k \in \mathsf{T}$, but at least one opener can not generate valid proof on the opening result.

Definition 7 (Traceability). *A multi-group signature scheme $\mathcal{MGS}$ provides traceability if for all PPT adversary $\mathcal{A}$, the following advantage function is negligible in λ:*

$$\mathbf{Adv}_{\mathcal{MGS},\mathcal{A}}^{\mathsf{trace}}(\lambda) = \Pr[\mathbf{Expt}_{\mathcal{MGS},\mathcal{A}}^{\mathsf{trace}}(\lambda) = 1]$$

Non-frameability. This property requires that it is infeasible for the adversary to generate a tuple of message M, signature Σ, tag T, an identity i with proofs $\{\tau^k\}_{k \in \mathsf{T}}$, which satisfies the following conditions, even if all issuers and openers are fully corrupted.

1. Σ is a valid MGS on M with T;
2. Σ traces to i which is an honest member in $\mathsf{G^T}$;
3. τ^k is an acceptable proof on i by Judge algorithm for all $k \in \mathsf{T}$;
4. The adversary has never obtained the valid MGS on (i, M, T) through signing oracle.

Definition 8 (Non-frameability). *A multi-group signature scheme $\mathcal{MGS}$ provides Non-frameability if for all PPT adversary $\mathcal{A}$, the following advantage function is negligible in λ:*

$$\mathbf{Adv}_{\mathcal{MGS},\mathcal{A}}^{\mathsf{nf}}(\lambda) = \Pr[\mathbf{Expt}_{\mathcal{MGS},\mathcal{A}}^{\mathsf{nf}}(\lambda) = 1]$$

Anonymity. This property requires that given two members in the same group (intersection) and a valid MGS generated by one of them, nobody can guess the correct signer with probability even negligibly bigger than $1/2$ except related openers.

Definition 9 (Anonymity). *A multi-group signature scheme $\mathcal{MGS}$ provides anonymity if for all PPT adversary $\mathcal{A}$, the following advantage function is negligible in λ:*

$$\mathbf{Adv}_{\mathcal{MGS},\mathcal{A}}^{\mathsf{anon}}(\lambda) = \left| \Pr[\mathbf{Expt}_{\mathcal{MGS},\mathcal{A}}^{\mathsf{anon}-0}(\lambda) = 1] - \Pr[\mathbf{Expt}_{\mathcal{MGS},\mathcal{A}}^{\mathsf{anon}-1}(\lambda) = 1] \right|$$

5 Lattice-Based Multi-Group Signature Scheme

In this section, we give the concrete multi-group signature scheme in the lattice setting based on our underlying ZKAoK system in Sect. 3.2.

- MGKg(1^λ): On the security parameter λ, the trusted party chooses the public parameters $\mathsf{pp} = \{n, q, k, R, R_q, \ell, m, \overline{m}, \chi, d, c_0, c_1, \cdots, c_d, B, \beta, \kappa, \mathcal{H}, \mathsf{COM}\}$ where $n, q, k, R, R_q, \ell, m, \overline{m}, \chi, d, c_0, c_1, \cdots, c_d, B, \beta$ are parameters in Ducas-Micciancio signature scheme as described in Sect. 2.4, and $\mathcal{H} : \{0, 1\}^* \rightarrow$

$\{1, 2, 3\}^\kappa$ is a collision-resistant hash function, $\kappa = \omega(\log \lambda)$, COM is a statistically hiding and computationally binding commitment scheme from [13]. It produces following keys independently

$$\mathsf{gpk}^k = \{\mathsf{pp}, \mathbf{B}^k, \mathbf{A}^k, \{\mathbf{A}^k_{[j]}\}_{j=0}^d, \mathbf{F}^k, \mathbf{F}^k_0, \mathbf{F}^k_1, u^k, \mathbf{a}^k, \mathbf{b}^k_1, \mathbf{b}^k_2\}, \quad \mathsf{ik}^k = \mathbf{R}^k, \quad \mathsf{ok}^k = (s^k_1, \mathbf{e}^k_1),$$

where $\mathbf{B}^k \in R_q^{1 \times m}$ is a uniformly random matrix. $\{\mathbf{A}^k \in R_q^{1 \times \overline{m}}, \{\mathbf{A}^k_{[j]}\}_{j=0}^d \in R_q^{1 \times k}, \mathbf{F}^k_0 \in R_q^{1 \times \overline{m}}, \mathbf{F}^k, \mathbf{F}^k_1 \in R_q^{1 \times \ell}, u^k \in R_q\}$ is verification key and $\mathbf{R}^k \in R_q^{m \times k}$ is signing key of the Ducas-Micciancio signature scheme [10]. $(\mathbf{a}^k, \mathbf{b}^k_1, \mathbf{b}^k_2) \in (R_q^\ell)^3$ is encryption key and $(s^k_1, \mathbf{e}^k_1) \in R_q \times R_q^\ell$ is decryption key of the extended LPR encryption scheme [23].
Let $\mathsf{mgpk} = \{\mathsf{gpk}^1, \mathsf{gpk}^2\}$ and makes it public, gives $\mathsf{ik}^1, \mathsf{ik}^2$ and $\mathsf{ok}^1, \mathsf{ok}^2$ to issuers and openers in different groups respectively.

- MUKg(mgpk): For any potential user i who intends to join multiple groups, firstly she generates her $\mathbf{x} \in R^m$ whose coefficients are uniformly random in the set $\{-1, 0, 1\}$ and computes syndromes $p^1 = \mathbf{B}^1 \cdot \mathbf{x}, p^2 = \mathbf{B}^2 \cdot \mathbf{x} \in R_q$. Let $\mathsf{usk}[i] = \mathbf{x}, \mathsf{upk}^1[i] = p^1, \mathsf{upk}^2[i] = p^2$.
- $\langle\mathsf{Join}, \mathsf{Issue}\rangle$: This protocol contents $\langle\mathsf{Join}^1, \mathsf{Issue}^1\rangle$ and $\langle\mathsf{Join}^2, \mathsf{Issue}^2\rangle$ which are independent of each other. For each $k \in \{1, 2\}$, the user i sends a joining request with $\mathsf{upk}^k[i] = p^k$ to the issuer in group G^k. If that p^k has been used, the issuer aborts, otherwise, he generates a Ducas-Micciancio signature $(t^k, \mathbf{r}^k, \mathbf{v}^k)$ on $\mathsf{rdec}(p^k)$ and gives it to the user. The user sets her multi-group signing key as $\mathsf{mgsk}[i] = (t^1, \mathbf{r}^1, \mathbf{v}^1, t^2, \mathbf{r}^2, \mathbf{v}^2, \mathbf{x})$. Accordingly, the issuer stores $\mathbf{reg}^k[i] = p^k$ and updates S^k to $S^k + 1$.
- MGSign($\mathsf{mgpk}, \mathsf{mgsk}[i], M$): With the multi-group signing key $\mathsf{mgsk}[i]$, the member generates an MGS $\Sigma = (\Pi_{\mathsf{mgs}}, \mathbf{c}^1_1, \mathbf{c}^1_2, \mathbf{c}^2_1, \mathbf{c}^2_2)$ on message $M \in \{0, 1\}^*$ where:
  (a) $\mathbf{c}^1_1, \mathbf{c}^1_2$ are ciphertexts of $\mathsf{rdec}(p^1)$, $\mathbf{c}^2_1, \mathbf{c}^2_2$ are ciphertexts of $\mathsf{rdec}(p^2)$
  (b) Π_{mgs} is a simulation-sound NIZKAoK proving the possession of a witness $(\mathbf{x}, \{p^k, t^k, \mathbf{r}^k, \mathbf{v}^k, \{g^k_i, \mathbf{e}^k_{i,1}, \mathbf{e}^k_{i,2}\}_{i=1,2}\}_{k=1,2})$ satisfying Eqs. (7), (8), (9) for $k = 1, 2$.
  This is done by running the protocol in Sect. 3.2 with public input $\xi = (\{\mathbf{B}^k, \mathbf{A}^k, \{\mathbf{A}^k_{[j]}\}_{j=0}^d, \mathbf{F}^k, \mathbf{F}^k_0, \mathbf{F}^k_1, u^k, \mathbf{a}^k, \mathbf{b}^k_1, \mathbf{b}^k_2, \mathbf{c}^k_1, \mathbf{c}^k_2\}_{k=1,2})$ and secret witness defined as above. The protocol is repeated $\kappa = \omega(\log \lambda)$ times to realize negligible soundness error and made non-interactive $\Pi_{\mathsf{mgs}} = (\{\mathrm{CMT}_i\}_{i=1}^\kappa, \mathrm{CH}, \{\mathrm{RSP}_i\}_{i=1}^\kappa)$ by the Fiat-Shamir heuristic [11] where $\mathrm{CH} = (Ch_1, Ch_2, \cdots, Ch_\kappa) = \mathcal{H}(M, \{\mathrm{CMT}_i\}_{i=1}^\kappa, \xi) \in \{1, 2, 3\}^\kappa$.
- MGVf(mgpk, M, Σ): On the message-signature pair (M, Σ), anybody has access to mgpk can verify its validity as follows:
  (a) Parse Σ as $(\{\mathrm{CMT}_i\}_{i=1}^\kappa, (Ch_1, Ch_2, \cdots, Ch_\kappa), \{\mathrm{RSP}_i\}_{i=1}^\kappa, \mathbf{c}^1_1, \mathbf{c}^1_2, \mathbf{c}^2_1, \mathbf{c}^2_2)$. Return 0 if $(Ch_1, Ch_2, \cdots, Ch_\kappa) \neq \mathcal{H}(M, \{\mathrm{CMT}_i\}_{i=1}^\kappa, \xi)$
  (b) For each $i \in [\kappa]$, run the verification phase of the protocol in Sect. 3.2. Return 0 if any of them is invalid.
  (c) Return 1.

- Open($\mathsf{gpk}^k, \mathsf{ok}^k, M, \Sigma, \mathsf{reg}^k$): On a valid $(M, \Sigma = (\Pi_{\mathsf{mgs}}, \mathbf{c}_1^1, \mathbf{c}_2^1, \mathbf{c}_1^2, \mathbf{c}_2^2))$, this algorithm proceeds as follows:
  (a) Decrypt $\mathbf{c}_1^k = (\mathbf{c}_{1,1}^k, \mathbf{c}_{1,2}^k)$ with $\mathsf{ok}^k = (s_1^k, \mathbf{e}_1^k)$ as follows.
      i. Compute $\mathbf{p}^{k''} = (\mathbf{c}_{1,2}^k - \mathbf{c}_{1,1}^k \cdot s_1^k)/\lfloor q/4 \rfloor$
      ii. Round each efficient of $\mathbf{p}^{k''}$ to its closest integer of $\{-1, 0, 1\}$ and obtain $\mathbf{p}^{k'} \in R_q^{\ell}$.
      iii. Return $p^{k'} \in R_q$ such that $\tau(p^{k'}) = \mathbf{H} \cdot \tau(\mathbf{p}^{k'})$
  (b) Return $(\perp, \perp)$ if $p^{k'}$ is not included in reg^k.
  (c) Otherwise, generate a NIZKAoK Π_{open}^k to demonstrate the correctness of the decryption result. The associated relation is $R_{\mathsf{open}} = \{(\mathbf{c}_{1,1}^k, \mathbf{c}_{1,2}^k, \mathbf{a}^k, \mathbf{b}_1^k \in R_q^{\ell}, p^{k'} \in R_q); s_1^k \in R_q, \mathbf{e}_1^k, \mathbf{y} \in R_q^{\ell}\}$ satisfying the following conditions:
      i. $\|s_1^k\|_\infty \le B$; $\|\mathbf{e}_1^k\|_\infty \le B$; $\|\mathbf{y}^k\|_\infty \le \lceil q/10 \rceil$;
      ii. $\mathbf{a}^k \cdot s_1^k + \mathbf{e}_1^k = \mathbf{b}_1^k$;
      iii. $\mathbf{c}_{1,2}^k - \mathbf{c}_{1,1}^k \cdot s_1^k = \mathbf{y}^k + \mathsf{rdec}(p^{k'})$
      Follow the similar method in Sect. 3, a statistical ZKAoK can be obtained and it is repeated $\kappa = \omega(\log \lambda)$ times to achieve negligible soundness error and made non-interactive $\Pi_{\mathsf{open}}^k = (\{\mathrm{CMT}_i\}_{i=1}^\kappa, \mathrm{CH}, \{\mathrm{RSP}_i\}_{i=1}^\kappa)$ by the Fiat-Shamir heuristic [11] where $\mathrm{CH} = (Ch_1, Ch_2, \cdots, Ch_\kappa) = \mathcal{H}(M, \Sigma, \{\mathrm{CMT}_i\}_{i=1}^\kappa, p^{k'}, \mathbf{a}^k, \mathbf{b}_1^k) \in \{1, 2, 3\}^\kappa$.
  (d) Return $(p^{k'}, \Pi_{\mathsf{open}}^k)$.
- Judge($\mathsf{gpk}^k, M, \Sigma, p^{k'}, \Pi_{\mathsf{open}}^k$): Based on the $(p^{k'}, \Pi_{\mathsf{open}}^k)$ produced by the opener in G^k, anyone can judge it following the method in MGVf algorithm with common input $(M, \Sigma, p^{k'}, \mathbf{a}^k, \mathbf{b}_1^k)$.

5.1 Analysis of the Scheme

Efficiency. On the security parameter λ and the number of groups $t = |\mathsf{T}| = \mathsf{poly}(\lambda)$. The public key mgpk has bit-size $\mathcal{O}(t \cdot \lambda \cdot \log^2 \lambda) = \widetilde{\mathcal{O}}(\lambda)$. The signing key $\mathsf{mgsk}[i]$ has bit-size $\mathcal{O}(t \cdot \lambda \cdot \log^2 \lambda) = \widetilde{\mathcal{O}}(\lambda)$. The size of a signature Σ is mainly determined by the NIZKAoK Π_{mgs} with bit-size $\mathcal{O}(L \cdot \log q) \cdot \omega(\log \lambda)$, where $\mathcal{O}(L \cdot \log q) = \mathcal{O}(t \cdot \lambda \cdot \log^4 \lambda)$ is the communication cost of our underlying ZKAoK system in Sect. 3.2. Thus, Σ has bit-size $\widetilde{\mathcal{O}}(\lambda)$. The Stern-like NIZKAoK Π_{open}^k has bit-size $\mathcal{O}(\lambda \cdot \log^3 \lambda) \cdot \omega(\log \lambda) = \widetilde{\mathcal{O}}(\lambda)$.

Correctness. The correctness of algorithms MGVf and Judge follows directly from the perfect completeness of the argument system, and the correctness of Open depends on the correctness of the extended version of LPR encryption scheme [23].

Security Analysis. In the following theorem, we prove that our scheme is secure according to the requirements in Sect. 4.

Theorem 4. *Suppose that the Stern-like argument system used in our scheme are simulation-sound, then in the random oracle, the given $\mathcal{MGS}$ scheme provides traceability, non-frameability, and anonymity under the RSIS and RLWE assumptions.*

We prove this theorem through the following Lemma 1–3. Due to the limitation of pages, the complete proofs are given in the full version.

Lemma 1. *Suppose that the* $\mathsf{RSIS}^{\infty}_{n,\overline{m},q,\widetilde{\mathcal{O}}(n^2)}$ *problem is hard. The given* $\mathcal{MGS}$ *scheme provides traceability in the random oracle model.*

Lemma 2. *Suppose that the* $\mathsf{RSIS}^{\infty}_{n,m,q,1}$ *problem is hard. The given* $\mathcal{MGS}$ *scheme provides non-frameability in the random oracle model.*

Lemma 3. *Suppose that the* $\mathsf{RLWE}_{n,\ell,q,\chi}$ *problem is hard. The given* $\mathcal{MGS}$ *scheme provides anonymity in the random oracle model.*

6   Conclusions

This paper described the first lattice-based multi-group signature scheme, which is also the first quantum-resistant construction for multi-group signature. In such scheme, the user can join in various groups and generates multi-group signatures on behalf of them, and the verifier is convinced that it was produced by the same member in different groups. Moreover, we formalized the model for MGS under which the security of our scheme was proved.

Acknowledgments. The authors would like to thank the anonymous reviewers of ICICS 2019 for helpful comments. This work is supported by the National Natural Science Foundation of China (Grant No. 61872359 and Grant No. 61936008).

References

1. Ajtai, M.: Generating hard instances of lattice problems (extended abstract). In: Proceedings of the Twenty-eighth Annual ACM Symposium on Theory of Computing, STOC 1996, pp. 99–108. ACM, New York (1996)
2. Ateniese, G., Camenisch, J., Joye, M., Tsudik, G.: A Practical and provably secure coalition-resistant group signature scheme. In: Bellare, M. (ed.) CRYPTO 2000. LNCS, vol. 1880, pp. 255–270. Springer, Heidelberg (2000). https://doi.org/10. 1007/3-540-44598-6_16
3. Ateniese, G., Tsudik, G.: Some open issues and new directions in group signatures. In: Franklin, M. (ed.) FC 1999. LNCS, vol. 1648, pp. 196–211. Springer, Heidelberg (1999). https://doi.org/10.1007/3-540-48390-X_15
4. Bellare, M., Shi, H., Zhang, C.: Foundations of group signatures: the case of dynamic groups. In: Menezes, A. (ed.) CT-RSA 2005. LNCS, vol. 3376, pp. 136–153. Springer, Heidelberg (2005). https://doi.org/10.1007/978-3-540-30574-3_11
5. Benjumea, V., Choi, S.G., Lopez, J., Yung, M.: Fair traceable multi-group signatures. In: Tsudik, G. (ed.) FC 2008. LNCS, vol. 5143, pp. 231–246. Springer, Heidelberg (2008). https://doi.org/10.1007/978-3-540-85230-8_21
6. Boneh, D., Boyen, X., Shacham, H.: Short group signatures. In: Franklin, M. (ed.) CRYPTO 2004. LNCS, vol. 3152, pp. 41–55. Springer, Heidelberg (2004). https:// doi.org/10.1007/978-3-540-28628-8_3

7. Boyen, X., Waters, B.: Compact group signatures without random oracles. In: Vaudenay, S. (ed.) EUROCRYPT 2006. LNCS, vol. 4004, pp. 427–444. Springer, Heidelberg (2006). https://doi.org/10.1007/11761679_26

8. Camenisch, J.: Efficient and generalized group signatures. In: Fumy, W. (ed.) EUROCRYPT 1997. LNCS, vol. 1233, pp. 465–479. Springer, Heidelberg (1997). https://doi.org/10.1007/3-540-69053-0_32

9. Chaum, D., van Heyst, E.: Group signatures. In: Davies, D.W. (ed.) EUROCRYPT 1991. LNCS, vol. 547, pp. 257–265. Springer, Heidelberg (1991). https://doi.org/10.1007/3-540-46416-6_22

10. Ducas, L., Micciancio, D.: Improved short lattice signatures in the standard model. In: Garay, J.A., Gennaro, R. (eds.) CRYPTO 2014, Part I. LNCS, vol. 8616, pp. 335–352. Springer, Heidelberg (2014). https://doi.org/10.1007/978-3-662-44371-2_19

11. Fiat, A., Shamir, A.: How to prove yourself: practical solutions to identification and signature problems. In: Odlyzko, A.M. (ed.) CRYPTO 1986. LNCS, vol. 263, pp. 186–194. Springer, Heidelberg (1987). https://doi.org/10.1007/3-540-47721-7_12

12. Gordon, S.D., Katz, J., Vaikuntanathan, V.: A group signature scheme from lattice assumptions. In: Abe, M. (ed.) ASIACRYPT 2010. LNCS, vol. 6477, pp. 395–412. Springer, Heidelberg (2010). https://doi.org/10.1007/978-3-642-17373-8_23

13. Kawachi, A., Tanaka, K., Xagawa, K.: Concurrently secure identification schemes based on the worst-case hardness of lattice problems. In: Pieprzyk, J. (ed.) ASIACRYPT 2008. LNCS, vol. 5350, pp. 372–389. Springer, Heidelberg (2008). https://doi.org/10.1007/978-3-540-89255-7_23

14. Kiayias, A., Tsiounis, Y., Yung, M.: Traceable signatures. In: Cachin, C., Camenisch, J.L. (eds.) EUROCRYPT 2004. LNCS, vol. 3027, pp. 571–589. Springer, Heidelberg (2004). https://doi.org/10.1007/978-3-540-24676-3_34

15. Laguillaumie, F., Langlois, A., Libert, B., Stehlé, D.: Lattice-based group signatures with logarithmic signature size. In: Sako, K., Sarkar, P. (eds.) ASIACRYPT 2013, Part II. LNCS, vol. 8270, pp. 41–61. Springer, Heidelberg (2013). https://doi.org/10.1007/978-3-642-42045-0_3

16. Libert, B., Ling, S., Mouhartem, F., Nguyen, K., Wang, H.: Signature schemes with efficient protocols and dynamic group signatures from lattice assumptions. In: Cheon, J.H., Takagi, T. (eds.) ASIACRYPT 2016, Part II. LNCS, vol. 10032, pp. 373–403. Springer, Heidelberg (2016). https://doi.org/10.1007/978-3-662-53890-6_13

17. Libert, B., Ling, S., Nguyen, K., Wang, H.: Zero-knowledge arguments for lattice-based accumulators: logarithmic-size ring signatures and group signatures without trapdoors. In: Fischlin, M., Coron, J.-S. (eds.) EUROCRYPT 2016, Part II. LNCS, vol. 9666, pp. 1–31. Springer, Heidelberg (2016). https://doi.org/10.1007/978-3-662-49896-5_1

18. Ling, S., Nguyen, K., Stehlé, D., Wang, H.: Improved zero-knowledge proofs of knowledge for the ISIS problem, and applications. In: Kurosawa, K., Hanaoka, G. (eds.) PKC 2013. LNCS, vol. 7778, pp. 107–124. Springer, Heidelberg (2013). https://doi.org/10.1007/978-3-642-36362-7_8

19. Ling, S., Nguyen, K., Wang, H.: Group signatures from lattices: simpler, tighter, shorter, ring-based. In: Katz, J. (ed.) PKC 2015. LNCS, vol. 9020, pp. 427–449. Springer, Heidelberg (2015). https://doi.org/10.1007/978-3-662-46447-2_19

20. Ling, S., Nguyen, K., Wang, H., Xu, Y.: Constant-size group signatures from lattices. In: Abdalla, M., Dahab, R. (eds.) PKC 2018, Part II. LNCS, vol. 10770, pp. 58–88. Springer, Cham (2018). https://doi.org/10.1007/978-3-319-76581-5_3

21. Lysyanskaya, A., Ramzan, Z.: Group blind digital signatures: a scalable solution to electronic cash. In: Hirchfeld, R. (ed.) FC 1998. LNCS, vol. 1465, pp. 184–197. Springer, Heidelberg (1998). https://doi.org/10.1007/BFb0055483
22. Lyubashevsky, V., Micciancio, D.: Generalized compact knapsacks are collision resistant. In: Electronic Colloquium on Computational Complexity (2005)
23. Lyubashevsky, V., Peikert, C., Regev, O.: On ideal lattices and learning with errors over rings. In: Gilbert, H. (ed.) EUROCRYPT 2010. LNCS, vol. 6110, pp. 1–23. Springer, Heidelberg (2010). https://doi.org/10.1007/978-3-642-13190-5_1
24. Micciancio, D.: Generalized compact knapsacks, cyclic lattices, and efficient one-way functions. Compil. Constr. **16**(4), 365–411 (2007)
25. Nguyen, P.Q., Zhang, J., Zhang, Z.: Simpler efficient group signatures from lattices. In: Katz, J. (ed.) PKC 2015. LNCS, vol. 9020, pp. 401–426. Springer, Heidelberg (2015). https://doi.org/10.1007/978-3-662-46447-2_18
26. Peikert, C., Rosen, A.: Efficient collision-resistant hashing from worst-case assumptions on cyclic lattices. In: Halevi, S., Rabin, T. (eds.) TCC 2006. LNCS, vol. 3876, pp. 145–166. Springer, Heidelberg (2006). https://doi.org/10.1007/11681878_8
27. del Pino, R., Lyubashevsky, V., Seiler, G.: Lattice-based group signatures and zero-knowledge proofs of automorphism stability. In: Proceedings of the 2018 ACM SIGSAC Conference on Computer and Communications Security, pp. 574–591. ACM (2018)
28. Stern, J.: A new paradigm for public key identification. IEEE Trans. Inf. Theory **42**(6), 1757–1768 (1996)
29. Trolin, M., Wikström, D.: Hierarchical group signatures. In: Caires, L., Italiano, G.F., Monteiro, L., Palamidessi, C., Yung, M. (eds.) ICALP 2005. LNCS, vol. 3580, pp. 446–458. Springer, Heidelberg (2005). https://doi.org/10.1007/11523468_37
30. Yang, R., Au, M.H., Lai, J., Xu, Q., Yu, Z.: Lattice-based techniques for accountable anonymity: composition of abstract Stern's protocols and weak PRF with efficient protocols from LWR. IACR Cryptol. ePrint Arch. **2017**, 781 (2017)

Ciphertext Policy Attribute-Based Encryption for Circuits from LWE Assumption

Geng Wang[✉], Zhen Liu, and Dawu Gu

School of Electronic Information and Electrical Engineering,
Shanghai Jiao Tong University, Shanghai, China
{wanggxx,liuzhen,dwgu}@sjtu.edu.cn

Abstract. Attribute-based encryption (ABE) is a standard method for achieving access control using cryptography, and is related to many other powerful primitives such as functional encryption. While classical pairing based ABE schemes support only boolean formulas as access policy, the first ABE scheme for arbitrary polynomial size circuits is given in [GVW13], and its security is based on LWE assumption. However, the GVW13 scheme is a key policy ABE (KP-ABE), and whether their method can be used to construct a ciphertext policy ABE (CP-ABE) scheme is currently unknown.

In this paper, we present the first direct construction (not from universal circuits) of CP-ABE scheme for circuits. Similar to the two-to-one recoding technique used in GVW13, we introduce three-to-one recoding, and use it to construct our scheme, which can be proved for selective security assuming that LWE problem is hard, for arbitrary polynomial size circuits. Compared with universal circuit based constructions, our scheme is simpler and has lesser decryption cost.

Keywords: Ciphertext policy attribute-based encryption · ABE for circuits · LWE · Lattice-based cryptography

1 Introduction

Attribute-based Encryption (ABE for short), first brought by Sahai and Waters [30], is a powerful cryptographic primitive in which decryption is correct only if the provided attribute set satisfies a certain access policy. By using different types of access policies, ABE can handle flexible access control matters, without using complex key distribution techniques. Also, ABE is highly related to other hot topics in cryptography, such as identity-based encryption (IBE), predicate encryption (PE) and functional encryption (FE).

This work is supported by the National Key Research and Development Program of China (No. 2016QY071401).

J. Zhou et al. (Eds.): ICICS 2019, LNCS 11999, pp. 378–396, 2020.
https://doi.org/10.1007/978-3-030-41579-2_22

There are mainly two types of ABE schemes, called key policy attribute-based encryption (KP-ABE) [23] and ciphertext policy attribute-based encryption (CP-ABE) [7]. The former embeds the access policy in the decryption key, while the ciphertext is related to a set of attributes; the latter does the opposite, the access policy is embedded in the ciphertext, and attributes are related to the decryption key, held by the users. In practical use, CP-ABE is considered more flexible than KP-ABE for access control model such as role-based access control (RBAC), since roles can be naturally assigned to users as attributes.

The early ABE schemes are mostly based on pairing in elliptic curves [7, 13, 14, 16, 22–25, 27, 29, 32], which are vulnerable to quantum attacks. As lattice-based cryptography gains more and more interest in the post-quantum background, many ABE constructions occur based on lattice, such as [3, 10, 33, 35]. These early schemes support various types of access policy, such as threshold gates, non-monotonic AND gates, or LSSS matrices, but most of them can be captured by boolean formulas, which represent the complexity class NC^1, and cannot support the access policy of polynomial size circuits. In 2013, Gorbunov et al. [21] presented the first ABE scheme for arbitrary polynomial size circuits of every a-priori bounded depth, by constructing reusable garbled circuits. Like other lattice-based schemes, their scheme is based on the hardness of LWE assumption [28], which security can be reduced to worst-case lattice problems.

However, since their scheme is only a KP-ABE scheme, their is still an open problem that whether similar methods can be used to construct CP-ABE schemes. In this paper, we solve this problem by presenting the first direct construction of CP-ABE scheme for arbitrary polynomial size circuits, not from universal circuits (UC). Our scheme cannot be naturally extended from the KP-ABE scheme in [21], though. Unlike in the case of KP-ABE, where each secret key is only related to a certain access policy circuit, for CP-ABE, the master public key and user secret keys must be able to handle *any* polynomial size circuits. So what we need is not only constructing a reusable garbled circuit, but a *programmable* reusable garbled circuit.

To solve this problem, we extend the two-to-one recoding in [21] into a new primitive we called *three-to-one recoding*. Each output for a "garbled" circuit gate is the recoding of 3, not 2 encodings: two encodings for input values, and one encoding for the description of the circuit gate itself. We also need to set the maximal circuit size a-priori, and construct recoding keys for every possible gate, each key labeled by the index and value of incoming/outgoing wires of the gate. Although that makes the public key and secret keys in our scheme a bit overloaded, we will show that the size of keys is still polynomial bounded. Also by using random oracle, the public key size can be further reduced to linear in the attribute size.

1.1 Related Works

Lattice-Based IBE/ABE/FE Schemes. It was first proven in [19] that lattice-based IBE schemes can be generated through lattice trapdoors [5]. By using trapdoor delegation, further constructions of IBE and hierarchical IBE

[1,2,6,12] are presented. Similar techniques are then used to construct KP-ABE/FE schemes based on LWE assumption with various access policies, such as inner product in [4], threshold function in [3] (which was extended to the ring settings in [35] for a better efficiency), and LSSS matrices in [10]. For CP-ABE schemes, Zhang et al. [33] and Wang [31] presented CP-ABE schemes for multi-valued functions, and the former was also extended to ring settings in [15]. These schemes cannot handle arbitrary circuits.

ABE for Circuits. There are mainly two methods of constructing ABE for arbitrary polynomial size circuits: from lattice assumption, or from multilinear map. Since almost all multilinear map candidates have been attacked by now, ABE constructed from multilinear maps [17,18] can not be considered as reliable as lattice-based schemes. Boneh et al. [9] provided two ABE schemes, one based on LWE assumption, another based on multilinear map, for arithmetic circuits which can also be used to implement boolean circuits. Their schemes are built upon a primitive called fully key-homomorphic encryption, which is an extension of the famous fully homomorphic encryption [20]. In [11], their LWE-based scheme was extended to support unbounded attribute size and semi-adaptive security.

All existing LWE-based ABE for circuits are KP-ABE schemes. However, the authors claimed in [17] that by using universal circuits, one can construct a CP-ABE scheme from a KP one. This can be applied to all existing KP-ABE schemes for circuits. However, there are some drawbacks for UC-based constructions:

(1) UC for $O(n)$ circuits has a larger size of $O(n \log n)$, which means that decryption cost is $O(n \log n)$.
(2) UC needs circuits as input, which means that public key size is at least linear in the circuit size.
(3) Construction of UC is difficult.

Compared with UC-based constructions, our scheme has a lower decryption time of $O(n)$, and our public key size is only linear to the attribute size if we consider random oracle model. Our scheme is also simpler. However, our secret key is much larger than UC-based constructions.

It was noticeable that a recent work in [34] has also discussed on direct construction of CP-ABE for circuits. However, their scheme is under a very weak security model, which cannot be considered secure in real applications.

1.2   Organization

This paper is organized as follows: in Sect. 2, we introduce some basic notions which are useful in our discussion. In Sect. 3, we give the definition of three-to-one recoding scheme, its correctness and security, also a construction from LWE assumption. In Sect. 4, we construct our CP-ABE scheme for circuits from three-to-one recoding, and prove its security. Finally in Sect. 5, we draw the conclusion.

2   Preliminary

Notations. Let PPT denote probabilistic polynomial-time. For any integer $q \geq 2$, we let $\mathbb{Z}_q$ denote the ring of integers modulo q and we represent $\mathbb{Z}_q$ as integers in $(-q/2, q/2]$. We let $\mathbb{Z}_q^{n \times m}$ denote the set of $n \times m$ matrices with entries in $\mathbb{Z}_q$. We use bold capital letters (e.g. $\mathbf{A}$) to denote matrices, bold lowercase letters (e.g. $\mathbf{x}$) to denote vectors. The notation $\mathbf{A}^T$ denotes the transpose of the matrix $\mathbf{A}$.

If $\mathbf{A}_1$ is an $n \times m_1$ matrix and $\mathbf{A}_2$ is an $n \times m_2$ matrix, then $[\mathbf{A}_1 \| \mathbf{A}_2]$ denotes the $n \times (m_1 + m_2)$ matrix formed by concatenating $\mathbf{A}_1$ and $\mathbf{A}_2$. A similar notation applies to vectors. When doing matrix-vector multiplication we always view vectors as column vectors. $\|.\|$ denotes the Euclidean norm, and $\|.\|_\infty$ denotes the infinity norm. When applied to matrix, it means the maximal norm among all its column vectors.

We say a function $f(n)$ is negligible if it is $O(n^{-c})$ for all $c > 0$, and we use $\mathsf{negl}(n)$ to denote a negligible function of n. We say $f(n)$ is polynomial if it is $O(n^c)$ for some $c > 0$, and we use $\mathsf{poly}(n)$ to denote a polynomial function of n. We say an event occurs with overwhelming probability if its probability is $1 - \mathsf{negl}(n)$. The function $\log x$ is the base 2 logarithm of x. The notation $\lfloor x \rceil$ denotes the nearest integer to x, rounding towards 0 for half-integers. $[j]$ denotes the set $\{1, 2, ..., j\}$ and $[i, j]$ denotes the set $\{i, i+1, ..., j\}$.

2.1   Ciphertext Policy Attribute-Based Encryption

We define ciphertext policy attribute-based encryption (CP-ABE), following [7]. A CP-ABE scheme for a class of predicate circuits $\mathcal{C}$ (namely, circuits with a single bit output) consists of four algorithms (Setup, Enc, KeyGen, Dec):

- Setup($1^\lambda, 1^l$) $\to$ (pp, mpk, msk): The setup algorithm gets as input the security parameter λ, the length l of the index, and outputs the public parameter (pp, mpk), and the master key msk. All the other algorithms get pp as part of its input.
- Enc(mpk, C, m) $\to$ ct$_C$: The encryption algorithm gets as input mpk, a predicate specified by $C \in \mathcal{C}$, and a message $m \in \mathcal{M}$. It outputs a ciphertext ct$_C$. Note that C is known if we know ct$_C$.
- KeyGen(msk, ind) $\to$ sk$_{\mathsf{ind}}$: The key generation algorithm gets as input msk and an index ind $\in \{0, 1\}^l$. It outputs a secret key sk$_{\mathsf{ind}}$.
- Dec(sk$_{\mathsf{ind}}$, ct$_C$) $\to$ m: The decryption algorithm gets as input sk$_{\mathsf{ind}}$ and ct$_C$, and outputs either $\perp$ or a message $m \in \mathcal{M}$.

For correctness, we require that for all (ind, C) such that $C(\mathsf{ind}) = 1$, all $m \in \mathcal{M}$ and ct$_C \leftarrow$ Enc(mpk, C, m), Dec(sk$_{\mathsf{ind}}$, ct$_C$) = m.

The selective security of a CP-ABE scheme is defined by the advantage of a stateful adversary $\mathcal{A}$ in an interactive game as follows:

Init. The adversary chooses the challenge circuit C^* and gives it to the challenger.

Setup. The challenger runs the **Setup** algorithm and gives the adversary pp, mpk.

Phase 1. The adversary submits an index ind for a **KeyGen** query. If $C^*(\text{ind}) = 0$, the challenger answers with a secret key sk_{ind} for ind. These queries can be repeated adaptively.

Challenge. The adversary submits two messages m_0 and m_1 of equal length. The challenger chooses a random bit $b \in \{0, 1\}$, and encrypts m_b under C^*. The encrypted ciphertext ct_{C^*} is returned to the adversary.

Phase 2. The adversary repeats **Phase 1** to get more secret keys.

Guess. The adversary outputs a guess b' for b.

The advantage of an adversary $\mathcal{A}$ in the CPA-CP-ABE game is defined by $\text{Adv}_{\mathcal{A}}^{\text{PE}}(\lambda) = |Pr[b' = b] - 1/2|$. If we omit the **Init** phase, and let the adversary $\mathcal{A}$ to choose the challenge circuit C^* at the **Challenge** phase, we get the definition for adaptive security (or called full security).

2.2 Learning with Errors (LWE) Assumption

The LWE problem was introduced by Regev [28], who showed that solving it on the average is as hard as (quantumly) solving the GapSVP and SIVP problems in the worst case. There are search version and decision version of LWE problem. In this paper, we use the decision version of LWE problem (or called dLWE).

Definition 1 (dLWE problem). *For an integer $q = q(n) \geq 2$ and an error distribution $\chi = \chi(n)$ over $\mathbb{Z}_q$, the learning with errors problem $\text{dLWE}_{n,m,q,\chi}$ is to distinguish between the following pairs of distributions:*

$$\{\mathbf{A}, \mathbf{As} + \mathbf{x}\} \text{ and } \{\mathbf{A}, \mathbf{u}\}$$

where $\mathbf{A} \xleftarrow{\$} \mathbb{Z}_q^{n \times m}$, $\mathbf{s} \xleftarrow{\$} \mathbb{Z}_q^n$, $\mathbf{x} \xleftarrow{\$} \chi^m$, $\mathbf{u} \xleftarrow{\$} \mathbb{Z}_q^m$.

Parameter Selection. We say that the distribution χ is B-bounded, if $Pr(|\chi| \leq B) = 1$. In this paper, we require that χ is B-bounded for some integer B. For the hardness of LWE problem, χ is usually chosen to be B-bounded discrete Gaussian, which definition can be found in the next section.

For parameter selection, we let χ be $\text{poly}(n)$-bounded, $m = \text{poly}(n)$ and $q = 2^{n^\epsilon}$ for $0 < \epsilon < 1$. We have strong evidence that the problem $\text{dLWE}_{n,m,q,\chi}$ is hard. Often, we omit m, and write the problem as $\text{dLWE}_{n,q,\chi}$.

2.3 Lattice Trapdoors

Lattice trapdoors [5,19,26] are used to sample short vectors on any coset of lattice, which its distribution is discrete Gaussian. In this paper, we require the distribution of the sampled vector to be "truncated", that is, the length of the vector is bounded. Sampling truncated vectors is easy: what we need is only to sample again if the sampled vector is out of bound.

We give the formal definition of truncated ($\sigma\sqrt{m}$-bounded) discrete Gaussian distribution for vector $\mathbf{x} \in \mathbb{Z}^m$ with parameter σ. First, we define a Gaussian function $\rho_\sigma : \mathbb{Z}^m \to \mathbb{R}^+$:

$$\rho_\sigma(\mathbf{x}) := \exp(-\pi\|\mathbf{x}\|^2/\sigma^2).$$

Now, we define the distribution $D_{\mathbb{Z}^m,\sigma}$ as:

$$D_{\mathbb{Z}^m,\sigma}(\mathbf{x}) \propto \begin{cases} \rho_\sigma(\mathbf{x}), & \text{if } \|\mathbf{x}\| \leq \sigma\sqrt{m}; \\ 0, & \text{otherwise.} \end{cases}$$

Lemma 1 ([19,26]). *There is an efficient randomized algorithm* TrapSamp(1^n, $1^m, q$) *that, given any integers* $n \geq 1$, $q \geq 2$, *and sufficiently large* $m = \Omega(n \log q)$, *outputs a parity check matrix* $\mathbf{A} \in \mathbb{Z}_q^{n \times m}$ *and a "trapdoor" matrix* $\mathbf{T} \in \mathbb{Z}^{m \times m}$ *such that the distribution of* $\mathbf{A}$ *is* negl(n)-*close to uniform.*

Moreover, there is an efficient algorithm SampleD *that with overwhelming probability over all random choices, does the following: For any* $\mathbf{u} \in \mathbb{Z}_q^n$, *and large enough* $\sigma = \Omega(\sqrt{n \log q})$, *the randomized algorithm* SampleD($\mathbf{A}, \mathbf{T}, \mathbf{u}, \sigma$) *outputs a vector* $\mathbf{r} \in \mathbb{Z}^m$ *with norm* $\|\mathbf{r}\|_\infty \leq \|\mathbf{r}\| \leq \sigma\sqrt{n}$ *(with probability 1). Furthermore, the following distributions of the tuple* $(\mathbf{A}, \mathbf{T}, \mathbf{U}, \mathbf{R})$ *are within* negl(n) *statistical distance of each other for any polynomial* $k \in \mathbb{N}$:

- $(\mathbf{A}, \mathbf{T}) \leftarrow$ TrapSamp($1^n, 1^m, q$); $\mathbf{U} \xleftarrow{\$} \mathbb{Z}_q^{n \times k}$, $\mathbf{R} \leftarrow$ SampleD($\mathbf{A}, \mathbf{T}, \mathbf{U}, \sigma$).
- $(\mathbf{A}, \mathbf{T}) \leftarrow$ TrapSamp($1^n, 1^m, q$); $\mathbf{R} \xleftarrow{\$} D_{\mathbb{Z}^m,s}^k$, $\mathbf{U} := \mathbf{A}\mathbf{R} \bmod q$.

3 Three-to-One Recoding

3.1 Definition

Similar to [21], our three-to-one recoding scheme consists of six polynomial-time algorithms (Params, Keygen, Encode, ReKeyGen3, SimReKeyGen3, Recode3) and a symmetric-key encryption scheme (E, D).

The first three algorithms are the same as two-to-one recoding in [21]:

- Params($1^\lambda, d_{\max}$) is a probabilistic algorithm that takes as input the security parameter λ and an upper bound $d_{\max}$ on the number of nested recoding operations (written in binary), outputs "global" public parameters pp.
- Keygen(pp) is a probabilistic algorithm that outputs a public/secret key pair (pk, sk).
- Encode(pk, s) is a probabilistic algorithm that takes pk and an input $s \in \mathcal{S}$, and outputs an encoding $\phi \in \mathcal{K}$.

The following three algorithms are for three-to-one recoding, and can be viewed as a recoding mechanism together with two ways to generate recoding keys: given one of the three secret keys, or by programming the output public key.

- ReKeyGen3($\mathsf{pk}_0, \mathsf{pk}_1, \mathsf{pk}_2, \mathsf{sk}_i, \mathsf{pk}_{\mathrm{tgt}}$), $i \in \{0, 1, 2\}$ is a probabilistic algorithm that takes a public keys pair ($\mathsf{pk}_i, \mathsf{sk}_i$) and two other public keys, a "target" public key $\mathsf{pk}_{\mathrm{tgt}}$, and outputs a recoding key $\mathsf{rk}^{\mathrm{tgt}}_{0,1,2}$.
- SimReKeyGen3($\mathsf{pk}_0, \mathsf{pk}_1, \mathsf{pk}_2$) is a probabilistic algorithm that takes three public keys pk_0, pk_1, pk_2 and outputs a recoding key $\mathsf{rk}^{\mathrm{tgt}}_{0,1,2}$ together with a "target" public key $\mathsf{pk}_{\mathrm{tgt}}$.
- Recode3($\mathsf{rk}^{\mathrm{tgt}}_{0,1,2}, \phi_0, \phi_1, \phi_2$) is a deterministic algorithm that takes the recoding key $\mathsf{rk}^{\mathrm{tgt}}_{0,1,2}$, three encodings ϕ_0, ϕ_1, ϕ_2, and outputs an encoding ϕ_{tgt}.

Correctness. Correctness of a TOR scheme requires two things. First, for every pk and $s \in \mathcal{S}$, there exists a family of sets $\Phi_{\mathsf{pk}, s, j}$, $j = 0, 1, \ldots d_{\max}$ such that:

- $Pr[\mathsf{Encode}(\mathsf{pk}, s) \in \Phi_{\mathsf{pk}, s, 0}] = 1$, where the probability is taken over the coin tosses of Encode;
- $\Phi_{\mathsf{pk}, s, 0} \subseteq \Phi_{\mathsf{pk}, s, 1} \subseteq \cdots \subseteq \Phi_{\mathsf{pk}, s, d_{\max}}$;
- For all $\phi, \phi' \in \Phi_{\mathsf{pk}, s, d_{\max}}$ and all $m \in \mathcal{M}$, $\mathsf{D}(\phi', \mathsf{E}(\phi, m)) = m$.

To understand this definition, consider $\phi \in \Phi_{\mathsf{pk}, s, j}$ to be an LWE sample with noise level j. As in other LWE-based cryptosystems, the decryption is correct as long as the noise is bounded by $q/4$ at the maximal noise level $d_{\max}$.

Secondly, the correctness of recoding requires that for any quadruple of key pairs ($\mathsf{pk}_0, \mathsf{sk}_0$), ($\mathsf{pk}_1, \mathsf{sk}_1$), ($\mathsf{pk}_2, \mathsf{sk}_2$), ($\mathsf{pk}_{\mathrm{tgt}}, \mathsf{sk}_{\mathrm{tgt}}$), and any encodings $\phi_0 \in \Phi_{\mathsf{pk}_0, s, j_0}$, $\phi_1 \in \Phi_{\mathsf{pk}_1, s, j_1}$ and $\phi_2 \in \Phi_{\mathsf{pk}_2, s, j_2}$, there is:

$$\mathsf{Recode3}(\mathsf{rk}^{\mathrm{tgt}}_{0,1,2}, \phi_0, \phi_1, \phi_2) \in \Phi_{\mathsf{pk}_{\mathrm{tgt}}, s, \max(j_0, j_1, j_2) + 1}.$$

for $\mathsf{rk}^{\mathrm{tgt}}_{0,1,2} \leftarrow \mathsf{ReKeyGen3}(\mathsf{pk}_0, \mathsf{pk}_1, \mathsf{pk}_2, \mathsf{sk}_0, \mathsf{pk}_{\mathrm{tgt}})$.

Security Properties

Key Indistinguishability: Let ($\mathsf{pk}_i, \mathsf{sk}_i$) $\leftarrow \mathsf{Keygen}(\mathsf{pp})$ for $i = 0, 1, 2$ and ($\mathsf{pk}_{\mathrm{tgt}}, \mathsf{sk}_{\mathrm{tgt}}$) $\leftarrow \mathsf{Keygen}(\mathsf{pp})$. Then, for $i \in \{0, 1, 2\}$, the statistical distance between $\mathsf{ReKeyGen3}(\mathsf{pk}_0, \mathsf{pk}_1, \mathsf{pk}_2, \mathsf{sk}_i, \mathsf{pk}_{\mathrm{tgt}})$ must be negligible in λ.

Recoding Simulation. Let ($\mathsf{pk}_i, \mathsf{sk}_i$) $\leftarrow \mathsf{Keygen}(\mathsf{pp})$ for $i = 0, 1, 2$. Then, the statistical distance between the following two distributions is negligible in λ:

- $\mathsf{pk}_{\mathrm{tgt}}, \mathsf{rk}$: ($\mathsf{pk}_{\mathrm{tgt}}, \mathsf{sk}_{\mathrm{tgt}}$) $\leftarrow \mathsf{Keygen}(\mathsf{pp}); \mathsf{rk} \leftarrow \mathsf{ReKeyGen}(\mathsf{pk}_0, \mathsf{pk}_1, \mathsf{pk}_2, \mathsf{sk}_0, \mathsf{pk}_{\mathrm{tgt}})$;
- $\mathsf{pk}_{\mathrm{tgt}}, \mathsf{rk}$: ($\mathsf{pk}_{\mathrm{tgt}}, \mathsf{rk}$) $\leftarrow \mathsf{SimReKeyGen}(\mathsf{pk}_0, \mathsf{pk}_1, \mathsf{pk}_2)$.

The properties above show that all four methods for generating the recoding key: using ReKeyGen with $\mathsf{sk}_0, \mathsf{sk}_1, \mathsf{sk}_2$ and using SimReKeyGen are statistically indistinguishable.

One-time Semantic Security. For all $m_0, m_1 \in \mathcal{M}$, the statistical distance between $\mathsf{E}(\phi, m_0) : \phi \xleftarrow{\$} \mathcal{K}$ and $\mathsf{E}(\phi, m_1) : \phi \xleftarrow{\$} \mathcal{K}$ must be negligible.

Correlated Pseudorandomness. The pseudorandomness of three-to-one recoding scheme is defined by the advantage of an adversary $\mathcal{A}$ as follows:

(1) The challenger runs $\mathsf{Params}(1^\lambda, d_{\max})$ and returns pp to the adversary.
(2) The challenger runs $\mathsf{Keygen}(\mathsf{pp})$ for $l + 1$ times, and gets $(\mathsf{pk}_i, \mathsf{sk}_i)$, $i = 1, ..., l, l + 1$. pk_i, $i = 1, ..., l + 1$ are returned to the adversary.
(3) The challenger chooses $s \xleftarrow{\$} \mathcal{S}$, calculates $\phi_i = \mathsf{Encode}(\mathsf{pk}_i, s)$ for $i = 1, ..., l$. Let $\phi_0' = \mathsf{Encode}(\mathsf{pk}_{l+1}, s)$ and $\phi_1' \xleftarrow{\$} \mathcal{K}$. The challenger chooses a random bit $b \in \{0, 1\}$, and returns $(\phi_1, ..., \phi_l, \phi_b')$ to the adversary.
(4) The adversary outputs a guess b' for b.

The advantage for $\mathcal{A}$ is defined by: $\mathsf{Adv}_{\mathcal{A}}^{\mathrm{CP}}(\lambda) := |\Pr(b = b') - 1/2|$. We require that for all PPT $\mathcal{A}$, the advantage $\mathsf{Adv}_{\mathcal{A}}^{\mathrm{CP}}(\lambda)$ is negligible in λ.

Note that if the recoding simulation property holds, all recoding keys have essentially no information about the secret keys. So recoding keys need not to be included in the security game.

3.2 Construction of Three-to-One Recoding from LWE

We construct a three-to-one recoding scheme from LWE assumption:

- $\mathsf{Params}(1^\lambda, d_{\max})$: First choose the LWE dimension $n = n(\lambda)$. Let the error distribution $\chi = \chi(n) = D_{\mathbb{Z}, \sqrt{n}}$, the error bound $B = B(n) = O(n)$, the modulus $q = q(n) = \tilde{O}(n^2 d_{\max})^{d_{\max}} n$, the number of samples $m = m(n) = O(n \log q)$ and the Gaussian parameter $\sigma = \sigma(n) = O(\sqrt{n \log q})$. Output the global public parameters $\mathsf{pp} = (n, \chi, B, q, m, \sigma)$. Define the domain $\mathcal{S}$ of the encoding scheme to be $\mathbb{Z}_q^n$.
- $\mathsf{Keygen}(\mathsf{pp})$: Run the trapdoor generation algorithm $\mathsf{TrapGen}(1^n, 1^m, q)$ to obtain a matrix $\mathbf{A} \in \mathbb{Z}_q^{n \times m}$ together with the trapdoor matrix $\mathbf{T} \in \mathbb{Z}^{m \times m}$. Output $\mathsf{pk} := \mathbf{A}$ and $\mathsf{sk} := \mathbf{T}$.
- $\mathsf{Encode}(\mathsf{pk}, s)$: Sample an error vector $\mathbf{e} \xleftarrow{\$} \chi^m$ and output the encoding $\phi := \mathbf{A}^T s + \mathbf{e} \in \mathbb{Z}_q^m$.

The recoding algorithms work as follows:

- $\mathsf{ReKeyGen3}(\mathsf{pk}_0, \mathsf{pk}_1, \mathsf{pk}_2, \mathsf{sk}_i; \mathsf{pk}_{\mathrm{tgt}})$: Let $\mathsf{pk}_0 = \mathbf{A}_0$, $\mathsf{pk}_1 = \mathbf{A}_1$, $\mathsf{pk}_2 = \mathbf{A}_2$, $\mathsf{sk}_i = \mathbf{T}_i$, $i \in \{0, 1, 2\}$ and $\mathsf{pk}_{\mathrm{tgt}} = \mathbf{A}_{\mathrm{tgt}}$. Compute the matrix $\mathbf{R} \in \mathbb{Z}^{3m \times m}$ in the following way:
  - For each $j \in \{0, 1, 2\}, j \neq i$, choose a (truncated) discrete Gaussian matrix $\mathbf{R}_j \in (D_{\mathbb{Z}, \sigma})^{m \times m}$. Namely, each entry of the matrix is an independent sample from the discrete Gaussian distribution $D_{\mathbb{Z}, \sigma}$.
  - Compute $\mathbf{U} := \mathbf{A}_{\mathrm{tgt}} - \sum_{j \in \{0,1,2\}}^{j \neq i} \mathbf{A}_j \mathbf{R}_j \in \mathbb{Z}_q^{n \times m}$.
  - Compute the matrix $\mathbf{R}_i$ by running the algorithm $\mathsf{SampleD}$ to compute a matrix $\mathbf{R}_i \in \mathbb{Z}^{m \times m}$ as follows:

$$\mathbf{R}_i \leftarrow \mathsf{SampleD}(\mathbf{A}_i, \mathbf{T}_i; \mathbf{U}, \sigma).$$

Output

$$\mathsf{rk}_{0,1,2}^{\mathrm{tgt}} := \begin{bmatrix} \mathbf{R}_0 \\ \mathbf{R}_1 \\ \mathbf{R}_2 \end{bmatrix} \in \mathbb{Z}^{3m \times m}.$$

Note that $\mathbf{A}_i\mathbf{R}_i = \mathbf{U} = \mathbf{A}_{\text{tgt}} - \sum_{j\in\{0,1,2\}}^{j\neq i} \mathbf{A}_j\mathbf{R}_j$, so $\sum_{j\in\{0,1,2\}} \mathbf{A}_j\mathbf{R}_j = \mathbf{A}_{\text{tgt}}$.

- SimReKeyGen3($\mathsf{pk}_0, \mathsf{pk}_1, \mathsf{pk}_2$): Let $\mathsf{pk}_0 = \mathbf{A}_0$, $\mathsf{pk}_1 = \mathbf{A}_1$, and $\mathsf{pk}_2 = \mathbf{A}_2$.
  - Sample matrices $\mathbf{R}_0, \mathbf{R}_1, \mathbf{R}_2 \in (D_{\mathbb{Z},\sigma})^{m\times m}$ by sampling each entry from the discrete Gaussian distribution $D_{\mathbb{Z},\sigma}$, and let $\mathbf{R} = [\mathbf{R}_0^T \| \mathbf{R}_1^T \| \mathbf{R}_2^T]^T$.
  - Define:
  $$\mathbf{A}_{\text{tgt}} = [\mathbf{A}_0 \| \mathbf{A}_1 \| \mathbf{A}_2]\mathbf{R} \in \mathbf{Z}_q^{n\times m}.$$

Output the pair ($\mathsf{pk}_{\text{tgt}} := \mathbf{A}_{\text{tgt}}, \mathsf{rk}_{0,1,2}^{\text{tgt}} := \mathbf{R}$).

- Recode($\mathsf{rk}_{0,1,2}^{\text{tgt}}, \phi_0, \phi_1, \phi_2$): Let $\mathsf{rk}_{0,1,2}^{\text{tgt}} = \mathbf{R}$. Compute the recoded ciphertext

$$\phi_{\text{tgt}} = [\phi_0^T \| \phi_1^T \| \phi_2^T]\mathbf{R}.$$

The one-time symmetric encryption scheme (E, D) used in the three-to-one recoding scheme is similar to other LWE-based cryptosystems, and can be viewed as an error-tolerant version of the one-time pad. We set $\mathcal{K} = \mathbb{Z}_q^m$ and $\mathcal{M} = \{0,1\}^m$. The formal definition is as follows:

- E($\phi, \mathbf{m}$) takes as input a vector $\phi \in \mathcal{K}$ and a bit string $\mathbf{m} \in \mathcal{M}$ and outputs the encryption:
$$\tau := \phi + \lceil q/2 \rceil \mathbf{m} \pmod q.$$

- D(ϕ', τ): First we define the rounding function Round(x), $x \in \mathbb{Z}_q = [-(q-1)/2, (q-1)/2]$ as follows:

$$\mathsf{Round}(x) = \begin{cases} 0, & \text{if } |x| \leq q/4; \\ 1, & \text{otherwise.} \end{cases}$$

Let the input of D be written as $\phi' = (\phi_1', ..., \phi_m') \in \mathbb{Z}_q^m$ and $\tau = (\tau_1, ..., \tau_m) \in \mathbb{Z}_q^m$. Then, D outputs:

$$\mathbf{m} = (\mathsf{Round}(\tau_1 - \phi_1'), ..., \mathsf{Round}(\tau_m - \phi_m')).$$

The security of (E, D) directly follows from that of one-time pad.

We give the correctness and security properties of three-to-one recoding from LWE in Appendix A.

4   CP-ABE for Circuits

Description on Circuits. We suppose that the maximal depth of all possible access policy circuits is $d_{\max}$, and the maximal number of gates is $c_{\max} = \text{poly}(\lambda)$. Each gate is binary gate which has two incoming wires and one outgoing wire. There are l input wires indexed from 1 to l, the i-th input is the i-th attribute in the attribute set, and exactly one output wire. We fix the output wire index to $c_{\max}$. (Note that the size of a certain circuit C may be less than $c_{\max}$, so some indexes may have no corresponding wires in C.) Each gate with input wires indexed u, v and output wire indexed w must satisfy $u < v < w$.

4.1   CP-ABE Construction

Setup($1^\lambda, 1^l, d_{\max}, c_{\max}$): For each input wire $i \in [l]$, generate 2 different public/secret key pairs, $(\mathsf{pk}_b^i, \mathsf{sk}_b^i) \leftarrow \mathsf{Keygen}(\mathsf{pp})$, for $b \in \{0, 1\}$. For each $u < v < w \leq c_{\max}$, generate 8 different public/secret key pairs, $(\mathsf{pk}_{b_u,b_v,b_w}^{u,v,w}, \mathsf{sk}_{b_u,b_v,b_w}^{u,v,w}) \leftarrow \mathsf{Keygen}(\mathsf{pp})$, for $b_u, b_v, b_w \in \{0, 1\}$. Finally, generate an additional public/secret key pair $(\mathsf{pk}_{\mathrm{out}}, \mathsf{sk}_{\mathrm{out}}) \leftarrow \mathsf{Keygen}(\mathsf{pp})$.

Output $\mathsf{mpk} := (\{\mathsf{pk}_b^i : i \in [l], b \in \{0, 1\}\}, \{\mathsf{pk}_{b_u,b_v,b_w}^{u,v,w} : u < v < w \leq c_{\max}, b_u, b_v, b_w \in \{0, 1\}\}, \mathsf{pk}_{\mathrm{out}})$; $\mathsf{msk} := (\{\mathsf{sk}_b^i : i \in [l], b \in \{0, 1\}\}, \{\mathsf{sk}_{b_u,b_v,b_w}^{u,v,w} : u < v < w \leq c_{\max}, b_u, b_v, b_w \in \{0, 1\}\})$.

Enc(mpk, C, m): The restriction on C is mentioned above. First, choose a uniformly random $s \xleftarrow{\$} \mathcal{S}$. For each input wire $i \in [l]$, calculate $\phi_b^i = \mathsf{Encode}(\mathsf{pk}_b^i, s)$ for $b \in \{0, 1\}$. For each gate $g_w \in C$ with incoming wires u, v and outgoing wire w, calculate $\phi_{b_u,b_v}^w = \mathsf{Encode}(\mathsf{pk}_{b_u,b_v,g_w(b_u,b_v)}^{u,v,w})$ for $b_u, b_v \in \{0, 1\}$. Finally, encrypt the message m as $\tau \leftarrow \mathsf{E}(\mathsf{Encode}(\mathsf{pk}_{\mathrm{out}}, s), m)$.

Output the ciphertext $\mathsf{ct}_C = (C, \{\phi_b^i : i \in [l], b \in \{0, 1\}\}, \{\phi_{b_u,b_v}^w : g_w \in C, b_u, b_v \in \{0, 1\}\}, \tau)$.

KeyGen($\mathsf{msk}, \mathsf{ind}$):

1. For each w such that $w \in [l + 1, c_{\max}]$ (w is the index of a non-input wire), generate public/secret key pairs: $(\mathsf{pk}_b^w, \mathsf{sk}_b^w) \leftarrow \mathsf{Keygen}(\mathsf{pp})$ if $w < c_{\max}$ or $b = 0$, and set $\mathsf{pk}_1^{c_{\max}} := \mathsf{pk}_{\mathrm{out}}$.
2. Let $\mathsf{ind} \in \{0, 1\}^l$. For each $u < v < w \leq c_{\max}$, generate:

$$\mathsf{rk}_{b_u,b_v,b_w}^{u,v,w} = \mathsf{ReKeyGen3}(\mathsf{pk}_{b_u,b_v,b_w}^{u,v,w}, \mathsf{pk}_{b_u}^u, \mathsf{pk}_{b_v}^v, \mathsf{sk}_{b_u,b_v,b_w}^{u,v,w}, \mathsf{pk}_{b_w}^w),$$

for $\begin{cases} b_u = \mathsf{ind}_u, & \text{if } u \in [l]; b_u \in \{0, 1\}, \text{otherwise}; \\ b_v = \mathsf{ind}_v, & \text{if } v \in [l]; b_v \in \{0, 1\}, \text{otherwise}; \\ b_w \in \{0, 1\}. \end{cases}$

Output all recoding keys as secret key:

$$\mathsf{sk}_{\mathsf{ind}} := (\mathsf{rk}_{b_u,b_v,b_w}^{u,v,w} : u < v < w \leq c_{\max}, b_u, b_v, b_w \in \{0, 1\}).$$

Dec($\mathsf{sk}_{\mathsf{ind}}, \mathsf{ct}_C$): For each $w = 1, ..., l$, wire w carries the value ind_l. For each $w = l + 1, ..., c_{\max}$, if there is a gate g_w indexed w in C, we let u, v be the two incoming wires for g_w, and b_u, b_v be the values carried by u, v. Then the value carries by w should be $b_w = g_w(b_u, b_v)$. Then, compute $\phi_{b_w}^w = \mathsf{Recode3}(\mathsf{rk}_{b_u,b_v,b_w}^{u,v,w}, \phi_{b_u}^u, \phi_{b_v}^v, \phi_{b_u,b_v}^w)$.

If $C(\mathsf{ind}) = 1$, we must have computed $\phi_1^{c_{\max}}$. Then output the message $m \leftarrow \mathsf{D}(\phi_1^{c_{\max}}, \tau)$.

If $C(\mathsf{ind}) = 0$, output $\perp$.

Discussion. Since we cannot predetermine the topology structure of the access policy circuit, we must construct public keys and secret keys for *any* possible wires, and that makes our secret key size $(O(c_{\max}^3))$ quite overloaded. However, each decryption procedure only use part of them, so the large secret key size does not increase the decryption time cost.

Correctness

Lemma 2. *Let the CP-ABE scheme above be constructed from a correct three-to-one recoding scheme for $d_{\max}$ levels. Then for $\mathsf{ct}_C \leftarrow \mathsf{Enc}(\mathsf{mpk}, C, m)$ and $\mathsf{sk}_{\mathsf{ind}} \leftarrow \mathsf{KeyGen}(\mathsf{msk}, \mathsf{ind})$, if $C(\mathsf{ind}) = 1$, we have $\mathsf{Dec}(\mathsf{sk}_{\mathsf{ind}}, \mathsf{ct}_C) = m$.*

Proof. For each wire indexed by w, we let b_w be the value it carries. We only need to show that for any gate g_w indexed by w, if g_w is depth i, then $\phi_{b_w}^w \in \Phi_{\mathsf{pk}_{b_w}^w, s, i}$, so that $\phi_1^{c_{\max}} \in \Phi_{\mathsf{pk}_{\mathsf{out}}, s, d_{\max}}$. We prove it by induction.

First, for each gate g_w of depth 1, its incoming wires u, v are from input wires, so that $\phi_{b_u}^u$ and $\phi_{b_v}^v$ are generated from Encode, and we have $\phi_{b_u}^u \in \Phi_{\mathsf{pk}_{b_u}^u, s, 0}$ and $\phi_{b_v}^v \in \Phi_{\mathsf{pk}_{b_v}^v, s, 0}$. Also $\phi_{b_u, b_v, b_w}^{u,v,w}$ is generated from Encode, so $\phi_{b_u, b_v, b_w}^{u,v,w} \in \Phi_{\mathsf{pk}_{b_u, b_v, b_w}^{u,v,w}, s, 0}$. Then from the correctness of $\mathsf{Recode3}$, we have $\phi_{b_w}^w \in \Phi_{\mathsf{pk}_{b_w}^w, s, 1}$.

Suppose that the result holds for all gates of depth $k \leq i$. For gate g_w of depth $i+1$ with incoming wires indexed u, v, we have that $\phi_{b_u}^u \in \Phi_{\mathsf{pk}_{b_u}^u, s, i}$, $\phi_{b_v}^v \in \Phi_{\mathsf{pk}_{b_v}^v, s, i}$, and $\phi_{b_u, b_v, b_w}^{u,v,w} \in \Phi_{\mathsf{pk}_{b_u, b_v, b_w}^{u,v,w}, s, 0}$. Then from the correctness of $\mathsf{Recode3}$, we have $\phi_{b_w}^w \in \Phi_{\mathsf{pk}_{b_w}^w, s, i+1}$. Thus the result holds for any $k \in [d_{\max}]$ by induction.

So we have $\phi_{c_{\max}, 1} \in \Phi_{\mathsf{pk}_{\mathsf{out}}, s, d_{\max}}$. By the correctness of encryption E, D, $\mathsf{Dec}(\mathsf{sk}_{\mathsf{ind}}, \mathsf{ct}_C) = \mathsf{D}(\phi_1^{c_{\max}}, \tau) = m$. □

4.2   Security Proof

In this section, we consider selective security of our scheme above. As it was mentioned in [21], using the technique from [8], it can be transformed into a fully secure scheme based on the subexponential hardness of LWE. We shall not discuss the details here.

Lemma 3. *For any adversary $\mathcal{A}$ against selective security of the attribute-based encryption scheme, there exists an adversary $\mathcal{B}$ against correlated pseudorandomness of three-to-one recoding scheme whose running time is essentially the same as that of $\mathcal{A}$, such that:*

$$\mathsf{Adv}_{\mathcal{A}}^{\mathsf{PE}}(\lambda) \leq \mathsf{Adv}_{\mathcal{B}}^{\mathsf{CP}} + \mathsf{negl}(\lambda)$$

where $\mathsf{negl}(\lambda)$ captures the statistical security terms in three-to-one recoding scheme.

Alternative Algorithms. First, we shall describe alternative algorithms Setup^*, Enc^* and KeyGen^*, given the three-to-one recoding challenge:

$$\mathsf{pp}, (\mathsf{pk}_i, \phi_i)_{i \in [4c_{\max} - 2l + 1]},$$

and use it to generate the challenge ciphertext $\mathsf{ct}_{C^*} = (C^*, \{\phi_b^i : i \in [l], b \in \{0, 1\}\}, \{\phi_{b_u, b_v, b_w}^{u,v,w} : u < v < w \leq c_{\max}, b_u, b_v, b_w \in \{0, 1\}\}, \tau)$. These algorithms are simulations of real algorithms in the CP-ABE scheme. Note that we cannot deduce s from the challenge ciphertext, nor the secret keys below: $\mathsf{sk}_b^i : i \in [l], b \in \{0,1\}$; $\mathsf{sk}_{b_u,b_v,g_w(b_u,b_v)}^{u,v,w}$ for each $g_w \in C^*$, and $\mathsf{sk}_{\mathrm{out}}$. Still, we can generate all other sk in the master secret key.

$\mathsf{Setup}^*(C^*, 1^\lambda, 1^l, d_{\max}, b_{\max})$: Let $\mathsf{pk}_{i,0} := \mathsf{pk}_{2i-1}$ and $\mathsf{pk}_{i,1} := \mathsf{pk}_{2i}$ for $i \in [l]$; for each $g_w \in C^*$, let u, v be its incoming wire indexes, let:

$$\mathsf{pk}_{0,0,g_w(0,0)}^{u,v,w} := \mathsf{pk}_{4w-2l-3}; \quad \mathsf{pk}_{0,1,g_w(0,1)}^{u,v,w} := \mathsf{pk}_{4w-2l-2};$$

$$\mathsf{pk}_{1,0,g_w(1,0)}^{u,v,w} := \mathsf{pk}_{4w-2l-1}; \quad \mathsf{pk}_{1,1,g_w(1,1)}^{u,v,w} := \mathsf{pk}_{4w-2l}$$

and $\mathsf{pk}_{\mathrm{out}} := \mathsf{pk}_{4c_{\max}-2l+1}$.

All other keys are generated from Keygen algorithm. For each $g_w \in C^*$, let

$$(\mathsf{pk}_{b_u,b_v,1-g_w(b_u,b_v)}^{u,v,w}, \mathsf{pk}_{b_u,b_v,1-g_w(b_u,b_v)}^{u,v,w}) \leftarrow \mathsf{Keygen}(\mathsf{pp})$$

for all $b_u, b_v \in \{0,1\}$, and for each $u < v < w \leq c_{\max}$ such that either there is no gate g_w in C^* or the incoming wires of g_w are not u, v, let

$$(\mathsf{pk}_{b_u,b_v,b_w}^{u,v,w}, \mathsf{sk}_{b_u,b_v,b_w}^{u,v,w}) \leftarrow \mathsf{Keygen}(\mathsf{pp})$$

for all $b_u, b_v, b_w \in \{0,1\}$.

Output $\mathsf{mpk} :=$

$$(\{\mathsf{pk}_b^i : i \in [l], b \in \{0,1\}\}, \{\mathsf{pk}_{b_u,b_v,b_w}^{u,v,w} : u < v < w \leq c_{\max}, b_u, b_v, b_w \in \{0,1\}\}, \mathsf{pk}_{\mathrm{out}}).$$

$\mathsf{Enc}^*(\mathsf{mpk}, C^*, m)$: Set $\tau \leftarrow \mathsf{E}(\phi_{4c_{\max}-2l+1}, m)$, and return:

$$\mathsf{ct}_{C^*} = (C^*, \{\phi_i : i \in [2l]\}, \{\phi_i : i \in [2l+1, 4c_{\max} - 2l]\}, \tau).$$

$\mathsf{KeyGen}^*(\mathsf{msk}, \mathsf{ind})$: If $C^*(\mathsf{ind}) = 1$ returns $\perp$. We first set $b_i = \mathsf{ind}_i$ for $i \in [l]$. For each $w \in [l+1, c_{\max}]$, if there is a gate g_w in C^*, and its incoming wires are u, v, we set $b_w = g_w(b_u, b_v)$, and generate:

$$(\mathsf{rk}_{b_u,b_v,b_w}^{u,v,w}, \mathsf{pk}_{b_w}^w) \leftarrow \mathsf{SimReKeyGen3}(\mathsf{pk}_{b_u,b_v,b_w}^{u,v,w}, \mathsf{pk}_{b_u}^u, \mathsf{pk}_{b_v}^v).$$

It is easy to see that each b_w is the value of wire w when running the circuit C^* with input ind. Since $C^*(\mathsf{ind}) = 0$, the procedure above finally generates $\mathsf{pk}_0^{c_{\max}}$, and does not contradict with existing keys.

Now that we have the value of $\mathsf{pk}_{b_w}^w$ for all $g_w \in C^*$. For each $w \in [l+1, c-1]$, if there is no g_w in C^*, generate $(\mathsf{pk}_b^w, \mathsf{sk}_b^w) \leftarrow \mathsf{Keygen}(\mathsf{pp})$ for $b \in \{0,1\}$. If $g_w \in C^*$, then the value of b_w is set, we generate $(\mathsf{pk}_{1-b_w}^w, \mathsf{sk}_{1-b_w}^w) \leftarrow \mathsf{Keygen}(\mathsf{pp})$.

For all other $u < v < w \leq c_{\max}$, if there is no gate g_w in C^* or the incoming wires of g_w are not u, v, then $\mathsf{sk}_{b_0,b_1,b_2}^{u,v,w}$ is generated in Setup^*, so for any $b_0, b_1, b_2 \in \{0,1\}$, we can set:

$$\mathsf{rk}_{b_0,b_1,b_2}^{u,v,w} \leftarrow \mathsf{ReKeyGen3}(\mathsf{pk}_{b_0,b_1,b_2}^{u,v,w}, \mathsf{pk}_{b_0}^u, \mathsf{pk}_{b_1}^v, \mathsf{sk}_{b_0,b_1,b_2}^{u,v,w}, \mathsf{pk}_{b_2}^w).$$

For $g_w \in C^*$ with incoming wires u, v, $\mathsf{sk}_{b_u,b_v,1-b_w}^{u,v,w}$ is also generated in Setup^*, so we can set

$$\mathsf{rk}_{b_u,b_v,1-b_w}^{u,v,w} \leftarrow \mathsf{ReKeyGen3}(\mathsf{pk}_{b_u,b_v,1-b_w}^{u,v,w}, \mathsf{pk}_{b_u}^u, \mathsf{pk}_{b_v}^v, \mathsf{sk}_{b_u,b_v,1-b_w}^{u,v,w}, \mathsf{pk}_{1-b_w}^w).$$

Next, we set:

$$\mathsf{rk}^{u,v,w}_{1-b_u,b_v,b} \leftarrow \mathsf{ReKeyGen3}(\mathsf{pk}^{u,v,w}_{1-b_u,b_v,b}, \mathsf{pk}^u_{1-b_u}, \mathsf{pk}^v_{b_v}, \mathsf{sk}^u_{1-b_u}, \mathsf{pk}^w_b) \qquad \text{if } u > l;$$

$$\mathsf{rk}^{u,v,w}_{b_u,1-b_v,b} \leftarrow \mathsf{ReKeyGen3}(\mathsf{pk}^{u,v,w}_{b_u,1-b_v,b}, \mathsf{pk}^u_{b_u}, \mathsf{pk}^v_{1-b_v}, \mathsf{sk}^v_{1-b_v}, \mathsf{pk}^w_b) \qquad \text{if } v > l;$$

$$\mathsf{rk}^{u,v,w}_{1-b_u,1-b_v,b} \leftarrow \mathsf{ReKeyGen3}(\mathsf{pk}^{u,v,w}_{1-b_u,1-b_v,b}, \mathsf{pk}^u_{1-b_u}, \mathsf{pk}^v_{1-b_v}, \mathsf{sk}^u_{1-b_u}, \mathsf{pk}^w_b) \text{ if } u,v > l$$

for $b \in \{0,1\}$.

Finally, we gather all the required recoding keys, and return:

$$\mathsf{sk}_{\mathsf{ind}} := (\mathsf{rk}^{u,v,w}_{b_0,b_1,b_2} : u < v < w \le c_{\max}, b_0, b_1, b_2 \in \{0,1\}).$$

Informally, all recoding keys generated from SimReKeyGen look the same as in KeyGen because of the recoding simulation property, and all other recoding keys look the same as in KeyGen because key indistinguishability.

Game Sequence. Next, consider the following sequence of games. We use Adv_0, $\mathsf{Adv}_1,\ldots$ to denote the advantage of the adversary $\mathcal{A}$ in Games 0, 1, etc. Game 0 is the real experiment.

Game i for $i = 1, 2, \ldots Q$, Q is the maximal number of KeyGen queries. As in Game 0, except the challenger answers the first $i - 1$ key queries using KeyGen* and the remaining $Q - i$ key queries using KeyGen. For the i-th key query ind_i, we consider sub-Games $i.w$ as follows:

Game $i.w$, for $w = l + 1, \ldots, c_{\max}$. The challenger switches $(\mathsf{rk}^{u,v,w}_{b_0,b_1,b_2} : u < v < w, b_0, b_1, b_2 \in \{0,1\})$ from KeyGen to KeyGen*. If there is no gate g_w indexed w in C^*, there is no difference between KeyGen and KeyGen*. Otherwise, let the incoming wires of g_w be labeled u, v, and b_u, b_v, b_w be the values of wire u, v, w in C^* with input ind_i. We do the following:

- First, we switch $(\mathsf{pk}^w_{b_w}, \mathsf{rk}^{u,v,w}_{b_u,b_v,b_w})$ from KeyGen to KeyGen*. This relies on recoding simulation.
- Next, we switch $\mathsf{rk}^{u,v,w}_{1-b_u,b_v,b}, \mathsf{rk}^{u,v,w}_{b_u,1-b_v,b}, \mathsf{rk}^{u,v,w}_{1-b_u,1-b_v,b}$ for $b \in \{0,1\}$ from KeyGen to KeyGen*. This relies on key indistinguishability.
- All other recoding keys are generated the same way in both KeyGen and KeyGen*.

We have $|\mathsf{Adv}_{i,w} - \mathsf{Adv}_{i,w+1}| \le \mathsf{negl}(\lambda)$ by key indistinguishability and recoding simulation for all i, w. Since $c_{\max}$ is polynomial in λ, we have $|\mathsf{Adv}_i - \mathsf{Adv}_{i+1}| \le \mathsf{negl}(\lambda)$ for all i.

Note that in Game Q, the challenger runs Setup* and answers all key queries using KeyGen* with the selective challenge C^* and generates the challenge ciphertext using Enc.

Game $Q + 1$. Same as Game Q, except the challenger generates the challenge ciphertext using Enc* with $\phi_{4c_{\max}-2l+1} = \mathsf{Encode}(\mathsf{pk}_{4c_{\max}-2l+1}, s)$. Clearly, $\mathsf{Adv}_{Q+1} = \mathsf{Adv}_Q$.

Game $Q + 2$. Same as Game $Q + 1$, except $\phi_{4c_{\max}-2l+1} \xleftarrow{\$} \mathcal{K}$. It is straightforward to construct an adversary $\mathcal{B}$ such that $|\mathsf{Adv}_{Q+1} - \mathsf{Adv}_{Q+2}| \le \mathsf{Adv}^{\mathsf{CP}}_{\mathcal{B}}(\lambda)$.

Finally, $\mathsf{Adv}_{Q+2} \le \mathsf{negl}(\lambda)$ by the one-time semantic security of (E, D). The lemma then follows readily.

4.3   Reducing Public Key Size in Random Oracle Model

In this section, we give an additional construction which can be proven secure in the random oracle model. Compared with our scheme above, this scheme has a much smaller public key size of $O(l)$, which has more advantages compared with universal circuit based constructions (further analysis can be found in the full paper).

Setup($1^\lambda, 1^l, d_{max}, c_{max}$): For each input wire $i \in [l]$, generate 2 different public/secret key pairs, $(\mathsf{pk}_b^i, \mathsf{sk}_b^i) \leftarrow \mathsf{Keygen(pp)}$, for $b \in \{0,1\}$, and an additional public/secret key pair $(\mathsf{pk_{out}}, \mathsf{sk_{out}}) \leftarrow \mathsf{Keygen(pp)}$. Moreover, output a hash function $H : \{0,1\}^{3\lceil \log c_{max} \rceil + 3} \rightarrow \mathcal{P}$ modeled as a random oracle, where $\mathsf{pk}' \xleftarrow{\$} \mathcal{P}$ and pk in $(\mathsf{pk}, \mathsf{sk}) \leftarrow \mathsf{Keygen(pp)}$ have negligible statistical distance. (For example, $\mathcal{P} = \mathbb{Z}_q^{n \times m}$ for the LWE-based construction of three-to-one recoding scheme).

Output $\mathsf{mpk} := (\{\mathsf{pk}_b^i : i \in [l], b \in \{0,1\}\}, \mathsf{pk_{out}}, H)$; $\mathsf{msk} := \{\mathsf{sk}_b^i : i \in [l], b \in \{0,1\}\}$.

Enc(mpk, C, m): The restriction on C is mentioned above. First, choose a uniformly random $s \xleftarrow{\$} \mathcal{S}$. For each input wire $i \in [l]$, calculate $\phi_b^i = \mathsf{Encode}(\mathsf{pk}_b^i, s)$ for $b \in \{0,1\}$. For each gate $g_w \in C$ with incoming wires u, v and outgoing wire w, calculate $\phi_{b_u,b_v}^w = \mathsf{Encode}(H(u\|v\|w\|b_u\|b_v\|g_w(b_u,b_v)), s)$ for $b_u, b_v \in \{0,1\}$. (Each u, v, w is considered as a $\lceil \log c_{max} \rceil$-bit string.) Finally, encrypt the message m as $\tau \leftarrow \mathsf{E}(\mathsf{Encode}(\mathsf{pk_{out}}, s), m)$.

Output the ciphertext $\mathsf{ct}_C = (C, \{\phi_b^i : i \in [l], b \in \{0,1\}\}, \{\phi_{b_u,b_v}^w : g_w \in C, b_u, b_v \in \{0,1\}\}, \tau)$.

KeyGen($\mathsf{msk}, \mathsf{ind}$):

1. For each w such that $w \in [l+1, c_{max}]$ (w is the index of a non-input wire), generate public/secret key pairs: $(\mathsf{pk}_b^w, \mathsf{sk}_b^w) \leftarrow \mathsf{Keygen(pp)}$ if $w < c_{max}$ or $b = 0$, and set $\mathsf{pk}_1^{c_{max}} := \mathsf{pk_{out}}$.
2. Let $\mathsf{ind} \in \{0,1\}^l$. For each $u < v < w \leq c_{max}$, generate:

$$\mathsf{rk}_{b_u,b_v,b_w}^{u,v,w} = \mathsf{ReKeyGen3}(H(u\|v\|w\|b_u\|b_v\|b_w), \mathsf{pk}_{b_u}^u, \mathsf{pk}_{b_v}^v, \mathsf{sk}_{b_u}^u, \mathsf{pk}_{b_w}^w),$$

$$\text{for} \begin{cases} b_u = \mathsf{ind}_u, & \text{if } u \in [l]; b_u \in \{0,1\}, \text{otherwise}; \\ b_v = \mathsf{ind}_v, & \text{if } v \in [l]; b_v \in \{0,1\}, \text{otherwise}; \\ b_w \in \{0,1\}. \end{cases}$$

Dec remains the same.

The security proof is essentially the same as the scheme in standard model. However, since the secret key corresponded with the random oracle output $H(u\|v\|w\|b_u\|b_v\|b_w)$ must be given in the proof, we can program the output of the oracle to set $H(u\|v\|w\|b_u\|b_v\|b_w) := \mathsf{pk}_{b_u,b_v,b_w}^{u,v,w}$ where $(\mathsf{pk}_{b_u,b_v,b_w}^{u,v,w}, \mathsf{sk}_{b_u,b_v,b_w}^{u,v,w}) \leftarrow \mathsf{Keygen(pp)}$. We omit the details here.

5   Conclusion

In this paper, we present a CP-ABE scheme for arbitrary polynomial size circuits based on LWE assumption. We note that there is currently no direct construction other than ours, and constructions from universal circuits are more complex and have higher decryption cost. However, the performance of our scheme, especially the secret key size is still nonapplicable for practice, which need further improvement. We shall consider it in our future work.

The duality between KP-ABE and CP-ABE has not been well studied in lattice as in pairing based cryptography. Many believe that the method used to construct KP-ABE in lattice cannot be used in CP-ABE construction as well. However, in this paper, based on the KP-ABE scheme in [21], we give a similar (although slightly different) construction for CP-ABE scheme. We hope that this work can spread some light into the further study of lattice-based ABE and FE schemes, and finally give birth to a universal framework for ABE/FE in lattice like the dual system framework in pairing based cryptography.

A Correctness and Security of Three-to-One Recoding from LWE

Correctness. We define the sets $\Phi_{\mathbf{A},\mathbf{s},j}$ for $\mathsf{pk} := \mathbf{A} \in \mathbb{Z}_q^{n \times m}$, $\mathbf{s} \in \mathbb{Z}_q^n$ and $j \in [0, d_{\max}]$ as follows:

$$\Phi_{\mathbf{A},\mathbf{s},j} = \mathbf{A}^T \mathbf{s} + \mathbf{e} : \|\mathbf{e}\|_\infty \leq B \cdot (3\sigma m \sqrt{m})^j.$$

Given this definition:

- Observe that when $\mathbf{e} \in \chi^m$, $\|\mathbf{e}\|_\infty \leq B$ by the definition of χ and B. So $\Pr[\mathsf{Encode}(\mathbf{A}, \mathbf{s}) \in \Phi_{\mathbf{A},\mathbf{s},0}] = 1$.
- $\Phi_{\mathbf{A},\mathbf{s},0} \subseteq \Phi_{\mathbf{A},\mathbf{s},1} \subseteq \ldots \subseteq \Phi_{\mathbf{A},\mathbf{s},d_{\max}}$, by definition of the sets above.
- For any two encodings $\phi = \mathbf{A}^T \mathbf{s} + \mathbf{e}$, $\phi' = \mathbf{A}^T \mathbf{s} + \mathbf{e}' \in \Phi_{\mathbf{A},\mathbf{s},d_{\max}}$:

$$\|\phi - \phi'\|_\infty = \|\mathbf{e} - \mathbf{e}'\|_\infty \leq 3 \cdot B \cdot (3\sigma m \sqrt{m})^{d_{\max}} < q/4,$$

  which holds as long as $n \cdot O(n^2 \log q)^{d_{\max}} < q/4$. Thus, ϕ and ϕ' are "close", and by the correctness property of the symmetric encryption scheme (E, D) described above, $\mathsf{D}(\phi', \mathsf{E}(\phi, \mu)) = \mu$ for any $\mu \in \{0,1\}^m$.
- Consider three encodings $\phi_0 \in \Phi_{\mathbf{A}_0,\mathbf{s},j_0}$, $\phi_1 \in \Phi_{\mathbf{A}_1,\mathbf{s},j_1}$ and $\phi_2 \in \Phi_{\mathbf{A}_2,\mathbf{s},j_2}$, for any $j_0, j_1, j_2 \in [0, d_{\max} - 1]$, any $\mathbf{A}_0, \mathbf{A}_1, \mathbf{A}_2 \in \mathbb{Z}_q^{n \times m}$ and $\mathbf{s} \in \mathbb{Z}_q^n$. Then, $\phi_0 = \mathbf{A}_0^T \mathbf{s} + \mathbf{e}_0$, $\phi_1 = \mathbf{A}_1^T \mathbf{s} + \mathbf{e}_1$ and $\phi_2 = \mathbf{A}_2^T \mathbf{s} + \mathbf{e}_2$, where $\|\mathbf{e}_0\|_\infty \leq B(3\sigma m \sqrt{m})^{j_0}$, $\|\mathbf{e}_1\|_\infty \leq B(3\sigma m \sqrt{m})^{j_1}$ and $\|\mathbf{e}_2\|_\infty \leq B(3\sigma m \sqrt{m})^{j_2}$. Then, the recoding ϕ_{tgt} is computed as follows:

$$\begin{aligned}
\phi_{\mathrm{tgt}}^T &:= [\phi_0^T \| \phi_1^T \| \phi_2^T] \mathbf{R}_{0,1,2}^{\mathrm{tgt}} \\
&= [\mathbf{s}^T \mathbf{A}_0 + \mathbf{e}_0^T \| \mathbf{s}^T \mathbf{A}_1 + \mathbf{e}_1^T \| \mathbf{s}^T \mathbf{A}_2 + \mathbf{e}_2^T] \mathbf{R}_{0,1,2}^{\mathrm{tgt}} \\
&= \mathbf{s}^T [\mathbf{A}_0 \| \mathbf{A}_1 \| \mathbf{A}_2] \mathbf{R}_{0,1,2}^{\mathrm{tgt}} + [\mathbf{e}_0^T \| \mathbf{e}_1^T \| \mathbf{e}_2^T] \mathbf{R}_{0,1,2}^{\mathrm{tgt}} \\
&= \mathbf{s}^T \mathbf{A}_{\mathrm{tgt}} + \mathbf{e}_{\mathrm{tgt}}^T
\end{aligned}$$

where $\mathbf{e}_{\text{tgt}} := [\mathbf{e}_0^T \| \mathbf{e}_1^T \| \mathbf{e}_2^T]\mathbf{R}_{0,1,2}^{\text{tgt}}$. Thus, we have:

$$\|\mathbf{e}_{\text{tgt}}\|_\infty := m \cdot \|\mathbf{R}_{0,1,2}^{\text{tgt}}\|_\infty \cdot (\|\mathbf{e}_0\|_\infty + \|\mathbf{e}_1\|_\infty + \|\mathbf{e}_0\|_\infty)$$
$$\leq m \cdot \sigma\sqrt{m} \cdot (B \cdot (3\sigma m\sqrt{m})^{j_0} + B \cdot (3\sigma m\sqrt{m})^{j_1} + B \cdot (3\sigma m\sqrt{m})^{j_2})$$
$$\leq B \cdot (3\sigma m\sqrt{m})^{\max(j_0,j_1,j_2)+1}$$

and we complete the proof.

Key Indistinguishability. Let $(\mathbf{A}_1, \mathbf{T}_1), (\mathbf{A}_2, \mathbf{T}_2) \leftarrow \mathsf{TrapSamp}(1^n, 1^m, q)$, and $\mathbf{R}_1, \mathbf{R}_2 \xleftarrow{\$} D_{\mathbb{Z}^m,\sigma}^m$. By the property of lattice trapdoors, we can see that the following two distribution $(\mathbf{U}, \mathbf{R}_0)$:

- $(\mathbf{A}_0, \mathbf{T}_0) \leftarrow \mathsf{TrapSamp}(1^n, 1^m, q); \mathbf{U} \xleftarrow{\$} \mathbb{Z}_q^{n \times m}, \mathbf{R} \leftarrow \mathsf{SampleD}(\mathbf{A}, \mathbf{T}, \mathbf{U}, \sigma);$
- $(\mathbf{A}_0, \mathbf{T}_0) \leftarrow \mathsf{TrapSamp}(1^n, 1^m, q); \mathbf{R_0} \xleftarrow{\$} D_{\mathbb{Z}^m,\sigma}^m, \mathbf{U} := \mathbf{A}_0\mathbf{R}_0.$

are statistically indistinguishable. Thus for the two distributions, $(\mathbf{A}_{\text{tgt}} := \mathbf{U} + \mathbf{A}_1\mathbf{R}_1 + \mathbf{A}_2\mathbf{R}_2 \bmod q, \mathbf{R} = [\mathbf{R}_0^T \| \mathbf{R}_1^T \| \mathbf{R}_2^T]^T)$ are statistically indistinguishable. In the first distribution, we change the sampling of $\mathbf{U}$ into: $\mathbf{A}_{\text{tgt}} \xleftarrow{\$} \mathbb{Z}_q^{n \times m}$, $\mathbf{U} := \mathbf{A}_{\text{tgt}} - \mathbf{A}_1\mathbf{R}_1 - \mathbf{A}_2\mathbf{R}_2 \bmod q$, which does not change the distribution, and $\mathbf{R}$ is generated from $\mathsf{ReKeyGen3}(\mathbf{A}_0, \mathbf{A}_1, \mathbf{A}_2, \mathbf{T}_0, \mathbf{A}_{\text{tgt}})$ in the first distribution. Also $(\mathbf{A}_{\text{tgt}}, \mathbf{R})$ are generated from $\mathsf{SimReKeyGen3}(\mathbf{A}_0, \mathbf{A}_1, \mathbf{A}_2)$ in the second distribution. Thus we have the recoding simulation property.

Similarly, each recoding key generated from $\mathsf{ReKeyGen3}(\mathbf{A}_0, \mathbf{A}_1, \mathbf{A}_2, \mathbf{T}_i, \mathbf{A}_{\text{tgt}})$ for $i \in \{0, 1, 2\}$ is statistically indistinguishable from the recoding key generated from $\mathsf{SimReKeyGen3}(\mathbf{A}_0, \mathbf{A}_1, \mathbf{A}_2)$. So the recoding keys generated from all four methods are statistically indistinguishable.

Correlated Pseudorandomness

We construct the following interactive games. Let **Game 0** be the original game.

Game 1: Instead of letting $(\mathsf{pk}_i, \mathsf{sk}_i) \leftarrow \mathsf{Keygen}(\mathsf{pp})$, we let $\mathsf{pk}_i \xleftarrow{\$} \mathbb{Z}_q^{n \times m}$. Game 1 is statistically indistinguishable from Game 0 because of the property of lattice trapdoors.

Game 2: Instead of letting $\phi_i = \mathsf{Encode}(\mathsf{pk}_i, s)$ for $i = 1, ..., l$ and $\phi_0' = \mathsf{Encode}(\mathsf{pk}_{l+1}, s)$, we let $\phi_1, ..., \phi_l, \phi_0' \xleftarrow{\$} \mathbb{Z}_q^m$. Game 2 is computationally indistinguishable from Game 1 because of LWE assumption.

In Game 2, ϕ_0' and ϕ_1' are both uniformly distributed, so the adversary cannot do better than random guess. Thus we prove the pseudorandomness of the scheme.

References

1. Agrawal, S., Boneh, D., Boyen, X.: Efficient lattice (H)IBE in the standard model. In: Gilbert, H. (ed.) EUROCRYPT 2010. LNCS, vol. 6110, pp. 553–572. Springer, Heidelberg (2010). https://doi.org/10.1007/978-3-642-13190-5_28

2. Agrawal, S., Boneh, D., Boyen, X.: Lattice basis delegation in fixed dimension and shorter-ciphertext hierarchical IBE. In: Rabin, T. (ed.) CRYPTO 2010. LNCS, vol. 6223, pp. 98–115. Springer, Heidelberg (2010). https://doi.org/10.1007/978-3-642-14623-7_6

3. Agrawal, S., Boyen, X., Vaikuntanathan, V., Voulgaris, P., Wee, H.: Functional encryption for threshold functions (or fuzzy IBE) from lattices. In: Fischlin, M., Buchmann, J., Manulis, M. (eds.) PKC 2012. LNCS, vol. 7293, pp. 280–297. Springer, Heidelberg (2012). https://doi.org/10.1007/978-3-642-30057-8_17

4. Agrawal, S., Freeman, D.M., Vaikuntanathan, V.: Functional encryption for inner product predicates from learning with errors. In: Lee, D.H., Wang, X. (eds.) ASIACRYPT 2011. LNCS, vol. 7073, pp. 21–40. Springer, Heidelberg (2011). https://doi.org/10.1007/978-3-642-25385-0_2

5. Ajtai, M.: Generating hard instances of the short basis problem. In: Wiedermann, J., van Emde Boas, P., Nielsen, M. (eds.) ICALP 1999. LNCS, vol. 1644, pp. 1–9. Springer, Heidelberg (1999). https://doi.org/10.1007/3-540-48523-6_1

6. Bert, P., Fouque, P.-A., Roux-Langlois, A., Sabt, M.: Practical implementation of ring-SIS/LWE based signature and IBE. In: Lange, T., Steinwandt, R. (eds.) PQCrypto 2018. LNCS, vol. 10786, pp. 271–291. Springer, Cham (2018). https://doi.org/10.1007/978-3-319-79063-3_13

7. Bethencourt, J., Sahai, A., Waters, B.: Ciphertext-policy attribute-based encryption. In: IEEE Symposium on Security and Privacy, pp. 321–334 (2007)

8. Boneh, D., Boyen, X.: Efficient selective-ID secure identity-based encryption without random oracles. In: Cachin, C., Camenisch, J.L. (eds.) EUROCRYPT 2004. LNCS, vol. 3027, pp. 223–238. Springer, Heidelberg (2004). https://doi.org/10.1007/978-3-540-24676-3_14

9. Boneh, D., et al.: Fully key-homomorphic encryption, arithmetic circuit ABE and compact garbled circuits. In: Nguyen, P.Q., Oswald, E. (eds.) EUROCRYPT 2014. LNCS, vol. 8441, pp. 533–556. Springer, Heidelberg (2014). https://doi.org/10.1007/978-3-642-55220-5_30

10. Boyen, X.: Attribute-based functional encryption on lattices. In: Sahai, A. (ed.) TCC 2013. LNCS, vol. 7785, pp. 122–142. Springer, Heidelberg (2013). https://doi.org/10.1007/978-3-642-36594-2_8

11. Brakerski, Z., Vaikuntanathan, V.: Circuit-ABE from LWE: unbounded attributes and semi-adaptive security. In: Robshaw, M., Katz, J. (eds.) CRYPTO 2016. LNCS, vol. 9816, pp. 363–384. Springer, Heidelberg (2016). https://doi.org/10.1007/978-3-662-53015-3_13

12. Cash, D., Hofheinz, D., Kiltz, E., Peikert, C.: Bonsai trees, or how to delegate a lattice basis. In: Gilbert, H. (ed.) EUROCRYPT 2010. LNCS, vol. 6110, pp. 523–552. Springer, Heidelberg (2010). https://doi.org/10.1007/978-3-642-13190-5_27

13. Chase, M.: Multi-authority attribute based encryption. In: Vadhan, S.P. (ed.) TCC 2007. LNCS, vol. 4392, pp. 515–534. Springer, Heidelberg (2007). https://doi.org/10.1007/978-3-540-70936-7_28

14. Chen, C., Zhang, Z., Feng, D.: Efficient ciphertext policy attribute-based encryption with constant-size ciphertext and constant computation-cost. In: Boyen, X., Chen, X. (eds.) ProvSec 2011. LNCS, vol. 6980, pp. 84–101. Springer, Heidelberg (2011). https://doi.org/10.1007/978-3-642-24316-5_8

15. Chen, Z., Zhang, P., Zhang, F., Huang, J.: Ciphertext policy attribute-based encryption supporting unbounded attribute space from R-LWE. KSII Trans. Internet Inf. Syst. 11(4), 2292–2309 (2017)

16. Cheung, L., Newport, C.C.: Provably secure ciphertext policy ABE. In: Proceedings of the 14th ACM Conference on Computer and Communications Security, pp. 456–465 (2007)
17. Garg, S., Gentry, C., Halevi, S., Sahai, A., Waters, B.: Attribute-based encryption for circuits from multilinear maps. In: Canetti, R., Garay, J.A. (eds.) CRYPTO 2013. LNCS, vol. 8043, pp. 479–499. Springer, Heidelberg (2013). https://doi.org/10.1007/978-3-642-40084-1_27
18. Garg, S., Gentry, C., Sahai, A., Waters, B.: Witness encryption and its applications. In: Symposium on the Theory of Computing, pp. 467–476 (2013)
19. Gentry, C., Peikert, C., Vaikuntanathan, V.: Trapdoors for hard lattices and new cryptographic constructions. In: Symposium on the Theory of Computing, pp. 197–206 (2007)
20. Gentry, C., Sahai, A., Waters, B.: Homomorphic encryption from learning with errors: conceptually-simpler, asymptotically-faster, attribute-based. In: Canetti, R., Garay, J.A. (eds.) CRYPTO 2013. LNCS, vol. 8042, pp. 75–92. Springer, Heidelberg (2013). https://doi.org/10.1007/978-3-642-40041-4_5
21. Gorbunov, S., Vaikuntanathan, V., Wee, H.: Attribute-based encryption for circuits. In: Symposium on the Theory of Computing, pp. 545–554 (2013)
22. Goyal, V., Jain, A., Pandey, O., Sahai, A.: Bounded ciphertext policy attribute based encryption. In: Aceto, L., Damgård, I., Goldberg, L.A., Halldórsson, M.M., Ingólfsdóttir, A., Walukiewicz, I. (eds.) ICALP 2008. LNCS, vol. 5126, pp. 579–591. Springer, Heidelberg (2008). https://doi.org/10.1007/978-3-540-70583-3_47
23. Goyal, V., Pandey, O., Sahai, A., Waters, B.: Attribute-based encryption for fine-grained access control of encrypted data. In: Proceedings of the 13th ACM Conference on Computer and Communications Security, pp. 89–98 (2006)
24. Lewko, A., Okamoto, T., Sahai, A., Takashima, K., Waters, B.: Fully secure functional encryption: attribute-based encryption and (hierarchical) inner product encryption. In: Gilbert, H. (ed.) EUROCRYPT 2010. LNCS, vol. 6110, pp. 62–91. Springer, Heidelberg (2010). https://doi.org/10.1007/978-3-642-13190-5_4
25. Lewko, A., Waters, B.: New proof methods for attribute-based encryption: achieving full security through selective techniques. In: Safavi-Naini, R., Canetti, R. (eds.) CRYPTO 2012. LNCS, vol. 7417, pp. 180–198. Springer, Heidelberg (2012). https://doi.org/10.1007/978-3-642-32009-5_12
26. Micciancio, D., Peikert, C.: Trapdoors for lattices: simpler, tighter, faster, smaller. In: Pointcheval, D., Johansson, T. (eds.) EUROCRYPT 2012. LNCS, vol. 7237, pp. 700–718. Springer, Heidelberg (2012). https://doi.org/10.1007/978-3-642-29011-4_41
27. Ostrovsky, R., Sahai, A., Waters, B.: Attribute-based encryption with non-monotonic access structures. In: Proceedings of the 14th ACM Conference on Computer and Communications Security, pp. 195–203 (2007)
28. Regev, O.: On lattices, learning with errors, random linear codes, and cryptography. J. ACM 56(6), 34 (2009)
29. Rouselakis, Y., Waters, B.: Practical constructions and new proof methods for large universe attribute-based encryption. In: Proceedings of the 2013 ACM SIGSAC Conference on Computer and Communications Security, pp. 463–474 (2013)
30. Sahai, A., Waters, B.: Fuzzy identity-based encryption. In: Cramer, R. (ed.) EUROCRYPT 2005. LNCS, vol. 3494, pp. 457–473. Springer, Heidelberg (2005). https://doi.org/10.1007/11426639_27
31. Wang, Y.: Lattice ciphertext policy attribute-based encryption in the standard model. Int. J. Netw. Secur. 16, 444–451 (2014)

32. Waters, B.: Ciphertext-policy attribute-based encryption: an expressive, efficient, and provably secure realization. In: Catalano, D., Fazio, N., Gennaro, R., Nicolosi, A. (eds.) PKC 2011. LNCS, vol. 6571, pp. 53–70. Springer, Heidelberg (2011). https://doi.org/10.1007/978-3-642-19379-8_4

33. Zhang, J., Zhang, Z., Ge, A.: Ciphertext policy attribute-based encryption from lattices. In: Proceedings of the 7th ACM Symposium on Information, Computer and Communications Security, pp. 16–17 (2012)

34. Zhao, J., Gao, H., Hu, B.: Ciphertext-policy attribute-based encryption for circuits from lattices under weak security model. In: Zhang, H., Zhao, B., Yan, F. (eds.) CTCIS 2018. CCIS, vol. 960, pp. 1–15. Springer, Singapore (2019). https://doi.org/10.1007/978-981-13-5913-2_1

35. Zhu, W., Jianping, Y., Wang, T., Zhang, P., Xie, W.: Efficient attribute-based encryption from R-LWE. China J. Electron **23**(4), 778–782 (2014)

Using Equivalent Class to Solve Interval Discrete Logarithm Problem

Bin Qi[1,2,3], Jie Ma[1,2,3], and Kewei Lv[1,2,3(✉)]

[1] State Key Laboratory of Information Security,
Institute of Information Engineering, Chinese Academy of Sciences,
Beijing 100093, China
{qibin,majie,lvkewei}@iie.ac.cn
[2] Data Assurance Communication Security Research Center,
Chinese Academy of Sciences, Beijing 100093, China
[3] School of Cyber Security, University of Chinese Academy of Sciences,
Beijing 100093, China

Abstract. The interval discrete logarithm problem (IDLP) is to find a solution n such that $g^n = h$ in a finite cyclic group $G = <g>$, where $h \in G$ and n belongs to a given interval. In this paper, we assume that computing the inverse of an element is easier than the multiplication of two elements in a group, and define an equivalent class to be the pair consisting of element and its inverse. So, a kangaroo jump can be performed between equivalent classes through pre-computation on these classes. To accelerate solving IDLP, we first introduce the concept of jumping distance and expanding factor to decide whether to perform the class operation or not. When the value of the expanding factor is greater than a given value, the class operation will be performed, such that each decision on jumps is locally optimal. The improved method takes an average of $(1 + o(1))\sqrt{N}$ times of class operation, where N is the size of a given interval.

Keywords: Interval discrete logarithm algorithm · Pollard kangaroo algorithm · Equivalent class

1 Introduction

The interval discrete logarithm problem (IDLP) is to find n such that $g^n = h$, for a given h and g in a finite cyclic group G, where g represents a generator of G, $n \in (0, N]$, and $G \subseteq \mathbb{Z}_p^*$. As a special case of a discrete logarithm problem, the IDLP is more proper to be used in the analysis and design of cryptosystem, as presented in [3] and [1]. To find a faster algorithm for IDLP is significant and useful in practice.

This work is partially supported by National Key R&D Program of China(no. 2017YFB0802500), The 13th Five-Year National Cryptographic Development Foundation(no. MMJJ20180208), Beijing Science and Technology Commission (no. Z181100002718001) and NSF (no. 61272039).

© Springer Nature Switzerland AG 2020
J. Zhou et al. (Eds.): ICICS 2019, LNCS 11999, pp. 397–412, 2020.
https://doi.org/10.1007/978-3-030-41579-2_23

To solve IDLP, new methods and techniques have been used continuously. In [8], a classical collision-based algorithm, called Pollard's kangaroo algorithm, was proposed for solving the DLP with the complexity of $O(\sqrt{q})$, which requires only $O(1)$ of storage space. There are two approaches to improve the Pollard kangaroo algorithm. One is to increase the number of kangaroos to improve efficiency. As for the first approach, in [4], the kangaroo algorithm is optimized by increasing the number of kangaroos, and the optimal state is that when four kangaroos jumped at the same time, which reduced the average group operation times to $(1.714 + o(1))\sqrt{N}$. The jumping of four kangaroos are $z_1 = hg^y, z_2 = h^{-1}g^y, z_3 = h^2g^y, z_4 = h^{-2}g^y$, respectively, and then combined with the Four-set Gaudry-Schost method to reduce the complexity to $(1.719 + o(1))\sqrt{N}$. In addition, in [5], the equivalence classes is used to solve the discrete logarithm problem in a short interval under the assumption that computing the inverse of a class element is faster than the general group operation. For convenience, the method in [5] is called the GR algorithm.

The other approach to improve the kangaroo algorithm is to increase the storage space. In [9], the authors improved the Pollard kangaroo algorithm by increasing the storage space size to the polynomial size, and the average number of group operations of the discrete logarithm problem was $(2 + o(1))\sqrt{N}$. In [2], the precomputation and decomposition of large integer multiplications are used to improve the computational efficiency in the iterative process. For convenience, here we denote the algorithm presented in [2] as the CHK algorithm. The CHK algorithm requires storing the value of the modular exponentiation in the form of g^y. Since the modular exponentiation requires at least one large integer multiplication when $y > 1$, it can improve the algorithm efficiency and avoid additional calculation by storing the value of g^y. Thus, the CHK algorithm accelerates the Pollard algorithm at least 10 times, but it also requires the preprocessing space size of $O((\log p)^{r+1} \cdot \log \log p)$. In [10], the method presented in [2] was used to solve the interval discrete logarithm. In [7], the authors also used the periodicity of trigonometric function to substitute the sum of small integers in [2].

Our Techniques. In this paper, we assume that computing the inverse of an element is easier than the multiplication of two elements in a group. In order to solve IDLP, over the interval $[0, N]$, we define the pairs consisting of an element and its inverse to be an equivalent class as GR algorithm, so that kangaroo jumps can be performed between the equivalent classes. We precompute a multiplication table of size $O((\log N)^{2\eta+1} \cdot \log \log N)$ so that we can inquire it to save the number of class operations, where η is small integer.

Then, we propose the concept of jumping distance and expanding factor to determine whether to perform the class operation or not. Here, we set a threshold of the expanding factor so that when the expanding factor is larger than the threshold, a class operation is performed. The greater the expanding factor is, the higher the probability of collision is. A class operation is done if the value of the expanding factor is larger than a given threshold. In the experiment, the average class operation times is $(1 + o(1))\sqrt{N}$, which is faster than the $(1.714 + o(1))\sqrt{N}$ class operation of the GR algorithm.

Organization. The rest of the paper is organized as follows. In Sect. 2, we introduce the methods proposed in [2,5,8]. In Sect. 3, we explain the expanding factor and its construction. An improved algorithm based on expanding factor is presented and evaluated experimentally. The heuristics complexity analysis of the improved algorithm is given in Sect. 4. The conclusions are drawn in Sect. 5.

2 Preliminaries and Related Algorithms

In this section, we briefly present the Pollard's kangaroo algorithm, the CHK algorithm, and the GR algorithm. The list of the symbols is presented in Table 1.

Table 1. The list of symbols.

Symbols	Meaning
$\mathbb{N}^*$	Positive integer set
η, ε	Small integer
S	$\{1, 2, \cdots, \eta\}$
$[q]$	$\{1, 2, \cdots, q\}$
Γ	$\Gamma = \{\pm u_1, \pm u_2, \cdots, \pm u_\eta\}$
M	$M = \{g^{u_s} : u_s \in \Gamma\}$
M^l	$M^l = \{M \bigcup \{1\}\}^l$
j_k^T	k^{th} jumping positon of kangaroo T
j_k^W	k^{th} jumping positon of kangaroo W
J^T	$J^T = \{j_k^T : k = 1, 2, \cdots\}$
J^W	$J^W = \{j_k^W : k = 1, 2, \cdots\}$
$d_{(k,s)}$	Jumping distance
D_k^T	Jumping distance set of kangaroo T
D_k^W	Jumping distance set of kangaroo W
D	$D = \bigcup_k D_k^T = \bigcup_k D_k^W$
$ListD$	$ListD = \bigcup_{i=1}^{k-1} D_i^T = \bigcup_{i=1}^{s-1} D_i^W$
R^T	Expanding factor of kangaroo T
R^W	Expanding factor of kangaroo W
$s \xleftarrow{\$} \psi$	s is chosen from set ψ uniformly at random
b	Boundary of expanding factor

2.1 Pollard's Kangaroo Algorithm

The Pollard's kangaroo algorithm [8] and its variants [2,4,5,7,10] generate a sequence of elements from a group G with a random walk of kangaroos.

A specific function $F : G \to G$ is defined, and a random walk is generated by iteratively applying F starting from a random group element. The function F is constructed in such a way that the solution is obtained when a random walk revisits an element it has already passed over. Every time an element is revisited, the collision happens.

More precisely, the Pollard's kangaroo algorithm is to use g and h as the starting elements to perform the iterated multiplications of elements of a group G respectively, which are denoted as kangaroos T and W, respectively. Two kangaroos jump independently to traverse the cyclic group G. When both jumps meet the same element of G, we can compute the solution of the discrete logarithm. The function F is $g_i = F(g_{i-1}) = g_{i-1} \cdot g^{f(g_{i-1})}$, where f denotes a random function.

For a kangaroo T having an initial value of $g_0 = g^{\alpha} \in G$, we calculate $f(g_0)$ based on the random function f, and then we obtain the value $g_1 = g_0 \cdot g^{f(g_0)}$ and use the next jump value $f(g_1)$ to calculate $g_2 = g_1 \cdot g^{f(g_1)}$. Finally, we obtain the sequence $\{g_i\}_{i \in \mathbb{N}^*}$, where $\mathbb{N}^*$ is denoted as positive integer set. Correspondingly, for kangaroo W having an initial value $g_0' = h$, we first calculate $g_1' = g_0' \cdot g^{f(g_0')}$ and then obtain the sequence $\{g_i'\}_{i \in \mathbb{N}^*}$. Finally, it is checked whether the two sequences share the same value and if there exists i, j such that $g_i = g_j'$, then, the correct solution is given by $\alpha + \sum_{s=1}^{i-1} f(g_s) - \sum_{t=1}^{j-1} f(g_t')$.

2.2   GR Algorithm

The GR algorithm [5] represents a variant of Pollard's kangaroo algorithm, but it makes kangaroos jump between equivalent classes $\{\{g^a, g^{-a}\} : a \in (-N/2, N/2] \cap \mathbb{Z}\}$ instead of in a group G. Thus, every time a sequence of elements from the group G is generated using the function F, the inverse of the elements needs to be computed. The GR algorithm is constructed under the assumption that computing the inverse of group elements is faster than the general group operation. So, GR algorithm can be applied in groups with fast inversion such as a group on the elliptic curve.

More precisely, in the GR algorithm, $\{hg^{\alpha}, h^{-1}g^{-\alpha}\}$ and $\{h^2g^{\beta}, h^{-2}g^{-\beta}\}$ are used as the starting elements to traverse the equivalent class $\{\{g^a, g^{-a}\} : a \in (-N/2, N/2] \cap \mathbb{Z}\}$, respectively. When both jumps meet the same element, we can compute the solution of the discrete logarithm.

The GR algorithm first calculates $h \cdot g^{-N/2}$, and translates the interval in which the solution is located from $(0, N] \cap \mathbb{Z}$ to $(-N/2, N/2] \cap \mathbb{Z}$. The binary tuple sequence $\{(g_i, g_i^{-1})\}_{i \in \mathbb{N}^*}$ can be obtained by inverting the value of g_i after each jump to get g_i^{-1}. Similarly, we can get the binary sequence $\{(g_i', g_i'^{-1})\}_{i \in \mathbb{N}^*}$. After each sequence $\{(g_i, g_i^{-1})\}_{i \in \mathbb{N}^*}$ and $\{(g_i', g_i'^{-1})\}_{i \in \mathbb{N}^*}$ increases with new pairs being added, we need to check whether the two sequences have the same value; if they share the same value, the solution can be found.

2.3   CHK Algorithm

In the CHK algorithm [2], precomputation is to avoid modular exponentiation operations in the iteration. Since the modular exponentiation value can be directly obtained by the table lookup operation, the CHK algorithm saves the running time compared with Pollard's kangaroo algorithm.

g and h are used as the starting elements to perform the iterated multiplications of elements of a group G respectively. When both jumps meet the same element of G, we can obtain the solution. The function F in CHK Algorithm is computed as $g_{i+j} = F(g_i) = g_i \cdot m$, where m is the element that can be read from the precomputed table M^l. In the process of constructing the function F, to reduce the number of large integer multiplication, the index function $\bar{s}(x, y) = s(xy)$ is used.

Function F in the CHK algorithm is implemented in the following way. First, index set $S = \{0, 1, \cdots, r-1\}$ and jump set $S' = \{s_0, s_1, \cdots, s_{r-1}\}$ are defined. Then, let $M = \{g^{s_i} : s_i \in S'\}$, and $M^l = \{M \cup \{1\}\}^l$, which denotes the multiplications of no more than l elements in a set $M \cup \{1\}$. Both kangaroos are required to jump and calculate two sequences, $\{g_i\}_{i\in\mathbb{N}^*}$ and $\{g_i'\}_{i\in\mathbb{N}^*}$. Once g_i is calculated, the function $s : \mathbb{Z} \to S$ is used to calculate the next jump value $s(g_i) \in S$. Then, we can get $g_{i+1} = g_i \cdot M_{s(g_i)}$, where $M_{s(g_i)}$ is the $s(g_i)^{th}$ element of M. Also, we can calculate g_{i+2} directly instead of calculating g_{i+1} first, that is:

$$g_{i+2} = g_{i+1} \cdot M_{s(g_{i+1})} = g_i \cdot M_{s(g_i)} \cdot M_{s(g_i \cdot M_{s(g_i)})} = g_i \cdot M_{s(g_i)} \cdot M_{\bar{s}(g_i, M_{s(g_i)})} \quad (1)$$

The value of $M_{s(g_i)} \cdot M_{\bar{s}(g_i, M_{s(g_i)})}$ can be determined directly from M^l; it only needs to do a big integer multiplication with g_i to get g_{i+2}. Similarly, we can obtain g_{i+3} directly instead of calculating g_{i+1} and g_{i+2}, but we can skip $(l-1)$ values at most because M^l is a multiplication of no more than l elements from a set $M \cup \{1\}$. Therefore, the random function $\bar{s}$ can make the kangaroo realize a farther and more flexible jump by using M^l, giving the kangaroo more jumping options.

However, it should be noted that only the values that are actually calculated can be stored in a sequence $\{g_i\}_{i\in\mathbb{N}^*}$. Namely, if values g_{i+1} and g_{i+2} are skipped, it is impossible to compare them with $\{g_i'\}_{i\in\mathbb{N}^*}$ since they are not stored in $\{g_i\}_{i\in\mathbb{N}^*}$. Similarly, we can compute a sequence $\{g_i'\}_{i\in\mathbb{N}^*}$. In order to decide whether to calculate certain values, the CHK algorithm constructs a function τ to control evenly whether to skip the calculation or not. After each sequence $\{g_i\}_{i\in\mathbb{N}^*}$ and $\{g_i'\}_{i\in\mathbb{N}^*}$ increases with new pairs being added, we need to compare whether the two sequences have the same value; if they share the same value in common, the solution is obtained.

3   Improved Algorithm Based on Expanding Factor

The previously described algorithms set the distinguished points based on a uniform distribution, but that does not guarantee that kangaroos always collide with a high probability. Furthermore, when the CHK algorithm and Pollard's kangaroo algorithm are used to solve the interval discrete logarithm, it is very likely to make the jumping distance beyond the range of interval, which will decrease efficiency. So, in this section, we propose the concepts of jumping distance and expanding factor to improve the algorithm.

We first need to compute $hg^{-\frac{N}{2}}$ and shift the interval of a solution to $(-\frac{N}{2}, \frac{N}{2}] \cap \mathbb{Z}$. Here, we assume that computing an inverse element is easier in a group G, and the concept of equivalent class is introduced.

We define the interval equivalent relation $\{g^a, g^{-a}\} = \{g^{-a}, g^a\}$, where $a \in (-\frac{N}{2}, \frac{N}{2}] \cap \mathbb{Z}$. This interval equivalent relation satisfies reflexivity, transitivity, and symmetry. Then, the interval equivalent class of a kangaroo T is given as $G^T = \{\{g^a, g^{-a}\} : a \in (-\frac{N}{2}, \frac{N}{2}] \cap \mathbb{Z}\}$.

Similarly, we define the interval equivalent relation $\{g^{n-\frac{N}{2}+b}, g^{n-\frac{N}{2}-b}\} = \{g^{n-\frac{N}{2}-b}, g^{n-\frac{N}{2}+b}\}$, where $b \in (-\frac{N}{2}, \frac{N}{2}] \cap \mathbb{Z}$. Then, the interval equivalent class of a kangaroo W's is given as $G^W = \{\{g^{n-\frac{N}{2}+b}, g^{n-\frac{N}{2}-b}\} : b \in (-\frac{N}{2}, \frac{N}{2}] \cap \mathbb{Z}\}$.

With the definition of equivalent classes, we define the multiplication operations between the equivalent classes as follows: $\{g^i, g^{i'}\} \cdot \{g^j, g^{j'}\} = \{g^{i+j}, g^{i'+j'}\}$. Assume that the ith jumps of kangaroos T and W are $\{g_i, \widehat{g_i}\}$ and $\{g'_i, \widehat{g'_i}\}$, respectively. After a given next jump distance a_i and b_i, the $(i+1)^{th}$ jump value of T and W can be calculated as $\{g_{i+1} = g_i \cdot g^{a_i}, \widehat{g_{i+1}} = \widehat{g_i} \cdot g^{-a_i}\}$ and $\{g'_{i+1} = g'_i \cdot g^{b_i}, \widehat{g'_{i+1}} = \widehat{g'_i} \cdot g^{-b_i}\}$, respectively.

We obtain $g^{\pm a_i}$ and $g^{\pm b_i}$ from the precomputed set in each jump. Therefore, the process of computing $\{g_{i+1}, \widehat{g_{i+1}}\}$ and $\{g'_{i+1}, \widehat{g'_{i+1}}\}$ requires only two large integer multiplications. For convenience, the process of obtaining $\{g_{i+1}, \widehat{g_{i+1}}\}$ from $\{g_i, \widehat{g_i}\}$ is called the class operation. In order to make T and W jump between the equivalent classes, the concept of jumping distance is introduced in the following.

3.1   Jumping Distance

The Pollard's kangaroo algorithm is to find the collision between $\{g^{\alpha} g^{\alpha_1} g^{\alpha_2} \cdots g^{\alpha_{t_1}}\}_{t_1 \in \mathbb{N}*}$ and $\{hg^{\beta_1} g^{\beta_2} \cdots g^{\beta_{t_2}}\}_{t_2 \in \mathbb{N}*}$ by jumps $\alpha_1, \alpha_2 \cdots \alpha_{t_1} \cdots$ and $\beta_1, \beta_2 \cdots \beta_{t_2} \cdots$, which have to be calculated respectively. If for some k and s, $g^{\alpha} g^{\alpha_1} g^{\alpha_2} \cdots g^{\alpha_k} = hg^{\beta_1} g^{\beta_2} \cdots g^{\beta_s}$, then the solution is $n = \alpha + \sum_{i=1}^{k} \alpha_i - \sum_{i=1}^{s} \beta_i$; that is, if a collision occurs, the solution is equal to the difference between the jump value $\alpha + \sum_{i=1}^{k} \alpha_i$ of a kangaroo T and the jump value $\sum_{i=1}^{s} \beta_i$ of a kangaroo W. When the collision occurs, the solution to IDLP is $n \in \{\alpha + \sum_{i=1}^{k} \alpha_i - \sum_{i=1}^{s} \beta_i\}_{k \in \mathbb{N}*, s \in \mathbb{N}*}$. The more value the set $\{\alpha + \sum_{i=1}^{k} \alpha_i - \sum_{i=1}^{s} \beta_i\}_{k \in \mathbb{N}*, s \in \mathbb{N}*}$ contains, the more efficient the algorithm is. For convenience, the following definitions are given.

Definition 1. The 1th jumping positions of kangaroos T and W are $\{j_1^T = \alpha, \widehat{j_1^T} = -\alpha\}$ and $\{j_1^W = \beta, \widehat{j_1^W} = -\beta\}$, respectively. The kth jumping position of a kangaroo T is $\{j_k^T = \alpha + \sum_{i=1}^{k-1} \alpha_i, \widehat{j_k^T} = -\alpha - \sum_{i=1}^{k-1} \alpha_i\}$, where $k \geq 2$. The sth jumping position of a kangaroo W is $\{j_s^W = \beta + \sum_{i=1}^{s-1} \beta_i, \widehat{j_s^W} = -\beta - \sum_{i=1}^{s-1} \beta_i\}$, where $s \geq 2$. We denote the jumping position sets of kangaroos T and W to be $J^T = \{\{j_k^T, \widehat{j_k^T}\} : k = 1, 2, \cdots\}$ and $J^W = \{\{j_s^W, \widehat{j_s^W}\} : s = 1, 2, \cdots\}$ respectively, in which the elements are arranged in the order in which they are added.

Definition 2. Let the kth jumping position of a kangaroo T be $\{j_k^T, \widehat{j_k^T}\}$, and the sth jumping position of a kangaroo W be $\{j_s^W, \widehat{j_s^W}\}$; then, the corresponding jumping distance is defined to be $d_{(k,s)} = \{j_k^T - j_s^W, \widehat{j_k^T} - \widehat{j_s^W}, \widehat{j_k^T} - j_s^W, j_k^T - \widehat{j_s^W}\} \cap (-\frac{N}{2}, \frac{N}{2}]) = \{j_k^T - j_s^W, j_k^T + j_s^W, j_s^W - j_k^T, -j_k^T - j_s^W\} \cap (-\frac{N}{2}, \frac{N}{2}])$.

Definition 3. We define the kth jumping distance set to be a set of the jumping distances between the kth jumping position of one kangaroo and all the jumping positions of the other kangaroo. Specifically, for the kth jump of a kangaroo T, the jumping distance set is expressed as $D_k^T = \bigcup_{i=1}^{s} d_{(k,i)}$, where s is the current number of jumps of W. And for the kth jump of a kangaroo W, the jumping distance set is expressed as $D_k^W = \bigcup_{i=1}^{s} d_{(i,k)}$, where s is the current number of jumps of a kangaroo T. Obviously, for $\forall d_{(i,j)} \in D_i^T \subset \bigcup_k D_k^T$, there exist D_j^W, s.t. $d_{(i,j)} \in D_j^W \subset \bigcup_k D_k^W$. So we have $\bigcup_k D_k^T = \bigcup_k D_k^W$. For convenience, we denote $D = \bigcup_k D_k^T = \bigcup_k D_k^W$.

Example. In Table 2, the first three jumping positions of the kangaroo T are $\{10, -10\}$, $\{12, -12\}$, and $\{x, -x\}$ respectively, where x is unknown, and the first three jumping positions of the kangaroo W are $\{1, 1\}$, $\{6, -6\}$, and $\{13, -13\}$ respectively.

Table 2. Example.

	j_i^T	j_i^W
$i = 1$	$\{2, -2\}$	$\{1, -1\}$
$i = 2$	$\{8, -8\}$	$\{4, -4\}$
$i = 3$	$\{x, -x\}$	$\{13, -13\}$

Table 3. Jumping distance set of the first three jumps.

$d_{(k,s)}$	$s = 1$	$s = 2$	$s = 3$
$k = 1$	$\{\pm 1, \pm 3\}$	$\{\pm 2, \pm 6\}$	$\{\pm 11, \pm 15\}$
$k = 2$	$\{\pm 7, \pm 9\}$	$\{\pm 4, \pm 12\}$	$\{\pm 5, \pm 21\}$
$k = 3$	$\{\pm(x-1), \pm(x+1)\}$	$\{\pm(x-4), \pm(x+4)\}$	$\{\pm(x-13), \pm(x+13)\}$

We can calculate the jumping distance set as:

$d_{(1,1)} = \{\pm1, \pm3\}$ $d_{(1,2)} = \{\pm2, \pm6\}$ $d_{(1,3)} = \{\pm11, \pm15\}$

$d_{(2,1)} = \{\pm7, \pm9\}$ $d_{(2,2)} = \{\pm4, \pm12\}$ $d_{(2,3)} = \{\pm5, \pm21\}$

$d_{(3,1)} = \{\pm(x-1), \pm(x+1)\}$ $d_{(3,2)} = \{\pm(x-4), \pm(x+4)\}$ $d_{(3,3)} = \{\pm(x-13), \pm(x+13)\}$

Then, the jumping distance set is given as:

$$
\begin{aligned}
D =& \{d_{(1,1)}, d_{(1,2)}, d_{(1,3)}, d_{(2,1)}, d_{(2,2)}, d_{(2,3)}, d_{(3,1)}, d_{(3,2)}, d_{(3,3)}\} \\
=& \{\pm1, \pm3, \pm2, \pm6, \pm11, \pm15, \pm7, \pm9, \pm4, \pm12, \pm5, \pm21, \pm(x-1) \\
& , \pm(x+1), \pm(x-4), \pm(x+4), \pm(x-13), \pm(x+13)\}
\end{aligned}
$$

For the kangaroo T, we have the first three jumping distance set as follows.

$$
\begin{aligned}
D_1^T =& \{d_{(1,1)}, d_{(1,2)}, d_{(1,3)}\} = \{\pm1, \pm3, \pm2, \pm6, \pm11, \pm15\} \\
D_2^T =& \{d_{(2,1)}, d_{(2,2)}, d_{(2,3)}\} = \{\pm7, \pm9, \pm4, \pm12, \pm5, \pm21\} \\
D_3^T =& \{d_{(3,1)}, d_{(3,2)}, d_{(3,3)}\} = \{\pm(x-1), \pm(x+1), \pm(x-4), \pm(x+4), \pm(x-13), \pm(x+13)\}
\end{aligned}
$$

Accordingly, for the kangaroo W, we have the first three jumping distance set as follows.

$$
\begin{aligned}
D_1^W =& \{d_{(1,1)}, d_{(2,1)}, d_{(3,1)}\} = \{\pm1, \pm3, \pm7, \pm9, \pm(x-1), \pm(x+1)\} \\
D_2^W =& \{d_{(1,2)}, d_{(2,2)}, d_{(3,2)}\} = \{\pm2, \pm6, \pm4, \pm12, \pm(x-4), \pm(x+4)\} \\
D_3^W =& \{d_{(1,3)}, d_{(2,3)}, d_{(3,3)}\} = \{\pm11, \pm15, \pm5, \pm21, \pm(x-13), \pm(x+13)\}
\end{aligned}
$$

It can be seen that D_t^T is the set of numbers in the tth row in Table 3, and D_t^W is the set of numbers in the tth column in Table 3.

Assume the jumping distance set is D. When $x = 16$, then $D = \{\pm1, \pm3, \pm2, \pm6, \pm11, \pm15, \pm7, \pm9, \pm4, \pm12, \pm5, \pm21, \pm17, \pm20, \pm29\}$, thus D has 30 elements; and when $x = 21$, then $D = \{\pm1, \pm3, \pm2, \pm6, \pm11, \pm15, \pm7, \pm9, \pm4, \pm12, \pm5, \pm21, \pm20, \pm22, \pm17, \pm25, \pm8, \pm34\}$, thus D has 36 elements. In the third jump, if $x=16$, then that jump is inefficient because the values $\pm15, \pm12, \pm3$ of the jumping distance $d_{(3,1)} = \{\pm15, \pm17\}, d_{(3,2)} = \{\pm12, \pm20\}, d_{(3,3)} = \{\pm3, \pm29\}$ have been contained in D. And, the new distance actually is only the values $\pm17, \pm20, \pm29$. However, when $x=21$, there will be 12 new jump distances: $D_3^T = \{\pm20, \pm22, \pm17, \pm25, \pm8, \pm34\}$, which will be added to D. If $n \in D$, we can find the solution.

If first two jumps do not collide with the solution, that is, the jumping difference between both kangaroos is not equal to n. Then, when $x=21$, the probability of finding the solution is $12/N$, but when $x=16$, the probability of finding the solution becomes $6/N$. So, by selecting the position of the next jump, we can increase the probability of solution finding. Since the solution n is an unknown element of a set $(0, N] \cap \mathbb{Z}$, the more elements in the jumping distance set of a jump are different from the previous ones, the more efficient the jump is, and the solution can be obtained easier.□

Assume that two kangaroos T and W jump at time $s(\leq t + 1)$ and time t, respectively. In order to give the improved algorithm, we present Algorithm 1 to compute D_{t+1}^T or D_{t+1}^W first. In Algorithm 1, *position* denotes the $(t + 1)^{th}$ position given in advance, and J^T and J^W denote the jumping position set of kangaroos T and W, respectively.

Algorithm 1. Computing Jumping Distance Set

    Input: $J^T, J^W, position = \{ps, ps' = -ps\}$, where *position* is given in advance
    Output: D_{t+1}^T, D_{t+1}^W
1   **for** $i = 1, \cdots, t$ **do**
2     $t_1 = ps - j_i^W, t_2 = ps + j_i^W, t_3 = -ps - j_i^W, t_4 = j_i^W - ps$;
3   store t_1, t_2, t_3, t_4 in D_{t+1}^T;
4   **end**
5   **for** $i = 1, \cdots, s$ **do**
6     $t_1 = ps - j_i^T, t_2 = ps + j_i^T, t_3 = -ps - j_i^T, t_4 = j_i^T - ps$;
7   store t_1, t_2, t_3, t_4 in D_{t+1}^W;
8   **end**
9   **return** D_{t+1}^T, D_{t+1}^W;

In Algorithm 1, the jumping position sets J^T and J^W of kangaroos T and W can be obtained by input J^T, J^W. We only need to use the $(t + 1)^{th}$ position of the kangaroo to make a difference between all the positions of the other kangaroo and store it in the D_{t+1}^T and D_{t+1}^W. Finally, Algorithm 1 has the complexity of $O(t)$.

3.2 Expanding Factor

Assume a kangaroo T has jumped $(k - 1)$ times, and kangaroo W has jumped $(s - 1)$ times; then, calculate the jump distance set D_i^T $(i = 1, 2, \cdots, k - 1)$ or D_i^W $(i = 1, 2, \cdots, s - 1)$ after each jump, and store the elements in a $ListD$; duplicate values should be saved only once in the $ListD$, i.e., $ListD = \bigcup_{i=1}^{k-1} D_i^T = \bigcup_{i=1}^{s-1} D_i^W$.

Definition 4. The expanding factor R is a ratio of the number of new jumps produced at the new jumping position to the maximum number of jumping differences, where these new jumping differences belong to the interval $(-N/2, N/2]$ and are not equal to any of the previous jumping difference. The expanding factors R_T and R_W of kangaroos T and W are respectively defined as:
$$R^T = \frac{|(D_k^T \setminus ListD) \cap (-\frac{N}{2}, \frac{N}{2}]|}{4s},$$ where $s(\leq k)$ is the number of current jump times of the kangaroo W;
$$R^W = \frac{|(D_s^W \setminus ListD) \cap (-\frac{N}{2}, \frac{N}{2}]|}{4k},$$ where $k(\leq s)$ is the number of current jump times of the kangaroo T.

Also, $R^T, R^W \in [0,1]$ because $0 \leq |D_k^T| \leq 4s$ and $0 \leq |D_s^W| \leq 4k$. Since the expanding factor denotes a ratio of the actual value to the theoretical maximum, the larger the expanding factor is, the more new jumping differences can be generated at a given jumping position.

If the expanding factor of a jumping position given in advance is smaller than a given boundary, another jumping position will be chosen. Thus, kangaroos will choose to jump such that the expanding factor is relatively large, so the class operation will be performed. We use Algorithm 2 to calculate R^T (or R^W), where D_k^T (or D_s^W) is calculated by Algorithm 1.

Algorithm 2. Computing Expanding Factor

Input: $ListD, D_k^T (or\ D_s^W)$
Output: $R^T (or\ R_W)$
1 $i_1 = 0, i_2 = 0$;
2 Kangaroo T: For all $d \in D_k^T$, if $d \notin ListD$ and $d \in (-\frac{N}{2}, \frac{N}{2}]$, then $i_1 = i_1 + 1$;
3 Kangaroo W: For all $d \in D_s^W$, if $d \notin ListD$ and $d \in (-\frac{N}{2}, \frac{N}{2}]$, then $i_2 = i_2 + 1$;
4 $R^T = \frac{i_1}{4s}, R^W = \frac{i_2}{4k}$;
5 **return** $R^T (or\ R^W)$;

By step 2 in Algorithm 2, we can get the number of elements in the difference sets which belong to the interval $(-N/2, N/2]$ and differ from any of the previous jumping differences. Then, we can calculate R^T (or R^W). Since s (or k) is the current number of jumps of the other kangaroo, we can get $|D_k^T| \leq 4s$ and $|D_s^W| \leq 4k$ according to Definition 2. Finally, Algorithm 2 has the complexity of $O(max\{s, k\})$.

3.3   Improved Algorithm

Based on the concept of the expanding factor, an improved algorithm is presented. By storing an inverse element, the kangaroo can jump back and forth, avoiding the kangaroo jumping all the way in one direction and needing to initialize the jumping position when expanding factor is particularly small.

Define the jump set $\Gamma = \{\pm u_1, \pm u_2, \cdots, \pm u_\eta\}$, where η is an integer. For convenience, denote $\Gamma_t = u_t, \Gamma_{-t} = -u_t, M = \{g^{u_i} : u_i \in \Gamma\}, M_t = g^{u_t}, M_{-t} = g^{u_{-t}}$. Let $M^l = \{M \cup \{1\}\}^l$, which denotes a multiplication of no more than l elements from set $M \cup \{1\}$. It should be noted that here, M^l contains inverse values and the original values of the jump process can be determined directly from M^l. Generally, the exponential parts of the elements in M^l are indexed to improve the algorithm efficiency.

We define the set $\psi = \{\pm 1, \pm 2, \cdots, \pm \eta\}$. Then $s \xleftarrow{\$} \psi$ denotes that an element s is sampled uniformly according to the set ψ, namely, s is chosen from $\{\pm 1, \pm 2, \cdots, \pm \eta\}$ uniformly at random. In practical application, the method called linear congruential generator (LCG) can be used to generate elements from ψ. LCG is one of the oldest and best-known pseudorandom number generator algorithms that yields a sequence of pseudorandomized numbers calculated with a discontinuous piecewise linear equation [11–13].

For the given initial jump values $\{g_1 = g^\alpha, \widehat{g}_1 = g^{-\alpha}\}$ and $\{g'_1 = hg^\beta, \widehat{g'_1} = hg^{-\beta}\}$ of T and W, the corresponding initial jumping positions are $j_1^T = \{\alpha, -\alpha\}$ and $j_1^W = \{\beta, -\beta\}$, respectively.

We set the boundary of the expanding factor to be $b \in (0, 1]$. For the kangaroo T, we generate the next jumping position $j_2^T = \{\alpha + \Gamma_{s_1}, -\alpha - \Gamma_{s_1}\}$, where $s_1 \xleftarrow{\$} \psi$. Thus, we can obtain the jumping distance D_2^T. Then, we can compute the expanding factor R^T, and check whether $R^T > b$; if this is true, then, we compute $g_2 = g_1 \cdot M_{s_1}$, $\widehat{g}_2 = \widehat{g}_1 \cdot M_{-s_1}$, and store the jumping distances in the $ListD$; else, we regenerate the value of s_1 form ψ to obtain another jumping position, and recalculate R^T. If there are $k(\leq \eta)$ times that $R^T < b$, then use ψ to regenerate two random values s_1 and s_2. Then, the next jumping position given in advance is $j_2^T = \{\alpha + \Gamma_{s_1} + \Gamma_{s_2}, -\alpha - \Gamma_{s_1} - \Gamma_{s_2}\}$. Similarly, if $R^T > b$, then $g_2 = g_1 \cdot M_{s_1} \cdot M_{s_2}$ and $\widehat{g}_2 = \widehat{g}_1 \cdot M_{-s_1} \cdot M_{-s_2}$. Correspondingly, if there are k times that $R^T < b$, then use ψ to generate 3 random values. Note that $M_{s_1} \cdot M_{s_2} \cdots M_{s_t} (t \leq \eta)$ can be determined directly from M^l and we can only read l consecutive products form M^l at most. Therefore, if the condition $R^T > b$ is not satisfied by continuously generating l random numbers from ψ, then the jumping position with the largest R^T is chosen as the next jumping position, and the corresponding jumping distances is stored in the $ListD$. Continuously, we get a series $\{(g_i, \widehat{g}_i)\}_{i \in \mathbb{N}^*}$.

Similarly, we obtain a series $\{(g'_i, \widehat{g'_i})\}_{i \in \mathbb{N}^*}$ of the kangaroo W. Then, we check whether the same value exists in $\{(g_i, \widehat{g}_i)\}_{i \in \mathbb{N}^*}$ and $\{(g_i, \widehat{g}_i)\}_{i \in \mathbb{N}^*}$. If there exists $g_t = g'_s$, where $g_t \in \{g_i\}_{i \in \mathbb{N}^*}$ and $g'_s \in \{g'_i\}_{i \in \mathbb{N}^*}$, then, we have $n = N/2 + j_t^T - j_s^W$. If there exists $g_t = \widehat{g'_s}$, where $g_t \in \{g_i\}_{i \in \mathbb{N}^*}$ and $\widehat{g'_s} \in \{\widehat{g'_i}\}_{i \in \mathbb{N}^*}$, then, we have $n = N/2 + j_t^T - j_s^{\widehat{W}} = N/2 + j_t^T + j_s^W$. If there exists $\widehat{g}_t = g'_s$, where $\widehat{g}_t \in \{\widehat{g}_i\}_{i \in \mathbb{N}^*}$ and $g'_s \in \{g'_i\}_{i \in \mathbb{N}^*}$, then, we have $n = N/2 + j_t^{\widehat{T}} - j_s^W = N/2 - j_t^T - j_s^W$. Lastly, if there exists $\widehat{g}_t = \widehat{g'_s}$, where $\widehat{g}_t \in \{\widehat{g}_i\}_{i \in \mathbb{N}^*}$ and $\widehat{g'_s} \in \{\widehat{g'_i}\}_{i \in \mathbb{N}^*}$, then, we have $n = N/2 + j_t^{\widehat{T}} - j_s^{\widehat{s}} = N/2 - j_t^T + j_s^W$.

Based on the above discussion, the improved algorithm is given in Algorithm 3, where kangaroos jump synchronously. Since the definition of M^l is similar to [2], $O((\log N)^{2\eta+1} \cdot \log \log N)$ of space is needed for M^l; see, e.g., [2,10] for the full details.

Correctness. In step 2 to 4, we first compute $h' = hg^{-\frac{N}{2}}$ and shift the interval of the solution to $(-\frac{N}{2}, \frac{N}{2}] \cap \mathbb{Z}$. Then we initialize the value of $g_1, \widehat{g}_1, g'_1, \widehat{g'_1}, j_1^T$ and j_1^W. Since the first jump is initialized, the kangaroos will make a 2th jump. Denote t as the tth jump that kangaroos are going to make, namely, $t = 2$ is initialized. Then we compute D_1^T, D_1^W and store them in $ListD$.

Kangaroo T makes a jump between steps 4 and 24, with a maximum of kl cycles. When $R^T > b$ is not satisfied by continuously generating l random numbers from ψ, PS and RS is used to select the *position* corresponding to the maximum R, where PS and RS are vectors of length kl, denoted as $PS_{1 \times kl}$ and $RS_{1 \times kl}$. Note that PS and RS are indexed by the number of iterations of step 4 to 24, namely, position ps and its corresponding expanding factor R^T have the same index. Let the ith value of PS and RS be PS_i and RS_i, respectively.

Algorithm 3. Solve IDLP with Equivalent Class

Input: $g, h, N, p, \alpha, \beta, l, S, k, b$
Output: ans

1 precompute M^l;
2 $h' = hg^{-N/2}, g_1 = g^{\alpha}, \widehat{g_1} = g^{-\alpha}, g_1' = h'g^{\beta}, \widehat{g_1'} = h'g^{-\beta}, j_1^T = \alpha, j_1^W = \beta, t = 2$;
3 compute D_1^T, D_1^W and store them in $ListD$, add j_1^T in J^T, add j_1^W in J^W;
4 **for** $i = 1, \cdots, l$ **do**
5   **for** $j = 1, \cdots, k$ **do**
6   **if** $i = 1$ and $j = 1$, **then** $PS_{1 \times kl} = \mathbf{0}_{1 \times kl}, RS_{1 \times kl} = \mathbf{0}_{1 \times kl}$;
7          $ps = j_t^T$;
8   **for** $m = 1, \cdots, i$ **do**
9              $ps = ps + \Gamma_s, s \xleftarrow{\$} \psi, position = \{ps, -ps\}$;
10   **end**
11         $D_{t+1}^T = \text{Algorithm1}(J^T, J^W, position); R^T = \text{Algorithm2}(ListD, D_{t+1}^T)$;
12         $PS_{(i-1)l+j} = ps, RS_{(i-1)l+j} = R^T$;
13   **if** $R^T > b$ **then**
14             $j_{t+1}^T = ps$, add j_{t+1}^T in J^T;
15   store D_{t+1}^T in $ListD$, read $g^{\pm(j_{t+1}^T - j_t^T)}$ from M^l;
16             $g_{t+1} = g_t \cdot g^{j_{t+1}^T - j_t^T}, \widehat{g_{t+1}} = \widehat{g_t} \cdot g^{j_t^T - j_{t+1}^T}$, store $\{g_{t+1}, \widehat{g_{t+1}}\}$ in G, goto 25;
17   **end**
18   **if** $i = l$ and $j = k$ **then**
19             $j_{t+1}^T = PS_{arg \max\{RS\}}$, add j_{t+1}^T in J^T;
20   store D_{t+1}^T in $ListD$, read $g^{\pm(j_{t+1}^T - j_t^T)}$ from M^l;
21             $g_{t+1} = g_t \cdot g^{j_{t+1}^T - j_t^T}, \widehat{g_{t+1}} = \widehat{g_t} \cdot g^{j_t^T - j_{t+1}^T}$, store $\{g_{t+1}, \widehat{g_{t+1}}\}$ in G, goto 25;
22   **end**
23   **end**
24 **end**
25 **for** $i = 1, \cdots, l$ **do**
26   **for** $j = 1, \cdots, k$ **do**
27   **if** $i = 1$ and $j = 1$, **then** $PS_{1 \times kl} = \mathbf{0}_{1 \times kl}, RS_{1 \times kl} = \mathbf{0}_{1 \times kl}$;
28         $ps = j_t^W$;
29   **for** $m = 1, \cdots, i$ **do**
30             $ps = ps + \Gamma_s, s \xleftarrow{\$} \psi, position = \{ps, -ps\}$;
31   **end**
32         $D_{t+1}^W = \text{Algorithm1}(J^T, J^W, position), R^W = \text{Algorithm2}(ListD, D_{t+1}^W)$;
33         $PS_{(i-1)l+j} = ps, RS_{(i-1)l+j} = R^W$;
34   **if** $R^W > b$ **then**
35             $j_{t+1}^W = ps$;
36   store D_{t+1}^W in $ListD$, read $g^{\pm(j_{t+1}^W - j_t^W)}$ from M^l;
37             $g_{t+1}' = g_t' \cdot g^{j_{t+1}^W - j_t^W}, \widehat{g_{t+1}'} = \widehat{g_t'} \cdot g^{j_t^W - j_{t+1}^W}$, store $\{g_{t+1}', \widehat{g_{t+1}'}\}$ in G', goto 46;
38   **end**
39   **if** $i = l$ and $j = k$ **then**
40             $j_{t+1}^W = PS_{arg \max\{RS\}}$, add j_{t+1}^W in J^W;
41   store D_{t+1}^W in $ListD$, read $g^{\pm(j_{t+1}^W - j_t^W)}$ from M^l;
42             $g_{t+1}' = g_t' \cdot g^{j_{t+1}^W - j_t^W}, \widehat{g_{t+1}'} = \widehat{g_t'} \cdot g^{j_t^W - j_{t+1}^W}$, store $\{g_{t+1}', \widehat{g_{t+1}'}\}$ in G', goto 46;
43   **end**
44   **end**
45 **end**
46 **if** $G \cap G' \neq \emptyset$ **then**
47   goto 51;
48 **else**
49     $t = t+1$, goto 4;
50 **end**
51 **if** there exist $g_x = g_s'$, **return** $ans = N/2 + j_x^T - j_s^W$;
52 **if** there exist $g_x = \widehat{g_s'}$, **return** $ans = N/2 + j_x^T + j_s^W$;
53 **if** there exist $\widehat{g_x} = g_s'$, **return** $ans = N/2 - j_x^T - j_s^W$;
54 **if** there exist $\widehat{g_x} = \widehat{g_s'}$, **return** $ans = N/2 - j_x^T + j_s^W$;

We first initialize PS and RS as zero vectors. Then in step 12, we add the position ps and its corresponding expanding factor R^T to PS and RS, respectively. If $R^T > b$ is not satisfied kl times, we select the positon corresponding to the maximum R^T by $PS_{arg\,max\{RS\}}$ in step 19, where $arg\,max\{RS\}$ is the index corresponding to the maximum value in RS. Besides, position ps is generated in advance in step 7 to 10. If the expanding factor R^T corresponding to ps grate than the given boundary b, then let jumping position $j_{t+1}^T = ps$ and compute the $(t+1)^{th}$ jump value as described in step 15 to 16. Or else, another position will be given again. Note that at most kl positions can be given. If $R^T > b$ is not satisfied kl times, we let the jumping position j_{t+1}^T be the ps corresponding to the largest R^T in RS as described above. Every time the jump value is computed, we store the jump value in G and end the loop in step 4–24 by the command of goto 25.

Similarly, kangaroo W makes a jump at step 25 to 45. Every time the jump value is computed, we store the jump value in G' and end the loop in step 25–45 by the command of goto 46. If the kangaroos jump t times, it needs at most kl cycles in $(t+1)^{th}$ jumps. Also, it takes at most $2(2t-1)$ subtractions to calculate the jumping distances for each jump, and it is judged whether these values existed in $ListD$. Therefore, the time required for each iteration is polynomial with complexity of $O(t)$. Finally, we check whether G and G' share the same value in step 46. If it is true, we have the answer by step 51–54. Or else, let $t = t + 1$ and make kangaroos jump again.

If $G \cap G' \neq \emptyset$, then one of the following equations is true.

$$\begin{aligned}
g^{j_x^T} &= hg^{-N/2}g^{j_s^W} = g^n g^{-N/2}g^{j_s^W} \\
g^{-j_x^T} &= hg^{-N/2}g^{j_s^W} = g^n g^{-N/2}g^{j_s^W} \\
g^{j_x^T} &= hg^{-N/2}g^{-j_s^W} = g^n g^{-N/2}g^{-j_s^W} \\
g^{-j_x^T} &= hg^{-N/2}g^{-j_s^W} = g^n g^{-N/2}g^{-j_s^W}
\end{aligned} \tag{2}$$

So we have $n - N/2 \in \{\pm j_x^T, \pm j_s^W\} \subset ListD$. On the contrary, if $n - N \in ListD$, there exist j_x^T and j_s^W such that one of the following equations is true.

$$\begin{aligned}
j_x^T &= n - N/2 + j_s^W \\
-j_x^T &= n - N/2 + j_s^W \\
j_x^T &= n - N/2 - j_s^W \\
-j_x^T &= n - N/2 - j_s^W
\end{aligned} \tag{3}$$

Then we have $G \cap G' \neq \emptyset$. So $G \cap G' \neq \emptyset$ if and only if $n - N/2 \in ListD$, namely, $\Pr[G \cap G' \neq \emptyset] = \Pr[n - N/2 \in ListD] = \frac{|ListD|}{N}$. Note that $|ListD|$ can reach N eventually, since $|ListD|$ increases with the number of iterations. Consequently when $|ListD| = N$, we have $\Pr[G \cap G' \neq \emptyset] = \Pr[n - N/2 \in ListD] = \frac{|ListD|}{N} = 1$, namely, the solution can be found finally, i.e. Algorithm 3 will end in a finite time.

3.4 Experimental Evaluation of Improved Algorithm

We selected large prime numbers of 521 bits in the DSS [6], where the prime number was $p = 6864797660130609714981900799081393217269435300143305409$ $3944634591855431833976553942450577463332171975329639963713633211113864$ $7686124403803403728088927070005449.$

Also, $g = 19$ was a generator of $\mathbb{Z}_p^*$. Then, the order of g was $p - 1$. The parameters were set as $\alpha = 100$, $\beta = 5$, $l = 15$, and $k = 8$. Let jump set $\Gamma = \{\pm 2, \pm 3,$ $\pm 5, \pm 6, \pm 8, \pm 9, \pm 11, \pm 12, \pm 14, \pm 15, \pm 17, \pm 18, \pm 20, \pm 21, \pm 23, \pm 25, \pm 26, \pm 28, \pm 29,$ $\pm 31, \pm 32, \pm 34, \pm 35, \pm 37, \pm 38, \pm 40, \pm 41, \pm 43, \pm 44, \pm 46, \pm 47, \pm 49, \pm 50, \pm 53, \pm 55,$ $\pm 56, \pm 58\}$, $l = 15$, $k = 8$, and $b = 0.8$. Also, $N = 2000, 5000, 8000$, and h was generated randomly. The average number of class operations is given in Table 4.

Table 4. Experiment results

N	Number of experiments	The average number of class operations
2000	1000	$0.9838\sqrt{N}$
5000	2000	$1.0182\sqrt{N}$
8000	3000	$1.0062\sqrt{N}$

From the results presented in Table 4, it can be concluded that the improved algorithm achieved a significant improvement in the number of class operations compared to the GR algorithm and other Pollard-kangaroo-like algorithms.

4 Heuristics and Analysis of Efficiency

Applying the process of the Algorithm 3, the average number of class operations of the improved algorithm is obtained, and it is shown in Table 5.

Table 5. The number of jumping distances.

Jump times	$\{j_i^T, j_i^{-T}\}$	$\{j_i^W, j_i^{-W}\}$	Number of increased elements in D	Number of elements in D
1th	$\{j_1^T, j_1^{-T}\}$	$\{j_1^W, j_1^{-W}\}$	4	4
2th	$\{j_2^T, j_2^{-T}\}$	$\{j_2^W, j_2^{-W}\}$	12	16
$\dots$	$\dots$	$\dots$	$\dots$	$\dots$
k^{th}	$\{j_k^T, j_k^{-T}\}$	$\{j_k^W, j_k^{-W}\}$	$4(2k-1)$	$4k^2$

Since the value of jumping distances can easily repeat in practical applications, we provide the definition of expanding factor as follows:

Definition 5. The total expanding factor of a jumping distance r is a ratio of the real number of elements in D to the theoretical maximum number of elements in D.

Then, we estimate the expected times of large integer multiplication, estimating it in the worst case. According to the total expanding factor, we assume the number of values of a new jumping distance of the kth jump is $4r(2k-1)$ in average. So, the total number of jumping distances of the kth jump is $4rk^2$. In the extreme situation, two kangaroo cannot collide every time, and jumping up to $\sqrt{N/(4r)}$ times can cover the entire range of required solutions set $(-N/2, N/2] \cap \mathbb{Z}$ (i.e., by solving $rk^2 > N$, we get $k > \sqrt{N/(4r)}$). Since it is needed to calculate two class operation for each jump, in the worst case, the cumulative total jump will be $(1/\sqrt{r} + o(1))\sqrt{N}$.

Also, since the jumping distance increases during the kth jump for $4r(2k-1)$ on average, the probability of getting a solution is $\frac{4r(2k-1)}{N}$. Besides, it is needed to compute the class operation for each jump, and the expected value of the number of class operations is $E = 2 \cdot \sum_{s=1}^{\sqrt{N/r}} \frac{2kr(2k-1)}{N} = 2/3\sqrt{N/r} + 1 - 2/3\sqrt{r/N}$. Therefore, the numbers of class operations are approximately $(2/(3\sqrt{r}) + o(1))\sqrt{N}$. In particular, $(2/3 + o(1))\sqrt{N}$ is the optimal complexity of the algorithm when $r = 1$.

In the 6000 experiments of Sect. 3.4, the average value of r is 0.44. So, the improved algorithm with time complexity of $(2/(3\sqrt{0.44}) + o(1))\sqrt{N} = (1.005 + o(1))\sqrt{N}$ is more efficient than the algorithms in [2–5,7] described in introduction.

5   Conclusions

In this paper, we present a new algorithm for computing the discrete logarithm using class operations. The improved algorithm uses the expanding factor to determine the next jump of a kangaroo and selects a local optimal position with the highest expanding factor in each jump so that the kangaroo can collide with higher efficiency.

In addition, the concept of expanding factor and jumping difference provides another perspective for understanding the kangaroo algorithm. As a heuristic, it would lead to some method by improving the expanding factor which can be used as an indicator to evaluate the superiority of the kangaroo algorithm and its improved algorithm.

References

1. Boneh, D., Goh, E.-J., Nissim, K.: Evaluating 2-DNF formulas on ciphertexts. In: Kilian, J. (ed.) TCC 2005. LNCS, vol. 3378, pp. 325–341. Springer, Heidelberg (2005). https://doi.org/10.1007/978-3-540-30576-7_18
2. Cheon, J.H., Hong, J., Kim, M.: Speeding up the Pollard rho method on prime fields. In: Pieprzyk, J. (ed.) ASIACRYPT 2008. LNCS, vol. 5350, pp. 471–488. Springer, Heidelberg (2008). https://doi.org/10.1007/978-3-540-89255-7_29
3. Fowler, A., Galbraith, S.: Kangaroo methods for solving the interval discrete logarithm problem. arXiv preprint arXiv:1501.07019 (2015)
4. Galbraith, S., Pollard, J., Ruprai, R.: Computing discrete logarithms in an interval. J. Math. Comput. **82**, 1181–1195 (2013)
5. Galbraith, S.D., Ruprai, R.S.: Using equivalence classes to accelerate solving the discrete logarithm problem in a short interval. In: Nguyen, P.Q., Pointcheval, D. (eds.) PKC 2010. LNCS, vol. 6056, pp. 368–383. Springer, Heidelberg (2010). https://doi.org/10.1007/978-3-642-13013-7_22
6. Gallagher, W.P.: Digital signature standard (DSS). Federal Information Processing Standards Publications. 186-3 (2013)
7. Liu, J., Lv, K.: Solving discrete logarithm problem in an interval using periodic iterates. In: Qing, S., Mitchell, C., Chen, L., Liu, D. (eds.) ICICS 2017. LNCS, vol. 10631, pp. 75–80. Springer, Cham (2018). https://doi.org/10.1007/978-3-319-89500-0_6
8. Pollard, J.M.: Monopoly and discrete logarithms. J. Cryptol. **13**, 437–447 (2000)
9. van Oorschot, P.C., Wiener, M.J.: On Diffie-Hellman key agreement with short exponents. In: Maurer, U. (ed.) EUROCRYPT 1996. LNCS, vol. 1070, pp. 332–343. Springer, Heidelberg (1996). https://doi.org/10.1007/3-540-68339-9_29
10. Wang, Y., Lv, K.: Improved method on the discrete logarithm problem in an interval. J. Cryptologic Res. **1**, 570–582 (2015)
11. Park, S.K., Miller, K.W.: Random number generators: good ones are hard to find. Commun. ACM **31**, 1192–1201 (1988)
12. L'ecuyer, P.: Tables of linear congruential generators of different sizes and good lattice structure. J. Math. Comput. Am. Math. Soc. **68**, 249–260 (1999)
13. Press, W.H., Teukolsky, S.A., Vetterling White, W.T.: Numerical Recipes: The Art of Scientific Computing. Cambridge University Press, Cambridge (2007)

Parallel Steepest Ascent Hill-Climbing for High Nonlinear Boolean and Vectorial Boolean Functions (S-Boxes)

Athmane Seghier$^{(\boxtimes)}$ and Jianxin Li

Beijing Advanced Innovation Center of Big data and Brain Computing,
Beihang University, Beijing, China
{seghierathmane,lijx}@act.buaa.edu.cn

Abstract. Boolean functions and their generalization Vectorial Boolean functions or Substitution Boxes (S-Boxes) have attracted much attention in the domain of modern block ciphers that use only these elements to provide the necessary confusion against the cryptanalysis attacks. Thus, a significant number of research has been done to construct cryptographically strong Boolean functions and S-Boxes. Among these researches, several heuristics were applied and therefore the hill climbing heuristic was largely investigated. In this paper, we propose a new variant of Hill Climbing heuristic called Parallel Steepest Ascent Hill Climbing to construct Boolean functions and $n \times m$ S-Boxes through the progressive construction and incorporation of their m coordinate Boolean functions. The obtained results demonstrate that this new variant provides solutions with high cryptographic properties.

Keywords: Boolean functions · S-Boxes · Hill Climbing · Cost function

1 Introduction

Cryptographic design of Boolean functions and S-Boxes is guided by three main directions: pseudo-random or exhaustive search, algebraic constructions and heuristic techniques.

Random search was the first technique explored for the Boolean functions. However, it is well known that the number of Boolean functions achieving optimal cryptographic properties is very small compared to the extremely large set of Boolean functions. Thus, it is difficult to find cryptographically good Boolean functions, only from random search, especially for functions with a large number n of inputs. Exhaustive search over a particular subset of the Boolean function space provides an alternative to the full search and is therefore possible for functions of higher n, depending on the range of functions to be examined. This modified exhaustive search has been relatively successful [1].

Supported by NSFC program (No. 61872022, 61421003), SKLSDE-2018ZX-16 and partly by the Beijing Advanced Innovation Center for Big Data and Brain Computing.

© Springer Nature Switzerland AG 2020
J. Zhou et al. (Eds.): ICICS 2019, LNCS 11999, pp. 413–429, 2020.
https://doi.org/10.1007/978-3-030-41579-2_24

The algebraic techniques have been used to develop the methodologies for the construction of cryptographically strong Boolean functions. There are several basic approaches to the algebraic design of Boolean function, the most common of which is a recursive construction, as well as numerous variants and more recently a linear transformation method. Many specific algorithms exist for the construction of Boolean functions that possess particular levels of cryptographically important properties including nonlinearity, algebraic order, autocorrelation and resilience, or specific combinations of these. Algebraic construction techniques are usually designed to achieve a specific property.

The major alternative to algebraic construction techniques are heuristic techniques. Heuristic techniques involve a process of iteratively improving a given function with respect to more than one property. They provide the ability to find Boolean functions that are superior to those generated using algebraic techniques. Specific heuristic techniques include the genetic algorithm, hill climbing, simulated annealing or their combinations.

Hill climbing [2] technique involves repeated application of small modifications to, for example, the truth table with the view to improve one or more properties. Genetic algorithms [3] work with a population of candidate functions. They involve the application of three fundamental operations that are inspired by natural evolution (selection, crossover and mutation), with the aim of producing future populations containing functions with the desired properties. Simulated Annealing [4,5] provides an extension to hill climbing techniques in which the search process is able to move out of local maximum in order to continue.

Similarly to the Boolean functions construction, S-Box construction is also guided by the three aforementioned directions. The first direction is based on the random or pseudo-random search. Good cryptographic properties can hardly be found following the random generation for a large size S-Boxes [6,7]. The second direction is based on the construction of S-Box guided by mathematical models. The AES S-Box design, based on the inverse mapping and the affine transformation in the finite field, is the best example of such methods [8]. This S-Box has the best practical cryptographic properties known. However, it was reported by Fuller et al. in [9,10], that the component Boolean functions forming the S-Boxes constructed with this kind of method are completely linearly dependent. The third direction based on the evolutionary or heuristic model, is known to be efficient in both software and hardware implementations. However, previous research has proven the limit of their direct modelling to find competitive S-Boxes (104 as maximum nonlinearity) [11].

Several Heuristics have been used for the S-Box generation task, such as Hill Climbing [12], Genetic Algorithm [13], Simulated Annealing [14], practical Swarm Optimisation [15], Ant Colony Optimisation [16] and Bee Waggle Dance algorithm [17]. However, As it was stated by Picek in [18], it is not entirely fair to compare between methods that start from random population or individual and those that start from a cryptographically good S-Box (reverse based construction). In addition to these three main directions, other construction methods can be followed such as, chaotic maps [19] or combination between Chaos solutions and heuristics [20–22].

In this paper, we introduce a new variant of the Hill Climbing heuristic called Parallel Steepest Ascent Hill Climbing and summarises its application to the Boolean functions and S-Boxes construction. Thus, the 2-bits tweaking process, previously introduced in [23] for the reverse construction of S-Box is applied to the Boolean functions, as well as the S-Boxes construction through the progressive construction and incorporation of its coordinate Boolean functions, contrarily to the conventional methods that handle the lookup table of the S-Box instead of its coordinate Boolean functions.

The remainder of the paper is organised as follows. Section 2 provides the preliminary knowledge around Boolean functions and S-Boxes. The proposed method is introduced in Sect. 3. Section 4 describes some experimental results on the cryptographic properties of the Boolean functions and S-Boxes obtained by this method. Finally, a brief conclusion is given in Sect. 5.

2 Preliminaries

2.1 Boolean Function

Let a Boolean function (BF) f, explicitly noted $f(x_1, \cdots, x_n)$, an n-variable Boolean function, $f : F_{2^n} \rightarrow F_2$ is a mapping from n-dimensional vector space to F_2, in the finite field. (Only 8-variables Boolean functions $(n = 8)$ are considered, here and everywhere below).

Several forms are available to represent a Boolean function. Each form is more suitable than the others to express or compute a given Boolean function property. In this paper only the used ones will be defined. Algebraic Normal Form (ANF) is the XOR sum of ANDed input variables representation for a given Boolean function represented by: $f(x_1, \cdots, x_n) = \oplus_{I \subseteq S} a_I \prod_{i \in I} x_i$, where $S = \{x_1, x_2, \cdots, x_n\}$ is the set of all possible terms of n variable and I the set of terms composing f. Truth table (TT) is the simplest representation of an n-variable Boolean function, where each element of a binary vector of length 2^n reflects the image corresponding to a unique element in F_{2^n} of the function inputs $(x_1, \cdots, x_n)$. The Walsh Hadamard Transform (WHT) denoted by $\hat{F}_f(w)$, is the most important representation in this document. It reflects the correlation between the function f and all the linear functions $l_w(x) = <w, x>$. It is defined by:

$$\hat{F}_f(w) = \sum_{x \in \mathbb{B}^n} \hat{f}(w) \cdot (-1)^{<w,x>} = \sum_{x \in \mathbb{B}^n} (-1)^{f(x) \oplus <w,x>}$$

$$\hat{F}_f(w) = \sum_{x \in \mathbb{B}^n} \hat{f}(x) \cdot \hat{l}_w(x) \tag{1}$$

The maximum absolute value of the WHT is denoted by:

$$WHD_{max}(f) = max_{w \in \mathbb{B}^n} |\hat{F}_f(w)| \tag{2}$$

Boolean function is defined by several properties that can be summarized on the following ones. The Hamming weight denoted by $wt(f)$, represents the number of ones in the truth table representation of f. The Hamming Distance d is the measure that gives the distance between two Boolean functions $f(x)$ and $g(x)$, which means the number of times that the two Boolean functions differ in their truth table representation, such as: $d(f(x), g(x)) = \#\{x : f(x) \neq g(x)\}$, where $\#\{\}$ indicates the number of occurrences of the set.

An n-variable Boolean function f is said to be balanced if it's Hamming weight $wt(f)$ is equal to 2^{n-1}. The algebraic degree or order, denoted by $deg(f)$ is the term(s) degree of the ANF with the largest product term which refers to the number of variables it includes, knowing that the functions with an algebraic degree inferior or equal to 1 are called affine functions. In the case of Vectorial Boolean function, the Algebraic degree is the minimum AD of all component functions.

The Nonlinearity Nl_f of a Boolean function f defined by the maximum absolute value of the WHT such as:

$$NL_f = (2^n - WHT_{max}(f))/2 \tag{3}$$

The Autocorrelation function (AC), denoted by $\hat{r}_f(\alpha)$, provides an indication of the imbalance of all first order derivatives $D_\alpha \hat{f}(x) = \hat{f}(x) \oplus \hat{f}(x \oplus \alpha)$ of a polarity form $\hat{f}$ of a Boolean function f, with respect to a vector $\alpha \in \mathbb{B}^n$. It is defined as: $\hat{r}_f(\alpha) = \sum_{x \in \mathbb{B}^n} f(x) \oplus f(x \oplus \alpha)$. The maximum AC value or absolute indicator of the polarity form $\hat{f}$ of f, denoted by $AC_{max}(f)$ is given by:

$$AC_{max}(f) = max_{(\alpha \in \mathbb{B}^n \setminus \{0\})} |\hat{r}_f(\alpha)| \tag{4}$$

2.2   Vectorial Boolean Function (S-Box)

The cryptographic properties of the $n \times m$ S-Box are not only reflected by the properties of its m coordinate Boolean functions, but by all its $2^m - 1$ non-zero component Boolean functions [24]. In this subsection, we define only the properties considered in this paper.

An $n \times m$ S-Box with $n \geq m$, is said **regular** if and only if all its m-bits output vectors occur with an equal number of times, namely 2^{n-m}. An S-Box with this property is known to satisfy the balance criterion for the m component and all their nonzero linear combinations.

The nonlinearity of an S-Box $S \in F_m^n$, is extended from the Boolean function case to the $2^m - 1$ component Boolean functions as:

$$Nl(S) = min_{\alpha \in F_2^m, \alpha \neq 0)} Nl(\alpha \cdot f) \tag{5}$$

The Differential Uniformity examines for a given S, the number of solutions of the equation: $S(x \oplus a) \oplus S(x) = b$, for every pair of input a and output b. S is said differentially $\delta - unifom$ if:

$$\delta = max_{a \in \mathbb{B}^n \setminus \{0\}} max_{b \in \mathbb{B}^n} |\{x \in \mathbb{B}^n | S(x) \oplus S(x \oplus a) = b\}| \tag{6}$$

The algebraic degree, denoted by $AD(S)$, called also minimum degree, is the minimum algebraic degree of all the component Boolean function.

$$AD(S) = min_{\alpha \in F_{2^n}, \alpha \neq 0} AD(\alpha \cdot f) \tag{7}$$

Where $(\alpha \cdot f)$ is a non-zero linear combination of the coordinate Boolean function $f_1, f_2, \cdots, f_n$ of S.

Autocorrelation $(AC)_{max}$ is determined by the maximum absolute indicator among the absolute indicators of all non-trivial component Boolean functions of S. That is:

$$AC(S)_{max} = max_{c=(c_1,c_2,\cdots,c_m) \in B^m \setminus \{0\}} |\hat{r}_{c_1 f_1 \oplus c_2 f_2 \oplus \cdots \oplus c_m f_m}(\alpha)| \tag{8}$$

An S-Box S represented by the component Boolean functions $B_0, B_1, \cdots, B_{2^n-2}$. B_i and $B_j, i \neq j \wedge i, j \in [0, 1, \cdots, 2^n - 2]$ are said to be linearly redundant or (affine equivalent), if it exists an affine transformation that maps between them such as:

$$B_i(x) = B_j(Dx^T \oplus a^T) \oplus b \cdot x^T \oplus c \tag{9}$$

Where D: non-singular binary matrix, a and b: two n-element binary vectors, c: a binary constant and $b \cdot x^T$ denotes a linear function of x selected by b [9]. Furthermore, An S-Box S is said to be R-Linearly Redundant, if R of its $2^m - 1$ component Boolean functions belong to m distinct extended affine equivalence classes. Thus, if $R = 1$, then S is completely linearly redundant, else if $R = 2^m - 1$, then S is non-linearly redundant S-Box.

3 Proposed Method

The Parallel Steepest Ascent Hill Climbing (PSAHC) Algorithm consists on the parallel version of the Steepest Ascent Hill Climbing. In this section we investigate the construction of Boolean function and S-Box using this enhanced version of the Hill Climbing heuristic.

Similarly to the Steepest Ascent Hill climbing variant, the proposed method takes into account all possible neighbours from each solution of the N elements composing the current population, then the N best elements are picked no matters their predecessor. In other words, the N best elements can come from the same or different predecessors. However, Similarly to Tabu Search (TS), PSAHC uses a list of previously visited neighbours. This list avoids the algorithm to explore or to select again during the search neighbours already explored.

The main idea behind the use of the parallel hill climbing is to deal with the treated problem as climbing an unknown hill by a group of climbers who challenge them-selves to reach the top of the hill as quickly as possible. Thus, instead of taking only one path to reach the top of the hill, the climbers borrow from the beginning different paths from different positions of the foothill simultaneously, in order to cover as much as possible and proportionally the foothill. In this case, the chances of taking the best path and consequently of reaching the top are improved. However, the main challenge of this technique is to find the proper way to define these paths in such a way that the foothill is as much as possible and proportionally covered. Algorithm 1 shows the different steps of the PSAHC method.

Algorithm 1. PSAHC algorithm for Boolean functions construction

---

Data: Void
Result: highly nonlinear Boolean function
begin
 $Max\_Eval \leftarrow 1000$;
 $P \leftarrow Generate\_N\_initial\_solutions$;
 $Counter \leftarrow 0$;
 $Already\_Explored\_Neighbours \leftarrow P$;
 while $Counter < Max\_Eval$ **do**
  for $solution x$ **in** P **do**
   $Neighbourhood \leftarrow Explore\_Two\_Local\_Neighbourhood(x)$;
   for $Neighbour$ **in** $Neighbourhood$ **do**
    if $Neighbour$ **not in** $Already\_Explored\_Neighbours$ **then**
     $Global\_Neighbourhood \leftarrow Neighbour$

  for $Neighbour$ **in** $Global\_Neighbourhood$ **do**
   $Compute\_Cost\_function(Neighbour)$;
   if $Neighbour = Targeted\_Solution$ **then**
    return $Neighbour$

  $Sort\_by\_Cost\_function(Global\_Neighbourhood)$;
  $P \leftarrow Global\_Neighbourhood[0 \cdot \cdot N]$;
  $Counter \leftarrow Counter + 1$;
 return $Global\_Neighbourhood[0]$

3.1 PSAHC for Boolean Function Construction

In this subsection we use the PSAHC algorithm to construct High nonlinear Boolean functions. Thus, we start from a random population of Balanced Boolean functions having nonlinearity $108 \leq NL \leq 110$ and respecting a minimum Hamming Distance between them, then we apply SAHC algorithm for each Boolean function of the population, which means the exploration of all neighbourhood through the 2-bits tweaking process, where the neighbourhood is defined by all Boolean function equal to: $2^{n-1} \times 2^{n-1} = 2^{2n-2}$ obtained by all possible tweaks between the 2^{n-1} zeros and 2^{n-1} ones. Once the entire population is treated, we sort the Boolean functions of the Neighbourhoods resulting from all the population according to their Cost function score. Such as, the used cost function represents the simplified version of the one proposed in [18], which is based on the reduction of the number of maximum absolute value coefficients of the Walsh Hadamard Distribution.

$$CF(f) = \sum_{i=0}^{N-1} \frac{WHD_{coef}[l-i]}{2^i} \tag{10}$$

With WHD_{coef} is the absolute Walsh Hadamard Distribution coefficient and l the last considered coefficient (if $l > 10$ then $N = 10$ else $N = l$).

The proposed method allows increasing the nonlinearity of an initial set of Balanced Boolean functions, randomly generated until obtaining nonlinearity equal to 116. Concretely, PSAHC method is somehow a hybrid method which mixes between the two heuristics: Steepest Ascent hill climbing and genetic algorithm, such as it takes the concept of breeding from the genetic algorithm by using a population instead of an individual. The new generation is obtained by choosing the best Boolean functions forming the 2-Local Specific Neighbourhood $(2 - LSN)$ of each Boolean functions of the current population, while accepting the non-improving solutions, so that the new population is formed by the best new functions obtained from the $2 - LSN$ that were not previously chosen, even if contrarily to the genetic algorithm that uses the conventional breading operation such as selection, mutation and crossover. It is important to note that the PSAHC method accepts no improving solutions when the best solutions obtained of the current set have worst score for the used cost function comparing to the previous set.

The advantage of this method is that ensures obtaining a nonlinearity equal to 116, which represents the maximum nonlinearity that can be obtained for an 8-variables balanced Boolean functions [25]. Moreover, comparing to the existing methods, this one gives the best absolute Walsh Hadamard distribution. This results is an improvement to the simple Hill Climbnig heuristic proposed in [2], that gives a nonlinearity equal to 114. However, there are some other methods based on a modified Hill Climbing that gives the same nonlinearity and better results for other cryptographic properties. Such as, in the modified Hill Climbing, but their construction starts from initial bent function instead of random Balanced Boolean function, where the nonlinearity is decreased until obtaining a balanced Boolean function [26,27].

3.2   PSAHC for S-Box Construction

In this subsection, the main idea is the exploration of the PSAHC algorithm through the 2-bits tweaking method for the progressive construction of the m (n-variables) coordinate Boolean functions composing the $n \times m$ S-Box.

The numerous researches on the Boolean functions and in particular those based on the application of the different heuristics have achieved remarkable results concerning the nonlinearity, with a nonlinearity equal to 114 for the hill climbing heuristic and 116 for Genetic algorithms and its combination with hill climbing. In this research these results will represent an interesting starting point or base for a progressive construction of Vectorial Boolean functions (S-Boxes). Thus, the S-Box construction is investigated, through the construction based on the progressive incorporation of the coordinate Boolean functions.

The construction will be confined to s-boxes with $n \geq m$ that satisfy the balance property which is reflected by balancing the number of occurrences of all possible m-bit output vectors to be equal to 2^{n-m}. Such as, an S-box with this property is called regular. In this paper only $n \times m$ regular S-Boxes with input $n = 8$ and output $m \in \{2, \cdots, 8\}$ are considered.

In this work the truth table representation is used contrarily to the majority of existing methods that use the look up table representation of the S-Box. To do so, a progressive construction is needed which allows to add progressively a new Boolean function to an initial $n \times (m-1)$ regular S-Box, in order to obtain $n \times m$ regular S-Box. However, to maintain a good quality of the cryptographic properties, it's important that the new Boolean function possesses good cryptographic properties and also all its nonzero combinations with the $m-1$ coordinate Boolean functions forming the initial $n \times (m-1)$ S-Box. This progressive construction is initiated by the construction of a single Boolean function. For that, any existing technique for the construction of cryptographically strong Boolean function can be used. However, the new technique called Parallel Hill Climbing is adopted during our experiment. Once the first Boolean function obtained, the remaining Boolean functions are progressively constructed using the same technique, but the search space will be restricted to the Boolean functions that satisfy the regular property of the resulting S-Box.

Solution Representation. The first step in implementing any Heuristic model is to choose the appropriate solution representation. The one used in this method is the truth table of the output Boolean function where 2^n represents the length of a single Boolean function.

Search Space. The search space is defined by the balanced Boolean functions that satisfy the regular property of $n \times m$ S-Box resulting from the incorporation of the Balanced Boolean function called "candidate Boolean function" to an initial regular $n \times (m-1)$ S-Box. As for each Local Search Algorithm heuristic, rules that define the neighbourhood of a candidate Boolean function are required. In this work this neighbourhood is defined by all solutions that are obtained by swapping two dissimilar bits (2-bits tweaking) according to the generation process defined below.

Generation Process. Before defining the generation process, we need first to define the **move function** between the individuals within this search space. The move function is the function that transforms an element from the search space to another. The move function here consists to swap two dissimilar bits that maintain the regular property. In the proposed method, the generation process is based on the moves that define the whole neighbourhood of a given Boolean function containing the Boolean function resulting from applying the move function called **two-bits tweaking** which consists to tweak two complementary bits (one and zero) of the truth table representation, in such a way that only Neighbours that maintain the regular property of the resulting S-Box are retained.

2-Bit Tweaking. The 2-bits tweaking technique is the swapping operation between two bits of the treated Boolean function f_i for $i = \{1, m\}/m \leq n$ that maintains the regular property of the resulting $n \times m$ S-Box S. to do so, these two bits to tweak must be carefully selected. For a given Vectorial Boolean Function S:

$$S : S_{2^n} \to S_{2^m}/S(f_1, \cdots, f_m) \tag{11}$$

The Boolean Function to tweak, f_i for $i \in \{1, m\}$ is defined as: $f_i : F_{2^n} \to F_2$ and G the remainder Boolean function (for $i = 2$) or Vectorial Boolean function $(2 < i \leq m)$, formed without the function to tweak f_i such as:

$$G = S - f_i = G(f_1, \cdots, f_{i-1}) : G_{2^n} \to G_{2^{m-1}} \tag{12}$$

The concept of Local Neighbourhood is adopted. Such as, the neighbour Nf_i of the 2-Local Neighbourhood $(2 - LN)$ of the balanced function f_i is obtained by swapping any two dissimilar bits $x, y \in \mathbb{Z}_2^n$ such as:

$$\begin{cases} f_i(x) = f_i(y) \\ Nf_i(x) = f_i(y) \\ Nf_i(y) = f_i(x) \\ Nf_i(z) = f_i(z), \forall z \in \mathbb{Z}_2^n/\{x, y\} \end{cases} \tag{13}$$

The above conditions maintain the balance property of the coordinate Boolean functions f_i of the treated S-Box S during the tweak process. However, in the Vectorial Boolean case, these conditions are not sufficient to ensure that the 2-Local Neighbours obtained by 13 maintain the regular property of the Vectorial Boolean function S. For that, additional conditions are required. To maintain the regular property of the S-Box S, the set of $2 - LN$ is restricted to the elements resulting from the tweak operation between the two positions i, j satisfying the regular property defined by the following conditions: Let take f the coordinate Boolean function of S to tweak, then:

$$\begin{cases} x_i, x_j \in \{0, 2^n - 1\} \ and \ x_i \neq x_j \\ G(x_i) = G(x_j) \\ f(x_i) \neq f(x_j) \end{cases} \tag{14}$$

These constraints are applied for each coordinate Boolean function f_i of S. Thus, the $2-LN$ set is reduced to the 2-Local Specific Neighbourhood $(2-LSN)$. Concretely, the 2-bits to tweak should be carefully selected to maintain the balance and regular properties of the S-Box, which means the identification of the set of 2^{n-m} tweakable 2-bits-pairs forming the $2 - LSN$, for the n-variable coordinate Boolean function to tweak, in relation to the $m - 1$ already accepted coordinate Boolean functions. For that, the first step consists to extract the positions of zeros (i) and ones (j) of the identical combinations formed by the $\frac{2^n}{2^{n-(m-1)}}$ combinations of the $(m - 1)$ remaining coordinate functions, for $I, j \in [0, 2^n - 1]$. Then, construct a set that regroups these $n-(m-1)$ bits combinations with their positions. Thus, As shown in Fig. 1, if the current Coordinate Boolean function to climb is $b_7(m = 7)$ then for each combination of the $\frac{2^n}{2^{n-(m-1)}}$ combinations, (in this case $\frac{2^8}{2^{8-(7-1)}} = 64$ different combinations of $2^{n-(m-1)} = 2^{8-(7-1)} = 4$ occurrences for each combination, such as, half of these occurrences match with zeros and half of them match with ones of b_m, which means that set of same combination is matching with 2 zeros and two ones of b_7). Then if the combination $[b_1, b_2, b_3, b_4, b_5, b_6] = [1, 1, 0, 0, 0, 1]$ is taken as example, then four 2-bits tweak are possible ($[b_{7_0}, b_{7_{71}}], [b_{7_0}, b_{7_{101}}], [b_{7_{71}}, b_{7_{234}}], [b_{7_{101}}, b_{7_{234}}]$), since each one has two zeros as possible moves. Furthermore, the same operation is repeated for each combination. So, the number of 2-bits tweaks possible for b_7 is: (number of ones corresponding to a given combination × the number of zeros corresponding to the same combination) × number of combinations = $(2 \times 2) \times 64$ combinations = 256 solutions. With: Possible moves of a combination = number of ones × number of zeros.

$$2 - LSN(BF_i) = \text{Possible\_moves\_combination} \times \text{number\_combinations}$$
$$2 - LSN(BF_i) = (2^{i-1} \times 2^{i-1}) \times 2^{n-i} = 2^{2i-2+n-i}$$

$$2 - LSN(BF_i) = 2^{i+n-2}, i \in \{1, \cdots, 8\} \qquad (15)$$

Position/BFs	b1	b2	b3	b4	b5	b6	b7
0	1	1	0	0	0	1	1
⋮	⋮	⋮	⋮	⋮	⋮	⋮	⋮
71	1	1	0	0	0	1	0
⋮	⋮	⋮	⋮	⋮	⋮	⋮	⋮
101	1	1	0	0	0	1	0
⋮	⋮	⋮	⋮	⋮	⋮	⋮	⋮
234	1	1	0	0	0	1	1
⋮	⋮	⋮	⋮	⋮	⋮	⋮	⋮
255	0	1	1	0	1	0	1

Fig. 1. Two-bits-tweaking method

Initial Population. The generation of an initial population requires a method to generate uniformly at random Balanced Boolean functions which maintain the regular property when added to an initial regular s-box. In this method, the generation of an initial population consists to generate randomly N Balanced Boolean functions with a nonlinearity NL defined to be $108 \leq NL \leq 110$. These Boolean functions which are added to an $n \times m - 1$ initial S-Box, must satisfy the regular property of the resulting $n \times m$ S-Box.

Cost Function. Cost function plays an important role in the selection of the best individuals during the generation process of any Heuristic model. Thus, the more computation accuracy can give the used cost function on the targeted property, the more this property can be improved and with a higher speed. Several Cost functions were proposed to improve the search accuracy of different heuristics applied on Boolean functions and S-Box construction. Among these cost functions the one proposed by Clark in [14] is the most famous. However, Picek in [18] proposed an interesting cost function that gives better results whatever the heuristic applied. Thus, to select the best neighbour according to its WHT or NL, a good cost function is required. In this paper the cost function used is the one proposed in [18].

$$CF(S) = \sum_{i=0}^{N-1} \frac{H(S)_{l-i}}{2^i} \tag{16}$$

With $H(S)$ is the histogram of absolute values of the Walsh-Hadamard Coefficients for an S-box S (if $l > 10$ then $N = 10$ else $N = l$).

4 Experimental Results

4.1 Boolean Function Construction

The experiment done for Boolean functions was the construction of Boolean functions using PSAHC algorithm, with as a stop condition not only reaching a nonlinearity $NL = 116$, but reaching the minimum value that the cost function can obtains before a certain number of evaluations. The Boolean function proposed below under the hexadecimal format, represents one of thousands similar results that reach the maximum optimisation following this method, for a Nonlinearity, an Autocorrelation and an algebraic degree that respectively correspond to $NL = 116, AC - 24, AD = 7$. The proposed Boolean function is:

66B482572291238CEE681DA0E075F63C3CDA4B9F315FA560313FBAAE6016E3ED

Table 1. Cryptographic properties comparison

Methods	Properties									
	NL	AD	AC	AWHD						
				0	4	8	12	16	20	24
PSAHC	116	7	24	16	0	16	64	80	64	16
In [27]	116	7	24	4	8	38	60	60	60	26
In [26]	116	7	16	4	16	28	48	76	64	20

Table 1 shows that the PSAHC method gives good results for the cryptographic properties even if it starts from a random balanced Boolean function. Moreover, PSAHC reaches the lowest Absolute Walsh Hadamard Distribution (AWHD), meaning that the distance from a nonlinearity equal to 118 is the lowest [16,24].

4.2   S-Box Construction

S-Box Nonlinearity with Coordinate Boolean Functions. In this experiment, the PSAHC is used to construct progressively 8 × 8 S-Boxes by considering only the nonlinearity of the Boolean functions climbed (coordinate Boolean functions). We call this version **PSAHC1**. The sample size is conducted by 150 S-Boxes.

Table 2. Absolute Walsh Hadamard Transform Distribution Comparison

No BF	2-LSN	Avg. iterations	Avg. number evaluations
BF_1	16384	12.1466	3 932 160
BF_2	8192	6.96	1 146 880
BF_3	4096	7.9333	655 360
BF_4	2048	9.1333	368 640
BF_5	1024	10.9	225 280
BF_6	512	14.1933	143 360
BF_7	256	21.6733	112 640
BF_8	128	75.5266	194 560

Table 2 aims to enumerate the average number of evaluations Avg_{Num_Eval} needed for the PSAHC1 version to obtain an S-Box with a Nonlinearity of its coordinate Boolean functions equal to 116, starting from a random BF with a $108 \leq NL \leq 110$. To do so, this average number of evaluations is computed for each Coordinate Boolean Function, according to its $2 - LSN$ obtained by Eq. 15, with the following formula:

$$Avg_{Num\_Eval_{(BF_i)}} = 2 - LSN(BF_i) \times P \times Avg\_Iter(BF_i), i \in \{1, \cdots, 8\} \quad (17)$$

From Table 2, it is concluded that the average number of evaluation needed to construct 8 × 8 S-Box by PSAHC1 is 6778880 evaluations.

Table 3 represents the proposed S-Box obtained by the PSAHC1 version. The proposed S-Box has a $NL = 96, AC = 88, \delta = 10, AD = 6$ and $LR = 255$. For its coordinate Boolean functions, the minimum, the maximum and the Average nonlinearity are all equal to 116.

S-Box Nonlinearity with Component Boolean Functions. In this experiment, the PSAHC is used to construct progressively 8 × 8 S-Boxes by considering the nonlinearity of all component Boolean functions. We call this version **PSAHC2**. Table 4 represents the proposed S-Box obtained by the PSAHC2 version. The proposed S-Box has a $NL = 102, AC = 96, \delta = 10, AD = 6$ and $LR = 255$.

The Absolute Walsh Hadamard Distribution in Table 5 regroups the WHD of the BF_i and all the component Boolean functions involving BF_i. The PSAHC2

Table 3. Proposed S-Box using PSAHC1

	0	1	2	3	4	5	6	7	8	9	A	B	C	D	E	F
0	05	9E	CB	51	15	F9	85	21	BD	74	F5	9D	0C	8A	5C	67
1	C1	6A	63	75	28	06	5A	3B	3C	E5	22	9C	64	93	92	F4
2	50	54	B5	71	4E	4A	8B	02	1D	1F	0D	F0	72	1E	1A	CF
3	33	49	A7	07	3E	25	A1	D6	C0	6C	73	7C	90	DA	60	68
4	FF	A0	F6	20	F3	F7	91	36	27	BC	BE	6B	C7	52	29	56
5	2F	12	7E	A8	E6	B8	2D	D3	CC	62	E9	5D	30	57	69	5B
6	DD	DB	F2	04	66	58	61	4C	5F	DE	94	FE	26	9A	BA	F1
7	95	AD	B9	E1	48	CD	E8	44	65	1C	A3	B6	E7	E0	34	6E
8	19	7B	FB	AB	DC	BF	24	43	88	BB	18	EC	D9	4B	FD	4F
9	37	CA	6D	C8	97	11	E4	FC	8D	2E	77	89	D2	9F	C3	EF
A	3D	55	AE	8F	10	13	4D	B3	47	A6	2B	AF	C5	6F	A2	D8
B	96	17	A4	16	39	AC	76	C2	32	DF	81	53	14	3F	1B	3A
C	31	38	99	D5	35	41	0F	D4	7D	0A	A5	C4	9B	FA	ED	84
D	87	59	B2	98	EE	B0	AA	01	8E	23	B1	70	D1	B4	CE	42
E	79	A9	D0	2A	2C	03	00	0E	08	0B	7F	B7	5E	82	D7	40
F	80	83	C6	46	78	09	86	C9	F8	8C	EA	7A	E3	E2	45	EB

Table 4. Proposed S-Box using PSAHC2

	0	1	2	3	4	5	6	7	8	9	A	B	C	D	E	F
0	72	83	C2	C4	C8	C1	DD	1B	C6	25	80	9C	26	F0	18	6F
1	2C	FB	FC	A6	28	4A	29	F5	DE	24	0E	9E	A8	44	95	8E
2	47	85	32	3E	A5	E3	02	A3	A2	75	B0	53	37	E4	EF	E9
3	0C	BF	1C	58	42	01	CF	56	AF	67	90	43	93	6E	3F	0A
4	D0	6C	9D	6B	C0	5E	F3	9F	ED	BE	DF	76	65	51	22	86
5	78	13	87	2A	0F	C7	35	07	91	D2	73	5B	9A	AA	CD	59
6	79	63	66	FD	A0	1E	4F	30	E7	C9	E1	C5	C3	19	F7	6D
7	62	34	11	97	2F	AD	F8	D5	84	D6	D4	EB	D3	DA	21	B1
8	6A	A7	D9	AB	82	81	96	10	0B	B3	8B	70	8A	7D	F6	EE
9	1D	D1	E0	F4	4D	3B	39	CB	17	BB	FE	5F	E5	B9	1F	7C
A	03	D8	46	3D	A1	B2	1A	A4	50	FF	69	E8	88	3A	4C	5D
B	F2	BD	7F	64	7E	71	B4	0D	36	8C	74	9B	52	E6	E2	B7
C	4B	2B	BC	12	CC	5A	92	B6	77	7B	F9	AE	8F	D7	EC	08
D	16	05	8D	5C	09	FA	04	15	33	31	CA	94	14	2E	68	AC
E	41	38	45	99	B5	23	3C	49	20	61	48	7A	98	CE	55	A9
F	DB	54	4E	B8	06	89	BA	DC	60	57	F1	40	27	2D	EA	00

Table 5. Absolute walsh hadamard distribution of component boolean functions for progressive construction

BF_i	NL	S-NL	AWHD													
			0	2	4	6	8	10	12	14	16	18	20	22	24	26
BF_1	116	116	16	0	16	64	80	64	16							
BF_2	114	114	40	60	53	82	96	98	67	16						
BF_3	112	112	74	143	144	151	170	153	120	65	4					
BF_4	112	110	222	291	343	260	286	230	233	113	68	2				
BF_5	110	108	361	698	672	621	550	441	326	228	137	60	2			
BF_6	112	106	799	1507	1383	1231	962	812	618	403	271	142	60	2		
BF_7	106	104	1616	3126	2706	2359	2107	1612	1127	760	500	276	135	59	1	
BF_8	108	102	3424	6147	5646	4775	4031	3058	2238	1489	926	526	316	132	59	1

results show that the for $n \times m$ S-Box ($n = 8, m \in \{1, \cdots, 8\}$), the $n \times m$ S-Boxes nonlinearity ($S\text{-}NL$) decreases progressively by one level for each value of m, starting with $NL = 116$ and ending with $NL = 102$ when $m = 8$.

Table 6. Comparison on the coordinates boolean functions nonlinearity

S-Box	1	2	3	4	5	6	7	8	Avg.
PSAHC 1	116	116	116	116	116	116	116	116	116
AES-S-Box	112	112	112	112	112	112	112	112	112
PSAHC 2	116	114	112	112	110	112	106	108	111.25
In [22]	110	110	110	110	112	112	110	110	110.5
In [21]	108	108	108	110	110	110	110	108	109
In [20]	108	108	108	108	108	108	108	108	108

It is clear from the comparison of the proposed method with the existing ones in Table 6, that the PSAHC1 version proposes the highest nonlinearity that can be obtained for the coordinate Boolean functions of an S-Box and their average nonlinearity.

5   Conclusion and Future Work

Through the preliminary tests, we conclude that the proposed method is very efficient for the both Boolean functions and S-Boxes construction cases. Thus, the PSAHC method ensures to get deterministically a nonlinearity equal to 116 for 8-variables Boolean functions and the lowest AWHD for the best results. While for the S-Box case, the maximum nonlinearity obtained with the PSAHC1 version is 96. However, to the best of our knowledge, it is the first method that can propose an unlimited number of S-Boxes with a nonlinearity of their coordinate Boolean functions equal to 116. Furthermore, the nonlinearity is not more than 102 with the PSAHC2 version. In addition, this nonlinearity of 102 is achieved deterministically for PSAHC2 with a best case, having a distance of only one Affine Boolean function from a 104 nonlinearity (with only one component BF with $NL = 102$, which has only one value in the highest coefficient of AWHD [26,1]), which is close to the maximum nonlinearity (104) that can be obtained by the existing approaches based on heuristics over a random initial start[1] population or individual.

Moreover, S-Box construction technique proposed in this paper, which is based on the progressive incorporation of coordinates Boolean functions highlights the previous research done around the construction of Boolean functions with good cryptographic properties. Thus, existing methods can be used to construct the first coordinate Boolean function of the S-Box.

As future work, this method can be examined with other cryptographic properties, like the autocorrelation.

References

1. Maitra, S., Pasalic, E.: Further constructions of resilient Boolean functions with very high nonlinearity. In: Helleseth, T., Kumar, P.V., Yang, K. (eds.) Sequences and their Applications. DISCMATH, pp. 265–280. Springer, London (2002). https://doi.org/10.1109/TIT.2002.1013128
2. Millan, W., Clark, A., Dawson, E.: Smart hill climbing finds better boolean functions. In: Workshop on Selected Areas in Cryptology 1997, Workshop Record, pp. 50–63 (1997)
3. Millan, W., Clark, A., Dawson, E.: An effective genetic algorithm for finding highly nonlinear boolean functions. In: Han, Y., Okamoto, T., Qing, S. (eds.) ICICS 1997. LNCS, vol. 1334, pp. 149–158. Springer, Heidelberg (1997). https://doi.org/10.1007/BFb0028471
4. Clark, J.A., Jacob, J.L.: Two-stage optimisation in the design of boolean functions. In: Dawson, E.P., Clark, A., Boyd, C. (eds.) ACISP 2000. LNCS, vol. 1841, pp. 242–254. Springer, Heidelberg (2000). https://doi.org/10.1007/10718964_20
5. Clark, J.A., Jacob, J.L., Stepney, S., Maitra, S., Millan, W.: Evolving boolean functions satisfying multiple criteria. In: Menezes, A., Sarkar, P. (eds.) INDOCRYPT 2002. LNCS, vol. 2551, pp. 246–259. Springer, Heidelberg (2002). https://doi.org/10.1007/3-540-36231-2_20
6. Millan, W.: How to improve the nonlinearity of bijective S-boxes. In: Boyd, C., Dawson, E. (eds.) ACISP 1998. LNCS, vol. 1438, pp. 181–192. Springer, Heidelberg (1998). https://doi.org/10.1007/BFb0053732
7. Millan, W., Burnett, L., Carter, G., Clark, A., Dawson, E.: Evolutionary heuristics for finding cryptographically strong S-boxes. In: Varadharajan, V., Mu, Y. (eds.) ICICS 1999. LNCS, vol. 1726, pp. 263–274. Springer, Heidelberg (1999). https://doi.org/10.1007/978-3-540-47942-0_22

---

[1] Random initial start means that the initial population or individual is not algebraically constructed (base function) like the finite field inversion based S-Box.

8. Daemen, J., Rijmen, V.: The Design of Rijndael. AES - The Advanced Encryption Algorithm. Springer, Berlin (2002)
9. Fuller, J., Millan, W.: Linear redundancy in S-boxes. In: Johansson, T. (ed.) FSE 2003. LNCS, vol. 2887, pp. 74–86. Springer, Heidelberg (2003). https://doi.org/10. 1007/978-3-540-39887-5_7
10. Fuller, J., Millan, W.: On linear Redundancy in the AES S-Box (2002)
11. Tesař, P.: A new method for generating high non-linearity S-boxes. Radioengineering **19**, 23–26 (2010)
12. Gao, S., Ma, W., Feng, J., Guo, N., Yan, Y.: Improved hill-climbing methods in the design of bijective S-boxes. In: 2010 Sixth International Conference on Natural Computation (ICNC), pp. 2378–2380 (2010). https://doi.org/10.1109/ICNC.2010. 5584026
13. Ivanov, G., Nikolov, N., Nikova, S.: Reversed genetic algorithms for generation of bijective S-boxes with good cryptographic properties. Cryptogr. Commun. **8**, 247–276 (2016). https://doi.org/10.1007/s12095-015-0170-5
14. Clark, J.A., Jacob, J.L., Stepney, S.: The design of S-boxes by simulated annealing. New Gener. Comput. **23**, 219–231 (2005). https://doi.org/10.1007/BF03037656
15. Xiangyang, X.: The block cipher for construction of S-boxes based on particle swarm optimization. In: 2010 2nd International Conference on Networking and Digital Society (ICNDS), pp. 612–615 (2010). https://doi.org/10.1109/ICNDS.2010. 5479283
16. Ahmad, M., Bhatia, D., Hassan, Y.: A novel ant colony optimization based scheme for substitution box design. Procedia Comput. Sci. **57**, 572–580 (2015). https:// doi.org/10.1016/j.procs.2015.07.394
17. Isa, H., Jamil, N., Z'aba, M.R.: Construction of cryptographically strong S-boxes inspired by bee waggle dance. New Gener. Comput. **34**, 221–238 (2016). https:// doi.org/10.1007/s00354-016-0302-2
18. Picek, S., Cupic, M., Rotim, L.: A new cost function for evolution of S-boxes. Evol. Comput. **24**, 695–718 (2016). https://doi.org/10.1162/EVCO_a_00191
19. Hussain, I., Shah, T., Gondal, M.A., Mahmood, H.: An efficient approach for the construction of LFT S-boxes using chaotic logistic map. Nonlinear Dyn. **71**, 133–140 (2013). https://doi.org/10.1007/s11071-012-0646-1
20. Wang, Y., Wong, K., Li, C., Li, Y.: A novel method to design S-box based on chaotic map and genetic algorithm. Phys. Lett. A **376**, 827–833 (2012). https:// doi.org/10.1016/j.physleta.2012.01.009
21. Yong, W., Peng, L., Yong, W.: An improved method to obtaining S-box based on chaos and genetic algorithm. 3733 (2015). https://doi.org/10.1080/1023697X. 2012.10669006
22. Wang, Y., Lei, P.: A method for constructing bijective S-box with high nonlinearity based on chaos and optimization. **25**, 1–15 (2015). https://doi.org/10.1142/ S0218127415501278
23. Seghier, A.: Progressive two-bits tweak for linear redundancy reduction from finite field S-boxes. In: Proceedings of the 8th International Conference on Communication and Network Security, pp. 50–55 (2018). https://doi.org/10.1145/3290480. 3290490
24. Carlet, C.: Vectorial boolean function Cryptography. In: Boolean Models and Methods in Mathematics, Computer Science, and Engineering (2010)
25. Picek, S., Santana, R., Jakobovic, D.: Maximal nonlinearity in balanced boolean functions with even number of inputs, revisited. In: 2016 IEEE Congress on Evolutionary Computation (CEC), pp. 3222–3229 (2016). https://doi.org/10.1109/CEC. 2016.7744197

26. Burnett, L., Millan, W., Dawson, E., Clark, A.: Simpler methods for generating better boolean functions with good cryptographic properties. Australas. J. Comb. **29**, 231–248 (2004)
27. Izbenko, Y., Kovtun, V., Kuznetsov, A.: The design of boolean functions by modified hill climbing method. In: 2009 Sixth International Conference on Information Technology: New Generations, pp. 356–361 (2009). https://doi.org/10.1109/ITNG.2009.102

Accelerating SM2 Digital Signature Algorithm Using Modern Processor Features

Long Mai[1,2]($\boxtimes$), Yuan Yan[1,2], Songlin Jia[1,2], Shuran Wang[1,2],
Jianqiang Wang[1,2], Juanru Li[1], Siqi Ma[2], and Dawu Gu[1]

[1] Shanghai Jiao Tong University, Shanghai, China
{root_mx,turing,jsl_713,wshuran,jarod,
dwgu}@sjtu.edu.cn,wjq.sec@gmail.com
[2] Data 61, CSIRO, Eveleigh, Australia
siqimslivia@gmail.com

Abstract. The public key cryptographic algorithm SM2 is now widely used in electronic authentication systems, key management systems, and e-commercial applications systems. As an asymmetric cryptographic algorithm is based on elliptic curves cryptographic (ECC), the SM2 algorithm involves many complex calculations and is expected to be sufficiently optimized. However, we found existing SM2 implementations are less efficient due to the lack of proper optimization. In this paper, we propose `Yog-SM2`, an optimized implementation of SM2 digital signature algorithm, that uses features of modern desktop processors such as extended arithmetic instructions and the large cache. `Yog-SM2` utilizes new features provided by modern processors to re-implement functions of big number arithmetic, prime field modular, elliptic curve point calculation, and random number generation. The use of these new hardware features significantly improves the performance of both SM2 signing and verifying. Our experiments demonstrated that the execution speed of `Yog-SM2` exceeds four mainstream SM2 implementations in state-of-the-art cryptographic libraries such as `OpenSSL` and `Intel ippcp`. In addition, `Yog-SM2` also achieves a better performance (97,475 sign/s and 18,870 verify/s) against the OpenSSL's optimized implementation of ECDSA-256 (46,753 sign/s and 16,032 verify/s, OpenSSL-1.1.1b x64) on a mainstream desktop processor (Intel i7 6700, 3.4 GHz). It indicates that SM2 digital signature is promising in a widespread application scenarios.

Keywords: SM2 Digital Signature Algorithm · Instruction set extensions · Elliptic curve cryptography

This work was partially supported by the Key Program of National Natural Science Foundation of China (Grant No. U1636217), the General Program of National Natural Science Foundation of China (Grant No. 61872237), the National Key Research and Development Program of China (Grant No. 2016QY071401), and the Major Project of Ministry of Industry and Information Technology of China (Grant No. 2018-36). We especially thank Ant Financial Services Group for the support of this research within the *SJTU-AntFinancial Security Research Centre*.

© Springer Nature Switzerland AG 2020
J. Zhou et al. (Eds.): ICICS 2019, LNCS 11999, pp. 430–446, 2020.
https://doi.org/10.1007/978-3-030-41579-2_25

1   Introduction

Issued by the State Cryptography Administration of China on December 17th, 2010, SM2 public key cryptographic algorithm is an asymmetric cryptography algorithm based on elliptic curves cryptography (ECC) and can be used to implement digital signature algorithm (DSA), key exchange protocol, and public key encryption. Later, SM2 digital signature algorithm was officially defined as an international standard in ISO/IEC14888-3/AMD1 on November 3rd, 2017. In reality, SM2 has been widely adopted in various application scenarios especially for financial industries (e.g., the bank transaction system [7]), industrial systems (e.g., PetroChina [2]), blockchain [8], and data protection (e.g., video conference program [13]).

Theoretically, elliptic curve based digital signature algorithms not only achieve a better security but also requires a smaller storage compared to the RSA digital signature algorithm. Thus, existing software products are recommended to update their crypto components in using such digital signature algorithms such as SM2DSA (SM2 Digital Signature Algorithm) and ECDSA (Elliptic Curve Digital Signature Algorithm). However, this implementation scheme significantly affects the actual execution speed of digital signature algorithms in real-world crypto libraries. For SM2DSA, it is generally more complex than the state-of-the-art ECDSA due to its structure and chosen parameters. In response, a series of researches [30,36–38] focus on improving the performance of SM2DSA. Previous researches [32,39] mainly study how to optimize SM2 at the hardware level. From the perspective of software optimization, Gueron *et al.* [29] aimed at optimizing two crucial operations–point-addition (*PA* for short) and point-doubling (*PD* for short) by implementing them in different coordinates. A more comprehensive work introduced by Brown *et al.* [28] is to optimize *PD* operation in *Jacobian* coordinates, *PA* in mixed *Affine-Jacobian* coordinates, fixed-point scalar multiplication by *comb method with two tables*, and free-point scalar multiplication by *window NAF* (non-adjacent form) method.

Unfortunately, we observed that seldom research considers how to exploit features of modern processors (e.g., instruction set extensions of Intel core and AMD Ryzen) to improve the execution speed of SM2DSA, although such features have being utilized by many state-of-the-art cryptographic libraries to achieve a highly-optimized version of ECDSA. For instance, in the latest OpenSSL (i.e., OpenSSL-1.1.1+), the optimized version of ECDSA executes three times faster than the compatible version (i.e., the one without involving new features of processors), and 23 times faster than its SM2DSA implementation (i.e., the one without involving new features of processors). If similar features of modern processors can be utilized by SM2DSA, the performance is expected to be improved significantly.

In response, in this paper we propose Yog-SM2, an optimized SM2DSA implementation by utilizing various hardware features of modern desktop processors. In detail, Yog-SM2 customizes functions of **big number arithmetic, modular operations, scalar multiplication,** and **random number generator** using extended arithmetic instructions provided by cutting-edge processors. Through applying such hardware based optimizations, Yog-SM2 achieves a considerable execution speed (97,475 sign/s and 18,870 verify/s) against its counterpart ECDSA of OpenSSL-1.1.1b x64 (46,753 sign/s and 16,032 verify/s) on an Intel i7 6700 processor. Moreover, Yog-SM2 outperforms four mainstream implementations of SM2DSA in state-of-the-art open source cryptographic libraries. To the best of our knowledge, Yog-SM2 is the most efficient SM2DSA implementation with nowadays desktop processors.

In summary, this paper achieves the following three contributions:

- We built Yog-SM2, a processor level optimized SM2DSA implementation. It fully utilizes various features of modern processors and thus significantly reduces the execution overhead of both signature and verification.
- Yog-SM2 re-implement many low-level functions such as a novel fixed-point scalar multiplication scheme which only consumes 31 PA operations to implement a 256-bit scalar multiplication for a specify base point on target elliptic curve, and a specific random number generator with only 82 instructions executed. This guarantees that Yog-SM2 is highly compact and efficient.
- Yog-SM2 not only outperforms existing SM2DSA implementations but also ECDSA implementations. The design and implementation of Yog-SM2 are expected to help designers of cryptographic algorithms to optimize other ciphers especially public key ciphers.

2   Background

2.1   SM2 Implementation

SM2 is an elliptic curve public key cryptographic algorithm issued by Chinese State Cryptography Administration on December 17th, 2010 [12]. Later, it was officially included in ISO/IEC14888-3/AMD1 on November 3rd, 2017. SM2 can be used for key-exchanging, data encryption and decryption, digital signature and verification [19–23]. In this paper, we only focus on digital signature.

To implement a SM2DSA algorithm, a series of complex calculations with both big numbers and elliptic curves are required. In practice, a typical implementation of SM2 requires the following functions as illustrated in Fig. 1. In the following, we introduce key functions in SM2 implementation:

- **Big Number Arithmetic Functions:** Big number arithmetic functions are fundamental for SM2. Those functions perform the basic arithmetic calculation (e.g., add, mod) of big number (e.g., 256-bit). Cryptographic libraries (e.g., OpenSSL [17] and Botan [5]) often implement their own big number arithmetic functions, or refer to some big number library such as the GNU MP (GMP) Bignum Library [9]. They usually support any length of big number for compatibility.
- **Prime Modular Functions:** Prime modular functions implements the operations of *modular multiplication, modular square, modular inversion*, etc. In addition, modular operations are usually used with arithmetic operations.

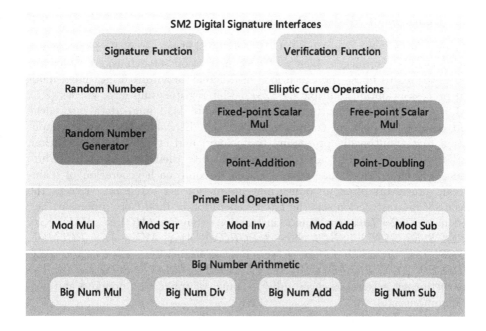

Fig. 1. Overview of SM2DSA algorithm

For example, a modular multiplication contains two operations: a multiplication and a modular reduction. Another feature for prime modular functions is that they will be involved when we convert a point from *Jacobian* coordinates to *Affine* coordinates. Note that most modular functions are time-consuming operations and thus directly influence the performance of both signature and verification functions.

– **Elliptic Curve Functions:** As the basic calculation of Elliptic Curve points, the *PA* and *PD* operations are basis of the elliptic curve point scalar multiplication. Scalar multiplication is classified to two types: *fixed-point scalar multiplication* and *free-point scalar multiplication*. Fixed-point scalar multiplication is used in both signature function and verification function, while free-point scalar multiplication is only used in verification function.

– **Random Number Functions:** The generation of an SM2 digital signature requires a random number to prove its security. To obtain a secure random number, traditional implementations usually need to collect information about the current environment to first generate a seed with high entropy, and then use a pseudo random number generator (PRNG) to extend the seed to a random number (e.g., 256-bit).

In addition to those functions, most SM2 implementations would provide high-level *sign* and *verify* interfaces to help generate digital signatures as well as verify them.

2.2   Features of Modern Processors

Modern processors (e.g., Intel CPUs with Skylake or CoffeeLake micro-architecture) introduces a plenty of new instruction set extensions and hardware features to boost the executions of different programs. First, most modern processors obtain multiple 64/128/256-bit registers and large caches (e.g., 8M L3 cache). These features allow software to load more data into cache and registers to perform complex computation. Especially for vector computation (e.g., multimedia processing technology) and cryptographic algorithm, and those new features can efficiently accelerate their processing procedure and speed the performance of application. Second, each generation of mainstream processors often introduce new instruction set extensions. Except the basic x86/64 instruction set, the latest generation of Intel Core processor (i.e., codename *Coffee Lake*) contains 30 instruction extensions (*MOVBE, MMX, SSE, SSE2, SSE3, SSSE3, SSE4.1, SSE4.2, POPCNT, AVX, AVX2, AES, PCLMUL, FSGSBASE, RDRND, FMA3, F16C, BMI, BMI2, VT-x, VT-d, TXT, TSX, RDSEED, ADX, PREFETCHW, CLFLUSHOPT, XSAVE, SGX, MPX*). The instruction set extensions cover a diverse range of application domains and programming usages.

3   Yog-SM2

In this section we present Yog-SM2, a highly-optimized implementation of the SM2DSA algorithm. Yog-SM2 fully utilizes several features of modern processors such as Intel Core and AMD Ryzen, and achieves a considerable performance increase in comparison with its counterpart (i.e., the optimized ECDSA in OpenSSL). In detail, Yog-SM2 leverages both new instruction extensions of modern processors and hardware characteristics (e.g., larger cache) to optimize functions of **big number arithmetic, modular operations, scalar multiplication**, and **random number generator**. In addition, Yog-SM2 adopts a **redundant instruction removal** policy to implement instruction-level efficient operations. In the following, we elaborate how Yog-SM2 implements each optimization.

3.1   Optimization Strategies

Extended Arithmetic Instructions. Since the calculations of elliptic curve involves a large number of arithmetic operations, Yog-SM2 utilizes extended arithmetic instructions to boost the execution (see Sects. 3.2 and 3.3). In detail, Yog-SM2 utilizes three instructions including *mulx, adcx* and *adox*. Table 1 gives a detailed descriptions about the mentioned instructions. These instructions are alternative versions of existing x86 instruction (*mul,* and *adc*) and fulfil the operations of multiple and addition, respectively. However, these three instructions are designed to support two separate carry chains and thus are used to speed up large integer arithmetic [34]. For instance, the *mulx* instruction does not affect any flag when executing, and the operating results can be saved in any common registers, which is more convenient than the original *mul* instruction. Moreover, this instruction does not overwrite the source operands.

Large Capacity On-Chip Storage. Nowadays processors often carry larger cache (e.g., 16 MB L3 cache) and registers with 64 to 512 bits. These features are leveraged to optimize our Yog-SM2. First, Yog-SM2 adopt a large look-up table (i.e., 512 KB) to accelerate the computation of fixed-point scalar multiplication (see Sect. 3.4). The look-up table contains 8,192 elliptic curve points in *Affine* coordinates. Traditionally, this occurs a frequent memory access and may introduce performance penalty. However, on modern processors the use of this table benefits from the large cache. Second, since most modern processors support 64-bit registers, the arithmetic operations in Yog-SM2 are fully optimized using 64-bit instead of 32-bit registers. In this way, the calculation is sufficiently boosted.

Table 1. Extended instructions used by Yog-SM2 to optimize arithmetic operations

Instruction	Instruction set	Description
mulx r64a, r64b, r/m64	BMI2	Unsigned multiply of r/m64 with RDX without affecting arithmetic flags
adcx r64, r/m64	ADX	Unsigned addition of r64 with CF, r/m64 to r64, writes CF
adox r64, r/m64	ADX	Unsigned addition of r64 with OF, r/m64 to r64, writes OF

3.2 Big Number Arithmetic Optimization

To optimize the big number arithmetic, we fully utilized 64-bit registers and the extended arithmetic instructions in modern processors.

Big Number Multiplication. When preforming big number multiplication $c = a * b$ (a, b and c are 256 bits number), Yog-SM2 separates the multiplication procedure into several rounds with each round calculate $a[i]*b[j]$ (i and j between 0 and 3, and each $a[i]$ or $b[j]$ is 64 bits and store in a single 64-bit register). In each round, Yog-SM2 first performs a multiplication operation with *mulx* instruction, followed by a serial of addition operations with *adcx* or *adox* instruction. Those serial addition operations are to add the product that the *mulx* instruction produces to the final result c. By using new instructions, only the *CF* flag or *OF* flag would be affected, and thus the overhead is much lower.

Big Number Modular. When performing modular operation, Yog-SM2 does not use the traditional "conditional subtraction" method (e.g, calculating $c = a \bmod b$ to judge the condition $a > b$, if satisfied, performs a subtraction). Instead, it uses a non-branch and sequential execution method to execute the modular subtraction. The idea for non-branch and sequential execution benefits from two instructions: *cmovz* and *cmovnz* [6]. These two instructions are the variants of *mov* instruction which performs different actions (e.g., move data or not) according to the zero flag ZF of EFLAGS register. By utilizing these instructions, we avoid the penalty of execution prediction failure and thus make better use of the CPU resources.

Another optimization for modular operation is to merge it with other operations. Aiming at higher performance, merging modular operation with other operations could reduce unnecessary instructions as well as extra memory accesses. For example, Yog-SM2 implements a big number modular addition operation *modAdd* instead of two separated functions (a modular operation and a addition operation). When it is frequently invoked, the cost of function call and return is reduced from twice to once.

3.3   Modular Operation Optimization

The implementation of Yog-SM2 adopts optimized modular multiplication and modular inversion, which benefit from the extended arithmetic instructions. Moreover, we improve the Montgomery modular multiplication by integrating multiplication operation into modular operation to reduce memory access operations and increase the efficiency of register usage. At the same time, we inline all sub functions of modular inversion to accelerate its procedure.

Modular Multiplication. We optimized the traditional Word-by-Word Montgomery Friendly Multiplication (*WW-MF*) algorithm used in modular multiplication with the *mulx*, *adcx*, and *adox* instructions. For two 256-bit numbers a and b (both can be saved by four 64-bit registers), the calculation of multiplication can be divided into four rounds:

1. Calculate $a * b[0]$, ($b[0]$ is the less signification 64 bits of b)
2. Calculate $a * b[1]$,
3. Calculate $a * b[2]$,
4. Calculate $a * b[3]$, ($b[3]$ is the most signification 64 bits of b)

Here we utilize extended arithmetic instructions to fulfil the multiplication and addition operations. Moreover, we notice that the original *WW-MF* algorithm is first to calculate the multiplication of a and b, storing the result into a temporary 512-bit variable T (which costs eight registers to store it), and then to reduce T from 512 bits to 256 bits by four rounds. In order to optimize the use of registers, we customized this algorithm to integrate four rounds of multiplication operation with four rounds of reduction operation. In other words, we perform one round of reduction operation after one round of multiplication operation. By this way, only **six** instead of **eight** registers are needed to save the intermediate results. Moreover, since the modular P used by SM2 is a Montgomery friendly modular (satisfying $-P^{-1}mod\ 2^s = 1$, s is the word size of current machine, in our environment, $s = 64$), the reduction steps can be further optimized from five steps to four steps.

Modular Inversion. To optimize the modular inversion operation of SM2DSA, we re-implement big number (256-bit) *shift-left, shift-right, addition,* and *subtraction* functions, which are used by the Almost Montgomery Inversion [35] (*AlmMonInv* for short) algorithm, a core algorithm for modular inversion (*AlmMonInv* algorithm is used to support both modular N inversion operation and modular P inversion operation, where N is the order of the base point G in elliptic curve and P is the prime number). We re-implement those functions with *adcx* and *adox* instructions, and inline all sub function in modular inversion to avoid function call and unnecessary memory access operations. In this way, the modular inversion operation is significantly optimized.

3.4   Scalar Multiplication Optimization

The optimization of scalar multiplication is divided into two steps: we first generate a look-up table for fixed-point scalar multiplication and reduce the complexity to only 31 *PA* operations; then we use an adaptive window NAF method to determine the best window for free-point scalar multiplication.

Fixed-Point Scalar Multiplication. We proposed a look-up table based fixed-point scalar multiplication that reduces the complexity to exactly 31 *PA* operations for a 256-bit scalar. The signing of SM2 requires a product of G (the base point of the elliptic curve of SM2 algorithm) with a 256-bit random scalar k. By splitting k into 32 bytes ($k = (k_{31}, ..., k_0)$) and pre-computing 256 possible elliptic curve points $P_i = k_i * 2^{8i} * G$, we generate 8,192 pre-computed points as a look-up table. Note that it consumes less storage space to represent the elliptic curve point in *Affine* coordinates than in *Jacobian* coordinates (i.e., 64 bytes for one point). Our table stores each elliptic curve point using the *Affine* coordinates. In total, the size of the look-up table is 512 KB.

When the signing process needs to compute $k * G$ for arbitrary k, it inquires the look-up table according to certain value of k_i and directly obtains the point P_i. Then it only conducts 31 *PA* operations to add these pre-computed points to get the result of $k * G$. As a result, we speed up the SM2 algorithm substantially.

Free-Point Scalar Multiplication. We found that traditional window method wNAF to optimize the free-point scalar multiplication fails to set the most optimized parameter (i.e., the window size w) for different processors. In Yog-SM2, the best value of w is determined at runtime. Yog-SM2 will choose different value of w used by wNAF and find the best one. In detail, Yog-SM2 evaluate the following runtime metrics–modular multiplication, modular square, and modular inversion. For instance, on a platform with Intel i7 6700 (3.4 GHz) processor, the result shown in Table 2 demonstrates that Yog-SM2 should set w to 3 to obtain the best performance. In comparison, GmSSL [10] and Intel-ippcp [11] both adopt a wNAF with fixed $w = 5$, which are not adaptive to various processors.

Table 2. Performance of wNAF method for different window

Window w	Complexity			Running-time (us)
	M	S	I	
2	1,712	1,282	-	47.85
3	**1,551**	**1,224**	**1**	**45.36**
4	1,477	1,196	3	46.66
5	1,449	1,185	7	56.02

M: modular multiplication; S: modular square; I: modular inversion.

3.5   Random Number Generator

Random number is crucial to SM2 algorithm. During an SM2 signing, it needs a 256-bit random k to help compute the signature. In addition, the random number generator is also used to generate the private key for the digital signature. We observe that generating a random number is usually time-consuming. Traditionally, to generate a (pseudo) random number, a large number of information about the current environment (e.g., memory usage statistics, current process ID, system performance counter, etc.) is collected. Hence, a software pseudo random number generator often executes tens of thousands of instructions to generate a random number.

To optimize the generation of random number, Yog-SM2 utilizes the Intel *RDRAND* hardware instruction [24] to generate random number for SM2 Signing. *RDRAND* is an instruction to obtain random numbers from an on-chip hardware random number generator. It is part of the Intel 64 and IA-32 instruction set architectures and is available in Intel Ivy Bridge processors and the successors. AMD also added support for the instruction in June 2015. By using this feature, Yog-SM2 only needs to execute 82 instructions (including the *RDRAND* instruction) to get a 256-bit random number securely.

3.6   Redundant Instruction Removal

We observe that the implementation of *PD* and *PA* functions contain many redundant instructions. We can remove those unnecessary instructions and thus significantly improve the performance. Figure 2 demonstrate a concrete example of redundant instruction removal. In Fig. 2(a) the function *foo* follows the convention of parameter passing follows the Windows x64 Application Binary

Interface (Windows x64 ABI) standard [3]. However, its function prologue (top box in dashed line) and function epilogue (bottom box in dashed line) are redundant and can be removed. Usually, function prologue and epilogue are necessary to save and restore the execution context of the caller at the invoking site. In our case, however, if the caller and the callee function (i.e., (foo)) DO NOT share registers and stacks. we can remove those unnecessary function prologue and epilogue to reduce memory accesses and thus significantly improve the performance.

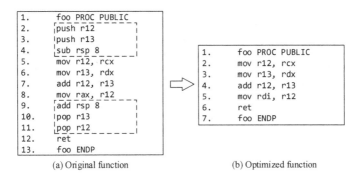

(a) Original function   (b) Optimized function

Fig. 2. Function prologue and epilogue comparison in assembly form

Figure 2(b) shows the optimized form of the original function. The memory access operations (instructions in the box with dashed line) are removed in the optimized version while the functionality is equivalent to the original version. Note that this redundant instruction removal only works if certain requirements are satisfied: (1) Except for RSP and RIP registers, all other registers are inherently volatile in callee functions (e.g., function foo). The optimized convention gives the callee functions the ability to use any common registers without storing them in function prologue and restoring them in function epilogue. (2) All common registers (except RSP and RIP registers) should be saved in callers (functions who call the foo). Only by this way can we use all registers in callee functions freely. (3) The way to pass parameters is different from the original convention. Fortunately, in our SM2 implementation the PD and PA functions are suitable for applying such instruction removal. As a result, Yog-SM2 could benefit from a more compact version of primitive functions.

4   Evaluation

To evaluate Yog-SM2, we first analyzed its **computation complexity** and then tested its actual **execution performance**. For computation complexity, we counted numbers of executed modular multiplication (M), modular squaring (S), modular inversion (I), and division (D). For execution performance, we counted instructions executed for signing and verifying, respectively. In addition, we compared the performance of Yog-SM2 to that of other four libraries including GmSSL, OpenSSL, Botan, and Intel-ippcp.

Our experiments were conducted on a workstation with an Intel core i7 6700 processor (3.4 GHz), 16 GB DDR4 memory, and 512 GB SSD. The operating system is Windows 7 (x64) and the compiler to generate binary code is Visual C++ 2015.

Table 3. Complexity analysis of popular SM2 implementations

Library	Sign				Verify		
	M	S	I	D	M	S	I
GmSSL-2.5.0	290	109	2	-	2,061	1,401	1
OpenSSL-1.1.1b	3,871	1,802	1	-	2,641	1,569	1
Botan-2.10.0	903	338	2	-	4,105	2,820	1
Intel-ippcp_2019u3	301	109	2	1	2,049	1,397	1
Yog-SM2	**263**	**97**	**2**	-	**1,905**	**1,333**	**1**

4.1 Complexity Analysis

We first analyzed the computation complexity of SM2 algorithm implemented in Yog-SM2 and other four mainstream cryptographic libraries. The results are shown in Table 3. Apparently, Yog-SM2 is the most efficient implementation for both signature operations and verification operations. Because of the optimized look-up table, fixed-point scalar multiplication reduces the needed calculations. To sign a message, Yog-SM2 only required 263 modular multiplication, 97 modular squaring, and two modular inversion. While performing a signature verification, Yog-SM2 proceeded 1,905 modular multiplication, 1,333 modular squaring, and one modular inversion. We also observed that OpenSSL has the highest complexity for the signature operation. Consider the verification operation, Botan has the highest complexity. By manually inspected their code, we found the root cause of such a high complexity: (1) OpenSSL adopts the Montgomery ladder algorithm [16], a constant time algorithm, to sign messages. This significantly increases the complexity. (2) Botan uses the Binary algorithm for both free-point scalar multiplication and fixed-point scalar multiplication in verification. Although code reuse makes the SM2 implementation of Botan more concise, it raises the computation complexity.

4.2 Execution Performance

We first used the number of executed instructions to evaluate the performance of different SM2 implementations. Results are depicted in Fig. 3. Comparing

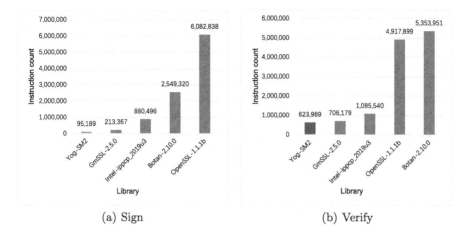

Fig. 3. Performance comparison of SM2 algorithm for each library

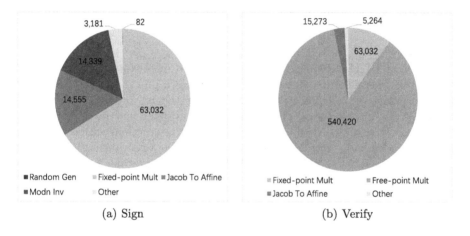

Fig. 4. Instruction consumption of each module in Yog-SM2

with the other SM2 implementations, Yog-SM2 averagely executed only 95,189 instructions for each signature operation, and 623,989 instructions for a verification operation. The other implementations operated more instructions. Specifically, the instructions executed by the SM2 implementation of OpenSSL is 63.9 times higher for signing and 7.9 times higher for verification. The low efficiency might be caused by its applicable security and compatibility for most platforms.

We also noticed that OpenSSL provides a specialized version of ECDSA that can be used on latest processors. To compare our optimization strategies and that of OpenSSL-ECDSA, we tested Yog-SM2 against OpenSSL's optimized implementation of ECDSA-256 on a mainstream desktop processor (Intel i7 6700, 3.4 GHz). Yog-SM2 achieves the speed of 97,475 sign/s and 18,870 verify/s against a 46,753 sign/s and 16,032 verify/s speed of OpenSSL-1.1.1b x64. The result proves that Yog-SM2 is also scalable to be extended to a specific platform for performance improvement.

In order to analyze the instruction composition of Yog-SM2 in detail, we divided Yog-SM2 into different modules and separately analyzed instruction consumption. Figure 4 describes results of instruction consumption, in which Fig. 4(a) and (b) show the consumption of signature instruction component and verification component, respectively. For each round of signature, the random number generator of Yog-SM2 only consumes 82 instructions on average. The fixed-point scalar multiplication operation contains consumption of *PA* operations, which consumes 66.22% of all instructions, The conversion from *Jacobian* coordinates to *Affine* coordinates is also involved whose consumption is almost the same as the modular inversion operation. To execute the modules in verification instruction component, on average, fixed-point scalar multiplication and free-point scalar multiplication executes 10.10% and 86.61% of instructions, respectively. It is worth pointing out that fixed-point scalar multiplication consumes the same for both signature and verification because branches are not created if there is no infinity-point (zero point) for fixed-point scalar multiplication operation.

Comparison of Hardware Improvement. To quantitatively measure the effect of using new features in hardware (i.e., modern processors), we compared the performance of Yog-SM2 with its compatible version–Yog-SM2/C. To make Yog-SM2/C be suitable for all platforms without utilizing new features in modern processors, we replaced all hardware-dependant instructions with compatible x86 instructions and removed all assembly code. The experiment showed that Yog-SM2/C only signs 13,079 times and verifies 1,993 times per second, respectively.

Table 4. Instruction consumption of each core module for Yog-SM2/C and Yog-SM2

Module name	Yog-SM2/C	Yog-SM2	Percentage of instruction reduction
Modp Sqr	610	185	69.7%
Modp Mult	694	223	67.9%
Modp Inv	107,170	14,391	86.6%
Random Gen	5,492	82	98.5%
Fixed-point Mult	365,068	62,475	82.9%

The comparison result of Yog-SM2/C and Yog-SM2 is shown in Table 4. The instruction consumption of modular squaring and modular multiplication in Yog-SM2 reduce 69.7% and 67.9% of instructions while comparing with Yog-SM2/C. Modular inversion in Yog-SM2 consumes 223 instructions, which achieves 86.6% reduction of instruction consumption. For the random number generator, we used $BCryptGenRandom$ provided by Microsoft in Yog-SM2/C and implemented *rdrand* provided by Intel in Yog-SM2. As a result, generating a 256-bit random number costs 5,492 instructions for Yog-SM/C, but only 82 instructions for Yog-SM2. In total, Yog-SM2 reduces 98.5% instructions.

We also tested the SM2 implementation of OpenSSL-1.1.1b and found the similar result. The SM2 implementation of OpenSSL-1.1.1b can only sign 1,988 times and verify 2,326 times per second, respectively. In comparison, the ECDSA-256 (46,753 sign/s and 16,032 verify/s, OpenSSL-1.1.1b x64) achieves a much better speed. Without the accelerating of hardware features, SM2DSA can hardly replace ECDSA in high-performance computation scenarios.

5 Discussion

Since the core operations in Yog-SM2, including PA operation, PD operation and all the called sub functions (e.g., modular multiplication, modular square etc.), were implemented in assembly form, the following optimizations are brought:

- Since the assembly code is not generated relying on source code compilation, a number of unnecessary instructions are eliminated.
- Redundant instructions such as unnecessary *push* and *pop* are removed by the method *redundant instruction removal*.
- As the core operations can fully utilize the extensive register resources by calling new instructions in modern processors in Windows x64 platform, data transfers are mainly carried in registers to speed up the calculation.

Nonetheless, this implementation also causes a scalability limitation. Because the assembly code may vary in different platforms, Yog-SM2 is hard to be directly applied to another platform. For example, the assembly code for Windows cannot run on Linux directly.

Note that cryptographic libraries (e.g., OpenSSL, Libreswan [14]), that rely on certain hardware features for cryptographic algorithms acceleration [4,15, 18], can only be applied to block ciphers and hash function. For instance, in OpenSSL, Intel Advanced Encryption Standard Instructions [1] have been used to accelerate the AES algorithm, and Intel SHA Extensions [25] are used for SHA1 and SHA-256 algorithms. However, these cryptographic instructions can only be applied to block ciphers and hash functions. Unlike those cryptographic libraries, Yog-SM2 utilizes a general-purpose hardware feature to optimize public key ciphers.

6 Related Work

SM2 algorithm can be optimized through two aspects, hardware and software. For SM2 hardware optimization, previous works focused on implementing SM2 algorithm in FPGA and on ASIC chip respectively. Existing software implementation mainly concerned about *PA* and *PD* operations,·modular inversion, and modular multiplication operations are commonly used instead.

PA and PD Operations. Brown *et al.* analyzed the operations *PA* and *PD* in different coordinates. Specifically, they assessed the complexity and running-time overhead of the fixed-point scalar multiplication with difference implementations including binary methods, binary NAF methods, window NAF methods, fixed-based windows methods, and fixed-based comb methods. Nonetheless, new features in modern processors (e.g., large caches) are not utilized. To speed up the operations of *PA* and *PD*, Gueron *et al.* converted the point representation from *Affine* coordinates to *Jacobian* coordinates. The operations *PA* and *PD* are carried to *Jacobian* coordinates, in which the calculations of *PA* and *PD* is faster than those in *Affine* coordinates.

Modular Inversion Optimization. Kaliski *et al.* [31] proposed a method for modular inversion in Montgomery domain, which helps modular inversion operation avoid trial of division operation. To improve the efficiency of the above mentioned Montgomery modular inversion algorithm, both Savas *et al.* [35] and Xu *et al.* [36] proposed optimized algorithms. Savas *et al.* boosted the second phase of the algorithm. Comparing with the original algorithm, the second phase achieves 6.69 times of increase while giving 160 bits of data and the whole algorithm improves 1.36 times of increase. Besides, Sen Xu *et al.* proposed an efficient constant-time implementation of modular inversion, which relies on the prime field base on the Fermat's little theorem. Their implementation improved 89% of the modular inversion operation for 256 bits prime number.

Modular Multiplication Operations. Montgomery [33] proposed an algorithm to calculate modular multiplication without trial division. However, the implementation is not fully optimized. Barrett [27] proposed Barrett reduction algorithm to reduce a number. The above works are further improved by Brown *et al.* They proposed an algorithm that is suitable for any modular without considering whether a number is a prime. However, this algorithm requires that a product of two numbers are calculated first. The algorithm is then applied to reduce the product, which is not efficient in our case. Adalier *et al.* [26] compared the above mentioned algorithms and concluded that Montgomery modular multiplication algorithm performs the best for 256 bits prime number. Unfortunately, those algorithms do not fully consider characteristics of each modular and new features of modern processors.

7   Conclusion

We present `Yog-SM2`, an optimized implementation of SM2DSA algorithm. `Yog-SM2` utilizes features of modern processors such as extended arithmetic instructions and large cache to fulfil efficient signing and verifying. The evaluation of `Yog-SM2` demonstrated that the performance of SM2 signing and verifying boosts significantly in modern desktop processors such as Intel core i7 processor. Compared with state-of-the-art cryptographic libraries, Yog-SM2 also achieves better performance with less instructions executed.

References

1. AES-NI. https://software.intel.com/en-us/articles/intel-advanced-encryption-standard-instructions-aes-ni
2. Anydef. http://www.anydef.com/?page_id=18
3. Application Binary Interface (ABI) for x64. https://docs.microsoft.com/en-us/cpp/build/x64-calling-convention?view=vs-2019
4. AVX instruction acceleration. https://software.intel.com/en-us/articles/improving-openssl-performance
5. Botan library. https://botan.randombit.net/
6. CMOVcc instruction. https://www.felixcloutier.com/x86/cmovcc
7. DONGJIN. http://www.donjin.com/fangan/375.shtml
8. FISCO BCOS. https://fisco-bcos-documentation.readthedocs.io/zh_CN/latest/docs/design/features/guomi.html
9. GMP library. https://gmplib.org/
10. GMSSL library. http://gmssl.org/
11. Intel IPPCP library. https://github.com/intel/ipp-crypto
12. Issued SM2. http://www.oscca.gov.cn/sca/xxgk/2010-12/17/content_1002386.shtml
13. KEDACOM. https://www.kedacom.com/cn/newskd/4800.jhtml
14. Libreswan library. https://libreswan.org/
15. Libreswan library acceleration. https://libreswan.org/wiki/Cryptographic_Acceleration
16. Montgomery Ladder Algorithm. https://hyperelliptic.org/EFD/g1p/auto-shortw-xz.html#doubling-dbl-2002-it-2
17. OpenSSL library. https://www.openssl.org/
18. OpenSSL library acceleration. https://software.intel.com/en-us/articles/improving-openssl-performance
19. Public key cryptographic algorithm SM2 based on elliptic curves part 1: General
20. Public key cryptographic algorithm SM2 based on elliptic curves part 2: Digital signature algorithm
21. Public key cryptographic algorithm SM2 based on elliptic curves part 3: Key exchange protocol
22. Public key cryptographic algorithm SM2 based on elliptic curves part 4: Public key encryption
23. Public key cryptographic algorithm SM2 based on elliptic curves part 5: Parameter definition
24. RDRAND instruction. https://software.intel.com/en-us/articles/intel-digital-random-number-generator-drng-software-implementation-guide
25. SHA extensions. https://software.intel.com/en-us/articles/intel-sha-extensions
26. Adalier, M., et al.: Efficient and secure elliptic curve cryptography implementation of Curve P-256. In: Workshop on Elliptic Curve Cryptography Standards, vol. 66 (2015)

27. Barrett, P.: Implementing the rivest shamir and adleman public key encryption algorithm on a standard digital signal processor. In: Odlyzko, A.M. (ed.) CRYPTO 1986. LNCS, vol. 263, pp. 311–323. Springer, Heidelberg (1987). https://doi.org/10.1007/3-540-47721-7_24

28. Brown, M., Hankerson, D., López, J., Menezes, A.: Software implementation of the NIST elliptic curves over prime fields. In: Naccache, D. (ed.) CT-RSA 2001. LNCS, vol. 2020, pp. 250–265. Springer, Heidelberg (2001). https://doi.org/10.1007/3-540-45353-9_19

29. Gueron, S., Krasnov, V.: Fast prime field elliptic-curve cryptography with 256-bit primes. J. Cryptograph. Eng. 5(2), 141–151 (2015)

30. Hu, X., Zheng, X., Zhang, S., Li, W., Cai, S., Xiong, X.: A high-performance elliptic curve cryptographic processor of SM2 over GF (p). Electronics 8(4), 431 (2019)

31. Kaliski, B.S.: The montgomery inverse and its applications. IEEE Trans. Comput. 44(8), 1064–1065 (1995)

32. Liu, Y., Guo, W., Tan, Y., Wei, J., Sun, D.: An efficient scheme for implementation of SM2 digital signature over GF(p). In: Khachidze, V., Wang, T., Siddiqui, S., Liu, V., Cappuccio, S., Lim, A. (eds.) iCETS 2012. CCIS, pp. 250–258. Springer, Heidelberg (2012). https://doi.org/10.1007/978-3-642-34447-3_23

33. Montgomery, P.L.: Modular multiplication without trial division. Math. Comput. 44(170), 519–521 (1985)

34. Ozturk, E., Guilford, J., Gopal, V., Feghali, W.: New instructions supporting large integer arithmetic on intel architecture processors. Intel white paper (2012)

35. Savas, E., Koç, C.K.: The montgomery modular inverse-revisited. IEEE Trans. Comput. 49(7), 763–766 (2000)

36. Xu, S., et al.: Efficient and constant time modular inversions over prime fields. In: 2017 13th International Conference on Computational Intelligence and Security (CIS), pp. 524–528. IEEE (2017)

37. Zhang, D., Bai, G.: Ultra high-performance ASIC implementation of SM2 with power-analysis resistance. In: 2015 IEEE International Conference on Electron Devices and Solid-State Circuits (EDSSC), pp. 523–526. IEEE (2015)

38. Zhang, D., Bai, G.: High-performance implementation of SM2 based on FPGA. In: 2016 8th IEEE International Conference on Communication Software and Networks (ICCSN), pp. 718–722. IEEE (2016)

39. Zhao, Z., Bai, G.: Ultra high-speed SM2 ASIC implementation. In: 2014 IEEE 13th International Conference on Trust, Security and Privacy in Computing and Communications, pp. 182–188. IEEE (2014)

Improved Differential Attacks on GIFT-64

Huaifeng Chen[1]($\boxtimes$), Rui Zong[2]($\boxtimes$), and Xiaoyang Dong[2]($\boxtimes$)

[1] The 6-th Research Institute of China Electronics Corporation,
Beijing, People's Republic of China
chenhf@ncse.com.cn
[2] Institute for Advanced Study, Tsinghua University,
Beijing, People's Republic of China
{zongrui,xiaoyangdong}@tsinghua.edu.cn

Abstract. GIFT is a new lightweight PRESENT-like block cipher, proposed by Banik et al. at CHES 2017. There are two versions, *i.e.*, GIFT-64 and GIFT-128, with block size 64 and 128 respectively. Both versions have a 128-bit key. The Sbox and the linear layer of GIFT are chosen carefully to avoid single difference bit or linear mask bit path in 2 consecutive rounds. This improves the security of GIFT against differential, linear and linear hull attacks. In this paper, we implement a new automatic search algorithm of differential characteristics on GIFT-64. Considering the situations that some characteristics have the same input and output difference, we find a few of improved differentials with longer rounds or higher probabilities. Among them, the best probability for 12-round differential is $2^{-56.5737}$, while that for 13-round differential is $2^{-61.3135}$. In addition, we find 52 13-round differentials with the same output differences. Based on them, we mount a multiple differential attack on 20-round GIFT-64 with 2^{62} chosen plaintexts, which attacks one more round than the best previous result. Also, we can attack 21-round GIFT-64 with the full codebook, using one differential with probability $2^{-62.0634}$. This is the longest attack as far as we know.

Keywords: Differential · Multiple differential · GIFT-64 · Key-recovery · Single-key

1 Introduction

GIFT lightweight block cipher is designed by Banik et al. [BPP+17], which includes two versions: GIFT-64 and GIFT-128. Both of them have a 128-bit key size and inherit the design framework from PRESENT [BKL+07], but correcting the well-known weakness of PRESENT about linear attacks.

PRESENT [BKL+07] is among the most important lightweight block ciphers, which has been standardized by ISO/IEC [Int11]. PRESENT adopts the well-known SPN structure. The design strategy of round function is very simple, the substitute layer is composed of 16 4-bit Sboxes in parallel and the linear layer is a bit-wise permuation. After years of cryptanalysis on PRESENT by researchers, it remains secure. However, the security margin becomes small. One of the most effective attacks is the linear hull attack [BN14, Cho10].

© Springer Nature Switzerland AG 2020
J. Zhou et al. (Eds.): ICICS 2019, LNCS 11999, pp. 447–462, 2020.
https://doi.org/10.1007/978-3-030-41579-2_26

GIFT not only maintains all the design advances of PRESENT, but also gains more efficiency in various domains, *i.e.*, much smaller hardware implementation, faster encryptions and more secure against the known attacks. Specially, by a dedicated selection of Sbox and bit permutation, it avoids the single active bit transitions for two consecutive rounds in both differential and linear characteristics, which stops the very effective linear hull attacks. Moreover, the hardware cost of the GIFT Sbox is smaller than that of PRESENT Sbox and its key schedule is much simpler than PRESENT, which makes GIFT more lightweight. In addition, in the round based hardware implementation, the area of GIFT is even smaller the recently proposed lightweight block ciphers SKINNY [BJK+16] and SIMON [BSS+15].

GIFT has received much attention from cryptography communities. At CT-RSA 2019, Zhu et al. [ZDY19] gave the first third-party cryptanalysis on GIFT, including a 19-round and a 22-round key-recovery attack on GIFT-64 and GIFT-128, respectively. Sasaki et al. [Sas18] improved the meet-in-the-middle (MitM) attack on 15-round GIFT-64. Zhou et al. [ZZDX19] listed some best differential characteristics for GIFT-64. Li et al. [LWZZ19] extend the key-recovery attack on GIFT-128 to 26 rounds. All the above are about attacks in single-key setting. Liu et al. [LLL+19] found a 21-round differential characteristic on GIFT-128. In related-key setting, Liu and Sasaki [LS19] gave a 23-round and a 21-round boomerang attack on GIFT-64 and GIFT-128, respectively. Chen et al. [CWZ] gave a 23-round related-key rectangle attack on GIFT-64, and Zhao et al. [ZDM+19] improved it to a 24-round attack.

Due to the nice performance and high security level, many lightweight designs choose GIFT as their basic primitives, such as SUNDAE-GIFT [BBP+], TGIF [IKM+], GIFT-COFB [BCI+] Elastic-Tweak [CDJ+19]. Notably, SUNDAE-GIFT [BBP+], GIFT-COFB [BCI+] have been recently selected as the second round candidates of the ongoing NIST Lightweight Cryptography (LWC) standardization project [NIS]. Hence, it is quit important to understand the security level of GIFT block cipher.

In this paper, we focus on the security of GIFT-64 against differential attack [BS91]. All the previous differential attacks on GIFT are based on automatic tools, such as MILP [ZDY19,ZZDX19,LWZZ19], SAT [Sas18] or STP [LLL+19]. In this paper, following Matsui's branch and bound [Mat94] method, we design a new automatic program to find the differentials of GIFT-64. Based on our new tool, we can find a cluster of 12-round or 13-round characteristics with the same input and output difference, hence the probabilities of the differentials are improved. Concretely, we find the best probability for 12-round differential is $2^{-56.5737}$, while the best previous one is 2^{-58}, and the best probability of 13-round differential is $2^{-61.3135}$, while the best previous one is 2^{-62}. In addition, we find 52 13-round differentials with the same output differences. Based on them, we mount a multiple differential attack on 20-round GIFT-64 with 2^{62} chosen plaintexts, which attacks one more round than the best previous result. Also, we can attack 21-round GIFT-64 with the full codebook, using a 13-round differential with probability $2^{-62.0634}$.

At ToSC 2019, Zhao et al. [ZDJ19] fully considered the impact of the input and output differences of a distinguisher on the differential attack and took this condition into account when programming the the differential search algorithm. They showed that a differential distinguisher with smaller probability may derive better key-recovery attack than that with larger probability, if the distinguisher causes fewer active bytes when extending several rounds in both sides. Inspired by Zhao et al. [ZDJ19], we do not use the 13-round differential with the largest probability, but as shown in Table 4 of Sect. 3.3, we use the differential whose hamming weight of the input difference is only 2 to launch our key-recovery attacks. Hence, when adding several rounds at the beginning, the difference will propagate to fewer bits. We summarize the related results and our attacks in Table 1.

Table 1. Cryptanalysis results of GIFT-64

Single-key setting						
Rounds	Approach	Setting	Time	Data	Memory	Ref.
14	IC	SK	2^{97}	2^{63}	–	[BPP+17]
15	MITM	SK	2^{120}	2^{64}	–	[BPP+17]
15	MITM	SK	2^{112}	–	–	[Sas18]
19	Differential	SK	2^{112}	2^{63}	–	[ZDY19]
20	**Multiple differential**	**SK**	$\mathbf{2^{112.68}}$	$\mathbf{2^{62}}$	$\mathbf{2^{112}}$	Sect. 4
20	**Differential**	**SK**	$\mathbf{2^{101.68}}$	$\mathbf{2^{64}}$	$\mathbf{2^{96}}$	Sect. 5
21	**Differential**	**SK**	$\mathbf{2^{107.61}}$	$\mathbf{2^{64}}$	$\mathbf{2^{96}}$	Sect. 5
Related-key setting[†]						
Rounds	Approach	Setting	Time	Data	Memory	Ref.
23	Boomerang	RK	$2^{126.6}$	$2^{63.3}$	–	[LS19]
23	Rectangle	RK	2^{107}	2^{60}	2^{60}	[CWZ]
24	Rectangle	RK	$2^{91.58}$	2^{60}	$2^{60.32}$	[ZDM+19]

[†]: Note that there is no security claim of GIFT under the related-key setting.

Outlines of the Paper

This paper is organised as follows. Section 2 gives the definition of symbols used in this paper and describes the lightweight block cipher GIFT-64. Section 3 illustrates the search algorithm and gives some new differential distinguishers. Then we make the multiple differential and differential attacks in Sects. 4 and 5. Finally, we conclude this paper in Sect. 6.

2   Preliminaries

2.1   Notations and Definitions of GIFT

In this section, the notations are defined as follows:

ΔP : the difference in plaintext,
Δ_S^i : the difference after SubCells operation in Round i, $0 \leq i \leq r-1$,
Δ_P^i : the difference after PermBits operation in Round i, $0 \leq i \leq r-1$,
Δ_K^i : the difference after AddRoundKey operation in Round i, $0 \leq i \leq r-1$,
$X[j \cdots k]$: j^{th} bit, $\cdots$, k^{th} bit of state X, note that $X[0]$ is the LSB of X.
$\ggg i$: an i-bit right rotation within a 16-bit word.
RK_i' : equal to PermBits$^{-1}(RK_i)$.

2.2   GIFT Block Cipher

GIFT [BPP+17] lightweight block cipher is proposed by Banik *et al.* at CHES 2017. The framework of GIFT is based on the design of PRESENT [BKL+07], but more secure and lightweight due to dedicated design of the Sboxes, bit permutation and the key schedule. GIFT has an SPN structure. There are two versions for GIFT according to the block size *i.e.*, GIFT-64 and GIFT-128. Both two versions adopt a 128-bit key. The numbers of rounds for GIFT-64 and GIFT-128 are 28 and 40, respectively.

There are three operations in each round function, *i.e.*, SubCells, PermBits and AddRoundKey, whose details are defined as follows:

1. SubCells: Apply 16 (or 32) 4-bit Sboxes in parallel to every nibble of the internal state of GIFT-64 (or GIFT-128). Both the two versions adopt the same Sbox shown in Table 2.

Table 2. The Sbox of GIFT

x	0	1	2	3	4	5	6	7	8	9	a	b	c	d	e	f
$GS(x)$	1	a	4	c	6	f	3	9	2	d	b	7	5	0	8	e

2. PermBits: Linear bit permutations $b_{P(i)} \leftarrow b_i$, $\forall i \in \{0, 1, \ldots n-1\}$, where the $P(i)$s are

$$P_{64}(i) = 4\lfloor \frac{i}{16} \rfloor + 16\left(3\lfloor \frac{i \bmod 16}{4} \rfloor + (i \bmod 4)\bmod 4\right) + (i \bmod 4),$$

$$P_{128}(i) = 4\lfloor \frac{i}{16} \rfloor + 32\left(3\lfloor \frac{i \bmod 16}{4} \rfloor + (i \bmod 4)\bmod 4\right) + (i \bmod 4),$$

for GIFT-64 and GIFT-128 respectively.

3. AddRoundKey: The round keys RK is $n/2$-bit, which is extracted from the key state (note that n is the state size and $n = 64$ or 128). Let $RK = U||V = u_{s-1}...u_0||v_{s-1}v_0$, where $s = n/4$.
For GIFT-64, the round key is XORed to the state as

$$b_{4i+1} \leftarrow b_{4i+1} \oplus u_i, \ b_{4i} \leftarrow b_{4i} \oplus v_i, \ \forall i \in \{0, ..., 15\}.$$

For GIFT-128, the round key is XORed to the state as

$$b_{4i+2} \leftarrow b_{4i+2} \oplus u_i, \ b_{4i+1} \leftarrow b_{4i+1} \oplus v_i, \ \forall i \in \{0, ..., 31\}.$$

For both versions, a single bit "1" and a 6-bit constant C are XORed into the internal state at positions $n - 1$, 23, 19, 15, 11, 7 and 3 respectively.

The 128-bit master key is initialized as $K = k_7||k_6||...||k_0$, where $|k_i| = 16$. For GIFT-64, the round key $RK = U||V = k_1||k_0$. For GIFT-128, the round key RK is $RK = U||V = k_5||k_4||k_1||k_0$. And for both versions, the key state is updated as follows,

$$k_7||k_6||...||k_0 \leftarrow (k_1 \ggg 2)||(k_0 \ggg 12)||...||k_3||k_2.$$

For more details of GIFT, we refer to [BPP+17].

3   Search for Differential Trails of GIFT-64

3.1   Our Search Algorithm

Our search algorithm is inspired by Matsui's work on DES in 1994 [Mat95]. It's a recursive algorithm that can search for the best differential characteristic and the best linear expression of S-box based ciphers. Specifically, it derives the best n-round characteristic with probability B_n from knowledge of the best i-round characteristic with probability B_i ($1 \leq i \leq n - 1$).

GIFT-64 is also a S-box based block cipher, Matsui's algorithm can be well applied to search for the best differential characteristic of it. Meanwhile, we add some dedicated constraints. For GIFT-64, every round function has 16 S-boxes, the searching process will be very slow when no constraints about the number of active S-boxes are set, as the algorithm needs to traverse all possible differentials. And also, the probability of a n-round differential is very related with the number of active S-boxes. In our search algorithm, we set up a upper bound of active S-boxes in each round function to be 3, *i.e.*, $t = 3$ in Procedure 2. For the initial state, the upper bound is set to be 2. In this process, the search algorithm traverse all possible difference values. Our algorithm also adopts the depth-first strategy and when the searching process covers enough rounds, it outputs the qualified results.

- **Procedure 1: Determine the initial state**
  1. Let $S_{in} = \{\Delta \in (\mathbb{F}_2^4)^{16}|\Delta \neq 0, wt(\Delta) \leq 2\}$.
  2. We choose the input difference $\Delta X_0 \in S_{in}$ and set the initial probability as $p_0 = 1$.

3. Initialize t as the upper bound of the number of active sboxes in each round and r as the number of searched rounds.
- **Procedure 2: Recursive Search** ($search(i)$)
  1. For each $(i-1)$-round differential characteristic, we get the difference ΔX_{i-1} and corresponding probability p_{i-1}.
  2. Set ΔX_{i-1} as the input difference and get each possible output difference Δ_i (suppose all Δ_is make up the set $S_i(\Delta X_{i-1})$) and extra probability $p_e \neq 0$ after one GIFT-64 round.
  3. Choose $\Delta X_i \in S_i(\Delta X_{i-1}), wt(\Delta X_i) \leq t$, we can get several (suppose m) i-round differential characteristics with probability $p_i = p_{i-1} * p_e$.
  4. If $i < r$, call $search(i+1)$.
  5. If $i = r$, we output all these m differential characteristics represented as $(\Delta X_0, p_0), (\Delta X_1, p_1), \ldots, (\Delta X_r, p_r)$.
  6. We also store a list of probabilities, with $(\Delta X_0, \Delta X_r)$ for indexing, to search the differentials with best probabilities.

3.2   The 12-Round Differentials of GIFT-64

Using the search strategy in Sect. 3.1, we get the best differential trail which covers 12 rounds with the probability of 2^{-58}. It's the longest differential trail that we found with probability larger than 2^{-64}. This is consistent with the probability of the best 12-round differential in [LWZZ19]. In total, we find 864 12-round differential characteristics with the best probability 2^{-58}.

Table 3. 12-round differential characteristic of GIFT-64

Round	State difference	Probability(log_2)	Round	State difference	Probability(log_2)
0	0000000600000006	0	0	0000000600000006	0
1	0000000002020000	−4	1	0000000002020000	−4
2	0000005000000050	−8	2	0000005000000050	−8
3	0000000000000202	−14	3	0000000000000202	−14
4	0000000500000005	−18	4	0000000500000005	−18
5	0000000002020000	−24	5	0000000002020000	−24
6	0000005000000050	−28	6	00a0000000a00000	−30
7	0000000000000202	−34	7	1010000000000000	−34
8	0000000500000005	−38	8	0000a0000000a000	−40
9	0000000002020000	−44	9	0000000001010000	−44
10	0000005000000050	−48	10	0000005000000050	−50
11	0000000000000202	−54	11	0000000000000202	−56
12	0000000500000005	−58	12	0000000500000005	−60

We find 10 12-round differential characteristics with the input difference 0000000600000006 and the output difference 0000000500000005. One characteristic is with probability 2^{-58}, six characteristics with probability 2^{-60}, and the others are with probability 2^{-62}. Thus, the total probability of this differential is $2^{-56.5737}$. Two of them are shown in Table 3.

3.3   The 13-Round Differentials of GIFT-64

Following the search strategy in Sect. 3.1, the best 13-round differential characteristics we found are with probability 2^{-64}. Thus, it is impossible to mount an attack using one single characteristic. In [LWZZ19], a 13-round differential characteristic with probability 2^{-62} is given. We point out that this is because there are 4 active nibbles in the last round of this characteristic. Recall our constraints of the search procedure in Sect. 3.1, the upper bound of the number of active S-boxes in each round is set to 3, this can explain the probability of that characteristic is larger than ours. As the nonzero difference bits in the output difference will diffuse very fast, the characteristic in [LWZZ19] is weaker when used to attack more rounds.

As a result, we consider about the cluster of trails with same input and output differences and search out some qualified 13-round differentials that can be used to mount key recovery attacks. Some of them are shown in Table 4.

Table 4. 13-round differentials of GIFT-64

Index	Input difference	Output difference	Probability(log_2)
1	000000c000000060	0000004000000011	-61.3135
2	000000e0000000e0	0000000000001010	-61.7857
3	00c0000000c00000	0000000000001010	-61.8102
4	0000000000000202	0000000500000005	-62.0634

As shown in Table 4, Differential 1 has the greatest probability. However, its output difference has three active nibbles. This will include too many key bits when it is used to mount attacks. All the other three differentials have two active S-boxes in the output difference. And for Differential 4, there are also only two active S-boxes when reverse the input difference one more round, this feature can be utilized to attack more rounds of GIFT-64.

What's more, we found a few of differentials that have same input difference patterns and same output difference with Differential 2 or Differential 3, which are listed in Tables 10 and 11. The sum of the probabilities of the 16 differentials in Table 10 is $2^{-58.0099}$, while that of the 36 differentials in Table 11 is $2^{-57.8102}$. These 52 differentials has a total probability $2^{-56.9066}$, leading to a significant 13-round multiple differential distinguisher of GIFT-64.

4   Multiple Differential Attack on GIFT-64

In this section, we use 52 13-round differentials to mount the multiple differential cryptanalysis on GIFT-64. When expanded backward several rounds, these differentials have common active sboxes. So we just guess the keys in the backward rounds and sieve the wrong states at the same time for all differentials which help improving the time complexity. See Tables 5 and 6 for the details of the expansion.

By adding three rounds before and four rounds after the distinguisher, we can attack 20-round GIFT-64. Table 5 illustrates the state and subkey details. The first column gives the symbols of state difference and subkeys. The second column gives the difference pattern and the involved subkeys. For the difference pattern, the '0', '1' and '2' denotes one bit 0 difference, 1 difference and undetermined difference respectively. We should point out that there are two '2's in Δ_P^2. In fact, according to the propagation rules of difference patterns, these two bits should have undetermined differences. However, for the target of controlling the data complexity, we forced them to be 0 (represented as $\underline{2}$ in Δ_P^2 and then represented as $\underline{0}$ in Δ_S^2 after the inverse of bit permutation). For involved subkey bits, '1' means that we must guess the corresponding key bits and '0' means we can omit them.

Table 5. Multiple differential cryptanalysis of GIFT-64

ΔP	2222	2222	2222	2222	2222	2222	2222	2222	2222	2222	2222	2222	2222	2222	2222	2222
Δ_S^1	0220	0022	2002	2200	2222	2222	2222	2222	2222	2222	2222	2222	2222	2222	2222	2222
Δ_P^1	2222	2222	2222	2222	2222	2222	2222	2222	0000	2222	2222	2222	0000	2222	2222	2222
RK_1	11	11	11	11	11	11	11	11	00	11	11	11	00	11	11	11
Δ_S^2	0002	2000	0200	0020	0002	2000	0200	0020	000$\underline{0}$	2000	0200	0020	000$\underline{0}$	2000	0200	0020
Δ_P^2	0000	0000	0000	0000	0000	0000	0000	0000	2222	2222	222$\underline{2}$	222$\underline{2}$	0000	0000	0000	0000
RK_2	00	00	00	00	00	00	00	00	00	11	11	11	00	00	00	00
Δ_S^3	0000	0000	0000	0000	0000	0000	0000	0000	2020	0202	2020	0202	0000	0000	0000	0000
Δ_P^3	0000	0000	0000	0000	0000	0000	2222	0000	0000	0000	0000	0000	0000	2222	0000	0000
RK_3	00	00	00	00	00	00	00	00	00	00	00	00	00	00	00	00
Δ_K^3	0000	0000	0000	0000	0000	0000	2222	0000	0000	0000	0000	0000	0000	2222	0000	0000
...							$\sum p_i \approx 2^{-56.9066}$									
Δ_P^{16}	0000	0000	0000	0000	0000	0000	0000	0000	0000	0000	0000	0000	0001	0000	0001	0000
Δ_S^{17}	0000	0000	0000	0000	0000	0000	0000	0000	0000	0000	0000	0000	2222	0000	2222	0000
RK'_{17}	00	00	00	00	00	00	00	00	00	00	00	00	11	00	11	00
Δ_P^{17}	0000	0000	0000	0202	0000	0000	0000	2020	0000	0000	0000	0202	0000	0000	0000	2020
Δ_S^{18}	0000	0000	0000	2222	0000	0000	0000	2222	0000	0000	0000	2222	0000	0000	0000	2222
RK'_{18}	00	00	00	11	00	00	00	11	00	00	00	11	00	00	00	11
Δ_P^{18}	2000	2000	2000	2000	0200	0200	0200	0200	0020	0020	0020	0020	0002	0002	0002	0002
Δ_S^{19}	2222	2222	2222	2222	2222	2222	2222	2222	2222	2222	2222	2222	2222	2222	2222	2222
RK'_{19}	11	11	11	11	11	11	11	11	11	11	11	11	11	11	11	11
Δ_P^{19}	2222	2222	2222	2222	2222	2222	2222	2222	2222	2222	2222	2222	2222	2222	2222	2222
Δ_S^{20}	2222	2222	2222	2222	2222	2222	2222	2222	2222	2222	2222	2222	2222	2222	2222	2222
RK'_{20}	11	11	11	11	11	11	11	11	11	11	11	11	11	11	11	11
Δ_P^{20}	2222	2222	2222	2222	2222	2222	2222	2222	2222	2222	2222	2222	2222	2222	2222	2222

The attack procedure and time complexity estimation are as follows.

1. Data Collection:
   (a) Structure Construction. Since there is no whitening key at the top of GIFT, we can construct structures at X_P^1, just before the first subkey

Table 6. Expand the input differences in Table 11 backward by one round

Δ_P^2	0000	0000	0000	0000	0000	0000	0000	0000	2222	2222	222̲2	222̲2	0000	0000	0000	0000
RK_2	00	00	00	00	00	00	00	00	00	11	11	11	00	00	00	00
Δ_S^3	0000	0000	0000	0000	0000	0000	0000	0000	0202	2020	0202	2020	0000	0000	0000	0000
Δ_P^3	0000	0000	2222	0000	0000	0000	0000	0000	0000	0000	2222	0000	0000	0000	0000	0000
RK_3	00	00	00	00	00	00	00	00	00	00	00	00	00	00	00	00
Δ_K^3	0000	0000	2222	0000	0000	0000	0000	0000	0000	0000	2222	0000	0000	0000	0000	0000

involved. By setting $X_P^1[12 - 15, 28 - 31]$ as const and iterating all the other bits, we get one structure with 2^{56} elements, in which about 2^{111} pairs with difference pattern Δ_P^1 could be obtained.

(b) Choose 2^t structures and we can get $N_1 = 2^{111+t}$ data pairs.

(c) Choose the plaintext-ciphertexts (P, P^*) and (C, C^*). For each state pair (X_P^1, X_P^{1*}) constructed, we can get the plaintexts (P, P^*) by applying the `PermBits`$^{-1}$ and `SubCells`$^{-1}$ operations. Then we obtain the corresponding ciphertext pairs (C, C^*).

2. Key Recovery:

In the procedure of subkey recovery, early distillation skill can be used to optimize the time complexity. The subkeys that need to be guessed are shown in Table 5. Considering one specific differential with probability p_i, one of the multiple differentials constituting the distinguisher, the detailed procedure of counting the right data pairs is as follows.

(a) Guess $RK_1[0, 1]$ and make the first Sbox substitution (the Sbox at $X_P^1[0 - 3]$). Select the pairs with difference $\Delta_S^2[0] = \Delta_S^2[2] = \Delta_S^2[3] = 0$ and about $N_1 * 2^{-3}$ candidates remain. Similarly, guess another 2 subkey bits and select the right candidate pairs until all $RK_1[0 - 5, 8 - 13, 16 - 31]$ are guessed. So, in this step, a similar procedure is processed 14 times and each distillation has a probability 2^{-3}. After this step, about $N_2 = N_1 * 2^{-3*14}$ pairs remain.

(b) Guess $RK_2[8, 9]$ and make the fifth Sbox substitution (the Sbox at $X_P^2[16 - 19]$). Select the pairs with difference $\Delta_S^3[17] = \Delta_S^3[19] = 0$ and about $N_2 * 2^{-2}$ candidates remain. There are 4 active sboxes in this step and a similar procedure is processed 4 times with distillation probability 2^{-2}. After this step, about $N_3 = N_2 * 2^{-2*4}$ pairs remain.

(c) Select the pairs that are consistent with the input difference of the specific differential and about $N_4 = N_3 * 2^{-8}$ pairs remain.

(d) Guess $RK_{20}'[0, 1, 8, 9, 16, 17, 24, 25]$ and make the corresponding inverse Sbox operations. We can get the output difference of the 1-th, 2-th, 3-th and 4-th Sbox at Δ_S^{19}. Since the corresponding input differences for these four Sboxes should be '0002', we select the possible pairs according to the difference distribution table. For each Sbox, half pairs would remain on average. So the probability of this 8-bits guess and distillation is expected to be 2^{-4}. Another three sub-procedures with distillation probability 2^{-4} similar to that can be done. After this step, about $N_5 = N_4 * 2^{-16}$ pairs remain.

(e) Guess $RK'_{19}[0,1]$ and make the first inverse Sbox operation at X_S^{19}. Select the pairs with difference $\Delta_P^{18}[1] = \Delta_P^{18}[2] = \Delta_S^{18}[3] = 0$. The distillation probability should be $2^{-3}/2^{-1} = 2^{-2}$, since the probability 2^{-1} has been considered in the above step. A similar guess and distillation procedure is processed 16 times in this step and about $N_6 = N_5 * 2^{-2*16}$ right pairs remain.

(f) Guess $RK'_{18}[0,1]$ and make the first inverse Sbox operation at X_S^{18}. Select the pairs with difference $\Delta_P^{17}[0] = \Delta_P^{17}[2] = 0$. The distillation probability is 2^{-2}. A similar procedure is processed 4 times in this step and after that about $N_7 = N_6 * 2^{-2*4}$ pairs remain.

(g) Guess $RK'_{17}[2,3]$ and make the second inverse Sbox operation at X_S^{17}. Select the pairs with difference $'0001'$ and the distillation probability is 2^{-4}. Similarly, guess $RK'_{17}[6,7]$ and make the distillation. At last about $N_8 = N_7 * 2^{-8}$ pairs remain for the wrong key guesses while about $N_8^* = N_4 * p_i$ pairs remain for the right key guess.

3. Complexity Estimation:

We list the details of time complexity estimation in Table 7. For the right key guess, the final counter of the right pairs for the differential with probability p_i is expected to be $2^{t+53} * p_i$, while that for the wrong key guesses would be 2^{t-11}. In our multiple differential procedure, we set $t = 6$ and use 64 structures to distinguish the right key and wrong keys, which leads to that about $2^{59} * \sum p_i \approx 4.29$ pairs remain in total for the right key and about $2^{-5} * 52 \approx 1.63$ pairs remain for the wrong keys on average. So the data complexity is $2^{56+6} = 2^{62}$ chosen plaintexts.

Table 7. Time complexity in each step

Step	#Remained	#Keys	Time($\frac{1}{16}-$R)	Pr
a	$N_1 = 2^{t+111}$	$2^{2\times14}$	$2^{t+1} \times (2^{113} + 2^{112} + \ldots + 2^{100})$	$2^{-3\times14}$
b	$N_2 = 2^{t+69}$	$2^{2\times4}$	$2^{t+1} \times (2^{99} \times 4)$	$2^{-2\times4-8}$
c	$N_3 = 2^{t+61}$	–	–	2^{-8}
d	$N_4 = 2^{t+53}$	$2^{8\times4}$	$2^{t+1} \times (2^{97} + 2^{101} + 2^{105} + 2^{109})$	$2^{-4\times4}$
e	$N_5 = 2^{t+37}$	$2^{2\times16}$	$2^{t+1} \times (2^{107} \times 16)$	$2^{-2\times16}$
f	$N_6 = 2^{t+5}$	$2^{2\times4}$	$2^{t+1} \times (2^{107} \times 4)$	$2^{-2\times4}$
g	$N_7 = 2^{t-3}$	$2^{2\times2}$	$2^{t+1} \times (2^{107} + 2^{105})$	$2^{-4\times2}$
Finished	$N_8 = 2^{t-11}$			

Step (a) and (b) can be done only one time for all the 52 differentials while step (c) to step (g) would be processed independently. Since Step (a) dominates the time, the total time complexity is about $2^{121} \times \frac{1}{16} \times \frac{1}{20} = 2^{112.68}$ times 20-round GIFT-64 encryptions. The memory complexity for storing the guessed key bits is 2^{112}.

5   Differential Cryptanalysis on GIFT-64

In this section, we use a 13-round differential

$$0000000000000202 \rightarrow 0000000500000005$$

with probability $2^{-62.0634}$. When expanded backward or forward by one round, there are only 2 active sboxes in both sides, which helps decreasing the number of guessed key bits.

5.1   20-Round Differential Attack on GIFT-64

By adding three rounds before and four rounds after the 13-round distinguisher, we can attack 20-round GIFT-64. Table 8 illustrates the state and subkey details of the attack.

Table 8. 20-round differential cryptanalysis of GIFT-64

ΔP	2222	2222	2222	2222	2222	2222	2222	2222	2222	2222	2222	2222	2222	2222	2222	2222
Δ^1_S	0002	2000	0200	0020	0002	2000	0200	0020	0002	2000	0200	0020	0002	2000	0200	0020
Δ^1_P	0000	0000	0000	0000	0000	0000	0000	0000	2222	2222	2222	2222	0000	0000	0000	0000
RK_1	00	00	00	00	00	00	00	00	11	11	11	11	00	00	00	00
Δ^2_S	0000	0000	0000	0000	0000	0000	0000	0000	2020	0202	2020	0202	0000	0000	0000	0000
Δ^2_P	0000	0000	0000	0000	0000	0000	2222	0000	0000	0000	0000	0000	0000	0000	2222	0000
RK_2	00	00	00	00	00	00	11	00	00	00	00	00	00	00	11	00
Δ^3_S	0000	0000	0000	0000	0000	0000	0010	0000	0000	0000	0000	0000	0000	0000	0010	0000
Δ^3_P	0000	0000	0000	0000	0000	0000	0000	0000	0000	0000	0000	0000	0000	0010	0000	0010
RK_3	00	00	00	00	00	00	00	00	00	00	00	00	00	00	00	00
Δ^3_P	0000	0000	0000	0000	0000	0000	0000	0000	0000	0000	0000	0000	0000	0010	0000	0010
$\cdots$								$p \approx 2^{-62.0634}$								
Δ^{16}_P	0000	0000	0000	0000	0000	0000	0000	0101	0000	0000	0000	0000	0000	0000	0000	0101
Δ^{17}_S	0000	0000	0000	0000	0000	0000	0000	2222	0000	0000	0000	0000	0000	0000	0000	2222
RK'_{17}	00	00	00	00	00	00	00	11	00	00	00	00	00	00	00	11
Δ^{17}_P	0000	2000	0000	2000	0000	0200	0000	0200	0000	0020	0000	0020	0000	0002	0000	0002
Δ^{18}_S	0000	2222	0000	2222	0000	2222	0000	2222	0000	2222	0000	2222	0000	2222	0000	2222
RK'_{18}	00	11	00	11	00	11	00	11	00	11	00	11	00	11	00	11
Δ^{18}_P	2020	2020	2020	2020	0202	0202	0202	0202	2020	2020	2020	2020	0202	0202	0202	0202
Δ^{19}_S	2222	2222	2222	2222	2222	2222	2222	2222	2222	2222	2222	2222	2222	2222	2222	2222
RK'_{19}	11	11	11	11	11	11	11	11	11	11	11	11	11	11	11	11
Δ^{19}_P	2222	2222	2222	2222	2222	2222	2222	2222	2222	2222	2222	2222	2222	2222	2222	2222
Δ^{20}_S	2222	2222	2222	2222	2222	2222	2222	2222	2222	2222	2222	2222	2222	2222	2222	2222
RK'_{20}	11	11	11	11	11	11	11	11	11	11	11	11	11	11	11	11
Δ^{20}_P	2222	2222	2222	2222	2222	2222	2222	2222	2222	2222	2222	2222	2222	2222	2222	2222

The 20-round attack procedure and complexity estimation are as follows.

1. Data Collection:
   (a) Structure Construction. Like the above attack, we also construct structures at X^1_P. By setting $X^1_P[0 - 15, 32 - 63]$ as const and iterating all the other bits, we get one structure with 2^{16} elements, in which about 2^{31} pairs with difference pattern Δ^1_P could be obtained.

(b) Choose 2^t structures and we can get $N_1 = 2^{31+t}$ data pairs.

(c) Choose the plaintext-ciphertexts (P, P^*) and (C, C^*).

2. Key Recovery:

The details of the key guess and data distillation are similar to the above multiple differential attack. So here we simplify the description of the attack and just give the basic steps.

(a) Guess RK_1 and about $N_2 = N_1 * 2^{-8}$ pairs remain.

(b) Guess RK_2 and about $N_3 = N_2 * 2^{-8}$ pairs remain.

(c) Guess RK_{20} and decrypt the pairs by one round.

(d) Guess RK_{19} and about $N_4 = N_3 * 2^{-32}$ pairs remain.

(e) Guess RK_{18} and about $N_5 = N_4 * 2^{-24}$ pairs remain.

(f) Guess RK_{17} and about $N_6 = N_5 * 2^{-8}$ pairs remain.

3. Complexity Estimation:

We list the details of time complexity estimation in Table 9. In our differential procedure, we set $t = 48$ and use 2^{48} structures to distinguish the right key and wrong keys, which leads to that about 2 pairs remain for the right key and about 2^{-1} pairs remain for the wrong keys. So the data complexity is 2^{64} chosen plaintexts. According to Table 9, Step (d) dominates the time and the attack needs about $2^{110} \times \frac{1}{16} \times \frac{1}{20} = 2^{101.68}$ 20-round GIFT-64 encryptions. The memory complexity for storing the guessed key bits is 2^{96}.

Table 9. Time complexity in each step

Step	#Remained	#Keys	Time($\frac{1}{16}$–R)	Pr
a	2^{t+31}	$2^{2\times4}$	$2^{t+1} \times (2^{33} \times 8)$	$2^{-2\times4}$
b	2^{t+23}	$2^{2\times2}$	$2^{t+1} \times (2^{29} + 2^{27})$	$2^{-4\times2}$
c	2^{t+15}	2^{32}	$2^{t+1} \times 2^{55}$	1
d	2^{t+15}	$2^{2\times16}$	$2^{t+1} \times (2^{57} \times 16)$	$2^{-2\times16}$
e	2^{t-17}	$2^{2\times8}$	$2^{t+1} \times (2^{57} + 2^{56} + 2^{55} + \ldots + 2^{50})$	$2^{-3\times8}$
f	2^{t-41}	$2^{2\times2}$	$2^{t+1} \times (2^{47} + 2^{45})$	$2^{-4\times2}$
Finished	2^{t-49}			

5.2 21-Round Differential Attack on GIFT-64

Using the same 13-round differential distinguisher and with the help of key schedule, we can add one more round before the 20-round attack to make the 21-round attack possible. In the 21-round attack, the subkeys involved in the first and last rounds are linear dependent, which means when we guess one subkey, the another one is also determined.

Using the structure constructed above and for each difference pair, we guess the first subkey and decrypt the pairs by one round to obtain the corresponding plaintext-ciphertext pairs. The other attack details are same with the 20-round attack and we omit them here. This attack takes about $2^{48+1+31} \times 2^{32} = 2^{112}$ one round encryptions more than the above attack, leading to that the total time complexity is smaller than $2^{112} \times \frac{1}{21} + 2^{101.68} \times \frac{20}{21} \approx 2^{107.61}$ 21-round encryptions.

6   Conclusion

In this paper, we give a recursive search algorithm of the differential trails for GIFT-64 and several improved differential attack results. With the multiple differential cryptanalysis model, we can attack 20-round GIFT-64, using 2^{62} chosen plaintexts and about $2^{112.68}$ encryptions. Also, using the differential cryptanalysis model, we analyse the 20-round and 21-round GIFT-64. Both attacks need 2^{64} plaintext-ciphertext pairs and the time complexities are $2^{101.68}$ and $2^{107.61}$ respectively. All these attacks cover 1 or 2 more rounds compared with the existing results.

Acknowledgement. The authors thank the anonymous reviewers for helpful comments. This paper is supported by the National Key Research and Development Program of China (No. 2017YFA0303903), the National Natural Science Foundation of China (No. 61902207), the National Cryptography Development Fund (No. MMJJ20180101, MMJJ20170121).

A   Multiple Differentials of GIFT-64

Table 10. 13-round multiple differentials of GIFT-64 (1)

Index	Input difference	Output difference	Probability(log_2)
1	000000e0000000e0	0000000000001010	-61.7857
2	000000f0000000e0	0000000000001010	-61.9312
3	000000e0000000f0	0000000000001010	-61.9312
4	000000e0000000d0	0000000000001010	-61.9312
5	000000d0000000e0	0000000000001010	-61.9312
6	000000f0000000f0	0000000000001010	-62.0099
7	000000f0000000d0	0000000000001010	-62.0099
8	000000d0000000f0	0000000000001010	-62.0099
9	000000d0000000d0	0000000000001010	-62.0099
10	000000f0000000c0	0000000000001010	-62.0931
11	000000e0000000c0	0000000000001010	-62.0931
12	000000d0000000c0	0000000000001010	-62.0931
13	000000c0000000f0	0000000000001010	-62.0931
14	000000c0000000e0	0000000000001010	-62.0931
15	000000c0000000d0	0000000000001010	-62.0931
16	000000c0000000c0	0000000000001010	-62.0931
			$\sum = -58.0099$

Table 11. 13-round multiple differentials of GIFT-64 (2)

Index	Input difference	Output difference	Probability(log_2)
1	0060000000600000	0000000000001010	-61.8102
2	0060000000c00000	0000000000001010	-61.8102
3	00c0000000c00000	0000000000001010	-61.8102
4	00c0000000600000	0000000000001010	-61.8102
5	0070000000600000	0000000000001010	-62.8102
6	0060000000700000	0000000000001010	-62.8102
7	0060000000500000	0000000000001010	-62.8102
8	0050000000600000	0000000000001010	-62.8102
9	0070000000c00000	0000000000001010	-62.8102
10	0060000000f00000	0000000000001010	-62.8102
11	0060000000d00000	0000000000001010	-62.8102
12	0050000000c00000	0000000000001010	-62.8102
13	00f0000000c00000	0000000000001010	-62.8102
14	00f0000000600000	0000000000001010	-62.8102
15	00d0000000c00000	0000000000001010	-62.8102
16	00d0000000600000	0000000000001010	-62.8102
17	00c0000000f00000	0000000000001010	-62.8102
18	00c0000000d00000	0000000000001010	-62.8102
19	00c0000000700000	0000000000001010	-62.8102
20	00c0000000500000	0000000000001010	-62.8102
21	0070000000700000	0000000000001010	-63.8102
22	0070000000500000	0000000000001010	-63.8102
23	0050000000700000	0000000000001010	-63.8102
24	0050000000500000	0000000000001010	-63.8102
25	0070000000f00000	0000000000001010	-63.8102
26	0070000000d00000	0000000000001010	-63.8102
27	0050000000f00000	0000000000001010	-63.8102
28	0050000000d00000	0000000000001010	-63.8102
29	00f0000000f00000	0000000000001010	-63.8102
30	00f0000000d00000	0000000000001010	-63.8102
31	00f0000000700000	0000000000001010	-63.8102
32	00f0000000500000	0000000000001010	-63.8102
33	00d0000000f00000	0000000000001010	-63.8102
34	00d0000000d00000	0000000000001010	-63.8102
35	00d0000000700000	0000000000001010	-63.8102
36	00d0000000500000	0000000000001010	-63.8102
			$\sum = -57.8102$

References

[BBP+]   Banik, S., et al.: Sundae-gift. Submission to Round 1 of the NIST Lightweight Cryptography Standardization process (2019)

[BCI+]   Banik, S., et al.: GIFT-COFB. Submission to Round 1 of the NIST Lightweight Cryptography Standardization process (2019)

[BJK+16] Beierle, C., et al.: The SKINNY family of block ciphers and its low-latency variant MANTIS. In: Robshaw, M., Katz, J. (eds.) CRYPTO 2016. LNCS, vol. 9815, pp. 123–153. Springer, Heidelberg (2016). https://doi.org/10.1007/978-3-662-53008-5_5

[BKL+07] Bogdanov, A., et al.: PRESENT: an ultra-lightweight block cipher. In: Paillier, P., Verbauwhede, I. (eds.) CHES 2007. LNCS, vol. 4727, pp. 450–466. Springer, Heidelberg (2007). https://doi.org/10.1007/978-3-540-74735-2_31

[BN14]   Blondeau, C., Nyberg, K.: Links between truncated differential and multi-dimensional linear properties of block ciphers and underlying attack complexities. In: Nguyen, P.Q., Oswald, E. (eds.) EUROCRYPT 2014. LNCS, vol. 8441, pp. 165–182. Springer, Heidelberg (2014). https://doi.org/10.1007/978-3-642-55220-5_10

[BPP+17] Banik, S., Pandey, S.K., Peyrin, T., Sasaki, Y., Sim, S.M., Todo, Y.: GIFT: a small present. In: Fischer, W., Homma, N. (eds.) CHES 2017. LNCS, vol. 10529, pp. 321–345. Springer, Cham (2017). https://doi.org/10.1007/978-3-319-66787-4_16

[BS91]   Biham, E., Shamir, A.: Differential cryptanalysis of DES-like cryptosystems. In: Menezes, A.J., Vanstone, S.A. (eds.) CRYPTO 1990. LNCS, vol. 537, pp. 2–21. Springer, Heidelberg (1991). https://doi.org/10.1007/3-540-38424-3_1

[BSS+15] Beaulieu, R., Shors, D., Smith, J., Treatman-Clark, S., Weeks, B., Wingers, L.: The SIMON and SPECK lightweight block ciphers. In: Proceedings of the 52nd Annual Design Automation Conference, San Francisco, CA, USA, 7–11 June 2015, pp. 175:1–175:6 (2015)

[CDJ+19] Chakraborti, A., Datta, N., Jha, A., Mancillas-Lopez, C., Nandi, M., Sasaki, Y.: Elastic-Tweak: a framework for short tweak tweakable block cipher. Cryptology ePrint Archive, Report 2019/440 (2019). https://eprint.iacr.org/2019/440

[Cho10]   Cho, J.Y.: Linear cryptanalysis of reduced-round PRESENT. In: Pieprzyk, J. (ed.) CT-RSA 2010. LNCS, vol. 5985, pp. 302–317. Springer, Heidelberg (2010). https://doi.org/10.1007/978-3-642-11925-5_21

[CWZ]   Chen, L., Wang, G., Zhang, G.: MILP-based related-key rectangle attack and its application to GIFT, Khudra, MIBS. Comput. J. **62**, 1805–1821 (2019)

[IKM+]   Iwata, T., et al.: Thank goodness it's Friday (TGIF). Submission to Round 1 of the NIST Lightweight Cryptography Standardization process (2019)

[Int11]   International Standardization of Organization (ISO): International Standard-ISO/IEC 29192-2, Information technology-Security techniques-Lightweight cryptography -Part 2: Block ciphers (2011)

[LLL+19] Liu, Y., et al.: STP models of optimal differential and linear trail for S-box based ciphers. Cryptology ePrint Archive, Report 2019/025 (2019). https://eprint.iacr.org/2019/025

[LS19]   Liu, Y., Sasaki, Y.: Related-key boomerang attacks on gift with automated trail search including BCT effect. Cryptology ePrint Archive, Report 2019/669 (2019). https://eprint.iacr.org/2019/669

[LWZZ19] Li, L., Wu, W., Zheng, Y., Zhang, L.: The relationship between the construction and solution of the MILP models and applications. Cryptology ePrint Archive, Report 2019/049 (2019). https://eprint.iacr.org/2019/049

[Mat94] Matsui, M.: Linear cryptanalysis method for DES cipher. In: Helleseth, T. (ed.) EUROCRYPT 1993. LNCS, vol. 765, pp. 386–397. Springer, Heidelberg (1994). https://doi.org/10.1007/3-540-48285-7_33

[Mat95] Matsui, M.: On correlation between the order of S-boxes and the strength of DES. In: De Santis, A. (ed.) EUROCRYPT 1994. LNCS, vol. 950, pp. 366–375. Springer, Heidelberg (1995). https://doi.org/10.1007/BFb0053451

[NIS]   NIST: Lightweight cryptography (LWC) standardization process (2019). https://csrc.nist.gov/Projects/Lightweight-Cryptography/Round-1-Candidates

[Sas18] Sasaki, Y.: Integer linear programming for three-subset meet-in-the-middle attacks: application to GIFT. In: Inomata, A., Yasuda, K. (eds.) IWSEC 2018. LNCS, vol. 11049, pp. 227–243. Springer, Cham (2018). https://doi.org/10.1007/978-3-319-97916-8_15

[ZDJ19] Zhao, B., Dong, X., Jia, K.: New related-tweakey boomerang and rectangle attacks on Deoxys-BC including BDT effect. IACR Trans. Symmetric Cryptol. **2019**(3), 121–151 (2019)

[ZDM+19] Zhao, B., Dong, X., Meier, W., Jia, K., Wang, G.: Generalized related-key rectangle attacks on block ciphers with linear key schedule. Cryptology ePrint Archive, Report 2019/714 (2019). https://eprint.iacr.org/2019/714

[ZDY19] Zhu, B., Dong, X., Yu, H.: MILP-based differential attack on round-reduced GIFT. In: Matsui, M. (ed.) CT-RSA 2019. LNCS, vol. 11405, pp. 372–390. Springer, Cham (2019). https://doi.org/10.1007/978-3-030-12612-4_19

[ZZDX19] Zhou, C., Zhang, W., Ding, T., Xiang, Z.: Improving the MILP-based security evaluation algorithms against differential cryptanalysis using divide-and-conquer approach. Cryptology ePrint Archive, Report 2019/019 (2019). https://eprint.iacr.org/2019/019

Adaptively Secure Puncturable Pseudorandom Functions via Puncturable Identity-Based KEMs

Xin Wang[1,2], Shimin Li[1,2], and Rui Xue[1,2(✉)]

[1] State Key Laboratory of Information Security, Institute of Information Engineering, Chinese Academy of Sciences, Beijing, China
{wangxin9076,lishimin,xuerui}@iie.ac.cn
[2] School of Cyber Security, University of Chinese Academy of Sciences, Beijing, China

Abstract. In this paper, we are interested in constructing Puncturable Pseudorandom Functions (PPRFs), a special class of constrained PRFs. While selectively secure PPRFs can be constructed from GGM tree-based PRFs, the adaptive counterpart is tricky to deal with. Inspired by previous works, we investigate on the possibility of directly obtaining adaptively-secure PPRF from Puncturable Identity-based Key Encapsulation Mechanism (PIB-KEM). Our contributions can be summarized as follows: (i) we show that one could derive adaptively-secure PPRFs very naturally originating from PIB-KEM satisfying two necessary conditions. (ii) we define t-puncturable IB-KEM (t-PIBKEM) and show its existence by an efficient conversion basing on Hierarchical IB-KEM (HIB-KEM). Furthermore, we demonstrate its application to constructing t-puncturable PRFs, a generalized notion of PPRFs.

Keywords: Puncturable PRF · Identity-based KEM · HIB-KEM

1 Introduction

Pseudorandom functions (PRFs) are fundamental in contemporary cryptography both from a theoretical and a practical point of view. Briefly, PRFs are a family of key-induced functions F associated with a key space $\mathcal{K}$, demanding that for a randomly sampled $k \in \mathcal{K}$, the function value $F(k, x)$ should be computationally indistinguishable from truly random values in the range of the function. A newly emerged notion of *constrained pseudorandom functions* was proposed by Boneh and Waters [4], concurrently defined by Kiayias et al. [9] and by Boyle et al. [6]. The novel aspect of a constrained PRF is that apart from a master key capable of evaluating the function at any points within the input space $\mathcal{X}$, it additionally allows for generating constrained keys from the master key. A constrained key is indexed by a set $S \subseteq \mathcal{X}$ (or a predicate f), and can be used to evaluate the function $F(k, \cdot)$ at any point $x \in S$ (or any point satisfying $f(x) = 1$). The security of

© Springer Nature Switzerland AG 2020
J. Zhou et al. (Eds.): ICICS 2019, LNCS 11999, pp. 463–481, 2020.
https://doi.org/10.1007/978-3-030-41579-2_27

constrained PRF, usually called pseudorandomness, is defined by a game played between a challenger and a distinguisher. We first give a brief overview of the *selective* pseudorandomness game. Ahead of time, the distinguisher should commit to a point x^* it wishes to be challenged. It then could issue two kinds of queries: evaluation query or key query. The evaluation query allows it to acquire function value at any points different from x^*. The key query permits it to hold polynomial many constrained keys, but under the restriction that they should be unable to evaluate at x^*. After these queries, the challenger sends a function value of x^* or a value picked uniformly at random from the range of the PRF and the goal of the distinguisher is to tell which is the case. An *adaptive* pseudorandomness game is defined analogously except the committing point could be decided by the distinguisher after all the queries have been issued. Constrained PRFs are very powerful and once their inception have been found applicable for building broadcast encryption [4], multiparty key exchange [5] and so forth. It is deserved to be mentioned that Sahai and Waters [10] developed "punctured programming" technique using constrained PRFs as a core ingredient together with indistinguishability obfuscation which leads to many appealing results.

Adaptively-Secure Puncturable PRF. Previous works are dedicated to giving concrete constructions of constrained PRFs for different function families, as initiated by Boneh and Waters [4]. Among these, *puncturable* PRFs (PPRFs) [10], a special class of constrained PRFs have aroused wide concern. A system of PPRF associates a constrained key with an element x in the input space. This key allows evaluation at all points $x' \neq x$, thus often named as punctured key since its functionality is removed at a single point. Currently, many relatively efficient constructions of PPRF can only achieve selective security. One can argue adaptive security for these constructions using complexity leveraging, but this causes exponential security loss. Technically, adaptively-secure constrained PRFs turned out tougher to construct than their selective counterpart. The work of Hohenberger, Koppula, and Waters [8] can offer adaptive security, but heavily depends on somewhat hard-to-implement indistinguishability obfuscation. In this work we are interested in constructing adaptively secure puncturable PRFs through other lightweight primitives. We provide a generic approach to neatly transform puncturable identity-based key encapsulation mechanism (PIB-KEM) scheme into adaptively-secure PPRFs.

Our Contributions. In this work, we focus on constructing adaptively secure PPRF from identity-based key encapsulation mechanism (IB-KEM). Our idea is inspired by the creative work of Abdalla et al. [1], which first investigated the relationship between verifiable random functions (VRF) and IB-KEM. We follow their work and aim to find other potential usages of an IB-KEM to build other cryptographic primitives (e.g. PPRFs) which seems hard to construct in their own sight.

Our constructions are centered around a primitive named puncturable IB-KEM (PIB-KEM). We note that it was previously defined as puncturable identity-based encryption which is utilized to give counterexample for n-circular security [7]. In a nutshell, a PIB-KEM scheme is a special IB-KEM scheme whose master secret key allows for efficient puncturing. Given a master secret key msk, one could derive a punctured key $msk(\{id'\})$ that is capable of producing any secret key sk_{id} associated with an identity id except the key $sk_{id'}$ corresponding to the punctured identity id'.

As our main contribution, we establish the connection between PIB-KEM and PPRFs. Our basic result shows that one could derive a system of adaptively-secure PPRF very naturally originating from PIB-KEM satisfying two necessary conditions.

As another contribution, we show the possibility to extend the aforementioned connection. We consider a more general case of PIB-KEM that the master secret key holder can derive a t-punctured key which allows for puncturing a set S containing polynomially many points and the size of S is at most t. Note that PIB-KEM is a special case that $t = 1$. We formalize the general case as t-puncturable IB-KEM (t-PIBKEM) and show a very efficient conversion from any ℓ-depth HIB-KEM scheme to a t-PIBKEM scheme with identity space $\{0,1\}^\ell$. Previously a transformation from HIB-KEM to PIB-KEM was proposed in [7], but no explicit construction was given to indicate the existence of t-PIBKEM. Furthermore, we demonstrate the application of t-PIBKEM to construct t-puncturable PRFs (t-PPRFs), defined as a generalized notion of PPRFs [8], as an extension to our basic result.

Our Techniques. We give a description of our construction here which shows how to construct PPRFs from PIB-KEM. The case for transforming t-PIB-KEM into t-PPRFs is almost the same. The PPRF is setup by first running $(mpk, msk) \leftarrow \mathsf{PIBKEM.Setup}(1^\lambda)$. Then it picks an arbitrary identity id_0 in ID space and generate an encapsulated ciphertext $C_0 = \mathsf{PIBKEM.Encap}(mpk, id_0)$. The master key k is composed of (msk, C_0). The evaluation on input x is defined by $F(k, x) = \mathsf{PIBKEM.Decap}(C_0, sk_x)$ where $sk_x \leftarrow \mathsf{PIBKEM.KeyDer}(msk, x)$. We assume the input space $\mathcal{X}$ of the PRF is equal to the ID space, so that the evaluation is meaningful with respect to any point. To derive a punctured key for a single point x^*, simply invoke $msk(\{x^*\}) \leftarrow \mathsf{PIBKEM.Puncture}(msk, x^*)$ and assign it as k_{x^*}. With this key in hand, one can generate $sk_x \leftarrow \mathsf{PIBKEM.Derive}(msk(\{x^*\}), x)$ and use this to decapsulate C_0. Note that evaluation can be done using k_{x^*} on input x as long as $x \neq x^*$ as required. For now the construction is not adequate to be a PPRF, as there is no pseudorandomness promise of the underlying PIB-KEM. To make a PIB-KEM scheme be qualified for building PPRFs, we need the following interesting property: if a ciphertext encapsulated under an identity id_0 is decapsulated by an unrelated secret key sk_{id}, i.e. $id \neq id_0$, the result (if meaningful) should look like a random value in the range of the session key space to a poly-time adversary even given out a punctured master key $msk(\{id\})$.

We notice that in [1] this property was defined as *pseudorandom decapsulation* in terms of an IB-KEM scheme and examples were given to prove that some existing IB-KEMs have already achieved this property. But unfortunately, there are no handy IB-KEMs can both achieve this property and have punctured keys as well. A very natural question is whether this property could also be adapted to hierarchical IB-KEM (HIB-KEM) and how to make use of it to build PIB-KEM satisfying pseudorandom decapsulation. In this paper, we put forth the notion of *pseudorandom decapsulation* in the HIB-KEM setting and formally prove that a PIB-KEM scheme can inherit this property from a HIB-KEM scheme. We also give an example to show that a well-known HIB-KEM scheme proposed by Boneh et al. [3] already achieves this property. Therefore, the existence of PIB-KEM with pseudorandom decapsulation is ensured. Thereby, our transformation from PIB-KEM to adaptively secure PPRFs naturally holds.

2   Preliminaries

We will denote with λ a security parameter. We say a function $\mathsf{negl} : \mathbb{N} \to \mathbb{R}$ is negligible if $|\mathsf{negl}(\lambda)| < 1/\mathrm{poly}(\lambda)$ holds for any polynomial $\mathrm{poly}(\lambda)$ and sufficiently large λ. We write $x \leftarrow X$ for sampling x from the set X uniformly at random and $x \twoheadleftarrow X$ for sampling x according to arbitrary distribution on X. We denote by $x \leftarrow A$ if x is the output of an algorithm A. We use $[n]$ for an integer n to denote the set $\{1, \ldots, n\}$. Let $\bar{b}$ denote the inversion of a single bit b.

2.1   Puncturable Pseudorandom Functions

In this section, we recall the syntax and security properties of a puncturable pseudorandom function family [10]. Puncturable pseudorandom functions (PPRFs) are a special class of constrained pseudorandom functions. A PRF $F : \mathcal{K} \times \mathcal{X} \to \mathcal{Y}$ is a puncturable pseudorandom function if there exists an additional key space $\mathcal{K}_p$ and three PPT algorithms $F.\mathsf{Setup}, F.\mathsf{Puncture}, F.\mathsf{Eval}$ as follows:

- $F.\mathsf{Setup}(1^\lambda)$ is a randomized algorithm that takes the security parameter λ as input and outputs a description of the key space $\mathcal{K}$, the punctured key space $\mathcal{K}_p$ and the PRF F.
- $F.\mathsf{Puncture}(k, x)$ is a randomized algorithm that takes as input a PRF key $k \in \mathcal{K}$ and $x \in \mathcal{X}$, and outputs a key $k_x \in \mathcal{K}_p$.
- $F.\mathsf{Eval}(k_x, x')$ is a deterministic algorithm that takes as input a punctured key $k_x \in \mathcal{K}_p$ and $x' \in \mathcal{X}$. Let $k \in \mathcal{K}, x \in \mathcal{X}$ and $k_x \leftarrow F.\mathsf{Puncture}(k, x)$. For correctness, we need the following property:

$$F.\mathsf{Eval}(k_x, x') = \begin{cases} F(k, x') & \text{if } x' \neq x \\ \bot & \text{otherwise} \end{cases}$$

Adaptive Pseudorandomness of PPRFs: The security game between the challenger and the adversary $\mathcal{A}$ consists of the following phases:

- **Setup Phase** The challenger chooses uniformly at random a PRF key $k \leftarrow \mathcal{K}$ and a bit $b \leftarrow \{0, 1\}$.

- **Evaluation Query Phase** $\mathcal{A}$ queries for polynomially many evaluations. For each evaluation query x, the challenger sends $F(k, x)$ to $\mathcal{A}$.
- **Challenge Phase** $\mathcal{A}$ chooses a challenge $x^* \in \mathcal{X}$. The challenger computes $k_{x^*} \leftarrow F.\mathsf{Puncture}(k, x^*)$. If $b = 0$, the challenger outputs k_{x^*} and $F(k, x^*)$. Else, it outputs k_{x^*} and $y \leftarrow \mathcal{Y}$.
- **Guess** $\mathcal{A}$ outputs a guess b' of b.

Let $E \subset \mathcal{X}$ be the set of evaluation queries. $\mathcal{A}$ wins if $b' = b$ and $x^* \notin E$. The advantage of $\mathcal{A}$ is defined to be $\mathsf{Adv}_{\mathcal{A}}^F(\lambda) = |\Pr[\mathcal{A} \text{ wins}] - \frac{1}{2}|$.

Definition 1. *The PRF F is an adaptively secure PPRF if for all PPT adversaries $\mathcal{A}$, $\mathsf{Adv}_{\mathcal{A}}^F(\lambda)$ is negligible in λ.*

2.2 t-Puncturable Pseudorandom Functions

Let $t(\cdot)$ be a polynomial. A PRF $F_t : \mathcal{K} \times \mathcal{X} \to \mathcal{Y}$ is a t-puncturable pseudorandom function (t-PPRF) if there is an additional key space $\mathcal{K}_p$ and three polynomial time algorithms $F_t.\mathsf{Setup}, F_t.\mathsf{Eval}, F_t.\mathsf{Puncture}$ defined as follows.

- $F_t.\mathsf{Setup}(1^\lambda)$ is a randomized algorithm that takes the security parameter λ as input and outputs a description of the key space $\mathcal{K}$, the punctured key space $\mathcal{K}_p$ and the PRF F_t.
- $F_t.\mathsf{Puncture}(k, S)$ is a randomized algorithm that takes as input a PRF key $k \in \mathcal{K}$ and $S \subset \mathcal{X}$ where $|S| \leq t(\lambda)$, and outputs a t-punctured key $k_S \in \mathcal{K}_p$.
- $F_t.\mathsf{Eval}(k_S, x')$ is a deterministic algorithm that takes as input a t-punctured key $k_S \in \mathcal{K}_p$ and $x' \in \mathcal{X}$. Let $k \in \mathcal{K}, S \subset \mathcal{X}$, and $k_S \leftarrow F_t.\mathsf{Puncture}(k, S)$. For correctness, we need the following property:

$$F_t.\mathsf{Eval}(k_S, x') = \begin{cases} F_t(k, x') & \text{if } x' \notin S \\ \bot & \text{otherwise} \end{cases}$$

The security of t-PPRFs is defined analogously to the adaptive pseudorandomness game for PPRFs.

Adaptive Pseudorandomness of t-PPRFs: The security game is as follows:

- **Setup Phase** The challenger chooses uniformly at random a PRF key $k \leftarrow \mathcal{K}$ and a bit $b \leftarrow \{0, 1\}$.
- **Evaluation Query Phase** $\mathcal{A}$ queries for polynomially many evaluations. For each evaluation query x, the challenger sends $F_t(k, x)$ to $\mathcal{A}$.
- **Key Query Phase** $\mathcal{A}$ queries for polynomially many keys. For each query, it sends a set $S \subset \mathcal{X}$, and receives $F_t.\mathsf{Puncture}(k, S)$.
- **Challenge Phase** $\mathcal{A}$ chooses a challenge $x^* \in \mathcal{X}$. If $b = 0$, the challenger outputs $F_t(k, x^*)$. Else, it outputs $y \leftarrow \mathcal{Y}$.
- **Guess** $\mathcal{A}$ outputs a guess b' of b.

Let $E \subset \mathcal{X}$ be the set of evaluation queries and $S_1, \ldots, S_q \subset \mathcal{X}$ be the t-punctured key queries. $\mathcal{A}$ wins if $b' = b$, $x^* \notin E$ and $x^* \in \bigcap_{i=1}^q S_i$. The advantage of $\mathcal{A}$ is defined to be $\mathsf{Adv}_{\mathcal{A}}^{F_t}(\lambda) = |\Pr[\mathcal{A} \text{ wins}] - \frac{1}{2}|$.

Definition 2. *The PRF F_t is an adaptively secure t-PPRF if for all PPT adversaries $\mathcal{A}$, $\mathsf{Adv}_{\mathcal{A}}^{F_t}(\lambda)$ is negligible in λ.*

2.3 (Hierarchical) Identity-Based Key Encapsulation

An identity-based encapsulation mechanism (IB-KEM) allows a sender and a receiver to agree on a random session key K in such a way that the sender can create K from public parameters and the receiver's identity and the receiver can recover K using his secret key. This notion was first formalized by Bentahar et al. [2].

Definition 3 (Identity-based Key Encapsulation Scheme). *An IB-KEM scheme* IBKEM *is defined by four algorithms* (Setup, KeyDer, Encap, Decap) *with following specifications:*

- Setup(1^λ) *is a randomized algorithm that takes as input a security parameter λ and outputs a master public key* mpk *and a master secret key* msk. *We assume* mpk *defines the identity space $\mathcal{ID}$, the key space $\mathcal{K}$ and the ciphertext space $\mathcal{C}$.*
- KeyDer(msk, id) *computes a secret key* $\mathsf{sk}_{\mathsf{id}}$ *for identity* id.
- Encap(mpk, id) *returns a random session key $K \in \mathcal{K}$ and a corresponding ciphertext $C \in \mathcal{C}$ encapsulating K under the identity* id.
- Decap(C, $\mathsf{sk}_{\mathsf{id}}$) *decapsulates C to get back a session key $K \in \mathcal{K}$ or a symbol $\perp$.*

The correctness of the scheme requires that for all $\lambda \in \mathbb{N}$, all (mpk, msk) *produced by* Setup(1^λ), *all identities* id $\in \mathcal{ID}$, *and* $(K, C) \leftarrow$ Encap(mpk, id), $\mathsf{sk}_{\mathsf{id}} \leftarrow$ KeyDer(msk, id), $\Pr[\mathsf{Decap}(C, \mathsf{sk}_{\mathsf{id}}) = K] = 1$.

Next, we recall the concept of Hierarchical IB-KEM (HIB-KEM). Every user in an HIB-KEM system has an id consisting of a vector such as $\mathsf{id} = (I_1, \ldots, I_k)$ where k means user's position in the hierarchy. We use $\mathsf{id}|_t$ to denote the t-prefix of $\mathsf{id} = (I_1, \ldots, I_t, \ldots, I_k)$, i.e. $\mathsf{id}|_t = (I_1, \ldots, I_t)$ where $t \leq k$. The root node of hierarchy is Private Key Generator (PKG), denoted by $\mathsf{id}|_0$.

Definition 4 (Hierarchical identity-based key encapsulation mechanism). *A hierarchical identity-based key encapsulation mechanism (HIB-KEM) consists of five algorithms:* (Setup, KeyGen, Derive, Encap, Decap). *For a HIB-KEM of depth ℓ, any identity is represented by a vector* id $= (I_1, \ldots, I_j)$ *where $1 \leq j \leq \ell$.*

- Setup(1^λ, ℓ) *takes as input a security parameter λ and outputs a master public key* mpk *and a master secret key* msk $= \mathsf{sk}_{\mathsf{id}|_0}$. *We assume* mpk *defines a hierarchical identity space $\mathcal{ID}$, a key space $\mathcal{K}$ and ciphertext space $\mathcal{C}$.*

- KeyGen(msk, id) *takes as input* msk *and* id, *and returns user secret key* sk_{id} *for identity* id.
- Derive(id, $sk_{id|_{k-1}}$) *takes as input a k-level identity* id $= (I_1, \ldots, I_k)$ *and the private key* $sk_{id|_{k-1}}$ *of its (k − 1)-level prefix, outputs a private key* sk_{id} *for identity* id.
- Encap(mpk, id) *takes as input* mpk *and* id, *returns* (C, K), *where ciphertext* C *is an encapsulation of* K *under the identity* id.
- Decap(C, sk_{id}) *decapsulates* C *to get back a session key* $K \in \mathcal{K}$.

The correctness of the scheme requires that for all $\lambda \in \mathbb{N}$, *all* (mpk, msk) *produced by* Setup(1^λ), *all identities* id $= (I_1, \ldots, I_k)$ *for* $k \in [\ell]$, *and* $(K, C) \leftarrow$ Encap(mpk, id), $sk_{id} \leftarrow$ KeyGen(msk, id), $\Pr[\text{Decap}(C, sk_{id}) = K] = 1$. *Moreover, it is required that the distribution of* $sk_{id} \leftarrow$ Derive(id, $sk_{id|_{k-1}}$) *is identical to the distribution of* KeyGen(msk, id).

3 (*t*-) Puncturable Identity-Based Key Encapsulation

Chen et al. [7] first defined the notion of puncturable IBE, which is a special IBE where the master secret key could be "punctured" with respect to a singleton {id}. With this key, one could generate a secret key $sk_{id'}$ corresponding to any identity id' $\in \mathcal{ID}$ except the punctured one id. We adapt their definition to the setting of KEM as follows:

3.1 Puncturable IB-KEM

Definition 5 (Puncturable IB-KEM). *A puncturable IB-KEM (PIB-KEM) scheme is an IB-KEM scheme whose master secret key allows for efficient puncturing at a single identity. The syntax of PIB-KEM is similar to standard IB-KEM except it equips two additional algorithms as follows:*

- Puncture(msk, id): *on input* msk *and an identity* id $\in \mathcal{ID}$, *output a punctured master secret key* msk({id}).
- Derive(msk({id}), id'): *on input* msk({id}) *and an identity* id' $\in \mathcal{ID}$, *output a secret key* $sk_{id'}$ *for* id' *if* id' $\neq$ id *and* $\perp$ *otherwise. The correctness of the algorithm demand that for all* id' $\neq$ id, *the outputs of* KeyDer(msk, id') *and* Derive(msk({id}), id') *have the same distribution.*

Puncturable IB-KEM from HIB-KEM. As noted in [7], a PIB-KEM scheme with certain length identity can be transformed from a HIB-KEM scheme with depth ℓ. Suppose we have an ℓ-level HIB-KEM scheme HIBKEM with identity space $(\{0,1\}^*)^\ell$, then a PIB-KEM scheme PIBKEM with identity space $\{0,1\}^\ell$ could be obtained as:

- Setup(λ): (mpk, msk) $\leftarrow$ HIBKEM.Setup(λ, ℓ).
- KeyDer(msk, id): On input msk and an identity id $\in \{0,1\}^\ell$, parse id as a vector $v = (\text{id}[1], \ldots, \text{id}[\ell])$ where id[i] denotes the i-th bit of id, then compute $sk_v \leftarrow$ HIBKEM.KeyGen(msk, v), output $sk_{id} := sk_v$.

- Puncture(msk, id*): On input msk and id* $\in \{0,1\}^\ell$: for $1 \leq i \leq \ell$, set $v_i = (\text{id}^*[1], \ldots, \text{id}^*[i-1], \overline{\text{id}^*[i]})$, then compute $\text{sk}_{v_i} \leftarrow \text{HIBKEM.KeyGen}(\text{msk}, v_i)$, output $\text{msk}(\{\text{id}^*\}) = (\text{sk}_{v_1}, \ldots, \text{sk}_{v_\ell})$.
- Derive(msk($\{\text{id}^*\}$), id): on input $\text{msk}(\{\text{id}^*\}) = (\text{sk}_{v_1}, \ldots, \text{sk}_{v_\ell})$ and an identity id $\in \{0,1\}^\ell$, if id $\neq$ id*, find v_j that is a prefix of id and output $\text{sk}_{\text{id}} \leftarrow \text{HIBKEM.Derive}(\text{sk}_{v_j}, \text{id})$; otherwise, output $\perp$.
- Encap(mpk, id): On input mpk and an identity id, parse id as a vector $v = (\text{id}[1], \ldots, \text{id}[\ell])$, output $C \leftarrow \text{HIBKEM.Encap}(\text{mpk}, v)$.
- Decap(C, sk_{id}): On input ciphertext C and sk_{id}, output $K \leftarrow \text{HIBKEM.Decap}(C, \text{sk}_{\text{id}})$.

3.2 t-Puncturable IB-KEM

In this subsection, we generalize the notion of PIB-KEM to obtain t-puncturable IB-KEM, where t is an arbitrary polynomial, and show its existence by carefully deriving from HIB-KEM. It is easy to see that PIB-KEM is a special case when $t = 1$.

Definition 6 (t-Puncturable IB-KEM). *Let $t(\cdot)$ be a polynomial. An IB-KEM scheme is a t-puncturable IB-KEM (t-PIBKEM) scheme whose master secret key allows for efficient puncturing at any set S of size at most t. The additional syntax of t-PIBKEM is as follows:*

- Puncture(msk, S): *on input* msk *and an identity set* $S \subset \mathcal{ID}$, $|S| \leq t(\lambda)$ *output a t-punctured master secret key* msk(S).
- Derive(msk(S), id): *on input a t-punctured master secret key* msk(S) *and an identity* id $\in \mathcal{ID}$, *output a secret key* sk_{id} *for* id *if* id $\notin S$ *and* $\perp$ *otherwise. The correctness of the algorithm demand that for all* id $\notin S$, *the outputs of* KeyDer(msk, id) *and* Derive(msk(S), id) *have the same distribution.*

t-**PIBKEM from HIB-KEM.** Suppose we have an ℓ-level HIB-KEM scheme HIBKEM with identity space $(\{0,1\}^*)^\ell$, then a t-PIBKEM scheme t-PIBKEM with identity space $\{0,1\}^\ell$ could be obtained as follows. Suppose S is a set of identities to be punctured, namely $S = \{\text{id}_1, \ldots, \text{id}_t\}$.

- Setup(λ): (mpk, msk) $\leftarrow$ HIBKEM.Setup(λ, ℓ).
- KeyDer(msk, id): On input msk and an identity id $\in \{0,1\}^\ell$, parse id as a vector $v = (\text{id}[1], \ldots, \text{id}[\ell])$ where $\text{id}[i]$ denotes the i-th bit of id, then compute $\text{sk}_v \leftarrow \text{HIBKEM.KeyGen}(\text{msk}, v)$, output $\text{sk}_{\text{id}} := \text{sk}_v$.
- Puncture(msk, S): On input msk and a set $S = \{\text{id}_1, \ldots, \text{id}_t\}$, follow the four steps below.
  - Run algorithm getList (see Table 1) and obtain t lists $L_{\text{id}_1}, \ldots, L_{\text{id}_t}$.
  - Compute the complement of each list, namely $\overline{L_{\text{id}_j}} := [\ell] \backslash L_{\text{id}_j}, j \in [t]$.
  - Run algorithm getKeyString (see Table 1) taking each $\overline{L_{\text{id}_j}}, j \in [t]$ as input and get t sets $K_{\text{id}_1}, \ldots, K_{\text{id}_t}$. The union of these sets is denoted by $K = \bigcup_{i=1}^{t} K_{\text{id}_i}$.

- Suppose that $K = \{v_1, \ldots, v_n\}$. For each $i \in [n]$, compute $\mathsf{sk}_{v_i} \leftarrow$ HIBKEM.KeyGen(msk, v_i), output $\mathsf{msk}(S) = (\mathsf{sk}_{v_1}, \ldots, \mathsf{sk}_{v_n})$.
- Derive($\mathsf{msk}(S), \mathsf{id}$): On input $\mathsf{msk}(S) = (\mathsf{sk}_{v_1}, \ldots, \mathsf{sk}_{v_n})$ and an identity $\mathsf{id} \in \{0,1\}^\ell$, if $\mathsf{id} \notin S$, find v_j that is a prefix of id and output $\mathsf{sk}_{\mathsf{id}} \leftarrow$ HIBKEM.Derive($\mathsf{sk}_{v_j}, \mathsf{id}$); otherwise, output $\perp$.
- Encap($\mathsf{mpk}, \mathsf{id}$): On input mpk and an identity id, parse id as a vector $v = (\mathsf{id}[1], \ldots, \mathsf{id}[\ell])$, output $C \leftarrow$ HIBKEM.Encap(mpk, v).
- Decap($C, \mathsf{sk}_{\mathsf{id}}$): On input ciphertext C and $\mathsf{sk}_{\mathsf{id}}$, output $K \leftarrow$ HIBKEM. Decap($C, \mathsf{sk}_{\mathsf{id}}$).

id	id$_1$	id$_2$	id$_3$	id$_4$	id$_5$
$S = \{$	0 0 0 0	0 1 0 0	0 0 1 0	0 0 0 1	1 0 0 0$\}$
List	$\{2,3,4,1\}$	$\{2,1\}$	$\{3,1,2\}$	$\{4,2,3,1\}$	$\{1\}$
4	~~0,0,0,1~~	0,1,0,1	0,0,1,1	~~0,0,0,0~~	1,0,0,1
3	~~0,0,1,·~~	0,1,1,·	~~0,0,0,·~~	~~0,0,1,·~~	1,0,1,·
2	~~0,1,·,·~~	0,0,·,·	0,1,·,·	0,1,·,·	1,1,·,·
1	~~1,·,·,·~~	1,·,·,·	1,·,·,·	1,·,·,·	~~0,·,·,·~~

Fig. 1. An example illustrating the process of Puncture algorithm. Actually, the algorithm does not list all the items below the third line of the table. We do so since it would be helpful to understand the principle of the algorithm.

To make it clear how the Puncture algorithm works, we show a toy example (Fig. 1) when the identity space of a PIB-KEM scheme consists of 4-bit strings, namely $\mathcal{ID} = \{0,1\}^4$. Ahead of time, we have a HIB-KEM scheme with identity space $(\{0,1\}^*)^4$. Suppose that we wish to puncture a set of 5 identities: $S = \{0000, 0100, 0010, 0001, 1000\}$. Our goal is to create a punctured key $\mathsf{msk}(S)$ with which we could generate secret key of any identity (there are 11 altogether in this example) not in S.

Table 1. Algorithms used in Puncture.

Algorithm getList	Algorithm getKeyString
Input: A puncturing set $S = \{\mathsf{id}_1, \ldots, \mathsf{id}_t\}$	**Input:** A set $\mathsf{Ind}_{\mathsf{id}_i} = \{i_1, i_2, \ldots, i_n\}$ recording
Output: t lists $L_{\mathsf{id}_1}, \ldots, L_{\mathsf{id}_t}$	$\quad$ id_i's indices
$\quad c \leftarrow 1.$	**Output:** A set K_{id_i} of ID-vectors $v_{i_1}, \ldots, v_{i_n}$
while $c \neq t$	$\quad K_{\mathsf{id}_i} \leftarrow \emptyset, c \leftarrow 1.$
$\quad$ **for all** $c+1 \leq j \leq t$ **do**	**while** $c \leq n$
$\quad\quad$ 1: Find an index i s.t. $\mathsf{id}_j[i] \neq \mathsf{id}_c[i]$	$\quad$ **for all** $1 \leq j \leq n$ **do**
$\quad\quad$ 2: If $i \notin L_{\mathsf{id}_c}$, add i to L_{id_c}	$\quad\quad$ 1: $v_{i_j} = (\mathsf{id}_i[1], \ldots, \mathsf{id}_i[i_j-1], \overline{\mathsf{id}_i[i_j]})$
$\quad\quad$ 3: If $i \notin L_{\mathsf{id}_j}$, add i to L_{id_j}	$\quad\quad$ 2: Add v_{i_j} to K_{id_i}
$\quad$ **end for**	$\quad$ **end for**
$\quad c \leftarrow c+1$	$\quad c \leftarrow c+1$
end while	**end while**

4 Main Constructions

In this section, we give two main constructions. The basic construction shows that one could derive adaptively-secure PPRFs from PIB-KEM satisfying two conditions. And the extended construction demonstrates the way of constructing t-PPRFs from a t-PIBKEM. To make use of PIB-KEM to construct PPRF, we need the underlying PIB-KEM scheme to be *PPRF-compatible*.

4.1 PPRF-Compatible (t-)PIB-KEM

A PIB-KEM scheme is said to be PPRF-compatible if satisfying:

1. **Unique and perfect derivation**
   - *Unique derivation.* The output of Derive algorithm taking as input a punctured master key msk{id} and an identity $id' \neq id$ is unique. There is only one secret key $sk_{id'}$ matched with id'. Note that this implicitly requires that the KeyDer algorithm is deterministic.
   - *Perfect derivation.* The output of Derive algorithm taking as input a punctured master key msk{id} and an identity $id' \neq id$ is equal to the output of KeyDer algorithm taking as input the master secret key and id'. That is, $\mathsf{Derive}(\mathsf{msk}\{id\}, id') = \mathsf{KeyDer}(\mathsf{msk}, id')$ for all $id' \neq id$.
2. **Pseudorandom decapsulation.** Let C be an encapsulation under identity id, it is required that if C is decapsulated by a secret key corresponding to any other identity $\overline{id}$, the result should be computationally indistinguishable from a uniformly random value. Formally, we define a game (Fig. 2) played between a challenger and a PPT adversary $\mathcal{A} = (\mathcal{A}_1, \mathcal{A}_2)$:

Similarly, we can define these properties in terms of a t-PIBKEM. The property of unique and perfect derivation is essentially the same. We additionally define

---

GAME PIB-KEM-RDECAP$_{\mathsf{PIBKEM}}^{\mathcal{A}}(\lambda)$:

$(\mathsf{mpk}, \mathsf{msk}) \leftarrow \mathsf{Setup}(1^\lambda)$

$id^* \twoheadleftarrow \mathcal{ID}$

$C^* \leftarrow \mathsf{Encap}(\mathsf{mpk}, id^*)$

$(\overline{id}, st) \leftarrow \mathcal{A}_1^{\mathsf{KeyDer}(\mathsf{msk}, \cdot)}(\mathsf{mpk}, C^*, id^*)$

$sk_{\overline{id}} \leftarrow \mathsf{KeyDer}(\mathsf{msk}, \overline{id}); \ \mathsf{msk}(\{\overline{id}\}) \leftarrow \mathsf{Puncture}(\mathsf{msk}, \overline{id})$

$b \leftarrow \{0, 1\}; \ K_0 \leftarrow \mathsf{Decap}(C^*, sk_{\overline{id}}); \ K_1 \leftarrow \mathcal{K}$

$b' \leftarrow \mathcal{A}_2(st, \mathsf{msk}(\{\overline{id}\}), K_b)$

If $b' = b$, return 1, else return 0

Fig. 2. The pseudorandom decapsulation property of a PIB-KEM scheme. The oracle KeyDer(msk, id) returns sk_{id} with the restriction that $\mathcal{A}$ is not allowed to query KeyDer(msk, $\cdot$) for identity $\overline{id}$.

a pseudorandom decapsulation game for a t-PIBKEM scheme as in Fig. 4 in the appendix.

Having all these properties, we are ready to give our main constructions of transforming $(t\text{-})$PIB-KEM into $(t\text{-})$PPRFs. The methods to provide a PIB-KEM scheme with these two properties are argued later in Sect. 5.

4.2   From PIB-KEM to Puncturable PRFs

In this section, we show our construction of PPRF $F : \mathcal{K} \times \mathcal{X} \rightarrow \mathcal{Y}$ and corresponding algorithms $F.\mathsf{Setup}, F.\mathsf{Puncture}, F.\mathsf{Eval}$ from a PIB-KEM scheme $\mathsf{PIBKEM} = (\mathsf{Setup}, \mathsf{KeyDer}, \mathsf{Encap}, \mathsf{Decap}, \mathsf{Puncture}, \mathsf{Derive})$. Let $\mathcal{ID}$ be the identity space, $\mathcal{K}$ the session key space, defined by PIBKEM. F maps from input space $\mathcal{X} = \mathcal{ID}$ to output space $\mathcal{Y} = \mathcal{K}$.

- $F.\mathsf{Setup}(1^{\lambda})$: Run $(\mathsf{mpk}, \mathsf{msk}) \leftarrow \mathsf{PIBKEM}.\mathsf{Setup}(1^{\lambda})$. Choose a random $\mathsf{id}_0 \leftarrow \mathcal{ID}$ and compute $C_0 \leftarrow \mathsf{Encap}(\mathsf{mpk}, \mathsf{id}_0)$. Set $k = (\mathsf{msk}, C_0)$. The function is described as:
$$F(k, x) = \mathsf{PIBKEM}.\mathsf{Decap}(C_0, \mathsf{sk}_{\mathsf{id}}),$$
where $\mathsf{id} := x$ and $\mathsf{sk}_{\mathsf{id}} = \mathsf{PIBKEM}.\mathsf{KeyDer}(\mathsf{msk}, \mathsf{id})$.
- $F.\mathsf{Puncture}(k, x)$: Let $\mathsf{id} := x$. First run $\mathsf{msk}(\{\mathsf{id}\}) \leftarrow \mathsf{PIBKEM}.\mathsf{Puncture}(\mathsf{msk}, \mathsf{id})$ using msk within k. Then set $k_x = (\mathsf{msk}(\{\mathsf{id}\}), C_0)$.
- $F.\mathsf{Eval}(k_x, x')$: Let $\mathsf{id} := x$ and $\mathsf{id}' := x'$. The function value y is acquired by first computing:
$$\mathsf{sk}_{\mathsf{id}'} = \begin{cases} \mathsf{PIBKEM}.\mathsf{Derive}(\mathsf{msk}(\{\mathsf{id}\}), \mathsf{id}') & \text{if } \mathsf{id}' \neq \mathsf{id} \\ \bot & \text{otherwise} \end{cases}$$
and then computing $y := \mathsf{PIBKEM}.\mathsf{Decap}(C_0, \mathsf{sk}_{\mathsf{id}'})$.

Correctness: It is required $F.\mathsf{Eval}(k_x, x') = F(k, x')$ when $x' \neq x$. This is promised by perfect derivation of Derive algorithm: $\mathsf{Derive}(\mathsf{msk}(\{\mathsf{id}\}), \mathsf{id}') = \mathsf{KeyDer}(\mathsf{msk}, \mathsf{id}') = \mathsf{sk}_{\mathsf{id}'}$ as long as $\mathsf{id}' \neq \mathsf{id}$. Thus, $F.\mathsf{Eval}(k_x, x') = \mathsf{PIBKEM}.\mathsf{Decap}(C_0, \mathsf{sk}_{\mathsf{id}'}) = F(k, x')$.

Adaptive Pseudorandomness: We next focus on the security of constructed PPRFs.

Theorem 1. *Assume* PIBKEM *is PPRF-compatible, then the construction above is an adaptively secure puncturable pseudorandom function.*

Proof. First it is promised to be PRF by unique derivation as multiple executions of $F.\mathsf{Eval}(k_x, \cdot)$ on the same input x' will give the same function value y. Suppose there exists an adversary $\mathcal{A}$ that breaks the adaptive pseudorandomness of PPRF with probability $\frac{1}{2} + \epsilon(\lambda)$, where $\epsilon(\lambda)$ is non-negligible, we build an algorithm $\mathcal{B}$ which has advantage $\epsilon(\lambda)$ in the PIB-KEM-RDECAP game.

$\mathcal{B}$ gets as input $(\mathsf{mpk}, C^*, \mathsf{id}^*)$ and simulates the adaptive pseudorandomness game with $\mathcal{A}$. When receiving an evaluation query $x \in \mathcal{ID}$ from $\mathcal{A}$, $\mathcal{B}$

queries its own KeyDer($\cdot$) oracle and obtains sk_x. Then it uses sk_x to compute Decap(C^*, sk_x). That is, $F(k, x) = \mathsf{Decap}(C^*, \mathsf{KeyDer}(\mathsf{msk}, x))$. When $\mathcal{A}$ sends the challenge point $x^* \in \mathcal{ID}$, $\mathcal{B}$ sends the same point to the challenger and gets back K_b together with $\mathsf{msk}(\{x^*\}) \leftarrow \mathsf{Puncture}(\mathsf{msk}, x^*)$ and returns $(K_b, k_{x^*} := \mathsf{msk}(\{x^*\}))$ to $\mathcal{A}$. Eventually, $\mathcal{B}$ outputs whatever $\mathcal{A}$ outputs to its own challenger as b'.

Since $\mathcal{B}$ simulates perfectly the adaptive pseudorandomness game to $\mathcal{A}$, the advantage of $\mathcal{B}$ is the same as $\mathcal{A}$, namely $\epsilon(\lambda)$. $\square$

4.3   Extension: From t-PIBKEM to t-Puncturable PRFs

From a t-PIBKEM scheme t-PIBKEM = (Setup, KeyDer, Encap, Decap, Puncture, Derive), we could derive a t-PPRF F_t with associated algorithms (Setup, Puncture, Eval). Let $\mathcal{ID}$ be the identity space, and $\mathcal{K}$ the session key space, defined by t-PIBKEM scheme. F_t maps from input space $\mathcal{X} = \mathcal{ID}$ to output space $\mathcal{Y} = \mathcal{K}$.

- F_t.Setup(1^λ) first runs (mpk, msk) $\leftarrow$ t-PIBKEM.Setup(1^λ), then chooses a random $\mathsf{id}_0 \leftarrow \mathcal{ID}$ and computes $C_0 \leftarrow \mathsf{Encap}(\mathsf{mpk}, \mathsf{id}_0)$. It sets $k = (\mathsf{msk}, C_0)$. The function value is:

$$F_t(k, x) = t\text{-PIBKEM.Decap}(C_0, \mathsf{sk}_{\mathsf{id}}),$$

  where $\mathsf{id} := x$ and $\mathsf{sk}_{\mathsf{id}} = t$-PIBKEM.KeyDer(msk, id).
- F_t.Puncture(k, S) runs $\mathsf{msk}(S) \leftarrow$ t-PIBKEM.Puncture(msk, S) using msk within k, then sets $k_S = (\mathsf{msk}(S), C_0)$.
- F_t.Eval(k_S, x') first computes

$$\mathsf{sk}_{x'} = \begin{cases} t\text{-PIBKEM.Derive}(\mathsf{msk}(S), x') & \text{if } x' \notin S \\ \bot & \text{otherwise} \end{cases}$$

and then computes $y = t$-PIBKEM.Decap($C_0, \mathsf{sk}_{x'}$).

Correctness: It is required that F_t.Eval(k_S, x') = $F_t(k, x')$ when $x' \notin S$. This is promised by perfect derivation of t-PIBKEM.Derive algorithm, which tells that t-PIBKEM.Derive($\mathsf{msk}(S), \mathsf{id}'$) = t-PIBKEM.KeyDer($\mathsf{msk}, \mathsf{id}'$) = $\mathsf{sk}_{\mathsf{id}'}$ as long as $\mathsf{id}' \notin S$. Thus by definition, F_t.Eval(k_S, x') = t-PIBKEM.Decap($C_0, \mathsf{sk}_{\mathsf{id}'}$) = $F_t(k, x')$.

Adaptive Pseudorandomness: The adaptive pseudorandomness is promised by:

Theorem 2. *Assume t-PIBKEM is PPRF-compatible, then the construction above is an adaptively secure t-puncturable pseudorandom function.*

The proof process is similar with Theorem 1. We give the full proof in the appendix.

5   Discussion of PPRF-Compatible PIB-KEM

In this section, we discuss the existence of PPRF-compatible PIB-KEM. We first show that the transformation from HIB-KEM to PIB-KEM can be modified to have unique and perfect derivation property using some derandomization techniques. Then we define the notion of *pseudorandom decapsulation* in the HIB-KEM setting, and give formal proofs to show that some existing HIB-KEM schemes already satisfy this property. Finally, we demonstrate that a PIB-KEM scheme deriving from a HIB-KEM scheme could inherit pseudorandom decapsulation.

5.1   PIB-KEM with Unique and Perfect Derivation

Suppose we have an ℓ-level HIB-KEM scheme HIBKEM with identity space $(\{0,1\}^*)^\ell$ and the randomness space of its Derive algorithm is $\mathcal{R}$, then a puncturable IB-KEM scheme PIBKEM with identity space $\{0,1\}^\ell$ with unique and perfect derivation could be obtained as follows.

- Setup(λ): $(\mathsf{mpk}_1, \mathsf{msk}_1) \leftarrow$ HIBKEM.Setup(λ, ℓ). Also generate a random key τ for a pseudorandom function $F_\tau : \{0,1\}^\ell \times [\ell] \to \mathcal{R}$. Then output $\mathsf{mpk} := \mathsf{mpk}_1$ and $\mathsf{msk} = (\mathsf{msk}_1, \tau)$.
- KeyDer($\mathsf{msk}, \mathsf{id}$): On input msk and an identity $\mathsf{id} \in \{0,1\}^\ell$, parse id as a vector $v = (\mathsf{id}[1], \ldots, \mathsf{id}[\ell])$ where $\mathsf{id}[i]$ denotes the i-th bit of id (conforming to Definition 4), then compute sk_v as follows: for $1 \leq i \leq \ell$, compute $\mathsf{sk}_{v|_i} =$ HIBKEM.Derive($\mathsf{sk}_{v|_{i-1}}, v|_i; F_\tau(\mathsf{id}, i)$), where $\mathsf{sk}_{v|_0} = \mathsf{msk}_1$ and $\mathsf{sk}_v = \mathsf{sk}_{v|_\ell}$, output $\mathsf{sk}_{\mathsf{id}} := \mathsf{sk}_v$.
- Puncture($\mathsf{msk}, \mathsf{id}^*$): On input msk and $\mathsf{id}^* \in \{0,1\}^\ell$: for $1 \leq i \leq \ell$, set $v^*|_i = (\mathsf{id}^*[1], \ldots, \mathsf{id}^*[i-1], \mathsf{id}^*[i]), v^*|_{\overline{i}} = (\mathsf{id}^*[1], \ldots, \mathsf{id}^*[i-1], \overline{\mathsf{id}^*[i]})$, and compute $\mathsf{sk}_{v^*|_i} =$ HIBKEM.Derive($\mathsf{sk}_{v^*|_{i-1}}, v^*|_i; F_\tau(\mathsf{id}^*, i)$), $\mathsf{sk}_{v^*|_{\overline{i}}} =$ HIBKEM.Derive($\mathsf{sk}_{v^*|_{i-1}}, v^*|_{\overline{i}}; F_\tau(\mathsf{id}^*, i)$), output $\mathsf{msk}(\{\mathsf{id}^*\}) = (\{\mathsf{sk}_{v^*|_{\overline{1}}}, \ldots, \mathsf{sk}_{v^*|_{\overline{\ell}}}\}, \tau)$.
- Derive($\mathsf{msk}(\{\mathsf{id}^*\}), \mathsf{id}$): On input $\mathsf{msk}(\{\mathsf{id}^*\}) = \{\mathsf{sk}_1, \ldots, \mathsf{sk}_\ell\}$ and an identity $\mathsf{id} \in \{0,1\}^\ell$, if $\mathsf{id} \neq \mathsf{id}^*$, parse id as a vector $v = (\mathsf{id}[1], \ldots, \mathsf{id}[\ell])$ and id^* as $v^* = (\mathsf{id}^*[1], \ldots, \mathsf{id}^*[\ell])$, find the longest common prefix of v and v^*, denote its length as j ($0 \leq j < \ell$). Let $\mathsf{sk}_{v|_{j+1}} := \mathsf{sk}_{j+1}$, for $j+1 < i < \ell$, compute $\mathsf{sk}_{v|_i} =$ HIBKEM.Derive($\mathsf{sk}_{v|_{i-1}}, v|_i; F_\tau(\mathsf{id}, i)$), output $\mathsf{sk}_{\mathsf{id}} := \mathsf{sk}_{v|_\ell}$; otherwise, output $\bot$.
- Encap($\mathsf{mpk}, \mathsf{id}$): On input mpk and an identity id, parse id as a vector $v = (\mathsf{id}[1], \ldots, \mathsf{id}[\ell])$, output $C \leftarrow$ HIBKEM.Encap(mpk, v).
- Decap($C, \mathsf{sk}_{\mathsf{id}}$): On input ciphertext C and $\mathsf{sk}_{\mathsf{id}}$, output $K \leftarrow$ HIBKEM. Decap($C, \mathsf{sk}_{\mathsf{id}}$).

One can verify that for any $\mathsf{id} \in \{0,1\}^\ell$, KeyDer($\mathsf{msk}, \mathsf{id}$) = Derive($\mathsf{msk}\{\mathsf{id}^*\}, \mathsf{id}$) for a punctured key $\mathsf{msk}(\{\mathsf{id}^*\})$ generated by Puncture($\mathsf{msk}, \mathsf{id}^*$).

Remark 1. The construction binds the three algorithms KeyDer, Puncture, Derive by consistently using HIBKEM.Derive algorithm and then derandomizes it through a unified way of letting the randomness be the output of a "global" PRF.

5.2   Pseudorandom Decapsulation of HIB-KEM

Abdalla et al. [1] have discussed the exact meaning of pseudorandom decapsulation in the setting of an IB-KEM. It is quite natural to consider whether this notion is also suitable for its hierarchical counterpart. We thus put forth the notion of *pseudorandom decapsulation* in the HIB-KEM setting.

Definition. Let C^* be an encapsulation under $id^* = (I_1, \ldots, I_\ell)$, it is required that if C^* is decapsulated by a secret key corresponding to any identity $\overline{id} = (I'_1, \ldots, I'_k)$ that is not a prefix of id^* for $k \leq \ell$, the result should look like a random bitstring. Formally, we define a game played between a challenger and a PPT adversary $\mathcal{A} = (\mathcal{A}_1, \mathcal{A}_2)$:

GAME HIB-KEM-RDECAP$_{\text{HIBKEM}}^{\mathcal{A}}(\lambda)$:

$(\text{mpk}, \text{msk}) \leftarrow \text{Setup}(1^\lambda)$

$id^* \twoheadleftarrow \mathcal{ID}$

$C^* \leftarrow \text{Encap}(\text{mpk}, id^*)$

$(\overline{id}, st) \leftarrow \mathcal{A}_1^{\text{KeyGen}(\text{msk}, \cdot)}(\text{mpk}, C^*, id^*)$

$sk_{\overline{id}} \leftarrow \text{KeyGen}(\text{msk}, \overline{id})$

$b \leftarrow \{0, 1\}; \; K_0 \leftarrow \text{Decap}(C^*, sk_{\overline{id}}); \; K_1 \leftarrow \mathcal{K}$

$b' \leftarrow \mathcal{A}_2^{\text{KeyGen}(\text{msk}, \cdot)}(st, K_b)$

If $b' = b$, return 1, else return 0

Fig. 3. The pseudorandom decapsulation property of a HIB-KEM scheme. The oracle KeyGen(msk, id) returns sk_{id} with the restriction that $\mathcal{A}$ is not allowed to query KeyGen(msk, $\cdot$) for identity $id^*, \overline{id}$ or an identity that is a prefix of either of them.

Existence of HIB-KEMs that satisfy pseudorandom decapsulation

In the following part, we give formal proofs to show that some existing HIB-KEM schemes already have the property of pseudorandom decapsulation.

BBG HIB-KEM achieves Pseudorandom Decapsulation. We prove that the HIB-KEM scheme proposed by Boneh, Boyen and Goh [3] satisfies the property of pseudorandom decapsulation. The KEM version of the scheme (BBG-KEM) is as follows:

Let $\mathbb{G}$ be a bilinear group of prime order p and let $e : \mathbb{G} \times \mathbb{G} \to \mathbb{G}_1$ be a bilinear map.

Setup(1^ℓ): Select a generator $g \in \mathbb{G}$, a random $\alpha \in \mathbb{Z}_p$, set $g_1 = g^\alpha$. Pick $g_2, g_3, h_1, \ldots, h_\ell \in \mathbb{G}$. Output $\text{mpk} = (g, g_1, g_2, g_3, h_1, \ldots, h_\ell)$, $\text{msk} = g_2^\alpha$.

KeyGen(msk, id): Suppose that $id = (I_1, \ldots, I_k) \in (\mathbb{Z}_p^*)^k$, output a private key sk_{id} as $sk_{id} = \left(g_2^\alpha \cdot (h_1^{I_1} \cdots h_k^{I_k} \cdot g_3)^r, g^r, h_{k+1}^r, \ldots, h_\ell^r \right)$.

Derive($\mathsf{sk}_{\mathsf{id}|k-1}$, id): Suppose that id $= (I_1, \ldots, I_k) \in (\mathbb{Z}_p^*)^k$, and let

$$\mathsf{sk}_{\mathsf{id}|k-1} = \left(g_2^\alpha \cdot (h_1^{I_1} \cdots h_{k-1}^{I_{k-1}} \cdot g_3)^{r'}, g^{r'}, h_k^{r'}, \ldots, h_\ell^{r'}\right) = (a_0, a_1, b_k, \ldots, b_\ell).$$

To generate $\mathsf{sk}_{\mathsf{id}}$, first pick a random $r'' \in \mathbb{Z}_p$ and then output private key $\mathsf{sk}_{\mathsf{id}}$ as:

$$\mathsf{sk}_{\mathsf{id}} = \left(a_0 \cdot b_k^{I_k} \cdot (h_1^{I_1} \cdots h_k^{I_k} \cdot g_3)^{r''}, a_1 \cdot g^{r''}, b_{k+1} \cdot h_{k+1}^{r''}, \ldots, b_\ell \cdot h_\ell^{r''}\right).$$

Encap(mpk, id): On input an identity id $= (I_1, \ldots, I_k) \in (\mathbb{Z}_p^*)^k$, pick a random $s \in \mathbb{Z}_p$, and output (C, K) as $C = \left(g^s, (h_1^{I_1} \cdots h_k^{I_k} \cdot g_3)^s\right)$, $K = e(g_1, g_2)^s$.

Decap($C, \mathsf{sk}_{\mathsf{id}}$): Parse $C = (A, B)$. Using $\mathsf{sk}_{\mathsf{id}} = (a_0, a_1, \ldots)$, compute $K = \frac{e(A, a_0)}{e(a_1, B)}$.

Boneh et al. put forth the following assumption which is helpful for our proof:

Decisional Weak BDHI Assumption. Let g and h be two generators of $\mathbb{G}$. Let α be a random number in $\mathbb{Z}_p^*$. Let $\boldsymbol{y}_{g,\alpha,\ell} = (y_1, \ldots, y_\ell)$ where $y_i = g^{(\alpha^i)}$. An algorithm $\mathcal{B}$ that outputs $b \in \{0,1\}$ has advantage ϵ in solving Decision ℓ-wBDHI* if

$$\left| \Pr[\mathcal{B}(g, h, \boldsymbol{y}_{g,\alpha,\ell}, e(g,h)^{(\alpha^{\ell+1})}) = 0] - \Pr[\mathcal{B}(g, h, \boldsymbol{y}_{g,\alpha,\ell}, T) = 0] \right| \geq \epsilon,$$

where the probability is taken over the random choices of generators g, h, α, T and random bits consumed by $\mathcal{B}$. The decisional ℓ-wBDHI* assumption posits that any PPT algorithm has only negligible advantage.

Theorem 3. *Assuming that the Decision ℓ-wBDHI* assumption holds in a bilinear group $\mathbb{G}$, then the BBG-KEM satisfies pesudorandom decapsulation.*

Proof. Suppose that $\mathcal{A} = (\mathcal{A}_1, \mathcal{A}_2)$ is a PPT adversary attacking the pseudorandom decapsulation of BBG-KEM and it has advantage ϵ. We construct a simulator $\mathcal{B}$ who has advantage ϵ to break the ℓ-wBDHI* assumption.

$\mathcal{B}$ takes as input a random tuple $(g, h, y_1, \ldots, y_\ell, T)$ from its challenger where $T = e(g, h)^{(\alpha^{\ell+1})}$ or $T \leftarrow \mathbb{G}_1$. $\mathcal{B}$ interacts with $\mathcal{A}$ as follows:

First $\mathcal{B}$ simply chooses $\mathsf{id}^* = (1, 1, \ldots, 1) \in (\mathbb{Z}_p^*)^\ell$ and we denote by $\overline{\mathsf{id}}$ the identity outputs by $\mathcal{A}$. Then $\mathcal{B}$ samples a random $w \in \mathbb{Z}_p$ and sets $g_1 = y_1 = g^\alpha$ and $g_2 = y_\ell \cdot g^w = g^{w + \alpha^\ell}$. Then $\mathcal{B}$ takes $w_1, w_2, \ldots, w_\ell \leftarrow \mathbb{Z}_p$ and sets $h_i = g^{w_i}/y_{\ell-i+1}$ for $i = 1, \ldots, \ell$. Next $\mathcal{B}$ picks random $u \leftarrow \mathbb{Z}_p$ and sets $g_3 = g^u \cdot \prod_{i=1}^\ell y_{\ell-i+1}$. The public key is $\mathsf{mpk} = (g, g_1, g_2, g_3, h_1, \ldots, h_\ell)$. The master secret key is $\mathsf{msk} = g_2^\alpha = g^{\alpha(w+\alpha^\ell)} = y_{\ell+1} \cdot y_1^w$, which is hidden from $\mathcal{B}$ since it does not know the value of $y_{\ell+1}$. Meanwhile, $\mathcal{B}$ produces the ciphertext $C^* = (A, B) = (h, h^{\sum_{i=1}^\ell w_i + u})$. It is a properly generated ciphertext for identity id^* with randomness s if $h = g^s$ since that

$$(h_1 \cdots h_\ell \cdot g_3)^s = \left(\frac{\prod_{i=1}^\ell g^{w_i}}{\prod_{i=1}^\ell y_{\ell-i+1}} \cdot g^u \prod_{i=1}^\ell y_{\ell-i+1} \right)^s = h^{\sum_{i=1}^\ell w_i + u}$$

$\mathcal{B}$ runs $\mathcal{A}_1$ on input $(\mathsf{mpk}, C^*, \mathsf{id}^*)$. When $\mathcal{A}$ queries for the private key of an identity $\mathsf{id} = (I_1, \ldots, I_n) \in (\mathbb{Z}_p^*)^n$ where $n \le \ell$, It must be the case that id is not id^* or a prefix of id^*. This ensures that there must exist a $k \in [n]$ such that $I_k \ne 1$. To answer the query, $\mathcal{B}$ first derives a private key for identity $(I_1, \ldots, I_k)$ and then construct a key for $\mathsf{id} = (I_1, \ldots, I_k, \ldots, I_n)$ using the Derive algorithm. To generate a key for $(I_1, \ldots, I_k)$, $\mathcal{B}$ first picks a random $\tilde{r} \in \mathbb{Z}_p$. Let $r = \frac{\alpha^k}{I_k - 1} + \tilde{r} \in \mathbb{Z}_p$. Then $\mathcal{B}$ hopes to generated the well-distributed key as $(g_2^\alpha \cdot (h_1^{I_1} \cdots h_k^{I_k} g_3)^r, g^r, h_{k+1}^r, \ldots, h_\ell^r)$, the only difficult is to compute the first term in outer brackets. Note that $y_i^{(\alpha^j)} = y_{i+j}$ and then:

$$g_2^\alpha \cdot (h_1^{I_1} \cdots h_k^{I_k} g_3)^r = g_2^\alpha \cdot \left(\prod_{i=1}^{k-1} y_{\ell-i+1}^{1-I_i} \cdot y_{\ell-k+1}^{1-I_k} \cdot \prod_{i=k+1}^{\ell} y_{\ell-i+1}^{1-I_i} \cdot g^{u+\sum_{i=1}^k I_i w_i} \right)^r.$$

We assume that k is the smallest number which meets the condition $I_k \ne 1$. So the first term in brackets $\prod_{i=1}^{k-1} y_{\ell-i+1}^{1-I_i}$ equals 1. The third and fourth terms could be computed by $\mathcal{B}$. Next we concentrate on the second term $(y_{\ell-k+1}^{1-I_k})^r$:

$$(y_{\ell-k+1}^{1-I_k})^r = (y_{\ell-k+1}^{1-I_k})^{\tilde{r}} \cdot y_{\ell-k+1}^{(1-I_k)\frac{\alpha^k}{I_k-1}} = (y_{\ell-k+1}^{1-I_k})^{\tilde{r}} / y_{\ell+1},$$

so $g_2^\alpha \cdot (y_{\ell-k+1}^{1-I_k})^r = y_{\ell+1} \cdot y_1^w \cdot (y_{\ell-k+1}^{1-I_k})^{\tilde{r}} / y_{\ell+1} = y_1^w (y_{\ell-k+1}^{1-I_k})^{\tilde{r}}$, which can be computed by $\mathcal{B}$ through its knowledge of $w, \tilde{r}$ and values of $y_1, y_{\ell-k+1}$ for $k \ge 1$.

Let $\overline{\mathsf{id}} = (I_1, \ldots, I_t)$ where $t \le \ell$ and suppose the private key for $\overline{\mathsf{id}}$ is $\mathsf{sk}_{\overline{\mathsf{id}}} = (a_0, a_1, \ldots)$. Concretely, suppose that $a_0 = g_2^\alpha (h_1^{I_1} \cdots h_t^{I_t} g_3)^v$ and $a_1 = g^v$. If $\mathcal{B}$ chooses a random value $v \in \mathbb{Z}_p$, this key is correctly distributed even though $\mathcal{B}$ cannot derive a_0. $\mathcal{B}$ computes the session key K as $T \cdot e(h, y_1^w) \cdot e\left(h, (h_1^{I_1} \cdots h_t^{I_t} g_3)^v\right) / e(g^v, h^{\sum_{i=1}^\ell w_i + u})$ and finally gives it to $\mathcal{A}_2$. Upon receiving K, $\mathcal{A}_2$ will output a guess bit b' of b. $\mathcal{B}$ returns whatever $\mathcal{A}$ outputs to its challenger. Notice that if $T = e(g, h)^{(\alpha^{\ell+1})}$, K is perfectly distributed because: $K = e(h, g_2^\alpha) e\left(h, (h_1^{I_1} \cdots h_t^{I_t} g_3)^v\right) / e(a_1, B) = \frac{e(A, a_0)}{e(a_1, B)}$. Otherwise if $T \leftarrow \mathbb{G}_1$, then K is uniformly distributed in $\mathbb{G}_1$. This concludes the theorem that BBG-KEM achieves pseudorandom decapsulation. $\square$

Remark 2. The above proof is reminiscent of the process to prove selective security of BBG HIB-KEM scheme. We believe that other examples could be given similarly as long as the underlying HIB-KEM scheme is provably secure in the selective-ID model.

5.3   Inheriting Pseudorandom Decapsulation from HIB-KEM

The following theorem tells that a PIB-KEM scheme deriving from a HIB-KEM scheme could inherit pseudorandom decapsulation.

Theorem 4. *If an ℓ-level HIB-KEM scheme* HIBKEM *with identity space* $(\{0,1\}^*)^\ell$ *satisfies the property of pseudorandom decapsulation, then so does a PIB-KEM scheme* PIBKEM *with identity space* $\{0,1\}^\ell$ *constructed in Sect. 3.1.*

Proof. Suppose there exists an adversary $\mathcal{A} = (\mathcal{A}_1, \mathcal{A}_2)$ attacking the decapsulation pseudorandomness of PIBKEM with identity space $\mathcal{ID} = \{0,1\}^\ell$, we use it as a subroutine to construct an algorithm $\mathcal{B}$ to break the decapsulation pseudorandomness of the underlying HIBKEM with identity space $\mathcal{ID} = (\{0,1\}^1)^\ell$. Initially, $\mathcal{B}$ takes as input $(\mathsf{mpk}, C^*, \mathsf{id}^*)$ and forwards this to $\mathcal{A}_1$. Upon receiving a KeyDer$(\mathsf{msk}, \cdot)$ query on identity $\mathsf{id} \in \{0,1\}^\ell$, $\mathcal{B}$ first parses this id as a vector $v = (\mathsf{id}[1], \ldots, \mathsf{id}[\ell])$ where $\mathsf{id}[i]$ denotes i-th bit of id and then answers by querying its own oracle KeyGen(msk, v). When $\mathcal{A}_1$ outputs an identity $\overline{\mathsf{id}} \in \{0,1\}^\ell$, $\mathcal{B}$ considers it as an ℓ-length vector $\overline{v}$ and outputs this vector. Later on it gets back a K_b from its challenger. Remember the task of $\mathcal{B}$ is to tell $b = 0$ if $K_b = \mathsf{Decap}(C^*, \mathsf{sk}_{\overline{v}})$ or $b = 1$ if $K_b \leftarrow \mathcal{K}$. Then it does the following: for $1 \leq i \leq \ell$, set $v_i = (\overline{\mathsf{id}}[1], \ldots, \overline{\mathsf{id}}[i-1], \overline{\mathsf{id}}[i])$, then query its KeyGen$(\mathsf{msk}, \cdot)$ oracle for each v_i. Note that these queries are valid since none of v_i is a prefix of $\overline{v}$. $\mathcal{B}$ constructs $\mathsf{msk}(\{\overline{\mathsf{id}}\}) := (\mathsf{sk}_{v_1}, \ldots, \mathsf{sk}_{v_\ell})$ and gives it to $\mathcal{A}_2$. It also gives K_b to $\mathcal{A}_2$. When $\mathcal{A}_2$ outputs a bit b', $\mathcal{B}$ outputs the same b'. By observation, $\mathcal{B}$ simulates perfectly the view of $\mathcal{A}$ in game PIB-KEM-RDECAP. So the probability of $\mathcal{B}$ guessing correctly is equal to the probability of $\mathcal{A}$'s output b' satisfying $b' = b$. $\qquad\square$

The following theorem indicates that same result is applicable for a t-PIB-KEM scheme. The proof proceeds analogously, we omit it here.

Theorem 5. *If an ℓ-level HIB-KEM scheme* HIBKEM *with identity space* $(\{0,1\}^*)^\ell$ *satisfies the property of pseudorandom decapsulation, then so does a t-PIB-KEM scheme t-*PIBKEM *with identity space* $\{0,1\}^\ell$ *constructed in Sect. 3.2.*

Acknowledgments. The authors would like to thank anonymous reviewers for their helpful comments and suggestions. This work was supported by National Natural Science Foundation of China (Grants 61772514,61602061), and National Key R&D Program of China (2017YFB1400700).

A   Pseudorandom decapsulation of t-PIB-KEM (Fig. 4)

GAME t-PIB-KEM-RDECAP$^{\mathcal{A}}_{t\text{-PIBKEM}}(\lambda)$:

$(\mathsf{mpk}, \mathsf{msk}) \leftarrow \mathsf{Setup}(1^{\lambda})$

$\mathsf{id}^* \twoheadleftarrow \mathcal{ID}$

$C^* \leftarrow \mathsf{Encap}(\mathsf{mpk}, \mathsf{id}^*)$

$(\overline{\mathsf{id}}, st) \leftarrow \mathcal{A}_1^{\mathsf{KeyDer}(\mathsf{msk}, \cdot), \mathsf{Puncture}(\mathsf{msk}, \cdot)}(\mathsf{mpk}, C^*, \mathsf{id}^*)$

$\mathsf{sk}_{\overline{\mathsf{id}}} \leftarrow \mathsf{KeyDer}(\mathsf{msk}, \overline{\mathsf{id}})$

$b \leftarrow \{0, 1\}; \ K_0 \leftarrow \mathsf{Decap}(C^*, \mathsf{sk}_{\overline{\mathsf{id}}}); \ K_1 \leftarrow \mathcal{K}$

$b' \leftarrow \mathcal{A}_2^{\mathsf{KeyDer}(\mathsf{msk}, \cdot), \mathsf{Puncture}(\mathsf{msk}, \cdot)}(st, K_b)$

If $b' = b$, return 1, else return 0

Fig. 4. The pseudorandom decapsulation property of a t-PIB-KEM scheme. The oracle $\mathsf{KeyDer}(\mathsf{msk}, \mathsf{id})$ returns $\mathsf{sk}_{\mathsf{id}}$ with the restriction that $\mathcal{A}$ is not allowed to query $\mathsf{KeyDer}(\mathsf{msk}, \cdot)$ for identity $\overline{\mathsf{id}}$. Meanwhile, the oracle $\mathsf{Puncture}(\mathsf{msk}, S)$ returns a punctured key $\mathsf{msk}(S)$ where S is a set with size at most t and $\mathcal{A}$ is only allowed to query $\mathsf{Puncture}(\mathsf{msk}, \cdot)$ for any set that *contains* the target identity $\overline{\mathsf{id}}$.

B   Proof of Theorem 2

Proof. The property of unique derivation obviously ensures it to be PRF.

Suppose there exists an adversary $\mathcal{A}$ that breaks the adaptive pseudorandomness of t-puncturable PRF with probability $\frac{1}{2} + \epsilon(\lambda)$, where $\epsilon(\lambda)$ is non-negligible, we build an algorithm $\mathcal{B}$ which has advantage $\epsilon(\lambda)$ in the t-PIB-KEM-RDECAP game.

$\mathcal{B}$ gets as input $(\mathsf{mpk}, C^*, \mathsf{id}^*)$ and simulates the adaptive pseudorandomness game with $\mathcal{A}$. On receiving an evaluation query $x \in \mathcal{ID}$ from $\mathcal{A}$, $\mathcal{B}$ queries its own $\mathsf{KeyDer}(\cdot)$ oracle and obtains sk_x. Then it uses sk_x to compute $\mathsf{Decap}(C^*, \mathsf{sk}_x)$. That is, $F(k, x) = \mathsf{Decap}(C^*, \mathsf{KeyDer}(\mathsf{msk}, x))$. When $\mathcal{A}$ issues a key query of a set S, $\mathcal{B}$ submits this set to oracle $\mathsf{Puncture}(\mathsf{msk}, \cdot)$ and gets back $\mathsf{Puncture}(\mathsf{msk}, S)$. Then it returns $k_S := (\mathsf{msk}(S), C^*)$ to $\mathcal{A}$. When $\mathcal{A}$ sends the challenge point $x^* \in \bigcap_{i=1}^q S_i$, $\mathcal{B}$ sends the same point to its challenger and gets back K_b where $K_b = \mathsf{Decap}(C^*, \mathsf{sk}_{x^*})$ or $K_b \leftarrow \mathcal{K}$. It returns this K_b to $\mathcal{A}$. Eventually, $\mathcal{B}$ outputs whatever $\mathcal{A}$ outputs to its challenger as b'.

Since $\mathcal{B}$ simulates perfectly the adaptive pseudorandomness game to $\mathcal{A}$, the advantage of $\mathcal{B}$ is the same as $\mathcal{A}$, namely $\epsilon(\lambda)$.   □

References

1. Abdalla, M., Catalano, D., Fiore, D.: Verifiable random functions: relations to identity-based key encapsulation and new constructions. J. Cryptol. **27**(3), 544–593 (2014)

2. Bentahar, K., Farshim, P., Malone-Lee, J., Smart, N.P.: Generic constructions of identity-based and certificateless kems. J. Cryptol. **21**(2), 178–199 (2008)
3. Boneh, D., Boyen, X., Goh, E.-J.: Hierarchical identity based encryption with constant size ciphertext. In: Cramer, R. (ed.) EUROCRYPT 2005. LNCS, vol. 3494, pp. 440–456. Springer, Heidelberg (2005). https://doi.org/10.1007/11426639_26
4. Boneh, D., Waters, B.: Constrained pseudorandom functions and their applications. In: Sako, K., Sarkar, P. (eds.) ASIACRYPT 2013. LNCS, vol. 8270, pp. 280–300. Springer, Heidelberg (2013). https://doi.org/10.1007/978-3-642-42045-0_15
5. Boneh, D., Zhandry, M.: Multiparty key exchange, efficient traitor tracing, and more from indistinguishability obfuscation. In: Garay, J.A., Gennaro, R. (eds.) CRYPTO 2014. LNCS, vol. 8616, pp. 480–499. Springer, Heidelberg (2014). https://doi.org/10.1007/978-3-662-44371-2_27
6. Boyle, E., Goldwasser, S., Ivan, I.: Functional signatures and pseudorandom functions. In: Krawczyk, H. (ed.) PKC 2014. LNCS, vol. 8383, pp. 501–519. Springer, Heidelberg (2014). https://doi.org/10.1007/978-3-642-54631-0_29
7. Chen, Y., Zhang, J., Deng, Y., Chang, J.: KDM security for identity-based encryption: constructions and separations. Inf. Sci. **486**, 450–473 (2019)
8. Hohenberger, S., Koppula, V., Waters, B.: Adaptively secure puncturable pseudorandom functions in the standard model. In: Iwata, T., Cheon, J.H. (eds.) ASIACRYPT 2015. LNCS, vol. 9452, pp. 79–102. Springer, Heidelberg (2015). https://doi.org/10.1007/978-3-662-48797-6_4
9. Kiayias, A., Papadopoulos, S., Triandopoulos, N., Zacharias, T.: Delegatable pseudorandom functions and applications. In: Sadeghi, A., Gligor, V.D., Yung, M. (eds.) CCS 2013, pp. 669–684. ACM, New York (2013). https://doi.org/10.1145/2508859.2516668
10. Sahai, A., Waters, B.: How to use indistinguishability obfuscation: deniable encryption, and more. In: Shmoys, D.B. (ed.) STOC 2014, pp. 475–484. ACM (2014). https://doi.org/10.1145/2591796.2591825

Towards Blockchain-Enabled Searchable Encryption

Qiang Tang[✉]

Luxembourg Institute of Science and Technology, 5 Avenue des Hauts-Fourneaux,
4362 Esch-sur-Alzette, Luxembourg
qiang.tang@list.lu

Abstract. Distributed Leger Technologies (DLTs), most notably Blockchain technologies, bring decentralised platforms which eliminate a single trusted third party and avoid the notorious single point of failure vulnerability. Since Nakamoto's Bitcoin cryptocurrency system, an enormous number of decentralised applications have been proposed on top of these technologies, aiming at more transparency and trustworthiness than their traditional counterparts. Unfortunately, Blockchain introduces very subtle implications for other desirable properties such as privacy. In this work, we demonstrate these subtle implications for Blockchain-based searchable encryption solutions, which are one specific use case of cloud computing services. These solutions build on top of Blockchain and attempt to achieve both the standard privacy property and the new fairness property, which requires that search operations are carried out faithfully and are rewarded accordingly. We show that directly replacing the server in an existing searchable encryption solution with a Blockchain will cause undesirable operational cost, privacy loss, and security vulnerabilities. The analysis results indicate that a dedicated server is still needed to achieve the desired privacy guarantee. To this end, we propose two frameworks which can be instantiated based on most existing searchable encryption schemes. Through analysing these two frameworks, we affirmatively show that a carefully engineered Blockchain-enabled solution can achieve the desired fairness property while preserving the privacy guarantee of the original searchable encryption scheme simultaneously.

1 Introduction

With the prevalence of cloud computing, many organizations are outsourcing their data and services to the cloud. By doing so, an organization or individual can enjoy a wide spectrum of benefits such as agileness and cost-saving. Moreover, the cloud service provider can deploy sophisticated cybersecurity solutions to meet the requirements from the relevant security regulations. It is widely perceived that the big cloud service providers, such as Amazon and Microsoft, provide better protection in practice than most organizations if they do it by themselves. However, there are indeed drawbacks for the outsourced data and corresponding operations, among which *loss of privacy* is the most significant

© Springer Nature Switzerland AG 2020
J. Zhou et al. (Eds.): ICICS 2019, LNCS 11999, pp. 482–500, 2020.
https://doi.org/10.1007/978-3-030-41579-2_28

one. As the cloud service provider can observe the data usage patterns and potentially have access to the plain data, it becomes a concern when the data contains sensitive information. The issue becomes more complex when the services are cross-border and need to comply with privacy regulations from different regimes. Besides privacy, the verifiability of outsourced computing tasks might also be a serious concern. In order to save cost, the cloud service provider might not carry out the promised tasks faithfully. At the end, the incomplete or even flawed computing results might damage the client's business severely. Therefore, how to guarantee privacy and verifiability in outsourcing has been an active research area for many years.

Regarding the potential computing tasks on outsourced data, search is the most fundamental one. To cater to the privacy needs, searchable encryption is a category of cryptographic primitives that allows data to be outsourced in an encrypted form while still being able to be searched over. Searchable encryption typically assumes a standard client-server setting, where a client outsources its encrypted data to a cloud server, which can then search on the client's behalf without decrypting the data. Existing searchable encryption schemes can be broadly classified into two settings. In the asymmetric setting [2], the client can publish a public key, by which anybody can generate searchable encrypted data and store it on the server. Later, the client, who has access to the private key, can let the server search on its behalf by issuing a trapdoor. In the symmetric setting [16], a client uses symmetric keys to encrypt its own data and stores the ciphertexts on the server. Later on, as in the asymmetric setting, the client can let the server search on its behalf by issuing a trapdoor. Compared to the symmetric setting, the asymmetric setting poses higher challenges to data privacy, as shown in [1]. This implies that asymmetric searchable encryption schemes leak much more information in reality, and potentially make such schemes very undesirable facing strong attackers.

In this paper, we focus on symmetric searchable encryption schemes and show how to properly leverage Blockchain to achieve verifiability and more properties without sacrificing privacy.

1.1 Preliminary on Symmetric Searchable Encryption

We assume the client has a database $\mathcal{DB}$, which contains the files which will be searched based on an inverted index. We assume a basic version of symmetric searchable encryption scheme which only consists of two stages Setup and Search, with an example shown in Sect. 3.1. In the Setup stage, the client extracts a keyword set $\mathcal{W}$ from the files in the $\mathcal{DB}$ and builds an encrypted inverted index, which is then stored on the server. In the Search stage, the client interacts with the server to search for the files which contain any keyword $w \in \mathcal{W}$.

To facilitate our discussions, we provide a high-level workflow of both stages. Existing schemes might optimize their performances or security with very specific tricks, e.g. index data structure. Nevertheless, most of them follow the workflow. In the Setup stage, the following operations will occur.

1. Run by the client, it first generates the key materials, namely private key(s).
2. Given the database $\mathcal{DB}$, a keyword set $\mathcal{W}$ is extracted and a plaintext inverted index is built. The index is informally a table [18], where each row contains the file identifiers associated with a specific keyword. Note that the client might choose to pad the rows so that they contain certain number of file identifiers, e.g. all rows can be padded to contain the same number of file identifiers.
3. Using the private key(s), the client *encrypts* the inverted index and obtains an encrypted form of it. Note that the *encryption* here means not only the hiding of keyword and identifier information but also can be the hiding of other pattern information such as the ordering of the encrypted keywords and identifiers. Finally, the encrypted index is stored on the server.

In the Search stage, if the client wants to find all the file identifiers associated with a keyword w, the following operations will occur.

1. Using the private key(s), the client generates a trapdoor T_w based on its private keys(s) and w, and sends it to the server.
2. With the trapdoor T_w, the server can go through the encrypted index and match those elements which contain the same keyword (i.e. w) as that embedded in the trapdoor.
3. For the matched elements, the server recovers the associated file identifiers, denoted as a set $\mathcal{ID}_w$ and return them to the client.

1.2 Privacy and Fairness Challenges

Searchable encryption can be seen as a derivative of standard encryption primitives, but it is more complex due to the fact that, concerning privacy, we need to consider not only the encrypted index but also the trapdoors. If there is a secure channel between the client and the server, then the server is the main privacy attacker. Intuitively, we will expect at least the encrypted index or trapdoors alone do not leak any information about the embedded keywords. This can be formulated in a similar way to the semantic security property of encryption schemes [9], and easy to achieve. However, the situation is more complex for searchable encryption, due to the fact that search operations link the encrypted index and trapdoors so that more information will be leaked. In more detail, there are concerns of access pattern leakage and search pattern leakage. Informally, access pattern is the file identifier information resulted from the client's search queries. While, search pattern is about whether two trapdoors contain the same keywords or not. These two types of leakages are clearly closely related. After receiving several trapdoors, even if the server might not learn the keywords, it can derive statistical information about the keywords based on access pattern. In practice, the statistical information can disclose the search pattern and even lead to full recovery of the keywords. Besides privacy, the other practical concern related to searchable encryption is the verifiability of search results. As we have mentioned before, it is desirable for the server to assure the client that the search results have come from a faithful execution of the protocol. On the other side, it is also desirable that the server is rewarded properly for the faithful execution of the search protocol. Follow the literature work, if a searchable encryption solution satisfies both requirements simultaneously, we say it is *fair*.

So far, very little has been done to design privacy-preserving and fair searchable encryption solutions, except for some recent solutions that leverage on Blockchain to achieve fairness [4,10]. We note that there are verifiable schemes, e.g. [3], which however only guarantee that a semi-honest server will follow the protocol. Being a technology that brings *trust* as many believe, Blockchain causes very subtle tradeoffs among the desirable properties, e.g. privacy and verifiability. It is not clear how well these recent searchable encryption solutions have addressed the privacy and fairness requirements.

1.3   Contribution and Organisation

Our contribution in this paper is two-fold. We start by examining some recent Blockchain-based searchable encryption solutions, i.e. [4,10]. We show that directly replacing the server of a searchable encryption scheme with a Blockchain is a very undesirable solution. First of all, it introduces considerable cost with respect to storing the encrypted index and executing the smart contract which implements the search operation. Secondly, these solutions suffer from the inherent issues of Blockchain, e.g. the forking problem. This might cause serious usability issues for these solutions. Thirdly, the privacy concerns of the underlying scheme are amplified by the Blockchain platform. The access pattern and search pattern leakages are exposed to all entities who can access the Blockchain. To mitigate the identified issues in our analysis, we then propose two frameworks that can be instantiated based on most existing searchable encryption schemes. In both frameworks, search operations are carried out by the server(s) as in the traditional schemes, while Blockchain is leveraged to achieve the fairness property only.

The rest of this paper is organised as follows. In Sect. 2, we present a brief summary of Blockchain technologies. In Sect. 3, we present and analyse the existing Blockchain-based solutions. In Sect. 4, we present our new frameworks and provide corresponding analysis. In Sect. 5, we conclude the paper.

2   Blockchain in a Nutshell

Since the seminal report from Nakamoto [11], the concept of Blockchain has become very popular not only in the research community but also in the society at large. Its popularity largely comes from the fact that it is the key enabling technology for the variety of cryptocurrency systems, including Bitcoin [11] and the altcoins, even though the history of both the idea of cryptocurrency and the techniques in Blockchain can be traced back to much earlier era [13]. As a matter of fact, today there are over 1600 such systems according to Wikipedia.

2.1 Blockchain Overview

Informally, the data on a Blockchain is organized in the form shown in Fig. 1. Depending on who maintains the chain (i.e. generate and approve new blocks), Blockchain systems can be roughly divided into two categories. If anyone can publish and approve a new block, it is permissionless. Otherwise, if only particular nodes are allowed to do it, it is permissioned. More details about the categorisation can be found in the NIST report [19]. From now on, we refer to these particular privileged nodes as *miners* in the paper.

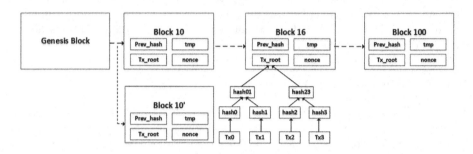

Fig. 1. Blockchain structure

As the core characteristic of Blockchain, repeatedly, a certain number of new data entries (e.g. transactions) will be packed into a new block and appended to the existing (longest) chain. In the case of Bitcoin Blockchain, a new block also includes the hash value of the last block of the current chain. The block is formed with some specific features, e.g. a proof of work (PoW) needs to be carried out so that the hash value of the new block contains some number of consecutive zeros. The new block will be broadcast to the whole network, and it will be accepted in the network after everything being validated. Depending on the variants and implementations, there are many subtle details on how a block is formed and accepted to the chain, we refer the readers to the corresponding technical specifications for the precise information.

Besides cryptocurrencies, Blockchain systems act as the key foundation platform for *smart contracts*, which facilitate automated execution of software programs in a verifiable manner. One of the notable examples is Ethereum, which is the second largest cryptocurrency system after Bitcoin and gains the popularity because of its powerful smart contracts functionality. In practice, smart contracts can enable a variety of trustworthy distributed applications, e.g. building digital Decentralized Autonomous Organizations (DAOs).

It is worth noting that Blockchain represents one special case of the broader distributed ledger technologies (DLTs), which are decentralised databases that rely on independent computers to record, share and synchronize digital transactions. Despite the different forms, a DLT can possess similar properties to those from a Blockchain. For a more comprehensive review of cryptocurrencies,

Blockchain and DLT technologies, we refer the readers to the comprehensive books such as [8,12,17].

2.2 Properties of Blockchain

Regardless of the forms of a Blockchain or DLT in general, the following useful properties can be expected.

- *Democracy and Decentralised Control.* Everyone can potentially act as a miner and has the same privilege to generate blocks and approve blocks to the Blockchain. This is generally true for systems employing the PoW as the consensus mechanism in the permissionless scenario, while it can be different in other cases. Regardless, Blockchain eliminates a single fully trusted party and avoids the single point of failure vulnerability.
- *Integrity and Immutability.* If an attacker or a group of colluded attackers does not dominate the consensus process, e.g. in the case of Bitcoin Blockchain more than 51% of the computing power is at the hands of semi-honest miners (see the explanation below for the semi-honest assumption), then it will not be able to modify the existing blocks that have been agreed on by the consensus.
- *Consistency.* There is a single consistent view of the chain even facing strong attackers, based on assumptions mentioned above. However, note that when nodes deviate from the predefined rules, forks could be generated and there will be different views from different players.

These properties further provide certain levels of auditability and transparency, and generally increase the trustworthiness of the system. These aforementioned properties or even a subset of them can be very desirable for many applications from different sectors. Some people have considered Blockchain as a trust machine for the society. The trust that users have towards Blockchain systems is mainly from the fact that the majority of miners will be semi-honest from the cryptographic perspective. The semi-honest assumption basically says that these miners will follow the predefined protocols to perform what has been specified and programmed in the Blockchain software, and particularly this excludes the possibility that they will collude to interfere with the normal Blockchain operations. For PoW-based Blockchain, the trust depends on the common assumption that 51% of the computing power lies at the hands of semi-honest miners. While for other types of Blockchain, corresponding assumptions need to be made. For example, for Proof of Stake (PoS)-based DLTs, we need to assume that the parties that possess the majority of stakes will behave honestly.

Besides cryptocurrencies, Blockchain has been widely promoted in designing decentralised protocols, e.g. fair secure multiparty computation protocols [6], confidentiality-preserving smart contracts [5], double auction [20], and the Blockchain-based searchable encryption schemes [4,10]. In most of these works, Blockchain is treated as a trusted platform that achieves some of the aforementioned properties persistently. However, we observe a dilemma with this trust assumption and raise concerns about the feasibility of (some) existing solutions. Let's suppose a client originally deploys a service at a dedicated cloud server, and now it wants to leverage Blockchain to improve the security.

– On one hand, all the promises of a Blockchain come from the holy assumption that no single entity can significantly influence the operations of the system and everything should be based on a consensus. In reality, it is more complex when it comes to questions such as how the evolution of a Blockchain platform should proceed, see the case of Bitcoin Blockchain. This means that a normal user like the client, will not play any significant role, particularly the client may not be able to determine the miners or even know them.
– On the other hand, from the perspective of the client, it may desire absolute certainty regarding the status of the Blockchain, the promised properties, and other aspects such as efficiency and cost. Unfortunately, the satisfaction of these requirements will depend on the consensus of some entities, which are not supposed to be influenced by the client.

Clearly, there is a governance dilemma facing the client when it wants to deploy its service on Blockchain. More consequences of this dilemma can be found in Sects. 3.2 and 3.3. Nowadays, this dilemma is hindering the deployment of Blockchain-based services.

3   Blockchain-Enabled Searchable Encryption

In this section, we first briefly recap the Blockchain-based searchable solutions from [4,10], and then present our analysis results from the economical, security and privacy aspects.

3.1   Description of the Existing Solutions

The central idea of solutions from [4,10] is to treat Blockchain (that supports smart contracts) as a transparent and neutral platform. Intuitively, these solutions just replace the server in traditional scenarios with a Blockchain, which interacts with the client via a smart contract. All search and fairness-related logics are programmed into the smart contract. Based on the transparency and neutrality assumptions, the following notion of "fairness" can be achieved: (1) search operations will be performed in the pre-defined manner if we assume that a majority of the miners will not collude with each other; (2) the miner(s) will be rewarded for their search operations due to the fact that deposits are required before any search operation is carried out.

Let the client's database be denoted as $\mathcal{DB}$. Next we review the solution from [10]. For simplicity, we only review the *Setup* and *Search* stages, while skipping the *add* and *delete* stages as they do not affect our analysis.

– Setup($\mathcal{DB}, \lambda$): run by the client, the following operations are performed.

1. Initialize an empty list L, an empty dictionary σ, a counter c, and a block size p.
2. Extract a keyword set $\mathcal{W}$ from $\mathcal{DB}$.
3. Select two pseudorandom functions F and G; Generate a secret key $K \xleftarrow{\$} \{0,1\}^\lambda$.
4. For every keyword $w \in \mathcal{W}$, do the following
   (a) Compute $K_1 = \mathsf{F}(K, 1||w)$ and $K_2 = \mathsf{F}(K, 2||w)$, where $||$ is a concatenation operator.
   (b) Set $\alpha = \lfloor \frac{|\mathsf{DB}(w)|}{p} \rfloor$ and $c = 0$, where $\mathsf{DB}(w)$ is the file identifier set associated with w and $|\mathsf{DB}(w)|$ indicates the number of identifiers in the set.
   (c) Divide $\mathsf{DB}(w)$ into $\alpha + 1$ blocks, and pad the last block into p entries if necessary.
   (d) For each block in $\mathsf{DB}(w)$, do the following
       i. Set $\tilde{id} = id_1|| \cdots ||id_p$, $r \xleftarrow{\$} \{0,1\}^\lambda$, $d = \tilde{id} \oplus \mathsf{G}(K_2, r)$, $l = \mathsf{F}(K_1, c)$.
       ii. Add (l, d, r) to the list L in lex order.
       iii. Set $c = c + 1$.
5. Set $EDB = L$, partition EDB into n blocks EDB_i ($1 \le i \le n$) and send them to the smart contract.
6. For each received EDB_i, the smart contract parses each entry in EDB_i into (l, d, r) and add it to the Blockchain.

- $\mathsf{Search}(K, w; *)$: run between the client and the Blockchain (via the smart contract), the following steps are followed.
1. The client computes $K_1 = \mathsf{F}(K, 1||w)$, $K_2 = \mathsf{F}(K, 2||w)$.
2. The client sets $c = 0$, and sets an iteration number R and step size $step$.
3. For $0 \le i \le R$, do the following
   (a) The client sets $ST_i = (K_1, K_2, c)$ and sends it to the smart contract.
   (b) The smart contract asserts the gas cost is lower than the balance, and then performs the following steps for $i = 0$ until $i \ge step$. Note that the solution assumes an Ethereum platform.
       i. Set $\ell = \mathsf{F}(K_1, c)$.
       ii. If $\mathsf{Get}(\ell) = \perp$ stop; otherwise, set the result to be (d, r). The Get function simply retrieves the tuple with the same ℓ.
       iii. Compute $\tilde{id} = d \oplus \mathsf{G}(K_2, r)$;
       iv. Parse and save $\tilde{id}$.
       v. Set $c = c + 1$.
       vi. Set $i = i + 1$.

The solution from [4] is pretty the same as the above solution. The main difference is that it assumes a specific electronic health record (EHR) application scenario and the keyword is in the form of an expression like "(disease = 'disease name') AND (num1 $\le$ age $\le$ num2)".

3.2   General Analysis w.r.t. Blockchain Usage

From an economical perspective, in comparison to a dedicated server based solution, it is clear that a Blockchain-based solution will incur more costs regarding storage and computations, because several miners will need to perform the same tasks in parallel. The computational cost might become a more significant concern if a PoW-based consensus is employed by the underlying Blockchain platform. In connection to *fairness*, one hidden concern is about the cost model for the miners of the Blockchain. By default, it is common to estimate the cost of operations based on the computations incurred by the smart contract executions. However, the real cost for the miners goes beyond that. For example, there is also cost for the communication and storage. In addition, the miners need to guarantee their availability for the searchable encryption services, which means investment in security and disaster recovery countermeasures. In the proposed solutions [4,10], it is not clear how the client should estimate these costs and include them in the offer.

Contrary to the common belief that Blockchain could act as a "trust" machine to build secure applications, it actually brings its inherent security risks that can be fatal to the applications on top. One prominent security issue is around smart contracts, where one well-known example is the decentralized autonomous organization (DAO) attack in 2016, which has exploited some software bugs in the underlying Ethereum smart contracts, that leads to the transfer of 3.6 million Ether to the attacker's account. As a result of the attack, the Ethereum Blockchain had to make a hard fork due to the lack of a unanimous consensus on the solution. Besides smart contracts, Blockchain systems in general are also subject to other attacks, e.g. those against consensus mechanisms and distributed denial-of-service (DDoS) attacks [15]. In the traditional setting, these issues might be easier to avoid or solve, or at least they can be solved much more quickly.

3.3   Specific Analysis w.r.t. Privacy Guarantee

As noted in Sect. 1.2, almost all searchable encryption schemes leak certain information to the server. Although a symmetric searchable encryption scheme leaks less than its asymmetric counterpart, the leakage might still be considered to be non-negligible. Take the scheme from Sect. 3.1 as an example, there are (at least) two kinds of leakages, which are commonly shared by other similar schemes.

- *search pattern leakage.* The Search algorithm is a deterministic function. This means that if the client searches the same keyword more than once, then the Blockchain miners will notice it. Based on such information, statistics such as frequency of searched keywords can be established. In turn, such statistics may allow the miners to recover the underlying keywords.
- *access pattern leakage.* In the Setup($\mathcal{DB}$) algorithm, DB(w) will be padded to guarantee that every block has exactly p entries. However, this padding operation does not anonymize the index length very well. Let's assume DB(w_1)

has $p + 1$ entries and $\mathsf{DB}(w_2)$ has $2p + 1$ entries. In this case, even after the padding, the keyword w_2 will result in p more entries on the Blockchain than the keyword w_1. As a result, the Search operation may reveal the size relationship of the file identifier sets associated with the searched keywords.

Specific to this scheme, it is undesirable to reveal $\tilde{id}$ to the smart contract. Nevertheless, this can be easily resolved by not sending K_2 to the smart contract and instead the client decrypts d by itself to recover $\tilde{id}$ at the end of the search operation.

In comparison to the traditional scenario without using a Blockchain, where the privacy information leakage is only limited to a single server, the leakage is amplified in Blockchain-based solutions. For searchable encryption applications, the immutability property of Blockchain might not be really necessary. In the contrary, this property might be undesirable concerning privacy protection. If the encrypted index and search histories live forever on a Blockchain, then it will stay as a persistent attack surface for any (emerging) attackers.

3.4   Summary and Roadmap

So far, we have analysed the advantages as well as disadvantages of Blockchain-based solutions. Our analysis indicates that a solution built directly based on a Blockchain, either permissioned or permissionless, causes issues from different aspects, including cost, security and privacy. For the studied solutions, it seems that the disadvantages will outweigh the advantages in practice. Nevertheless, this does not imply that Blockchain is useless for these applications, rather we believe that Blockchain will be a very useful tool to guarantee the fairness property. Without it, it will be a very sophisticated task to design fair and privacy-preserving searchable encryption solutions, and it may need to make significant changes to existing privacy-preserving searchable encryption schemes.

Based on our analysis, towards designing privacy-preserving and fair searchable encryption solutions, a modular approach seems more appropriate: exploiting Blockchain for the fairness guarantee and relying on dedicated server(s) for the actual search operations on the basis of an existing searchable encryption scheme. The key challenge is to guarantee that the involvement of Blockchain does not affect the privacy guarantees of the underlying searchable encryption scheme. This leads to two new frameworks in the next section.

4   New Generic Blockchain-Based Frameworks

In this section, we propose two generic Blockchain-based frameworks, that can be instantiated based on most symmetric searchable encryption schemes. In both frameworks, there are three types of entities involved.

- *Client:* The client is the party that wants to outsource its encrypted index.
- *Server(s):* As in the traditional setting, the server(s) store the encrypted index and carry out the search operations.

– *Blockchain:* The Blockchain acts as a semi-trusted platform to ensure fairness.

We assume there is a secure communication channel (for confidentiality and integrity) between the client and all server(s), while there is no such a link between any entity and the Blockchain but we do assume that only the legitimate entity can communicate with the smart contract (which means a channel with integrity protection only).

4.1 Initial Framework Design

In this design, the client needs to choose multiple servers for the sake of facilitating fairness while limiting information leakage to the Blockchain. Suppose there is a symmetric searchable encryption scheme (Setup, Search), which can be abstracted in the manner of Sect. 1.1. Shown in Fig. 2, leveraging on a Blockchain, the new construction consists of two stages $(\mathsf{Setup}^{\dagger}, \mathsf{Search}^{\dagger})$.

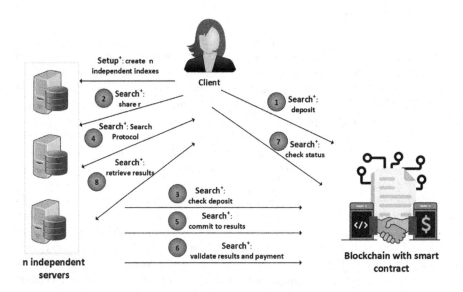

Fig. 2. Initial design

– $\mathsf{Setup}^{\dagger}$ Stage: The client chooses n servers which will not collude all together by assumption. The client then runs Setup n times to generate n independent encrypted indexes for its database. Finally, the client stores the indexes on the servers, where every server receives a unique index.
– $\mathsf{Search}^{\dagger}$ Stage: Given any keyword w, the search operation goes with the following phases.

1. *Request* phase: The client deposits a certain amount of money on the Blockchain. The money should cover the cost of search operations of the servers and the operational cost of Blockchain for the whole workflow (i.e. this and next phases). Simultaneously, the client chooses a random number r and sends it to all the servers to initiate a search operation.
2. *Search* phase: Every server verifies that sufficient money has been deposited on the Blockchain. If the verification passes, it runs the Search protocol with the client. Regarding the abstraction of Search in Sect. 1.1, the server skips Step 3, and, instead, it does the following.
   (a) Compute a hash value of the form: $H(\mathcal{ID}_w\|r)$, where $\mathcal{ID}_w$ contains the matched file identifiers and H is a cryptographic hash function.
   (b) Run a commitment scheme (e.g. that from [14]) to generate a commitment *commit* for $H(\mathcal{ID}_w\|r)$.
   (c) Store *commit* on the Blockchain.
3. *Validation* phase: Every server checks that all other servers have sent their commitments to the Blockchain. If so, it sends its key, which is related to the commitment scheme, to the Blockchain. The smart contract opens all the commitments with the corresponding keys and stores $H(\mathcal{ID}_w\|r)$ on the Blockchain. If all the opened results are the same, then the smart contract makes a payment using the deposited money to every server. Otherwise, the smart contract stops and leaves the client and servers to solve the dispute offline.
4. *Retrieval* phase: If payments have been made, the client requests all the servers to send back the file identifiers $\mathcal{ID}_w$. It can validate the received $\mathcal{ID}_w$ based on the hash value $H(\mathcal{ID}_w\|r)$ and the random number r.

It is easy to check that if the client and servers are semi-honest, then the searchable encryption solution will work properly. Comparing with the solution from Sect. 3.1, it is clear that the Blockchain has very light involvement here: mainly storing deposit and validating the hashed search results, i.e. the hash values $H(\mathcal{ID}_w\|r)$. Next, we evaluate the overall security of this design by answering the following questions.

How has the privacy guarantee of the original searchable encryption scheme been affected? From the perspective of an individual server, it is easy to see that adapting a searchable encryption scheme to the new framework does not affect the privacy properties of the original scheme. In another word, the information leakage to an individual server remains the same. When several servers collude, it becomes quite tricky, at least for those schemes which can only be proven secure in the indistinguishability-based security models. Nevertheless, if the underlying searchable encryption scheme adopts a simulation-based security definition, e.g. [7], we conjecture that the collusion of all servers leaks the same amount of information as in the case of a single server.

How does the Blockchain affect the privacy and other security properties? As to data storage related to the index and search results, the Blockchain only stores $H(ID\|r)$ which is a random value if H is modelled as a random oracle. Therefore, the Blockchain does not affect the privacy guarantee regarding all potential attackers: one server, multiple servers, and even all servers.

How has the fairness property been achieved? We analyse the fairness property from perspectives of the client and servers, respectively.

- It is easy to check that if at least one server is semi-honest then any misbehaved server will be detected and no payment will be made. Here, the misbehaviour mainly means that a server does not commit to the right $\mathcal{ID}_w$. It is left as an offline task to figure out who are the cheated servers and how to compensate for the semi-honest ones.
- *Let's assume the indexes have been generated faithfully by the client in the* Setup† *Stage and the random number r and trapdoors issued to the servers are properly generated in the* Search† *Stage.* If all servers carry out the search honestly then they will be paid by the smart contract in the *Validation* Phase, regardless of the client's decision at that point. However, if the client is malicious and deviates from the protocol specification, e.g. issuing a wrong trapdoor to a specific server, then even if a server is honest it might not be paid.

In summary, the above design does not provide a full-fledged solution for fairness because offline operations need to be carried out to solve the dispute and compensate for all honest behaviours. It tells us that employing multiple servers does not necessarily lead to a straightforward achievement of fairness. This is due to the fact that we do not want the client and servers to make their operations transparent and publicly verifiable for the sake of privacy protection, in contrast to the analysed Blockchain-based solutions.

4.2   Improved Framework Design

In the initial design, it is easy to check that if all the servers collude then they can fake the $\mathcal{ID}_w$ together so that the validation by the Blockchain will not detect the cheating. In practice, it might be difficult to decide how many servers should be chosen to fulfill the assumption, i.e. setting the n parameter. If we simply assume all the servers are semi-honest, a common assumption in many papers, then both caveats will not be an issue. However, it is desirable to get rid of them technically. In addition, the client might misbehave in the protocol, e.g. sends a wrong index or trapdoor to a specific server, so that fairness will not be achieved even if all servers are semi-honest. Although this is very unlikely to occur for a rational client in practice, but it remains as a potential concern.

To eliminate these caveats with technical countermeasures, we propose an improved design, shown in Fig. 3. Since we do not intend to improve or affect the security guarantee of the original searchable encryption scheme, this improved design aims at achieving the fairness property while avoiding the caveats in the initial design. To this end, we let the client sign the encrypted index and the trapdoors so that no entity can misbehave and deny its misbehaviour. Public-key encryption and zero-knowledge proofs are employed to preserve the privacy guarantee of the original scheme. We require also the server to deposit money on the Blockchain to deter its cheating incentives.

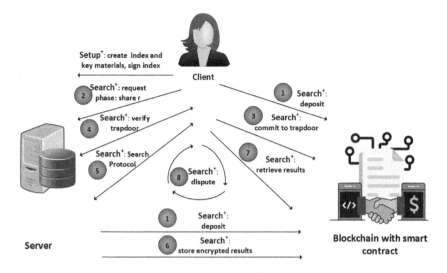

Fig. 3. Improved design

Suppose there is a symmetric searchable encryption scheme (Setup, Search), which can be abstracted in the manner of Sect. 1.1. The improved construction has two new stages (Setup†, Search†).

1. **Setup†** Stage: The client runs Setup to generate a searchable index for its database $\mathcal{DB}$, with the following deviations.
   - For each keyword $w \in \mathcal{W}$, besides the associated file identifier set $\mathcal{ID}_w$, the client generates a private key K_w and adds an additional virtual identifier $id_w^* = \mathsf{H}(K_w \| \mathcal{ID}_w)$ where H is a cryptographic hash function and $\mathcal{ID}_w$ denotes the concatenation of file identifiers in lex order. We further assume that id_w^* can be easily distinguished from those identifiers in $\mathcal{ID}_w$.
   - The client chooses an EU-CMA (Existential Unforgeability under a Chosen Message Attack) secure signature scheme (KeyGen$_s$, Sign, Verify) and runs KeyGen$_s$ to generate a sign/verification key pair (sk_s, vk_s). It also chooses an IND-CPA (Indistinguishability under chosen-plaintext attack) secure public key encryption scheme (KeyGen$_e$, Enc, Dec) and runs KeyGen$_e$ to generate an encryption/decryption key pair (pk_e, sk_e).

   Besides the required activities in the original Setup procedure, the client stores K_w $(w \in \mathcal{W})$, sk_s, and ske locally, and stores the public keys on the Blockchain. The client also generates a signature sig_I for the encrypted index and stores it on the Blockchain.

   We assume the smart contract on the Blockchain platform has been deployed with the following functions.
   - **Deposit:** the client or the server can call this function to deposit money which can be used to make payments.
   - **Dispute:** the client can call this function to resolve cheating activities.

– SearchOK: the client explicitly validates the search result and makes a payment.

2. Search† Stage: Given any keyword w, the search operation goes with the following phases.

(a) *Request* phase: Both the client and the server deposit a certain amount of money on the Blockchain, by invoking the Deposit function of the smart contract. The client's money should cover the cost of search operation of the server, the operational cost of Blockchain for the whole workflow (i.e. this and next steps excluding dispute resolution), and the cost of dispute resolution function Dispute. While the server's money should cover the operational cost of Blockchain for the whole workflow, the cost of dispute resolution function Dispute, plus a pre-agreed amount for punishing its potential cheating behaviour.

At the end of this phase, the smart contract verifies the deposits and indicates the client and the server to proceed or not.

(b) *Search* Phase: The server runs the Search protocol with the client. Referring to the abstraction of Search in Sect. 1.1, we add the following extra operations.

– At the end of Step 1, the client chooses a random number r and generates a signature $sig_w = \mathsf{Sign}(\mathsf{H}(r\|T_w), sk_s)$. It stores sig_w on the Blockchain and shares r with the server.

– At the beginning of Step 2, the server retrieves the sig_w from the Blockchain and verifies it according to the received trapdoor and random number r by the Verify algorithm. It also verifies the signature sig_I for the encrypted index. If the verifications pass, it continues the operations; otherwise it aborts.

– In Step 3, after recovering the file identifiers $id_w^*, \mathcal{ID}_w$, the server encrypts them with pk_e and stores the ciphertext C_w on the Blockchain.

(c) *Retrieval & Validation* Phase: Before going to the details, we define two actions first.

– **Action type-1**: the smart contract (1) makes a payment to the server; (2) return the server's deposit back.

– **Action type-2**: the smart contract (1) pays the server's deposit to the client by deducing the amount for smart contract execution and the server's deposit for dispute resolution function Dispute.

In this phase, the client retrieves the ciphertext C_w and obtains the plaintext: $id_w^*, \mathcal{ID}_w$. Then the client verifies the search results by checking $id_w^* = \mathsf{H}(K_w\|\mathcal{ID}_w)$.

– If the verification passes, the client invokes the SearchOK function which will carry out **Action type-1** and return the client's deposit for dispute resolution function Dispute.

– If the verification fails, the client invokes the Dispute function, by providing $id_w^*, \mathcal{ID}_w$ and a zero-knowledge proof $\mathcal{P}_1$ showing that $id_w^*, \mathcal{ID}_w$ are the plaintext of the ciphertext C_w; the server is required to provide r, T_w. The Dispute function does the following.

   i. Verify the signature sig_w based on the received r and T_w. If the verification passes, it continues; otherwise it carries out **Action type-2** in favor of the client.

   ii. Request the server to upload a copy of encrypted index, denoted as $\mathcal{I}$, and verify its signature sig_I which has been stored on the Blockchain. If the verification passes, it continues; otherwise it carries out **Action type-2** in favor of the client.

   iii. Verify the proof $\mathcal{P}_1$. If the verification passes, it continues; otherwise it carries out **Action type-1** in favor of the server.

   iv. Execute the Search procedure with T_w to obtain $id_w^{*\prime}, \mathcal{ID}_w'$. If these values are different from $id_w^*, \mathcal{ID}_w$, it carries out **Action type-2** in favor of the client. Otherwise, it carries out **Action type-1** in favor of the server.

If the Dispute function is not invoked, the smart contract carries out **Action type-1** and returns the client's deposit for dispute resolution function Dispute.

It is easy to check that if the client and the server are semi-honest, then the searchable encryption solution will work properly. Unless there is a dispute to be resolved, the Blockchain has very light involvement in the new solution: mainly storing deposits, public keys, the signatures, encrypted search results, and so on. As to setting up of the client's signature scheme and encryption scheme in the Setup† Stage, EU-CMA security is necessary to prevent other entities (e.g. the server) from forging the client's signature, while IND-CPA is adequate to protect the confidentiality of the encrypted data due to the fact that no outsider attacker is allowed to commit ciphertext to the Blockchain and get access to decryption oracle (see our unilateral integrity assumption made in the beginning of this section).

Next, we evaluate the overall security of this design by answering the same questions as those for the initial design.

How has the privacy guarantee of the original searchable encryption scheme been affected? The main change to the original searchable encryption scheme is adding the virtual identifier id_w^* for every keyword, and this clearly does not change any privacy guarantee of the scheme. From the view of the server, the Blockchain does not provide any new information about the trapdoor and encrypted index. Therefore, the new design leaks exactly the same amount of information to the server as in the original scheme.

How does the Blockchain affect the privacy and other security properties? Due to the fact that the Blockchain only stores the signatures, encrypted search results and other public information, therefore it does not affect security guarantee of the original searchable encryption scheme, regardless of the category of the underlying Blockchain. When a dispute occurs, it will expose more information such as encrypted index and trapdoor. However, this will not cause any privacy problem, because it does not amplify the privacy concerns as in the case of solutions analysed in Sect. 3, due to the fact that only the encrypted index and one trapdoor is made public on the Blockchain.

How has the fairness property been achieved? Compared with the initial design, fairness is guaranteed without relying on any assumption on the client.

- We first analyse the fairness property for the client. Note that the added virtual identifiers id_w^* in the Setup† Stage is a HMAC (hash-based message authentication code) for the file identifiers associated with the keyword w. Therefore, after recovering $id_w^*, \mathcal{ID}_w$ in the *Retrieval & Validation* Phase, the client can determine whether the result is correct or not by verifying this value. If it is not correct, then the server must have misbehaved because applying legitimate T_w to legitimate $\mathcal{I}$ will result in the correct $id_w^*, \mathcal{ID}_w$. With respect to the dispute resolution procedure in the *Retrieval & Validation* Phase, the server will be punished in either step i, ii, or iv.
- We then analyse the fairness property for the server. For any search query, if the server honestly carries out the operation, then the following will hold: (i) a random number r, a trapdoor T_w, and a valid signature sig_w stored on the Blockchain; (ii) the searchable index $\mathcal{I}$ is the original one with a valid signature sig_I stored on the Blockchain; (iii) a ciphertext C_w stored on the Blockchain where the plaintext $id_w^*, \mathcal{ID}_w$ are the results of applying T_w to $\mathcal{I}$. With respect to the definition of the *Retrieval & Validation* Phase, it is straightforward to verify that the server will receive a payment for its work.

As a quick remark, this improved solution incurs less cost than the initial solution, which multiple servers need to perform search operations in parallel.

5 Conclusion

In this paper, we analysed two Blockchain-based searchable encryption solutions and identified a number of issues with respect to economical, security and privacy issues. We demonstrated that Blockchain is not a silver bullet that can be used straightforwardly to solve fairness issues in reality. Based on the analysis, we presented two Blockchain-enabled frameworks which can be applied to most existing symmetric searchable encryption schemes to achieve fairness while preserving the original privacy guarantees. We provided corresponding analysis to the new designs, and showed that the improved construction achieves the same level of fairness as the existing Blockchain-based solutions without suffering their privacy problems. It was also shown that, as long as there is no dispute, the overhead of involving the Blockchain is very low. As an immediate next step, we plan to implement the improved framework and demonstrate its performances with respect to concrete searchable encryption schemes and Blockchain platforms.

References

1. Arriaga, A., Tang, Q., Ryan, P.: Trapdoor privacy in asymmetric searchable encryption schemes. In: Pointcheval, D., Vergnaud, D. (eds.) AFRICACRYPT 2014. LNCS, vol. 8469, pp. 31–50. Springer, Cham (2014). https://doi.org/10.1007/978-3-319-06734-6_3
2. Boneh, D., Di Crescenzo, G., Ostrovsky, R., Persiano, G.: Public key encryption with keyword search. In: Cachin, C., Camenisch, J.L. (eds.) EUROCRYPT 2004. LNCS, vol. 3027, pp. 506–522. Springer, Heidelberg (2004). https://doi.org/10.1007/978-3-540-24676-3_30
3. Chai, Q., Gong, G.: Verifiable symmetric searchable encryption for semi-honest-but-curious cloud servers. In: Proceedings of IEEE International Conference on Communications (ICC 2012), pp. 917–922 (2012)
4. Chen, L., Lee, W., Chang, C., Choo, K.R., Zhang, N.: Blockchain based searchable encryption for electronic health record sharing. Future Gener. Comp. Syst. **95**, 420–429 (2019)
5. Cheng, R., et al.: Ekiden: a platform for confidentiality-preserving, trustworthy, and performant smart contracts. In: IEEE European Symposium on Security and Privacy (EuroS&P 2019), pp. 185–200 (2019)
6. Choudhuri, A.R., Green, M., Jain, A., Kaptchuk, G., Miers, I.: Fairness in an unfair world: fair multiparty computation from public bulletin boards. In: Proceedings of the 2017 ACM SIGSAC Conference on Computer and Communications Security, pp. 719–728 (2017)
7. Curtmola, R., Garay, J., Kamara, S., Ostrovsky, R.: Searchable symmetric encryption: improved definitions and efficient constructions. In: Proceedings of the 13th ACM conference on Computer and Communications Security, pp. 79–88. ACM (2006)
8. Diedrich, H.: Ethereum: Blockchains, Digital Assets, Smart Contracts, Decentralised Autonomous Organisations. CreateSpace Independent Publishing Platform, Scotts Valley (2016)
9. Goldwasser, S., Micali, S.: Probabilistic encryption. J. Comput. Syst. Sci. **28**(2), 270–299 (1984)
10. Hu, S., Cai, C., Wang, Q., Cong, W., Luo, X., Ren, K.: Searching an encrypted cloud meets blockchain: a decentralized, reliable and fair realization. In: 2018 IEEE Conference on Computer Communications (INFOCOM 2018), pp. 792–800. IEEE (2018)
11. Nakamoto, S.: Bitcoin: A Peer-to-Peer Electronic Cash System (2018). https://bitcoin.org/bitcoin.pdf
12. Narayanan, A., Bonneau, J., Felten, E., Miller, A., Goldfeder, S.: Bitcoin and Cryptocurrency Technologies: A Comprehensive Introduction. Princeton University Press, Princeton (2016)
13. Narayanan, A., Clark, J.: Bitcoin's academic pedigree. Commun. ACM **60**(12), 36–45 (2017)
14. Pedersen, T.P.: Non-interactive and information-theoretic secure verifiable secret sharing. In: Proceedings of the 11th Annual International Cryptology Conference on Advances in Cryptology, pp. 129–140 (1992)
15. Saad, M., et al.: Exploring the attack surface of blockchain: a systematic overview (2019). http://arxiv.org/abs/1904.03487
16. Song, D.X., Wagner, D., Perrig, A.: Practical techniques for searches on encrypted data. In: IEEE Symposium on Security and Privacy, pp. 44–55. IEEE Computer Society (2000)

17. Swan, M.: Blockchain: Blueprint for a New Economy. O'Reilly, Sebastopol (2015)
18. Tang, Q.: Towards Blockchain-Enabled Searchable Encryption (full paper) (2019). https://arxiv.org/abs/1908.09564
19. Yaga, D., Mell, P., Roby, N., Scarfone, K.: Blockchain Technology Overview (2018). https://nvlpubs.nist.gov/nistpubs/ir/2018/NIST.IR.8202.pdf
20. Zavodovski, A., Bayhan, S., Mohan, N., Wong, W., Zhou, P., Kangasharju, J.: DeCloud: truthful decentralized double auction for edge clouds. In: International Conference on Distributed Computing Systems (ICDCS) (2019) (page to appear)

Internet Security

DTGuard: A Lightweight Defence Mechanism Against a New DoS Attack on SDN

Jianwei Hou, Ziqi Zhang, Wenchang Shi$^{(\boxtimes)}$, Bo Qin, and Liang Bin

Renmin University of China, Beijing 100872, People's Republic of China
{houjianwei,zhangziqi,wenchang,bo.qin,liangb}@ruc.edu.cn

Abstract. The decoupling of the control plane and the data plane in Software-Defined Networking (SDN) enables the flexible and centralized control of networks. The two planes communicate via the southbound interface. However, the limited communication bandwidth on the southbound interface is exposed to potential denial of services (DoS) threats that may compromise the functions of southbound interface and even affect the whole SDN network. Some research has already focused on DoS attacks on the southbound interface and explored some countermeasures. Most of them are primarily concerned with the risk of malicious uplink traffic from the data plane to the control plane while few work expresses concern about downlink traffic from the control plane to the data plane. However, the threat of downlink traffic is also severe. In this paper, we reveal a DoS threat of amplified downlink traffic and implement a novel DoS attack, called control-to-data plane saturation attack, to demonstrate the threat. To mitigate such threats, we propose a lightweight defence mechanism called DTGuard that can monitor and identify abnormal ports based on a random forest classifier and migrate abnormal traffic along with a low-load link timely. The design of DTGuard conforms to the OpenFlow protocol without introducing additional modifications on the devices. The experimental results show that DTGuard can effectively mitigate the control-to-data plane saturation attack with a minor overhead on the controller.

Keywords: SDN · Network security · DoS attack · Mitigation

1 Introduction

Software-Defined Networking (SDN) is a networking architecture that decouples the control logic from the forwarding logic in a network providing high flexibility

This work is partially supported by the Natural Science Foundation of China under grant No. 61472429, Natural Science Foundation of Beijing Municipality under grant No. 4122041, and National High Technology Research and Development Program of China under grant No. 2007AA01Z414. The first two authors contributed equally to this research.

© Springer Nature Switzerland AG 2020
J. Zhou et al. (Eds.): ICICS 2019, LNCS 11999, pp. 503–520, 2020.
https://doi.org/10.1007/978-3-030-41579-2_29

and programmability. A typical SDN architecture consists of a logically central-ized controller in the control plane, a set of network devices (such as switches) in the data plane and various applications in the application plane [7]. The control plane dictates the whole network behavior. It issues control messages to switches to specify their actions via the southbound interface.

The limited bandwidth of the southbound interface could be a bottleneck of an SDN network, which opens a new venue for attackers [11]. Attackers can launch a Denial of Service (DoS) attack against SDN by overloading the south-bound interface. Since the core control information of an SDN network is deliv-ered via the southbound interface, such as device management, link discovery and topology management, the dysfunction of the southbound interface may significantly downgrade the performance of the whole SDN network.

Previous work on DoS threats to the southbound interface focused on uplink traffic from the data to control planes [6,10,12,14,15,17,18]. The successful attacks can fingerprint match fields of the flow rules [19], thus to craft mas-sive table-miss packets that may trigger massive Packet-In messages from the switch to the controller, exhausting computing or networking resources. How-ever, to our knowledge, few work is concerned with the threat of downlink traffic from the control to data planes, which also needs to be taken seriously.

In the paper, we focus on the DoS threat of amplified downlink traffic that may overload the southbound interface and even eventually lead to the whole SDN network dysfunction. To demonstrate that the threat does exist in SDN, we propose and implement a new SDN-aimed DoS attack, called control-to-data plane saturation attack. The attack can leverage a handful of crafted packets that can trigger the Flood operation of the controller to generate amplified downlink traffic, which will increase the load on the southbound interface and may finally compromise the whole network performance. This raises a serious alarm because it is an effective attack that can leverage a small amount of traffic to incur significant performance degradation on an SDN network.

To mitigate the DoS threat of downlink traffic to SDN networks, we present an efficient and lightweight defence mechanism, called DTGuard, to provide automatic and real-time detection of control-to-data plane saturation attack. Utilizing a pre-trained random forest classifier, DTGuard can classify normal and abnormal ports of the switch based on traffic-based features. It can detect the attack timely under the low attack rate and migrate the abnormal traffic on the southbound interface to the data plane to effectively mitigate the attack.

The main contributions of this work can be summarized as follows:

- We reveal the risk of denial of services introduced by amplified downlink traffic that it can overload the southbound interface and even paralyze the whole network.
- We present a novel DoS attack, control-to-data plane saturation attack, to demonstrate the threat we have revealed. The attack can leverage a few crafted packets to generate amplified traffic, overloading the southbound interface and exhausting the bandwidth in the data plane. We implemented the attack on an SDN simulation environment under different SDN con-trollers to demonstrate the feasibility and generality of it.

– We propose a lightweight defence system against the downlink DoS attack based on a random forest model, called DTGuard. DTGuard is protocol-independent without additional modifications on switches. Experimental results show that DTGuard can efficiently identify the abnormal port of the switch and migrate malicious traffic with a negligible performance overhead.

The rest of the paper is organized as follows. We discuss the related work in Sect. 2. In Sect. 3, we illustrate the design and implementation of the control-to-data plane saturation attack to demonstrate the threat exists indeed. To mitigate the DoS threat of downlink traffic, we propose a defence system, called DTGuard. The detailed design of DTGuard is presented in Sect. 4. The implementation and evaluation of DTGuard are illustrated in Sect. 5. Finally, the paper is concluded in Sect. 6.

2 Related Work

The southbound interface that supports the interaction between the control and data planes may pose a potential new attack surface, leading to severe threats to SDN security [16]. Attackers can launch DoS attacks to exhaust the limited bandwidth on the southbound interface. There is already much research on the DoS threat of uplink traffic to explore mitigation methods. The mitigation methods mainly fall into three groups: (i) those based on traffic caching/migration (ii) those based on traffic feature extraction (iii) those based on traffic filtering.

The core idea of the mitigation methods based on traffic migration is to migrate malicious traffic to non-critical links or caches to reduce the load on the southbound interface. AVANT-GUARD [17] introduced a proxy to sift failed TCP sessions in the data plane prior to being sent to the control plane, which can reduce interaction times between the data and control planes. AVANT-GUARD is a protocol-dependent defence system against SYN flood attacks. FloodGuard [18] prevented the controller from overload by installing proactive flow rules and temporarily caching table-miss packets in a data-plane cache. Table-miss packets in the cache would be sent as Packet-In messages to the controller later at a low rate. FloodGuard breaks the protocol-dependent limitation in AVANT-GUARD but may lead to long delay and high packet loss rate for some flows. FloodDefender [6] proposed to offload malicious traffic to neighbor switches to migrate the load of the compromised link, and employed an Support Vector Machine (SVM) model to identify the attack traffic.

Some mitigation mechanisms of DoS attacks try to distinguish malicious traffic from normal traffic based on traffic-based features. Hu et al. [14] proposed an entropy-based detection scheme to identify whether a DDoS attack occurs by calculating the entropy of the IP address for each new stream. Mousavi et al. [10] also proposed an entropy-based method to measure the change of network features (include source and destination IP addresses, source and destination IP ports) and used an SVM classifier to classify the network traffic. Peng et al. [15] utilized DPTCM-KNN algorithm to measure the difference between abnormal traffic and normal traffic to identify the anomalies.

There are also some research efforts on defending SDN-aimed DoS attacks by filtering abnormal traffic. Kotani and Okabe [12] proposed a defence mechanism that it could filter out less important Packet-In messages without dropping important ones to keep a low level of load on switches. The switches record the values of the header fields before sending the packets to the controller. When the following packets with the same header fields arrive, the switch would temporarily cache the packets before the corresponding flow rule of these packets was installed on the flow table, which can prevent a large number of Packet-In messages from being sent to the controller in a short time.

All of the above work focused on the mitigation strategies to SDN-aimed DoS attacks of uplink traffic. However, the severe DoS threat of downlink traffic to the southbound interface also needs much attention. We implement a novel attack to reveal this threat and explore countermeasures to mitigate the threat.

3   Control-to-Data Plane Saturation Attack

In this section, to illustrate the DoS risk introduced by downlink traffic on the southbound interface, we present a new DoS attack on SDN networks, called control-to-data plane saturation attack. We first introduce the basic knowledge on "OpenFlow" [13], which is the most widely accepted southbound protocol. In this paper, we focus on the SDN networks that use OpenFlow protocol. Then we present the adversary model and details of the attack. We implement and evaluate the feasibility and effects of the attack in an SDN simulation environment under different SDN controllers.

3.1   Packet Processing in SDN

SDN separates the control and data planes by defining an open and standardized southbound interface and a protocol (e.g., the OpenFlow protocol) to access such interface. All traffic between the two planes passes through this interface.

Each OpenFlow-enabled switch maintains one or more flow tables and handles flows depending on the flow rules in the flow table. When a packet arrives, if there is a matched rule, the switch will directly deal with the packet according to the rule. If there is no matched rule, the packet will be sent to the controller in the form of a Packet-In message. The controller parses the Packet-In packet to make appropriate decisions and installs a corresponding flow rule on the switch. Controllers usually deliver the following three types of decisions via the southbound interface:

- Forward: forwarding the packet along a path to the specified port. The controller calculates the forwarding path based on the information of source and destination hosts, and then sends Flow-Mod messages to all the switches on the path to establish a connection between the source and destination hosts.
- Flood: flooding the packets in the data plane. The controller will send Packet-Out messages to all switches.

– Drop: dropping the packet. The controller sends a Flow-Mod message to the switch that reports this packet and installs a drop rule for packets of this flow on the switch.

3.2   Adversary Model

We assume that an adversary can control one or more hosts or virtual machines to craft packets and generate attack traffic. However, we do not assume the adversary can compromise the controller, applications or switches.

Based on the analysis presented in Sect. 3.1, there remains a possibility for adversaries to craft a few packets that can trigger amplified traffic from the control to the data plane. We analyze the number of triggered packets downward via the southbound interface according to the three decisions of the controller:

– Case-1: when a packet triggers a Drop decision, there are 2 packets generated on the southbound interface, that is, 1 Packet-In packet and 1 Flow-Mod packet.
– Case-2: when a packet triggers a Forward decision, there are $1 + P$ packets generated on the southbound interface, that is, 1 Packet-In packet and P Flow-Mod packets (P is the number of switches on the forwarding path).
– Case-3: when a packet triggers a Flood decision, there will be $N + N$ or $N + 1$ (based on control logic of different controllers) packets generated on the southbound interface. For some controllers (such as RYU, Floodlight), all switches will send Packet-In messages to the controller and the controller will issue Packet-Out messages to all switches to flood the packets to all the hosts in the network. That is, N Packet-In packets and N Packet-Out packets (N is the number of all switches in the network). For some other controllers (such as OpenDayLight), only one switch will send a Packet-In message to the controller and the controller will send Packet-Out messages to all the switches. That is, 1 Packet-In packet and N Packet-Out packets.

In general, Case-1 and Case-2 generate little traffic, having little impact on the network. However, when a Flood decision is triggered, the controller needs to communicate with all switches in the network, which opens a door for attackers to generate overwhelming downlink traffic by crafting a few crafted packets.

3.3   Attack Method

When an adversary is going to launch an attack with overwhelming downlink traffic, the key issue that he/she concerns most is **how to craft a packet that can trigger the Flood decision of the controller**.

On one hand, based on TCP/IP protocol, the controller will send broadcast packets (e.g., ARP request packets, DHCP request) to all hosts in the network by default, which triggers the Flood decision.

On the other hand, the controller maintains a list of known hosts in the SDN network. When a Packet-In message arrives, the controller will extract the source address and the location of the host (i.e., the ID and port of the switch connected with the host) from the message and add this information into the host list. Therefore, when receiving a packet whose destination address is not included in the host list, the controller need to send packets to all hosts in the network, which also triggers the Flood decision. After the destination host replies to this packet, the controller can learn its location and add the destination host to its host list.

We implemented experiments on three popular SDN controllers (i.e., Floodlight, RYU, and OpenDaylight) to verify whether the controller will make the Flood decision on these two kinds of packets. The results show that all the three controllers make Flood decision on the two kinds of packets and send packets to all hosts in the network.

Based on the analysis above, we design a new SDN-based DoS attack, called control-to-data plane saturation attack. The attack crafts the packets that can trigger the Flood decision of a controller to generates amplified downlink traffic, overloading the southbound interface. Compared with existing SDN-based DoS attack on the southbound interface, this attack has two characteristics. One is that adversaries only need to send a handful of packets at a low rate, so it is difficult to detect the active malicious host. The other characteristic of the attack is good concealment because the amplified traffic is generated by the controller which is highly trusted by the devices in the data plane.

3.4   Attack Evaluation

To demonstrate the DoS threat of downlink traffic exists indeed, we implement the control-to-data plane saturation attack on a simulation testbed using Mininet [1]. We adopt the Fat-tree topology, a common topology for data center networks [3], with pod = 4 and host density = 2 (that is, each edge switch connects with 2 terminal hosts). The experimental topology is shown in Fig. 2.

We select a host in the data plane to craft the UDP packets whose destination addresses are not in the host list of the controller by randomizing destination IP addresses of the packets. These packets can trigger the Flood decision of the controller, generating the amplified traffic.

The amplification factors of the attack traffic under the three controllers are shown in Table 1. When there is no attack traffic, the load of the southbound interface keeps a lower state. There is communication between switches and the controller for some normal tasks, such as transferring heartbeat packets and sending LLDP packets for link discovery. When the attack occurs, based on the analysis in Sect. 3.2, the amplification factors of RYU and Floodlight should be two times of the number of switches in theory, that is 40 in our testbed. As shown in Table 1, the practical amplification factors reach about 25, which are lower than the theoretical value, restricted by network environment and network resources. And in the testbed under OpenDaylight controller, because only one switch will send Packet-In message to the controller and all switch will receive Packet-Out message for Flood, the theoretical value of the amplification factor is $N + 1$ (that is 21 in our testbed) while the experimental value is about 13.

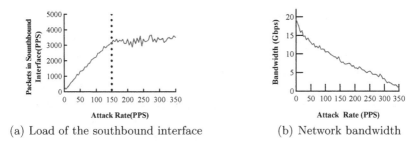

(a) Load of the southbound interface   (b) Network bandwidth

Fig. 1. Effects of different attack rates on SDN under Floodlight controller

Table 1. Summary of amplification factors in the networks under three controllers

Controller	Attack rate (PPS)	The load of southbound interface (PPS)	Amplification factor
RYU	0	56	25.56
	50	1334	
Floodlight	0	68	24.94
	50	1315	
OpendayLight	0	112	13.32
	50	778	

We use TCPDUMP to evaluate the relationship between the attack rate and the load of the southbound interface while using iperf to measure the network bandwidth of host communication in the data plane under different attack rate. The test results are shown in Fig. 1 (Floodlight as an example).

As shown in Fig. 1(a), the crafted packets have amplification effects on the traffic of the southbound interface. The load of southbound interface multiplies with the increase of attack rate and tends to saturate when the attack rate reaches around 150 pps. It can be seen from Fig. 1(b) that the network bandwidth between hosts decreases from 20 Gbps with the increase of the attack rate. The attack rate at around 50 pps can lead to network fluctuation, and the network bandwidth tends to 0 when the attack rate reaches around 350 pps.

Therefore, we can draw a conclusion that the control-to-data plane saturation attack can overload the southbound interface and also lead to network collapse in the data plane, affecting the normal communication between hosts.

4   Proposed Countermeasure

The control-to-data plane saturation attack is an SDN-aimed DoS attack rooted in the SDN architecture because of the decoupling of the control and data planes. To detect and mitigate this attack, we introduce DTGuard, an efficient, lightweight, and protocol-independent defence mechanism. We present the detailed design of DTGuard in this section.

4.1   System Architecture

The basic idea of DTGuard is to distinguish the abnormal port from the normal by a machine learning method to detect the attack. The switch's port that connected with the attack host is an abnormal port. And DTGuard migrates the overwhelming traffic concentrated on the southbound interface to the data plane when the attack occurs. DTGuard mainly consists of four modules including an attack detection module, a traffic statistics module, a path calculation module, and a flow rule generation module, as shown in Fig. 3.

The attack detection module keeps active after the controller starts up to detect whether there is an abnormal port. When an abnormal port is detected, DTGuard activates the other three modules to handle the attack.

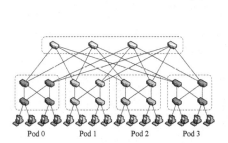

Fig. 2. Experimental topology

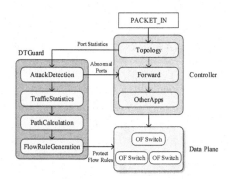

Fig. 3. The architecture of DTGuard

4.2   Attack Detection Module

The attack detection module executes regularly at a period of time T to monitor the traffic on each port of the switch connected with hosts and extract traffic features of the port. It leverages a pre-trained classifier based on a random forest model [9] to classify the traffic on the port either as normal or abnormal based on six traffic-based features. The six features of the traffic on a port will be discussed in more detail below.

Success Rate of Flow Rule Matching (SRf): To generate control-to-data plane traffic, attackers need to craft the packets with no matched flow rules in the switches' flow tables. Therefore, when the attack occurs, the success rate of flow rule matching may decrease. We use Eq. (1) to compute SRf.

$$SRf = \frac{Num_{matched}}{Num_{received}} \tag{1}$$

$Num_{received}$ represents the total number of packets received by a port of the switch in the period T while $Num_{matched}$ represents the number of packets that match the flow rule successfully.

Rate of Bidirectional Flows (RBf)**:** Normally, the dataflow between hosts in the network is bidirectional. That is, one host sends packets to other hosts, and other hosts respond after receiving the packets. When an attack occurs, the number of unidirectional dataflows may increase because attackers send packets with fake destination IP addresses. Therefore, the rate of bidirectional flows may decrease [8]. We use Eq. (2) to compute RBf.

$$RBf = \frac{Num_{pair}}{FlowNum} \tag{2}$$

Num_{pair} is the number of bidirectional flows passing through a port in the period T, and $FlowNum$ is the number of all flows passing through the port.

Trigger Rate of Flood Action (TRf)**:** In a normal network environment, most traffic will be forwarded directly according to the flow rules on switches. Only a small amount of traffic is reported to the controller and triggers the Flood action. However, when the attack occurs, the number of packets triggering the Flood decision increases, resulting in a significant increase in trigger rate of Flood action. We use Eq. (3) to calculated the trigger rate.

$$TRf = \frac{Num_{Flood}}{PacketInNum} \tag{3}$$

$PacketInNum$ is the number of all Packet-In messages received by the controller from a port during the period T, and Num_{Flood} is the number of Packet-In messages that trigger the Flood decision.

The Entropy of Destination IP Address: Usually, the destination address for host communication keeps stable. But when an attack occurs, a large number of packets with random destination IP addresses are generated, which increases the uncertainty of the corresponding destination IP address of a certain source IP address [10]. The entropy is a measure of the uncertainty of random variables in information theory. Therefore, we use the entropy of destination IP address to measure the changes of destination IP addresses that correspond to a source IP address. The calculation method is as follows:

We define the Map L between the destination IP address $dstIP_i$ and the occurrences c_i of this IP on a port in T period as Eq. (4):

$$L = \{(dstIP_1, c_1), (dstIP_2, c_2)...(dstIP_n, c_n)\} \tag{4}$$

The $dstIP$ is the hash value of the destination IP address, and the c_i is the number of occurrences of the destination IP address. The appearing probability of each destination IP address is as Eq. (5):

$$p_i = \frac{c_i}{\sum_{i=1}^{n} c_i} \tag{5}$$

According to the definition of entropy, the entropy of each destination IP address can be calculated as Eq. (6):

$$H = -\sum_{i=1}^{n} p_i \log p_i \tag{6}$$

Trigger Rate of Flow-Mod ($TRfd$)**:** When an attack occurs, a large number of packets with random destination IP addresses are generated. There may be a decrease in the number of Flow-Mod messages sent to the switch because the controller does not know the location of the destination host. We use Eq. (7) to calculate $TRfd$.

$$TRfd = \frac{Num_{FlowMod}}{PacketInNum} \tag{7}$$

$PacketInNum$ is the number of all Packet-In messages received by the controller from a port during the period T, and $Num_{FlowMod}$ is the number of Packet-In messages that trigger Flow-Mod messages.

Average of Packets per Flow (APf)**:** We define the data flow that can trigger the rule installation as a valid data flow. When an attack occurs, the attack packets are directly flooded to the data plane by the controller without installing new rules on the switches, so that no valid flow is formed. As a result, during an attack, the number of packets $PacketNumber$ may increases while the number of valid flows $FlowCount$ may remain unchanged, which eventually leads to an increase in the average number of packet per flow. The average of packets per flow is calculated as Eq. (8).

$$APf = \frac{PacketNumber}{FlowCount} \tag{8}$$

These six traffic-based features constitute a 6-tuple to be the input of the classifier to classify network traffic either as normal or abnormal. We use the random forest model to train the classifier. The random forest is an easy-implemented classification method with low computational overhead and strong generalization ability. The implementation of the classifier is described in Sect. 5.1.

4.3 Traffic Statistics Module

The traffic statistics module obtains the traffic information of each port of all switches from the detection module. Leveraging this information, it maps the traffic information of the port to the corresponding link based on the network topology and constructs a weighted graph of the network traffic.

The traffic of each link changes rapidly in a network. To reduce the impact of network fluctuations on the sampling results, we divide the link load into multiple levels. The granularity of the level can be adjusted according to the actual network environment. For example, if the granularity is set as 100, the level of the load ranged from 0–100 can be labeled as level 1, the level of the load ranged from 101–200 can be labeled as level 2, and so on. An example of a weighted graph of the network traffic is shown in Fig. 4(a).

(a) A weighted graph of network traffic (b) The forwarding path in data plane

Fig. 4. A weighted graph of network traffic and the corresponding forwarding path

4.4   Path Calculation Module

Path calculation module aims to select an optimistic forwarding path to migrate abnormal traffic. The path selection follows the principles of low load and no repetition. The forwarding path can be obtained by calculating a Minimum spanning tree (MST) of the weighted graph of the network traffic. When an attack is detected, the controller sends one Packet-Out message to the root node of the MST. The switch at the root node forwards the packet step by step along each edge of the MST to achieve flood function. An example of the forwarding path is shown in Fig. 4(b).

We use Prim algorithm to calculate the MST of the network, and the time complexity of the first calculation is $O(n \log n)$. When the load of some links in the network changes, it would not always bring changes to the MST. In this case, to reduce computational overhead, it is usually not necessary to recalculate the entire MST. Only when the link topology changes or when the change of link load have an impact on the MST, the MST will dynamically update according to the result generated by the previous calculation. Based on four cases of the load update, we detailedly discuss the update process of MST.

Given the weighted graph G, the vertex set V, and the set of edges E, calculate the current MST T. When the weight of an edge e changes, w_{old} represents the weight before the update, and w represents the updated weight.

- Case-1: $w_{old} < w$ and $e \notin T$, the weight of e increases. Since e does not belong to T, the increase of its weight does not affect the current MST, T remains unchanged;
- Case-2: $w_{old} > w$ and $e \in T$, the weight of e decreases. Since e is a part of T, the decrease of its weight does not change the current MST, T remains unchanged;
- Case-3: $w_{old} > w$ and $e \notin T$, the weight of e decreases. A new tree may be constructed with a smaller weight because of the decrease of e. First, edge e can be added to the current MST T to get T'. Therefore, there is a loop C in T', as shown in Fig. 5(a). The red edge in the figure is e. According to the loop theorem of the minimum spanning tree, the edge with the largest weight in loop C should be removed from T' to get the new MST. The time complexity of the algorithm for this case is $O(n)$.

– Case-4: $w_{old} < w$ and $e \in T$, the weight of e increases. There may be another edge with a lower weight than e to construct a new MST because of the increase of e. First, the edge e can be deleted from the current MST T to obtain T'. Therefore, there are two independent subtrees in T'. a and b are vertexes of $e(a, b)$. A is the set of vertexes that can be reached from vertex a in T' and B is the set of vertexes that can be reached from vertex b in T', $A \cap B = \emptyset$ and $A \cup B = V$. C is a cut-set of edges in graph G. As shown in Fig. 5(b), e is the blue edge, $C = \{s_1, s_2, s_3, e\}$ is the set of edges connecting the two subtrees. When the weight of e increases, according to the cut property of the minimum spanning tree, the edge with the smallest weight in C should be added to T' to get the new MST. The time complexity of the algorithm for this case is $O(n)$.

Therefore, the change of load on the link may not always lead to the change of MST. When the load update changes the MST, the new MST is recalculate based on the previous calculation without introducing too much overhead.

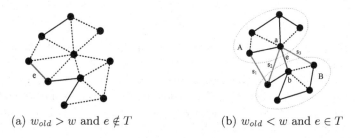

(a) $w_{old} > w$ and $e \notin T$ (b) $w_{old} < w$ and $e \in T$

Fig. 5. Dynamic updating of minimum spanning tree (Color figure online)

4.5   Flow Rule Generation Module

Flow rule generation module generates and installs the corresponding flow rules on the switches in the MST based on the forwarding path obtained from the path calculation module. When the controller makes a Flood decision, there are two ways to execute the Flood action for two cases.

– Case-1: if the source port of the packet that triggers the Flood is an abnormal port, the controller will send a Packet-OUT message only to the switch at the root of the MST. The root node forwards the packet along the MST until the packet is delivered to all ports of all switches in the network.
– Case-2: if the source port of the packet that triggers the Flood is a normal port, the controller will flood the packets to all switches directly.

We use a reserved field of the IP header field, ToS, to enable the switch to distinguish whether a packet is from a normal host or an abnormal host. For Case-1, the match field IP_TOS keeps as defaults, IP_TOS = 0b00000000. For Case-2, the controller sets the match field IP_TOS = 0b00000011 before sending out the Packet-Out message to the root switch of the MST.

5   Implementation and Evaluation

In this section, we implement the prototype of DTGuard on Floodlight in a simulated SDN environment to evaluate its performance and overhead.

5.1   Implementation

TestBed. Using Mininet-2.3.0 and Open vSwitch-2.0.2 to simulate the underlying network, we deploy the controller and the underlying network on a single physical machine with 7.7 GB memory, 4 cores at 2.13 GHz. The controller communicates with switches via OpenFlow 1.3 protocol. The experimental topology is a fat tree topology with pod $= 4$ and host density $= 2$, as shown in Fig. 2.

We implement the prototype of DTGuard on an open source SDN controller Floodlight without additional modifications on the data plane. The four modules of DTGuard are implemented in Java language. The Attack Detection module is mounted on the Packet-In processing chain of Floodlight and starts up at the same time as the controller startup. The other three modules are activated when an abnormal port is detected by the Attack Detection module.

Traffic Generation. To generate the traffic similar to the real traffic in the real network environment, we have extended the Mininet so that hosts can communicate with each other to simulate normal traffic. The simulated normal traffic falls into two parts, one is the random traffic between hosts, and the other is the traffic of common services.

- Traffic between hosts: The $No.m$ host in the network sends packets to the $No.(m+i)$ host, the $No.(m+j)$ host, the $No.(m+k)$ host with probabilities of P_t, P_a, and P_c, respectively. The legitimate traffic generated during tests is a composition of several different protocols (TCP (85%), UDP (10%), ICMP (5%)) based on the statistics of network traffic in the real world [4,5].
- Traffic of common services: to simulate the network traffic based on the C/S model, we have selected some hosts as servers that are deployed with some common services(e.g., FTP, HTTP) while other hosts as clients request these services at a random probability.

Training Classifier Model. To generate training samples, we set a time window of the controller to 10 s and calculate traffic-based 6-tuple of the 10 s for each port. To generate abnormal traffic, we use Scapy [2] to craft the UDP packets with random destination IP addresses which can trigger the Flood decision of the controller. The attack rate increases at a step of 25 pps, starting from 0 pps to 350 pps. We have collected 1,000 samples at each attack rate from abnormal ports and normal ports, respectively. We totally collected 30,000 samples to train the classifier, 70% of the sample as the training set and 30% as the test set.

5.2   Results and Evaluation

Attack Detection Effects. The effectiveness of our detection mechanism is evaluated through Detection Rate (DR) and False Alarm rate (FA) measurement. DR and FA are defined as Eq. (9):

$$DR = \frac{TP}{TP + FN} \qquad FA = \frac{FP}{TN + FP} \tag{9}$$

TP (True Positives) represents the number of abnormal ports that are classified as abnormal, and FN (False Negatives) represents the number of abnormal ports that are classified as normal. TN (True Negatives) represents the number of normal ports that are classified as normal and FP (False Positives) represents the number of normal ports that are classified as abnormal.

The attack detection effect of the classifier is depicted in Fig. 6. As the attack rate increases, the difference between the features of normal and abnormal traffic becomes more and more obvious, so that the DR increases. When the attack rate reaches 25 pps, the DR keeps stable at 98% or more. The FA is stable below 1%, as shown in Fig. 7. The results demonstrate the classifier can distinguish the abnormal traffic at both high attack rate and low attack rate with high accuracy. Therefore, DTGuard can detect the DoS attack at an early stage under a low attack rate, preventing the network from significant performance degradation.

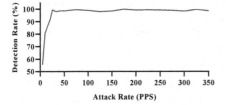   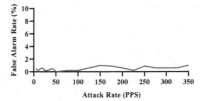

Fig. 6. Detection rate   **Fig. 7.** False alarm rate

Defence Effects. To demonstrate the defence effect of DTGuard, we have launched control-to-data plane saturation attacks in two environments with: (i) an original Floodlight controller, or (ii) a Floodlight controller with DTGuard.

We use TCPDUMP to measure the load of southbound interface in both two environments. As shown in Fig. 8, in (i) environment, as the attack rate increases, the load of the southbound interface multiplies, which tends to saturate at about 150 pps attack rate. In (ii) environment, because the malicious traffic is migrated to the data plane, eliminating the amplification effect of traffic, the load of the southbound interface is significantly reduced. The statistics results of the test in Fig. 8 show that DTGuard reduces the southbound interface load by an average of 74.2%, which demonstrates the effectiveness of DTGuard.

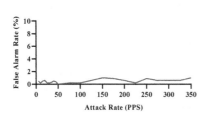

Fig. 8. Load of southbound interface

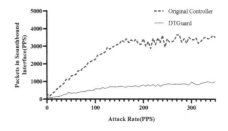

Fig. 9. Network bandwidth

We use iperf to measure the network bandwidth of host communication in both two environments, as shown in Fig. 9. The normal network bandwidth is about 20 Gbps when there is no attack. As the attack rate increases, the malicious traffic gradually overwhelms the southbound interface in (i) environment, so that the network bandwidth is significantly reduced. In (ii) environment, although the network bandwidth also decreases with the increase of the attack rate, the declining trend of network bandwidth slows down. The statistics results of the test in Fig. 9 show that DTGuard prevents network bandwidth against the decline by about 41.7% on average at the same attack rate.

Overhead Analysis. Each module of Floodlight chains together to deal with the received packets. When a Packet-In message arrives, it will be processed along the chain of modules. To evaluate the extra processing time brought by DTGuard, we use Floodlight's PacketIn Processing Time Service to measure the running time of each module.

Table 2. PacketIn processing time of each module

Module	Normal network	Network under attack	
		init-stage	following-stage
DTGuard	4.90%	15.62%	9.71%
Forwarding	80.85%	72.19%	76.25%
DeviceManagerImpl	8.93%	7.92%	9.63%
LinkDiscoveryManager	3.94%	2.71%	2.87%
Others	1.37%	1.56%	1.54%

When there is no abnormal port detected, DTGuard only activates the Attack Detection module. As shown in Table 2, in this situation, DTGuard takes only 4.9% of the time of the processing chain. When an abnormal port is detected, the other three modules are also activated. It takes 15.62% of the time of the processing chain at the initial execution after the attack because DTGuard needs to construct the entire MST. The following cost of DTGuard accounts for 9.71%

of the time of the processing chain to update the MST. Compared with the Forwarding module, DTGuard takes little processing time, which may not bring much delay to the controller.

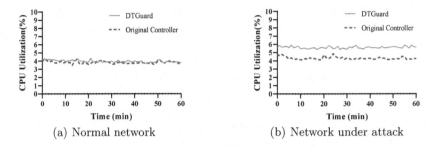

(a) Normal network   (b) Network under attack

Fig. 10. CPU load of original controller and DTGuard

We used JProfiler to measure the CPU utilization of the controllers in environments (i), (ii) before and after the attack, as shown in Fig. 10. Figure 10(a) shows the CPU utilization of the controllers when there is no attack. In this situation, the CPU utilization curve of the controller with DTGuard almost coincides with that of the original controller. Note that there is only the attack detection module of the DTGuard starting up at this point. Figure 10(b) shows the CPU utilization of controllers when an attack occurs. Note that all four modules of the DTGuard start up at this point. The CPU utilization increases by about 1.3% in this situation. Overall, the overhead of DTGuard on the controller is very little.

6   Conclusion

The southbound interface that provides communication between the control and data planes in an SDN faces potential DoS threats. In this paper, we have revealed a severe DoS threat of amplified downlink traffic to SDN security. To demonstrate the threat indeed exists in general SDN networks, we implement a new SDN-aimed DoS attack called control-to-data plane saturation attack on the testbed under three different SDN controllers. The experimental results demonstrate that the attack can leverage a handful of crafted packets to generate more than the 13 times amplification effect of the attack traffic, exhausting the costly network bandwidth and downgrading the network performance.

To mitigate the control-to-data plane saturation threat in SDN, we propose a lightweight mitigation mechanism, called DTGuard. DTGuard can efficiently detect and identify the abnormal ports by a random forest classifier without modifications in the data plane. Once an attack is detected, it can migrate the attack traffic timely to the data plane along a path with a low load. The experimental results show that DTGuard can precisely detect the control-to-data plane saturation attack and effectively mitigate the abnormal traffic with minimal overheads.

References

1. Mininet. http://mininet.org/
2. Scapy. http://www.secdev.org/projects/scapy/
3. Bari, M.F., et al.: Data center network virtualization: a survey. IEEE Commun. Surv. Tutor. **15**(2), 909–928 (2013)
4. Borgnat, P., Dewaele, G., Fukuda, K., Abry, P., Cho, K.: Seven years and one day: sketching the evolution of internet traffic. In: 28th IEEE International Conference on Computer Communications, Joint Conference of the IEEE Computer and Communications Societies (INFOCOM 2009), 19–25 April 2009, Rio de Janeiro, Brazil, pp. 711–719 (2009)
5. Braga, R., de Souza Mota, E., Passito, A.: Lightweight DDoS flooding attack detection using NOX/OpenFlow. In: Proceedings of the 35th Annual IEEE Conference on Local Computer Networks (LCN 2010), 10–14 October 2010, Denver, Colorado, USA, pp. 408–415 (2010)
6. Gao, S., Peng, Z., Xiao, B., Hu, A., Ren, K.: FloodDefender: protecting data and control plane resources under SDN-aimed DoS attacks. In: 2017 IEEE Conference on Computer Communications (INFOCOM 2017), 1–4 May 2017, Atlanta, GA, USA, pp. 1–9 (2017)
7. Gude, N., et al.: NOX: towards an operating system for networks. ACM SIGCOMM Comput. Commun. Rev. **38**(3), 105–110 (2008)
8. Guo, R., Yin, H., Wang, D., Zhang, B.: Research on the active DDoS filtering algorithm based on IP flow. IJCNS **2**(7), 600–607 (2009)
9. Ho, T.K.: Random decision forests. In: Proceedings of 3rd International Conference on Document Analysis and Recognition, vol. 1, pp. 278–282. IEEE (1995)
10. Hu, D., Hong, P., Chen, Y.: FADM: DDoS flooding attack detection and mitigation system in software-defined networking. In: 2017 IEEE Global Communications Conference (GLOBECOM 2017), 4–8 December 2017, Singapore, pp. 1–7 (2017)
11. Imran, M., Durad, M.H., Khan, F.A., Derhab, A.: Toward an optimal solution against denial of service attacks in software defined networks. Future Gener. Comp. Syst. **92**, 444–453 (2019)
12. Kotani, D., Okabe, Y.: A packet-in message filtering mechanism for protection of control plane in OpenFlow networks. In: Proceedings of the Tenth ACM/IEEE Symposium on Architectures for Networking and Communications Systems (ANCS 2014), 20–21 October 2014, Los Angeles, CA, USA, pp. 29–40 (2014)
13. McKeown, N., et al.: OpenFlow: enabling innovation in campus networks. Comput. Commun. Rev. **38**(2), 69–74 (2008)
14. Mousavi, S.M., St-Hilaire, M.: Early detection of DDoS attacks against SDN controllers. In: International Conference on Computing, Networking and Communications (ICNC 2015), 16–19 February 2015, Garden Grove, CA, USA, pp. 77–81 (2015)
15. Peng, H., Sun, Z., Zhao, X., Tan, S., Sun, Z.: A detection method for anomaly flow in software defined network. IEEE Access **6**, 27809–27817 (2018)
16. Shin, S., Gu, G.: Attacking software-defined networks: a first feasibility study. In: Proceedings of the Second ACM SIGCOMM Workshop on Hot Topics in Software Defined Networking (HotSDN 2013), The Chinese University of Hong Kong, Hong Kong, China, Friday, 16 August 2013, pp. 165–166 (2013)
17. Shin, S., Yegneswaran, V., Porras, P.A., Gu, G.: AVANT-GUARD: scalable and vigilant switch flow management in software-defined networks. In: 2013 ACM SIGSAC Conference on Computer and Communications Security (CCS 2013), 4–8 November 2013, Berlin, Germany, pp. 413–424 (2013)

18. Wang, H., Xu, L., Gu, G.: FloodGuard: a DoS attack prevention extension in software-defined networks. In: 45th Annual IEEE/IFIP International Conference on Dependable Systems and Networks (DSN 2015), 22–25 June 2015, Rio de Janeiro, Brazil, pp. 239–250 (2015)
19. Zhang, M., Hou, J., Zhang, Z., Shi, W., Qin, B., Liang, B.: Fine-grained fingerprinting threats to software-defined networks. In: 2017 IEEE Trustcom/BigDataSE/ICESS, 1–4 August 2017, Sydney, Australia, pp. 128–135 (2017)

Towards Comprehensive Security Analysis of Hidden Services Using Binding Guard Relays

Muqian Chen[1,2], Xuebin Wang[1,2(✉)], Jinqiao Shi[1,3(✉)], Yue Gao[1,2], Can Zhao[1,2], and Wei Sun[4]

[1] Institute of Information Engineering, Chinese Academy of Sciences, Beijing, China
wangxuebin@iie.ac.cn, shijinqiao@bupt.edu.cn
[2] School of Cyber Security, University of Chinese Academy of Sciences, Beijing, China
[3] Beijing University of Posts and Telecommunications, Beijing, China
[4] School of Computer and Information Technology, Beijing Jiaotong University, Beijing, China

Abstract. Tor Hidden Service is a widely used tool designed to protect the anonymity of both client and server. In order to prevent the predecessor attacks, Tor introduces the guard selection algorithms. While the long-term binding relation between hidden service and guard relay increases the cost of existing predecessor attacks, it also gives us a new perspective to analyze the security of hidden services.

We utilize a novel method which can reveal guard relays for multiple hidden services. The method helps us to reveal guard relays for 13604 hidden services, and observe their binding relations for 7 months. Based on the binding relations, we conduct the first protocol-level measurement and family analysis of hidden services, and discover two types of families about hidden services, named onion family and onion-node family.

Our measurement reveals 263 onion families in Tor network, and the analysis shows that onion addresses in these families tend to use common prefixes or meaningful prefixes. By analyzing the webpage of these hidden services, we surprisingly find a super onion family that contains 121 hidden services, most of which runs a fraudulent website of bitcoin. Additionally, we also discover 49 onion-node families which have abnormal binding relations between hidden services and their guard relays, including expire bindings, bridge bindings and middle node bindings.

1 Introduction

Tor makes it possible for users to hide their locations while offering various kinds of services, such as web publishing or an instant messaging server. Using Tor hidden services, users can connect to these onion services each without knowing

The original version of this chapter was revised: the affiliation of the authors' names corrected. The correction to this chapter is available at https://doi.org/10.1007/978-3-030-41579-2_48

J. Zhou et al. (Eds.): ICICS 2019, LNCS 11999, pp. 521–538, 2020.
https://doi.org/10.1007/978-3-030-41579-2_30

the other's network identity. However, the anonymity of Tor network has been threatened by various attacks.

To improve anonymity and reduce the risk of traffic correlation attacks, Tor never delivers users' traffic through more than two nodes from the same node family. Generally, a node family is a set of Tor nodes that are under the administrative control of the same person or organization. Besides the traffic correlation attacks, node families can also conduct multiple attacks on Tor, including exit traffic tampering [13,14], bridge address collecting [15], onion address harvesting [7]. In order to identify the node family, Tor project provide the explicit declaration when the Tor relay runs at the beginning. Additionally, Tor project also developed several methods [10,23] to detect the implicit node family, which is never declared in the consensus file.

The conventional researches about family phenomenon focus mostly on relay nodes. However, the family phenomenon about hidden services are existing theoretically and never be studied before. This is the consequence of the strong anonymity of hidden services, leading to the hidden services unlinkable by the third-party researchers. Assume that the family phenomenon of hidden services (e.g. onion family) can be discovered, then the hidden services will be clustered according to the same owner. Or if the family phenomenon between hidden services and relay nodes (e.g. onion-node family) can be discovered, then the owner of hidden service can be tracked alongside the relay nodes. Once one hidden service in the cluster being de-anonymized, all of the other hidden services are de-anonymized. Additionally, applications through hidden services such as Bitcoin or TorChat are also affected by this, the wallet addresses or user account may be clustered when the user use multiple identities.

According to the protocol, multiple hidden services deployed on the same Tor process use same guard relays, and guard relays are selected as Tor relays randomly according to their bandwidth and flags. Therefore, hidden services binding with same group of guard relays can be regarded as onion families, which means that they are deployed by the same person. Additionally, the onion-node family also can be observed when a hidden service binds with its guard relay without following the protocol (e.g. abnormal binding relations).

Note that we should monitor guard relays of hidden services for a long time if we want to reveal families in Tor network. Although existing guard discovery attacks [7,12,18] can be used to help us achieve the goal by taking our controlled relays become the second hop of HS-RP circuits (referred to as middle relay). They are not suitable for the scenario with multiple targets. Existing attacks can only embed HS-irrelevant traffic signals into HS-RP circuits for every hidden service, as the Rend-Points (Rendezvous Point) cannot identify which hidden service creates the HS-RP circuit. As a result, in the case of multiple targets, the controlled relays cannot identify which hidden service creates HS-RP circuit through them by detecting the traffic signals. So we utilize a novel method to address the problem. Different from existing methods, we further embed the hidden service's identifier into the Rendezvous Cookie (Rend-Cookie) and the circuit watermark, thus our controlled middle relays can identify which hidden service creates HS-RP circuit through them by detecting the circuit watermark.

We use the method to reveal guard relays for 13604 hidden services and observe their binding relations for 7 months.

Based on the obtained binding relations, we conduct the first protocol-level measurement and family analysis of hidden services. 263 onion families are revealed in Tor by correlating the binding guard relays of each hidden services. And we also discover a super onion family, which contains 121 hidden services.

Second, we discover 49 onion-node families in Tor network, which have abnormal binding relations between hidden service and guard relay. It can be divided into three types: namely expire binding (a guard relay is used more than 120 days), bridge binding and middle binding. All of these three types of onion-node families are not configured by default, and can only be achieved by modifying the configuration or even source code. Thus, that is a very definite possibility that these hidden services may have the same owner of their guard relays, whose IP addresses are already revealed. The contributions of this paper are listed as follows:

- We are the first to observe the onion family phenomenon, and find 263 onion families that cannot be obtained by simply measuring the content and page structure similarity. Additionally, we also find a super onion family that controls 121 hidden services. The owner of the family utilizes 6 Tor processes to run his hidden services, which are related to bicoin fraudulent, hacker hiring and live streaming services.
- Apart from the onion family, we also find three types of onion-node families in the Tor network, with different abnormal binding relations. There are 34 hidden services of expire binding, 14 hidden services of bridge bindings and 1 hidden service of middle binding in Tor network. We argue that these abnormal binding relations increase the risk of leaking the privacy of hidden services.

Organization. The rest of the paper is organized as follows. In Sect. 2, we illustrate the background and motivation. Section 3 details our measurement method to reveal guard relays of hidden services. We also have some interesting findings which are described in Sect. 4. Section 5 discusses the privacy implications of our previous findings and gives our suggestion for improvement. We introduce the related work in Sect. 6 and the conclusion in Sect. 7.

2   Background

2.1   Guard Selection Algorithm

In order to prevent the predecessor attack, Tor project designed and updated the guard selection algorithm. According to the guard selection algorithm, each client randomly selects a small set of relays as their guard set, and chooses guard relay only from this set whenever creating circuits, which tremendously mitigates the impact of predecessor attack.

The current guard selection algorithm can be described as follow:

(i) At the first bootstrap stage, the client randomly selects 20–60 relays with the Guard flag in its *Sampled Guard Set* weighted by bandwidth.

(ii) The client selects relays which appear in current consensus and are not disabled by path bias issue from *Sampled Guard Set*, and adds these relays into *Filtered Guard Set*.

(iii) For the reachable relays in *Filtered Guard Set*, the client adds them into *Usable Filtered Guard Set*. If the size of *Usable Filtered Guard Set* is less than 20, the client must add new relays into *Sampled Guard Set*.

(iv) Once the client creates circuits successfully through the guard relay, the client adds it into *Confirmed Guard Set* and orders the guard relays according to their added time.

(v) At last, the client calculates the ordered intersection of *Confirmed Guard Set* and *Filtered Guard Set*, regarding the first 3 elements as *Primary Guard Set*.

Every time the client creates a common circuit, it firstly chooses the first reachable guard relay from *Primary Guard Set*. If the *Primary Guard Set* is empty, then it selects guard relays from the ordered intersection set of *Confirmed Guard Set* and *Filtered Guard Set*. If the size of *Primary Guard Set* is less than 3, then the client chooses nodes randomly from *Filtered Guard Set - Confirmed Guard Set*, and adds the nodes into *Primary Guard Set*. Otherwise, it randomly selects a relay from *Usable Filtered Guard Set*.

Guard relays are fast and stable compared to other relays in the Tor network. Consequently, the binding relations between hidden services and their guard relays are relatively stable. Moreover, all the hidden services deployed on one client have the same guard sequence. Thus, we argue the hidden services with the same guard sequence in a long time may be deployed on the same client.

2.2   Components in Hidden Service

Hidden service was introduced in 2004 as a feature of Tor, enabling the anonymity of responders. As shown in Fig. 1, the hidden service architecture consists of the following five components:

Hidden Server (Hidden Service): Hidden Server is the information publisher which can hosts various services, such as SSH, WEB, IRC. Apart from providing the stable service, the hidden server can also hide its location.

Client-OP: Tor client is run by users who want to connect into the Tor network. Generally it is run as an Onion Proxy (OP), so we will mark it as Client-OP in the following.

Rendezvous Point (Rend-Point): Rendezvous Point is the Tor relay which is chosen by the Client-OP randomly, for the purpose to conceal the location of client-OP.

Introduction Point (Intro-Point): Introduction Point is the Tor relay which is chosen by the hidden service. It maintains a long-term circuit with the hidden service and forwards the requests from clients to the hidden service.

Hidden Service Directories (HSDir): Hidden Service Directory is a Tor relay which has the flag **HsDir**. The Hidden Service publishes its descriptor which contains the information of Intro-Point on corresponding HSDir using DHT addressing technique. The Client-OP fetches the descriptor from HsDir before it accesses the Hidden Service.

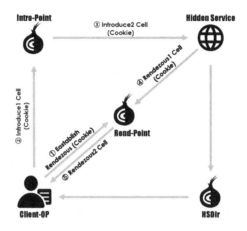

Fig. 1. Hidden service architecture

It should be noted that users can run multiple hidden services on a single Tor process.For these hidden services, they use the same guard relays of the Tor process in each circuit. And this may be a design flaw of Tor which can make these hidden services linkable by the attacker.

3   Measurement Methodology

In this section, we describe in detail the methodology which is utilized to obtain the binding relations. The method is proposed to reveal guard relays of multiple hidden service in parallel, in order to probe the global guard binding relations in Tor network.

3.1   Revealing Guard Relays of Hidden Services

The mechanism of the hidden service is described by the previous work extensively [3]. It should be noticed that the Rendezvous Cookie (Rend-Cookie) is an arbitrary 20-byte value, generated randomly by Client-OP. First, it is sent to the Rend-Point by Client-OP and the Rend-Point record the circuit which delivers the Rend-Cookie. Then, the Rend-Cookie is delivered to the hidden service through *introduce1* and *introduce2* cell. When the hidden service receives the designed Rend-Cookie, it will create a HS-RP circuit to the Rend-Point, and send the Rend-Point a *rendezvous1* cell with the Rend-Cookie. Afterwards, the Rend-Point binds up two circuits with the same Rend-Cookie, and delivers messages for these two circuits. At last, the Rend-Point sends the Client-OP a *rendezvous2* cell to start the communication.

In this attack, we assume that the attacker controls a Client-OP, a Rend-Point as well as some Tor relays. Our attack utilizes a design flaw of the hidden service's protocol, that the Client-OP can send messages to the collusion Rend-Point through the Rend-Cookie, because the Rend-Cookie is randomly generated by Client-OP and delivered to the Rend-Point through HS-RP circuit. Our attack embeds the hidden services' identifiers into the Rend-Cookies and delivers them to our Rend-Points. Then our Rend-Points embed the identifiers into the HS-RP circuits as circuit watermarks, so that the controlled relays can identify which hidden service creates HS-RP circuit through them, and achieve to attack multiple hidden services in parallel.

The attacker should conduct the attack round by round, until one of its controlled relays is selected as the second hop of the HS-RP circuit. Figure 2 depicts the three phases of each round of SignalCookie attack.

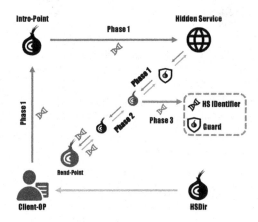

Fig. 2. Details of our guard discovery methods

Phase 1: Rend-Cookie Delivery. Before sending requests to the hidden service, the Client-OP will first generate a designed Rend-Cookie. The designed Rend-Cookie consists of three parts: *Cookie Header, HS Identifier* and *Random Content. Cookie Header* is a fixed content designed to distinguish the malicious cookies from other common cookies; *HS Identifier* is random value that indicates the identity of target hidden service, which can let the Rend-Point associate the HS-RP circuits with hidden services after receiving Rend-Cookies; And *Random Content* is designed to distinguish the Rend-Cookies with the same target. After generating the Rend-Cookie, each Client-OP picks a controlled relay as the Rend-Point. Then the Client-OP generates a *introduce1* cell including the designed Rend-Cookie and the fingerprint of the selected malicious Rend-Point, and sends the cell to a Intro-Point. The Rend-Cookie will be sent to the selected malicious Rend-Point through Intro-Point and hidden service. When the Rend-Points receive designed Rend-Cookies, they will verify the Cookie Header and extract *HS Identifiers*. As a result, they can identify which hidden service creates the HS-RP circuits to them.

Phase 2: Hidden Service Identifier Modulation. After recognizing the hidden service which created the HS-RP circuit, Rend-Points will send circuit watermarks containing the received *HS Identifiers* along with the HS-RP circuits. Each *HS Identifier* is modulated to the number of *drop* cells[1] in each time window (2 s). In each window, three *drop* cells represent signal 1, and one *drop* cell is signal 0. For instance, the message 5 ($[101]_2$) can be delivered in 6 s as [3 cells, 1 cell, 3 cells].

Phase 3: Circuit Watermark Detection. When the controlled relays are selected on the HS-RP circuits, they can recognize the circuit watermarks embedded by Rend-Points. Each controlled relay records the number of received inbound cells in every time window, and generates the cell sequence ordering by time. Next, controlled relays restore the *HS Identifiers* from the cell sequence according to the modulating schema and recognize the hidden services which create the HS-RP circuits through them. Additionally, the number of relay cells before the start of the watermark can be used to figure out their position on HS-RP circuits. The second hop of a HS-RP circuit would receive two outbound relay cells (*extend* cell and *rendezvous1* cell) before the signal starts. Consequently, if a controlled relay is selected on the second hop of the HS-RP circuit, the previous hop will be the guard relay of the target hidden service.

Compared with the previous work, our method has an extra phase (phase 1), which makes the Rend-Points can identify the hidden services which create HS-RP circuits to them. Hence Rend-Points can embed unique circuit watermarks relevant to hidden services. When one of our controlled relays detects the circuit watermark, it can identify the target hidden service which creates the HS-RP circuit according to the *HS Identifier* in the watermark. Therefore, controlled relays will not be interfered when discovering guard relays of multiple hidden services and the attack can be conducted in parallel. And the evaluation about the accuracy and efficiency of this method is shown by the previous work [8].

3.2   Data Collection

In order to collect data more efficiently, we first utilize 7 Virtual Machines (VMs) on cloud environment provided by Vultr [1]. Each VM is configured with 2 CPUs and 4 GB of RAM, and 15 malicious Client-OPs which is designed to generate requests of hidden services are deployed on every VM. Additionally, we also operate 10 Tor relays on 10 VMs with 1 CPU and 2 GB of RAM. These VMs are

---

[1] *drop* cells are long-range paddings, the OR or OP must drop it when receiving such a cell.

located in different countries, including Japan, Singapore, Australia, Germany, France, the Netherlands and the United States. The running Tor relays are based on a modified Tor version 0.3.1.7, which can act as the malicious Rend-Point and the malicious middle relay at the same time. It should be noted that our Tor relays have no Guard and Exit flags, On the one hand, this type of relays has a larger catch probability to be chosen as the middle relays than relays with Guard or Exit flags. On the other hand, in order to comply the ethical measurements, our relays will not be selected as guard relays, which prevents the real IP addresses of hidden services from being de-anonymized. During the experimenting, we discover 13604 onion addresses through aggregating the result in multiple directory websites (e.g., hidden wiki, TorLinks). Taking the discovered hidden services as targets, we monitored the guard relays of these hidden services from 2017-11-21 to 2018-06-21.

However, in our seven consecutive attacking attempts, we discovered that only 3756 hidden services were active in all seven months. This is a consequence of the short lifespan of onion websites and of the fact that the majority of onion domains collected from public sources often become unreachable after a short amount of time. Therefore, public directories contain a very large amount of outdated material, which wrongly contributes to the image of Tor hidden services.

4   Structure Analysis

In this section, we analyze the two types of family phenomenon, which are named *onion family* and *onion node family*.

4.1   Onion Family

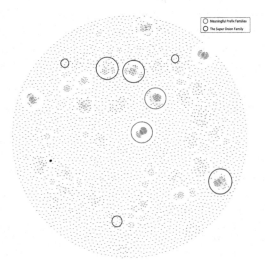

Fig. 3. Onion Families in Tor[6] (We also give a more clear picture in Appendix A)

In this part, we focused on the onion family phenomenon in the Tor network. Onion family is a group of hidden services run by the same person. These hidden services may seem unrelated. However, after a long time observation, we can cluster these hidden services through their guard sequence. This is the result of that hidden services on a same Tor process use the same guard relay.

After monitoring the guard relays of these hidden services in 7 months, we cluster hidden services which are on same Tor processes. First we list guard relays for every hidden service in each months separately, i.e. $G_{hs,m}$ represents the guard relays used by the hidden service hs in the whole month m. For each pair of hidden services, we intersect their guard lists $(G_{hs_1,m}, G_{hs_2,m})$ in each month, and get the list of common guard relays $(ComG_m = G_{hs_1,m} \cap G_{hs_2,m})$ in the month. Then we can model the probability of this situation as the following question.

Question: *Two hidden services separately choose their guard nodes in Tor network. How can we distinguish whether they are in the same process or just happen to choose the same node?*

Suppose the choose probability of each relay i can be expressed as θ_i, which is the fraction of the weighed bandwidth to the whole network. The probability in each month can be largely calculated as $P(hs_1, hs_2, m) = \prod_{i \in ComG_m} \theta_i$, and we then use the average probability of each month as the final probability. We argue to set the threshold as 0.3, which means that we regard two hidden services running on the same Tor process when their probability is lower than 0.3.

Family Analysis: To better show the relation of onion family, we map the relations of hidden services into a graph. We denote each hidden service as node, and the edge between two nodes means that the probability of two hidden services is less than the threshold. We visualize the relations into a graph through `Gephi` `(0.9.2)`, and show the structure in Fig. 3. By checking the connected components in the graph through `NetworkX (2.3)`, 263 onion families can be discovered in Tor network.

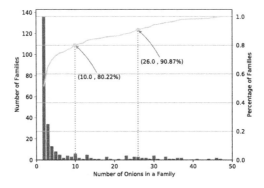

Fig. 4. Family size distribution

As shown in Fig. 4, the size of each family is quite small. 51.71% of families only have 2 hidden services, 80.22% of families have less than 10 hidden services. Each family has 7.52 hidden services in average, and has 47 hidden services at most.

By analyzing the onion address of these families, we discover two kinds of families, which have common prefix or meaningful prefixes. Additionally, combining with the content of hidden services, we also discover a super onion family, which have both meaningful prefix addresses and common prefix addresses.

Table 1. Meaningful prefix family

The largest meaningful prefix family (46 hidden services)					
amazingv7h*	amazonfkuu*	armoryohaj*	bitphar76n*	blenderri3*	btcwash7jm*
carddumpa3*	cardsm4fgc*	cardsunwqr*	ccpalym5nu*	cfactoryxe*	chbetterat*
cmarketsiu*	counterfxh*	djn4mhmbbq*	drugszun7t*	eucannapgg*	ezuwnhj5j6*
fakebillke*	fakeids5bp*	fakeidskhf*	fogwalletg*	footballth*	grhacheapd*
gunsdtk47t*	gunsganjki*	hackrentew*	hosting6ia*	kplatypxb2*	limaconzru*
loundryslz*	maghrebwzb*	market77w4*	marketdfts*	mghreb4l5h*	mollyworup*
moneyplheq*	mystorea4m*	passporxak*	payshielgj*	plasticmav*	plasticmrj*
replicasuw*	russianyhl*	storess4s5*	vendorcugc*		

Meaningful Prefix Family: Our artificial analysis discovers 6 families whose onion addresses start with a meaningful prefix. Generally, the meaningful prefixes are 'card', 'bitcoin', 'drugs' and so on. And each hidden service is a specific type of commodity trading platform. Table 1 shows the onion address of the largest onion families, which contains 46 hidden services. Considering about the privacy, each hidden services just shows the first 10 characters.

Common Prefix Family: We also discovered 86 families whose onion addresses with a common prefix. The size of families ranges 2 to 44. These families have onion addresses start with the same prefix. 70 families have the common prefix with a single character, e.g. 'b', '6', 'e'. And other 16 families have the common prefix with meaningful string, such as '222222', 'bitcoi', 'hydra'.

Case Study - *Super Onion Family*: It should be noticed that, 'bitcoi' is a popular prefix in Tor network. Most of these hidden services are running a fraudulent website of bitcoin, whose title is '100x Your Coins in 24 H'. We find that the deposit wallet address of most of these website are *'1Q4w6StJWn8mwtSbb4UiBtDkGtcDpvogvd'*, which means that these websites are all belong to the same owner. Surprisingly, these websites, which have the same deposit wallet address, appear in 6 onion families. This result implies that the owner of the website runs 6 Tor processes, and controls 121 hidden services in total. Three of the processes deploy more than 30 onion addresses, and the other three deploy less than 10 onion address. All of these hidden services can be considered as a super onion family. Apart from these fraudulent websites, the owner also runs other two types of websites, one is the website about hiring hackers, and the other is called redroom, which is a famous live-streaming service.

4.2   Onion-Node Family

Onion-node Family contains a hidden service and its guard node which have an abnormal binding relation. In living Tor network, Tor relays run by volunteers, which means that every Tor relay can be evil. Consequently, in order to prevent being compromised by a evil node for a long time, hidden services choose stable nodes as their guard nodes, and change their guard nodes periodically. In another word, a hidden service cannot have more trust in any relays, unless the owner of hidden service is familiar to the relay. In our opinion, this trust relation may imply the hidden service and its guard relay belong to the same owner. Based our analysis, there are three types of onion-node families, which named expire bindings, bridge bindings and middle node bindings.

Expire Binding: We analyzed the onion-node family phenomenon with *expire bindings*. Tor protocol [2] shows that guard nodes of hidden services are rotated as the duration of 120 days, which means that the binding duration is no longer than 120 days by default. According to our measurement (Fig. 5), the average binding duration is 37.45 days, and 99.68% of the hidden services have the binding duration which is less than 120 days. It should be noticed that 34 (0.29%) individual hidden services have the expire binding relations with their guard relays (Table 2). Additionally, the last two hidden services is also an onion family that pin their guard relay for a long time. Apparently, both of their addresses have a meaningful prefix, and their content is entirely same after our artificial analysis.

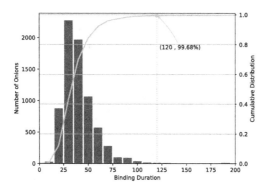

Fig. 5. Distribution of binding duration

We argue that owners of these hidden services (both of individual hidden services and onion family hidden services) deploy guard relays in advance and config their hidden services connecting into Tor network through the deployed guard relays, and thus, form groups of onion-node family. Considering about their anonymity, we recommend that these hidden services bind their own guard relays with a duration between 40 to 80 days to improve their anonymity. Our result shows that 37.17% of the hidden service have the binding duration in this interval, which is much more than the interval larger than 120 days.

Bridge Binding: Our analysis shows 14 hidden services binding with their guard relays which never appears in the consensus in these 7 months (Table 3). We guess that these hidden services connect into the Tor network through a bridge relay, including the common bridge, obfs3, obfs4. In order to verify our conjecture, we analyze the bridge information in this 7 months, with the help of current bridge discovery techniques [16,17]. According to the bridge information, we find that there are 2 hidden services connecting into the Tor network through private bridges, and we regard these hidden services and their guard relays as *bridge binding* onion-node families. Another 12 hidden services connecting into the Tor network through public bridges. We do not recommend the first way to use hidden services (private bridge). Because no other people can use the private bridge except the owner of the bridge. The attacker can immediately find the owner of hidden service through the private bridge.

Table 2. Expire binding individual hidden services

Onion	Guard	Onion	Guard	Onion	Guard
swnwd**	85.230.184.93	anthi**	79.172.193.32	jabbe**	185.34.33.2
7ep7a**	217.182.198.95	g3plb**	213.32.119.219	zazoi**	23.252.105.31
j7zby**	213.239.217.18	3topn**	23.81.66.90	megam**	198.98.62.56
vini4**	195.154.164.243	2lebt**	54.201.127.175	ih4xe**	163.172.94.119
recip**	208.80.154.39	zdla6**	178.132.0.6	bznjt**	212.47.234.192
evz2f**	79.137.112.4	iamje**	172.241.140.26	egy2b**	130.225.254.103
unshe**	38.229.33.141	sq4le**	178.254.19.101	dox6b**	37.187.30.78
goaw7**	163.172.149.155	hackc**	198.50.191.95	gv4ax**	93.104.209.61
zngbg**	94.23.29.204	iqij3**	89.163.225.115	ecleg**	134.19.177.109
lcvks**	204.11.50.131	xfmro**	51.254.101.242	cwu7e**	37.59.118.7
hss33**	80.158.19.228	cpsto**	213.152.168.27	zg7i2**	91.233.116.119
pkmld**	37.187.103.15				

Middle Node Binding: We discover 1 hidden service binds with a relay which is never assigned the guard flag, named *middle node binding* family. This is also a deprecated configuration of the hidden service, because binding with a middle node needs to modify the source code of Tor, which means the owner of hidden service gives much more trust to this middle nodes.

Table 3. Abnormal guard relays

Type	Onion address	Guard	Onion address	Guard
Private bridge	anone**	198.204.*.*	agart**	178.17.*.*
Public bridge	syuoa**	138.68.*.*	2dhgq**	109.105.*.*
	unshe**	38.229.*.*	baker**	185.47.*.*
	5z6gi**	193.205.*.*	zazoi**	23.252.*.*
	2lebt**	54.218.*.*	t25zy**	51.254.*.*
	s4p52**	62.141.*.*	22222**	151.80.*.*
	sfiop**	24.106.*.*	offic**	192.36.*.*
	ts4w7**	188.40.*.*		
Middle node (no guard flag)	kmh7s**	195.201.*.*		

5 Discussion

5.1 Anonymity Analysis of Onion Family

According to the content and the number of Tor processes, there should be four ways of users to deploy hidden services:

- Same content deploys on single Tor process.
- Same content deploys on multiple Tor processes.
- Different content deploys on single Tor process.
- Different content deploys on multiple Tor processes.

However, considering about their anonymity, we strongly recommend that users should neither deploy hidden services with the same content on multiple Tor processes nor different content on single Tor process. The risk analysis of these two manners is listed in the following: Denote that the owner has n hidden services with the same content, and the web page has the vulnerabilities with p_v probability. She deploys them on m Tor processes. In the meantime, suppose that an attacker deploys malicious guard relays into the Tor network with p_c catch probability.

Risks on Same Content with Multiple Tor Processes: Denote that the safe probability of the owner to prevent from de-anonymizing by the webpage vulnerability and predecessor attack can be expressed as S_v and S_c separately.

$$S_v = 1 - p_v, S_c = (1 - p_c)^m \tag{1}$$

So the safe probability of the owner is S.

$$S = S_v * S_c = (1 - p_v)(1 - p_c)^m \tag{2}$$

Formula 2 shows that the safe probability S of the owner decreases with the increasing of m, which means that, the owner of hidden service faces more anonymity risks when she uses more Tor processes.

Risks on Different Content with Single Tor Processes: As same as the previous analysis, the safe probability of the owner from preventing de-anonymize from the webpage vulnerability or from predecessor attacks can be expressed as S_v and S_c.

$$S_v = (1 - p_v)^n, S_c = 1 - p_c \qquad (3)$$

So the safe probability of the owner can be expressed as S.

$$S = S_v * S_c = (1 - p_v)^n(1 - p_c) \qquad (4)$$

From the formula 4, we can see that the safe probability S of the owner decreases with the increasing of n, which means that, the owner of hidden service faces more anonymity risks when she has more hidden services with different content on a single Tor process.

As a result, we recommend that the owner of hidden services should deploy hidden services with the same content on the same Tor process, and deploy hidden services with different content on multiple Tor processes.

5.2   Ethical Discussion

In order to evaluate the family phenomenon in Tor network, we conducted our experiment in living Tor network. However, conducting researches on the living anonymity networks must be performed in a responsible manner. One could be considered as a potential violation of user privacy is the collection of guard relays of hidden services. However, for an attacker without AS-level capability, she cannot track any hidden service's location only through its guard relay. Therefore de-anonymizing hidden services cannot be covered in our study. Additionally, we securely delete all collected data after statistically analyzing them, only publish aggregated statistics about the collected data.

Another factor may also be considered as a potential violation is that, we deploy 10 relays which can record the meta-data for each cell in the living Tor network. However, this is a standard approach in the context of Tor's researches, as it is adopted by the previous work frequently [6, 7, 22]. Additionally, our relays have no Guard or Exit flags, and the meta-data of this kind of relays do not support any of the existing attacks against the anonymity. At last, our experiments are conducted over a period of seven months, and each relays under our control is configured to contribute at least a shared bandwidth of 2 Mb/s, which means that we also contribute additional routing capacity to the Tor network.

6   Related Work

Predecessor Attack: The first published predecessor attack against Tor hidden services were presented by Overlier [18]. The attacker repeatedly connects to the hidden service and verifies whether controlled relays on the HS-RP circuit with the support of traffic correlation. However, it suffers from the low speed and accuracy because it is based on the traffic analysis. To solve this problem, Biryukov [7] and Ling [12] separately proposed a new method through generating a signature (50 Paddings and circuit destroy) to de-anonymize the hidden service. The attacker's controlled relays can recognize the signature when the relays are on the HS-RP circuit. So that the attacker can reveal the guard relays of the target hidden service. However, controlled relays cannot recognize the hidden service through the signature, because the signature is too simple to carry the identifiers of hidden services.

Hidden Service Measurement: Content analysis of Tor hidden services had been extensively analyzed for a long time. One of the very first works that studied the nature of the hidden service was presented by Bergman [5]. In his work, the author introduced and analyzed for the first time different characteristics of the Tor hidden services. Afterwards, plenty of work [6,7,19] measures the various properties of Tor hidden services, including size, content, popularity or their ability to remain anonymous. Furthermore, there is also some work that focuses on the criminals in Tor hidden services. Soska [21] presented a long-term analysis of 16 anonymous marketplaces, providing a comprehensive understanding of their nature and their evolution over time. Analysis of the marketplace entities such as customers and vendors in Tor hidden services is also a prevalent point [4,9,11]. Closest among these papers to our work, Iskander [20] measures the link relation between hidden services in the Tor network, and performed a link structure and presents a privacy analysis of the Tor hidden services.

In this paper, we utilize a novel method which can reveal the guard relays for multiple hidden services at the same time. By means of our method, we are the first to give a comprehensive analysis of the binding relation between hidden service and their guard relays. At last, we also put forward two suggestions to improve the security of hidden services.

7 Conclusion

In this paper, we focus on the security of the binding relations between hidden services and their guard relays. We utilize a novel method to reveal the guard relays of hidden services, and monitor guard relays of 13604 hidden services for 7 months. By analyzing the binding relations, we discover 2 kinds of families in Tor network, which are named onion family and onion-node family.

We first discover 263 onion families through correlating the guard sequence of each hidden service in the Tor network and dozens of families deploy hidden services with common prefix or meaningful prefix. Additionally, by analyzing contents of these onion families, we also discover a super onion family which controls 121 hidden services. The super onion family is deployed on 6 Tor processes, and the theme of its hidden services are related to bicoin fraudulent, hacker hiring and live streaming services. Additionally, we also discover 49 onion-node families which have abnormal binding relations. The abnormal binding relation can be divided into three groups, which are long-term binding duration, binding with private bridges and binding with relays without Guard flag. We consider that these abnormal binding relations leak the privacy of hidden services because the hidden services have too much trusts on its guard relays. At last, we give a risk analysis of onion families in detail and put forward suggestions on the current Tor protocol in order to improve the security.

Acknowledgments. This work was supported by the National Key Research and Development Program of China (Grant No. 2017YFC0820700) and National Defense Science and Technology Innovation Special Zone Project.

Appendix A. Onion Families in a Vector Graph

The structure of onion families in Tor is shown in the following figure. For some reason, the previous figure (Fig. 3) is not a vector graph. So we put a vector graph here (Fig. 6). The graph do not have any annotations, but it could see the address of hidden services clearly. We can find onion families with common prefixes and meaningful prefixes through enlarging the graph.

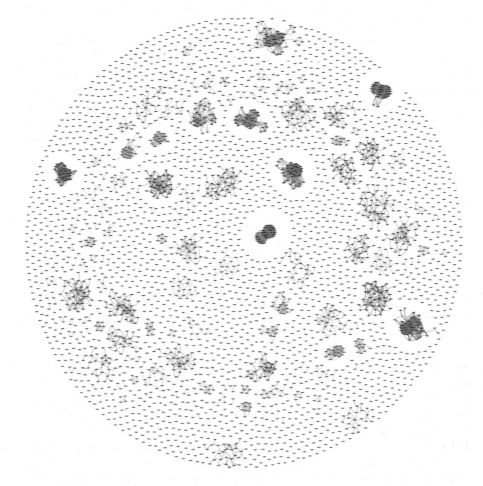

Fig. 6. Onion families in Tor

References

1. http://www.vultr.com/
2. https://gitweb.torproject.org/torspec.git/tree/guard-spec.txt
3. Tor specification. https://gitweb.torproject.org/torspec.git/tree/rend-spec-v2.txt
4. Barratt, M.J., Ferris, J.A., Winstock, A.R.: Use of silk road, the online drug marketplace, in the United Kingdom, Australia and the United States. Addiction **109**(5), 774–783 (2014)
5. Bergman, M.K.: White paper: the deep web: surfacing hidden value. J. Electron. Publishing **7**(1) (2001)
6. Biryukov, A., Pustogarov, I., Thill, F., Weinmann, R.P.: Content and popularity analysis of tor hidden services. In: IEEE International Conference on Distributed Computing Systems Workshops, pp. 188–193 (2014)
7. Biryukov, A., Pustogarov, I., Weinmann, R.P.: Trawling for tor hidden services: detection, measurement, deanonymization. In: 2013 IEEE Symposium on Security and Privacy (SP), pp. 80–94. IEEE (2013)
8. Chen, M., Wang, X., Liu, T., Shi, J., Yin, Z., Fang, B.: Signalcookie: discovering guard relays of hidden services in parallel. In: 2019 IEEE Symposium on Computers and Communications (ISCC). IEEE (2019)
9. Christin, N.: Traveling the silk road: a measurement analysis of a large anonymous online marketplace. Arch. Neurol. **2**(3), 293 (2012)
10. Danner, N., Defabbia-Kane, S., Krizanc, D., Liberatore, M.: Effectiveness and detection of denial-of-service attacks in Tor. ACM Trans. Inf. Syst. Secur. (TISSEC) **15**(3), 11 (2012)
11. Hout, M.C.V., Bingham, T.: 'Silk road', the virtual drug marketplace: a single case study of user experiences. Int. J. Drug Policy **24**(5), 385–391 (2013)
12. Ling, Z., Luo, J., Wu, K., Fu, X.: Protocol-level hidden server discovery. In: International Conference on Computer Communications, pp. 1043–1051 (2013)
13. Ling, Z., Luo, J., Wu, K., Yu, W., Fu, X.: TorWard: discovery of malicious traffic over Tor. In: IEEE INFOCOM 2014-IEEE Conference on Computer Communications, pp. 1402–1410. IEEE (2014)
14. Ling, Z., Luo, J., Wu, K., Yu, W., Fu, X.: TorWard: discovery, blocking, and traceback of malicious traffic over Tor. IEEE Trans. Inf. Forensics Secur. **10**(12), 2515–2530 (2015)
15. Matic, S., Troncoso, C., Caballero, J.: Dissecting tor bridges: a security evaluation of their private and public infrastructures. In: Network and Distributed Systems Security Symposium, pp. 1–15. The Internet Society (2017)
16. Matic, S., et al.: Dissecting tor bridges: a security evaluation of their private and public infrastructures. In: Network and Distributed System Security Symposium (2017)
17. McLachlan, J., Hopper, N.: On the risks of serving whenever you surf: vulnerabilities in Tor's blocking resistance design. In: Proceedings of the 8th ACM Workshop on Privacy in the Electronic Society, pp. 31–40. ACM (2009)
18. Overlier, L., Syverson, P.F.: Locating hidden servers. In: IEEE Symposium on Security and Privacy, pp. 100–114 (2006)
19. Owen, G., Savage, N.: Empirical analysis of tor hidden services. IET Inf. Secur. **10**(3), 113–118 (2016)
20. Sanchez-Rola, I., Balzarotti, D., Santos, I.: The onions have eyes: a comprehensive structure and privacy analysis of tor hidden services. In: Proceedings of the 26th International Conference on World Wide Web, pp. 1251–1260. International World Wide Web Conferences Steering Committee (2017)

21. Soska, K., Christin, N.: Measuring the longitudinal evolution of the online anonymous marketplace ecosystem. In: USENIX Conference on Security Symposium, pp. 33–48 (2015)
22. Sun, Y., Edmundson, A., Vanbever, L., Li, O.: RAPTOR: routing attacks on privacy in Tor. In: USENIX Security Symposium, pp. 271–286 (2015)
23. Winter, P., Ensafi, R., Loesing, K., Feamster, N.: Identifying and characterizing Sybils in the Tor network. In: USENIX Security Symposium, pp. 1169–1185 (2016)

Context-Aware IPv6 Address Hopping

Matthias Marx[(⊠)], Monina Schwarz, Maximilian Blochberger, Frederik Wille,
and Hannes Federrath

Department of Informatics, University of Hamburg,
Vogt-Kölln-Str. 30, 22527 Hamburg, Germany
{marx,schwarz,blochberger,3wille,federrath}@informatik.uni-hamburg.de

Abstract. Different web browsers have developed approaches to better
isolate the activities of users on different websites. However, those only
work on the application-level and using the user's IP address, all actions
of the users can be linked. We present a context-aware IP address alteration scheme that utilizes the large IPv6 address space to protect against
IP-address-based tracking.

We propose a scheme where a distinct outbound IPv6 address is used
for each visited website and its dependencies. A prototype has been
implemented and support for several web protocols and applications has
been ensured. We evaluated the impact of the prototype on browsing performance. The results indicate that the impact is negligible. In combination with existing application-level measures, effective protection against
tracking can be achieved.

Keywords: Browser · Privacy · Tracking · IPv6 · Address hopping

1 Introduction

The spread of IPv6 has continued to increase in recent years. Today, more than
26% of all autonomous systems announce IPv6 prefixes [32]. The most upheld
feature of IPv6 is the huge 128 bit address space. With IPv6, each device could
be assigned a lifelong unique IP address and by that IP-address-based tracking opportunities arise. We present a context-aware address alteration scheme
that utilizes the large IPv6 address space to protect against IP-address-based
tracking.

The IPv6 Privacy Extension recommends lifetimes for IP addresses and
encourages changing the source IP address regularly. However, IP addresses are
usually used for one day for new connections [25]. 24 h is too long for effective
protection of the users' privacy [4]. We will use many IP addresses at the same
time and on a per-destination basis.

RFC 6177 (IPv6 Address Assignment to End Sites) recommends Internet Service Providers (ISPs) to pass subnets with at most 64 bit long prefixes, to home
users [24]. Any customer, from large businesses to small households, receives
more IPv6 addresses than the whole IPv4 address space. However, only a fraction of these addresses is used. We show how to use a new IP address for each

© Springer Nature Switzerland AG 2020
J. Zhou et al. (Eds.): ICICS 2019, LNCS 11999, pp. 539–554, 2020.
https://doi.org/10.1007/978-3-030-41579-2_31

website visited and take the context in which a request is made into account to maintain compatibility.

A prototype is designed and developed to show the feasibility of our approach[1]. We compare our concept to the Tor Browser [28]. Considering a clearly weaker adversary model, we can achieve much better performance. This makes our approach interesting for common users who need protection against ad networks but not against global observers and who do not want to sacrifice browsing performance or invest more time in preserve their privacy.

The remainder of this paper is organized as follows. In Sect. 2, we survey related works. In Sect. 3, we detail the design and implementation of context-aware IPv6 address hopping. In Sect. 4, we evaluate privacy enhancement and performance of our implementation. We discuss the results in Sect. 5 and, finally, conclude in Sect. 6.

2 Preliminaries and Related Work

In this section, preliminaries of context-aware IPv6 address hopping and related work are discussed. First, we introduce IPv6 and the Tor Browser in Sect. 2.1 because our prototype takes advantage of it. Then, we present related work that utilizes IPv6 addresses to enhance privacy or security in Sects. 2.2 and 2.3. Approaches to isolate contexts in web browsers are presented in Sect. 2.4.

2.1 Preliminaries

IPv6. Internet Protocol version 6 (IPv6) is the successor to IPv4. With IPv6 there are a lot more IP addresses, since addresses now have 128 bit instead of 32 bit as with IPv4. IPv6 addresses have usually two parts of 64 bit each: a subnet prefix and an interface identifier. The adresses are written as eight groups of hexadecimal digits, leading zeros can be omitted and consecutive groups of zeros can be replaced with a double colon. Figure 1 shows two representations of the same address. The subnet prefix is used for routing, the interface identifier specifies an interface in a given subnet [6,14].

Fig. 1. Two representations of the same IPv6 address.

---

[1] The source code can be found at [39].

ISPs should assign at least one 64 bit prefix to home users and will assign in most cases significantly more addresses [24]. An IPv6 prefix is represented by the notation `ipv6-address/prefix-length`, where `prefix-length` specifies how many of the leftmost contiguous bits of the address comprise the prefix [14]. A subnet defined by a n bit prefix has 2^{128-n} addresses. This means that a typical home user's IPv6 subnet has at least 2^{32} times more addresses than the entire IPv4 address space.

Tor Browser. The Tor Browser is a browser that takes various measures to protect the privacy of its users. All user traffic is routed through the Tor anonymization network. This hides users' IP addresses and allows bypassing censorship. Browser fingerprinting is made more difficult and all visited websites are isolated from each other. This prevents third-party trackers from creating user profiles [28].

Different websites are isolated from each other by their URL bar origin. URL bar origin means at least the second-level DNS name. For example, the origin of `mail.google.com` would be `google.com` [28]. In practice, different origins are differentiated by means of the Public Suffix List [23]. This list contains all effective top level domains under which Internet users can or could directly register names. For example, it lists `dyndns.org`. This means that the domains `alice.dyndns.org` and `bob.dyndns.org` could belong to different entities and should be isolated from each other.

The Tor Browser also takes various measures to further isolate different URL bar origins, for example in relation to HTTP Keep-Alive connections or Cookies [28].

Our implementation is based on the Tor Browser, however, we make use of browser's website isolation features only and do not route traffic through the Tor network.

2.2 Address Hopping for Enhanced Privacy

IPv6 Stateless Address Autoconfiguration introduced a static interface identifier that enabled device tracking across networks. RFC 4941 [25] (Privacy Extensions for Stateless Address Autoconfiguration in IPv6) deals with this problem and proposed that a device should use temporary, random addresses for outbound connections. However, the randomly generated IP addresses are usually used for one day for new connections. It has been shown that sessions of 24 h length can be linked to the same user [4]. Therefore, Privacy Extensions are not a sufficient protection against tracking.

Lindqvist and Tapio proposed to alter identifiers on all layers of the protocol stack [18]. Instead of using a single system-wide protocol stack, each process would access the network through a virtual protocol stack. Besides IP addresses, the virtual protocol stack would also alter MAC addresses. The authors noted that IPv6 is more suitable than IPv4 for address changing schemes and suggested that each connection could use its own IP address. However, this would mean that a very large number of IP addresses are used which could lead to unexpected side effects. Lindqvist and Tapi focus on mobile computers and local adversaries, we also consider privacy issues with global IPv6 addresses. We extend their approach and consider the context of each request. For requests that can be easily linked at the application-level, we use the same address. Requests triggered by different contexts use different addresses.

Raghavan et al. describe a scenario where an ISP mixes the IP addresses of packets that are sent by their customers [29]. The IP address of each outgoing packet would be changed, similar to network address translation (NAT). The goal of the proposed technology is to enhance privacy of all customers of an ISP by default. In this paper, the approach of Raghavan et al. to form an anonymity set with all customers of an ISP is further discussed to prevent an adversary from linking several addresses to a single user.

Herrmann et al. [13] discuss the privacy issues of long-lived IPv6 prefixes and propose several prefix changing schemes: prefix hopping, prefix bouquets and prefix sharing. Prefix hopping is similar to IPv6 privacy extensions but instead of changing the IP address every day, it changes the prefix more frequently, e. g., every few seconds. Prefix bouquets suggests the ISP to delegate a number of prefixes to each customer instead of a single one. The customer's device would then choose a prefix either per destination or for each connection. However, one prefix per IP destination does not provide unlinkability against ad networks and address hopping over connections could impede compatibility and therefore usability. With prefix sharing, an ISP would assign one prefix to several customers. This scheme is similar to Raghavan et al.'s approach.

Unlike Herrmann et al. we do not change the IP addresses per destination or connection, but make the IP address dependent on the application context. Context-specific assignment is an improvement over prior work that assigned IP addresses per connection or per destination IP. In contrast to preceding approaches, context-aware address hopping only requires modifications to one communication partner.

2.3 Address Hopping for Enhanced Security

IPv6 address hopping schemes have also been discussed in other contexts than user privacy. Sifalakis et al. presented an approach to obscure the data exchange between two peers by spreading a data stream across multiple end-to-end connections [34]. Dunlop et al. suggested to repeatedly rotate the addresses of both, sender and receiver, to maintain user privacy and protect against targeted network attacks [8]. Judmayer et al. presented an address hopping scheme that defends IoT devices against reconnaissance and denial-of-service attacks as well as address-based correlation [15].

2.4   Context Isolation in Web Browsers

All major web browsers implement isolation mechanisms. These aim not only at security [7], but also at privacy [26], robustness and performance [30]. The mechanisms include memory isolation, separate processes and separate storages for cookies or HTML5 web storage data [22].

Pan et al. [26] suggested to partition client-side state into multiple isolation units (contexts) so that identifiers that could be used for tracking are not unique anymore. Protection against browser fingerprinting or IP-address-based tracking was not subject of their paper, as this has already been covered by the Tor Browser [28]. However, using Tor has disadvantages for browsing performance. Our approach makes use of the Tor browser's isolation features only and does not route traffic through the Tor network.

3   Context-Aware Address Hopping

Mozilla describes in its anti tracking policy web tracking practices that should be blocked by default by web browsers. These tracking techniques include third-party cookie-based and URL parameter-based cross-site tracking, browser fingerprinting and supercookies [21]. The mentioned techniques work on the application-level and can be prevented by application-level measures. However, even if we defeat all possible application-level tracking techniques, users' actions can still be linked at the network-level. For effective tracking protection, network-level and application-level defenses should be combined.

In Sect. 3.1, we describe our design goals and adversary model. Then, we explain various address generation options in Sect. 3.2. After that, we describe details of our implementation in Sect. 3.3.

3.1   Design Goals and Adversary Model

There are tools like Tor that provide network-level unlinkability with respect to strong adversaries. However, when using Tor, the browsing performance decreases. VPNs have a performance and cost overhead as well [27,31]. We will utilize the huge IPv6 address space to protect against network-level tracking with respect to relatively weak adversaries. Our concept should protect against website operators and ad networks. A third party included in two or more websites must not be able to link visitors on different websites to the same user. We consider the users' ISP as trusted. Our concept should have no perceptible

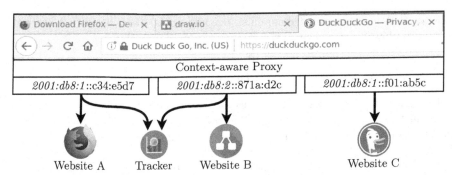

(a) With context-aware IPv6 address hopping, each request is send to the proxy and assigned an outbound IP address based on the tab it originates from.

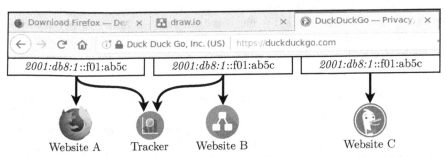

(b) Without context-aware IPv6 address hopping, all requests are send with the same outbound IP address.

Fig. 2. Three tabs are opened in a browser and sending requests to websites A, B and C. Websites A and B include the same third-party tracker. Prefixes are in italics.

influence on the browsing performance. Furthermore, it should be transparent to the user, and backwards compatible to existing web applications and Internet infrastructure.

To achieve our goals, an HTTP request must not use the same outbound IP address as another request belonging to another URL bar origin. Also, all requests within one URL bar origin should use the same outbound IP address to reduce possible compatibility issues. The desired behavior is illustrated in Fig. 2a. Each request passes the context-aware proxy and uses an outbound IP address that depends on the URL bar origin of the corresponding tab. Note that different IP addresses are used to contact the tracker. In contrast, Fig. 2b illustrates the current state. The adversary can link the requests to a single user, based on the IP address.

3.2   Address Generation

A requirement for protecting users' privacy is that an adversary can not easily link multiple IPv6 addresses to a single user. Without changing the current Internet infrastructure, users can use any addresses in the subnet assigned to them by their ISP. Thus, interface identifiers can be varied easily. However, the prefix can not be varied easily without changing the infrastructure. This is shown in Fig. 2a, the prefixes are in italics. If the prefix is not varied and not shared with other users, address- or rather prefix-based tracking remains possible. In the following section, three prefix changing variants are described.

Prefixes of Variable Length. When ISPs delegate prefixes of fixed length to their users as suggested by RFC 6177 [24], adversaries could easily link all IP addresses that belong to a single user if the size of the subnets is known. To prevent this simple mapping, ISPs could delegate prefixes of variable length. Still, adversaries might be able to detect the length of those prefixes by cluster analysis.

The similarity between two IPv6 addresses can be seen as the difference from 128 to the number of matching sequential bits starting with the most significant bit. The longer a shared prefix is, the shorter is the distance between two addresses [17]. The IP addresses "2a08::13ff" and "2a08::1300" have a distance of 32 bit while the IP addresses "2f08::1337" and "2018::1337" have a distance of 112 bit. IP addresses from smaller subnets will form tighter clusters than those from larger subnets.

Prefix Bouquets. Following Herrmann et al. [13], an ISP could provide prefix bouquets. However, many prefixes would be required if each prefix is to be used only once. If prefixes were used multiple times, an attacker could possibly link some activities.

ISPs could then tend to build prefix bouquets out of smaller prefixes or even specific IP addresses. This would break the current IPv6 auto-configuration as it relies on 64 bit interface identifiers [35].

Prefix Sharing. Alternatively, prefixes could be shared over larger groups of users. As with NAT, prefix sharing could conceal the individual user's behavior [9]. Though, NAT users can be fingerprinted [37]. Two approaches for prefix sharing are discussed below.

Unique IP Addresses. When sharing a prefix among several home networks, packets might be routed to a wrong host if uniqueness of IP addresses is not guaranteed. Herrmann et al. [13] suggest three variants for prefix sharing that guarantee uniqueness. First, the ISP could deploy central DHCP servers which receive requests from user devices. The ISP would learn which websites are accessed by which device. However, even without address hopping, the ISP learns which websites are visited, e. g., if the ISP's DNS servers are used, if the traffic is unencrypted, if server name indication is used or if only one web page is using a destination's IP address. Second, the customer's router could receive a pre-allocated set of IP addresses by the ISP. The IP addresses are then distributed by the router without the ISP learning which device allocated a specific IP address. This would require changes to software on both ISP and consumer end. The third option suggests the ISP to apply NAT to all consumer traffic.

Probabilistic IP Address Generation. Alternatively to ensuring IP address uniqueness, one could gamble that a randomly generated IP address is not used by another host on the network. This could lead to collisions. In the following, we examine how likely collisions would be.

Based on the birthday problem, Eq. (1) approximates the probability p of at least one collision for n generated and d possible IP addresses:

$$p(n,d) \approx 1 - e^{\frac{-(n^2-n)}{2d}} \tag{1}$$

Table 1. Number of addresses that can be generated before causing a collision at a probability of 10^{-6} in subnets of differenz sizes.

Prefix length	Generated addresses
/48	1,554,944,645
/56	97,184,040
/64	6,074,003
/72	379,625
/80	23,727

For example, a collision occurs with a probability of 50% when generating about $5.05 \cdot 10^9$ IP addresses within a /64 prefix. Probabilities for /64 and other prefix lengths are shown in Fig. 3. Table 1 shows the number of IP addresses that can be generated with a collision probability of 10^{-6} for different subnet sizes.

Assuming that one hundred users visit one hundred websites each, results in ten thousand generated IP addresses. Using Eq. (1), the probability of a collision of two of these IP addresses in a /64 is only about $2.71 \cdot 10^{-12}$. Even with one million generated addresses, the probability is only about $2.71 \cdot 10^{-8}$.

For the unlikely case that two hosts generate the same IP address, a router would need to decide to which of the two hosts it sends a packet. The hosts would have to detect when responses are not received and then generate a new IP address.

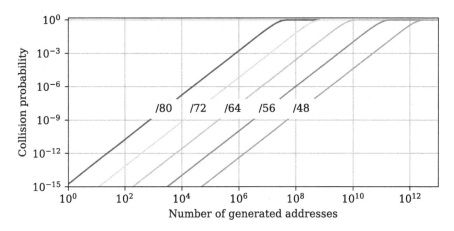

Fig. 3. Each graph shows the collision probability when generating a number of addresses for a prefix length. The x-axis describes the number of addresses and the y-axis the collision probability.

3.3 Implementation

We implement our prototype in the Go programming language as an alternative proxy for the Tor Browser and do not route traffic through the Tor network. We make use of the browser's website isolation feature only.

By default, Tor isolates streams for which different SOCKS usernames and passwords were provided. Thus, the Tor Browser uses a set of SOCKS credentials per URL bar origin to isolate different origins. We replace Tor's SOCKS proxy with our prototype which uses different outbound IPv6 addresses for different sets of SOCKS credentials. Thus, for connections to different URL bar origins different IPv6 addresses will be used.

When receiving previously unknown credentials, the proxy generates, based on the procedures defined in RFC 4941 [25], a new outbound IPv6 address and saves the mapping. Then, the proxy establishes a TCP connection to the destination. If the connection is established, the client may start sending data as it would without a proxy.

The working principle of the prototype is illustrated in Fig. 4. The browser requests the HTML content of *mozilla.org* and *draw.io*. Both websites include a common third-party resource. Different outbound IP addresses are used for the different contexts.

4 Evaluation

We evaluate our approach from three different perspectives. In Sect. 4.1, we study the privacy improvement for users. In Sect. 4.2, we investigate the com-

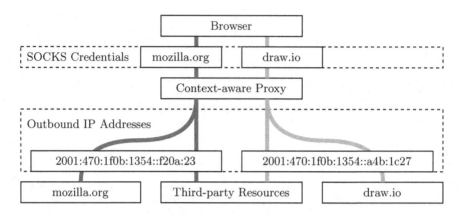

Fig. 4. Two websites include common third-party resources. With context-aware address hopping, different outbound IP addresses are used in different contexts.

patibility with today's web protocols. In Sect. 4.3, we measure the performance overhead.

4.1   Privacy

With the help of the URL bar origins and the Public Suffix List [23], we achieve that different outbound IP addresses are used for different (effective) top-level domains. As a result, a third party can not link visitors on different websites based on their IP adresses to the same user.

In addition to the IP address, cookies, various cache-based, fingerprinting-based and other mechanisms can be used to track users [5]. That means that context-aware IP address hopping alone does not protect against tracking. Our concept can be effective only in combination with tools like ad blockers that prevent application-level tracking or like Multi-Account Containers for the Firefox browser that allow users to separate different contexts [22]. However, if we assume that actions against those other tracking mechanisms have been taken, then context-aware IP address hopping will be an effective complement.

4.2   Compatibility

Our prototype is able to forward outbound TCP connections opened by the browser. The prototype's behavior is not dependent on the payload of the packets as the proxy only forwards binary data from either side. Therefore, it can be assumed that any TCP-based protocol is supported. Modern web browsers support a variety of protocols in addition to and on top of HTTP and JavaScript. In the following, we will take a closer look at two widely used protocols.

The WebSocket Protocol [11] provides a two-way communication instead of the strict client-server architecture of HTTP. It uses the HTTP Upgrade header to upgrade a HTTP connection to a WebSocket connection. The procedure is designed to be interoperable with the existing HTTP infrastructure such as prox-ies. It is also intended to be used with a single TCP connection. Following this, the prototype can be expected to be compatible with WebSockets. A *WebSocket Echo Test* [16] was used to successfully test this compatibility.

WebRTC [2] allows real-time communication like video conferences. It defines a framework for peer-to-peer applications in the browser. It is already supported by various browsers including Firefox [19]. It allows to add additional protocols to the mandatory set of the standard. These protocols may use both TCP and UDP as transport protocols [3]. However, the Tor Browser disables WebRTC at com-pile time [28]. Therefore, it is not easily testable whether WebRTC would work with the prototype. Still, the ability of WebRTC to open connections through NAT might also work with the prototype. Yet, WebRTC might leak the client's IP addresses to other peers [36]. In the future, our prototype could be extended to support incoming connections and bidirectional UDP relaying since the SOCKS protocol supports both.

In order to test more sophisticated web services, we manually tested the third-party authentication services of Google [12] and Facebook [10]. No restrictions were noted. Also the Shibboleth service of the Hamburg University of Technology could be used with our prototype.

Some web applications force a logout on IP address change. Thus, choosing the client's IP address based on the destination's IP address may lead to a compatibility issue. Since we are choosing the client's IP address based on the URL bar origin, we expect that no sessions will be terminated by our address hopping scheme.

4.3 Performance

Privacy enhancing techniques that require an overlay network, such as Tor, have significant impact on browsing performance [27,31]. Context-aware IPv6 address hopping does not require an overlay network. To evaluate the perfor-mance impact caused by our prototype, we compare it against two different browsers: the original Firefox web browser and the Tor Browser. For a variety of reasons, we compare our prototype to the Tor Browser, although Tor has a much stronger adversary model. First, our prototype builds on top of the Tor Browser. As a consequence, overhead induced by the Tor Browser (not Tor) evens out when comparing our solution with the performance of the Tor Browser. Sec-ond, the Tor Browser is the only widespread tool that achieves unlinkability on the network layer. We show that much better performance can be achieved by weakening the adversary model. This might lead to higher acceptance among users. We argue that there must also be lightweight techniques that are easy to use and protect against relatively weak adversaries. These techniques might reach those users who otherwise would not be protected at all. Thus, we have the following three configurations:

1. **Firefox:** A default installation of Firefox (version 65.0.1), which acts as a baseline for browsing without additional privacy protection.

2. **Tor Browser:** A default installation of Tor Browser (version 8.0.6), which offers additional privacy protection by reducing browser fingerprintability and onion routing.
3. **Prototype:** Our prototype, which consists of an unmodified Tor Browser (version 8.0.6) connecting through our prototype SOCKS proxy.

For obvious reasons, we expect our solution to perform faster than the Tor Browser. When IPv6 is available on the local network, address hopping can use the native, direct connection to the destination. In particular, packets can be routed on the same path as without address hopping, resulting in similar latencies. Thus, we expect that our protoype achieves about the same performance as Firefox and users would notice no difference.

We measure the performance of the Alexa Top 100 global sites [1]. The list was retrieved on February 26, 2019, and is reduced to websites that are reachable by IPv6 so that address hopping can be employed. The data set was divided in two parts:

1. **Top 10:** Out of the top 10 domains, five had IPv6 support. For these domains, 50 measurements were taken for each configuration.
2. **Top 100:** Out of the top 100 domains, 27 domains had IPv6 support. For these domains, 10 measurements were taken for each configuration.

We use Selenium [33] to start the three configurations independently and retrieve each web page several times. The browser caches have been disabled. We utilize the Performance API [38] to measure the timings of the different stages while retrieving and displaying a web page[2]. For each measurement we took the time it required for the HTML document and all its dependent resources to be retrieved over the network, i.e., the `loadEventStart` key of the Performance API [20]. The Performance API returns timestamps with millisecond precision. The measurements has been taken sequentially on the same computer using a DSL connection with 100 Mibit/s download and 20 Mibit/s upload.

The mean and standard deviation of the time needed to retrieve and render an HTML document and its dependent resources is displayed in Table 2. Details for the five websites remaining of the top 10 Alexa global sites for all three configurations are further highlighted in Fig. 5. The mean values give an impression of the speed of the client and the standard deviation can be interpreted as a measure of steadiness. The results indicate that the prototype performs nearly identical to the unmodified Firefox browser, while having a similar standard deviation. Using the prototype is significantly faster than using Tor, whose values also show a high standard deviation. This order is not only represented by the overall values but also by the website specific mean and standard deviation values. The native uplink is on average slightly faster than the prototype which

---

[2] The browser profiles of the The Browser and our protoype had to be configured to allow accessing Firefox's Performance API: `privacy.resistFingerprinting = false`.

in turn is on average faster than Tor. Some values of prototype and native uplink are very close, especially when taking the standard deviation into consideration.

The results indicate that our technique can be used without a significant impact on browsing performance.

Table 2. Mean and standard deviation of the time in seconds needed to retrieve and render an HTML document and its dependent resources as well as the number of third-party resources.

Website	Firefox		Prototype		Tor browser		3rd-party
	Mean	SD	Mean	SD	Mean	SD	Resources
google.com	0.43	0.11	0.42	0.06	7.96	4.09	3
youtube.com	1.78	0.68	1.91	0.49	8.79	2.16	10
facebook.com	1.07	0.16	1.23	0.20	9.55	2.27	1
wikipedia.org	0.19	0.10	0.22	0.05	1.76	0.50	0
yahoo.com	0.51	0.25	0.48	0.13	3.88	1.49	1
Alexa Top 10	0.27	0.49	0.28	0.51	2.13	3.32	3
Alexa Top 100	0.30	0.72	0.64	0.39	2.28	4.74	12.26

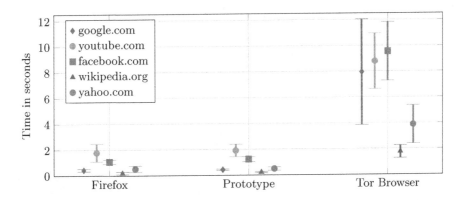

Fig. 5. Mean and standard deviation of the time in seconds needed to retrieve and render an HTML document and its dependent resources. The five domains are the subset of the Alexa Top 10 domains with IPv6 support. 50 measurements were taken for each configuration.

5 Discussion

By using URL bar origins, we achieve that a third party included in two or more websites is not be able to link visitors on different websites to the same user. Moreover, by involving the ISP, we achieve that our concept is transparent to the user and has no perceptible influence on browsing performance. That we consider the ISP as trustworthy is not a disadvantage. After all, the ISP does not learn more about users' browsing behavior than it does today. The concept is backwards compatible to existing web applications, but can be integrated into today's infrastructure to a limited extent only. Regarding the prefix changes, ISPs will have to deviate from today's standards.

Context-aware IPv6 Address Hopping is a good complement to existing application-level protection. Our concept has a clearly weaker attacker model compared to Tor, but there are no perceptible performance penalties. Hence, on the network level, we could protect the privacy of people who today do not use Tor.

6   Conclusion

This paper introduced context-aware IPv6 address hopping to prevent IP address-based linking of users' activities. The proposed address hopping scheme uses a distinct outbound IPv6 address for each visited website and its dependencies. In combination with application-level measures, effective protection against tracking can be achieved.

A prototype of context-aware IPv6 address hopping has been implemented. For this the Tor Browser was used, whereby Tor's SOCKS proxy was exchanged for our implementation. Support for several web protocols and applications has been ensured. We evaluated the impact of the prototype on browsing performance. The results indicate that the impact is negligible.

Future work is needed to examine how ISPs can provide users with multiple and frequently changing IPv6 prefixes. Also, the context-aware approach could be extended to other applications and the operating system. Furthermore, it could be examined how existing anonymous communication networks such as Tor can be made more context-aware and what advantages and disadvantages that would have.

Acknowledgment. We thank the anonymous reviewers for their insightful comments and suggestions. This work is supported in part by the German Federal Ministry of Education and Research under the reference number 16KIS0368 and the German Federal Ministry for Economic Affairs and Energy under the reference number 03SIN432.

References

1. Alexa Internet Inc.: The Top 500 Sites on the Web (2019). https://www.alexa.com/topsites
2. Alvestrand, H.: Overview: real time protocols for browser-based applications. Internet-Draft draft-ietf-rtcweb-overview-19, November 2017
3. Alvestrand, H.T.: Transports for WebRTC. Technical report, draft-ietf-rtcweb-transports-17, Internet Engineering Task Force, October 2016. Work in Progress
4. Banse, C., Herrmann, D., Federrath, H.: Tracking users on the internet with behavioral patterns: evaluation of its practical feasibility. In: Gritzalis, D., Furnell, S., Theoharidou, M. (eds.) SEC 2012. IAICT, vol. 376, pp. 235–248. Springer, Heidelberg (2012). https://doi.org/10.1007/978-3-642-30436-1_20

5. Bujlow, T., Carela-Español, V., Solé-Pareta, J., Barlet-Ros, P.: Web Tracking: Mechanisms, Implications, and Defenses. arXiv preprint arXiv:1507.07872 (2015)
6. Carpenter, B., Chown, T., Gont, F., Jiang, S., Petrescu, A., Yourtchenko, A.: Analysis of the 64-bit Boundary in IPv6 Addressing. RFC 7421, RFC Editor, January 2015
7. Chen, E.Y., Bau, J., Reis, C., Barth, A., Jackson, C.: App isolation: get the security of multiple browsers with just one. In: ACM Conference on Computer and Communications Security, pp. 227–238. ACM (2011)
8. Dunlop, M., Groat, S., Urbanski, W., Marchany, R., Tront, J.: MT6D: a moving target IPv6 defense. In: Military Communications Conference 2011, pp. 1321–1326. IEEE (2011)
9. Egevang, K.B., Francis, P.: The IP Network Address Translator (NAT). RFC 1631, RFC Editor, May 1994
10. Facebook: Facebook Login (2019). https://developers.facebook.com/docs/facebook-login/web
11. Fette, I., Melnikov, A.: The WebSocket protocol. RFC 6455, RFC Editor, December 2011
12. Google LLC: Google Sign-In for Websites (2019). https://developers.google.com/identity/sign-in/web/
13. Herrmann, D., Arndt, C., Federrath, H.: IPv6 Prefix Alteration: An Opportunity to Improve Online Privacy. CoRR abs/1211.4704 (2012)
14. Hinden, R., Deering, S.: IP Version 6 Addressing Architecture. RFC 4291, RFC Editor, February 2006
15. Judmayer, A., Ullrich, J., Merzdovnik, G., Voyiatzis, A.G., Weippl, E.: Lightweight address hopping for defending the IPv6 IoT. In: International Conference on Availability, Reliability and Security, p. 20. ACM (2017)
16. Kaazing Corporation: WebSocket echo test (2019). https://www.websocket.org/echo.html
17. Krishnamurthy, B., Wang, J.: On network-aware vclustering of web clients. ACM SIGCOMM Comput. Commun. Rev. **30**(4), 97–110 (2000)
18. Lindqvist, J., Tapio, J.M.: Protecting privacy with protocol stack virtualization. In: Workshop on Privacy in the Electronic Society, pp. 65–74. ACM, New York (2008). https://doi.org/10.1145/1456403.1456416
19. Mozilla: Firefox 22.0 releasenotes (2013). https://website-archive.mozilla.org/www.mozilla.org/firefox_releasenotes/en-US/firefox/22.0/releasenotes/
20. Mozilla: PerformanceNavigationTiming - Web APIs — MDN (2018). https://developer.mozilla.org/en-US/docs/Web/API/PerformanceNavigationTiming
21. Mozilla: Anti tracking policy (2019). https://wiki.mozilla.org/Security/Anti_tracking_policy#1._Cross-site_tracking
22. Mozilla: Multi-Account Containers (2019). https://support.mozilla.org/en-US/kb/containers
23. Mozilla Foundation: Public Suffix List (2019). https://publicsuffix.org
24. Narten, T., Huston, G., Roberts, L.: IPv6 Address Assignment to End Sites. BCP 157, RFC Editor, March 2011
25. Narten, T., Draves, R., Krishnan, S.: Privacy Extensions for Stateless Address Autoconfiguration in IPv6. RFC 4941, RFC Editor, September 2007
26. Pan, X., Cao, Y., Chen, Y.: I do not know what you visited last summer: protecting users from third-party web tracking with trackingfree browser. In: Network and Distributed System Security Symposium (2015)

27. Panchenko, A., Pimenidis, L., Renner, J.: Performance analysis of anonymous communication channels provided by Tor. In: International Conference on Availability, Reliability and Security, pp. 221–228, March 2008. https://doi.org/10.1109/ARES.2008.63
28. Perry, M., Clark, E., Murdoch, S., Koppen, G.: The design and implementation of the Tor browser [DRAFT] (2018). https://www.torproject.org/projects/torbrowser/design/
29. Raghavan, B., Kohno, T., Snoeren, A.C., Wetherall, D.: Enlisting ISPs to improve online privacy: IP address mixing by default. In: Goldberg, I., Atallah, M.J. (eds.) PETS 2009. LNCS, vol. 5672, pp. 143–163. Springer, Heidelberg (2009). https://doi.org/10.1007/978-3-642-03168-7_9
30. Reis, C., Gribble, S.D.: Isolating web programs in modern browser architectures. In: ACM European Conference on Computer Systems, pp. 219–232. ACM (2009)
31. Ries, T., Panchenko, A., State, R., Engel, T.: Comparison of low-latency anonymous communication systems: practical usage and performance. In: Australasian Information Security Conference, pp. 77–86 (2011)
32. RIPE NCC: IPv6 Enabled Networks (2018). http://v6asns.ripe.net/v/6?s=_ALL;s=_RIR_RIPE_NCC
33. Selenium - Web Browser Automation (2019). https://docs.seleniumhq.org
34. Sifalakis, M., Schmid, S., Hutchison, D.: Network address hopping: a mechanism to enhance data protection for packet communications. In: International Conference on Communications, vol. 3, pp. 1518–1523. IEEE (2005)
35. Thomson, S., Narten, T., Jinmei, T.: IPv6 Stateless Address Autoconfiguration. RFC 4862, RFC Editor, September 2007
36. Uberti, J., Shieh, G.: WebRTC IP Address Handling Requirements. Internet-Draft draft-ietf-rtcweb-ip-handling-04, July 2017
37. Verde, N.V., Ateniese, G., Gabrielli, E., Mancini, L.V., Spognardi, A.: No NAT'd user left behind: fingerprinting users behind NAT from NetFlow records alone. In: International Conference on Distributed Computing Systems, pp. 218–227. IEEE (2014)
38. W3C: A Primer for Web Performance Timing APIs (2018). http://w3c.github.io/perf-timing-primer/
39. Wille, F.: IPv6 Address Hopping - SOCKS5 Proxy: Version 1, February 2018. https://doi.org/10.5281/zenodo.1184149

Towards Homograph-Confusable Domain Name Detection Using Dual-Channel CNN

Guangxi Yu[1,2], Xinghua Yang[1(✉)], Yan Zhang[1,2], Huajun Cui[1,2], Huiran Yang[1], and Yang Li[1,2]

[1] Institute of Information Engineering, Chinese Academy of Sciences, Beijing, China
yangxinghua@iie.ac.cn
[2] School of Cyber Security, University of Chinese Academy of Sciences, Beijing, China

Abstract. Homograph attack is a common way of phishing attacks, which aims to generate visual spoofing domain names by replacing a single character or combinations of characters. To analyze and detect homograph domain names, former works mainly consider about distance based methods, analyzing edit distance or Euclidean distance between two domain names, or utilize OCR (Optical Character Recognition) technique. However, these methods may not only have a large number of false positive cases, but they also increase processing overhead. In this paper, we proposed a dual-channel CNN classifier with retrieving algorithm of minimum hash (MinHash) and locality sensitive hash (LSH) to detect homograph domain names. The dual-channel CNN classifier was trained to analyze dual-channel domain images. The MinHash and LSH were designed to search domain name with similar characters, which can reduce the large data efficiently. By comparing with other detection methods, our method can distinguish homograph domain names from normal ones effectively, which can achieve 98.5% detection rates. Experiments on DNS real log datasets indicate that MinHash and LSH scheme can perform well in reducing the large data.

Keywords: Domain name · Homograph · CNN · MinHash · LSH

1 Introduction

Phishing attack is one of the greatest and most serious threats against the Internet currently. Phishing refers to the network criminal act that steals users' personal information including username and password. Generally, to achieve this criminal purpose, attacker first registers fake domain names by imitating well-known websites, and then delivers them to victims to lure users into clicking these elaborate fraud websites, resorting to every possible method of attack.

In phishing, attacker can structure and generate fake domain names in various ways, such as homograph attack [1], typosquatting [2], soundsquatting [3], combosquatting [4], etc. Homograph attack is a common way, which aims to generate visual spoofing domain names by replacing some of the characters with other visually similar ones. For example, the character 'l' is similar to the figure '1', and the combination 'rn' (*i.e.*, r and n) is similar to 'm'. In addition, because IDNs (International Domain Names) have been widely

© Springer Nature Switzerland AG 2020
J. Zhou et al. (Eds.): ICICS 2019, LNCS 11999, pp. 555–568, 2020.
https://doi.org/10.1007/978-3-030-41579-2_32

used, attackers can also impersonate domain names of trusted entities via homograph techniques in Unicode character set, which greatly expands the homographic area and increases the difficulty of detection. Typosquatting is an another way to generate fake domain names using character-replacement, character-omission, character-permutation, character-insertion and missing-dot [2]. However, compared with homograph domain names, typosquatting domain names are commonly used by online advertisement and domain parking [2]. Due to the similarity between these phishing domain names and well-known domain names, prior researches proposed many detection methods to detect phishing domain names based on similarity analysis of domain names.

In detail, for homograph domain name analysis, former researches mainly consider about edit distance (*i.e.*, Levenshtein distance) between two domain names, and regard the pair of domain names with small distance as homograph domains. However, methods only based on edit distance will have a large number of false positive cases, especially for domain names with few characters. For example, (*bbc.com*, *msn.com*) and (*bloodhorse.com*, *bl00dh0rse.com*) have the same edit distance, however, domain names in former pair are normal ones. In addition to edit distance, some detection methods such as OCR (Optical Character Recognition) [5, 6] are proposed to detect the similarities of domain names and web contents. Obviously, these methods will increase processing overheads when grabbing and analyzing a large number domain names or web pages, which makes it hard to meet the demand of fast detection. Deep learning based detection method has also been proposed, such as siamese CNN (Convolutional Neural Network) [7]. It may take much more time for training and also has a relatively low detection rate by using Euclidean distance.

In this paper, we propose a dual-channel CNN based detection method to analyze and detect homograph domain name. Firstly, we convert a pair of domain names into dual-channel domain images. In detail, each channel corresponds to a domain name. Secondly, we design and train a CNN based classifier to analyze these dual-channel domain images. Thirdly, considering the large number of domain name in real network, we utilize minimum hash (MinHash) and locality sensitive hashing (LSH) to search domain name with similar characters, which can reduce the large data efficiently. Our experiment results show that the proposed method can detect homograph domain name effectively. In detail, the dual-channel CNN based classifier could achieve a high detection rate of 98.5%; by analyzing detection results, the retrieving algorithm of MinHash and LSH could narrow detection scope and reduce the large data efficiently. Compared with other methods, our method can achieve a higher detection rate and consume less time for training.

The remainder of this paper is organized as follows. The related work in relevant field is reviewed briefly in Sect. 2. Section 3 provides an overview of the proposed detection method. Section 4 introduces the detailed CNN classifier. Section 5 introduces the MinHash and LSH algorithm. Section 6 introduces the datasets and discusses the performance results using real-world DNS log data. Finally, Sect. 7 presents some brief concluding remarks.

2 Related Works

Holgers *et al.* [1] studied homograph domain names and homograph attack in an early time, their measurement results suggest that homograph attacks seem like an attractive future method for attackers to lure users to spoofed sites. Particularly, homograph attacks do have the potential to become more common and malicious with the use of IDNs. Besides, in an extensive measurement study, Quinkert *et al.* [8] found that more and more technology companies and financial institutions are targeted by homograph attacks.

To effectively distinguish homograph domain names from normal ones, researchers have proposed many approaches, which can be classified into two categories: distance based analysis and character or visual similarity analysis.

For distance analysis, researchers mainly regard a pair of domain names with small edit distance as homograph domain names. However, methods only based on edit distance will have a large number of false positive cases, especially for domain names with few characters. Meanwhile, conventional methods based on edit distance do not take into account visual confusion on characters. Therefore, for quantifying visual similarity of domain names, Liu *et al.* [9] proposed a novel quantitative method to measure the visual similarity of two given domains. Based on generalized edit distance that takes insights of novel visual characteristics, this method can search the maximum visual similarity of a domain over a given popular website set. Similarly, Black [10] also proposed a method of visual similarity. However, visual distance is still edit distance with a weight of character and operation. Nowadays, in addition to the conventional methods, deep learning algorithms, such as CNN, LSTM, have also been used to detect homograph domain names. Woodbridge *et al.* [7] presented a solution to analyze homographic problem using a siamese CNN. The siamese CNN first extracts feature vectors of domain name images, and then distinguishes similar strings or dissimilar strings by using Euclidean distance. Similarly, Ya *et al.* [11] proposed an LSTM based siamese network to analyze sequences of characters of squatting domain names, and calculate the distance between vectors in Euclidean space as well.

For similarity analysis, it was theorized that OCR technique could be used to detect homograph domain names. Sawabe *et al.* [5] leveraged OCR technique to recognize similarities between IDNs and legitimate domain names automatically. This OCR method can generate corresponding mappings with ASCII characters, which are on the basis of the input IDNs containing non-ASCII characters. Then if there are legitimate domains in these candidate mappings, the corresponding input IDN is detected as being a homograph domain name. In addition, Tian *et al.* [6] built a novel machine learning classifier that takes advantage of image analysis and OCR technique to detect squatting phishing pages and domain names. However, when generating domain images, the OCR method must perform a series of preliminary image processing. Meanwhile, this method also has a relatively lower detection rate. For another strategy, Roshanbin *et al.* [12] explored a mathematical approach to define the visual similarity between Unicode glyphs, which utilizes Normalized Information Distance and Kolmogorov Complexity theory.

Additionally, to detect homograph attack, some researches [13, 14] also generate candidate homograph domain names from popular ones, and then analyze behaviors of these domain names based on WHOIS records, DNS records and web pages, etc. Although these proposed solutions can analyze the behaviors of homograph domain names well, they cannot meet the demand of homograph detection in real network traffic.

3 Detection System Overview

In order to detect homograph domain names, we utilize a CNN based classifier as a key component, which can analyze visual similarities between a query domain name and a domain name in whitelist. The domain whitelist is obtained from Alexa domain list[1]. In this section, we make an overview of our detection method, which is shown in Fig. 1.

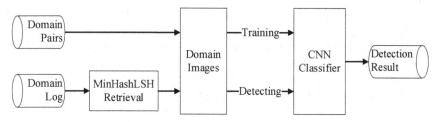

Fig. 1. Overview of detection system

In training stage, we first select homograph domain names and non-homograph domain names to create a truth marked training dataset. Then we convert pairs of domain names into domain images, and train a CNN classifier to distinguish these domain images.

In detecting stage, we first combine a real domain name queried by network user with a target domain name, then we use the well-trained classifier to analyze the pair of domain names. Due to the large number domain names in DNS real logs, we use the pre-retrieval process with MinHash and LSH algorithm to narrow the target image list, which can also decrease time of processing and increase detection rate.

4 CNN Classifier Model

In this section, we introduce the main parts of CNN classification model, including training dataset, CNN classification model and performance of classification.

4.1 Training Dataset

As mentioned before, in this paper, the training dataset consists of benign domain names and homograph domain names. For benign domain names, they were all selected from Alexa 1M domain list and regarded as negative samples. We first randomly matched any two domain names, and then selected 500K pairs of domain names whose edit distance are less than or equal to 6. For positive samples, we constructed pairs of homograph domain names based on Alexa top 10K domain names using the *typofinder*[2] tool. Finally,

---

[1] https://www.alexa.com/topsites.

[2] https://github.com/nccgroup/typofinder.

we also randomly selected 500K cases. Specially, because edit distance based methods are completely dependent on the distance between every two domain strings, we attempt to make positive samples have the same distribution as negative samples, which aims to prove the validity of the proposed CNN method. Meanwhile, considering the real distribution of data in DNS logs, we set our training dataset as shown in Fig. 2.

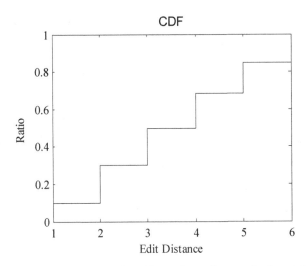

Fig. 2. Edit distance distribution of positive and negative samples in training dataset

In this paper, a CNN classifier is intended to produce a binary value from an input image transformed from an input text. In our model, we constructed images of size $16 \times 120 \times 2$ with white text on black background using CODE2000 font. In our experiments, we set the image size according to the length of domain names. Images could accommodate horizontal space for 25 Unicode characters with image size 16×120, which could cover almost all domain names in training dataset. The figure '2' refers to two channels, and each channel consists of a domain name in detail. Finally, we classified our training set with percentage split, where 70% of the dataset was used for training, and the rest was used to check the correctness.

Note that we only analyze domain names with second level domain (SLD), because a large number of homograph domain names are registered under SLD [15], and in this paper we use domain names in Alexa list as target domain names, which only contain SLDs. Besides, we omit the part of top level domains (TLDs), because homograph TLDs cannot be used arbitrarily. Although a homograph TLD can achieve an effective deception, it may not be resolved by authoritative servers.

4.2 Classification Model

In this subsection, we build a dual-channel CNN based classification model, which consists of two convolutional layers and two full-connected layers, as shown in Fig. 3.

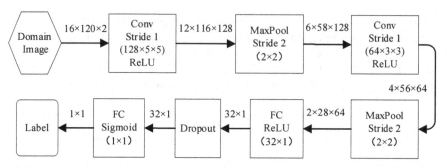

Fig. 3. Dual-channel CNN based classification model

We first transform our dataset of domain names into dataset of images, and then select important features from input data via convolutional and maxpooling layers followed a full-connected layer with 32 neural units, finally we utilize a sigmoid layer to concatenate them into a compact label value. In detail, we label the number of convolution kernel and kernel size in the corresponding convolutional layer. Different from other methods, we can avoid various calculations about edit distance or Euclidean distance. What's more, complicated pre-processing on images is unnecessary.

4.3 Performance and Comparison

To maximize the performance of classification, we trained the CNN classification model using our training dataset with a batch size of 128. And we used *Adam* as optimizer penalized via cross entropy loss. In detail, the training experiment was run using ten-fold cross validation, on a physical server with 12 cores CPU and 128G RAM. Finally, fewer than 30 epochs were required for convergence, and each training epoch took about 18 min. Evaluation is accomplished with a detailed F1 score, True Positive Rate (TRP), False Positive Rate (FPR) and False Negative Rate (FNR), which is shown in Table 1.

Table 1. Performance of CNN based classifier.

F1	TPR	FPR	FNR	AUC
98.5%	98.3%	1.2%	1.5%	99%

To further analyze the effectiveness of our detection method, we made a comparison with some other methods by using our training dataset. First, we analyzed methods of edit distance and visual distance. Specially, we used public homograph character list[3] to analyze visual distance. Then we performed OCR technique to recognize similarities among domain names in training dataset automatically. Here, we utilized *Tesseract-OCR*[4] as a tool to perform OCR detection. Next we also analyzed the siamese CNN,

---

[3] https://www.unicode.org/Public/security/8.0.0/confusables.txt.
[4] https://github.com/tesseract-ocr/.

which is a pair of identical convolutional neural networks [7]. At its core, each branch represents a domain image separately, and outputs of these two branches are merged by a similarity function. The differences between our model and siamese model are depicted in Fig. 4. In the comparative experiment, we used *Adam* as optimizer penalized via contrastive loss, and trained siamese CNN with a batch size of 128. Finally we show the ROC of different methods in Fig. 5.

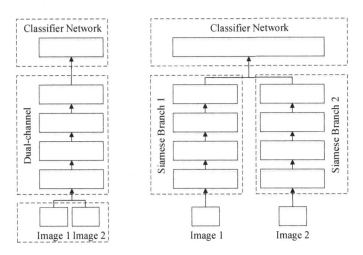

Fig. 4. Dual-channel model and siamese network model

Compared with dual-channel CNN, method based on edit distance can hardly detect homograph domain names in our dataset. This result indicates that the method with conventional edit distance does not have ability to distinguish homograph domains from normal ones when they have a similar edit distance distribution, even though there exists a great difference in characters. Method based on visual distance performs much better than that based on conventional edit distance. However, to achieve the desired result, this detection method has to depend on a manually maintained mapping list of homograph characters.

OCR technique only performs a little better than edit distance method. Note that we just use OCR to detect homograph domain names directly. Although it may perform well when analyzing Unicode characters in domain strings one by one, here we do not make a series of preliminary image processing, which is also not the focus in this paper.

Compared with dual-channel CNN, siamese CNN can also achieve high performance. However, siamese CNN still depends on distance analysis which is Euclidean distance. And it also takes longer to train a detection model. For example, in our experiment, each training epoch of dual-channel CNN took about 18 min, each training epoch of siamese CNN took about 1 h under the same training setting. What's more, dual-channel CNN could make full use of hidden features of domain images by coupling two image channels after the first convolutional layer, which could further improve detection rate.

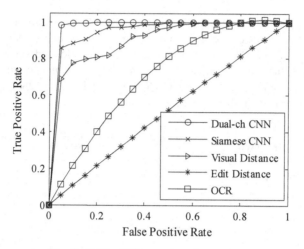

Fig. 5. ROC of different detection methods

From above results and analysis, we can conclude that the proposed dual-channel based CNN method is an effective solution to detect homograph domain names.

5   MinHash and LSH Algorithm

To reduce the amount of data efficiently, we utilize an algorithm of MinHash and LSH to search domain names with similar characters. In this section, we first introduce some definition of MinHash and LSH, and then we describe the detailed algorithm proposed in our detection method.

5.1   MinHash and LSH

MinHash. MinHash is widely used to analyze the similarity of text based on Jaccard similarity function [16]. In detail, Jaccard function represents the probability of two sets having the same value (*i.e.*, the ratio of the cardinalities of the intersection and union of the two sets). To simplify the notation and terminology, let A and B be sets of domain names, Jaccard similarity is defined as:

$$Jaccard(A, B) = \frac{|A \cap B|}{|A \cup B|}$$

Next, in order to simplify the calculation process and improve the computation efficiency, let $H(A)$ and $H(B)$ represent hash values of A and B separately, which are calculated by hash function H. And let $H_{min}(A)$ and $H_{min}(B)$ represent MinHash signature of these two sets. Then to estimate the similarity of two sets, we can use

MinHash based Jaccard function. This function has the same expected value as original Jaccard function, which is defined as [16]:

$$E\left(\frac{H_{min}(A) \cap H_{min}(B)}{H_{min}(A) \cup H_{min}(B)}\right) = E(\text{Jaccard}(A, B))$$

It has been shown that MinHash function can present the highly efficient method for computation. To generate MinHash signature, multiple ways can be used. First, by using only one hash function we can generate and select first K hash values as MinHash signature. Or second, we can also use K hash functions and select the minimum hash value of each function to generate a MinHash signature. In detail, we choose the later way in this paper.

Locality Sensitive Hashing. The basic idea behind MinHash is to project the data into a low-dimensional space. If this projection is performed appropriately, we can compare every two domain sets easily. However, when comparing and analyzing large amount of data, MinHash has also a disadvantage of high complexity. To overcome this shortcoming, LSH provides an idea to find approximate nearest neighbors in time sub-linear in n.

Assume that our database is a set of vectors $\mathbf{X} = \{x_1, x_2, \ldots, x_n\}$. Given a query vector q, we are interested in finding the most similar items in the database to the query. To achieve this goal, LSH projects each vector in database into a corresponding hash vector, which satisfies the locality sensitive hashing property [17]:

$$\Pr\big(h(x_i) = h(x_j)\big) = \text{sim}\big(x_i, x_j\big).$$

Where, $\text{sim}(x_i, x_j)$ is the similarity function of interest. Finally, by searching highly similar cases colliding together in the hash table, we can find the nearest neighbors quickly.

5.2 Algorithm

Based on the algorithm of MinHash and LSH, we give our retrieval algorithm, as shown in Algorithm 1.

Algorithm 1: MinHashLSH

Input: detect_domain: Domain names in DNS log
          object_domain: Domain names in object dataset
          jaccard_threshold
Output: homograph_pairs

1.   **for** *each domain in object_domain* **do**
2.   bigram = Bigram(domain)
3.   obj_minhash = MinHash(bigram)
4.   obj_lsh = LSHInsert(obj_minhash)
5.   **end**
6.   **for** *each domain in detect_domain* **do**
7.   bigram = Bigram(domain)
8.   dec_minhash = MinHash(bigram)
9.   homograph_pairs = LSHQuery(obj_lsh, dec_minhash, jaccard_threshold)
10.**end**
11.**return** homograph_pairs

First, we set up a hash table, which consists of hash vectors about Alexa top domain names projected by LSH function. In practice, there are a lot of domain names with similar hash vectors, because they are generated by MinHash function, which only relies on several key hash values. Therefore, we separate each domain into several bigram units to decrease the number of false positive cases. Second, after constructing hash table, we retrieve objected domain names in this table, and get their similar domain names finally.

6   Evaluation

6.1   Dataset Collection

DNS Log. We measure homograph domain names by analyzing DNS real logs, which are generated by local DNS servers operated by a large ISP in China. These logs record the interactive information between local DNS servers and client hosts. As shown in Fig. 6, each record in the logs consists of five fields. For the log data size, take a middle level province as an example, it is over 1.9 TB per day. In this paper, we collected DNS logs on April 1, 2018. Note that we only considered the queries with SLDs. Finally, we obtained about 7.2M distinct domain names with different SLD zones. Therefore, it will bring a great pressure to the classifier, if we do not consider reducing the total number of domain names by using hash method.

Note that almost all domain names in DNS logs are composed of alphanumeric characters. And almost all IDNs are related to Chinese domain name, which have already been converted into Punycode in our DNS logs. So, in practice, we might fail to find homograph domain names. Next, we mainly make a further analysis about the efficiency of performance of MinHash and LSH algorithm.

Source IP	Domain name	Query time	Destination IP	RCODE

Fig. 6. The form of a record in DNS logs

6.2 MinHash and LSH Performance

To analyze performance of MinHash and LSH algorithm, we first set a series of experiments with gradually scaled datasets, and then recorded data retrieving time of these experiments based on Algorithm 1. The results are shown in Fig. 7.

In detail, the legend numbers in Fig. 7, *i.e.*, 10K, 100K, 1M, correspond to the number of Alexa domain names in retrieving database constructed by LSH. The X-axis is gradually scaled domain names in DNS logs. In experiment, we separately selected four control groups with 100, 1K, 10K, 100K domain names collected from DNS logs. The results show that the time consuming grows linearly along with the increase of number of domain names. From the results, we may take about the same length of time when retrieving the same group of domain names in retrieving database with different sizes. For example, it took about 202.91 s when we retrieved 100K domain names in the hash database with 10K hash vectors; similarly, it took about 210.62 s when we retrieved 100K domain names in database with 1M vectors. The average length of retrieving time is 0.2 ms per domain name.

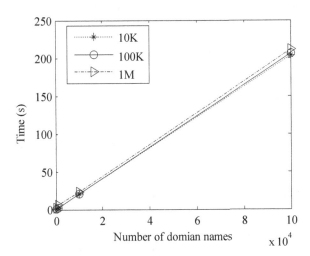

Fig. 7. Retrieving performance of MinHash and LSH

After retrieving all domain names in DNS logs using the 100K hash database, we could obtain 19,440 domain names with Jaccard similarity 0.6, which account for about 0.27% of the total domain names. And we also obtained about 45K pairs of domain names needed to be further confirmed. According to this result, we can conclude that the algorithm of MinHash and LSH can heavily reduce the number of domain names and remarkably reduce the computational tasks.

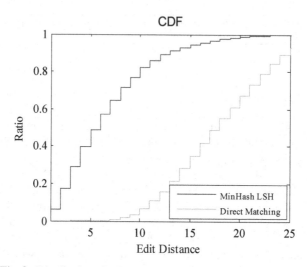

Fig. 8. Distribution of edit distance after using MinHash and LSH

To analyze effectiveness of MinHash and LSH, we display the distribution of edit distance after using hash algorithm in Fig. 8. From this figure, we can see that domain names with edit distance less than 10 accounts for about 80% after using the algorithm of MinHash and LSH. However, edit distance of domain names obtained by direct matching is scattered. Therefore, by using MinHash and LSH, we can narrow the retrieval scope and improve processing efficiency.

6.3 Detection Performance

In experiment, we finally found about 2K homograph domain names after using dual-channel CNN classifier. As shown in Table 2, most of detected domain names are composed of alphanumeric characters, left part of Table 2 represents homograph domain names, and right part represents original domain names. What's more, these homograph domain names are more likely to be constructed by replacing one or more visual spoofing characters. As mentioned before, almost all IDNs have already been converted into Punycode in our DNS logs, so we do not consider homograph domains of IDNs especially.

Table 2. Cases of homograph domain pairs

tsinfhua.edu.cn	tsinghua.edu.cn
kin8tenqoku.com	kin8tengoku.com
fujifllm-dsc.com	fujifilm-dsc.com
flyflv.com	flyfly.cc

To determine whether the detected domain names are phishing domains or not, we attempt to crawl their web content. First, we randomly selected about 200 domain names, accounting for about 10% of all domain names. Then we requested and recorded their corresponding response one by one. Finally, we find that 58.5% detected domain names cannot be requested, but the impersonated domain names can be accessed normally. Therefore, these detected domain names may belong to misspelled domains or belong to abandoned phishing domains. Besides, we also find that about 15% domain names were related to pornographic content. And their domain names are generated using some similar words or characters.

7 Conclusion

In this paper, we proposed a deep learning based homograph domain names detection method, which is based on a dual-channel CNN classifier with retrieving algorithm of minimum hash and locality sensitive hash. The dual-channel CNN classifier was trained to detect dual-channel domain images. MinHash and LSH were designed to reduce the large data of DNS logs. Compared with existing approaches and systems, experiment results show that the proposed method can effectively detect homograph domain names, which could achieve high detection rate of 98.5%. Additionally, the MinHash and LSH search could also efficiently narrow detection scope and reduce the large data. Future work will continually analyze the detection results with several datasets and more entries.

Acknowledgments. The work was supported in part by Innovative Project of Cutting-edge Science and Technology (Grant No. Y750171201).

References

1. Holgers, T., Watson, D.E., Gribble, S.D.: Cutting through the confusion: a measurement study of homograph attacks. In: USENIX Annual Technical Conference, General Track, pp. 261–266 (2006)
2. Wang, Y.-M., Beck, D., Wang, J., Verbowski, C., Daniels, B.: Strider typo-patrol: discovery and analysis of systematic typo-squatting. SRUTI **6**, 2.2–2.3 (2006)
3. Nikiforakis, N., Balduzzi, M., Desmet, L., Piessens, F., Joosen, W.: Soundsquatting: uncovering the use of homophones in domain squatting. In: Chow, S.S.M., Camenisch, J., Hui, L.C.K., Yiu, S.M. (eds.) ISC 2014. LNCS, vol. 8783, pp. 291–308. Springer, Cham (2014). https://doi.org/10.1007/978-3-319-13257-0_17
4. Kintis, P., et al.: Hiding in plain sight: a longitudinal study of combosquatting abuse. In: CCS 2017 (2017)
5. Sawabe, Y., Chiba, D., Akiyama, M., Goto, S.: Detecting homograph IDNs using OCR. Proc. Asia Pac. Adv. Netw. **46**, 56–64 (2018)
6. Tian, K., Jan, S.T., Hu, H., Yao, D., Wang, G.: Needle in a haystack: tracking down elite phishing domains in the wild. In: Proceedings of the Internet Measurement Conference 2018, pp. 429–442. ACM (2018)
7. Woodbridge, J., Anderson, H.S., Ahuja, A., Grant, D.: Detecting homoglyph attacks with a Siamese neural network. In: 2018 IEEE Security and Privacy Workshops (SPW), pp. 22–28. IEEE (2018)
8. Quinkert, F., Lauinger, T., Robertson, W., Kirda, E., Holz, T.: It's not what it looks like: measuring attacks and defensive registrations of homograph domains. In: 2019 IEEE Conference on Communications and Network Security (CNS), pp. 259–267. IEEE (2019)

9. Liu, T., Zhang, Y., Shi, J., Ya, J., Li, Q., Guo, L.: Towards quantifying visual similarity of domain names for combating typosquatting abuse. In: MILCOM 2016 - 2016 IEEE Military Communications Conference, pp. 770–775. IEEE (2016)

10. Black, P.E.: Compute visual similarity of top-level domains (2014). https://hissa.nist.gov/~black/GTLD/

11. Ya, J., Liu, T., Li, Q., Lv, P., Shi, J., Guo, L.: Fast and accurate typosquatting domains evaluation with Siamese networks. In: MILCOM 2018 - 2018 IEEE Military Communications Conference (MILCOM), pp. 58–63. IEEE (2018)

12. Roshanbin, N., Miller, J.: Finding homoglyphs - a step towards detecting unicode-based visual spoofing attacks. In: Bouguettaya, A., Hauswirth, M., Liu, L. (eds.) WISE 2011. LNCS, vol. 6997, pp. 1–14. Springer, Heidelberg (2011). https://doi.org/10.1007/978-3-642-24434-6_1

13. Le Pochat, V., Van Goethem, T., Joosen, W.: Funny accents: exploring genuine interest in internationalized domain names. In: Choffnes, D., Barcellos, M. (eds.) PAM 2019. LNCS, vol. 11419, pp. 178–194. Springer, Cham (2019). https://doi.org/10.1007/978-3-030-15986-3_12

14. Elsayed, Y., Shosha, A.: Large scale detection of IDN domain name masquerading. In: 2018 APWG Symposium on Electronic Crime Research (eCrime), pp. 1–11. IEEE (2018)

15. Levine, J., Hoffman, P.: Variants in second-level names registered in top-level domains (2013)

16. Broder, A.Z., Charikar, M., Frieze, A.M., Mitzenmacher, M.: Min-wise independent permutations. J. Comput. Syst. Sci. **60**, 630–659 (2000)

17. Kulis, B., Grauman, K.: Kernelized locality-sensitive hashing for scalable image search. In: ICCV, pp. 2130–2137 (2009)

FraudJudger: Fraud Detection on Digital Payment Platforms with Fewer Labels

Ruoyu Deng[1], Na Ruan[1(✉)], Guangsheng Zhang[2], and Xiaohu Zhang[2]

[1] Moe Key Lab of Artificial Intelligence, Department of CSE,
Shanghai Jiao Tong University, Shanghai, China
{dengruoyu,naruan}@sjtu.edu.cn
[2] China Telecom Bestpay Co., Ltd., Beijing, China
{zhangguangsheng,zhangxiaohu}@bestpay.com.cn

Abstract. Automated fraud detection on electronic payment platforms is a tough problem. Fraud users often exploit the vulnerability of payment platforms and the carelessness of users to defraud money, steal passwords, do money laundering, etc., which causes enormous losses to digital payment platforms and users. There are many challenges for fraud detection in practice. Traditional fraud detection methods require a large-scale manually labeled dataset, which is hard to obtain in reality. Manually labeled data cost tremendous human efforts. In our work, we propose a semi-supervised learning detection model, FraudJudger, to analyze user behaviors on digital payment platforms and detect fraud users with fewer labeled data in training. FraudJudger can learn the latent representations of users from raw data with the help of Adversarial Autoencoder (AAE). Compared with other state-of-the-art fraud detection methods, FraudJudger can achieve better detection performance with only 10% labeled data. Besides, we deploy FraudJudger on a real-world financial platform, and the experiment results show that our model can well generalize to other fraud detection contexts.

Keywords: Fraud detection · Adversarial autoencoder · Semi-supervised learning

1 Introduction

Digital payment refers to transactions that consumers pay for products or services on the Internet. With the explosive growth of electronic commerce, more and more people choose to purchase on the Internet. Different from traditional face-to-face payments, digital transactions are ensured by a third-party digital payment platform. The security of the third-party platform is the primary concern. Digital payment platforms bring huge convenience to people's daily life, but it is vulnerable to cybercrime attacks [22,24]. Attackers have many kinds of fraud behaviors to attack digital payment platforms. For example, fraudsters may pretend to be a staff in a digital payment platform and communicate with

© Springer Nature Switzerland AG 2020
J. Zhou et al. (Eds.): ICICS 2019, LNCS 11999, pp. 569–583, 2020.
https://doi.org/10.1007/978-3-030-41579-2_33

normal users to steal valuable information. Some fraudsters will use fake identities to transact in these platforms. An estimated 73% of enterprises report some form of suspicious activity that puts around $7.6 of every $100 transacted at risk [1]. Those frauds cause tremendous damage to companies and consumers.

Automatic detection for fraud payments is a hot topic in companies and researchers. Many researchers focus on understanding fraud users' behavior patterns. It is believed that fraud users have different habits compared with benign users. The first challenge is how to find useful features to distinguish fraud users with benign users. Sun et al. [17] use the clickstream to understand user's behavior and intentions. Some other features like transaction records [28], time patterns [8], geolocation information [6] and illicit address information [11], etc., are also proved useful in fraud detection. Fraud users have inner social connections. They always conduct fraud actions together and have relations with each other. Some researchers focus on analyzing user's social networks to find suspicious behaviors [4,19] by graph models. They believe fraud users have some common group behaviors. The limitation of the above methods is that it is hard to find appropriate features to detect frauds manually. In traditional fraud detection methods, researchers should try many features until the powerful features are found, and these features may be partial in practice. Some information may be omitted in chosen features, and new features should be found when fraud contexts change. A proper method to learn useful features automatically is needed.

Another challenge is lacking sufficient and convincing manually labeled data in the real world. Manually labeled data are always hard to obtain in reality. It costs a vast human resource to identify fraud users manually [21]. Lacking enough labeled data to train models is a common phenomenon for many platforms. Some researchers use unsupervised learning or semi-supervised learning models to detect frauds [16]. However, for unsupervised learning, it is hard to set targets and evaluate the performance in training models. Some researchers focus on one-class detection methods which only require benign users in training [9,27]. However, it omits information of fraud users. These works always comprise on detection performance.

In our work, we aim at overcoming these real-world challenges in fraud detection. We tackle the problem in fraud detection when insufficient labeled data are provided.

For the first challenge, we can automatically learn the best "feature" to distinguish fraud users and benign users with the help of Autoencoder [15]. Autoencoder is an unsupervised model to learn efficient data codings. It can get rid of "noise" features and only leave essential features. Origin features are encoded to latent representations by autoencoder. Makhzani et al. [14] combine autoencoder and generative adversarial network (GAN) [7], and propose a novel model called "adversarial autoencoder (AAE)". AAE can generate data's latent representations matching the aggregated posterior in an adversarial way from unlabeled data.

We propose a novel fraud detection model named FraudJudger to detect digital payment frauds automatically. FraudJudger can learn efficient features from users' operations and transaction records on digital payment platforms. In this process, FraudJudger makes full use of information in the unlabeled data. With the help of some labeled data, FraudJudger can learn how to classify users based on their latent features.

In summary, our work makes the following main contributions:

1. We propose a digital payment fraud detection model FraudJudger to overcome the shortcomings of real-world data. Our model requires fewer labeled data and can learn efficient latent features of users.
2. Our experiment is based on a real-world payment platform. The experiment result shows that our detection model achieves better detection performance with only 10% labeled data compared with other well-known supervised methods.
3. Our detection model shows strong adaptability in different contexts.

The remainder of the paper is organized as follows. In Sect. 2, we present related work. Our detection paradigm is provided in Sect. 3. Section 4 presents the details of FraudJudger. We deploy our model on a real-world payment platform, and the evaluation is in Sect. 5. Finally, we conclude our research in Sect. 6.

2   Related Work

Recently, fraud detection on digital payment platforms becomes a hot issue in the finance industry, government, and researchers. There is currently no sophisticated monitoring system to solve such problems since the digital payment platforms have suddenly emerged in recent years. Researchers often use financial fraud detection methods to deal with this problem. The types of financial fraud including credit card fraud, telecommunications fraud, insurance fraud. Many researchers regard these detection problems as a binary classification problem. Traditional detection methods use rule-based systems [3] to detect abnormal behavior, which is eliminated by the industry environment where financial fraud is becoming more diverse and updated quickly. With the gradual maturity of machine learning and data mining technologies, some artificial intelligence models have gradually been applied to the field of fraud detection. The models most favored by researchers are Naive Bayes (NB), Support Vector Machines (SVM), Decision Tree, etc. However, these models have a common disadvantage that it is easy to overfit the training data for them. In order to overcome this problem, some models based on bagging ensemble classifier [25] and anomaly detection [2] are used in fraud detection. Besides, some researchers use an entity relationship network [18] to infer possible fraudulent activity. In recent years, more and more deep learning models are proposed. Generative adversarial network (GAN) [7] is proposed to generate adversarial samples and simulate the data distribution to improve the classification accuracy, and new deep learning methods are applied in this field. Zheng et al. [28] use a GAN based on a deep denoising autoencoder architecture to detect telecom fraud.

Many researchers focus on the imbalanced data problem. In the real world, fraud users account for only a small portion, which will lower the model's performance. Traditional solutions are oversampling minority class [5]. It does not fundamentally solve this problem. Zhang et al. [26] construct a clustering tree to consider imbalanced data distribution. Li et al. [12] propose a Positive Unlabeled Learning (PU-Learning) model that can improve the performance by utilizing positive labeled data and unlabeled data in detecting deceptive opinions.

Some researchers choose unsupervised learning and semi-supervised learning [23] due to the lack of enough labeled data in the real-world application. Unsupervised learning methods require no prior knowledge of users' labels. It can learn data distributions and have the potential to find new fraud users. Roux et al. [20] proposed a cluster detection based method to detect tax fraud without requiring historic labeled data.

In our work, we use semi-supervised learning to detect fraud users, and an unsupervised method is applied in analyzing fraud user patterns and finding potential fraud users.

3   Fraud Detection Paradigm

Our fraud detection paradigm is designed based on existing payment platforms' fraud detection workflows.

Many digital payment platforms have been devoted to fraud detection for many years. These platforms have their own fraud users blacklists, and they track and analyze fraud users on the blacklists continuously. Payment platforms have concluded many rules based on years of experience. As shown in Fig. 1, platforms can use these detection rules to manually detect new fraud users and build fraud users blacklists and benign users lists. However, these labeled users only make up a small portion of all users. Most users on the platforms are unlabeled. FraudJudger is trained based on these labeled users and unlabeled users, which can make full use of every user's information. Once the detection model is trained, it can be used to classify new unknown users.

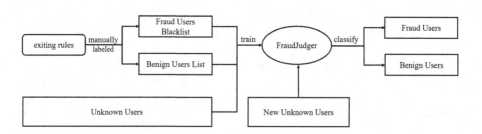

Fig. 1. Fraud detection paradigms of FraudJudger

4   FraudJudger: Fraud Detection Model

4.1   Model Overview

FraudJudger can learn the latent representations of input features and classify users. Figure 2 shows the architecture of our detection model. Each blue square box in Fig. 2 corresponds to a neural network. There are four networks in Fraud-Judger: encoder E, decoder E' and two discriminators D_1 and D_2. The inputs of the model are user features x, and the outputs are predicted labels y and users' latent features z.

4.2   The Structure of FraudJudger

In this section, we will explain each part of FraudJudger in detail.

Encoder: First, FraudJudger learns the latent representations of origin user features x by the encoder. The dimension of origin user features x is too high to analyze directly for the following reasons:

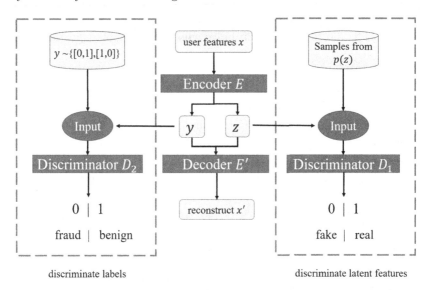

Fig. 2. The architecture of FraudJudger

1. Raw data contain irrelevant information, which is noise from our perspective. These irrelevant features will waste computation resources and affect the model's performance.
2. High dimension features will weaken the model's generalization ability. Detection model will be easily overfitted.

   The encoder part reduces the dimension of features and only leave essential features. For an input merged feature x, encoder E will learn the latent representation z of x. The dimension of the latent variables z is less than the dimension of the input x, and it is determined by the output layer of the encoder's network. The encoding procedure can be regarded as dimensionality reduction. Besides, it will output an extra one-hot variable y to indicate the class of input value, which is a benign user or fraud user in our model. Our model uses y to classify an unknown user. 0 means fraud user and 1 is the benign user. The inner structure of the encoder is a multi-layer network.

$$E(x) = (y, z) \tag{1}$$

Decoder: The purpose of the decoder is learning how to reconstruct the input of the encoder from encoder's outputs. The decoder's procedure is the inverse of the encoder. Inputs of the decoder E' are outputs of the encoder E. The decoder will learn how to reconstruct inputs x from y and z. The output of the decoder is x'. The inner structure of the decoder is also the inverse of the inner structure of the encoder.

$$E'(y, z) = x' \tag{2}$$

Discriminator: Like the discriminator of GAN, we use discriminators in our model to judge whether a variable is real or not. Since the encoder has two outputs, y and z, we need two discriminators D_1 and D_2 to discriminate them, respectively. The discriminators will judge whether a variable is in the real distribution.

4.3   Loss Function

Loss functions are used to measure the inconsistency between the model's outputs and expected outputs. There are four loss functions to be optimized in FraudJudger.

Encoder-Decoder Loss: The loss of the encoder and the decoder L_{e-d} is defined by mean-square loss between the input x of the encoder and output x' of the decoder. It measures the similarity between x and x'.

$$L_{e-d} = \mathbb{E}((x - x')^2) \tag{3}$$

Generator Loss: Encoding the class y and latent vectors z from x can be regarded as the generator in GAN. Let $p(y)$ be the prior distributions of y, which are the distributions of fraud users and benign users in the real world. And $p(z)$ is the prior distribution of z, which is assumed as Gaussian distribution: $z \sim \mathcal{N}(\mu, \sigma^2)$. The generator tries to generate y and z in their prior distributions to fool the discriminators. The loss function of the generator L_G is:

$$L_G = -\mathbb{E}(log(1 - D_1(z)) + log(1 - D_2(y))) \tag{4}$$

Discriminator Loss: The loss of two discriminators are defined to measure the ability in discriminating fake values.

$$L_{D_1} = -\mathbb{E}(a_z log(D_1(z)) + (1 - a_z)log(1 - D_1(z)))$$
$$L_{D_2} = -\mathbb{E}(a_y log(D_2(y)) + (1 - a_y)log(1 - D_2(y))) \tag{5}$$
$$L_D = L_{D_1} + L_{D_2}$$

where a_z, a_y are the true labels (fake samples or real) of inputs z and y. The total loss of the discriminator part is the sum of each discriminator.

Classifier Loss: We can teach the encoder to output the right label y with the help of a few samples with labels. And the loss function L_C is:

$$L_C = -\mathbb{E}(a'_y log(y) + (1 - a'_y)log(1 - y)) \tag{6}$$

where a'_y means the right label (fraud or benign) for a sample, and y is the output label from the encoder. When the encoder outputs a wrong label, the classifier will back-propagate the classification loss and teach the encoder how to predict labels correctly.

4.4   Training Procedure

The model learns how to optimize loss functions in the training procedure. In the training phase, the generator generates like the real label information y and latent representations z by the encoder network. Two discriminators try to judge whether the inputs are fake or real. It is a two-player min-max game. The generator tries to generate true values to fool discriminators, and discriminators are improving discrimination accuracy. Both of the generator and discriminators will improve their abilities simultaneously by optimizing loss functions L_{e-d}, L_G and L_D. Samples with labels can help to increase the classification ability of our model by optimizing the classifier loss L_C. The algorithm for training the FraudJudger model is shown in Algorithm 1.

Algorithm 1. Training FraudJudger

Input: Set of labeled users $\mathbf{U_l} = \{u_{l1}, u_{l2}, ..., u_{ln}\}$;
Set of labels of labeld users $\mathbf{a_{yl}} = \{a_{y1}, a_{y2}, ..., a_{yn}\}$;
Set of unlabeled users $\mathbf{U_n} = \{u_{n1}, u_{n2}, ..., u_{nm}\}$;
Number of epochs ep;
Output: Well-trained FraudJudger model;

1 Initialize parameters in FraudJudger;
2 **for** $i = 1, ..., ep$ **do**
3   **foreach** *user in U_l* **do**
4   Compute latent representations y,z of the user;
5   Optimize L_{e-d},L_G,L_D and L_C;
6   **end**
7   **foreach** *user in U_n* **do**
8   Compute latent representations y,z of the user;
9   Optimize L_{e-d},L_G and L_D;
10   **end**
11 **end**

Algorithm 2. Classify unknown users by FraudJudger

Input: Set of unknown users $\mathbf{U} = \{u1, u2, ..., un\}$;
Well-trained FraudJudger model;
Output: The classes of users $\mathbf{Y} = \{y1, y2, ..., yn\}$;

1 **foreach** *user in U* **do**
2   compute latent representations y,z of the user by FraudJudger;
3     $Y \mathrel{+}= y$;
4 **end**
5 **return** *Labels of users Y*;

Once the training of our model finishes, we can use it to classify unknown users. The algorithm for classifying unknown users is shown in Algorithm 2.

5   Experiment

5.1   Platform Description

We deploy FraudJudger on a real-world payment platform. The payment platform we choose is Bestpay[1], which operates the payment and finance businesses. Bestpay is the third-largest payment platform in China, and there are more than 200 million users in Bestpay. Bestpay stores user's operation records and transaction records, and these records can be regarded as the raw features of users. These data in the platform have been anonymized before we use in case of privacy leakage. The data contains more than 29,000 user's operation behaviors and transaction behaviors in 30 days. All users in the data are manually labeled as benign or fraud. The fraud behavior in this dataset is illegal bonus-getting. We regard labels of these users as ground truth. In this data, the amount of fraud users is 4,046, which accounts for 13.78% of total users. Each user contains two kinds of data, one is operation data, and the other one is transaction data. There are 20 features in operation data and 27 features in transaction data. Some important operation features and transaction features arc listcd in Table 1.

As shown in Table 1, there are some common features in both operation data and transaction data. We first merge operation features and transaction features by the key feature, which is "user id". It means that features belong to the same user will be merged. Each pair of features in operation features set and transaction features set will produce new features which contain their statistic properties. After merging features, and filtering out features with a high missing rate, we get 940-dimensional merged features for each user. FraudJudger will analyze the 940-dimensional merged features to detect frauds.

---

[1] https://www.bestpay.com.cn/.

Table 1. Part features in operation data and transaction data

Operation feature	Explanation	Transaction feature	Explanation
mode	User's operation type	time	Transaction time
time	Operation time	device	Transaction device
device	Operation device	tran_amt	Transaction amount
version	Operation version	channel	Platform type
IP	Device's IP address	IP	Device's IP address
MAC	Device's MAC address	acc_id	Account id
os	Device's operation system	balance	Balance after transaction
geo_code	Location information	trains_type	Type of transaction

5.2   Hyperparameters

The structure of the encoder, decoder, and discriminator in FraudJudger is a five-layer network, which contains three hidden layers. The number of neurons in each hidden layer is 1024, 512, 512, respectively. The dimension of the latent representation z is 128, and the training epoch is 500. Fraudjudger takes the 940 dimensions of user's features as input, and learn latent representations whose dimensions are 128. We randomly choose 20,000 users in training and another 6,000 users for evaluation.

5.3   Compared with Supervised Models

Many traditional semi-supervised algorithms sacrifice on model's performance comparing with supervised models. We compare our model's classification performance with other supervised classification models to evaluate the detection performance of FraudJudger. Three different excellent supervised machine learning models are chosen: Linear Discriminant Analysis (LDA), Random Forest, and Adaptive Boosting model (AdaBoost). All of these models' inputs are users with labels. Besides, we set three groups of FraudJudger models with 5% labels, 10% labels, and 20% labels, respectively, to evaluate FraudJudger's performance with different requirements of labeled data. The inputs to each model are the 940-dimensional merged features.

We use accuracy, precision, recall, and F1 score to measure the detecting performance of models. Precision is the fraction of true detected fraud users among all users classified as fraud users. Accuracy is the proportion of users who are correctly classified. Recall is intuitively the ability of the model to

Table 2. AUC of FraudJudger and supervised models

Models	FraudJudger -5%labels	**FraudJudger -10%labels**	**FraudJudger -20%labels**	LDA	Random Forest	AdaBoost
AUC	0.944	**0.983**	**0.985**	0.946	0.930	0.975

find all the fraud samples. F1 score is a weighted harmonic mean of precision and recall. We also use the ROC (Receiver Operating Characteristic) curve and AUC (Area Under Curve) to evaluate the result. ROC and AUC are another two measurements of the detection ability.

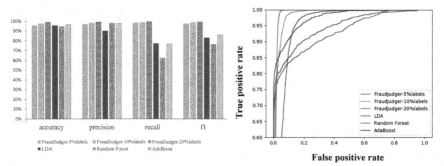

(a) Accuracy, Precision, Recall and F1   (b) ROC of FraudJudger and other models
Score of models

Fig. 3. Comparing FraudJudger with supervised detection models (Color figure online)

Figure 3(a) shows the accuracy, precision, recall, and F1 score of each model. FraudJudger outperforms other supervised models in recall and F1 score even with only 5% labeled data in training. It demonstrates that FraudJudger is good at detecting fraud users. And Fig. 3(b) and Table 2 show the ROC and AUC results. As we can see from the results, the model's detection accuracy increases with more labeled training data. When the proportion of labeled data is larger than 10%, FraudJudger outperforms all other supervised classification models in AUC. It is reasonable because FraudJudger can automatically learn essential features and omit noisy features from raw inputs rather than using features from raw data directly like other supervised detection models. If we use fewer labels, FraudJudger still has a satisfying performance. Compared with other supervised algorithms, FraudJudger saves more than 90% work on manually labeling data and achieves better performance.

In conclusion, FraudJudger has an excellent performance on fraud users detection even with a small ratio of labeled data. Comparing with other supervised fraud detection methods, FraudJudger has a low requirement for the amount of labeled data and can learn effective features. Our model can be applied in realistic situations.

5.4   Visualization of Latent Representation

FraudJudger uses learned latent representations to detect fraud users. In order to have an intuitively understanding of the latent representations, we use t-SNE [13] to visualize the latent representations learned from FraudJudger. T-SNE is a practical method to visualize high-dimensional data by giving each data point a location in a two-dimensional map. We visualize the latent features of users learned from FraudJudger when the ratio of labeled data is 10% in training. The dimension of learned latent representations is 100.

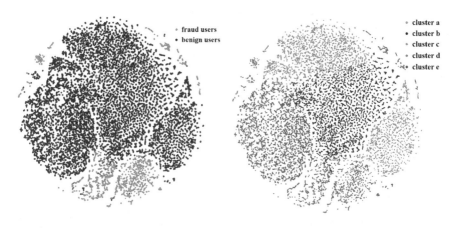

(a) Visualization of latent representations by t-SNE

(b) Visualization of cluster result of latent representations

Fig. 4. Visualization of latent representation

Figure 4(a) is the visualization of latent representations by t-SNE. The red points represent fraud users, and blue points represent benign users. Fraud users and benign users are well separated by latent representations in the t-SNE map. Benign users gather together, and fraud users are isolated to benign users. It means that the latent representations learned from FraudJudger can well separate benign users and fraud users.

Furthermore, we cluster users' latent representations into five groups by K-means, and plot each group with different colors in Fig. 4(b). Figure 4(b) contains five different colors, and each color represents each group of users after clustering. It is hoped that benign users and fraud users will form different groups after clustering, and the clustering result verifies it. The dividing lines between different groups are quite apparent.

Comparing Fig. 4(b) with Fig. 4(a), most fraud users are clustered into the same group in Fig. 4(b). The fraud users in Fig. 4(a) are corresponding to the purple group in Fig. 4(b). Benign users with different behavior patterns are clustered into four different groups. Fraud users and benign users are well separated by cluster analysis. Since no label information is used in clustering, it verifies that the fraud users and benign users have distinct latent features learned from FraudJudger.

5.5   Evaluation on Other Contexts

In order to evaluate FraudJudger's generalization ability in other contexts, we test FraudJudger on vandals detection. Vandals are widespread on many social networks, especially on Wikipedia.

Dataset Description. This evaluation is based on the UMDWikipedia dataset [10]. It contains about 33,000 Wikipedia users and 770,000 edits from Jan 2013 to July 2014. Users in the dataset are listed in the white lists or blacklists. Each user has a sequence of edit records on Wikipedia pages. The dimension of each user's feature is 200. Zheng et al. [27] choose users with the lengths of the edit sequence range from 4 to 50. After the preprocessing, the dataset contains 10528 benign users and 11495 vandals, and the dataset is available at https://github.com/PanpanZheng/OCAN/.

Comparison. We compare FraudJudger with following state-of-art fraud detection methods:

(a) One-class Gaussian process (OCGP) [9] is a one-class classification model derived from the Gaussian process framework.
(b) One-class adversarial nets (OCAN) [27] builds LSTM-Autoencoder to learn the latent representation of users and uses a complementary GAN model to detect fraud users.
(c) Label Propagation (LP) [23] is a semi-supervised learning model which uses an iterative algorithm to propagate labels through the dataset along with high-density areas defined by unlabeled data.

Both of the first two methods, OVGP and OCAN, are one-class classification models, which only use positive labeled data while training. In our evaluation, we randomly choose 7,000 benign users as the training dataset to train the two models.

For group (c), we randomly choose 7,000 users, and 2.5% of them are labeled to train the LP model.

We set three other groups of experiments with different proportions of labeled samples for training FraudJudger:

(d) 2.5% labeled data. 175 labeled and 6,825 unlabeled users for training.
(e) 5.0% labeled data. 350 labeled and 6,650 unlabeled users for training.
(f) 10.0% labeled data. 700 labeled and 6,300 unlabeled users for training.

The total number of users used for training FraudJudger is also 7,000. It should be noted that in our concern, it is harder to get 7,000 reliable benign users than get 175 labeled users, which means the requirements for training data of group (c)(d)(e)(f) are more strict than group (a)(b). We randomly choose another 3,000 benign users and 3,000 vandals as the testing dataset. The measurements are precision, accuracy, recall, and F-1 score. Each model is evaluated on 10 different runs to avoid randomness. The result of each measurement is presented by the mean value and standard deviation of the 10 runs. The dimension of latent representations is 8 in FraudJudger.

Table 3. Vandal detection results (mean± std.) of models

Algorithm	Precision	Recall	F1 score	Accuracy
OCGP	0.838 ± 0.023	0.829 ± 0.037	0.833 ± 0.016	0.834 ± 0.014
OCAN	0.907 ± 0.062	0.922 ± 0.035	0.901 ± 0.023	0.897 ± 0.024
LP-2.5%	0.878 ± 0.030	0.860 ± 0.046	0.861 ± 0.046	0.864 ± 0.044
FraudJudger-2.5%	$\mathbf{0.975 \pm 0.011}$	0.865 ± 0.023	0.917 ± 0.015	0.917 ± 0.015
FraudJudger-5.0%	0.947 ± 0.015	0.908 ± 0.016	0.927 ± 0.009	0.925 ± 0.009
FraudJudger-10.0%	0.950 ± 0.016	$\mathbf{0.926 \pm 0.023}$	$\mathbf{0.938 \pm 0.011}$	$\mathbf{0.935 \pm 0.012}$

The result is in Table 3. Fraudjudger achieves better performance than the other three state-of-the-art detection algorithms. Fraudjudger has higher values in the four measurements and fewer standard deviation. It means that FraudJudger can be used in fraud detection and can have excellent performance even with a small ratio of labeled data. The model's detection accuracy and F1 score increase with more labeled training data. We find that when training with 2.5% labeled data, the precision is the highest. We argue that this is because if a model is not sensitive in classifying a user as a vandal, the model will have higher precision, but the recall will be lower. A better-trained model will have good performance both on precision and recall.

In conclusion, FraudJudger can save more work on manually labeling data and achieve better performance in vandal detection with a lower requirement for training data. It is demonstrated that FraudJudger has excellent performance in different scenarios.

6 Conclusion

In this paper, we proposed a novel fraud users detection model FraudJudger, which requires fewer labeled data in training. FraudJudger can learn latent features of users from raw data and classify users based on the learned latent features. We overcome restrictions of real-world data that it is hard to obtain enough labeled data. Our experiment is based on two different real-world contexts, and the result demonstrates that FraudJudger has a good performance in fraud detection. Compared with other well-known methods, FraudJudger has advantages in learning latent representations of fraud users and saves more than 90% manually labeling work. Our model achieves high performance on different platforms. We have seen broad prospects of deep learning in fraud detection.

Acknowledgments. Our work is supported by National Nature Science Foundation of China (NSFC) No. 61702330; China Telecom Bestpay Co., Ltd.

References

1. Aerospike: Enabling digital payments transformation (2019). https://www.aerospike.com/lp/enabling-digital-payments-transformation-ebook
2. Ahmed, M., Mahmood, A., Islam, M.R.: A survey of anomaly detection techniques in financial domain. Future Gener. Comput. Syst. **55**, 278–288 (2015)
3. Bahnsen, A.C., Aouada, D., Stojanovic, A., Ottersten, B.: Feature engineering strategies for credit card fraud detection. Expert Syst. Appl. **51**, 134–142 (2016)
4. Beutel, A., Xu, W., Guruswami, V., Palow, C., Faloutsos, C.: CopyCatch: stopping group attacks by spotting lockstep behavior in social networks. In: Proceedings of the 22nd International Conference on World Wide Web (WWW), pp. 119–130. ACM (2013)
5. Chawla, N.V., Bowyer, K.W., Hall, L.O., Kegelmeyer, W.P.: SMOTE: synthetic minority over-sampling technique. J. Artif. Intell. Res. **16**, 321–357 (2002)
6. Deng, R., et al.: SpamTracer: manual fake review detection for O2O commercial platforms by using geolocation features. In: Guo, F., Huang, X., Yung, M. (eds.) Inscrypt 2018. LNCS, vol. 11449, pp. 384–403. Springer, Cham (2019). https://doi.org/10.1007/978-3-030-14234-6_21
7. Goodfellow, I., et al.: Generative adversarial nets. In: Proceedings of the Advances in Neural Information Processing Systems (NIPS), pp. 2672–2680 (2014)
8. Santosh, K.C., Mukherjee, A.: On the temporal dynamics of opinion spamming: case studies on yelp. In: Proceedings of the 25th International Conference on World Wide Web (WWW), pp. 369–379. ACM (2016)
9. Kemmler, M., Rodner, E., Wacker, E.S., Denzler, J.: One-class classification with Gaussian processes. Pattern Recogn. **46**(12), 3507–3518 (2013)
10. Kumar, S., Spezzano, F., Subrahmanian, V.: VEWS: a wikipedia vandal early warning system. In: Proceedings of the 21th ACM SIGKDD International Conference on Knowledge Discovery and Data Mining. ACM (2015)
11. Lee, S., et al.: Cybercriminal minds: an investigative study of cryptocurrency abuses in the dark web. In: Network and Distributed Systems Security Symposium (NDSS) (2019)
12. Li, H., Chen, Z., Liu, B., Wei, X., Shao, J.: Spotting fake reviews via collective positive-unlabeled learning. In: Proceedings of the IEEE International Conference on Data Mining (ICDM), pp. 899–904. IEEE (2014)
13. van der Maaten, L., Hinton, G.: Visualizing data using t-SNE. J. Mach. Learn. Res. **9**(Nov), 2579–2605 (2008)
14. Makhzani, A., Shlens, J., Jaitly, N., Goodfellow, I., Frey, B.: Adversarial autoencoders. arXiv preprint arXiv:1511.05644 (2015)
15. Ng, A., et al.: Sparse autoencoder. CS294A Lect. Notes **72**(2011), 1–19 (2011)
16. de Roux, D., Perez, B., Moreno, A., del Pilar Villamil, M., Figueroa, C.: Tax fraud detection for under-reporting declarations using an unsupervised machine learning approach. In: Proceedings of the 24th ACM SIGKDD International Conference on Knowledge Discovery & Data Mining, pp. 215–222. ACM (2018)
17. Sun, J., et al.: FraudVis: understanding unsupervised fraud detection algorithms. In: Proceedings of the IEEE Pacific Visualization Symposium (PacificVis), pp. 170–174. IEEE (2018)
18. Van Vlasselaer, V., Eliassi-Rad, T., Akoglu, L., Snoeck, M., Baesens, B.: Gotcha! Network-based fraud detection for social security fraud. Manag. Sci. **63**(9), 3090–3110 (2016)

19. Varol, O., Ferrara, E., Davis, C.A., Menczer, F., Flammini, A.: Online human-bot interactions: detection, estimation, and characterization. In: Proceedings of the Eleventh International AAAI Conference on Web and Social Media (ICWSM) (2017)
20. Vincent, P., Larochelle, H., Lajoie, I., Bengio, Y., Manzagol, P.A.: Stacked denoising autoencoders: learning useful representations in a deep network with a local denoising criterion. J. Mach. Learn. Res. **11**(Dec), 3371–3408 (2010)
21. Viswanath, B., et al.: Towards detecting anomalous user behavior in online social networks. In: Proceedings of the 23rd USENIX Security Symposium (USENIX Security), pp. 223–238 (2014)
22. West, J., Bhattacharya, M.: Intelligent financial fraud detection: a comprehensive review. Comput. Secur. **57**, 47–66 (2016)
23. Xiaojin, Z., Zoubin, G.: Learning from labeled and unlabeled data with label propagation. Technical report, Technical Report CMU-CALD-02-107, Carnegie Mellon University (2002)
24. Yao, Y., Viswanath, B., Cryan, J., Zheng, H., Zhao, B.Y.: Automated crowdturfing attacks and defenses in online review systems. In: Proceedings of the 2017 ACM SIGSAC Conference on Computer and Communications Security (CCS 2017), pp. 1143–1158. ACM (2017)
25. Zareapoor, M., Shamsolmoali, P., et al.: Application of credit card fraud detection: based on bagging ensemble classifier. Procedia Comput. Sci. **48**(2015), 679–685 (2015)
26. Zhang, Y., Liu, G., Zheng, L., Yan, C., Jiang, C.: A novel method of processing class imbalance and its application in transaction fraud detection. In: Proceedings of the IEEE/ACM 5th International Conference on Big Data Computing Applications and Technologies (BDCAT), pp. 152–159. IEEE (2018)
27. Zheng, P., Yuan, S., Wu, X., Li, J., Lu, A.: One-class adversarial nets for fraud detection. In: Proceedings of the AAAI Conference on Artificial Intelligence, vol. 33, pp. 1286–1293 (2019)
28. Zheng, Y.J., Zhou, X.H., Sheng, W.G., Xue, Y., Chen, S.Y.: Generative adversarial network based telecom fraud detection at the receiving bank. Neural Netw. **102**, 78–86 (2018)

Cloudcot: A Blockchain-Based Cloud Service Dependency Attestation Framework

Zhenyu Zhao[1], Qingni Shen[1(✉)], Wu Luo[1], and Anbang Ruan[2]

[1] Peking University, Beijing, China
{1701210343,qingnishen,lwyeluo}@pku.edu.cn
[2] Octa Innovations Ltd., Beijing, China
ar@8lab.cn

Abstract. The security of cloud infrastructure is an important issue. Many solutions have been proposed to protect the integrity of cloud infrastructure through integrating Trusted Computing hardware. However, these existing solutions suffer from high complexity, repetition and latency. In this paper, we propose a blockchain based cloud service dependency attestation framework–CloudCoT (Cloud Chain-of-Trust). With CloudCoT which combines trusted computing and blockchain technology, cloud users are able to automatically extract the valid dependency of their applications deployed on cloud. And they can attest the valid dependency with low latency through its measurement mechanism and verification mechanism. In addition to the decentralized features, we can see that CloudCoT has higher efficiency while maintaining strong safety in experimental evaluation.

Keywords: Trusted computing · Cloud computing · Blockchain · Decentralized

1 Introduction

With cloud computing infiltrating our daily life, its security [16] has become an issue for academics and industry. Cloud Infrastructure is a "black box" for users, which means they have no control over their own data and resources but to believe that the cloud service provider is credible. However, this assumption can easily fail because of single-node failure, administrators misuse, internal attack [12] and vulnerabilities of security mechanism. Therefore, it's vital to build trust for cloud infrastructure. Many attempts have been made to build trusted cloud based on Trusted Computing. Trusted Computing is a hardware-based integrity protection scheme. A Root-of-Trust (RoT) is implemented by a hardware device embedded in the platform, i.e. the Trusted Platform Module (TPM) [6]. It builds a chain-of-trust (CoT) from hardware to operating system, to application layers (after IMA proposed [20]), and protects the chain through hardware-protected registers (platform configuration registers, PCR). Its remote

© Springer Nature Switzerland AG 2020
J. Zhou et al. (Eds.): ICICS 2019, LNCS 11999, pp. 584–599, 2020.
https://doi.org/10.1007/978-3-030-41579-2_34

attestation (RA) technology [21] allows remote users to verify the integrity of platforms. Specifically, the validity of the TPM is determined by the certificate written by the TPM manufacturer. The validity of the PCRs is determined by the signature of the TPM and the validity of the trust chain is determined by PCRs. Users can determine the integrity of the verified platform by comparing the result with expected values.

When attesting to cloud services for a cloud application (app), traditional central attestation (CA) approaches [10,13,14,23] require users to verify all the nodes in cloud, which is a waste of time and resources. Decentralized Attestation (DA) approaches [18,19] were brought up to establish the cloud Trusted Computing Base (cTCB) and the cloud Root-of-Trust (cRoT). These methods define the dependencies of cloud services and propose the corresponding attestation schemes. Even so, some challenges remain:

(1) Invalid Dependency: CA approaches attest all nodes of the entire cloud. DA approaches narrow the verification range to the nodes that interact with the cloud application. However, it still contains invalid dependencies. For example, if a node interacts with a cloud app only at time t, then the measurement information of this node after t is this cloud app's invalid dependency.
(2) Repetition: nodes in the cloud are actually homogeneous to some extent [7, 17]. These nodes have the same operating system and run same services, so the measurement logs (MLs) of them will be similar to a large extent. So it's redundant to directly combine all the integrity evidence of all dependencies like what the scheme before did.
(3) Verification Latency: A big problem in RA is the time delay. The huge delay prevents the verifier from responding in time. There is a lot of work focused on reducing the latency of RA such as [11,25]. With so many cloud nodes, the delay caused by the attestation of cloud application could be very huge.

In this paper, a CloudCoT solution was proposed to solve the challenges mentioned above. (1) We define the valid dependency of cloud app, and design a strategy to exclude the useless dependency. (2) We design a deduplication mechanism to remove the repeated ML when measuring the nodes. (3) To reduce the verification latency, an obvious way is to complete all or partial verification in advance. Since the WhiteList (WL) of target nodes should be decided by the user himself, it's necessary to complete the measurement and partial verification (before matching WL) in advance. Thus, we need to save the intermediate verification results safely and efficiently. For traditional databases such as mySQL, the single-node failure and internal attack are unsolvable so that users cannot trust the verification results. Because of blockchain's tamper-proof and distributed characteristics [15], it's reasonable to integrate blockchain to save the intermediate results. However, the storage capability of blockchain is limited, so the InterPlanetary File System (IPFS) [4] is introduced. IPFS is aprotocol designed to create acontent-addressable,peer-to-peermethod of storing and sharinghypermediain adistributed file system. Therefore, this paper designs a measurement mechanism and a verification mechanism to save the integrity evidence measured by TPM on the IPFS, and save the hash value of integrity evidence on blockchain via smart contract. This method solves the above three challenges and ensures high security. In summary, the **contributions** of this paper are:

- We propose the CloudCoT, a blockchain based cloud service dependency attestation framework combining trusted computing and blockchain to attest cloud service valid dependency with no-repetition and low verification latency.
- We design a measurement mechanism which stores the TPM measurement results in the blockchain to reduce redundant measurement. We design a verification mechanism which separates traditional verification process to pre-attestation and last challenge. It reduces verification latency significantly.
- We implement CloudCoT in experimental environment and the experiments show that besides achieving fine-grained cloud service dependency attestation, CloudCoT improves user attestation efficiency significantly with very low overhead incurred.

In the following text: Sect. 2 introduces the related work. Sect. 3 introduces motivation and architecture of CloudCoT. Sect. 4 presents the valid dependency definitions. In Sect. 5, we introduce the design of CloudCoT framework including measurement mechanism and verification mechanism. Our implementation and experiments are presented in Sect. 6. Finally, we conclude our paper and discuss the future work in Sect. 7.

2   Related Work

Trusted Computing. Trusted Computing contributes to verifying the trustworthiness of prover. Verifier can determine the current integrity state of prover due to remote attestation. Considering the large cost of transmitting and calculating ML, Jaeger et al. [11] present Policy-Reduced Integrity Measurement Architecture (PRIMA) which leverages the information flow and SELinux to measure the code and data related to the target application. This limits the scope of the attestation target applications, and hence reduces the size of ML. Some other work such as [25] also achieves ML reduction.

Blockchain and Cloud Security. Alansari et al. [8,9] propose a novel identity and access management system for cloud federations. They use blockchain technology and Intel SGX trusted hardware to guarantee the integrity of the policy evaluation process. ProvChain [15] collects and verifies cloud data provenance by embedding the provenance data into blockchain transactions. Comparing to above work which uses blockchain to enhance cloud privacy and assure cloud data source trustworthy, this paper uses blockchain to verify cloud nodes' integrity state.

Cloud Trustworthiness. Santos [22] and Schiffman [24] attempted to apply trusted computing technology to cloud systems. Cloud nodes (i.e. physical servers) are equipped with built-in TPMs. A central attestation delegate uses the confirmed evidence generated by the TPM to verify other nodes. This mechanism assumes that cloud nodes are basically isomorphic. At the same time, users can only rely on this central delegate to verify the whole cloud. A critical step to prove the trustworthiness is to verify the central delegate. However, the complexity, heterogeneity, and dynamism of the cloud will affect the function of these mechanisms. Repcloud [19] considers the cloud as a P2P network, uses the remote attestation of trusted computing to establish a reputation mechanism similar to the P2P network for the cloud, and constructs a global reputation based on the local reputation maintained by the cloud node, thereby establishes a trusted cloud. This scheme uses each cloud node as a provider and a verifier of an adjacent node. However, it only uses PCR as evidence for each verification, but not a WL to verify the trust of the node (in fact, how to store WL is also a problem to be solved in the establishment of trusted cloud). But giving consideration that PCR only records the ML summary (20 bytes), different loading sequences of ML will produce different PCRs. Maintaining a large and good PCR list itself is a very difficult problem. In addition, directly regarding cloud as a P2P network also has certain drawbacks, since the cloud is generally a centralized structure.

3 Motivation and Architecture Overview

3.1 Scenario

There are many management nodes in the actual cloud environment scenario that carry the basic services of the cloud infrastructure, such as the schedule service, the storage service and the network service. Infrastructure as a Service (IaaS) cloud provide services in form of virtual machine (VM) hosted by the compute node in the cloud. The compute service runs on the compute node to manage the VM. When attesting to cloud application APP1 deployed by company A, A needs to attest the trust of all the VMs contained in APP1, the hosts hosting the VMs, services running on these compute nodes and the services on which these compute nodes depend [19].

3.2 Security Model

Here we provide a brief overview of our security model for CloudCoT. More details are given in later sections. We assume the following:

- All nodes in the cloud platform are equipped with TPM and each VM has vTPM. TPM is safe, has not been tampered with and behaves honestly.
- Attackers may have control of one or several cloud nodes' kernels. However, a certain proportion of nodes (depending on the consensus algorithm used by the blockchain, such as proof-of-work algorithm [2] requiring at least 51% of the nodes are trusted to resist collusion attacks) in the cloud environment remain trustworthy.

More security mechanism details about how to defend malicious attack such as replay attack and impersonation attack will be introduced in Sect. 5.

3.3 Motivation

As shown in Fig. 1, we use an example to show what's the valid dependency of a node. Based on the services included in Openstack's official website [5], it includes basic components such as Nova, Swift, Cinder, Neutron, Glance, Keystone, etc., providing services such as computing, network and storage, etc. In Fig. 1, *node*1 to 4 represent Nova, Glance, Neutron, Cinder nodes respectively.

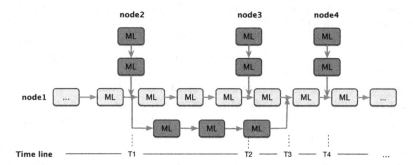

Fig. 1. Cloud Chain-of-Trust

1. *node*1 interacts with *node*2 node at time $T1$, requesting to obtain the image required to create the virtual machine $VM1$, and *node*2 sends the image *Image*1 to *node*1;
2. *node*1 interacts with *node*3 at time $T2$, requesting to acquire the network information required to create the virtual machine, and *node*3 sends the virtual machine network information to *node*1;
3. *node*1 needs to establish another virtual machine $VM2$ at time $T3$, so it starts another thread and interacts with *node*2 to request the image needed for the new virtual machine. *node*2 sends the new image *Image*2 to *node*1;
4. In the previous process of creating the virtual machine $VM1$, *node*1 requests *node*4 to obtain the persistent storage information required to create the virtual machine $VM1$;

Obviously, the valid dependency of one node is dynamic with constantly communication, not to mention an APP. For the valid dependency of every moment in this case, we will explain in detail in Sect. 4 after the definition.

Under the security model and challenges in Sect. 1, what we need to consider is how to enable users to verify the trust of the cloud nodes' valid dependency. So the goals of our framework are as follows: (1) Identify the valid dependency of a cloud APP during each communication; (2) Design a measurement mechanism to measure the valid dependency and save the measurement results without repetition for verification; (3) Design a verification mechanism to verify the measurement results with low latency.

3.4   Architecture Overview

Our architecture is based on trusted computing and blockchain. It requires that every node is in a blockchain network including management nodes and compute nodes. As Fig. 2 shows, compared to the native IaaS cloud, we add three functional modules to cloud nodes: (1) The Network Monitor module on cloud node to confirm the valid dependency itself. (2) The Pre-attestation module extracts integrity information protected by the TPM, makes a preliminary attestation and sends results to Blockchain Service. (3) The Blockchain Service module further verifys the integrity information and stores them on the chain. Besides, we designed a challenge module for cloud users to complete the final verification by matching integrity information with WL.

Our architecture contains two parts: *measurement mechanism* and *verification mechanism* (Sect. 5). The *measurement mechanism* is implemented by Pre-attestation module and Blockchain module. Pre-attestation module extracts integrity information protected by the TPM and completes the first half part of attestation. Blockchain Service module saves the integrity evidence to IPFS and blockchain. To assure the trustworthiness of integrity evidence, we design generating transaction and vote transaction protocol. By designing the transaction content and voting mechanism, blockchain can protect the CoT after *merge* (defined in Sect. 4). In the meantime, the *measurement mechanism* determines the valid dependency of one node through the *merge* operation.

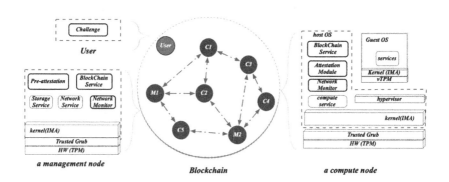

Fig. 2. Architecture of CloudCOT

The *verification mechanism* is implemented by combining Pre-attestation, Blockchain Service and Challenge module. Verification includes the verification of TPM signature, PCR value and ML essentially. In CloudCoT, the former two are completed by generating transaction and vote transaction protocol through Pre-attestation module and Blockchain Service module. The only remaining verification which needs to match ML with user's WL is completed by Challenge module.

4 Definition of Valid Dependency

In this part, we introduce traditional CoT of single node and our CloudCoT according to cloud nodes' valid dependency.

Traditional CoT. In the field of trusted computing, it's believed that trust can be passed step-by-step without delivery loss. For example, the trust chain of node A from the start time (time $\perp$) to the current time (time t) is expressed as:

$$CoT^A_{\perp \to t} = \{RoT_A, seq\} = \{ROT_A, <x_{t_0}, x_{t_1}, ..., x_t> \\ \mid RoT_A \ is \ trusted \wedge t_0 < t_1 < ... < t \} \tag{1}$$

RoT_A is the trusted root of a trusted node A. Seq represents a series of hardware and software components loaded after node A starts. x_{t_0} is the component loaded at time t_0.

The platform configuration registers (PCR) in the TPM is used to protect the integrity of the CoT. The loading of any of the hardware and software components will trigger the TPM_Extend operation of the PCR, which concatenates the current PCR value with the component's measurement value (usually the result of the hash) and hashes the concatenated result.

$$PCR = TPM\_Extend(PCR, newMeasurement) \tag{2}$$

Through this iterative TPM_Extend operation, the PCR records a summary of the CoT. After obtaining the trusted PCR and the CoT to be verified, the verifier can simulate the TPM_Extend operation on the CoT, and compare the result with the PCR to verify the trust of the CoT.

CloudCoT. For a cloud node in the cloud, due to network communication between cloud nodes, the state of node A at a certain time may depend on the data sent by node B. Therefore, we believe that the cloud CoT of A should include two parts: the CoT of A itself and the CoT of the nodes on which A depends when the dependency exists (that is what we call valid dependencies). In order to handle this dependency automatically, we define that at time t, when A generates a dependency on B, a $merge$ operation occurs:

$$CoT^A_{\perp \to t} = merge(CoT^A_{\perp \to t}, CoT^B_{\perp \to t}) \\ = \begin{cases} CoT^A_{\perp \to t} \cup \{t, refer(CoT^B_{t' \to t})\}, & if \ B \ has \ merged \ to \ A \ in \ t' \\ CoT^A_{\perp \to t} \cup \{t, refer(CoT^B_{\perp \to t})\}, & otherwise \end{cases} \tag{3}$$

If a $merge$ operation occurs between A and B at a previous time (such as t'), the component information from time t' to time t in B's CoT will be merged into A's CoT, otherwise we $merge$ the entire CoT of B into A. The time t will be used as a metadata for the CoT to characterize the $merge$ operation at time t. In addition, due to the homogeneous characteristic of cloud nodes (such as the hardware and software components loaded between two computing nodes are highly repetitive), we need to exclude the same part of A and B's CoT to reduce redundancy in the *merge* process. We call this operation as *refer*. We define the VMs as all VMs hosting user's APP, and the Host (VM) is the cloud node hosting this VM. When the cloud APP is verified at time t, its CoT is:

$$CoT_{\perp \to t}^{APP} = \{CoT_{\perp \to t}^{Host(VM_i)} \cup CoT_{\perp \to t}^{VM_i} \mid VM_i \in VMs\} \qquad (4)$$

According to the definition of formula (3), in our hypothetical scenario in motivation, if *node*1 is the master node, we can obtain cloud CoT of *node*1 at different moment:

$$CoT_{\perp \to T1}^{N1} = merge(CoT_{\perp \to T1}^{N1}, CoT_{\perp \to T1}^{N2}) \qquad (5)$$

where N1 and N2 stand for node1 and node2 respectively. That is, the CloudCoT at $T1$ should be CoT of *node*1 and *node*2 before T1;

$$CoT_{\perp \to T2}^{N1} = merge(CoT_{\perp \to T2}^{N1}, CoT_{\perp \to T1}^{N2}, CoT_{\perp \to T2}^{N3}) \qquad (6)$$

Because *node*1 and *node*2 didn't communicate between $T1$ and $T2$, so this part of $node2's$ CoT will not be the dependency of *node*1 at T2;

$$COT_{\perp \to T3}^{N1} = merge(COT_{\perp \to T3}^{N1}, COT_{\perp \to T3}^{N2}, COT_{\perp \to T2}^{N3}) \qquad (7)$$

It's worth pointing out that $COT_{\perp \to T3}^{N2} = merge(COT_{\perp \to T1}^{N2}, COT_{T1 \to T3}^{N2})$;

$$COT_{\perp \to T4}^{N1} = merge(COT_{\perp \to T4}^{N1}, COT_{\perp \to T3}^{N2}, COT_{\perp \to T2}^{N3}, \\ COT_{\perp \to T4}^{N4}) \qquad (8)$$

The CoT at $T4$ is the sum of the previous ones.

5   Design of CloudCoT

To verify $CoT_{\perp \to t}^{APP}$, the direct way is to provide the verifier with the PCR value corresponding to each sub-CoT, and then the verifier verifies all PCR signatures and all PCR pairs of sub-CoTs. However, as we mentioned before, trusted computing is an active defense mechanism, and the discovery of an attack depends on the verifier's match of the trusted CoT to the expected WL. For each TPM signature verification and CoT verification based on PCRs, it will inevitably cause a large verification delay. Therefore, our architecture uses Blockchain technology to translate the verifier's validation to the time when the event occurs, thus allowing user to liberate from the verification delay. The corresponding measurement mechanism and verification mechanism are as follows.

5.1   Measurement Mechanism

Generating Transactions. The blockchain stores data through data blocks and chain structures. Each data block includes a block head and a block body, with a unique hash value as a corresponding block address. The hash value of the previous block is connected to the successive block, thus forming a chain structure. Each completed transaction will be permanently recorded in the block body for all users to query. At the same time, each block will be marked with a time stamp when the it's generated. As the time stamp increases, the block will extend to form a chain with a timeline. Thus, data can be traced in time. In our CloudCoT architecture, we pack each measurement information into a single transaction and verify it by multiple nodes in the blockchain when it's uplinked. We use the smart contract [1] to write transaction content because smart contract is executed by multiple nodes on the blockchain. We define the node that sends data as *Sender*, such as the management node that sends the image to the VM in the cloud. The node accepting the data is defined as *Receiver*. The protocol of generating a transaction is listed in Fig. 3.

1. At the beginning of interaction, sender generates message (msg) and sends it to receiver. Then, receiver determines if msg changes its ML. According to IMA's measurement strategy [21], only scripts, user-level executables, dynamically loadable libraries and kernel modules are measured. So only they can change ML, other files that do not affect Receiver's security will be directly released. If ML is changed by msg, receiver will verify sender with a random number to prevent replay attacks. Here $nonce = Hash<msg, ts>$, ts is the timestamp.

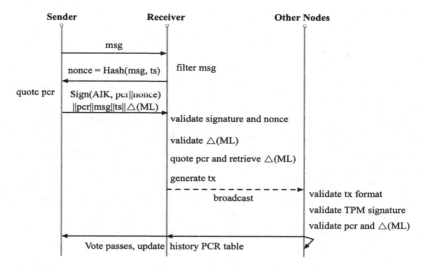

Fig. 3. Generating and vote transaction protocol

2. Sender loads the AIK generated by its own TPM to sign its own PCR (here we use PCR10) with nonce as sender's signature. We call this operation *quote*. If sender's ML was updated, then sender would retrieve its own $\Delta(ML)$ (the portion of the ML between *ts* and the time ML last submitted). Otherwise, all MLs from the machine power-up to the current time will be submitted.

3. After receiving evidence from sender, receiver validates its signature and nonce firstly. Secondly, receiver validates the PCR with $\Delta(ML)$. If all legal, receiver will *quote* its own PCR and retrieve its $\Delta(ML)$.

4. Finally, receiver generates a six-tuple <s-name/d-name, s-pcr/d-pcr, s-payload/d-payload>, and broadcasts it as a transaction (tx) to let other nodes vote. Here, s-name/d-name is the node identifier of Sender and Receiver; *s-pcr/d-pcr* is the signed PCR value of the Sender and Receiver. *s-payload* includes the nonce of sender, *ts* and its Δ(ML) what we call $s - \Delta(ML)$. d-payload includes Receiver's nonce', *ts* and its $\Delta(ML)$ what we call $d - \Delta(ML)$.

Deduplication Mechanism. We designed a deduplication mechanism for two situations: *(1) Single Node Duplication:* we record the number of ML rows per measurement, so that each time the *delta* (ML) which needs to be measured is the portion of the current ML row minus the number of ML rows from the last measurement. *(2) Multi-Nodes Duplication:* Many cloud nodes are highly homogenous with same ML and PCR. We record initial PCR values as standard after actual measurement. Nodes whose PCR values equal to standard will be considered safe. Assuming that the initial $PCR_{compute} = \alpha$ for all initialized compute nodes then, in the measurement, all nodes with PCR equal to α can be regarded as a secure computing node that just booted and has not been tampered with.

Vote Transactions. Vote transaction protocol is depicted in Fig. 3. After a transaction is generated, a vote will be initiated. Each node (including Sender and Receiver) needs to maintain a history PCR table to record nodes's PCRs value at different time. After receiving the transaction to be attested, a vote node validates the transaction format and signature firstly. Then it validates the TPM signature and the correctness of *s-pcr/d-pcr* value with history PCR table and *s-payload/d-payload*. If validation succeeds, it will vote in favour. If other nodes also vote in favour then the consensus is reached according to the consensus algorithm. The transaction will be written into blockchain, which can be queried anytime. After that every node updates local historical PCR Table.

5.2 Verification Mechanism

Verification includes the verification of TPM signature, PCR value and ML essentially. But in CloudCoT, the former two have been completed by Generate Transaction and Vote protocol, only remaining ML to be matched with user WL. The measurement information including the label of source node, the target node, their communication time, and the state of the two nodes has uplinked when nodes communicated. When users attest a cloud APP (or VM), they can directly get the results from the blockchain and compare them with their expected WL. We assume users have downloaded the latest blockchain information already. Then they can use Algorithm 1 to finish the last step of verification.

When users use an IaaS service provided by mainstream suppliers such as AWS, Azure and AliCloud, the hostnames and IPs of VMs which run their cloud APPs can be easily gotten. Thus, according to the algorithm, users give a certain period $(t1 \sim t2)$ and one or more target nodes' labels (consist of hostnames and IPs) as input parameters. The challenge mechanism will search all the communication information of target nodes including nodes' measurement information, communication time and etc., meaning that Cloud Chain-of-Trust is generated. Last, users match ML to WL if PCR value is the expected value.

Algorithm 1. Challenge Mechanism

Input: time range t_1, t_2, one target node *Node1* of APP
Output: verification result
  1: Search all the information of *Node1* in range of t1 t2
  2: Obtain the PCRs, MLs of all nodes communicated with *Node1* including *Node1's*
  3: **if** MLs match UserWhiteList **then**
  4:     return true;
  5: **end if**
  6: return false;

---

6   Implementation and Evaluation

6.1   Implementation

To implement CloudCoT architecture, we assembled some open source projects such as Ethereum and IPFS and wrote the rest of the code ourselves. Due to resource constraints, we built five virtual machines on the server. All of them were connected to a Blockchain (modified Ethereum) with a network monitoring and attestation module. The model of the server CPU is Intel(R) Xeon(R) CPU E3-1230 V5 @3.40 GHz with 4 cores. Each virtual machine has 2 cores with 4 GB memory. The operating system version is Ubuntu 14.04 with kernel version 4.2.0.

We chose Ethereum (whose consensus mechanism is proof-of-work (PoW) algorithm) due to its popularity, wide applicability and mature smart contract technology. However, due to limited transaction size of Ethereum smart contract [2] (A total of 8,000,029, about 8 million (from https://ethstats.net/) for each transaction, and the size of one line of our ML is 152 bytes or so. After calculation, we have to ensure that the log size can only be within 700 lines each time data upload to blockchain), we chose IPFS to support our framework whose storage cost is significantly lower than Ethereum. We hash the ML, then store the hash of the ML on the blockchain, and store the corresponding real ML on the IPFS. This can greatly reduce the overhead of the blockchain and achieve decentralization at the same time. This treatment's benefit can be seen in evaluation.

Table 1. ML of two schemes/lines

	$CCoT_{first}$	FRA_{first}	$CCoT_{avg}$	FRA_{avg}
Running	96526	96526	64	100374
Reboot	1631	1631	64	5811

6.2   Evaluation

Efficiency of Deduplication Mechanism (1) ML Size: In order to prove the effectiveness of our deduplication mechanism, we used Full Remote Attestation (FRA) scheme as a control group. For each attestation, the FRA scheme attested integrity evidence of node from the boot process to application layers. As Table 1 indicates, a huge reduction on ML needed to be transmitted and verified was recorded for CloudCoT. We chose two kinds of environment to evaluate our framework efficiency objectively: the environment after a period of normal operation and the environment after restart. Measurement was made every 5 min and in total 120 measurements were performed.

FRA_{first} represents the time of first attestation and FRA_{avg} represents the average time of attestation, $CloudCoT_{first}$ represents the time of first attestation while $CloudCoT_{avg}$ represents the average time of attestation. It can be seen that CloudCoT performed far better than traditional integrity measurement FRA except for the first measurement. This is because that we introduce deduplication mechanism as mentioned in Sect. 5. In this way, the efficiency is significantly improved when the correctness is guaranteed. It's worth mentioning that the reduction of ML means reducing overhead of verification, storage and transmission.

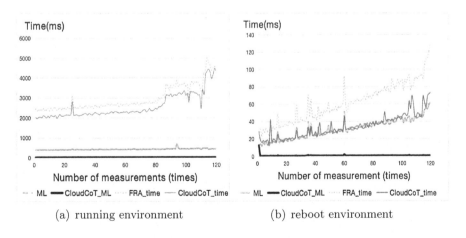

(a) running environment   (b) reboot environment

Fig. 4. Measurement overhead in verification

(2) Time Usage of Attestation: We recorded the time usage of attestation of FRA and CloudCoT respectively to show the reduction of attestation time usage. In Fig. 4(a) and (b), FRA_time and $CloudCoT\_time$ represent the time usage of the entire verification process of the two solutions. ML and $CloudCoT\_ML$ represent the time taken to process the ML respectively. In the reboot environment, FRA average time is 37.16 ms, $CloudCoT$ average time is 1.31 ms; in the running environment, FRA average time is 423.27 ms, and $CloudCoT$ average time is 0.53 ms. It can be seen that with the increase of ML, $CloudCoT$ improve the time efficiency than FRA by nearly a thousand times.

Efficiency of Measurement and Verification Mechanism. In the traditional verification scheme (including CA and DA), every node needs to be verified separately. For example, 5 attestations need to be done to verify 5 different nodes in total. In CloudCoT, the time cost was distributed to every communication. The final time cost would be the sum of verification cost (5x), uplink cost and challenge cost. The time cost of introducing CloudCoT including uplink time and challenge time under different ML sizes is listed in Table 2. It can be seen CloudCoT's uplink time and challenge time is acceptable compared to the verification time.

Table 2. Time cost of measurement mechanism

ML lines	ML size/byte	Verification/s	Uplink/s	Challenge time/s	
				Select	IPFS read
10	1.14 K	1.28	0.783	0.006	0.261
100	11.59 K	1.38	0.983	0.007	0.328
1000	116.0 K	2.54	1.018	0.013	0.339
10000	1.13 M	3.19	1.048	0.015	0.349
100000	10.5 M	8.26	1.060	0.016	0.354

* The challenge time includes the time to filter the user's specified information, read the original content from the IPFS using hash value, and the time to match WL (we didn't measure this time because the WL is provided by users themselves).

Efficiency of Storage (1) Time Efficiency: The time cost of storing MLs of different sizes in the central server database (MySQL, Ver 14.14 Distrib 5.6.35), blockchain (Ethereum 1.6.7) and IPFS (Ver 0.4.13) was measured separately. In Table 3, central server, blockchain and IPFS refer to the time needed to write information into corresponding position. There was no significant increase in time cost between writing in IPFS and in the central server, even faster to write in IPFS when the ML is large, because the relational database takes time to establish relationships.

(2) Space Efficiency: IPFS is a content-addressable storage protocol means reducing the redundancy of resource storage (Same resource has the same hash value). As a result, when nodes are enough, IPFS saves a lot of storage space compared to central storage server. However, there are problems with storage incentive mechanism, storage data security and privacy protection. Filecoin incentive mechanism [3] has been proposed to encourage people to share the storage cost with cloud servers.

Table 3. Time usage of storage

ML lines	ML size/byte	Central server/s	Blockchain/s	IPFS/s
10	1.14 K	0.054	12.64	1.347
100	11.59 K	0.063	14.62	1.425
1000	116.0 K	0.091	*	1.442
10000	1.13 M	0.745	*	1.507
100000	10.5 M	5.366	*	1.619

* Blockchain cannot store ML of these sizes via smart contract.

Security Analysis. Under our security model in Sect. 3, CloudCoT can defend most of attack scenarios.

(1) **Single Malicious Node Attack:** The first attack we need to consider is that the attacker has the ability to directly attack the cloud service provider's virtual machines even infrastructure. But under the protect of TPM, when an attacker can only attack the cloud service nodes or users' application running on VMs, but does not have the privilege to tamper with the underlying layer kernel and TPM, his behavior will be identified by the remote attestation. So CloudCoT remains high security.

(2) **Malicious Cooperative Attack:** As a decentralized scheme, the second attack way is malicious cooperative. The malicious cooperative attack means that attackers have the control of several nodes and these tampered nodes cooperate to achieve attack goals. For example, in blockchain, the consensus mechanism requires nodes to vote. If a lot of tampered nodes vote maliciously, they will change the consensus result and thus benefit the attacker. CloudCoT's defense capabilities in this area depend entirely on the blockchain it used. For example, we are currently using Ethereum as our blockchain, which supports PoW as its consensus mechanism. So if we ensure that no more than 51% of the nodes have been tampered with, the collusion attack can be defended.

(3) **Other Attacks:** For other attacks, CloudCoT also has corresponding defense methods. For example, we use nonce in our protocol to avoid replay attacks and use session keys to resist man-in-the-middle attack. On the other hand, the runtime attacks to Trusted Computing mechanisms and hardware-based attacks are not considered. However, it is worth pointing

out that because we have adopted a consensus mechanism, the attack of a single node or a small number of nodes cannot change the consensus result. Therefore, even if some nodes are attacked by the method we cannot defend, our mechanism can still run normally, and the user can still obtain the true attestation result from CloudCoT.

7   Conclusion and Future Work

In this paper, we propose the CloudCoT framework to achieve cloud service dependency identification and attestation. It can automatically identify the cloud APP's valid dependency and record dependent nodes' integrity evidence to blockchain after deduplication. Moreover, by our measurement mechanism user can directly obtain tamper-proof CoT record of his APP (or VM). By the challenge mechanism, he can finish the attestation. We implemented CloudCoT in our simulated cloud environment. The evaluation showed that CloudCoT has higher efficiency than the current fine-grained cloud service attestation schemes.

Even our framework is highly secured under most of the attack scenarios such as single malicious node and malicious cooperative nodes attack, it's vulnerable under certain situations. For example, we didn't take the network routing channel attack and memory overflow attack into consideration. Furthermore, for highly frequent malicious measurement request (Such as initiate 10 uplink requests per second with one-line ML), we consider adopting a more detailed measurement strategy. For example, after detecting high frequency communication, the time interval between each measurement will be increased to balance the cost and security. Privacy protection in CloudCoT is also a key point for our future work. Moreover, CloudCoT should be evaluated in a production infrastructure, which we could not currently achieve due to the lack of resource.

Acknowledgements. This work was supported by National Natural Science Foundation of China under Grant No. 61672062 and No. 61232005.

References

1. Ethereum project. https://www.ethereum.org
2. Ethereum yellow paper. https://ethereum.github.io
3. Filecoin: A decentralized storage network. https://filecoin.io/filecoin.pdf
4. IPFS wiki. https://en.wikipedia.org/wiki/InterPlanetary_File_System
5. Openstack services. https://www.openstack.org/software/project-navigator/openstack-components/#openstack-services
6. Trusted computing group, TPM 2.0 library specification (2016). https://trustedcomputinggroup.org/resource/tpm-library-specification/
7. Abbadi, I.M.: Clouds trust anchors. In: IEEE International Conference on Trust (2012)
8. Alansari, S., Paci, F., Margheri, A., Sassone, V.: Privacy-preserving access control in cloud federations. In: IEEE International Conference on Cloud Computing (2017)

9. Alansari, S., Paci, F., Sassone, V.: A distributed access control system for cloud federations. In: IEEE International Conference on Distributed Computing Systems (2017)
10. Berger, S., Goldman, K., Pendarakis, D., Safford, D., Valdez, E., Zohar, M.: Scalable attestation: a step toward secure and trusted clouds. In: IEEE International Conference on Cloud Engineering (2015)
11. Jaeger, T., Sailer, R., Shankar, U.: Prima: policy-reduced integrity measurement architecture. In: Proceedings of the Eleventh ACM Symposium on Access Control Models and Technologies, pp. 19–28 (2006)
12. Kandias, M., Virvilis, N., Gritzalis, D.: The insider threat in cloud computing. In: Bologna, S., Hämmerli, B., Gritzalis, D., Wolthusen, S. (eds.) CRITIS 2011. LNCS, vol. 6983, pp. 93–103. Springer, Heidelberg (2013). https://doi.org/10.1007/978-3-642-41476-3_8
13. Khan, I., Rehman, H., Anwar, Z.: Design and deployment of a trusted eucalyptus cloud. In: IEEE International Conference on Cloud Computing (2011)
14. Lee, R.B.: CloudMonatt: an architecture for security health monitoring and attestation of virtual machines in cloud computing. ACM SIGARCH Comput. Archit. News **43**(3), 362–374 (2015)
15. Liang, X., Shetty, S., Tosh, D., Kamhoua, C., Kwiat, K., Njilla, L.: ProvChain: a blockchain-based data provenance architecture in cloud environment with enhanced privacy and availability. In: IEEE/ACM International Symposium on Cluster (2017)
16. Mogull, R., Arlen, J., Lane, A., Mortman, D., Gilbert, F.: Security guidance for critical areas of focus in cloud computing v4.0 (2017)
17. Reiss, C., Tumanov, A., Ganger, G.R., Katz, R.H., Kozuch, M.A.: Heterogeneity and dynamicity of clouds at scale: Google trace analysis. In: ACM Symposium on Cloud Computing (2012)
18. Ruan, A., Martin, A.: NeuronVisor: defining a fine-grained cloud root-of-trust. In: Yung, M., Zhu, L., Yang, Y. (eds.) INTRUST 2014. LNCS, vol. 9473, pp. 184–200. Springer, Cham (2015). https://doi.org/10.1007/978-3-319-27998-5_12
19. Ruan, A., Martin, A.: RepCloud: attesting to cloud service dependency. IEEE Trans. Serv. Comput. **10**(5), 675–688 (2017)
20. Sailer, R., Zhang, X., Jaeger, T., Doorn, L.V.: Design and implementation of a TCG-based integrity measurement architecture. In: Proceedings of the 13th USENIX Security Symposium, San Diego, CA, USA, 9–13 August 2004 (2004)
21. Sailer, R., Zhang, X., Jaeger, T., Doorn, L.V.: Design and implementation of a TCG-based integrity measurement architecture. In: Conference on USENIX Security Symposium (2004)
22. Santos, N., Gummadi, K.P., Rodrigues, R.: Towards trusted cloud computing. In: Conference on Hot Topics in Cloud Computing (2009)
23. Schiffman, J., Sun, Y., Vijayakumar, H., Jaeger, T.: Cloud verifier: verifiable auditing service for IaaS clouds (2013)
24. Schiffman, J., Moyer, T., Vijayakumar, H., Jaeger, T., Mcdaniel, P.: Seeding clouds with trust anchors. In: ACM Cloud Computing Security Workshop (2010)
25. Wu, L., Wei, L., Yang, L., Ruan, A., Wu, Z.: Partial attestation: towards cost-effective and privacy-preserving remote attestations. In: TrustCom/BigDataSE/ISPA (2017)

Machine Learning Security

An Adversarial Attack Based on Multi-objective Optimization in the Black-Box Scenario: MOEA-APGA II

Chunkai Zhang, Yepeng Deng, Xin Guo, Xuan Wang, and Chuanyi Liu[✉]

Department of Computer Science and Technology,
Harbin Institute of Technology, Shenzhen, Shenzhen, China
{ckzhang,liuchuanyi}@hit.edu.cn

Abstract. Various approaches have been proposed to exploit the vulnerability to challenge the robustness of victim models, in the black-box scenario, it is difficult to generate barely noticeable adversarial examples while guaranteeing the attack success rate. Although some methods could solve this problem to some extent, the imperceptibility of the generated perturbations is still far from that of the most advanced attack, worse still, it is infeasible to attack the color image datasets due to its inefficiency. In MOEA-APGA II, We propose the new objective function and the novel population evolution strategies to reduce the average distortion without sacrificing the attack success rate, and compared to the state-of-the-art black-box attack (ZOO), our method achieves a better attack success rate under fewer queries on the benchmark datasets.

Keywords: Adversarial examples · Black-box attack · Multi-objective optimization

1 Introduction

Even the state-of-the-art artificial neural network in deep learning was tended to suffer from misclassification when the input samples have been tainted by small perturbations [1]. Various approaches have been proposed to exploit this vulnerability to challenge the robustness of victim models [2], called as adversarial attacks, and the perturbed samples called as adversarial examples. In the adversarial attack, the attack capability and visual quality are two main evaluating indicators, the former may refer to success rate, which indicates the percentage of the label of the original images are successfully changed to hopeful labels by overlying the perturbations [3], the latter is negatively related to the distortion degree of the perturbation of adversarial examples.

Assuming the complete knowledge of the victim model [4], the white-box attack can directly generate adversarial examples by using internal information. However, in most actual attack scenes the black-box attack [5,6] is much more

© Springer Nature Switzerland AG 2020
J. Zhou et al. (Eds.): ICICS 2019, LNCS 11999, pp. 603–612, 2020.
https://doi.org/10.1007/978-3-030-41579-2_35

realistic. Some methods take advantage of the transferability of the adversarial example to attack models that have never been touched [5,7], but they have the poor success rate. Some methods train the substitute model based on the information in the process of attacking the victim model [8], which can greatly improve the success rate, but it is necessary to fit a new approximation for each victim model. Different from the above ideas, in some methods the victim model merely provides a measurement of the quality of the perturbed samples, so these methods is more general, such ZOO and one-pixel. ZOO attack [9] and its variants can consider both the attack capability and visual quality using the weighted sum method, which increase the success rate within a low average distortion, but how to select the weights become a challenge. Su et al. [10] optimized the adversarial perturbations using the Differential Evolutionary algorithm [11], but the number of pixels to be perturbed should be specified in advance. MOEA-APGA [12] was based on the multi-objective evolutionary algorithm MOEA/D [13] to simultaneously optimizes the prediction probability and the distortion of perturbations, and generate representative perturbations set of Pareto optimal solutions [14], and then a final perturbation is select to execute finally attack. However, due to the diversity of the Pareto set, part of the evolutionary resources could be occupied by individuals with low distortion but unsuccessful attacks.

In this paper, we proposed some strategies aim to improve the visual quality of generated adversarial examples and the convergence speed of MOEA-APGA, so could carry out an attack on the color image datasets.

2   Related Work

In this section, we first present problem formulations about adversarial attacks and some existing algorithms and then offer some preliminaries about the basic algorithm MOEA-APGA.

2.1   Problem Formulation

Let $x \in \mathcal{X} := [0,1]^{n \times d}$ be an original sample of n pixels and d color channels with the ground truth label $l \in \mathbb{R}^k$. In order to craft adversarial example $\hat{x}$ similar to x, a minimizer (perturbation) r is overlayed on the original sample.

As a attacker, we intend to change the prediction result of $C_\theta(\cdot)$ to achieve the goal of fooling the networks. $\hat{y}$ is the result of $C_\theta(\cdot)$ based on the input $\hat{x}$. Attack methods are divided into two categories for different adversarial goals: targeted attacks (targeted fooling) and non-target attacks (misclassification) [1]. The definition of 'targeted attack to a target class t' can be formulated as $\hat{y} = t$, $t \in \mathbb{R}^k$, and the problem of 'non-target attack', can be defined as $\hat{y} \neq l$.

Most existing attacks are not optimal because they do not solve the problem of succeeding under minimal distortion as a priori,

$$\min_{\hat{x} \in \mathcal{X}: f(\hat{x}) \neq l} \|\hat{x} - x\|. \tag{1}$$

---

[1] In some works, 'non-target attack' is also called 'misclassification', but in this paper, 'misclassification' covers the 'targeted attack' and the 'non-target attack'.

Szegedy et al. [1] approximate this constrained minimization problem by a Lagrangian formulation

$$\min_{\hat{x} \in \mathcal{X}} \lambda \|\hat{x} - x\|^2 + \ell(f(\hat{x}), t). \tag{2}$$

Parameter λ controls the balance between the distortion and the classification loss. Szegedy et al. [1] carry out this optimization by box-constrained L-BFGS.

2.2 MOEA-APGA

MOEA-APGA owns two objectives: (i) the prediction probability (PP) is the output of the Softmax layer $\sigma(z)$ of the attacked classifier, which denotes the classification probabilities of an adversarial example; (ii) the perturbation metric (PM) measures the distortion of perturbation, the smaller it is, the better the imperceptibility is.

$$PP(\hat{x}) = \begin{cases} 1 - \sigma[C_\theta(\hat{x})]_t, & for\ targeted\ attack \\ \sigma[C_\theta(\hat{x})]_l, & for\ non\ target\ attack \end{cases}, \tag{3}$$

$$PM(r) = \begin{cases} \|r\|_0 = \sqrt[0]{\sum_{i=1}^{mn} d_i^0}, & for\ pixel\ level \\ \|r\|_2 = \sqrt{\sum_{i=1}^{mn} d_i^2}, & for\ global\ level \end{cases}. \tag{4}$$

The non-targeted attack is realized by minimizing the prediction probability of the original class, conversely, the targeted attack is realized by minimizing that opposite number of the target class. It is shown that global-level has a better imperceptibility, thus, only the global-level disturbances are compared in the experimental.

Random perturbations r is set as the initial individuals in the population, and new perturbations are generated by population evolution. The population evolution module of MOEA-APGA decomposes a multi-objective optimization problem into a number of different simple optimization subproblems by Tchebycheff [14] and then bases on the evolutionary algorithm to optimize those subproblems simultaneously. The problem is converted to a minimum optimization problem with two objectives. The Tchebycheff value is calculated by

$$\min g^{te}\left(r|\overrightarrow{\lambda_i}\right) = \max\left\{\lambda_i^1 PP(\hat{x}), \lambda_i^2 PM(r)\right\}. \tag{5}$$

where $\left\{\overrightarrow{\lambda_1}, \cdots, \overrightarrow{\lambda_n}\right\}$ is a set of evenly spread weight vectors, the dimension is the same as the population size n.

3 MOEA-APGA II

Algorithm 1 shows the pseudo-code of MOEA-APGA II.

Algorithm 1. MOEA-APGA II

Input: The serialized image, img; Adversarial goals, $goal$; Ground truth label, y or Target label, t; Maximum number of generations, $maxgen$; Population size, n; Weight vector, $\{\lambda_1, \cdots, \lambda_n\}$; The size of neighbours, ns; Crossover probability, pc;

Output: Adversarial perturbation for crafting adversarial example, AP;

Step1: Population initialization.

1: $P \leftarrow Initial\,(n)$ // Randomly generate a batch of individuals as the initial population;

2: **for** $i = 1$ to n **do**

3:     $N_i \leftarrow$ get the ns individuals from P with the nearest Euclidean distance between any individual in P, and the weight vector λ_i;

4: **end for**

Step2: Population evolution.

5: **for** $gen_t = 1$ to $maxgen$ **do**

6:     **for** $i = 1$ to n **do**

7:         $P_i' \leftarrow$ Randomly select an parent individual from N_i or P;

8:         $child_{cross} \leftarrow Crossover\left(P_i', P_i, pc\right)$;

9:         $Mutation\ Position\ (MP) \leftarrow$ Select a series of positions for mutation based on the mutation probability distribution function of each position, which is calculated by the 'Mutate the Key Positions First' strategy;

10:         $Mutation\ Amplitude_{max}\ (MA_{max}) \leftarrow$ Determining the maximum amplitude of mutation based on 'Adaptive Adjustment Strategy of Disturbance Amplitude' strategy;

11:         $child_{new} \leftarrow Mutation\,(child_{cross}, MP, MA_{max})$;

12:         $\min g^{te}\left(child_{new} | \overrightarrow{\lambda_i}\right) \leftarrow$ Calculate an adaptive assessment for each new individual by (8);

13:         Update population;

14:     **end for**

15: **end for**

Step3: Perturbation Filter.

16: $AP \leftarrow SelectNonDominatedItemsets\,(P)$;//Select the non-dominated individuals from the final population P by fast non-dominated sorting strategy. Then get the final solution according to the needs of the problem;

3.1   Definition of the Objective Function

On the one hand, since the result of multi-objective optimization is a Pareto set, and the samples in the set are diverse, there is no guarantee that the samples in the result set will make the attack successful. MOEA-APGA proposed the filtering strategy to solve the problem, however, those samples that could not be successfully attack still occupy a lot of computing resources. On the other hand, there is a situation that some individuals with low absolute prediction probability are still the largest among the C_θ^i and can successfully attack. In the previous work, such individuals are punished, which is not reasonable. Therefore, we proposed the following improved strategy, replacing the objective function prediction probability (PP) with the new optimized objective F: (1) targeted attack

$$F(x,t) = \begin{cases} \alpha + (1 - \sigma\,[C_\theta^t]) \cdot \alpha^{index_t} & for\ (1 - \sigma\,[C_\theta^t]) > 1 - \frac{1}{k} & (a) \\ \alpha + (1 - \sigma\,[C_\theta^t]) \cdot 10^{index_t} & for\ index_t > 0 & (b) \\ (1 - \sigma\,[C_\theta^t]) & for\ others & (c) \end{cases}$$

$$(6)$$

(2) non-target attack

$$F(x,l) = \begin{cases} \alpha \cdot \sigma\,[C_\theta^l] & for\ \sigma\,[C_\theta^l] > 0.5\ or\ index_l = 0 & (a) \\ \sigma\,[C_\theta^l] \cdot \beta^{k - index_l - 1} & for\ others & (b) \end{cases}$$

$$(7)$$

$\sigma\,[C_\theta^t]$ represents the prediction probability of target label $t \in \mathbb{R}^k$ from the Softmax layer of C_θ with the input sample x. We sort all the prediction probabilities in descending order, and $index_t$ represents the sequence index of target label t among the sorted prediction probabilities C_θ^i. When the Top-1 result is t, $index_t = 0$, when the predicted result is the least likely to be t, then $index_t = k - 1$, k is the total number of labels. α represents a larger value, usually be 1e10; β is a relatively smaller value, satisfied $\beta \geq 1$, set as 1.3 in this paper. After replacing (5) with $F(x,t)$, the adaptive evaluation function is shown as:

$$\min g^{te}\left(r|\overrightarrow{\lambda_i}\right) = \max\left\{\lambda_i^1 F\left(\hat{x}\right), \lambda_i^2 PM\left(r\right)\right\}. \tag{8}$$

3.2 Mutate the Key Positions First

In the process of generating adversarial example, we found that the positions of some pixels would significantly affect the classification results, even slightly disturbed. We defined these pixel positions as key positions, and the 'Mutate the key positions first' strategy expects to have a higher mutation probability for these key positions, while the mutation probability of the pixels with less impact on classification is smaller. The specific formula is as follows:

$$P\left(x_d = \text{Ind}_{ijd}\right) = \partial \cdot \left(|G(i,j)| + \Theta\|\,\text{Ind}\,\|_\infty\right)\ \sum_{i=1}^{d} P\left(x_d\right) = 1 \tag{9}$$

$$G(i,j) = (I * K)_{ij} = \sum_{m=0}^{k_1-1}\sum_{n=0}^{k_2-1} I(i - m, j - n)K(m,n) \tag{10}$$

$$K(m,n) = \partial \cdot \frac{1}{2\pi\sigma^2}e^{-\frac{m^2+n^2}{2\sigma^2}} \tag{11}$$

Where d represents the d-th channel, $G(i,j)$ means to perform the smoothing operation on the two-dimensional image of the perturbation individual. According to three-sigma rule, we set $\sigma = \frac{1}{6}*image_{width}$. $\Theta\|Ind\|_\infty$ is the base probability, composed of the base probability coefficient Θ and the maximum amplitude of current individual $\|Ind\|_\infty = \max\left(|Ind|\right)$. ∂ is the normalization coefficient, guaranteeing that the sum of probability equals to 1.

3.3 Adaptive Adjustment Strategy of Disturbance Amplitude

In the process of the iterations in MOEA-APGA, the range of mutation disturbance was decreasing to help the convergence of the evolutionary algorithm, but
it cannot adapt to the attack difficulty of each sample. In order to solve this
problem, we propose an adaptive adjustment strategy of disturbance amplitude.

$$\text{pm}_{num} = \begin{cases} C_1 \cdot Ind_{len} & Attack \; failure \\ C_1 \cdot Ind_{len} \cdot G\,(iter) + num_{\min} & other \end{cases} \tag{12}$$

$$\text{pm}_{amp} = \begin{cases} C_2 Ind_{\max} + amp_{\min} & Attack \; failure \\ C_3 \cdot Ind_{\max} \cdot G\,(iter) + amp_{\min} & other \end{cases} \tag{13}$$

pm_{num} and pm_{amp} indicate the mutation disturbance number of perturbed
pixels of individual and the mutation disturbance range of the perturbation
respectively. Where $G\,(i_{ratio})$ is a monotonically decreasing function; Ind_{len},
$Ind_{\max}$ are the dimension and maximum perturbation value of the current individual; C_1, C_2, and C_3 are the proportional constant coefficient; $num_{\min}$, $amp_{\min}$
are the minimum number of perturbed pixels and the minimum perturbation
amplitude.

4 Evaluation and Results

In this paper, the experiments are verified on MNIST ($28 \times 28 \times 1$) and Cifar-10
($32 \times 32 \times 3$), each data set has 10 classes. We randomly select 200 samples
from the test set of each dataset as original samples for the attack. There are
200 attacks for the non-target attack, as for targeted attack, each class will be
attacked to another k-1 class, and thus there are 1800 attacks in total for each
of the data set. On the MNIST, the victim model is the same DNN model with
MOEA-APGA, while on Cifar-10, it is consistent with that of C&W attack [15]
and ZOO attack.

Targeted and non-target attacks follow the same environment settings during
the experiment. MOEA-APGA II perform 100 initial population and 20 neighborhood, which is same as MOEA-APGA. Convenient for us to observe the
improvement of our algorithm, we adopt the best imperceptible perturbation
type, the global-level perturbation, denoted as MOEA-APGA (GP). For evaluation function, we set $\alpha = 1e10$, $\beta = 1.3$; For the strategy of 'Mutate the Key
Positions First', we set $\Theta = 10$ at the beginning, $k_1 = k_2 = 0.25 * 28$ for Mnist
and $k_1 = k_2 = 0.25 * 32$ for Cifar; For the strategy of 'Adaptive Adjustment
Strategy of Disturbance Amplitude', we set $C_1 = 0.035$, $C_2 = 0.5$, and $C_3 = 0.2$,
$num_{\min} = 1$, $amp_{\min} = 0.01$, $G\,(i_{ratio}) = 1 - i_{ratio}$.

C&W attack performs 20 iterations of binary search over λ. For each selected
value of λ, it runs 2,000 iterations of gradient descent with the Adam optimizer.
ZOO attack carry-over its original settings, it performs a binary search up to 9
times to find the best λ, For each selected value of λ, it runs 3,000 max iterations
($iter_{max}$) for MNIST and 1,000 max iterations for Cifar-10, and it terminates the

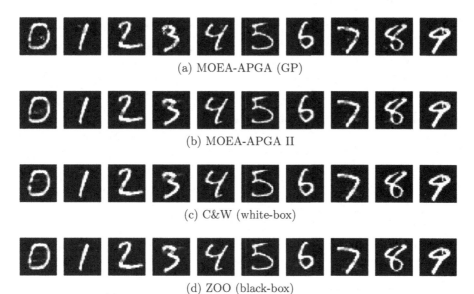

(a) MOEA-APGA (GP)

(b) MOEA-APGA II

(c) C&W (white-box)

(d) ZOO (black-box)

Fig. 1. The result of non-target attack based on the MNIST. Each column represents input classes 0 to 9, while each row represents the perturbation method. From top to bottom are MOEA-APGA (GP), MOEA-APGA II, C&W (white-box) and ZOO (black-box).

optimization process early if the loss does not decrease for 100 early stop iterations ($iter_{es}$). For each iteration updates 128 pixels (*batch size*) with the Adam optimizer. In addition, we also perform 100 iterations and 50 iterations under 9 times binary search ($time_{bs}$) separately to observe the influence of limiting the number of queries of the victim model on the algorithm.

The successful adversarial samples over MNIST and Cifar-10 under the goal of targeted attack and there are non-target attack shown in Figs. 1, 2, 3 and 4 separately. We use following three metrics to evaluate the performances of the improved algorithm: Success Rate, Average Distortion, and Average Visiting Time. The results are shown in Table 1.

Success Rate (SR). The success rate, referring to fooling rate [10, 16], indicates that the trained model changes the percentage of its predicted labels after the image was tainted. In the case of misclassification fooling rate (MR) is defined as the percentage of adversarial images that were successfully classified by the target system as an arbitrary target class, and targeted fooling rate (TFR) is defined as the probability of perturbing a natural image to a specific target class. In order to ensure visual quality, we regard the case of $L_2 > 20$ as an attack failure.

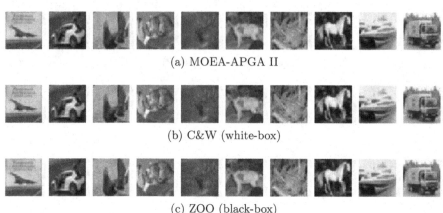

(a) MOEA-APGA II

(b) C&W (white-box)

(c) ZOO (black-box)

Fig. 2. The result of non-target attack based on the Cifar-10. Each column represents ten input classes, while each row represents the perturbation method. From top to bottom are MOEA-APGA II, C&W (white-box) and ZOO (black-box).

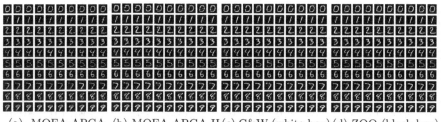

(a) MOEA-APGA (b) MOEA-APGA II (c) C&W (white-box) (d) ZOO (black-box)

Fig. 3. The result of targeted attack based on MNIST. Each row represents input classes 0 to 9, while each column represents target classes 0 to 9, and the diagonal is the original image.

Average Distortion (Avg.L_2). The average L_2 norm for all successful adversarial examples is used to estimate the distortion between adversarial images and the original ones. The smaller the value is, the harder it is to perceive the difference between the rogue image and the original image.

Average Visiting Time (Avg.VT). It refers to the average times of queries to the victim model required for generating each adversarial example [5]. The access to the victim model is useful for our attack behavior, it helps to the fitting of the internal information of the model.

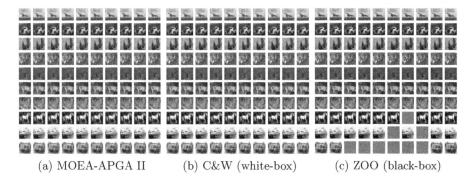

| (a) MOEA-APGA II   (b) C&W (white-box)   (c) ZOO (black-box) |

Fig. 4. The result of targeted attack based on Cifar-10. Each row represents ten input classes, while each column represents ten target classes, and the diagonal is the original image. Empty part indicates attack failure.

Table 1. Experimental results.

Method	Dataset					
	Non-Target Attack			*Targeted Attack*		
	SR	*Avg.L_2*	*Avg. VT*	*SR*	*Avg.L_2*	*Avg. VT*
MNIST						
MOEA-APGA(GP)	100%	1.8323	40,000	100%	3.1712	40,000
MOEA-APGAII	100%	1.4736	40,000	100%	2.5081	40,000
C&W (white-box)	100%	1.3751	40,000	100%	2.2614	40,000
ZOO (black-box)	23.5%	0.8344	57,600	4.83%	0.9379	57,600
	87.5%	1.4472	115,200	45.27%	1.7931	115,200
	100%	1.3778	>486,400	100%	2.2713	>486,400
Cifar-10						
MOEA-APGAII	100%	0.3204	40,000	100%	0.6343	40,000
C& W (white-box)	100%	0.1424	40,000	100%	0.3492	40,000
ZOO (black-box)	99.5%	0.2721	57,600	77.44%	0.4674	57,600
	100%	0.2555	115,200	95.38%	0.4836	115,200
	100%	0.2026	>230,400	97.5%	0.4075	>230,400

5 Conclusion

In this paper, we proposed the objective function and several novel strategies to improve the efficiency and performance of attacks. Experimental results on both grayscale and color image data sets show that the success rate outperforms the other methods, such as the C&W attack and the ZOO attack. When the number of queries to the victim model is not a primary consideration, our attack attains comparable performance in terms of distortion to the state-of-the-art white-box attack (C&W attack), and in the case of limited queries, we still maintain the distortion within an acceptable range.

Acknowledgment. This study was supported by the National Key Research and Development Program of China (No.2016YFB0800900) and the Shenzhen Research Council (Grant No.JSGG20170822160842949,GJHZ20180928155209705).

References

1. Szegedy, C., et al.: Intriguing properties of neural networks. arXiv preprint arXiv:1312.6199 (2013)
2. Nguyen, A., Yosinski, J., Clune, J.: Deep neural networks are easily fooled: high confidence predictions for unrecognizable images. In: Proceedings of the IEEE Conference on Computer Vision and Pattern Recognition, Boston, pp. 427–436 (2014)
3. Akhtar, N., Mian, A.: Threat of adversarial attacks on deep learning in computer vision: a survey. IEEE Access **6**, 14410–14430 (2018)
4. Goodfellow, I.J., Shlens, J., Szegedy, C.: Explaining and harnessing adversarial examples. In: International Conference on Machine Learning, pp. 1–10 (2015)
5. Papernot, N., Mcdaniel, P., Goodfellow, I., Jha, S., Celik, Z.B., Swami, A.: Practical black-box attacks against deep learning systems using adversarial examples. In: ACM Asia Conference on Computer and Communications Security (2016)
6. Tu, C.C., et al.: Autozoom: autoencoder-based zeroth order optimization method for attacking black-box neural networks. In: Proceedings of the AAAI Conference on Artificial Intelligence, vol. 33, pp. 742–749 (2019)
7. Liu, Y., Chen, X., Liu, C., Song, D.: Delving into transferable adversarial examples and black-box attacks. arXiv preprint arXiv:1611.02770 (2016)
8. Narodytska, N., Kasiviswanathan, S.: Simple black-box adversarial attacks on deep neural networks. In: Computer Vision and Pattern Recognition Workshops, pp. 1310–1318 (2017)
9. Chen, P.Y., Zhang, H., Sharma, Y., Yi, J., Hsieh, C.J.: Zoo: zeroth order optimization based black-box attacks to deep neural networks without training substitute models. In: Proceedings of the 10th ACM Workshop on Artificial Intelligence and Security, pp. 15–26. ACM (2017)
10. Su, J., Vargas, D.V., Sakurai, K.: One pixel attack for fooling deep neural networks. IEEE Trans. Evol. Comput. **23**(5), 828–841 (2019)
11. Das, S., Suganthan, P.N.: Differential evolution: a survey of the state-of-the-art. IEEE Trans. Evol. Comput. **15**(1), 4–31 (2011)
12. Deng, Y., Zhang, C., Wang, X.: A multi-objective examples generation approach to fool the deep neural networks in the black-box scenario. In: IEEE International Conference on Data Science in Cyberspace, pp. 92–99. IEEE (2019)
13. Zhang, Q., Li, H.: MOEA/D: a multiobjective evolutionary algorithm based on decomposition. IEEE Trans. Evol. Comput. **11**(6), 712–731 (2007)
14. Hillermeier, C.: Nonlinear Multiobjective Optimization: A Generalized Homotopy Approach, vol. 135. Springer, Berlin (2001). https://doi.org/10.1007/978-3-0348-8280-4
15. Carlini, N., Wagner, D.: Towards evaluating the robustness of neural networks. In: IEEE Symposium on Security and Privacy, pp. 39–57. IEEE (2017)
16. Sarkar, S., Bansal, A., Mahbub, U., Chellappa, R.: UPSET and ANGRI : Breaking high performance image classifiers. arXiv preprint arXiv:1707.01159 (2017)

Neuron Selecting: Defending Against Adversarial Examples in Deep Neural Networks

Ming Zhang, Hu Li, Xiaohui Kuang[(⊠)], Ling Pang, and Zhendong Wu

National Key Laboratory of Science and Technology on Information System Security,
Beijing 100101, China
xiaohui_kuang@163.com

Abstract. Recent studies have demonstrated that deep neural networks
are vulnerable to adversarial examples, i.e. inputs crafted by applying
small but intentionally perturbations to legitimate examples to mislead
the models. Adversarial examples pose a serious threat to the application of deep neural networks in safety-critical scenarios. Inspired by
human visual system, we propose a novel method called Neuron-Selecting
to defend against adversarial examples. The main idea of the Neuron-
Selecting is to select the vital few neurons that contribute to the final
right predictions and filter out the trivial many neurons that are activated by perturbations. Experiments on MNIST and CIFAR-10 models
show that the Neuron-Selecting can effectively defend against the state-
of-the-art attacks, especially ones that have small perturbations but high
attack success rate. We believe our work provides a new perspective to
defend against adversarial examples.

Keywords: Neuron Selecting · Adversarial examples · Defense method

1 Introduction

Deep Neural Networks (DNNs) have recently led to dramatic performance
improvements in a wide range of applications, such as image classification [12]
and speech recognition [10]. While focusing on how to improve DNNs' accuracy and efficiency, researchers have gradually paid great attention to the safety
of DNNs. In safety-critical scenarios, unsecure models may bring devastating
consequences. Specifically, the main threat for DNNs comes from adversarial
examples, i.e. inputs crafted by making slight perturbations to legitimate inputs
with the intent of misleading machine learning models [25].

Adversarial examples can be formally defined as follows: given the deep learn-
ing model $f : \mathbb{R}^N \to L_1, L_2, ..., L_m$, there exists x such that $f(x) = L_i$ and $\hat{x}$
such that $\|\hat{x} - x\|_p < \epsilon$, where $f(\hat{x}) = L_j$ and $i \neq j$. Then $\hat{x}$ is an adversarial
example with perturbation constraint ϵ.

Plenty of researches show that only a small change to the original example
can successfully attack the target model [3,8,9,21,25]. Therefore, it is necessary and urgent to study the defense techniques for machine learning models,

© Springer Nature Switzerland AG 2020
J. Zhou et al. (Eds.): ICICS 2019, LNCS 11999, pp. 613–629, 2020.
https://doi.org/10.1007/978-3-030-41579-2_36

especially for DNNs which are vulnerable to tiny perturbations. This problem has received considerable research attention in recent years, but there seems no perfect solution so far and things appear to be worse than initially thought. Adversarial examples have been shown to be robust to physical world transformations to some extent, e.g. 3D objects will be misclassified under a wide distribution of angles and viewpoints [2].

We think the reason an adversarial example is misclassified is that perturbations activate some neurons that should not be activated. Taking digital recognition as an example, humans can easily identify a digit as long as the digit has its own specific shape. Digits should be recognized without being affected by the background elements. "0" is "0" not because "0" is written in black on white paper. It should be recognized as "0" even with a particularly complicated background. The most probable cause for a perturbed "0" being misidentified by DNNs is that the perturbations activate some irrelevant neurons. Thus, is it possible to filter out those wrongly activated neurons by adversarial examples? To answer this question, we propose a novel defense method, called the Neuron-Selecting, to defend against adversarial examples in DNNs, which selects the vital few neurons that contribute to the final right predictions and filters out the trivial many neurons that are activated by perturbations. The main contributions of the paper are as follows:

(1) We found that the activations of normal examples follow the law of "Vital few and trivial many", while adversarial examples change the distribution of "vital few" and "trivial many".
(2) We proposed the Neuron-Selecting method for defending against adversarial examples in DNNs.
(3) We also empirically evaluated our defense method on MNIST and CIFAR-10 models and verified that it can defend against the state-of-the-art attacks. The rest of the paper is organized as follows: the related work is discussed in Sect. 2. We analyze the neuron activations distribution and describe the Neuron-Selecting defense method in Sect. 3. In Sect. 4, we evaluate the effectiveness of the proposed method against the state-of-the-art attacks. Finally, the conclusion is presented in Sect. 5.

2   Related Work

The attack-and-defense game on DNNs has last for several years. There are many methods on how to generate and defend against adversarial examples.

2.1   Attack Methods

The L-BFGS method introduced by Szegedy et al. [25] aims to crafting adversarial examples by solve a box-constrained optimization problem, i.e. minimize $\|\hat{x} - x\|_2^2$, such that $C(\hat{x}) = l$ where $\hat{x} \in [0, 1]^m$.

Goodfellow et al. [9] proposed Fast Gradient Sign Method (FGSM). The adversarial example $\hat{x}$ corresponding to the original input x is computed as

$\hat{x} \leftarrow \epsilon \cdot sign(\nabla_x J(\theta, x, y))$, with θ being the parameters of the model, x the input to the model, y the target associated with x and $J(\theta, x, y)$ the cost used to train the neural network.

The Carlini-Wagner (C&W) attack [5] also take generation of adversarial example as an optimal problem. C&W aims to find small valid change δ that can be made to an input x that will change its classification result. C&W instantiates the distance metric with a L_p norm and defines an objective function f such that $f(x + \delta) \leq 0$ if and only if the model misclassifies $\hat{x} \leftarrow x + \delta$.

Inspired by C&W attack, Chen et al. [6] proposed the Elastic Net Method (EAD). Compared with C&W which uses L_p norm, EAD performs elastic-net regularization with β controlling the trade-off between L_1 and L_2. When $\beta = 0$, EAD attack can be viewed as C&W L_2 attack.

The Basic Iterative Method (BIM) introduced by Kurakin et al. [14] applies FGSM multiple times with small step size and clips intermediate results after each step to ensure that they are in an ϵ-neighborhood of the original input, i.e. $\hat{x}_0 = x, \hat{x}_{t+1} = Clip_{x,\epsilon}\{\hat{x}_t - \alpha \cdot sign(\nabla_x J(\hat{x}_t, y_L))\}$, where y_L is the target class.

Slightly different from BIM, Madry et al. [17] proposed to use Projected Gradient Descent (PGD) on the negative loss function. PGD is also a multi-step variant FGSM and can be written as $x^{t+1} = \prod_{x+S}(x^t + \alpha \cdot sign(\nabla_x L(\theta, x, y)))$, where $S \subseteq \mathbb{R}^d$ is a set of allowed perturbations that formalize the manipulative power of the adversary.

Based on BIM, Dong et al. [7] introduced the Momentum Iterative Method (MIM). MIM accelerates gradient descent algorithms by accumulating a velocity vector in the gradient direction of the loss function across iterations. It can be simply written as $g_0 = 0, \hat{x}_0 = x, g_{t+1} = \mu \cdot g_t + \nabla_x J(\hat{x}_t, y)/\|\nabla_x J(\hat{x}_t, y)\|_1$, $\hat{x}_{t+1} = \hat{x} + \alpha \cdot sign(g_{t+1})$, where g_t gathers the gradients of the first t iterations with a decay factor μ.

Aforementioned methods mainly rely on computing the gradient of each example, but the Jacobian-based Saliency Map Approach (JSMA) introduced by Papernot et al. [21] stems from another view, which iteratively perturbs features of the input that have large adversarial saliency scores. The scores are computed based on Jacobian of the model. For candidate adversarial example $\hat{x}_c$, the derivative of class j with respect to input feature i is computed using $[\partial f_j(\hat{x}_c)/\partial x_i]_{i,j}$.

DeepFool introduced by Moosavi-Dezfooli et al. [20] can only ensure that the model classifies the adversarial example to a class different from the original one. Similar as other attacks, DeepFool also iteratively computes the perturbation. It can be simply written as $\hat{x}_0 = x, r_t \leftarrow -\nabla f(\hat{x}_t) \cdot f(\hat{x}_t)/\|\nabla f(\hat{x}_t)\|_2^2, \hat{x}_{t+1} \leftarrow \hat{x}_t + \hat{r}_t$, where r is the perturbation added in each iteration and $\hat{r} = \sum_t \hat{r}_t$ is the sum perturbation added to the original example x.

There have been many other attack methods proposed in recent years [23,27]. For space limitations, we did not review them here and one can find details in references.

2.2   Defense Methods

Network distillation introduced by Papernot et al. [22] tries to defend DNNs by making use of class probability knowledge outputted by initial network. The knowledge is transferred to the distilled network, thus improving generalization capabilities of DNNs and enhancing its resilience to perturbations.

Adversarial training [9,15,25,28] is another wildly used defense method which injects adversarial examples during training to improve the generalization of the model. The most important work in adversarial training is to generate enough high-quality adversarial examples. Since the retraining is commonly accepted, it is often used as a basic method to enhance DNNs.

Different from those defense methods which focus on designing a more robust algorithm, adversarial detecting [11,16,19] aims to detect adversarial examples before they are inputted to DNNs. Relevant work in this area either perform density estimation in the subspace of deep features learned by the model, or use statistical tests or Principal Components Analysis (PCA).

Input reconstruction is another kind of defense method focusing on the property of adversarial example, and tries to pre-process the input data to improve the robustness of DNNs. For example, MagNet [18] uses detector networks to learn how to differentiate normal and adversarial examples by approximating the manifold of normal examples, and reformer network to move adversarial examples towards the manifold of normal examples. Similarly, PixelDefend [24] purifies maliciously perturbed image based on statistical hypothesis testing.

Another kind of defense method can be summarized as classifier robustifying. Ensemble Adversarial Training (EAT) [26] augments training data with perturbations transferred from other models. Ensemble of Diverse Specialists (EDS) [1] defines specialty using confusion matrix to identify and reject fooling instances. However, those method were proved not strong enough later by He et al. [13].

The aforementioned defense methods can be selected to protect DNNs. However, as stated in [4], most of these methods can be easily bypassed by carefully crafted adversarial examples. The current methods defend against adversarial examples usually by using regularizations, data augmentation or input preprocessing. However, in many cases the network cannot be retrained and the examples are difficult to be augmented or preprocessed. To tackle this situation, we propose a novel defense method that is just carried out in the testing stage and the neural network is trained as usual.

3   Neuron-Selecting Defense Method

3.1   Inspiration from Human Visual System

Humans can easily recognize a digit and are hardly interfered by other elements as long as the digit has its own specific shape and outline, even if the surrounding elements are particularly complicated. That is not because we have not seen the surrounding elements but because we do not let them be involved in the decision-making of recognizing digits. Figure 1 shows humans' recognition results of a perturbed "0". We can easily recognize the perturbed digit as "0". We should nevertheless acknowledge that we also see some noise while seeing a "0". But why do we recognize a "0 + noise" image as "0"? The reason is that we just make use of the signals activated by pixels inside the red contour to make the final decision. Contrarily, the signals activated by pixels outside the red contour (noise) are ignored. After all, the noise is not a component of the "0". We believe that humans have the ability to select necessary neurons to make a certain decision. The artificial neural networks do not seem to have such ability. The DNNs rudely eat all the elements in the input space. We think one reason for the DNNs being vulnerable to adversarial examples is that the perturbed elements in adversarial examples activate some irrelevant neurons and what's worse, these irrelevant neurons are involved in the decision-making. There is a strong need to make the DNNs have the ability of selecting specific neurons to perform the specific task.

Fig. 1. Humans' recognition results of a perturbed "0". (Color figure online)

3.2   Preliminary Analysis of Neuron Activations

We trained a network called the MNIST-CNN model for preliminary analysis. The MNIST-CNN is used to perform the MNIST[1] classification task. The architecture of the model is shown in Fig. 2, which is identical to those presented in [5] and [22]. The model has 4 convolutional layers, 2 max pooling layers and 3 fully connected layers. For convenience, we sequentially call these layers CONV1, CONV2, POOL3, CONV4, CONV5, POOL6, FC7 and FC8. We choose the layer FC7 to observe the activation changes by inputting the network normal and adversarial examples. Firstly, we randomly select 200 normal examples that are correctly classified as class 0 from the test set and obtain the activations from layer FC7. The activations are stacked together to form a graph as shown in Fig. 3(a). The x-axis is the neuron No. (Indices of 200 neurons) in layer FC7 and the y-axis is the corresponding activations of normal examples. The brighter the point is, the greater the activation's value. The values in the darkest area are all zero, which means that the neurons are not activated. It is pretty obvious that the activations of normal examples present high regularity and consistency. For normal examples, only some few neurons are significantly

---

[1] http://yann.lecun.com/exdb/mnist/.

activated and the examples of the same class usually activate the same neurons. We find that neurons activated by normal examples follow the rule of "Vital few and trivial many".

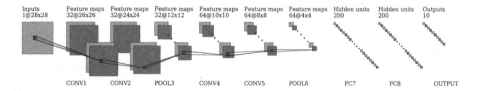

Fig. 2. Architecture of the MNIST-CNN model.

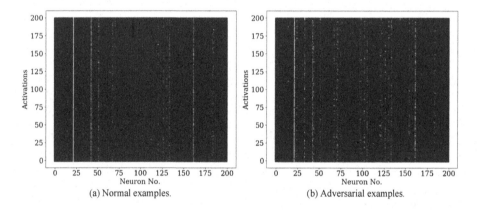

(a) Normal examples.   (b) Adversarial examples.

Fig. 3. Activations of layer FC7.

On the contrary, the activations of adversarial examples exhibit different distributions. Similarly, we randomly select 200 adversarial examples generated by the CWL2 [5] untargeted attack method, where CWL2 is a special case of C&W attack with L2 as distance metric. These examples should be classified as class 0, but now all misclassified by MNIST-CNN. The results are shown in Fig. 3(b). We can see that the activations of adversarial examples differ from that of normal examples. Compared with normal examples, the activations of adversarial examples present less regularity and consistency. Adversarial examples activate some neurons that have never been activated by normal examples. We find that adversarial examples change the distribution of "vital few" and "trivial many".

3.3   Neuron Selecting Method

Compared with human visual system, the DNNs lack the ability of selecting specific neurons to perform the specific task. We find that for a specific model, normal examples usually activate some specific neurons but adversarial examples activate some irrelevant ones. Accordingly, we design a Neuron-Selecting method to help the DNNs select specific neurons to make right decisions and filter out irrelevant neurons activated by perturbations, thus can effectively defending against adversarial examples. The Neuron-Selecting is just carried out in the testing stage and the neural network is trained as usual. The framework of the Neuron-Selecting is illustrated in Fig. 4.

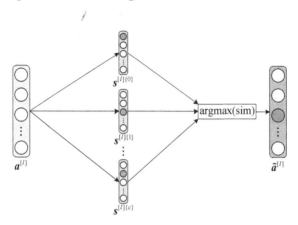

Fig. 4. Neuron-Selecting framework for defending against adversarial examples.

In Fig. 4, $a^{[l]}$ represents the activations of layer l on which the Neuron-Selecting will be implemented. $s^{[l]\{0\}}$, $s^{[l]\{1\}}$,..., $s^{[l]\{c\}}$ are called neuron selectors. $\tilde{a}^{[l]}$ represents the activations of layer l after implementing the Neuron-Selecting. In the training stage, the activations of layer l are used to construct neuron selectors. In the testing stage, the neuron selectors are used to map $a^{[l]}$ to the selected outputs $\tilde{a}^{[l]}$. The selected outputs are then input to the next layer.

We first describe how to construct neuron selectors. For layer l, we need to construct a corresponding neuron selector for every class of examples. Here we take how to construct $s^{[l]\{c\}}$ as an example, which represents the selector on layer l for class c. Firstly, the neural network is trained until achieving a testing accuracy comparable to the state-of-the-art, for instance 98% for the MNIST-CNN model. Then we collect activations of n (n can be considered as a hyper-parameter. In our experiments, $n = 100$.) examples that are correctly classified as class c. Suppose $a^{[l]\{c\}(j)}$ is the activation from layer l of the j-th example that is classified as class c. Then the average is calculated.

$$\bar{a}^{[l]\{c\}} = \frac{1}{n} \sum_{j=0}^{n-1} a^{[l]\{c\}(j)} \tag{1}$$

$\bar{a}^{[l]\{c\}}$ is a vector and it represents the average of activations in the layer l for a given class c computed over the n examples. We denote the number of neurons in layer l as $n^{[l]}$. Obviously, $\bar{a}^{[l]\{c\}}$ has $n^{[l]}$ elements, and the i-th element is denoted as $\bar{a}_i^{[l]\{c\}}$. Based on the analysis in Subsect. 3.2, the activations of normal examples follow the rule of "Vital few and trivial many". Naturally, only vital few elements of $\bar{a}^{[l]\{c\}}$ have significantly large values. We denote the approach of finding the vital few elements of $\bar{a}^{[l]\{c\}}$ as $VitalFew(\ )$. In experiment, we use the Pareto chart[2], which is widely used to highlight the most important among a set of factors, to select the vital few neurons. The approach of using the Pareto chart can be formalized as follows and the details are in Appendix A.

$$VF_{\bar{a}} = VitalFew(\bar{a}^{[l]\{c\}},\ p) \tag{2}$$

Here, p is a hyper-parameter that defines the contribution rate of the vital few elements, $VF_{\bar{a}}$ represents the vital few set.

Finally, the elements of the neuron selector $s^{[l]\{c\}}$ are defined as follows.

$$s_i^{[l]\{c\}} = \begin{cases} 1, if\ \bar{a}_i^{[l]\{c\}} \in VF_{\bar{a}} \\ 0, otherwise \end{cases} \tag{3}$$

Similarly, we can construct neuron selectors for other classes and layers.

In the testing stage, suppose $a^{[l]\{unk\}}$ is the activation of an example whose class is unknown. We have different neuron selectors for different classes. The mapped activation is calculated as follows.

$$\tilde{a}^{[l]\{unk\}} = a^{[l]\{unk\}} * s^{[l]\{t\}};\ where\ t = \underset{c \in \{0,1,...,n^{\{c\}}-1\}}{\arg\max} \{sim(a^{[l]\{unk\}},\ s^{[l]\{c\}})\} \tag{4}$$

Here $*$ denotes an element-wise product. $n^{\{c\}}$ represents the number of classes. $sim()$ is a similarity function. In the experiment, we use the cosine similarity function. The formula implies that first calculate similarities between $a^{[l]\{unk\}}$ and all the selectors $s^{[l]\{c\}}$, $c \in \{0, 1, ..., n^{\{c\}} - 1\}$, and then choose the selector corresponding to the largest similarity as the targeted selector. Finally, do the element-wise product between $a^{[l]\{unk\}}$ and the targeted selector $s^{[l]\{t\}}$ to get the mapped activation $\tilde{a}^{[l]\{unk\}}$.

For a trained network, the vital few neurons in each layer are fixed. The Neuron-Selecting is designed to be started from the last layer (the output layer excluded) of the neural network. As for the neural network, the deeper the layer is, the more abstract and more regular the features, i.e. the activations. Thus, the difference between the "vital few" and the "trivial many" is more significant. Accordingly the Neuron-Selecting is more operational and effective. For the MNIST-CNN model, we recommend implementing the Neuron-Selecting on layer FC8 first, and then going back to layers FC7, POOL6, and CONV5 etc. as needed.

---

[2] https://en.wikipedia.org/wiki/Pareto_chart.

4   Experiments

We empirically evaluated the Neuron-Selecting defense method on the MNIST-CNN and CIFAR10-CNN models. CIFAR10-CNN has a similar architecture with MNIST-CNN but is trained with CIFAR-10^3 dataset.

4.1   Experimental Setup

The model architectures of MNIST-CNN and CIFAR10-CNN are identical to those presented in [5] and [22]. The models are implemented with Tensorflow (v1.12.0). We achieve 98.65% testing accuracy on MNIST-CNN and 77.05% testing accuracy on CIFAR10-CNN.

We use CleverHans (v2.1.0)[4] to generate different kinds of adversarial examples. CleverHans provides lots of the state-of-the-art attack methods, of which FGSM, BIM, JSMA, DeepFool, CWL2, PGD and MIM are chosen in our experiments. These are typical attack methods on DNNs. For MNIST-CNN, the hyper-parameters of attack methods except the CWL2 all take the default values in CleverHans. As default values would results in low attack success rate for CWL2, we use the values proposed in [4]. For CIFAR10-CNN, the default values cause so large perturbations to adversarial examples that humans can hardly recognize correctly. So the values of some hyper-parameters especially the "*eps*" are decreased for CIFAR10-CNN.

4.2   Defending Against CWL2 Untargeted Adversarial Examples

We first evaluated the defense effect on the CWL2 untargeted attacks to MNIST-CNN. CWL2 is considered one of the most efficient attacks with small perturbations but high attack success rate.

The selecting operations are first implemented on layer FC8. After achieving the best effect on layer FC8, we take the selecting operations backward to layer FC7. The rest selecting operations can be done in the same manner until the defense effect is no longer improved or up to the satisfactory level. We take the accuracy and the confidence as evaluating criteria for defense effect. This is principally because some attacks allege that they can not only make DNNs misclassify adversarial examples, but also with high confidences. Naturally, we hope our defense method can not only correctly classify adversarial examples, but also with high confidences.

A key implementation for the Neuron-Selecting is to select the vital few neurons that contribute to the final decision-making. The number of vital few neurons is decided by the parameter p in formula (2). In experiments we find that for MNIST-CNN, no matter which class the normal examples belong to, only one vital neuron in layer FC8 is significantly activated. So for layer FC8, we simply take the neuron with the maximum activation value as vital. Because

---

[3] http://www.cs.toronto.edu/~kriz/cifar.html.
[4] https://github.com/tensorflow/cleverhans.

the confidences of different classes are different, here we just present the confidences of the class-0 examples. Moreover, we take the average confidence value for evaluation. After implementing the Neuron-Selecting on FC8, the accuracy is 63.57% and the confidence is 0.8160.

We apply the Neuron-Selecting backward to more layers. For further-back layers, we use the approach in formula (2) to select the vital neurons. So accuracy and confidence will vary with p. The results are shown in Fig. 5. We can see that when the selected layers are "FC7&FC8", which means the layer FC7 is selected after the selecting on FC8 is finished, the defense effect is improved. When $p \approx 0.95$ for layer FC7, it can achieve the best result with accuracy 70.52% and confidence 0.9405. Similarly, when the selected layers are "POOL6&FC7&FC8", the defense effect is further improved. When $p \approx 0.7$ for layer POOL6, it achieves the best result with accuracy 84.55% and confidence 0.9924. When the selected layers are "CONV5&POOL6&FC7&FC8" and $p \approx 0.8$ for layer CONV5, it achieves the best result with accuracy 88.11% and confidence 0.9930. When the selected layers are "CONV4&CONV5&POOL6&FC7&FC8" and $p \approx 0.9$ for layer CONV4, it achieves the best result with accuracy 91.98% and confidence 0.9966. It is obvious that as more layers join the team of the Neuron-Selecting, both the accuracy and the confidence are greatly improved.

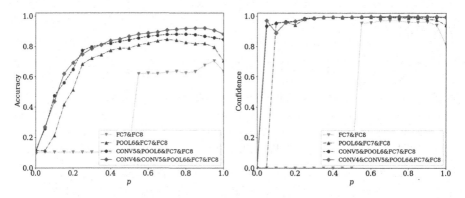

Fig. 5. Accuracy and confidence of CWL2 adversarial examples after the Neuron-Selecting.

We do not implement the Neuron-Selecting backward to layers POOL3, CONV2 or CONV1, as we find that the Neuron-Selecting on these layers decreases the defense effect. It is because POOL3, CONV2 and CONV1 are the beginning layers of MNIST-CNN that all the neurons in these layers are activated and the activations show no regularity. There are no vital neurons, thus the Neuron-Selecting does not work.

The Neuron-Selecting defense method should not sacrifice the accuracy of normal examples largely while defending against adversarial examples. The results on normal examples are shown in Fig. 6. We can see that after applying the Neuron-Selecting on layers "CONV4&CONV5&POOL6&FC7&FC8",

the accuracy of adversarial examples reaches the highest value 91.98% and the accuracy of normal examples decreases from 98.65% to 94.84%. The confidence of normal examples has few changes and is even slightly improved.

We believe that it inevitably influences the accuracy of normal examples while defending against adversarial examples. There is usual tradeoff between normal and adversarial examples.

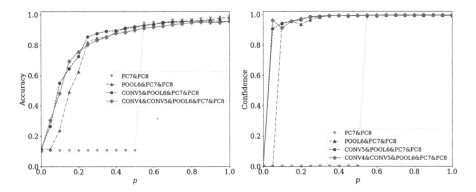

Fig. 6. Accuracy and confidence of normal examples after the Neuron-Selecting.

4.3 Delicate Changes to Activations Brought by Neuron-Selecting

To explain why the Neuron-Selecting can defend against adversarial examples, we illustrated the delicate changes to the activations of MNIST-CNN brought by the Neuron-selecting. We randomly chose 200 normal class-0 examples and the corresponding CWL2 untargeted adversarial examples and presented the activations of the selected layers as Fig. 7 shows. For space limitations, we just presented the first and the last 200 neurons in layers CONV4, CONV5 and POOL6. In Fig. 7, the first and the second rows represent the activations of 200 normal examples before and after the Neuron-Selecting. The third and the last rows represent the activations of 200 adversarial examples before and after the Neuron-Selecting. The x-axis is the neuron indices and the y-axis is the activations. The activation values are scaled and presented as grey images. The darker the point is, the larger the activation's value. It can be seen that before the Neuron-Selecting the activations of adversarial examples are different from that of normal ones. The differences are increasing layer by layer. Finally the differences mislead the network into wrong classifications of adversarial examples. However, after applying the Neuron-Selecting, the differences between activations of adversarial and normal examples are decreasing. As the input propagates forward, the activations of adversarial examples tend to consistent with that of normal ones. This is why the network can correctly classify the adversarial examples again.

To present the differences more intuitively, we calculate the average L2 distances (Euclidean distances) of adversarial and normal examples on different

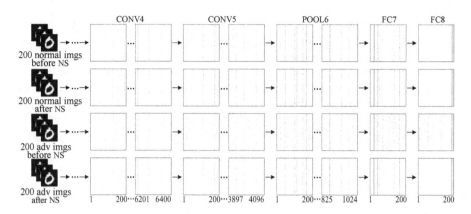

Fig. 7. Activations of normal and adversarial examples before and after the Neuron-Selecting.

layers. As Fig. 8 shows, before the Neuron-Selecting, there is very large L2 distance between activations of adversarial and normal examples. But after the Neuron-Selecting, the distance is reduced significantly.

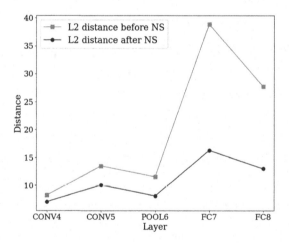

Fig. 8. Distances of normal and adversarial examples before and after Neuron-Selecting.

4.4   Defending Against Adversarial Examples on MNIST-CNN

We evaluated the defense effect of the Neuron-Selecting against other typical attacks on the MNIST-CNN model. For simplicity, we use the same defense strategies as on the CWL2 untargeted adversarial examples. In Table 1, "+FC7" represents the selected layers are "FC7&FC8", and "+POOL6" represents the selected layers are "POOL6&FC7&FC8", and so on. We evaluated both the untargeted and targeted adversarial examples if the attack supports. The targeted attacks here refer to the targeted-next ($L_t = (L_i+1) \bmod n^{\{c\}}$). We use the average L2 distance (Euclidean distance) between adversarial and normal examples to measure the degree of perturbations. It can be seen from Table 1 that the Neuron-Selecting can effectively defend against various types of adversarial examples. Overall, as more layers join the Neuron-Selecting team, the defense effect is improved. The best case is defending against CWL2 targeted/untargeted attacks, with accuracy 91.98% and 92.75%. The worst case is defending against MIM untargeted attacks and JSMA targeted/untargeted attacks, with accuracy 73.78%, 76.81% and 76.94% respectively. Remarkably, among all these attacks, CWL2 produces the smallest perturbations and MIM/JSMA does relatively much more. We find that the Neuron-Selecting excels at defending against attacks that have small perturbations but high attack success rate. Such attacks are usually imperceptible for humans and are more likely to cause heavy damages to the application of DNNs.

Table 1. Accuracy of adversarial examples on MNIST-CNN.

Normal/adversarial		L2 distance	Accuracy (before NS)	Accuracy (after NS)				
				FC8 (max)	+FC7 ($p=0.95$)	+POOL6 ($p=0.7$)	+CONV5 ($p=0.8$)	+CONV4 ($p=0.9$)
Normal	/	0.0000	0.9865	0.9861	0.9812	0.9542	0.9565	0.9485
FGSM	Untargeted	4.0214	0.7367	0.7565	0.7334	0.7423	0.7939	0.8694
	Targeted	4.0264	0.7458	0.7661	0.7399	0.7569	0.8121	0.8781
BIM	Untargeted	2.6043	0.3430	0.3572	0.3828	0.6450	0.7206	0.8145
	Targeted	2.5266	0.6853	0.7027	0.6761	0.8003	0.8439	0.8854
JSMA	Untargeted	**4.3213**	0.6040	0.6227	0.6203	0.6371	0.6792	**0.7681**
	Targeted	**4.3211**	0.6064	0.6247	0.6205	0.6407	0.6876	**0.7694**
DeepFool	Untargeted	2.5677	0.3440	0.5812	0.6059	0.7464	0.8100	0.8705
CWL2	Untargeted	**1.4666**	0.0733	0.6357	0.7052	0.8455	0.8811	**0.9198**
	Targeted	**0.6395**	0.5848	0.7598	0.7677	0.8817	0.9036	**0.9275**
PGD	Untargeted	3.8463	0.2147	0.2261	0.2544	0.6129	0.7139	0.8359
	Targeted	3.7971	0.6134	0.6537	0.6266	0.8006	0.8524	0.8991
MIM	Untargeted	**4.9036**	0.2389	0.2441	0.2618	0.4634	0.5496	**0.7378**
	Targeted	4.8994	0.5514	0.5689	0.5457	0.6787	0.7370	0.8398

4.5 Defending Against Adversarial Examples on CIFAR10-CNN

We also evaluated the Neuron-Selecting defense method on the CIFAR10-CNN model. As well, we first conducted experiments on the CWL2 untargeted attacks and found that it would be best to implement the Neuron-Selecting on layers FC8, FC7, POOL6 and CONV5. The p values for these layers are 0.95, 0.7, 0.75

and 0.75 respectively. Then we evaluated on other types of attacks and the results are presented in Table 2. It can be seen that after applying the Neuron-Selecting, the defense ability of the model against different types of attacks is greatly improved. However, it is obvious that CIFAR10-CNN itself has not achieved a high accuracy on the classification of CIFAR-10 dataset. When the model itself has poor performance, the defense effect of the Neuron-Selecting will be compromised. We think that if the network is deeper, more layers can be implemented the Neuron-Selecting on and the defense effect will be better. The experimental results on CIFAR10-CNN also demonstrate that the Neuron-Selecting excels at defending against attacks like CWL2 that have small perturbations but high attack success rate.

Table 2. Accuracy of adversarial examples on CIFAR10-CNN.

Normal/adversarial		L2 distance	Accuracy (before NS)	Accuracy (after NS)			
				FC8 ($p = 0.95$)	+FC7 ($p = 0.7$)	+POOL6 ($p = 0.75$)	+CONV5 ($p = 0.75$)
Normal	/	0.0000	0.7705	0.7710	0.7445	0.7052	0.7015
FGSM	Untargeted	1.6470	0.5180	0.5191	0.5145	0.5293	0.5399
	Targeted	1.6469	0.5131	0.5141	0.5181	0.5306	0.5405
BIM	Untargeted	1.4992	0.3390	0.3454	0.3712	0.4508	0.4700
	Targeted	1.4965	0.4590	0.4602	0.4653	0.5175	0.5263
JSMA	Untargeted	3.4022	0.3461	0.4184	0.4666	0.5062	0.5184
	Targeted	3.2663	0.3099	0.3866	0.4536	0.5044	0.5142
DeepFool	Untargeted	0.9913	0.1346	0.3069	0.4041	0.4832	0.4998
CWL2	Untargeted	**0.6707**	0.1213	0.4973	0.5829	0.6304	**0.6441**
	Targeted	**1.1843**	0.0013	0.3639	0.5223	0.6051	**0.6234**
PGD	Untargeted	1.2856	0.2210	0.2405	0.3066	0.4599	0.4914
	Targeted	1.2687	0.3321	0.3549	0.4317	0.5545	0.5730
MIM	Untargeted	1.6480	0.2250	0.2343	0.2741	0.4061	0.4349
	Targeted	1.6479	0.3255	0.3377	0.3852	0.4903	0.5050

5 Conclusion

We proposed a Neuron-Selecting method to defend against adversarial examples in DNNs. The Neuron-Selecting is designed to select the right decision-making neurons and filter out the irrelevant neurons activated by perturbations, thus adversarial examples can be correctly classified. We evaluated our defense method both on MNIST and CIFAR-10 models. The results show that the Neuron-Selecting can effectively defend against various types of adversarial examples, especially ones that have small perturbations but high attack success rate.

We have not compared the Neuron-Selecting to other defense methods. The reason is that current defense methods, e.g. adversarial training, usually employ the network retraining, data augmentation or input preprocessing. Our Neuron-Selecting defense method applies well to the situation that the network cannot be retrained and the data is difficult to be augmented or preprocessed. So it is very difficult to provide a fair comparison. We hope our work could provide a new perspective to defend against adversarial examples, i.e. while concentrating on eliminating the perturbations in adversarial examples, we might as well take efforts to get rid of the "perturbations" of the model itself brought by adversarial examples.

A   Pareto Chart for Selecting the Vital Few Neurons

The Pareto chart, named after Vilfredo Pareto, is to highlight the most important among a set of factors and is widely used in economics, engineering and sociology. As shown in Fig. 9, in the Pareto chart for selecting the vital few neurons, the activation values are represented in descending order by bars, and the cumulative percentage of the activation values is represented by the line. The left vertical axis is the activation values and the right vertical axis is the cumulative percentage. The horizontal axis is the neuron No. that identifies the different neurons in the layer. p is the value of the cumulative percentage. Then we can easily find the vital few neurons based on the value of p. For example, when $p = 0.8$, the neurons associated with the cumulative percentage 0.8 are the vital few neurons.

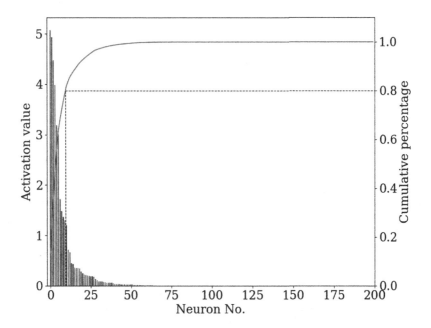

Fig. 9. Pareto chart for selecting the vital few neurons.

References

1. Abbasi, M., Gagné, C.: Robustness to adversarial examples through an ensemble of specialists. In: 5th International Conference on Learning Representations (2017)
2. Athalye, A., Engstrom, L., Ilyas, A., Kwok, K.: Synthesizing robust adversarial examples. In: Proceedings of the 35th International Conference on Machine Learning, pp. 284–293 (2018)
3. Carlini, N., et al.: Hidden voice commands. In: 25th USENIX Security Symposium, pp. 513–530 (2016)
4. Carlini, N., Wagner, D.A.: Adversarial examples are not easily detected: bypassing ten detection methods. In: Proceedings of the 10th ACM Workshop on Artificial Intelligence and Security, pp. 3–14 (2017)
5. Carlini, N., Wagner, D.A.: Towards evaluating the robustness of neural networks. In: 2017 IEEE Symposium on Security and Privacy, pp. 39–57 (2017)
6. Chen, P., Sharma, Y., Zhang, H., Yi, J., Hsieh, C.: EAD: elastic-net attacks to deep neural networks via adversarial examples. In: Proceedings of the Thirty-Second AAAI Conference on Artificial Intelligence, pp. 10–17 (2018)
7. Dong, Y., et al.: Boosting adversarial attacks with momentum. In: 2018 IEEE Conference on Computer Vision and Pattern Recognition, pp. 9185–9193 (2018)
8. Eykholt, K., et al.: Robust physical-world attacks on deep learning visual classification. In: 2018 IEEE Conference on Computer Vision and Pattern Recognition, pp. 1625–1634 (2018)
9. Goodfellow, I.J., Shlens, J., Szegedy, C.: Explaining and harnessing adversarial examples. In: 3rd International Conference on Learning Representations (2015)
10. Graves, A., Mohamed, A., Hinton, G.E.: Speech recognition with deep recurrent neural networks. In: IEEE International Conference on Acoustics, Speech and Signal Processing, pp. 6645–6649 (2013)
11. Grosse, K., Manoharan, P., Papernot, N., Backes, M., McDaniel, P.D.: On the (statistical) detection of adversarial examples. CoRR. arXiv:1702.06280 (2017)
12. He, K., Zhang, X., Ren, S., Sun, J.: Deep residual learning for image recognition. In: 2016 IEEE Conference on Computer Vision and Pattern Recognition, pp. 770–778 (2016)
13. He, W., Wei, J., Chen, X., Carlini, N., Song, D.: Adversarial example defense: ensembles of weak defenses are not strong. In: 11th USENIX Workshop on Offensive Technologies (2017)
14. Kurakin, A., Goodfellow, I.J., Bengio, S.: Adversarial examples in the physical world. In: 5th International Conference on Learning Representations (2017)
15. Kurakin, A., Goodfellow, I.J., Bengio, S.: Adversarial machine learning at scale. In: 5th International Conference on Learning Representations (2017)
16. Lu, J., Issaranon, T., Forsyth, D.A.: SafetyNet: detecting and rejecting adversarial examples robustly. In: IEEE International Conference on Computer Vision, pp. 446–454 (2017)
17. Madry, A., Makelov, A., Schmidt, L., Tsipras, D., Vladu, A.: Towards deep learning models resistant to adversarial attacks. In: 6th International Conference on Learning Representations (2018)
18. Meng, D., Chen, H.: MagNet: a two-pronged defense against adversarial examples. In: Proceedings of the 2017 ACM SIGSAC Conference on Computer and Communications Security, pp. 135–147 (2017)
19. Metzen, J.H., Genewein, T., Fischer, V., Bischoff, B.: On detecting adversarial perturbations. In: 5th International Conference on Learning Representations (2017)

20. Moosavi-Dezfooli, S., Fawzi, A., Frossard, P.: DeepFool: a simple and accurate method to fool deep neural networks. In: 2016 IEEE Conference on Computer Vision and Pattern Recognition, pp. 2574–2582 (2016)
21. Papernot, N., McDaniel, P.D., Goodfellow, I.J., Jha, S., Celik, Z.B., Swami, A.: Practical black-box attacks against deep learning systems using adversarial examples. CoRR. arXiv:1602.02697 (2016)
22. Papernot, N., McDaniel, P.D., Wu, X., Jha, S., Swami, A.: Distillation as a defense to adversarial perturbations against deep neural networks. In: IEEE Symposium on Security and Privacy, pp. 582–597 (2016)
23. Sabour, S., Cao, Y., Faghri, F., Fleet, D.J.: Adversarial manipulation of deep representations. In: 4th International Conference on Learning Representations (2016)
24. Song, Y., Kim, T., Nowozin, S., Ermon, S., Kushman, N.: PixelDefend: leveraging generative models to understand and defend against adversarial examples. In: 6th International Conference on Learning Representations (2018)
25. Szegedy, C., et al.: Intriguing properties of neural networks. In: 2nd International Conference on Learning Representations (2014)
26. Tramèr, F., Kurakin, A., Papernot, N., Goodfellow, I.J., Boneh, D., McDaniel, P.D.: Ensemble adversarial training: attacks and defenses. In: 6th International Conference on Learning Representations (2018)
27. Uesato, J., O'Donoghue, B., Kohli, P., van den Oord, A.: Adversarial risk and the dangers of evaluating against weak attacks. In: Proceedings of the 35th International Conference on Machine Learning, pp. 5032–5041 (2018)
28. Wu, Y., Bamman, D., Russell, S.J.: Adversarial training for relation extraction. In: Proceedings of the 2017 Conference on Empirical Methods in Natural Language Processing, pp. 1778–1783 (2017)

Capturing the Persistence of Facial Expression Features for Deepfake Video Detection

Yiru Zhao[1], Wanfeng Ge[1], Wenxin Li[1], Run Wang[1], Lei Zhao[1,2(✉)], and Jiang Ming[3]

[1] School of Cyber Science and Engineering, Wuhan University, Wuhan, China
leizhao@whu.edu.cn
[2] Key Laboratory of Aerospace Information Security and Trusted Computing, Ministry of Education, Wuhan, China
[3] University of Texas at Arlington, Arlington, USA

Abstract. The security of the Deepfake video has become the focus of social concern. This kind of fake video not only infringes copyright and privacy but also poses potential risks to politics, journalism, social trust, and other aspects. Unfortunately, fighting against Deepfake video is still in its early stage and practical solutions are required. Currently, biological signal based and learning-based are two major ways in detecting Deepfake video. We explore that facial expression between two adjacent frames appears significant differences in generative adversarial network (GAN)-synthesized fake video, while in a real video the facial expression looks naturally and transforms in a smooth way across frames. In this paper, we employ optical flow to capture the obvious differences of facial expressions between adjacent frames in a video and incorporate the temporal characteristics of consecutive frames into a convolutional neural network (CNN) model to distinguish the Deepfake video. In our experiments, we evaluate the effectiveness of our approach on a publicly fake video dataset, FaceForensics++. Experimental results show that our proposed approach achieves an accuracy higher than 98.1% and the AUC score reaches more than 0.9981.

Keywords: Deepfake Detection · Temporal features · Spatial features · Optical flow

1 Introduction

With the remarkable progress of GANs in image synthesis, we cannot believe our eyes in the AI era. Fake videos can be easily generated with tools such as FaceSwap [2], Deepfacelab [1], FaceApp [5] by touching a few keys on devices. These tools leverage the power of GANs in image synthesis and provide quite interesting functionalities to users, for instance, users can swap one's face to others and create a nearly realistic fake video. As shown in Fig. 1, A physically

© Springer Nature Switzerland AG 2020
J. Zhou et al. (Eds.): ICICS 2019, LNCS 11999, pp. 630–645, 2020.
https://doi.org/10.1007/978-3-030-41579-2_37

discordant person can do a great dance by changing faces with someone from dance video. However, this also brings some security concerns and privacy issues to users when the image synthesis techniques are abused.

Everyone will be the victims including celebrities and politicians. A celebrity's face could be swapped to a naked body and an illusory official statement can be announced by a politician in an AI-synthesized fake video. Thus, it is crucial to call for effective ways for spotting these AI-synthesized fake videos which are also known as Deepfake [3]. There are three common types of Deepfake, namely face swapping, lip-sync, and puppet-master [11]. In our work, we mainly focus on face swapping which is widely used in free tools (e.g. ZAO [9]) and could easily incur misinformation dissemination in social networks.

Detecting manipulated media content is a longstanding research focus. However, traditional techniques face many challenges for detecting the Deepfake video. These techniques extract pix-level or color-level statistical features [15,18,19], which can be easily suffered by compression, resizing, etc. In generating videos, compression and resizing is common operations, thus traditional image forensics techniques failed in fake video detection.

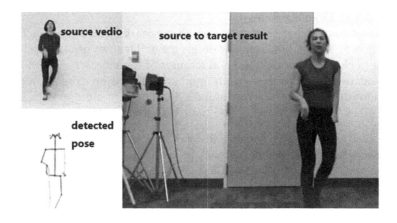

Fig. 1. Deepfake video

Existing work on detecting Deepfake videos can be summarized into two categories, biological signal based and learning-based. Agarwal et al. [11] observed that individual exhibits distinct patterns of facial and head movement when speaking, while Deepfake video tends to disrupt these particular patterns. Yang et al. [24] investigated that current neural network synthesized faces appear mismatched facial landmarks. Li et al. [16] distinguished fake videos by capturing the frequency of eye blinking. Some researchers [17] noticed that the synthesized faces in Deepfake video always in a fixed size. Afshar et al. [10] proposed detecting Deepfake video with the basic insight that some frames in Deepfake video exhibit large blurred areas or a double facial contour. These work pay attention to extract obvious biological signal features that are unrealistic in real videos. Some work leverage the power of neural networks in feature representation. The basic insight of these work is that the inconsistencies are introduced across frames in synthesizing fake videos, particularly temporal discrepancies across frames [14,21].

In our work, we explore another biological signal features which can be applied in distinguishing Deepfake videos. Facial expression in adjacent frames should be transformed naturally and has strong correlations, while it is hard to be overcome in synthesizing fake videos as facial expression patterns are always inadequate for individuals. In the meantime, we find optical flow can capture the subtle facial expression variations in consecutive frames effectively.

In this work, we employ optical flow to characterize the temporal changes of facial expressions, that is, the temporal features proposed in this paper. Then we use the convolutional neural network to extract the spatial features of the original images. According to the Spatial-temporal characteristics consistency of subtle expressions, we use the convolutional neural network to extract the features at a deep level to detect the Deepfake video. Our contributions are:

1. In this paper, we observed that facial expression between two adjacent frames in the Deepfake videos appears significant differences, which can be used to better detect Deepfake videos.
2. We employ optical flow to capture the differences of facial expression between two adjacent frames based on our observation. Then we use the optical flow graphs to characterize the temporal features of the videos.
3. We evaluate the effectiveness of our approach on FaceForensics++, a publicly fake video dataset. The experimental results show that our approach achieves an accuracy higher than 98.1% and the AUC score reaches more than 0.9981.

The rest of this paper is organized as follows. Section 2 introduces the background. Section 3 describes our approach in detail. Section 4 presents the implementation and evaluation of our method, Sect. 5.

2   Background

In this section, we firstly introduce the generation of Deepfake videos. Then we further analyze its vulnerabilities.

2.1   Deepfake Video Generation

One way to generate Deepfake videos is to use an encoder-decoder model based on AI, which consists of two processes, the training process as well as the generation process. In the training process, two neural networks are trained, each of which is composed of an encoder network and a decoder network. For input pictures of two different faces A and B, the encoder network first compresses the face data in each picture into a low-dimensional vector and then uses the decoder network to decode the low-dimensional vector obtained in the previous step to generate the decoded picture. Then the network is optimized by minimizing the difference between the decoded image and the input image. The encoder network of the two images must remain consistent during the training phase, in order to extract the consistency of the features in these two pictures. In the generation process, we use the trained decoder B to decode the encoded low-dimensional vector of A, so that we get the face-changing image of A.

In general, the overall process of the training process is to extract the features of two different faces (original face and target face) with the encoder of the same parameters and then recover the target face image with the decoder trained from the target face. The encoder is a convolutional neural network that extracts features such as facial features, expressions and so on from the image input. The decoder recovers the original image from the extracted features according to the parameters of the encoder [14]. The encoder contains a general method for extracting the typical features of human faces, and different decoders can recover different faces from the extracted features.

Another more common way to generate Deepfake videos is based on Generative Adversarial Network (GAN)[13]. As is shown in Fig. 2. A Generative Adversarial Network consists of two parts: the generator and the discriminator. The generator takes face samples that need to be swapped as input to generate false video. The discriminator is simply a classifier trained with supervised learning techniques to check if the video is real or fake. The generator and the discriminator are rivals of each other. All the parameters are trained until convergence.

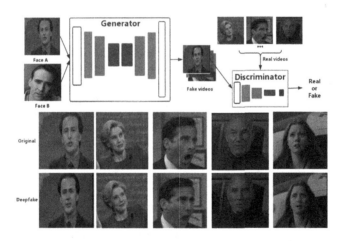

Fig. 2. The procedure of face swapping with GANs

2.2 Vulnerability of Deepfake Videos

Through the above analysis, we can see that when generating Deepfake videos, the face is replaced frame by frame, and then the complete video is synthesized. As is well known, video differs from images in that video is composed of many consecutive frames. For real video, successive frames represent continuous changes in the target object over time, so they have strong consistency. In contrast, a Deepfake video will inevitably break the consistency between adjacent frames by processing each frame and then combining them. In other words, the facial expression of the target area in the Deepfake video will have a certain degree of distortion and anomalies. Therefore, extracting the characteristics of the variation between adjacent frames helps us to get a more comprehensive Deepfake video feature.

3   Our Approach

In order to extract the characteristics of the variation between adjacent frames, we need to get the change of pixels within the image sequence in the time domain and the correlation between adjacent frames to find the correspondence between the previous frame and the current frame. Calculating optical flow is such a method. In this paper, we characterize the temporal features by calculating the optical flow fields of the facial images in two consecutive frames.

However, we want to extract deeper features. We use a convolutional neural network (CNN) to obtain the spatial features of the frame and combine them with the temporal features. Based on the consistency of space-temporal characteristics, our CNN-based deep learning model can acquire deeper features.

We build a model that consists of four parts: data preprocessing, spatial feature extraction, temporal feature extraction, and deep learning model.

At first, we processed video data set into pictures frame by frame and intercepted the faces in the pictures. Then, we use CNN to extract the spatial features of human faces. At the same time, we calculate the optical flow between two continuous pictures of human faces to obtain the optical flow diagrams. After that, the powerful self-extraction ability of CNN is used to extract the temporal features of optical flow diagrams. According to the consistency of space-temporal characteristics, we combine the temporal and spatial characteristics so that CNN can acquire deeper features. Finally, we train the deep learning model to implement Deepfake video detection. The entire process is shown in Fig. 3.

3.1   Data Preprocessing

In general, data preprocessing is a common requirement for many learning algorithms and models. Data preprocessing describes any type of processing performed on raw data to prepare it for another processing procedure. In this paper, the data preprocessing stage mainly consists of three steps: extracting image frames from the video, extracting the face region from the image, and sequentially storing the images.

First, we selected training data sets and verification data sets from real videos and Deepfake videos. Then we separate frames from the original video data sets frame by frame. We do video segmentation and then extract the face region of every frame. At last, the processed face images are stored in the order of the video frame sequence number.

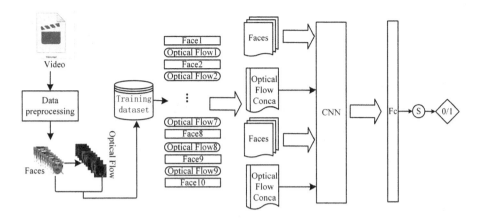

Fig. 3. Overall framework of the model

3.2 Temporal Feature Extraction Based on Optical Flow

We know that when generating Deepfake videos, the face is replaced frame by frame, and then the complete video is synthesized. Such a process neglects the consistency of slight changes in facial expressions between frames in the original video, which is likely to bring about disharmonious cases. In most cases, the emotions of people do not change suddenly, in other words, the expressions of human beings change continuously in normal videos. That is to say, the emotions reflected by their facial expressions between adjacent frames should be consistent. However, since each frame is independent, videos generated by the Deepfake technique do not always take into account this kind of situation, leading to inconsistent facial expressions between adjacent frames. It may be hard to tell with the naked eye, but it is not difficult for the machine to recognize.

Therefore, we need to find the correspondence between the previous frame and the current frame. Calculating optical flow is a method of calculating the change of pixels within image sequence in the time domain and the correlation between adjacent frames, thereby calculating the motion of the object between adjacent frames. Optical flow is the instantaneous velocity of a moving pixel within the image. If the time interval is small enough, the velocity can be expressed by displacement. In simple terms, assuming that the angle of observation is constant, the optical flow represents the movement of a point from the first frame to the second frame. For example, for two adjacent frames in a video, or frames extracted from a video at a small-time interval, the instantaneous velocity of pixel movement can be expressed by displacement. We usually regard it as a two-dimensional vector $u = (u,v)$ describing the instantaneous velocity of the pixel, which is also called the optical flow vector.

Optical flow can be divided into two types, dense optical flow, and sparse optical flow [22]. The dense optical flow performs point-by-point matching on the image to calculate the offset of all points on the image, while the sparse optical flow only needs to specify a set of points with obvious characteristics for tracking. In contrast, due to the denser optical flow vector, dense optical flow is significantly better than the sparse optical flow at the registration effect, but at the same time, the calculation amount is larger because the offset of each point is calculated. In our work, we select dense optical flow because the amount of image pixels that need to be calculated is limited and the demand for accuracy is high.

OpenCV [22] provides an algorithm for calculating dense optical flows: the Farneback dense optical flow algorithm. The principle is briefly described below [16]. The working principle of the optical flow method is based on the following assumptions [23]:

1. The brightness of the target pixel does not change between two consecutive frames of images.
2. There is a similar motion between adjacent pixels.

We define $X = [x, y]$ as one pixel position in the image and t as time. We note the brightness of $X = [x, y]$ at time t as $I(x, y, t)$.

For two consecutive frames in the image, since the brightness of the target pixel does not change, the brightness of the same pixel in these two frames does not change, which is expressed as:

$$I(x, y, t) = I(x + \Delta x, y + \Delta y, t + \Delta t) \tag{1}$$

We use the first order Taylor expansion at $I(x, y, t)$ of formula (1), and get formula (2):

$$I(x + \Delta x, y + \Delta y, t + \Delta t) = I(x, y, t) + \frac{\partial I}{\partial x} dx + \frac{\partial I}{\partial y} dy + \frac{\partial I}{\partial t} dt + \xi \tag{2}$$

In formula (2), ξ is the second order infinitesimal in Taylor's expansion, which can be ignored. Substituting formula 2 into formula 1, and divide both sides by dt, we get:

$$\frac{I(x, y, t)}{dt} = \frac{\partial I}{\partial x}\frac{dx}{dt} + \frac{\partial I}{\partial y}\frac{dy}{dt} + \frac{\partial I}{\partial t} = 0 \tag{3}$$

It is obvious that $\frac{dx}{dt}$ and $\frac{dy}{dt}$ represent the motion vectors of the tracked pixel points in the x-axis direction and the y-axis direction. Let $u = \frac{dx}{dt}$, $v = \frac{dy}{dt}$, then (u, v) is the desired optical flow. This feature is very suitable for the temporal feature extraction in this paper.

3.3   Spatial Feature Extraction Based on CNN

According to the consistency of space-temporal features, we want to extract the spatial features of adjacent frames. Considering that the convolutional neural network (CNN) has a strong self-learning ability, we hope to build our own network to learn and capture the characteristics such as low-level features, contour, grayscale, texture, and other features. These features can well reflect some subtle abnormalities of the human face in Deepfake videos, such as edge stiffness, jitter, distortion, color and so on.

3.4   Deep Learning Model

We obtain the optical flow diagram by calculating the optical flow and extract the spatial features between adjacent frames through the convolutional neural network. We combine the two features and use the convolutional neural network to further extract the deeper features. Considering the excellent performance of CNN in image classification, we decided to use this type of network to implement our detection. The general structure is shown in Fig. 4. Then we trained and verified the model on the data set, adjusted and modified the network structure with poor verification performance, and finally got the model that performed well on both the training set and the verification set.

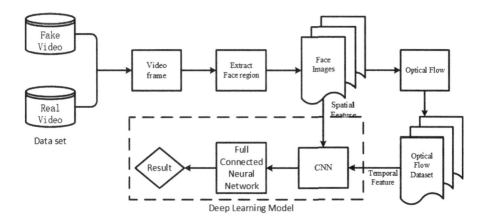

Fig. 4. The Structure of our deep learning model

The neural network has one input layer, four convolutional layers, four batch normalization layers, four pooling layers, one flatten layer, two dropout layers, and three dense layers. The specific information of each part is as follows:

1. Input layer: This layer accepts ten 256*256*3 original frames and two 256*256*8 optical flow diagrams as input at a time.
2. The parameters of convolutional layers and pooling layers, as well as the processing results of each layer, are shown in Table 1.
3. Batch normalization layer: This layer normalizes the data of each batch to ensure the rapid convergence of the model.
4. flatten layer: This layer is mainly used to "flatten" the data input from the convolutional layer, that is, to convert multidimensional data to one-dimensional input.
5. Dropout layer 1: Whenever parameters are updated each the time during training, the input neurons are randomly disconnected with a probability of 0.5.

6. Dense layer 1: Fully connected layer with 16 units. It calculates the dot product between the input vector and the weight vector to obtains 16 outputs, and inputs the result to the Leaky ReLU activation function for nonlinear processing.
7. Dropout layer 2: The input neurons are randomly disconnected with a probability of 0.5 each time the parameters are updated during the training.
8. Dense layer 2: Fully connected layer with 1 unit. It calculates the dot product between the input vector and the weight vector to get 1 output.
9. Dense layer 3: Fully connected layer with 1 unit. This layer accepts the processing result of 10 video frames and 2 optical flow pictures as input, and then output the final classification result.

Table 1. Parameters and results of convolutional layers and pooling layers

Layers	Filter size	Step length	Number of convolutional kernels	Activation function	Feature map
Convolutional layer C1	3*3	1	8	Relu	256*256*8
Pooling layer M1	Pooling window size: 2*2				128*128*8
Convolutional layer C2	5*5	1	8	Relu	128*128*8
Pooling layer M2	Pooling window size: 2*2				64*64*8
Convolutional layer C3	5*5	1	16	Relu	64*64*16
Pooling layer M3	Pooling window size: 2*2				32*32*16
Convolutional layer C4	5*5	1	16	Relu	32*32*16
Pooling layer M4	Pooling window size: 4*4				8*8*16

Each layer of CNN plays its role. The convolutional layer extracts the features of the image, and its weight sharing and partial connection structure reduces the number of parameters that need to be optimized. The batch normalization layer speeds up the convergence of the model. The pooling layer compresses the data, reducing memory consumption. The Dropout layer helps avoid over-fitting. After the network completes the training, the obtained CNN model and its parameters can be used for verification and testing. We modify and adjust the structure of the model several times according to the verification performance. Finally, we choose the neural network with the highest accuracy. Figure 5 show the feature map of the input optical flow map after every convolutional layer.

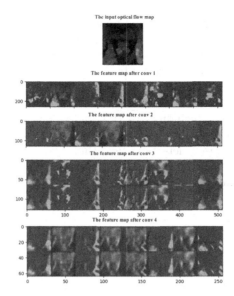

Fig. 5. The intermediate results

4 Implementation and Evaluation

In this section, we briefly introduce our dataset and experimental process. Finally, we evaluate our model's performance and analyze the experiment results.

4.1 Experimental Setup

To evaluate our method, we use the FaceForensics++ Datasets published on github [1], which is an open dataset containing 1000 Deepfake standard-definition videos and 1000 real standard-definition videos collected from several social media platforms. Since the dataset is open source and diverse, evaluation based on it ensures that our method is effective and robust.

The experiments in this paper were performed on a Windows 10 desktop computer with an Intel(R) Core(TM) i7-8700CPU@3.20 GHz, a memory of 16 GB, and a GPU for the Nvidia GTX1080ti. The deep learning model was built using Keras 2.2.4 [7] and used Tensorflow 1.8.0 [8] as the backend engine.

4.2 Experiment Process

Our experiment contains several steps.

Firstly, we randomly select 850 videos from 1000 real videos and 850 from 1000 Deepfake videos as the training dataset. As for the testing dataset, we randomly select 100 videos from each category respectively.

Secondly, we separate frames from the original video data set frame by frame. In this paper, we use FFmpeg [6] to separate frames from the original video data set frame by frame. FFmpeg is the leading multimedia framework, able to decode, encode, transcode, mux, demux, stream, filter and play pretty much anything that humans and machines have created. We use the Python language to call the FFmpeg program for video framing.

Thirdly, we do video segmentation and then extract the face region of every frame. We use Dlib [4], which is a modern C++ toolkit containing machine learning algorithms and tools, including the HOG-SVM algorithm for face detection and multiple detection algorithms based on CNN. Through experiments, we found that the CNN-based detection algorithms are better, so we choose the latter to get face position information. Then we use OpenCV [22] to crop the obtained face position information and save it as a 256*256 3-channel .png format image. The number of images in the dataset is shown in Table 2.

Table 2. Experimental data

Class	Training	Verification
Deepfake frames	**17116**	1924
Real frames	**17191**	1962
Total frames	**34307**	3886

Then, we calculate the optical flow fields of the facial images in two consecutive frames. We use OpenCV, which provides a function called calcOpticalFlow-Farneback to implement the Farneback dense optical flow algorithm. The image of the human facial area extracted from the video is an RGB image, but the Farneback dense optical flow algorithm can only calculate a grayscale image. So it is necessary to first convert the RGB image into a grayscale image. Besides, we need to take care that the input of this function is an 8-bit single-channel picture of 256*256 pixels of two consecutive frames, while the output is a CV_32FC2 format optical flow image of the same size as the input picture which is a two-channel image. We calculate 4 optical flow maps between 5 frames, and we define the combination of the above-mentioned pictures as a group. We use two continuous groups as an input as is shown in Fig. 6, and then mark it with 1 for fake video or 0 for real video.

At last, we incorporate the temporal features with spatial features of consecutive frames into a convolutional neural network (CNN) model to distinguish the Deepfake video.

4.3 Experimental Result

In the experiment, we set the iteration of the model to 80 times, and the loss function of the deep learning model to MSE (mean square error). The calculation method is as follows:

$$Loss = \frac{1}{2m} \sum_{i=1}^{m} (\hat{y_i} - y_i)^2 \tag{4}$$

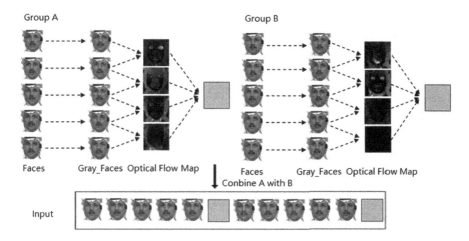

Fig. 6. The generation of input sequence

$\hat{y}_i$ is the predicted value of the model, and y_i is the label of the sample. Loss function can well represent the fitting degree between the predicted results of the model and the real label, and the smaller the value, the better. As shown in Fig. 7, With the increase of training times, the loss function value of the model gradually decreases.

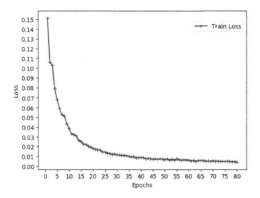

Fig. 7. The changing curve of loss

Accuracy is an important evaluation index for the classification model. The accuracy is defined in a standard way as formula 5. TP stands for True Positive, the number of Deepfake images correctly classified. TN is True Negative, referring to the number of True images correctly classified. FP is False Positive and refers to the number of Deepfake images misclassified. FN is False Negative and is the number of true images wrongly classified. The higher the accuracy, the better the accuracy of the model.

$$accuracy = \frac{TP + TN}{TP + FP + TN + FN} \tag{5}$$

Besides, the ROC curve is also selected as the evaluation standard, which can well describe the generalization performance of the model. The ROC curve plots the TPR (True Positive Rate) against the FPR (False Positive Rate) for every test case. We then calculate the AUC (Area Under the ROC curve) to characterize how well the model performs. The closer is AUC to 1, the better the model performance. The formula of TPR, FPR, and AUC is as follows:

$$TPR = \frac{TP}{TP + FN} \tag{6}$$

$$FPR = \frac{FP}{FP + TN} \tag{7}$$

$$AUC = \frac{1}{2} \sum_{i=1}^{m-1} (FPR_{i+1} - FPR_i)(TPR_i + TPR_{i+1}) \tag{8}$$

Figure 8 shows the system accuracy on both training sets and test set as the epoch number grows. It indicates that our method could achieve accuracy greater than 98% on the training set and 96% on the testing set after 40 iterations. Figure 9 shows the ROC curve. In paper [20], the author compares many models using the FaceForensics++ data set. We chose the two models MesoNet [10] and XceptionNet [12] to compare with our model, because only MesoNet and XceptionNet are the detection models for Deepfake. Then we reproduce these two models and experiment with our models on the same training and validation sets. Since some parameters in the experiment are different from those in Paper [20], such as data set division and CPU parameters. In order to compare the effects of models in various aspects, AUC is also selected as the comparison standard. our experimental results are shown in the Table 3. It is obvious that our method achieves far higher accuracy on the standard definition dataset than other deep learning models.

In contrast, our model has achieved ideal results in all indicators while maintaining a simple model structure. Since fake videos detecting applications always require detecting algorithm to be low time and computation consumed, our system meets the demand with high practicality and accuracy.

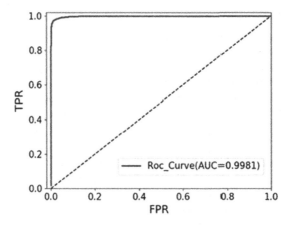

Fig. 8. ROC curve

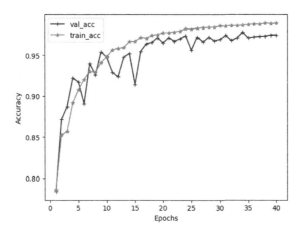

Fig. 9. The changing curve of model accuracy

Table 3. Comparison of accuracy results

Deep learning model	Accuracy (%)	AUC results
MesoNet [10]	**92.00%**	**0.9859**
XceptionNet [12]	**95.73%**	**0.6653**
Our model	**98.10%**	**0.9981**

5   Conclusion

Nowadays, fighting against Deepfake videos has become more and more important. In this paper, by analyzing the generation process of video, we find that
facial expressions between adjacent frames are inevitably abnormal. In response

to this phenomenon, we propose a Deepfake video detection method base on subtle facial expressions. We employ optical flow to capture the obvious differences of facial expressions between adjacent frames in a video and incorporate the temporal characteristics of consecutive frames into a convolutional neural network (CNN) model to distinguish the Deepfake video.

According to experiment results, our model achieves great performance, with an accuracy much higher than most of the existing models, and at the same time, the complexity of the model can be greatly reduced.

In conclusion, our method can ensure both effectiveness and practicability. Our future work includes doing further research on deep fake videos with different quality levels, and realize automatic adjustment of parameters.

Acknowledgment. This work is partly supported by National Natural Science Foundation of China under Grant No.61672394 and 61872273. Any opinions, findings, and conclusions or recommendations expressed in this paper are those of the authors and do not necessarily reflect the views of the funding agencies.

References

1. Deepfacelab. http://deepfakes.com.cn/. Accessed 22 Apr 2019
2. Deepfake github. http://github.com/deepfakes/faceswap. Accessed 20 Apr 2019
3. Deepfake wikipedia. https://en.wikipedia.org/wiki/Deepfake. Accessed 12 Sept 2019
4. Dlib. http://dlib.net/. Accessed 20 Mar 2019
5. Fakeapp. http://www.fakeapp.com/. Accessed 22 Apr 2019
6. Ffmpeg. http://ffmpeg.org/. Accessed 20 Mar 2019
7. Keras. http://keras.io/. Accessed 10 July 2018
8. Tensorflow. http://tensorflow.google.cn/. Accessed 10 July 2018
9. Zao. https://apps.apple.com/cn/app/zao/id1465199127. Accessed 12 Sept 2019
10. Afchar, D., Nozick, V., Yamagishi, J., Echizen, I.: Mesonet: a compact facial video forgery detection network. In: 2018 IEEE International Workshop on Information Forensics and Security, WIFS 2018, Hong Kong, China, 11–13 December 2018, pp. 1–7 (2018). https://doi.org/10.1109/WIFS.2018.8630761
11. Agarwal, S., Farid, H., Gu, Y., He, M., Nagano, K., Li, H.: Protecting world leaders against deep fakes. In: Proceedings of the IEEE Conference on Computer Vision and Pattern Recognition Workshops, pp. 38–45 (2019)
12. Chollet, F.: Xception: deep learning with depthwise separable convolutions. In: 2017 IEEE Conference on Computer Vision and Pattern Recognition, CVPR 2017, Honolulu, HI, USA, 21–26 July 2017, pp. 1800–1807 (2017). https://doi.org/10. 1109/CVPR.2017.195
13. Goodfellow, I.J., et al.: Generative adversarial networks. CoRR abs/1406.2661 (2014). http://arxiv.org/abs/1406.2661
14. Güera, D., Delp, E.J.: Deepfake video detection using recurrent neural networks. In: 2018 15th IEEE International Conference on Advanced Video and Signal Based Surveillance (AVSS), pp. 1–6 (2018). https://doi.org/10.1109/AVSS.2018.8639163
15. Li, H., Li, B., Tan, S., Huang, J.: Detection of deep network generated images using disparities in color components. arXiv preprint arXiv:1808.07276 (2018)

16. Li, Y., Chang, M., Lyu, S.: In ictu oculi: exposing AI created fake videos by detecting eye blinking. In: 2018 IEEE International Workshop on Information Forensics and Security, WIFS 2018, Hong Kong, China, 11–13 December 2018, pp. 1–7 (2018). https://doi.org/10.1109/WIFS.2018.8630787

17. Lyu, Y.L.S.: Exposing deepfake videos by detecting face warping artifacts. CoRR abs/1811.00656 (2018). http://arxiv.org/abs/1811.00656

18. McCloskey, S., Albright, M.: Detecting GAN-generated imagery using color cues. arXiv preprint arXiv:1812.08247 (2018)

19. Nataraj, L., et al.: Detecting GAN generated fake images using co-occurrence matrices. arXiv preprint arXiv:1903.06836 (2019)

20. Rössler, A., Cozzolino, D., Verdoliva, L., Riess, C., Thies, J., Nießner, M.: Faceforensics: a large-scale video dataset for forgery detection in human faces. CoRR abs/1803.09179 (2018). http://arxiv.org/abs/1803.09179

21. Sabir, E., Cheng, J., Jaiswal, A., AbdAlmageed, W., Masi, I., Natarajan, P.: Recurrent convolutional strategies for face manipulation detection in videos. Interfaces (GUI) **3**, 1 (2019)

22. Taheri, S., Veidenbaum, A.V., Nicolau, A., Hu, N., Haghighat, M.R.: Opencv.js: computer vision processing for the open web platform. In: Proceedings of the 9th ACM Multimedia Systems Conference, MMSys 2018, Amsterdam, The Netherlands, 12–15 June 2018, pp. 478–483 (2018). https://doi.org/10.1145/3204949.3208126

23. Wang, L., et al.: Temporal segment networks: towards good practices for deep action recognition. In: Leibe, B., Matas, J., Sebe, N., Welling, M. (eds.) ECCV 2016. LNCS, vol. 9912, pp. 20–36. Springer, Cham (2016). https://doi.org/10.1007/978-3-319-46484-8_2

24. Yang, X., Li, Y., Lyu, S.: Exposing deep fakes using inconsistent head poses. In: IEEE International Conference on Acoustics, Speech and Signal Processing, ICASSP 2019, Brighton, United Kingdom, 12–17 May 2019, pp. 8261–8265 (2019). https://doi.org/10.1109/ICASSP.2019.8683164

Machine Learning Privacy

Differentially Private Frequent Itemset Mining Against Incremental Updates

Wenjuan Liang[1,2], Hong Chen[1(✉)], Yuncheng Wu[1], and Cuiping Li[1]

[1] Key Lab of Data Engineering and Knowledge Engineering of MOE,
Renmin University of China, Beijing, China
{liangwenjuan,chong,yunchengwu,licuiping}@ruc.edu.cn
[2] College of Computer and Information Engineering,
Henan University, Kaifeng, China

Abstract. Differential privacy has recently been applied to frequent itemset mining (FIM). Most existing works focus on promoting result utility while satisfying differential privacy. However, they all focus on "one-shot" release of a static dataset, which do not adequately address the increasing need for up-to-date sensitive information. In this paper, we address the problem of differentially private FIM for dynamic datasets, and propose a scheme against infinite incremental updates which satisfies ϵ-differential privacy in any sliding window. To reduce the increasing perturbation error against incremental updates, we design an adaptive budget allocation scheme combining with transactional dataset change. To reduce the high sensitivity of one-shot release, we split long transactions and analyze its information loss. Then we privately compute the approximate number of frequent itemsets. Based on the above results, we design a threshold exponential mechanism to privately release frequent itemsets. Through formal privacy analysis, we show that our scheme satisfies ϵ-differential privacy in any sliding window. Extensive experiment results on real-world datasets illustrate that our scheme achieves high utility and efficiency.

Keywords: FIM · Incremental updates · w-event privacy · Differential privacy

1 Introduction

Frequent itemset mining is a fundamental component in many important data mining applications, such as web log mining, trend analysis and fraud detection etc. Since transactions in the database are changing, it is necessary to update frequent itemsets as time goes on. Directly releasing frequent itemsets and their support may breach the privacy of individuals. In particular, continually updating statistics over time leaks more and more information to the attackers. If a subset of history transactions for some user is available to the attacker, with the updated frequent itemsets in the outputs, an inference attack is successful [1,2],

© Springer Nature Switzerland AG 2020
J. Zhou et al. (Eds.): ICICS 2019, LNCS 11999, pp. 649–667, 2020.
https://doi.org/10.1007/978-3-030-41579-2_38

which can be seen in Fig. 1. So how to protect the privacy of individuals while getting a continuously updated statistics is important. Differential privacy [3] is a strong and rigorous standard privacy guarantee against adversaries with any background knowledge. In this paper, we focus on differentially private frequent itemset mining against infinite incremental updates.

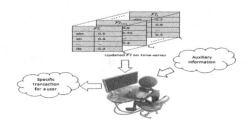

Fig. 1. An attack scenario

By adding a carefully chosen amount of noise, differential privacy assures that the output of a computation is insensitive to any individual tuple in the input, and thus privacy is protected. The magnitude of added noise is determined by the privacy budget ϵ and the sensitivity of the computation. The greater the privacy budget, the less the added noise, vice versa. For the same privacy budget ϵ, the greater the sensitivity, the more the added noise.

To the best of our knowledge, there is no literature on differentially private FIM on dynamic scenario. Due to the inherent dynamics and high-dimensionality of transactional dataset, there are **two challenges** to apply differential privacy to our problem: First, with the number (N) of updates increasing, noise increases due to the composition theorem [3] of differential privacy. The perturbation error achieves to $O(N)$. To reduce this error, some works [19,23] propose sampling representative points to privately release or only consider the privacy of recent release. These methods are proposed to protect the continual release of simple statistics, and can not directly be used in our problem. To solve this challenge, we design an adaptive privacy budget allocation scheme for FIM on a dynamic scenario. We consider how to protect the privacy in every sliding window (w snapshots) of continually updated transactional datasets. Our scheme can reduce the perturbation error against incremental updates to $O(w)$.

Second, since long transactions cause the space of candidate frequent itemsets very large, the sensitivity of "one-shot" release is very high. For example, suppose the maximal length of transaction is l and the total size of items is $|I|$, it is not hard to show that the sensitivity is $O(\sum_{i=1}^{l} \binom{|I|}{l})$. The magnitude of noise added is too large, which reduces the utility of the release results. To solve this problem, existing works [5–8,10] of differentially private FIM on a static dataset present some schemes. For example, TT [8] first proposes truncating long transactions, and then it designs a private release scheme based on Apriori algorithm. PFP [5] first proposes splitting long transactions based on the relation of all items found in advance, and then it designs a private release scheme based on FP-growth algorithm. The preprocessing processes of the above schemes consume too much time, and their private release schemes are designed for the static scenario, which can not be used for the continual release. For the above reasons, we make the following contributions:

- For the first time we put forward a scheme for differentially private FIM against infinite incremental updates, which satisfies ϵ-differentially privacy in any sliding window. To reduce the increasing perturbation error against incremental updates and maximize the utility of privacy budget in the sliding window, we design an adaptive budget allocation scheme in the sliding window combining with transactional dataset change.
- To reduce the high sensitivity of one-shot release, we split long transactions based on random sampling and analyze its information loss. Then we privately calculate the approximate number of frequent itemsets. Based on the split dataset and the approximate number, we design a threshold exponential mechanism to privately release frequent itemsets at t_i. In the release process, we promote the result utility by offsetting the information loss and using the support threshold to further reduce the space of candidate frequent itemsets.
- Formal privacy analysis proves that our scheme satisfies ϵ-differential privacy in any sliding window. Extensive experiments on real datasets show our scheme achieves high data utility and efficiency.

The rest of the paper is organized as follows. Section 2 presents necessary background on differential privacy and problem statement. Section 3 proposes a private release scheme and gives a detailed privacy analysis. Comprehensive experimental results are reported in Sect. 4. Section 5 discusses the related works, and Sect. 6 concludes our work.

2   Preliminaries

2.1   Differential Privacy

In the definition of differential privacy [3], a randomized mechanism is differentially private if its outcome on any neighboring datasets (D, D') is almost the same. D can be attained from D' by adding(removing) one individual's record. In our problem, an adversary should learn approximately the same information about any individual user from two w-neighboring datasets D_w, D'_w. D'_w can be obtained from D_w by adding or removing one individual's transactions in any window of w snapshots.

Definition 1 *(w-event ϵ-**differential privacy**) [3,22]. A randomized mechanism M provides w-event ϵ-differential privacy, iff for any output O of M and for any two w-neighboring series of dynamic datasets D_w, D'_w, we have:*

$$Pr[M(D_w) \in O] \leq Pr[M(D'_w) \in O] \times e^\epsilon \tag{1}$$

ϵ is the privacy budget which reflects the level of the privacy.

Definition 2 (LM) [3]. *Given a query function* $f = <f_1, ..., f_d>$, *a mechanism M that adds i.i.d. Laplace noise to query result* $f(D)$ *can achieve* ϵ-*differential privacy, which is referred to as Laplace mechanism (LM).*

$$M(D) = f(D) + <\Delta_1, ..., \Delta_d> \tag{2}$$

where $\Delta_i \sim Lap(\frac{GS(f)}{\epsilon})$ $(1 \leq i \leq d)$, $GS(f) = max(\|f(D) - f(D')\|_1)$, *which is the sensitivity and reflects greatest impact on the result while adding or deleting one record in D.*

Definition 3 (EM) [4]. *Given the output domain R, the exponential mechanism (EM) requires a user-specified quality function* $u : (D \times O) \to R$, *u outputs a real-valued score that measures how desirable r is to the user (larger scores are preferred). To ensure* ϵ-*differential privacy, EM samples r from R with probability:*

$$Pr[r \in R] \propto exp(\frac{\epsilon u(D, r)}{2\Delta u}) \tag{3}$$

Where Δu *denotes the sensitivity of the quality function* u.

Theorem 1 (Sequential Composition) [3]. *Let* $M_1, \cdots, M_m$ *be m randomized algorithms, where* M_i *provides* ϵ_i-*differential privacy* $(1 \leq i \leq m)$. *A sequence of* $M_i(D)$ *over database D provides* $(\sum \epsilon_i)$-*differential privacy.*

2.2   Problem Formulation

Let N (N is an infinite number) denote the total number of incremental updates. Let $D = \{D_1, \cdots, D_N\}$ denote a series of dynamic transactional datasets, D_i is a snapshot at t_i, D_1 is the initial database. Let $\{\Delta D_1, \cdots, \Delta D_{N-1}\}$ denote the incremental datasets from t_2. For each t_i $(2 \leq i \leq N)$, $D_i = D_1 + \sum_{j=1}^{i-1} \Delta D_j$, and we aim to release a private frequent itemsets $\widehat{FI}_i$, which is a set of patterns whose support is greater than λ (support threshold). Over N time points, the series of noisy frequent itemsets $\widehat{FI} = \{\widehat{FI}_1, \cdots, \widehat{FI}_N\}$ should guarantee w-event ϵ-differential privacy in any sliding window of w snapshots.

3   Core Strategies

Our publishing mechanism M is composed of N sub mechanisms $M_1, \cdots, M_N$ (N is an infinite integer). Each $M_i(1 \leq i \leq N)$ is a random mechanism that operates on D_i and outputs a private frequent itemsets $\widehat{FI}_i$ at timestamps t_i. It contains the following two processes: the first one is privately computing the dissimilarity of the transactional datasets at adjacent timestamps. The second one is one-shot private release based on threshold exponential mechanism at t_i.

3.1   Adaptive Budget Allocation in a Sliding Window

To achieve ϵ-differential privacy in the sliding window, we can uniformly distribute ϵ to each release within any window of w consecutive timestamps. However, it results in a low utility. This motivates us to design an adaptive budget allocation scheme: Only when the change of transactional datasets between two consecutive timestamps is large enough will a private release be made. Otherwise the budget is saved to promote the subsequent release. We distribute the release budget in an exponentially decreasing fashion, and recycle the release budget spent in the time points falling outside the active window. In the above way, the sum of budgets of each release in any sliding window is at most ϵ and the overall utility can be improved. Detailed scheme is as follows: for each t_i, we use $\epsilon_{i,1} = \alpha\epsilon/w$ $(0 \leq \alpha \leq 1)$ to make a private dissimilarity computation (lines 2–4). If the dissimilarity is less than θ (dissimilarity threshold), we set $\epsilon_{i,2} = 0$, and make a passive release (lines 5–7), which means release $\widehat{FI}_{i-1}$ instead of $\widehat{FI}_i$. Otherwise, we compute the remaining budget ϵ_{rm} for the active window $[i - w + 1, i]$, $\epsilon_{rm} = (1 - \alpha)\epsilon - \sum_{k=i-w+1}^{i-1} \epsilon_{i,2}$, which means ϵ minus the dissimilarity budget spent in window $[i - w + 1, i]$ and the release budget spent in window $[i - w + 1, i - 1]$, and allocate ϵ_{rm} to $\epsilon_{i,2}$ in an exponentially decreasing fashion, $\epsilon_{i,2}$ is set to be $\epsilon_{rm}/2$. We use $\epsilon_{i,2}$ to make a private one-shot release at t_i (lines 9–11). Detailed privacy analysis can be seen in Sect. 3.3.

To capture the change of transactional datasets, a direct solution is computing the difference between $\widehat{FI}_i$ of the current time unit and $\widehat{FI}_{i-1}$ of the previous time unit. However, it is inefficient and the budget cannot be saved. We propose the following solution: we capture the change of transactional datasets by computing the dissimilarity of noisy frequent 1-items $\widehat{F}_i$ instead of noisy frequent itemsets $\widehat{FI}_i$, since according to Downward Closure Property, the change of $\widehat{F}_i$ can reflect the change of $\widehat{FI}_i$. To evaluate the difference of frequent 1-items, we modify the metric F-score [8]: $precision = |\widehat{F}_i \cap \widehat{F}_{i-1}|/|\widehat{F}_i|$, $recall = |\widehat{F}_i \cap \widehat{F}_{i-1}|/|\widehat{F}_{i-1}|$, $\widehat{F}_i$ is the frequent 1-items at t_i, $\widehat{F}_{i-1}$ is the frequent 1-items at t_{i-1}. To achieve differential privacy, before computing the dissimilarity, we add $Lap(\frac{l_{opt}}{\epsilon_{i,1}})$ to F_i, since the budget allocated here is $\epsilon_{i,1}$ and the sensitivity is l_{opt} (See the definition in Sect. 3.2). Detailed process can be seen in Algorithm 1.

3.2   Release Based on Threshold Exponential Mechanism

To reduce the sensitivity of one-shot release, we design a threshold exponential mechanism to privately release $\widehat{FI}_i$. According to exponential mechanism [4], the curial factors affecting utility are the privacy budget and the sensitivity of the release task. In our one-shot release, the budget allocated here is $\epsilon_{i,2}$, and the sensitivity is the number of all possible candidate frequent itemsets generated in the release process. If we design the private release scheme based on the original high sensitivity, it will result in a low utility. To improve the utility, we need to reduce the space of candidate frequent patterns set. The strategies

---

Algorithm 1. Adaptive Budget Allocation in Sliding Window

Input: D_i, $\widehat{F}_{i-1}$, $\widehat{FI}_{i-1}$, $(\epsilon_{i-w+1,2}, ..., \epsilon_{i-1,2})$, ϵ, w, l_{opt}, λ, θ;
Output: $\widehat{FI}_i$
1: Find the true frequent 1-items F_i based on D_i^- and λ.
2: Distribute the dissimilarity budget at t_i: $\epsilon_{i,1} = \alpha\epsilon/w(0 \leq \alpha \leq 1)$.
3: Compute noisy frequent 1-items: $\widehat{F}_i$ = Add $Lap(\frac{l_{opt}}{\epsilon_{i,1}})$ to F_i.
4: Compute the similarity between t_{i-1} and t_i:F-score=$2 \times \frac{precision \times recall}{precision + recall}$,
    where $precision = \frac{|\widehat{F}_i \cap \widehat{F}_{i-1}|}{|\widehat{F}_i|}$; $recall = \frac{|\widehat{F}_i \cap \widehat{F}_{i-1}|}{|\widehat{F}_{i-1}|}$.
5: Compute the dissimilarity between t_{i-1} and t_i: dis_i = 1-F-score.
6: **if** $dis_i < \theta$ **then**
7:     $\epsilon_{i,2} = 0$; Return $\widehat{FI}_{i-1}$.
8: **else**
9:     Distribute the release budget at t_i: $\epsilon_{i,2} = \frac{(1-\alpha)\epsilon - \sum_{k=i-w+1}^{i-1} \epsilon_{i,2}}{2}$.
10:     $\widehat{FI}_i$=Release based on Threshold Exponential Mechanism$(D_i, \epsilon_{i,2}, \lambda, l_{opt})$.
11:     Return $\widehat{FI}_i$.
12: **end if**

---

are designed as follows: first we split long transactions to reduce the number of candidate patterns. Then based on the split transactions, we design a threshold exponential mechanism to further reduce the sensitivity.

(1) Split long transactions. From work [8], we know that given the maximal length l, where $l = O(1)$, the geometric noise algorithm is ϵ-differentially private provided $\epsilon \geq log(|I|)$, $|I|$ is the number of distinct Items of a dataset. This means that the constraint on the maximal length of transactions has a significant impact on the utility of the private release result. If most transactions in a dataset are short and a few are long, then these few long transactions have a large effect on the sensitivity, while having little impact on frequent itemsets. Therefore, the utility can be improved by limiting the maximal length of transactions. Existing related work [5] has proposed a private splitting method to reduce the sensitivity of frequent itemset mining. However, their splitting method requires several times of dataset scanning. It is designed for the static dataset release and cannot be applied to continual release because of inefficiency. In our continual release process, we will use random sampling to split long transactions efficiently, which is more suitable for the dynamic release. Since random splitting may cause information loss, we analyzed it and make an offset in the subsequent release.

Let l_{opt} denote the optimal splitting length, how to set l_{opt} is important for the utility of our scheme. Our method is as follows: first, let $Z = <z_1,, z_n>$ where z_i denotes the percentage of transactions with length i in the dataset. To achieve differential privacy, $\epsilon_{i,2,1} = \beta\epsilon_{i,2}/2$ is allocated to this process and $Lap(\frac{1}{n\epsilon_{i,2,1}})$ is added to z_i. l_{opt} is set to the smallest integer such that $\sum_{i=1}^{l_{opt}} z_i \geq \eta$ $(0 < \eta < 1)$, which means the percentage of the transactions with length no greater than l_{opt} is at least η percentage.

Splitting may cause information loss, because the support of some itemsets decreases after splitting. We approximate information loss by analyzing random splitting. Suppose the length of a long transaction T is $l(l > l_{opt})$ and t contains an itemset X. The length constraint on transactions is l_{opt}. From work [8] we know the probability of X remaining in the truncation transaction is:

$$Pr_{truncate(|X|,l)}(X) = \frac{\binom{l-|X|}{l_{opt}-|X|}}{\binom{l}{l_{opt}}}$$

Based on the above equation, we analyze the probability that X remains in $\lceil l/l_{opt} \rceil$ short transactions after splitting. After splitting T, there are $\lfloor l/l_{opt} \rfloor$ short transactions whose length is l_{opt} and one short transaction whose length may be smaller than l_{opt}. Let $a = l - \lfloor l/l_{opt} \rfloor$ be the number of items in the short transaction with length smaller than l_{opt}.

If $a < |X|$, the probability of an itemset X remaining in one of $\lfloor l/l_{opt} \rfloor$ short transactions is

$$Pr_{split(|X|,l,a<|X|)}(X) = \binom{\lfloor l/l_{opt} \rfloor}{1} \frac{\binom{l-|X|}{l_{opt}-|X|}}{\binom{l}{l_{opt}}} = \frac{\lfloor l/l_{opt} \rfloor \binom{l-|X|}{l_{opt}-|X|}}{\binom{l}{l_{opt}}}$$

If $a \geq |X|$, the probability that X remains in the last short transaction whose length is smaller than l_{opt} is $\frac{\binom{l-|X|}{a-|X|}}{\binom{l}{a}}$, so the total probability that X remains in all short transactions of t is

$$Pr_{split(|X|,l,a\geq|X|)}(X) = \frac{\lfloor l/l_{opt} \rfloor \binom{l-|X|}{l_{opt}-|X|}}{\binom{l}{l_{opt}}} + \frac{\binom{l-|X|}{a-|X|}}{\binom{l}{a}}$$

We assume a uniform distribution among transactions with different cardinality containing the itemset X. Suppose the total number of transactions in database is n. Let g_k be the number of transactions of length k containing itemset X. The remaining information rate (the probability retained in the split dataset after splitting) of X after splitting is

$$R_m(X) = \sum_{k=|X|}^{l_{opt}} \frac{g_k}{\sum_{j=1}^{n} g_j} + \sum_{k=l_{opt}+1}^{n} \frac{g_k}{\sum_{j=1}^{n} g_j} \cdot Pr_{split(|X|,l)}(X)) \qquad (4)$$

(2) Release based on Threshold Exponential Mechanism. After splitting long transactions, we will design a private release scheme to select frequent itemsets from Cantree based on exponential mechanism. CanTree (canonical-order tree) [9] is designed for incremental mining of frequent patterns. To achieve differential privacy, when mining of Cantree, we need to add random noises to this process. The amount of added noise is proportionate to the size of candidate set. Although splitting long transactions has reduced the size of candidate set, it is still large and will affect the efficiency and utility of the release. To this end, we propose a threshold exponential mechanism to further improve the utility. The main idea is before sampling frequent itemsets we compare the support threshold and the noisy support of candidate frequent itemsets, and prune those obviously infrequent candidate itemsets. Then according to the true support of each candidate frequent, we use exponential mechanism to sampling frequent itemsets. Since the space of candidate set is further reduced, the amount of added noise is also reduced and the utility of the sampling result is improved.

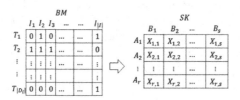

Fig. 2. Sketch matrix example

The key to design the threshold exponential mechanism is privately calculate the number of frequent itemsets $\hat{n}_i$. This is because $\hat{n}_i$ is the sensitivity of one-shot private release based on threshold exponential mechanism, it determines the magnitude of added noise. To get this number, we transform an existing no-private calculation method [11] to a private one. The principle of the transformation is designing a sketch matrix to estimate the approximate number of frequent itemsets, in the calculation process, Laplace noise is added to guarantee differential privacy. Detailed process is given as follows: Based on D_i, we can get a binary matrix BM representing D_i, each row of BM corresponds to a transaction and each column corresponds to an item. So BM has $|D_i| \times |I|$ elements $b_{p,q}$, $b_{p,q}$ is one if the p-th transaction contains item q. Randomly partition the transactions into r groups, and randomly partition the items into s groups. Based on the partition results, we can generate a sketch matrix SK based on BM. SK has r rows and s columns. We can see an example of SK in Fig. 2. Let $A_p(1 \le p \le r)$ be the set of transactions being represented by the p-th row of SK, and $B_q(1 \le q \le s)$ denotes the set of items represented by the q-th column. So $\sum_{p=1}^{r} |A_p| = |D_i|$, and $\sum_{q=1}^{s} |B_q| = |I|$. Each cell $X_{p,q}$ of the sketch matrix SK is derived from the submatrix of the binary matrix BM, it is a binary block with $|A_p|$ rows and $|B_q|$ columns. Each column of $X_{p,q}$ can be regard as a random variable $Y_{p,q}$ with a binomial distribution $Bin(|A_p|, d_{pq})$, where $|A_p|$ is the number of cells in a column of the block and d_{pq} is the probability that the cell is 1. Since any subset of frequent columns is also frequent, the estimated number of frequent itemsets which are subsets of $B_q(1 \le q \le s)$ is as follows:

$$\sum_{m=1}^{|B_q|} C_{|B_q|}^m Pr(\sum_{p=1}^{r} Y[m]_{pq}) \ge \lambda |D_i|) \tag{5}$$

where $Y[m]_{pq}(1 \leq p \leq r)$ is a random variable with binomial distribution Bin $(|A_p|, d^m_{pq})$. Based on Eq. (5), the expected number of all frequent itemsets of D_i is

$$n_i = \sum_{m_1=1}^{|B_1|} \cdots \sum_{m_s=1}^{|B_s|} C^{m_1}_{|B_1|} \times \cdots \times C^{m_s}_{|B_s|} Pr(\sum_{p=1}^{r}(Y[m_1, \cdots, m_s]_{p[q_1, \cdots, q_s]}) \geq \lambda |D_i|) \quad (6)$$

where $Y[m_1, \cdots, m_s]_{p[q_1, \cdots, q_s]}$ is a random variable with binomial distribution Bin $(|A_p|, d^{m_1}_{p1} \times \cdots \times d^{m_s}_{ps})$. To achieve differential privacy, we allocate this process the privacy budget $\epsilon_{i,2,2} = \beta\epsilon_{i,2}/2$ $(0 \leq \beta \leq 1)$. The sensitivity of this process is $min(r \times l_{opt}, r \times s)$, since adding (or deleting) one transaction in the split database D_i may affect the calculation of $min(r \times l_{opt}, r \times s)$ blocks. According to the budget allocated here and the sensitivity of this calculation, we add $Lap(\frac{min(r \times l_{opt}, r \times s)}{\epsilon_{i,2,2}})$ noise to n_i, which is

$$\hat{n}_i = n_i + Lap(\frac{min(r \times l_{opt}, r \times s)}{\epsilon_{i,2,2}}) \quad (7)$$

Therefore, the estimated number of frequent itemsets depends on two parts: one is the probability that the sum of random variables, each one with binomial distribution and no less than $\lambda|D_i|$, the other is Laplace noise.

Based on the private number calculated in the previous step, the detailed release scheme is given in Algorithm 2. First we divide the privacy budget $\epsilon_{i,2}$ into three parts: $\epsilon_{i,2,1} = \epsilon_{i,2,2} = \beta\epsilon_{i,2}/2$ and $\epsilon_{i,2,3} = (1 - \beta)\epsilon_{i,2}$ (line 1); $\epsilon_{i,2,1}$ is used to splitting long transactions, $\epsilon_{i,2,2}$ is used to privately estimate the number of frequent itemsets described in previous step (lines 4–7); $\epsilon_{i,2,3}$ is used to privately select frequent itemsets using threshold exponential mechanism (lines 8–19). We first split long transactions of D_i based on $\epsilon_{i,2,1}$ and l_{opt} (line 2); Based on the split database we generate or update Cantree at t_i (line 3); The threshold exponential mechanism contains the following steps: Given the updated Cantree, we first add Laplace noise to the true support of each candidate itemset, and offset the information loss of each candidate frequent itemset based on Eq. (4) (lines 10–11), then we prune candidate frequent itemsets whose updated noisy supports smaller than the threshold (lines 12–14); Next for each candidate frequent itemsets in $CSet$, we sampling a frequent itemset according to its utility function: $Pr[e|D_i] \propto exp(\frac{\epsilon_{i,2,3}C(e, D_i)}{4\hat{n}_i})$ (lines 16–18). Repeating the above steps until we choose $\hat{n}_i$ itemsets from $CSet$. Using our threshold exponential Mechanism, the amount of noise added to the support of each candidate itemset is proportionate to $\hat{n}_i$, the utility is improved.

Theorem 2. *Algorithm 2 satisfies $\epsilon_{i,2}$ differential privacy.*

Proof. First, we analyze the privacy of lines 1–7 in Algorithm 2 . It consists of two processes: random splitting of long transactions and privately calculate the approximate number of frequent itemsets. The splitting process satisfies $\epsilon_{i,2,1}$-differential privacy. The calculation process satisfies $\epsilon_{i,2,2}$-differential privacy.

Let $C(e, D_i)$ denote the true support of the pattern e, $\hat{C}(e, D_i)$ denote the noise support, $\hat{C}(e, D_i) = C(e, D_i) + Lap(4\hat{n}_i/\epsilon_{i,2,3})$. The utility score we set to each candidate pattern e is as follows: if $\hat{C}(e, D_i) < \lambda$, the utility score of e is $f_1(e, D_i) = 0$, Otherwise, the utility score of e is $f_2(e, D_i) = exp(\frac{\epsilon_{i,2,3}C(e,D_i)}{4\hat{n}_i})$.

$$
\begin{aligned}
Pr[e|D_i] &= \frac{f_1(e,D_i) \times Pr[\hat{C}(e,D_i)<\lambda] + f_2(e,D_i) \times Pr[\hat{C}(e,D_i)\geq\lambda]}{\sum_{e \in CandidateSet} f_1(e,D_i) \times Pr[\hat{C}(e,D_i)<\lambda] + f_2(e,D_i) \times Pr[\hat{C}(e,D_i)\geq\lambda]} \\
&= \frac{f_2(e,D_i) \times Pr[(C(e,D_i)+Lap_{noise})\geq\lambda R_m(e)]}{\sum_{e \in CSet} f_2(e,D_i) \times Pr[(C(e,D_i)+Lap_{noise})\geq\lambda R_m(e)]} \\
&= \frac{f_2(e,D_i) \times Pr[Lap_{noise}\geq(\lambda R_m(e)-(C(e,D_i))]}{\sum_{e \in CSet} f_2(e,D_i) \times Pr[Lap_{noise}\geq(\lambda R_m(e)-(C(e,D_i)))]} \\
&= \frac{f_2(e,D_i) \times \int_{\lambda R_m(e)-C(e,D_i)}^{\infty} Pr[Lap_{noise}=x]dx}{\sum_{e \in CSet} f_2(e,D_i) \times \int_{\lambda R_m(e)-C(e,D_i)}^{\infty} Pr[Lap_{noise}=x]dx} \quad (8) \\
&\leq \frac{f_2(e,D_i) \times \int_{\lambda R_m(e)-C(e,D'_i)-1}^{\infty} Pr[Lap_{noise}=x]dx}{\sum_{e \in CSet} f_2(e,D_i) \times \int_{\lambda R_m(e)-C(e,D'_i)-1}^{\infty} Pr[Lap_{noise}=x]dx} \\
&= \frac{f_2(e,D_i) \times \int_{\lambda R_m(e)-C(e,D'_i)}^{\infty} Pr[Lap_{noise}=x-1]dx}{\sum_{e \in CSet} f_2(e,D_i) \times \int_{\lambda R_m(e)-C(e,D'_i)}^{\infty} Pr[Lap_{noise}=x-1]dx}
\end{aligned}
$$

$$
\begin{aligned}
\frac{Pr[Lap_{noise}=x-1]}{Pr[Lap_{noise}=x]} &= \frac{exp(-\frac{|x-1|\epsilon_{i,2,3}}{4\hat{n}_i})}{exp(-\frac{|x|\epsilon_{i,2,3}}{4\hat{n}_i})} = exp(-\frac{(|x-1|-|x|)\epsilon_{i,2,3}}{4\hat{n}_i}) \leq e^{\frac{\epsilon_{i,2,3}}{4n\hat{n}_i}} \\
exp(-\frac{\epsilon_{i,2,3}}{4\hat{n}_i}) &\leq \frac{f_2(e,D_i)}{f_2(e,D'_i)} \leq exp(\frac{\epsilon_{i,2,3}}{4\hat{n}_i})
\end{aligned}
\quad (9)
$$

Algorithm 2. Release based on Threshold Exponential Mechanism

Input: D_i, $\epsilon_{i,2}$, λ, l_{opt}.
Output: Frequent itemsets $\widehat{FI}_i$
1: $\epsilon_{i,2,1} = \epsilon_{i,2,2} = \beta\epsilon_{i,2}/2$; $\epsilon_{i,2,3} = (1-\beta)\epsilon_{i,2}$; $(0 \leq \beta \leq 1)$.
2: Splitting long transactions in D_i based on $\epsilon_{i,2,1}$ and l_{opt}.
3: Generate or update Cantree based on the split D_i at t_i.
4: Generate BM(Binary Matrix) of D_i;
5: Derive SK(Sketch Matrix) from BM;
6: Calculate n_i based on SK according to equation(6);
7: $\hat{n}_i = n_i + Lap(\frac{min(r \times l_{opt}, r \times s)}{\epsilon_{i,2,2}})$.
8: Set $CSet = \emptyset$.
9: **for** each pattern e in Cantree **do**
10:     Calculate the information loss of $R_m(e)$ according to equation(4).
11:     $\hat{C}(e, D_i) = \frac{C(e,D_i)+Lap(4\hat{n}_i/\epsilon_{i,2,3})}{R_m(e)}$.
12:     **if** $\hat{C}(e, D_i) \geq \lambda$ **then**
13:         Add e to $CSet$.
14:     **end if**
15: **end for**
16: **for** j=1 to $\hat{n}_i$ **do**
17:     $\widehat{FI}_i$ += Sampling e from $CSet$ with $Pr[e|D_i] \propto exp(\frac{\epsilon_{i,2,3}C(e,D_i)}{4\hat{n}_i})$.
18: **end for**
19: Return $\widehat{FI}_i$.

According to Eq. (9)

$$(8) \leq \frac{e^{\frac{\epsilon_{i,2,3}}{4\hat{n}_i}} \times f_2(e,D_i') \times e^{\frac{\epsilon_{i,2,3}}{4\hat{n}_i}} \times \int_{\lambda R_m(e)-C(e,D_i')}^{\infty} Pr[Lap_{noise}=x]dx}{\sum_{e \in CSet} e^{-\frac{\epsilon_{i,2,3}}{4\hat{n}_i}} \times f_2(e,D_i') \times e^{-\frac{\epsilon_{i,2,3}}{4n_i}} \times f_2(e,D_i') \times \int_{\lambda R_m(e)-C(e,D_i')}^{\infty} Pr[Lap_{noise}=x]dx}$$

$$= \frac{e^{\frac{\epsilon_{i,2,3}}{2\hat{n}_i}} \times f_2(e,D_i') \times Pr[\hat{C}(e,D_i') \geq \lambda]}{\sum_{e \in CSet} e^{-\frac{\epsilon_{i,2,3}}{2\hat{n}_i}} \times f_2(e,D_i') \times Pr[\hat{C}(e,D_i') \geq \lambda]} \qquad (10)$$

$$= exp(\frac{\epsilon_{i,2,3}}{\hat{n}_i})Pr[e|D'].$$

From Eq. (10), sampling $\hat{n}_i$ frequent itemsets based on threshold exponential mechanism satisfies $\epsilon_{i,2,3}$ differential privacy. According to Theorem 1, Algorithm 2 satisfies $\epsilon_{i,2}$ differential privacy.

3.3 Privacy Analysis

Theorem 3. *The privacy budget spent in any sliding window(w) is less than ϵ.*

Proof. We need to prove $\forall i \in [w,N]$, $\sum_{k=i-w+1}^{i} \epsilon_k \leq \epsilon$, which means the privacy budget spent in any window of w timestamps is less than ϵ. For each time stamp i, we allocate $\epsilon_{i,1} = \alpha\epsilon/w(0 \leq \alpha \leq 1)$ to dissimilarity computation. The total privacy budget spent for dissimilarity computation in a sliding widow is $\sum_{k=i-w+1}^{i} \epsilon_{k,1} = \alpha\epsilon$. For each i, if the dissimilarity is greater than θ, we distribute the privacy budget $\epsilon_{i,2} = \epsilon_{rm}/2$ in an exponentially decreasing fashion to this point, otherwise distribute $\epsilon_{i,2} = 0$ to this point. Suppose the release budget spent on the first sampling point in a window is $\epsilon_{rm}/2$, the release budget spent on the second sampling point is $\epsilon_{rm}/2^2$, and so on. So a series of the release budget in a window is an approximate geometric sequence. Since the maximum value of ϵ_{rm} is $(1-\alpha)\epsilon$, the first item of the geometric sequence is less than $(1-\alpha)\epsilon/2$. Suppose the number of sampling points in a window is δ, the total privacy budget in a window is $\frac{\frac{(1-\alpha)\epsilon}{2} \cdot (1-(1/2)^{\delta})}{1/2} \leq (1-\alpha)\epsilon$. That means the total privacy budget spent for $M_{i,2}$ for any sliding window of length w is less than $(1-\alpha)\epsilon$. So, $\forall i \in [w,N]$, $\sum_{k=i-w+1}^{i} \epsilon_k = \sum_{k=i-w+1}^{i} \epsilon_{k,1} + \sum_{k=i-w+1}^{i} \epsilon_{k,2} \leq \alpha\epsilon + (1-\alpha)\epsilon = \epsilon$.

Theorem 4. *Let M be a mechanism that takes as dynamic database $D = \{D_1, \cdots, D_N\}$ over N time points, and outputs $\widehat{FI} = \{\widehat{FI}_i : 1 \leq i \leq N\}$. We can decompose M into N mechanisms $M_1, \cdots, M_N$, such that $M_i(D_i) = \widehat{FI}_i$. If $\forall i \in [w,N]$, $\sum_{k=i-w+1}^{i} \epsilon_k \leq \epsilon$, then M satisfies ϵ-differential privacy in any sliding window.*

Proof. Let D_w, D_w' be two neighboring series of dynamic datasets in a silding window. $\forall i \in [w,N]$, for any output $\widehat{FI}$ and any datasets D_w, D_w', we need to prove the probability ratio of an adversary learns the information from D_w and D_w' is less than e^{ϵ}, which means $\ln \frac{Pr[M(D_w)=\widehat{FI}]}{Pr[M(D_w')=\widehat{FI}]} \leq \epsilon$.

Since $\forall i \in [w,N]$, $\ln \frac{Pr[M(D_w)=\widehat{FI}]}{Pr[M(D_w')=\widehat{FI}]} = \sum_{k=i-w+1}^{i} \ln \left(\frac{Pr[M_k(D_k)=\widehat{FI}_k]}{Pr[M_k(D_k')=\widehat{FI}_k]} \right).$

Let S denote the set of all sampling points, and S^C denote the set of non-sampling points in the active window $[i - w + 1, i]$. We have

$$\sum_{k=i-w+1}^{i} \ln\left(\frac{Pr[M_k(D_k) = \widehat{FI}_k]}{Pr[M_k(D'_k) = \widehat{FI}_k]}\right) = \sum_{k \in S} \ln\left(\frac{Pr[M_k(D_k) = \widehat{FI}_k]}{Pr[M_k(D'_k) = \widehat{FI}_k]}\right) + \sum_{k \in S^C} \ln\left(\frac{Pr[M_k(D_k) = \widehat{FI}_k]}{Pr[M_k(D'_k) = \widehat{FI}_k]}\right).$$

Since the budget spent at each time point in S^C is $\epsilon_{i,1}$, the total privacy budget spent for S^C is $\sum_{k \in S^C} \ln\left(\frac{Pr[M_k(D_k)=\widehat{FI}_k]}{Pr[M_k(D'_k)=\widehat{FI}_k]}\right) = |S^C| \cdot \epsilon_{i,1}$.

The privacy budget spent at each time point in S is $\epsilon_{i,1} + \epsilon_{i,2}$, the total privacy budget spent for S is $\sum_{k \in S} \ln\left(\frac{Pr[M_k(D_k)=\widehat{FI}_k]}{Pr[M_k(D'_k)=\widehat{FI}_k]}\right) = |S| \cdot \epsilon_{i,1} + |S| \cdot \epsilon_{i,2}$.

The total privacy budget spent for the window $[i - w + 1, i]$ is

$\sum_{k=i-w+1}^{i} \ln\left(\frac{Pr[M_k(D_k)=\widehat{FI}_k]}{Pr[M_k(D'_k)=\widehat{FI}_k]}\right) = (|S^C| + |S|) \cdot \epsilon_{i,1} + |S| \cdot \epsilon_{i,2}$.

According to Theorem 2, $(|S^C| + |S|) \cdot \epsilon_{i,1} + |S| \cdot \epsilon_{i,2} \leq w \cdot \alpha\epsilon/w + (1 - \alpha)\epsilon = \epsilon$.

So $\forall i \in [w, N]$, $\ln\frac{Pr[M(D_w)=\widehat{FI}]}{Pr[M(D'_w)=\widehat{FI}]} \leq \epsilon$, we complete the proof.

4   Experiments

In this section, we evaluate the utility and efficiency of our scheme. We conduct all experiments on a PC with Intel® Core™ i7-3540M CPU(3.00 Ghz) and 8G RAM. All algorithms are implemented with Java.

Comparison. Since in the absence of direct competitors in the literature, we devise two comparison algorithms by adopting existing related methods. Let DDFIM denote our scheme, Solution1 and Solution2 denote two comparison algorithms. Solution1 comprises of BA (Budget Absorption) [22] and TT (Transaction Truncation) [8]. Solution2 comprises of DSAT (Distance-based Sampling with Adaptive Threshold) [21] and PFP (Private release based on FPGrowth) [5]. DSAT and BA are used as budget allocation methods against infinite updates in our comparison algorithms; TT and PFP are used as one shot release methods in our comparison algorithms.

Metrics. To compare the utility of our scheme, we employ the standard metrics to measure the utility: F-score [8] and RE [10]. F-score is used to measure the utility of generated frequent itemsets. RE is used to measure the error with respect to the actual supports of itemsets. We use the running time to measure the efficiency of algorithms.

Datasets. Real datasets we used in experiments are MSNBC [12], Kosaarak [13] and BMS-POS (POS) [13], which record the URL categories visited by users in time order, click stream data and commercial sale data used in KDDCUP 2000 respectively. Detailed information of datasets is shown in Table 1. $|D|$ is the number of records of a dataset, $|I|$ is the number of distinct items, Max$|t|$ and Avg$|t|$ denote the maximal and the average record length respectively. In the following experiments, we randomly choose $10\% \times |D|$ records as the initial dataset D_1 from the selected dataset and choose another $5\% \times |D|$ records

Table 1. Detailed information of datasets

Dataset	$|D|$	$|I|$	Max$|t|$	Avg$|t|$
MSNBC	989,818	17	14,975	1.72
Kosaarak	990,002	41270	699	8.1
POS	515597	1657	164	6.5

without replacement as each incremental update database ΔD_i. The parameters α, β are set to 0.2, since a small value results in a higher utility.

4.1 Effect of ϵ on Utility

In this set of experiments, we examine the utility by varying ϵ from 0.5 to 2.5 on three datasets.

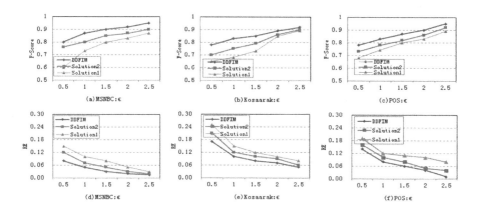

Fig. 3. Effect of ϵ on utility

The threshold θ for dissimilarity computation is set to 0.6; η is 0.8; λ is 0.005 on kosaarak, 0.003 on MSNBC and 0.008 on POS, w is 5. From Fig. 3, DDFIM always performs better than the other two comparison algorithms. After employing the threshold exponential mechanism, the sensitivity of DDFIM has been reduced greatly. Benefiting from the adaptive budget allocation, the budget allocated to each sampling release has been enlarged. For the above two reasons, the utility of DDFIM is highest. Solution2 always performs better than Solution1 in all cases. Because Solution2 samples the release points based on an adaptive allocation scheme, which maximizes the budget utility; it splits long transactions instead of truncation, which also promotes the utility. With the increase of ϵ, we can see the values of F-score on three datasets are all increasing, and the values of RE on three datasets are all decreasing; this is because the average budget allocated for each release becomes larger, which results in less laplace noise.

4.2   Effect of w on Utility

In this set of experiments, we examine F-score and RE of the three algorithms on three datasets with the change of w from 3 to 11.

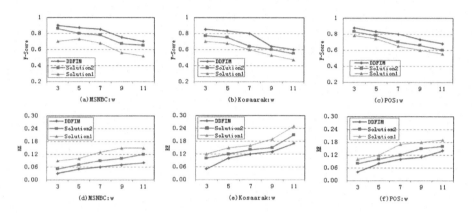

Fig. 4. Effect of w on utility

The threshold θ for dissimilarity computation is set to 0.6; η is 0.8; ϵ is 1; λ is 0.005 on kosaarak, 0.003 on MSNBC and 0.008 on POS. From Fig. 4, DDFIM always performs better than the other two comparison algorithms. Because benefitting from the threshold exponential mechanism, the sensitivity of DDFIM is lowest. Solution2 always performs better than Solution1 in all cases. Because Solution2 samples the release points based on an adaptive allocation scheme, which maximizes the budget utility; it splits long transactions instead of truncation, which also promotes the utility. With the increase of w, we can see the values of F-score on three datasets are all decreasing, and the values of RE on three datasets are all increasing; this is because the average budget allocated for each release becomes smaller, which results in more laplace noise. The average utility on MSNBC is higher than the other two datasets, because fewer items contained in MSNBC and more short transactions result in less information loss.

4.3   Effect of θ on Utility

In this set of experiments, we examine the F-score and relative error (RE) of DDFIM and Solution1 on three datasets by varying the dissimilarity threshold (θ) from 0.2 to 0.8. Since Solution2 sampled based on an adaptive threshold, there is no need to observe the utility of Solution2 with the change of θ. The parameters are set as: w is 5; η is 0.8; ϵ is 1; λ is 0.005 on Kosaarak, 0.003 on MSNBC λ and 0.008 on POS.

Figure 5 shows the utility (F-score and RE) of two algorithms with respect to different θ on three datasets. DDFIM always performs better than Solution1. Since DDFIM employs the threshold exponential mechanism to make a one shot

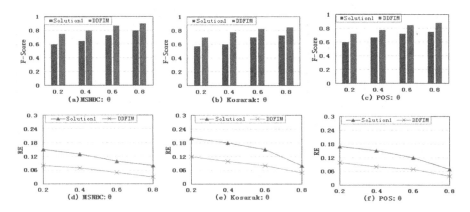

Fig. 5. Effect of θ on utility

release, which reduce the number of candidate frequent itemsets greatly and the noise is also reduced. With the increase of θ, the F-scores of DDFIM and Solution1 are increasing, and the values of RE are all decreasing. Because the average number becomes smaller, the budget spent at each sampling point is increased, which causes less noise to the results and the utility is improved.

4.4 Effect of λ on Utility

In this set of experiments, we examine the F-score and relative error (RE) of three algorithms by varying the support threshold (λ) from 0.001 to 0.013 on MSNBC, from 0.001 to 0.007 on Kosarak and from 0.004 to 0.016 on POS. The parameters are set as: w is 5, η is 0.8, ϵ is 1, θ is 0.6.

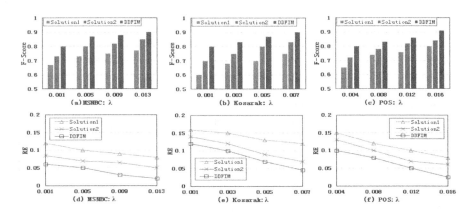

Fig. 6. Effect of λ on utility

Figure 6 shows the utility with respect to different λ on three datasets. We can see DDFIM performs best. By using threshold exponential mechanism, the sensitivity of DDFIM equals to the size of $CSet$. Since Solution1 performs the mining based on Apriori, when mining l-frequent itemsets, its sensitivity is all number of candidate l-frequent itemsets, which equals to possible combination number of its $(l-1)$-frequent itemsets. Since Solution2 performs the mining based on FP-Growth; when mining l-frequent itemsets, its sensitivity equals to the number of support computations of l-frequent itemsets; the sensitivity of DDFIM is lower than that of the other two algorithms, it is closest to the true number of frequent itemsets. With the increase of λ, the values of F-score of all three algorithms are increasing and the values of RE of three algorithms are decreasing. This is because the number of candidate frequent itemsets becomes smaller, the sensitivity of each algorithm is reduced, which results in less noise.

4.5   Efficiency

In this set of experiments, we examine the efficiency of three algorithms. The running time is used as our performance metric. We evaluate the efficiency of the three algorithms by varying the dataset size from 500k to 900k. The parameters we used here are set as: θ is set to 0.6, η is 0.8, $\epsilon = 1.0$ and $w = 5$, λ is 0.005 on Kosaarak, 0.003 on MSNBC and 0.008 on POS.

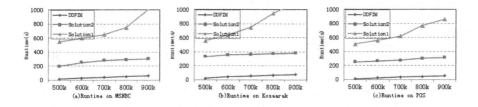

Fig. 7. Efficiency on datasets

Figure 7 shows the runtime of the three algorithms under three datasets. As dataset size grows, the values of the runtime of three algorithms are all increasing. Because the number of the transactions becomes larger, all algorithms consume much more time. The runtime of Solution1 is higher than that of DDFIM. Because in each release, Solution1 needs to truncate long transactions several times, which consumes too much time; moreover, Solution1 performs mining based on Apriori, which also consumes too much time. The runtime of Solution2 is always high on three datasets. Because Solution2 needs to find the correlation of all items in advance and uses the result to guide the splitting, it is too inefficient.

5   Related Works

Differentially Private FIM on a Static Dataset. Recently, several studies [5–8,10] start to address the issue of performing FIM while satisfying differential privacy. Since the challenge of high dimensionality of long transactions, the sensitivity of the private release of frequent patterns is very high. To reduce the sensitivity, several schemes are proposed to promote the result utility. Bhaskar et al. [7] propose two kinds of schemes based on LM [3] and EM [4] by considering candidate frequent patterns with length no greater than l. Zeng et al. [8] propose a scheme based on Apriori, which contains a transaction truncation method to reduce sensitivity. Li et al. [10] propose to find a basis set, and project long transactions to the basis set to reduce sensitivity. The latest work PriSuper [6] uses SEM mechanism to release top-k frequent patterns based on the maximum frequent itemsets found in advance. Su et al. [5] propose transaction splitting to reduce sensitivity, first they find the relationship of all items and then split long transactions based on the above results. Based on the ideas of sampling and transaction truncation, [27,28] propose two schemes for high-dimensional databases and large-scale data. The above works suppose the sever is trusted. Wang et al. [26] propose a method based on locally differential privacy, they suppose the sever is untrusted. All methods are designed for static scenario.

Differentially Private Continual Release on Dynamic Scenario. These works can be classified into two categories: (1) Partition or tree structure: Dwork et al. [14,15] first propose how to employ differential privacy in a dynamic scenario, and they employ a tree structure to reduce the perturbing error. The subsequent works [16,17] employ partition or improved tree structure to promote the utility. Bolot et al. [23] propose releasing decayed sums based on a binary tree. (2) Adaptive sampling: the following works design adaptive sampling methods to maximize the utility of the privacy budget on time-series. Fan et al. [20] propose a framework FAST to reduce the perturbed error against updates, its core idea is adaptive sampling based on Kalman filtering. Li et al. [21] design an adaptive sampling method with adaptive threshold (DSAT) to release the statistics of dynamic datasets. Kellaris et al. [22] propose two budget allocation methods on time-series based on sampling. Cao et al. [25] propose a continually release scheme for trajectory data, to reduce the perturbed error, they quantify the privacy leakage caused by temporal correlations. The above methods cannot be directly used in our problem, since all of them are designed for continual release of simple statistics.

6   Conclusions

In this paper, we have studied the problem of differentially private frequent itemsets mining against infinite incremental updates. Firstly we promote an adaptive budget allocation scheme combining with transactional dataset change. Then we design a private release scheme based on threshold exponential mechanism. We have proved our scheme satisfies ϵ-differential privacy in any sliding window. Experiments on real datasets show that our scheme achieves high utility and efficiency. As the future work, we will investigate how to preserve ϵ-differential privacy against infinite updates for other application scenarios (e.g., releasing sequential data).

Acknowledgements. This work is supported by National Natural Science Foundation of China (No. 61532021, 61772537, 61772536, 61702522).

References

1. Calandrino, J.A., et al.: You might also like: privacy risks of collaborative filtering. In: IEEE Symposium on Security and Privacy, pp. 231–246 (2011)
2. Soria-Comas, J., Domingo-Ferrer, J.: Big data privacy: challenges to privacy principles and models. Data Sci. Eng. 1(1), 25–36 (2016)
3. Dwork, C., McSherry, F., Nissim, K., Smith, A.: Calibrating noise to sensitivity in private data analysis. In: Halevi, S., Rabin, T. (eds.) TCC 2006. LNCS, vol. 3876, pp. 265–284. Springer, Heidelberg (2006). https://doi.org/10.1007/11681878_14
4. McSherry, F., Talwar, K.: Mechanism design via differential privacy. In: FOCS, pp. 94–103 (2007)
5. Su, S., Xu, S., et al.: Differentially private frequent itemset mining via transaction splitting. In: ICDE, pp. 1564–1565 (2016)
6. Wang, N., et al.: PrivSuper: a superset-first approach to frequent itemset mining under differential privacy. In: ICDE, pp. 809–820 (2017)
7. Bhaskar, R., Laxman, S., Smith, A., Thakurta, A.: Discovering frequent patterns in sensitive data. In: KDD, pp. 503–512 (2010)
8. Zeng, C., Naughton, J.F., et al.: On differentially private frequent itemset mining. In: PVLDB, vol. 6, no. 1, pp. 25–36 (2012)
9. Leung, C.K.-S., et al.: CanTree: a tree structure for efficient incremental mining of frequent patterns. In: ICDM, pp. 274–281 (2005)
10. Li, N., Qardaji, W.H., et al.: PrivBasis: frequent itemset mining with differential privacy. In: PVLDB, vol. 5, no. 11, pp. 1340–1351 (2012)
11. Jin, R., McCallen, S.: Estimating the number of frequent itemsets in a large database. In: EDBT, pp. 505–516 (2009)
12. UCI machine learning repository. http://archive.ics.uci.edu/ml
13. Frequent itemset mining dataset repository. http://fimi.ua.ac.be/data
14. Dwork, C.: Differential privacy in new settings. In: SODA, pp. 174–183 (2010)
15. Dwork, C., Naor, M., Pitassi, T., Rothblum, G.N.: Differential privacy under continual observation. In: STOC, pp. 715–724 (2010)
16. Hubert Chan, T.-H., Shi, E., Song, D.: Private and continual release of statistics. In: Abramsky, S., Gavoille, C., Kirchner, C., Meyer auf der Heide, F., Spirakis, P.G. (eds.) ICALP 2010. LNCS, vol. 6199, pp. 405–417. Springer, Heidelberg (2010). https://doi.org/10.1007/978-3-642-14162-1_34
17. Chen, Y., Machanavajjhala, A., et al.: PeGaSus: data-adaptive differentially private stream processing. In: CCS, pp. 1375–1388 (2017)
18. Chen, R., Shen, Y., Jin, H.: Private analysis of infinite data streams via retroactive grouping. In: CIKM, pp. 1061–1070 (2015)
19. Fan, L., Xiong, L., et al.: FAST: differentially private real-time aggregate monitor with filtering and adaptive sampling. In: SIGMOD, pp. 1065–1068 (2013)
20. Fan, L., Xiong, L.: An adaptive approach to real-time aggregate monitoring with differential privacy. In: TKDE, vol. 26, no. 9, pp. 2094–2106 (2014)
21. Li, H., Xiong, L., et al.: Differentially private histogram publication for dynamic datasets: an adaptive sampling approach. In: CIKM, pp. 1001–1010 (2015)
22. Kellaris, G., Papadopoulos, S., et al.: Differentially private event sequences over infinite streams. In: PVLDB, vol. 7, no. 12, pp. 1155–1166 (2014)

23. Bolot, J., Fawaz, N., Muthukrishnan, S., Nikolov, A., Taft, N.: Private decayed predicate sums on streams. In: ICDT, pp. 284–295 (2013)
24. Dwork, C., Naor, M., Reingold, O., Rothblum, G.N.: Pure differential privacy for rectangle queries via private partitions. In: Iwata, T., Cheon, J.H. (eds.) ASIACRYPT 2015. LNCS, vol. 9453, pp. 735–751. Springer, Heidelberg (2015). https://doi.org/10.1007/978-3-662-48800-3_30
25. Cao, Y., Yoshikawa, M., et al.: Quantifying differential privacy under temporal correlations. In: ICDE, pp. 821–832 (2017)
26. Wang, T., Li, N., Jha, S.: Locally differentially private frequent itemset mining. In: IEEE Symposium on Security and Privacy, pp. 127–143 (2018)
27. Xu, J., Han, K., Song, P., Xu, C., Gui, F.: PrivBUD-wise: differentially private frequent itemsets mining in high-dimensional databases. In: Shao, J., Yiu, M.L., Toyoda, M., Zhang, D., Wang, W., Cui, B. (eds.) APWeb-WAIM 2019. LNCS, vol. 11641, pp. 110–124. Springer, Cham (2019). https://doi.org/10.1007/978-3-030-26072-9_8
28. Xiong, X., Chen, F.: Frequent itemsets mining with differential privacy over large-scale data. IEEE Access **6**, 28877–28889 (2018)

Differentially Private Reinforcement Learning

Pingchuan Ma[1], Zhiqiang Wang[1,2,3(✉)], Le Zhang[1], Ruming Wang[4], Xiaoxiang Zou[5(✉)], and Tao Yang[3]

[1] Beijing Electronic Science and Technology Institute, Beijing, China
wangzq@besti.edu.cn
[2] State Information Center, Beijing, China
[3] Key Lab of Information Network Security,
Ministry of Public Security, Shanghai, China
[4] Hainan University, Haikou, China
[5] National Computer Network Emergency Response
Technical Team/Coordination Center of China, Beijing, China

Abstract. With remarkable performance and extensive applications, reinforcement learning is becoming one of the most popular learning techniques. Often, the policy π^* released by reinforcement learning model may contain sensitive information, and an adversary can infer demographic information through observing the output of the environment. In this paper, we formulate differential privacy in reinforcement learning contexts, design mechanisms for ϵ-greedy and Softmax in the K-armed bandit problem to achieve differentially private guarantees. Our implementation and experiments illustrate that the output policies are under good privacy guarantees with a tolerable utility cost.

Keywords: Differential privacy · Reinforcement learning · Privacy preserving

1 Introduction

Recent years have witnessed a boom in artificial intelligence, which contributes to a wide range of applications, such as face recognition, self-driving, medical diagnosis, etc. [17,25]. Notably, the success of AlphaGo[1] speeds up the development of reinforcement learning. Nevertheless, the security and privacy issues combined with artificial intelligence also draw full attention from researchers in the meantime. In real-world scenarios, trained reinforcement learning policies are released to client-side and often contain sensitive information, from which adversaries may infer demographic information. As AI models have millions of parameters, some sensitive information are contained in the model parameters implicitly. Recently, model inversion and membership inference attacks has shown it effectiveness on

---

[1] https://deepmind.com/research/alphago/.

© Springer Nature Switzerland AG 2020
J. Zhou et al. (Eds.): ICICS 2019, LNCS 11999, pp. 668–683, 2020.
https://doi.org/10.1007/978-3-030-41579-2_39

some AI models [10,22,23,28]. Although there are not any well-known attacks performs on the data privacy of reinforcement learning models (to the best of our knowledge), we still think the environment should be protected since it contains sensitive information.

As a promising privacy-preserving technique, differential privacy introduced a strong privacy model which provides formal privacy guarantees that do not depend on the background knowledge or computational power of an adversary [11]. Apple Inc. integrated differential privacy for collecting sensitive data in its operating systems, iOS and macOS, respectively. Google released a framework for local differentially private data aggregation and deployed it in Chrome [9]. While differential privacy for reinforcement learning in specific cases has been conveyed in some work [2,19,27], our definitions and methods are different from theirs which adapt the features of generic reinforcement learning models.

Typically, the question of how to combine differential privacy with reinforcement learning can be divided into two parts, (1) how to formulate the privacy issues in reinforcement learning and (2) how to design mechanisms that achieve differential privacy in reinforcement learning contexts.

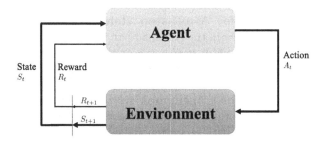

Fig. 1. Structure of reinforcement learning.

In this paper, the first objective is to define the formal privacy model in reinforcement learning contexts. However, differing from learning models with initial datasets, as is shown in Fig. 1, reinforcement learning does not have the notion of dataset or data tuples and only learns from the feedbacks of environments. Therefore, the traditional definition of differential privacy is not applicable for reinforcement learning. Luckily, we notice that the functions of states, actions and reward in reinforcement learning are similar to samples and labels in supervised learning to some extent. We thereby define reinforcement learning differential privacy based on this observation.

The second objective is to design a mechanism that achieves differential privacy guarantees. However, today's reinforcement learning models usually adopt deep neural networks to approximate action values or policies, and it is a common belief that these neural networks are hard to be analyzed theoretically. So in this paper, we illustrate the ideas of the mechanism achieving differential privacy in a simplified setting, i.e., the K-armed bandit problem, which still preserves the important features distinguishing reinforcement learning from other types of learning.

Contribution. In summary, our main contributions are as follows:

- (ϵ, δ)-**Differentially Private Reinforcement Learning.** We extend the definition of differential privacy in reinforcement learning contexts. To be precise, our definition no longer adopts the notion of databases in traditional differential privacy models and utilizes the environments instead.
- **Exponential Mechanism for ϵ-greedy.** We analyze the sensitivity of utility function, adopt the exponential mechanism for achieving differentially private ϵ-greedy algorithm in the K-armed bandit problem (it can be simply transferred to similar algorithms, such as Q-Learning, Sarsa.), and finally, prove it.
- **Laplace Mechanism for Softmax with Fine-grained Sensitivity.** Different from ϵ-greedy, Softmax does not output an optimal policy, but a p.d.f. denoting the probability of each action. Additionally, the high global sensitivity of Softmax algorithm results in damage to data utility. We analyze the smooth sensitivity of Softmax, utilize more fine-grained noise to perturb output, and achieve (ϵ, δ)-differentially private reinforcement learning.

Future Direction. We present two prospective future directions.

- **Differential Privacy for Multi-step Reinforcement Learning.** We address differential privacy in the K-armed bandit problem in this paper. It is of great significance to study how to achieve differential privacy in multi-step reinforcement learning models, which are much more popular in real-world scenarios.
- **Differential Privacy for Continuous Action Reinforcement Learning.** While the problem of privacy-preserving discrete action model is solved in this paper, how to perturb a continuous action in reinforcement learning models is an important topic as well.

The next section reviews preliminaries on reinforcement learning and differential privacy, respectively. Section 3 demonstrates our formal definition. Section 4 presents the mechanism design for ϵ-greedy and Softmax, respectively. Section 5 describes our experimental results. Section 6 discusses related work, and Sect. 7 concludes.

2 Preliminaries

In this section, we briefly introduce notions of reinforcement learning and differential privacy.

2.1 Reinforcement Learning

Reinforcement learning is a set of machine learning methods concerned with how agents take actions in an environment for maximising cumulative reward [25]. Typically, the reinforcement learning problem can be cast as a Markov Decision Process (MDP) [13]. For agents in the environment E, the state space

$\mathcal{X}$, where each $x \in \mathcal{X}$ denotes the stage of an agent in the environment E, when an action $a \in \mathcal{A}$ is taken, reward will be given by the environment E based on the reward function $\mathcal{R}$. To summarise, a quaternion $E = \langle \mathcal{X}, \mathcal{A}, P, R \rangle$ denote the reinforcement learning model, where $P : \mathcal{X} \times \mathcal{A} \times \mathcal{X} \to \mathbb{R}$ denotes the state transition probability, $R : \mathcal{X} \times \mathcal{A} \times \mathcal{X} \to \mathbb{R}$ denotes the reward function of the environment E.

Unlike other supervised learning techniques, the output of reinforcement learning can only be invested after multi-step. In this article, we utilize the K-armed bandit problem with ϵ-greedy and Softmax algorithms to convey our research [16].

K-armed Bandit. To be precise, the K-armed bandit is a problem where the reward is allocated by choices for maximizing it when each choice's properties are only partially known at the time of allocation, and players may become better understood as time passes [3,12]. Occasionally, the bandit algorithms tend to be trapped into Exploration-Exploitation dilemma, where the agents strive to balance sufficiently exploring the variant space and exploiting the optimal action.

ϵ-**greedy.** Intuitively, a common policy is to take the optimal action with the probability of $1 - \epsilon$ and randomly choose an action with the probability of ϵ. After an initial period, the agents can solve the optimal action π^* under which most reward is given, but will still randomly try action with the probability of ϵ.

Softmax (Boltzmann Exploration). Softmax is based on Luce's choice axiom and picks an arm with the probability given by Boltzmann distribution according to its average reward [16]. Following is the p.d.f. of each action.

$$P(k) = \frac{\exp(\frac{Q(k)}{\tau})}{\sum_{i=0}^{K} \exp(\frac{Q(i)}{\tau})} \tag{1}$$

where τ is temperature parameter which controls the randomness. When $\tau = 0$, the algorithm is pure greedy. By the contrast, when $\tau \to +\infty$, the algorithm selects actions randomly.

2.2 Differential Privacy

With the growth of data aggregation and mining, the threats to data privacy also increase. Roughly speaking, *differential privacy* is a mathematical model of data privacy guarantees in a statistical dataset [4–7]. The objective of differential privacy is to perturb the output of queries to prevent adversaries infer the demographic information. The noise is controlled by the privacy budget ϵ^2.

We let a vector $D = [D_1, D_2, \cdots, D_n]$ to denote a statistical database, where D_i for each $i \in \{1, 2, \cdots, n\}$ is a tuple. The notion of (ϵ, δ)-differential privacy can be defined as:

---

[2] To distinguish the ϵ in differential privacy and ϵ-greedy, the ϵ in ϵ-greedy will be replaced by ϵ_{rl} in the remainder of the article, namely ϵ_{rl}-greedy.

Definition 2.1 $((\epsilon, \delta)$-differential privacy) [4]. *A randomized function $\mathcal{K}$ gives (ϵ, δ)-differential privacy if for all data sets D_1 and D_2 differing on at most one element, and all $S \subseteq Range(\mathcal{K})$,*

$$Pr[\mathcal{K}(D_1) \in S] \leq exp(\epsilon) \times Pr[\mathcal{K}(D_2) \in S] + \delta \tag{2}$$

where $\mathcal{K}(D_1)$ (resp. $\mathcal{K}(D_2)$) is the output of randomized function $\mathcal{K}(\cdot)$ on input D_1 (resp. D_2) and ϵ is the privacy budget. Specially, ϵ-differential privacy is achieved when $\delta = 0$.

To achieve differential privacy, researchers have proposed many mechanisms. Laplace Mechanism is proposed in [7] for numeric queries (e.g., How many students got A in the last quiz?). The mechanism is to add noise from zero-mean Laplace distribution to the query output. To reduce the noise in our case, we utilize smooth sensitivity instead of ΔQ in traditional Laplace Mechanism, which also achieves differential privacy. (See proof in [20]) Formally, we have the following definition and theorem.

Definition 2.2 (Local sensitivity) [20]. *The local sensitivity of a query function $Q : D^n \to \mathbb{R}^d$ is*

$$LS_Q(D) = \max_{D':\|D-D'\|_0=1} \|Q(D) - Q(D')\|_1 \tag{3}$$

Definition 2.3 (Smooth upper bound) [20]. *$S(\cdot)$ is a β-smooth upper bound on the local sensitivity if,*

$$\begin{aligned} &\forall D, S_Q(D) \geq LS_Q(D) \\ &\forall D, D' : \|D - D'\|_0, S_Q(D) \leq e^{-\beta} S_Q(D') \end{aligned} \tag{4}$$

Definition 2.4 (β-smooth sensitivity) [20]. *For $\beta > 0$, the β-smooth sensitivity of a query function $Q : D^n \to \mathbb{R}^d$ is*

$$S_{Q,\beta}^*(D) = \max_{D' \in D^n} (LS_Q(D') \cdot e^{-\beta\|D-D'\|_0}) \tag{5}$$

Theorem 2.1. *For $\epsilon, \delta \in (0, 1)$, the d-dimensional Laplace distribution, $h(z) = \frac{1}{2^d} \cdot e^{-\|z\|_1}$, is (α, β)-admissible with $\alpha = \frac{\epsilon}{2}$, and $\beta = \frac{\epsilon}{4(d+\ln(2/\delta))}$, where $Z \sim h(z)$. (See proof in [20]).*

Theorem 2.2. *Denote h be (α, β)-admissible noise p.d.f., and Z be sampled from h. For a query function $Q : D^n \to \mathbb{R}^d$, let $S_Q^* : D^n \to \mathbb{R}$ be a β-smooth sensitivity on the local sensitivity of Q. The following mechanism achieves (ϵ, δ)-differential privacy. (See proof in [20]).*

$$\mathcal{M}(D)^n = Q(D)^n + Z \cdot \frac{S_Q^*(D)}{\alpha} \tag{6}$$

The goal of ϵ-greedy is to choose an optimal policy among a range of policies. Hence, it seems impossible to directly add numeric noise to the arbitrary utilities. To address the problem, researchers proposed the exponential mechanism, which is regarded as the natural building block for answering queries with arbitrary utilities [8]. To achieve the exponential mechanism, we need to have a utility function $u : \mathbb{N}^{|\mathcal{X}|} \times \mathcal{R} \to \mathbb{R}$ and consider the sensitivity of u, where $\mathcal{R}$ is the arbitrary range. We have the following definition.

Definition 2.5 (Sensitivity of utility function) [8].

$$\Delta u = \max_{r \in \mathcal{R}} \max_{x,y:\|x-y\|_1 \leq 1} \|u(x,r) - u(y,r)\| \tag{7}$$

where x, y are neighbouring databases.

The exponential mechanism is to output $r \in \mathcal{R}$ with probability proportional to $\exp(\epsilon u(x,r)/2\Delta u)$. Formally, we have the following theorem thereby.

Theorem 2.3 (Exponential Mechanism). *ϵ-differential privacy can be achieved by Exponential Mechanism $\mathcal{M}(x, u, \mathcal{R})$, that satisfies*

$$Pr[\mathcal{M}(x, u, \mathcal{R}) = r] \propto \exp(\frac{\epsilon u(x,r)}{2\Delta u}) \tag{8}$$

where Δu is the sensitivity utility function. (See proof in [8]).

3 (ϵ, δ)-Differentially Private Reinforcement Learning

The above definition of differential privacy is based on the assumption that each tuple in the database is aggregated from individuals, aiming at protecting the demographic information of each tuple. However, in the reinforcement model, it seems hard to find an object relevant to the database.

The situation can change when we have an insight into the reinforcement learning model. Enormous tuples are generated in the runtime of the model. These tuples contain some information about the environment, and some of the data may be inherently sensitive. What we want to protect in this article is, therefore, the environments. Different environments result in the difference between optimal policy. For the seek of preventing inference attacks, our goal is to perturb the optimal policy.

In traditional differential privacy, we have the notion of neighboring databases, which only differ in one tuple. We can use the quaternion $\langle x_0, a, x, r \rangle$ to denote the tuple, where x_0 refers to the original state, a refers to the action, x refers to the transited state, and r refers to the reward given by the environment. Similarly, we can define the neighboring environment.

Definition 3.1 (Neighbouring Environment). *The neighbouring environments E, E' have exactly one case $\langle x_0^*, a^*, x^* \rangle$ satisfy*

$$\mathbb{E}[R_{E_0}(x_0^*, a^*, x^*)] \neq \mathbb{E}[R_{E_0'}(x_0^*, a^*, x^*)], \tag{9}$$

and for any $\langle x_0, a, x \rangle \neq \langle x_0^*, a^*, x^* \rangle$ satisfies

$$\mathbb{E}[R_{E_0}(x_0, a, x)] = \mathbb{E}[R_{E_0'}(x_0, a, x)], \tag{10}$$

and for any $\langle x_0, a, x \rangle$ satisfies

$$\begin{aligned} 0 \leq R_{E_0}(x_0, a, x) \leq \Lambda \\ 0 \leq R_{E_0'}(x_0, a, x) \leq \Lambda \end{aligned} \tag{11}$$

where $R_{E_0}, R_{E_0'}$ are the reward function of E, E' respectively, $\mathbb{E}[R_E(x_0, a, x)]$ denotes the mean of reward function and Λ denotes the upper bound of $\mathbb{E}[R_{E_0}(x_0, a, x)]$.

In other words, an environment E denotes a set of tuples in traditional differential privacy models. Hence, the definition of neighboring environments is similar to neighboring databases. A notable point in the definition is that $\mathbb{E}[R_E(x_0, a, x)] \leq \Lambda$. In non-numeric cases, the utility function u equals to $\arg\max_{\langle x_0, a, x \rangle} \mathbb{E}[R_{E_0}(x_0, a, x)]$. Without any constraints on E, the maximal difference between $u_{E_0}, u_{E_0'}$ is going to be very high. In the same way, in numeric cases, $\|Q(D) - Q(D')\|$ goes high as well. Hence, it is pointless to consider an environment E has an infinite reward, which results in an uncontrolled sensitivity.

Since we have neighboring environments E, E', we are now ready to define the (ϵ, δ)-differentially private reinforcement learning, which will guarantee a randomized reinforcement learning model output similarly in neighboring environments. We formulate the (ϵ, δ)-differentially private reinforcement learning thereby.

Definition 3.2 ((ϵ, δ)-differentially private reinforcement learning). *A reinforcement learning model $\mathcal{M}$ achieves ϵ-differentially private reinforcement learning, iff. for neighbouring environments $E, E' \in \mathcal{E}$ and $\pi \in \Pi$*

$$Pr[\mathcal{M}(E) = \pi] \leq \exp(\epsilon) \times Pr[\mathcal{M}(E') = \pi] + \delta \tag{12}$$

where $\mathcal{M}(E)$ (resp. $\mathcal{M}(E')$) denotes the optimal policy of $\mathcal{R}$ under the environment E (resp. E'), and π denotes the optimal policy of the model. Specially, ϵ-differentially private reinforcement learning is achieved when $\delta = 0$.

4   Mechanism Design

4.1   Exponential Mechanism for ϵ_{rl}-greedy

In ϵ_{rl}-greedy, the optimal policy $\pi^* = \arg\max_a \mathbb{E}[R(\cdot)]$. In other words, the best policy is to take the action under which the agent can be rewarded most. It is true that the reinforcement learning model does not choose the action with the most reward in all cases. In ϵ_{rl}-greedy, the model will explore other actions with the probability of ϵ_{rl}. After vast turns, $Q(a)$ equals to $\mathbb{E}[R(a)]$ at that time under the strong law of large numbers.

Hence, the utility function $u(E,r) = Q_E(a) = \mathbb{E}[R(a)]$, when $t \to +\infty$, where $Q_E(a)$ refers to $Q(a)$ under environment E. Since we have the utility function, we can analyse the sensitivity of u. Similarly, the definition of Δu denotes the maximal difference of $u(E,r)$ due to one change in the environment. We have the sensitivity of $u(E,r)$.

$$
\begin{aligned}
\Delta u &= \max_{a \in \mathcal{A}} \max_{E,E'} \| u(E,a) - u(E',a) \| \\
&= \max_{a \in \mathcal{A}} \max_{E,E'} \| \mathbb{E}[R_E(a)] - \mathbb{E}[R_{E'}(a)] \| \\
&= \max_{a \in \mathcal{A}} \| \max(\mathbb{E}[R_E(a)], \mathbb{E}[R_{E'}(a)]) \| \\
&= \Lambda
\end{aligned}
\tag{13}
$$

where E, E' are neighbouring environments, Λ denotes the upper bound of reward for all actions.

Algorithm 1. Differentially private ϵ_{rl}-greedy for the K-armed bandit

---

Input: Reward Function R; Number of Arms K; Exploration Rate ϵ_{rl}; Privacy Budget
    ϵ; Reward Upper Bound Λ.
1: $r \leftarrow 0$
2: **for all** $i \in \{1, 2, \cdots, K\}$ **do**
3:     $Q(i) \leftarrow 0$
4:     $count(i) \leftarrow 0$
5: **end for**
6: **repeat**
7:     $t \leftarrow t + 1k$
8:     **if** $rand() < \epsilon_{rl}$ **then**
9:         $a \leftarrow \lceil K \times rand() \rceil$
10:    **else**
11:        $a \leftarrow \arg\max_i Q(i)$
12:    **end if**
13:    $v = R(a)$
14:    $Q(a) \leftarrow \frac{Q(a) \times count(a) + v}{count(a) + 1}$
15:    $count(a) \leftarrow count(a) + 1$
16:    $\pi \leftarrow \arg\max_i Q(i)$ //update policy
17: **until** $t \to +\infty$
18: **for all** $i \in \{1, 2, \cdots, K\}$ **do**
19:    $P(i) \leftarrow \exp(\frac{\epsilon Q(a)}{2\Lambda})$
20: **end for**
21: Choose an action a based on probability distribution P
22: $\pi^* = \arg\max_i Q(i)$
Output: Optimal Policy π^*

Algorithm 1 describes the differentially private ϵ_{rl}-greedy in the K-armed bandit problem, where $rand()$ returns the randomized real number in $[0,1]$, $count(a)$

refers to the times of action a being taken, $Q(a)$ refers to the mean reward of an action a. We perturb the final output, which may not return the optimal policy. But with high probability, the algorithm will output a relatively optimal policy. The probability distribution can be managed by modifying the parameter ϵ. Greater ϵ always combines with better privacy guarantees. In an extreme case, if $\epsilon = 0$, the algorithm will randomly choose a policy. And we also present the proof for achieving differential privacy in Appendix A.

Selection of T. Theoretically, the loop will never break in the algorithm due to the unfulfillable terminate condition. Instead, the terminate condition can be set to a value, where each action can well test. For a K-armed bandit, if the reward of each action obeys distribution $\mathcal{D}$. The mean test time of each action $\mathbb{E}(t_a) \geq \frac{\epsilon_{rl}T}{K}$. Since that all outputs in $R(\cdot)$ are i.i.d. and follows a certain distribution, we can attain an approximate bound for estimating $\mathbb{E}(R(\cdot))$. To improve the readability, the detailed analysis is presented in Appendix B. Nevertheless, to achieve the estimation with high accuracy and confidence, the bound is still too high for the algorithm, especially with a small ϵ_{rl}. In practice, $T = \gamma \times \frac{K}{\epsilon_{rl}}$, where γ is a constant. According to our experiments, in most cases, it suffices to take $\gamma = 20$ (γ will be discussed in the next section).

4.2 Laplace Mechanism for Softmax

Instead of outputting an optimal policy, Softmax outputs a p.d.f. denoting probability of each actions being taken. Basically, the allocation of probabilities follows the Boltzmann distribution.

$$P(k) = \frac{\exp(\frac{Q(k)}{\tau})}{\sum_{i=0}^{K} \exp(\frac{Q(i)}{\tau})} \tag{14}$$

similarly, where $Q(k)$ denotes the mean reward of k and τ is a parameter in Boltzmann distribution. For the reason that Softmax outputs the p.d.f. of actions, the query f can be formulated as follows.

$$f(E) = P = [\frac{\exp(\frac{Q(1)}{\tau})}{\sum_{i=0}^{K} \exp(\frac{Q(i)}{\tau})}, \cdots, \frac{\exp(\frac{Q(k)}{\tau})}{\sum_{i=0}^{K} \exp(\frac{Q(i)}{\tau})}] \tag{15}$$

The local sensitivity are attained thereby.

$$
\begin{aligned}
LS_f &= \max_{E':\|E-E'\|_0=1} \|Q_E(a) - Q_{E'}(a)\|_1 \\
&= \max_{E'} \sum_{i}^{K} \frac{h_E(k)}{\sum_{i=0}^{K} h_E(i)} - \frac{h_{E'}(k)}{\sum_{i=0}^{K} h_{E'}(i)} \\
&= \max_{E'} \frac{2(\sum h_E(i) - h_{E'}(i^*))(h_E(i^*) - h_{E'}(i^*))}{\sum h_E(i) \sum h_{E'}(i)} \\
&= \frac{2h_E(i^*)}{\sum h_E(i)} \text{ when } h_{E'}(i^*) = 0 \\
&= \max_{a \in \mathcal{A}} \frac{2h_E(a)}{\sum h_E(i)}
\end{aligned}
\tag{16}
$$

where $h(i)$ denotes $\exp(\frac{Q(i)}{\tau})$, $i^* = \arg\max h_E(i)$.

Assume for simplicity that $0 \leq \frac{2f_E(1)}{\sum f_E(i)} \leq \cdots \leq \frac{2f_E(|\mathcal{A}|)}{\sum f_E(i)} \leq \Lambda$. Then we have the β-smooth sensitivity.

$$S^*_{f,\beta}(E) = \max_{E' \in E^n} (LS_f(E') \cdot e^{-\beta\|E-E'\|_0})$$
$$= \max_{k=0,\cdots,|\mathcal{A}|} \left(\max_{a \in \mathcal{A}} \frac{2h_E(a)}{\sum h_E(i)} \cdot e^{-\beta k}\right) \tag{17}$$

Since we have the above $S^*_{Q,\beta}(E)$, we can traverse all prospective k and find the maximal sensitivity.

Algorithm 2. Differentially private Softmax for the K-armed bandit

---

Input: Reward Function R; Number of Arms K; Temperature τ; Privacy Parameters
ϵ, δ; Reward Upper Bound Λ.
1: $r \leftarrow 0$
2: $\alpha \leftarrow \epsilon/2$, $\beta \leftarrow \frac{\epsilon}{4(K+\ln(2/\delta))}$ Apply **Theorem 2.1**
3: **for all** $i \in \{1, 2, \cdots, K\}$ **do**
4: $\quad Q(i) \leftarrow 0$
5: $\quad count(i) \leftarrow 0$
6: **end for**
7: $t \leftarrow 0$
8: **repeat**
9: $\quad t \leftarrow t+1$
10: $\quad$ Choose an action a based on **Eq. 14**
11: $\quad v = R(a)$
12: $\quad Q(a) \leftarrow \frac{Q(a)\times count(a)+v}{count(a)+1}$
13: $\quad count(a) \leftarrow count(a) + 1$
14: **until** $t \to +\infty$
15: Traverse all k for $S^*_f(E)$
16: $\widetilde{P} = P + Z^K \cdot \frac{S^*_f(E)}{\alpha}$ Apply **Theorem 2.2**
17: Normalise $\widetilde{P}$
Output: Optimal Policy Probability Density Function $\widetilde{P}$

Algorithm 2 describes the differentially private Softmax for the K-armed bandit, where the output is p.d.f. With smooth sensitivity, a more fine-grained noise is attained. To simplify, we present the traversing algorithm in Appendix C. The detailed proof is too long to be conveyed in this paper, but a similar proof on traditional differential privacy can be found in [20].

5 Experiments

To compare the privacy and utility in our method, we design a series of experiments on synthetic data.

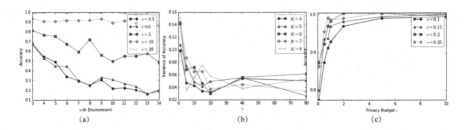

Fig. 2. Comparison of (a) accuracy in different environments with different privacy budget ϵ, (b) variance of accuracy under different γ in different environments in ϵ-greedy algorithm, and accuracy in different privacy budget ϵ with different τ in Softmax algorithm.

Synthetic Dataset. We design a set of synthetic tuples to simulate the situation in real-world scenarios. As in illustrated in Eq. 18, we generate some datasets which vary in scale and reward distribution which obeys the following equation.

$$\mathbb{E}^K(R_{E_K}(a)) = [\underbrace{\frac{1}{2}^1, \frac{1}{2}^2, \cdots, \frac{1}{2}^{K-2}, \frac{1}{2}^{K-1}, \frac{1}{2}^{K-1}}_{K \text{ items}}] \tag{18}$$

where K denotes the arms of the bandit. The probability distribution of the reward function for each input action obeys the following equation.

$$Pr(R_E(a) = r) = \begin{cases} 0.5 \; r = 2\mathbb{E}[R_E(a)] \\ 0.5 \; r = 0 \end{cases} \tag{19}$$

Configuration. Denoting π^* and $\widetilde{\pi^*}$ as the true optimal policy and the perturbed policy, we define the accuracy for publishing $\widetilde{\pi^*}$ as $\frac{\sum^t R(\widetilde{\pi^*})}{\sum^t R(\pi^*)}$ in ϵ-greedy, where t denotes the repeat time and equals to 50 in our experiments. For Softmax, $\delta = 0.01$, $T = 200K$, $K = 3$. And the accuracy equals to $\frac{E^T \widetilde{P}}{E^T P}$, where P denotes the p.d.f. of actions and E denotes the mean reward of actions.

Result. Given are Fig. 2(a), (b) and (c) that compares the accuracy in different environments with different privacy budget ϵ, γ and τ. From Fig. 2(a), we observe that our mechanism has high performance on synthetic datasets. In small privacy budget ϵ cases, the accuracy begins to fall as the number of arms increases. And, for $\epsilon > 10$, the proposed mechanism maintains a tolerable error rate regardless of the scale of environments. Comparing lines in Fig. 2(b), it is evident that for small γ, the accuracy holds a high variance. As γ grows, for all environments in the experiments, the accuracy becomes steady. Figure 2(c) illustrates the performance of the differentially private Softmax algorithm. The accuracy is strong enough when $\epsilon > 1$ for all values of τ in the experiments.

Summary of the Experimental Analysis

- Our mechanisms provide sufficient privacy and utility in reinforcement learning contexts (both ϵ-greedy and Softmax). Appropriate privacy budget can be selected to achieve privacy-utility trade-off based on the scale of environments.
- The growth on the scale of environments in ϵ-greedy may result in the sharp reduction of accuracy (with more than 10x accurate with different privacy budget in the same environment), but the exponential mechanism works well on small scale environments even in small privacy budget.
- The accuracy is fluctuating in ϵ-greedy for a small γ and becomes steady when the number increases. We select γ as 20 for utility-efficiency trade-off.
- The smooth sensitivity greatly improves the accuracy in Softmax. To be precise, smooth sensitivity saves about 15% of noise to achieve the same level of privacy in this case when compared with global sensitivity.

6   Related Work

Machine learning/deep learning is one of the most popular queries in this era, which enables people to discover the inherent property and connection among tuples [24]. However, the models, as well as corresponding training data, are under threats from various perspective [18].

Privacy-Preserving Machine Learning. [21] proposed privacy-preserving distributed reinforcement learning. [15] then introduced the sample complexity of differentially private learning. [14] carefully reviewed the state-of-the-art methods of differentially private machine learning (supervised learning, unsupervised learning, dimensionality reduction, statistical estimators, respectively). [1] developed a differentially private deep learning model based on TensorFlow. [26] proposed a privacy-preserving scheme for ML called Heda combined homomorphic cryptosystem with differential privacy and a set of methods for determining appropriate privacy budget and reducing sensitivity.

Comparison to [2,19,27]**.** For differentially private reinforcement learning, [2,19,27] did extensive work in this field. But their approaches still adopted traditional differential privacy, which is not applicable in the generic reinforcement learning contexts. Their works perturbed the trajectory series which may result in global reward degradation. We extend the notion in reinforcement learning contexts that distinguish our work from theirs.

7   Conclusion

As ML/DL techniques are widely used, the security and privacy of these systems are of great significance. While enormous methods were proposed in recent years, a formal model for privacy guarantees for reinforcement learning remains to be studied. Though most reinforcement learning approaches do not require initial training data, the environments may contain sensitive information and be attacked in some scenarios.

In this paper, we discuss the privacy models in both traditional queries and reinforcement learning contexts, define the notion of neighboring environments, propose (ϵ, δ)-differentially private reinforcement learning model and develop mechanisms for privacy-preserving ϵ_{rl}-greedy and Softmax algorithms in the K-armed bandit problem. Our implementation and experiments illustrate that the policies given by our model are under good privacy guarantees with a tolerable utility cost.

Acknowledgement. This research was financially supported by the National Key Research and Development Plan (2018YFB1004101), China Postdoctoral Science Foundation Funded Project (2019M650606), Key Lab of Information Network Security, Ministry of Public Security (C19614), Special Fund on Education and Teaching Reform of BESTI (jy201805), the Fundamental Research Funds for the Central Universities (328201910), Key Laboratory of Network Assessment Technology of Institute of Information Engineering, Chinese Academy of Sciences.

Appendices

A. Proof of Algorithm 1

$$
\begin{aligned}
\frac{Pr[\mathcal{M}(E) = \pi]}{Pr[\mathcal{M}(E') = \pi]} &= \frac{\frac{\exp(\frac{\epsilon}{2}Q_E(\pi)/\Lambda)}{\int_{a \in \mathcal{A}} \exp(\frac{\epsilon}{2}Q_E(a)/\Lambda)da}}{\frac{\exp(\frac{\epsilon}{2}Q_{E'}(\pi)/\Lambda)}{\int_{a \in \mathcal{A}} \exp(\frac{\epsilon}{2}Q_{E'}(a)/\Lambda)da}} \\
&= \frac{\frac{\exp(\frac{\epsilon}{2}\mathbb{E}[R_E(\pi)]/\Lambda)}{\int_{a \in \mathcal{A}} \exp(\frac{\epsilon}{2}\mathbb{E}[R_E(a)]/\Lambda)da}}{\frac{\exp(\frac{\epsilon}{2}\mathbb{E}[R_{E'}(\pi)]/\Lambda)}{\int_{a \in \mathcal{A}} \exp(\frac{\epsilon}{2}\mathbb{E}[R_{E'}(a)]/\Lambda)da}} \quad \text{For } T \to +\infty \\
&= \frac{\exp(\frac{\epsilon}{2}(\mathbb{E}[R_E(\pi)] - \mathbb{E}[R_{E'}(\pi)])/\Lambda)}{\int_{a \in \mathcal{A}} \exp(\frac{\epsilon}{2}(\mathbb{E}[R_E(a)] - \mathbb{E}[R_{E'}(a)])/\Lambda)da} \\
&\leq \frac{\exp(\frac{\epsilon}{2}\Delta u/\Lambda)}{\exp(-\frac{\epsilon}{2}\Delta u/\Lambda)\int_{a \in \mathcal{A}} da} \quad \text{Apply } \textbf{Eq. 8} \\
&\leq \exp(\epsilon) \quad \text{If } \int_{a \in \mathcal{A}} da \geq 1
\end{aligned}
\tag{20}
$$

B. Analysis on Total Time Steps

We analyze the total time steps n needed to get a *accurate* approximation of $q_*(a) = \mathbb{E}_t[R_t \mid A_t = a]$ for every action a. The analysis is presented in two aspects. The first aspect is to consider how many times m we need to select action a to get an accurate approximation of $q_*(a)$. The second aspect is to analyze the value of n needed to guarantee m times sampling of a. We start with the first aspect.

Recall that w.l.o.g. R_t is assumed to be within $[0, \Lambda]$. Consider the Doob martingale $B_i = \mathbb{E}[\frac{1}{m}(X_1 + X_2 + \cdots + X_m) \mid X_1, X_2, \ldots, X_i]$, where X_i is the numerical reward received when we select action a. Note that X_i's are i.i.d. The stochastic process $B_0, B_1, \ldots$ is a martingale w.r.t. X_i as $\mathbb{E}(|B_j|) \leq \Lambda < \infty$ and

$$
\begin{aligned}
&\mathbb{E}[B_{j+1} \mid X_1, \ldots, X_j] \\
&= \mathbb{E}\left[\mathbb{E}\left(\frac{1}{m}(X_1 + \cdots + X_m) \mid X_1, \cdots, X_{j+1}\right) \mid X_1, \cdots, X_j\right] \\
&= \mathbb{E}\left[\frac{1}{m}(X_1 + X_2 + \cdots + X_m) \mid X_1, \ldots, X_j\right] \\
&= B_j
\end{aligned}
\tag{21}
$$

holds. Note that $B_0 = \mathbb{E}[\frac{1}{m}(X_1 + X_2 + \cdots + X_m)] = q_*(a)$ and $B_m = \frac{1}{m}(X_1 + X_2 + \cdots + X_m)$, which is just $Q(a)$ in the algorithm. We also have $|B_{j+1} - B_j| \leq \frac{\Lambda}{m}$ as X_i's are independent and

$$
\left|\frac{1}{m}(x_1 + \cdots + x_j + \cdots + x_m) - \frac{1}{m}(x_1 + \cdots + x'_j + \cdots + x_m)\right| \leq \frac{\Lambda}{m}
\tag{22}
$$

holds. According to the Azuma-Hoeffding inequality, we then have $P(|Q(a) - q_*(a)| \geq \lambda\Lambda) \leq 2\exp\left(-\frac{(\lambda\Lambda)^2}{2\Lambda^2/m}\right) = 2\exp\left(-\frac{\lambda^2 m}{2}\right)$, where $\lambda \in (0, 1)$.

Now we consider the second aspect. Instead of counting the number of times a particular action a is selected, we consider the number of times selecting a when $rand() < \epsilon_{rl}$, which servers as a lower bound of the actual counting. Denote the latter as Y_i. So in every time step, action a is selected with probability $\frac{\epsilon_{rl}}{K}$. Applying Chernoff bound, if the total time steps $n = \frac{2mK}{\epsilon_{rl}}$ we have $P(Y_i < m) \leq \exp\left(-\frac{m}{4}\right)$. Applying the union bound we have the probability that every action is selected at least m times is at least $1 - K\exp\left(-\frac{m}{4}\right)$. With conditional probability the final probability that every estimate $Q(a)$ is within $\lambda\Lambda$ of $q_*(a)$ is

$$
\begin{aligned}
&\left(1 - K \cdot 2e^{-\frac{\lambda^2 m}{2}}\right)\left(1 - Ke^{-\frac{m}{4}}\right) \\
&\geq 1 - K\left(2e^{-\frac{\lambda^2 m}{2}} + e^{-\frac{m}{4}}\right) \\
&\geq 1 - \frac{3}{K^{c'}} \geq 1 - \frac{1}{K^c}
\end{aligned}
\tag{23}
$$

if we choose $m = \frac{2}{\lambda^2}(c' + 1)\ln K$, where c', c are constants. In a word if the total time steps $n \geq \frac{4K}{\epsilon_{rl}\lambda^2}(c' + 1)\ln K$ then w.h.p. every action value estimate is within a preferable range of the true action value.

C. Traverse in Algorithm 2

Algorithm 3. Traverse for S_f^*

Input: Number of Arms K; Privacy Parameter β; Upper Bound Λ.

1: $S_f^*(E) \leftarrow -\infty$
2: **for all** $k \in \{1, 2, \cdots, K\}$ **do**
3:     $S_f(E) \leftarrow \frac{\Lambda}{\sum^{K-k} h_E(i) + \Lambda} \cdot e^{-\beta k}$
4:     **if** $S_f^*(E) < S_f(E)$ **then**
5:         $S_f^*(E) \leftarrow S_f(E)$
6:     **end if**
7: **end for**
Output: Smooth Sensitivity $S_f^*(E)$

References

1. Abadi, M., et al.: Deep learning with differential privacy. In: Proceedings of the 2016 ACM SIGSAC Conference on Computer and Communications Security, pp. 308–318. ACM (2016)
2. Balle, B., Gomrokchi, M., Precup, D.: Differentially private policy evaluation. In: International Conference on Machine Learning, pp. 2130–2138 (2016)
3. Berry, D.A., Fristedt, B.: Bandit Problems: Sequential Allocation of Experiments (Monographs on Statistics and Applied Probability), vol. 5, pp. 71–87. Chapman and Hall, London (1985)
4. Dwork, C.: Differential privacy: a survey of results. In: Agrawal, M., Du, D., Duan, Z., Li, A. (eds.) TAMC 2008. LNCS, vol. 4978, pp. 1–19. Springer, Heidelberg (2008). https://doi.org/10.1007/978-3-540-79228-4_1
5. Dwork, C.: Differential privacy. In: van Tilborg, H.C.A., Jajodia, S. (eds.) Encyclopedia of Cryptography and Security, pp. 338–340. Springer, Boston (2011). https://doi.org/10.1007/978-1-4419-5906-5
6. Dwork, C.: A firm foundation for private data analysis. Commun. ACM **54**(1), 86–95 (2011)
7. Dwork, C., McSherry, F., Nissim, K., Smith, A.: Calibrating noise to sensitivity in private data analysis. In: Halevi, S., Rabin, T. (eds.) TCC 2006. LNCS, vol. 3876, pp. 265–284. Springer, Heidelberg (2006). https://doi.org/10.1007/11681878_14
8. Dwork, C., Roth, A., et al.: The algorithmic foundations of differential privacy. Found. Trends® Theoret. Comput. Sci. **9**(3–4), 211–407 (2014)
9. Erlingsson, Ú., Pihur, V., Korolova, A.: RAPPOR: randomized aggregatable privacy-preserving ordinal response. In: Proceedings of the 2014 ACM SIGSAC Conference on Computer and Communications Security, pp. 1054–1067. ACM (2014)
10. Fredrikson, M., Jha, S., Ristenpart, T.: Model inversion attacks that exploit confidence information and basic countermeasures. In: Proceedings of the 22nd ACM SIGSAC Conference on Computer and Communications Security, pp. 1322–1333. ACM (2015)

11. Friedman, A., Schuster, A.: Data mining with differential privacy. In: Proceedings of the 16th ACM SIGKDD International Conference on Knowledge Discovery and Data Mining, KDD 2010, pp. 493–502. ACM, New York (2010)

12. Gittins, J., Glazebrook, K., Weber, R.: Multi-Armed Bandit Allocation Indices. Wiley, Hoboken (2011)

13. Jaakkola, T., Singh, S.P., Jordan, M.I.: Reinforcement learning algorithm for partially observable Markov decision problems. In: Advances in Neural Information Processing Systems, pp. 345–352 (1995)

14. Ji, Z., Lipton, Z.C., Elkan, C.: Differential privacy and machine learning: a survey and review. arXiv preprint arXiv:1412.7584 (2014)

15. Kasiviswanathan, S.P., Lee, H.K., Nissim, K., Raskhodnikova, S., Smith, A.: What can we learn privately? SIAM J. Comput. 40(3), 793–826 (2011)

16. Kuleshov, V., Precup, D.: Algorithms for multi-armed bandit problems. arXiv preprint arXiv:1402.6028 (2014)

17. LeCun, Y., Bengio, Y., Hinton, G.: Deep learning. Nature 521(7553), 436 (2015)

18. Liu, Q., Li, P., Zhao, W., Cai, W., Yu, S., Leung, V.C.M.: A survey on security threats and defensive techniques of machine learning: a data driven view. IEEE Access 6, 12103–12117 (2018). https://doi.org/10.1109/ACCESS.2018.2805680

19. Mishra, N., Thakurta, A.: (Nearly) optimal differentially private stochastic multi-arm bandits. In: Proceedings of the Thirty-First Conference on Uncertainty in Artificial Intelligence, pp. 592–601. AUAI Press (2015)

20. Nissim, K., Raskhodnikova, S., Smith, A.: Smooth sensitivity and sampling in private data analysis. In: Proceedings of the Thirty-ninth Annual ACM Symposium on Theory of Computing, pp. 75–84. ACM (2007)

21. Sakuma, J., Kobayashi, S., Wright, R.N.: Privacy-preserving reinforcement learning. In: Proceedings of the 25th International Conference on Machine learning, pp. 864–871. ACM (2008)

22. Salem, A., Zhang, Y., Humbert, M., Berrang, P., Fritz, M., Backes, M.: ML-Leaks: model and data independent membership inference attacks and defenses on machine learning models. arXiv preprint arXiv:1806.01246 (2018)

23. Shokri, R., Stronati, M., Song, C., Shmatikov, V.: Membership inference attacks against machine learning models. In: 2017 IEEE Symposium on Security and Privacy (SP), pp. 3–18. IEEE (2017)

24. Sun, S.: A survey of multi-view machine learning. Neural Comput. Appl. 23(7–8), 2031–2038 (2013)

25. Sutton, R.S., Barto, A.G.: Reinforcement Learning: An Introduction. MIT Press, Cambridge (2018)

26. Tang, X., Zhu, L., Shen, M., Du, X.: When homomorphic cryptosystem meets differential privacy: training machine learning classifier with privacy protection. arXiv preprint arXiv:1812.02292 (2018)

27. Tossou, A.C., Dimitrakakis, C.: Algorithms for differentially private multi-armed bandits. In: Thirtieth AAAI Conference on Artificial Intelligence (2016)

28. Wu, X., Fredrikson, M., Jha, S., Naughton, J.F.: A methodology for formalizing model-inversion attacks. In: 2016 IEEE 29th Computer Security Foundations Symposium (CSF), pp. 355–370. IEEE (2016)

Privacy-Preserving Distributed Machine Learning Based on Secret Sharing

Ye Dong[1,2], Xiaojun Chen[1(✉)], Liyan Shen[1,2], and Dakui Wang[1]

[1] Institute of Information Engineering, Chinese Academy of Sciences, Beijing, China
{dongye,chenxiaojun,shenliyan,wangdakui}@iie.ac.cn
[2] School of Cyber Security, University of Chinese Academy of Sciences,
Beijing, China

Abstract. Machine Learning has been widely applied in practice, such as disease diagnosis, target detection. Commonly, a good model relies on massive training data collected from different sources. However, the collected data might expose sensitive information. To solve the problem, researchers have proposed many excellent methods that combine machine learning with privacy protection technologies, such as secure multiparty computation (MPC), homomorphic encryption (HE), and differential privacy. In the meanwhile, some other researchers proposed distributed machine learning which allows the clients to store their data locally but train a model collaboratively. The first kind of methods focuses on security, but the performance and accuracy remain to be improved, while the second provides higher accuracy and better performance but weaker security, for instance, the adversary can launch membership attacks from the gradients' updates in plaintext.

In this paper, we join secret sharing to distributed machine learning to achieve reliable performance, accuracy, and high-level security. Next, we design, implement, and evaluate a practical system to jointly learn an accurate model under semi-honest and servers-only malicious adversary security, respectively. And the experiments show our protocols achieve the best overall performance as well.

Keywords: Secret sharing · Distributed machine learning · Privacy-preserving

1 Introduction

Recent advances in machine learning have produced exciting achievements both in academia and industry, the machine learning systems are approaching or even surpassing human-level accuracy in speech, image and text recognition. That thanks to algorithmic breakthroughs and hardware developments, which help our systems process massive amounts of data.

However, massive data collection, which is a key step in learning an accurate model, has caused public panic about privacy breaches. As a consequence, the useful but sensitive data such as medical records, are forbidden to be shared

© Springer Nature Switzerland AG 2020
J. Zhou et al. (Eds.): ICICS 2019, LNCS 11999, pp. 684–702, 2020.
https://doi.org/10.1007/978-3-030-41579-2_40

among different institutes due to proprietary reasons or compliance requirements [20,32]. Privacy-preserving machine learning via MPC provides a promising solution by allowing different institutions to train various models based on their joint data without revealing any sensitive information beyond the outcome.

The state-of-the-art solutions for privacy-preserving machine learning based on MPC, i.e. [22,26,28], are many orders of magnitude slower than training on plaintext. The main source of inefficiency is that the bulk of computation in the training phase takes place within a secure manner such as garbled circuits or HE. It is well-known that computing complex function, especially non-linear function, in secure form is very expensive.

To improve the efficiency, we design our protocols based on distributed machine learning and instead of joining the secure computation technologies to these expensive computations in our protocols, we join secret sharing to the gradients' sharing phase which only consists of simple arithmetics, i.e. addition. In this way, we can improve efficiency greatly while still meet the security requirements. Finally, each client can learn no information beyond the trained model, and the parameter servers can learn no sensitive information.

1.1 Our Contribution

In this paper, We design two new and efficient protocols for privacy-preserving linear regression, Multilayer perceptron (MLP), and Convolutional neural network (CNN) in the distributed machine learning settings assuming the data are distributed across the clients. Then we give the security analysis of our protocols. And lastly, we implement, evaluate our protocols and compare them with other latest results in a comparable environment.

Resistance to Semi-honest and Servers-Only Malicious Adversary. In the semi-honest setting, we use Shamir's Secret Sharing to design protocol Γ_{sash}. As long as no more than $t - 1$ (t is the threshold) servers can collude and at least two clients are honest, Γ_{sash} can against users-only, servers-only and users-servers threat models.

In the malicious setting, to resist servers-only malicious modifications, we design a verifiable protocol Γ_{sam} via a variant of Secret Sharing with information-theoretic Message Authentication Code (MAC) [12]. In Γ_{sam}, besides sharing the gradients g, each client computes g's information-theoretic MAC and shares it among parameter servers. In addition to protecting privacy like Γ_{sash}, Γ_{sam} can prevent servers from malicious modifications as long as no more than $t-1$ servers can collude and no client colludes with servers.

Performances. Our privacy-preserving machine learning protocols are more efficient than state-of-the-art solutions. For example, for a dataset with 60,000 samples and 784 features, our protocol is 30× faster than the protocols implemented in [27] for CNN in the semi-honest setting. And even our malicious protocol can achieve 25× improvement.

As discussed above, our protocols can be divided into two phases, offline and online phase. In a comparable experimental environment, our protocols are at the same efficiency level with [24] in the online phase, but we can achieve 5×–10× improvement in the offline phase. Note that vectorization, i.e. operating on matrices and vectors, is critical in the efficiency of training on plaintext, we can benefit from this technique here. For instance, we find that the vectorized protocols improve our efficiency around 7.5–10× in the online phases and 5–10× in the offline phases.

As experiments show, our protocols are even more competitive with training on plaintext. For instance, for the MNIST[1], our protocols can achieve the same level of accuracy at a total time of 40.2 s for linear regression, 205.2 s for MLP and 723.6 s for CNN.

1.2   Related Work

In the earlier stage, the work on privacy-preserving machine learning mainly focused on traditional machine learning models such as linear regression [3–5], logistic regression [8], decision trees [2], k-means clustering [6,9] and SVM [7,10]. These papers proposed solutions based on MPC but were limited to a particular kind of model. For example, Nikolaenko et al. [13] and Gascon et al. [19] presented secure computation protocols for linear regression on mega datasets via leveled-HE (LHE) and garbled circuits. However, both papers are limited to linear regression and the key problems are both reduced to solving a linear system using Yao's garbled circuits. And the efficiency overheads appear to be very high.

For the logistic regression, Wu et al. [14] chose to approximate the sigmoid function using polynomials and train the model using LHE, but the complexity is too high and accuracy is poor. Mohassel et al. [22] presented a solution that can be applied to linear regression, logistic regression and neural networks on the two-server setting where data owners distribute their private data among two non-collude servers and proposed a new method based on piecewise linear function for the non-linear function to improve efficiency. However, there is still a big gap compared to training on plaintext.

Meanwhile, Liu et al. [23] proposed a secure inference framework that can protect the server's model and client's data at the same time. Privacy-preserving predictions were also studied by Galad-Bachrach et al. [21,31]. But the models in this setting need to be trained on plaintext ahead of time.

Shokri and Shmatikov [17] proposed a solution by sharing the model's gradients among the clients during the training via a parameter server. They improve the efficiency greatly, but the leaks of gradients could weaken the security [29]. Phon et al. [27] extended the result against semi-honest adversaries using LHE, but the performance is too poor. Recently, Bonawitz et al. [24] proposed a protocol to secure aggregate gradients. But their offline phase is very complex, and if some clients dropped out, the efficiency would be reduced.

---

[1] MNIST database, http://yann.lecun.com/exdb/mnist/. Accessed: 2017-09-24.

So it is urgent and challenging to propose a secure framework to train complex and huge machine learning models efficiently.

An orthogonal and complementary work considers the differential privacy of machine learning algorithms [15,18]. In this setting, the key point is to introduce an additive noise to the data or the update function, so as to prevent the adversary from inferring the data from the released model. Our system can be combined with such technology to provide stronger security.

1.3 Roadmap

In Sect. 2, we introduce the preliminaries. In Sect. 3, we give our system architecture and the design of our protocols. We also analyze the correctness and privacy of our protocols. In Sect. 4, we give the results of our experiments, and in Sect. 5, we conclude our paper.

2 Preliminaries

In this paper, the notations we used are as below:

a denotes a scalar, g denotes a vector and g_i denotes the i-th element of g. $\mathbf{X}$ denotes a matrix and $\mathbf{X}_{ij}$ denotes the element in row i and column j. $\langle a \rangle_i$ denotes the i-th shares of a, and the same as to vector and matrix. And N denotes the number of servers and M denotes the number of clients.

2.1 Machine Learning

In this section, we briefly review the distributed machine learning and some machine learning algorithms: linear regression, MLP, CNN. All these algorithms are classic and can be found in standard machine learning papers or textbooks.

Distributed Machine Learning is a new kind of settings of machine learning, there exist many different settings [25,30] and we adopt the Parameter-Server (PS) setting [16] in this paper. As shown in Fig. 1, in the P-S setting there are many clients and one parameter server. Each client has a private dataset. Note that the data between different clients are of the same type, i.e. medical records. In general, there are five phases in the P-S setting, local training phase, upload phase, aggregate phase, download phase, and update phase.

Before training, all the clients negotiate a unified model and everyone stores a replica and initializes it. In the local training phase, each client trains the model locally and computes the gradients $g = (g_0, g_1, ..., g_{n-1})$, where g_i is the gradient for coefficient w_i. Next, the clients will upload g to the parameter server. On the other hand, the parameter server will wait a while to receive enough gradients and then aggregate them as sum $g_s = \sum g$ or average $g_{avg} = \frac{1}{M} g_s$. Finally, the clients will download the aggregated gradients and update the local model for the next training epoch.

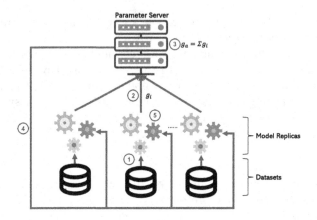

Fig. 1. Distributed machine learning, parameter-server setting. ① local training, ② upload gradients, ③ aggregate gradients, ④ download gradients, ⑤ update the local model.

Distributed Selective SGD. Learning the parameters of a model is not easy, especially for a complex model, i.e. neural networks. The methods that solve this problem are typically variants of gradient descent algorithm (GD) [11]. Among these algorithms, stochastic gradient descent (SGD) is a drastic simplification that computes the gradients over a subset (mini-batch) of the whole dataset while maintains high accuracy.

Let w be the vector of all parameters in a model, w_i is the i-th element of w. Let E be the error function which can be based on L^2 norm or cross-entropy. The update rule of SGD for a parameter w_i is

$$w_i = w_i - \alpha \frac{\partial E_i}{\partial w_i} \tag{1}$$

where α is the learning rate and E_i is the error computed over the mini-batch i.

Note that the update of each parameter is independent, so that the client can send a portion of gradients which are important instead of all gradients to reduce communication [17], which we use in this paper.

Linear Regression. Given n training data samples x_i, each contains d features and the corresponding labels y_i, where $y_i = \pm 1$. Training a linear regression model is a process to learn a function f such that $f(x_i) = y_i$. Linear regression has many applications in real life, i.e. detecting diseases in medical research.

In linear regression, the function f is a linear operation and can be represented as the inner product of x_i and the coefficient vector w:

$$f(x_i) = \sum_{j=1}^{d} x_{ij} w_j = x_i \cdot w \tag{2}$$

where $\cdot$ denote the inner product of two vectors.

Multi-layer Perceptron. Deep Learning aims to extract more complex features than traditional machine learning models. MLP is one basic form of deep learning models.

Figure 2(a) shows a typical MLP with two hidden layers, each node represents a neuron, it receives the output of the neurons of previous layers plus a bias from a special neuron. Then it computes a weighted average of its inputs. Finally, the neuron applies a non-linear function to the weighted average.

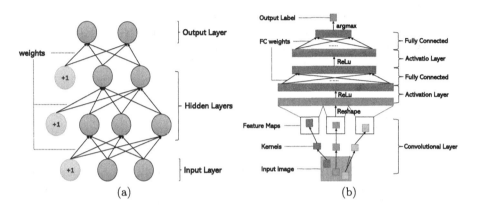

Fig. 2. Neural networks. (a) is for MLP, (b) is for CNN.

Convolutional Neural Networks. CNN has gained much more attention in the past decades owing to its superb accuracy. While there are many different CNNs, they all share a similar structure.

As shown in Fig. 2(b), the input to a CNN is represented as a matrix $\mathbf{X}$ where each element corresponds to the value of a pixel. Pictures can have multiple color channels, i.e. RGB, in which case the picture is represented as a multidimensional matrix, i.e. tensor. Compared to MLP, CNN has additive layers: (i) Convolution layer, (ii) (Mean or Max)-Pooling layer, both play important roles.

2.2   Secure Computation

Secret-Sharing. Shamir's Secret Sharing [1] is a powerful cryptographic primitive which allows a client to split a secret into n shares, so that any less than t shares reveal no information about the original secret while any t shares can recover the secret.

Definition 1. *Shamir's Secret Sharing scheme consists of a sharing algorithm $\mathcal{S}$ and a reconstruct algorithm $\mathcal{R}$.*

$\mathcal{S}$ takes a secret s, a threshold t, and n as inputs, outputs n shares of s

$$\mathcal{S}(s, t, n) \rightarrow \{\langle s \rangle_0, \langle s \rangle_1, ..., \langle s \rangle_n\} \tag{3}$$

with $t \leq n$.

$\mathcal{R}$ takes the threshold t, a subset of the shares with size m as inputs, and recovers the secret s

$$\mathcal{R}(\{\langle s\rangle_0, \langle s\rangle_1, ..., \langle s\rangle_m\}, t) \rightarrow s \tag{4}$$

with $m \geq t$.

Correctness requires that $\forall s \in \mathbb{F}$, $\forall t$, $n(t \leq n)$, if $\{\langle s\rangle_0, \langle s\rangle_1, ..., \langle s\rangle_n\}$ are shares of s, then any subsets of size $m(m \geq t)$ could reconstruct the original secret s.

Security requires that any subsets of shares of size $m'(m' \leq t-1)$ disclose no information about s, which means that $\forall s, s' \in \mathbb{F}$ and two subsets of shares with size $m'(m' \leq t-1)$, no polynomial-time adversary $\mathcal{A}$ can distinguish the distribution of the two subsets

$$|Pr[\mathcal{A}(\{\langle s\rangle_0, ..., \langle s\rangle_{m'}\}) = 1] - Pr[\mathcal{A}(\{\langle s'\rangle_0, ..., \langle s'\rangle_{m'}\}) = 1]| \leq \frac{1}{p(x)} \tag{5}$$

where $p(\cdot)$ is a positive polynomial and x is sufficiently large.

Secret Sharing with Information-Theoretic MAC. The Shamir's Secret Sharing scheme can only against semi-honest adversaries, but not resist malicious modifications. So we import a variant of information-theoretic Message Authentication Code (MAC) [12].

Definition 2. *Secret Sharing scheme with information-theoretic MAC consists of a sharing algorithm $\mathcal{S}$, a reconstruct algorithm $\mathcal{R}$, an authentication function δ, a verification function v, and a global key α.*

$\mathcal{S}$ takes a secret s, the function δ, the threshold t, and n as inputs, and outputs their shares

$$\mathcal{S}(s, \delta, t, n) \rightarrow \{(\langle s\rangle_0, ..., \langle s\rangle_n), (\langle \delta(s)\rangle_0, ..., \langle \delta(s)\rangle_n)\} \tag{6}$$

$\mathcal{R}$ takes the threshold t, the function v and the subsets of shares as inputs, and outputs s

$$\mathcal{R}((\{\langle s\rangle_0, ..., \langle s\rangle_m\}), (\{\langle \delta(s)\rangle_0, ..., \langle \delta(s)\rangle_m\}), v, t) \rightarrow s \tag{7}$$

if $v(s, \delta(s), \alpha) = 1$, else $\mathcal{R}(\cdot)$ returns $\perp$.

Note $\delta(s) = \alpha \cdot s \mod p$ and $v(\cdot) = 1$ if and only if the reconstructed s and $\delta(s)$ satisfy $\delta(s) = \alpha \cdot s \mod p$.

Correctness and privacy against the semi-honest adversary are identical to what we have mentioned in Shamir's Secret Sharing scheme.

Since we require that the global key α is unknown to the adversary $\mathcal{M}$. So $\forall \langle s\rangle_i$, even $\mathcal{M}$ modifies it with only one bit, the possibility that $\mathcal{M}$ can construct a valid share of its MAC is negligible.

3   System Architecture

Our scheme is based on distributed machine learning except that we introduce two or more non-collude servers like [22,28], to protect the privacy. However, the servers in our protocols are not responsible for storing data or training the model but aggregating the gradients.

Instead of uploading the plain gradients to one parameter server in distributed machine learning, the clients share gradients after each training epoch and upload these shares to corresponding servers in our protocols.

In this paper, we propose two protocols, Γ_{sash} and Γ_{sam}. In Γ_{sash}, we require the servers are semi-honest or honest-but-curious and at most $t-1$ servers can collude. In Γ_{sam}, we enhance our security capabilities to against servers-only malicious adversary via Secret Sharing with information-theoretic MAC (Fig. 3).

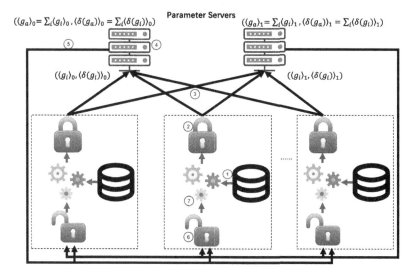

Fig. 3. Architecture for our protocols with two parameter servers. ① local training, ② share the gradients (and MACs), ③ upload gradients' shares (and MACs' shares), ④ aggregate gradients' shares (and MACs' shares), ⑤ download aggregated gradients' shares (and MACs' shares), ⑥ reconstruct aggregated gradients (MACs and verify), ⑦ update the local model and train it again (or abort). Note that MACs are for malicious security.

3.1 Γ_{sash} −Protocol for Semi-honest Security

In the offline phase, the clients communicate with each other to agree on a common secret sharing scheme, a machine learning model, i.e. a neural network, through secure channels. Also, clients need to generate random numbers independently. The parameter servers initialize the shares of g_a as all zeros. Then each client establishes a TLS/SSL secure channel with each server to protect the integrity of the shares.

Next, each client trains the model using private data locally and computes the gradients g as Eq. 1.

The elements of g are all float-point decimal numbers, which are not suitable for arithmetic operations in secure computations. So we have to encode all the elements of g as integers in a large finite field.

For instance, we can multiply them by a large scaling factor and truncate the results as integers modulo p, p is a big prime. When decode, we could determine the sign of an encoded element and divide the scaling factor[2]. As shown in the experiments, the errors introduced by truncation are so small that have little impacts on the final model.

Note that the clients can only encode and share a portion of gradients which are important, and we use $s_i^{(up)}$ to indicate them.

Next, the client i shares g_i as $\langle g_i \rangle_0, \langle g_i \rangle_1, ..., \langle g_i \rangle_{N-1}$, sends $\langle g_i \rangle_j$ and $s_i^{(up)}$ to the j-th server. Note that both encoding and secret sharing can be accelerated via vectorization.

On the other hand, the servers would wait a while to receive enough secret shares, i.e. all the secret shares, and then compute the secret shares of the aggregated gradients according to $\{s_i^{(up)}\}$

$$\langle g_a \rangle_j = \sum_i \langle g_i \rangle_j \tag{8}$$

After the aggregation, the servers will reply to clients' requests $s_i^{(down)}$ with the aggregated shares, $s_i^{(down)}$ indicates the elements to be downloaded. The details are in Fig. 4. We will prove the correctness and security below.

Correctness. In Γ_{sash}, the parameter servers are responsible for aggregating the gradients' shares, which is in secret sharing form. To prove our protocol's correctness, we import Lemma 1, which we prove in Appendix A.1.

Lemma 1. *The addition of secret shares is the secret shares of the sum. For example, $\{\langle x \rangle_i\}$ are the secret shares of x and $\{\langle y \rangle_i\}$ are the secret shares of y, then $\{\langle z \rangle_i = \langle x \rangle_i + \langle y \rangle_i\}$ are the secret shares of $z = x + y$.*

According to Lemma 1, we know that each server aggregates one of the secret shares of g_a rightly. So in the end, the clients will receive enough secret shares and reconstruct the g_a.

Security. In Γ_{sash}, we consider the security of the training protocol against semi-honest adversaries with three different threat models, namely users-only threat model where some users are corrupted, servers-only threat model where some servers are corrupted, and users-servers threat model where some users and servers are controlled by adversary.

---

[2] https://mortendahl.github.io/2017/04/17/private-deep-learning-with-mpc/.

Theorem 1 (Privacy in Semi-honest Adversary). *The protocol Γ_{sash} is secure in presence of semi-honest adversaries, meaning they leak no sensitive information about the honest clients' gradients, as long as the adversary can only corrupt no more than $t - 1$ servers and $M - 2$ clients.*

In the users-only threat model, what the adversary $\mathcal{A}$ can get about honest clients is the sum of their gradients.

$$\sum_{j \in honest.} \boldsymbol{g}_j = \sum_{i \in all} \boldsymbol{g}_i - \sum_{k \in corrupted} \boldsymbol{g}_k \tag{9}$$

Even the number of corrupted clients are $M - 2$, $\mathcal{A}$ get no information about the gradients towards a particular client. So we can protect the honest clients' privacy.

In the servers-only threat model, we require $\mathcal{A}$ can only corrupt up to $t - 1$ servers. So $\mathcal{A}$ can not distinguish the gradients' shares from pseudorandom numbers under Shamir's Secret Sharing scheme, which means $\mathcal{A}$ can not violate clients' privacy.

From users-only threat model and servers-only threat model, we can know that even $\mathcal{A}$ corrupt $t - 1$ servers and $M - 2$ clients, what $\mathcal{A}$ can get is as in the users-only threat model since the corrupted servers leak no private information.

3.2 Γ_{sam} −Protocol for Servers-only Malicious Security

Protocol Γ_{sash} can against semi-honest adversary, but not ensure that servers will sum up the gradients honestly, which means if a server is controlled by a malicious adversary $\mathcal{M}$, he can launch an attack,i.e. poisoning attack. For instance, $\mathcal{M}$ can replace the gradients' shares with random values to reduce the performance of the final model.

In order to prevent this kind of attacks, we propose Γ_{sam}, a protocol based on Secret Sharing with information-theoretic MAC, which can detect servers' malicious behaviors. So in Γ_{sam}, in addition to sharing the gradients, the clients have to compute and share the gradients' MAC $\boldsymbol{\delta}(\boldsymbol{g})$. And the servers have to aggregate the shares of $\boldsymbol{\delta}(\boldsymbol{g})$. The details are in Fig. 4.

Correctness. In protocol Γ_{sash} we have proved that the sum of secret shares is the secret shares of the sum. Now we bring in Lemma 2, we give its proof in Appendix A.2.

Lemma 2. *The sum of homomorphic MACs is the MAC of the sum. For example, $\boldsymbol{\delta}(\boldsymbol{x})$ and $\boldsymbol{\delta}(\boldsymbol{y})$ are homomorphic MACs of $\boldsymbol{x}$ and $\boldsymbol{y}$, respectively, then $\boldsymbol{\delta}(\boldsymbol{x}) + \boldsymbol{\delta}(\boldsymbol{y})$ is the homomorphic MAC of $\boldsymbol{x} + \boldsymbol{y}$.*

As long as the clients compute homomorphic MACs of gradients, we have that the sum of the MACs is the MAC of the sum of gradients on the basis of Lemma 2. So combining with Lemma 1, we can prove the correctness of Γ_{sam}.

Security. The privacy of Γ_{sam} is the same as Γ_{sash}, and we can prevent the corrupted servers from malicious modification with a servers-only threat model.

Theorem 2 (Resistance to Malicious Adversary in servers-only threat model). *The protocol Γ_{sam} is secure against malicious adversaries in the servers-only threat model, meaning the adversary can not launch active poisoning attacks without detection, as long as the adversary can only corrupt no more than $t-1$ servers.*

As long as the global secret key α is only known to clients, the possibility that $\mathcal{M}$ can construct a valid MAC for an arbitrary secret s is equal to the possibility that $\mathcal{M}$ can get α. So we have

$$Pr(\mathcal{M}(\boldsymbol{\delta}, s) = 1) = \frac{1}{2^{\lceil \log p \rceil}} \tag{10}$$

As long as the prime p is sufficient large, the possibility is negligible.

Assuming $\mathcal{M}$ modifies the $\langle g \rangle_u$ to launch a poisoning attack. So he would add the modified shares to aggregated shares, which denoted as $\langle g_a \rangle'_u$. If $\langle g_a \rangle'_u$

Secure Training Protocol

Input: M local datasets and replicas of a model
Output: a trained model

if *Server* **then**
    Initialize. Initializing $\langle g_a \rangle_j$ and $\langle \boldsymbol{\delta}(g)_a \rangle_j$ as all-zeros;
    Update. After receiving gradients' secret shares, MACs' secret shares and $s_i^{(up)}$ from each client, each server will add these secret shares to $\langle g_a \rangle_j$ and $\langle \boldsymbol{\delta}(g)_a \rangle_j$ according to $s_i^{(up)}$, usually $s_i^{(up)} \subset g$;
    Response. For each downloading request, each server will reply with the gradients' shares and MACs' shares according to $s_i^{(down)}$;

if *Client* **then**
    Initialize. Initializing models according to the same policy;
    Local training. Each client gets a mini-batch from the local dataset, trains the model and computes the gradients g;
    Secret Sharing. The clients encode g and generate the secret shares of g as $\{\langle g \rangle_j\}$, compute $\boldsymbol{\delta}(g)$ and share it as $\{\langle \boldsymbol{\delta}(g) \rangle_j\}$ (or only processing the top k of g with the largest absolute value, where we use $s_i^{(up)}$ to indicate the corresponding elements);
    Upload. Sending the gradients' secret shares, MACs' secret shares and $s_i^{(up)}$ to corresponding servers;
    Download. Sending a downloading request along with $s_i^{(down)}$, which indicates the elements to be downloaded, to all servers;
    Reconstruct. After sending the request, the client will wait until receiving enough secret shares to reconstruct the aggregated gradients, aggregated MACs and verify the validity, update the local model and go to **Local training** or abort if the verification failed;

Fig. 4. Details for our protocol. Note that the red-and-underlined parts are only required for malicious protocol Γ_{sam} (not necessary for semi-honest protocol Γ_{sash}). (Color figure online)

is downloaded and the client would try using it to reconstruct the $\boldsymbol{g}_a$

$$\boldsymbol{g}'_a = \mathcal{R}(\{\langle \boldsymbol{g}_a \rangle_i\}_{i \in \{t\}, i \neq u} \cup \{\langle \boldsymbol{g}_a \rangle'_u\}) \tag{11}$$

Also, the client can reconstruct $\boldsymbol{\delta}(\boldsymbol{g}_a)$ at the same time.

It is obvious that the possibility $\boldsymbol{v}(\alpha, \boldsymbol{g}'_a, \boldsymbol{\delta}(\boldsymbol{g}_a)) = 1$ is negligible as long as α is unknown to the $\mathcal{M}$ and no more than $t - 1$ servers could collude.

So in Γ_{sam}, we can avoid disclosing any particular client's gradients under the assumption of Shamir's Secret Sharing scheme. Moreover, we could detect corrupted servers' malicious behaviors via information-theoretic MAC.

4 Experiments

4.1 Environment

Our experiments are executed on three Intel(R) Xeon(R) CPU E5-2650 v3@ 2.30 GHz servers with each has 64G RAM in the LAN setting.

We simulate 2 parameter servers and 32 clients. All protocols have been implemented in Python3 language, and we use Tensorflow 1.13.1[3] library, this popular machine-learning library has been used by major Internet companies such as Google.

4.2 Experiments Setup

In our experiments, we use MNIST as our training set. And we compare all results with two baseline scenarios. The first is the basic federate learning Γ_{fl}, which consists of one parameter server and 32 clients with no secure techniques. The other scenario is Google's Secure Aggregation protocol Γ_{sag} [24], which masks the gradients before uploading[4]. All the protocols are executed synchronously.

For all the scenarios, we implement linear regression, MLP, and CNN. We compare them in accuracy, convergence rate and performance in detail below.

4.3 Experiments Results

Accuracy. We compare the same model in different scenarios, we find that our accuracies in the semi-honest and malicious setting are both nearly to the accuracy of Γ_{fl}. The highest accuracy's drop is within 0.01 for CNN and MLP, and 0.02 for linear regression.

We plot the accuracy changes along with the training epochs. And we show that with the increasing of the training epochs, the influence produced by encoding a float-number as a big integer is being smaller and smaller. For instance, Fig. 5(a) shows that in a CNN, the curve for Γ_{sash} almost coincides with the curve for Γ_{fl}. And we get similar results for linear regression and MLP, we plot them in Appendix B due to the space limit.

The best accuracies for each model in all protocols are shown in Table 1.

---

[3] https://github.com/tensorflow/tensorflow/releases/tag/v1.13.1.
[4] We only implement the basic secure aggregation with no dropouts.

Table 1. Accuracy for each model in all protocols.

Model	Protocol			
	Γ_{fl}	Γ_{sag}	Γ_{sash}	Γ_{sam}
Linear regression	0.929	0.924	0.918	0.913
MLP	0.979	0.977	0.978	0.974
CNN	0.997	0.994	0.995	0.991

Convergence Rate. Our experiments also illustrate that the convergence rates in all protocols over training epochs are at the same level, the secure techniques do not influence the results much.

For instance, the convergence rates of Γ_{sash} and Γ_{sam} are almost the same as Γ_{fl} for CNN. From Fig. 5(a), it is obvious that the models all approach 0.95 at around 50 epochs and reach 0.99 at around 100 epochs in different protocols.

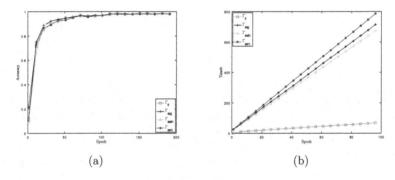

(a)   (b)

Fig. 5. Experimental results of CNN. (a) is for accuracy, (b) is for performance.

Performance. Our protocols can be divided into offline phase and online phase naturally. In the offline phase, the clients mainly generate random numbers independently. We run the process 10 times for each model and take the average as the result. The details are in Table 2. Note that protocol Γ_{sag} needs around 22.81 s in our setting to negotiate keys between clients, and we do not include it in Table 2.

From Table 2 we can see that Γ_{sash} is around 10× faster than Γ_{sag}, and Γ_{sam} is around 5× faster than Γ_{sag}.

As for the online phase, we plot the running time along with the epochs for CNN in Fig. 5(b). It is illustrated that our semi-honest protocol Γ_{sash} is faster than Γ_{sag} even Γ_{sag} is in the best situation. For example, the running time for Γ_{sash} is 701.85 s, while Γ_{sag} needs 744.68 s, both run 100 epochs. As for our malicious protocol Γ_{sam}, the running time is a little longer, which is around 819.99 s.

Table 2. Offline performances (seconds, 100 epochs).

Model	Protocol			
	Γ_{fl}	Γ_{sag}	Γ_{sash}	Γ_{sam}
Linear regression	0	11.90	0.60	1.19
MLP	0	110.53	14.24	27.47
CNN	0	243.92	21.77	41.44

However, we know that Γ_{sag} needs extra time to deal with the masking elements if some clients dropped out in the training process, this reduces their efficiency greatly, while our protocols do not need this extra operation even if the same misfortune happens. This is because the clients in our protocols are independent of each other, which means the dropped clients do not impact other online clients. Combining offline and online, we can see that our protocol's whole performance is better than Γ_{sag}, both semi-honest and malicious. And compared to privacy-preserving deep learning methods based on HE [27], our improvements are dramatically where they need 2.25 h for MLP and 7.3 h for CNN. Note that we plot the figures for linear regression and MLP in Appendix B.

On the other hand, Γ_{sag} only needs one parameter server, but Γ_{sash} and Γ_{sam} need two or more parameter servers, and we require that at most $t-1$ servers could collude. However, import two or more servers is a common method for distributing machine learning, and it is easy to satisfy this security requirement in practice. Meanwhile, in Γ_{sag} the parameter server would learn the aggregated gradients and even the trained model, but in Γ_{sash} and Γ_{sam} the parameter servers can learn nothing. What's more, our protocols are more robust than Γ_{sag}, since we allow $n-t$ servers to halt at worst but Γ_{sag} must ensure the parameter server runs normally.

5   Conclusion

We introduce a novel secure computation framework for distributed machine learning that achieves high accuracy and performance by combining distributed machine learning with secret sharing. In contrast to previous state-of-the-art frameworks, we improve the efficiency of more than 10× and maintain the required security in semi-honest. Besides, we propose a verifiable protocol against servers-only malicious modifications based on information-theoretic MAC. We evaluated our framework on linear regression, MLP, and CNN and achieve excellent results both in accuracy and performance. What's more, combining differential privacy with distributed machine learning is a promising solution against inferring attacks, which can enhance our security as well. We leave it for future work.

Acknowledgements. We are grateful to the anonymous reviewers for their comprehensive comments. And we thank Xiangfu Song, Yiran Liu from Shandong University for helpful discussions on MPC, and Junming Ke from Singapore University of Technology and Design for his help. This work was supported by the Strategic Priority Research Program of Chinese Academy of Sciences, Grant No. XDC02040400.

A   Proof of Correctness

A.1   Lemma 1

Proof. Suppose we have two secrets, s_0 and s_1, and we share both in Shamir's Secret Sharing scheme with two polynomial-functions

$$
\begin{aligned}
f(x) &= a_0 + a_1 \cdot x + ... + a_{t-1} \cdot x^{t-1} \quad \mod p \\
g(x) &= b_0 + b_1 \cdot x + ... + b_{t-1} \cdot x^{t-1} \quad \mod p
\end{aligned}
\tag{12}
$$

where $f(0) = a_0 = s_0$, $g(0) =. b_0 = s_1$ and p is a large prime.

In order to compute the shares, we can evaluate $f(x)$ and $g(x)$ at n different points $f(x_0), f(x_1), ..., f(x_{n-1})$ and $g(x_0), g(x_1), ..., g(x_{n-1})$ respectively.

Then we will turn to getting the shares of $s_0 + s_1$. We define a new polynomial-function

$$
h(x) = (a_0 + b_0) + (a_1 + b_1) \cdot x + ... + (a_{t-1} + b_{t-1}) \cdot x^{t-1} \quad \mod p \tag{13}
$$

Obviously, $h(x)$ is a polynomial-function of degree $t - 1$ with t coefficients and $h(0) = s_0 + s_1$. On the one hand, $h(x_i)$ is the shares for $s_0 + s_1$, and on the other hand, we can confirm

$$
\begin{aligned}
h(x_i) &= (a_0 + b_0) + (a_1 + b_1) \cdot x_i + ... + (a_{t-1} + b_{t-1}) \cdot x_i^{t-1} \\
&= (a_0 + a_1 \cdot x_i + ... + a_{t-1} \cdot x_i^{t-1}) + (b_0 + b_1 \cdot x_i + ... + b_{t-1} \cdot x_i^{t-1}) \\
&= f(x_i) + g(x_i) \quad \mod p, \ 0 \le i \le n - 1
\end{aligned}
\tag{14}
$$

So that the shares of $s_0 + s_1$ can be computed by adding the corresponding shares of s_0 and s_1.

A.2   Lemma2

Proof. Suppose we have $x_0, x_1, ..., x_{n-1}$ and a secret key α. We could the compute the MAC of x_i

$$
\delta(x_i) = \alpha \cdot x_i \quad \mod p, \ 0 \le i \le n - 1 \tag{15}
$$

Then we can also compute the MAC of x_i's sum:

$$
\delta(\sum_{i=0}^{n-1} x_i) = \alpha \cdot (\sum_{i=0}^{n-1} x_i) \quad \mod p \tag{16}
$$

Then it is easy to confirm

$$\delta(\sum_{i=0}^{n-1} x_i) = (\alpha \cdot x_0) + (\alpha \cdot x_1) + \ldots + (\alpha \cdot x_{n-1}) \mod p$$

$$= \delta(x_0) + \delta(x_1) + \ldots + \delta(x_{n-1}) \mod p \qquad (17)$$

$$= \sum_{i=0}^{n-1} \delta(x_i) \mod p$$

For a more concrete proof, please refer to [12].

B Accuracy and Performance for Linear Regression and MLP

B.1 Linear Regression

See Fig. 6.

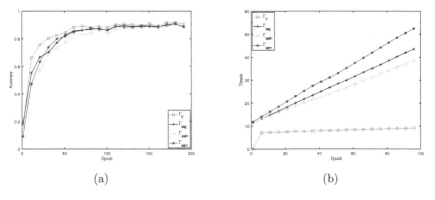

(a)   (b)

Fig. 6. Experimental results of linear regression. (a) is for accuracy, (b) is for performance.

B.2   MLP

See Fig. 7.

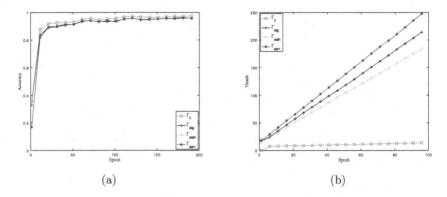

(a)   (b)

Fig. 7. Experimental results of MLP. (a) is for accuracy, (b) is for performance.

References

1. Shamir, A.: How to share a secret. Commun. ACM **22**(11), 612–613 (1979). https://doi.org/10.1145/359168.359176
2. Lindell, Y., Pinkas, B.: Privacy preserving data mining. In: Bellare, M. (ed.) CRYPTO 2000. LNCS, vol. 1880, pp. 36–54. Springer, Heidelberg (2000). https://doi.org/10.1007/3-540-44598-6_3
3. Du, W., Atallah, M.J.: Privacy-preserving cooperative scientific computations. In: CSFW. IEEE (2001). 0273. https://doi.org/10.1109/CSFW.2001.930152
4. Du, W., Han, Y.S., Chen, S.: Privacy-preserving multivariate statistical analysis: linear regression and classification. In: Proceedings of the 2004 SIAM International Conference on Data Mining. Society for Industrial and Applied Mathematics, pp. 222–233 (2004). https://doi.org/10.1137/1.9781611972740.21
5. Sanil, A.P., Karr, A.F., Lin, X., et al.: Privacy-preserving regression modelling via distributed computation. In: Proceedings of the Tenth ACM SIGKDD International Conference on Knowledge Discovery and Data Mining, pp. 677–682. ACM (2004). https://doi.org/10.1145/1014052.1014139
6. Jagannathan, G., Wright, R.N.: Privacy-preserving distributed k-means clustering over arbitrarily partitioned data. In: Proceedings of the Eleventh ACM SIGKDD International Conference on Knowledge Discovery in Data Mining, pp. 593–599. ACM (2005). https://doi.org/10.1145/1081870.1081942
7. Yu, H., Vaidya, J., Jiang, X.: Privacy-preserving SVM classification on vertically partitioned data. In: Ng, W.-K., Kitsuregawa, M., Li, J., Chang, K. (eds.) PAKDD 2006. LNCS (LNAI), vol. 3918, pp. 647–656. Springer, Heidelberg (2006). https://doi.org/10.1007/11731139_74

8. Slavkovic, A.B., Nardi, Y., Tibbits, M.M.: "Secure" logistic regression of horizontally and vertically partitioned distributed databases. In: Seventh IEEE International Conference on Data Mining Workshops (ICDMW 2007), pp. 723–728. IEEE (2007). https://doi.org/10.1109/ICDMW.2007.114
9. Bunn, P., Ostrovsky, R.: Secure two-party k-means clustering. In: Proceedings of the 14th ACM Conference on Computer and Communications Security, pp. 486–497. ACM (2007). https://doi.org/10.1145/1315245.1315306
10. Vaidya, J., Yu, H., Jiang, X.: Privacy-preserving SVM classification. Knowl. Inf. Syst. **14**(2), 161–178 (2008). https://doi.org/10.1007/s10115-007-0073-7
11. Bottou, L.: Large-scale machine learning with stochastic gradient descent. In: Lechevallier, Y., Saporta, G. (eds.) Proceedings of COMPSTAT 2010, pp. 177–186. Physica-Verlag HD, Heidelberg (2010). https://doi.org/10.1007/978-3-7908-2604-3_16
12. Damgård, I., Pastro, V., Smart, N., Zakarias, S.: Multiparty computation from somewhat homomorphic encryption. In: Safavi-Naini, R., Canetti, R. (eds.) CRYPTO 2012. LNCS, vol. 7417, pp. 643–662. Springer, Heidelberg (2012). https://doi.org/10.1007/978-3-642-32009-5_38
13. Nikolaenko, V., Ioannidis, S., Weinsberg, U., et al.: Privacy-preserving matrix factorization. In: Proceedings of the 2013 ACM SIGSAC Conference on Computer & Communications Security, pp. 801–812. ACM (2013). https://doi.org/10.1145/2508859.2516751
14. Wu, S., Teruya, T., Kawamoto, J.: Privacy-preservation for stochastic gradient descent application to secure logistic regression. In: The 27th Annual Conference of the Japanese Society for Artificial Intelligence, vol. 27, pp. 1–4 (2013)
15. Song, S., Chaudhuri, K., Sarwate, A.D.: Stochastic gradient descent with differentially private updates. In: 2013 IEEE Global Conference on Signal and Information Processing, pp. 245–248. IEEE (2013). https://doi.org/10.1109/GlobalSIP.2013.6736861
16. Li, M., Andersen, D.G., Park, J.W., et al.: Scaling distributed machine learning with the parameter server. In: 11th USENIX Symposium on Operating Systems Design and Implementation (OSDI 14), pp. 583–598 (2014). https://doi.org/10.1145/2640087.2644155
17. Shokri, R., Shmatikov, V.: Privacy-preserving deep learning. In: Proceedings of the 22nd ACM SIGSAC Conference on Computer and Communications Security, pp. 1310–1321. ACM (2015). https://doi.org/10.1145/2810103.2813687
18. Abadi, M., Chu, A., Goodfellow, I., et al.: Deep learning with differential privacy. In: Proceedings of the 2016 ACM SIGSAC Conference on Computer and Communications Security, pp. 308–318. ACM (2016). https://doi.org/10.1145/2976749.2978318
19. Gascó, A., Schoppmann, P., Balle, B., et al.: Secure linear regression on vertically partitioned datasets. IACR Cryptology ePrint Archive 2016, 892 (2016)
20. Regulation (EU) 2016/679 of the European Parliament and of the Council of 27 April 2016 on the protection of natural persons with regard to the processing of personal data and on the free movement of such data, and repealing Directive 95/46/EC (GDPR). Official J. Eur. Union, L119 (2016)
21. Gilad-Bachrach, R., Dowlin, N., Laine, K., et al.: CryptoNets: applying neural networks to encrypted data with high throughput and accuracy. In: International Conference on Machine Learning, pp. 201–210 (2016)
22. Mohassel, P., Secureml, Z.Y.: A system for scalable privacy-preserving machine learning. In: 2017 IEEE Symposium on Security and Privacy (SP), pp. 19–38. IEEE (2017). https://doi.org/10.1109/SP.2017.12

23. Liu J, Juuti, M., Lu, Y., et al.: Oblivious neural network predictions via miniONN transformations. In: Proceedings of the 2017 ACM SIGSAC Conference on Computer and Communications Security, pp. 619–631. ACM (20170. https://doi.org/10.1145/3133956.3134056

24. Bonawitz, K., Ivanov, V., Kreuter, B., et al.: Practical secure aggregation for privacy-preserving machine learning. In: Proceedings of the 2017 ACM SIGSAC Conference on Computer and Communications Security, pp. 1175–1191. ACM (2017). https://doi.org/10.1145/3133956.3133982

25. Lin, Y., Han, S., Mao, H., et al.: Deep gradient compression: reducing the communication bandwidth for distributed training. arXiv preprint arXiv:1712.01887 (2017)

26. Riazi, M.S., Weinert, C., Tkachenko, O., et al.: Chameleon: a hybrid secure computation framework for machine learning applications. In: Proceedings of the 2018 on Asia Conference on Computer and Communications Security, pp. 707–721. ACM (2018). https://doi.org/10.1145/3196494.3196522

27. Phong, L.T., Aono, Y., Hayashi, T., et al.: Privacy-preserving deep learning via additively homomorphic encryption. IEEE Trans. Inf. Forensics Secur. **13**(5), 1333–1345 (2018). https://doi.org/10.1109/TIFS.2017.2787987

28. Wagh, S., Gupta, D., Chandran, N.: SecureNN: 3-party secure computation for neural network training. Proc. Priv. Enhancing Technol. **1**, 24 (2019). https://doi.org/10.2478/popets-2019-0035

29. Nasr, M., Shokri, R., Houmansadr, A.: Comprehensive privacy analysis of deep learning: stand-alone and federated learning under passive and active white-box inference attacks. arXiv preprint arXiv:1812.00910 (2018)

30. Yang, Q., Liu, Y., Chen, T., et al.: Federated machine learning: concept and applications. ACM Trans. Intell. Syst. Technol. (TIST) **10**(2), 12 (2019). https://doi.org/10.1145/3298981

31. Juvekar, C., Vaikuntanathan, V., Chandrakasan, A.: GAZELLE: a low latency framework for secure neural network inference. In: 27th USENIX Security Symposium (USENIX Security 18), pp. 1651–1669 (2018)

32. Centers for Medicare & Medicaid Services. The Health Insurance Portability and Accountability Act of 1996 (HIPAA) (1996). http://www.cms.hhs.gov/hipaa/

Privacy-Preserving Decentralised Singular Value Decomposition

Bowen Liu and Qiang Tang$^{(\boxtimes)}$

Luxembourg Institute of Science and Technology (LIST),
5, Avenue des Hauts-Fourneaux, 4362 Esch-sur-Alzette, Luxembourg
{bowen.liu,qiang.tang}@list.lu

Abstract. With the proliferation of data and emerging data-driven applications, how to perform data analytical operations while respecting privacy concerns has become a very interesting research topic. With the advancement of communication and computing technologies, e.g. the FoG computing concept and its associated Edge computing technologies, it is now appealing to deploy decentralized data-driven applications. Following this trend, in this paper, we investigate privacy-preserving singular value decomposition (SVD) solutions tailored for these new computing environments. We first analyse a privacy-preserving SVD solution by Chen et al., which is based on the Paillier encryption scheme and some heuristic randomization method. We show that (1) their solution leaks statistical information to an individual player in the system; (2) their solution leaks much more information when more than one players collude. Based on the analysis, we present a new solution, which distributes the SVD results into two different players in a privacy-preserving manner. In comparison, our solution minimizes the information leakage to both individual player and colluded ones, via randomization and threshold homomorphic encryption techniques.

1 Introduction

Internet of Things (IoT) is increasingly appearing in our lives, which promises to connect everyone with everything from everywhere. In practice, IoT generates a large amount of data that is closely related to the human users (or, owners) of the devices. On the positive side, such data can be used for many useful purposes such as building smart services. However, on the other side, it brings huge privacy risks [15]. In most applications, the root of the privacy issue lies in the fact that data needs to be aggregated to a must-to-be trusted service provider before any service can be provided.

To mitigate the privacy concerns resulted from privacy-invasive data aggregation in general, information security researchers and cryptographers have been advocating privacy-preserving distributed protocols for decades. Unfortunately, these protocols do not appeal to the real-world applications, which are often designed for the cloud computing paradigm that essentially requires data aggregation to a central third-party server. Recently, with the advancement of communication infrastructure (e.g. 5G) and computing technologies such as the

© Springer Nature Switzerland AG 2020
J. Zhou et al. (Eds.): ICICS 2019, LNCS 11999, pp. 703–721, 2020.
https://doi.org/10.1007/978-3-030-41579-2_41

FoG computing concept and its associated Edge computing technologies, it has become a trend to design and deploy decentralised applications, which push computations to the edge so that it avoids data aggregation to some extent. Coined by Numhauser in 2011 [1], there are many (similar) definitions for FoG computing. For example, Cisco [5] defines FoG computing as a paradigm that extends cloud computing [9] and services to the edge of the network. In reality, FoG computing can process its services at different nodes in the network as opposed to a central server. It significantly decreases the data movement across the network, so as to reduce the congestion, cost, and latency, and it also provides a decentralised infrastructure that naturally facilitates privacy protection. While many FoG-based applications are emerging, it is becoming an interesting research topic to design privacy-preserving solutions for the data exploitation tasks in these applications.

1.1 Related Work and Problem Statement

In this paper, we are interested in how to perform Singular Value Decomposition (SVD) based on data from decentralized IoT devices. In machine learning and data mining, SVD is a powerful and fundamental matrix factorization technique. It provides a means to decompose a matrix into a product of three simpler matrices, so that one may discover useful and interesting properties of the original matrix [7]. It finds many applications in reality. One prominent example is recommender systems [10].

Chen et al. [3] proposed a privacy-preserving FoG computing framework for SVD computation. In their solution, the result of SVD is separated into two parts and stored at two different nodes. As a result, if an attacker compromises only one node, then it does not learn everything. Unfortunately, there is no formal analysis in [3]. Han et al. [7] provided a solution for performing SVD in partitioned dataset, where two players collaborate with each other to perform SVD based on their joint dataset. Their solution is based on a number of cryptographic primitives, and the authors concluded that it is a challenge to reduce the complexity when their solution is used for large dataset. For privacy-preserving matrix factorization (MF) in general, Nikolaenko et al. [12] proposed a garbled circuit-based protocol and Kim et al. [8] proposed a protocol based on homomorphic encryption. In both solutions, the factorization operation is decentralized to two non-colluding servers, one of them controls key materials while the other carries out the factorization operation. When the two servers are compromised at the same time, then everything is leaked.

Despite the literature work, it remains an open problem to design an efficient privacy-preserving SVD (or MF in general) protocol that provides rigorous security even when several players are compromised simultaneously.

1.2 Contribution and Organization

In this paper, we aim at rigorous privacy-preserving SVD solutions in the FoG computing paradigm. Firstly, we review the solution by [3] in Sect. 3 and demonstrate several privacy risks in Sect. 4. Our analysis covers a number of scenarios, including individual player/attacker and more colluded players/attackers. Moreover, we also briefly analyse the recommender use case. Based on the analysis, we simplify the FoG architecture from [3] and present a stronger security model, which captures scenarios where several players may collude. We then propose a new solution based on threshold homomorphic encryption and push some of the heavy computation workloads to the edge. We further analyse the security properties and the asymptotic complexities, as well as benchmarking results on a PC. These results appear in Sect. 5. In addition, we present some preliminary in Sect. 2 and draw some conclusions in Sect. 6.

2   Preliminary on Singular Value Decomposition

Let $\mathbb{M}$ be a $m \times n$ matrix. As shown in Fig. 1, the SVD of $\mathbb{M}$ is a factorization of the form $\mathbb{U}\Sigma\mathbb{V}^T$, where $\mathbb{U}$ is an $m \times m$ left-singular matrix of $\mathbb{M}$, Σ is an $m \times n$ singular matrix of $\mathbb{M}$, $\mathbb{V}$ is a $n \times n$ right-singular matrix of $\mathbb{M}$, and T means conjugate transpose. In addition, there are also two relations:

$$\mathbb{M}\cdot\mathbb{M}^T = \mathbb{U}\Sigma\mathbb{V}^T\cdot\mathbb{V}\Sigma^T\mathbb{U}^T = \mathbb{U}\Sigma\Sigma^T\mathbb{U}^T; \ \mathbb{M}^T\cdot\mathbb{M} = \mathbb{V}\Sigma^T\mathbb{U}^T\cdot\mathbb{U}\Sigma\mathbb{V}^T = \mathbb{V}\Sigma^T\Sigma\mathbb{V}^T$$

The columns of $\mathbb{U}$ (left-singular vectors) and $\mathbb{V}$ (right-singular vectors) are, respectively, eigenvectors of $\mathbb{M} \cdot \mathbb{M}^T$ and $\mathbb{M}^T \cdot \mathbb{M}$. The non-zero elements of Σ are the square roots of the non-zero eigenvalues of $\mathbb{M} \cdot \mathbb{M}^T$ and $\mathbb{M}^T \cdot \mathbb{M}$.

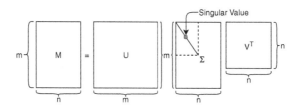

Fig. 1. Singular value decomposition

A prominent application of SVD is recommender systems. Using the users' rating data, a service provider can recommend other films that they might like. As a toy example, suppose we have 3 users' score records for 4 movies (0 for the case of not being rated), see Table 1.

For this toy example, after applying SVD to the rating matrix, we can obtain three singular matrices denoted as $\mathbb{U}$, Σ and $\mathbb{V}^T$.

$$\mathbb{U} = \begin{pmatrix} -0.784 & 0.243 & 0.571 \\ -0.588 & 0.000 & -0.809 \\ -0.196 & -0.970 & 0.143 \end{pmatrix} \quad \Sigma = \begin{pmatrix} 5.831 & 0.000 & 0.000 & 0.000 \\ 0.000 & 5.000 & 0.000 & 0.000 \\ 0.000 & 0.000 & 2.828 & 0.000 \end{pmatrix} \quad \mathbb{V}^T = \begin{pmatrix} -0.807 & -0.135 & -0.202 & -0.538 \\ 0.146 & -0.776 & -0.582 & 0.194 \\ -0.538 & 0.202 & -0.135 & 0.807 \\ 0.000 & 0.137 & -0.158 & 0.727 \end{pmatrix}$$

Table 1. Rating matrix

	Movie A	Movie B	Movie C	Movie D
User 1	3	0	0	4
User 2	4	0	1	0
User 3	0	4	3	0

In practice, a dimensionality reduction procedure can be applied to generate small-rank feature matrices. Note that the eigenvalue 2.828 is smaller than the other two values, so that we can choose to suppress it and have a truncated variant of Σ, namely

$$\Sigma^* = \begin{pmatrix} 5.831 & 0.000 \\ 0.000 & 5.000 \end{pmatrix}$$

Accordingly, we generate a variant of $\mathbb{U}$ by removing its last column and a variant of $\mathbb{V}^T$ by removing its last two rows. Let the variants be denoted as $\mathbb{U}^*$ and $\mathbb{V}^{*T}$ respectively. By computing $\mathbb{U}^* \Sigma^{*\frac{1}{2}}$ and $\Sigma^{*\frac{1}{2}} \mathbb{V}^{*T}$, we obtain the user and item feature matrices shown in Tables 2 and 3.

Table 2. User feature matrix

User 1	-1.893	0.543
User 2	-1.420	0.000
User 3	-0.473	-2.169

Table 3. Movie/Item feature matrix

Movie A	Movie B	Movie C	Movie D
-1.949	-0.326	-0.488	-1.299
0.326	-1.735	-1.301	0.434

Based on these feature matrices, a recommender service provider can serve users with predictions on the movies they have not rated.

3   Overview of Chen et al.'s Solution

By assuming a FoG architecture, shown in Fig. 2, Chen et al. [3] designed a privacy-preserving SVD solution based on some heuristic randomization techniques and the Paillier scheme, described in our full paper [11]. This FoG computing architecture consists of the following types of entities:

- *Server*: The initialization of the whole system is generated and operated by the server, it is considered as fully trusted node in the FoG architecture. Once, the initialisation is done, the server will not get involved anymore. So, we omit it in Fig. 2.
- *Edge Devices ED*: Each edge device is the original collector of the data and represents the human user behind it.
- *First-layer FoG Device FD*: The FoG device is responsible for collecting the data from edge devices and coordinating the SVD operations.

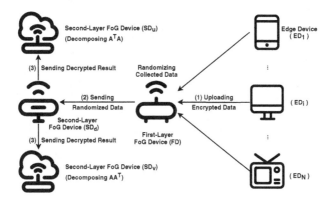

Fig. 2. Fog computing architecture

– *Second-layer FoG Devices SDs*: There are three different devices in this category. SD_d decrypts the received information and obtains the randomized data matrix, and prepares data for SD_u and SD_v, who will perform the decomposition.

3.1 Description of the Solution

Initialisation. The trusted server will setup the parameters for the system, shown in Table 4. In terms of Paillier cryptosystem [13], the server generates the public key $(n = pq, g)$, and the private key (λ, μ). In the meanwhile, the server generates

Table 4. Initialization parameters

Parameter	Propose
N	*Number of Edge Devices (ED)*
l	*Dimension of data vector*
x	*Range of value in data vector: $[0, x]$*
k_1	*For generating $t = 2^{k_1}$*
W	*Randomized $W > max(N, l) \cdot x^2$*
S	*Randomized $S > max(N, l) \cdot (x^2 + 2tWx + t^2W^2)$*
k_2	*Bit length of W*
k_3	*Bit length of S*
$\vec{a}$	*For transforming vector into number*
k	*Length of p, q in Paillier cryptosystem*
(n, g)	*Public key of Paillier cryptosystem*
(λ, μ)	*Private key of Paillier cryptosystem*

two random coprime numbers W and S respectively. Additionally, a super-increasing vector $\vec{a} = (a_1 = 1, a_2, ..., a_l)^T$ is generated, and each value needs to conform to the following conditions: $\sum_{j=1}^{i-1} a_j \cdot (x + tW + tS) < a_i$, $i \in [2, l]$ and $\sum_{j=1}^{l} a_j \cdot (x + tW + tS) < n$. The Paillier private key (λ, μ) is assigned to SD_d, and the private randomization parameters W and S are assigned to FD, SD_u, SD_v. All other parameters are public.

Privacy-Preserving Protocol. The privacy-preserving protocol runs in four steps.

1. ED_i's data is expressed in vector form $\vec{d_i} = (d_{1i}, d_{2i}, ..., d_{li})^T$. Note that the data from EDs forms a matrix $\mathbb{A}$ as follows.

$$\mathbb{A} = \begin{bmatrix} d_{11} & d_{12} & \cdots & d_{1N} \\ d_{21} & d_{22} & \cdots & d_{2N} \\ \vdots & \vdots & \ddots & \vdots \\ d_{l1} & d_{l2} & \cdots & d_{lN} \end{bmatrix} \tag{1}$$

By using the public vector $\vec{a}$, ED_i first converts its vector into an integer.

$$m_i = \vec{d_i}^T \cdot \vec{a} = a_1 d_{1i} + a_2 d_{2i} + ... + a_l d_{li}$$

It then encrypts this integer with Paillier public key to obtain c_i. At the end of this step, ED_i, for every $1 \leq i \leq N$, sends c_i to FD.

2. After receiving every c_i, FD chooses two vectors $\vec{z_i} = (z_{1i}, z_{2i}, ..., z_{li})^T$ and $\vec{r_i} = (r_{1i}, r_{2i}, ..., r_{li})^T$, where each element is randomly chosen from $[1, t]$. It then computes the randomization parameter $R_i = \sum_{k=1}^{l} a_k \cdot (z_{ki} \cdot W + r_{ki} \cdot S)$, and sets the randomized ciphertext c_i' as

$$\begin{aligned} c_i' &= c_i \cdot g^{R_i} \ mod \ n^2 \\ &= (g^{m_i} \cdot r_i^n) \cdot g^{R_i} \ mod \ n^2 \\ &= (g^{\sum_{k=1}^{l} a_k \cdot d_{ki}} \cdot r_i^n) \cdot g^{\sum_{k=1}^{l} a_k \cdot (z_{ki} \cdot W + r_{ki} \cdot S)} \ mod \ n^2 \\ &= g^{\sum_{k=1}^{l} a_k \cdot (d_{ki} + z_{ki} \cdot W + r_{ki} \cdot S)} \cdot r_i^n \ mod \ n^2 \end{aligned}$$

At the end of this step, FD sends c_i' $(1 \leq i \leq N)$ to SD_d.

3. After receiving every c_i', SD_d decrypts it to obtain

$$m_i' = \sum_{k=1}^{l} a_k \cdot (d_{ki} + z_{ki} \cdot W + r_{ki} \cdot S) \ mod \ n$$

Next, by applying Algorithm 1, the randomized non-encrypted data in vector form can be computed.

Algorithm 1. Recover Vector from Integer

Input: m_i' and $\vec{a} = (a_1, a_2, ..., a_l)^T$

Output: randomized non-encrypted data $\vec{d_i'}$

1: let $tmp = (t_{a_1}, t_{a_2}, ..., t_{a_l})^T$ within empty value inside

2: $X_l \leftarrow m_i' = \sum_{j=1}^{l} a_k \cdot (d_{ji} + z_{ji} \cdot W + r_{ji} \cdot S) \bmod n$

3: **for** $k = l$ to 2 **do**

4:    $X_{k-1} \leftarrow X_k \bmod a_k$

5:    $t_{ak} \leftarrow \frac{X_k - X_{k-1}}{a_k} = d_{ki} + z_{ki} \cdot W + r_{ki} \cdot S$

6: **end for**

7: $t_{a_1} \leftarrow X_1 = d_{1i} + z_{1i} \cdot W + r_{1i} \cdot S$

8: **return** $\vec{d_i'} = (t_{a_1}, t_{a_2}, ..., t_{a_l})^T$

Now, SD_d has the matrix $\mathbb{A}'$ made up by N different randomized non-encrypted vectors $\vec{d_i'} = (d_{1i}', d_{2i}', ..., d_{li}')^T$.

$$\mathbb{A}' = \begin{bmatrix} \vec{d_1'} & \vec{d_2'} & ... & \vec{d_N'} \end{bmatrix} = \begin{bmatrix} d_{11}' & d_{12}' & ... & d_{1N}' \\ d_{21}' & d_{22}' & ... & d_{2N}' \\ \vdots & \vdots & \ddots & \vdots \\ d_{l1}' & d_{l2}' & ... & d_{lN}' \end{bmatrix} \tag{2}$$

At last, SD_d sends $res_u = \mathbb{A}' \cdot \mathbb{A}'^T$ and $res_v = \mathbb{A}'^T \cdot \mathbb{A}'$ to SD_u and SD_v respectively.

4. With res_u, SD_u derandomizes every entry e_{ij}' as follows.

$$e_{ij}' \bmod S \bmod W$$
$$= (d_{ij} + z_{ij} \cdot W + r_{ij} \cdot S) \bmod S \bmod W$$
$$= (d_{ij} + z_{ij} \cdot W) \bmod W$$
$$= d_{ij}$$

The resulting matrix is $\mathbb{A} \cdot \mathbb{A}^T$. Then, SD_u performs eigenvalue decomposition to obtain $\mathbb{U}$ and Σ of $\mathbb{A} \cdot \mathbb{A}^T$, referring to Sect. 2. Similarly, SD_v can obtain $\mathbb{V}$ and Σ of $\mathbb{A}^T \cdot \mathbb{A}$. At the end, SD_u and SD_v will store $\mathbb{U}\Sigma^{\frac{1}{2}}$ and $\mathbb{V}\Sigma^{\frac{1}{2}}$ respectively. Note that they might apply the dimension reduction procedure, as mentioned in Sect. 2, to store smaller feature matrices.

3.2 Recommender Use Case

Referring to the recommender use case described in Sect. 2, Chen et al. [3] presented a procedure to extend the privacy-preserving SVD protocol to compute predictions of unrated items for the user of any edge device ED. Assuming this use case, the information that SD_u obtains at the end of privacy-preserving SVD protocol, namely $\mathbb{U}\Sigma^{\frac{1}{2}}$, can be regarded as the user feature matrix, where the i-th row is the feature vector of the user of ED_i. Correspondingly, the information that SD_v obtains at the end of privacy-preserving SVD protocol, namely

$\mathbb{V}\Sigma^{\frac{1}{2}}$, can be regarded as the item feature matrix, where the j-th row is the feature vector of the j-th item.

If the user of ED_i wants to retrieve the prediction on the j-th item, the procedure is detailed below.

1. SD_u and SD_v randomize $InfoUi$ and $InfoIj$ with W and S, respectively, and send the randomized data to SD_d. Here, as described above, $InfoUi$ stands for the user feature vector of ED_i, while $InfoIj$ stands for the item feature vector of item j. As an example, the randomization of $InfoUi$ is shown in Algorithm 2.

Algorithm 2. Randomize data with W and S

Input: $InfoUi$, W, S and range of random number $[1, t]$
Output: randomized vector $InfoUi'$
1: **for** every element h_{zi} of $InfoUi$ where $1 \leq z \leq l$ **do**
2:　　Generate random integer x, y from $[1, t]$
3:　　$h'_{z1} \longleftarrow = h_{z1} + x \cdot W + y \cdot S$
4: **end for**
5: **return** $InfoUi' = (h'_{1i}, h'_{2i}, ..., h'_{li})$

---

2. After receiving the randomized feature vectors $InfoUi'$ and $InfoIj'$, SD_d computes a randomized score $Score' = InfoUi'\{InfoIj'\}^T$, and sends it to FD.
3. After receiving $Score'$, FD can derandomize it with W and S to obtain the plaintext prediction for ED_i:

$$Score = Score' \bmod S \bmod W = InfoUi \cdot InfoIj^T$$

4　Analysis of Chen et al.'s Solution

In [3], Chen et al. analysed all devices of the system, and claimed that none of them has the ability to learn private data under normal operations. However, we show that their solution has a number of vulnerabilities, it leaks information not only to an individual device but also colluded devices (more seriously).

4.1　Information Leakage to Individual Device

At the end of the privacy-preserving protocol, SD_v obtains $\mathbb{A}^T \cdot \mathbb{A}$ with following notation.

$$\mathbb{A}^T \cdot \mathbb{A} = \begin{bmatrix} v_{11} & v_{12} & \cdots & v_{1N} \\ v_{21} & v_{22} & \cdots & v_{2N} \\ \vdots & \vdots & \ddots & \vdots \\ v_{N1} & v_{N2} & \cdots & v_{NN} \end{bmatrix} \tag{3}$$

Leakage 1. We note that the values v_{ii}, for $i \in [1, N]$, are in the following form.

$$\begin{cases} v_{11} = d_{11}^2 + d_{21}^2 + \dots + d_{l1}^2 \\ \quad \dots \\ v_{NN} = d_{1N}^2 + d_{2N}^2 + \dots + d_{lN}^2 \end{cases}$$

According to Cauchy-Schwarz inequality [14], based on v_{ii}, SD_v can deduce the upper bound about the average of the elements in $\vec{d_i}$ for each device ED_i, namely $\frac{\sum_{j=1}^{l} d_{ji}}{l} \le (\frac{v_{ii}}{l})^{\frac{1}{2}}$.

Leakage 2. Taking the elements related to ED_1 as an example, SD_v possesses the following values.

$$\begin{cases} v_{11} = d_{11}^2 + d_{21}^2 + \dots + d_{l1}^2 \\ \quad \dots \\ v_{N1} = d_{1N}d_{11} + d_{2N}d_{21} + \dots + d_{lN}d_{l1} \end{cases}$$

Adding all of them, SD_v can obtain $\sum_{j=1}^{N} v_{j1} = \sum_{j=1}^{N} d_{1j} \cdot d_{11} + \sum_{j=1}^{N} d_{2j} \cdot d_{21} + \dots + \sum_{j=1}^{N} d_{lj} \cdot d_{l1}$. Based on the fact that every $d_{ji} \in [0, x]$, according to the law of large numbers [2], the above equality can be approximately written as

$$\frac{\sum_{j=1}^{N} v_{j1}}{N} = \frac{1+x}{2} \cdot d_{11} + \frac{1+x}{2} \cdot d_{21} + \dots + \frac{1+x}{2} \cdot d_{l1}$$

Based on this, SD_v can obtain the approximate average of the elements in $\vec{d_1}$ for device ED_1, namely $\frac{2\sum_{j=1}^{N} v_{j1}}{N \cdot (1+x) \cdot l}$. Clearly, the same analysis applies to ED_i $(2 \le i \le N)$.

4.2 When Two Devices Collude

If SD_u and SD_v collude, they possess $\mathbb{U}$, Σ and $\mathbb{V}$ which are the singular matrices of $\mathbb{A}$. It means they can restore all private data as $\mathbb{U} \cdot \Sigma \cdot \mathbb{V}^T = \mathbb{A}$. If SD_d and FD collude, they will possess W, S, and the Paillier private key (μ, λ). With this information, they can recover the private data of all EDs. Clearly, if SD_u or SD_v colludes with SD_d, they can also recover everything in the same way.

Next, we investigate the case that SD_v and one ED collude. Generally, let's assume if SD_v and ED_i collude. They possess $\vec{d_i}$ and $\mathbb{A}^T \cdot \mathbb{A}$ as defined in Eq. (3). The elements from the i-th column of $\mathbb{A}^T \cdot \mathbb{A}$ are defined as follows.

$$\begin{cases} v_{1i} = d_{11}d_{1i} + d_{21}d_{2i} + \dots + d_{l1}d_{li} \\ \quad \dots \\ v_{(i-1)i} = d_{1(i-1)}d_{1i} + d_{2(i-1)}d_{2i} + \dots + d_{l(i-1)}d_{li} \\ \quad \dots \\ v_{(i+1)i} = d_{1(i+1)}d_{1i} + d_{2(i+1)}d_{2i} + \dots + d_{l(i+1)}d_{li} \\ \quad \dots \\ v_{Ni} = d_{1N}d_{1i} + d_{2N}d_{2i} + \dots + d_{lN}d_{li} \end{cases}$$

Below, we describe two simple active attacks.

Attack 1. Being an active attacker, ED_i can set its vector to be $\vec{d_i} = (1, 1, ..., 1)$. As a result, from the value v_{ji} where $j \in [1, N]$ and $j \neq i$, SD_v and ED_i can learn the average of the elements in the vector of ED_j.

$$\frac{v_{ji}}{l} = \frac{d_{1j} + d_{2j} + ... + d_{lj}}{l}$$

Attack 2. Similarly, ED_i can set its vector to be $\vec{d_i} = (0, ..., 1, ..., 0)$ where the y-th element is 1 and all others are 0. In this case, from the value v_{ji}, SD_v and ED_i can learn the the element d_{yj} in the vector of ED_j.

$$v_{ji} = d_{1j}d_{1i} + d_{2j}d_{2i} + ... + d_{yj}d_{yi} + ... + d_{lj}d_{li} = d_{yj}$$

4.3   When More Participants Collude

Attack 1. Suppose that SD_v and l (or more) EDs collude. If this case, they will possess $A^T \cdot A$ defined by Eq. (3) and for example the following l $\vec{d}$s.

$$\begin{cases} \vec{d_i} = (d_{1i}, d_{2i}, ..., d_{li})^T \\ \quad \cdots \\ \vec{d}_{(i+l-1)} = (d_{1(i+l-1)}, d_{2(i+l-1)}, ..., d_{l(i+l-1)})^T \end{cases}$$

With the information, SD_v may recover the data of any ED_j, for $j \notin [i, i+l-1]$. Note that the i-th to $i+l-1$-th elements from the j-th column of $A^T \cdot A$ are defined as follows. The attack is simply to solve the system of l-variable linear equations.

$$\begin{cases} v_{ij} = d_{1i}d_{1j} + d_{2i}d_{2j} + ... + d_{li}d_{lj} \\ \quad \cdots \\ v_{N(i+l-1)} = d_{1(i+l-1)}d_{1j} + d_{2(i+l-1)}d_{2j} + ... + d_{l(i+l-1)}d_{lj} \end{cases}$$

By solving the system of equation, the attacker can obtain all the value of d_{aj} where $a \in [1, l]$.

Attack 2. Suppose SD_d and h EDs collude, where h is an integer, they will process A' as defined by Eq. (2). For example, consider the following h $\vec{d}$s.

$$\begin{cases} \vec{d_i} = (d_{1i}, d_{2i}, ..., d_{li})^T \\ \quad \cdots \\ \vec{d}_{(i+h-1)} = (d_{1(i+h-1)}, d_{2(i+h-1)}, ..., d_{l(i+h-1)})^T \end{cases}$$

For ED_j, where $j \in [i, i+h-1]$, the relevant elements in A' lie in the j-th column which can be expressed as:

$$\begin{cases} d'_{1j} = d_{1j} + z_{j1} \cdot W + r_{j1} \cdot S \\ \quad \cdots \\ d'_{lj} = d_{lj} + z_{jl} \cdot W + r_{jl} \cdot S \end{cases}$$

These equations can be transformed into the following form shown in Eq. (4), where zs, rs, and W, S are the unknowns.

$$\begin{cases} d'_{1j} - d_{1j} = z_{j1} \cdot W + r_{j1} \cdot S \\ \qquad \cdots \\ d'_{lj} - d_{lj} = z_{jl} \cdot W + r_{jl} \cdot S \end{cases} \tag{4}$$

Since rs and zs are random integers chosen from $[1, t]$, according to the law of large numbers [2], we can get an approximated form of the following equation.

$$\frac{1}{l} \cdot \sum_{i=1}^{l}(d'_{ij} - d_{ij}) = \frac{1+t}{2} \cdot W + \frac{1+t}{2} \cdot S$$

Since the computation is based on data from ED_j, we let P_j denote the approximated estimation for $W + S$.

$$P_j = W + S = \frac{2}{(1+t) \cdot l} \cdot \sum_{i=1}^{l}(d'_{ij} - d_{ij})$$

Based on P_j for all $j \in [i, i + h - 1]$, SD_d can try to recover W and S by a brute-force attack, shown in Algorithm 3.

Algorithm 3. Brute-force the value of W and S

Input: P, Range of W
Output: Value of W and S
1: Let LC denote the set of all results of $d'_{ij} - d_{ij}$ where $i \in [1, l]$ and $j \in [1, N]$
   (i.e. Equation (4) for ED_j)
2: **for each** f in range of W **do**
3:    $S_{BF} \leftarrow P - f$
4:    **for each** LC_k in LC **do**
5:       $ModS_k \leftarrow LC_k \mod S_{BF}$
6:    **end for**
7:    Let $ModS$ denote the set of all $ModS_k$
8:    **if** $GCD(ModS) > 1$ and $coprime(GCD(ModS), S_{BF})$ **then**
9:       **return** $W = GCD(ModS)$, $S = S_{BF}$
10:   **end if**
11: **end for**

Once W and S are found, the whole matrix $\mathbb{A}$ can be recovered. We emphasize that a brute-force attack has been analyzed in [3], where the attacker tries each possible value of S. The complexity of their attack is $O(2^{k_3})$. In contrast, our attack enumerates the parameter W which is much smaller than S (as shown in Table 4, $S > max(N, l) \cdot (x^2 + 2tWx + t^2W^2)$). The complexity of current brute-force method is only $O(2^{k_2}) + 2lh$.

4.4   Analysis of the Recommender Use Case

Regarding the recommender use case from Sect. 3.2, we observe that it has two privacy vulnerabilities. One is that FD obtains the prediction score for the edge devices. The score indicates the interest of the human user behind the device, so that it may be considered as private information. Disclosing such information may be considered undesirable by many. The other is that SD_d obtains the randomized feature vectors for all prediction queries. Considering the attack from Sect. 4.3, SD_d may recover W and S, and then recover the plaintext data from all the devices.

5   New Privacy-Preserving SVD Solution

In this section, we first simplify the FoG architecture shown in Fig. 2 and propose a stronger security model. Then, we present a new solution and provide detailed security and performance analysis.

5.1   Security Model

Our new FoG architecture is shown in Fig. 3. In comparison to that in Fig. 2, we get rid of the involvement of the second-layer SD_d device. With this new architecture, the second-layer devices SD_u and SD_v will store the decomposed matrices, while the first-layer device FD is responsible for interacting with the edge devices and coordinating the SVD operations.

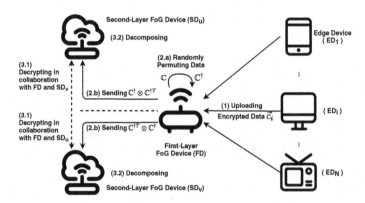

Fig. 3. Simplified FoG architecture

The purpose of our solution is to perform SVD based on the private data from all edge devices ED_i $(1 \leq i \leq N)$, where ED_i's input is a data vector $\vec{d_i}$. Note that we assume every data vector is in a column form and all these data vectors form a data matrix $\mathbb{A}$, as defined in Eq. (1). As the output, SD_u and

SD_v should learn $(\mathbb{U}, \Sigma)$ and $(\mathbb{V}, \Sigma)$ respectively. Any other disclosure about the private information, including ED_i's data, $(\mathbb{U}, \Sigma)$ and $(\mathbb{V}, \Sigma)$, will be considered as an information leakage. Referring to the description of SVD in Sect. 2, the legitimate information disclosure is equivalent to disclosing $\mathbb{A} \cdot \mathbb{A}^T$ and $\mathbb{A}^T \cdot \mathbb{A}$ to SD_u and SD_v respectively.

Comparing with [3] and other distributed machine learning solutions, we will not make a general semi-honest assumption to ask all participants to follow the protocol specification and not to collude with each other. As we have put in our analysis, such an assumption is not realistic in practice, particularly some edge devices can be compromised or forged easily. Instead, we assume some players may collude and try to figure out information that they are not supposed to learn. Next, we enumerate all the attack scenarios and our privacy expectations.

1. When a group of edge devices is regarded as the attacker, it should learn nothing about the private data of other edge devices. This implies that the attacker learns nothing about $(\mathbb{U}, \Sigma)$ and $(\mathbb{V}, \Sigma)$ more than what it can infer from its own data.
2. When SD_u is regarded as the attacker, it only learns $(\mathbb{U}, \Sigma)$. When SD_v is regarded as the attacker, it only learns $(\mathbb{V}, \Sigma)$. When FD is regarded as the attacker, it learns nothing.
3. When SD_u and FD are regarded as the attacker (i.e. they collude), it only learns $(\mathbb{U}, \Sigma)$. When SD_v and FD are regarded as the attacker (i.e. they collude), it only learns $(\mathbb{V}, \Sigma)$. When SD_u and SD_v are regarded as the attacker (i.e. they collude), it learns a randomly permuted data matrix $\mathbb{A}^\dagger$, which is obtained by randomly permuting the rows and columns of $\mathbb{A}$. This means the attacker cannot trivially link a data vector to an edge device and cannot trivially recover the order of the elements in a data vector.
4. When FD and a group of edge devices are regarded as the attacker, it should learn nothing about the private data of other edge devices. This implies that the attacker learns nothing about $(\mathbb{U}, \Sigma)$ and $(\mathbb{V}, \Sigma)$ more than that it can infer from its own data.
5. When SD_u and a group of edge devices are regarded as the attacker, it should learn nothing more than what can be inferred from $\mathbb{A}^\dagger \cdot \mathbb{A}^{\dagger^T}$ and the data vectors of these edge devices. When SD_v and a group of edge devices are regarded as the attacker, it should learn nothing more than what can be inferred from $\mathbb{A}^{\dagger^T} \cdot \mathbb{A}^\dagger$ and the data vectors of these edge devices. Recall that $\mathbb{A}^\dagger$ is defined in bullet 3.

Note that we do not consider the scenarios, where all edge devices collude or all FoG devices (SD_u, SD_v and FD) collude, because in both cases the attacker will know everything by default in our setting.

In our construction, we will use threshold homomorphic encryption as the main building block, which guarantees that only the legitimate information will be decrypted and delivered to the corresponding parties. As such, when we say the solution does not leak any information about some private data α, it meant that if another piece data β will generate the same output as α then the attacker cannot determine whether α or β has been used as the input. It has the same flavor as the semantic security of the underlying homomorphic encryption scheme.

5.2   Description of the New Solution

Our main tool is a homomorphic encryption scheme, which supports partial homomorphic multiplication (between plaintext and ciphertext) and a polynomial number of homomorphic additions. In addition, we also require the scheme to allow us to support threshold decryption. To this end, the threshold Paillier scheme [6], described in Appendix B of our full paper [11], satisfies our needs. This leads to the following initialisation for our new solution.

In the initialization stage, SD_u, SD_v and FD jointly set up the parameters of the threshold homomorphic encryption scheme. We assume the public key is pk, while the private key shares for the FoG devices are denoted as sk_u, sk_v and sk_f respectively. We require a $(3,3)$ threshold decryption setting, namely all three FoG devices need to collaborate in order to recover a plaintext message.

For the privacy-preserving SVD protocol, we will keep every data vector in encrypted form after leaving the edge devices, and threshold decryption is only carried out to recover the legitimate matrices for SD_u and SD_v respectively. Depicted in Fig. 3, the protocol consists of four phases.

1. *Edge Computing* Phase: ED_i ($1 \leq i \leq N$) uses the public key pk to encrypt its vector $\vec{d_i} = (d_{1i}, d_{2i}, ..., d_{li})^T$ into a ciphertext vector $\vec{c_i} = (c_{1i}, c_{2i}, ..., c_{li})^T$ where $c_{1i} = \mathbf{Enc}(d_{1i}, pk)$ and so on. Then, ED_i sends $\vec{c_i}$, an encrypted inner product $\mathbf{Enc}(\vec{d_i}^T \cdot \vec{d_i}, pk)$, and $\frac{l(l+1)}{2}$ encrypted scalar values $\mathbf{Enc}(d_{xi}d_{yi}, pk)$ ($1 \leq x \leq l, x \leq y \leq l$) to FD. Note that these encryption operations can be done offline.

   After receiving $\vec{c_i}$ ($1 \leq i \leq N$), FD will possess a ciphertext matrix $\mathbb{C}$, which is an encrypted counterpart of $\mathbb{A}$ defined in Eq. (1).

$$\mathbb{C} = \begin{bmatrix} c_{11} & c_{12} & \cdots & c_{1N} \\ c_{21} & c_{22} & \cdots & c_{2N} \\ \vdots & \vdots & \ddots & \vdots \\ c_{l1} & c_{l2} & \cdots & c_{lN} \end{bmatrix}$$

   Next, FD computes the encrypted forms of $\mathbb{A}\mathbb{A}^T$ and $\mathbb{A}^T\mathbb{A}$, generally denoted as $\mathbb{C} \otimes \mathbb{C}^T$ and $\mathbb{C}^T \otimes \mathbb{C}$ respectively. For the sake of notation simplicity, if two ciphertexts encrypt the same plaintext, then we consider them the same.
   - We note that, for $1 \leq x, y \leq l$, the element on x-th row and y-th column of $\mathbb{C} \otimes \mathbb{C}^T$ is in the form $\sum_{i=1}^{N} c_{xi} \otimes c_{yi}$, which can be computed by FD based on the encrypted scalar values from all edge devices. For each such element, FD needs to perform $N-1$ homomorphic additions based on the received encrypted scalar values, and it also needs to perform a ciphertext rerandomization for security reasons.

- FD obtains $\mathbb{C}^T \otimes \mathbb{C}$ by pushing the computing task back to the edge devices as follows. For $1 \leq x, y \leq N$, the element on x-th row and y-th column of $\mathbb{C}^T \otimes \mathbb{C}$ is in the form of an encrypted inner products $\vec{c_x}^T \otimes \vec{c_y}$. Note that, if the edge device ED_x is given $\vec{c_y}$, then it can compute $\vec{c_x}^T \otimes \vec{c_y}$ more efficiently by replacing $\vec{c_x}^T$ with the plaintext, namely $\vec{d_x}^T$, and the complexity is l partial homomorphic multiplications, $l-1$ homomorphic additions and a ciphertext rerandomization (to prevent the leakage of the plaintext data). As the values on the diagonal have been sent by the edge devices, there are only $\frac{(N-1)(N-2)}{2}$ encrypted inner products to be computed, every edge device needs to compute $\frac{(N-1)(N-2)}{2N}$ on average.

2. *Randomization* Phase: FD chooses two random permutations. PU randomly permutes the edge device indexes: for any $1 \leq i \leq N$, $\mathsf{PU}(i) \in \{1, 2, \cdots, N\}$. PI permutes the index of elements in data vectors: for any $1 \leq i \leq l$, $\mathsf{PU}(i) \in \{1, 2, \cdots, l\}$. In this phase, based on $\mathbb{C} \otimes \mathbb{C}^T$ and $\mathbb{C}^T \otimes \mathbb{C}$, FD generates their variants corresponding to the following permuted plaintext data matrix.

$$\mathbb{A}^\dagger = \begin{bmatrix} d_{\mathsf{PU}(1)\mathsf{PI}(1)} & d_{\mathsf{PU}(1)\mathsf{PI}(2)} & \cdots & d_{\mathsf{PU}(1)\mathsf{PI}(N)} \\ d_{\mathsf{PU}(2)\mathsf{PI}(1)} & d_{\mathsf{PU}(2)\mathsf{PI}(2)} & \cdots & d_{\mathsf{PU}(2)\mathsf{PI}(N)} \\ \vdots & \vdots & \ddots & \vdots \\ d_{\mathsf{PU}(l)\mathsf{PI}(1)} & d_{\mathsf{PU}(l)\mathsf{PI}(2)} & \cdots & d_{\mathsf{PU}(l)\mathsf{PI}(N)} \end{bmatrix}$$

Let $\mathbb{C}^\dagger$ denote a ciphertext of $\mathbb{A}^\dagger$. Then, FD can generate $\mathbb{C}^\dagger \otimes \mathbb{C}^{\dagger T}$ and $\mathbb{C}^{\dagger T} \otimes \mathbb{C}^\dagger$ as follows.

(a) Clearly, PI does not affect $\mathbb{C}^\dagger \otimes \mathbb{C}^{\dagger T}$, which can be generated based on PU by rearranging the elements in $\mathbb{C} \otimes \mathbb{C}^T$.

(b) Clearly, PU does not affect $\mathbb{C}^{\dagger T} \otimes \mathbb{C}^\dagger$, which can be generated based on PI by rearranging the elements in $\mathbb{C}^T \otimes \mathbb{C}$.

At the end, FD sends $\mathbb{C}^\dagger \otimes \mathbb{C}^{\dagger T}$ to SD_u, and sends $\mathbb{C}^{\dagger T} \otimes \mathbb{C}^\dagger$ to SD_v.

3. *Ephemeral SVD* Phase: After receiving $\mathbb{C}^\dagger \otimes \mathbb{C}^{\dagger T}$, SD_u can request the help from SD_v and FD to decrypt all the elements to obtain $\mathbb{A}^\dagger \mathbb{A}^{\dagger T}$. It can then perform decomposition and obtain $\mathbb{U}^\dagger$ and $\Sigma^\dagger$. Similarly, SD_v can obtain $\mathbb{V}^\dagger$ and $\Sigma^\dagger$.

4. *Secure Storage* Phase (optional): Based on some predefined rule, SD_u and SD_v can truncate $\Sigma^\dagger$ in a certain way (see Sect. 2), and then store an encrypted product instead of the plaintext matrices. For example, if they do not truncate $\Sigma^\dagger$ at all, they store $\mathbf{Enc}(\mathbb{U}^\dagger (\Sigma^\dagger)^{\frac{1}{2}}, pk)$ and $\mathbf{Enc}((\Sigma^\dagger)^{\frac{1}{2}} (\mathbb{V}^\dagger)^T, pk)$ respectively.

The permutations, namely PU and PI, only affects the location of device indexes and data elements in the data matrix, so that they do not affect the functionality of SVD in any manner. Referring to the recommender use case, FD can easily determine the feature vectors for a specific user and item in $\mathbb{U}^\dagger (\Sigma^\dagger)^{\frac{1}{2}}$ and $(\Sigma^\dagger)^{\frac{1}{2}} (\mathbb{V}^\dagger)^T$. If the optional *Secure Storage* Phase is adopted, then when an outsider attacker compromises any two of the FoG devices (i.e. SD_u,

SD_v and FD) at the end of the solution, it learns nothing due to the threshold decryption requirement.

5.3   Security and Performance Analysis

Security Analysis. We show that the solution satisfies our privacy expectations defined in Sect. 5.1.

1. When a group of edge devices are regarded as the attacker, it does not learn anything about the private data of other edge devices because it only receives encrypted data and has no access to the decryption oracle.
2. When SD_u (or SD_v) is regarded as the attacker, it only learns $(\mathbb{U}^\dagger, \Sigma^\dagger)$ (or, $(\mathbb{V}^\dagger, \Sigma^\dagger)$) because that is the only information disclosed in the *Ephemeral SVD* Phase. When FD is regarded as the attacker, it clearly learns nothing because of the threshold decryption constraint.
3. When SD_u and FD are regarded as the attacker, it possesses $(\mathbb{U}^\dagger, \Sigma^\dagger)$ and the permutations. As a result, it only learns $(\mathbb{U}, \Sigma)$ because of the threshold decryption constraint. Similarly, when SD_v and FD are regarded as the attacker, it only learns $(\mathbb{V}, \Sigma)$. When SD_u and SD_v are regarded as the attacker, it learns a randomly permuted data matrix $\mathbb{A}^\dagger$, which is equivalent to $(\mathbb{U}^\dagger, \Sigma^\dagger)$ and $(\mathbb{V}^\dagger, \Sigma^\dagger)$.
4. When FD and a group of edge devices are regarded as the attacker, it does not learn anything about the private data of other edge devices because it only receives encrypted data and does not receive any decryption output.
5. Due to the threshold decryption constraint, when SD_u and a group of edge devices are regarded as the attacker, it only learns $\mathbb{A}^\dagger \cdot \mathbb{A}^{\dagger T}$ and the data vectors of these edge devices. Similarly, when SD_v and a group of edge devices are regarded as the attacker, it only learns $\mathbb{A}^{\dagger T} \cdot \mathbb{A}^\dagger$ and the data vectors of these edge devices.

Asymptotic Performance Analysis. Regarding the complexity of the new solution, we summarize the number of main cryptographic operations in Table 5. It excludes offline and optional operations. As to notation, Dec, $\oplus$, $\otimes$, rand denote threshold decryption, homomorphic addition, homomorphic multiplication, and ciphertext rerandomization respectively. Regarding the threshold Paillier scheme described in Appendix B of our full paper [11], referring to the cryptographic operations, we make the following note: a partial $\otimes$ is an exponentiation, a $\oplus$ is a modulo multiplication, and a rand is a modulo multiplication.

Optimised Benchmarking. In order to learn the actual running time of different parties, we implement our solution based on the threshold Paillier scheme. For the benchmarking, we choose a 2048-bit n, set $s = 2$, and split the key into three shares and require the decryption to involve all three key shares. We assume there are 1000 devices and every data vector has 100 elements. In addition, as in the recommender use case, every element of the data vector is a small number from 0 to 5.

Table 5. Asymptotic complexity

Player	Complexity
ED_i	$\frac{l(N-1)(N-2)}{2N}$ partial $\otimes$, $\frac{(l-1)(N-1)(N-2)}{2N}$ $\oplus$, $\frac{(N-1)(N-2)}{2N}$ rand
FD	$\frac{l(l+1)(N-1)}{2}$ $\oplus$, $\frac{l(l+1)+N(N+1)}{2}$ Dec, $\frac{l(l+1)}{2}$ rand
SD_u	$\frac{l(l+1)+N(N+1)}{2}$ Dec
SD_v	$\frac{l(l+1)+N(N+1)}{2}$ Dec

To reduce the number of threshold decryption operations, we propose to pack multiple ciphertexts into one and decrypt all of them at once.

– Every ciphertext in the matrix $\mathbb{C}^\dagger \otimes \mathbb{C}^{\dagger^T}$ encrypts a number in the range $[0, 2^{15})$. Since the message space for threshold Paillier is $(0, n^2)$, we can pack around 270 ciphertexts C_i $(1 \leq i \leq 270)$ into a single one as $C_1 \cdot (C_2)^{2^{15}} \cdots (C_{270})^{2^{15 \times 269}}$. Note that operations are modulo n^{2+1}. The packing incurs $269 + 15 + 30 + \cdots + 15 \times 269 = 544944$ ciphertext multiplications. Recovering individual plaintext is trivial based on modulo operations with respect to $2^{15 \times 269}, 2^{15 \times 268}, \cdots, 2^{15}$ sequentially.
– Every ciphertext in the matrix $\mathbb{C}^{\dagger^T} \otimes \mathbb{C}^\dagger$ encrypts a number in the range $[0, 2^{12})$. Similar to the above case, we can pack around 340 ciphertexts C_i $(1 \leq i \leq 340)$ into one as $C_1 \cdot (C_2)^{2^{12}} \cdots (C_{340})^{2^{12 \times 339}}$. The packing incurs $339 + 12 + 24 + \cdots + 12 \times 339 = 691899$ ciphertext multiplications.

After the optimisation, based on Table 5, we derive the new asymptotic complexity in Table 6. Note that mul is a modulo multiplication, Dec and Dec (comb) refer to the *Share decryption* and *Combination* algorithms respectively described in Appendix B of our full paper [11]. Based on our implementation on a PC with 3.40 GHz CPU and 16 GB memory, we obtain the actual running time in the last column.

Table 6. Optimised complexity ($N = 1000, l = 100$)

Player	Complexity	Time
ED_i	49850 partial $\otimes$, 49850 mul	3 s
FD	5050000 mul, 1491 Dec	189 s
SD_u	$\mathbb{C}^\dagger \otimes \mathbb{C}^{\dagger^T}$: 19 Dec (comb), 10353936 mul; $\mathbb{C}^{\dagger^T} \otimes \mathbb{C}^\dagger$: 1472 Dec	267 s
SD_v	$\mathbb{C}^\dagger \otimes \mathbb{C}^{\dagger^T}$: 19 Dec; $\mathbb{C}^{\dagger^T} \otimes \mathbb{C}^\dagger$: 1472 Dec (comb), 1018475328 mul	15061 s

In order to further reduce the running time for SD_v, there are two more ways to further optimise the computations. The first one is to check the density of the dataset and pack more ciphertexts into one, and the other is to outsource the computations to the edge devices.

6 Conclusion

In this paper, we analysed the privacy-preserving SVD solution by Chen et al. [3], and demonstrated several privacy vulnerabilities. Based on our analysis, we presented an enhanced solution and provided analysis on both security and efficiency. As an immediate future work, we would like to further optimize its efficiency by exploiting fine-grained packing and computation outsourcing. It is also an interesting work to study the performances with larger datasets and improve the efficiency a step further (e.g. by pushing more computations back to the edge devices [4]). In addition, it is an important work to compare the performances of the (optimised) solutions to those in the literature. To this end, the comparison should also take into account the potential application requirements. One of them is that the SVD might be carried out frequently based on the new data constantly generated by the edge devices. We conjecture that the garbled circuit based solutions such as [12] will have a disadvantage in such situations.

References

1. Bar-Magen Numhauser, J.: Fog computing introduction to a new cloud evolution. University of Alcalá (2012)
2. Barbour, A.D., Luczak, M.J.: A law of large numbers approximation for Markov population processes with countably many types. Probab. Theor. Relat Fields **153**(3), 727–757 (2012). https://doi.org/10.1007/s00440-011-0359-2
3. Chen, S., Lu, R., Zhang, J.: A flexible privacy-preserving framework for singular value decomposition under internet of things environment. In: Steghöfer, J.-P., Esfandiari, B. (eds.) IFIPTM 2017. IAICT, vol. 505, pp. 21–37. Springer, Cham (2017). https://doi.org/10.1007/978-3-319-59171-1_3
4. Chen, X., Li, J., Ma, J., Tang, Q., Lou, W.: New algorithms for secure outsourcing of modular exponentiations. IEEE Trans. Parallel Distrib. Syst. **25**(9), 2386–2396 (2014)
5. Cisco: Fog Computing and the Internet of Things: Extend the Cloud to where the things are (2015)
6. Damgård, I., Jurik, M.: A generalisation, a simplication and some applications of Paillier's probabilistic public-key system. In: Kim, K. (ed.) PKC 2001. LNCS, vol. 1992, pp. 119–136. Springer, Heidelberg (2001). https://doi.org/10.1007/3-540-44586-2_9
7. Han, S., Ng, W.K., Philip, S.Y.: Privacy-preserving singular value decomposition. In: 2009 IEEE 25th International Conference on Data Engineering, pp. 1267–1270. IEEE (2009)
8. Kim, S., Kim, J., Koo, D., Kim, Y., Yoon, H., Shin, J.: Efficient privacy-preserving matrix factorization via fully homomorphic encryption. In: Proceedings of the 11th ACM on Asia Conference on Computer and Communications Security, pp. 617–628. ACM (2016)
9. Knorr, E., Gruman, G.: What cloud computing really means. InfoWorld **7**, 20 (2008)
10. Koren, Y., Bell, R., Volinsky, C.: Matrix factorization techniques for recommender systems. Computer **42**(8), 30–37 (2009)

11. Liu, B., Tang, Q.: Privacy-preserving decentralised singular value decomposition. Cryptology ePrint Archive: 2019/1346 (2019)
12. Nikolaenko, V., Ioannidis, S., Weinsberg, U., Joye, M., Taft, N., Boneh, D.: Privacy-preserving matrix factorization. In: Proceedings of the 2013 ACM SIGSAC Conference on Computer & Communications Security, pp. 801–812. ACM (2013)
13. Paillier, P.: Public-key cryptosystems based on composite degree residuosity classes. In: Stern, J. (ed.) EUROCRYPT 1999. LNCS, vol. 1592, pp. 223–238. Springer, Heidelberg (1999). https://doi.org/10.1007/3-540-48910-X_16
14. Wu, H.H., Wu, S.: Various proofs of the Cauchy-Schwarz inequality. Octogon Math. Mag. 17(1), 221–229 (2009)
15. Yang, Y., Wu, L., Yin, G., Li, L., Zhao, H.: A survey on security and privacy issues in Internet-of-Things. IEEE Internet Things J. 4(5), 1250–1258 (2017)
16. Zhou, J., Cao, Z., Dong, X., Lin, X.: Security and privacy in cloud-assisted wireless wearable communications: challenges, solutions, and future directions. IEEE Wirel. Commun. 22(2), 136–144 (2015)
17. Zhuo, G., Jia, Q., Guo, L., Li, M., Li, P.: Privacy-preserving verifiable data aggregation and analysis for cloud-assisted mobile crowdsourcing. In: IEEE INFOCOM 2016-The 35th Annual IEEE International Conference on Computer Communications, pp. 1–9. IEEE (2016)

Web Security

WSLD: Detecting Unknown Webshell Using Fuzzy Matching and Deep Learning

Zihao Zhao[1,2], Qixu Liu[1,2(✉)], Tiantian Song[3], Zhi Wang[1,2], and Xianda Wu[1]

[1] Institute of Information Engineering, Chinese Academy of Sciences, Beijing, China
{zhaozihao,liuqixu,wangzhi,wuxianda}@iie.ac.cn
[2] School of Cyber Security, University of Chinese Academy of Sciences, Beijing, China
[3] Tsinghua-Berkeley Shenzhen Institute, Tsinghua University, Beijing, China
songtt18@mails.tsinghua.edu.cn

Abstract. Web applications have become one of the most common targets for attackers to exploit vulnerabilities in recent years. After successfully attacking the webserver, hackers upload webshell to maintain long-term and secret access to the server. Nowadays, webshell written by various script languages leads more and more security researchers to focus on how to detect it efficiently and automatically. Therefore, we classify multiple classes of webshell based on the implementation of webshell and then propose a heuristic detection method based on fuzzy matching and recurrent neural network. We analyze the behavioral characteristics of suspicious files by driving the known malicious samples, extract system call sequence, and perform automatic detection based on the recurrent neural network. Through feature learning and model training, the experimental results show that our method has high accuracy for webshell detection whether it written by various languages, obfuscated or encrypted. The prototype system WSLD has been well designed and implemented based on our method. With a total of 5541 samples trained and 2100 samples tested, the result shows that the webshell recognition rate of WSLD can reach 98.86%, which proves it is an effective and feasible method.

Keywords: Fuzzy match · Webshell · Recurrent neural network · Heuristic detection

1 Introduction

With the rapid development of Internet technology, the network is increasingly connected with people's lives, and the security of Web applications has received more and more attention. According to the 2018 website security situation analysis report released by Qihoo 360 [1], there were a total of 703,000 websites that suffered from attack throughout the year, and more than 8,040,000 webshell were uploaded during the whole year, ranking second among the top ten website security risks. Server-side security issues are becoming more and more serious, and even seriously threaten the normal operation of network services. Therefore, it is important to discover and detect server vulnerabilities and backdoors in time to ensure server-side security.

© Springer Nature Switzerland AG 2020
J. Zhou et al. (Eds.): ICICS 2019, LNCS 11999, pp. 725–745, 2020.
https://doi.org/10.1007/978-3-030-41579-2_42

Webshell is often seen as a remote access Trojan on a compromised webserver during a network attack. Because it is a command execution environment written in a server-side dynamic scripting language, it is easier to bypass intrusive security products from external and traffic perspectives. Therefore, how to go deep into the server and analyze the malicious code in the website asynchronously with the most accurate and timely methods to know the security status of the website server has become an urgent problem.

Traditional webshell detection methods are mostly based on regular matching, which analyzes and matches keywords such as dangerous functions and malicious signatures of common webshell. Since stealth webshell usually has similar features to normal web scripts, such detection methods cannot accurately detect stealth webshell. In addition, this kind of method will also generate more false negatives for the unknown webshell. The filtered webshell usually needs further technical verification by website maintainer, which puts higher demands on the administrator. Detection methods based on log analysis, traffic analysis and behavior analysis have been proposed in order to detect highly obfuscated and encrypted webshell timely. However, there are problems such as single detection dimension, long detection time, and detection requiring intrusion in the implementation process of these methods.

With the development of artificial intelligence, deep learning has been fully applied in solving network security problems. As for webshell detection, when selecting a large number of samples, suitable sample features and detection methods, machine learning based methods can get better detection results than traditional detection methods. In this paper, we present a method for detecting webshell based on fuzzy matching and deep learning. The main contributions of this paper are as follows:

(1) We summarize the latest developments in the field of webshell detection in recent years, and then we classify different variants of webshell into four categories based on the analysis of the principle of webshell implementation.

(2) We propose a heuristic method to detect webshell based on fuzzy matching and deep learning. Through the fuzzy matching, the normal and the high-risk webshell are divided into two classes, then the system will detect the suspicious class through the recurrent neural network (RNN) algorithm based on the system call sequence driven by a large number of malicious samples, and finally the classified webshell is merged and identified. Experiments show that this approach can be used to make up for the shortcomings of traditional detection technology and existing machine learning detection methods, which effectively detects webshell and provides good experience for users.

(3) We design and implement a system named WSLD (Webshell Detector), which is a prototype system for detecting webshell. WSLD can automate the analysis and detection of uploaded samples, and it can not only achieve a cost-sensitive classification of webshell, but also can accurately predict unknown and specially constructed webshell. WSLD has a good ability to recognize malicious samples written in different languages, encrypted or highly obfuscated. In terms of performance, the system can detect webshell asynchronously till all files are detected.

The rest of this paper is arranged as follows. The second section summarizes the existing webshell detection methods and their existing problems. The third section analyzes the implementation of webshell, classifies different variants of webshell into four categories and proposes a detection method based on fuzzy matching and deep learning. The fourth section presents the design of WSLD and elaborates the three modules in the detection framework. The fifth section implements the prototype system WSLD and explains the implementation details of each module. The sixth section lists the experimental setup, conducts two experiments to test and compare WSLD with some popular webshell detection tools, and finally explains the test results; the seventh section summarizes the full paper.

2 Related Work

The detection of malicious code on web pages has always been a hotspot of security research. Because webshell is seriously harmful, threatening and far-reaching in web malicious code, security researchers have carried out extensive and in-depth research on how to detect webshell-related malicious code more effectively. The summary of the research work on webshell detection in all directions is shown in Table 1.

The static feature matching detection mainly focuses on the data execution to extract features from high-risk functions and feature codes. The detection results are closely related to the feature library. Piotr and Thornton [2] collected a large number of samples to form a rich feature library and develop a php-webshell-detector. Subsequently, Truong et al. [3] proposed a static detection webshell method for real-time updating of the feature library by scanning decoding, encryption function and statistical behavior information. Hu [4] conducted feature extraction based on properties of webshell and detected webshell using decision tree. Later, Meng et al. [5] extracted the attributes of web pages as features and used the SVM method to detect the webshell. It's easy to find that the static feature detection is generated from the existing feature database of webshell and can't detect unknown webshell effectively. Because it is easy to bypass, the encoded webshell causes more false positives and false negatives.

Subsequently, dynamic webshell detection based on abnormal traffic was successively proposed. Starov used dynamic analysis in the research of webshell [6] to quantify common features of webshell, such as authentication mechanisms, interface features, and so on. From the perspective of usability, the dynamic method can realize real-time detection from the implementation of webshell, but it is usually expensive to deploy during the implementation and requires a list of routine maintenance rules.

As a method of threat identification and analysis, log analysis can provide complete event tracking for webshell detection. Shi [7] analyzed the logs and performed text feature matching to detect webshell. Deng et al. [8] realized the detection of webshell by extracting log text features and establishing a request model. It can be found that webshell detection based on logs is difficult to touch the nature of webshell, and the detection efficiency is lower for a large number of access logs.

Detection of webshell behavior analysis is based on the parsing process of website scripts in the system environment. Cui [9] extracted the opcode sequence of PHP and used the random forest to identify webshell. Besides, some work [10] attempted to

Table 1. Webshell detection related research work summary

Research interests	Research advances	Research team	Remaining problems
Detection technology based on static feature	Build a webshell feature library to detect webshell	ShellDetector Inc.	Hard to identify encrypted, obfuscated shell; Unable to detect unknown webshell
	Webshell detection by updating the feature library in real time	Southeast University	
	Detection by webshell attributes	IIE, CAS	
	Detection based on attributes and operations	Peking University	
Traffic-based analysis	Analysis the features of webshell by traffic	Stony Brook University	High deployment costs; Hard to detect encrypted traffic
Detection technology based on log analysis	Log-based feature matching detection	Sichuan University	Hard to touch the nature; A large number of useless logs
	Detect webshell based on logging and lexical analysis techniques	St. John's University	
Detection technology based on behavioral analysis	Webshell detection model with PHP opcode sequence features	Sichuan University	Cannot detect stealth or content scenes-based webshell
	Random forest based on dynamic feature selection	Electronic Engineering Institute	
Detection technology based on statistics	Statistical indicators to compare webshell with normal files	Cisco	Distinguish obfuscated from normal files
	Logistic regression based on statistical features to detect webshell	Sichuan University	
Detection technology based on deep learning	CNN model based on HTTP requests to detect webshell	Army Engineering University	Single feature type; Only one deep learning algorithm
	SVDD algorithm to detect webshell	One scorpion Technology	
	BP neural network to detect webshell based on semantic analysis	Peking University	

construct feature vectors for different webshell types and built a random forest model to detect webshell.

Nowadays, webshell is often obfuscated to bypass the firewall. Meanwhile, the obfuscated webshell often presents specific statistical characteristics. NeoPI [11] mainly identified the obfuscated files. The main work of the detection was to calculate the statistical range of normal files by statistical methods and compare the hidden malicious code with the files to be detected. Ma [12] built a supervised classification model based on logistic regression to detect webshell. However, this method relied on statistical features in the process of identifying webshell and could not provide the basis for discriminating whether the files were webshell. Therefore, the method leads some false positives which have to be classified by manual analysis.

With the development of artificial intelligence, the neural network algorithms are gradually applied to webshell detection. Tian [13] proposed a method to convert the HTTP request into a fixed-size word vector matrix and built a CNN model to perform feature learning on the webshell request to detect webshell. Wu [14] proposed using the chi-squared test and deep learning algorithm to obtain the text features of webshell, using the incremental learning SVDD model to build the classifier. Zhang [15] proposed semantic analysis on the compiled files and built a BP neural network to detect unknown samples.

From the above analysis, we can see that although many efforts are focused on webshell detection, most of the existing methods have problems such as limited detection dimensions, single features, and detection methods that need to perform intrusion. Compared with other algorithms, the detection method proposed in this paper has rich detection dimensions, and all the test indicators performed well.

3 Proposed Methodology

With the development of webshell, more and more webshell is obfuscated to bypass WAF filters and signatures. In this section, we analyze the nature of webshell based on its implementation, classify webshell into four categories and propose a webshell detection method based on fuzzy matching and deep learning.

3.1 Webshell Overview

Starov [6] proposed a comprehensive study of webshell by using different static and dynamic analysis methods to analyze the function of webshell from the principle of webshell and how the attacker use these functions to complete the attack. Inspired by the analysis of webshell, in order to effectively detect webshell, we have effectively analyzed the implementation process of webshell.

This section analyzes the principle and implementation of webshell. Table 2 lists webshell written in different languages. By contrast, we can find that although webshell can be written in different languages, it is essentially the same in its implementation, which can be divided into two parts: data transmission and data execution.

Subsequently, we organized webshell to data transmission and data execution in accordance with webshell implementation, as shown in Table 3. When the webshell

Table 2. Webshell written by different script languages

Scripts	Examples of Webshell
ASP	<%eval request("pass")%>
ASPX	<%@ Page Language="Jscript"%><%eval(Request.Item["cmd"],"unsafe");%>
JSP	<%Runtime.getRuntime().exec(request.getParameter("i"));%>
PHP	<?php assert($_REQUEST["c"]);?>

is uploaded to the vulnerable website, the attacker connects to the webshell for data transmission. After receiving the transmitted data part, the server interprets and executes the transmission content, thereby completing the process of remotely controlling the target server.

Table 3. Components of webshell

Scripts	Data transmission (DT)	Data execution (DE)
ASP	request("pass")	eval(DT)
ASPX	Request.Item["cmd"]	eval(DT)
JSP	request.getParameter("i")	exec(DT)
PHP	$_REQUEST["c"]	assert(DT)

3.2 Webshell Classification Based on Webshell Implementation

According to the analysis of webshell principle in Sect. 3.1, this section presents the research on webshell variations, analyzes the nature of different variants of webshell, and summarizes the classification of unknown webshell confrontation techniques.

From the attacker's point of view, if you want to successfully upload and connect to the webshell, you need to bypass all kinds of protection tools. Taking the detection-bypass webshell leaked into the Internet as a starting point, we divide all webshell into two parts: data transmission and data execution. And then we mainly classify it into four categories.

(1) Modifications in commands and functions based on data execution and data transmission. In the implementation of webshell, data connection and command execution are often involved. Some static detection methods [2, 3] build feature libraries and match them around these unique high-risk functions. In order to effectively avoid static feature killing, webshell uses function name split and reorganization, dynamic execution technology to bypass the specific features of static protection tools, and thus successfully executed.

(2) Confusion variation based on data execution and data transmission. This type of variation uploads webshell to the vulnerable website by encrypting webshell code, obfuscating it into coded fragments without a fixed behavior pattern, bypassing web detection limit. During the data transmission process, webshell can decode the payload encoded in the transmission process to perform further penetration behavior of attackers.

(3) A variation based on web server data execution and data transmission configuration. The variation requires the server to have some support in the configuration and thus execute successfully. If you use the short format script to bypass detection, you need to enable the short format support in advance. This type of detection-bypass webshell uses a certain pre-condition, which is accidental.

(4) Data execution and data transmission deformation methods based on language characteristics. This variation uses the language features of various scripting languages to hide the webshell. For example, webshell is directly inserted into the normal script of the vulnerable website by using the callback feature of the php function. Also, when variables are controllable, webshell can cause code execution by using serialization and deserialization to bypass detection, et al.

According to the above four classifications, it can be found that the webshell variations are constantly changing and updating, and all are based on the webshell principle for data execution and data transmission.

3.3 Webshell Detection Method

In the analysis of the second section, it can be found that the existing detection methods mostly use webshell detection as the starting point, and webshell samples are used as the carrier to obtain the instant and effective webshell detection model. We take the nature of webshell as the starting point, analyze the variant behavior of the samples, and propose a detection method based on fuzzy matching and deep learning.

(1) **Webshell heuristic detection method based on fuzzy matching**. For code snippets of data execution and data transmission in webshell, we build a multi-dimensional detection model that heuristically detects and prevents webshell. The method constructs a three-dimensional stereo detection method, using webshell itself to build a fuzzy hash sample library, webshell data execution and data transmission as the main rules of the fine-grained regular feature library, and building the random forest algorithm by statistical features of variant webshell.

(2) **Webshell detection method based on deep learning**. We construct a deep learning detection based on system call sequence. No matter how webshell is obfuscated, the system call sequence can touch the nature of webshell according to data execution and data transmission. For the purpose of detecting unknown webshell, the effective webshell system call sequence is used as a feature to drive a large number of normal/webshell samples for effective parameter training and data tuning, and finally to obtain the final model with the best detection effect.

4   WSLD Design

Based on the above strategy, we design a framework for webshell detection based on heuristic fuzzy matching and deep learning, as shown in Fig. 1. The framework mainly includes three parts: heuristic fuzzy matching module, recurrent neural network detection module and cloud analysis module. The first two modules can be directly invoked by the user; the cloud analysis module is deployed in the cloud server and communicates with the webshell detection engine regularly and synchronizes the latest webshell feature library.

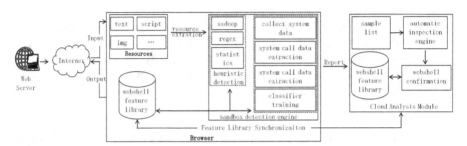

Fig. 1. WSLD framework

The framework first recursively resolves the user-uploaded folder. The upload files are first input into the heuristic fuzzy matching module which adopts a combination of static detection, statistical detection and heuristic detection. Then, the resources are initially identified and classified into high-risk samples and suspicious samples. When all techniques in the module detect that a sample is webshell, the file is output directly as high-risk sample. Otherwise, the file is considered as suspicious sample.

The suspicious sample is preprocessed by sandbox, and each system call function is extracted based on the behavior of system to form a host system call sequence. The sample sequence is eigen vectorized using the ADFA system call sequence table [17, 18]. Subsequently, the suspicious samples of the feature engineering are imported into a deep learning detection driven by a large number of normal/webshell samples. Suspicious samples are further detected by a recurrent neural network with long short-term memory cells, and the input samples are finally identified. After the detection is completed, heuristic fuzzy matching module and recurrent neural network detecting module timely report the detected high-risk webshell to the user, and report to the cloud analysis module for confirmation. Finally, the framework can detect and identifie malicious samples through local passive and cloud-active dual-engine webshell detectors, synchronize webshell signatures, and isolate webshell execution on key functions.

4.1   Heuristic Fuzzy Matching Module

After the analysis of webshell and existing detection technology, considering the variations of webshell and the disadvantages of various existing detection techniques mentioned before, WSLD framework uses a three-dimensional stereo detection strategy based on data transmission and data execution in the heuristic fuzzy matching module, as shown in Fig. 2.

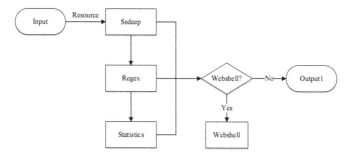

Fig. 2. Heuristic fuzzy matching module

The system will traverse all the files to be detected according to the uploaded folder path, collect related information of the included file, and extract attribute features such as file name, file suffix, and file authority after the uploaded file is obtained, in order to be used for policy detection for the part of the regular matching in this module.

After obtaining the standardized input, the module first calculates the fuzzy hashes of all the files through the library of ssdeep and generates a fuzzy hash table. The series of fuzzy hashes are then compared to the fuzzy hashes in the webshell feature library to determine the similarity of the samples. A high-risk webshell is detected based on the threshold range obtained by the training of known samples. The remaining samples are entered into the feature regular matching section.

From the analysis of the webshell implementation process, the characteristics of regular matching include the high-risk behavior function of fine-grained webshell, the low-false positive webshell feature, the codec function call, the source code feature and the webshell developer information, et al. By performing regular matching in the file to be detected, the common high-risk webshell is efficiently detected, and the remaining samples are then input to the statistical method detection part.

The statistical detection method is further tested for obfuscated and encrypted webshell. Entropy, compression, the longest word, index of coincidence and the specific webshell feature are selected as conditional attributes. And then we use random forest algorithm to build the statistical webshell detection based on the optimal parameters.

Finally, the thresholds of the heuristic detection module are defined based on the results of the detection methods mentioned above. By analyzing the comprehensive index of the uploaded file, the abnormal webshell can be detected through the threshold comparison. The remaining Output1 to be further detected will be input into the deep learning detection module.

4.2 Detection Engine Based on Multi-layer RNN

In order to detect unknown webshell more effectively, based on the webshell detection method of data transmission and data execution, we built up a deep learning webshell detection method based on system call sequence.

Algorithm 1 Pseudocode of Multi-layer RNN

---

begin

    file := loadFileSyscall(Output1)

    testX := replace(file)

    net := RNN.Webshell()

    ws_model := DNN(net)

    predictY := ws_model.predict(testX)

    if predictY = IsWebshell **then**

        #move file to temp folder

        #send file info to cloud

        return file is webshell

    end if

end

Namely, as the pseudocode in Algorithm 1 shows, the deep learning module of WSLD framework collects the system call sequence generated by the samples during the loading process through auditd unix, and sequentially performs data cleansing and feature vector generation. Subsequently, the module loads the multi-layer RNN algorithm based on the system call sequence driven by a large number of normal/webshell samples for webshell detection of the samples to be tested. After the samples pass the algorithm, the framework will perform binary classification (normal/webshell) on all samples.

After the detection is completed, the system directly returns to users the result combining heuristic fuzzy matching module and deep learning algorithm module.

4.3 Cloud Analysis Module

The cloud analysis module includes a webshell cloud feature library that is updated in real time and process of uploading webshell by a client. The feature library is uploaded to the cloud by the detection process which is updated in real time.

When the host completes the requested webshell detection process, the client asynchronously reports the detected webshell to the cloud analysis module for confirmation. The cloud analysis module performs feature processing on the uploaded samples, compares and identifies with the existing cloud feature library.

The cloud adds the newly confirmed webshell static features to the feature library and periodically updates to all users feature libraries by further comparing the webshell in the cloud feature library (Fig. 3).

5 WSLD Implementation

In this section, we describe the implementation details of WSLD. We elaborate on how we collect webshell and normal scripts for the detection, how WSLD is implemented, and how WSLD automatically detect webshell in different modules.

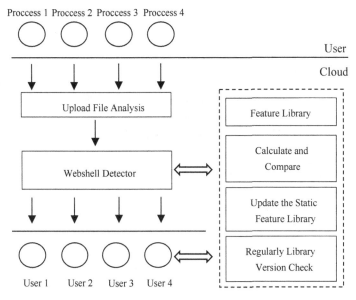

Fig. 3. Overview of the design of cloud analysis module

5.1 Webshell Feature Library

In the early stage of the experiment, we mainly collected the open source webshell and the leaked webshell. After the process of deduplication, we covered 5541 samples including 3496 webshell written by various scripting languages [19, 20] and 2045 open source CMS samples for the training set. The detailed distribution is shown in Fig. 4.

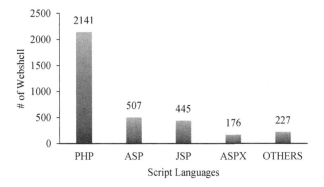

Fig. 4. Scripts distribution of webshell

In order to enhance the generalization of the deep learning training model, we use the crawler to index webshell, run the webshell samples, record the system call sequence and vectorize the samples in the webshell feature library according to the ADFA-LD data set rules. The data in the sample set that conflicts with the dataset rules is directly discarded, and the same formatted data as the ADFA-LD dataset is finally obtained to ensure the validity of the retained samples.

5.2 Fuzzy Hash Extraction

Fuzzy hash is based on hash algorithm, which is a context-triggered segmentation hash that applies a rolling hash. The fuzzy hash algorithm first blocks the file, calculates the hash value of each block, and then compares the obtained hash values with the others to determine the similarity, which is different from the hash algorithm. Fuzzy hash is mainly used to find homology files. Jesse Kornblum developed ssdeep [21, 22] to generate and calculate the similarity of two files.

For the method proposed here, we construct a fuzzy hash webshell library. All the files to be detected traversed by the directory are calculated by ssdeep to calculate the fuzzy hash value, compare the similarity between the files and known webshell, and detect the webshell effectively.

Since ssdeep can calculate the similarity between two files, the fuzzy hashes of the files to be detected are compared with the webshell databases. The higher the calculated percentage, the higher the similarity of the files. In the process of finding the best similarity threshold for detecting webshell, we use 90% of webshell to construct feature libraries, 10% webshell (350) and 350 normal CMS samples as test data to test specific thresholds. With the ratio of webshell train data to test data is 9:1 in the experiment, the threshold of webshell similarity is finally determined to be 90%. At this time, the false positives and false negatives in the test data are the least, the normal sample false positive is 0, and the webshell sample false negative rate is 1.43%.

5.3 Regex Match

We construct a fine-grained regular feature library with webshell data execution and data transmission as the main rules by analyzing the implementation process of webshell. The selected webshell features are mainly divided into high-risk behavior functions of fine-grained webshell, low-false positive sentence trojan regular feature, codec function call, source code feature and webshell developer information. Take the high-risk behavior functions of fine-grained webshell as an example, the details of them are shown in Table 4.

In addition, for the unique features, we also collected the following parts:

a. Webshell developer email, user's email, such as xb5@hotmail.com and so on.
b. Developer's personal website, organization website URL, such as Kockaf52.com, www.hkmjj.com, etc.
c. Developer nickname, attacker nickname or webshell name, such as phpspy, c99, etc.
d. Webshell unique features, such as an intrinsic function name c99_buff_prepare, an intrinsic variable name c99sh_surl, and so on.

Based on the main features and specific feature rules of webshell mentioned, we have compiled 202 webshell rules that conform to Python regular expressions and form webshell feature database. Some rules are shown in Fig. 5.

Table 4. Webshell features and function details

Features	Function details
Data execution	assert/eval/shell_exec/shell/exec/curl_exec/proc_open/system/python_eval
File operation	file_get_contents/curl/posix_getpwuid/fileowner/filegroup/posix_getgrgid
Database operation	Mssql_fetch_array/mysql_fetch_assoc/mysql_fetch_array/mysql_result
Codec function call	str_rot13/base64_encode/base64_decode/gzencode/gzdeflat/gzcompress

lostDC.php=(shellexec\s*\(\$command\))

cmd1.php=((system|passthru|shell_exec|exec|eval|proc_open|popen|ass ert|include|require|include_once|require_once|array_map|array_walk)\ s*\(\s*(str_rot13|base64_decode|gzinflate))

aspshell.asp=(eval\s*\(eval\s*\(|exs\(exs\(dec\(|Replace\(Replace\(StrRe verse\(|6877656D2B736972786677752B237E232C2A)

Fig. 5. Regex for webshell features

We match the input files with the constructed regular feature library, efficiently filter out common high-risk webshell and mark them. The rest of the samples are then input into the statistical method detection part.

5.4 Statistical Indicators

According to the analysis in the third section, variant webshell is often obfuscated and encrypted to show some special statistical features. Therefore, in order to detect unknown webshell effectively, we construct a random forest algorithm based on the statistical characteristics of webshell.

For the feature selection, entropy, the longest word, compression ratio, index of coincidence and specific webshell feature are selected as condition attributes.

a. Entropy. Entropy measures the uncertainty of a file by using an ASCII code table. Generally, the higher the entropy, the more disordered the information is. The formula is as follows, N represents possible sources of information.

$$E(X) = \sum_{k=1}^{N} P_i \log P_i \tag{1}$$

b. Index of coincidence. Index of coincidence can be used to assess the probability of finding two same letters by randomly selecting two letters from a file. Usually, the low coincidence index indicates that the file code is potentially encrypted or hashed. The formula is as follows: N is the length of a file; n_i represents the frequency of letter I and there are a total of m different letters.

$$IC(X) = \frac{\sum_{i=1}^{m} n_i n_{i-1}}{N(N-1)} \tag{2}$$

c. Longest word. An encrypted webshell always have strings with extremely huge length. Thus, we can conclude whether it is suspicious to be a webshell by measuring the length of the longest word from a file.
d. Compression. The compression is the ratio of uncompressed size to compressed size of a file. An encoded webshell usually has a higher data compression ratio. Therefore, data compression can be treated as a feature to detect webshell.
e. Webshell feature. we choose two specific webshell features as the file feature. One is shown as Fig. 6, and the other feature is the regex database of the previous section.

```
eval\(|file_put_contents|base64_decode|python_eval|exec\
(|passthru|popen|proc_open|pcntl|assert\(|system\(|shell
```

Fig. 6. One of the specific webshell features

Here, a total of 3496 webshell samples and 2045 normal samples are randomly divided into two parts. The ratio of training data to test data is 1:1. The random forest algorithm is used to train webshell to obtain the best training indicators for the decision tree. The final indicator is that the number of weak learners (*n_estimators*) is 21, the minimum number of subtrees (*min_samples_split*) is 10, the minimum number of samples in the leaf node (*min_samples_leaf*) is 1, the maximum depth of decision tree (*max_depth*) is 7, and the maximum number of features in random forest (*max_features*) is 40%. While *n_estimators* is trained separately and the rest of the indicators are by default, the accuracy rate is shown in Fig. 7. When *n_estimators* is 21, the accuracy is the highest. The training process for the remaining indicators is consistent with *n_estimators*.

Finally, the best parameters of the random forest are combined to train and obtain a statistical webshell detection model.

5.5 Feature Extraction

In the neural network detection module, the sample input is system call sequence. The system calls include all behaviors from opening a web page to establishing a connection which is generated by auditd Unix and filtered according to the size of the file.

By collecting and recording the system call sequence over a period of time, each system call function is converted into a sequence vector according to the ADFA-LD data set rules [17, 18], and finally a total of 1080 system call records are organized. Excluding sample data that conflicts with the rules, the same formatted data as the ADFA-LD data set is obtained to ensure the validity of retained samples.

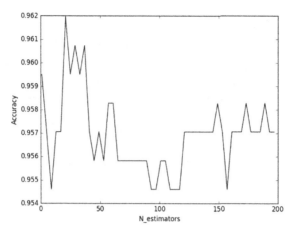

Fig. 7. N_estimators parameter selection

5.6 RNN Detection

RNN is a neural network that models sequence data. The actual performance of RNN is that each neuron in the network memorizes the information output by the last timestamp and applies it to the calculation of the current output. Compared to traditional methods, RNN introduces directed loops with the ability to handle context-related problems well.

In this paper, the deep learning detection method based on the system call sequence can detect unknown webshell more effectively than the method based on the heuristic fuzzy matching module. To predict unknown webshell, the effective webshell call sequence is used as a feature to drive a large number of normal/webshell samples for effective parameter training and data tuning. The final model for obtaining the best detection effect is shown in Fig. 8.

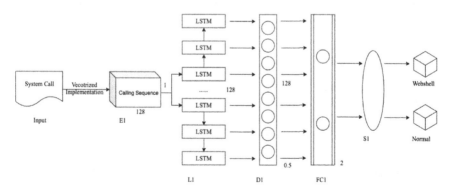

Fig. 8. Design of multi-layer RNN structure

The structure of multi-layer RNN designed by WSLD to detect unknown webshell is shown as follows:

a. Embed layer E1. The input is a sequence of 100 tensors, and after embedding, it outputs to a 128-dimensional vector space.
b. LSTM layer L1. The vector is input to the 128-dimensional LSTM, and the hidden layer is also processed in 128 layers.
c. Dropout layer D1. The random mechanism prevents over-fitting caused by too many parameters and insufficient data, and it is retained with a probability of 0.5.
d. Fully connected layer FC1. The number of input nodes is 128, the number of hidden nodes is 128, and the total number of output nodes is 2.
e. Softmax layer S1. The Softmax layer contains two neurons, which classify the features of the full-connected layer output and classify them into two categories: normal and webshell malicious code.
f. Classifier Selection. Defining the Adam optimizer, setting the learning rate to 0.1%, and setting cross-entropy to assess the difference between the probability distribution and the true distribution of the current model prediction.

6   Experiments and Evaluation

In order to verify the effects of the prototype system, we evaluated WSLD with two experiments. The first experiment was a performance test to verify whether WSLD can detect the webshell in the production environment. In the second experiment, we conducted the test with a case study of TwoFace Family webshell to verify the detection effect on unknown webshell.

6.1   Experimental Setup

The webserver environment in the experiment is Ubuntu16.04 with 8 GB of memory, Intel GMA HD 4000 graphics; the cloud server is Ubuntu 16.04 with 16 GB of memory, NVIDIA GeForce GTX 960 graphics. It deploys an automatically detection system and updates the webshell feature database synchronously.

6.2   Performance Test

As for the test data set, we collected 2100 samples with no duplication to the training set, including open source webshell samples [24] and CMS samples [25–28]. Webshell is a random selection of 1050 malicious samples taken from a 638 stars project in GitHub. Meanwhile, a total of 1050 normal samples were randomly selected from open source CMS.

In the evaluation of WSLD, we adopt the confusion matrix to evaluate the prediction results. The evaluation results are shown in Table 5.

Based on the confusion matrix, we use accuracy, recall, precision and F1 to evaluate WSLD effectively. Then we choose some popular webshell detection tools to compare the recognition effect of WSLD. Here we also input the test samples to BAIDU WEBDIR+ [29], Chaitin CloudWalker [30], Shell-Detector [31] and 360 TOTAL SECURITY [32]. The result is shown in Table 6 (unit: %).

Table 5. Confusion matrix

Confusion matrix	Predicted condition	
True condition	Webshell	Normal
Webshell	1034 (True Positive)	16 (False Negative)
Normal	8 (False Positive)	1042 (True Negative)

Table 6. Recognition effect

Method	Accuracy	Precision	Recall	F1-Score
WSLD	98.86	99.23	98.48	98.85
BAIDU WEBDIR+ [29]	84.05	100	68.10	81.02
Chaitin CloudWalker [30]	81.52	100	63.05	77.34
Shell-detector [31]	75.14	80.70	66.10	72.67
360 TOTAL SECURITY [32]	61.00	100	22.00	36.07

It can be seen that the precision of BAIDU WEBDIR+, Chaitin CloudWalker and 360 TOTAL SECURITY has reached 100%, which indicates that there is no false positive for the prediction of normal documents. However, recall of the three tools is not good, that is, the detection is not enough to identify webshell. Shell-Detector is a good tool for webshell detection, but it introduces more false positives from normal samples, resulting in an overall accuracy that does not achieve the desired results.

As shown in Table 6, accuracy of WSLD is 98.86%, recall is 98.48%, and F1 is 98.85%. Among them, WSLD missed 16 webshell and misreported 8 normal files. It can be seen that the webshell detection method we proposed can effectively classify the normal/webshell samples. Also, WSLD has strong detection capabilities for the exposed webshell in the production environment. At the same time, this method has false positives for normal samples within an acceptable range.

In the performance test of the system, the same 2100 samples were used as test samples. We tested the duration of WSLD, BAIDU WEBDIR+, Chaitin CloudWalker, Shell-Detector and 360 TOTAL SECURITY to measure the detection efficiency and user experience. The comparison of performance is shown in Table 7.

Table 7. Detection time comparison

Method	BAIDU WEBDIR+	Chaitin CloudWalker	Shell-Detector	360 total security	WSLD
Time (s)	580	181	513	59	123

From the running time of this experiment, WSLD has a longer duration of detection than 360 Total Security and it is more efficient than the other three tools. This also shows that WSLD proposed in this paper sacrifices some performance, which improves the detection efficiency of webshell. Overall, WSLD also provides a good experience.

6.3   Unknown Webshell Case Study: TwoFace Family Webshell

The main purpose of the second experiment was to analyze and evaluate the performance of WSLD in the detection of unknown webshell.

In April 2019, a data [16] of OilRig (also known as APT 34 by FireEye) was published on Twitter by an unknown group. The leaked data contains hundreds of credentials of the infected organization, webshell source code, et al.

The leaked data contains three webshell, HyperShell, HighShell and Minion. Hyper-Shell and HighShell are variations of TwoFace. Minion is a variation of HighShell which overlaps HighShell in code, file name and functions. The tags in HyperShell are shown in the Fig. 9. The string in the pre tag is exactly what the webshell uses to encrypt the embedded payload.

```
<pre><%= Server.HtmlEncode("NxKK<TjWN^lv-$*UZ|Z-H;cG-
L(O>7a") %></pre>
```

Fig. 9.   Component of HyperShell

In this experiment, we found that the other four tools in the comparison can not detect the unknown webshell based on TwoFace Family, but WSLD can effectively detect this kind of variant webshell.

During the analysis of the samples, we found that the implementation of TwoFace Family is to splice the generated password with a hard-coded salt string, calculate its SHA-1, and then use Base64 to encode and form a password for authentication. After authentication, TwoFace generates its SHA-256 using the initial password mentioned above, and then uses Base64 to encode it to output a new string. The first 24 bits of the string are used as the 3DES key, and the authenticated webshell is decrypted to remotely control the infected host. The process is shown in Fig. 10.

The reason why WSLD can effectively detect the TwoFace family is that the samples use the encryption and encoding mentioned in the third section to generate a new variant of webshell. When the sample files are input to the system, the fuzzy matching module calculates the statistical features of the sample files such as entropy, the longest word, index of coincidence, and compression ratio. Then the sample files are input into the random forest algorithm for detection. The features selected in this module can effectively distinguish between webshell and normal files that are obfuscated and encrypted on file attributes. In addition, in the deep learning module, system calls that are repeatedly encoded and encrypted can also be effectively detected by multi-layer RNN.

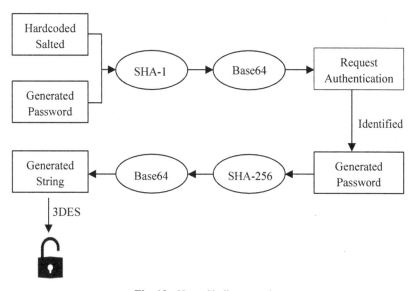

Fig. 10. HyperShell connection

7 Conclusion

In this paper, we classify the variant webshell based on the implementation analysis of webshell. We summarize the recent research progress on webshell detection. During the analysis of webshell, we propose a heuristic webshell detection method based on fuzzy matching and deep learning. Then we develop a webshell detection system WSLD based on the method. Among them, the accuracy of WSLD can reach 98.86%. In the case of unknown webshell detection, WSLD can accurately detect the TwoFace webshell family, which also provides a better user experience in performance. In the future work, we will conduct fine-grained sample analysis for false positives and perform more accurate detection on webshell.

We believe that a better understanding of webshell will lead to better detection techniques. Therefore, we hope that the webshell detection method proposed in this paper can be used to promote the research of web application malware.

Acknowledgements. This work is supported by the Key Laboratory of Network Assessment Technology at Chinese Academy of Sciences, Beijing Key Laboratory of Network Security and Protection Technology, the National Key Research and Development Program of China (No. 2016YFB0801604, No. 2016YFB0801603, No. 2016QY071405), the Youth Innovation Promotion Association CAS, and the Strategic Priority Research Program of Chinese Academy of Sciences (Grant No. XDC02040100).

References

1. China Website Security Vulnerability Analysis Report (2018). http://zt.360.cn/1101061855. php?dtid=1101062368&did=490995546
2. Piotr, Thornton: PHP-Shell-Detector: A PHP Script help you find webshell (2007). https:// github.com/emposha/PHP-Shell-Detector
3. Truong, D., Cheng, G., Guo, X., Pan, W.: Webshell detection techniques in web applications. In: Proceedings of the 5th International Conference on Computing Communications and Networking Technologies, pp. 1–7. IEEE, Hefei (2014)
4. Hu, J., Xu, Z., Ma, D., Yang, J.: Research of webshell detection based on decision tree. J. Netw. New Media **6**, 15–19 (2012)
5. Meng, Z., Mei, R., Zhang, T., Wen, W.: Research of Linux WebShell detection based on SVM classifier. Netinfo Secur. **5**, 5–9 (2014)
6. Starov, O., Dahse, J., Ahmad, S., Holz, T., Nikiforakis, N.: No honor among thieves: a large-scale analysis of malicious web shells. In: Proceedings of the 25th International Conference on World Wide Web, pp. 1021–1032. ACM, Montreal (2016)
7. Shi, L., Fang, Y.: Webshell detection method research based on web log. Inf. Secur. Res. **2**, 66–73 (2016)
8. Deng, L.Y., Lee, D., Chen, Y., Yann, L.: Lexical analysis for the WebShell attacks. In: Proceedings of the 3th International Symposium on Computer, Consumer and Control, pp. 579–582. IEEE, Xian (2016)
9. Cui, H., Huang, D., Fang, Y., Liu, L., Huang, C.: Webshell detection based on random forest–gradient boosting decision tree algorithm. In: Proceedings of the 3rd International Conference on Data Science in Cyberspace, pp. 153–160. IEEE, Guangzhou (2018)
10. Jia, W., Qi, L., Shi, F., Hu, R.: Webshell detection method based on random forest improved algorithm. Appl. Res. Comput. **35**, 1558–1561 (2018)
11. NeoPI: Detection of Web Shells Using Statistical Methods (2014). https://github.com/ Neohapsis/NeoPI
12. Ma, Z.: Research on webshell detection method based on logistic regression algorithm. J. Inf. Secur. Res. **5**, 298–302 (2019)
13. Tian, Y., Wang, J., Zhou, Z., Zhou, S.: CNN-webshell: malicious web shell detection with convolutional neural network. In: Proceedings of the 6th International Conference on Network, Communication and Computing, pp. 75–79. ACM, Kunming (2017)
14. Wu, B., Zhao, L.: Webshell detection method based on deep learning and semi-supervised learning. Netw. Inf. Secur. **37**, 19–22 (2018)
15. Zhang, H.: A method for WebShell detection based on semantics analysis and neural network. Cyberspace Secur. **10**, 17–23 (2019)
16. Bryan, L., Robert, F.: Behind the Scenes with OilRig (2019). https://unit42.paloaltonetworks. com/behind-the-scenes-with-oilrig
17. Creech, G., Hu, J.: A semantic approach to host-based intrusion detection systems using contiguous and discontiguous system call patterns. IEEE Trans. Comput. **63**, 807–819 (2013)
18. Creech, G., Hu, J.: Generation of a new IDS test dataset: time to retire the KDD collection. In: Proceedings of the Wireless Communications and Networking Conference, pp. 4487–4492. IEEE, Shanghai (2013)
19. Webshell Open Source Project (2019). https://github.com/tennc/webshell
20. Webshell Samples (2018). https://github.com/ysrc/webshell-sample
21. Digital Ninja: Fuzzy clarity: using fuzzy hashing techniques to identify malicious code (2007). https://docplayer.net/37815300-Fuzzy-clarity-using-fuzzy-hashing-techniques-to-identify-malicious-code-fuzzy-clarity-using-fuzzy-hashing-techniques-to-identify-malicious-code. html

22. Kornblum, J.: ssdeep - Fuzzy hashing program (2010). http://ssdeep.sourceforge.net/
23. Li, Y., Huang, J., Ikusan, A., Mitchell, M., Zhang, J., Dai, R.: ShellBreaker: automatically detecting PHP-based malicious web shells. Comput. Secur. (2019). https://doi.org/10.1016/j.cose.2019.101595
24. Webshell && Backdoor Collection (2017). https://github.com/xl7dev/WebShell
25. Wordpress (2019). https://github.com/WordPress/WordPress
26. Joomla (2019). https://github.com/joomla/joomla-cms
27. October CMS (2019). https://github.com/octobercms/october
28. OpenCMS (2019). https://github.com/alkacon/opencms-core
29. BAIDU WEBDIR+Webshell Detector (2019). https://scanner.baidu.com
30. CloudWalker Platform (2018). https://github.com/chaitin/cloudwalker
31. Shell-Detector (2016). http://www.shelldetector.com
32. Total Security (2019). https://www.360totalsecurity.com

A Character-Level BiGRU-Attention for Phishing Classification

Lijuan Yuan[1], Zhiyong Zeng[2], Yikang Lu[1], Xiaofeng Ou[3], and Tao Feng[2(✉)]

[1] School of Statistics and Mathematics, Yunnan University of Finance
and Economics, Kunming 650221, Yunnan, China
[2] School of Information, Yunnan University of Finance and Economics,
Kunming 650221, Yunnan, China
vonpower@ynufe.edu.cn
[3] Shanghai Jiao Tong University Yunnan Research Institute,
Dali 671000, Yunnan, China

Abstract. Online phishing usually tricks victims by showing fake information which is similar to the legitimate one, so that the phishers could elevate their privileges. In order to guard users from fraudulent information and minimize the loss caused by visiting phishing websites, a variety of methods have been developed to filter out phishing websites. At present, there are several phishing detection methods continually being updated, but the experimental results of them are not enough satisfactory. To fill these gaps, an improved model based on attention mechanism bi-directional gated recurrent unit, named BiGRU-Attention model, will be introduced. The basic mechanism of this model is that it obtains the characters before and after a particular character through the BiGRU, and then calculates score for that character by the Attention. Since the final score depends on the composition of the input, the more similar between phishing and legitimate websites, the more difficult it is to be distinguished. By utilizing this model, most of the phishing URLs will be tested out. Also, an explanation of why phishing and legal websites can be distinguished will be given. Based on the experimental results, the BiGRU-Attention model achieves an accuracy of 99.55%, and the F1-score is 99.54%. Besides, the effectiveness of deep neural network in anti-phishing application and cybersecurity will be demonstrated. Keywords Phishing Detection, BiGRU-Attention Model, Important Characters, The Difference Between similar URLs.

Keywords: Phishing detection · BiGRU-Attention model · Important characters · The difference between similar URLs

1 Introduction

Phishing is a form of cybercrime that uses "internet baits" such as emails, website links to induce victims to do some dangerous operations. As long as the victims click on those malicious website links, the phishers can easily conduct

© Springer Nature Switzerland AG 2020
J. Zhou et al. (Eds.): ICICS 2019, LNCS 11999, pp. 746–762, 2020.
https://doi.org/10.1007/978-3-030-41579-2_43

further attacks, such as modifying passwords and defrauding [1]. According to the APWG [2], there is a significant growth in phishing, which increased 50% in the third quarter of 2018. More than that, the cumulative growth rate reached to 260% in the fourth quarter of 2018. In this period, the number of new phishing websites increased by an average of 40,109 per month.

Since the number of phishing activities and the accrued loss have a rapid rise, numerous methods have been developed to automatically detect phishing websites [3]. There are mainly three types of technical methods including blacklist mechanisms, classification algorithms based on machine learning and based on deep learning either. The earliest method of phishing detection is blacklist mechanisms mainly rely on individual identification and report of phishing links [4]. This kind of detection method can achieve high accuracy, but it requires a large amount of manpower and time, still the websites must be in the blacklist. With the development of artificial intelligence, machine learning has been widely applied in phishing detection. Traditional machine learning has made great progress in phishing detection, however, they mainly rely on feature engineering, which based on manual design and vast trials, which requires a large amount of labor and domain expertise. Given the increasing complexity of the problem, the existing methods may fail to detect new domains or patterns and therefore limit the system performance. Deep learning, which is a subfield of machine learning, can extract and learn features from the inputs. It highly eliminates the time spent on manual feature extraction and excavates some potential features.

In machine learning, detection of phishing URLs is regarded as a classification problem, because phishing websites aim to disguise themselves by designed to be merely a few characters different from the legitimate ones. The small difference makes it difficult to differentiate correctly. In this paper, the BiGRU-Attention (Bi-directional Gated Recurrent Unit) model, which is to obtain the key information from characters themselves, is an attention mechanism based on Bi-directional Gated Neural Network. Traditionally, the whole URLs are used as input of a model to detect phishing websites, however, when the URLs are very long or the differences between fake and true websites are small, deep learning models might forget important information. As a matter of fact, this shortcoming can be surmounted by BiGRU-Attention, which accuracy achieves 99.55%, the recall is 99.43%, and F1-score is 99.54%.

In this paper, the related work about phishing URL detection will be introduced. Subsequently, the BiGRU-Attention neural networks classification model will be demonstrated. After that, the dataset and experimental design will be described. Followed by the introduction about how the BiGRU-Attention model distinguish similar URLs, the experimental results of different models will be discussed. In the last section, this paper will be concluded.

2 Related Work

In this section, the research on phishing detection in caber security will be summarized. We Blacklist-based phishing detection methods, traditional machine learning and deep learning methods will be mainly described.

2.1 Blacklist Detection

The earliest method of phishing detection is blacklist search, which principle is preventing victims from visiting phishing websites recorded in the blacklist. Blacklists for different browsers are constructed by different technologies, including manual reporting, ranking search and some other methods [5,6]. At present, the two well-known phishing websites are Phish Tank and Open Phish, which are Manual Reporting. This kind of detection based on the existing blacklist has a higher accuracy, but its shortcoming is that the website URL must be within the blacklist.

2.2 Traditional Machine Learning

Since blacklist updated by Manual Reporting is too slow to identify URLs that are not belonging to the blacklist [7]. Methods of identifying phishing URLs are usually classified as machine learning [8–13] and deep learning [14]. Zouina and his partner [15] use the SVM algorithm to detect phishing websites and the results show that the accuracy rate reaches to 95.80%. Chiew and Tan et al. [9] propose a hybrid integrated development algorithm based on data perturbation and function perturbation for feature screening. In this work, Random Forest, SVM, C4.5 and other traditional machine learning methods are used to predict these features. They conclude that random forest is producing the highest accuracy. Sahingoz et al. compare the results of Decision Tree, Adaboost, KNN and Random Forest, SMO and Nave Bayes models, which they find Random Forest has the highest accuracy which reaches 97.89% [16]. Although the traditional machine learning methods have achieved excellent results in phishing detection, it takes a lot of time to extract features manually and requires domain experts knowledge. With the development of the Internet, the complexity and volumes of URLs make it increasingly difficult to conduct feature engineering.

2.3 Deep Learning

Deep learning can automatically extract features, reduce the time for manual feature extraction, and identify some potential features. Alejandro and his co-workers compare the traditional machine learning method with LSTM (Long short-term memory) method, and the result shows that the LSTM method is superior to machine learning methods, with an accuracy rate of 98.7% [10]. Saxe and Berlin propose a character-level CNN (convolutional neural network) deep learning method for malicious URLs detection, which reduces the error rate by

0.1% comparing to the basic features [17]. Le and Pham et al. use CNN to classify and predict the word-level URLs, and achieve good results [18]; some researchers [18,19] use CNN, CNN-LSTM, CNN-GRU and other methods to study the classification of malicious websites. In terms of detection of phishing attacks, a lot of researchers use the combination of URLs string information and extract page content features as input, and then consider deep learning methods, such as LTSM, CNN.

2.4 Summary of Related Work

For the existing phishing detection methods, the traditional machine learning is based on manual features to improve the accuracy of the model. The deep learning method can achieve to the automatic feature extraction to improve the model recognition rate. However, few people have learned how to present them by the perspective of the similarity between phishing websites and legitimate websites. Then classification is performed by the differences they present. In this paper, a method to learn how to present URL characters is proposed. The model is able to improve the recognition rate comparing to the previous models.

3 The Proposed Model

In this paper, there is a comparison between legal and phishing websites that is marked by 0 and 1 respectively. Therefore, we can regard the problem as dichotomous classification problem. In terms of the BiGRU-Attention model with the URLs' characters as input, there is a better performance of extracting URL information, which means that this model can detect phishing websites better. In the next part, the design of this model will be described in detail.

3.1 Overview of the Proposed Model

To solve the problem of phishing classification, BiGRU-Attention model is introduced in this section. First of all, characters pretreatment, which output acts as the input, needs to be implemented. Secondly, word vector for each character needs to be extracted. After that, BiGRU-Attention is used to capture the most important character information in a URL sequence. Lastly, the classification models will be trained to detect phishing. The process of phishing detection is presented in Fig. 1.

(1) Input processing: According to the data we collected, there are only 0.6% of the URL longer than 150 characters which are HTTP domains or HTTPs domains. Therefore, we capture the first 150 characters of the URLs, so that all the inputs of our model are fixed-length. The components of the URL include protocol, domain name, port, virtual directly, file name, anchor and parameter, among which the information of domain name and port is very important. Therefore, the URL, which characters are more than 150, is proceed to extract the first 150 characters as input information. Besides, we are interpolated with zero in front of characters, if their length is less 150.

(2) Feature extraction: Feature extraction embeds the input vector. Each character is presented by a vector associated with whole characters, which means the corresponding vector of each character is associated with all characters.

(3) Information representation: Features are information representation that determine the upper limit of this model. The results, which are from embedding layer, obtain the forward and backward position information representation of each character by BiGRU. URL is a sign for a resource available on the Internet which presented as a line of string. Therefore, the characters in different positions of the URL represent different Internet resources. The previous or next character position of a particular character can be figured out by BiGRU. After obtaining the location information of the URL characters, the attention layer has a function that is giving different score for each character according to the importance of the character. The mechanism is that each character is assigned a specific weight, specially a larger weight will be assigned to a more important character. Then, the similar legitimate websites and phishing can be presented with different weights.

(4) Classification model: This model is for classifying the URLs. Firstly, The cross-entropy function is considered as the loss function of model. Then, The adaptive gradient descent method is utilized to update the parameters and optimize the model. Lastly, Some indexes including accuracy, precision, recall and F1-score are chosen to evaluate this model.

In BiGRU-Attention model, The representation information of URL characters is considered. Since the characters within a URL are in order, The forward and backward information of the URL characters is taken into account in the information representation of characters. Considering that most of the character information is identical and visually similar between similar legal URL and phishing URL, it is difficult to distinguish them correctly if we only consider the location information of the characters and the sequence of those characters.

In other words, in terms of two URLs with same length and one different character, it is difficult to get a clearly differential representation based on the character sequence. Therefore, this model assigns different weights to different characters to detect better phishing.

3.2   Attention Model Based on Bigru Unit

In this model, the original URL input length should be limited to 150. If it is out of this situation, it needs to be truncated or complemented. The processed URL sequence is labeled by $[c_1, c_2, ..., c_t]$, while input the embedded layer and map each character as a word vector, that is:

$$x_t = [x_{t1}, x_{t2}, ..., x_{te}], t \in [1, E] \tag{1}$$

In this case, x_t denotes the vector of the t character. e represents the dimensions of the t character.

BIGRU is bi-directional GRU (Gated Recurrent unit) which is an improved version of recurrent neural network. It is known that recurrent neural network

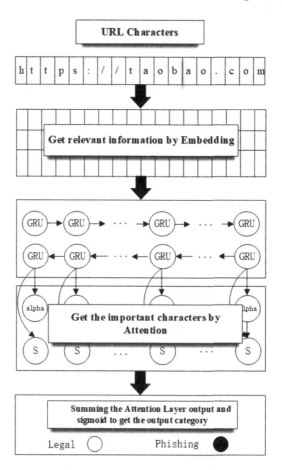

Fig. 1. Process of phishing website detection.

is used to process time series data. In theory, RNN (Recurrent Neural Network) can learn the unit information representation of the current time. As the back-propagation process, gradient calculation may have the situation of gradient explosion or disappearance, it reduces the effect of unit learning in the earlier time. LSTM is designed to solve this problem. LSTM, which is controlling input, forget and output units in RNN, is composed by input gate, forget gate and output gate. The GRU (Gated Recurrent Unit) is proposed by Cho et al. [21] in 2014. It combines the forget gate and input gate as renewal gate, the calculation of state unit is adjusted. The structure of GRU is simpler than LSTM. When the data scale is small, the effect of GRU training is similar to LSTM, while in some cases, it might be better.

The GRU model only calculates the correlation between t time and the previous time. However, the t character in URLs characters is not only related to the previous character, but also affected by the latter character. Therefore,

BiGRU (Bidirectional-GRU) is introduced to obtain the forward and backward information of the t character. In this part, it obtains the location information of the URL sequence. On this basis, Attention layer can get the information of different character importance.

BiGRU is including forward and backward GRU sequences. Each state in each GRU layer marked by h_t, which is determined by both gate r_t and update gate z_t:

$$
\begin{cases}
h_t = (1 - z_t)eh_t + z_t e\tilde{h}_t \\
z_t = s(W_h x_t + U_z h_{t-1} + b_z) \\
\tilde{h}_t = tanh(W_h x_t + r_t e U_z h_{t-1} + b_h) \\
r_t = s(W_r x_t + U_r h_{t-1} + b_r)
\end{cases}
\tag{2}
$$

The state unit is the output unit of GRU. The output at t time marked by h_t is directly related to the update gate z_t and hidden state $\tilde{h}_t$, which depends on the forgetting gate r_t and input unit x_t. Tensor of BiGRU is labeled by $h_t = [\overrightarrow{h_t}, \overleftarrow{h_t}]$, which $\overrightarrow{h_t}$ and $\overleftarrow{h_t}$ represent position and reverse GRU output tensor.

Attention to the development of the network layer in the field of natural language has achieved remarkable results [22–26]. Attention network layer gives higher weight to the words related to the target. In other words, this model pays attention to important information. Our work introduces Attention Network Layer into the research of phishing website detection, which means the special characters in URLs strings gain more attention in order to express information better.

Combining with BiGRU model, the time attributes of sequence data can be figured out. Besides the weight of the information represented by the character t in the whole sequence is calculated, and the representation information of character t is updated according to the weight. The vector representing the character t not only contains the relevant information between the URL characters and the location information, but also includes the information of the importance of the characters fed back by different categories. In below, the Attention layer design is shown in Fig. 2, which is calculated as follows:

$$
\begin{cases}
u_t = tanh(W_w h_t + b_w) \\
a_t = \dfrac{exp(u_t^T u_w)}{\sum_t exp(u_t^T u_w)} \\
s_t = \sum_t a_t h_t
\end{cases}
\tag{3}
$$

In these expressions, u_w is the vector of each character which is computed by linear transformation and tanh function after the BiGRU layer, and a_t presents the weight of each character. Besides, s_t is the calculation of c_t after the attention layer, and $[s_1, s_2, ..., s_n]$ shows the final information representation of the URL sequence.

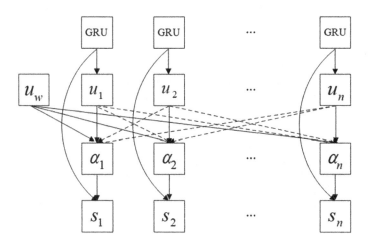

Fig. 2. The structure of attention layer.

After the BiGRU layer, the location information of each character in the URL sequence is obtained. The weight of the vector for each character is calculated and the new vector representation of the character is obtained.

Finally, when data is processed at attention level, the score of each character which is labeled as s_t is the output, the comprehensive representation of URL string information by cumulative summation of fractions can be obtained as well:

$$y^* = \sum_t s_t \tag{4}$$

The sigmoid function is used to classify the result, and it makes $y*$ translate into the range of $[0,1]$:

$$y_{prob} = sigmoid(y^*) \tag{5}$$

$$y_{label} = \begin{cases} 0, y_{prob} < 0.5 \\ 1, y_{prob} >= 0.5 \end{cases} \tag{6}$$

where 0 and 1 represents Legal and phishing website respectively.

4 Experimental Analysis and Evaluation

In this section, the related events such as our data, experimental parameters and model evaluation indicators will be described. Also, the results of our models and other models on legitimate websites and similar phishing sites will be analyzed. At the end of this section, there will be a comparison between the results of our models and other models.

4.1 Datasets and Description

Phish Tank is an open community where anyone can submit, verity and share phishing websites. At the same time, a suspicious URL is audited by at least two members [27]. When it is identified as a phishing site, it would be published in time, and statistically, 759,361 phishing websites has been submitted between December 2011 and January 2018. In addition, Common Crawl that stored a great deal of websites is an open website for crawler learners. There are 800,000 websites provided as legitimate websites data.

The collected normal and phishing websites are merged into data called dataset, which is written by Bahnsen [10]. The dataset is randomly divided into train, validation and test category. The proportion of these three categories is 8:1:1, in which 50% of each dataset is legal websites and the other 50% is phishing websites. In Table 1, the domain name distribution of the dataset is calculated.

In Table 1, the source of dataset and the time period of collection of websites are presented, while the information of general domain name and independent domain name are mainly counted. Domain names are composed of groups of ASCII and national language characters. At the same time, group of characters

Table 1. The statistics of our dataset

	Phish urls		Legal urls	
Data sources	Phish Tank		Common Crawl	
Date	2011/12/22–2018/1/9		2017/12	
	Count	Percent	Count	Percent
TLDs	576	100%	234	100%
gTLDs	429	74.48%	165	70.51%
ccTLDs	147	25.52%	69	29.49%
Unique Domains	237999	100%	5341	100%
.com	110885	46.59%	2984	55.87%
Other gTLDs	79346	33.33%	1832	34.30%
ccTLDs	38406	16.14%	525	9.83%
IP address	9347	3.93%	0	0%
Domains others	18	0.008%	0	0%
ULRs	759361	100%	800000	100%
.com	358891	47.26%	540375	67.55%
Other gTLDs	263579	34.71%	203290	25.41%
ccTLDs	113121	14.90%	56335	7.04%
IP address	23749	3.13%	0	0%
Domains others	22	0.003%	0	0%
https	19354	2.55%	294230	36.77%
http	74007	97.45%	505770	63.23%

is separated by dots. From right to left, the character groups are respectively called top-level domain name, second-level domain name, third-level domain name, and so on. Top-level domains (TLDs) are divided into three categories: country code top-level domains (ccTLDs), generic top-level domains (gTLDs), and new top-level domains.

The top-level domain names within the datasets of websites, the number of them and generic top-level domain names occupied by countries or regions are counted. In this dataset, the registered areas of phishing websites are from 429 cities or regions, and legal websites are from 165 cities or regions. There are 147 registered phishing websites and 69 legal websites with top-level domain names. In comparison, the dataset distribution of phishing websites is more extensive than legal websites, which means, the data distribution of legal websites is more centralized.

In addition, the domain names of all websites are counted. Among the addresses from Phish Tank, the number of unique domain names is 237,999 in total, of which 46.59% are first-class domain names with "com", while 33.33% are some other general top-level domain names, about 16.14% are national or regional top-level domain names, and 3.93% are IP addresses. The unique domain name of legitimate website is 5,341. In percentage, 55.87% are ".com", 34.30% and 9.83% are other top-level domain names and national or regional top-level domain names respectively. There is no IP addresses are as domain name in the dataset. Compared with the two datasets, the number of unique domain names and the composition of domain names of phishing websites are significantly larger than those of legal websites, which may make it easier for the model to identify legal websites.

The number of the websites with different domain names are calculated. From the statistical results, the distribution is similar to the websites with a unique domain name. Overall, the data distribution of legal websites is more centralized than that of phishing websites.

4.2   Experiment Design and Evaluation

In the embedding layer, the URLs string information is regarded to be uniformly distributed. The dimension of embedding is set to be 128, which means a character is represented by a vector of 128 dimensions. Features of URLs in the bidirectional GRU layer can be extracted from the forward and backward directions. The merging effect can be applied to make the URLs information to be more completed, and the important characters are decided by attention mechanism. Moreover, the BiGRU-Attention model is processed by a special method, so the results are decided by the score of characters summation, rather than adding a fully connected layer (Table 2).

Table 2. The best performance of the model on the validation set

Parameter	Settings
Word embedding dimension	128
GRU dimension	60
LSTM dimension	60
Attention size	80
Batch size	256
Epoch	20
Learning rate	0.001
Optimizer	Adam

To evaluate this model, parameters such as Accuracy, Precision, Recall, F1 score, FP and FN are applied.

$$\begin{cases} Accuracy = \frac{TP+TN}{TP+TN+FP+FN} \\ Recall = \frac{TP}{TP+FN} \\ Precision = \frac{TP}{TP+FP} \\ F_1 - Score = 2\frac{Precision*Recall}{Precision+Recall} \end{cases} \tag{7}$$

In the evaluation process, TP, TN, FP and FN respectively represent the number of positive classes being correctly predicted, the number of negative classes being correctly predicted, the number of positive classes being correctly predicted and the number of negative classes being incorrectly predicted.

4.3 BiGRU-Attention Model Experiment Result

After training the model, the best model parameters from the verification set are applied. The accuracy rate is 99.55%, and the recall rate and F1 score are also reaching higher. The number of misjudged phishing and legitimate websites are also lower than 269 and 430 respectively. In Table 3, the misjudgment rate is reduced by 0.34%, and the missing report rate is 0.57%. Although the distribution of domain names of phishing and normal website datasets are being doubted, the distribution of normal website domain-name is more centralized, which is more feasible to identify legitimate websites. This is also very consistent with the results of the model.

Figure 3 shows the change in accuracy of the model during the 20 rounds of training. The accuracy rate of the initial training verification set is 98.18%, which is much higher than the training dataset. During the first three rounds, the accuracy of the training set skyrocket to around 99% and be adjacent to the validation set. After that, both of these two sets come to be smooth.

Table 3. The best performance of the model on the validation set

Model	Validation					
	Accuracy %	Precision %	Recall %	F1-score %	FP	FN
BiGRU-Attention	99.55	99.64	99.43	99.54	269	430

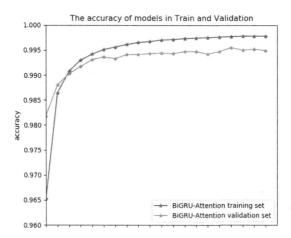

Fig. 3. Accuracy curve of the BiGRUAttention model on the training set and validation set.

Table 4. The similar URLs between Legal and Phish

Index	Begin	Phish	Character minimum difference
1	https://www.taobao.com/	https://www.ta0ba0.com/	2
2	https://www.apple.com/	https://www.apple.com/	5
3	http://www.google.com/	http://www.google.com/	1

The difference between Taobao and the corresponding phishing is to replace "o" in "Taobao" with "0". The characters in the URL of the apple's official website are all English characters, but the phishing URL uses "apple", which are Silvan characters. Similarly, the Google phishing URL replaces character "l" to "1".

4.4   Model Information Representation

There are similar pages or links between phishing and legitimate websites. These websites disguise themselves through some small modifications, for instance, a character is replaced by a similar one or simply add some characters to the legitimate domain name, so that victims may not notice the differences. Examples are shown in Table 4.

A series of similar legal and phishing URLs are listed in Table 4. The phishing websites are very similar to the legitimate websites. Since the small differences among themselves, it increases the difficulty of how the deep learning model learns the sequence of URL. The representation of this BiGRU-Attention model is improved to be better by distinguishing the URL characters of legal websites and phishing ones. GRU and BiGRU get unidirectional and bidirectional information for URL characters. They only get the order information in the URL sequence, which can achieve limited effect. In addition to obtaining the order information of the sequence, our model also obtained important character information. GRU, BiGRU and our model can be used to represent URL characters and then plot them into graphs to make it easier for observing differences Fig. 4.

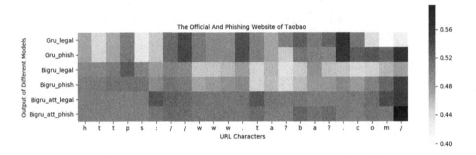

Fig. 4. The output representation of URLs in different models: The vertical ordinate shows models in the experiment, and the horizontal ordinate shows the characters in URL. In the URLs, character "?" indicates that the replaced characters in legal URLs. Gru_legal, Bigru_legal and Bigru_att_legal respectively represent the output of GRU, BiGRU and BiGRU-Attention models.

Gru_legal and Gru_ respectively represent URL character representations of "Taobao" legitimate and phishing websites. Two URL characters are represented, starting with the first "?" and ending with the string. Comparing to GRU, BiGRU has the characteristics of considering characters information in two directions. The two URL characters are completely different. Comparing to BiGRU, our model BiGRU-Attention captures important characters from legitimate websites and phishing, and learn to distinguish different URLs from the domain name part. It indicates that URL sequence information can be better represented by BiGRU-Attention model.

Aiming to other URLs, we can get similar information. The stronger the model representation ability, the higher the accuracy of its prediction. Our model's ability to characterize is better than GRU and BiGRU, according to more correctly predictions this model do for the "Taobao" phishing website and the "Google" phishing website.

4.5   Result From Different Models

All models in Table 5 are trained to be using the same data set, and all of them use the string of the URL as the input to get the classification results. In the experiments, some models are used to compared with the BiGRU-Attention model. For example, the model "LSTM" proposed in [10], which performs character embedding on input data, uses Long Short-Term Memory neural networks for feature extraction in the time dimension, and uses the fully-connected layer for classification. During all the experiments, the full connection layer is discarded for the classification model, while a more concise way is selected to support the classification. After the feature extraction is completed, the URL string sequence is directly summed and classified.

Table 5. Performance of the different models on the test

Model	Test					
	Accuracy%	Precision%	Recall%	F1-score%	FP	FN
LSTM [10]	99.13	99.06	99.15	99.11	710	645
GRU	99.05	98.88	99.17	99.02	853	630
BiGRU	99.39	99.61	99.14	99.37	297	650
BiLSTM-Attention	99.54	99.63	99.42	99.53	288	439
BiGRU-Attention(our model)	99.55	99.64	99.43	99.54	269	430
BiGRU-Attention-fully	99.49	99.59	99.37	99.48	306	478

After the training, the results of all the models within the test sets are shown in Table 5. The accuracy of GRU, BiGRU and BiGRU-Attention model keep increasing. The accuracy of the BiGRU-Attention-fully model is 0.05% lower than our model, and the number of misjudged samples is 66, which is more than our model. This shows that our model is better than BiGRU-Attention-fully. At the same time, it is not necessary for the last layer to use a fully connected layer as a classification model. Comparing to the BiLSTM-Attention one, the effect is almost the same with our model. Specially, the accuracy of it is only 0.01% lower, and the number of misjudged samples is only 20 samples more than our model, which is a small number for the entire sample set. But the BiLSTM-Attention model requires more parameters than our model which could be shown in Table 6.

Table 6. The complexity description of model

Model parameter	Count (only BiLSTM and BiGRU)	Model storage space (MB)
BiLSTM-Attention	288000	1.29
BiGRU-Attention	162000	1.03

In terms of the number of parameters required and the storage space needed, our model performs greater than BiLSTM-Attention. The BiLSTM-Attention model has 288,000 parameters in BiLSTM portion, which requires 126,000 more than the BiGRU portion of the BiGRU-Attention model. Besides, after the training of the parameter, storage accounts for 1.29 MB of memory, which is 0.26 MB more than our model. Therefore, our model performs better as a whole.

5   Conclusion

In this paper, the BiGRU-Attention model is used to detect phishing URL in the field of cyber security. There is also a comparison among the BiGRU-Attention and other models. The experimental results show that this model has a higher accuracy rate, which indicates that it is more suitable for phishing URL detection.

There are some design tips for this model. In the design part, bi-directional GRU is used for feature extraction in the time dimension, on the other hand, Attention layer is used to calculate URL characters sequence score. They supports this model to learn the differences between URLs from domain names. Furthermore, comparing to traditional classification model, a fully connected layer is set to classify the features. However, the fully connected layer is discarded and the feature are directly summed in this model, which means its parameters are reduced and the accuracy of it is improved.

By analyzing the experimental results, this model has been proved to have a good performance in phishing detection. The reason is that BiGRU-Attention improves the accuracy of the model to detect phishing websites by learning the vector that is representing the domain name information better.

By analyzing the experimental results, this model has been proved to have a good performance in phishing detection. The BiGRU-Attention mechanism improves the accuracy of our model in detecting phishing websites by learning the vector that has a good domain-name information representation. In this paper, due to the limitation of the experiment, several problems in this paper are listed as follows. There is no cross-validation in the experiment considering the possibility of over-fitting. At the same time, there is no comparisons of the experimental results between using a particular length of the URL and using the domain part of the URL. According to these problems, improvements will be done in further research. Besides, we will focus on improving the information representation, and proving the importance of it for phishing detection by using numerous different data sources.

References

1. Dhamija, R., Tygar, J.D., Hearst, M.: Why phishing works. In: Proceedings of the SIGCHI Conference on Human Factors in Computing Systems, vol. 1–2, pp. 581–590. ACM (2006)
2. APWG: Phishing Activity Trends Report, 4rd Quarter 2018, Technical report. December 2018
3. Jeeva, S.C., Rajsingh, E.B.: Intelligent phishing url detection using association rule mining. Hum. Centric Comput. Inf. Sci. 6(1), 10 (2016)
4. Fang, Y., Zhang, C., Huang, C., et al.: Phishing email detection using improved RCNN model with multilevel vectors and attention mechanism. IEEE Access 7, 56329–56340 (2019)
5. Zhang, J., Porras, P.A., Ullrich J.: Highly predictive blacklisting. In: Proceedings of USENIX Security Symposium, pp. 107–122 (2008)

6. Zhuang, W.W., Jiang, Q.S., Xiong T.K.: An intelligent antiphishing strategy model for phishing website detection. In: Proceedings of 32nd International Conference on Distributed Computing Systems Workshops, pp. 51–56. IEEE (2012)

7. Sheng, S., Wardman, B., Warner, G., Cranor, L., Hong, J., Zhang, C.: An empirical analysis of phishing blacklists. In: Proceedings of 6th Conference Email Anti-Spam (CEAS), Sacramento, CA, USA, pp. 59–78 (2009)

8. Zouina, M., Outtaj, B.: A novel lightweight URL phishing detection system using SVM and similarity index. Hum. Centric Comput. Inf. Sci. **7**(1), 1–13 (2017). https://doi.org/10.1186/s13673-017-0098-1

9. Chiew, K.L., Tan, C.L., Wong, K., Yong, K.S., Tiong, W.K.: A new hybrid ensemble feature selection framework for machine learning-based phishing detection system. Inf. Sci. **484**, 153–166 (2019)

10. Bahnsen, A.C., Bohorquez, E.C., Villegas, S., Vargas, J., Gonzlez, F.A.: Classifying phishing URLs using recurrent neural networks. In: Proc of 2017 APWG Symposium on Electronic Crime Research (eCrime), pp. 1–8. IEEE (2017)

11. Marchal, S., Saari K., Singh N., Asokan, N.: Know your phish: novel techniques for detecting phishing sites and their targets. In: Proceedings of 36th International Conference on Distributed Computing Systems (ICDCS), pp. 323–333. IEEE (2016)

12. Feroz, M.N., Menge,l.S.: Phishing URL detection using URL ranking. In: Proceedings IEEE International Congress on Big Data, pp. 635–638. IEEE (2015)

13. Aydin, M., Baykal, N.: Feature extraction and classification phishing websites based on URL. In: Proceedings of IEEE Conference on Communications and Network Security (CNS), pp. 769–770. IEEE (2015)

14. Kp, S., et al.: A short review on applications of deep learning for cyber security. arXiv preprint arXiv:1812.06292 (2018)

15. Zouina, M., Outtaj, B.: A novel lightweight URL phishing detection system using SVM and similarity index. Human-centric Computing and Information Sciences, vol. 7, p. 17. Springer Open, Netherlands (2017)

16. Sahingoz, O.K., Buber, E., Demir, O., Diri, B.: Machine learning based phishing detection from URLs. Expert Syst. Appl. **117**, 345–357 (2019)

17. Saxe J., Berlin K.: eXpose: a character-level convolutional neural network with embeddings for detecting malicious URLs, file paths and registry keys. arXiv preprint arXiv: 1702.08568 (2017)

18. Le, H., Pham, Q., Sahoo, D., Hoi, S.C.: URLNet: learning a URL representation with deep learning for malicious URL detection, arXiv preprint arXiv:1802.03162 (2018)

19. Vazhayil, A., Vinayakumar, R., Soman, K.P.: Comparative study of the detection of malicious urls using shallow and deep networks. In: Proceedings of 9th International Conference on Computing, Communication and Networking Technologies (ICCCNT), pp. 1–6. IEEE (2018)

20. Yang, W., Zuo, W., Cui, B.: Detecting malicious URLs via a keyword-based convolutional gated-recurrent-unit neural network. IEEE Access **7**, 29891–29900 (2019)

21. Cho, K., vanMerrienboer, B., Bahdanau, D., Bengio, Y.: On the properties of neural machine translation: encoder-decoder approaches (2014). arXiv:1409.1259

22. Cui, B., He, S., Yao, X., Shi, P.: Malicious URL detection with feature extraction based on machine learning. Int. J. High Perform. Comput. Netw. **12**, 166–178 (2018)

23. Bahdanau, D., Cho, K., Bengio, Y.: Neural machine translation by jointly learning to align and translate, arXiv preprint arXiv:1409.0473 (2014)

24. Yang, Z., Yang, D., Dyer, C., He, X., Smola, A., Hovy, E.: Hierarchical attention networks for document classification. In: Proceedings of the Conference of the North American Chapter of the Association for Computational Linguistics, vol. 2016, pp. 1480–1489. Human Language Technologies, North American (2016)
25. Li, H., Min, M.R., Ge, Y., Kadav, A.: A context-aware attention network for interactive question answering. In: Proceedings of the 23rd ACM SIGKDD International Conference on Knowledge Discovery and Data Mining, pp. 927–935. ACM (2017)
26. Wang, X., et al.: Dynamic attention deep model for article recommendation by learning human editors demonstration. In: Proceedings of the 23rd ACM SIGKDD International Conference on Knowledge Discovery and Data Mining, pp. 2051–2059. ACM (2017)
27. Mnih, V., Heess, N., Graves, A. et al.: Recurrent models of visual attention. In: Proceedings of Advances in Neural Information Processing Systems, pp. 2204–2212 (2014)

Tear Off Your Disguise: Phishing Website Detection Using Visual and Network Identities

Zhaoyu Zhou[1,2]($\boxtimes$), Lingjing Yu[1,2], Qingyun Liu[1], Yang Liu[1], and Bo Luo[3]

[1] Institute of Information Engineering, Chinese Academy of Sciences, Beijing, China
{zhouzhaoyu,yulingjing,liuqingyun,liuyang}@iie.ac.cn
[2] School of Cyber Security, University of Chinese Academy of Sciences, Beijing, China
[3] Department of EECS, The University of Kansas, Lawrence, KS 66045, USA
bluo@ku.edu

Abstract. Adversaries create *phishing websites* that spoof the visual appearances of frequently used legitimate websites in order to trick victims into providing their private information, such as bank accounts and login credentials. Phishing detection is an ongoing combat between the defenders and the attackers, where various defense mechanisms have been proposed, such as blacklists, heuristics, data mining, etc. In this paper, we present a new perspective on the identification of phishing websites. The proposed solution, namely PhishFencing, consists of three main steps: (1) filtering: a list of trusted and non-hosting websites is used to eliminate pages from legitimate hosts; (2) matching: a sub-graph matching mechanism is developed to determine if an unknown webpage contains logo images of whitelisted legitimate websites–once a match is detected, the unknown webpage is considered a *suspicious page*; (3) identification: host features are utilized to identify whether a suspicious webpage is hosted on the same cluster of servers as the corresponding legitimate pages–if not, the suspicious page is tagged as *phishing*. Compared with existing approaches in the literature, PhishFencing introduces an autonomous mechanism to replace the manual process of collecting and refreshing groundtruth data. As a in-network solution, PhishFencing could also partially detect phishing pages hosted on HTTPS servers, without requiring any support from clients. Through intensive experiments, we show that PhishFencing is very effective in comparing with the literature.

Keywords: Phishing · Phishing identification · Website fingerprints

1 Introduction

Phishing websites forge frequently used, legitimate sites to lure users to submit their sensitive personal data or account credentials. Statistics from the Anti-Phishing Working Group [3] show that most of the phishing websites target

---

Z. Zhou and L. Yu are co-first authors of this paper.

© Springer Nature Switzerland AG 2020
J. Zhou et al. (Eds.): ICICS 2019, LNCS 11999, pp. 763–780, 2020.
https://doi.org/10.1007/978-3-030-41579-2_44

at payment (33.0%) or financial (14.3%) sites. Meanwhile, with the increasing popularity of online shopping and banking over the last two decades, their client base has grown from technophiles to normal users, who are less capable of recognizing well-designed phishing sites. Victims deceived by phishing websites often suffer from serious consequences such as identity thefts and huge property losses. Therefore, from both security research and practice perspectives, it is crucial to efficiently and effectively identify and block phishing websites over the Internet.

Online phishing has been an active research area in the last 10 to 15 years [16,17], during which both the attack and defense techniques evolve simultaneously. Existing phishing detection methods could be roughly classified into three categories: (1) URL-based (e.g., identifying cloaked URLs), (2) network-based (e.g., detecting DNS poisoning or abnormal DNS registrations), and (3) content-based (e.g., identifying suspicious websites that are visually similar to benign sites). In the battle of online phishing between attackers and defenders, phishing identification methods proposed in the literature may soon become ineffective, for instance, when adversaries purposefully modify page contents or further tampering with phishing URL, such as using "squatting" domains [26].

In this paper, we present a phishing website detection mechanism, named PhishFencing, which attempts to detect discrepancies among a set of relatively robust network and content features. In particular, we identify the "visual identity" of the unknown page, which is often the forged identity, from visual features such as the logos on the page screenshots. We also identify the "network identity" of the unknown page based on its host features, such as IP, AS and geolocation. When both identities are inconsistent, the unknown page is highly likely to be a phishing webpage. The proposed mechanism does not require any support or software installation on the client side. PhishFencing will be deployed at primary exit routers of enterprise networks or at the ISPs, to monitor incoming traffic and to block any phishing pages from flowing into the network.

The proposed approach consists of three main steps, namely *filtering*, *matching*, and *identification*. We first collect the logos of the legitimate websites on the whitelist and generate a fingerprint of visual features for each logo. When a user inside the network visits a webpage, we first invoke the filters to identify if the user is visiting a known trusted website (not necessarily the whitelisted sites). If the visited page comes from a unknown site or web hosting site, we move to the matching step to render the page from passively eavesdropping the data stream. Sub-image matching is invoked to compute the visual similarities between the unknown page and all logos in the local fingerprint database and then compare with a threshold. In this step, the unknown page may trigger matches with fingerprints of multiple legitimate pages, since some legitimate sites may use slightly different logos across several (entry) pages, such as https://www.amazon.com/ and https://www.amazon.co.jp/. In this situation, we pass all the matched legitimate sites as the target websites to the next step. In the identification step, we first extract the network attributes of the hosts of the unknown website and the target websites. After clustering the hosts of the target sites, we finally identify whether the unknown webpage comes from an outlier host, compared to all the clusters of legitimate hosts.

In practice, it is difficult for visual-similarity-based detectors to maintain a complete and up-to-date database/whitelist of all protected legitimate sites, especially consider the fact that the visual layout of the legitimate websites may change. It is tedious and labor-intensive to ask system administrators to manually monitor all the sites on the whitelist and keep an updated image database. To tackle this challenge, we propose to utilize search engines to collect and update the groundtruth data. With this method, we are able to collect a larger groundtruth set with more comprehensive coverage of the visual appearances of the whitelist sites.

The main contributions of this paper are three-fold: (1) we propose a novel and highly practical approach to autonomously collect/refresh logo images and visual features from the whitedlisted legitimate websites; (2) we propose the first approach that is able to partially identify phishing websites hosted on HTTPS servers without requiring any interaction with the client computer/browser; and (3) we have developed a three-stage approach, namely PhishFencing, to identify phishing webpages based on the visual and network features that show higher reliability in practice. Through intensive experiments, we demonstrate the superior performance of PhishFencing.

The rest of this paper is organized as follows: we first define the problem and discuss the design goals in Sect. 2. We introduce the core algorithms and the implementation details of PhishFencing in Sects. 3 and 4. We then present the experiment results and performance analysis in Sect. 5. Finally, we discuss the related works in Sect. 7 and conclude the paper in Sect. 8.

2   Problem and Objectives

In this paper, we tackle the problem of discovering and identifying phishing websites, given a whitelist of legitimate websites. Formally, we have a collection of whiltlisted websites as $T = \{T_1, T_2, ..., T_n\}$, in which T_i denotes a *known legitimate website*[1]. In the **threat model**, the adversaries would imitate the visual appearances of a legitimate site T_i, and attempt to trick victims (users) to visit the phishing page and provide their credentials. A user from within the enterprise network visits an external page S_i (i.e., the *unknown page*), which could be a phishing page that might bring potential damage to the enterprise network. The objective of this project is to design a phishing detection mechanism $M(S, T)$ that, giving a new website S_x, identifies whether it is a phishing website imitating T_x: $M(S_x, T_x) = \{0, 1\}$.

In this project, we aim to tackle two practical challenges: (1) Groundtruth data collection and refresh: the whitelist of legitimate websites usually contains a list of site names (e.g., Bank of America) and/or their entry URLs (e.g., https://www.bankofamerica.com/). Moreover, each legitimate website may have multiple entry points besides the root page, e.g., BoA have pages like https://www.bankofamerica.com/credit-cards/manage-your-credit-card-account/. It is practically impossible to manually visit all these sites to generate visual fingerprints,

---

[1] In this paper, we use whitelisted sites and legitimate sites interchangeably.

and to keep all the fingerprints up to date. In PhishFencing, we employ web search engines to crawl a set of logos of legitimate pages for each whitelist entry, with the hypothesis that the top results from the largest commercial search engine are *trustworthy*. (2) Encrypted traffic: to the best of our knowledge, all existing phishing detection mechanisms for HTTPS phishing sites require collaboration from the client side, such as installation of browser add-ons, or local detection mechanisms. However, it is impractical to require and enforce that all the devices connected to the network to have anti-phishing software/client installed. Especially, with the growing popularity of BYOD (bring your own device) programs in the industry, more personal devices are connected to corporate networks. In PhishFencing, we present the first mechanism to (partially) detect phishing pages hosted on HTTPS sites without requiring any assistance from the client computer/browser.

3   Features and Algorithms

In this section, we first introduce features utilized in PhishFencing, and then describe the core algorithms for image matching and phishing detection.

3.1   Features

We aim to extract features which are easily obtained and difficult to manipulate by attackers. For example, URLs and content of webpages (HTML codes and resources) are not stable enough and easy to be bypassed by attackers. For URLs, adversaries may use squatting domain [26] to imitate target sites' URLs, while others construct normal but totally irrelevant URLs to overpass detection [2]. In the case of content of webpages, some adversaries use exactly the same HTML structures and resources as the target websites, while others carefully manipulate those content to overpass detection. At the same time, most of legitimate websites, such as Amazon, change texts and pictures on their webpages frequently, which also makes content features less reliable. Features used in PhishFencing are listed in Table 1. Next, we will describe each feature in detail.

Table 1. Features used for PhishFencing.

#	Feature	Step	#	Feature	Step
1	Domain	Filtering	5	IP prefix	Identification
2	Form	Filtering	6	AS number	Identification
3	Logo	Matching	7	Geolocation	Identification
4	Webpage screenshot	Matching			

Domain Features. PhishFencing takes the host names of HTTP pages or Server Name Indication extensions (SNI) of HTTPS sites as the domain feature.

We assume that pages from Alexa top sites are benign. In practice, we crawl the domain names of Alexa top 3000 sites, and denote them as the list of *trusted websites* (not to be confused with the whitelist of legitimate websites). Note that pages from web hosting service providers, such as https://sites.google.com, are not all trustworthy, since they have been found to be utilized to host phishing webpages in the literature [26]. Therefore, we exclude all web hosting services from the trusted site list. Except for the web hosting services, we can safely assume that adversaries are unable to allocate sub-domains of the highly popular, heavily monitored, and better managed sites to host phishing pages. Compromised domains, as exceptions to this assumption, are discussed in Sect. 6.

Form Features. Forms, including INPUT and FORM tags, are used to collect information from the client side. When an HTML file does not contain any form element, it cannot be used to harvest personal information [28].

Logo Features. Logos are used in phishing detection in the literature, such as PhishZoo [4]. However, it is tedious and labor-intensive to manually discover and refresh all logo images of whitelisted sites. To overcome this drawback, Phish-Fencing automatically collects and updates logo images using search engines. In practice, a query consists of the websites' name plus the keyword "logo", e.g., "paypal.com logo", is sent to the search engine. The top n results from picture search are crawled to enhance the diversity of the result set, since a site may have multiple versions of logos and they may be presented differently in images.

Webpage Screenshot Features. Different from PhishZoo [4], PhishFencing uses the screenshot of an unkown webpage in matching with logos from whitelisted sites, rather than exhaustively comparing with every image on the webpage, for two reasons: (1) repetitively invoking the matching algorithm to compare every image from the unknown page against the fingerprint of every logo is computationally expensive; and more importantly (2) adversaries may use tricks to avoid using full/original logo images to avoid detection, e.g., splitting the logo into small images, or overlay layers of images. However, they still need to preserve the overall visual presentation of the spoofed page. Hence, we render the full pages and utilize sub-image matching to compare them with logo fingerprints. In practice, we use Selenium to capture a 1920×1080 screenshot for each unknown page. Note that the identities (logos) of spoofed sites are always presented at the top of the page, hence, it is not necessary to capture the entire page.

Host Features. We treat all IP prefix features, Autonomous System number (AS number) features, and geolocation features as host features. Host features are also widely adopted in phishing webpage detection. Host features are considered as relatively reliable. It is difficult for attackers to compromise servers hosting legitimate websites, hence, the host distribution of phishing websites should be different from that of legitimate websites. Note that PhishFencing passively collects IP addresses of unknown and legitimate sites from the same channel, i.e. an ISP or a gateway of enterprise network. This ensures the consistency of observed IP distribution. For a given IP address, PhishFencing collects its AS number and the server's geographic location using the *MAXMIND* database [1]. The IP prefix is extracted to represent the class C network the IP belongs to, for the reason that prefixes contain IP addresses association information [27]. For a whitelisted legitimate website, we collect IP address prefixes, AS numbers, latitudes and longitudes features, to be used to train a model for outlier detection.

3.2 Algorithms

In this paper, we employ a graph matching algorithm to decide whether a logo image is a sub-graph of a screenshot, as well as an classification algorithm to identify phishing websites.

Graph Matching Algorithm. As the phishing webpage can be self-defined, attackers can use different scales of logo images to deceive users and to evade logo detection methods which are not robust enough on image scale variation. So we applied Scale Invariant Feature Transform (SIFT) algorithm [19] which can generate scale-invariant keypoint descriptors.

The major steps are briefly explained as follows. The first step is to detect extrema in the scale-space. To achive this goal, *SIFT* generates smoothed images in different scale, defined as $L(x, y, \sigma)$. Given a 2D image $I(x, y)$, $L(x, y, \sigma)$ is computed from the convolution of a variable-scale Gaussian $G(x, y, \sigma)$ and $I(x, y)$:

$$L(x, y, \sigma) = G(x, y, \sigma) * I(x, y), \tag{1}$$

where $*$ refers to the convolution operation, x and y are the spatial coordinates of a plane and:

$$G(x, y, \sigma) = \frac{1}{2\pi\sigma^2} e^{-(x^2+y^2)/2\sigma^2}. \tag{2}$$

Then through difference-of-Gaussian function, scale-space extrema, which is regarded as potential interest points, can be detected. The second step focus on locating keypoints accurately. From potential interest points extracted in the first step, *SIFT* rejects the points which have low contrast and are poorly localized along an edge for stability. Next, based on local image gradient directions, *SIFT* assigns one or more orientations to each keypoint location. In the last step, *SIFT* set a region around each keypoint's location where some points sampled and the gradient magnitude and orientation of these points are computed to form a 4*4*8 vector as the keypoint descriptor.

In particular, when using different background colors, such as white or black, attackers need to invert the color of logo images accordingly for users to recognize. When color inverted, the keypoints' positions could still match but the keypoints orientation and descriptor vector would change, which will reduce our matching performance. So we use both original image and color inverted image for matching. To be specific, we firstly convert a BGR image to a GRAY image, then for all x and y in the image plane, we compute $I'(x, y) = 255 - I(x, y)$. So for a logo image, we generate two sets of keypoint descriptors for matching. We will compare the performance of using color inverted images or not in Sect. 5.

After keypoint descriptors generated, we applied Fast Library for Approximate Nearest Neighbors (FLANN) algorithm [24] which will build up index trees (multiple randomized kd-trees in practice) for screenshots' keypoints to find the nearest neighbor in a screenshot for each keypoint in logo image. The nearest neighbor refers to the keypoint with minimum Euclidean distance from the keypoint descriptor vector. For each keypoint in logo image P_{logo}, the index tree is used to locate it's nearest keypoint in the screenshot $P_{screenshot}$. In order to evaluate the matchness between P_{logo} and the corresponding $P_{screenshot}$, we utilize the secondary neighbor keypoint $P'_{screenshot}$, to calculate the ratio $R_{matching}$ of distances:

$$R_{matching} = \frac{D(P_{logo}, P_{screenshot})}{D(P_{logo}, P'_{screenshot})} \tag{3}$$

where D refers to the Euclidean distance.

As the correct matches need to make the nearest neighbor significantly closer than the secondary neighbor which refers to the closest incorrect match, we can reject matches with low distance ratio R [19]. Then we calculate the percentage of keypoints in logo images, which own correct matches Sim, to decide whether the logo image is the sub-graph of the screenshot. Higher Sim means that more keypoints are correctly matched and so logo images have higher possibility as the sub-graph of the screenshot. So when the Sim is higher than a threshold, we say the match between a logo image and a screenshot is achieved.

Phishing Website Identification Algorithm. To identify phishing websites, we apply host features of both target websites and suspecious websites to One Class Support Vector Machine (one-class SVM) [9] to detect outliers, which are host features of phishing websites. One-class SVM uses only positive data, i.e. host features from the target website, as input to estimate the support vector of a high-dimensional distribution. Given a target website, our training vectors can be constructed as $\mathbf{h}_i = f_{1,i}, \ldots, f_{3,i}$ where $i = 1, \ldots, m$, m is the number of webpages, $f_{t,i}$ denotes the tth feature in host features and $\mathbf{h}_i \in R^n$ presents the host features extracted from the ith webpage. During the training process, we need to find out ω and $\mathbf{b}$ satisfied:

$$\min_{\omega, \mathbf{b}} \frac{1}{2}||\omega||^2 + \frac{1}{\nu m} \sum_{i=1}^{m} \epsilon_i$$
$$s.t.\ \omega^T \mathbf{h}_i + \mathbf{b} \geq 1 - \epsilon_i \tag{4}$$
$$\epsilon_i \geq 0, i = 1, 2, \ldots, m$$

where ω and $\mathbf{b}$ are used to construct the *hyperplane* which is the boundary of positive data. Since our training data can not be linearly separated, kernel function Radial Basis Function kernel (RBF kernel) is employed to map the data to a higher dimension feature space, in which data can be linearly separated. For two samples $\mathbf{h}, \mathbf{h}'$, the RBF kernel $K(\mathbf{h}, \mathbf{h}')$ can be defined as:

$$K(\mathbf{h}, \mathbf{h}') = exp\left(\frac{||\mathbf{h} - \mathbf{h}'||_2^2}{-2\sigma^2}\right) \tag{5}$$

Once ω and $\mathbf{b}$ are optimized, given a new vector $\mathbf{h} = f_1, \ldots, f_3$, if $\mathbf{h}$ satisfied:

$$\omega^T \mathbf{h} + \mathbf{b} < 0 \tag{6}$$

then we regard this new vector as an outlier, i.e. host features from a phishing website.

4   Design of PhishFencing

4.1   Overview of PhishFencing

As shown in Fig. 1, PhishFencing consists of three steps: (1) in the filtering step, we apply domain features (Alexa top 3000 domains) and form check to filter out trusted and harmless websites. The remaining pages are called the *unknown webpages*. (2) In the matching step, PhishFencing checks whether the whitelisted legitimate websites' logo images are sub-graphs of screenshots of unknown webpages. If a logo image is identified as a sub-graph of the screenshot of a webpage, we regard the webpage as a *suspicious webpage*. (3) Finally, PhishFencing applies outlier detection on host features of these *suspicious webpages* to identify phishing webpages.

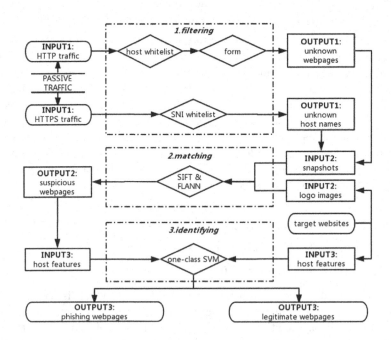

Fig. 1. Model of PhishFencing

4.2   Filtering

In filtering step, PhishFencing attempts to employ simple heuristics to eliminate websites that are definitely not phishing websites. First, PhishFencing collects HTTP/HTTPS streams passively. From HTTP packets, host names, HTML files and URLs can be extracted. Hence, domain features and form check can be applied directly to filter out trusted websites in two heuristics: (1) Suffix matching is applied on domain features to identify if the unknown page comes from a trusted website, as introduced in Sect. 3.1. (2) The HTML page and all sub-frames are scanned to identify forms. When a webpage does not contain any form, it cannot be a phishing page. In practice, these two heuristics eliminate majority of the unknown pages with very small computation cost. Note that this step is only introduced to save computation. In an environment where computing resource is not a concern, we can reduce size of the trusted sites list, just in case an adversary compromises an Alexa top domain (or its sub-domain) to host phishing pages. On the other hand, for HTTPS streams, we can neither access the complete URLs nor the HTML source files since they are all encrypted. Hence, PhishFencing only applies domain-based filtering on the SNI field, which indicates the host name of a website, to eliminate trusted websites from going into future steps.

4.3   Matching

In the matching step, PhishFencing identifies suspicious webpages based on the similarities between the rendered unknown pages and logo images of whitelisted websites. HTTP and HTTPS pages are handled differently in this step.

For HTTP pages, PhishFencing renders the *unknown webpage* fetched from passive HTTP streams, and then captures a screenshot image of the fully rendered page. Simultaneously, PhishFencing fetches logo images of whitelisted websites as described in Sect. 3.1, and pass them to SIFT matching.

For HTTPS pages, PhishiFencing could only extract host names from the packets, not the complete URL or any file name/content, hence, PhishFencing cannot directly obtain the corresponding webpages. To (partially) solve this problem, for each host name from the HTTPS streams, PhishFencing searches it on search engines and crawls all the returned URLs within the domain. For example, we search "https://bit.ly" which is extracted from the SNI field of the HTTPS packet, and we can see URLs such as "https://bit.ly/2kIChZC" shown up in results. All the returned URLs are actively crawled to obtain the screenshots of the corresponding webpages[2]. At the same time, PhishFencing also visits the host name directly to crawl the default (root) page of the domain, and follows any link on the page to collect all accessible pages in the domain. All pages are rendered and screenshots are captured. The rationale of these operations is that the attackers often post phishing URLs on other websites (such as online

---

[2] An upper limit of crawled URLs is set just in case the domain is huge, however, it is rarely reached in our experiments.

forums) so that they can reach out to a larger audience of potential victims. Such URLs are likely to be captured by web search engines. Meanwhile, we also see that many (sub)domains are only created for phishing purposes–once a confirmed phishing page is found from the domain, especially as the root page of the domain or accessible from the root page, other pages in the same domain become highly suspicious.

Next, the SIFT algorithm is invoked to generate keypoint descriptors of both logo images and screenshots. The keypoint descriptors of each logo image and screenshot pair are further sent to the FLANN algorithm to determine whether the logo image matches a sub-graph of the screenshot image. When a screenshot contains sub-graphs that are similar to a logo image in the whitelist, the corresponding page is then marked as *suspicious*, which is sent to the next step for further identification.

4.4   Identification

In the previous step, PhishFencing has discovered suspicious webpages, whose visual identities carry significant similarity with whitelisted sites. In the identification step, PhishFencing attempts to finally determine whether a suspicious page is a phishing page based on the host features, i.e., by comparing the host distribution of the suspicious page and the whitelisted legitimate pages.

As described in Sect. 3.1, PhishFencing collects the IP addresses of the websites which host suspicious webpages, and the IP addresses of the corresponding legitimate websites. We then employ *MAXMIND* to obtain the AS numbers and geolocation of these IP addresses. Finally, we utilize `one-class` `SVM` on the host features of both the suspicious websites and their corresponding legitimate websites to discover outliers. All outliers are then labeled as phishing webpages, which should be blocked at the firewalls.

5   Experimental Evaluation

In this section, we empirically evaluate PhishFencing and demonstrate its performance. We first describe our dataset. Then we define the evaluation metrics and present the experiment results.

5.1   Dataset

Logo Fetching Mechanism. We chose domains of Alexa top 1600 sites to evaluate the effectiveness of our logo fetching mechanism. We deployed *Google Images Download* to obtain the first 10 images for each domain from Google. At the same time we took screenshot of the root page (the landing page when directly visit a domain) for each domain by *Selenium*. Since some websites apply bot detection technologies such as reCaptcha to avoid crawlers, we verified the correctness of logos manually.

PhishFencing. We use *PhishTank* as the source of phishing pages. URLs from *PhishTank* are manually verified to exclude links that land on irrelevant webpages or with 404 errors. To obtain the groundtruth dataset, we visited verified *PhishTank* URLs from computers inside our institutional network. We captured the traffic using *tcpdump* at the gateway, and used them as positive (phishing) samples. Similarly, we visited the corresponding legitimate websites to generate negative (non-phishing) samples. For each legitimate site, we intended to visit multiple webpages in different content, HTML structures, languages, and background colors to increase the diversity of the negative samples, and to accumulate IP address features of the legitimate sites.

The groundtruth dataset has been collected for 7 days continuously with 77,539 phishing URLs verified by *PhishTank*, among which 13,902 were labelled with target brands. We followed SquatPhish [26] to select 8 most frequently targeted brands, which cover 68.98% of the phishing webpages in our groundtruth dataset. They are *paypal, microsoft, facebook, google, amazon, apple, dropbox,* and *yahoo*. Since PhishFencing uses an autonomous mechanism to collect groundtruth data, it could easily scale up to handle thousands of whitelisted sites. After manually verified these phishing webpages based on the method mentioned in [26], only 772 URLs remained as valid phishing URLs (majority of the phishing websites went offline after a very short lifespan), in which 48.7% are hosted on HTTP and 51.3% are hosted on HTTPS.

For each brand, we chose its primary website(s) from Alexa as our target website(s). For brands like Amazon, multiple target site have been identified, such as amazon.com, amazon.cn, amazon.jp, etc. Note that in our paper, if two host names have the same second-level domain (SLD) and the same top-level domain (TLD), they are considered to belong to the same site. For example, "*scholar.google.com*" and "*www.google.com*" belong to the same website "*google.com*" according to our definition. For each target website, PhishFencing crawled the top 10 logo images using *Selenium* with *chromedriver*, and eliminated duplicate logos (logos with similar SIFT features), to generate the set of logo images. Meanwhile, for all the target websites, 461 different IP addresses were extracted by PhishFencing to build host features.

5.2 Evaluation Metrics

The overall performance is measured in terms of precision ($P_{overall}$) and recall ($R_{overall}$) where

$$P_{overall} = \frac{|\{phising\ webpages\} \cap \{identified\ webpages\}|}{|\{identified\ webpages\}|}, \tag{7}$$

$$R_{overall} = \frac{|\{phising\ webpages\} \cap \{identified\ webpages\}|}{|\{phishing\ webpages\}|}. \tag{8}$$

We also employed the F1-score to combine both precision and recall to evaluate the overall effectiveness of different approaches. The F1-score is defined as:

$$F_1 = \frac{2 \times P_{overall} \times R_{overall}}{P_{overall} + R_{overall}} \tag{9}$$

At the same time, since PhishFencing consists of three primary steps, we also want to evaluate each steps separately to see their best performance. In the filtering step, we can simply adjust the list of trusted websites to ensure all potential phishing webpages are passed to the following steps. In the matching step, we first evaluate the reliability of our automatic logo fetching mechanism, we define the accurate rate (A_{logo}) on logo retrieving as:

$$A_{logo} = \frac{|\{websites\ with\ logo\ correctly\ fetched\}|}{|\{websites\}|}. \tag{10}$$

As for PhishFencing's matching performance, we define *matching precision* ($P_{matching}$) and *matching recall* ($R_{matching}$) to describe the performance of subgraph matching.

$$P_{matching} = \frac{|\{webpages\ with\ certain\ logo\} \cap \{matched\ webpages\}|}{|\{matched\ webpages\}|}, \tag{11}$$

$$R_{matching} = \frac{|\{webpages\ with\ certain\ logo\} \cap \{matched\ webpages\}|}{|\{webpages\ with\ certain\ logo\}|}. \tag{12}$$

Last, we evaluate the performance of the identification step with samples that are correctly matched. We define identification precision as $P_{identify}$ and identification recall as $R_{identify}$ in a very similar way as Eqs. 7 and 8.

5.3   Performance Evaluation

In this section, we first present the reliability of our logo fetching mechanism. Then we evaluate PhishFencing's performance on groundtruth dataset.

Effectiveness of Logo Retrieval. We evaluated the performance of our automatic logo fetching mechanism through manual verification: (1) we utilized the logo fetching mechanism to retrieve the logo images of Alexa's top 1600 websites; (2) we also downloaded the screenshots of each domain's landing page; (3) for each of the top 1600 sites, we manually verified if the fetched logo appears in the landing page. For domains which we were unable to retrieve the right logo images, we further examine the errors and categorized them, as shown in Fig. 2.

As shown in Fig. 2, for 4.43% of the websites, the fetched logos do not appear on the domains' landing pages, while the landing pages appear to be legitimate (Error type #1). Meanwhile, we were unable to download legitimate landing pages for some domains: (Error type #2) the landing pages are not reachable due to DNS error, 404 page not found error, or connection time-out. (Error type #3) Landing pages of some domains behave maliciously such as browser hijacking. (Error type #4) Some domains instantly redirect the browser to other domains, hence, the original domains do not host any service. (Error type #5) Some domains were shut down while sale or notification pages were reached. (Error type #6) There are also domains used for ad serving, which work as connectors between website owners and advertisers. And (Error type #7) some

#	Error type	Error rate
1	Logo mismatch	4.43%
2	Domain unreachable	3.56%
3	Browser hijacker	2.75%
4	Redirect	2.75%
5	Shut down	1.06%
6	Ad serving	0.44%
7	No logo	0.25%

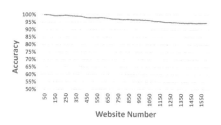

Fig. 2. Causes and frequency of failed/wrong logo image retrieval.

Fig. 3. Accuracy of logo fetching on Alexa's top k websites.

websites do not have any logo. Domains that generate errors #2 to #6 do not provide web services, hence, we eliminated them in our further evaluations.

After we eliminated the domains mentioned above (error types #2 to #6), we calculated the accuracy of our logo fetching mechanism for Alexa's top k sites. As shown in Fig. 3, PhishFencing correctly fetched the logo images of at least 95% of the top 1600 sites. PhishFencing performs better on websites that rank higher, for example, logo fetching accuracy reaches 98% for top 650 sites.

PhishFencing Evaluation. To present the performance of PhishFencing in matching step, we compared our mechanism with *SIFT* and *SURF* which were employed in *PhishZoo* [4] as shown in Fig. 4(a). F1-scores with *SIFT* were much higher than those with *SURF*. And with our improved algorithm, we can slightly outperform the recall and precision of original SIFT. To be more specific, we calculated both precision ($P_{matching}$) and recall ($R_{matching}$) rate of PhishFencing as shown in Fig. 4(b). We can see that when $Sim = 0.09$, we can obtain 99.27% precision and 97.90% recall in the matching step. Note that we used names of websites to fetch logo images which is more reliable than using brand names. For example, logo images of "*amazon.cn*" and "*amazon.com*" are different. If we simply use "*amazon logo*" to fetch logo images, the logo of "*amazon.cn*" would not shown up in the top results.

In the identification step, PhishFencing achieved 97.8% ($P_{identify}$) precision and 100% recall ($R_{identify}$) on 8 target brands on average using host features from webpages which had been successfully matched. Note that legitimate IP addresses were collected in nearly 2–3 h for each target website. In Fig. 5, we list the number of IP addresses collected on each of the 8 target brands. The number of IP addresses are not necessarily massive which suggest that our mechanism is not depending on large amount of prior data and can be used on client side as well.

As for the overall performance, we compared PhishFencing with the Squat-Phish approach [26], which is the state of art solution for identifying phishing webpages with specific target brand. We applied SquatPhish which is open sourced on github on our groundtruth dataset. As shown in Fig. 6, we first compare the performance of both approaches installed on the gateway to capture

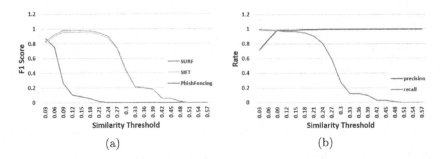

Fig. 4. Matching performance: (a) F1 -score comparison of SIFT, SURF and the matching mechanism in PhishFencing approach on groudtruth data. (b) Precision and Recall rate with different similarity threshold selected using PhishFencing on groundtruth data.

target website	# of IP addresses
amazon.com	138
apple.com	98
microsoft.com	67
google.com	51
yahoo.com	50
dropbox.com	42
paypal.com	8
facebook.com	7

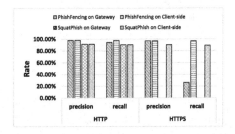

Fig. 5. Number of legitimate IP addresses collected for each target website in groundtruth data

Fig. 6. Overall performance comparison of SquatPhish on HTTP, PhishFencing on HTTP and PhishFencing on HTTPS tested on groundtruth data.

HTTP streams. PhishFencing reaches 97.8% precision and 97.7% recall which are both higher than SquatPhish. Then we evaluate the performance of Phish-Fencing on HTTPS streams. Since SquatPhish utilizes webpage's screenshot and HTML source code which cannot be obtained from encrypted packets, Squat-Phish cannot handle HTTPS streams when it is deployed at the gateway. The results show that PhishFencing achieved 26.32% recall on HTTPS-hosted phishing websites, when it is deployed at the gateway and only relies on two side channels to infer if the host domain is suspicious. Although there is still room to improve the recall, PhishFencing is the first solution of its kind to partially detect HTTPS-hosted phishing at the gateway.

Last, we also like to note that PhishFencing performs well on small size of host features. Therefore, it can be deployed on the client side, which only has limited data for the host features of the legitimate sites. In the experiments, Phish-Fencing's performance on HTTP streams remains high when it is deployed at the client side. Meanwhile, the recall rate on HTTPS-hosted phishing increased dramatically since we are now able to obtain the full URLs from HTTPS packets.

6   Discussions

PhishFencing is effective in phishing detection in the experiments, however, we still recognize its limitations and opportunities for future improvements.

First, as we have explained in Sect. 4.3, PhishFencing could only obtain the domain name, not the full URL, from HTTPS streams. Therefore, we rely on two side channels to find (other) pages hosted in this domain. This method appears to be effective on a portion of the HTTPS-hosted phishing websites. However, when no phishing pages are detected through the two side channels, PhishFencing is unable to discover any "hidden" phishing page. While the problem of detecting HTTPS-hosted phishing without the support from the client side is very challenging, we believe there is still space to improve.

We have applied suffix matching on domains of websites to filter out trusted websites, with the assumption that pages hosted on trusted sites (excluding any web-hosting service providers) are trustworthy. However, this assumption may be violated, especially when the adversary compromises a trusted site to host phishing webpages. In response, PhishFencing could cache the visits to trusted domains, and use the non-utilized server cycles to evaluate the (sampled) cached pages. When phishing is identified, *ex post facto* repairing mechanism is invoked, while the corresponding site would be removed from the trusted site list.

For HTTPS-hosted unknown pages, PhishFencing relies on correct host names in SNI fields. However, *domain fronting*, a versatile censorship circumvention technique, can be employed to show one domain in SNI field while using another domain in the HTTP host field [14]. In this way, attackers can replace the host name in the SNI field with a legitimate host name to evade our detection.

Some logo images may be shown on irrelevant websites. For example, the *Visa* logo may be shown on retailers' homepages to show that visa cards are accepted, or on a check-out/payment pages. In the first case, the pages are highly likely to be eliminated from phish detection since they usually do not contain any form. In the second case, a legitimate HTTPS-hosted payment page is unlikely to be misclassified, since the page itself is not accessible to PhishFencing, while the domain is likely to be benign. However, HTTP-hosted pages carrying Visa logos and containing forms (e.g., a retailer's homepage with a input box for search) may be misclassified as phishing. Fortunately, such cases are very rare in our experiments and they can be fixed by adding those sites to the trusted list.

Last, PhishFencing evaluates the visual identities of webpages by comparing the logos of whitelisted sites and the phishing webpages. In the very rare case where a whitelisted site do not have a logo or the logo image is not shown on the phishing webpages, PhishFencing's recall would be impacted. However, in our groundtruth dataset, all the sites in the whitelist have logo images and there are only 2.19% known phishing webpages that do not have any logo on them.

7   Related Works

Phishing website detection mechanisms can be roughly categorized into target-independent and target-dependent approaches. Target-independent approaches extract common features from all the phishing websites to train a model for phishing websites identification [21,23]. Target-dependent approaches, which PhishFencing belongs to, identify phishing websites mainly through comparing the similarity between target websites and on-identifying websites [28,31].

For target-independent approaches, the most commonly used features are URL features (i.e. structures and lengths of an URL) [5,15,18], webpage features (i.e. links, keywords, and HTML DOM extracted from a webpage) [20] and host features (i.e. IP addresses, AS numbers and geolocation of a website's hosts). Mechanisms in [8,11,22,25,27,30] combine large amount of features mentioned above and employ different machine learning algorithms to detect phishing websites. Apart from these machine learning methods, [10,13,29] make use of websites' identities as well as search engines. They try to figure out identities of a website at first. For example, [29] uses Term Frequency Inverse Document Frequency (TF-IDF) to extract terms with highest weight as a website's identities. [13] applies Optical Character Recognition (OCR) on a webpage's screenshot and regards the text generated by OCR as the webpage's identity. [10] uploads segmented screenshot of a webpage to Google Image Search engine and regards the keywords returned as the webpage's identities. Then they query the identities of a website through search engine. If the domain name of the on-identifying website does not match any of N top search result, they would classify the website as a phishing one. However, target-independent approaches use generic characteristics which can be constructed by attackers to evade the detection systems.

For target-dependent methods, visual features such as screenshot and logo image are most commonly used. Meerkat [6] trains deep learning models to detect phishing webpages hosted on compromised websites via visual elements in webpages. Apart from visual elements on the webpages, [26] applies OCR on URLs to detect squatting phishing domains. Besides visual features, [7] compares the layout and HTML text between target webpage and on-identifying webpage. [4,12] combines HTML features and visual features for identifying.

PhishFencing is different from existing approaches that: (1) PhishFencing chooses visual and network features which are representative and difficult to be manipulated compared to the target-independent methods. (2) PhishFencing utilizes search engines to autonomously collect/refresh logo images and visual features of HTTPS websites. Existing target-dependent approaches either identify logo manually or segmented the screenshot to locate logo which is less reliable than the approach in our mechanism. (3) PhishFetching can deal with phishing websites hosted on HTTPS which, to the best of our knowledge, has not been mentioned by other works.

8 Conclusion

In this paper, we present a phishing website identification approach named PhishFencing. The core idea is to detect if an unknown webpage carries the visual identity (logo) of a whitelisted legitimate site, while its host features deviate from the distribution of the known hosts of the legitimate site. PhishFencing consists three major steps: filtering, matching, and identification. As a network-based solution, PhishFencing will be deployed at the gateways of enterprise networks or at the ISPs' network backbones, to block phishing pages from being transmitted to end users. In the experiments, we demonstrate that PhishFencing outperforms state-of-art phishing detection solutions in the literature.

Acknowledgements. Zhaoyu Zhou, Lingjing Yu, Qingyun Liu, and Yang Liu were supported in part by Y8YY041101 and Y9W0013401. The authors also like to thank the anonymous reviewers for their constructive suggestions.

References

1. Maxmind. https://www.maxmind.com/en/geoip2-databases
2. Phishtank. https://www.phishtank.com/index.php
3. Phishing activity trends report. Technical report 2nd Quarter, APWG (2018)
4. Afroz, S., Greenstadt, R.: Phishzoo: detecting phishing websites by looking at them. In: IEEE ICSC, pp. 368–375 (2011)
5. Blum, A., Wardman, B., Solorio, T., Warner, G.: Lexical feature based phishing url detection using online learning. In: ACM AISec Workshop, pp. 54–60 (2010)
6. Borgolte, K., Kruegel, C., Vigna, G.: Meerkat: detecting website defacements through image-based object recognition. In: USENIX Security, pp. 595–610 (2015)
7. Britt, J., Wardman, B., Sprague, A., Warner, G.: Clustering potential phishing websites using deepmd5. In: USENIX LEET (2012)
8. Canali, D., Cova, M., Vigna, G., Kruegel, C.: Prophiler: a fast filter for the large-scale detection of malicious web pages. In: WWW Conference, pp. 197–206 (2011)
9. Chang, C.C., Lin, C.J.: Libsvm: a library for support vector machines. ACM TIST **2**(3), 27 (2011)
10. Chang, E.H., Chiew, K.L., Tiong, W.K., et al.: Phishing detection via identification of website identity. In: IEEE ICITCS, pp. 1–4 (2013)
11. Choi, H., Zhu, B.B., Lee, H.: Detecting malicious web links and identifying their attack types. WebApps **11**(11), 218 (2011)
12. Corona, I., et al.: Deltaphish: detecting phishing webpages in compromised websites. In: ESORICS, pp. 370–388 (2017)
13. Dunlop, M., Groat, S., Shelly, D.: Goldphish: using images for content-based phishing analysis. In: IEEE ICIMP, pp. 123–128 (2010)
14. Fifield, D., Lan, C., Hynes, R., Wegmann, P., Paxson, V.: Blocking-resistant communication through domain fronting. PETS **2015**(2), 46–64 (2015)
15. Garera, S., Provos, N., Chew, M., Rubin, A.D.: A framework for detection and measurement of phishing attacks. In: ACM workshop on Recurring malcode (2007)
16. Jagatic, T.N., Johnson, N.A., Jakobsson, M., Menczer, F.: Social phishing. Commun. ACM **50**(10), 94–100 (2007)
17. Khonji, M., Iraqi, Y., Jones, A.: Phishing detection: a literature survey. IEEE Commun. Surv. Tutorials **15**(4), 2091–2121 (2013)
18. Le, A., Markopoulou, A., Faloutsos, M.: Phishdef: url names say it all. In: INFOCOM, pp. 191–195 (2011)
19. Lowe, D.G.: Distinctive image features from scale-invariant keypoints. Int. J. Comput. Vis. **60**(2), 91–110 (2004)
20. Ludl, C., McAllister, S., Kirda, E., Kruegel, C.: On the effectiveness of techniques to detect phishing sites. In: DIMVA, pp. 20–39 (2007)

21. Ma, J., Saul, L.K., Savage, S., Voelker, G.M.: Beyond blacklists: learning to detect malicious web sites from suspicious URLs. In: ACM KDD, pp. 1245–1254 (2009)
22. Marchal, S., Armano, G., Gröndahl, T., Saari, K., Singh, N., Asokan, N.: Off-the-hook: an efficient and usable client-side phishing prevention application. IEEE Trans. Comput. **66**(10), 1717–1733 (2017)
23. Marchal, S., François, J., State, R., Engel, T.: Phishstorm: detecting phishing with streaming analytics. IEEE Trans. Netw. Serv. Manage. **11**(4), 458–471 (2014)
24. Muja, M., Lowe, D.G.: Fast approximate nearest neighbors with automatic algorithm configuration. VISAPP (1) **2**(331–340), 2 (2009)
25. Thomas, K., Grier, C., Ma, J., Paxson, V., Song, D.: Design and evaluation of a real-time url spam filtering service. In: IEEE S&P, pp. 447–462 (2011)
26. Tian, K., Jan, S.T., Hu, H., Yao, D., Wang, G.: Needle in a haystack: tracking down elite phishing domains in the wild. In: ACM IMC, pp. 429–442 (2018)
27. Whittaker, C., Ryner, B., Nazif, M.: Large-scale automatic classification of phishing pages (2010)
28. Xiang, G., Hong, J., Rose, C.P., Cranor, L.: Cantina+: a feature-rich machine learning framework for detecting phishing web sites. ACM TISSEC **14**(2), 1–28 (2011)
29. Xiang, G., Hong, J.I.: A hybrid phish detection approach by identity discovery and keywords retrieval. In: WWW Conference, pp. 571–580 (2009)
30. Zhang, W., Jiang, Q., Chen, L., Li, C.: Two-stage ELM for phishing web pages detection using hybrid features. World Wide Web **20**(4), 797–813 (2017)
31. Zhang, Y., Hong, J.I., Cranor, L.F.: Cantina: a content-based approach to detecting phishing web sites. In: WWW Conference, pp. 639–648 (2007)

Steganography and Steganalysis

Hierarchical Representation Network for Steganalysis of QIM Steganography in Low-Bit-Rate Speech Signals

Hao Yang, Zhongliang Yang, Yongjian Bao, and YongFeng Huang$^{(\boxtimes)}$

Department of Electronic Engineering, Tsinghua University, Beijing, China
yfhuang@tsinghua.edu.cn

Abstract. With the volume of Voice over IP (VoIP) traffic rising shapely, more and more VoIP-based steganography methods have emerged in recent years, which poses a great threat to the security of cyberspace. Low bit-rate speech codecs are widely used in the VoIP application due to its powerful compression capability. Previous steganalysis methods mostly focus on capturing the inter-frame correlation or intra-frame correlation features in code-words ignoring the hierarchical structure which exists in speech frame. In this paper, motivated by the complex multi-scale structure, we design a Hierarchical Representation Network (HRN) to tackle the steganalysis of Quantization Index Modulation (QIM) steganography in low-bit-rate speech signal. In the proposed model, Convolution Neural Network (CNN) is used to model the hierarchical structure in the speech frame, and three levels of attention mechanisms are applied at different convolution blocks, enabling it to attend differentially to more and less important contents in speech frame. Experiments demonstrated that the steganalysis performance of the proposed method outperform the state-of-the-art methods especially in detecting both short and low embeded speech samples. Moreover, our model needs less computation and has higher time efficiency to be applied to real online services.

Keywords: Convolution Neural Network · Attention mechanisms · Voice over IP (VoIP) · Steganalysis

1 Introduction

Steganalysis and steganography are different sides of the same coin. Steganography tries to hide messages in plain sight while steganalysis tries to detect their existence or even more to retrieve the embedded data from suspicious carriers. In recent years, the fast growth of Internet services has provided a multimedia

This work was supported in part by the National Key Research and Development Program of China underGrant SQ2018YGX210002 and in part by the National Natural Science Foundation of China under Grants U1536207, U1705261, and U1636113.

© Springer Nature Switzerland AG 2020
J. Zhou et al. (Eds.): ICICS 2019, LNCS 11999, pp. 783–798, 2020.
https://doi.org/10.1007/978-3-030-41579-2_45

transfer which can share enormous volumes of data over the Internet. Enormous network traffic makes it suitable for steganography [3,24,25,29]. VoIP enables the digitalisation, compression and transmission of analogue audio signals from a sender to a receiver using IP packets in multimedia transfer. Due to its real-time and large-scale characteristics, more and more VoIP-based covert communication systems have been brought up in recent years [8,17,33]. This type of covert communication has become a major threat to security monitoring of network communication. Thus, it is important to develop a powerful steganalysis tool to analyze VoIP streams.

VoIP is a typical streaming media technology. In general, VoIP streams are dynamic chunks of a series of packets that consist of IP headers, UDP headers, RTP headers and numbers of carrier frames. All of these fields can be used to embed secret information. However, information hiding based on network protocols including IP, UDP and RTP fields can be easily detected since all of the protocols are public and data in these fields are fixed mostly [21]. On the contrary, embedding information into carrier data field or payload filed which varies with time can achieve a relatively high level of concealment making them hard to detect [24]. Low bit-rate speech coding algorithms which have powerful compression capability such as G.729 and G.723.1 standard are specially defined by the International Telecommunication Union (ITU) for VoIP and are widely used to compress speech segment in VoIP streams. They try to minimize the decoding error by Analysis-by-Synthesis (AbS) framework and can achieve high compression ratio while preserving superb voice quality [5].

The QIM steganography [1] achieves information embedding by modifying the Vector Quantization (VQ) codeword search in the process of the speech encoder. The QIM method is a very common steganography scheme which can offer higher concealment capability and better robustness. Previous research on steganalysis of QIM-based steganography in low-bit-rate speech always focuses on inter-frame correlation or intra-frame correlation features but neglects the hierarchical structure which exists in speech frame. An interesting observation is that many natural sequences such as language, handwriting and speech have the capacity to recursively combine smaller units into hierarchically organized larger ones which is a fundamental property [4]. For example, in speech sequence, the phoneme, a basic phonology unit, can make up sub-words and words are composed of sub-words. The information contained in each acoustic unit is limited, but their combination leads to expressions that can flexibly convey infinite nuances and meanings. Having noticed that all the previous methods have neglected this property of speech, we try to construct a model to capture these hierachical features for steganalysis of the QIM steganography because QIM steganography can bring slight distortion to the hierarchical structure in speech. In the proposed model, CNN, regarded as a proper architecture to model hierachical structure, is stacked to capture different levels of features [35]. The attention mechanism [26] is used after every convolution block to select important components. All of the features selected from different levels of convolution blocks are concatenated and fed into fully connected layers which will serve as a classifier to indicate whether the sample speech is 'stego' or 'cover'. Experiments show that our model can effectively achieve the state-of-art results in both low and short samples which are the hardest parts in detecting QIM steganography in VoIP streams. Moreover, our models need less computation and has higher time efficiency to be applied to real online services.

We summarize our main contributions as follow:

(1) We first pointed out that speech steganalysis can make full use of the semantic hierarchical structure of speech itself, and design a reasonable network structure to model this hierarchical structure in speech carriers.
(2) The end-to-end model we proposed has two distinctive characteristics: (i) it uses a convolution network to model the hierarchical structure in the speech carrier, which mirrors the hierarchical structure of speech; (ii) it has different levels of attention mechanisms applied at different levels of features, enabling it to attend differentially to more and less steganalysis contents when constructing the speech representation for classification.
(3) The experiment on public dataset shows the proposed method can outperform all the state-of-the-art methods especially in low embeded and short samples. Meanwhile, time efficiency of the proposed model is also excellent compared with other methods.

The rest of this paper is organized as follows. In Sect. 2, we introduce some background knowledge of the research. Section 3 summarizes the related work. In Sect. 4, we introduce and describe the details of the proposed hierarchical representation network architecture. In Sect. 5, we introduce the experiment setting and benchmark. The experimental results and models are also discussed in this part. In Sect. 6, the concluding remarks are given.

2   Preliminaries

2.1   Linear Predictive Coding

Linear Predictive Coding (LPC) is mostly used for representing the spectral envelope of a digital signal of speech in compressed form, using the information of a linear predictive model. It is very useful for encoding speech at a low-bit rate and provides accurate estimates of speech parameters. Speech codecs such as G.729 and G.723.1 are based on the linear predictive coding (LPC) model, which uses an LPC filter to analyze and synthesize acoustic signals between the encoding and decoding endpoints. LPC filter can expressed as follow:

$$H(z) = \frac{1}{A(z)} = \frac{1}{1 - \sum_{i=1}^{n} a_i z^{-i}}, \tag{1}$$

where a_i is the ith coefficient of the LPC filter. The short-time stationary nature of the voice signal requires the entire signal sample to be divided into frames and the LPC filter's coefficients are then computed for each frame. During the speech coding, the LPC filter's coefficients of each frame are first computed and converted to line spectrum frequency (LSF) coefficients. Subsequently, the LSF coefficients are encoded by using vector quantization (VQ). Speech codecs adopt split VQ and use different split vectors to quantify the LSF coefficients and then Quantization Index Sequence (QIS) is generated, which can be formulated as:

$$S = [s_1, s_2, \cdots, s_T] = \begin{bmatrix} s_{1,1} & s_{2,1} & s_{T,1} \\ s_{1,2} & s_{2,2} & \cdots\cdots & s_{T,2} \\ s_{1,3} & s_{2,3} & s_{T,3} \end{bmatrix}, \tag{2}$$

where T is the total frame numbers in the sample window of the speech, s_i denotes the vector in i-th frame of the speech segment, and $s_{i,j}$ denotes the j-th code-word in the i-th frame respectively.

2.2   QIM-Based Steganography

Quantization index modulation techniques have been gaining popularity in the data hiding community because of their robustness and information-theoretic optimality against a large class of attacks. The QIM-based VoIP steganography hides the secret data during the VQ process by embedding information in the choice of quantizers [1]. For example if we want to embed bit stream, a standard scalar QIM with two sub-codebooks L_1 and L_2 can be simply expressed as follow:

$$s_i = Q_m(x_i) = \begin{cases} Q_0(x_i) & if\ m_i = 0, \\ Q_1(x_i) & if\ m_i = 1. \end{cases}$$

where x_i represents the input signal, and m is the message bit we want to embedded. Q_i is the quantizers which choose quantitative vector from sub-codebook of L_i. L_i is the sub-codebook of L in VQ process. For a two division of codebook L, the sub-codebook should satisfy the following conditions:

$$L1 \cap L2 = \emptyset \quad and \quad L1 \cup L2 = L. \tag{3}$$

The receiver can recover the secret information by judging to which sub-codebook the quantitative vector belongs.

For VoIP frames, QIM steganography is used to quantify the LSF coefficients. Obviously, QIM steganography will have an impact on the elements of QIS. Thus, QIS is a proper clue for steganalysis of QIM steganography. Another advantage of using QIS is that we can conduct steganalysis directly in the compressed domain, which will have little impact on user experiences of VoIP service [31,32].

3   Related Work

In this section, we introduce conventional steganalysis method in VoIP and deep learning based models in this field.

3.1   Conventional Steganalysis Method in VoIP

Conventional steganalysis method always focuses on extracting statistical features. For example, there are some audio steganalysis methods that can be utilized for detecting the QIM-based VoIP steganography by extracting statistical features in the uncompressed domain [7,12]. Nevertheless, these methods are not effective in detecting QIM steganography VoIP streams which are integrated with low bit-rate speech codecs. The reason is that these methods introduce minimal additional distortion in decoded speech signals. Thus it is difficult to obtain features in uncompressed domain for steganalysis. Besides, some researchers try to conduct steganalysis in the transform domain, where the statistical characteristics of elements in transform domain can be distorted during QIM steganography in speech encoding process. Therefore, the corresponding steganalysis methods usually exploit the statistical characteristics of the carrier, such as Mel-frequency features [13], statistic features [7], codewords correlations [15] and so on. Most of these traditional methods either have low accuracy or require a lot of computation to extract features which made them hard to reach the requirements of VoIP scenario. For example, Li et al. [15] extracted the modified codewords into a data stream, and used Markov chain to model the transition pattern between successive code-words which was very time consuming and was hard to apply at real scenarios.

3.2   Deep Learning Based Steganalysis Method in VoIP

Deep learning techniques have been well applied in image [6], speech [30] and natural language processing [2]. Application of deep learning techniques in the field of steganalysis has also be further explored [34]. In the steganalysis of audio. Paulin et al. [19] presents a steganalysis method that used a deep belief network (DBN) as a classifier for audio files. In another work, Paulin et al. [20] presented a new method to train Restricted Boltzmann Machines (RBMs) using Evolutionary Algorithms (EAs), where RBMs are used in the first step of a steganalysis tool for audio files and the vector they used to train the model was MFCC. Rekik et al. [22] advocated a powerful and sophisticated classifier called Autoregressive Time Delay Neural Network (AR-TDNN). The approach uses LSF (line spectral frequencies) parameters as a cue of audio type. Wang et al. [27] presents an effective steganalytic scheme based on CNN for detecting MP3 steganography in the entropy code domain. The above all focused on static audio file and can't be directly applied to stream media carrier.

There are also several attempts to apply deep learning methods to steganalysis of VoIP. Lin et al. [16] found there are four strong codeword correlation patterns in VoIP streams, which will be distorted after embedding with hidden data. Thus, to extract those correlation features, they propose the codeword correlation model, which is based on recurrent neural network (RNN). Yang et al. [34] defined multi-channel sliding detection windows to extract feature from raw speech stream. Then, they used two feature extraction channels with CNN to extract correlations features of the input signal between neighborhood frames. The method they proposed can achieve almost real-time detection of VoIP speech signals. Although the above methods had significantly improved the performance of VoIP steganalysis, they all neglected the hierarchical structure in speech carrier which has great potential to improve the performance of steganalysis.

4   Methodology

4.1   Problem Definition

Steganalysis of speech streams in this paper is to judge whether there wes extra information embeded in the raw speech frame. For the online real-time speech service network system, it is unlikely to get a complete voice sample, because it will seriously affect the quality of network voice services. In general, we can only use a small window to sample a small segment of the network voice stream as our test sample. Assume that the sample window size is N and C category in total, the corresponding speech sequence can be written as $S^t = [s_1^t, s_2^t, ..., s_N^t]$, where S_i^t represents speech frame code-words at time step t. The label for a sequence is denoted as y, $1 \leq y \leq C$. Our goal is to construct an end-to-end model $\phi(S^t)$ to predict a label $\hat{y}$.

4.2   Model Structure

The architecture of proposed model is shown in Fig. 1. In the proposed model, raw speech is first sampled by a sliding window and QIM sequences generated after this step. Then, the sequences are fed into the proposed model. In the proposed model, there are two main parts including feature extraction module, feature fusion and classification module. In feature extraction module, convolution layers are cascaded to model the hierarchical structure, and attention mechanism [26] is used to select important features from different levels. In feature fusion and classification module, features from different level are concatenated for final classification and two fully connected layers serve as classification in these parts. Moreover, parameters in the proposed model are trained on a supervised learning framework. In the following part, we will introduce the detail parts of each module.

4.3   Convolution Layers

Convolution layers are the backbone of the feature extraction module. We cascade three convolution blocks to capture different levels of features. Convolution layers in our model all used one-dimensional convolution [10]. In the module, a filter m convolves with the window vectors at each position in a valid way to generate a feature map h, each element h_i of the feature map for window vector h_j is produced as follows:

$$h_j = f(s_{j:j+k-1} \odot m + b), \tag{4}$$

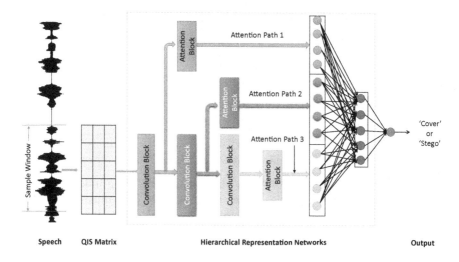

Fig. 1. Structure of proposed hierarchical representation network

where $s_{j:j+k-1}$ means a vector with k consecutive frame vector in S, $\odot$ is element-wise multiplication, b is a bias term and f is a nonlinear transformation function where ReLU [18] is used in our model. The structure of the second and third convolution blocks is essentially similar to the first one but with different convolution kernel sizes.

4.4 Attention Mechanism

In the proposed model, attention mechanism [26] is used for selecting different features in each layer. It is generally believed that the more the neural network layers in a model, the more abstract the features will be extracted [35]. In the feature extraction module, we use a 3-layer convolutional layer to extract hierarchical features. For steganalysis, the impact of steganography on speech stream may occur at each level of the hierarchical structure. Therefore, we believe that features in each layer of the model are useful and they are all used for final classification. However, in each steganography sample, the importance of different levels are not equal. Thus, we introduce attention mechanism in our model to select important feature in each sample. In the attention block of Fig. 1, inputted data which generated by each convolution block can be denoted as $h = [h_1, h_2, \cdots, h_j]$, and for $h_i \in h$, its attention weight α_i can be formulated as follows:

$$
\begin{aligned}
m_{\mathrm{i}} &= \tanh(h_i), \\
\hat{\alpha}_i &= w_i m_i + b_i, \\
\alpha_i &= \frac{\exp(\hat{\alpha}_i)}{\sum_j \exp(\hat{\alpha}_i)},
\end{aligned}
\tag{5}
$$

where w and b are the parameters of the attention layer. Therefore, the output representation r in every attention path is given by:

$$r = \sum_i \alpha_i h_i. \tag{6}$$

Based on such transformation, the features from convolution layers will be assigned with different attention weights. Thus, important information can be identified more easily.

4.5   Feature Fusion and Classification Layer

After the sample has been processed by the feature extraction module, we will get features from different levels. These features were concatenated for final classification and the compound feature vector z can be denoted as follow:

$$z = [r_1, r_2, r_3], \tag{7}$$

where r_i is the representative feature from the i-th attention block. Generally, the dimension of z is still very high, which is under the risk of over-fitting. Therefore, we take a two-layer fully-connected layers to compress it. The compress process can be expressed as follow:

$$z_c = f_2(w_2 f_1(w_1 z + b_1) + b_2), \tag{8}$$

where w_i and b_i is the parameters of the i-th fully-connected layer. f_i is the activation function in i-th fully-connected layer and we use ReLu [18] in our model. The compressed feature vector z_c is then sent to a softmax classifier to generate the probability distribution over the label set Y. The soft-max classifier can be denoted as:

$$p_t(i) = \frac{\exp(w_i \cdot z_c + b_i)}{\sum\limits_{k=1}^{C} \exp(w_k \cdot z_c + b_k)}, \tag{9}$$

where $p_t(i)$ is the probability of the category i at time step t, the total category number is C. w_k and b_k are the parameters in soft-max classifier. After these step, we can get predicted label $\hat{y}$, which is the element position with the maximum probability in the distribution p_t and the label value decides the speech sample belongs to 'Cover' or 'Stego'.

4.6   Loss Function

The whole proposed model is trained under a supervised learning framework where cross entropy error loss is chosen as loss function of the network. Given a training sample s^i and its true label $y^i \in \{1, 2, ..., k\}$ where k is the number of possible labels and the estimated probabilities $\hat{y}_j^i \in [0, 1]$ for each label $j \in \{1, 2, ..., k\}$, the error is defined as:

$$L(s^i, y^i) = \sum_{j=1}^{k} 1\{y^i = j\} \log(\hat{y}_j^i), \tag{10}$$

where 1{condition} is an indicator such that 1{condition is true} = 1 otherwise 1{condition is false} = 0. Moreover, in order to mitigate overfitting, we apply dropout technique [23] and Batch Normalization [9] to regularize our model.

5   Model Evaluation and Discussion

5.1   Dataset

Our experiments were conducted in a public dataset[1] that has been published by Lin *et al.* [16]. Samples in this dataset have different types of native speakers. Each speech file in the datasets was encoded according to the G.729a standard. Speech clips without hidden information were assigned the category label 'cover' which made up the cover speech dataset, while, secret data were embedded using CNV-QIM [28] steganography in split vector quantization process. Those speech samples with hiding data were assigned the category label 'stego' and make up the stego speech dataset. When we conducted experiment, samples in cover speech dataset and stego speech dataset were cut into different lengths to test the model performance with different duration. Segments of the same length were successive and not overlapped. For the training set with 0.1s clips, there were 2,486,708 samples with the 1:1 ratio of cover clips and stego clips.

5.2   Experimental Setting

Baselines. In order to validate the effectiveness of the proposed model, we compared the performance of our model with several baseline methods. Methods to be compared include:

IDC [7]: This method tries to exploit the Index Distribution Characteristics (IDC). The model extracted vector variation rate to measure the change of a vector and used first-order Markov chain for quantifying the correlated features. Then, they used Support Vector Machine (SVM) for classification.

QCCN [15]: The authors constructed a model called the Quantization code-word correlation network (QCCN) based on split VQ code-words from adjacent speech frames. They used high order Markov to model correlation characteristics of split VQ code-words and they also used SVM for classification.

RNN-SM [16]: This method indicated four strong code-word correlation patterns in VoIP streams, which will be distorted after embedding with hidden data. To extract those correlation features, the author proposed the codeword correlation model, which was based on Recurrent Neural Network (RNN).

CSW [34]: In order to exploit the correlations between frames and different neighborhood frames in a VoIP signal, the method combines sliding windows and convolution neural network to conduct steganalysis in compressed domains.

---

[1] https://github.com/fjxmlzn/RNN-SM.

Setting of the Proposed Model. The hyperparameters in our model were selected via cross-validation on the trail set. More specifically, the convolution kernel sizes of CNN filters were 1, 3, 5 from the first convolution block to the third convolution block. The number of each CNN filter in each convolution block was 256. The dimension of fully connected layer was 64, and the dropout rate was 0.6 for fully connected layer. The batch size in training process was 256, and the maximal training epoch was set to 200 which was large enough for convergence of all the models. We used Adam [11] as the optimizer for network training. Our model was implemented by Keras. We train all networks on GeForce GTX 1080 GPU with 16G graphics memory. The prediction process is done both on previous GPU and on Intel(R) Xeon(R) CPU E5-2683 v3 2.00 GHz.

Evaluation metric we chose to validate our model performance was classification accuracy, defined as the ratio of the number of samples that were correctly classified to the total number of samples.

5.3   Evaluation Results and Discussion

Table 1. Detection accuracy of 10s samples under different embedding rate

Language	Method	Embedding rate									
		10%	20%	30%	40%	50%	60%	70%	80%	90%	100%
EN	IDC [7]	51.60	58.55	63.65	71.50	76.25	83.50	87.25	91.60	95.55	97.20
	QCCN [15]	54.40	75.45	92.45	97.35	99.15	99.60	100.00	100.00	99.95	**99.30**
	RNN-SM [16]	59.64	92.44	94.56	96.90	97.76	98.77	99.24	99.71	99.79	98.78
	CSW [34]	83.48	94.15	97.76	99.17	99.71	99.91	99.95	99.98	100.00	99.05
	Ours	**86.83**	**95.08**	**98.25**	**99.53**	**99.84**	**99.95**	99.99	100.00	100.00	99.13
CH	IDC [7]	52.75	59.25	65.55	71.40	78.50	82.60	89.15	93.60	96.05	98.05
	QCCN [15]	57.35	75.00	92.00	98.25	99.50	99.85	100.00	99.95	99.90	**99.75**
	RNN-SM [16]	55.14	74.19	90.12	95.24	98.05	98.25	99.09	99.51	99.76	99.55
	CSW [34]	77.18	92.05	96.58	98.70	99.64	99.87	99.94	99.98	100.00	99.51
	Ours	**86.54**	**95.24**	**98.28**	**99.38**	**99.81**	**99.92**	100.00	100.00	100.00	99.61

Influence of Embeding Rate. The embedding rate is an important factor influencing detecting accuracy. At first, we fixed the sample length at 10s, and changed embedding rate from 10% to 100% with step size of 10% to test different models. English and Chinese speeches were tested separately. As Table 1 shows, when the embedding rate is low, the detection accuracy is also low. The reason is that when the embedding rate is small, the statistical distribution of the carrier before and after steganography is small, making it more difficult to be detected. Furthermore, all the models increase remarkably with the increase of the embedding rate when the embedding rate is low, but it is not obvious when the embedding rate is high. Because as the embedding rate increases, the samples have more clues for steganalysis leading to higher detection accuracy but it doesn't benefit more when the embedding rate is high relatively. Besides, we can see that when the embedding rate is 10%, the proposed model outperforms the CSW method by more than 11% in testing Chinese samples. Overall, our model significantly improves the detection accuracy in low embedding rate.

Influence of Sample Length. The duration of voice is another factor which has great impact when detecting QIM based steganography in VoIP streams. The detection of short steganography samples is challenging. To test the performance of the proposed algorithm against different lengths of samples, we fixed the embedding rate at 100%. As for the sample length, we tested 10 samples whose lengths are equally spaced in the range of 0.1 s to 1 s with step equals to 0.1 s.

According to the results shown in Table 2, we can see that when the sample length increases, the detection accuracy increases. This phenomenon is easy to explain. Longer sequence provides more observations on code-word correlations, which can therefore be modeled more accurately. Thus, the difference between the code-word correlation patterns of stego speech and cover speech is more distinct, leading to easier classification. Moreover, when the sample is short, increasing sample length significantly benefits the accuracy. As the sample length increases, the benefit of increasing sample length diminishes. Most importantly, we can come to the conclusion that our model is better than all the previous methods when the samples are short. It means that our method can effectively detect the QIM steganography in low bit rate speech only by capturing a small segment speech stream of a monitored VoIP session, which is very important for VoIP corresponding censoring.

Table 2. Detection accuracy of 100% embedding rate samples under different lengths

Language	Method	Sample length (s)									
		0.1	0.2	0.3	0.4	0.5	0.6	0.7	0.8	0.9	1
EN	IDC [7]	85.40	88.00	88.50	89.25	90.10	91.45	91.40	92.40	92.95	93.70
	QCCN [15]	82.00	88.85	92.15	95.00	95.70	96.15	96.25	96.90	96.90	98.00
	RNN-SM [16]	90.40	95.50	97.38	97.81	98.16	98.23	98.38	98.48	98.49	98.54
	CSW [34]	91.59	95.63	97.40	97.85	98.21	98.36	98.40	98.43	98.49	98.47
	Ours	**92.63**	**96.41**	**97.85**	**98.25**	**98.53**	**98.71**	**98.80**	**98.82**	**98.93**	**98.95**
CH	IDC [7]	86.80	88.65	90.20	90.50	91.20	92.25	93.10	94.25	94.70	94.05
	QCCN [15]	81.20	90.05	93.75	95.25	96.50	97.45	97.60	98.30	98.10	98.50
	RNN-SM [16]	90.91	95.91	97.03	97.72	98.09	98.12	98.51	98.69	99.06	98.86
	CSW [34]	91.84	96.12	97.70	98.32	98.56	98.40	98.99	98.80	99.13	98.95
	Ours	**92.33**	**96.79**	**98.20**	**98.82**	**99.11**	**99.24**	**99.34**	**99.41**	**99.42**	**99.43**

Besides, we also tested our algorithm under different lengths and different embedding rates. From the Table 3 we can see, the proposed model output perform all the state-of-the art method in both short and low embedded samples.

5.4 Time Efficiency of Different Model

Time efficiency is also an important factor in determining whether a model can actually be applied to an online scenario. Yang *et al.* [34] have demonstrated in their article that CSW significantly outperforms other methods in terms of time efficiency. Thus, our experiments only compare the time efficiency of our model with the CSW method. The results are shown in the Table 6 and Fig. 2.

Table 3. Classification accuracy under different length and different embedding rate

Language.	Embed. rates	0.3 s					0.5 s				
		IDC	QCCN	RNN-SM	CSW	Ours	IDC	QCCN	RNN-SM	CSW	Ours
Chinese	10	54.50	53.15	57.61	59.66	**60.73**	56.55	53.65	71.43	62.45	**64.03**
	20	60.10	58.25	66.81	70.02	**71.76**	59.60	61.85	71.29	74.21	**76.21**
	30	65.70	62.90	74.60	77.87	**85.05**	65.45	67.35	78.42	82.19	**84.09**
	40	70.05	71.45	80.08	82.75	**85.11**	70.15	75.20	84.39	86.83	**90.03**
English	10	54.55	53.15	59.68	61.23	**62.81**	51.85	53.65	62.46	64.33	**66.57**
	20	58.15	58.25	70.05	70.61	**73.50**	59.85	61.85	72.45	75.72	**79.23**
	30	63.65	62.90	77.17	78.21	**81.16**	64.05	67.35	80.38	83.80	**85.83**
	40	69.50	71.45	77.27	84.43	**86.66**	72.30	75.20	86.22	89.49	**91.26**

Obviously, from the Table 6, our model performs significantly better than the CSW method in various sample lengths. Especially, when the sample length is short, such as 0.1s, inference time of the proposed model is only 2/3 of the CSW method. In addition, we also noticed that because the CSW model uses multi-channel convolution to extract features and our model used share convolution with single convolution path, parameters of proposed model have been significantly reduced. For instance, when the sample length is 1s, parameters of proposed model are also 1/4 of the CSW method, which makes it easier to apply to real scenarios (Table 4).

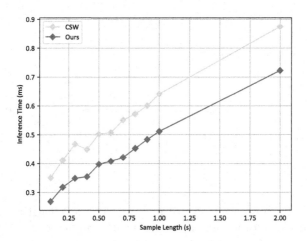

Fig. 2. Time efficiency of different models

5.5   Discussion of Model Variants

In this part, we try to investigate the function of different parts in the proposed model by comparing it with its several variants. Performances of different variants are shown in Table 5.

Table 4. Parameters of different model

Model	Total parameters
CSW [34]	567,041
Ours	157,825

First, comparing #0, #1, #2 and #3, we can see that features extracted from different aspects are beneficial to steganalysis. It is easy to explain that steganography will change the structure of speech in different aspects, and features from different shortcut connections provide abundant information for detection.

Table 5. The detection accuracy of various models

Index	Network description	Accuracy
#0	The proposed model	**87.14**
#1	Remove path 1	86.97
#2	Remove path 2	86.76
#3	Remove 1 and 2	86.82
#4	Replace attention with max pooling	79.63
#5	Reduce convolution block to 2	82.06
#6	Add convolution block to 4	85.59

Meanwhile, the attention mechanism is used in our model to select important information as well as to reduce dimensions. However, pooling [14] is the most common way to reduce the dimension of features which has a similar function attention mechanism. Hence, we replaced the attention mechanism with max pooling operation to show the effectiveness of attention mechanisms. It is obvious that giving different weights to different vectors is helpful to our model when #0 is compared with #4. Moreover, models in #0, #5 and #6 shows that three convolution blocks are proper in our experiments. In general, more features of the input data can be captured by a deeper network and the difference between model #0 and #6 proves that. However, performances of #0 and #6

Table 6. Detection performance of different model under different lengths

Method	Metric	Sample length (s)										
		0.1	0.2	0.3	0.4	0.5	0.6	0.7	0.8	0.9	1	2
CSW	Mean (ms)	0.3509	0.4113	0.4671	0.4494	0.5023	0.5073	0.5512	0.5718	0.6005	0.6413	0.8749
	Std	0.1490	0.1957	0.2033	0.1637	0.1829	0.1446	0.1806	0.2000	0.2059	0.2160	0.2913
Ours	Mean (ms)	**0.2683**	**0.3181**	**0.3488**	**0.3542**	**0.3975**	**0.4078**	**0.4212**	**0.4530**	**0.4833**	**0.5115**	**0.7225**
	Std	0.1322	0.1613	0.1581	0.1594	0.1636	0.1406	0.1292	0.1492	0.1609	0.1563	0.2373

demonstrate that it doesn't mean that the deeper the network is, the better the model performance will be, since deeper networks may result in over-fitting and vanishing gradient problems.

6   Conclusions

VoIP is a very popular streaming media for steganography. Detecting short and low embeded QIM steganography samples in VoIP stream remains an unsolved challenge in real circumstances. Potential VoIP-based covert communications based on QIM steganography pose a great threat to the security of cyberspace. Previous methods in steganalysis of QIM based steganography always pay much attention to the correlations in inter-frames and intra-frames but ignore the hierarchical structure in speech frames. In this paper, motivated by the complex multi-scale structure which appears in speech, we proposed hierarchical representative network to address this steganalysis problem in VoIP streams. In our model, CNN is stacked to model hierarchical structure in speech and attention mechanisms are applied to select import information. Experiments demonstrate that our model is effective and can achieve state-of-the-art results. Besides, our model needs less computation and has higher time efficiency to be applied to real online services. Although our model performs well enough, detection accuracy in low embedded rate still needs improvement.

References

1. Chen, B., Wornell, G.: Quantization index modulation: a class of provably good methods for digital watermarking and information embedding. IEEE Trans. Inf. Theory **47**(4), 1423–1443 (2002)
2. Devlin, J., Chang, M.W., Lee, K., Toutanova, K.: Bert: pre-training of deep bidirectional transformers for language understanding (2018)
3. Dora, M.B.L., Juan, M.M.A.: Highly transparent steganography model of speech signals using efficient wavelet masking. Expert Syst. Appl. **39**(10), 9141–9149 (2012)
4. Fine, S., Singer, Y., Tishby, N.: The hierarchical hidden Markov model: analysis and applications. Mach. Learn. **32**(1), 41–62 (1998)
5. Goode, B.: Voice over internet protocol (VoIP). Proc. IEEE **90**(9), 1495–1517 (2002)
6. He, K., Zhang, X., Ren, S., Sun, J.: Deep residual learning for image recognition (2015)
7. Huang, Y.F., Tang, S., Zhang, Y.: Detection of covert voice-over internet protocol communications using sliding window-based steganalysis. IET Commun. **5**(7), 929–936 (2011)
8. Huang, Y.F., Tang, S., Yuan, J.: Steganography in inactive frames of voip streams encoded by source codec. IEEE Trans. Inf. Forensics Secur. **6**(2), 296–306 (2011)
9. Ioffe, S., Szegedy, C.: Batch normalization: accelerating deep network training by reducing internal covariate shift. In: International Conference on International Conference on Machine Learning, pp. 448–456. JMLR.org (2015)

10. Kim, Y.: Convolutional neural networks for sentence classification. Eprint Arxiv (2014)
11. Kingma, D., Ba, J.: Adam: a method for stochastic optimization (2014)
12. Kocal, O.H., Yuruklu, E., Avcibas, I.: Chaotic-type features for speech steganalysis. IEEE Trans. Inf. Forensics Secur. **3**(4), 651–661 (2008)
13. Kraetzer, C., Dittmann, J.: Mel-cepstrum-based steganalysis for VoIP steganography. In: Security, Steganography, and Watermarking of Multimedia Contents IX, pp. 650505–650505-12 (2007)
14. Krizhevsky, A., Sutskever, I., Hinton, G.E.: Imagenet classification with deep convolutional neural networks. In: International Conference on Neural Information Processing Systems (2012)
15. Li, S., Jia, Y., Kuo, C.C.J.: Steganalysis of qim steganography in low-bit-rate speech signals. IEEE/ACM Trans. Audio Speech Lang. Process. **25**(99), 1–1 (2017)
16. Lin, Z., Huang, Y., Wang, J.: RNN-SM: fast steganalysis of VoIP streams using recurrent neural network. IEEE Trans. Inf. Forensics Secur. **13**(7), 1854–1868 (2018)
17. Mazurczyk, W.: Voip steganography and its detection - a survey. ACM Comput. Surv. **46**(2), 1–21 (2013)
18. Nair, V., Hinton, G.E.: Rectified linear units improve restricted boltzmann machines. In: International Conference on International Conference on Machine Learning (2010)
19. Palaz, D., Magimai.-Doss, M., Collobert, R.: Convolutional neural networks-based continuous speech recognition using raw speech signal. In: IEEE International Conference on Acoustics (2015)
20. Paulin, C., Selouani, S.A., Hervet, E.: Speech steganalysis using evolutionary restricted Boltzmann machines. In: Evolutionary Computation (2016)
21. Pelaez, J.C.: Using misuse patterns for voip steganalysis. In: International Workshop on Database & Expert Systems Application (2009)
22. Rekik, S., Selouani, S.A., Guerchi, D., Hamam, H.: An autoregressive time delay neural network for speech steganalysis. In: International Conference on Information Science, Signal Processing and Their Applications, pp. 54–58 (2012)
23. Srivastava, N., Hinton, G., Krizhevsky, A., Sutskever, I., Salakhutdinov, R.: Dropout: a simple way to prevent neural networks from overfitting. J. Mach. Learn. Res. **15**(1), 1929–1958 (2014)
24. Tian, H., Liu, J., Li, S.: Improving security of quantization-index-modulation steganography in low bit-rate speech streams. Multimedia Syst. **20**(2), 143–154 (2014)
25. Tian, H., Zhou, K., Jiang, H., Huang, Y., Liu, J., Feng, D.: An adaptive steganography scheme for voice over IP. In: IEEE International Symposium on Circuits and Systems, pp. 2922–2925 (2009)
26. Vaswani, A., et al.: Attention is all you need (2017)
27. Wang, Y., Yang, K., Yi, X., Zhao, X., Xu, Z.: CNN-based steganalysis of MP3 steganography in the entropy code domain. In: Proceedings of the 6th ACM Workshop on Information Hiding and Multimedia Security, Innsbruck, Austria, 20–22 June 2018, pp. 55–65 (2018)
28. Xiao, B., Huang, Y., Tang, S.: An approach to information hiding in low bit-rate speech stream. In: IEEE GLOBECOM Global Telecommunications Conference, pp. 1–5 (2008)
29. Xu, E., Liu, B., Xu, L., Wei, Z., Zhao, B., Su, J.: Adaptive VoIP steganography for information hiding within network audio streams. In: International Conference on Network-Based Information Systems, pp. 612–617 (2011)

30. Yang, H., Yang, Z., Bao, Y., Huang, Y.: Fast steganalysis method for VoIP streams (2019)
31. Yang, H., Yang, Z., Bao, Y., Liu, S., Huang, Y.: FCEM: a novel fast correlation extract model for real time steganalysis of VoIP stream via multi-head attention (2019)
32. Yang, H., Yang, Z., Huang, Y.: Steganalysis of VoIP streams with CNN-LSTM network. In: Proceedings of the ACM Workshop on Information Hiding and Multimedia Security, pp. 204–209. ACM (2019)
33. Yang, Z., Peng, X., Huang, Y.: A sudoku matrix-based method of pitch period steganography in low-rate speech coding. In: Lin, X., Ghorbani, A., Ren, K., Zhu, S., Zhang, A. (eds.) SecureComm 2017. LNICST, vol. 238, pp. 752–762. Springer, Cham (2018). https://doi.org/10.1007/978-3-319-78813-5_40
34. Yang, Z., Yang, H., Hu, Y., Huang, Y., Zhang, Y.: Real-time steganalysis for stream media based on multi-channel convolutional sliding windows (2019). http://arxiv.org/abs/1902.01286
35. Zeiler, M.D., Fergus, R.: Visualizing and understanding convolutional networks. In: Fleet, D., Pajdla, T., Schiele, B., Tuytelaars, T. (eds.) ECCV 2014. LNCS, vol. 8689, pp. 818–833. Springer, Cham (2014). https://doi.org/10.1007/978-3-319-10590-1_53

Convolutional Neural Network Based Side-Channel Attacks with Customized Filters

Man Wei[1,2,3(✉)], Danping Shi[1,2,3], Siwei Sun[1,2,3], Peng Wang[1,2,3], and Lei Hu[1,2,3]

[1] State Key Laboratory of Information Security, Institute of Information Engineering, Chinese Academy of Sciences, Beijing, China
{weiman,shidanping,sunsiwei,wpeng,hulei}@iie.ac.cn
[2] Data Assurance and Communication Security Research Center, Chinese Academy of Sciences, Beijing, China
[3] School of Cyber Security, University of Chinese Academy of Sciences, Beijing, China

Abstract. Deep learning is progressively gaining attention as a powerful tool for conducting profiling side-channel attacks. In particular, convolutional neural network (CNN) is one of the mostly employed learning techniques in the context of side-channel analysis. The first layer of a standard CNN always performs a set of convolutions between the input and some finite impulse response filters. In this work, we substitute the standard filter by a customized filter borrowed from the domain of speaker recognition due to the resemblance between the power traces and speech signals. In contrast to standard filters, the new filter only depends on parameters with a clear physical meaning, where only low and high cutoff frequencies are learned from the training data. Experimental results obtained from public datasets show that the side-channel attacks based on CNNs equipped with this new filter are more effective and robust than attacks based on standard CNNs. The results of this work open new perspective and encourage further research on the effect of the filters of the CNN-based side-channel attacks.

Keywords: Side-Channel Analysis · Machine Learning · Deep learning · Convolutional Neural Networks

1 Introduction

Side-Channel Analysis (SCA) has been a serious concern as it is able to retrieve secret information from real cryptographic devices by exploiting physical leakages like power consumptions [22], timing information [21], and electromagnetic radiations [6]. Generally, SCA can be divided into *non-profiling* attacks and *profiling* attacks. In non-profiling attacks, the attacker can only use the physical leakages captured on the target device to extract its secret key. This class

© Springer Nature Switzerland AG 2020
J. Zhou et al. (Eds.): ICICS 2019, LNCS 11999, pp. 799–813, 2020.
https://doi.org/10.1007/978-3-030-41579-2_46

of attacks includes Differential Power Analysis (DPA) [22], Correlation Power Analysis (CPA) [11] and Mutual Information Analysis (MIA) [16]. While in profiling attacks, the attacker is in possession of a *profiling device*, which has similar leakage characteristics of the target device with a *configurable* key. Therefore, the attacker can play with the profiling device to learn the characteristic of its physical leakages (the profiling phase). Based on the knowledge obtained from the profiling device and the physical leakages captured on the target device, the attacker can perform an attack on the target device (the attack phase). This class of attacks includes Template Attacks [13] and Stochastic Attacks (*a.k.a.*, Linear Regression Analysis) [15,33,34].

Due to its very nature, profiling attacks have successfully borrowed techniques from Machine Learning (*e.g.*, the Support Vector Machine [14,36], the Random Forest [32], *etc.*) to defeat both protected [17,26] and unprotected cryptographic implementations [8,19,20,25,27]. In particular, the discovery of techniques for learning in so-called deep neural networks in year 2006 known as deep learning [1,9,24] has further stimulated the endeavor of automatic learning from data in all scientific and industrial domains. To the best of our knowledge, Maghrebi et al. was the first to perform profiling attacks with deep learning techniques [28], which confirmed the overwhelming advantages compared to template attacks in certain cases. Moreover, unlike template attacks which typically suffer from the difficulty to deal with the misalignment and high dimensionality of the data, the deep learning based approach was shown to be quite robust to trace misalignment especially when enhanced by data augmentation techniques [12]. It is also possible to apply the deep learning technique in the time-frequency domain. In [37], Yang et al. proposed a deep learning based side-channel attack where Convolutional Neural Network (CNN) was employed to learn time-frequency 2D patterns and extract high level key-related features in the spectrograms. More and more evidence indicates that the deep learning based approach is a promising way for side-channel analysis, and this line of research is developed rapidly [18,35].

Contribution. In this work, we use a set of parameterized sinc functions that implement band-pass filters as the convolution filters of the CNNs employed in deep learning based side-channel attacks. This technique is first successfully applied in the domain of speaker recognition, which inspires us to try it out in the context of deep learning based side-channel attacks since the power traces are quite similar to speech signals in nature. We perform experiments on several public datasets include traces captured on both unprotected and protected (masking and jitter-based countermeasures) implementations, which demonstrate that the new CNNs are more effective than the standard ones. For example, in the attack on a masked AES implementation with simulated jitter, our CNNs perform much better than the standard ones. Along the way, we also discuss the impact of the size of the customized filter on the network performance for each dataset. The architecture can not only improve the convergence speed over a standard CNN, but also save the computation in the first layer. Our work opens new perspective and encourages further investigations on the effect of the filters of the CNN-based side-channel attacks.

Organization. In Sect. 2, we give a brief introduction of convolutional neural network based side-channel attack together with the so-called sinc filter that will be used in the following sections. Then in Sect. 3, we perform experimental attacks on several public datasets with both protected and unprotected AES implementations. A comparison is made between CNNs with sinc filters and standard CNNs. Section 4 concludes the paper.

2 Preliminaries

In this section, we give a brief introduction of profiling side-channel attacks, convolutional neural networks, and the filter that will be applied in our CNN-based side-channel attacks.

2.1 Profiling Side-Channel Attacks

A profiling side-channel attack is composed of two phases: a profiling phase (*i.e.*, training in the machine learning context) and an attack phase (*i.e.*, matching). During the profiling phase, the adversary has fully control of a copy of the target device, and can set the input and secret key with desired values. Thus he can acquire a set of N_p side-channel traces $\mathcal{D}_{profiling} = \{\mathbf{x}_i : i = 1, 2, \ldots, N_p\}$. Every trace $\mathbf{x}_i$ corresponds to a computation $v_i = f(p_i, k_i)$, which represents the value of a target sensitive variable $V = f(P, K)$, where P stands for the input information (plaintext or ciphertext), and K is the secret key. In the context of machine learning, the value of the sensitive variable V is computed as a label to construct a classifier. The adversary aims at building a discriminative model for each possible value of the label with the training set $\mathcal{D}_{profiling}$.

During the attack phase, the adversary acquires a new set of N_a traces $\mathcal{D}_{attack} = \{\mathbf{x}_i : i = 1, 2, \ldots, N_a\}$ from the real target device, where the secret key k^* is fixed and unknown. With the established model, the most likely key (deduced from the label) can be output for a trace $\mathbf{x}_i$ in $\mathcal{D}_{attack}$. To retrieve the correct key, the maximum likelihood approach can be used to compute $d_{N_a}[k]$ with N_a traces for every key candidate $k \in \mathcal{K}$:

$$d_{N_a}[k] = \prod_{i=1}^{N_a} \Pr[v_i = f(p_i, k) | \mathbf{x} = \mathbf{x}_i], \qquad (1)$$

the hypothesis key which maximizes $d_{N_a}[k]$ is supposed to be the correct key.

Evaluation Metrics. In machine learnings, the *accuracy* is used to assess the efficiency of a model, which is defined as the percentage of the number of correct predictions in the total number of input samples. In the context of side-channel analysis, it corresponds to the proportion of correct secret key predictions in the total input traces, where a correct key prediction for a given trace $\mathbf{x}_i$ is fulfilled when the actual key equals to k such that $d_1[k] = \Pr[v_i = f(p, k)|\mathbf{x} = \mathbf{x}_i]$ is maximized. That is, the event of a correct prediction is defined in the situation where only one single trace is available in the key-recovery attack. However, in many practical cases, it is difficult to recover the key with only one trace, which leads to the following more reasonable metric for the multiple traces matching.

In side-channel analysis, the so-called *rank* is commonly used to evaluate the effectiveness of an attack. Let $\mathcal{D}_{profiling}$ and $\mathcal{D}_{attack}$ be the profiling and attack dataset respectively. The model $\hat{g}$ is trained with traces in $\mathcal{D}_{profiling}$, and tested with traces in $\mathcal{D}_{attack}$. A rank is defined as the amount of hypothetical key values $k \in \mathcal{K}$ providing with higher probabilities than that of the true key k^*:

$$\text{rank}(\hat{g}, \mathcal{D}_{profiling}, \mathcal{D}_{attack}, i) = |\{k \in K : d_i[k] > d_i[k^*]\}|,$$

where $d_i[k]$ is the likelihood of the candidate k estimated from the first i traces in $\mathcal{D}_{attack}$. The rank quantifies the difficulty of correct key recovery under a given number of available traces.

2.2   Convolutional Neural Networks

Convolutional Neural Networks (CNNs) are a kind of popular neural networks in image processing and speaker recognitions. A general CNN architecture includes convolutional blocks and one or more fully-connected layers. The convolutional block studied in this paper is composed of a convolutional layer followed by activation functions, and a pooling layer. We refer the reader to [23,29] for a more systematic exhibition of the topic, and only give a brief description of the key components which are relevant to our work.

Convolutional Layer. A convolutional layer extracts the local features of the input by performing a set of time domain convolutions between the input data and convolution filters. A convolutional operation can be defined as:

$$y[n] = (x * h)[n] = \sum_{l=1}^{L} x[l] \cdot h[n - l],$$

where x is a chunk of the input signal, and h is the convolution filter of size L. The convolution filter slides over the input data with its step length controlled by the *stride*.

The input data can be padded with 0 such that the output keeps the same shape as the input, called the same padding, or the data is not padded, resulting in a smaller output, called the valid padding. During the training phase in a standard convolution filter, all the L elements of the filter are learned from data. Followed the convolutional layer, a non-linear activation function is applied to each input neuron, where Sigmoid, TanHyperbolic (Tanh), and Rectified Linear Unit (ReLU) functions are commonly used.

Pooling Layer. A pooling layer can decrease the amount of neurons by discarding unnecessary details while reserving useful features [10]. The pooling layer also makes filters slide over the input. However, different from the convolutional layer, the pooling filter is controlled by the pooling function without trainable weight. The max pooling function outputs the maximum values within the slide window, and the average pooling function outputs the average values within the slide window.

Fully Connected Layer. Commonly, several so-called fully-connected (FC) layers are connected to the CNN blocks to obtain a global result after the features derived from the previous layers. For the classification problem, the last FC layer is usually activated by the so-called softmax function.

2.3 The Sinc Filter

The sinc filter was first successfully employed in speaker recognitions [31]. The sinc filter is based on parametrized sinc function and the convolutional operation with a sinc filter g, defined as:

$$y[n] = (x * g)[n, f_1, f_2] = \sum_{l=1}^{L} x[l] \cdot g[n - l, f_1, f_2],$$

where only f_1, and f_2 are the trainable parameters, and g implements a rectangular bandpass filter. In the frequency domain, the magnitude of a bandpass filter can be written as the difference between two lowpass filter:

$$G[f, f_1, f_2] = rect(\frac{f}{2f_2}) - rect(\frac{f}{2f_1}),$$

where f_1 and f_2 are the low and high cut-off frequencies, and $rect()$ is the rectangular function in the magnitude frequency domain. The function g transforms the bandpass filter from the frequency domain to the time domain using the inverse Fourier transform. Thus the function g can be expressed by the following equation:

$$g[n, f_1, f_2] = 2f_2 sinc(2\pi f_2 n) - 2f_1 sinc(2\pi f_1 n), \tag{2}$$

where the *sinc* function is defined as $sinc(x) = sin(x)/x$. Since the cut-off frequencies f_1, f_2 are learnable during the training phase, they can be initialized randomly in the range $[0, f_s/2]$, where f_s represents the sampling frequency of the input signal. To ensure $f_1 \geq 0$ and $f_2 \geq f_1$, we replace f_1 and f_2 in Equation (2) by $|f_1|$ and $|f_1| + |f_2 - f_1|$ respectively in practice.

Moreover, due to the limited number of elements in the time domain, the function g should be truncated. To smooth out the abrupt discontinuities of g, a Hamming window function $w[n] = 0.54 - 0.46 \cdot cos(\frac{2\pi n}{L})$ is applied:

$$g_w[n, f_1, f_2] = g[n, f_1, f_2] \cdot w[n].$$

Note that function g is symmetric. Therefore, the input only needs to be convoluted with half of the filter and inherits the results for the other half.

3   Experimental Analysis of the CNN-based Attack with the Sinc Filter

In this work, our experiments are conducted on a computer equipped with one NVIDIA GeForce GTX 1080Ti GPU. The deep-learning based algorithms are implemented with the Keras library [4] and the Tensorflow library [5].

Datasets. We consider three public datasets commonly used in the community to study deep-learning based attacks: DPA contest V4 [3], DPA contest V2 [2], and ASCAD [7].

- DPA contest V4 (DPAv4) provides a set of power traces which were collected from a masked software implementation of AES-256 on an Atmel ATMega-163 smart-card connected to a SASEBO-W FPGA board. Each measurement has 125 points per clock cycle with a sampling rate of 500M samples per second. In our case, we focus on the output of the first round S-box, and use the first byte of the output $V = \mathrm{Sbox}(p[1] \oplus k^*[1])$ as the label during the training phase, where $p[1]$ is the first byte of a plaintext p. Thus the label contains 256 classes. We use 30000 traces of the dataset as the training set, and 5000 traces as the matching set.

- DPA contest V2 (DPAv2) targets on an unprotected hardware implementation of AES-128 on SASEBO GII FPGA board. The sampling rate is 5G samples per second, and each acquisition has approximately 213 points per clock cycles. We analyse the leakage of the register updating in the last round: $V = \mathrm{Sbox}^{-1}(c[1] \oplus k^*[1]) \oplus c[1]$, where $c[1]$ is the first byte of ciphertext c. The training set contains 90000 traces, and the matching set contains 10000 traces.

- ASCAD is an open database which is exclusively used for the deep learning analysis [30]. The raw traces were obtained from a software protected AES implementation on an ATMega-8515. Each one was acquired with a sampling rate of 2G samples per second, and has 500 points per clock cycle. The database includes three processed datasets with corresponding labeled datasets: ASCAD.h5, ASCAD_desync50.h5 and ASCAD_desync100.h5, which are composed of traces without jitter, traces with a 50 samples window maximum jitter, and traces with a 100 samples window maximum jitter, respectively. Each dataset is divided into a training set with 50000 traces and a matching set with 10000 traces. The corresponding label is the value of the third byte of the masked S-box output $V = \mathrm{Sbox}(p[3] \oplus k^*[3])$ in the first round.

Remark. Except ASCAD, both DPAv4 and DPAv2 need certain preprocessing to be successful attacked in the open literature. In this work, a min-max normalization $\frac{x - x_{min}}{x_{max} - x_{min}}$ is performed to rescale a measurement x. The scaling plays a key role in the gradient problem such that the model becomes more susceptible in the training phase (Table 1).

Table 1. Data splitting size in datasets

Dataset	Profiling traces	Attack traces
DPAv4	30000	5000
DPAv2	90000	10000
ASCAD	50000	10000
ASCAD_desync50	50000	10000
ASCAD_desync100	50000	10000

3.1 Evaluation Method

In this paper, we split the tenth of the training dataset as a validation dataset. The candidate SincNet is trained and validated on the given dataset of $\mathcal{D}_{profiling}$, and the model with the best validation accuracy will be saved during the training phase. Then the algorithm performs an attack on the given dataset of $\mathcal{D}_{attack}$ and are evaluated with metrics like the accuracy, the top-5 accuracy (*i.e.*, the proportion where the correct label is amongst the best 5 predictions in the matching set), and the rank. Based on these evaluation metrics, the suitable hyperparameters are determined through synthetical consideration. We also compare the performances of SincNet based attack and CNN based attack on each dataset respectively according to these metrics.

3.2 CNN Architecture

We establish our CNN model with sinc filters in the first convolutional layer, which is called SincNet in [31]. The convolution stride is set to 1, and the same-padding is used to preserve the size of the output. Each convolutional layer is followed by the ReLU activation function. The pooling layer uses the average pooling function, and the stride is set 2. After the feature extraction, several fully-connected layers are added, which include a flatten layer, one or more dense layers activated by the ReLU function, and the output layer activated by the softmax function. Indeed, the main purpose of our experiments is to determine the validity of SincNet, not to find the optimal model for each dataset. Therefore we do not spend much effort to determine these architecture parameters of CNN.

However, due to the differences of the targeted datasets, we make some adjustments in the detailed architecture for each one. For DPAv4 which targets on a software implementation, the complete architecture is illustrated in Fig. 1, which contains one convolutional block with 32 sinc filters, one convolutional block with 64 standard filters of length 11, and one dense layer of 512 neurons.

While DPAv2 refers to an FPGA implementation and needs much more traces to perform training, more convolutional operations are employed. Based on the architecture for DPAv4, we add a third convolutional block which has 128 standard convolution filters of length 11, and the rest of the architecture remains the same.

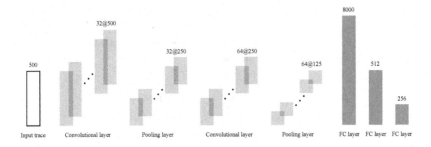

Fig. 1. The CNN architecture for DPAv4

As for ASCAD, a CNN model called CNN$_{\text{best}}$ was proposed in [30]. The architecture consists of 5 convolutional blocks where each block has a convolutional layer with respectively 64, 128, 256, 512, and 512 filters of length 11, and two dense layers of 4096 neurons. We directly replace the standard CNN filters in the first convolutional layer with the sinc filters.

These models will be trained with a batch size of 200 using the RMSprop optimizer, and the initial learning rates are set to 0.00001 except for DPAv4 whose learning rate is set to 0.0001. According to previous work on these datasets, 75 epochs are sufficient for training. During the training phase, the network filter weights are recorded for the best validation accuracy. Then the size of the sinc filter in each model will be tuned for each target in the next section.

On the Size of the Sinc Filters. Note that the increased bandpass filter size does not change the number of trainable parameters. Thus larger filter size will put no extra burdens on the optimization problem. Following the previous experiments in [37], we select the filter size of 1/8, 1/4, and 1/2 percentage of one clock cycle respectively. Then we do the training and attack with all these different filter sizes for each dataset.

The ranking convergence of the experimental attacks can be seen in Fig. 2, and a comparison is made with respect to some important metrics in Table 2. We report the minimum number of traces when the rank first achieves 0, and also report the minimum number of traces where the rank reaches 0 and remains the same till all traces traversed in $\mathcal{D}_{attack}$.

In DPAv4, according to Table 2, all the architectures with different filter sizes of 31 (1/8 clock cycle), 63 (1/4 clock cycle), and 125 (1/2 clock cycle) result in the rank 0 with only one challenge trace, where the filter size of 125 archives the best accuracy 26.22%. In DPAv2, when the filter size is set to 27 (1/8 clock cycle), the rank first achieves 0 with 398 traces and is stabilized at 0 after 569 traces. Although the accuracy results are around the probability of the random guessing, the correct key can be distinguished from other key guesses when plenty of traces are combined. Thus we are more concerned with the rank to evaluate the effectiveness of an attack. In ASCAD, only 37 traces can stabilize a rank 0 with a filter size of 63 (1/8 clock cycle). As for ASCAD_desync50 and

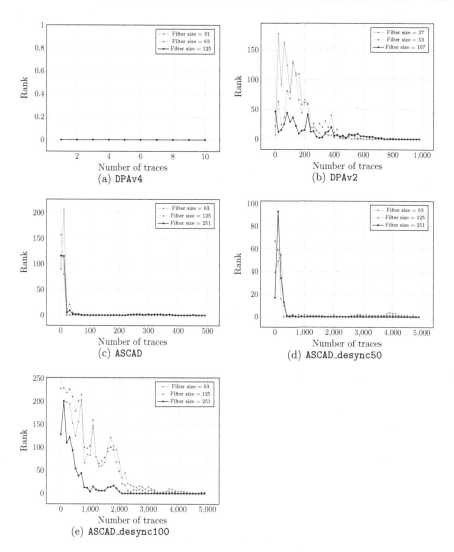

Fig. 2. Ranking convergence with different filter sizes

ASCAD_desync100, we find that less traces are needed to recover the correct key when the fiter size is larger.

These experimental results suggest that sinc filter size from 1/4 clock cycle to 1/2 clock cycle is a appropriate range for some practical cases. In particular, for the desynchronized dataset, larger filter size like 1/2 clock cycle can be a preference.

Table 2. Results for different filter sizes of SincNet-based attack

Dataset	Filter size	Accuracy	Top-5 accuracy	Rank = 0	Rank ≡ 0
DPA v4	31 (1/8)	25.26%	67.72%	1	1
	63 (1/4)	24.12%	66.84%	1	1
	125 (1/2)	**26.22%**	**67.72%**	**1**	**1**
DPA v2	27 (1/8)	**0.35%**	**2.13%**	**398**	**569**
	53 (1/4)	0.50%	2.37%	585	815
	107 (1/2)	0.43%	2.41%	741	776
ASCAD	63 (1/8)	0.59%	3.16%	52	91
	125 (1/4)	**0.58%**	**3.00%**	**21**	**37**
	251 (1/2)	0.70%	2.98%	71	468
ASCAD_desync50	63 (1/8)	0.45%	2.34%	718	4725
	125 (1/4)	0.56%	2.17%	237	4213
	251 (1/2)	**0.55%**	**2.43%**	**403**	**738**
ASCAD_desync100	63 (1/8)	0.53%	2.35%	4521	6439
	125 (1/4)	0.38%	2.41%	3931	5361
	251 (1/2)	**0.48%**	**2.38%**	**2034**	**2055**

Remark. Indeed, results not reported here reveals that larger filter size more than 1/2 clock cycle such as one clock cycle may bring a gradient vanish. During the training phase, the accuracy stops rising in the early phase, and probably leads a profiling failure.

3.3   Comparisons with Standard CNNs

In this section, we compared the performance of our SincNet architecture with the classical CNN architecture in SCA. For each dataset, we considered a standard CNN architecture based on the same architecture as the best-behaved SincNet and only replacing the sinc filter in the first convolutional layer with standard CNN filter of the same size.

The ranking convergence is presented in Fig. 3, and the evaluation results are summarized in Table 3. They show that our SincNet perform successful attacks with different datasets. In DPAv4, only one single trace can recover the correct key in SincNet, which is one less than in CNN. As for DPAv2, the rank score stabilized at 0 only after 569 traces in SincNet, while 1191 traces in CNN. As for ASCAD, SincNet performs better than CNN both in the top-5 accuracy and rank. In particular for ASCAD_desync50 and ASCAD_desync100, SincNet significantly outperforms CNN in all metrics.

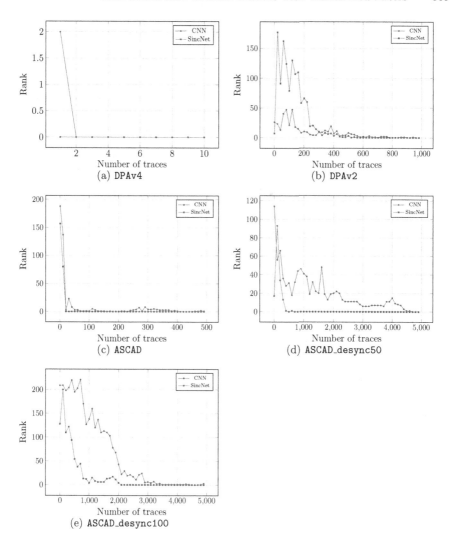

Fig. 3. Ranking convergence of SincNet and CNN model

As it is observed from Fig. 4, the SincNet has some other advantages. The accuracy curve of SincNet converges faster in the training phase over the standard CNN. Since the first layer only focus the filter parameters with major impact on performance, the meanful filters learn the characteristics much easier. Besides, SincNet reduces not only the number of parameters, but also half of computations in the first convolutional layer.

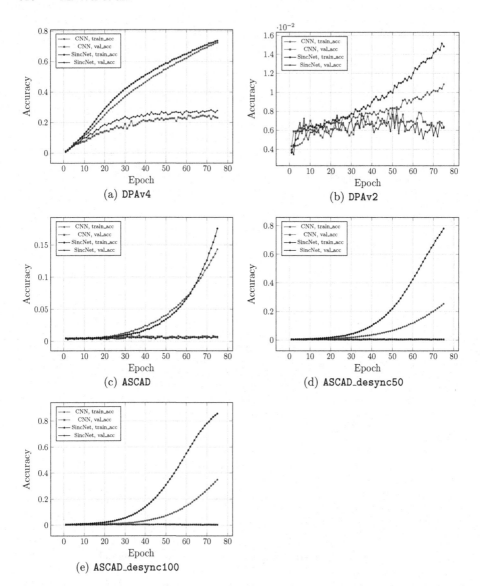

Fig. 4. Accuracy and validation accuracy of SincNet and CNN model over different training epoches

Table 3. Results of CNN-based attack and SincNet-based attack

Dataset	Model	Accuracy	Top-5 accuracy	Rank = 0	Rank ≡ 0
DPA v4	CNN	22.56%	63.46%	2	2
	SincNet	26.22%	67.22%	1	1
DPA v2	CNN	0.42%	2.43%	578	1191
	SincNet	0.35%	2.13%	398	569
ASCAD	CNN	0.71%	2.93%	148	612
	SincNet	0.58%	3.00%	21	37
ASCAD_desync50	CNN	0.39%	1.93%	4576	>10000
	SincNet	0.55%	2.43%	403	738
ASCAD_desync100	CNN	0.41%	2.04%	4471	>10000
	SincNet	0.48%	2.38%	2034	2055

4 Conclusion

In this work, by using CNNs with customized filters borrowed from the domain of speaker recognitions, we show that the first layer of CNNs (the filters) has an important effect on the overall performance of CNN-based side-channel analysis. In particular, CNNs with the sinc filters outperforms standard CNNs on several public datasets. This work serves to motivate further research on the design and selection of convolution filters.

Acknowledgements. The authors thank the anonymous reviewers for many helpful comments. The work is supported by the National Key R&D Program of China (Grant No. 2018YFA0704704), the Chinese Major Program of National Cryptography Development Foundation (Grant No. MMJJ20180102), the National Natural Science Foundation of China (61772519, 61732021, 61802400, 61802399), and the Youth Innovation Promotion Association of Chinese Academy of Sciences.

References

1. Deep Learning Tutorials. http://deeplearning.net/reading-list/tutorials/
2. DPA contest v2. http://www.dpacontest.org/v2/
3. DPA contest v4. http://www.dpacontest.org/v4/rsm_doc.php
4. Keras library. https://keras.io/
5. Abadi, M., et al.: TensorFlow: large-scale machine learning on heterogeneous distributed systems. CoRR abs/1603.04467 (2016)
6. Agrawal, D., Archambeault, B., Rao, J.R., Rohatgi, P.: The EM side-channel(s). In: Cryptographic Hardware and Embedded Systems - CHES 2002, 4th International Workshop, Redwood Shores, CA, USA, 13–15 August 2002, Revised Papers, pp. 29–45 (2002)
7. ANSSI: ASCAD database (2019). https://github.com/ANSSI-FR/ASCAD

8. Bartkewitz, T., Lemke-Rust, K.: Efficient template attacks based on probabilistic multi-class support vector machines. In: Mangard, S. (ed.) CARDIS 2012. LNCS, vol. 7771, pp. 263–276. Springer, Heidelberg (2013). https://doi.org/10.1007/978-3-642-37288-9_18

9. Bishop, C.M.: Pattern Recognition and Machine Learning. Springer, Heidelberg (2006)

10. Boureau, Y., Ponce, J., LeCun, Y.: A theoretical analysis of feature pooling in visual recognition. In: Proceedings of the 27th International Conference on Machine Learning (ICML 2010), Haifa, Israel, 21–24 June 2010, pp. 111–118 (2010)

11. Brier, E., Clavier, C., Olivier, F.: Correlation power analysis with a leakage model. In: Joye, M., Quisquater, J.-J. (eds.) CHES 2004. LNCS, vol. 3156, pp. 16–29. Springer, Heidelberg (2004). https://doi.org/10.1007/978-3-540-28632-5_2

12. Cagli, E., Dumas, C., Prouff, E.: Convolutional neural networks with data augmentation against jitter-based countermeasures. In: Fischer, W., Homma, N. (eds.) CHES 2017. LNCS, vol. 10529, pp. 45–68. Springer, Cham (2017). https://doi.org/10.1007/978-3-319-66787-4_3

13. Chari, S., Rao, J.R., Rohatgi, P.: Template attacks. In: Kaliski, B.S., Koç, K., Paar, C. (eds.) CHES 2002. LNCS, vol. 2523, pp. 13–28. Springer, Heidelberg (2003). https://doi.org/10.1007/3-540-36400-5_3

14. Cortes, C., Vapnik, V.: Support-vector networks. Mach. Learn. **20**(3), 273–297 (1995)

15. Doget, J., Prouff, E., Rivain, M., Standaert, F.: Univariate side channel attacks and leakage modeling. J. Cryptographic Eng. **1**(2), 123–144 (2011)

16. Gierlichs, B., Batina, L., Tuyls, P., Preneel, B.: Mutual information analysis. In: Oswald, E., Rohatgi, P. (eds.) CHES 2008. LNCS, vol. 5154, pp. 426–442. Springer, Heidelberg (2008). https://doi.org/10.1007/978-3-540-85053-3_27

17. Gilmore, R., Hanley, N., O'Neill, M.: Neural network based attack on a masked implementation of AES. In: IEEE International Symposium on Hardware Oriented Security and Trust, HOST 2015, Washington, DC, USA, 5–7 May 2015, pp. 106–111 (2015)

18. Hettwer, B., Gehrer, S., Güneysu, T.: Profiled power analysis attacks using convolutional neural networks with domain knowledge. In: Selected Areas in Cryptography - SAC 2018–25th International Conference, Calgary, AB, Canada, 15–17 August 2018, Revised Selected Papers, pp. 479–498 (2018)

19. Heuser, A., Zohner, M.: Intelligent machine homicide. In: Schindler, W., Huss, S.A. (eds.) COSADE 2012. LNCS, vol. 7275, pp. 249–264. Springer, Heidelberg (2012). https://doi.org/10.1007/978-3-642-29912-4_18

20. Hospodar, G., Gierlichs, B., Mulder, E.D., Verbauwhede, I., Vandewalle, J.: Machine learning in side-channel analysis: a first study. J. Cryptographic Eng. **1**(4), 293–302 (2011)

21. Kocher, P.C.: Timing attacks on implementations of Diffie-Hellman, RSA, DSS, and other systems. In: Koblitz, N. (ed.) CRYPTO 1996. LNCS, vol. 1109, pp. 104–113. Springer, Heidelberg (1996). https://doi.org/10.1007/3-540-68697-5_9

22. Kocher, P., Jaffe, J., Jun, B.: Differential power analysis. In: Wiener, M. (ed.) CRYPTO 1999. LNCS, vol. 1666, pp. 388–397. Springer, Heidelberg (1999). https://doi.org/10.1007/3-540-48405-1_25

23. LeCun, Y., Bengio, Y.: Convolutional networks for images, speech, and time series. In: The Handbook of Brain Theory and Neural Networks, pp. 255–258 (1998)

24. LeCun, Y., Bengio, Y., Hinton, G.E.: Deep learning. Nature **521**(7553), 436–444 (2015)

25. Lerman, L., Bontempi, G., Markowitch, O.: Power analysis attack: an approach based on machine learning. IJACT **3**(2), 97–115 (2014)
26. Lerman, L., Medeiros, S.F., Bontempi, G., Markowitch, O.: A machine learning approach against a masked AES. In: Smart Card Research and Advanced Applications - 12th International Conference, CARDIS 2013, Berlin, Germany, 27–29 November 2013, Revised Selected Papers, pp. 61–75 (2013)
27. Lerman, L., Poussier, R., Bontempi, G., Markowitch, O., Standaert, F.-X.: Template attacks vs. machine learning revisited (and the curse of dimensionality in side-channel analysis). In: Mangard, S., Poschmann, A.Y. (eds.) COSADE 2014. LNCS, vol. 9064, pp. 20–33. Springer, Cham (2015). https://doi.org/10.1007/978-3-319-21476-4_2
28. Maghrebi, H., Portigliatti, T., Prouff, E.: Breaking cryptographic implementations using deep learning techniques. In: Carlet, C., Hasan, M.A., Saraswat, V. (eds.) SPACE 2016. LNCS, vol. 10076, pp. 3–26. Springer, Cham (2016). https://doi.org/10.1007/978-3-319-49445-6_1
29. O'Shea, K., Nash, R.: An introduction to convolutional neural networks. CoRR abs/1511.08458 (2015)
30. Prouff, E., Strullu, R., Benadjila, R., Cagli, E., Dumas, C.: Study of deep learning techniques for side-channel analysis and introduction to ASCAD database. IACR Cryptol. ePrint Archive **2018**, 53 (2018)
31. Ravanelli, M., Bengio, Y.: Speaker recognition from raw waveform with SincNet. In: 2018 IEEE Spoken Language Technology Workshop, SLT 2018, Athens, Greece, 18–21 December 2018, pp. 1021–1028 (2018)
32. Rokach, L., Maimon, O.Z.: Data Mining with Decision Trees: Theory and Applications, vol. 69. World scientific, Singapore (2008)
33. Schindler, W.: Advanced stochastic methods in side channel analysis on block ciphers in the presence of masking. J. Math. Cryptol. **2**(3), 291–310 (2008)
34. Schindler, W., Lemke, K., Paar, C.: A stochastic model for differential side channel cryptanalysis. In: Rao, J.R., Sunar, B. (eds.) CHES 2005. LNCS, vol. 3659, pp. 30–46. Springer, Heidelberg (2005). https://doi.org/10.1007/11545262_3
35. Timon, B.: Non-profiled deep learning-based side-channel attacks with sensitivity analysis. IACR Trans. Cryptogr. Hardw. Embed. Syst. **2019**(2), 107–131 (2019)
36. Weston, J., Watkins, C.: Multi-class support vector machines (1998)
37. Yang, G., Li, H., Ming, J., Zhou, Y.: Convolutional neural network based side-channel attacks in time-frequency representations. In: International Conference on Smart Card Research and Advanced Applications, pp. 1–17 (2018)

DLchain: A Covert Channel over Blockchain Based on Dynamic Labels

Jing Tian[1,2], Gaopeng Gou[1,2(✉)], Chang Liu[1,2], Yige Chen[1,2], Gang Xiong[1,2], and Zhen Li[1,2]

[1] Institute of Information Engineering, Chinese Academy of Sciences, Beijing, China
gougaopeng@iie.ac.cn
[2] University of Chinese Academy of Sciences, Beijing, China

Abstract. With the continuous improvement of the traffic analysis techniques, traditional network covert channels based on the TCP/IP architecture are facing many risks. Blockchain is a new kind of decentralized public network. The openness together with strong tamper resistance of the blockchain makes it become a natural platform to construct covert channel. However, the existing blockchain-based covert channels have a major drawback: the recipient identifies the transactions containing covert messages through the fixed labels, which significantly reduces the availability and concealment of the system. In this paper, we propose a new blockchain covert channel construction scheme, DLchain, which substitutes the fixed labels with dynamic labels. We design a dynamic label generation algorithm based on the statistical distribution of the real transaction data to ensure the concealment of the dynamic labels. We prove that DLchain has the features of undetectability, anti-traceability and strong robustness.

Keywords: Blockchain · Covert channel construction · Dynamic label

1 Introduction

When network users communicate on the Internet, they typically ensure the confidentiality of messages through encryption. However, the communication participants may expose their meta-data such as IP address, to the network eavesdroppers. The meta-data can be used to identify the users and discover communication links between them. Therefore, an outside observer with ulterior motives can easily monitor and analyze the traffic, and expose the identity information of communicators, which greatly threatens the user privacy and the freedom of communication. For example, malicious attacks from private organizations aimed at stealing confidential government data, such as GhostNet [14], ShadowNet [4] and Axiom [2], have emerged.

Research Supported by IIE, CAS international cooperation project.
Research Supported by the CAS/SAFEA International Partnership Program for Creative Research Teams.

In this context, the demand to construct network covert channels is increasing, and many covert communication systems have been proposed [15,27,37]. There are two main kinds of covert network channels [23], covert timing channels (CTCs) and covert storage channels (CSCs). CTCs include the covert messages into the timing behavior at the sender and then extract the covert messages at the receiver. CTCs are greatly influenced by network delay or jitters, so their robustness is not very well [23]. CSCs include the messages to storage objects at the sender and then reading them at the receiver. A typical CSC is Tor [15], which is an implementation of onion routing. Tor has about 8 million daily users [21]. However, storage-based mechanism is susceptible to traffic analysis attacks by adversaries who can monitor it. Many of the literatures show how to detect the channel and trace the traffic, including strong flow correlation attack [25], Low-resource routing attacks [26] and Torben attack [7]. A successful covert channel requires undetectability, anti-traceability and good robustness. However, the traditional covert channel cannot meet these requirements.

Blockchain is the representative of the new generation of information technology. It has the characteristics of participant-anonymity, flooding propagation mechanism and tampering resistance, which means it is a compelling platform for covert communication. The botchain [1] is the first mechanism that enables botmaster to communicate covertly with bots by embedding command & contro (C&C) instructions in Bitcoin transactions. Besides, chainchannels [16] and other similar systems [5,13] also use blockchains to prevent the traffic tracked by the observers. However, they all select the fixed labels such as public keys and wallet addresses to ensure that the receiver can identity the special transactions containing covert messages from thousands of transactions. Once these labels are exposed, the whole channel will be exposed and the communication will be broken, which significantly reduces the availability and concealment of the system.

For this reason, we reinvent blockchain-based covert transmission architecture, in the form of the DLchain. DLchain can generate labels dynamically, which alleviates the risk of channel exposure. Our dynamic labels are based on the probability distribution of true transaction data, which greatly increases the statistical undetectability of the channel. DLchain provides anti-traceability, including message indistinguishability, sender or receiver anonymous and unobservability. The blockchain feature of tamper resistance and the cryptographic characteristic of ECDSA (elliptic curve digital signature algorithm) [11] ensure the robustness of our channel.

Contributions. In this paper we make the following contributions:

1. We propose DLchain, a mechanism enabling the senders and receivers to covertly communicate over public blockchain. It can hide communication relationships and protect user privacy.
2. We present dynamic label generation algorithm. It can dynamicly generate labels that are statistically undetectable.
3. We show that DLchain satisfies the undetectability, anti-traceability and robustness. Moreover, compared with the existing systems, DLchain can resist

the message statistical analysis and the address association attack while still
ensuring high availability.

The remainder of this paper is organized as follows. In Sect. 2, we overview the
existing blockchain based covert channels and motivate our work. Section 3 introduces the DLchain architecture and Sect. 4 shows the dynamic label generation
algorithm. In Sect. 5, we assess and analyze our system. We compare DLchain to
previous covert channels in Sect. 6 and make a conclusion in Sect. 7. we discuss
future work in Sect. 8.

2   Review of the Existing Blockchain Based Covert Channels

There are three existing systems on blockchain based covert channel: zombiecoin [13], botchain [1] and chainchannel [16]. Brenner et al. [13] explored
the possibility of applying blockchain technology to the transmission of C&C
instructions in a secret way, and they described the prototypes of zombiecoin,
which are based on Ethereum. After that, Ali et al. [5] proposes zombiecoin2.0,
which validates the claims in [13] and deploys successfully over the Bitcoin network. Chainchannels [16] realizes a new way of embedding covert messages in
blockchain with key leakage and makes some cryptographic proofs. Botchain [1]
is a fully functional botnet which is based on Bitcoin protocol.

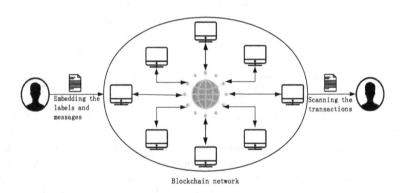

Fig. 1. The general framework of blockchain covert channel.

The designs of these three systems are very similar. Figure 1 shows the general framework of them. In the three systems, communication participants are
expected to covertly transmit messages through blockchain. They first apply to
be the client nodes of the blockchain network, and negotiate labels in advance so
that the receiver can identify the transactions containing covert messages from
thousands of transactions. To ensure security, both sides also need to negotiate
the encoding, encryption algorithm and the way of message embedding. Then

the sender encodes, encrypts, embeds the messages into certain transactions according to the negotiated algorithm, and sends them to the server nodes of blockchain. After the flooding propagation mechanism of blockchain network, the receiver identifies the special transactions through negotiated labels and extracts the covert messages.

The differences between the three systems lie in two aspects: how to insert covert messages and what the fixed labels used. In terms of the first aspect, Zombiecoin [13] and botchain [1] directly embed the messages in the output script function OP_RETURN[1], which is a field of particular blockchain implementation and originally used to carry additional transaction information. Chainchannels [16] is different from them at this aspect. It uses a subliminal channel to insert messages totally in digital signatures. In terms of the second aspect, Botchain [1], proposed by Cybaze, uses pre-negotiated virtual currency wallet addresses as the labels to scan transactions. However, in both zombiecoin [13] and chainchannels [16], scanning transactions that contain covert messages is done through a pair of pre-negotiated public-private keys. In the two systems, the receiver identifies these transactions by scanning the ScriptSig [2] which contains the sender's public-key and the digital signature (computed over the transaction) using private-key. The receiver verifies the signature and decodes the messages.

So labels are very important to identify covert messages in blockchain. Once the labels are detected or thwarted, the whole covert channel will expose and may be destroyed. There are methods that systematically detect and thwart unwanted data insertion on blockchain [22], indicating that the attackers can identify the messages by analyzing the label characteristics. However, none of the existing blockchain based covert channels addresses the concealment and privacy of the labels, which is the main motivation of our proposal. Unlike any of the existing schemes using fixed labels, DLchain functions with a dynamic label generation algorithm, making it more covertly to transmit messages.

3   DLchain Architecture

3.1   System Overview

We use Bitcoin [24] to illustrate DLchain. It consists of the senders, the receivers, Bitcoin network, message embedding and extracting, dynamic label embedding and scanning. The initial seed, signature scheme, and encoding are negotiated by both parties in advance, and the next seed will be transferred at the end of this communication. Then, the senders and receivers generate labels simultaneously using the seed and the algorithm mentioned in Sect. 3. The Fig. 2 gives an overview of the DLchain architecture.

---

[1] Available under https://en.bitcoin.it/wiki/OP_RETURN.

[2] The unlocking script in Bitcoin to verify whether a transaction is passed.

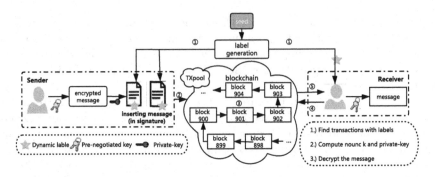

Fig. 2. DLchain architecture. 1. The senders and receivers generate dynamic labels at the same time. So the receivers can identity transactions from the senders. 2. The senders encrypt the messages using the pre-negotiated key. And the private-key used for signature is substituted by the encrypted messages. Then the senders sign two transactions using the special private-key and pack the label into the transactions. 3. The transactions are verified, propagated in the whole network and are recorded on blockchain. 4, 5. The receivers identify transactions according to the label, get the transactions and extract the covert message.

3.2   Embedding and Scanning Dynamic Labels

The labels should be directly embedded in an obvious location to facilitate rapid identification by the receivers. And labels need to be confused with a large number of normal data, which makes it difficult for the outside observers to identify them.

The output script function OP_RETURN allows users to insert up to 220 bytes of data in each transaction after it was expanded in May 2018 [6]. Many services plan to migrate to using that function, such as Proof of Existence [18]. An analysis in 2014 reveals that the OP_RETURN field was used in about a quarter of transactions in 80-block portion of the blockchain [12]. The amount of scripts increases dramatically around Nov. 2018 [3], indicating the feature is very popular now. So, we can use the OP_RETURN script to insert our labels.

The length of our label is the second consideration. If the length is too short, it may lead to duplication with real data. Conversely, too long will cause the increased cost of scanning. The first 3 bytes of the OP_RETURN data can indicate the protocol but it's not an enforced rule [10]. More than 40% of the first 3 bytes are a fixed protocol [3], which means the first 3 bytes in each transaction are easy to repeat. So the length of our labels should be greater than three bytes. In addition, the website [3] records the distribution of the sizes of the OP_RETURN scripts since the birth of the Bitcoin and the most two common script lengths until Aug.2019 are 23 (12078010 transactions) and 83 (12078010 transactions). Considering both concealment and the cost of scanning, we choose 23 as the length of the labels. The receivers identify the special transactions by scanning the OP_RETURN and extract the messages.

3.3   Embedding and Extracting Covert Messages

On the other hand, covert messages should be inserted indirectly in a hidden way, so that even if the labels are exposed, the messages will not be leaked.

Algorithm 1. Embedding Algorithm.

Input:

   Two transactions: tx_1, tx_2; Random factor: k; Covert message: d; The generator point, G; the order of the curve n.

Output:

1: $(x_1, y_1) = k \cdot G$
2: $r = x_1 \bmod n$
3: $t_1 = \text{SHA-1}(tx_1)$
4: $t_2 = \text{SHA-1}(tx_2)$
5: $s_1 \equiv k^{-1}(t_1 + dr) \bmod n$
6: $s_2 \equiv k^{-1}(t_2 + dr) \bmod n$
7: **return** $(r, s_1), (r, s_2)$

Algorithm 2. Extraction Algorithm.

Input:

   the order of the curve n; s_1, s_2; r; Two transactions: tx_1, tx_2.

Output:

   Determining random factor k from $sign_1, sign_2$ and using k to recover covert message d.

1: $k \cdot s_1 \equiv t_1 + dr \bmod n$
2: $k \cdot s_2 \equiv t_2 + dr \bmod n$
3: $k(s_1 - s_2) \equiv t_1 - t_2 \bmod n$
4: $k \equiv (s_1 - s_2)^{-1}(t_1 - t_2) \bmod n$
5: $d = r^{-1}(k \cdot s_1 - t_1) \equiv r^{-1}(k \cdot s_2 - t_2) \bmod n$

   Many blockchain-based virtual currencies use the ECDSA (elliptic curve digital signature algorithm) [11]. Simmons first expounds how to implement messages transmission in digital signature schemes [32,33]. We choose a subliminal channel in the signature as a covert approach to insert messages. The chainchannels [16] uses the subliminal channel technique too. It substitutes the nonce used in ECDSA with the covert message. Different from chainchannels, we substitute private-key with the covert message and use this special private-key to derive a public-key pk, which allows the pk to change based on the transmitted message. Then we sign two transactions carrying the covert message, just that the d represents the message instead of private-key. The embedding process is shown in Algorithm 1. Because the reuse of random factor will cause the private-key d in ECDSA to be recovered by an observer [11]. The receiver can recover the d as the Algorithm 2.

4   Dynamic Label Generation Algorithm

There are two basic requirements for the labels: one is dynamic, which means that labels must be constantly changing, and the other is consistency, which means that both sides must ensure the same labels in the same period of time. So we think of DGA (Domain Generation Algorithm), which is used in botnet communication. It is a technique that generates dynamic domains, thus avoiding the detection based on domain blacklists. In the DGA-based botnet, botmaster runs a certain DGA using a seed to generate a large number of AGDs (Algorithmically-generated Domains), and a small number of them are randomly selected for registration and point to the botnet C&C servers. Bots use the same seed to run the DGA and generate the same domains. Then they use these domains to make DNS request and get the C&C server addresses.

AGDs satisfy the basic requirements of label composition, namely, dynamic and consistency, but they do not meet the concealment: because the generation process of AGDs has nothing to do with benign domains, AGDs and benign domains have obvious differences in grammatical features, and they will be easily detected by statistical feature-based algorithms [31]. So we modify it and design a new algorithm for generating covert labels.

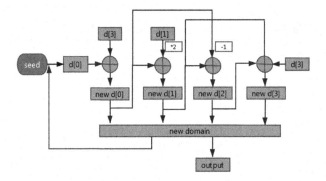

Fig. 3. Banjori domain production process: it uses a domain mutation scheme where a previously generated domain is used as input for the calculation of the subsequent domain, and it only modifies the first four positions of a given hard-coded seed domain. In addition, all AGDs of one seed have the same length.

The dynamic labels require the capability of concealment. To accomplish this, we utilize several tricks gleaned from a close reading of the study of DGA [28,29] and blockchain protocol format to allow the label to change over time and impersonate the real data in transactions. Our dynamic label generation algorithm uses the DGA algorithm Banjori [8] for reference, whose seeds are time-independent and deterministic, and the generation scheme is arithmetic-based [29]. The Fig. 3 illustrates its specific production process.

Not like Banjori [8], which only modifies the first four positions, our dynamic label generation algorithm modifies the entire string. In addition, the generation

---

Algorithm 3. Dynamic Label Generation Algorithm.

Input:

    The seed of length N, $S_n = \{s_i, 0 \leq i < N\}$;

    The character set of the first N positions of OP_RETURN, $C_n = \{c_i, 0 \leq i \leq n\}$;

    The frequency distribution of $C_n, F_n = \{f_i, 0 \leq i < n\}$;

Output:

1: Initialize a dictionary D;

2: Sorting F_n in descending order;

3: Sorting C_n in its corresponding f_n;

4: **for** each $f_i \in F_n$ **do**

5:     $v_i \Leftarrow f_i * N$;

6:     Rounding the value of v_i;

7:     Generating a term d_i in the dictionary $D, d_i \Leftarrow \{c_i : v_i\}$;

8: **end for**

9: $L_n \Leftarrow S_n$;

10: **for** each $v_i \in D_n$ **do**

11:     Selecting v_i positions from $S_n : P \Leftarrow \{p_j, 0 \leq j < v_i\}$;

12:     Replacing each position $p_j \in P$ in L_n with c_i;

13:     $S_n \Leftarrow S_n - c_i$;

14: **end for**

15: **return** L_n;

---

scheme is not based on the addition of some fixed position characters, but on the statistical distribution of the real transaction data on the OP_RETURN, which makes the label indistinguishable from the real data. We depict our algorithm in Algorithm 3. The length of seed N is 23, which is introduced in Sect. 3.2. The frequency distribution C_n in the algorithm is updated every day, so different labels are generated constantly. By calculating ER (entropy rate) and conducting KS test (Kolmogorov-smirnov D test) in Sect. 5.1, we prove that our transformation for Banjori is very successful.

5 Assessment and Analysis

In this section, we make a complete assessment for DLchain from the aspects of the undetectability, anti-traceability and robustness. In addition, we also show that our transformation for Banjori is very successful.

5.1 Undetectability

We assume an adversary can analyze transaction information to find suspicious data, then detects labels to expose the covert channels. We analyze the labels in two aspects, one is the regularity of change, the other is the difference of probability distribution.

The Regularity of the Change. Because covert channels will cause the change of ER, many literatures [17,34–36] use ER to detect covert channels. ER is the conditional entropy as the random variable sequence length $m \to \infty$, which describes the uncertainty of a random variable sequence. And the smaller the ER, the stronger the regularity. So we use the ER to measure the regularity of the change of dynamic labels. However, in practical applications, only limited samples can be used for estimation. Porta et al. [30] propose to use the entropy rate of finite samples to reflect the nature of random events by CCE (corrected conditional entropy), which is shown in Eq. 1. The estimated value of ER, which is calculated in Eq. 2, is the minimum value of CCE when m changes.

$$CCE\left(X_m | X_{m-1}\right) = H\left(X_m | X_{m-1}\right) + p\left(X_m\right) H\left(X_1\right) \tag{1}$$

$$\overline{ER} = \min_{i=1,m} \left(CCE\left(X_i | X_{i-1}\right)\right) \tag{2}$$

We use bitcoin-etl[3] to collect the OP_RETURN from Jan.2019 to Jul.2019 as the real data. Figure 4 shows the trends of the ER for real data and dynamic labels over time. As you can see, the trend of the ER of real data is almost the same as that of dynamic labels and the ER of Banjori almost remains unchanged. That is to say, our transformation for Banjori is very successful and dynamic labels can simulate the change regularity of the real data very well.

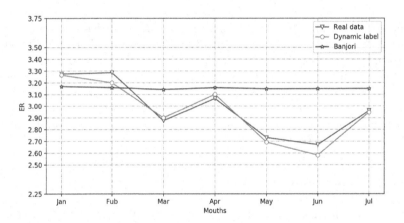

Fig. 4. Entropy rate for label and real data over the first half of this year, and use the Banjori as a comparison

The Difference of Probability Distribution. KS test [20], points an upper bound between the cumulative probability of experience and the cumulative probability of the target distribution at each data point. How to calculate the upper bound is shown as Eq. 3.

$$D_n = \max_{1 \leq k \leq n} \left\{ |F_n\left(x_k\right) - F_0\left(x_k\right)| , |F_0\left(x_{k+1}\right) - F_n\left(x_k\right)| \right\} \tag{3}$$

---

[3] ETL scripts for Bitcoin, available under https://twitter.com/BlockchainETL.

Now it usually uses the p-value to decide whether or not two sets of samples are drawn from the same distribution [19]. Generally speaking, if the p-value is greater than designated significance-level (generally set to 0.05), it is concluded that the two sets come from the same distribution. The first set we choosed is the distribution of characters in the real OP_RETURN data from Jan.2019 to Jul.2019. The second we consider is the distribution of character in labels generated by our algorithm introduced in Sect. 3. In addition, we replace the second distribution with Banjori domains to prove that our transformation for Banjori is successful.

The Fig. 6 in Sect. 6 shows that all KS p-values for Banjori domains are less than 10^{-6}, which shows the probability distribution of Banjori is very different from real data. However, all KS p-values for the dynamic labels over time are greater than 0.05, which proves the effectiveness of our transformation for Banjori and KS test will be not valid in detecting the covert labels.

5.2 Anti-traceability

Message Indistinguishability. There are two aspects of indistinguishability: one is indistinguishability in behavior. All network communication between the sender and receiver proceeds as the standard Bitcoin protocol specification, so the network behavior of both sides to an outside observer is indistinguishable from the traffic of genuine Bitcoin users. The other is indistinguishability in content. An adversary observing the network will not be able to distinguish covert messages from transactions without knowing the labels. Thus, he can not distinguish the messages from content.

Sender or Receiver Anonymous. For the sender's anonymity, Bitcoin provides pseudonymity, a weaker form of anonymity, which causes that the attackers can find the correlation between different Bitcoin addresses and infer the user identities. In Sect. 6, we show that DLchain resists address association attack and is superior to other fixed label systems in sender's anonymity. For the receiver's anonymity, because of the mechanism of flooding propagation in blockchain, senders and receivers can communicate without any direct connection. The number of receivers will not be known by monitors because who has received the messages will not be recorded. Messages are propagated to all nodes in the blockchain, and the receivers identify them according to the labels. This kind of indirect communication makes the adversaries unable to identify the receivers, so it can ensure the anonymity of the receivers.

Sender or Receiver Unobservability. Unobservability means that an adversary can not learn whether the senders or receivers are sending or receiving messages. For the senders, they will make normal transactions while sending covert messages. Thus, the adversaries cannot tell whether the transaction contains a covert message. For the receivers, Once the transaction is recorded in the blockchain by miners, anyone can view and scan the public transactions at any time. In the current standard protocol, blockchain nodes receive transactions and perform checks for correctness, such as whether the syntax and data structure of the transaction is correct, whether the input/output list is empty, etc. After that, the nodes forward the transaction on to other nodes. So even if the minors reject the transaction because of the low transaction fee or other reasons, the receivers have already got it, validated it, and received the messages. Adversaries have no way of knowing how many covert messages are in the blockchain or whether anyone is receiving them.

5.3   Robustness Analysis

We illustrate robustness in two aspects. The one is tamper resistance to ensure that the message is transmitted to the receivers correctly. The other is error analysis when the receivers extract the message.

Tamper Resistance. Each block in the blockchain contains the hash of previous block, corresponding time stamp and transaction data, which makes the content of block difficult to tamper with. The literature [36] discusses the probability of successful tampering, as shown in Eq. 4. The p is the probability that the next data is normally stored as a block, q is the probability that it is tampered with and stored as a block, and z is the number of blocks that need to be supplemented.

$$q_z = 1 - \sum_{k=0}^{z} \frac{\lambda^k e^{-\lambda}}{k!} \left(1 - \frac{q}{p^{(z-k)}} \right) \tag{4}$$

When $p = 0.9$ and $z = 5$, the calculation result is less than 0.001. In practical scenarios, p is much larger than q, because adversaries must have extremely strong computational power to calculate a long enough forked chain and obtain recognition from other nodes in order to achieve the propose of tampering with data. So there are almost no errors in the message transmission.

Error Analysis When Extracting Messages. The other aspect to illustrate robustness is from the perspective of message recovery. The more complete the message recovery is, the more robust the system will be. In our system, we mainly consider whether there will be errors in the process of extracting the final message after the original message is embedded through the subliminal channel. Since we use ECDSA, its cryptographic characteristics ensure that the private-key is unique. We use the covert message as the private-key. The extraction of private-key is accomplished by the attack of repeated use of random factor, so the private-key calculated in that process will not change. That is, no errors occur during the process of extracting the message.

6   Comparison

The covert channels share the common goal of hiding communication relationship from the outside observers, simultaneously ensuring the users' identity anonymity while still providing high availability. The comparison between the fixed label systems and DLchain is carried out from the following aspects (a summary is provided in Table 1).

Table 1. Comparing blockchain based covert channel systems. By †, we mean if the covert messages are embedded by the technique of subliminal channel.

	Zombiecoin	Botchain	Chainchannels	DLchain
Message indirectly embedding†	×	×	√	√
Channel availability	×	×	×	√
Address association attack resistant	×	×	×	√
Message statistical analysis resistant	×	×	√	√

The Channel Availability. The following Fig. 5 illustrates the blockchain protocol fields used by DLchain and a typical fixed label system, zombiecoin [13], to insert labels and covert messages. The zombiecoin [13] uses the public-key in TxIn as the fixed label and inserts covert messages in the OP_RETURN. If the label used in last communication is found by the outside observers, they can identify the specific transactions according the fixed label. This indicates that the channel has already exposed. The two parties of the communication can not continue to communicate, thus reducing the availability of the channel. This problem exists in all fixed label systems. But in DLchain the labels change all the time, which means they are used only once. The use of dynamic labels So the communication can continue.

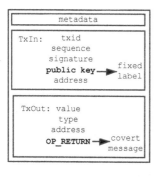
(a) Zombiecoin

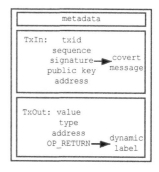
(b) DLchain

Fig. 5. Fields used by DLchain and zombiecoin

Address Association Attack Resistant. We assume in a period of time, n_u users, $\mathbf{U} = \{u_1, u_2, \ldots, u_{n_u}\}$, make transactions T. $H(U)$ represents the entropy of users. $H(U|T)$ represents the entropy under the condition of knowing T. The greater the entropy of users, the more uncertain the users' identity is. In the fixed label systems, the transactions made by the same sender have the same public-key and address in TxIn, so the observers can find the correlation between different Bitcoin addresses by analyzing the transactions related to the fixed address or public-key. These address relationships can be used for user identity association and traceability. So in all three fixed label systems, the entropy of users is $H(U|T)$.

Lemma 1. *(Non-negativity of the mutual information): for random variables U and T hold $I(U;T) = H(U) - H(U|T) \geq 0$*

But in DLchain, we substitute the private-key with the covert message. The public-key is derived from the special private-key. The transactions made by the same sender have different public-keys and addresses, thus leading to the failure of the correlation attack. So the entropy of users is $H(U)$. From the lemma 1, we can conclude that the DLchain is superior than the fixed label systems at user identity anonymity.

Defend Against Message Statistical Analysis. An observer can analyze the OP_RETURN data to find abnormal data. Some fixed label systems such as zombiecoin [13] and botchain [1], directly use the OP_RETURN to insert messages. We use the DDoS attack library for Agobot [9] as a C&C instruction set used in these fixed label systems. Because this instruction set will not change with time. The ER of it will be a fixed value. So we use this data and the real OP_RETURN data collected in Sect. 5.1 to do KS test (introduced in Sect. 5.1). The Fig. 6 shows the result of p-value of KS test.

We can know the p-value of C&C instructions used in the fixed label systems is low than 0.05, which means their probability distribution patterns are very different from real data in OP_RETURN. So the covert messages in zombiecoin and botchain have higher risk to be exposure by statistical analysis.

But in DLchain, the OP_RETURN field is inserted by the dynamical labels that are generated as the distribution of real transaction data, which makes the p-value of DLchain is much larger than 0.05, so the labels are statistically indistinguishable. In addition, the chainchannels [16] doesn't use the OP_RETURN field to insert messages or labels, so it doesn't have this problem too.

In summary, DLchain can effectively guarantee the channel availability. It provides the resistance against address association attack and message statistical analysis.

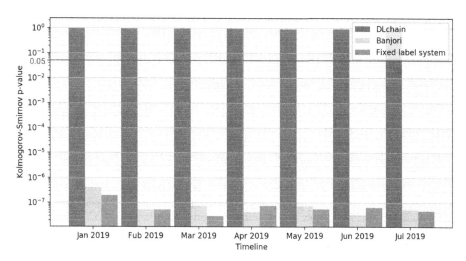

Fig. 6. p-value of Kolmogorov-Smirnov test. The ks test's first set is the distribution of characters in the real OP_RETURN data from Jan.2019 to Jul.2019. The second is dynamic labels used in DLchain, Banjori domains and the Agobot's C&C instructions, respectively.

7 Conclusion

In this paper, we propose DLchain for the first time. DLchain can hide the communication relationship. It is an effective method to decrease the risk of channel exposure and protect user privacy. DLchain uses dynamic and undetectable labels to construct the blockchain-based covert channel. We compare DLchain with other systems and demonstrate the undetectability, anti-traceability and robustness of it. We believe that DLchain poses a reliable method of covert message transmission, and we hope that our work will prompt further discussion about blockchain-based covert channels.

8 Future Work

DLchain can transmit different covert messages according to the application scenarios. For example, in order to avoid network filtering based on IP and port, we can use DLchain to transmit the network access points to Tor clients. However, if it is applied to malicious behavior, it will make malicious behavior more difficult to detect. For example, if DLchain is used for botnet communication, the botnet will be more difficult to be taken over or eradicated.

However, the Bitcoin community is not aware of the threat that this covert channel may be used for malicious behavior. We think it is necessary to make a research regarding discovering the abuse and regulating the network with traffic analysis or other techniques.

References

1. Botchain. https://botchain.network/
2. Identify Chinese cyber espionage group. https://tinyurl.com/pntdm64
3. A web about op_return. https://opreturn.org
4. Adair, S., Deibert, R., Rohozinski, R.: Shadows in the cloud: investigating cyber espionage 2.0. A joint report of the Information Warfare Monitor and Shadowserver Foundation (2010). http://shadows-in-the-cloud.net
5. Ali, S.T., McCorry, P., Lee, P.H., Hao, F.: ZombieCoin 2.0: managing next-generation botnets using bitcoin. Int. J. Inf. Secur. **17**(4), 411–422 (2018)
6. Apodaca, R.: Op_return and the future of bitcoin. Bitzuma (2014)
7. Arp, D., Yamaguchi, F., Rieck, K.: Torben: a practical side-channel attack for deanonymizing tor communication. In: Proceedings of the 10th ACM Symposium on Information, Computer and Communications Security, ASIA CCS 2015, Singapore, 14–17 April 2015, pp. 597–602 (2015). https://doi.org/10.1145/2714576. 2714627
8. BADER, J.: Domain generation algorithm analyses. Blog posts on various DGAs (2015). http://www.johannesbader.ch/tag/dga/
9. Barford, P., Yegneswaran, V.: An inside look at botnets. In: Christodorescu, M., Jha, S., Maughan, D., Song, D., Wang, C. (eds.) Malware Detection. Advances in Information Security, vol. 27, pp. 171–191. Springer, Boston (2007). https://doi. org/10.1007/978-0-387-44599-1_8
10. Bartoletti, M., Pompianu, L.: An analysis of bitcoin OP_RETURN metadata. In: Brenner, M., et al. (eds.) FC 2017. LNCS, vol. 10323, pp. 218–230. Springer, Cham (2017). https://doi.org/10.1007/978-3-319-70278-0_14
11. Bos, J.W., Halderman, J.A., Heninger, N., Moore, J., Naehrig, M., Wustrow, E.: Elliptic curve cryptography in practice. In: Christin, N., Safavi-Naini, R. (eds.) FC 2014. LNCS, vol. 8437, pp. 157–175. Springer, Heidelberg (2014). https://doi.org/ 10.1007/978-3-662-45472-5_11
12. Bradbury, D.: Blocksign utilises block chain to verify signed contracts. Coindesk (2014)
13. Brenner, M., Christin, N., Johnson, B., Rohloff, K. (eds.): FC 2015. LNCS, vol. 8976. Springer, Heidelberg (2015). https://doi.org/10.1007/978-3-662-48051-9
14. Deibert, R., Rohozinski, R., Manchanda, A.: Tracking GhostNet: investigating a cyber espionage network. Munk Centre for International Studies, University of Toronto (2009)
15. Dingledine, R., Mathewson, N., Syverson, P.F.: Tor: the second-generation onion router. In: Proceedings of the 13th USENIX Security Symposium, San Diego, CA, USA, 9–13 August 2004, pp. 303–320 (2004)
16. Frkat, D., Annessi, R., Zseby, T.: ChainChannels: private botnet communication over public blockchains. In: IEEE International Conference on Internet of Things (iThings) and IEEE Green Computing and Communications (GreenCom) and IEEE Cyber, Physical and Social Computing (CPSCom) and IEEE Smart Data (SmartData), iThings/GreenCom/CPSCom/SmartData 2018, Halifax, NS, Canada, 30 July–3 August 2018, pp. 1244–1252 (2018)
17. Gianvecchio, S., Wang, H.: Detecting covert timing channels: an entropy-based approach. In: Proceedings of the 14th ACM Conference on Computer and Communications Security, pp. 307–316. ACM (2007)
18. Kirk, J.: Could the bitcoin network be used as an ultrasecure notary service? ComputerWorld, 23 May 2013

19. Kordzakhia, N., Novikov, A., Ycart, B.: Approximations for weighted Kolmogorov-Smirnov distributions via boundary crossing probabilities. Stat. Comput. **27**(6), 1513–1523 (2017)
20. Lilliefors, H.W.: On the Kolmogorov-Smirnov test for normality with mean and variance unknown. J. Am. Stat. Assoc. **62**(318), 399–402 (1967)
21. Mani, A., Wilson-Brown, T., Jansen, R., Johnson, A., Sherr, M.: Understanding tor usage with privacy-preserving measurement. In: Proceedings of the Internet Measurement Conference 2018, IMC 2018, Boston, MA, USA, 31 October–02 November 2018, pp. 175–187 (2018)
22. Matzutt, R., Henze, M., Ziegeldorf, J.H., Hiller, J., Wehrle, K.: Thwarting unwanted blockchain content insertion. In: 2018 IEEE International Conference on Cloud Engineering, IC2E 2018, Orlando, FL, USA, 17–20 April 2018, pp. 364–370 (2018)
23. Millen, J.K.: 20 years of covert channel modeling and analysis. In: 1999 IEEE Symposium on Security and Privacy, Oakland, California, USA, 9–12 May 1999, pp. 113–114 (1999). https://doi.org/10.1109/SECPRI.1999.766906
24. Nakamoto, S., et al.: Bitcoin: A Peer-to-Peer Electronic Cash System (2008)
25. Nasr, M., Bahramali, A., Houmansadr, A.: DeepCorr: strong flow correlation attacks on tor using deep learning. In: Proceedings of the 2018 ACM SIGSAC Conference on Computer and Communications Security, CCS 2018, Toronto, ON, Canada, 15–19 October 2018, pp. 1962–1976 (2018)
26. Nikiforakis, N., Kapravelos, A., Joosen, W., Kruegel, C., Piessens, F., Vigna, G.: Cookieless monster: exploring the ecosystem of web-based device fingerprinting. In: 2013 IEEE Symposium on Security and Privacy, SP 2013, Berkeley, CA, USA, 19–22 May 2013, pp. 541–555 (2013). https://doi.org/10.1109/SP.2013.43
27. Piotrowska, A.M., Hayes, J., Elahi, T., Meiser, S., Danezis, G.: The Loopix anonymity system. In: 26th USENIX Security Symposium, USENIX Security 2017, Vancouver, BC, Canada, 16–18 August 2017, pp. 1199–1216 (2017)
28. Plohmann, D.: Dgaarchive: A deep dive into domain generating malware. https://www.botconf.eu/wp-content/uploads/2015/12/OK-P06-Plohmann-DGArchive.pdf
29. Plohmann, D., Yakdan, K., Klatt, M., Bader, J., Gerhards-Padilla, E.: A comprehensive measurement study of domain generating malware. In: 25th USENIX Security Symposium, USENIX Security 16, Austin, TX, USA, 10–12 August 2016, pp. 263–278 (2016)
30. Porta, A., et al.: Measuring regularity by means of a corrected conditional entropy in sympathetic outflow. Biol. Cybern. **78**(1), 71–78 (1998). https://doi.org/10.1007/s004220050414
31. Schüppen, S., Teubert, D., Herrmann, P., Meyer, U.: FANCI: feature-based automated NXdomain classification and intelligence. In: 27th USENIX Security Symposium, USENIX Security 2018, Baltimore, MD, USA, 15–17 August 2018, pp. 1165–1181 (2018)
32. Simmons, G.J.: The prisoners' problem and the subliminal channel. In: Chaum, D. (ed.) Advances in Cryptology, pp. 51–67. Springer, Boston (1983). https://doi.org/10.1007/978-1-4684-4730-9_5
33. Simmons, G.J.: The subliminal channel and digital signatures. In: Beth, T., Cot, N., Ingemarsson, I. (eds.) EUROCRYPT 1984. LNCS, vol. 209, pp. 364–378. Springer, Heidelberg (1985). https://doi.org/10.1007/3-540-39757-4_25
34. Wang, L., Dyer, K.P., Akella, A., Ristenpart, T., Shrimpton, T.: Seeing through network-protocol obfuscation. In: Proceedings of the 22nd ACM SIGSAC Conference on Computer and Communications Security, pp. 57–69. ACM (2015)

35. Wu, J.Z., Ding, L.P., Wang, Y.J.: Research on key problems of covert channel in cloud computing. J. China Inst. Commun. **32**(9) (2011)
36. Yanfeng, L., Liping, D., Jingzheng, W., Qiang, C., Xuehua, L., Bei, G.: Research on a new network covert channel model in blockchain environment. J. Commun. (2019)
37. Zhang, X., Zhu, L., Wang, X., Zhang, C., Zhu, H., Tan, Y.: A packet-reordering covert channel over volte voice and video traffics. J. Netw. Comput. Appl. **126**, 29–38 (2019). https://doi.org/10.1016/j.jnca.2018.11.001

Correction to: Towards Comprehensive Security Analysis of Hidden Services Using Binding Guard Relays

Muqian Chen, Xuebin Wang, Jinqiao Shi, Yue Gao, Can Zhao, and Wei Sun

Correction to:
Chapter "Towards Comprehensive Security Analysis of Hidden Services Using Binding Guard Relays" in: J. Zhou et al. (Eds.): *Information and Communications Security*, **LNCS 11999,** **https://doi.org/10.1007/978-3-030-41579-2_30**

In the version of this paper that was originally published, the affiliation of Muqian Chen, Xuebin Wang, Yue Gao, and Can Zhao has been changed to: 'School of Cyber Security, University of Chinese Academy of Sciences, Beijing, China'.

The updated version of this chapter can be found at
https://doi.org/10.1007/978-3-030-41579-2_30

Author Index

Printed in the United States
By Bookmasters